JOEL WHITBURN PRESENTS

SONGS & ARTISTS
2008

THE ESSENTIAL MUSIC GUIDE FOR YOUR IPOD™ AND OTHER PORTABLE MUSIC PLAYERS

Cover design by Eggert Creative, Inc.

ISBN 0-89820-171-3
ISBN 978-0-89820-171-0

Record Research Inc.
P.O. Box 200
Menomonee Falls, Wisconsin   53052-0200
U.S.A.

Phone: (262) 251-5408
Fax: (262) 251-9452
E-Mail: books@recordresearch.com
Web Site: www.recordresearch.com

TABLE OF CONTENTS

Each of the above playlists consists of 200 of the hottest hits of each half-decade of the rock era, except for 2005-2007. 2005 and 2006 cover those entire years, while 2007 covers the top hits for the first 8 months of the year.

Specialty Playlists

AUTHOR'S NOTE

Wow! It's amazing how much a small plastic case with some metal and circuits can impact a life, an industry, a culture! About three years ago, I bought my first iPod, a 30 gig. From the moment I hooked it up to my computer, I was hooked. I began the arduous process of downloading 55 years of record collecting on to this tiny computer hard drive. I am now on my third iPod, an 80 gig, and it still blows my mind that I can carry my favorite songs and artists, the essential recordings and a representative sampling from the history of recorded music in my pocket!

I very systematically built my electronic music collection. I started with my *Top Pop Singles* book and artist by artist added to my iPod, all songs that made Billboard's Hot 100 and pop singles charts from 1955 on. First, I downloaded all songs from the artists' CDs. If those were not available, I went to my collection of Various Artists CD compilations. And, if a song was never released on CD, I hooked up my turntable to my computer. I stipulated that each digitized recording was to be the original version of each song at the time of its popularity, not a re-recording or an alternate mix. (If you're at your wits end searching for a digital recording, consult with your local computer store for software and hardware that will allow you to download songs from your vinyl records or cassettes, directly on to your computer. Some of the titles in this book are not available on CD, but most can easily be found on vinyl or cassette at eBay, GEMM, or other online music sites.)

After I completed the "Hot 100" recordings, I also included many songs that hit the Bubbling Under charts, from #101 to 135. I moved on to the early pop hits back to 1900, then the top hits of Country, R&B, Adult Contemporary, Rock and Disco, and finally the songs that made the Grammy Hall Of Fame and Rolling Stone's list of the Top 500 Recordings. I have since completed those categories but each week brings new songs on the charts and I'll find new categories to download like Latin or World. As of this writing, my iPod contains 17,775 songs.

Another outcome of that first iPod purchase was the idea for *Songs & Artists*. This book is 180 degrees from our intensive data and chart research tomes, some which number 1,000+ pages. It is a simple song checklist, which reaches beyond the charts and spans many genres of music. *Songs & Artists* is a place where you can easily browse for tunes to add to your MP3 player, either by artist or by title. The playlists in the back are suggested songs to aid you in creating your own personal playlists.

This has been the impact of the portable MP3 player on my life. The influence of this device on the music industry has been revitalizing. And swiftly it has made its imprint on world culture. It's hard to believe that bits of plastic, metal and chips can affect so much. Maybe there really is a little genie in there.

JOEL WHITBURN

5

Joel Whitburn and Record Research: The Undisputed Experts on Recorded Music

What began simply as a teenager's record collection 56 years ago has today grown into the largest and most successful business of its kind anywhere in the world.

Joel Whitburn and his Record Research staff have been highlighting the hits, archiving the artists and tracking the trends in recorded music longer, deeper and more definitively than anyone else in the business. The result: there's no one better qualified or experienced to compile the definitive book of playlists for iPods and other portable music players – the hottest trend in recorded music.

Joel first began collecting records as a teenager growing up in the 1950s. As both his collection and his zeal for record collecting grew through the years, Joel began organizing his records according to the highest positions they reached on *Billboard* magazine's music charts. In 1970, with the encouragement of friends in the music industry, Joel turned his chart-watching hobby into a business with the publication of his first book – a slender volume titled simply *Record Research*.

Over the past 37 years, Joel's company, Record Research Inc., has published 112 reference books, which chronicle well over a century of American music, reaching as far back as 1890. Record Research publications cover virtually every charted music genre, including Pop, Rock, Country, R&B/Hip-Hop, Adult Contemporary, Dance/Disco and more.

These volumes, as well as Joel's books published by Billboard Books, are required reading for virtually anyone with a serious interest in music. Joel has also collaborated with Rhino Records on a series of over 150 *Billboard* CD compilations of America's top-charted hits. His own comprehensive charted music collection is the backbone of his research.

Songs & Artists 2008 is the third edition of a new line of books. With *Songs & Artists 2006*, Joel and his Record Researchers moved into new and somewhat "uncharted" territory.

"While there certainly are many charted hits in the book, *Songs & Artists 2008* looks beyond the charts – past just the commonly played hits," Joel notes. "I've included my personal picks of all the songs a listener needs to hear to fully appreciate the scope and impact of each artist's career and contribution to the legacy of recorded music."

"Here, and only here, are the detailed, 'must-have' playlists that comprehensively capture the essence of each artist, each era and each music genre," he adds.

From an eager record-collecting teenager in the 1950s to a world-renowned musicologist in the 21st century, Joel Whitburn's passion for recorded music is stronger than ever in the digital age.

ARTIST SECTION

Following are some basic guidelines for using this section:

ARTIST NAME is in bold, uppercase type. Artists are listed alphabetically.

Song Title is in lowercase type below artist name and is listed alphabetically.

Check Box to the far left is for your discretion. Check off the songs in your collection or check off the songs on your wishlist.

Year of the song's peak popularity appears to the immediate left of the song title.

★ to the right of a title indicates that the title appears in one of the half-decade Classic Songs Playlists in the back of the book.

A

AALIYAH
- '98 Are You That Somebody? ★
- '94 At Your Best (You Are Love)
- '94 Back & Forth ★
- '03 Come Over
- '02 I Care 4 U
- '00 I Don't Wanna
- '96 If Your Girl Only Knew
- '02 Miss You ★
- '02 More Than A Woman
- '97 One I Gave My Heart To, The ★
- '96 One In A Million
- '01 Rock The Boat
- '00 Try Again ★

ABBA
- '79 Chiquitita
- '76 Dancing Queen ★
- '79 Does Your Mother Know
- '76 Fernando
- '80 Gimme! Gimme! Gimme!
- '74 Honey, Honey
- '76 I Do, I Do, I Do, I Do, I Do
- '79 I Have A Dream
- '77 Knowing Me, Knowing You
- '81 Lay All Your Love On Me
- '76 Mamma Mia
- '77 Name Of The Game, The
- '75 SOS
- '78 Take A Chance On Me ★
- '74 Waterloo
- '82 When All Is Said And Done
- '80 Winner Takes It All, The

ABBOTT, Gregory
- '86 Shake You Down ★

ABC
- '85 Be Near Me
- '86 (How To Be A) Millionaire
- '82 Look Of Love, The
- '83 Poison Arrow
- '87 When Smokey Sings

ABDUL, Paula
- '91 Blowing Kisses In The Wind
- '89 Cold Hearted
- '89 Forever Your Girl ★
- '89 (It's Just) The Way That You Love Me
- '88 Knocked Out
- '95 My Love Is For Real
- '89 Opposites Attract ★
- '91 Promise Of A New Day, The ★
- '91 Rush, Rush ★
- '88 Straight Up ★
- '92 Vibeology
- '92 Will You Marry Me?

AC/DC
- '80 Back In Black
- '93 Big Gun
- '76 Dirty Deeds Done Dirt Cheap
- '81 For Those About To Rock (We Salute You)
- '95 Hard As A Rock
- '88 Heatseeker
- '80 Hells Bells
- '79 Highway To Hell
- '78 Jack, The
- '77 Let There Be Rock
- '90 Moneytalks
- '00 Stiff Upper Lip
- '76 T.N.T.
- '90 Thunderstruck
- '77 Whole Lotta Rosie
- '80 You Shook Me All Night Long ★

ACE
- '75 How Long

ACE, Johnny
- '55 Pledging My Love

ACE OF BASE
- '93 All That She Wants ★
- '95 Beautiful Life
- '98 Cruel Summer
- '94 Don't Turn Around
- '94 Living In Danger
- '96 Lucky Love
- '94 Sign, The ★

ACKLIN, Barbara
- '68 Love Makes A Woman

ADAMS, Bryan
- '93 All For Love [w/ Rod Stewart & Sting] ★
- '91 Can't Stop This Thing We Started ★
- '83 Cuts Like A Knife
- '92 Do I Have To Say The Words?
- '91 (Everything I Do) I Do It For You ★
- '95 Have You Ever Really Loved A Woman? ★
- '87 Hearts On Fire
- '87 Heat Of The Night
- '85 Heaven ★
- '96 I Finally Found Someone [w/ Barbra Streisand]
- '97 I'll Always Be Right There
- '85 It's Only Love [w/ Tina Turner]
- '84 Kids Wanna Rock
- '96 Let's Make A Night To Remember
- '82 Lonely Nights
- '85 One Night Love Affair
- '93 Please Forgive Me
- '84 Run To You
- '85 Somebody
- '83 Straight From The Heart
- '85 Summer Of '69 ★
- '91 There Will Never Be Another Tonight
- '83 This Time
- '92 Thought I'd Died And Gone To Heaven
- '87 Victim Of Love

ADAMS, Johnny
- '69 Reconsider Me

ADAMS, Oleta
- '90 Get Here

ADDERLEY, "Cannonball"
- ☐ '61 African Waltz
- ☐ '67 Mercy, Mercy, Mercy

ADDRISI BROTHERS, The
- ☐ '59 Cherrystone
- ☐ '77 Slow Dancin' Don't Turn Me On
- ☐ '72 We've Got To Get It On Again

ADKINS, Trace
- ☐ '96 Every Light In The House
- ▣ '06 Honky Tonk Badonkadonk ★
- ▣ '97 I Left Something Turned On At Home
- ▣ '07 Ladies Love Country Boys
- ☐ '97 (This Ain't) No Thinkin' Thing

AD LIBS, The
- ☐ '65 Boy From New York City, The ★

ADVENTURES OF STEVIE V
- ☐ '90 Dirty Cash (Money Talks)

AEROSMITH
- ▣ '93 Amazing
- ▣ '88 Angel
- ☐ '77 Back In The Saddle
- ☐ '75 Big Ten Inch Record
- ☐ '94 Blind Man
- ☐ '78 Come Together
- ▣ '94 Crazy
- ▣ '93 Cryin'
- ☐ '94 Deuces Are Wild
- ☐ '77 Draw The Line
- ▣ '73 Dream On
- ▣ '87 Dude (Looks Like A Lady)
- ☐ '93 Eat The Rich
- ☐ '97 Falling In Love (Is Hard On The Knees)
- ▣ '98 I Don't Want To Miss A Thing ★
- ☐ '01 Jaded
- ▣ '89 Janie's Got A Gun ★
- ☐ '77 Kings And Queens
- ☐ '76 Last Child
- ▣ '93 Livin' On The Edge
- ☐ '74 Lord Of The Thighs
- ▣ '89 Love In An Elevator
- ☐ '73 Mama Kin
- ☐ '90 Other Side, The
- ☐ '97 Pink
- ▣ '88 Rag Doll
- ☐ '79 Remember (Walking In The Sand)
- ▣ '74 Same Old Song And Dance
- ☐ '74 Seasons Of Wither
- ▣ '75 Sweet Emotion ★
- ☐ '97 Taste Of India
- ☐ '74 Train Kept A Rollin'
- ▣ '76 Walk This Way ★
- ☐ '90 What It Takes

AFI
- ▣ '06 Miss Murder

AFROMAN
- ▣ '01 Because I Got High

AFTER 7
- ☐ '90 Can't Stop
- ☐ '89 Heat Of The Moment
- ☐ '91 Nights Like This
- ☐ '90 Ready Or Not
- ☐ '95 'Til You Do Me Right

AFTER THE FIRE
- ☐ '83 Der Kommissar ★

AGUILERA, Christina
- ☐ '06 Ain't No Other Man ★
- ☐ '02 Beautiful ★
- ☐ '03 Can't Hold Us Down
- ☐ '07 Candyman
- ☐ '99 Christmas Song (Chestnuts Roasting On An Open Fire)
- ▣ '00 Come On Over Baby (all I want is you) ★
- ▣ '03 Fighter
- ▣ '99 Genie In A Bottle ★
- ☐ '06 Hurt
- ☐ '00 I Turn To You
- ☐ '01 Lady Marmalade *[w/ Lil' Kim, Mya & P!nk]* ★
- ▣ '01 Nobody Wants To Be Lonely *[w/ Ricky Martin]*
- ☐ '03 Voice Within, The
- ▣ '99 What A Girl Wants ★

A-HA
- ☐ '85 Sun Always Shines On T.V., The
- ▣ '85 Take On Me ★

AHMAD
- ☐ '94 Back In The Day

AIKEN, Clay
- ☐ '03 Invisible
- ☐ '04 Solitaire
- ▣ '03 This Is The Night ★

AIR SUPPLY
- ▣ '80 All Out Of Love ★
- ▣ '82 Even The Nights Are Better
- ▣ '80 Every Woman In The World
- ▣ '81 Here I Am (Just When I Thought I Was Over You)
- ▣ '85 Just As I Am
- ▣ '80 Lost In Love ★
- ▣ '83 Making Love Out Of Nothing At All
- ▣ '81 One That You Love, The
- ▣ '81 Sweet Dreams
- ▣ '82 Two Less Lonely People In The World
- ▣ '82 Young Love

AKENS, Jewel
- ☐ '65 Birds And The Bees, The ★

AKINS, Rhett
- ▣ '96 Don't Get Me Started
- ▣ '95 That Ain't My Truck

AKON
- ▣ '05 Belly Dancer (Bananza)
- ▣ '07 Don't Matter ★
- ▣ '06 I Wanna Love You ★
- ▣ '04 Locked Up
- ▣ '05 Lonely ★
- ▣ '06 Smack That ★
- ▣ '07 Sorry, Blame It On Me ★

ALABAMA
- ☐ '93 Angels Among Us
- ▨ '92 Born Country
- ▨ '83 Closer You Get, The
- ☐ '97 Dancin', Shaggin' On The Boulevard
- ☐ '83 Dixieland Delight
- ☐ '91 Down Home
- ▨ '81 Feels So Right
- ☐ '90 Forever's As Far As I'll Go
- ☐ '85 Forty Hour Week (For A Livin')
- ▨ '99 God Must Have Spent A Little More Time On You [w/ *NSYNC]
- ☐ '91 Here We Are
- ☐ '89 High Cotton
- ▨ '98 How Do You Fall In Love
- ▨ '92 I'm In A Hurry (And Don't Know Why)
- ▨ '84 If You're Gonna Play In Texas (You Gotta Have A Fiddle In The Band)
- ▨ '90 Jukebox In My Mind
- ▨ '81 Love In The First Degree
- ▨ '82 Mountain Music
- ☐ '80 My Home's In Alabama
- ☐ '90 Pass It On Down
- ☐ '93 Reckless
- ▨ '84 Roll On (Eighteen Wheeler)
- ☐ '97 Sad Lookin' Moon
- ☐ '95 She Ain't Your Ordinary Girl
- ▨ '89 Song Of The South
- ☐ '82 Take Me Down
- ▨ '85 There's No Way

ALARM, The
- ☐ '89 Sold Me Down The River

ALBERT, Morris
- ☐ '75 Feelings

AL B. SURE!
- ▨ '89 If I'm Not Your Lover
- ☐ '90 Misunderstanding
- ☐ '88 Nite And Day
- ☐ '88 Off On Your Own (Girl)
- ▨ '88 Rescue Me
- ☐ '92 Right Now

ALDEAN, Jason
- ▨ '06 Amarillo Sky
- ☐ '05 Hicktown
- ▨ '06 Why

ALEXANDER, Arthur
- ☐ '62 Anna (Go To Him)
- ☐ '75 Every Day I Have To Cry Some
- ☐ '62 You Better Move On

ALI, Tatyana
- ▨ '98 Daydreamin'

ALIAS
- ▨ '90 More Than Words Can Say ★
- ▨ '91 Waiting For Love

ALICE DEEJAY
- ☐ '00 Better Off Alone

ALICE IN CHAINS
- ☐ '96 Again
- ▨ '95 Heaven Beside You
- ☐ '94 I Stay Away
- ▨ '91 Man In The Box
- ☐ '94 No Excuses
- ☐ '93 Rooster
- ☐ '92 Them Bones

ALIEN ANT FARM
- ▨ '01 Smooth Criminal

ALIVE & KICKING
- ☐ '70 Tighter, Tighter

ALL-AMERICAN REJECTS, The
- ▨ '06 Dirty Little Secret ★
- ▨ '07 It Ends Tonight ★
- ▨ '06 Move Along ★

ALLAN, Davie, & The Arrows
- ☐ '67 Blue's Theme

ALLAN, Gary
- ☐ '06 Life Ain't Always Beautiful
- ▨ '02 Man To Man
- ▨ '04 Nothing On But The Radio
- ▨ '02 One, The
- ☐ '03 Tough Little Boys

ALLEN, Deborah
- ☐ '83 Baby I Lied

ALLEN, Donna
- ☐ '89 Joy And Pain
- ☐ '87 Serious

ALLEN, Lee
- ☐ '58 Walkin' With Mr. Lee

ALLEN, Rex
- ☐ '62 Don't Go Near The Indians

ALL-4-ONE
- ▨ '95 I Can Love You Like That
- ▨ '94 I Swear ★
- ▨ '94 So Much In Love ★
- ☐ '96 Someday

ALLISON, Gene
- ☐ '57 You Can Make It If You Try

ALLMAN, Gregg
- ☐ '87 I'm No Angel
- ☐ '73 Midnight Rider

ALLMAN BROTHERS BAND, The
- ☐ '72 Ain't Wastin' Time No More
- ☐ '72 Blue Sky
- ▨ '79 Crazy Love
- ☐ '70 Dreams
- ☐ '91 End Of The Line
- ☐ '90 Good Clean Fun
- ☐ '70 In Memory Of Elizabeth Reed
- ☐ '73 Jessica
- ☐ '72 Little Martha
- ☐ '72 Melissa
- ☐ '70 Midnight Rider
- ☐ '72 One Way Out
- ▨ '73 Ramblin Man ★
- ☐ '70 Revival (Love Is Everywhere)

ALLMAN BROTHERS BAND, The — cont'd
- '71 Statesboro Blues
- '81 Straight From The Heart
- '69 Whipping Post

ALL SAINTS
- '98 I Know Where It's At
- '98 Never Ever ★

ALLURE
- '97 All Cried Out
- '97 Head Over Heels

ALPERT, Herb/The Tijuana Brass
- '67 Banda, A
- '68 Carmen
- '67 Casino Royale
- '87 Diamonds [w/ Janet Jackson]
- '66 Flamingo
- '67 Happening, The
- '87 Keep Your Eye On Me
- '62 Lonely Bull, The
- '87 Making Love In The Rain
- '66 Mame
- '64 Mexican Shuffle, The
- '79 Rise ★
- '79 Rotation
- '82 Route 101
- '66 Spanish Flea
- '65 Taste Of Honey
- '68 This Guy's In Love With You ★
- '65 Tijuana Taxi
- '68 To Wait For Love
- '67 Wade In The Water
- '66 What Now My Love
- '66 Work Song, The
- '65 Zorba The Greek

ALSTON, Gerald
- '90 Slow Motion

ALTER BRIDGE
- '04 Open Your Eyes

ALY & AJ
- '06 Chemicals React
- '07 Potential Breakup Song
- '06 Rush

AMAZING RHYTHM ACES, The
- '76 End Is Not In Sight (The Cowboy Tune), The
- '75 Third Rate Romance

AMBER
- '99 Sexual (Li Da Di)
- '96 This Is Your Night

AMBOY DUKES, The
- '68 Journey To The Center Of The Mind

AMBROSIA
- '80 Biggest Part Of Me
- '75 Holdin' On To Yesterday
- '78 How Much I Feel
- '77 Magical Mystery Tour
- '80 You're The Only Woman (You & I)

AMERICA
- '83 Border, The
- '75 Daisy Jane
- '73 Don't Cross The River
- '72 Horse With No Name, A ★
- '72 I Need You
- '74 Lonely People
- '72 Sandman
- '75 Sister Golden Hair ★
- '74 Tin Man
- '76 Today's The Day
- '72 Ventura Highway
- '82 You Can Do Magic

AMERICAN BREED, The
- '67 Bend Me, Shape Me
- '68 Green Light
- '67 Step Out Of Your Mind

AMERICAN IDOL
- '03 God Bless The U.S.A.
- '05 When You Tell Me That You Love Me

AMERIE
- '05 1 Thing ★
- '02 Why Don't We Fall In Love

AMES, Ed
- '67 My Cup Runneth Over
- '67 Time, Time
- '65 Try To Remember
- '67 When The Snow Is On The Roses
- '67 Who Will Answer?

AMES BROTHERS, The
- '60 China Doll
- '56 Forever Darling
- '56 I Saw Esau
- '56 It Only Hurts For A Little While
- '57 Melodie D'Amour (Melody of Love)
- '55 My Bonnie Lassie
- '54 Naughty Lady Of Shady Lane, The
- '58 Pussy Cat
- '58 Red River Rose
- '57 Tammy
- '58 Very Precious Love, A

AMOS, Tori
- '94 Cornflake Girl
- '94 God
- '92 Me And A Gun
- '92 Silent All These Years
- '98 Spark

ANDERSON, Bill
- '63 8 X 10
- '66 I Get The Fever
- '67 For Loving You [w/ Jan Howard]
- '69 My Life (Throw It Away If I Want To)
- '75 Sometimes [w/ Mary Lou Turner]
- '63 Still

ANDERSON, John
- '93 Money In The Bank
- '92 Seminole Wind
- '83 Swingin'
- '91 Straight Tequila Night

ANDERSON, Laurie
- ☐ '82 O Superman (For Massenet)
- ☐ '84 Sharkey's Day

ANDERSON, Lynn
- ▣ '70 Rose Garden ★

ANDERSON, Sunshine
- ▣ '01 Heard It All Before

ANDREWS, Jessica
- ▣ '01 Who I Am

ANDREWS, Julie
- ☐ '56 I Could Have Danced All Night
- ☐ '65 My Favorite Things
- ☐ '65 Sound Of Music, The
- ☐ '65 Spoonful Of Sugar, A
- ☐ '65 Super-cali-fragil-istic-expi-ali-docious

ANDREWS, Lee, & The Hearts
- ☐ '57 Long Lonely Nights
- ☐ '57 Tear Drops
- ☐ '58 Try The Impossible

ANGEL, Ashley Parker
- ▣ '06 Let U Go

ANGELICA
- ▣ '91 Angel Baby

ANGELS, The
- ▣ '62 Cry Baby Cry
- ▣ '63 I Adore Him
- ▣ '63 My Boyfriend's Back ★
- ☐ '63 Thank You And Goodnight
- ☐ '61 'Til
- ☐ '64 Wow Wow Wee (He's The Boy For Me)

ANGELS & AIRWAVES
- ☐ '06 Adventure, The

ANIMALS, The
- ☐ '64 Boom Boom
- ☐ '65 Bring It On Home To Me
- ☐ '66 Don't Bring Me Down
- ☐ '65 Don't Let Me Be Misunderstood
- ☐ '66 Help Me Girl
- ▣ '64 House Of The Rising Sun, The ★
- ☐ '64 I'm Crying
- ☐ '66 Inside-Looking Out
- ☐ '65 It's My Life
- ☐ '67 Monterey
- ☐ '67 San Franciscan Nights
- ☐ '66 See See Rider
- ☐ '68 Sky Pilot
- ☐ '65 We Gotta Get Out Of This Place
- ☐ '67 When I Was Young

ANIMOTION
- ☐ '85 Let Him Go
- ☐ '85 Obsession
- ☐ '89 Room To Move

ANKA, Paul
- ☐ '60 Adam And Eve
- ☐ '58 (All of a Sudden) My Heart Sings
- ☐ '58 Crazy Love
- ☐ '61 Dance On Little Girl
- ☐ '57 Diana ★
- ☐ '62 Eso Beso (That Kiss!)
- ☐ '69 Goodnight My Love
- ☐ '60 Hello Young Lovers
- ☐ '83 Hold Me 'Til The Mornin' Comes
- ▣ '75 (I Believe) There's Nothing Stronger Than Our Love
- ☐ '75 I Don't Like To Sleep Alone
- ☐ '60 I Love You In The Same Old Way
- ▣ '59 I Miss You So
- ▣ '81 I've Been Waiting For You All Of My Life
- ☐ '59 It's Time To Cry
- ▣ '61 Kissin' On The Phone
- ☐ '58 Let The Bells Keep Ringing
- ▣ '59 Lonely Boy ★
- ☐ '63 Love (Makes the World Go 'Round)
- ▣ '62 Love Me Warm And Tender
- ☐ '60 My Home Town
- ☐ '72 My Way
- ☐ '74 One Man Woman/One Woman Man
- ▣ '60 Puppy Love ★
- ▣ '59 Put Your Head On My Shoulder ★
- ☐ '60 Something Happened
- ☐ '62 Steel Guitar And A Glass Of Wine, A
- ▣ '61 Story Of My Love, The
- ☐ '60 Summer's Gone
- ☐ '78 This Is Love
- ☐ '75 Times Of Your Life
- ☐ '61 Tonight My Love, Tonight
- ☐ '58 You Are My Destiny
- ▣ '74 (You're) Having My Baby ★

ANNETTE
- ☐ '59 First Name Initial
- ☐ '59 Lonely Guitar
- ☐ '60 O Dio Mio
- ▣ '60 Pineapple Princess
- ☐ '59 Tall Paul
- ▣ '60 Train Of Love

ANN-MARGRET
- ☐ '61 I Just Don't Understand

ANOTHER BAD CREATION
- ☐ '91 Iesha
- ☐ '91 Playground

ANT, Adam
- ☐ '82 Goody Two Shoes ★
- ☐ '90 Room At The Top
- ☐ '84 Strip
- ☐ '95 Wonderful

ANTHONY, Marc
- ▣ '99 I Need To Know ★
- ▣ '00 You Sang To Me ★

ANTHONY, Ray
- ☐ '59 Peter Gunn

APOLLO 100
- ☐ '72 Joy

APPLE, Fiona
- ☐ '97 Criminal

13

APPLEJACKS, The
- ☐ '58 Mexican Hat Rock
- ☐ '58 Rocka-Conga

APRIL WINE
- ☐ '82 Enough Is Enough
- ☐ '80 I Like To Rock
- ■ '81 Just Between You And Me
- ☐ '79 Roller
- ☐ '81 Sign Of The Gypsy Queen
- ☐ '72 You Could Have Been A Lady

AQUA
- ☑ '97 Barbie Girl
- ☑ '97 Lollipop (Candyman)

AQUATONES, The
- ☑ '58 You

ARBORS, The
- ☐ '69 Letter, The
- ☐ '66 Symphony For Susan, A

ARCADE FIRE
- ☐ '07 Keep The Car Running
- ☐ '04 Rebellion (Lies)

ARCADIA
- ☐ '85 Election Day
- ☐ '86 Goodbye Is Forever

ARC ANGELS
- ☐ '92 Too Many Ways To Fall

ARCHER, Tasmin
- ☐ '93 Sleeping Satellite

ARCHIES, The
- ■ '68 Bang-Shang-A-Lang
- ☐ '69 Jingle Jangle
- ☑ '69 Sugar, Sugar ★

ARDEN, Jann
- ☐ '96 Insensitive

ARDEN, Toni
- ☐ '58 Padre

ARENA, Tina
- ☐ '96 Chains

ARGENT
- ■ '72 Hold Your Head Up ★

ARMS, Russell
- ☐ '57 Cinco Robles (Five Oaks)

ARMSTRONG, Louis
- ☐ '56 Blueberry Hill
- ■ '64 Hello, Dolly! ★
- ☐ '56 Theme From The Threepenny Opera (Mack The Knife)
- ■ '88 What A Wonderful World

ARMY OF ANYONE
- ☐ '06 Goodbye

ARNOLD, Eddy
- ☐ '55 Cattle Call, The
- ■ '66 I Want To Go With You
- ☐ '66 Last Word In Lonesome Is Me, The
- ☑ '65 Make The World Go Away
- ☐ '66 Somebody Like Me
- ☐ '68 Then You Can Tell Me Goodbye
- ☐ '67 Turn The World Around
- ☐ '65 What's He Doing In My World

ARRESTED DEVELOPMENT
- ☑ '92 Mr. Wendal ★
- ☑ '92 People Everyday
- ☑ '92 Tennessee ★

ARTISTS AGAINST AIDS
- ☐ '01 What's Going On

ARTISTS UNITED AGAINST APARTHEID
- ☐ '85 Sun City

ART OF NOISE, The
- ☐ '88 Kiss
- ☐ '86 Paranoimia
- ☐ '86 Peter Gunn

ASHANTI
- ☑ '02 Baby
- ☑ '02 Foolish ★
- ☑ '02 Happy
- ☑ '04 Only U
- ☑ '03 Rain On Me
- ☑ '03 Rock Wit U (Awww Baby) ★

ASHFORD & SIMPSON
- ☐ '79 Found A Cure
- ■ '89 I'll Be There For You
- ☐ '78 It Seems To Hang On
- ☐ '84 Solid

ASHTON, GARDNER & DYKE
- ☐ '71 Resurrection Shuffle

ASIA
- ☐ '90 Days Like These
- ☐ '83 Don't Cry
- ☑ '82 Heat Of The Moment ★
- ■ '82 Only Time Will Tell
- ☐ '83 Smile Has Left Your Eyes, The

ASSEMBLED MULTITUDE, The
- ☐ '70 Overture From Tommy (A Rock Opera)

ASSOCIATION, The
- ☐ '66 Along Comes Mary
- ■ '66 Cherish ★
- ■ '68 Everything That Touches You
- ■ '67 Never My Love ★
- ☐ '66 Pandora's Golden Heebie Jeebies
- ☐ '68 Time For Livin'
- ■ '67 Windy ★

ASTLEY, Jon
- ☐ '88 Put This Love To The Test

ASTLEY, Rick
- ☐ '91 Cry For Help
- ☐ '89 Giving Up On Love
- ☐ '93 Hopelessly
- ☐ '88 It Would Take A Strong Strong Man

'87 Never Gonna Give You Up ★
'88 She Wants To Dance With Me
'88 Together Forever

ASTRONAUTS, The
'63 Baja

ATARIS, The
'03 Boys Of Summer, The

ATC
'01 Around The World (La La La La La)

ATKINS, Chet
'59 Boo Boo Stick Beat
'65 Yakety Axe

ATKINS, Rodney
'03 Honesty (Write Me A List)
'06 If You're Going Through Hell (Before
The Devil Even Knows) ★
'07 These Are My People
'07 Watching You

ATLANTA RHYTHM SECTION
'81 Alien
'78 Champagne Jam
'79 Do It Or Die
'74 Doraville
'78 I'm Not Gonna Let It Bother Me Tonight
'78 Imaginary Lover
'77 So In To You
'79 Spooky

ATLANTIC STARR
'87 Always ★
'82 Circles
'92 Masterpiece ★
'89 My First Love
'85 Secret Lovers ←

AUDIOSLAVE
'05 Be Yourself
'02 Cochise
'05 Doesn't Remind Me
'03 I Am The Highway
'03 Like A Stone
'06 Original Fire
'03 Show Me How To Live

AUGUSTANA
'06 Boston ★

AUSTIN, Patti
'82 Baby, Come To Me [w/ James Ingram] ★

AUSTIN, Sil
'56 Slow Walk

AUTOGRAPH
'84 Turn Up The Radio

AVALON, Frankie
'59 Bobby Sox To Stockings
'59 Boy Without A Girl, A
'58 DeDe Dinah
'60 Don't Throw Away All Those Teardrops
'58 Ginger Bread
'58 I'll Wait For You

'59 Just Ask Your Heart
'60 Togetherness
'59 Venus ★
'60 Where Are You
'59 Why
'62 You Are Mine

AVANT
'04 Don't Take Your Love Away
'06 4 Minutes
'02 Makin' Good Love
'00 My First Love
'03 Read Your Mind
'00 Separated

AVANT-GARDE, The
'68 Naturally Stoned

AVENGED SEVENFOLD
'06 Bat Country

AWB (AVERAGE WHITE BAND)
'75 Cut The Cake
'75 If I Ever Lose This Heaven
'74 Pick Up The Pieces ★
'76 Queen Of My Soul
'75 School Boy Crush

AZ
'95 Sugar Hill

AZAR, Steve
'01 I Don't Have To Be Me ('Til Monday)

AZ YET
'97 Hard To Say I'm Sorry
'96 Last Night

B

BABY BASH
'05 Baby I'm Back
'07 Cyclone ★
'03 Suga Suga

BABY / BIRDMAN
'02 Do That...
'06 Stuntin' Like My Daddy [w/ Lil Wayne]
'03 What Happened To That Boy

BABY BOY DA PRINCE
'07 Way I Live, The

BABYFACE
'94 And Our Feelings
'97 Every Time I Close My Eyes
'92 Give U My Heart [w/ Toni Braxton]
'89 It's No Crime
'90 My Kinda Girl
'93 Never Keeping Secrets
'89 Tender Lover
'01 There She Goes
'96 This Is For The Lover In You ★
'94 When Can I See You
'90 Whip Appeal

BABYS, The
- '80 Back On My Feet Again
- '79 Every Time I Think Of You
- '77 Isn't It Time

BACHELORS, The
- '65 Chapel In The Moonlight
- '64 Diane
- '64 I Believe
- '66 Love Me With All Of Your Heart
- '65 Marie
- '64 No Arms Can Ever Hold You

BACHMAN, Tal
- '99 She's So High

BACHMAN-TURNER OVERDRIVE
- '73 Blue Collar
- '75 Hey You
- '74 Let It Ride
- '75 Roll On Down The Highway
- '76 Take It Like A Man
- '74 Takin' Care Of Business
- '74 You Ain't Seen Nothing Yet ★

BACKSTREET BOYS
- '99 All I Have To Give
- '97 As Long As You Love Me ★
- '01 Drowning
- '98 Everybody (Backstreet's Back) ★
- '99 I Want It That Way ★
- '98 I'll Never Break Your Heart ★
- '05 Incomplete
- '99 Larger Than Life
- '01 More Than That
- '00 One, The
- '97 Quit Playing Games (With My Heart) ★
- '00 Shape Of My Heart
- '00 Show Me The Meaning Of Being Lonely ★

BACKUS, Jim
- '58 Delicious!

BAD COMPANY
- '74 Bad Company
- '77 Burnin' Sky
- '74 Can't Get Enough
- '82 Electricland
- '75 Feel Like Makin' Love
- '75 Good Lovin' Gone Bad
- '90 Holy Water
- '92 How About That
- '90 If You Needed Somebody
- '75 Movin' On
- '88 No Smoke Without A Fire
- '74 Ready For Love
- '79 Rock 'N' Roll Fantasy
- '76 Run With The Pack
- '75 Shooting Star
- '76 Silver, Blue & Gold
- '91 Walk Through Fire
- '76 Young Blood

BAD ENGLISH
- '89 Forget Me Not

- '90 Possession
- '89 Price Of Love
- '89 When I See You Smile ★

BADFINGER
- '72 Baby Blue
- '70 Come And Get It
- '71 Day After Day ★
- '70 No Matter What

BADU, Erykah
- '00 Bag Lady
- '02 Love of My Life (An Ode To Hip Hop)
- '97 Next Lifetime
- '97 On&On
- '97 Tyrone

BAEZ, Joan
- '75 Diamonds And Rust
- '71 Night They Drove Old Dixie Down ★
- '63 We Shall Overcome

BAHA MEN
- '00 Who Let The Dogs Out ★

BAILEY, Philip
- '84 Easy Lover [w/ Phil Collins]

BAILEY RAE, Corinne
- '06 Put Your Records On

BAINBRIDGE, Merril
- '96 Mouth ★

BAIRD, Dan
- '93 I Love You Period

BAKER, Anita
- '94 Body & Soul
- '86 Caught Up In The Rapture
- '88 Giving You The Best That I Got ─
- '89 Just Because
- '86 Sweet Love
- '90 Talk To Me

BAKER, George, Selection
- '70 Little Green Bag
- '75 Paloma Blanca

BAKER, LaVern
- '55 Bop-Ting-A-Ling
- '60 Bumble Bee
- '56 I Can't Love You Enough
- '58 I Cried A Tear
- '59 I Waited Too Long
- '56 Jim Dandy ★
- '57 Jim Dandy Got Married
- '55 Play It Fair
- '61 Saved
- '62 See See Rider
- '55 Tweedlee Dee

BALANCE
- '81 Breaking Away

BALIN, Marty
- '81 Atlanta Lady (Something About Your Love)
- '81 Hearts

BALL, David
- ☐ '01 Riding With Private Malone
- ☐ '94 Thinkin' Problem

BALL, Kenny, & His Jazzmen
- 🔳 '62 Midnight In Moscow ★

BALLARD, Hank, & The Midnighters
- ☐ '61 Continental Walk, The
- 🔳 '60 Finger Poppin' Time
- 🔳 '60 Hoochi Coochi Coo, The
- ☐ '61 Let's Go Again
- 🔳 '60 Let's Go, Let's Go, Let's Go
- 🔳 '61 Switch-A-Roo, The
- 🔳 '60 Twist, The

BALLOON FARM, The
- ☐ '68 Question Of Temperature, A

BALTIMORA
- ☐ '85 Tarzan Boy

BAMBAATAA, Afrika
- 🔳 '82 Planet Rock ★

BANANARAMA
- ☐ '84 Cruel Summer
- 🔳 '88 I Can't Help It
- ☐ '87 I Heard A Rumour
- 🔳 '88 Love In The First Degree
- ☐ '84 Robert DeNiro's Waiting
- 🔳 '86 Venus ★

BAND, The
- ☐ '73 Ain't Got No Home
- ☐ '68 Chest Fever
- ☐ '72 Don't Do It
- ☐ '71 Life Is A Carnival
- ☐ '68 I Shall Be Released
- 🔳 '69 Night They Drove Old Dixie Down, The
- ☐ '76 Ophelia
- ☐ '69 Rag Mama Rag
- ☐ '70 Shape I'm In
- ☐ '68 This Wheel's On Fire
- ☐ '70 Time To Kill
- ☐ '69 Up On Cripple Creek
- 🔳 '68 Weight, The ★

BAND AID
- ☐ '84 Do They Know It's Christmas?

B ANGIE B
- 🔳 '91 I Don't Want To Lose Your Love
- 🔳 '91 So Much Love

BANGLES
- 🔳 '89 Be With You
- 🔳 '89 Eternal Flame ★
- ☐ '87 Hazy Shade Of Winter ★
- ☐ '86 If She Knew What She Wants
- ☐ '88 In Your Room
- 🔳 '86 Manic Monday ★
- 🔳 '86 Walk Like An Egyptian ★
- ☐ '87 Walking Down Your Street

BANKS, Darrell
- ☐ '66 Open The Door To Your Heart

BANKS, Lloyd
- ☐ '05 Karma
- ☐ '04 On Fire

BANNER, David
- 🔳 '05 Play

BARBARIANS, The
- ☐ '65 Are You A Boy Or Are You A Girl
- ☐ '66 Moulty

BARBER('S), Chris, Jazz Band
- ☐ '59 Petite Fleur (Little Flower)

BARBOUR, Keith
- ☐ '69 Echo Park

BARCLAY, Eddie
- ☐ '55 Bandit, The

BARDEUX
- 🔳 '88 When We Kiss

BARE, Bobby
- 🔳 '58 All American Boy, The *[BILL PARSONS]* ★
- ☐ '74 Daddy What If
- ☐ '63 Detroit City
- ☐ '63 500 Miles Away From Home
- ☐ '74 Marie Laveau
- ☐ '64 Miller's Cave
- ☐ '62 Shame On Me

BARENAKED LADIES
- 🔳 '99 It's All Been Done
- 🔳 '98 One Week ★
- 🔳 '00 Pinch Me

BAR-KAYS
- ☐ '84 Freakshow On The Dance Floor
- ☐ '79 Move Your Boogie Body
- 🔳 '76 Shake Your Rump To The Funk
- ☐ '67 Soul Finger

BARNES, Jimmy
- 🔳 '87 Good Times *[w/ INXS]*
- 🔳 '88 Too Much Ain't Enough Love

BARNUM, H.B.
- 🔳 '61 Lost Love

BARRETTO, Ray
- 🔳 '63 El Watusi

BARRY, Joe
- ☐ '61 I'm A Fool To Care

BARRY, Len
- 🔳 '66 Like A Baby
- 🔳 '65 1-2-3
- ☐ '66 Somewhere

BARRY & THE TAMERLANES
- 🔳 '63 I Wonder What She's Doing Tonight

BARTLEY, Chris
- 🔳 '67 Sweetest Thing This Side Of Heaven

BASIA
- ☐ '90 Cruising For Bruising
- ☐ '88 Time And Tide

BASIE, Count
- ☐ '56 April In Paris
- ☐ '55 Every Day (I Have The Blues)

BASIL, Toni
- ▨ '82 Mickey ★

BASS, Fontella
- ☐ '65 Don't Mess Up A Good Thing [w/ Bobby McClure]
- ☐ '65 Recovery
- ☐ '65 Rescue Me

BASSEY, Shirley
- ☐ '65 Goldfinger

BAXTER, Les
- ☐ '56 Poor People Of Paris, The ★
- ☐ '55 Unchained Melody
- ☐ '55 Wake The Town And Tell The People

BAY CITY ROLLERS
- ▨ '76 I Only Want To Be With You
- ☐ '76 Money Honey
- ▤ '76 Rock And Roll Love Letter
- ▨ '75 Saturday Night ★
- ▨ '77 Way I Feel Tonight, The
- ☐ '77 You Made Me Believe In Magic

BAZUKA
- ▨ '75 Dynomite

BBMAK
- ☐ '00 Back Here

B. BUMBLE & THE STINGERS
- ▨ '61 Bumble Boogie
- ☐ '62 Nut Rocker

BEACH BOYS, The
- ☐ '66 Barbara Ann ★
- ☐ '63 Be True To Your School
- ☐ '81 Beach Boys Medley, The
- ▨ '65 California Girls ★
- ☐ '66 Caroline, No [BRIAN WILSON]
- ☐ '81 Come Go With Me
- ▨ '64 Dance, Dance, Dance
- ▨ '67 Darlin'
- ☐ '68 Do It Again
- ☐ '65 Do You Wanna Dance?
- ☐ '64 Don't Worry Baby
- ☐ '62 409
- ☐ '68 Friends
- ▨ '64 Fun, Fun, Fun ★
- ☐ '85 Getcha Back
- ▨ '66 God Only Knows ★
- ☐ '79 Good Timin'
- ▨ '66 Good Vibrations ★
- ☐ '65 Help Me, Rhonda ★
- ☐ '67 Heroes And Villains
- ☐ '69 I Can Hear Music
- ▨ '64 I Get Around ★
- ▨ '63 In My Room ★
- ☐ '76 It's O.K.
- ▨ '88 Kokomo ★
- ☐ '63 Little Deuce Coupe
- ☐ '65 Little Girl I Once Knew, The

- ☐ '64 Little Honda
- ☐ '63 Little Saint Nick
- ☐ '76 Rock And Roll Music
- ☐ '73 Sail On Sailor
- ☐ '63 Shut Down
- ☐ '66 Sloop John B ★
- ☐ '63 Surfer Girl
- ☐ '62 Surfin' Safari
- ▨ '63 Surfin' U.S.A. ★
- ☐ '63 Ten Little Indians
- ☐ '64 Wendy
- ☐ '64 When I Grow Up (To Be A Man)
- ▨ '67 Wild Honey
- ▨ '66 Wouldn't It Be Nice

BEASTIE BOYS
- ▨ '04 Ch-Check It Out
- ▨ '89 Hey Ladies
- ☐ '98 Intergalactic
- ☐ '94 Sabotage
- ▨ '86 (You Gotta) Fight For Your Right (To Party!) ★

BEATLES, The
- ☐ '70 Across The Universe
- ☐ '65 Act Naturally
- ☐ '64 Ain't She Sweet
- ☐ '64 All My Loving
- ▨ '67 All You Need Is Love ★
- ▨ '64 And I Love Her
- ☐ '67 Baby You're A Rich Man
- ☐ '68 Back In The U.S.S.R.
- ☐ '69 Ballad Of John And Yoko, The
- ☐ '82 Beatles' Movie Medley, The
- ☐ '68 Birthday
- ☐ '68 Blackbird
- ▨ '64 Can't Buy Me Love ★
- ▨ '69 Come Together ★
- ☐ '67 Day In The Life, A
- ☐ '65 Day Tripper
- ☐ '68 Dear Prudence
- ☐ '64 Do You Want To Know A Secret ★
- ☐ '69 Don't Let Me Down
- ☐ '66 Drive My Car
- ▨ '65 Eight Days A Week ★
- ☐ '66 Eleanor Rigby ★
- ☐ '67 Fool On The Hill
- ☐ '95 Free As A Bird
- ☐ '64 From Me To You
- ▨ '69 Get Back ★
- ☐ '68 Glass Onion
- ☐ '69 Golden Slumbers/Carry That Weight/The End/Her Majesty
- ☐ '66 Good Day Sunshine
- ☐ '76 Got To Get You Into My Life
- ▨ '64 Hard Day's Night, A ★
- ☐ '67 Hello Goodbye ★
- ▨ '65 Help! ★
- ☐ '68 Helter Skelter
- ☐ '69 Here Comes The Sun
- ▨ '68 Hey Jude ★
- ☐ '67 I Am The Walrus
- ☐ '65 I Don't Want To Spoil The Party
- ▨ '64 I Feel Fine ★
- ☐ '64 I Saw Her Standing There ★

- ☐ '64 I Should Have Known Better
- ■ '64 I Want To Hold Your Hand ★
- ☐ '64 I'll Be Back
- ☐ '64 I'll Cry Instead
- ☐ '65 I'm A Loser
- ☐ '64 If I Fell
- ☐ '65 In My Life ★
- ☐ '68 Lady Madonna ★
- ■ '70 Let It Be ★
- ☐ '70 Long And Winding Road, The ★
- ■ '64 Love Me Do ★
- ☐ '67 Lovely Rita
- ■ '67 Lucy In The Sky With Diamonds
- ☐ '67 Magical Mystery Tour
- ☐ '64 Matchbox
- ■ '69 Maxwell's Silver Hammer
- ☐ '65 Michelle
- ☐ '64 My Bonnie (My Bonnie Lies Over The Ocean)
- ☐ '65 No Reply
- ☐ '65 Norwegian Wood (This Bird Has Flown)
- ☐ '66 Nowhere Man ★
- ☐ '68 Ob-La Di, Ob-La-Da
- ☐ '69 Octopus's Garden
- ☐ '69 Oh! Darling
- ☐ '69 Old Brown Shoe
- ■ '64 P.S. I Love You
- ■ '66 Paperback Writer ★
- ☐ '67 Penny Lane ★
- ☐ '64 Please Please Me ★
- ☐ '66 Rain
- ■ '96 Real Love
- ☐ '68 Revolution
- ☐ '64 Rock And Roll Music
- ■ '68 Rocky Raccoon
- ☐ '64 Roll Over Beethoven
- ☐ '67 Sgt. Pepper's Lonely Hearts Club Band
- ☐ '69 She Came In Through The Bathroom Window
- ■ '64 She Loves You ★
- ☐ '64 She's A Woman
- ☐ '67 She's Leaving Home
- ☐ '64 Slow Down
- ☐ '69 Something ★
- ■ '67 Strawberry Fields Forever ★
- ☐ '66 Taxman
- ☐ '64 Thank You Girl
- ■ '65 Ticket To Ride ★
- ☐ '64 Twist And Shout ★
- ■ '65 We Can Work It Out ★
- ☐ '67 When I'm Sixty-Four
- ☐ '68 While My Guitar Gently Weeps
- ☐ '67 With A Little Help From My Friends
- ■ '66 Yellow Submarine ★
- ■ '65 Yesterday ★
- ☐ '64 You Can't Do That
- ☐ '65 You're Going To Lose That Girl
- ☐ '65 You've Got To Hide Your Love Away

BEATTY, E.C.
- ☐ '59 Ski King

BEAU BRUMMELS, The
- ☐ '65 Just A Little
- ☐ '65 Laugh, Laugh

- ☐ '65 You Tell Me Why

BECK
- ☐ '05 E-Pro
- ☐ '97 Jack-Ass
- ■ '93 Loser ★
- ☐ '96 Where It's At

BECK, Jeff
- ☐ '68 Beck's Bolero
- ☐ '85 People Get Ready *[w/ Rod Stewart]*
- ☐ '80 Pump, The
- ☐ '68 Shapes Of Things
- ☐ '89 Where Were You

BECKHAM, Bob
- ■ '60 Crazy Arms
- ☐ '59 Just As Much As Ever

BEDINGFIELD, Daniel
- ■ '02 Gotta Get Thru This
- ■ '03 If You're Not The One

BEDINGFIELD, Natasha
- ■ '05 These Words
- ■ '06 Unwritten ★

BEE GEES
- ☐ '72 Alive
- ☐ '97 Alone
- ☐ '77 Boogie Child
- ☐ '69 Don't Forget To Remember
- ☐ '77 Edge Of The Universe
- ☐ '75 Fanny (Be Tender With My Love)
- ☐ '69 First Of May
- ☐ '81 He's A Liar
- ☐ '67 Holiday
- ■ '71 How Can You Mend A Broken Heart ★
- ☐ '77 How Deep Is Your Love ★
- ☐ '68 I Started A Joke
- ☐ '68 I've Gotta Get A Message To You
- ■ '77 If I Can't Have You
- ☐ '75 Jive Talkin' ★
- ☐ '67 (Lights Went Out In) Massachusetts
- ☐ '70 Lonely Days ★
- ■ '76 Love So Right
- ■ '79 Love You Inside Out
- ■ '78 More Than A Woman
- ☐ '72 My World
- ☐ '67 New York Mining Disaster 1941 (Have You Seen My Wife, Mr. Jones)
- ■ '78 Night Fever ★
- ☐ '75 Nights On Broadway
- ☐ '89 One
- ■ '72 Run To Me
- ■ '77 Stayin' Alive ★
- ■ '67 To Love Somebody
- ■ '78 Too Much Heaven ★
- ☐ '79 Tragedy ★
- ■ '83 Woman In You, The
- ☐ '68 Words
- ☐ '67 World
- ■ '76 You Should Be Dancing ★

BEENIE MAN
- ☐ '04 Dude
- ☐ '02 Feel It Boy
- ☐ '98 Who Am I "Sim Simma"

BEGA, Lou
- ☑ '99 Mambo No. 5 (A Little Bit Of...) ★

BEGINNING OF THE END, The
- ☐ '71 Funky Nassau

BELAFONTE, Harry
- ☐ '57 Banana Boat (Day-O)
- ☐ '57 Cocoanut Woman
- ☐ '57 Don't Ever Love Me
- ☐ '57 Island In The Sun
- ☐ '56 Jamaica Farewell
- ☐ '57 Mama Look At Bubu
- ☐ '56 Mary's Boy Child

BELEW, Adrian
- ☐ '89 Oh Daddy
- ☑ '90 Pretty Pink Rose [w/ David Bowie]

BELL, Archie, & The Drells
- ☐ '68 I Can't Stop Dancing
- ☐ '68 There's Gonna Be A Showdown
- ☑ '68 Tighten Up ★

BELL, Benny
- ☐ '75 Shaving Cream

BELL, Madeline
- ☑ '68 I'm Gonna Make You Love Me

BELL, Vincent
- ☐ '70 Airport Love Theme (Gwen And Vern)

BELL, William
- ☐ '77 Tryin' To Love Two

BELLAMY BROTHERS
- ☑ '79 If I Said You Have A Beautiful Body Would You Hold It Against Me
- ☑ '76 Let Your Love Flow ★
- ☐ '85 Old Hippie
- ☐ '82 Redneck Girl

BELL & JAMES
- ☑ '79 Livin' It Up (Friday Night)

BELL BIV DeVOE
- ☐ '90 B.B.D. (I Thought It Was Me)?
- ☑ '90 Do Me!
- ☐ '92 Gangsta
- ☑ '90 Poison ★
- ☐ '93 Something In Your Eyes
- ☑ '90 When Will I See You Smile Again?
- ☐ '91 Word To The Mutha!

BELLE, Regina
- ☐ '89 All I Want Is Forever [w/ James "J.T. Taylor]
- ☐ '89 Baby Come To Me
- ☐ '89 Make It Like It Was
- ☐ '87 Show Me The Way
- ☐ '90 What Goes Around

- ☑ '92 Whole New World (Aladdin's Theme) [w/ Peabo Bryson] ★

BELLE STARS, The
- ☐ '89 Iko Iko

BELL NOTES, The
- ☐ '59 I've Had It

BELLS, The
- ☐ '71 Stay Awhile

BELLUS, Tony
- ☐ '59 Robbin' The Cradle

BELLY
- ☐ '93 Feed The Tree

BELMONTS, The
- ☑ '62 Come On Little Angel
- ☑ '61 Tell Me Why

BELVIN, Jesse
- ☐ '56 Goodnight My Love
- ☐ '59 Guess Who

BENATAR, Pat
- ☐ '88 All Fired Up
- ☐ '93 Everybody Lay Down
- ☐ '81 Fire And Ice
- ☐ '79 Heartbreaker
- ☐ '80 Hell Is For Children
- ☑ '80 Hit Me With Your Best Shot ★
- ☑ '79 I Need A Lover
- ☐ '85 Invincible
- ☐ '83 Little Too Late
- ☐ '83 Looking For A Stranger
- ☑ '83 Love Is A Battlefield
- ☑ '85 Ooh Ooh Song
- ☐ '81 Promises In The Dark
- ☐ '85 Sex As A Weapon
- ☐ '82 Shadows Of The Night
- ☑ '81 Treat Me Right
- ☑ '84 We Belong ★
- ☑ '80 We Live For Love
- ☐ '80 You Better Run

BENÉT, Eric
- ☑ '99 Spend My Life With You

BENNETT, Boyd, & His Rockets
- ☐ '55 My Boy-Flat Top
- ☐ '55 Seventeen

BENNETT, Joe, & The Sparkletones
- ☐ '57 Black Slacks

BENNETT, Tony
- ☐ '56 Autumn Waltz, The
- ☑ '60 Best Is Yet To Come, The
- ☐ '57 Ca, C'est L'amour
- ☐ '56 Can You Find It In Your Heart
- ☐ '60 Climb Ev'ry Mountain
- ☐ '58 Firefly
- ☑ '65 Fly Me To The Moon
- ☐ '67 For Once In My Life
- ☐ '56 From The Candy Store On The Corner To The Chapel On The Hill

□ '63 Good Life, The
□ '56 Happiness Street (Corner Sunshine Square)
□ '86 How Do You Keep The Music Playing
□ '62 I Left My Heart In San Francisco ★
☑ '63 I Wanna Be Around
☒ '65 If I Ruled The World
□ '57 In The Middle OF An Island
□ '56 Just In Time
□ '68 My Favorite Things
☑ '57 One For My Baby
☑ '65 Shadow Of Your Smile, The
☑ '59 Smile
□ '93 Steppin' Out With My Baby
□ '68 They Can't Take That Away From Me
□ '63 This Is All I Ask
☑ '66 Time For Love, A
☑ '66 Very Thought Of You, The
□ '64 Who Can I Turn To (When Nobody Needs Me)
□ '68 Yesterday I Heard The Rain
☑ '58 Young And Warm And Wonderful

BENSON, George
□ '80 Give Me The Night
☑ '77 Greatest Love Of All, The
☑ '83 Inside Love (So Personal)
☑ '83 Lady Love Me (One More Time)
☑ '79 Love Ballad
□ '78 On Broadway
□ '76 This Masquerade
☑ '81 Turn Your Love Around ⎯

BENTLEY, Dierks
☑ '05 Come A Little Closer
☑ '06 Every Mile A Memory
☑ '05 Lot Of Leavin' Left To Do
☑ '06 Settle For A Slowdown
☑ '03 What Was I Thinkin'

BENTON, Brook
□ '60 Baby (You've Got What It Takes)
     [w/ Dinah Washington] ★
□ '61 Boll Weevil Song, The
□ '59 Endlessly
□ '60 Fools Rush In (Where Angels Fear To Tread)
□ '61 For My Baby
□ '61 Frankie And Johnny
□ '64 Going Going Gone
□ '62 Hit Record
□ '60 Hither And Thither And Yon
□ '62 Hotel Happiness
□ '63 I Got What I Wanted
□ '59 It's Just A Matter Of Time ★
□ '60 Kiddio
□ '62 Lie To Me
□ '63 My True Confession
□ '70 Rainy Night In Georgia ★
□ '61 Revenge
□ '60 Rockin' Good Way (To Mess Around And Fall In Love) [w/ Dinah Washington]
□ '60 Same One, The

□ '62 Shadrack
□ '59 So Close
□ '59 So Many Ways
□ '59 Thank You Pretty Baby
□ '61 Think Twice
□ '60 Ties That Bind, The
□ '63 Two Tickets To Paradise
□ '62 Walk On The Wild Side

BERLIN
□ '83 Metro, The
☑ '84 No More Words
☑ '86 Take My Breath Away ★

BERMUDAS, The
□ '64 Donnie

BERNARD, Rod
□ '59 This Should Go On Forever

BERRY, Chuck
□ '59 Almost Grown
☑ '59 Back In The U.S.A.
□ '56 Brown Eyed Handsome Man
□ '58 Carol
☑ '58 Johnny B. Goode ★
☑ '55 Maybellene ★
□ '59 Memphis
□ '72 My Ding-A-Ling ★
□ '64 Nadine (Is It You?)
☑ '64 No Particular Place To Go
□ '58 Reelin' & Rockin'
□ '72 Reelin' & Rockin' [live]
□ '57 Rock & Roll Music ★
☑ '56 Roll Over Beethoven ★
☑ '57 School Day ★
☑ '58 Sweet Little Sixteen ★
□ '55 Thirty Days
□ '56 Too Much Monkey Business
□ '64 You Never Can Tell

BERRY, John
□ '96 She's Taken A Shine
□ '95 Standing On The Edge Of Goodbye
☑ '94 Your Love Amazes Me

BERTRAND, Plastic
□ '78 Ca Plane Pour Moi

BETTER THAN EZRA
□ '97 Desperately Wanting
□ '95 Good
□ '95 In The Blood

BEYONCÉ
☑ '03 Baby Boy ★
□ '07 Beautiful Liar ★ [w/ Shakira]
☑ '06 Check On It ★
☑ '03 Crazy In Love ★
☑ '06 Deja Vu
☑ '07 Get Me Bodied
☑ '06 Irreplaceable ★
☑ '03 Me, Myself And I
☑ '04 Naughty Girl ★
☑ '06 Ring The Alarm ★

B-52's, The
- ☐ '89 Channel Z
- ☐ '79 Dance This Mess Around
- ☐ '90 Deadbeat Club
- ☐ '92 Good Stuff
- ☐ '83 Legal Tender
- ☑ '89 Love Shack ★
- ☐ '80 Private Idaho
- ☐ '89 Roam
- ☐ '79 Rock Lobster
- ☐ '85 Summer Of Love

B.G.
- ☑ '99 Bling Bling

BICE, Bo
- ☑ '05 Inside Your Heaven

BIG & RICH
- ☑ '07 Lost In This Moment
- ☑ '04 Save A Horse (Ride A Cowboy)

BIG AUDIO DYNAMITE
- ☐ '91 Globe, The
- ☐ '89 James Brown
- ☐ '88 Just Play Music!
- ☐ '91 Rush

BIG BOPPER
- ☐ '58 Big Bopper's Wedding
- ☑ '58 Chantilly Lace ★

BIG BROTHER & THE HOLDING COMPANY
— see JOPLIN, Janis

BIG COUNTRY
- ☐ '83 In A Big Country

BIG MOUNTAIN
- ☑ '94 Baby, I Love Your Way ★
- ☐ '96 Get Together

BIG PUNISHER
- ☑ '97 I'm Not A Player
- ☑ '98 Still Not A Player

BIG STAR
- ☐ '74 September Gurls
- ☐ '72 Thirteen

BIG TYMERS
- ☑ '02 Still Fly

BILK, Mr. Acker
- ☐ '62 Stranger On The Shore ★

BILLY & LILLIE
- ☐ '58 La Dee Dah ★
- ☐ '58 Lucky Ladybug

BILLY JOE & THE CHECKMATES
- ☐ '62 Percolator (Twist)

BIMBO JET
- ☐ '75 El Bimbo

BINGOBOYS
- ☐ '91 How To Dance

BIRDMAN — see BABY

BISHOP, Elvin
- ☑ '76 Fooled Around And Fell In Love ★

BISHOP, Stephen
- ☐ '78 Everybody Needs Love
- ☐ '83 It Might Be You
- ☐ '77 On And On
- ☐ '76 Save It For A Rainy Day

BIZ MARKIE
- ☑ '90 Just A Friend ★

BJÖRK
- ☐ '94 Big Time Sensuality
- ☐ '93 Human Behaviour

BLACK('S), Bill, Combo
- ☐ '60 Blue Tango
- ☐ '60 Don't Be Cruel
- ☐ '61 Hearts Of Stone
- ☐ '60 Josephine
- ☐ '61 Ole Buttermilk Sky
- ☐ '59 Smokie
- ☐ '62 Twist-Her
- ☐ '60 White Silver Sands

BLACK, Cilla
- ☑ '64 You're My World

BLACK, Clint
- ☐ '93 Bad Goodbye, A *[w/ Wynonna]*
- ☐ '00 Been There
- ☑ '89 Better Man, A
- ☐ '94 Good Run Of Bad Luck, A
- ☐ '89 Killin' Time
- ☐ '96 Like The Rain
- ☐ '91 Loving Blind
- ☐ '90 Nobody's Home
- ☑ '97 Nothin' But The Taillights
- ☐ '95 One Emotion
- ☐ '98 Shoes You're Wearing, The
- ☐ '97 Something That We Do
- ☐ '93 State Of Mind
- ☐ '95 Summer's Comin'
- ☐ '90 Walkin' Away
- ☐ '92 We Tell Ourselves
- ☑ '99 When I Said I Do *[w/ Lisa Hartman Black]*
- ☐ '93 When My Ship Comes In
- ☑ '91 Where Are You Now

BLACK, Jeanne
- ☐ '60 He'll Have To Stay

BLACK BOX
- ☐ '90 Everybody Everybody
- ☐ '90 I Don't Know Anybody Else
- ☐ '91 Strike It Up

BLACKBYRDS, The   *Rock cReek pAAK*
- ☐ '76 Happy Music
- ☐ '75 Walking In Rhythm

BLACK CROWES, The
- ☐ '90 Hard To Handle
- ☐ '92 Hotel Illness
- ☐ '98 Kicking My Heart Around
- ☐ '92 Remedy

□ '91 Seeing Things
□ '91 She Talks To Angels
□ '92 Sting Me
□ '92 Thorn In My Pride

BLACK EYED PEAS
■ '05 Don't Lie
■ '05 Don't Phunk With My Heart ★
■ '04 Hey Mama
■ '04 Let's Get It Started
■ '05 My Humps ★
■ '06 Pump It ★
■ '03 Where Is The Love? ★

BLACKFLAG
□ '82 TV Party

BLACKFOOT
□ '79 Highway Song
□ '79 Train, Train

BLACKHAWK
□ '94 Every Once In A While
□ '95 I'm Not Strong Enough To Say No
□ '95 Like There Ain't No Yesterday
□ '99 There You Have It

BLACK OAK ARKANSAS
□ '73 Jim Dandy

BLACKOUT ALLSTARS, The
□ '96 I Like It

BLACK ROB
■ '01 Bad Boy For Life [w/ P. Diddy & Mark Curry]

BLACK SABBATH
■ '70 Black Sabbath
□ '71 Children Of The Grave
■ '71 Iron Man
□ '70 N.I.B.
□ '71 Paranoid
□ '98 Psycho Man
□ '71 War Pigs

BLACKstreet
□ '94 Before I Let You Go
■ '94 Booti Call
□ '97 Don't Leave Me
■ '96 No Diggity ★
■ '98 Take Me There [w/ Mya]

BLANCHARD, Jack, & Misty Morgan
□ '70 Tennessee Bird Walk

BLAND, Billy
□ '60 Let The Little Girl Dance

BLAND, Bobby
□ '64 Ain't Nothing You Can Do
■ '63 Call On Me
□ '61 Don't Cry No More
□ '57 Farther Up The Road
□ '61 I Pity The Fool
□ '74 I Wouldn't Treat A Dog (The Way You Treated Me)
■ '59 I'll Take Care Of You
■ '63 That's The Way Love Is

□ '74 This Time I'm Gone For Good
□ '61 Turn On Your Love Light

BLANE, Marcie
■ '62 Bobby's Girl ★

BLAQUE
■ '00 Bring It All To Me [w/ *NSYNC] ★
■ '99 808

BLENDERS, The
□ '63 Daughter

BLESSID UNION OF SOULS
■ '99 Hey Leonardo (She Likes Me For Me)
■ '95 I Believe ★
■ '97 I Wanna Be There
■ '95 Let Me Be The One

BLEU, Corbin
■ '07 Push It To The Limit

BLIGE, Mary J.
□ '94 Be Happy
■ '06 Be Without You ★
□ '06 Enough Cryin
□ '97 Everything
□ '01 Family Affair ★
■ '97 I Can Love You
□ '95 I'm Goin' Down
□ '03 Love @ 1st Sight
□ '01 No More Drama
□ '96 Not Gon' Cry ★
□ '04 Not Today
■ '03 Ooh!
□ '02 Rainy Dayz
■ '92 Real Love
□ '97 Seven Days
□ '93 Sweet Thing
□ '06 Take Me As I Am
■ '92 You Remind Me

BLIND FAITH
□ '69 Can't Find My Way Home
□ '69 Presence Of The Lord
□ '69 Sea Of Joy

BLIND MELON
□ '93 No Rain

BLINK-182
□ '00 Adam's Song
■ '99 All The Small Things ★
■ '03 Feeling This
■ '04 I Miss You
□ '00 Man Overboard
□ '01 Rock Show, The
■ '99 What's My Age Again?

BLONDIE
□ '80 Atomic
■ '80 Call Me ★
■ '79 Dreaming
■ '79 Heart Of Glass ★
□ '82 Island Of Lost Souls
□ '99 Maria
■ '79 One Way Or Another

BLONDIE — cont'd
- '81 Rapture ★
- '80 Tide Is High, The ★

BLOODROCK
- '71 D.O.A.

BLOODSTONE
- '73 Natural High
- '74 Outside Woman

BLOOD, SWEAT & TEARS
- '69 And When I Die
- '71 Go Down Gamblin'
- '69 God Bless The Child
- '70 Hi-De-Ho
- '70 Lucretia Mac Evil
- '69 Spinning Wheel ★
- '69 You've Made Me So Very Happy ★

BLOOM, Bobby
- '70 Montego Bay

BLOW, Kurtis
- '80 Breaks, The

BLOW MONKEYS, The
- '86 Digging Your Scene

BLUE CHEER
- '68 Summertime Blues

BLUE HAZE
- '72 Smoke Gets In Your Eyes

BLUE JAYS, The
- '61 Lover's Island

BLUE MAGIC
- '74 Sideshow
- '74 Three Ring Circus

BLUE OCTOBER
- '06 Hate Me
- '07 Into The Ocean

BLUE ÖYSTER CULT
- '81 Burnin' For You
- '76 (Don't Fear) The Reaper ★
- '77 Godzilla
- '79 In Thee

BLUES BROTHERS
- '80 Gimme Some Lovin'
- '79 Hey Bartender
- '79 Rubber Biscuit
- '78 Soul Man
- '80 Who's Making Love

BLUES IMAGE
- '70 Ride Captain Ride ★

BLUES MAGOOS
- '66 (We Ain't Got) Nothin' Yet

BLUE STARS
- '55 Lullaby Of Birdland

BLUES TRAVELER
- '96 But Anyway

BLUES TRAVELER
- '95 Hook
- '95 Run-Around ★

BLUE SWEDE
- '74 Hooked On A Feeling ★
- '74 Never My Love

BLUNT, James
- '06 You're Beautiful ★

BLUR
- '94 Girls & Boys
- '97 Song 2

BMU (BLACK MEN UNITED)
- '94 U Will Know

BOB & EARL
- '63 Harlem Shuffle

BOBBETTES, The
- '57 Mr. Lee ★

BOB B. SOXX & THE BLUE JEANS
- '63 Why Do Lovers Break Each Other's Heart?
- '62 Zip-A-Dee Doo-Dah

BoDEANS
- '96 Closer To Free
- '86 Fadeaway
- '91 Good Things

BOGGUSS, Suzy
- '92 Drive South

BOLTON, Michael
- '94 Ain't Got Nothing If You Aint' Got Love
- '95 Can I Touch You...There?
- '94 Completely
- '90 Georgia On My Mind
- '97 Go The Distance
- '89 How Am I Supposed To Live Without You ★
- '90 How Can We Be Lovers
- '91 Love Is A Wonderful Thing
- '92 Missing You Now
- '93 Said I Loved You...But I Lied
- '88 (Sittin' On) The Dock Of The Bay
- '89 Soul Provider
- '92 Steel Bars
- '87 That's What Love Is All About
- '91 Time, Love And Tenderness
- '92 To Love Somebody
- '91 When A Man Loves A Woman
- '90 When I'm Back On My Feet Again

BOND, Johnny
- '60 Hot Rod Lincoln

BONDS, Gary (U.S.)
- '61 Dear Lady Twist
- '60 New Orleans
- '82 Out Of Work
- '61 Quarter To Three ★
- '61 School Is In
- '61 School Is Out
- '62 Seven Day Weekend

□ '81 This Little Girl
□ '62 Twist, Twist Senora

BONE CRUSHER
■ '03 Never Scared

BONE THUGS-N-HARMONY
■ '96 Crossroads, Tha ★
□ '96 Days Of Our Livez
□ '95 1st Of Tha Month
□ '98 Ghetto Cowboy *[w/ Mo Thugs Family]*
■ '07 I Tried
□ '97 If I Could Teach The World
■ '97 Look Into My Eyes ★
□ '94 Thuggish-Ruggish-Bone

BONEY M
□ '78 Mary's Boy Child/Oh My Lord
□ '78 Rivers Of Babylon

BONHAM, Tracy
□ '96 Mother Mother

BON JOVI
■ '94 Always ★
■ '88 Bad Medicine ★
■ '93 Bed Of Roses
□ '90 Blaze Of Glory ★
□ '88 Born To Be My Baby
□ '87 Edge Of A Broken Heart
□ '89 I'll Be There For You ★
■ '93 In These Arms
■ '00 It's My Life
□ '92 Keep The Faith
□ '89 Lay Your Hands On Me
■ '86 Livin' On A Prayer ★
□ '89 Living In Sin
□ '90 Miracle
□ '87 Never Say Goodbye
□ '84 Runaway
□ '95 This Ain't A Love Song
■ '87 Wanted Dead Or Alive
■ '06 Who Says You Can't Go Home
□ '06 Who Says You Can't Go Home
   [w/ Jennifer Nettles]
■ '86 You Give Love A Bad Name ★
□ '07 (You Want To) Make A Memory

BONNIE LOU
□ '55 Daddy-O

BONNIE SISTERS
□ '56 Cry Baby

BONOFF, Karla
□ '82 Personally

BOOKER, Chuckii
□ '92 Games
□ '89 Turned Away

BOOKER, James
□ '60 Gonzo

BOOKER T. & THE MG'S
□ '62 Green Onions ★
□ '67 Groovin'
□ '68 Hang 'Em High

□ '67 Hip Hug-Her
□ '71 Melting Pot
□ '69 Mrs. Robinson
□ '68 Soul-Limbo
□ '69 Time Is Tight

BOOMTOWN RATS, The
□ '80 I Don't Like Mondays
□ '81 Up All Night

BOONE, Daniel
□ '72 Beautiful Sunday

BOONE, Debby
■ '77 You Light Up My Life ★

BOONE, Pat
□ '55 Ain't That A Shame
□ '57 Anastasia
□ '57 April Love ★
□ '55 At My Front Door (Crazy Little Mama)
□ '64 Beach Girl
□ '57 Bernardine
□ '61 Big Cold Wind
□ '56 Chains Of Love
□ '56 Don't Forbid Me
□ '48 Exodus Song, The (This Land Is Mine)
□ '59 Fools Hall Of Fame
□ '59 For A Penny
□ '58 For My Good Fortune
□ '56 Friendly Persuasion (Thee I Love)
□ '58 Gee, But It's Lonely
□ '55 Gee Whittakers!
□ '56 I Almost Lost My Mind ★
□ '56 I'll Be Home
□ '58 I'll Remember Tonight
■ '57 I'm Waiting Just For You
□ '58 If Dreams Came True
□ '58 It's Too Soon To Know
□ '61 Johnny Will
□ '56 Long Tall Sally
■ '57 Love Letters In The Sand ★
□ '61 Moody River ★
□ '57 Remember You're Mine
□ '62 Speedy Gonzales
□ '58 Sugar Moon
□ '57 There's A Gold Mine In The Sky
□ '56 Tutti' Frutti
□ '59 Twixt Twelve And Twenty
■ '55 Two Hearts
□ '60 (Welcome) New Lovers
□ '57 Why Baby Why
□ '59 With The Wind And The Rain In Your Hair
□ '58 Wonderful Time Up There, A

BOSTON
■ '86 Amanda ★
□ '87 Can'tcha Say (You Believe In Me)/Still In Love
□ '78 Don't Look Back
□ '78 Feelin' Satisfied
□ '76 Hitch A Ride
■ '76 Let Me Take You Home Tonight
□ '77 Long Time
□ '78 Man I'll Never Be, A

BOSTON — cont'd
- ■ '76 More Than A Feeling ★
- ☐ '77 Peace Of Mind
- ☐ '76 Rock & Roll Band
- ☐ '76 Smokin'
- ■ '76 Something About You
- ☐ '86 We're Ready

BOURGEOIS TAGG
- ■ '90 Dare To Fall In Love [BRENT BOURGEOIS]
- ☐ '87 I Don't Mind At All

BOWEN, Jimmy
- ■ '57 I'm Stickin' With You

BOWIE, David
- ☐ '80 Ashes To Ashes
- ☐ '84 Blue Jean
- ☐ '72 Changes
- ☐ '83 China Girl
- ■ '85 Dancing In The Street [w/ Mick Jagger]
- ☐ '87 Day-In Day-Out
- ☐ '74 Diamond Dogs
- ■ '75 Fame ★
- ☐ '80 Fashion
- ☐ '75 Golden Years
- ■ '77 Heroes ★
- ☐ '73 Jean Genie
- ■ '83 Let's Dance ★
- ☐ '83 Modern Love
- ☐ '87 Never Let Me Down
- ☐ '90 Pretty Pink Rose [w/ Adrian Belew]
- ☐ '74 Rebel Rebel
- ☐ '73 Space Oddity
- ☐ '72 Starman
- ☐ '72 Suffragette City
- ☐ '85 This Is Not America [w/ Pat Metheny Group]
- ☐ '76 TVC 15
- ■ '81 Under Pressure [w/ Queen] ★
- ☐ '75 Young Americans
- ☐ '72 Ziggy Stardust

BOWLING FOR SOUP
- ☐ '05 Almost
- ☐ '04 1985

BOW WOW
- ☐ '00 Bounce With Me [LIL BOW WOW]
- ☐ '00 Bow Wow (That's My Name) [LIL BOW WOW]
- ☐ '06 Fresh Azimiz
- ☐ '07 I'm A Flirt
- ■ '05 Let Me Hold You ★
- ☐ '03 Let's Get Down
- ■ '05 Like You ★
- ☐ '07 Outta My System
- ■ '06 Shortie Like Mine ★

BOW WOW WOW
- ■ '82 I Want Candy ★

BOX TOPS, The
- ☐ '68 Choo Choo Train
- ☐ '68 Cry Like A Baby ★
- ☐ '68 I Met Her In Church
- ■ '67 Letter, The ★
- ☐ '67 Neon Rainbow

- ■ '69 Soul Deep
- ☐ '68 Sweet Cream Ladies, Forward March

BOYCE, Tommy, & Bobby Hart
- ☐ '68 Alice Long (You're Still My Favorite Girlfriend)
- ■ '67 I Wonder What She's Doing Tonite

BOY GEORGE — see CULTURE CLUB

BOY KRAZY
- ■ '93 That's What Love Can Do

BOY MEETS GIRL
- ■ '88 Waiting For A Star To Fall

BOYS, The
- ■ '90 Crazy
- ■ '88 Dial My Heart
- ■ '89 Lucky Charm

BOYS CLUB
- ■ '88 I Remember Holding You

BOYS DON'T CRY
- ☐ '86 I Wanna Be A Cowboy

BOYS LIKE GIRLS
- ■ '07 Great Escape, The

BOYZ II MEN
- ■ '92 End Of The Road ★
- ☐ '97 4 Seasons Of Loneliness ★
- ☐ '99 I Will Get There
- ■ '94 I'll Make Love To You ★
- ☐ '92 In The Still Of The Nite (I'll Remember)
- ■ '91 It's So Hard To Say Goodbye To Yesterday ★
- ☐ '93 Let It Snow
- ☐ '91 Motownphilly
- ■ '94 On Bended Knee ★
- ■ '95 One Sweet Day [w/ Mariah Carey] ★
- ☐ '97 Song For Mama, A
- ☐ '95 Thank You
- ■ '92 Uhh Ahh
- ■ '95 Water Runs Dry

BRADLEY, Jan
- ☐ '63 Mama Didn't Lie

BRADLEY, Owen, Quintet
- ☐ '58 Big Guitar
- ☐ '57 White Silver Sands

BRAM TCHAIKOVSKY
- ☐ '79 Girl Of My Dreams

BRANCH, Michelle
- ■ '02 All You Wanted ★
- ☐ '03 Are You Happy Now?
- ■ '03 Breathe
- ☐ '01 Everywhere
- ☐ '02 Game Of Love, The [w/ Santana] ★
- ☐ '02 Goodbye To You
- ■ '06 I'm Feeling You [w/ Santana]

BRAND NEW HEAVIES, The
- ☐ '91 Never Stop

BRANDT, Paul
☐ '96 I Do

BRANDY
☐ '99 Almost Doesn't Count
☐ '95 Baby ★
☐ '95 Best Friend
☐ '98 Boy Is Mine, The *[w/ Monica]* ★
☐ '95 Brokenhearted
☐ '02 Full Moon
☐ '98 Have You Ever? ★
☐ '94 I Wanna Be Down ★
☐ '96 Missing You *[w/ Tamia, Gladys Knight & Chaka Khan]*
☐ '95 Sittin' Up In My Room ★
☐ '04 Talk About Our Love
☐ '02 What About Us?

BRANIGAN, Laura
☐ '82 Gloria ★
☐ '83 How Am I Supposed To Live Without You
☐ '84 Lucky One, The
☐ '87 Power Of Love
☐ '84 Self Control
☐ '83 Solitaire
☐ '85 Spanish Eddie

BRASS CONSTRUCTION
☐ '76 Movin'

BRASS RING, The
☐ '67 Dis-Advantages Of You, The
☐ '66 Phoenix Love Theme (Senza Fine)

BRAT PACK, The
☐ '90 You're The Only Woman

BRAUN, Bob
☐ '62 Till Death Do Us Part

BRAVE COMBO
☐ '93 Cielito Lindo
☐ '87 Happy Wanderer

BRAXTON, Toni
☐ '93 Another Sad Love Song
☐ '93 Breathe Again ★
☐ '92 Give U My Heart *[w/ Babyface]*
☐ '00 He Wasn't Man Enough ★
☐ '94 How Many Ways
☐ '94 I Belong To You
☐ '97 I Don't Want To
☐ '00 Just Be A Man About It
☐ '92 Love Shoulda Brought You Home
☐ '93 Seven Whole Days
☐ '96 Un-Break My Heart ★
☐ '94 You Mean The World To Me
☐ '96 You're Makin' Me High ★

BREAD
☐ '73 Aubrey
☐ '71 Baby I'm - A Want You
☐ '72 Diary
☐ '72 Everything I Own
☐ '72 Guitar Man, The
☐ '77 Hooked On You

☐ '71 If
☐ '70 It Don't Matter To Me
☐ '71 Let Your Love Go
☐ '76 Lost Without Your Love
☐ '70 Make It With You ★
☐ '71 Mother Freedom
☐ '72 Sweet Surrender

BREAKFAST CLUB
☐ '87 Right On Track

BREAKING BENJAMIN
☐ '07 Breath
☐ '06 Diary Of Jane, The
☐ '04 So Cold
☐ '05 Sooner Or Later

BREATHE
☐ '89 Don't Tell Me Lies
☐ '88 Hands To Heaven ★
☐ '88 How Can I Fall?
☐ '90 Say A Prayer

BREEDERS, The
☐ '93 Cannonball

BREMERS, Beverly
☐ '71 Don't Say You Don't Remember

BRENDA & THE TABULATIONS
☐ '67 Dry Your Eyes
☐ '71 Right On The Tip Of My Tongue

BRENNAN, Walter
☐ '60 Dutchman's Gold
☐ '62 Old Rivers

BREWER, Teresa
☐ '60 Anymore
☐ '55 Banjo's Back In Town, The
☐ '56 Bo Weevil
☐ '57 Empty Arms
☐ '58 Hula Hoop Song, The
☐ '55 Let Me Go, Lover!
☐ '56 Mutual Admiration Society
☐ '55 Pledging My Love
☐ '55 Silver Dollar
☐ '56 Sweet Old Fashioned Girl, A
☐ '56 Tear Fell, A
☐ '57 You Send Me

BREWER & SHIPLEY
☐ '71 One Toke Over The Line

BRICK
☐ '76 Dazz
☐ '77 Dusic

BRICKELL, Edie
☐ '88 What I Am

BRICKMAN, Jim
☐ '05 Beautiful *[w/ Wayne Brady]*
☐ '97 Gift, The
☐ '01 Simple Things

BRIDGES, Alicia
☐ '78 I Love The Nightlife (Disco 'Round)

BRIGGS, Lillian
- ☐ '55 I Want You To Be My Baby

BRIGHTER SIDE OF DARKNESS
- ☐ '72 Love Jones

BRILEY, Martin
- ☐ '83 Salt In My Tears, The

BRISTOL, Johnny
- ☐ '74 Hang On In There Baby

BROCK, Chad
- ☐ '99 Ordinary Life
- ☐ '00 Yes!

B-ROCK & THE BIZZ
- ☐ '97 MyBabyDaddy

BRONSKI BEAT
- ☐ '86 Hit That Perfect Beat
- ☐ '85 Smalltown Boy

BROOKLYN BRIDGE
- ☐ '69 Blessed Is The Rain
- ☐ '69 Welcome Me Love
- ☐ '68 Worst That Could Happen

BROOKLYN DREAMS — see SUMMER, Donna

BROOKS, Donnie
- ☐ '60 Doll House
- ☐ '60 Mission Bell

BROOKS, Garth
- ☐ '93 Ain't Going Down (Til The Sun Comes Up)
- ☐ '93 American Honky-Tonk Bar Association
- ☐ '95 Beaches Of Cheyenne, The
- ☐ '94 Callin' Baton Rouge
- ☐ '90 Dance, The
- ☐ '90 Friends In Low Places ★
- ☐ '05 Good Ride Cowboy
- ☐ '94 Hard Luck Woman
- ☐ '89 If Tomorrow Never Comes
- ☐ '97 In Another's Eyes *[w/ Trisha Yearwood]*
- ☐ '96 It's Midnight Cinderella
- ☐ '93 Learning To Live Again
- ☐ '97 Longneck Bottle
- ☐ '99 Lost In You *[GARTH BROOKS AS CHRIS GAINES]*
- ☐ '07 More Than A Memory
- ☐ '89 Much Too Young (To Feel This Damn Old)
- ☐ '90 Not Counting You
- ☐ '92 Papa Loved Mama
- ☐ '92 River, The
- ☐ '91 Rodeo
- ☐ '91 Shameless
- ☐ '95 She's Every Woman
- ☐ '97 She's Gonna Make It
- ☐ '92 Somewhere Other Than The Night
- ☐ '93 Standing Outside The Fire
- ☐ '93 That Summer
- ☐ '91 Thunder Rolls, The
- ☐ '98 To Make You Feel My Love

- ☐ '91 Two Of A Kind, Workin' On A Full House
- ☐ '97 Two Piña Coladas
- ☐ '90 Unanswered Prayers
- ☐ '92 What She's Doing Now
- ☐ '01 Wild Horses
- ☐ '02 Wrapped Up In You
- ☐ '98 You Move Me

BROOKS, Louis, & His Hi-Toppers
- ☐ '55 It's Love Baby (24 Hours a Day)

BROOKS, Meredith
- ☐ '97 Bitch ★

BROOKS & DUNN
- ☐ '01 Ain't Nothing 'Bout You
- ☐ '92 Boot Scootin' Boogie ★
- ☐ '91 Brand New Man
- ☐ '06 Building Bridges
- ☐ '97 He's Got You
- ☐ '97 Honky Tonk Truth
- ☐ '98 How Long Gone
- ☐ '98 Husbands And Wives
- ☐ '96 I Am That Man
- ☐ '98 If You See Him/If You See Her *[w/ Reba McEntire]*
- ☐ '05 It's Getting Better All The Time
- ☐ '95 Little Miss Honky Tonk
- ☐ '01 Long Goodbye, The
- ☐ '96 Man This Lonely, A
- ☐ '96 My Maria
- ☐ '91 My Next Broken Heart
- ☐ '92 Neon Moon
- ☐ '01 Only In America
- ☐ '05 Play Something Country
- ☐ '07 Proud Of The House We Built
- ☐ '03 Red Dirt Road
- ☐ '93 Rock My World (Little Country Girl)
- ☐ '93 She Used To Be Mine
- ☐ '94 She's Not The Cheatin' Kind
- ☐ '94 That Ain't No Way To Go
- ☐ '04 That's What It's All About
- ☐ '93 We'll Burn That Bridge
- ☐ '03 You Can't Take The Honky Tonk Out Of The Girl
- ☐ '95 You're Gonna Miss Me When I'm Gone

BROTHER CANE
- ☐ '95 And Fools Shine On
- ☐ '93 Got No Shame
- ☐ '98 I Lie In The Bed I Make

BROTHERHOOD OF MAN, The
- ☐ '76 Save Your Kisses For Me
- ☐ '70 United We Stand

BROTHERS FOUR, The
- ☐ '61 Frogg
- ☐ '60 Greenfields ★
- ☐ '60 My Tani
- ☐ '65 Try To Remember

BROTHERS JOHNSON, The
- ☐ '76 Get The Funk Out Ma Face
- ☐ '76 I'll Be Good To You
- ☐ '80 Stomp!

□ '77 Strawberry Letter 23

BROWN, Al
□ '60 Madison, The

BROWN, Arthur
□ '68 Fire

BROWN, Bobby
□ '88 Don't Be Cruel
□ '89 Every Little Step
□ '93 Get Away
□ '86 Girlfriend
▣ '92 Good Enough
□ '92 Humpin' Around
▣ '88 My Prerogative ★
▣ '89 On Our Own ★
□ '89 Rock Wit'cha ➝
□ '89 Roni ➝
□ '93 Something In Common [w/ Whitney Houston]

BROWN, Buster
□ '60 Fannie Mae

BROWN, Charles
□ '60 Please Come Home For Christmas

BROWN, Chris
▣ '06 Gimme That
▣ '07 Poppin'
▣ '05 Run It! ★
□ '06 Say Goodbye ★
▣ '06 Yo (Excuse Me Miss) ★

BROWN, Chuck, & The Soul Searchers
□ '79 Bustin' Loose

BROWN, Foxy
□ '97 Get Me Home
□ '97 I'll Be

BROWN, James
□ '69 Ain't It Funky Now
□ '61 Baby, You're Right
□ '61 Bewildered
□ '67 Bring It Up
□ '70 Brother Rapp
□ '67 Cold Sweat
□ '71 Escape-ism
□ '72 Get On The Good Foot
□ '71 Get Up, Get Into It, Get Involved
□ '70 Get Up (I Feel Like Being Like A) Sex Machine
□ '69 Give It Up Or Turnit A Loose
□ '71 Hot Pants (She Got To Use What She Got To Get What She Wants)
▣ '67 I Can't Stand Myself (When You Touch Me)
□ '69 I Don't Want Nobody To Give Me Nothing (Open Up The Door, I'll Get It Myself)
□ '72 I Got A Bag Of My Own
□ '73 I Got Ants In My Pants
□ '68 I Got The Feelin'
▣ '65 I Got You (I Feel Good) ★
□ '88 I'm Real

▣ '66 It's A Man's Man's Man's World
▣ '70 It's A New Day
□ '72 King Heroin
□ '69 Let A Man Come In And Do The Popcorn
□ '68 Licking Stick - Licking Stick
□ '85 Living In America
□ '61 Lost Someone
□ '71 Make It Funky
□ '69 Mother Popcorn (You Got To Have A Mother For Me)
□ '74 My Thang
□ '62 Night Train
□ '64 Oh Baby Don't You Weep
□ '64 Out Of Sight
□ '74 Papa Don't Take No Mess
▣ '65 Papa's Got A Brand New Bag ★
□ '74 Payback, The
▣ '56 Please, Please, Please ★
□ '69 Popcorn, The
□ '63 Prisoner Of Love
□ '68 Say It Loud - I'm Black And I'm Proud
□ '71 Soul Power
▣ '70 Super Bad
□ '72 Talking Loud And Saying Nothing
□ '68 There Was A Time
□ '60 Think
□ '58 Try Me

BROWN, Jocelyn
□ '84 Somebody Else's Guy

BROWN, Maxine
□ '60 All In My Mind
□ '61 Funny
□ '64 Oh No Not My Baby

BROWN, Nappy
□ '55 Don't Be Angry
□ '57 Little By Little

BROWN, Peter
□ '78 Dance With Me [w/ Betty Wright]
□ '77 Do Ya Wanna Get Funky With Me

BROWN, Polly
□ '75 Up In A Puff Of Smoke

BROWN, Roy
□ '57 Let The Four Winds Blow

BROWN, Ruth
□ '55 I Want To Do More
□ '57 Lucky Lips
□ '58 This Little Girl's Gone Rockin'

BROWN, Shirley
□ '74 Woman To Woman

BROWN, Sleepy
□ '04 I Can't Wait

BROWNE, Jackson
□ '80 Boulevard
▣ '72 Doctor My Eyes
□ '83 For A Rocker
□ '86 For America
□ '74 Fountain Of Sorrow

BROWNE, Jackson — cont'd
- ☐ '77 Here Come Those Tears Again
- ☐ '80 Hold On Hold Out
- ☐ '86 In The Shape Of A Heart
- ☐ '74 Late For The Sky
- ☐ '83 Lawyers In Love
- ☐ '78 Load-Out/Stay
- ☐ '76 Pretender, The
- ☐ '72 Redneck Friend
- ☐ '72 Rock Me On The Water
- ☐ '78 Running On Empty
- ☐ '82 Somebody's Baby
- ☐ '83 Tender Is The Night
- ☐ '80 That Girl Could Sing
- ☐ '73 These Days
- ☐ '78 You Love The Thunder
- ☐ '85 You're A Friend Of Mine *[w/ Clarence Clemons]*

BROWNE, Tom
- ☐ '80 Funkin' For Jamaica (N.Y.)

BROWNS, The
- ☐ '60 Old Lamplighter, The
- ☐ '59 Scarlet Ribbons (For Her Hair)
- ☐ '59 Three Bells, The ★

BROWNSTONE
- ☐ '97 5 Miles To Empty
- ☐ '94 If You Love Me

BROWNSVILLE STATION
- ☐ '74 Kings Of The Party
- ☒ '73 Smokin' In The Boy's Room

BRUBECK, Dave, Quartet
- ☐ '61 Take Five

BRYANT, Anita
- ☐ '60 In My Little Corner Of The World
- ☐ '60 Paper Roses
- ☐ '59 Till There Was You
- ☐ '60 Wonderland By Night

BRYANT, Ray, Combo
- ☐ '60 Madison Time

BRYNNER, Yul, & Deborah Kerr
- ☐ '56 Shall We Dance

BRYSON, Peabo
- ☒ '92 Beauty And The Beast *[w/ Celion Dion]* ★
- ☐ '93 By The Time This Night Is Over *[w/ Kenny G]*
- ☐ '91 Can You Stop The Rain
- ☒ '78 I'm So Into You
- ☒ '84 If Ever You're In My Arms Again
- ☐ '89 Show & Tell
- ☒ '83 Tonight, I Celebrate My Love *[w/ Roberta Flack]*
- ☒ '92 Whole New World (Aladdin's Theme) *[w/ Regina Belle]* ★

B.T. EXPRESS
- ☒ '74 Do It ('Til You're Satisfied) ★
- ☐ '75 Express
- ☐ '75 Give It What You Got
- ☐ '75 Peace Pipe

B2K
- ☒ '02 Bump, Bump, Bump *[w/ P. Diddy]* ★
- ☒ '03 Girlfriend
- ☐ '02 Gots Ta Be
- ☒ '02 Uh Huh

BUBBLE PUPPY, The
- ☐ '69 Hot Smoke & Sasafrass

BUBLÉ, Michael
- ☒ '07 Everything
- ☒ '05 Home ★
- ☒ '06 Save The Last Dance For Me

BUCHANAN & GOODMAN — see GOODMAN, Dickie

BUCHANAN BROTHERS
- ☐ '69 Medicine Man

BUCKCHERRY
- ☒ '06 Crazy Bitch
- ☐ '99 Lit Up

BUCKINGHAM, Lindsey
- ☐ '84 Go Insane
- ☐ '83 Holiday Road
- ☐ '81 Trouble

BUCKINGHAMS, The
- ☐ '67 Don't You Care
- ☐ '67 Hey Baby (They're Playing Our Song)
- ☐ '66 Kind Of A Drag ★
- ☐ '67 Mercy, Mercy, Mercy
- ☐ '67 Susan

BUCKLEY, Jeff
- ☐ '94 Hallelujah

BUCKNER & GARCIA
- ☐ '82 Pac-Man Fever

BUDDEN, Joe
- ☒ '03 Pump It Up

BUFFALO SPRINGFIELD, The
- ☐ '67 Bluebird
- ☐ '67 For What It's Worth ★
- ☐ '67 Mr. Soul
- ☐ '67 Rock 'N' Roll Woman

BUFFETT, Jimmy
- ☐ '79 Boat Drinks
- ☐ '76 Captain And The Kid, The
- ☐ '77 Changes In Latitudes, Changes In Attitudes
- ☐ '78 Cheeseburger In Paradise
- ☐ '74 Come Monday
- ☐ '79 Fins
- ☐ '78 Grapefruit/Juicy Fruit
- ☐ '76 Havana Daydreamin'
- ☒ '03 It's Five O'Clock Somewhere *[w/ Alan Jackson]*
- ☐ '85 Jolly Mon Sing
- ☐ '78 Mañana
- ☒ '77 Margaritaville ★
- ☐ '83 One Particular Harbor
- ☐ '74 Pencil Thin Mustache

- ☐ '75 Pirate Looks At Forty, A
- ☐ '78 Son Of A Son Of A Sailor
- ☐ '80 Volcano
- ☐ '78 Why Don't We Get Drunk

BUGGLES, The
- ☐ '79 Video Killed The Radio Star

BULLET
- ☐ '71 White Lies, Blue Eyes

BUOYS, The
- ☐ '71 Timothy

BURDON, Eric, & War
- ☐ '70 Spill The Wine ★

BURKE, Solomon
- ☐ '62 Cry To Me
- ☐ '64 Everybody Needs Somebody To Love
- ☐ '64 Goodbye Baby (Baby Goodbye)
- ☐ '65 Got To Get You Off My Mind
- ☐ '63 If You Need Me
- ☐ '61 Just Out Of Reach (Of My Two Open Arms)
- ☐ '65 Tonight's The Night
- ☐ '63 You're Good For Me

BURNETTE, Dorsey
- ☐ '60 (There Was A) Tall Oak Tree

BURNETTE, Johnny
- ☐ '60 Dreamin'
- ☐ '61 God, Country And My Baby
- ☐ '61 Little Boy Sad
- ☐ '57 Rockbilly Boogie [ROCK & ROLL TRIO]
- ☐ '59 Settin' The Woods On Fire
- ☐ '56 Train Kept A-Rollin', The [ROCK & ROLL TRIO]
- ☐ '60 You're Sixteen ★

BURNETTE, Rocky
- ☐ '80 Tired Of Toein' The Line

BUSCH, Lou
- ☐ '56 11th Hour Melody

BUSH
- ☐ '99 Chemicals Between Us, The
- ☐ '95 Comedown
- ☐ '94 Everything Zen
- ☐ '95 Glycerine ★
- ☐ '96 Greedy Fly
- ☐ '96 Machinehead
- ☐ '96 Swallowed

BUSH, Kate
- ☐ '85 Cloudbusting
- ☐ '87 Don't Give Up [w/ Peter Gabriel]
- ☐ '85 Hounds Of Love
- ☐ '89 Love And Anger
- ☐ '79 Man With The Child In His Eyes, The
- ☐ '85 Running Up That Hill
- ☐ '78 Wuthering Heights

BUSTA RHYMES
- ☐ '01 Break Ya Neck
- ☐ '98 Dangerous

- ☐ '03 I Know What You Want [w/ Mariah Carey] ★
- ☐ '02 Pass The Courvoisier
- ☐ '97 Put Your Hands Where My Eyes Could See
- ☐ '06 Touch It ★
- ☐ '98 Turn It Up [Remix]/Fire It Up
- ☐ '99 What's It Gonna Be?! ★
- ☐ '96 Woo-Hah!! Got You All In Check

BUSTERS, The
- ☐ '63 Bust Out

BUTLER, Jerry
- ☐ '71 Ain't Understanding Mellow [w/ Brenda Lee Eager]
- ☐ '68 Are You Happy
- ☐ '61 Find Another Girl
- ☐ '58 For Your Precious Love [w/ The Impressions]
- ☐ '60 He Will Break Your Heart
- ☐ '68 Hey, Western Union Man
- ☐ '64 I Stand Accused
- ☐ '61 I'm A Telling You
- ☐ '64 Let It Be Me [w/ Betty Everett]
- ☐ '62 Make It Easy On Yourself
- ☐ '69 Moody Woman
- ☐ '61 Moon River
- ☐ '67 Mr. Dream Merchant
- ☐ '63 Need To Belong
- ☐ '68 Never Give You Up
- ☐ '69 Only The Strong Survive
- ☐ '69 What's The Use Of Breaking Up

BUTLER, Jonathan
- ☐ '87 Lies

BUTTHOLE SURFERS
- ☐ '96 Pepper

BUZZCOCKS, The
- ☐ '78 Ever Fallen In Love
- ☐ '78 What Do I Get?

B*WITCHED
- ☐ '99 C'est La Vie

BYRD, Tracy
- ☐ '96 Big Love
- ☐ '93 Holdin' Heaven
- ☐ '98 I'm From The Country
- ☐ '95 Keeper Of The Stars, The
- ☐ '02 Ten Rounds With José Cuervo

BYRDS, The
- ☐ '65 All I Really Want To Do
- ☐ '70 Chestnut Mare
- ☐ '65 Chimes Of Freedom
- ☐ '66 Eight Miles High ★
- ☐ '65 He Was A Friend Of Mine
- ☐ '68 Hickory Wind
- ☐ '65 I'll Feel A Whole Lot Better
- ☐ '66 Mr. Spaceman
- ☐ '65 Mr. Tambourine Man ★
- ☐ '67 My Back Pages
- ☐ '67 So You Want To Be A Rock 'N' Roll Star

BYRDS, The — cont'd
- ▣ '65 Turn! Turn! Turn! (To Everything There Is A Season) ★

BYRNES, Edward
- ▨ '59 Kookie, Kookie (Lend Me Your Comb) *[w/ Connie Stevens]*

C

CABRERA, Ryan
- ☐ '04 On The Way Down
- ☐ '04 True

CADETS, The
- ☐ '56 Stranded In The Jungle

CADILLACS, The
- ▣ '58 Peek-A-Boo
- ☐ '55 Speedoo

CAESAR, Shirley
- ☐ '75 No Charge

CAFFERTY, John
- ☐ '85 C-I-T-Y
- ☐ '84 On The Dark Side
- ☐ '84 Tender Years
- ☐ '85 Tough All Over

CAGLE, Chris
- ▣ '02 I Breathe In, I Breathe Out
- ▣ '03 What A Beautiful Day

CAILLAT, Colbie
- ▣ '07 Bubbly ★

CAIOLA, Al, & His Orchestra
- ☐ '61 Bonanza
- ☐ '60 Magnificent Seven, The

CAKE
- ☐ '96 Distance, The
- ☐ '98 Never There

CALDWELL, Bobby
- ☐ '78 What You Won't Do For Love ▬

CALE, J.J.
- ▣ '72 After Midnight
- ☐ '72 Crazy Mama

CALL, The
- ☐ '89 Let The Day Begin

CALLING, The
- ▣ '01 Wherever You Will Go ★

CALLOWAY
- ☐ '90 I Wanna Be Rich ★

CAMEO
- ▣ '85 Attack Me With Your Love
- ☐ '87 Back And Forth
- ☐ '86 Candy
- ☐ '81 Freaky Dancin'
- ☐ '79 I Just Want To Be
- ☐ '84 She's Strange
- ☐ '85 Single Life
- ▣ '86 Word Up ★

CAMOUFLAGE
- ☐ '88 Great Commandment, The

CAMPBELL, Glen
- ▣ '70 All I Have To Do Is Dream *[w/ Bobbie Gentry]*
- ☐ '67 By The Time I Get To Phoenix
- ☐ '75 Country Boy (You Got Your Feet In L.A.)
- ☐ '71 Dream Baby (How Long Must I Dream)
- ☐ '68 Dreams Of The Everyday Housewife
- ☐ '70 Everything A Man Could Ever Need
- ☐ '69 Galveston
- ☐ '67 Gentle On My Mind
- ☐ '70 Honey Come Back
- ☐ '68 I Wanna Live
- ▣ '70 It's Only Make Believe
- ☐ '69 Let It Be Me *[w/ Bobbie Gentry]*
- ☐ '70 Oh Happy Day
- ▣ '75 Rhinestone Cowboy ★
- ☐ '77 Southern Nights ★
- ☐ '77 Sunflower
- ☐ '69 True Grit
- ☐ '69 Try A Little Kindness
- ☐ '69 Where's The Playground Susie
- ▣ '68 Wichita Lineman ★

CAMPBELL, Jo Ann
- ☐ '62 (I'm The Girl On) Wolverton Mountain
- ☐ '60 Kookie Little Paradise, A

CAMPBELL, Tevin
- ▣ '92 Alone With You
- ▣ '94 Always In My Heart
- ☐ '93 Can We Talk
- ☐ '92 Goodbye
- ☐ '94 I'm Ready
- ☐ '90 Round And Round
- ☐ '91 Tell Me What You Want Me To Do
- ☐ '90 Tomorrow (A Better You, Better Me) *[w/ Quincy Jones]*

CAMPER VAN BEETHOVEN
- ☐ '89 Pictures Of Matchstick Men

CAM'RON
- ▣ '02 Hey Ma ★
- ☐ '98 Horse & Carriage
- ▣ '02 Oh Boy ★

C & C MUSIC FACTORY
- ☐ '94 Do You Wanna Get Funky
- ▣ '90 Gonna Make You Sweat (Everybody Dance Now) ★
- ▣ '91 Here We Go
- ▣ '91 Things That Make You Go Hmmmm...

CANDLEBOX
- ▣ '94 Far Behind
- ▣ '98 It's Alright

CANDYMAN
- ☐ '90 Knockin' Boots

CANIBUS
- ☐ '98 Second Round K.O.

CANNED HEAT
- ☐ '68 Going Up The Country
- ☐ '70 Let's Work Together
- ▣ '68 On The Road Again

CANNIBAL & THE HEADHUNTERS
- ☐ '65 Land Of 1000 Dances

CANNON, Ace
- ☐ '62 Blues (Stay Away From Me)
- ☐ '61 Tuff

CANNON, Freddy
- ☐ '64 Abigail Beecher
- ☐ '65 Action
- ☐ '61 Buzz Buzz A-Diddle-It
- ☐ '60 Chattanooga Shoe Shine Boy
- ☐ '66 Dedication Song, The
- ☐ '60 Jump Over
- ☐ '62 Palisades Park ★
- ☐ '59 Tallahassee Lassie
- ☐ '61 Transistor Sister
- ☐ '59 Way Down Yonder In New Orleans

CANNON, Nick
- ▣ '03 Gigolo

CANTRELL, Blu
- ☐ '01 Hit 'Em Up Style (Oops!) ★

CAPALDI, Jim
- ☐ '83 Living On The Edge
- ▣ '83 That's Love

CAPITOLS, The
- ☐ '66 Cool Jerk

CAPRIS, The
- ☐ '60 There's A Moon Out Tonight ★

CAPTAIN & TENNILLE
- ☐ '77 Can't Stop Dancin'
- ▣ '79 Do That To Me One More Time ★
- ▣ '76 Lonely Night (Angel Face)
- ▣ '75 Love Will Keep Us Together ★
- ☐ '76 Muskrat Love
- ☐ '76 Shop Around
- ▣ '75 Way I Want To Touch You, The
- ☐ '78 You Never Done It Like That

CAPTAIN HOLLYWOOD PROJECT
- ☐ '93 More And More

CARA, Irene
- ☐ '84 Breakdance
- ▣ '80 Fame ★
- ▣ '83 Flashdance...What A Feeling ★
- ☐ '80 Out Here On My Own
- ☐ '83 Why Me?

CARAVELLES, The
- ☐ '63 You Don't Have To Be A Baby To Cry

CARDIGANS, The
- ▣ '96 Lovefool ★

CAREFREES, The
- ☐ '64 We Love You Beatles

CAREY, Mariah
- ▣ '94 All I Want For Christmas Is You
- ▣ '96 Always Be My Baby ★
- ☐ '94 Anytime You Need A Friend
- ▣ '97 Butterfly
- ☐ '91 Can't Let Go
- ☐ '00 Crybaby
- ▣ '05 Don't Forget About Us ★
- ▣ '93 Dreamlover ★
- ▣ '91 Emotions ★
- ▣ '94 Endless Love *[w/ Luther Vandross]*
- ▣ '95 Fantasy ★
- ▣ '96 Forever
- ☐ '99 Heartbreaker
- ▣ '93 Hero ★
- ▣ '97 Honey ★
- ☐ '91 I Don't Wanna Cry
- ▣ '03 I Know What You Want *[w/ Busta Rhymes]* ★
- ☐ '99 I Still Believe
- ▣ '92 I'll Be There ★
- ☐ '05 It's Like That
- ▣ '90 Love Takes Time ★
- ☐ '01 Loverboy
- ☐ '92 Make It Happen
- ▣ '98 My All ★
- ▣ '95 One Sweet Day *[w/ Boyz II Men]* ★
- ▣ '05 Shake It Off ★
- ▣ '91 Someday ★
- ☐ '99 Thank God I Found You ★
- ▣ '90 Vision Of Love ★
- ▣ '05 We Belong Together ★
- ☐ '98 When You Believe *[w/ Whitney Houston]*
- ▣ '94 Without You

CAREY, Tony
- ▣ '84 Fine Fine Day, A
- ☐ '84 First Day Of Summer, The

CARGILL, Henson
- ☐ '67 Skip A Rope

CARLISLE, Belinda
- ☐ '88 Circle In The Sand
- ▣ '87 Heaven Is A Place On Earth ★
- ☐ '88 I Get Weak
- ☐ '89 Leave A Light On
- ▣ '86 Mad About You
- ☐ '90 Summer Rain

CARLISLE, Bob
- ▣ '97 Butterfly Kisses ★

CARLTON, Carl
- ▣ '74 Everlasting Love
- ▣ '81 She's A Bad Mama Jama (She's Built, She's Stacked)

CARLTON, Vanessa
- ☐ '02 Ordinary Day
- ▣ '02 Thousand Miles, A ★

CARMEN, Eric
- ▣ '75 All By Myself ★
- ☐ '78 Change Of Heart
- ▣ '87 Hungry Eyes

CARMEN, Eric — cont'd
- ■ '85 I Wanna Hear It From Your Lips
- ■ '88 Make Me Lose Control
- □ '76 Never Gonna Fall In Love Again
- □ '77 She Did It
- □ '76 Sunrise

CARNE, Jean
- □ '86 Closer Than Close

CARNES, Kim
- ■ '81 Bette Davis Eyes ★
- □ '85 Crazy In The Night (Barking At Airplanes)
- □ '82 Does It Make You Remember
- ■ '80 Don't Fall In Love With A Dreamer
  [w/ Kenny Rogers]
- □ '81 Draw Of The Cards
- ■ '80 More Love
- □ '82 Voyeur
- ■ '84 What About Me? *[w/ Kenny Rogers & James Ingram]*
- ■ '78 You're A Part Of Me *[w/ Gene Cotton]*

CAROSONE, Renato
- □ '58 Torero

CARPENTER, Mary Chapin
- □ '91 Down At The Twist And Shout
- □ '93 He Thinks He'll Keep Her
- □ '92 I Feel Lucky
- □ '94 I Take My Chances
- □ '93 Passionate Kisses
- □ '94 Shut Up And Kiss Me

CARPENTERS
- □ '77 All You Get From Love Is A Love Song
- □ '77 Calling Occupants Of Interplanetary Craft
- □ '71 For All We Know
- □ '72 Goodbye To Love
- □ '72 Hurting Each Other
- □ '76 I Need To Be In Love
- ■ '74 I Won't Last A Day Without You
- □ '72 It's Going To Take Some Time
- □ '70 Merry Christmas Darling
- □ '75 Only Yesterday
- ■ '74 Please Mr. Postman
- □ '71 Rainy Days And Mondays ★
- □ '73 Sing
- □ '75 Solitaire
- □ '71 Superstar ★
- □ '76 There's A Kind Of Hush (All Over The World)
- ■ '70 (They Long To Be) Close To You ★
- ■ '73 Top Of The World ★
- □ '81 Touch Me When We're Dancing
- ■ '70 We've Only Just Begun ★
- □ '73 Yesterday Once More

CARR, Cathy
- □ '56 Ivory Tower ★

CARR, Joe "Fingers"
- □ '56 Portuguese Washerwomen

CARR, Valerie
- □ '58 When The Boys Talk About The Girls

CARR, Vikki
- □ '67 It Must Be Him
- □ '67 Lesson, The
- □ '69 With Pen In Hand

CARRACK, Paul
- □ '87 Don't Shed A Tear
- □ '89 I Live By The Groove
- □ '82 I Need You
- □ '88 One Good Reason

CARRADINE, Keith
- □ '76 I'm Easy

CARROLL, David, & His Orchestra
- □ '55 It's Almost Tomorrow
- □ '55 Melody Of Love
- □ '62 White Rose Of Athens, The

CARROLL, Jason Michael
- ■ '07 Alyssa Lies

CARS, The
- ■ '78 Bye Bye Love
- □ '79 Dangerous Type
- ■ '84 Drive ★
- ■ '78 Good Times Roll
- □ '84 Hello Again
- □ '86 I'm Not The One
- □ '79 It's All I Can Do
- □ '78 Just What I Needed
- ■ '79 Let's Go ★
- □ '84 Magic
- □ '78 Moving In Stereo
- □ '78 My Best Friend's Girl
- ■ '81 Shake It Up ★
- □ '82 Since You're Gone
- □ '85 Tonight She Comes
- □ '80 Touch And Go
- □ '85 Why Can't I Have You
- □ '87 You Are The Girl
- □ '84 You Might Think
- ■ '78 You're All I've Got Tonight

CARSON, Jeff
- □ '95 Car, The
- □ '95 Not On Your Love

CARSON, Kit
- □ '55 Band Of Gold

CARSON, Mindy
- □ '55 Wake The Town And Tell The People

CARTER, Aaron
- □ '00 Aaron's Party (Come Get It)

CARTER, Carlene
- □ '90 Come On Back
- ■ '93 Every Little Thing
- ■ '90 I Fell In Love

CARTER, Clarence
- □ '68 Looking For A Fox
- □ '70 Patches

☐ '68 Slip Away
☐ '69 Snatching It Back
☐ '89 Strokin'
☐ '68 Too Weak To Fight

CARTER, Deana
☐ '97 How Do I Get There
☐ '96 Strawberry Wine
☐ '96 We Danced Anyway

CARTER, Mel
☐ '66 Band Of Gold
☐ '65 Hold Me, Thrill Me, Kiss Me
☐ '63 When A Boy Falls In Love

CARTWRIGHT, Lionel
☐ '91 Leap Of Faith

CASCADA
☐ '06 Everytime We Touch ★

CASCADES, The
☐ '63 Last Leaf, The
☐ '63 Rhythm Of The Rain ★

CASE
☐ '98 Faded Pictures *[w/ Joe]*
☐ '99 Happily Ever After
☐ '01 Missing You ★
☐ '96 Touch Me Tease Me

CASEY, Al
☐ '63 Surfin' Hootenanny

CASH, Alvin, & The Crawlers
☐ '65 Twine Time

CASH, Johnny
☐ '58 All Over Again
☐ '58 Ballad Of A Teenage Queen
☐ '69 Boy Named Sue, A ★
☐ '55 Cry! Cry! Cry!
☐ '69 Daddy Sang Bass
☐ '59 Don't Take Your Guns To Town
☐ '56 Folsom Prison Blues
☐ '68 Folsom Prison Blues [live]
☐ '56 Get Rhythm
☐ '79 (Ghost) Riders In The Sky
☐ '57 Give My Love To Rose
☐ '58 Guess Things Happen That Way
☐ '85 Highwayman *[w/ Waylon Jennings, Willie Nelson & Kris Kristofferson]*
☐ '03 Hurt
☐ '59 I Got Stripes
☐ '56 I Walk The Line ★
☐ '70 If I Were A Carpenter *[w/ June Carter]*
☐ '67 Jackson *[w/ June Carter]*
☐ '71 Man In Black
☐ '76 One Piece At A Time
☐ '63 Ring Of Fire ★
☐ '70 Sunday Morning Coming Down
☐ '72 Thing Called Love, A
☐ '64 Understand Your Man
☐ '58 Ways Of A Woman In Love, The
☐ '70 What Is Truth

CASH, Rosanne
☐ '81 Seven Year Ache

CASHMAN & WEST
☐ '72 American City Suite

CASINOS, The
☐ '67 Then You Can Tell Me Goodbye

CASSIDY
☐ '03 Hotel ★
☐ '05 I'm A Hustla

CASSIDY, David
☐ '71 Cherish
☐ '72 Could It Be Forever
☐ '72 How Can I Be Sure
☐ '90 Lyin' To Myself
☐ '72 Rock Me Baby

CASSIDY, Shaun
☐ '77 Da Doo Ron Ron
☐ '78 Do You Believe In Magic
☐ '77 Hey Deanie
☐ '77 That's Rock 'N' Roll

CASSIE
☐ '06 Me & U ★

CASTAWAYS, The
☐ '65 Liar, Liar

CASTELLS, The
☐ '61 Sacred
☐ '62 So This Is Love

CASTING CROWNS
☐ '05 Praise You In This Storm
☐ '03 Voice Of Truth

CASTLEMAN, Boomer
☐ '75 Judy Mae

CAST OF RENT
☐ '05 Seasons Of Love

CASTOR, Jimmy
☐ '75 Bertha Butt Boogie, The
☐ '66 Hey, Leroy, Your Mama's Callin' You
☐ '72 Troglodyte (Cave Man)

CATE BROS.
☐ '76 Union Man

CATES, George, & His Orchestra
☐ '56 Moonglow And Theme From "Picnic"

CATHY JEAN & THE ROOMMATES
☐ '61 Please Love Me Forever

CAT MOTHER & THE ALL NIGHT NEWS BOYS
☐ '69 Good Old Rock 'N Roll

CAUSE & EFFECT
☐ '92 You Think You Know Her

CAVALIERE, Felix
☐ '80 Only A Lonely Heart Sees

C COMPANY Feat. TERRY NELSON
☐ '71 Battle Hymn Of Lt. Calley

CELEBRATION Feat. MIKE LOVE
- ☐ '78 Almost Summer

CERRONE
- ☐ '77 Love In 'C' Minor

CETERA, Peter
- ▣ '89 After All *[w/ Cher]*
- ▣ '93 Even A Fool Can See
- ▣ '86 Glory Of Love ★
- ▣ '86 Next Time I Fall, The *[w/ Amy Grant]*
- ▣ '88 One Good Woman
- ▣ '92 Restless Heart

CHAD & JEREMY
- ☐ '65 Before And After
- ☐ '66 Distant Shores
- ☐ '65 I Don't Wanna Lose You Baby
- ☐ '65 If I Loved You
- ☐ '64 Summer Song, A
- ☐ '64 Willow Weep For Me
- ☐ '64 Yesterday's Gone

CHAIRMEN OF THE BOARD
- ☐ '70 Everything's Tuesday
- ☐ '70 Give Me Just A Little More Time
- ☐ '70 Pay To The Piper
- ☐ '70 (You've Got Me) Dangling On A String

CHAKACHAS, The
- ☐ '72 Jungle Fever

CHAMBERLAIN, Richard
- ☐ '63 All I Have To Do Is Dream
- ☐ '62 Love Me Tender
- ☐ '62 Theme From Dr. Kildare (Three Stars Will Shine Tonight)

CHAMBERS BROTHERS, The
- ▣ '68 I Can't Turn You Loose
- ▣ '68 Time Has Come Today

CHAMILLIONAIRE
- ▣ '06 Ridin' ★
- ☐ '06 Turn It Up

CHAMPAIGN
- ▣ '81 How 'Bout Us
- ▣ '83 Try Again

CHAMPS, The
- ☐ '58 El Rancho Rock
- ☐ '62 Limbo Rock
- ▣ '58 Tequila ★
- ☐ '60 Too Much Tequila

CHANDLER, Gene
- ☐ '64 Bless Our Love
- ☐ '62 Duke Of Earl ★
- ☐ '78 Get Down
- ☐ '70 Groovy Situation
- ☐ '66 I Fooled You This Time
- ☐ '64 Just Be True
- ☐ '65 Nothing Can Stop Me
- ☐ '63 Rainbow
- ☐ '65 Rainbow '65 [live]
- ☐ '64 What Now

CHANGE
- ☐ '80 Lover's Holiday, A

CHANGING FACES
- ☐ '94 Foolin' Around
- ☐ '97 G.H.E.T.T.O.U.T.
- ☐ '94 Stroke You Up

CHANNEL, Bruce
- ▣ '62 Hey! Baby ★

CHANSON
- ☐ '78 Don't Hold Back

CHANTAY'S
- ☐ '63 Pipeline ★

CHANTELS, The
- ▣ '58 Every Night (I Pray)
- ☐ '57 He's Gone
- ▣ '58 I Love You So
- ☐ '61 Look In My Eyes
- ▣ '58 Maybe ★
- ☐ '61 Well. I Told You

CHAPIN, Harry
- ☐ '74 Cat's In The Cradle ★
- ☐ '80 Sequel
- ☐ '72 Taxi
- ☐ '74 WOLD

CHAPMAN, Steven Curtis
- ▣ '03 All About Love
- ☐ '04 All Things New
- ☐ '99 Dive
- ☐ '00 Fingerprints Of God
- ☐ '91 For The Sake Of The Call
- ☐ '92 Great Adventure, The
- ☐ '01 Live Out Loud
- ☐ '96 Lord Of The Dance
- ☐ '89 More To This Life
- ☐ '91 No Better Place
- ☐ '99 Speechless

CHAPMAN, Tracy
- ☐ '88 Baby Can I Hold You
- ▣ '88 Fast Car ★
- ▣ '96 Give Me One Reason ★

CHARLENE
- ☐ '82 I've Never Been To Me

CHARLES, Jimmy
- ☐ '60 Million To One, A

CHARLES, Ray
- ☐ '72 America The Beautiful
- ☐ '87 Baby Grand *[w/ Billy Joel]*
- ☐ '71 Booty Butt
- ☐ '62 Born To Lose
- ☐ '63 Busted
- ☐ '65 Crying Time
- ☐ '71 Don't Change On Me
- ☐ '63 Don't Set Me Free
- ☐ '56 Drown In My Own Tears
- ☐ '68 Eleanor Rigby
- ☐ '55 Fool For You, A
- ▣ '60 Georgia On My Mind ★

□ '67 Here We Go Again
□ '04 Here We Go Again *[w/ Norah Jones]*
□ '62 Hide 'Nor Hair
■ '61 Hit The Road Jack ★
■ '62 I Can't Stop Loving You ★
□ '66 I Chose To Sing The Blues
□ '59 I'm Movin' On
■ '55 I've Got A Woman
□ '71 If You Were Mine
■ '67 In The Heat Of The Night
□ '66 Let's Go Get Stoned
□ '64 My Heart Cries For You
□ '63 No One
□ '61 One Mint Julep
□ '60 Ruby
□ '85 Seven Spanish Angels *[w/ Willie Nelson]*
□ '57 Swanee River Rock (Talkin' 'Bout That River)
□ '63 Take These Chains From My Heart
□ '63 That Lucky Old Sun
□ '66 Together Again
□ '61 Unchain My Heart
■ '59 What'd I Say ★
□ '63 Without Love (There Is Nothing)
□ '67 Yesterday
□ '62 You Are My Sunshine
□ '62 You Don't Know Me
■ '62 Your Cheating Heart

CHARLES, Ray, Singers
□ '64 Al-Di-La
□ '64 Love Me With All Your Heart (Cuando Calienta El Sol)

CHARLES, Sonny
□ '69 Black Pearl *[w/ The Checkmates, Ltd.]*
□ '83 Put It In A Magazine

CHARLES & EDDIE
■ '92 Would I Lie To You?

CHARLIE
□ '83 It's Inevitable

CHARMS, The
□ '55 Hearts Of Stone
□ '56 Ivory Tower
□ '55 Ling, Ting, Tong

CHARTBUSTERS, The
■ '64 She's The One

CHASE
■ '71 Get It On

CHASEZ, JC
■ '03 Blowin' Me Up (With Her Love)

CHEAP TRICK
□ '79 Ain't That A Shame
■ '90 Can't Stop Fallin' Into Love
□ '88 Don't Be Cruel
□ '79 Dream Police
■ '88 Flame, The ★
□ '88 Ghost Town
■ '79 I Want You To Want Me ★
□ '78 Surrender

□ '79 Voices

CHECKER, Chubby
□ '63 Birdland
□ '59 Class, The
■ '61 (Dance The) Mess Around
□ '62 Dancin' Party
□ '61 Fly, The
□ '64 Hey, Bobba Needle
□ '63 Hooka Tooka
□ '60 Hucklebuck, The
■ '61 Jingle Bell Rock *[w/ Bobby Rydell]*
□ '64 Lazy Elsie Molly
□ '63 Let's Limbo Some More
□ '61 Let's Twist Again
□ '62 Limbo Rock ★
□ '63 Loddy Lo
□ '61 Pony Time ★
□ '62 Popeye (The Hitchhiker)
□ '62 Slow Twistin' *[w/ Dee Dee Sharp]*
□ '63 Twenty Miles
■ '60 Twist, The ★
□ '63 Twist It Up

CHEECH & CHONG
□ '73 Basketball Jones Featuring Tyrone Shoelaces
□ '74 Black Lassie
□ '78 Bloat On (Featuring The Bloaters)
□ '85 Born In East L.A.
□ '71 Dave
□ '74 Earache My Eye (Featuring Alice Bowie)
□ '76 Framed
□ '73 Sister Mary Elephant (Shudd-Up!)
□ '74 Three Little Pigs

CHEERS, The
□ '55 Black Denim Trousers ★

CHER
■ '89 After All *[w/ Peter Cetera]*
□ '66 Alfie
□ '65 All I Really Want To Do
□ '66 Bang Bang (My Baby Shot Me Down)
■ '98 Believe ★
□ '74 Dark Lady
□ '71 Gypsys, Tramps & Thieves ★
□ '73 Half-Breed
■ '90 Heart Of Stone
■ '87 I Found Someone
■ '89 If I Could Turn Back Time ★
■ '89 Just Like Jesse James
□ '72 Living In A House Divided
■ '91 Love And Understanding
■ '90 Shoop Shoop Song (It's In His Kiss)
■ '79 Take Me Home
□ '74 Train Of Thought
■ '72 Way Of Love, The
□ '88 We All Sleep Alone
■ '65 Where Do You Go
□ '67 You Better Sit Down Kids

CHERISH
■ '06 Do It To It

CHERRELLE
- ☐ '88 Everything I Miss At Home
- ☒ '88 Never Knew Love Like This [w/ Alexander O'Neal]
- ☐ '86 Saturday Love [w/ Alexander O'Neal]

CHERRY, Don
- ☐ '55 Band Of Gold ★
- ☐ '56 Ghost Town
- ☐ '56 Wild Cherry

CHERRY, Eagle-Eye
- ☒ '98 Save Tonight ★

CHERRY, Neneh
- ☐ '89 Buffalo Stance ★
- ☐ '89 Kisses On The Wind

CHERRY POPPIN' DADDIES
- ☐ '98 Zoot Suit Riot

CHESNEY, Kenny
- ☐ '05 Anything But Mine
- ☒ '07 Beer In Mexico
- ☐ '03 Big Star
- ☒ '07 Don't Blink ★
- ☒ '01 Don't Happen Twice
- ☐ '02 Good Stuff, The
- ☒ '99 How Forever Feels
- ☒ '04 I Go Back
- ☐ '00 I Lost It
- ☐ '06 Living In Fast Forward
- ☒ '96 Me And You
- ☒ '07 Never Wanted Nothing More
- ☒ '03 No Shoes, No Shirt, No Problems
- ☒ '00 She Thinks My Tractor's Sexy
- ☐ '97 She's Got It All
- ☐ '05 Summertime
- ☐ '98 That's Why I'm Here
- ☒ '03 There Goes My Life
- ☐ '96 When I Close My Eyes
- ☒ '04 When The Sun Goes Down [w/ Uncle Kracker]
- ☐ '05 Who You'd Be Today
- ☐ '04 Woman With You, The
- ☒ '99 You Had Me From Hello
- ☒ '06 You Save Me
- ☐ '01 Young

CHESNUTT, Mark
- ☐ '93 Almost Goodbye
- ☐ '90 Brother Jukebox
- ☐ '92 Bubba Shot The Jukebox
- ☐ '94 Goin' Through The Big D
- ☐ '95 Gonna Get A Life
- ☐ '98 I Don't Want To Miss A Thing
- ☐ '93 I Just Wanted You To Know
- ☐ '92 I'll Think Of Something
- ☐ '93 It Sure Is Monday
- ☐ '96 It's A Little Too Late
- ☐ '97 Thank God For Believers
- ☐ '90 Too Cold At Home
- ☐ '91 Your Love Is A Miracle

CHEVALIER, Maurice
- ☐ '58 Thank Heaven For Little Girls

CHEVELLE
- ☐ '02 Red, The
- ☐ '03 Send The Pain Below
- ☐ '04 Vitamin R (Leading Us Along)

CHIC
- ☐ '77 Dance, Dance, Dance (Yowsah, Yowsah, Yowsah)
- ☒ '79 Good Times ★
- ☒ '79 I Want Your Love ?
- ☒ '78 Le Freak ★

CHICAGO
- ☐ '78 Alive Again
- ☐ '85 Along Comes A Woman
- ☐ '77 Baby, What A Big Surprise
- ☐ '71 Beginnings
- ☐ '74 Call On Me
- ☒ '71 Colour My World
- ☐ '72 Dialogue
- ☐ '70 Does Anybody Really Know What Time It Is?
- ☐ '73 Feelin' Stronger Every Day
- ☐ '71 Free
- ☒ '84 Hard Habit To Break
- ☒ '82 Hard To Say I'm Sorry ★
- ☐ '75 Harry Truman
- ☒ '97 Here In My Heart
- ☒ '88 I Don't Wanna Live Without Your Love
- ☐ '69 I'm A Man
- ☐ '74 (I've Been) Searchin' So Long
- ☐ '87 If She Would Have Been Faithful...
- ☒ '76 If You Leave Me Now ★
- ☐ '73 Just You 'N' Me
- ☒ '88 Look Away
- ☐ '82 Love Me Tomorrow
- ☐ '71 Lowdown
- ☐ '70 Make Me Smile
- ☐ '78 No Tell Lover
- ☐ '75 Old Days
- ☐ '71 Questions 67 And 68
- ☐ '72 Saturday In The Park ★
- ☒ '84 Stay The Night
- ☐ '70 25 Or 6 To 4 ★
- ☒ '89 What Kind Of Man Would I Be?
- ☒ '86 Will You Still Love Me?
- ☐ '74 Wishing You Were Here
- ☐ '89 You're Not Alone
- ☒ '84 You're The Inspiration ★

CHICAGO BEARS SHUFFLIN' CREW
- ☐ '86 Superbowl Shuffle

CHICAGO LOOP, The
- ☒ '66 (When She Needs Good Lovin') She Comes To Me

CHIFFONS, The
- ☒ '63 He's So Fine ★
- ☐ '63 I Have A Boyfriend
- ☐ '63 Love So Fine, A
- ☒ '63 One Fine Day
- ☐ '66 Sweet Talkin' Guy

CHILD, Desmond
- ☐ '91 Love On A Rooftop

CHILD, Jane
☐ '90 Don't Wanna Fall In Love

CHI-LITES, The
☐ '71 (For God's Sake) Give More Power To The People
▣ '71 Have You Seen Her ★
☐ '73 Letter To Myself, A
▣ '72 Oh Girl ★
☐ '73 Stoned Out Of My Mind

CHILLIWACK
☐ '82 I Believe
☐ '81 My Girl (Gone, Gone, Gone)

CHIMES, The
☐ '61 I'm In The Mood For Love
☐ '60 Once In Awhile

CHINGY
☐ '04 Balla Baby
▣ '03 Holidae In ★
▣ '04 One Call Away ★
▣ '06 Pullin' Me Back
▣ '03 Right Thurr ★

CHIPMUNKS, The
☐ '62 Alvin Twist, The
☐ '59 Alvin's Harmonica
☐ '60 Alvin's Orchestra
☐ '58 Chipmunk Song, The
☐ '59 Ragtime Cowboy Joe
☐ '60 Rudolph The Red Nosed Reindeer

CHORDETTES, The
▣ '56 Born To Be With You
☐ '56 Eddie My Love
☐ '57 Just Between You And Me
☐ '56 Lay Down Your Arms
▣ '58 Lollipop ★
▣ '55 Mr. Sandman ★
☐ '61 Never On Sunday
▣ '59 No Other Arms, No Other Lips
☐ '58 Zorro

CHORDS, The
▣ '54 Sh-Boom

CHRISTIAN, Chris
▣ '81 I Want You, I Need You

CHRISTIE
☐ '70 Yellow River

CHRISTIE, Lou
☐ '63 Gypsy Cried, The
☐ '69 I'm Gonna Make You Mine
☐ '65 Lightnin' Strikes ★
☐ '66 Rhapsody In The Rain
☐ '63 Two Faces Have I

CHRISTOPHER, Gavin
▣ '86 One Step Closer To You

CHUMBAWAMBA
▣ '97 Tubthumping ★

CHURCH, The
☐ '90 Metropolis
☐ '88 Under The Milky Way

CHURCH, Eugene
☐ '58 Pretty Girls Everywhere

CIARA
☐ '07 Can't Leave 'Em Alone
☐ '06 Get Up
▣ '04 Goodies ★
▣ '07 Like A Boy
▣ '05 Oh ★
▣ '05 1,2 Step ★
☐ '06 Promise

CINDERELLA
☐ '89 Coming Home
▣ '88 Don't Know What You Got (Till It's Gone)
☐ '89 Last Mile, The
▣ '86 Nobody's Fool
☐ '90 Shelter Me

CITIZEN KING
☐ '99 Better Days (And The Bottom Drops Out)

CITY BOY
☐ '78 5.7.0.5.

CITY HIGH
☐ '01 Caramel
☐ '01 What Would You Do?

C.J. & CO.
☐ '77 Devil's Gun

CLANTON, Jimmy
☐ '60 Another Sleepless Night
☐ '60 Come Back
☐ '59 Go, Jimmy, Go
☐ '58 Just A Dream
☐ '58 Letter To An Angel, A
☐ '59 My Own True Love
☐ '58 Part Of Me, A
☐ '62 Venus In Blue Jeans
☐ '61 What Am I Gonna Do

CLAPTON, Eric
▣ '70 After Midnight
☐ '89 Bad Love
☐ '70 Bell Bottom Blues *[DEREK & THE DOMINOS]*
☐ '70 Blues Power
▣ '96 Change The World ★
▣ '77 Cocaine
☐ '80 Cocaine [live]
☐ '85 Forever Man
☐ '76 Hello Old Friend
☐ '81 I Can't Stand It
▣ '74 I Shot The Sheriff ★
☐ '83 I've Got A Rock N' Roll Heart
☐ '86 It's In The Way That You Use It
▣ '78 Lay Down Sally ★
▣ '72 Layla *[DEREK & THE DOMINOS]* ★
☐ '92 Layla [live]
☐ '70 Let It Rain

CLAPTON, Eric — cont'd
- ☐ '98 My Father's Eyes
- ☐ '89 Pretending
- ☒ '78 Promises
- ☐ '06 Say What You Will
- ☒ '85 See What Love Can Do
- ☐ '85 She's Waiting
- ☒ '92 Tears In Heaven ★
- ☐ '80 Tulsa Time
- ☐ '79 Watch Out For Lucy
- ☐ '74 Willie And The Hand Jive
- ☒ '78 Wonderful Tonight

CLARK, Claudine
- ☐ '62 Party Lights

CLARK, Dave, Five
- ☐ '64 Any Way You Want It
- ☐ '66 At The Scene
- ☐ '64 Because
- ☐ '64 Bits And Pieces
- ☐ '64 Can't You See That She's Mine
- ☐ '65 Catch Us If You Can
- ☐ '65 Come Home
- ☐ '64 Do You Love Me
- ☐ '67 Everybody Knows
- ☐ '64 Everybody Knows (I Still Love You)
- ☐ '64 Glad All Over
- ☐ '65 I Like It Like That
- ☐ '65 Over And Over ★
- ☐ '66 Please Tell Me Why
- ☐ '65 Reelin' And Rockin'
- ☐ '66 Try Too Hard
- ☐ '67 You Got What It Takes
- ☐ '67 You Must Have Been A Beautiful Baby

CLARK, Dee
- ☐ '59 Hey Little Girl
- ☐ '59 How About That
- ☐ '59 Just Keep It Up
- ☐ '58 Nobody But You
- ☐ '61 Raindrops ★
- ☐ '61 Your Friends

CLARK, Petula
- ☐ '66 Color My World
- ☐ '68 Don't Give Up
- ☐ '67 Don't Sleep In The Subway
- ☐ '64 Downtown ★
- ☐ '66 I Couldn't Live Without Your Love
- ☐ '65 I Know A Place
- ☐ '68 Kiss Me Goodbye
- ☐ '65 My Love ★
- ☐ '67 Other Man's Grass Is Always Greener, The
- ☐ '65 Round Every Corner
- ☐ '66 Sign Of The Times, A
- ☐ '67 This Is My Song
- ☐ '66 Who Am I
- ☐ '65 You'd Better Come Home

CLARK, Roy
- ☐ '73 Come Live With Me
- ☐ '69 Yesterday, When I Was Young

CLARK, Sanford
- ☐ '56 Fool, The ★

CLARK, Terri
- ☐ '95 Better Things To Do
- ☐ '97 Emotional Girl
- ☐ '04 Girls Lie Too
- ☐ '02 I Just Wanna Be Mad
- ☐ '03 I Wanna Do It All
- ☐ '98 Now That I Found You
- ☐ '96 Poor, Poor Pitiful Me
- ☐ '95 When Boy Meets Girl
- ☐ '98 You're Easy On The Eyes

CLARKE, Stanley
- ☐ '81 Sweet Baby [w/ George Duke]

CLARKE, Tony
- ☐ '65 Entertainer, The

CLARKSON, Kelly
- ☒ '05 Because Of You ★
- ☐ '07 Because Of You [w/ Reba McEntire]
- ☒ '05 Behind These Hazel Eyes ★
- ☒ '04 Breakaway ★
- ☐ '03 Miss Independent
- ☒ '02 Moment Like This, A ★
- ☐ '07 Never Again
- ☒ '05 Since U Been Gone ★
- ☐ '06 Walk Away

CLASH, The
- ☐ '79 Complete Control
- ☐ '80 London Calling ★
- ☒ '82 Rock The Casbah ★
- ☐ '82 Should I Stay Or Should I Go
- ☐ '80 Train In Vain (Stand By Me)
- ☐ '79 White Man In Hammersmith Palais
- ☐ '79 White Riot

CLASSICS, The
- ☐ '63 Till Then

CLASSICS IV
- ☒ '69 Everyday With You Girl
- ☒ '67 Spooky ★
- ☐ '68 Stormy
- ☐ '69 Traces
- ☐ '72 What Am I Crying For?

CLAY, Judy
- ☒ '68 Country Girl - City Man [w/ Billy Vera]

CLAY, Tom
- ☐ '71 What The World Needs Now Is Love/Abraham, Martin and John

CLAYTON, Adam, & Larry Mullen
- ☐ '96 Theme From Mission: Impossible

CLAYTON, Merry
- ☐ '75 Keep Your Eye On The Sparrow
- ☐ '73 Oh No, Not My Baby

CLEAN LIVING
- ☐ '72 In Heaven There Is No Beer

CLEFTONES, The
- ☐ '61 Heart And Soul
- ☐ '56 Little Girl Of Mine

CLEMONS, Clarence
- ☐ '85 You're A Friend Of Mine *[w/ Jackson Browne]*

CLEOPATRA
- ☐ '98 Cleopatra's Theme

CLIBURN, Van
- ☐ '58 Tchaikovsky: Piano Concerto No. 1

CLICK FIVE, The
- ☐ '05 Just The Girl ★

CLIFF, Jimmy
- ☐ '75 Harder They Come, The
- ☐ '93 I Can See Clearly Now
- ☐ '69 Many Rivers To Cross
- ☐ '69 Wonderful World, Beautiful People
- ☐ '75 You Can Get It If You Really Want

CLIFFORD, Buzz
- ☐ '61 Baby Sittin' Boogie

CLIFFORD, Linda
- ☐ '80 Red Light
- ☐ '78 Runaway Love

CLIFFORD, Mike
- ☐ '62 Close To Cathy

CLIMAX
- ☐ '72 Precious And Few

CLIMAX BLUES BAND
- ☐ '77 Couldn't Get It Right
- ☐ '81 I Love You

CLIMIE FISHER
- ☐ '88 Love Changes (Everything)

CLINE, Patsy
- ☐ '61 Crazy ★
- ☐ '61 I Fall To Pieces ★
- ☐ '62 She's Got You
- ☐ '63 Sweet Dreams (Of You)
- ☐ '57 Walkin' After Midnight

CLINTON, George
- ☐ '83 Atomic Dog

CLIPSE
- ☐ '02 Grindin'
- ☐ '02 When The Last Time

CLIQUE, The
- ☐ '69 Sugar On Sunday

CLOONEY, Rosemary
- ☐ '54 Hey There
- ☐ '54 Mambo Italiano
- ☐ '57 Mangos
- ☐ '56 Memories Of You *[w/ Benny Goodman]*
- ☐ '54 This Ole House

CLOVERS, The
- ☐ '56 Devil Or Angel
- ☐ '56 Love, Love, Love
- ☐ '59 Love Potion No. 9

CLUB NOUVEAU
- ☐ '87 Lean On Me ★
- ☐ '87 Why You Treat Me So Bad

COASTERS, The
- ☐ '59 Along Came Jones
- ☐ '59 Charlie Brown ★
- ☐ '59 I'm A Hog For You
- ☐ '61 Little Egypt (Ying-Yang)
- ☐ '72 Love Potion Number Nine
- ☐ '59 Poison Ivy
- ☐ '59 Run Red Run
- ☐ '57 Searchin' ★
- ☐ '61 Wait A Minute
- ☐ '58 Yakety Yak ★
- ☐ '57 Young Blood ★

COCHRAN, Anita
- ☐ '97 What If I Said *[w/ Steve Wariner]*

COCHRAN, Eddie
- ☐ '58 C'mon Everybody ★
- ☐ '59 Cut Across Shorty
- ☐ '57 Drive In Show
- ☐ '58 Jeannie Jeannie Jeannie
- ☐ '57 Sittin' In The Balcony
- ☐ '59 Somethin' Else
- ☐ '58 Summertime Blues ★
- ☐ '59 Teenage Heaven
- ☐ '60 Three Steps To Heaven
- ☐ '57 Twenty Flight Rock

COCHRANE, Tom
- ☐ '92 Life Is A Highway
- ☐ '92 No Regrets

COCKBURN, Bruce
- ☐ '80 Wondering Where The Lions Are

COCKER, Joe
- ☐ '70 Cry Me A River
- ☐ '69 Delta Lady
- ☐ '72 Feeling Alright
- ☐ '71 High Time We Went
- ☐ '70 Letter, The
- ☐ '72 Midnight Rider
- ☐ '69 She Came In Through The Bathroom Window
- ☐ '82 Up Where We Belong *[w/ Jennifer Warnes]* ★
- ☐ '89 When The Night Comes
- ☐ '69 With A Little Help From My Friends
- ☐ '75 You Are So Beautiful

COCK ROBIN
- ☐ '85 When Your Heart Is Weak

COFFEY, Dennis
- ☐ '71 Scorpio
- ☐ '72 Taurus

COHN, Marc
- ☐ '91 Walking In Memphis

COLDPLAY
- ☑ '03 Clocks ★
- ☐ '02 Scientist, The
- ☑ '05 Speed Of Sound ★
- ☐ '06 Talk
- ☐ '01 Yellow

COLE, Cozy
- ☐ '58 Topsy II ★
- ☐ '58 Turvy II

COLE, Jude
- ☐ '90 Baby, It's Tonight
- ☐ '92 Start The Car
- ☐ '90 Time For Letting Go

COLE, Keyshia
- ☑ '05 I Should Have Cheated
- ☑ '07 Let It Go ★
- ☑ '06 Love

COLE, Nat "King"
- ☐ '58 Angel Smile
- ☐ '56 Ask Me
- ☐ '57 Ballerina
- ☐ '55 Blossom Fell, A ★
- ☐ '58 Come Closer To Me
- ☐ '55 Darling Je Vous Aime Beaucoup
- ☐ '62 Dear Lonely Hearts
- ☐ '55 Forgive My Heart
- ☐ '64 I Don't Want To Be Hurt Anymore
- ☐ '64 I Don't Want To See Tomorrow
- ☐ '55 If I May *[w/ The Four Knights]*
- ☐ '58 Looking Back
- ☐ '57 My Personal Possession *[w/ The Four Knights]*
- ☐ '56 Night Lights
- ☐ '62 Ramblin' Rose ★
- ☐ '55 Sand And The Sea, The
- ☐ '57 Send For Me
- ☐ '55 Someone You Love
- ☐ '57 Stardust
- ☐ '63 That Sunday, That Summer
- ☐ '56 That's All There Is To That *[w/ The Four Knights]*
- ☐ '63 Those Lazy-Hazy-Crazy Days Of Summer
- ☐ '60 Time And The River
- ☐ '56 To The Ends Of The Earth
- ☐ '56 Too Young To Go Steady
- ☑ '91 Unforgettable *[w/ Natalie Cole]*
- ☐ '57 With You On My Mind

COLE, Natalie
- ☐ '87 I Live For Your Love
- ☑ '77 I've Got Love On My Mind
- ☐ '75 Inseparable
- ☐ '87 Jump Start
- ☑ '89 Miss You Like Crazy
- ☑ '78 Our Love
- ☐ '88 Pink Cadillac
- ☐ '80 Someone That I Used To Love
- ☐ '76 Sophisticated Lady (She's A Different Lady)
- ☐ '75 This Will Be
- ☑ '91 Unforgettable *[w/ Nat "King" Cole]*

- ☐ '90 Wild Women Do

COLE, Paula
- ☑ '97 I Don't Want To Wait
- ☐ '98 Me
- ☐ '97 Where Have All The Cowboys Gone?

COLLECTIVE SOUL
- ☐ '95 December
- ☐ '95 Gel
- ☐ '99 Heavy
- ☐ '97 Listen
- ☐ '97 Precious Declaration
- ☐ '94 Shine
- ☐ '95 Smashing Young Man
- ☐ '96 Where The River Flows
- ☐ '00 Why
- ☑ '95 World I Know, The

COLLIER, Mitty
- ☐ '64 I Had A Talk With My Man

COLLINS, Dave & Ansil
- ☐ '71 Double Barrel

COLLINS, Dorothy
- ☐ '55 My Boy - Flat Top
- ☐ '56 Seven Days

COLLINS, Edwyn
- ☑ '95 Girl Like You, A

COLLINS, Judy
- ☑ '70 Amazing Grace ★
- ☐ '68 Both Sides Now
- ☐ '73 Cook With Honey
- ☐ '75 Send In The Clowns

COLLINS, Lyn
- ☐ '72 Think (About It)

COLLINS, Phil
- ☑ '84 Against All Odds (Take A Look At Me Now) ★
- ☑ '89 Another Day In Paradise ★
- ☐ '93 Both Sides Of The Story
- ☑ '02 Can't Stop Loving You
- ☐ '90 Do You Remember?
- ☑ '85 Don't Lose My Number
- ☑ '84 Easy Lover *[w/ Philip Bailey]*
- ☐ '94 Everyday
- ☑ '88 Groovy Kind Of Love ★
- ☐ '90 Hang In Long Enough
- ☐ '93 Hero *[w/ David Crosby]*
- ☐ '81 I Missed Again
- ☐ '90 I Wish It Would Rain Down ★
- ☑ '81 In The Air Tonight
- ☑ '85 One More Night ★
- ☐ '85 Separate Lives *[w/ Marilyn Martin]* ★
- ☐ '90 Something Happened On The Way To Heaven
- ☐ '85 Sussudio ★
- ☐ '86 Take Me Home
- ☑ '98 True Colors
- ☑ '88 Two Hearts ★
- ☑ '82 You Can't Hurry Love
- ☑ '99 You'll Be In My Heart

COLLINS, Tyler
- ☐ '90 Girls Nite Out

COLLINS, William "Bootsy"
- ☐ '78 Bootzilla

COLOR ME BADD
- ☐ '91 All 4 Love ★
- ☐ '94 Choose
- ☐ '96 Earth, The Sun, The Rain, The
- ☐ '92 Forever Love
- ☐ '91 I Adore Mi Amor ★
- ☐ '91 I Wanna Sex You Up
- ☐ '92 Slow Motion
- ☐ '92 Thinkin' Back
- ☐ '93 Time And Chance

COLTER, Jessi
- ☐ '75 I'm Not Lisa

COLTRANE, Chi
- ☐ '72 Thunder And Lightning

COLVIN, Shawn
- ☐ '97 Sunny Came Home ★

COMMANDER CODY & HIS LOST PLANET AIRMEN
- ☐ '72 Hot Rod Lincoln

COMMODORES
- ☐ '77 Brick House
- ☐ '77 Easy
- ☐ '76 Just To Be Close To You
- ☐ '81 Lady (You Bring Me Up)
- ☐ '74 Machine Gun
- ☐ '85 Nightshift
- ☐ '81 Oh No
- ☐ '80 Old-Fashion Love
- ☐ '79 Sail On ◄
- ☐ '75 Slippery When Wet
- ☐ '79 Still
- ☐ '75 Sweet Love
- ☐ '78 Three Times A Lady ★
- ☐ '77 Too Hot Ta Trot
- ☐ '79 Wonderland

COMMON
- ☐ '00 Light, The

COMMUNARDS
- ☐ '87 Never Can Say Goodbye

COMO, Perry
- ☐ '55 All At Once You Love Her
- ☐ '73 And I Love You So
- ☐ '58 Catch A Falling Sta ★
- ☐ '62 Caterina
- ☐ '60 Delaware
- ☐ '56 Dream Along With Me
- ☐ '65 Dream On Little Dreamer
- ☐ '57 Girl With The Golden Braids, The
- ☐ '56 Glendora
- ☐ '56 Hot Diggity (Dog Ziggity Boom) ★
- ☐ '63 (I Love You) Don't You Forget It
- ☐ '70 It's Impossible
- ☐ '57 Ivy Rose

- ☐ '56 Juke Box Baby
- ☐ '57 Just Born (To Be Your Baby)
- ☐ '58 Kewpie Doll
- ☐ '55 Ko Ko Mo (I Love You So)
- ☐ '58 Love Makes The World Go 'Round
- ☐ '58 Magic Moments
- ☐ '58 Moon Talk
- ☐ '56 More
- ☐ '54 Papa Loves Mambo
- ☐ '57 Round And Round ★
- ☐ '69 Seattle
- ☐ '56 Somebody Up There Likes Me
- ☐ '67 Stop! And Think It Over
- ☐ '55 Tina Marie
- ☐ '67 You Made It That Way (Watermelon Summer)

COMPANY B
- ☐ '87 Fascinated

CONCRETE BLONDE
- ☐ '90 Joey ★

CONFEDERATE RAILROAD
- ☐ '92 Queen Of Memphis
- ☐ '93 Trashy Woman

CON FUNK SHUN
- ☐ '77 Ffun
- ☐ '81 Too Tight

CONLEY, Arthur
- ☐ '68 Funky Street
- ☐ '67 Shake, Rattle & Roll
- ☐ '67 Sweet Soul Music ★

CONNIFF, Ray, Sinters
- ☐ '66 Lookin' For Love
- ☐ '66 Somewhere, My Love

CONNOR, Chris
- ☐ '56 I Miss You So

CONNORS, Norman
- ☐ '76 You Are My Starship

CONTI, Bill
- ☐ '77 Gonna Fly Now

CONTOURS, The
- ☐ '62 Do You Love Me ★

CONWELL, Tommy, & The Young Rumblers
- ☐ '88 I'm Not Your Man
- ☐ '88 If We Never Meet Again

COOKE, Sam
- ☐ '63 Another Saturday Night
- ☐ '62 Bring It On Home To Me
- ☐ '60 Chain Gang ★
- ☐ '65 Change Is Gonna Come, A ★
- ☐ '64 Cousin Of Mine
- ☐ '61 Cupid
- ☐ '59 Everybody Likes To Cha Cha Cha
- ☐ '61 Feel It
- ☐ '63 Frankie And Johnny
- ☐ '64 Good News

COOKE, Sam — cont'd
- ☐ '64 Good Times
- ☐ '62 Having A Party
- ☐ '57 (I Love You) For Sentimental Reasons
- ☒ '57 I'll Come Running Back To You
- ☐ '63 Little Red Rooster
- ☐ '58 Lonely Island
- ☒ '58 Love You Most Of All
- ☒ '62 Nothing Can Change This Love
- ☒ '59 Only Sixteen
- ☐ '60 Sad Mood
- ☒ '63 Send Me Some Lovin'
- ☒ '65 Shake
- ☐ '62 Somebody Have Mercy
- ☐ '65 Sugar Dumpling
- ☐ '57 Summertime
- ☐ '61 That's It - I Quit - I'm Movin' On
- ☐ '62 Twistin' The Night Away
- ☐ '58 Win Your Love For Me
- ☐ '60 Wonderful World
- ☒ '57 You Send Me ★
- ☒ '58 You Were Made For Me

COOKIES, The
- ☐ '62 Chains
- ☐ '63 Don't Say Nothin' Bad (About My Baby)
- ☐ '63 Girls Grow Up Faster Than Boys

COOLEY, Eddie, & The Dimples
- ☐ '56 Priscilla

COOLIDGE, Rita
- ☐ '83 All Time High
- ☐ '79 I'd Rather Leave While I'm In Love
- ☒ '78 Way You Do The Things You Do, The
- ☐ '77 We're All Alone
- ☐ '78 You
- ☒ '77 (Your Love Has Lifted Me) Higher And Higher

COOLIO
- ☐ '97 C U When U Get There
- ☒ '94 Fantastic Voyage ★
- ☒ '95 Gangsta's Paradise ★
- ☐ '96 It's All The Way Live (Now)
- ☐ '96 1,2,3,4 (Sumpin' New)
- ☐ '95 Too Hot

COOPER, Alice
- ☐ '72 Be My Lover
- ☐ '73 Billion Dollar Babies
- ☐ '80 Clones (We're All)
- ☐ '71 Eighteen
- ☐ '72 Elected
- ☐ '73 Hello Hurray
- ☐ '78 How You Gonna See Me Now
- ☐ '76 I Never Cry
- ☐ '73 No More Mr. Nice Guy
- ☐ '75 Only Women
- ☐ '89 Poison
- ☒ '72 School's Out
- ☐ '72 Under My Wheels
- ☐ '75 Welcome To My Nightmare
- ☐ '77 You And Me

COOPER, Les, & The Soul Rockers
- ☒ '62 Wiggle Wobble

COOPER, Michael
- ☒ '87 To Prove My Love

COPE, Julian
- ☐ '87 World Shut Your Mouth

COPELAND, Ken
- ☒ '57 Pledge Of Love

COPPOLA, Imani
- ☐ '97 Legend Of A Cowgirl

COREY, Jill
- ☒ '56 I Love My Baby (My Baby Loves Me)
- ☒ '57 Love Me To Pieces

CORINA
- ☐ '91 Temptation

CORNELIUS BROTHERS & SISTER ROSE
- ☐ '72 Don't Ever Be Lonely (A Poor Little Fool Like Me)
- ☒ '72 I'm Never Gonna Be Alone Anymore
- ☐ '72 Too Late To Turn Back Now ★
- ☒ '71 Treat Her Like A Lady ★

CORNELL, Don
- ☐ '55 Bible Tells Me So, The
- ☐ '55 Love Is A Many-Splendored Thing
- ☐ '55 Most Of All
- ☐ '55 Young Abe Lincoln

CORONA
- ☒ '94 Rhythm Of The Night, The ★

CORRS, The
- ☒ '01 Breathless

CORSAIRS, The
- ☐ '61 Smoky Places

CORTEZ, Dave "Baby"
- ☐ '59 Happy Organ, The ★
- ☐ '62 Rinky Dink

COSBY, Bill
- ☐ '67 Little Ole Man (Uptight-Everything's Alright)

COSTA, Don, & His Orchestra
- ☐ '60 Never On Sunday
- ☐ '60 Theme From "The Unforgiven" (The Need For Love)

COSTELLO, Elvis
- ☐ '79 Accidents Will Happen
- ☐ '77 Alison
- ☐ '83 Everyday I Write The Book
- ☐ '80 I Can't Stand Up For Falling Down
- ☐ '79 Oliver's Army
- ☐ '91 Other Side Of Summer, The
- ☐ '78 Pump It Up
- ☐ '78 Radio, Radio
- ☐ '89 Veronica
- ☐ '77 Watching The Detectives ★

□ '79 (What's So Funny 'Bout) Peace, Love And Understanding

COTTON, Gene
□ '78 Before My Heart Finds Out
□ '78 Like A Sunday In Salem (The Amos & Andy Song)
□ '78 You're A Part Of Me *[w/ Kim Carnes]*
□ '76 You've Got Me Runnin'

COUNT FIVE
□ '66 Psychotic Reaction

COUNTING CROWS
▓ '04 Accidentally In Love
□ '96 Angels Of The Silences
□ '03 Big Yellow Taxi
□ '94 Einstein On The Beach (For An Eggman)
▓ '99 Hanginaround
▓ '96 Long December, A ★
▓ '93 Mr. Jones ★
▓ '94 Round Here

COUNTRY JOE & THE FISH
□ '67 I-Feel-Like-I'm-Fixin'-To-Die-Rag
□ '67 Not So Sweet Martha Lorraine
□ '68 Rock And Soul Music

COVAY, Don
□ '73 I Was Checkin' Out She Was Checkin' In
□ '64 Mercy, Mercy

COVEN
□ '71 One Tin Soldier, The Legend of Billy Jack

COVERDALE, David
□ '93 Pride And Joy *[w/ Jimmy Page]*

COVER GIRLS, The
▓ '87 Because Of You
▓ '89 My Heart Skips A Beat — M
▓ '88 Promise Me
▓ '89 We Can't Go Wrong
□ '92 Wishing On A Star

COWBOY CHURCH SUNDAY SCHOOL
□ '55 Open Up Your Heart (And Let The Sunshine In)

COWBOY JUNKIES
□ '94 Sweet Jane

COWSILLS, The
□ '69 Hair
□ '68 Indian Lake
□ '67 Rain, The Park & Other Things, The ★
□ '68 We Can Fly

COX, Deborah
▓ '98 Nobody's Supposed To Be Here ★
□ '95 Sentimental
▓ '99 We Can't Be Friends
▓ '96 Who Do U Love

COZIER, Jimmy
▓ '01 She's All I Got

CRABBY APPLETON
□ '70 Go Back

CRACKER
□ '93 Low

CRADDOCK, Billy "Crash"
□ '74 Rub It In
□ '74 Ruby, Baby

CRAMER, Floyd
□ '62 Chattanooga Choo Choo
□ '60 Last Date ★
□ '61 On The Rebound
□ '61 San Antonio Rose

CRANBERRIES, The
▓ '93 Linger ★
□ '95 Ode To My Family
□ '96 Salvation
□ '96 When You're Gone
□ '94 Zombie

CRANE, Les
□ '71 Desiderata

CRASH TEST DUMMIES
▓ '94 Mmm Mmm Mmm Mmm ★

CRAWFORD, Johnny
□ '62 Cindy's Birthday
□ '63 Proud
□ '62 Rumors
□ '62 Your Nose Is Gonna Grow

CRAY, Robert, Band
□ '86 Smoking Gun

CRAZY ELEPHANT
▓ '69 Gimme Gimme Good Lovin'

CRAZY FROG
▓ '05 Axel F

CRAZY TOWN
▓ '00 Butterfly ★

CREAM
□ '69 Badge
□ '69 Crossroads
□ '67 I Feel Free
□ '68 Spoonful
□ '67 Strange Brew
▓ '68 Sunshine Of Your Love ★
▓ '68 White Room

CREED
▓ '99 Higher ★
□ '97 My Own Prison
▓ '01 My Sacrifice ★
▓ '98 One
□ '02 One Last Breath
□ '98 Torn
□ '00 What If
□ '98 What's This Life For
▓ '00 With Arms Wide Open ★

CREEDENCE CLEARWATER REVIVAL
- ☐ '69 Bad Moon Rising ★
- ◪ '69 Born On The Bayou
- ☐ '69 Commotion
- ◪ '69 Down On The Corner ★
- ◪ '69 Fortunate Son
- ☐ '69 Green River ★
- ◪ '71 Have You Ever Seen The Rain ★
- ☐ '71 Hey Tonight
- ◪ '70 I Heard It Through The Grapevine
- ◪ '68 I Put A Spell On You
- ☐ '69 Lodi
- ☐ '70 Long As I Can See The Light
- ◪ '70 Lookin' Out My Back Door ★
- ◪ '69 Proud Mary ★
- ☐ '70 Run Through The Jungle
- ☐ '72 Someday Never Comes
- ☐ '68 Suzie Q.
- ☐ '71 Sweet Hitch-Hiker
- ◪ '70 Travelin' Band ★
- ☐ '70 Up Around The Bend ★
- ◪ '70 Who'll Stop The Rain ★

CRENSHAW, Marshall
- ☐ '82 Someday, Someway

CRESCENDOS, The
- ☐ '58 Oh Julie

CRESTS, The
- ☐ '59 Angels Listened In, The
- ☐ '61 Model Girl
- ☐ '59 Six Nights A Week
- ◪ '58 16 Candles ★
- ☐ '60 Step By Step
- ☐ '60 Trouble In Paradise
- ☐ '61 What A Surprise

CREW-CUTS, The
- ☐ '55 Angels In The Sky
- ☐ '55 Chop Chop Boom
- ☐ '55 Don't Be Angry
- ☐ '55 Earth Angel
- ☐ '55 Gum Drop
- ☐ '55 Ko Ko Mo (I Love You So)
- ☐ '55 Mostly Martha
- ☐ '56 Seven Days
- ◪ '54 Sh-Boom
- ☐ '55 Story Untold, A
- ◪ '57 Young Love

CREWE, Bob
- ☐ '66 Music To Watch Girls By

CRICKETS, The — see HOLLY, Buddy

CRIME MOB
- ◪ '07 Rock Yo Hips

CRITTERS, The
- ☐ '67 Don't Let The Rain Fall Down On Me
- ☐ '66 Mr. Dieingly Sad
- ☐ '66 Younger Girl

CROCE, Jim
- ◪ '73 Bad, Bad Leroy Brown ★
- ◪ '73 I Got A Name
- ◪ '74 I'll Have To Say I Love You In A Song
- ◪ '73 One Less Set Of Footsteps
- ◪ '72 Operator (That's Not the Way it Feels)
- ◪ '73 Time In A Bottle ★
- ◪ '74 Workin' At The Car Wash Blues
- ◪ '72 You Don't Mess Around With Jim

CROSBY, Bing
- ☐ '57 Around The World
- ◪ '56 True Love [w/ Grace Kelly] ★
- ◪ '55 White Christmas

CROSBY, David
- ◪ '93 Hero [w/ Phil Collins]
- ☐ '72 Immigration Man [w/ Graham Nash]

CROSBY, STILLS & NASH (& YOUNG)
- ☐ '70 Almost Cut My Hair
- ☐ '88 American Dream
- ☐ '70 Carry On
- ☐ '77 Dark Star
- ☐ '77 Fair Game
- ☐ '88 Got It Made
- ☐ '70 Helpless
- ☐ '69 Helplessly Hoping
- ☐ '77 Just A Song Before I Go
- ☐ '69 Marrakesh Express
- ☐ '70 Ohio ★
- ◪ '70 Our House
- ☐ '82 Southern Cross
- ☐ '69 Suite: Judy Blue Eyes
- ☐ '70 Teach Your Children
- ☐ '82 Wasted On The Way
- ☐ '69 Wooden Ships
- ☐ '70 Woodstock

CROSS, Christopher
- ◪ '83 All Right
- ◪ '81 Arthur's Theme (Best That You Can Do) ★ ━
- ☐ '80 Never Be The Same
- ◪ '80 Ride Like The Wind ★ ━
- ☐ '80 Sailing ★ ━
- ◪ '81 Say You'll Be Mine
- ☐ '83 Think Of Laura

CROSS COUNTRY
- ◪ '73 In The Midnight Hour

CROSSFADE
- ◪ '04 Cold

CROW
- ☐ '69 Evil Woman Don't Play Your Games With Me

CROW, Sheryl
- ◪ '94 All I Wanna Do ★
- ☐ '06 Always On Your Side [w/ Sting]
- ☐ '95 Can't Cry Anymore
- ☐ '97 Change Would Do You Good, A
- ◪ '97 Everyday Is A Winding Road
- ◪ '03 First Cut Is The Deepest, The
- ◪ '96 If It Makes You Happy ★
- ☐ '94 Leaving Las Vegas
- ☐ '98 My Favorite Mistake
- ◪ '02 Picture [w/ Kid Rock] ★

'02 Soak Up The Sun
'02 Steve McQueen
'94 Strong Enough ★

CROWDED HOUSE
'87 Don't Dream It's Over ★
'87 Something So Strong

CROWELL, Rodney
'80 Ashes By Now

CRUCIAL CONFLICT
'96 Hay

CRUSADERS, The
'79 Street Life

CRYAN' SHAMES, The
'66 Sugar And Spice

CRYSTALS, The
'63 Da Doo Ron Ron ★
'62 He's A Rebel ★
'62 He's Sure The Boy I Love
'63 Then He Kissed Me
'61 There's No Other (Like My Baby)
'62 Uptown

CUFF LINKS, The
'69 Tracy

CULT, The
'89 Fire Woman

CULTURE BEAT
'93 Mr. Vain

CULTURE CLUB
'83 Church Of The Poison Mind
'93 Crying Game, The [BOY GEORGE]
'82 Do You Really Want To Hurt Me ★
'83 I'll Tumble 4 Ya
'84 It's A Miracle
'83 Karma Chameleon ★
'87 Live My Life [BOY GEORGE]
'84 Miss Me Blind
'84 Mistake No. 3
'86 Move Away
'83 Time (Clock Of The Heart)
'84 War Song, The

CUMMINGS, Burton
'76 Stand Tall
'81 You Saved My Soul

CURB, Mike, Congregation
'70 Burning Bridges

CURE, The
'85 Boys Don't Cry
'89 Fascination Street
'92 Friday I'm In Love
'92 High
'85 In Between Days
'87 Just Like Heaven
'92 Letter To Elise, A
'89 Love Song
'90 Never Enough
'90 Pictures Of You

'93 Purple Haze
'87 Why Can't I Be You?

CURIOSITY KILLED THE CAT
'87 Misfit

CURRINGTON, Billy
'07 Good Directions
'05 Must Be Doin' Somethin' Right

CURTOLA, Bobby
'62 Fortuneteller

CUTTING CREW
'87 (I Just) Died In Your Arms ★
'87 I've Been In Love Before
'87 One For The Mockingbird

CYMARRON
'71 Rings ★

CYMBAL, Johnny
'63 Mr. Bass Man
'63 Teenage Heaven

CYPRESS HILL
'93 Insane In The Brain

CYRKLE, The
'66 Red Rubber Ball ★
'66 Turn-Down Day

CYRUS, Billy Ray
'92 Achy Breaky Heart ★
'98 Busy Man
'92 Could've Been Me
'93 In The Heart Of A Woman

D

DA BRAT
'94 Fa All Y'all
'94 Funkdafied
'97 Ghetto Love
'95 Give It 2 You
'03 In Love Wit Chu
'98 Party Continues, The [w/ Jermaine Dupri]
'96 Sittin' On Top Of The World
'00 What'Chu Like

DADDY DEWDROP
'71 Chick-A-Boom (Don't Ya Jes' Love It)

DADDY-O'S, The
'58 Got A Match?

DADDY YANKEE
'04 Gasolina ★
'06 Rompe

DALE, Alan
'55 Cherry Pink (And Apple Blossom White)
'55 Sweet And Gentle

DALE, Dick
'61 Let's Go Trippin'
'62 Misirlou
'62 Surf Beat

DALE & GRACE
- ☐ '63 I'm Leaving It Up To You
- ☐ '64 Stop And Think It Over

DALTREY, Roger
- ☐ '85 After The Fire
- ☐ '80 Without Your Love

DAMIAN, Michael
- ☐ '89 Cover Of Love
- ☐ '89 Rock On
- ☐ '89 Was It Nothing At All

DAMIAN DAME
- ☐ '91 Exclusivity
- ☐ '91 Right Down To It

DAMITA JO
- ☐ '61 I'll Be There
- ☐ '60 I'll Save The Last Dance For You

DAMNED, The
- ☐ '76 New Rose

DAMN YANKEES
- ☐ '90 Coming Of Age
- ☐ '92 Don't Tread On Me
- ☐ '90 High Enough ★
- ☐ '92 Mister Please
- ☐ '92 Where You Goin' Now

DAMON('S), Liz, Orient Express
- ☐ '70 1900 Yesterday

DAMONE, Vic
- ☐ '57 Affair To Remember (Our Love Affair)
- ☐ '56 On The Street Where You Live ★
- ☐ '65 You Were Only Fooling (While I Was Falling In Love)

DANA, Vic
- ☐ '66 I Love You Drops
- ☐ '70 If I Never Knew Your Name
- ☐ '61 Little Altar Boy
- ☐ '70 Red Red Wine
- ☐ '65 Red Roses For A Blue Lady
- ☐ '64 Shangri-La

DANCER, PRANCER & NERVOUS
- ☐ '59 Happy Reindeer, The

D'ANGELO
- ☐ '95 Brown Sugar
- ☐ '95 Cruisin'
- ☐ '96 Lady
- ☐ '00 Untitled (How Does It Feel)

DANIELS, Charlie, Band
- ☐ '79 Devil Went Down To Georgia, The ★
- ☐ '80 In America
- ☐ '80 Legend Of Wooley Swamp, The
- ☐ '75 Long Haired Country Boy
- ☐ '75 South's Gonna Do It, The
- ☐ '82 Still In Saigon
- ☐ '73 Uneasy Rider

DANITY KANE
- ☐ '06 Show Stopper

DANLEERS, The
- ☐ '58 One Summer Night

DANNY & THE JUNIORS
- ☐ '57 At The Hop ★
- ☐ '58 Dottie
- ☐ '58 Rock And Roll Is Here To Stay
- ☐ '60 Twistin' U.S.A.

DANNY WILSON
- ☐ '87 Mary's Prayer

DANTÉ & THE EVERGREENS
- ☐ '60 Alley-Oop

D'ARBY, Terence Trent
- ☐ '88 Dance Little Sister
- ☐ '88 Sign Your Name
- ☐ '88 Wishing Well ★

DARENSBOURGE, Joe
- ☐ '58 Yellow Dog Blues

DARIN, Bobby
- ☐ '60 Artificial Flowers
- ☐ '60 Beyond The Sea
- ☐ '60 Clementine
- ☐ '59 Dream Lover ★
- ☐ '58 Early In The Morning
- ☐ '63 18 Yellow Roses
- ☐ '62 If A Man Answers
- ☐ '66 If I Were A Carpenter
- ☐ '61 Irresistible You
- ☐ '61 Lazy River
- ☐ '59 Mack The Knife ★
- ☐ '66 Mame
- ☐ '61 Multiplication
- ☐ '61 Nature Boy
- ☐ '59 Plain Jane
- ☐ '58 Queen Of The Hop ★
- ☐ '58 Splish Splash ★
- ☐ '62 Things
- ☐ '62 What'd I Say
- ☐ '60 Won't You Come Home Bill Bailey
- ☐ '61 You Must Have Been A Beautiful Baby
- ☐ '63 You're The Reason I'm Living

DARREN, James
- ☐ '67 All
- ☐ '62 Conscience
- ☐ '59 Gidget
- ☐ '61 Goodbye Cruel World
- ☐ '62 Her Royal Majesty
- ☐ '62 Mary's Little Lamb

DARTELLS, The
- ☐ '63 Hot Pastrami

DARUDE
- ☐ '01 Sandstorm

DAS EFX
- ☐ '92 They Want EFX

DASHBOARD CONFESSIONAL
- ☐ '04 Vindicated

DAUGHTRY
- '07 Home ★
- '07 It's Not Over ★
- '07 Over You

DAVID, Craig
- '01 Fill Me In
- '01 7 Days

DAVID & DAVID
- '86 Welcome To The Boomtown

DAVID & JONATHAN
- '66 Michelle

DAVIDSON, Clay
- '00 Unconditional

DAVIS, Alana
- '97 32 Flavors

DAVIS, Linda — see McENTIRE, Reba

DAVIS, Mac
- '72 Baby Don't Get Hooked On Me ★
- '80 It's Hard To Be Humble
- '74 One Hell Of A Woman
- '74 Rock N' Roll (I Gave You The Best Years Of My Life)
- '74 Stop And Smell The Roses

DAVIS, Paul
- '81 Cool Night
- '80 Do Right
- '77 I Go Crazy
- '74 Ride 'Em Cowboy
- '82 '65 Love Affair
- '76 Superstar
- '78 Sweet Life

DAVIS, Sammy Jr.
- '72 Candy Man, The ★
- '67 Don't Blame The Children
- '68 I've Gotta Be Me
- '55 Love Me Or Leave Me
- '63 Shelter Of Your Arms, The
- '55 Something's Gotta Give
- '55 That Old Black Magic
- '62 What Kind Of Fool Am I

DAVIS, Skeeter
- '63 End Of The World, The ★
- '60 (I Can't Help You) I'm Falling Too
- '63 I Can't Stay Mad At You
- '60 My Last Date (With You)

DAVIS, Spencer, Group
- '66 Gimme Some Lovin' ★
- '67 I'm A Man

DAVIS, Tyrone
- '82 Are You Serious
- '68 Can I Change My Mind
- '76 Give It Up (Turn It Loose)
- '69 Is It Something You've Got
- '73 There It Is
- '70 Turn Back The Hands Of Time
- '75 Turning Point

DAWN — see ORLANDO, Tony

DAY, Bobby
- '58 Over And Over
- '58 Rock-in Robin ★

DAY, Doris
- '58 Everybody Loves A Lover
- '55 I'll Never Stop Loving You
- '55 Love Me Or Leave Me
- '56 Whatever Will Be, Will Be (Que Sera, Sera) ★

DAY, Howie
- '05 Collide

DAY, Morris
- '88 Fishnet
- '85 Oak Tree, The

DAYNE, Taylor
- '93 Can't Get Enough Of Your Love
- '88 Don't Rush Me
- '90 Heart Of Stone
- '88 I'll Always Love You
- '90 I'll Be Your Shelter
- '90 Love Will Lead You Back ★
- '88 Prove Your Love
- '87 Tell It To My Heart
- '89 With Every Beat Of My Heart

DAYS OF THE NEW
- '98 Down Town, The
- '99 Enemy
- '98 Shelf In The Room
- '97 Touch, Peel And Stand

DAZZ BAND
- '82 Let It Whip ★

DC TALK
- '95 Jesus Freak
- '96 Just Between You And Me

DEADEYE DICK
- '94 New Age Girl

DEAD OR ALIVE
- '86 Brand New Lover
- '85 You Spin Me Round (Like A Record)

DEAL, Bill, & The Rhondels
- '69 I've Been Hurt
- '69 May I
- '69 What Kind Of Fool Do You Think I Am

DEAN, Billy
- '92 If There Hadn't Been You
- '05 Let Them Be Little
- '90 Only Here For A Little While
- '91 Somewhere In My Broken Heart

DEAN, Jimmy
- '61 Big Bad John ★
- '62 Cajun Queen, The
- '62 Dear Ivan
- '76 I.O.U.
- '62 Little Black Book

DEAN, Jimmy — cont'd
- ☐ '62 P.T. 109
- ☐ '62 Steel Men
- ☐ '62 To A Sleeping Beauty

DEAN & JEAN
- ☐ '64 Hey Jean, Hey Dean
- ☐ '63 Tra La La La Suzy

DeANDA, Paula
- ☐ '06 Doing Too Much
- ☐ '07 Walk Away (Remember Me)

DEATH CAB FOR CUTIE
- ☐ '06 Soul Meets Body

DeBARGE
- ☐ '83 All This Love
- ☐ '83 I Like It
- ☐ '85 Rhythm Of The Night ★
- ☐ '83 Time Will Reveal
- ☐ '85 Who's Holding Donna Now

DeBARGE, Chico
- ☐ '86 Talk To Me

DeBARGE, El
- ☐ '86 Who's Johnny

DeBURGH, Chris
- ☐ '83 Don't Pay The Ferryman
- ☐ '84 High On Emotion
- ☐ '87 Lady In Red, The ★

DeCASTRO SISTERS, The
- ☐ '55 Boom Boom Boomerang
- ☐ '55 Teach Me Tonight

DEE, Jimmy
- ☐ '58 Henrietta

DEE, Joey, & the Starliters
- ☐ '62 Hey, Let's Twist
- ☐ '63 Hot Pastrami With Mashed Potatoes
- ☐ '61 Peppermint Twist ★
- ☐ '62 Shout
- ☐ '62 What Kind Of Love Is This

DEE, Kiki
- ☐ '76 Don't Go Breaking My Heart [w/ Elton John] ★
- ☐ '74 I've Got The Music In Me

DEE, Lenny
- ☐ '55 Plantation Boogie

DEE, Tommy
- ☐ '59 Three Stars

DEEE-LITE
- ☐ '90 Groove Is In The Heart

DEELE, The
- ☐ '83 Body Talk
- ☐ '88 Two Occasions

DEEP BLUE SOMETHING
- ☐ '95 Breakfast At Tiffany's ★

DEEP PURPLE
- ☐ '70 Black Night
- ☐ '72 Highway Star
- ☐ '68 Hush
- ☐ '68 Kentucky Woman
- ☐ '74 Might Just Take Your Life
- ☐ '69 River Deep-Mountain High
- ☐ '73 Smoke On The Water ★
- ☐ '72 Space Truckin'
- ☐ '71 Strange Kind Of Woman
- ☐ '73 Woman From Tokyo

DEES, Rick
- ☐ '76 Disco Duck

DEFAULT
- ☐ '01 Wasting My Time

DEF LEPPARD
- ☐ '87 Animal
- ☐ '88 Armageddon It
- ☐ '84 Bringin' On The Heartbreak
- ☐ '83 Foolin'
- ☐ '92 Have You Ever Needed Someone So Bad
- ☐ '88 Hysteria
- ☐ '92 Let's Get Rocked ★
- ☐ '88 Love Bites
- ☐ '92 Make Love Like A Man
- ☐ '93 Miss You In A Heartbeat
- ☐ '83 Photograph
- ☐ '88 Pour Some Sugar On Me ★
- ☐ '99 Promises
- ☐ '83 Rock Of Ages
- ☐ '89 Rocket
- ☐ '92 Stand Up (Kick Love Into Motion)
- ☐ '93 Two Steps Behind

DeFRANCO FAMILY
- ☐ '73 Abra-Ca-Dabra
- ☐ '73 Heartbeat - It's A Lovebeat
- ☐ '74 Save The Last Dance For Me

DEFTONES
- ☐ '00 Change (In The House Of Flies)

DeGARMO, Diana
- ☐ '04 Dreams

DeGRAW, Gavin
- ☐ '05 Chariot ★
- ☐ '05 I Don't Want To Be ★
- ☐ '06 We Belong Together

DÉJA
- ☐ '87 You And Me Tonight

DeJOHN SISTERS
- ☐ '55 (My Baby Don't Love Me) No More

DEKKER, Desmond, & The Aces
- ☐ '69 Israelites

DEL AMITRI
- ☐ '92 Always The Last To Know
- ☐ '90 Kiss This Thing Goodbye
- ☐ '95 Roll To Me

DELANEY & BONNIE & FRIENDS
- ☐ '70 Comin' Home
- ☐ '71 Never Ending Song Of Love
- ☐ '71 Only You Know And I Know
- ☐ '70 Soul Shake

DE LA SOUL
- ☐ '05 Feel Good Inc *[w/ Gorillaz]* ★
- ☐ '89 Me Myself And I

DELEGATES, The
- ☐ '72 Convention '72

DELFONICS, The
- ☐ '68 Break Your Promise
- ☐ '70 Didn't I (Blow Your Mind This Time)
- ☒ '68 La - La - Means I Love You
- ☐ '68 Ready Or Not Here I Come (Can't Hide From Love)
- ☐ '70 Trying To Make A Fool Of Me
- ☐ '69 You Got Yours And I'll Get Mine

DELINQUENT HABITS
- ☐ '96 Tres Delinquentes

DELLS, The
- ☒ '68 Always Together
- ☐ '68 Does Anybody Know I'm Here
- ☐ '73 Give Your Baby A Standing Ovation
- ☐ '69 I Can Sing A Rainbow/Love Is Blue
- ☐ '71 Love We Had (Stays On My Mind)
- ☒ '69 Oh, What A Night
- ☐ '68 Stay In My Corner
- ☐ '68 There Is

DELL-VIKINGS, The
- ☒ '57 Come Go With Me ★
- ☐ '57 Cool Shake
- ☐ '57 Whispering Bells

DeLORY, Al
- ☐ '70 Song From M*A*S*H

DeLUNA, Kat
- ☒ '07 Whine Up

DEMENSIONS, The
- ☐ '60 Over The Rainbow

DEM FRANCHIZE BOYZ
- ☒ '05 I Think They Like Me
- ☒ '06 Lean Wit It, Rock Wit It ★

DENNIS, Cathy
- ☐ '89 C'mon And Get My Love *[D MOB Introducing Cathy Dennis]*
- ☐ '90 Just Another Dream
- ☐ '91 Too Many Walls
- ☒ '91 Touch Me (All Night Long)
- ☐ '92 You Lied To Me

DENNY, Martin
- ☐ '59 Enchanted Sea, The
- ☐ '59 Quiet Village

DENVER, John
- ☒ '74 Annie's Song ★
- ☐ '74 Back Home Again

- ☐ '75 Calypso
- ☐ '75 Fly Away
- ☐ '77 How Can I Leave You Again
- ☐ '75 I'm Sorry
- ☐ '76 Looking For Space
- ☐ '77 My Sweet Lady
- ☒ '72 Rocky Mountain High
- ☐ '82 Shanghai Breezes
- ☐ '81 Some Days Are Diamonds (Some Days Are Stone)
- ☒ '74 Sunshine On My Shoulders ★
- ☐ '74 Sweet Surrender
- ☒ '71 Take Me Home, Country Roads ★
- ☐ '75 Thank God I'm A Country Boy ★

DEODATO
- ☐ '73 Also Sprach Zarathustra (2001)

DEPECHE MODE
- ☐ '90 Enjoy The Silence
- ☒ '93 I Feel You
- ☐ '97 It's No Good
- ☐ '87 Never Let Me Down Again
- ☒ '85 People Are People ★
- ☒ '89 Personal Jesus ★
- ☐ '90 Policy Of Truth
- ☒ '87 Strangelove
- ☐ '93 Walking In My Shoes

DEREK
- ☐ '68 Cinnamon

DEREK & THE DOMINOS — see CLAPTON, Eric

DERRINGER, Rick
- ☐ '74 Rock And Roll, Hoochie Koo

DeSARIO, Teri
- ☐ '79 Yes, I'm Ready *[w/ K.C.]*

DeSHANNON, Jackie
- ☐ '69 Love Will Find A Way
- ☒ '69 Put A Little Love In Your Heart
- ☐ '65 What The World Needs Now Is Love

DESMOND, Johnny
- ☐ '55 Play Me Hearts And Flowers (I Wanna Cry)
- ☒ '55 Sixteen Tons
- ☐ '55 Yellow Rose Of Texas, The

DES'REE
- ☒ '94 You Gotta Be ★

DESTINY'S CHILD
- ☒ '99 Bills, Bills, Bills ★
- ☒ '01 Bootylicious ★
- ☐ '99 Bug A Boo
- ☒ '05 Cater 2 U
- ☒ '01 Emotion
- ☐ '05 Girl
- ☐ '00 Independent Women ★
- ☒ '00 Jumpin', Jumpin' ★
- ☒ '04 Lose My Breath ★
- ☒ '97 No, No, No ★
- ☒ '99 Say My Name ★

DESTINY'S CHILD — cont'd
- 🎵 '05 Soldier ★
- 🎵 '01 Survivor ★

DETERGENTS, The
- ☐ '64 Leader Of The Laundromat

DETROIT EMERALDS
- 🎵 '72 Baby Let Me Take You (In My Arms)
- 🎵 '71 Do Me Right
- 🎵 '72 You Want It, You Got It

DeVAUGHN, William
- ☐ '74 Be Thankful For What You Got

DEVICE
- ☐ '86 Hanging On A Heart Attack

DEVO
- 🎵 '80 Whip It ★
- ☐ '81 Working In The Coal Mine

DeVORZON, Barry, & Perry Botkin, Jr.
- ☐ '76 Nadia's Theme (The Young And The Restless)

DEVOTIONS, The
- ☐ '64 Rip Van Winkle

DEXYS MIDNIGHT RUNNERS
- ☐ '83 Come On Eileen ★

DeYOUNG, Cliff
- ☐ '74 My Sweet Lady

DeYOUNG, Dennis
- ☐ '84 Desert Moon

D4L
- 🎵 '06 Laffy Taffy ★

D.H.T.
- 🎵 '05 Listen To Your Heart ★

DIAMOND, Neil
- ☐ '81 America
- ☐ '73 Be
- ☐ '76 Beautiful Noise
- ☐ '68 Brooklyn Roads
- ☐ '69 Brother Love's Travelling Salvation Show
- ☐ '66 Cherry, Cherry
- ☐ '73 "Cherry Cherry" from Hot August Night
- ☐ '70 Cracklin' Rosie ★
- ☐ '77 Desirée
- ☐ '70 Do It
- ☐ '71 Done Too Soon
- ☐ '79 Forever In Blue Jeans
- ☐ '67 Girl, You'll Be A Woman Soon
- ☐ '70 He Ain't Heavy...He's My Brother
- ☐ '82 Heartlight
- ☐ '81 Hello Again
- ☐ '69 Holly Holy
- ☐ '71 I Am...I Said
- ☐ '66 I Got The Feelin' (Oh No No)
- ☐ '71 I'm A Believer
- ☐ '83 I'm Alive
- ☐ '75 I've Been This Way Before
- ☐ '76 If You Know What I Mean

- ☐ '67 Kentucky Woman
- ☐ '74 Longfellow Serenade
- ☐ '80 Love On The Rocks ★
- ☐ '72 Morningside
- ☐ '82 On The Way To The Sky
- ☐ '72 Play Me
- ☐ '68 Red Red Wine
- ☐ '79 Say Maybe
- ☐ '79 September Morn'
- ☐ '70 Shilo
- ☐ '66 Solitary Man
- ☐ '72 Song Sung Blue ★
- ☐ '70 Soolaimón (African Trilogy II)
- ☐ '71 Stones
- ☐ '69 Sweet Caroline ★
- ☐ '67 Thank The Lord For The Night Time
- ☐ '72 Walk On Water
- ☐ '81 Yesterday's Songs
- ☐ '78 You Don't Bring Me Flowers [w/ Barbra Streisand] ★
- ☐ '67 You Got To Me

DIAMOND RIO
- 🎵 '02 Beautiful Mess
- 🎵 '97 How Your Love Makes Me Feel
- ☐ '02 I Believe
- ☐ '98 Imagine That
- ☐ '92 In A Week Or Two
- ☐ '94 Love A Little Stronger
- ☐ '91 Meet In The Middle
- ☐ '92 Norma Jean Riley
- ☐ '01 One More Day
- ☐ '98 Unbelievable
- 🎵 '95 Walkin' Away

DIAMONDS, The
- ☐ '56 Church Bells May Ring, The
- ☐ '58 High Sign
- ☐ '56 Ka-Ding-Dong
- ☐ '58 Kathy-O
- ☐ '57 Little Darlin' ★
- 🎵 '56 Love, Love, Love
- ☐ '61 One Summer Night
- ☐ '59 She Say (Oom Dooby Doom)
- ☐ '57 Silhouettes
- ☐ '56 Soft Summer Breeze
- ☐ '57 Stroll, The
- ☐ '58 Walking Along
- 🎵 '56 Why Do Fools Fall In Love
- 🎵 '57 Words Of Love
- ☐ '57 Zip Zip

DIBANGO, Manu
- ☐ '73 Soul Makossa

DICK & DEEDEE
- ☐ '61 Mountain's High, The ★
- ☐ '62 Tell Me
- ☐ '64 Thou Shalt Not Steal
- ☐ '63 Turn Around
- ☐ '63 Young And In Love

DICKENS, "Little" Jimmy
- ☐ '65 May The Bird Of Paradise Fly Up Your Nose

DICKY DOO & THE DON'TS
- '58 Click-Clack
- '58 Nee Nee Na Na Na Na Nu Nu

DIDDLEY, Bo
- '55 Bo Diddley ★
- '55 Diddley Daddy
- '57 Hey Bo Diddley
- '55 I'm A Man
- '60 Road Runner
- '59 Say Man
- '57 Who Do You Love?
- '62 You Can't Judge A Book By The Cover

DIDO
- '01 Thankyou ★
- '03 White Flag

DIESEL
- '81 Down In The Silvermine
- '81 Sausalito Summernight

DIFFIE, Joe
- '95 Bigger Than The Beatles
- '90 Home
- '91 If The Devil Danced (In Empty Pockets)
- '90 If You Want Me To
- '00 It's Always Somethin'
- '91 New Way (To Light Up An Old Flame)
- '99 Night To Remember, A
- '94 Pickup Man
- '93 Prop Me Up Beside The Jukebox (If I Die)
- '95 So Help Me Girl
- '94 Third Rock From The Sun

DIGABLE PLANETS
- '93 Rebirth Of Slick (Cool Like Dat)

DIGITAL UNDERGROUND
- '90 Humpty Dance, The ★
- '91 Kiss You Back

DINNING, Mark
- '59 Teen Angel ★

DINO
- '90 Gentle
- '89 I Like It
- '93 Ooh Child
- '90 Romeo
- '89 Sunshine
- '89 24/7

DINO, Kenny
- '61 Your Ma Said You Cried In Your Sleep Last Night

DINO, Paul
- '61 Ginnie Bell

DINO, DESI & BILLY
- '65 I'm A Fool
- '65 Not The Lovin' Kind
- '65 Rebel Kind, The

DINOSAUR JR.
- '94 Feel The Pain

DION
- '68 Abraham, Martin And John
- '63 Be Careful Of Stones That You Throw
- '63 Donna The Prima Donna
- '63 Drip Drop
- '61 Havin' Fun
- '62 (I Was) Born To Cry
- '62 Little Diane
- '60 Lonely Teenager
- '62 Love Came To Me
- '62 Lovers Who Wander
- '61 Majestic, The
- '63 Ruby Baby ★
- '61 Runaround Sue ★
- '63 Sandy
- '63 This Little Girl
- '61 Wanderer, The ★

DION & THE BELMONTS
- '58 Don't Pity Me
- '59 Every Little Thing I Do
- '58 I Wonder Why
- '60 In The Still Of The Night
- '58 No One Knows
- '59 Teenager In Love, A ★
- '60 When You Wish Upon A Star
- '59 Where Or When

DION, Celine
- '97 All By Myself
- '92 Beauty And The Beast *[w/ Peabo Bryson]* ★
- '96 Because You Loved Me ★
- '03 Have You Ever Been In Love
- '98 I'm Your Angel *[w/ R. Kelly]* ★
- '91 (If There Was) Any Other Way
- '92 If You Asked Me To ★
- '96 It's All Coming Back To Me Now ★
- '92 Love Can Move Mountains
- '94 Misled
- '98 My Heart Will Go On (Love Theme From 'Titanic') ★
- '02 New Day Has Come, A
- '92 Nothing Broken But My Heart
- '93 Power Of Love, The ★
- '99 That's The Way It Is
- '98 To Love You More
- '93 When I Fall In Love *[w/ Clive Griffin]*
- '90 Where Does My Heart Beat Now ★

DIRE STRAITS
- '91 Calling Elvis
- '91 Heavy Fuel
- '79 Lady Writer
- '85 Money For Nothing ★
- '86 So Far Away
- '79 Sultans Of Swing ★
- '80 Tunnel Of Love
- '85 Walk Of Life ★

DIRKSEN, Senator Everett McKinley
- '66 Gallant Men

DIRTY VEGAS
- '02 Days Go By ★

DISCO TEX & THE SEX-O-LETTES
- ☐ '74 Get Dancin'
- ☐ '75 I Wanna Dance Wit' Choo (Doo Dat Dance)

DISHWALLA
- ☐ '96 Counting Blue Cars

DISTURBED
- ☐ '06 Just Stop
- ☐ '06 Land Of Confusion
- ☐ '02 Prayer
- ☐ '05 Stricken

DIVINE
- ☒ '98 Lately ★
- ☐ '99 One More Try

DIVINYLS
- ☒ '91 I Touch Myself

DIXIEBELLES, The
- ☐ '63 (Down At) Papa Joe's
- ☐ '64 Southtown, U.S.A.

DIXIE CHICKS
- ☒ '99 Cowboy Take Me Away
- ☒ '00 Goodbye Earl
- ☐ '01 If I Fall You're Going Down With Me
- ☐ '02 Landslide
- ☐ '02 Long Time Gone
- ☒ '07 Not Ready To Make Nice ★
- ☐ '99 Ready To Run
- ☐ '98 There's Your Trouble
- ☐ '02 Travelin' Soldier
- ☒ '98 Wide Open Spaces
- ☒ '00 Without You
- ☒ '99 You Were Mine

DIXIE CUPS, The
- ☐ '64 Chapel Of Love ★
- ☐ '65 Iko Iko
- ☐ '64 People Say
- ☐ '64 You Should Have Seen The Way He Looked At Me

D.J. JAZZY JEFF & THE FRESH PRINCE
- ☐ '93 Boom! Shake The Room
- ☐ '88 Nightmare On My Street, A
- ☒ '88 Parents Just Don't Understand
- ☐ '91 Ring My Bell
- ☒ '91 Summertime

DJ KHALED
- ☒ '07 We Takin' Over

DJ KOOL
- ☒ '97 Let Me Clear My Throat

DJ SAMMY & YANOU
- ☒ '02 Heaven ★

DMX
- ☐ '98 Get At Me Dog
- ☐ '00 Party Up (Up In Here)
- ☒ '99 Ruff Ryders' Anthem
- ☒ '00 What You Want

D.N.A. — see VEGA, Suzanne

DOBKINS, Carl Jr.
- ☐ '59 Lucky Devil
- ☐ '59 My Heart Is An Open Book

DR. BUZZARD'S ORIGINAL SAVANNAH BAND
- ☐ '76 Whispering/Cherchez La Femme/Se Si Bon

DR. DRE
- ☐ '93 Dre Day *[w/ Snoop Doggy Dogg]*
- ☒ '00 Forgot About Dre
- ☐ '95 Keep Their Heads Ringin'
- ☐ '93 Let Me Ride
- ☒ '00 Next Episode, The *[w/ Snoop Doggy Dogg]*
- ☒ '93 Nuthin' But A "G" Thang *[w/ Snoop Doggy Dogg]* ★

DR. HOOK
- ☒ '82 Baby Makes Her Blue Jeans Talk
- ☐ '79 Better Love Next Time
- ☒ '72 Cover Of "Rolling Stone", The
- ☐ '80 Girls Can Get It
- ☐ '76 Little Bit More, A
- ☒ '76 Only Sixteen
- ☒ '80 Sexy Eyes
- ☒ '78 Sharing The Night Together
- ☒ '72 Sylvia's Mother
- ☒ '79 When You're In Love With A Beautiful Woman

DR. JOHN
- ☐ '73 Right Place Wrong Time

DOGGETT, Bill
- ☐ '58 Hold It
- ☐ '56 Honky Tonk ★
- ☐ '56 Slow Walk
- ☐ '57 Soft

DOG'S EYE VIEW
- ☐ '96 Everything Falls Apart

DOKKEN
- ☒ '85 Alone Again
- ☐ '83 Breaking The Chains

DOLBY, Thomas
- ☐ '83 She Blinded Me With Science

DOMINO
- ☐ '93 Getto Jam
- ☐ '94 Sweet Potato Pie

DOMINO, Fats
- ☐ '55 Ain't That A Shame ★
- ☐ '61 Ain't That Just Like A Woman
- ☐ '55 All By Myself
- ☐ '59 Be My Guest
- ☐ '57 Big Beat, The
- ☐ '57 Blue Monday ★
- ☐ '56 Blueberry Hill ★
- ☐ '56 Bo Weevil
- ☐ '60 Country Boy
- ☐ '60 Don't Come Knockin'
- ☐ '61 Fell In Love On Monday

- ☐ '56 Honey Chile
- ☐ '59 I Want To Walk You Home
- ☐ '57 I Want You To Know
- ☐ '59 I'm Gonna Be A Wheel Some Day
- ☐ '56 I'm In Love Again
- ☐ '59 I'm Ready
- ☐ '57 I'm Walkin'
- ☐ '61 It Keeps Rainin'
- ☐ '57 It's You I Love
- ☐ '61 Let The Four Winds Blow
- ☐ '56 My Blue Heaven
- ☐ '60 My Girl Josephine
- ☐ '60 Natural Born Lover
- ☐ '55 Poor Me
- ☐ '60 Put Your Arms Around Me Honey
- ☐ '63 Red Sails In The Sunset
- ☐ '61 Shu Rah
- ☐ '58 Sick And Tired
- ☐ '60 Three Nights A Week
- ☐ '57 Valley Of Tears
- ☐ '57 Wait And See
- ☐ '60 Walking To New Orleans ★
- ☐ '61 What A Party
- ☐ '61 What A Price
- ☐ '57 When I See You
- ☐ '56 When My Dreamboat Comes Home
- ☐ '58 Whole Lotta Loving
- ☐ '62 You Win Again

DONALDS, Andru
- ☐ '94 Mishale

DONALDSON, Bo, & The Heywoods
- ☐ '74 Billy, Don't Be A Hero ★
- ☐ '74 Heartbreak Kid, The
- ☐ '74 Who Do You Think You Are

DON & JUAN
- ☐ '62 What's Your Name

DON AND THE GOODTIMES
- ☐ '67 I Could Be So Good To You

DONEGAN, Lonnie, & His Skiffle Group
- ☐ '61 Does Your Chewing Gum Lose It's Flavor (On The Bedpost Over Night)
- ☐ '56 Rock Island Line ★

DONNER, Ral
- ☐ '61 Girl Of My Best Friend
- ☐ '61 Please Don't Go
- ☐ '61 She's Everything (I Wanted You To Be)
- ☐ '62 (What A Sad Way) To Love Someone
- ☐ '61 You Don't Know What You've Got (Until You Lose It)

DONNIE & THE DREAMERS
- ☐ '61 Count Every Star

DONOVAN
- ☐ '69 Atlantis
- ☐ '65 Catch The Wind
- ☐ '67 Epistle To Dippy
- ☐ '69 Goo Goo Barabajagal (Love Is Hot)
- ☐ '68 Hurdy Gurdy Man
- ☐ '68 Jennifer Juniper

- ☐ '68 Lalena
- ☐ '66 Mellow Yellow ★
- ☐ '66 Sunshine Superman ★
- ☐ '67 There Is A Mountain
- ☐ '69 To Susan On The West Coast Waiting
- ☐ '65 Universal Soldier
- ☐ '67 Wear Your Love Like Heaven

DOOBIE BROTHERS, The
- ☐ '74 Another Park, Another Sunday
- ☐ '74 Black Water ★
- ☐ '73 China Grove ★
- ☐ '91 Dangerous
- ☐ '79 Dependin' On You
- ☐ '89 Doctor, The
- ☐ '74 Eyes Of Silver
- ☐ '76 It Keeps You Runnin'
- ☐ '72 Jesus Is Just Alright
- ☐ '72 Listen To The Music
- ☐ '73 Long Train Runnin'
- ☐ '79 Minute By Minute
- ☐ '89 Need A Little Taste Of Love
- ☐ '80 One Step Closer
- ☐ '80 Real Love
- ☐ '72 Rockin' Down The Highway
- ☐ '73 South City Midnight Lady
- ☐ '75 Sweet Maxine
- ☐ '75 Take Me In Your Arms (Rock Me)
- ☐ '76 Takin' It To The Streets
- ☐ '79 What A Fool Believes ★
- ☐ '77 You Belong To Me

DO OR DIE
- ☐ '96 Po Pimp

DOORS, The
- ☐ '67 Alabama Song (Whiskey Bar)
- ☐ '67 Back Door Man
- ☐ '67 Break On Through (To The Other Side)
- ☐ '67 Crystal Ship
- ☐ '67 End, The
- ☐ '68 Five To One
- ☐ '68 Hello, I Love You ★
- ☐ '71 L.A. Woman
- ☐ '67 Light My Fire ★
- ☐ '71 Love Her Madly
- ☐ '67 Love Me Two Times
- ☐ '67 Moonlight Drive
- ☐ '67 People Are Strange
- ☐ '71 Riders On The Storm
- ☐ '70 Roadhouse Blues
- ☐ '67 Strange Days
- ☐ '69 Tell All The People
- ☐ '68 Touch Me
- ☐ '68 Unknown Soldier, The
- ☐ '67 When The Music's Over
- ☐ '69 Wishful Sinful
- ☐ '70 You Make Me Real

DORE, Charlie
- ☐ '80 Pilot Of The Airwaves

DORMAN, Harold
- ☐ '60 Mountain Of Love

DORSEY, Jimmy, Orchestra
- ☐ '57 June Night
- ☐ '57 So Rare ★

DORSEY, Lee
- ☐ '61 Do-Re-Mi
- ☐ '66 Holy Cow
- ☐ '65 Ride Your Pony
- ☐ '66 Working In The Coal Mine
- ☐ '61 Ya Ya

DORSEY, Tommy, Orchestra
- ☐ '58 Tea For Two Cha Cha

DOUBLE
- ☐ '86 Captain Of Her Heart, The

DOUGLAS, Carl
- 📼 '74 Kung Fu Fighting ★

DOUGLAS, Carol
- ☐ '74 Doctor's Orders

DOUGLAS, Mike
- ☐ '65 Men In My Little Girl's Life, The

DOVE, Ronnie
- ☐ '66 Cry
- ☐ '66 Happy Summer Days
- ☐ '66 I Really Don't Want To Know
- ☐ '65 I'll Make All Your Dreams Come True
- ☐ '65 Kiss Away
- ☐ '66 Let's Start All Over Again
- ☐ '65 Little Bit Of Heaven, A
- ☐ '65 One Kiss For Old Times' Sake
- ☐ '64 Right Or Wrong
- ☐ '64 Say You
- ☐ '66 When Liking Turns To Loving

DOVELLS, The
- ☐ '61 Bristol Stomp ★
- ☐ '62 Bristol Twistin' Annie
- ☐ '62 (Do The New) Continental
- ☐ '62 Hully Gully Baby
- ☐ '63 You Can't Sit Down

DOWELL, Joe
- ☐ '62 Little Red Rented Rowboat
- ☐ '61 Wooden Heart ★

ZDOWN AKA KILO
- ☐ '07 Lean Like A Cholo

DOZIER, Lamont
- ☐ '74 Fish Ain't Bitin'
- ☐ '73 Trying To Hold On To My Woman

DRAKE, Charlie
- ☐ '62 My Boomerang Won't Come Back

DRAKE, Pete
- ☐ '64 Forever

DRAMATICS, The
- ☐ '76 Be My Girl
- ☐ '73 Hey You! Get Off My Mountain
- ☐ '72 In The Rain
- ☐ '71 Whatcha See Is Whatcha Get ★

DRAPER, Rusty
- ☐ '55 Are You Satisfied?
- ☐ '57 Freight Train
- ☐ '56 In The Middle Of The House
- ☐ '57 Let's Go Calypso
- ☐ '55 Seventeen
- ☐ '55 Shifting, Whispering Sands, The

DREAM
- ☐ '00 He Loves U Not ★
- ☐ '01 This Is Me

DREAM ACADEMY, The
- ☐ '85 Life In A Northern Town ★
- ☐ '86 Love Parade, The

DREAMLOVERS, The
- ☐ '61 When We Get Married

DREAM WEAVERS, The
- ☐ '55 It's Almost Tomorrow

DREW, Patti
- ☐ '67 Tell Him

DRIFTERS, The
- ☐ '55 Adorable
- ☐ '59 Dance With Me
- ☐ '60 I Count The Tears
- ☐ '63 I'll Take You Home
- ☐ '64 I've Got Sand In My Shoes
- ☐ '59 (If You Cry) True Love, True Love
- ☐ '63 On Broadway
- ☐ '61 Please Stay
- ☐ '64 Saturday Night At The Movies
- ☐ '60 Save The Last Dance For Me ★
- ☐ '61 Some Kind Of Wonderful
- ☐ '61 Sweets For My Sweet
- 📼 '59 There Goes My Baby ★
- 📼 '60 This Magic Moment
- ☐ '64 Under The Boardwalk
- ☐ '62 Up On The Roof ★
- ☐ '55 What'cha Gonna Do
- ☐ '62 When My Little Girl Is Smiling
- ☐ '54 White Christmas

D.R.S.
- ☐ '93 Gangsta Lean

DRU HILL
- ☐ '98 How Deep Is Your Love ★
- ☐ '02 I Should Be...
- ☐ '97 In My Bed
- ☐ '97 Never Make A Promise
- ☐ '96 Tell Me
- ☐ '98 These Are The Times
- ☐ '97 We're Not Making Love No More

DRUSKY, Roy
- ☐ '61 Three Hearts In A Tangle

D12
- ☐ '04 How Come
- 📼 '04 My Band ★
- ☐ '01 Purple Hills [Pills]

DUALS
- ☐ '61 Stick Shift

DUBS, The
- ☐ '57 Could This Be Magic

DUDLEY, Dave
- ☐ '63 Six Days On The Road

DUFF, Hilary
- ☐ '04 Come Clean
- ☐ '03 So Yesterday
- ☐ '05 Wake Up
- ■ '07 With Love

DUICE
- ☐ '93 Dazzey Duks

DUKE, George
- ☐ '77 Reach For It
- ☐ '81 Sweet Baby [w/ Stanley Clarke]

DUKE, Patty
- ☐ '65 Don't Just Stand There
- ☐ '65 Say Something Funny

DUNDAS, David
- ☐ '76 Jeans On

DUNN, Holly
- ■ '86 Daddy's Hands
- ☐ '90 You Really Had Me Going

DUPREE, Robbie
- ☐ '80 Hot Rod Hearts
- ☐ '80 Steal Away

DUPREES, The
- ☐ '63 Have You Heard
- ☐ '62 My Own True Love
- ☐ '63 Why Don't You Believe Me
- ☐ '62 You Belong To Me

DUPRI, Jermaine
- ☐ '98 Money Ain't A Thang
- ☐ '98 Party Continues, The [w/ Da Brat]
- ☐ '01 Welcome To Atlanta [w/ Ludacris]

DURAN DURAN
- ☐ '88 All She Wants Is
- ☐ '93 Come Undone
- ☐ '83 Girls On Film
- ■ '82 Hungry Like The Wolf ★
- ☐ '88 I Don't Want Your Love
- ☐ '83 Is There Something I Should Know
- ☐ '84 New Moon On Monday
- ☐ '86 Notorious ★
- ■ '92 Ordinary World ★
- ☐ '84 Reflex, The ★
- ☐ '83 Rio
- ☐ '85 Save A Prayer
- ☐ '87 Skin Trade
- ☐ '83 Union Of The Snake
- ☐ '85 View To A Kill, A ★
- ☐ '84 Wild Boys, The ★

DURST, Fred — see LEWIS, Aaron

DYKE & THE BLAZERS
- ☐ '69 Let A Woman Be A Woman - Let A Man Be A Man
- ☐ '69 We Got More Soul

DYLAN, Bob
- ☐ '68 All Along The Watchtower
- ☐ '64 All I Really Want To Do
- ☐ '65 Ballad Of A Thin Man
- ☐ '63 Blowin' In The Wind ★
- ☐ '66 Can You Please Crawl Out Your Window?
- ☐ '65 Desolation Row
- ☐ '63 Don't Think Twice, It's All Right
- ☐ '89 Everything Is Broken
- ☐ '73 Fool Such As I
- ☐ '74 Forever Young
- ☐ '71 George Jackson
- ☐ '79 Gotta Serve Somebody
- ☐ '63 Hard Rain's A-Gonna Fall
- ☐ '65 Highway 61 Revisited
- ■ '75 Hurricane
- ☐ '71 I Shall Be Released
- ☐ '69 I Threw It All Away
- ■ '66 I Want You
- ■ '70 If Not For You
- ☐ '76 Isis
- ■ '64 It Ain't Me Babe
- ☐ '65 It's All Over Now, Baby Blue
- ☐ '66 Just Like A Woman
- ■ '73 Knockin' On Heaven's Door
- ☐ '69 Lay Lady Lay
- ☐ '67 Leopard-Skin Pill-Box Hat
- ■ '65 Like A Rolling Stone ★
- ☐ '65 Maggie's Farm
- ☐ '63 Masters Of War
- ☐ '74 Most Likely You Go Your Way (And I'll Go Mine)
- ☐ '76 Mozambique
- ☐ '65 Mr. Tambourine Man
- ☐ '64 My Back Pages
- ☐ '74 On A Night Like This
- ☐ '65 Positively 4th Street
- ☐ '67 Quinn The Eskimo (The Mighty Quinn)
- ☐ '66 Rainy Day Women #12 & 35 ★
- ☐ '65 She Belongs To Me
- ☐ '66 Stuck Inside Of Mobile With The Memphis Blues Again
- ☐ '65 Subterranean Homesick Blues
- ■ '84 Sweetheart Like You
- ☐ '75 Tangled Up In Blue
- ☐ '64 Times They Are A-Changin', The ★
- ☐ '66 Visions Of Johanna
- ☐ '71 Watching The River Flow
- ☐ '70 Wigwam
- ☐ '74 You Angel You

DYSON, Ronnie
- ☐ '70 (If You Let Me Make Love To You Then) Why Can't I Touch You?
- ☐ '73 One Man Band (Plays All Alone)

E

EAGLES
- ■ '75 After The Thrill Is Gone
- ☐ '74 Already Gone
- ■ '74 Best Of My Love ★
- ■ '73 Desperado
- ☐ '73 Doolin-Dalton

EAGLES — cont'd
- ☐ '94 Get Over It
- ◼ '79 Heartache Tonight ★
- ◼ '77 Hotel California ★
- ◼ '80 I Can't Tell You Why ★
- ☐ '79 In The City
- ☐ '74 James Dean
- ◼ '77 Life In The Fast Lane
- ☐ '79 Long Run, The
- ◼ '94 Love Will Keep Us Alive
- ◼ '75 Lyin' Eyes ★
- ◼ '76 New Kid In Town ★
- ☐ '05 No More Cloudy Days
- ◼ '75 One Of These Nights ★
- ☐ '73 Outlaw Man
- ◼ '72 Peaceful Easy Feeling
- ☐ '78 Please Come Home For Christmas
- ☐ '79 Sad Café
- ◼ '80 Seven Bridges Road
- ◼ '72 Take It Easy
- ◼ '75 Take It To The Limit ★
- ◼ '73 Tequila Sunrise
- ☐ '79 Those Shoes
- ☐ '77 Victim Of Love
- ☐ '77 Wasted Time
- ◼ '72 Witchy Woman

EAMON
- ◼ '03 F**k It (I Don't Want You Back)

EARL, Stacy
- ☐ '91 Love Me All Up
- ☐ '92 Romeo & Juliet

EARLE, Steve
- ☐ '86 Guitar Town

EARL-JEAN
- ☐ '64 I'm Into Somethin' Good

EARLS, The
- ☐ '62 Remember Then

EARTH, WIND & FIRE
- ◼ '79 After The Love Has Gone ★ ⸰
- ☐ '79 Boogie Wonderland [w/ The Emotions] ⸰
- ☐ '74 Devotion
- ☐ '83 Fall In Love With Me
- ☐ '78 Fantasy ⸰
- ☐ '76 Getaway
- ◼ '78 Got To Get You Into My Life
- ◼ '81 Let's Groove ★ ⸰
- ☐ '74 Mighty Mighty
- ☐ '76 Saturday Nite
- ◼ '78 September ⸰
- ☐ '77 Serpentine Fire
- ◼ '75 Shining Star ★
- ☐ '75 Sing A Song
- ☐ '87 System Of Survival
- ☐ '75 That's The Way Of The World
- ◼ '88 Thinking Of You

EASTON, Sheena
- ◼ '83 Almost Over You
- ☐ '89 Arms Of Orion, The [w/ Prince]
- ◼ '85 Do It For Love

- ☐ '81 For Your Eyes Only ★
- ☐ '88 Lover In Me, The
- ☐ '81 Modern Girl
- ☐ '81 Morning Train (Nine To Five) ★
- ☐ '84 Strut
- ☐ '84 Sugar Walls
- ◼ '83 Telefone (Long Distance Love Affair)
- ◼ '83 We've Got Tonight [w/ Kenny Rogers]
- ☐ '91 What Comes Naturally
- ☐ '82 When He Shines
- ☐ '81 You Could Have Been With Me

EASYBEATS, The
- ☐ '67 Friday On My Mind

ECHO & THE BUNNYMEN
- ☐ '86 Bring On The Dancing Horses
- ☐ '84 Killing Moon, The

ECHOES, The
- ☐ '61 Baby Blue

EDDIE, John
- ☐ '86 Jungle Boy

EDDY, Duane
- ☐ '62 Ballad Of Paladin, The
- ☐ '60 Because They're Young ★
- ☐ '59 Bonnie Came Back
- ☐ '63 Boss Guitar
- ☐ '58 Cannonball
- ☐ '62 (Dance With The) Guitar Man
- ☐ '59 Forty Miles Of Bad Road
- ☐ '59 Lonely One, The
- ☐ '58 Moovin' N' Groovin'
- ☐ '60 "Pepe"
- ☐ '60 Peter Gunn
- ☐ '58 Ramrod
- ☐ '58 Rebel-'Rouser ★
- ☐ '61 Ring Of Fire
- ☐ '60 Shazam!
- ☐ '59 Some Kind-A Earthquake
- ☐ '61 Theme From Dixie
- ☐ '59 "Yep!"

EDEN'S CRUSH
- ☐ '01 Get Over Yourself

EDISON LIGHTHOUSE
- ☐ '70 Love Grows (Where My Rosemary Goes)

EDMONDS, Kevon
- ☐ '99 24/7

EDMUNDS, Dave
- ☐ '70 I Hear You Knocking
- ☐ '83 Slipping Away

EDSELS, The
- ☐ '61 Rama Lama Ding Dong

EDWARD BEAR
- ☐ '73 Close Your Eyes
- ☐ '72 Last Song

EDWARDS, Bobby
- ☐ '61 You're The Reason

EDWARDS, Dennis
- ☐ '84 Don't Look Any Further

EDWARDS, Jonathan
- ☐ '71 Sunshine

EDWARDS, Tommy
- ☐ '60 I Really Don't Want To Know
- ☐ '58 It's All In The Game ★
- ☐ '58 Love Is All We Need
- ☐ '59 Morning Side Of The Mountain, The
- ☐ '59 My Melancholy Baby
- ☐ '59 Please Mr. Sun

EELS
- ☐ '96 Novocaine For The Soul

E-40
- ☐ '97 Rappers' Ball
- ☐ '06 Tell Me When To Go
- ☐ '97 Things'll Never Change
- ☐ '06 U And Dat

EGAN, Walter
- ☐ '78 Magnet And Steel

EIFFEL 65
- ☐ '99 Blue (Da Ba Dee) ★

8TH DAY, The
- ☐ '71 She's Not Just Another Woman
- ☐ '71 You've Got To Crawl (Before You Walk)

ELASTICA
- ☐ '95 Connection

ELBERT, Donnie
- ☐ '72 I Can't Help Myself (Sugar Pie, Honey Bunch)
- ☐ '71 Where Did Our Love Go

EL CHICANO
- ☐ '73 Tell Her She's Lovely
- ☐ '70 Viva Tirado

EL DORADOS, The
- ☐ '55 At My Front Door

ELECTRIC INDIAN, The
- ☐ '69 Keem-O-Sabe

ELECTRIC LIGHT ORCHESTRA
- ☐ '80 All Over The World
- ☐ '86 Calling America
- ☐ '74 Can't Get It Out Of My Head
- ☐ '79 Confusion
- ☐ '77 Do Ya
- ☐ '79 Don't Bring Me Down ★
- ☐ '75 Evil Woman
- ☐ '75 Fire On High
- ☐ '81 Hold On Tight
- ☐ '80 I'm Alive
- ☐ '81 Julie Don't Live Here
- ☐ '79 Last Train To London
- ☐ '76 Livin' Thing
- ☐ '78 Mr. Blue Sky
- ☐ '83 Rock 'N' Roll Is King
- ☐ '73 Roll Over Beethoven

- ☐ '79 Shine A Little Love
- ☐ '73 Showdown
- ☐ '76 Strange Magic
- ☐ '78 Sweet Talkin' Woman
- ☐ '77 Telephone Line
- ☐ '77 Turn To Stone
- ☐ '81 Twilight
- ☐ '80 Xanadu *[w/ Olivia Newton-John]* ★

ELECTRIC PRUNES, The
- ☐ '67 Get Me To The World On Time
- ☐ '66 I Had Too Much To Dream (Last Night)

ELECTRONIC
- ☐ '91 Get The Message
- ☐ '90 Getting Away With It

ELEGANTS, The
- ☐ '58 Little Star ★

ELEPHANT'S MEMORY
- ☐ '70 Mongoose

ELGART, Larry
- ☐ '82 Hooked On Swing

ELLEDGE, Jimmy
- ☐ '61 Funny How Time Slips Away

ELLIMAN, Yvonne
- ☐ '77 Hello Stranger
- ☐ '71 I Don't Know How To Love Him
- ☐ '78 If I Can't Have You ★ ══
- ☐ '76 Love Me
- ☐ '79 Love Pains

ELLINGTON, Duke
- ☐ '67 Mount Harissa

ELLIOTT, Missy "Misdemeanor"
- ☐ '01 Get Ur Freak On ★
- ☐ '02 Gossip Folks
- ☐ '99 Hot Boyz ★
- ☐ '05 Lose Control ★
- ☐ '01 One Minute Man
- ☐ '03 Pass That Dutch
- ☐ '97 Rain (Supa Dupa Fly)
- ☐ '97 Sock It 2 Me
- ☐ '02 Work It ★

ELLIS, Shirley
- ☐ '65 Clapping Song, The
- ☐ '64 Name Game, The
- ☐ '63 Nitty Gritty, The

ELLISON, Lorraine
- ☐ '66 Stay With Me

EMERSON DRIVE
- ☐ '02 Fall Into Me
- ☐ '02 I Should Be Sleeping
- ☐ '07 Moments

EMERSON, LAKE & PALMER
- ☐ '77 Fanfare For The Common Man
- ☐ '72 From The Beginning
- ☐ '72 Hoedown
- ☐ '73 Karn Evil 9
- ☐ '71 Lucky Man

EMF
- ☐ '91 Lies.
- ◩ '91 Unbelievable ★

EMINEM
- ◩ '02 Cleanin' Out My Closet ★
- ◩ '05 Encore
- ◩ '04 Just Lose It ★
- ◩ '05 Like Toy Soldiers
- ◩ '02 Lose Yourself ★
- ◩ '05 Mockingbird ★
- ◩ '99 My Name Is
- ◩ '00 Real Slim Shady, The ★
- ◩ '06 Shake That ★
- ◩ '03 Sing For The Moment
- ◩ '00 Stan ★
- ◩ '03 Superman
- ◩ '05 When I'm Gone
- ◩ '02 Without Me ★
- ◩ '06 You Don't Know

EMOTIONS, The
- ◩ '77 Best Of My Love ★ ⊙
- ☐ '79 Boogie Wonderland [w/ Earth, Wind & Fire]
- ☐ '69 So I Can Love You

ENCHANTMENT
- ☐ '77 Gloria
- ◩ '78 It's You That I Need
- ☐ '77 Sunshine

ENGLAND, Ty
- ☐ '95 Should've Asked Her Faster

ENGLAND DAN & JOHN FORD COLEY
- ☐ '77 Gone Too Far
- ◩ '76 I'd Really Love To See You Tonight ★
- ☐ '77 It's Sad To Belong
- ☐ '79 Love Is The Answer
- ☐ '76 Nights Are Forever Without You
- ☐ '78 We'll Never Have To Say Goodbye Again

ENGLISH BEAT
- ☐ '80 Ranking Full Stop
- ☐ '82 Save It For Later

ENGLISH CONGREGATION, The
- ◩ '72 Softly Whispering I Love You

ENGVALL, Bill
- ☐ '97 Here's Your Sign [w/ Travis Tritt]

ENIGMA
- ☐ '94 Return To Innocence ★
- ☐ '91 Sadeness

ENRIQUEZ, Jocelyn
- ☐ '96 Do You Miss Me

EN VOGUE
- ☐ '91 Don't Go
- ◩ '96 Don't Let Go (Love) ★
- ◩ '92 Free Your Mind
- ☐ '92 Give It Up, Turn It Loose
- ☐ '92 Giving Him Something He Can Feel
- ☐ '90 Hold On
- ☐ '90 Lies

- ☐ '93 Love Don't Love You
- ◩ '92 My Lovin' (You're Never Gonna Get It) ★
- ☐ '97 Too Gone, Too Long
- ◩ '94 Whatta Man [w/ Salt 'N' Pepa] ★
- ☐ '97 Whatever
- ☐ '90 You Don't Have To Worry

ENYA
- ☐ '91 Caribbean Blue
- ☐ '94 Oíche Chiún (Silent Night)
- ☐ '01 Only Time ★
- ☐ '89 Orinoco Flow (Sail Away) ★

EPPS, Preston
- ☐ '59 Bongo Rock

EQUALS, The
- ◩ '68 Baby, Come Back

ERASURE
- ☐ '94 Always
- ☐ '88 Chains Of Love
- ☐ '88 Little Respect, A

ERIC B & RAKIM
- ☐ '87 I Know You Got Soul
- ☐ '88 Paid In Full

ERUPTION
- ☐ '78 I Can't Stand The Rain

ESCAPE CLUB, The
- ☐ '91 I'll Be There
- ☐ '88 Shake For The Sheik
- ☐ '88 Wild, Wild West ★

ESPN Presents
- ☐ '97 Jock Jam, The

ESQUIRES, The
- ☐ '67 And Get Away
- ☐ '67 Get On Up

ESSEX, The
- ☐ '63 Easier Said Than Done ★
- ☐ '63 Walkin' Miracle, A

ESSEX, David
- ☐ '73 Rock On

ESTEFAN, Gloria/Miami Sound Machine
- ◩ '88 Anything For You ★
- ☐ '86 Bad Boy
- ☐ '87 Betcha Say That
- ☐ '91 Can't Forget You
- ☐ '87 Can't Stay Away From You
- ◩ '91 Coming Out Of The Dark ★
- ◩ '85 Conga
- ☐ '90 Cuts Both Ways
- ◩ '89 Don't Wanna Lose You ★
- ◩ '95 Everlasting Love
- ◩ '86 Falling In Love (Uh-Oh)
- ☐ '89 Get On Your Feet
- ☐ '98 Heaven's What I Feel
- ☐ '89 Here We Are
- ◩ '93 I See Your Smile
- ☐ '96 I'm Not Giving You Up

'91 Live For Loving You
'99 Music Of My Heart *[w/ *NSYNC]* ★
'88 1-2-3
'87 Rhythm Is Gonna Get You
'94 Turn The Beat Around
'86 Words Get In The Way

ESTUS, Deon
'89 Heaven Help Me *[w/ George Michael]*

ETERNAL
'94 Stay

ETHERIDGE, Melissa
'94 Come To My Window
'05 Cry Baby/Piece Of My Heart
'06 I Run For Life
'96 I Want To Come Over
'94 I'm The Only One ★
'95 If I Wanted To
'96 Nowhere To Go

E.U.
'88 Da'Butt

EUROPE
'87 Carrie
'87 Final Countdown, The ★
'87 Rock The Night
'88 Superstitious

EURYTHMICS
'89 Don't Ask Me Why
'84 Here Comes The Rain Again ★ ⚊
'83 Love Is A Stranger
'86 Missionary Man
'84 Right By Your Side
'85 Sisters Are Doin' It For Themselves
    [w/ Aretha Franklin]
'83 Sweet Dreams (Are Made of This) ★
'85 There Must Be An Angel (Playing With My Heart)
'84 Who's That Girl?
'85 Would I Lie To You?

EVAN & JARON
'00 Crazy For This Girl

EVANESCENCE
'03 Bring Me To Life ★
'06 Call Me When You're Sober ★
'04 My Immortal ★

EVANS, Faith
'05 Again
'99 All Night Long
'02 I Love You
'97 I'll Be Missing You *[w/ Puff Daddy]* ★
'98 Love Like This
'99 Never Gonna Let You Go
'95 Soon As I Get Home
'01 You Gets No Love
'95 You Used To Love Me

EVANS, Paul
'60 Happy-Go-Lucky-Me
'60 Midnite Special

'59 (Seven Little Girls) Sitting In The Back Seat

EVANS, Sara
'00 Born To Fly
'01 I Could Not Ask For More
'02 I Keep Looking
'98 No Place That Far
'03 Perfect
'05 Real Fine Place To Start, A
'04 Suds In The Bucket

EVE
'02 Gangsta Lovin' ★
'99 Gotta Man
'01 Let Me Blow Ya Mind *[w/ Gwen Stefani]* ★
'00 Love Is Blind
'02 Satisfaction
'07 Tambourine
'99 What Ya Want *[w/ Nokio]*

EVERCLEAR
'97 Everything To Everyone
'98 Father Of Mine
'98 I Will Buy You A New Life
'95 Santa Monica (Watch The World Die)
'00 Wonderful

EVERETT, Betty
'64 Let It Be Me *[w/ Jerry Butler]*
'64 Shoop Shoop Song (It's In His Kiss)
'69 There'll Come A Time

EVERLAST
'98 What It's Like

EVERLY BROTHERS, The
'58 All I Have To Do Is Dream ★
'60 Always It's You
'58 Bird Dog ★
'67 Bowling Green
'57 Bye Bye Love ★
'60 Cathy's Clown ★
'58 Claudette
'62 Crying In The Rain
'58 Devoted To You
'61 Don't Blame Me
'61 Ebony Eyes
'64 Gone, Gone, Gone
'62 I'm Here To Get My Baby Out Of Jail
'60 Let It Be Me
'60 Like Strangers
'60 Love Hurts
'58 Love Of My Life
'60 Lucille
'60 Memories Are Made Of This
'59 Poor Jenny
'58 Problems ★
'60 So Sad (To Watch Good Love Go Bad)
'61 Stick With Me Baby
'59 Take A Message To Mary
'61 Temptation
'62 That's Old Fashioned (That's The Way Love Should Be)
'58 This Little Girl Of Mine
'59 ('Til) I Kissed You ★

EVERLY BROTHERS, The — cont'd
- ☛ '57 Wake Up Little Susie ★
- ☐ '61 Walk Right Back
- ☒ '60 When Will I Be Loved

EVERY MOTHERS' SON
- ☐ '67 Come On Down To My Boat ★

EVERYTHING
- ☐ '98 Hooch

EVERYTHING BUT THE GIRL
- ☒ '95 Missing ★

EVE 6
- ☒ '01 Here's To The Night
- ☐ '98 Inside Out
- ☒ '00 Promise

EXCITERS, The
- ☐ '62 Tell Him

EXILE
- ☒ '78 Kiss You All Over ★
- ☐ '78 You Thrill Me

EXPOSÉ
- ☐ '87 Come Go With Me
- ☐ '92 I Wish The Phone Would Ring
- ☐ '93 I'll Never Get Over You (Getting Over Me)
- ☒ '87 Let Me Be The One ▬
- ☐ '87 Point Of No Return
- ☒ '87 Seasons Change ★ ▬
- ☐ '89 Tell Me Why
- ☐ '89 What You Don't Know
- ☐ '89 When I Looked At Him
- ☐ '90 Your Baby Never Looked Good In Blue

EXTREME
- ☐ '91 Hole Hearted
- ☒ '91 More Than Words ★
- ☐ '92 Rest In Peace

EYE TO EYE
- ☐ '82 Nice Girls

F

FABARES, Shelley
- ☐ '62 Johnny Angel ★
- ☐ '62 Johnny Loves Me

FABIAN
- ☒ '60 About This Thing Called Love
- ☐ '59 Come On And Get Me
- ☐ '59 Hound Dog Man
- ☐ '59 I'm A Man
- ☐ '60 String Along
- ☐ '59 This Friendly World
- ☒ '59 Tiger ★
- ☐ '59 Turn Me Loose

FABIAN, Lara
- ☐ '00 I Will Love Again

FABOLOUS
- ☒ '04 Breathe
- ☒ '01 Can't Deny It

- ☒ '03 Can't Let You Go ★
- ☒ '03 Into You ★
- ☒ '07 Make Me Better
- ☐ '02 Trade It All (Part 2)
- ☐ '01 Young'n (Holla Back)

FABRIC, Bent, & His Piano
- ☐ '62 Alley Cat

FABULOUS THUNDERBIRDS, The
- ☐ '88 Powerful Stuff
- ☐ '86 Tuff Enuff
- ☐ '86 Wrap It Up

FACENDA, Tommy
- ☐ '59 High School U.S.A.

FACES
- ☐ '71 (I Know) I'm Losing You *[w/ Rod Stewart]*
- ☐ '73 Ooh La La
- ☐ '72 Stay With Me

FACE TO FACE
- ☐ '84 10-9-8

FACTS OF LIFE
- ☐ '77 Sometimes

FAGEN, Donald
- ☐ '82 I.G.Y. (What A Beautiful World)
- ☐ '83 New Frontier

FAIRCHILD, Barbara
- ☐ '73 Teddy Bear Song

FAITH, Adam
- ☐ '65 It's Alright

FAITH, Percy, & His Orchestra
- ☐ '60 Theme For Young Lovers
- ☐ '60 Theme From "A Summer Place" ★

FAITHFULL, Marianne
- ☐ '64 As Tears Go By
- ☐ '65 Come And Stay With Me
- ☐ '65 Summer Nights
- ☐ '65 This Little Bird

FAITH, HOPE & CHARITY
- ☐ '75 To Each His Own

FAITH NO MORE
- ☒ '90 Epic

FALCO
- ☐ '86 Rock Me Amadeus ★
- ☐ '86 Vienna Calling

FALCON, Billy
- ☐ '91 Power Windows

FALCONS, The
- ☐ '59 You're So Fine

FALL OUT BOY
- ☒ '06 Dance, Dance ★
- ☒ '05 Sugar, We're Goin' Down ★
- ☒ '07 Thnks Fr Th Mmrs ★
- ☐ '07 This Ain't A Scene, It's An Arms Race ★

FALTERMEYER, Harold
- ☐ '85 Axel F ★

FÄLTSKOG, Agnetha
- ☐ '83 Can't Shake Loose

FAME, Georgie
- ☐ '68 Ballad Of Bonnie And Clyde, The
- ☐ '65 Yeh, Yeh

FANCY
- ▨ '74 Touch Me
- ▨ '74 Wild Thing

FANNY
- ☐ '75 Butter Boy
- ☐ '71 Charity Ball

FANTASIA
- ☐ '05 Free Yourself
- ▥ '04 I Believe ★
- ☐ '05 Truth Is
- ▥ '07 When I See U

FANTASTIC JOHNNY C, The
- ☐ '67 Boogaloo Down Broadway
- ☐ '68 Hitch It To The Horse

FARDON, Don
- ☐ '68 (The Lament Of The Cherokee) Indian Reservation

FARGO, Donna
- ▥ '72 Funny Face
- ☐ '72 Happiest Girl In The Whole U.S.A., The

FARRIS, Dionne
- ▥ '95 I Know ★

FASTBALL
- ▥ '99 Out Of My Head
- ☐ '98 Way, The ★

FASTER PUSSYCAT
- ▥ '90 House Of Pain

FATBACK
- ☐ '80 Backstrokin'
- ▨ '78 I Like Girls

FAT BOYS
- ☐ '84 Jail House Rap
- ☐ '88 Twist (Yo, Twist!) [w/ Chubby Checker]
- ☐ '87 Wipeout [w/ Beach Boys]

FATBOY SLIM
- ☐ '99 Praise You
- ☐ '98 Rockafeller Skank, The

FATHER MC
- ☐ '92 Everything's Gonna Be Alright
- ▨ '91 I'll Do 4 U

FAT JOE
- ▥ '05 Get It Poppin' ★
- ▥ '07 Make It Rain
- ☐ '01 We Thuggin
- ▥ '02 What's Luv? ★

FEIST
- ☐ '07 1, 2, 3, 4 ★

FELDER, Don
- ☐ '81 Heavy Metal (Takin' A Ride)

FELDER, Wilton
- ▣ '85 (No Matter How High I Get) I'll Still Be Lookin' Up To You

FELICIANO, José
- ☐ '70 Feliz Navidad
- ☐ '68 Hi-Heel Sneakers
- ☐ '68 Light My Fire

FELONY
- ☐ '83 Fanatic, The

FELTS, Narvel
- ☐ '75 Reconsider Me

FENDER, Freddy
- ▥ '75 Before The Next Teardrop Falls ★
- ☐ '75 Secret Love
- ☐ '75 Wasted Days And Wasted Nights
- ☐ '76 You'll Lose A Good Thing

FENDERMEN, The
- ☐ '60 Mule Skinner Blues ★

FERGIE
- ▣ '07 Big Girls Don't Cry ★
- ☐ '07 Fergalicious ★
- ▥ '07 Glamorous ★
- ▥ '06 London Bridge

FERGUSON, Jay
- ☐ '79 Shakedown Cruise
- ☐ '77 Thunder Island

FERGUSON, Johnny
- ☐ '60 Angela Jones

FERGUSON, Maynard
- ☐ '77 Gonna Fly Now (Theme From "Rocky")

FERKO STRING BAND
- ☐ '55 Alabama Jubilee

FERRANTE & TEICHER
- ☐ '60 Exodus ★
- ☐ '61 (Love Theme From) One Eyed Jacks
- ☐ '69 Midnight Cowboy
- ☐ '60 Theme From The Apartment
- ☐ '61 Tonight

FERRY, Bryan
- ☐ '88 Kiss And Tell
- ☐ '85 Slave To Love

FEVER TREE
- ☐ '68 San Francisco Girls (Return Of The Native)

FIELD MOB
- ☐ '06 Georgia [w/ Ludacris]
- ☐ '02 Sick Of Being Lonely
- ▥ '06 So What ★

FIELDS, Ernie, Orch.
- ☐ '59 In The Mood

FIELDS, Richard "Dimples"
- ☐ '82 If It Ain't One Thing...It's Another

FIESTAS, The
- ☐ '59 So Fine

5TH DIMENSION, The
- ☐ '69 Aquarius/Let The Sunshine In ★
- ☐ '70 Blowing Away
- ☐ '68 California Soul
- ☐ '68 Carpet Man
- ☐ '67 Go Where You Wanna Go
- ☐ '72 If I Could Reach You
- ☐ '72 (Last Night) I Didn't Get To Sleep At All
- ☐ '73 Living Together, Growing Together
- ☐ '71 Love's Lines, Angles And Rhymes
- ☐ '71 Never My Love
- ☐ '70 One Less Bell To Answer ★
- ☐ '67 Paper Cup
- ☐ '70 Puppet Man
- ☐ '70 Save The Country
- ☐ '68 Stoned Soul Picnic
- ☐ '68 Sweet Blindness
- ☐ '72 Together Let's Find Love
- ☐ '67 Up -- Up And Away
- ☐ '69 Wedding Bell Blues ★
- ☐ '69 Workin' On A Groovy Thing

FIFTH ESTATE, The
- ☐ '67 Ding Dong! The Witch Is Dead

50 CENT
- ☐ '07 Ayo Technology ★
- ☐ '06 Best Friend [w/ Olivia]
- ☐ '05 Candy Shop ★
- ☐ '05 Disco Inferno ★
- ☐ '03 In Da Club ★
- ☐ '05 Just A Lil Bit ★
- ☐ '05 Outta Control (Remix) [w/ Mobb Deep]
- ☐ '03 P.I.M.P. ★
- ☐ '07 Straight To The Bank
- ☐ '03 21 Questions ★
- ☐ '02 Wanksta
- ☐ '05 Window Shopper

FILTER
- ☐ '95 Hey Man Nice Shot
- ☐ '99 Take A Picture

FINE YOUNG CANNIBALS
- ☐ '89 Don't Look Back
- ☐ '89 Good Thing ★
- ☐ '89 She Drives Me Crazy ★

FINGER ELEVEN
- ☐ '04 One Thing
- ☐ '07 Paralyzer

FINNEGAN, Larry
- ☐ '62 Dear One

FIORILLO, Elisa
- ☐ '90 On The Way Up
- ☐ '87 Who Found Who [w/ Jellybean]

FIREBALLS, The/GILMER, Jimmy
- ☐ '67 Bottle Of Wine
- ☐ '60 Bulldog
- ☐ '63 Daisy Petal Pickin'
- ☐ '61 Quite A Party
- ☐ '63 Sugar Shack ★
- ☐ '59 Torquay
- ☐ '60 Vaquero

FIREFALL
- ☐ '77 Cinderella
- ☐ '80 Headed For A Fall
- ☐ '77 Just Remember I Love You
- ☐ '81 Staying With It
- ☐ '78 Strange Way
- ☐ '76 You Are The Woman

FIREFLIES
- ☐ '59 You Were Mine

FIREHOUSE
- ☐ '91 Don't Treat Me Bad
- ☐ '95 I Live My Life For You
- ☐ '91 Love Of A Lifetime
- ☐ '92 When I Look Into Your Eyes

FIRM, The
- ☐ '86 All The Kings Horses
- ☐ '85 Radioactive

FIRST CHOICE
- ☐ '73 Armed And Extremely Dangerous
- ☐ '77 Doctor Love

FIRST CLASS
- ☐ '74 Beach Baby

FISCHER, Lisa
- ☐ '91 How Can I Ease The Pain

FISHER, Eddie
- ☐ '56 Cindy, Oh Cindy
- ☐ '55 Dungaree Doll
- ☐ '55 Everybody's Got A Home But Me
- ☐ '66 Games That Lovers Play
- ☐ '55 Heart
- ☐ '54 I Need You Now
- ☐ '55 (I'm Always Hearing) Wedding Bells
- ☐ '55 Man Chases A Girl (Until She Catches Him)
- ☐ '56 On The Street Where You Live
- ☐ '55 Song Of The Dreamer

FISHER, Miss Toni
- ☐ '59 Big Hurt, The ★
- ☐ '62 West Of The Wall

FITZGERALD, Ella
- ☐ '60 How High The Moon
- ☐ '60 Mack The Knife

FIVE
- ☐ '98 When The Lights Go Out

FIVE AMERICANS, The
- ☐ '66 Evol-Not Love
- ☐ '66 I See The Light
- ☐ '67 Sound Of Love

'67 Western Union
'67 Zip Code

FIVE BLOBS, The
'58 Blob, The

FIVE FLIGHTS UP
'70 Do What You Wanna Do

FIVE FOR FIGHTING
'04 100 Years
'06 Riddle, The
'04 Silent Night
'01 Superman (It's Not Easy)

FIVE KEYS, The
'55 Ling, Ting, Tong
'56 Out Of Sight, Out Of Mind
'56 Wisdom Of A Fool

FIVE MAN ELECTRICAL BAND
'71 Absolutely Right
'71 Signs ★

504 BOYZ
'00 Wobble Wobble

FIVE SATINS, The
'56 In The Still Of The Nite ★
'57 To The Aisle

FIVE STAIRSTEPS, The
'70 O-o-h Child ★

FIVE STAR
'86 Can't Wait Another Minute
'85 Let Me Be The One

5000 VOLTS
'75 I'm On Fire

FIXX, The
'84 Are We Ourselves?
'84 Deeper And Deeper
'89 Driven Out
'91 How Much Is Enough
'83 One Thing Leads To Another ★
'83 Saved By Zero
'86 Secret Separation
'83 Sign Of Fire, The

FLACK, Roberta
'78 Closer I Get To You, The *[w/ Donny Hathaway]*
'74 Feel Like Makin' Love
'72 First Time Ever I Saw Your Face ★
'78 If Ever I See You Again
'73 Jesse
'73 Killing Me Softly With His Song ★
'82 Making Love
'88 Oasis
'91 Set The Night To Music *[w/ Maxi Priest]*
'83 Tonight, I Celebrate My Love
'72 Where Is The Love *[w/ Donny Hathaway]*
'71 You've Got A Friend

FLAMING EMBER, The
'70 I'm Not My Brothers Keeper
'69 Mind, Body and Soul
'70 Westbound #9

FLAMING LIPS, The
'94 She Don't Use Jelly

FLAMINGOS, The
'59 I Only Have Eyes For You ★
'59 Lovers Never Say Goodbye
'60 Nobody Loves Me Like You
'60 Your Other Love

FLARES, The
'61 Foot Stomping

FLASH
'72 Small Beginnings

FLASH CADILLAC & THE CONTINENTAL KIDS
'76 Did You Boogie (With Your Baby)

FLATT & SCRUGGS
'63 Ballad Of Jed Clampett, The
'68 Foggy Mountain Breakdown (Theme From Bonnie & Clyde)

FLEETWOOD MAC
'69 Albatross
'88 As Long As You Follow
'87 Big Love
'69 Black Magic Woman
'77 Chain, The
'77 Don't Stop ★
'77 Dreams ★
'87 Everywhere
'77 Go Your Own Way ★
'77 Gold Dust Woman
'82 Gypsy
'82 Hold Me ★
'73 Hypnotized
'77 I Don't Want To Know
'75 Landslide
'87 Little Lies
'82 Love In Store
'75 Monday Morning
'77 Never Going Back Again
'70 Oh Well
'75 Over My Head
'76 Rhiannon (Will You Ever Win)
'79 Sara
'90 Save Me
'76 Say You Love Me
'77 Second Hand News
'87 Seven Wonders
'77 Silver Springs
'80 Think About Me
'79 Tusk ★
'77 You Make Loving Fun

FLEETWOODS, The
'59 Come Softly To Me ★
'63 Goodnight My Love
'59 Graduation's Here

FLEETWOODS, The — cont'd
- ☐ '61 (He's) The Great Impostor
- ☐ '62 Lovers By Night, Strangers By Day
- ☒ '59 Mr. Blue ★
- ☐ '60 Outside My Window
- ☐ '60 Runaround
- ☐ '61 Tragedy

FLINT, Shelby
- ☐ '60 Angel On My Shoulder

FLIRTATIONS, The
- ☐ '69 Nothing But A Heartache

FLOATERS, The
- ☐ '77 Float On ★

FLOCK OF SEAGULLS, A
- ☒ '82 I Ran (So Far Away) ★
- ☐ '82 Space Age Love Song
- ☒ '83 Wishing (If I Had A Photograph Of You)

FLOETRY
- ☒ '03 Say Yes

FLOYD, Eddie
- ☐ '68 Bring It On Home To Me
- ☒ '68 I've Never Found A Girl (To Love Me Like You Do)
- ☐ '66 Knock On Wood

FLOYD, King
- ☒ '71 Baby Let Me Kiss You
- ☐ '70 Groove Me
- ☐ '72 Woman Don't Go Astray

FLYING BURRITO BROTHERS
- ☐ '69 Hot Burrito #1
- ☐ '69 Sin City

FLYING LIZARDS
- ☐ '80 Money

FLYING MACHINE, The
- ☒ '69 Smile A Little Smile For Me

FOCUS
- ☐ '73 Hocus Pocus

FOGELBERG, Dan
- ☐ '84 Believe In Me
- ☐ '81 Hard To Say
- ☐ '80 Heart Hotels
- ☒ '84 Language Of Love, The
- ☐ '81 Leader Of The Band
- ☐ '87 Lonely In Love
- ☒ '79 Longer
- ☒ '83 Make Love Stay
- ☒ '82 Missing You
- ☐ '77 Nether Lands
- ☐ '75 Part Of The Plan
- ☐ '78 Power Of Gold, The [w/ Tim Weisberg]
- ☐ '90 Rhythm Of The Rain/Rain
- ☐ '82 Run For The Roses
- ☐ '80 Same Old Lang Syne

FOGERTY, John
- ☐ '75 Almost Saturday Night
- ☐ '85 Centerfield
- ☐ '86 Change In The Weather
- ☐ '86 Eye Of The Zombie
- ☐ '73 Hearts Of Stone [BLUE RIDGE RANGERS]
- ☐ '72 Jambalaya (On the Bayou) [BLUE RIDGE RAINGERS]
- ☐ '84 Old Man Down The Road, The
- ☐ '85 Rock And Roll Girls
- ☒ '75 Rockin' All Over The World

FOGHAT
- ☐ '76 Drivin' Wheel
- ☐ '75 Fool For The City
- ☐ '77 I Just Want To Make Love To You [live]
- ☒ '75 Slow Ride
- ☐ '78 Stone Blue
- ☐ '79 Third Time Lucky (First Time I Was A Fool)

FOLDS, Ben, Five
- ☐ '97 Brick

FOLK IMPLOSION
- ☐ '95 Natural One

FONTANA, Wayne — see MINDBENDERS

FONTANE SISTERS, The
- ☐ '56 Banana Boat Song, The
- ☒ '58 Chanson D'Amour (Song Of Love)
- ☐ '55 Daddy-O
- ☐ '56 Eddie My Love
- ☐ '55 Hearts Of Stone
- ☐ '55 Rock Love
- ☐ '55 Rollin' Stone
- ☒ '55 Seventeen

FOO FIGHTERS
- ☐ '02 All My Life
- ☒ '05 Best Of You ★
- ☐ '96 Big Me
- ☐ '05 DOA
- ☐ '97 Everlong
- ☐ '99 Learn To Fly
- ☐ '06 No Way Back
- ☐ '07 Pretender, The
- ☐ '95 This Is A Call

FORBERT, Steve
- ☐ '79 Romeo's Tune

FORCE M.D.'S
- ☐ '87 Love Is A House
- ☒ '86 Tender Love ⚊

FORD, Frankie
- ☐ '59 Sea Cruise

FORD, Lita
- ☐ '89 Close My Eyes Forever [w/ Ozzy Osbourne]
- ☒ '88 Kiss Me Deadly

FORD, "Tennessee" Ernie
- ☐ '55 Ballad Of Davy Crockett
- ☐ '57 In The Middle Of An Island
- ☒ '55 Sixteen Tons ★
- ☐ '56 That's All

FORD, Willa
- ☒ '01 I Wanna Be Bad

FOREIGNER
- ☐ '78 Blue Morning, Blue Day
- ☐ '82 Break It Up
- ☑ '77 Cold As Ice
- ☐ '79 Dirty White Boy
- ☑ '78 Double Vision
- ☑ '77 Feels Like The First Time
- ☑ '79 Head Games
- ☑ '78 Hot Blooded ★
- ☑ '88 I Don't Want To Live Without You
- ☑ '84 I Want To Know What Love Is ★
- ☑ '81 Juke Box Hero
- ☐ '77 Long, Long Way From Home
- ☐ '87 Say You Will
- ☐ '85 That Was Yesterday
- ☐ '95 Until The End Of Time
- ☑ '81 Urgent
- ☑ '81 Waiting For A Girl Like You ★

FORT MINOR
- ☑ '06 Where'd You Go ★

FORTUNES, The
- ☐ '71 Here Comes That Rainy Day Feeling Again
- ☐ '65 Here It Comes Again
- ☐ '65 You've Got Your Troubles

FOSTER, David
- ☐ '85 Love Theme From St. Elmo's Fire

FOSTER, Radney
- ☐ '93 Nobody Wins

FOUNDATIONS, The
- ☑ '67 Baby, Now That I've Found You
- ☑ '69 Build Me Up Buttercup

FOUNTAINS OF WAYNE
- ☑ '03 Stacy's Mom

FOUR ACES
- ☐ '56 Friendly Persuasion (Thee I Love)
- ☐ '55 Heart
- ☑ '56 I Only Know I Love You
- ☑ '55 Love Is A Many-Splendored Thing ★
- ☐ '55 Melody Of Love
- ☑ '55 Mister Sandman
- ☐ '55 Woman In Love, A
- ☐ '56 You Can't Run Away From It

FOUR COINS, The
- ☑ '55 I Love You Madly
- ☐ '55 Memories Of You
- ☐ '57 My One Sin
- ☐ '57 Shangri-La
- ☐ '58 World Outside, The

FOUR ESQUIRES, The
- ☐ '58 Hideaway
- ☐ '56 Look Homeward Angel
- ☑ '57 Love Me Forever

FOUR FRESHMEN, The
- ☐ '56 Graduation Day

FOUR JACKS & A JILL
- ☐ '68 Master Jack

FOUR LADS, The
- ☐ '56 Bus Stop Song (A Paper Of Pins)
- ☐ '58 Enchanted Island
- ☐ '56 House With Love In It, A
- ☐ '57 I Just Don't Know
- ☐ '58 Mocking Bird, The
- ☑ '55 Moments To Remember ★
- ☑ '56 My Little Angel
- ☐ '56 No, Not Much! ★
- ☐ '57 Put A Light In The Window
- ☐ '56 Standing On The Corner ★
- ☑ '58 There's Only One Of You
- ☐ '57 Who Needs You

4 NON BLONDES
- ☑ '93 What's Up ★

FOURPLAY
- ☐ '91 After The Dance

4 P.M. (For Positive Music)
- ☐ '94 Sukiyaki

FOUR PREPS, The
- ☐ '62 Big Draft, The
- ☐ '58 Big Man
- ☐ '59 Down By The Station
- ☐ '56 Dreamy Eyes
- ☐ '60 Got A Girl
- ☐ '58 Lazy Summer Night
- ☐ '61 More Money For You And Me
- ☐ '58 26 Miles (Santa Catalina) ★

4 SEASONS, The
- ☐ '63 Ain't That A Shame!
- ☐ '64 Alone
- ☐ '67 Beggin'
- ☑ '62 Big Girls Don't Cry ★
- ☐ '64 Big Man In Town
- ☐ '65 Bye, Bye, Baby (Baby, Goodbye)
- ☑ '63 Candy Girl
- ☐ '67 C'mon Marianne
- ☐ '64 Dawn (Go Away) ★
- ☑ '75 December, 1963 (Oh, What a Night) ★
- ☐ '65 Don't Think Twice
- ☐ '66 I've Got You Under My Skin
- ☐ '65 Let's Hang On!
- ☐ '63 Marlena
- ☐ '63 New Mexican Rose
- ☐ '66 Opus 17 (Don't You Worry 'Bout Me)
- ☑ '64 Rag Doll ★
- ☐ '64 Ronnie
- ☐ '62 Santa Claus Is Coming To Town
- ☐ '64 Save It For Me
- ☑ '62 Sherry ★
- ☑ '64 Silence Is Golden
- ☐ '64 Stay
- ☐ '66 Tell It To The Rain
- ☑ '63 Walk Like A Man ★
- ☑ '75 Who Loves You ★
- ☐ '68 Will You Love Me Tomorrow
- ☐ '66 Working My Way Back To You

FOUR TOPS
- ☒ '73 Ain't No Woman (Like The One I've Got)
- ☐ '73 Are You Man Enough
- ☐ '65 Ask The Lonely
- ☒ '64 Baby I Need Your Loving
- ☐ '67 Bernadette
- ☒ '65 I Can't Help Myself ★
- ☐ '68 If I Were A Carpenter
- ☐ '88 Indestructible
- ☐ '70 It's All In The Game
- ☐ '65 It's The Same Old Song
- ☐ '72 Keeper Of The Castle
- ☐ '74 One Chain Don't Make No Prison
- ☒ '66 Reach Out I'll Be There ★
- ☒ '70 River Deep - Mountain High *[w/ The Supremes]*
- ☐ '67 7 Rooms Of Gloom
- ☐ '66 Shake Me, Wake Me (When It's Over)
- ☐ '65 Something About You
- ☐ '66 Standing In The Shadows Of Love
- ☒ '70 Still Water (Love)
- ☐ '73 Sweet Understanding Love
- ☐ '68 Walk Away Renee
- ☐ '81 When She Was My Girl
- ☐ '67 You Keep Running Away

FOUR VOICES, The
- ☐ '58 Dancing With My Shadow
- ☐ '56 Lovely One

FOX, Charles
- ☐ '81 Seasons

FOX, Samantha
- ☒ '89 I Only Wanna Be With You
- ☐ '88 I Wanna Have Some Fun
- ☒ '88 Naughty Girls (Need Love Too)
- ☒ '86 Touch Me (I Want Your Body)

FOXX, Inez, with Charlie Foxx
- ☐ '63 Mockingbird

FOXX, Jamie
- ☒ '06 DJ Play A Love Song
- ☒ '06 Unpredictable ★

FOXY
- ☐ '78 Get Off
- ☐ '79 Hot Number

FRAMPTON, Peter
- ☒ '76 Baby, I Love Your Way
- ☐ '76 Do You Feel Like We Do
- ☐ '79 I Can't Stand It No More
- ☒ '77 I'm In You ★
- ☒ '76 Show Me The Way ★
- ☒ '77 Signed, Sealed, Delivered (I'm Yours)

FRANCIS, Connie
- ☐ '59 Among My Souvenirs
- ☐ '61 Baby's First Christmas
- ☐ '64 Blue Winter
- ☐ '61 Breakin' In A Brand New Broken Heart
- ☒ '62 Don't Break The Heart That Loves You ★
- ☒ '60 Everybody's Somebody's Fool ★
- ☐ '63 Follow The Boys
- ☐ '59 Frankie
- ☐ '59 God Bless America
- ☐ '61 (He's My) Dreamboat
- ☐ '62 I'm Gonna' Be Warm This Winter
- ☐ '59 If I Didn't Care
- ☐ '63 If My Pillow Could Talk
- ☐ '60 Jealous Of You (Tango Della Gelosia)
- ☐ '59 Lipstick On Your Collar
- ☐ '60 Mama
- ☐ '60 Many Tears Ago
- ☒ '58 My Happiness ★
- ☐ '60 My Heart Has A Mind Of Its Own
- ☐ '62 Second Hand Love
- ☐ '58 Stupid Cupid
- ☐ '60 Teddy
- ☐ '61 Together
- ☐ '62 Vacation
- ☒ '61 When The Boy In Your Arms (Is The Boy In Your Heart)
- ☐ '61 Where The Boys Are
- ☐ '58 Who's Sorry Now
- ☐ '63 Your Other Love

FRANKE & THE KNOCKOUTS
- ☒ '81 Sweetheart
- ☐ '82 Without You (Not Another Lonely Night)
- ☒ '81 You're My Girl

FRANKIE GOES TO HOLLYWOOD
- ☐ '84 Relax ★
- ☐ '84 Two Tribes

FRANKIE J
- ☒ '03 Don't Wanna Try
- ☒ '05 How To Deal
- ☒ '05 More Than Words
- ☒ '05 Obsession [No Es Amor] ★

FRANKLIN, Aretha
- ☐ '68 Ain't No Way
- ☐ '72 All The King's Horses
- ☐ '73 Angel
- ☐ '86 Another Night
- ☐ '67 Baby I Love You
- ☐ '77 Break It To Me Gently
- ☐ '71 Bridge Over Troubled Water
- ☐ '70 Call Me
- ☐ '67 Chain Of Fools ★
- ☐ '72 Day Dreaming
- ☐ '67 Do Right Woman-Do Right Man
- ☐ '70 Don't Play That Song
- ☐ '69 Eleanor Rigby
- ☐ '85 Freeway Of Love
- ☐ '83 Get It Right
- ☐ '68 House That Jack Built, The
- ☐ '87 I Knew You Were Waiting (For Me) *[w/ George Michael]* ★
- ☒ '67 I Never Loved A Man (The Way I Love You)
- ☒ '68 I Say A Little Prayer
- ☒ '74 I'm In Love
- ☐ '86 Jimmy Lee
- ☐ '82 Jump To It
- ☐ '86 Jumpin' Jack Flash

68

- ☑ '67 Natural Woman (You Make Me Feel Like)
- ☑ '67 Respect ★
- ☐ '61 Rock-A-Bye Your Baby With A Dixie Melody
- ☐ '71 Rock Steady
- ☐ '98 Rose Is Still A Rose, A
- ☐ '68 See Saw
- ☐ '69 Share Your Love With Me
- ☐ '85 Sisters Are Doin' It For Themselves
  [w/ Eurythmics]
- ☐ '71 Spanish Harlem
- ☐ '70 Spirit In The Dark
- ☐ '68 (Sweet Sweet Baby) Since You've Been Gone
- ☐ '68 Think
- ☐ '89 Through The Storm *[w/ Elton John]*
- ☐ '80 United Together
- ☐ '73 Until You Come Back To Me (That's What I'm Gonna Do)
- ☐ '69 Weight, The
- ☐ '85 Who's Zoomin' Who
- ☐ '94 Willing To Forgive
- ☑ '71 You're All I Need To Get By

FRANKLIN, Kirk
- ☑ '06 Looking For You

FRANKS, Michael
- ☐ '76 Popsicle Toes

FRANZ FERDINAND
- ☐ '04 Take Me Out

FRAY, The
- ☑ '06 How To Save A Life ★
- ☑ '06 Over My Head (Cable Car) ★

FREAK NASTY
- ☑ '97 Da' Dip

FREBERG, Stan
- ☐ '57 Banana Boat (Day-O)
- ☐ '56 Heartbreak Hotel
- ☐ '57 Wun'erful, Wun'erful!
- ☐ '55 Yellow Rose Of Texas, The

FRED, John, & His Playboy Band
- ☐ '67 Judy In Disguise (With Glasses) ★

FREDDIE & THE DREAMERS
- ☐ '65 Do The Freddie
- ☐ '65 I Understand (Just How You Feel)
- ☑ '65 I'm Telling You Now ★
- ☑ '65 You Were Made For Me

FREE
- ☐ '70 All Right Now

FREEMAN, Bobby
- ☐ '58 Betty Lou Got A New Pair Of Shoes
- ☐ '64 C'mon And Swim
- ☐ '58 Do You Want To Dance
- ☑ '60 (I Do The) Shimmy Shimmy

FREEMAN, Ernie
- ☐ '57 Raunchy

FREE MOVEMENT, The
- ☐ '71 I've Found Someone Of My Own

FREEWAY
- ☐ '02 Rock The Mic

FREHLEY, Ace
- ☐ '78 New York Groove

FRENCH, Don
- ☐ '59 Lonely Saturday Night

FRENCH, Nicki
- ☑ '95 Total Eclipse Of The Heart ★

FRENTE!
- ☐ '94 Bizarre Love Triangle

FREY, Glenn
- ☑ '84 Heat Is On, The ★
- ☐ '82 I Found Somebody
- ☑ '82 One You Love, The
- ☑ '84 Sexy Girl
- ☐ '85 Smuggler's Blues
- ☑ '88 True Love
- ☑ '85 You Belong To The City ★

FRIDA
- ☐ '82 I Know There's Something Going On

FRIEDMAN, Dean
- ☐ '77 Ariel

FRIEND & LOVER
- ☐ '68 Reach Out Of The Darkness

FRIENDS OF DISTINCTION, The
- ☐ '69 Going In Circles
- ☐ '69 Grazing In The Grass
- ☐ '70 Love Or Let Me Be Lonely

FRIJID PINK
- ☐ '70 House Of The Rising Sun

FROGMEN, The
- ☐ '61 Underwater

FROST, Max, & The Troopers
- ☐ '68 Shape Of Things To Come

FUEL
- ☐ '01 Bad Day
- ☑ '00 Hemorrhage (In My Hands)
- ☐ '98 Shimmer

FUGEES
- ☐ '95 Fu-Gee-La
- ☑ '96 Killing Me Softly ★
- ☑ '96 No Woman, No Cry
- ☑ '96 Ready Or Not
- ☐ '97 Sweetest Thing, The

FULLER, Bobby, Four
- ☐ '66 I Fought The Law ★
- ☐ '66 Love's Made A Fool Of You

FUNKADELIC
- ☐ '71 Maggot Brain
- ☐ '79 (not just) Knee Deep
- ☐ '78 One Nation Under A Groove

FUNKY 4 + 1
- ☐ '01 That's The Joint

FURAY, Richie
- ☐ '79 I Still Have Dreams

FURTADO, Nelly
- ☐ '01 I'm Like A Bird
- ☐ '06 Maneater
- ☐ '06 Promiscuous ★
- ☐ '07 Say It Right ★
- ☐ '01 Turn Off The Light ★

FU-SCHNICKENS
- ☐ '93 What's Up Doc? (Can We Rock?)
  [w/ Shaquille O'Neal]

FUZZ, The
- ☐ '71 I Love You For All Seasons

G

GABLE, Eric
- ☐ '89 Remember (The First Time)

GABRIEL, Peter
- ☐ '86 Big Time
- ☐ '80 Biko
- ☐ '92 Digging In The Dirt
- ☐ '87 Don't Give Up *[w/ Kate Bush]*
- ☐ '80 Games Without Frontiers
- ☐ '86 In Your Eyes
- ☐ '86 Red Rain
- ☐ '82 San Jacinto
- ☐ '82 Shock The Monkey
- ☐ '86 Sledgehammer ★
- ☐ '77 Solsbury Hill
- ☐ '92 Steam

GABRIELLE
- ☐ '93 Dreams

GADABOUTS, The
- ☐ '56 Stranded In The Jungle

GALLERY
- ☐ '72 Big City Miss Ruth Ann
- ☐ '72 I Believe In Music
- ☐ '72 Nice To Be With You

GALLOP, Frank
- ☐ '66 Ballad Of Irving, The

GAME, The
- ☐ '05 Dreams
- ☐ '05 Hate It Or Love It ★
- ☐ '05 How We Do ★

GAP BAND, The
- ☐ '89 All Of My Love
- ☐ '84 Beep A Freak
- ☐ '80 Burn Rubber (Why You Wanna Hurt Me)
- ☐ '82 Early In The Morning
- ☐ '86 Going In Circles
- ☐ '82 Outstanding
- ☐ '83 Party Train
- ☐ '82 You Dropped A Bomb On Me

GARBAGE
- ☐ '96 #1 Crush
- ☐ '96 Stupid Girl

GARDNER, Don, & Dee Dee Ford
- ☐ '62 I Need Your Loving

GARFUNKEL, Art
- ☐ '73 All I Know
- ☐ '75 Break Away
- ☐ '75 I Only Have Eyes For You
- ☐ '73 I Shall Sing
- ☐ '74 Second Avenue
- ☐ '78 (What A) Wonderful World
  [w/ James Taylor & Paul Simon]

GARI, Frank
- ☐ '61 Lullaby Of Love
- ☐ '61 Princess
- ☐ '60 Utopia

GARLAND, Judy
- ☐ '61 For Me And My Gal [live]
- ☐ '61 Over The Rainbow [live]
- ☐ '61 Trolley Song, The [live]
- ☐ '61 You Made Me Love You [live]

GARNETT, Gale
- ☐ '64 We'll Sing In The Sunshine

GARRETT, Leif
- ☐ '78 I Was Made For Dancin'
- ☐ '77 Runaround Sue
- ☐ '77 Surfin' USA

GARY, John
- ☐ '67 Cold

GATES, David
- ☐ '73 Clouds
- ☐ '77 Goodbye Girl
- ☐ '75 Never Let Her Go
- ☐ '78 Took The Last Train

GAYE, Marvin
- ☐ '67 Ain't No Mountain High Enough *[w/ Tammi Terrell]*
- ☐ '68 Ain't Nothing Like The Real Thing *[w/ Tammi Terrell]*
- ☐ '65 Ain't That Peculiar
- ☐ '63 Can I Get A Witness
- ☐ '68 Chained
- ☐ '73 Come Get To This
- ☐ '74 Distant Lover
- ☐ '69 Good Lovin' Ain't Easy To Come By *[w/ Tammi Terrell]*
- ☐ '77 Got To Give It Up ★
- ☐ '63 Hitch Hike
- ☐ '64 How Sweet It Is To Be Loved By You
- ☐ '68 I Heard It Through The Grapevine ★
- ☐ '76 I Want You
- ☐ '65 I'll Be Doggone
- ☐ '67 If I Could Build My Whole World Around You *[w/ Tammi Terrell]*
- ☐ '71 Inner City Blues (Make Me Wanna Holler)

☑ '67 It Takes Two *[w/ Kim Weston]*
☐ '68 Keep On Lovin' Me Honey *[w/ Tammi Terrell]*
☑ '73 Let's Get It On ★
☑ '71 Mercy Mercy Me (The Ecology) ⚊
☐ '74 My Mistake (Was To Love You)
☐ '64 Once Upon A Time *[w/ Mary Wells]*
☐ '63 Pride And Joy
☐ '85 Sanctified Lady
☑ '82 Sexual Healing ★ ⚊
☐ '62 Stubborn Kind Of Fellow
☐ '69 That's The Way Love Is
☑ '69 Too Busy Thinking About My Baby
☐ '72 Trouble Man
☐ '64 Try It Baby
☑ '71 What's Going On ★ ⚊
☐ '64 What's The Matter With You Baby *[w/ Mary Wells]*
☐ '73 You're A Special Part Of Me *[w/ Diana Ross]*
☐ '64 You're A Wonderful One
☑ '68 You're All I Need To Get By *[w/ Tammi Terrell]*
☑ '67 Your Precious Love *[w/ Tammi Terrell]*

GAYLE, Crystal
☑ '77 Don't It Make My Brown Eyes Blue ★
☐ '79 Half The Way
☐ '78 Ready For The Times To Get Better
☑ '78 Talking In Your Sleep
☑ '82 You And I *[w/ Eddie Rabbitt]*

GAYNOR, Gloria
☑ '78 I Will Survive ★ ⚊
☐ '74 Never Can Say Goodbye

G-CLEFS, The
☐ '61 I Understand (Just How You Feel)
☐ '56 Ka-Ding Dong

GEDDES, David
☐ '75 Last Game Of The Season (A Blind Man In The Bleachers)
☐ '75 Run Joey Run

GEIGER, Teddy
☑ '06 For You I Will (Confidence)

GEILS, J., Band
☐ '82 Angel In Blue
☐ '81 Centerfold ★
☐ '80 Come Back
☐ '81 Flamethrower
☑ '82 Freeze-Frame ★
☐ '73 Give It To Me
☐ '82 I Do
☐ '71 Looking For A Love
☐ '80 Love Stinks
☐ '74 Must Of Got Lost
☑ '78 One Last Kiss

GENE & DEBBE
☐ '68 Playboy

GENE & EUNICE
☐ '59 Poco-Loco

GENE LOVES JEZEBEL
☐ '90 Jealous

GENERAL PUBLIC
☑ '94 I'll Take You There
☐ '84 Tenderness

GENESIS
☐ '81 Abacab
☐ '78 Follow You Follow Me
☐ '92 Hold On My Heart
☐ '91 I Can't Dance
☐ '87 In Too Deep
☑ '86 Invisible Touch ★
☑ '92 Jesus He Knows Me
☐ '83 Just A Job To Do
☐ '75 Lamb Lies Down On Broadway
☐ '86 Land Of Confusion
☐ '83 Mama
☐ '82 Man On The Corner
☐ '80 Misunderstanding
☐ '92 Never A Time
☐ '81 No Reply At All
☐ '91 No Son Of Mine
☐ '82 Paperlate
☐ '83 That's All!
☑ '86 Throwing It All Away ⚊
☐ '87 Tonight, Tonight, Tonight
☐ '80 Turn It On Again

GENTRY, Bobbie
☑ '70 All I Have To Do Is Dream *[w/ Glen Campbell]*
☐ '70 Cinnamon Girl
☐ '69 Fancy
☑ '69 Let It Be Me *[w/ Glen Campbell]*
☑ '67 Ode To Billie Joe ★

GENTRYS, The
☐ '65 Keep On Dancing

GEORGE, Barbara
☐ '61 I Know (You Don't Love Me No More)

GEORGIA SATELLITES
☑ '86 Keep Your Hands To Yourself ★

GERARDO
☐ '91 Rico Suave
☐ '91 We Want The Funk

GERRY & THE PACEMAKERS
☐ '64 Don't Let The Sun Catch You Crying
☐ '65 Ferry Cross The Mersey
☐ '66 Girl On A Swing
☐ '64 How Do You Do It?
☐ '64 I Like It
☐ '64 I'll Be There
☐ '65 It's Gonna Be Alright

GETO BOYS, The
☐ '91 Mind Playing Tricks On Me
☐ '93 Six Feet Deep

GETZ, Stan
- [ ] '62 Desafinado *[w/ Charlie Byrd]*
- [ ] '64 Girl From Ipanema, The *[w/ Astrud Gilberto]*

GHOST TOWN DJ'S
- [ ] '96 My Boo

GIANT
- [ ] '90 I'll See You In My Dreams

GIANT STEPS
- [ ] '88 Another Lover

GIBB, Andy
- [ ] '80 Desire
- [x] '78 Everlasting Love, An
- [x] '80 I Can't Help It *[w/ Olivia Newton-John]*
- [x] '77 I Just Want To Be Your Everything ★
- [ ] '77 (Love Is) Thicker Than Water ★
- [x] '78 (Our Love) Don't Throw It All Away
- [ ] '78 Shadow Dancing ★
- [ ] '80 Time Is Time

GIBB, Barry — see STREISAND, Barbra

GIBB, Robin
- [ ] '84 Boys Do Fall In Love
- [ ] '78 Oh! Darling

GIBBS, Georgia
- [ ] '55 Dance With Me Henry (Wallflower)
- [ ] '56 Happiness Street
- [x] '58 Hula Hoop Song, The
- [x] '55 I Want You To Be My Baby
- [ ] '56 Kiss Me Another
- [ ] '56 Rock Right
- [ ] '55 Sweet And Gentle
- [ ] '56 Tra La La
- [ ] '55 Tweedle Dee

GIBBS, Terri
- [ ] '81 Somebody's Knockin'

GIBSON, Debbie
- [ ] '90 Anything Is Possible
- [ ] '89 Electric Youth
- [ ] '88 Foolish Beat
- [x] '89 Lost In Your Eyes ★
- [ ] '89 No More Rhyme
- [ ] '87 Only In My Dreams
- [ ] '88 Out Of The Blue
- [ ] '87 Shake Your Love
- [ ] '88 Staying Together

GIBSON, Don
- [ ] '58 Blue Blue Day
- [ ] '60 Far, Far Away
- [ ] '58 Give Myself A Party
- [ ] '58 I Can't Stop Loving You
- [ ] '60 Just One Time
- [ ] '61 Lonesome Number One
- [ ] '59 Lonesome Old House
- [ ] '58 Oh Lonesome Me ★
- [ ] '61 Sea Of Heartbreak
- [ ] '59 Who Cares

GILDER, Nick
- [ ] '78 Hot Child In The City ★

GILKYSON, Terry, & The Easy Riders
- [ ] '57 Marianne

GILL, Johnny
- [ ] '90 Fairweather Friend
- [ ] '90 My, My, My
- [ ] '90 Rub You The Right Way
- [ ] '91 Wrap My Body Tight

GILL, Vince
- [ ] '92 Don't Let Our Love Start Slippin' Away
- [ ] '93 Heart Won't Lie, The *[w/ Reba McEntire]*
- [ ] '95 Go Rest High On That Mountain
- [ ] '96 High Lonesome Sound *[w/ Alison Krauss]*
- [ ] '94 House Of Love *[w/ Amy Grant]*
- [x] '92 I Still Believe In You
- [x] '95 I Will Always Love You *[w/ Dolly Parton]*
- [ ] '97 Little More Love, A
- [ ] '90 Never Knew Lonely
- [ ] '93 No Future In The Past
- [ ] '93 One More Last Chance
- [ ] '96 Pretty Little Adriana
- [ ] '92 Take Your Memory With You
- [ ] '94 Tryin' To Get Over You
- [ ] '94 What The Cowgirls Do
- [x] '90 When I Call Your Name
- [x] '94 When Love Finds You
- [ ] '94 Whenever You Come Around
- [x] '95 You Better Think Twice

GILLEY, Mickey
- [ ] '80 Stand By Me

GILMAN, Billy
- [ ] '00 One Voice

GILMER, Jimmy — see FIREBALLS

GILREATH, James
- [ ] '63 Little Band Of Gold

GINA G
- [x] '96 Ooh Aah...Just A Little Bit

GIN BLOSSOMS
- [ ] '94 Allison Road
- [ ] '96 Follow You Down ★
- [ ] '93 Found Out About You
- [ ] '93 Hey Jealousy
- [ ] '96 Til I Hear It From You
- [ ] '94 Until I Fall Away

GINO & GINA
- [ ] '58 (It's Been A Long Time) Pretty Baby

GINUWINE
- [x] '01 Differences
- [ ] '03 Hell Yeah
- [x] '02 I Need A Girl (Part Two) *[w/ P. Diddy]* ★
- [x] '03 In Those Jeans
- [x] '96 Pony ★
- [x] '99 So Anxious
- [ ] '02 Stingy

GIUFFRIA
- ☐ '84 Call To The Heart

GLADIOLAS, The
- ☐ '57 Little Darlin'

GLADSTONE
- ☐ '72 Piece Of Paper, A

GLAHÉ, Will, & His Orchestra
- ☐ '57 Liechtensteiner Polka

GLASS BOTTLE, The
- ☐ '71 I Ain't Got Time Anymore

GLASS TIGER
- ☐ '86 Don't Forget Me (When I'm Gone) ★
- ☐ '87 I Will Be There
- ☐ '88 I'm Still Searching
- ☐ '86 Someday

GLAZER, Tom
- ☐ '63 On Top Of Spaghetti

GLENCOVES, The
- ☐ '63 Hootenanny

GLITTER, Gary
- ☐ '72 Rock And Roll Part 2 ★

GNARLS BARKLEY
- ▥ '06 Crazy ★

GODLEY & CREME
- ☐ '85 Cry

GODSMACK
- ☐ '00 Awake
- ☐ '01 Greed
- ☐ '02 I Stand Alone
- ☐ '03 Re-Align
- ☐ '04 Running Blind
- ☐ '06 Speak
- ☐ '03 Straight Out Of Line

GODSPELL
- ☐ '72 Day By Day

GOD'S PROPERTY
- ☐ '97 Stomp

GO-GO'S
- ☐ '84 Head Over Heels
- ▥ '81 Our Lips Are Sealed ★
- ▥ '84 Turn To You
- ☐ '82 Vacation
- ▥ '82 We Got The Beat ★

GOLD, Andrew
- ☐ '77 Lonely Boy
- ▥ '78 Thank You For Being A Friend

GOLDEN EARRING
- ▥ '74 Radar Love
- ☐ '82 Twilight Zone

GOLDSBORO, Bobby
- ☐ '68 Autumn Of My Life
- ☐ '66 Blue Autumn
- ☐ '68 Honey ★

- ☐ '66 It's Too Late
- ☐ '65 Little Things
- ☐ '64 See The Funny Little Clown
- ☐ '68 Straight Life, The
- ☐ '73 Summer (The First Time)
- ☐ '65 Voodoo Woman
- ☐ '70 Watching Scotty Grow
- ☐ '64 Whenever He Holds You

GOMM, Ian
- ☐ '79 Hold On

GONE ALL STARS
- ☐ '58 "7-11" (Mambo No. 5)

GONZALEZ
- ☐ '79 Haven't Stopped Dancing Yet

GOOD CHARLOTTE
- ▥ '03 Anthem, The
- ☐ '03 Girls And Boys
- ☐ '05 I Just Wanna Live
- ▥ '02 Lifestyles Of The Rich And Famous
- ☐ '07 River, The

GOODIE MOB
- ☐ '95 Cell Therapy

GOODMAN, Dickie
- ☐ '66 Batman & His Grandmother
- ☐ '74 Energy Crisis '74
- ☐ '56 Flying Saucer, The
- ☐ '57 Flying Saucer The 2nd
- ☐ '75 Mr. Jaws
- ☐ '57 Santa And The Satellite
- ☐ '61 Touchables In Brooklyn, The

GOO GOO DOLLS
- ☐ '05 Better Days
- ☐ '99 Black Balloon
- ☐ '00 Broadway
- ☐ '04 Give A Little Bit
- ☐ '02 Here Is Gone
- ▥ '98 Iris ★
- ▥ '95 Name ★
- ▥ '98 Slide ★

GORDON, Barry
- ☐ '55 Nuttin' For Christmas

GORDON, Rosco
- ☐ '60 Just A Little Bit

GORE, Lesley
- ☐ '67 California Nights
- ☐ '64 I Don't Wanna Be A Loser
- ▥ '63 It's My Party ★
- ☐ '63 Judy's Turn To Cry
- ☐ '64 Look Of Love
- ☐ '64 Maybe I Know
- ☐ '65 My Town, My Guy And Me
- ☐ '63 She's A Fool
- ☐ '65 Sunshine, Lollipops And Rainbows
- ☐ '64 That's The Way Boys Are
- ☐ '63 You Don't Own Me

GORILLAZ
- ☐ '01 Clint Eastwood
- ☐ '05 Feel Good Inc *[w/ De La Soul]* ★

GORME, Eydie
- ☐ '63 Blame It On The Bossa Nova
- ☐ '63 I Can't Stop Talking About You *[w/ Steve Lawrence]*
- ☐ '63 I Want To Stay Here *[w/ Steve Lawrence]*
- ☐ '64 I Want You To Meet My Baby
- ☐ '57 Love Me Forever
- ☐ '56 Mama, Teach Me To Dance
- ☐ '56 Too Close For Comfort
- ☐ '58 You Need Hands

GOULET, Robert
- ☐ '64 My Love, Forgive Me (Amore, Scusami)

GO WEST
- ☐ '87 Don't Look Down - The Sequel
- ☐ '92 Faithful
- ☐ '90 King Of Wishful Thinking
- ☐ '85 We Close Our Eyes
- ☐ '93 What You Won't Do For Love

GQ
- ☐ '79 Disco Nights (Rock-Freak)
- ☐ '79 I Do Love You

GRACIE, Charlie
- ☒ '57 Butterfly ★
- ☐ '57 Fabulous

GRACIN, Josh
- ☐ '04 Nothin' To Lose

GRAHAM, Larry
- ☒ '80 One In A Million You

GRAMM, Lou
- ☐ '89 Just Between You And Me
- ☐ '87 Midnight Blue
- ☐ '90 True Blue Love

GRAMMER, Billy
- ☐ '58 Gotta Travel On

GRANAHAN, Gerry
- ☐ '58 No Chemise, Please

GRANATA, Rocco
- ☐ '59 Marina

GRAND FUNK RAILROAD
- ☐ '75 Bad Time
- ☐ '70 Closer To Home/I'm Your Captain
- ☐ '72 Footstompin' Music
- ☐ '70 Inside Looking Out
- ☒ '74 Loco-Motion, The
- ☐ '72 Rock 'N Roll Soul
- ☐ '74 Shinin' On
- ☒ '74 Some Kind Of Wonderful
- ☐ '73 Walk Like A Man
- ☐ '73 We're An American Band ★

GRANDMASTER FLASH & THE FURIOUS FIVE
- ☐ '82 Message, The ★

- ☐ '83 White Lines (Don't Don't Do It) *[w/ Melle Mel]*

GRANT, Amy
- ☐ '85 Angels
- ☒ '91 Baby Baby ★
- ☐ '82 El Shaddai
- ☒ '91 Every Heartbeat ★
- ☐ '85 Find A Way
- ☐ '92 Good For Me
- ☒ '94 House Of Love *[w/ Vince Gill]*
- ☒ '92 I Will Remember You
- ☐ '88 Lead Me On
- ☐ '94 Lucky One
- ☒ '86 Next Time I Fall, The *[w/ Peter Cetera]*
- ☐ '97 Takes A Little Time
- ☒ '91 That's What Love Is For
- ☐ '85 Thy Word

GRANT, Earl
- ☐ '58 End, The
- ☐ '62 Swingin' Gently

GRANT, Eddy
- ☒ '83 Electric Avenue ★
- ☐ '84 Romancing The Stone

GRANT, Gogi
- ☐ '55 Suddenly There's A Valley
- ☐ '56 Wayward Wind, The ★

GRANT, Janie
- ☐ '61 Triangle

GRASS ROOTS, The
- ☐ '70 Baby Hold On
- ☐ '68 Bella Linda
- ☐ '72 Glory Bound
- ☐ '69 Heaven Knows
- ☐ '69 I'd Wait A Million Years
- ☐ '67 Let's Live For Today
- ☐ '68 Midnight Confessions
- ☐ '69 River Is Wide, The
- ☐ '72 Runway, The
- ☐ '71 Sooner Or Later
- ☐ '70 Temptation Eyes
- ☐ '67 Things I Should Have Said
- ☐ '71 Two Divided By Love
- ☐ '66 Where Were You When I Needed You

GRATEFUL DEAD
- ☐ '80 Alabama Getaway
- ☐ '71 Bertha
- ☐ '70 Box Of Rain
- ☐ '70 Casey Jones
- ☐ '70 Dark Star
- ☐ '75 Franklin's Tower
- ☐ '70 Friend Of The Devil
- ☐ '87 Hell In A Bucket
- ☐ '75 Music Never Stopped
- ☐ '72 One More Saturday Night [live]
- ☐ '71 Playing In The Band
- ☐ '70 Ripple
- ☐ '78 Shakedown Street
- ☐ '69 St. Stephen
- ☐ '70 Sugar Magnolia
- ☐ '77 Terrapin Station

- ☐ '87 Touch Of Grey ★
- ☐ '70 Truckin'
- ☐ '69 Turn On Your Love Light
- ☐ '70 Uncle John's Band

GRAY, Dobie
- ▣ '73 Drift Away
- ☐ '65 "In" Crowd, The
- ☐ '78 You Can Do It

GRAY, Macy
- ▣ '00 I Try ★

GREAN, Charles Randolph, Sounde
- ☐ '69 Quentin's Theme

GREAT WHITE
- ☐ '89 Angel Song, The
- ☐ '89 Once Bitten Twice Shy

GREAVES, R.B.
- ☐ '70 Always Something There To Remind Me
- ☐ '69 Take A Letter Maria ★

GRECCO, Cyndi
- ☐ '76 Making Our Dreams Come True

GREEN, Al
- ▣ '73 Call Me (Come Back Home)
- ☐ '75 Full Of Fire
- ☐ '94 Funny How Time Slips Away [w/ Lyle Lovett]
- ☐ '73 Here I Am (Come And Take Me)
- ▣ '72 I'm Still In Love With You
- ☐ '76 Keep Me Cryin'
- ☐ '75 L-O-V-E (Love)
- ▣ '74 Let's Get Married
- ▣ '71 Let's Stay Together ★ ⚊
- ▣ '73 Livin' For You
- ☐ '72 Look What You Done For Me
- ▣ '72 Love And Happiness ⚊
- ▣ '88 Put A Little Love In Your Heart [w/ Annie Lennox]
- ☐ '74 Sha-La-La (Make Me Happy)
- ☐ '74 Take Me To The River
- ☐ '71 Tired Of Being Alone
- ▣ '72 You Ought To Be With Me

GREEN, Garland
- ☐ '69 Jealous Kind Of Fella

GREEN, Pat
- ☐ '03 Wave On Wave

GREEN, Vivian
- ☐ '03 Emotional Rollercoaster

GREENBAUM, Norman
- ☐ '70 Spirit In The Sky ★

GREEN DAY
- ▣ '04 American Idiot
- ☐ '94 Basket Case ★
- ▣ '05 Boulevard Of Broken Dreams ★
- ☐ '95 Brain Stew/Jaded
- ☐ '95 Geek Stink Breath
- ▣ '97 Good Riddance (Time Of Your Life)
- ▣ '05 Holiday ★
- ☐ '95 J.A.R. (Jason Andrew Relva)
- ☐ '94 Long View
- ▣ '00 Minority
- ☐ '06 Saints Are Coming, The [w/ U2]
- ▣ '05 Wake Me Up When September Ends ★
- ☐ '00 Warning
- ▣ '94 When I Come Around ★

GREENE, Lorne
- ☐ '64 Ringo

GREEN JELLY
- ☐ '93 Three Little Pigs

GREENWOOD, Lee
- ▣ '84 God Bless The USA

GREGG, Bobby
- ☐ '62 Jam, The

GRIFFITHS, Marcia
- ▣ '89 Electric Slide (Boogie) ★

GRIGGS, Andy
- ▣ '05 If Heaven
- ☐ '04 She Thinks She Needs Me
- ▣ '00 She's More
- ▣ '99 You Won't Ever Be Lonely

GROBAN, Josh
- ☐ '04 Believe
- ☐ '02 O Holy Night
- ☐ '02 To Where You Are
- ☐ '03 You Raise Me Up

GROCE, Larry
- ☐ '76 Junk Food Junkie

GROOVE THEORY
- ☐ '95 Tell Me

GROSS, Henry
- ☐ '76 Shannon
- ☐ '76 Springtime Mama

GTR
- ☐ '86 When The Heart Rules The Mind

GUARALDI, Vince, Trio
- ☐ '62 Cast Your Fate To The Wind
- ☐ '87 Linus And Lucy

GUESS WHO, The
- ☐ '71 Albert Flasher
- ▣ '70 American Woman ★
- ☐ '74 Clap For The Wolfman
- ☐ '74 Dancin' Fool
- ☐ '70 Hand Me Down World
- ☐ '69 Laughing
- ☐ '70 No Sugar Tonight
- ☐ '69 No Time
- ☐ '71 Rain Dance
- ☐ '65 Shakin' All Over
- ☐ '70 Share The Land
- ☐ '74 Star Baby
- ▣ '69 These Eyes
- ☐ '69 Undun

GUIDRY, Greg
- ☐ '82 Goin' Down

GUITAR, Bonnie
- ☐ '57 Dark Moon

GUNHILL ROAD
- ☐ '73 Back When My Hair Was Short

G-UNIT
- ☐ '03 Stunt 101
- ☐ '04 Wanna Get To Know You

GUNS N' ROSES
- ☐ '91 Don't Cry
- ▣ '90 Knockin' On Heaven's Door
- ▣ '91 Live And Let Die
- ▣ '92 November Rain ★
- ▣ '89 Paradise City
- ▣ '89 Patience ★
- ▣ '88 Sweet Child O' Mine ★
- ▣ '88 Welcome To The Jungle
- ▣ '91 You Could Be Mine

GUTHRIE, Arlo
- ☐ '69 Alice's Restaurant Massacree
- ☐ '72 City Of New Orleans, The

GUTHRIE, Gwen
- ☐ '86 Ain't Nothin' Goin' On But The Rent

GUY
- ☐ '99 Dancin'
- ☐ '91 Do Me Right
- ☐ '89 I Like
- ☐ '91 Let's Chill

GUY, Jasmine
- ▣ '91 Just Want To Hold You

GYM CLASS HEROES
- ▣ '07 Cupid's Chokehold/Breakfast In America ★

H

HADDAWAY
- ▣ '93 What Is Love ★

HAGAR, Sammy
- ☐ '87 Give To Live
- ▣ '84 I Can't Drive 55
- ▣ '82 I'll Fall In Love Again
- ☐ '97 Little White Lie
- ☐ '97 Marching To Mars
- ☐ '99 Mas Tequila
- ☐ '84 Two Sides Of Love
- ☐ '87 Winner Takes It All
- ☐ '82 Your Love Is Driving Me Crazy

HAGGARD, Merle
- ☐ '66 Bottle Let Me Down, The
- ☐ '66 Fugitive, The
- ☐ '73 If We Make It Through December
- ☐ '85 Kern River
- ☐ '68 Mama Tried
- ▣ '69 Okie From Muskogee

HAIRCUT ONE HUNDRED
- ☐ '82 Love Plus One

HALEY, Bill, & His Comets
- ☐ '55 Birth Of The Boogie
- ☐ '55 Burn That Candle
- ☐ '53 Crazy Man, Crazy
- ☐ '55 Dim, Dim The Lights
- ☐ '55 Mambo Rock
- ☐ '55 Razzle-Dazzle
- ☐ '56 Rip It Up
- ☐ '56 R-O-C-K
- ☐ '55 Rock-A-Beatin' Boogie
- ▣ '55 Rock Around The Clock ★
- ☐ '56 Rudy's Rock
- ☐ '56 Saints Rock 'N Roll, The
- ☐ '56 See You Later, Alligator ★
- ▣ '54 Shake, Rattle And Roll
- ☐ '58 Skinny Minnie

HALL, Aaron
- ▣ '98 All The Places (I Will Kiss You)
- ☐ '92 Don't Be Afraid
- ▣ '94 I Miss You

HALL, Daryl
- ☐ '86 Dreamtime
- ▣ '86 Foolish Pride

HALL, Daryl, & John Oates
- ☐ '84 Adult Education
- ▣ '77 Back Together Again
- ☐ '82 Did It In A Minute
- ▣ '02 Do It For Love
- ☐ '76 Do What You Want, Be What You Are
- ☐ '88 Downtown Life
- ☐ '88 Everything Your Heart Desires
- ☐ '83 Family Man
- ☐ '80 How Does It Feel To Be Back
- ☐ '81 I Can't Go For That (No Can Do) ▬
- ☐ '78 It's A Laugh
- ☐ '82 Italian Girls
- ▣ '81 Kiss On My List ★
- ▣ '82 Maneater ★ ▬
- ☐ '84 Method Of Modern Love
- ☐ '88 Missed Opportunity
- ☐ '85 Nite At The Apollo Live! The Way You Do The Things You Do/My Girl
- ☐ '83 One On One
- ▣ '84 Out Of Touch ★
- ☐ '85 Possession Obsession
- ▣ '81 Private Eyes ★
- ▣ '77 Rich Girl ★
- ▣ '76 Sara Smile
- ☐ '83 Say It Isn't So
- ☐ '74 She's Gone
- ☐ '90 So Close
- ☐ '85 Some Things Are Better Left Unsaid
- ☐ '79 Wait For Me
- ▣ '81 You Make My Dreams
- ▣ '80 You've Lost That Lovin' Feeling
- ▣ '82 Your Imagination

HALL, Jimmy
☒ '80 I'm Happy That Love Has Found You

HALL, Larry
☐ '59 Sandy

HALL, Tom T.
☒ '73 I Love
☐ '71 Year That Clayton Delaney Died, The

HALOS, The
☐ '61 "Nag"

HAMILTON, Anthony
☐ '04 Charlene

HAMILTON, Bobby
☒ '58 Crazy Eyes For You

HAMILTON, George IV
☐ '63 Abilene
☐ '58 Now And For Always
☐ '57 Only One Love
☐ '56 Rose And A Baby Ruth, A
☐ '57 Why Don't They Understand

HAMILTON, Roy
☐ '58 Don't Let Go
☐ '55 Unchained Melody
☐ '61 You Can Have Her

HAMILTON, Russ
☐ '57 Rainbow

HAMILTON, JOE FRANK & REYNOLDS
☐ '71 Don't Pull Your Love
☒ '75 Fallin' In Love ★
☐ '75 Winners And Losers

HAMLISCH, Marvin
☐ '74 Entertainer, The

HAMMEL, Karl Jr.
☐ '61 Summer Souvenirs

HAMMER, Jan
☐ '85 Miami Vice Theme ★

HAMMOND, Albert
☐ '73 Free Electric Band, The
☐ '74 I'm A Train
☐ '72 It Never Rains In Southern California
☐ '75 99 Miles From L.A.

HANCOCK, Herbie
☐ '83 Rockit

HANSON
☒ '97 I Will Come To You
☒ '97 MMMBop ★
☐ '00 This Time Around
☒ '97 Where's The Love

HAPPENINGS, The
☐ '66 Go Away Little Girl
☐ '67 I Got Rhythm
☐ '67 My Mammy
☐ '66 See You In September

HARDCASTLE, Paul
☐ '85 19

HARDEN TRIO, The
☐ '66 Tippy Toeing

HARDY, Hagood
☐ '76 Homecoming, The

HARNELL, Joe, & His Orchestra
☐ '62 Fly Me To The Moon - Bossa Nova

HARPERS BIZARRE
☐ '67 Chattanooga Choo Choo
☐ '67 Come To The Sunshine
☐ '67 59th Street Bridge Song (Feelin' Groovy)

HARPO, Slim
☐ '66 Baby Scratch My Back
☐ '57 I'm A King Bee
☐ '61 Rainin' In My Heart

HARPTONES, The
☐ '55 Life Is But A Dream
☐ '53 Sunday Kind Of Love, A

HARRIS, Betty
☐ '63 Cry To Me

HARRIS, Eddie
☐ '61 Exodus

HARRIS, Emmylou
☐ '75 Boulder To Birmingham
☐ '75 If I Could Only Win Your Love
☐ '81 Mister Sandman
☐ '75 One Of These Days
☐ '80 That Lovin' You Feelin' Again *[w/ Roy Orbison]*
☐ '76 Together Again

HARRIS, Major
☐ '75 Love Won't Let Me Wait

HARRIS, Richard
☐ '68 MacArthur Park

HARRIS, Rolf
☐ '63 Tie Me Kangaroo Down, Sport

HARRIS, Sam
☐ '84 Sugar Don't Bite

HARRIS, Thurston
☐ '57 Little Bitty Pretty One

HARRISON, George
☐ '81 All Those Years Ago ★
☐ '71 Bangla-Desh
☐ '79 Blow Away
☐ '77 Crackerbox Palace
☐ '74 Dark Horse
☐ '75 Ding Dong; Ding Dong
☐ '73 Give Me Love - (Give Me Peace On Earth) ★
☐ '87 Got My Mind Set On You ★
☐ '70 Isn't It A Pity
☐ '70 My Sweet Lord ★

HARRISON, George — cont'd
- ☐ '76 This Song
- ☐ '71 What Is Life
- ☐ '87 When We Was Fab
- ☐ '75 You

HARRISON, Wilbert
- ☐ '59 Kansas City ★
- ☐ '69 Let's Work Together

HART, Corey
- ☐ '85 Boy In The Box
- ▣ '86 Can't Help Falling In Love
- ☐ '85 Everything In My Heart
- ☐ '86 I Am By Your Side
- ☐ '88 In Your Soul
- ☐ '84 It Ain't Enough
- ☐ '90 Little Love, A
- ☐ '85 Never Surrender
- ▣ '84 Sunglasses At Night

HART, Freddie
- ▣ '71 Easy Loving

HARTMAN, Dan
- ☐ '84 I Can Dream About You
- ☐ '78 Instant Replay
- ☐ '85 Second Nature
- ☐ '84 We Are The Young

HARVEY, PJ
- ☐ '95 Down By The Water

HARVEY DANGER
- ☐ '98 Flagpole Sitta

HATFIELD, Juliana, Three
- ☐ '93 My Sister

HATHAWAY, Donny — see FLACK, Roberta

HATHAWAY, Lalah
- ☐ '90 Heaven Knows

HAVENS, Richie
- ☐ '71 Here Comes The Sun

HAWKES, Chesney
- ☐ '91 One And Only, The

HAWKINS, Dale
- ☐ '58 La-Do-Dada
- ▣ '58 My Babe
- ▣ '57 Susie-Q
- ☐ '59 Yea-Yea (Class Cutter)

HAWKINS, Edwin, Singers
- ☐ '70 Lay Down (Candles In The Rain)
  [w/ Melanie]
- ▣ '69 Oh Happy Day

HAWKINS, Ronnie
- ☐ '59 Forty Days
- ☐ '59 Mary Lou
- ▣ '63 Who Do You Love

HAWKINS, Screamin' Jay
- ▣ '56 I Put A Spell On You

HAWKINS, Sophie B.
- ▣ '95 As I Lay Me Down ★
- ☐ '92 Damn I Wish I Was Your Lover

HAYES, Bill
- ☐ '55 Ballad Of Davy Crockett, The ★
- ☐ '57 Wringle, Wrangle

HAYES, Isaac
- ☐ '69 By The Time I Get To Phoenix
- ☐ '72 Do Your Thing
- ☐ '79 Don't Let Go
- ☐ '73 "Joy" —
- ☐ '71 Never Can Say Goodbye
- ☐ '71 Theme From Shaft ★
- ☐ '72 Theme From The Men
- ☐ '69 Walk On By

HAYES, Wade
- ☐ '94 Old Enough To Know Better
- ☐ '96 On A Good Night

HAYMAN, Richard
- ☐ '56 Theme from "The Three Penny Opera" (Moritat) *[w/ Jan August]*

HAYWARD, Justin
- ☐ '78 Forever Autumn
- ☐ '75 I Dreamed Last Night *[w/ John Lodge]*

HAYWOOD, Leon
- ☐ '80 Don't Push It Don't Force It
- ▣ '75 I Want'a Do Something Freaky To You

HAZELWOOD, Lee — see SINATRA, Nancy

HEAD, Murray
- ▣ '85 One Night In Bangkok ★
- ☐ '70 Superstar

HEAD, Roy
- ☐ '65 Apple Of My Eye
- ☐ '65 Just A Little Bit
- ▣ '65 Treat Her Right ★

HEAD EAST
- ☐ '75 Never Been Any Reason
- ☐ '78 Since You Been Gone

HEADLEY, Heather
- ☐ '03 I Wish I Wasn't

HEALEY, Jeff, Band
- ▣ '89 Angel Eyes

HEART
- ▣ '90 All I Wanna Do Is Make Love To You ★
- ☐ '87 Alone ★
- ▣ '77 Barracuda
- ▣ '76 Crazy On You
- ☐ '79 Dog & Butterfly
- ☐ '76 Dreamboat Annie
- ☐ '80 Even It Up
- ☐ '78 Heartless
- ☐ '83 How Can I Refuse
- ☐ '90 I Didn't Want To Need You
- ☐ '77 Kick It Out
- ☐ '77 Little Queen
- ▣ '76 Magic Man

☐ '85 Never
☐ '86 Nothin' At All
☐ '78 Straight On
☐ '90 Stranded
☐ '80 Tell It Like It Is
☐ '87 There's The Girl
☒ '86 These Dreams ★
☐ '82 This Man Is Mine
☒ '85 What About Love?
☐ '87 Who Will You Run To
☒ '93 Will You Be There (In The Morning)

HEARTBEATS, The
☐ '56 Thousand Miles Away, A

HEARTLAND
☐ '06 I Loved Her First

HEATHERLY, Eric
☐ '00 Flowers On The Wall

HEATHERTON, Joey
☐ '72 Gone

HEATWAVE
☒ '78 Always And Forever
☒ '77 Boogie Nights ★
☐ '78 Groove Line, The

HEAVY D & THE BOYZ
☐ '97 Big Daddy
☐ '94 Got Me Waiting
☐ '91 Is It Good To You
☒ '91 Now That We Found Love
☐ '94 Nuttin' But Love

HEBB, Bobby
☐ '66 Satisfied Mind, A
☒ '66 Sunny ★

HEDGEHOPPERS ANONYMOUS
☐ '66 It's Good News Week

HEFTI, Neal
☐ '66 Batman Theme

HEIGHTS, The
☒ '92 How Do You Talk To An Angel ★

HELL, Richard, & The Voidoids
☐ '77 (I Belong To The) Blank Generation

HELLOGOODBYE
☒ '07 Here (In Your Arms)

HELMS, Bobby
☐ '57 Fraulein
☐ '57 Jingle Bell Rock
☒ '57 My Special Angel

HENDERSON, Joe
☐ '62 Snap Your Fingers

HENDERSON, Michael
☒ '78 Take Me I'm Yours

HENDRICKS, Bobby
☐ '58 Itchy Twitchy Feeling

HENDRIX, Jimi
☐ '68 All Along The Watchtower ★
☐ '71 Angel
☐ '67 Are You Experienced?
☐ '68 Bold As Love
☐ '68 Burning Of The Midnight Lamp
☐ '68 Castles Made Of Sand
☐ '68 Crosstown Traffic
☐ '71 Dolly Dagger
☐ '70 Drifting
☐ '67 Fire
☒ '67 Foxey Lady
☐ '71 Freedom
☐ '70 Hear My Train A Comin'
☐ '67 Hey Joe
☐ '68 If 6 Was 9
☐ '68 Little Wing
☐ '67 Manic Depression
☐ '70 Night Bird Flying
☒ '67 Purple Haze ★
☐ '67 Red House
☐ '68 Spanish Castle Magic
☐ '69 Star Spangled Banner [live]
☐ '66 Stone Free
☐ '67 Third Stone From The Sun
☐ '68 Up From The Skies
☐ '68 Voodoo Child (Slight Return)
☐ '67 Wind Cries Mary, The

HENLEY, Don
☒ '85 All She Wants To Do Is Dance
☒ '84 Boys Of Summer, The ★
☒ '82 Dirty Laundry ★
☐ '89 End Of The Innocence, The
☐ '90 Heart Of The Matter, The
☐ '89 I Will Not Go Quietly
☐ '89 Last Worthless Evening, The
☒ '81 Leather And Lace [w/ Stevie Nicks]
☐ '90 New York Minute
☐ '85 Not Enough Love In The World
☒ '92 Sometimes Love Just Ain't Enough
     [w/ Patty Smyth] ★
☐ '85 Sunset Grill
☐ '00 Taking You Home
☐ '92 Walkaway Joe [w/ Trisha Yearwood]
☐ '86 Who Owns This Place

HENRY, Clarence
☐ '56 Ain't Got No Home
☐ '61 But I Do
☐ '61 You Always Hurt The One You Love

HENSON, Jim
☐ '79 Rainbow Connection
☐ '70 Rubber Duckie

HERMAN'S HERMITS
☐ '65 Can't You Hear My Heartbeat
☐ '66 Dandy
☐ '67 Don't Go Out Into The Rain (You're
     Going To Melt)
☐ '66 East West
☐ '68 I Can Take Or Leave Your Loving
☐ '65 I'm Henry VIII, I Am ★
☐ '64 I'm Into Something Good

HERMAN'S HERMITS — cont'd
- '65 Just A Little Bit Better
- '66 Leaning On The Lamp Post
- '66 Listen People
- '65 Mrs. Brown You've Got A Lovely Daughter ★
- '65 Must To Avoid, A
- '67 No Milk Today
- '65 Silhouettes
- '67 There's A Kind Of Hush
- '66 This Door Swings Both Ways
- '65 Wonderful World

HERNANDEZ, Patrick
- '79 Born To Be Alive ★

HERNDON, Ty
- '98 It Must Be Love
- '96 Living In A Moment
- '97 Loved Too Much
- '95 What Mattered Most

HESITATIONS, The
- '68 Born Free

HEWETT, Howard
- '86 I'm For Real
- '90 Show Me

HEYWOOD, Eddie
- '56 Canadian Sunset [w/ Hugo Winterhalter] ★
- '56 Soft Summer Breeze

HIBBLER, Al
- '56 After The Lights Go Down Low
- '56 11th Hour Melody
- '55 He
- '56 Never Turn Back
- '55 Unchained Melody ★

HICKS, Taylor
- '06 Do I Make You Proud ★

HI-FIVE
- '91 I Can't Wait Another Minute
- '91 I Like The Way (The Kissing Game) ★
- '93 Never Should've Let You Go
- '92 Quality Time
- '92 She's Playing Hard To Get

HIGGINS, Bertie
- '81 Key Largo

HIGH INERGY
- '77 You Can't Turn Me Off (In The Middle Of Turning Me On)

HIGHLIGHTS, The
- '56 City Of Angels

HIGH SCHOOL MUSICAL CAST
- '06 Breaking Free ★
- '06 Get'cha Head In The Game
- '07 Gotta Go My Own Way
- '06 Start Of Something New
- '06 We're All In This Together
- '06 What I've Been Looking For
- '07 What Time Is It

- '07 You Are The Music In Me

HIGHWAYMEN, The
- '61 Cotton Fields
- '61 Michael ★

HILL, Bunker
- '62 Hide & Go Seek

HILL, Dan
- '87 Can't We Try [w/ Vonda Sheppard]
- '87 Never Thought (That I Could Love)
- '77 Sometimes When We Touch ★
- '89 Unborn Heart

HILL, Faith
- '99 Breathe ★
- '02 Cry
- '01 If My Heart Had Wings
- '95 It Matters To Me
- '97 It's Your Love [w/ Tim McGraw] ★
- '98 Just To Hear You Say That You Love Me [w/ Tim McGraw]
- '98 Let Me Let Go
- '00 Let's Make Love [w/ Tim McGraw]
- '05 Like We Never Loved At All [w/ Tim McGraw]
- '06 Lucky One, The
- '05 Mississippi Girl
- '94 Piece Of My Heart
- '96 Someone Else's Dream
- '94 Take Me As I Am
- '01 There You'll Be
- '98 This Kiss ★
- '00 Way You Love Me, The ★
- '93 Wild One

HILL, Jessie
- '60 Ooh Poo Pah Doo

HILL, Lauryn
- '98 Can't Take My Eyes Off Of You
- '98 Doo Wop (That Thing) ★
- '99 Everything Is Everything
- '99 Ex-Factor

HILLSIDE SINGERS, The
- '71 I'd Like To Teach The World To Sing

HILLTOPPERS, The
- '57 Joker (That's What They Call Me)
- '56 Ka-Ding-Dong
- '55 Kentuckian Song, The
- '57 Marianne
- '55 My Treasure
- '55 Only You (And You Alone)

HILTON, Paris
- '06 Stars Are Blind

HINDER
- '07 Better Than Me
- '06 Get Stoned
- '06 Lips Of An Angel ★

HINTON, Joe
- '64 Funny

HIPSWAY
- ☐ '87 Honeythief, The

HIRT, Al
- ☐ '64 Cotton Candy
- ☐ '64 Java
- ☐ '64 Sugar Lips

HITCHCOCK, Robyn, & The Egyptians
- ☐ '89 Madonna Of The Wasps
- ☐ '91 So You Think You're In Love

HODGES, Eddie
- ☐ '62 (Girls, Girls, Girls) Made To Love
- ☐ '61 I'm Gonna Knock On Your Door

HOFFS, Susanna
- ☐ '91 My Side Of The Bed

HOGAN, Brooke
- ☐ '06 About Us

HOKU
- ☐ '00 Another Dumb Blonde

HOLDEN, Ron
- ☐ '60 Love You So

HOLE
- ☐ '98 Celebrity Skin
- ☐ '94 Doll Parts
- ☐ '98 Malibu

HOLIDAY, J.
- ☐ '07 Bed ★

HOLLAND, Amy
- ☐ '80 How Do I Survive

HOLLAND, Eddie
- ☐ '62 Jamie

HOLLIDAY, Jennifer
- ☐ '82 And I Am Telling You I'm Not Going
- ☐ '83 I Am Love

HOLLIES, The
- ☐ '74 Air That I Breathe, The ★
- ☐ '66 Bus Stop
- ☐ '67 Carrie-Anne
- ☐ '69 He Ain't Heavy, He's My Brother
- ☐ '68 Jennifer Eccles
- ☐ '64 Just One Look
- ☐ '72 Long Cool Woman (In A Black Dress) ★
- ☐ '72 Long Dark Road
- ☐ '65 Look Through Any Window
- ☐ '67 On A Carousel
- ☐ '67 Pay You Back With Interest
- ☐ '83 Stop In The Name Of Love
- ☐ '66 Stop Stop Stop

HOLLISTER, Dave
- ☐ '99 My Favorite Girl
- ☐ '01 One Woman Man

HOLLOWAY, Brenda
- ☐ '64 Every Little Bit Hurts
- ☐ '65 When I'm Gone
- ☐ '67 You've Made Me So Very Happy

HOLLY, Buddy/The Crickets
- ☐ '58 Early In The Morning
- ☐ '57 Everyday
- ☐ '58 Heartbeat
- ☐ '58 I'm Gonna Love You, Too
- ☐ '59 It Doesn't Matter Anymore
- ☐ '58 It's So Easy
- ☐ '58 Maybe Baby
- ☐ '57 Not Fade Away
- ☐ '57 Oh, Boy! ★
- ☐ '57 Peggy Sue ★
- ☐ '59 Raining In My Heart
- ☐ '58 Rave On ★
- ☐ '58 Real Wild Child [IVAN]
- ☐ '57 That'll Be The Day ★
- ☐ '58 Think It Over
- ☐ '59 True Love Ways
- ☐ '57 Words Of Love

HOLLYWOOD ARGYLES
- ☐ '60 Alley-Oop ★

HOLLYWOOD FLAMES
- ☐ '57 Buzz-Buzz-Buzz

HOLMAN, Eddie
- ☐ '69 Hey There Lonely Girl ★

HOLMES, Clint
- ☐ '73 Playground In My Mind ★

HOLMES, Rupert
- ☐ '80 Answering Machine
- ☐ '79 Escape (The Pina Colada Song) ★
- ☐ '80 Him

HOLY, Steve
- ☐ '06 Brand New Girlfriend
- ☐ '01 Good Morning Beautiful

HOMBRES, The
- ☐ '67 Let It Out (Let It All Hang Out)

HOMER & JETHRO
- ☐ '59 Battle Of Kookamonga, The

HONDELLS, The
- ☐ '64 Little Honda ★

HONEYCOMBS, The
- ☐ '64 Have I The Right?

HONEY CONE, The
- ☐ '72 Day I Found Myself, The
- ☐ '71 One Monkey Don't Stop No Show
- ☐ '71 Stick-Up
- ☐ '71 Want Ads ★

HONEYDRIPPERS, The
- ☐ '85 Rockin' At Midnight
- ☐ '84 Sea Of Love ★

HONEYMOON SUITE
- ☐ '86 Feel It Again

HOOBASTANK
- ☐ '01 Crawling In The Dark
- ☐ '04 Reason, The ★
- ☐ '02 Running Away

HOODOO GURUS
- [ ] '89 Come Anytime

HOOKER, John Lee
- [ ] '62 Boom Boom

HOOTERS
- [ ] '85 All You Zombies
- [x] '85 And We Danced
- [ ] '85 Day By Day
- [ ] '87 Johnny B
- [ ] '86 Where Do The Children Go

HOOTIE & THE BLOWFISH
- [x] '94 Hold My Hand ★
- [x] '96 I Go Blind
- [ ] '98 I Will Wait
- [x] '95 Let Her Cry
- [ ] '96 Old Man & Me (When I Get To Heaven)
- [x] '06 One Love
- [x] '95 Only Wanna Be With You ★
- [ ] '95 Time
- [ ] '96 Tucker's Town

HOPKIN, Mary
- [ ] '69 Goodbye
- [ ] '70 Temma Harbour
- [ ] '68 Those Were The Days ★

HORNE, Jimmy "Bo"
- [ ] '78 Dance Across The Floor

HORNE, Lena
- [ ] '55 Love Me Or Leave Me

HORNSBY, Bruce, & The Range
- [ ] '90 Across The River
- [ ] '86 Every Little Kiss
- [ ] '88 Look Out Any Window
- [ ] '87 Mandolin Rain
- [ ] '88 Valley Road, The
- [x] '86 Way It Is, The ★

HORTON, Johnny
- [ ] '59 Battle Of New Orleans, The ★
- [ ] '60 North To Alaska ★
- [ ] '60 Sink The Bismarck

HOT
- [ ] '77 Angel In Your Arms

HOT BUTTER
- [ ] '72 Popcorn

HOT CHOCOLATE
- [ ] '75 Disco Queen
- [ ] '75 Emma
- [ ] '78 Every 1's A Winner
- [ ] '77 So You Win Again
- [x] '75 You Sexy Thing ★

HOTLEGS
- [ ] '70 Neanderthal Man

HOUSE OF PAIN
- [x] '92 Jump Around ★

HOUSTON
- [ ] '04 I Like That

HOUSTON, David
- [ ] '66 Almost Persuaded
- [x] '69 Baby, Baby (I Know You're A Lady)
- [ ] '67 My Elusive Dreams [w/ Tammy Wynette]
- [x] '67 You Mean The World To Me

HOUSTON, Marques
- [x] '03 Clubbin

HOUSTON, Thelma
- [x] '76 Don't Leave Me This Way ★
- [ ] '79 Saturday Night, Sunday Morning

HOUSTON, Whitney
- [x] '90 All The Man That I Need ★
- [ ] '96 Count On Me [w/ CeCe Winans]
- [ ] '87 Didn't We Almost Have It All ★
- [x] '95 Exhale (Shoop Shoop) ★
- [x] '86 Greatest Love Of All ★
- [x] '98 Heartbreak Hotel ★
- [x] '85 How Will I Know ★
- [ ] '96 I Believe In You And Me
- [ ] '93 I Have Nothing
- [ ] '00 I Learned From The Best
- [x] '87 I Wanna Dance With Somebody (Who Loves Me) ★
- [x] '92 I Will Always Love You ★
- [x] '93 I'm Every Woman
- [ ] '90 I'm Your Baby Tonight ★
- [ ] '99 It's Not Right But It's Okay ★
- [ ] '88 Love Will Save The Day
- [ ] '91 Miracle
- [x] '99 My Love Is Your Love ★
- [ ] '91 My Name Is Not Susan
- [ ] '88 One Moment In Time
- [ ] '93 Queen Of The Night
- [ ] '93 Run To You
- [x] '85 Saving All My Love For You ★
- [x] '87 So Emotional
- [ ] '93 Something In Common [w/ Bobby Brown]
- [ ] '91 Star Spangled Banner, The
- [ ] '97 Step By Step
- [x] '98 When You Believe [w/ Mariah Carey]
- [ ] '88 Where Do Broken Hearts Go ★
- [ ] '96 Why Does It Hurt So Bad
- [ ] '85 You Give Good Love

HOWARD, Adina
- [x] '95 Freak Like Me ★

HOWARD, Jan — see ANDERSON, Bill

HOWARD, Miki
- [ ] '92 Ain't Nobody Like You
- [ ] '89 Ain't Nuthin' In The World
- [ ] '90 Love Under New Management
- [ ] '90 Until You Come Back To Me (That's What I'm Gonna Do)

HOWE, Steve
- [ ] '80 Concerto In D

HOWLIN' WOLF
- [ ] '61 Back Door Man
- [ ] '61 Red Rooster
- [ ] '65 Killing Floor
- [ ] '56 Smoke Stack Lightnin'

□ '60 Spoonful

H-TOWN
- □ '93 Knockin' Da Boots
- □ '97 They Like It Slow
- □ '96 Thin Line Between Love & Hate, A

HUDSON & LANDRY
- □ '71 Ajax Liquor Store

HUDSON BROTHERS
- □ '75 Rendezvous
- ▨ '74 So You Are A Star

HUES CORPORATION, The
- ▨ '74 Rock The Boat ★
- □ '74 Rockin' Soul

HUEY
- ▨ '07 Pop, Lock And Drop It ★

HUGH, Grayson
- □ '89 Talk It Over

HUGHES, Fred
- ▨ '65 Oo Wee Baby, I Love You

HUGHES, Jimmy
- □ '64 Steal Away

HUGO & LUIGI
- ▨ '59 Just Come Home

HULLABALLOOS, The
- ▨ '65 I'm Gonna Love You Too

HUMAN BEINZ, The
- □ '67 Nobody But Me

HUMAN LEAGUE, The
- ▨ '82 Don't You Want Me ★
- ▨ '90 Heart Like A Wheel
- ▨ '86 Human ★ ▬
- □ '83 (Keep Feeling) Fascination
- □ '83 Mirror Man
- □ '95 Tell Me When

HUMBLE PIE
- ▨ '72 Hot 'N' Nasty
- □ '71 I Don't Need No Doctor
- □ '71 Stone Cold Fever
- □ '72 30 Days In The Hole

HUMPERDINCK, Engelbert
- □ '76 After The Lovin'
- □ '67 Am I That Easy To Forget
- □ '69 I'm A Better Man
- □ '67 Last Waltz, The
- □ '68 Les Bicyclettes De Belsize
- □ '68 Man Without Love, A
- □ '70 My Marie
- □ '68 Quando, Quando, Quando
- □ '67 Release Me (And Let Me Love Again)
- ▨ '70 Sweetheart
- □ '67 There Goes My Everything
- □ '78 This Moment In Time
- □ '71 When There's No You
- □ '69 Winter World Of Love

HUMPHREY, Paul
- □ '71 Cool Aid

HUNT, Tommy
- □ '63 I Am A Witness

HUNTER, Ivory Joe
- □ '57 Empty Arms
- ▨ '56 Since I Met You Baby ★

HUNTER, John
- □ '84 Tragedy

HUNTER, Tab
- □ '59 (I'll Be With You In) Apple Blossom Time
- □ '57 Ninety-Nine Ways
- □ '57 Young Love

HURRICANE CHRIS
- ▨ '07 Bay Bay, A ★

HÜSKER DÜ
- □ '84 Turn On The News

HUSKY, Ferlin
- □ '57 Gone
- □ '60 Wings Of A Dove

HYLAND, Brian
- □ '62 Ginny Come Lately
- □ '70 Gypsy Woman
- ▨ '60 Itsy Bitsy Teenie Weenie Yellow Polkadot Bikini ★
- □ '66 Joker Went Wild, The
- □ '61 Let Me Belong To You
- □ '66 Run, Run, Look And See
- ▨ '62 Sealed With A Kiss
- □ '62 Warmed Over Kisses (Left Over Love)

HYMAN, Dick
- □ '69 Minotaur, The
- □ '56 Moritat (A Theme from "The Three Penny Opera")

HYMAN, Phyllis
- □ '91 Don't Wanna Change The World

I

IAN, Janis
- □ '75 At Seventeen
- □ '67 Society's Child (Baby I've Been Thinking)

ICE CUBE
- □ '94 Bop Gun (One Nation)
- □ '93 Check Yo Self
- □ '93 It Was A Good Day
- □ '98 Pushin' Weight
- □ '98 We Be Clubbin'
- □ '99 You Can Do It
- □ '94 You Know How We Do It

ICEHOUSE
- □ '87 Crazy
- □ '88 Electric Blue

ICICLE WORKS
- ☐ '84 Whisper To A Scream (Birds Fly)

ICY BLU
- ☐ '92 I Wanna Be Your Girl

IDEAL
- ☐ '99 Get Gone

IDES OF MARCH, The
- ☐ '70 Vehicle ★

IDOL, Billy
- ☐ '90 Cradle Of Love ★
- ☐ '81 Dancing With Myself
- ☐ '87 Don't Need A Gun
- ☐ '84 Eyes Without A Face ★
- ☐ '84 Flesh For Fantasy
- ☐ '82 Hot In The City
- ☐ '81 Mony Mony
- ☐ '87 Mony Mony "Live" ★
- ☐ '83 Rebel Yell ★
- ☐ '87 Sweet Sixteen
- ☐ '86 To Be A Lover
- ☐ '83 White Wedding

IFIELD, Frank
- ☐ '62 I Remember You

IGLESIAS, Enrique
- ☐ '99 Bailamos ★
- ☐ '00 Be With You ★
- ☐ '07 Do You Know? (The Ping Pong Song)
- ☐ '02 Escape
- ☐ '01 Hero ★
- ☐ '99 Rhythm Divine

IGLESIAS, Julio
- ☐ '88 Ae, Ao
- ☐ '84 All Of You [w/ Diana Ross]
- ☐ '84 To All The Girls I've Loved Before
  [w/ Wilile Nelson] ★

IKETTES, The
- ☐ '62 I'm Blue (The Gong-Gong Song)
- ☐ '65 Peaches "N" Cream

ILLUSION, The
- ☐ '69 Did You See Her Eyes

IMAJIN
- ☐ '98 Shorty (You Keep Playin' With My
  Mind) [w/ Keith Murray]

IMBRUGLIA, Natalie
- ☐ '98 Torn ★
- ☐ '98 Wishing I Was There

IMMATURE
- ☐ '94 Constantly
- ☐ '94 Never Lie
- ☐ '96 Please Don't Go
- ☐ '99 Stay The Night
- ☐ '97 Watch Me Do My Thing
- ☐ '95 We Got It

IMPALAS, The
- ☐ '59 Sorry (I Ran All the Way Home) ★

IMPRESSIONS, The
- ☐ '64 Amen
- ☐ '70 Check Out Your Mind
- ☐ '69 Choice Of Colors
- ☐ '74 Finally Got Myself Together (I'm A
  Changed Man)
- ☐ '68 Fool For You
- ☐ '58 For Your Precious Love [w/ Jerry Butler]
- ☐ '61 Gypsy Woman
- ☐ '64 I'm So Proud
- ☐ '63 It's All Right
- ☐ '64 Keep On Pushing
- ☐ '65 People Get Ready ★
- ☐ '75 Same Thing It Took
- ☐ '75 Sooner Or Later
- ☐ '64 Talking About My Baby
- ☐ '68 This Is My Country
- ☐ '67 We're A Winner
- ☐ '65 Woman's Got Soul
- ☐ '64 You Must Believe Me
- ☐ '65 You've Been Cheatin'

INC., The
- ☐ '02 Down 4 U

INCUBUS
- ☐ '06 Anna-Molly
- ☐ '00 Drive
- ☐ '04 Megalomaniac
- ☐ '99 Pardon Me
- ☐ '00 Stellar
- ☐ '04 Talk Shows On Mute
- ☐ '02 Warning
- ☐ '01 Wish You Were Here

INDECENT OBSESSION
- ☐ '90 Tell Me Something

INDEPENDENTS, The
- ☐ '73 Leaving Me

INDIA.ARIE
- ☐ '02 Little Things
- ☐ '01 Video

INDIGO GIRLS
- ☐ '89 Closer To Fine
- ☐ '97 Shame On You

INFORMATION SOCIETY
- ☐ '90 Think
- ☐ '88 Walking Away
- ☐ '88 What's On Your Mind (Pure Energy)

INGMANN, Jorgen, & His Guitar
- ☐ '61 Apache ★

INGRAM, Jack
- ☐ '06 Wherever You Are

INGRAM, James
- ☐ '82 Baby, Come To Me [w/ Patti Austin] ★
- ☐ '90 I Don't Have The Heart ★
- ☐ '81 Just Once [w/ Quincy Jones]
- ☐ '81 One Hundred Ways [w/ Quincy Jones]
- ☐ '86 Somewhere Out There [w/ Linda
  Ronstadt] ★

■ '84 What About Me? *[w/ Kenny Rogers & Kim Carnes]*
☐ '83 Yah Mo B There *[w/ Michael McDonald]*

INGRAM, Luther
☐ '72 I'll Be Your Shelter (In Time Of Storm)
🎵 '72 (If Loving You Is Wrong) I Don't Want To Be Right

INNER CIRCLE
■ '93 Bad Boys ★
■ '93 Sweat (A La La La La Long)

INNOCENTS, The
☐ '60 Gee Whiz
☐ '60 Honest I Do

INOJ
■ '98 Love You Down
☐ '98 Time After Time

INSTANT FUNK
■ '79 I Got My Mind Made Up (You Can Get It Girl)

INTRIGUES, The
☐ '69 In A Moment

INTRO
☐ '93 Come Inside

INTRUDERS, The
☐ '68 Cowboys To Girls
☐ '73 I'll Always Love My Mama
☐ '68 (Love Is Like A) Baseball Game

INXS
☐ '87 Devil Inside ★
☐ '90 Disappear
☐ '83 Don't Change
☐ '97 Elegantly Wasted
☐ '87 Good Times *[w/ Jimmy Barnes]*
■ '92 Heaven Sent
☐ '85 Listen Like Thieves
■ '87 Need You Tonight ★
☐ '88 Never Tear Us Apart
☐ '88 New Sensation
☐ '92 Not Enough Time
☐ '83 One Thing, The
☐ '05 Pretty Vegas
☐ '90 Suicide Blonde
☐ '86 What You Need

IRBY, Joyce "Fenderella"
☐ '89 Mr. D.J.

IRIS, Donnie
☐ '80 Ah! Leah!
☐ '81 Love Is Like A Rock
☐ '82 My Girl

IRISH ROVERS, The
☐ '68 Unicorn, The
☐ '81 Wasn't That A Party

IRON BUTTERFLY
☐ '68 In-A-Gadda-Da-Vida ★

IRONHORSE
☐ '79 Sweet Lui-Louise

IRWIN, Big Dee
☐ '63 Swinging On A Star *[w/ Little Eva]*

IRWIN, Russ
☐ '91 My Heart Belongs To You

ISAAK, Chris
☐ '94 Baby Did A Bad Bad Thing
☐ '95 Somebody's Crying
☐ '90 Wicked Game ★

ISLANDERS, The
☐ '59 Enchanted Sea, The

ISLEY BROTHERS, The
■ '83 Between The Sheets —
☐ '01 Contagious
■ '80 Don't Say Goodnight (It's Time For Love)
☐ '75 Fight The Power
☐ '75 For The Love Of You
☐ '69 I Turned You On
■ '79 I Wanna Be With You
■ '69 It's Your Thing ★
☐ '77 Livin' In The Life
■ '71 Love The One You're With
☐ '72 Pop That Thang
☐ '77 Pride, The
■ '59 Shout ★
☐ '78 Take Me To The Next Phase
■ '73 That Lady
■ '66 This Old Heart Of Mine (Is Weak For You)
■ '62 Twist And Shout
☐ '76 Who Loves You Better

ISLEY, JASPER, ISLEY
☐ '85 Caravan Of Love

IT'S A BEAUTIFUL DAY
☐ '69 White Bird

IVAN — see HOLLY, Buddy

IVES, Burl
☐ '62 Call Me Mr. In-Between
☐ '62 Funny Way Of Laughin'
☐ '61 Little Bitty Tear, A
☐ '62 Mary Ann Regrets

IVY THREE, The
☐ '60 Yogi

J

JACKS, The
☐ '55 Why Don't You Write Me?

JACKS, Terry
☐ '74 Seasons In The Sun ★

JACKSON, Alan
☐ '97 Between The Devil And Me
☐ '90 Chasin' That Neon Rainbow
■ '93 Chattahoochee ★
☐ '92 Dallas

JACKSON, Alan — cont'd

- ☒ '91 Don't Rock The Jukebox
- ☐ '02 Drive (For Daddy Gene)
- ☒ '94 Gone Country
- ☐ '90 Here In The Real World
- ☒ '96 Home
- ☐ '95 I Don't Even Know Your Name
- ☐ '91 I'd Love You All Over Again
- ☒ '98 I'll Go On Loving You
- ☐ '95 I'll Try
- ☒ '00 It Must Be Love
- ☒ '03 It's Five O'Clock Somewhere [w/ Jimmy Buffett]
- ☐ '96 Little Bitty
- ☐ '99 Little Man
- ☒ '94 Livin' On Love
- ☐ '92 Love's Got A Hold On You
- ☐ '93 Mercury Blues
- ☐ '92 Midnight In Montgomery
- ☒ '99 Pop A Top
- ☒ '03 Remember When
- ☐ '98 Right On The Money
- ☒ '92 She's Got The Rhythm (And I Got The Blues)
- ☐ '91 Someday
- ☐ '94 Summertime Blues
- ☐ '95 Tall, Tall Trees
- ☐ '02 That'd Be Alright
- ☐ '97 There Goes
- ☐ '90 Wanted
- ☒ '01 Where I Come From
- ☒ '01 Where Were You (When The World Stopped Turning)
- ☒ '97 Who's Cheatin' Who
- ☒ '07 Woman's Love, A
- ☐ '02 Work In Progress

JACKSON, Chuck

- ☐ '62 Any Day Now (My Wild Beautiful Bird)
- ☐ '64 Beg Me
- ☐ '61 I Don't Want To Cry
- ☐ '63 Tell Him I'm Not Home

JACKSON, Deon

- ☒ '66 Love Makes The World Go Round

JACKSON, Freddie

- ☐ '91 Do Me Again
- ☒ '86 Have You Ever Loved Somebody
- ☐ '85 He'll Never Love You (Like I Do)
- ☐ '88 Hey Lover
- ☐ '92 I Could Use A Little Love (Right Now)
- ☐ '87 I Don't Want To Lose Your Love
- ☐ '87 Jam Tonight
- ☐ '86 Little Bit More, A
- ☐ '90 Love Me Down
- ☐ '91 Main Course
- ☐ '88 Nice 'N' Slow
- ☐ '85 Rock Me Tonight (For Old Times Sake)
- ☐ '86 Tasty Love
- ☒ '85 You Are My Lady

JACKSON, J.J.

- ☐ '66 But It's Alright

JACKSON, Janet

- ☒ '93 Again ★
- ☒ '01 All For You ★
- ☐ '90 Alright
- ☐ '94 And On And On
- ☐ '94 Any Time, Any Place
- ☐ '94 Because Of Love
- ☒ '92 Best Things In Life Are Free, The [w/ Luther Vandross]
- ☒ '90 Black Cat ★
- ☒ '06 Call On Me [w/ Nelly]
- ☒ '90 Come Back To Me
- ☐ '86 Control
- ☐ '87 Diamonds [w/ Herb Alpert]
- ☒ '00 Doesn't Really Matter ★
- ☒ '90 Escapade ★
- ☐ '98 Go Deep
- ☐ '97 Got 'Til It's Gone
- ☐ '98 I Get Lonely
- ☐ '93 If
- ☐ '87 Let's Wait Awhile
- ☐ '90 Love Will Never Do (Without You) ★
- ☐ '89 Miss You Much ★
- ☐ '86 Nasty
- ☐ '87 Pleasure Principle, The
- ☐ '89 Rhythm Nation ★
- ☐ '95 Runaway ★
- ☐ '95 Scream [w/ Michael Jackson]
- ☐ '01 Someone To Call My Lover ★
- ☐ '01 Son Of A Gun (I Betcha Think This Song Is About You)
- ☐ '91 State Of The World
- ☒ '93 That's The Way Love Goes ★
- ☐ '97 Together Again ★
- ☐ '86 What Have You Done For Me Lately
- ☒ '86 When I Think Of You ★
- ☐ '93 Where Are You Now
- ☐ '94 You Want This

JACKSON, Jermaine

- ☐ '72 Daddy's Home
- ☐ '84 Do What You Do
- ☐ '89 Don't Take It Personal
- ☐ '84 Dynamite
- ☐ '86 I Think It's Love
- ☐ '82 Let Me Tickle Your Fancy
- ☐ '80 Let's Get Serious
- ☐ '84 Tell Me I'm Not Dreamin' (Too Good To Be True) [w/ Michael Jackson]
- ☐ '80 You're Supposed To Keep Your Love For Me

JACKSON, Joe

- ☐ '83 Breaking Us In Two
- ☒ '79 Is She Really Going Out With Him?
- ☐ '82 Steppin' Out
- ☐ '84 You Can't Get What You Want (Till You Know What You Want)

JACKSON, Michael

- ☐ '88 Another Part Of Me
- ☒ '87 Bad ★
- ☒ '83 Beat It ★
- ☐ '72 Ben
- ☒ '83 Billie Jean ★

□ '91 Black Or White ★
□ '01 Butterflies
□ '88 Dirty Diana ★
□ '79 Don't Stop 'Til You Get Enough ★
□ '84 Farewell My Summer Love
□ '82 Girl Is Mine, The *[w/ Paul McCartney]* ★
□ '71 Got To Be There
□ '92 Heal The World
□ '83 Human Nature
□ '87 I Just Can't Stop Loving You *[w/ Siedah Garrett]* ★
□ '72 I Wanna Be Where You Are
□ '92 In The Closet
□ '92 Jam
□ '75 Just A Little Bit Of You
□ '88 Man In The Mirror ★
□ '80 Off The Wall
□ '83 P.Y.T. (Pretty Young Thing)
□ '92 Remember The Time ★
□ '79 Rock With You ★
□ '72 Rockin' Robin
□ '83 Say Say Say *[w/ Paul McCartney]* ★
□ '95 Scream *[w/ Janet Jackson]*
□ '80 She's Out Of My Life
□ '88 Smooth Criminal
□ '96 They Don't Care About Us
□ '84 Thriller ★
□ '83 Wanna Be Startin' Somethin'
□ '87 Way You Make Me Feel, The ★
□ '93 Who Is It
□ '93 Will You Be There
□ '95 You Are Not Alone
□ '01 You Rock My World

JACKSON, Millie
□ '72 Ask Me What You Want
□ '73 Hurts So Good

JACKSON, Rebbie
□ '84 Centipede

JACKSON, Stonewall
□ '59 Waterloo

JACKSON, Wanda
□ '61 In The Middle Of A Heartache
□ '60 Let's Have A Party
□ '61 Right Or Wrong

JACKSON 5/JACKSONS
□ '70 ABC ★
□ '78 Blame It On The Boogie
□ '72 Corner Of The Sky
□ '74 Dancing Machine
□ '76 Enjoy Yourself
□ '73 Get It Together
□ '73 Hallelujah Day
□ '80 Heartbreak Hotel
□ '75 I Am Love
□ '69 I Want You Back ★
□ '70 I'll Be There ★
□ '72 Little Bitty Pretty One
□ '72 Lookin' Through The Windows
□ '70 Love You Save, The ★
□ '80 Lovely One
□ '71 Mama's Pearl

□ '71 Maybe Tomorrow
□ '71 Never Can Say Goodbye
□ '79 Shake Your Body (Down To The Ground)
□ '77 Show You The Way To Go
□ '84 State Of Shock
□ '71 Sugar Daddy
□ '84 Torture
□ '74 Whatever You Got, I Want

JACOBS, Dick, & His Orchestra
□ '57 Fascination
□ '56 "Main Title" And "Molly-O"
□ '56 Petticoats Of Portugal

JADAKISS
□ '04 U Make Me Wanna
□ '04 Why?

JADE
□ '92 Don't Walk Away
□ '94 Every Day Of The Week
□ '92 I Wanna Love You
□ '93 One Woman

JAGGED EDGE
□ '98 Gotta Be
□ '99 He Can't Love U
□ '00 Let's Get Married
□ '00 Promise
□ '03 Walked Outta Heaven ★
□ '01 Where The Party At ★

JAGGER, Mick
□ '85 Dancing In The Street *[w/ David Bowie]*
□ '93 Don't Tear Me Up
□ '85 Just Another Night
□ '87 Let's Work
□ '85 Lucky In Love

JAGGERZ, The
□ '70 Rapper, The ★

JAHEIM
□ '02 Anything *[w/ Next]*
□ '00 Could It Be
□ '02 Fabulous *[w/ Tha Rayne]*
□ '03 Put That Woman First

JAM, The
□ '83 In The City
□ '81 That's Entertainment
□ '82 Town Called Malice, A

JAMES
□ '93 Laid

JAMES, Elmore
□ '61 Shake Your Moneymaker

JAMES, Etta
□ '60 All I Could Do Was Cry
□ '61 At Last
□ '61 Don't Cry, Baby
□ '55 Good Rockin' Daddy
□ '60 My Dearest Darling
□ '63 Pushover
□ '68 Security

JAMES, Etta — cont'd
- [ ] '62 Something's Got A Hold On Me
- [ ] '62 Stop The Wedding
- [ ] '67 Tell Mama
- [x] '61 Trust In Me
- [ ] '55 Wallflower, The

JAMES, Joni
- [ ] '56 Give Us This Day
- [ ] '55 How Important Can It Be?
- [ ] '59 Little Things Mean A Lot
- [ ] '60 My Last Date (With You)
- [ ] '58 There Goes My Heart
- [ ] '59 There Must Be A Way
- [x] '55 You Are My Love

JAMES, Rick
- [ ] '83 Cold Blooded
- [ ] '82 Dance Wit' Me
- [x] '81 Give It To Me Baby
- [ ] '88 Loosey's Rap
- [ ] '78 Mary Jane
- [x] '84 17
- [x] '81 Super Freak
- [x] '78 You And I

JAMES, Sonny
- [ ] '65 Behind The Tear
- [ ] '57 First Date, First Kiss, First Love
- [ ] '68 Heaven Says Hello
- [x] '67 I'll Never Find Another You
- [x] '67 It's The Little Things
- [ ] '68 World Of Our Own, A
- [x] '56 Young Love ★
- [x] '65 You're The Only World I Know

JAMES, Tommy
- [ ] '71 Draggin' The Line
- [ ] '71 I'm Comin' Home
- [x] '80 Three Times In Love

JAMES, Tommy, & The Shondells
- [ ] '69 Ball Of Fire
- [x] '68 Crimson And Clover ★
- [ ] '69 Crystal Blue Persuasion
- [ ] '68 Do Something To Me
- [ ] '67 Gettin' Together
- [x] '66 Hanky Panky ★
- [ ] '67 I Like The Way
- [x] '67 I Think We're Alone Now
- [x] '66 It's Only Love
- [ ] '67 Mirage
- [ ] '68 Mony Mony ★
- [x] '66 Say I Am (What I Am)
- [ ] '69 She
- [ ] '69 Sweet Cherry Wine

JAMES GANG
- [ ] '70 Funk #49
- [ ] '74 Must Be Love
- [ ] '71 Walk Away

JAMIES, The
- [ ] '58 Summertime, Summertime

JAN & DEAN
- [ ] '59 Baby Talk
- [ ] '64 Dead Man's Curve
- [ ] '63 Drag City
- [ ] '61 Heart And Soul
- [ ] '63 Honolulu Lulu
- [ ] '65 I Found A Girl
- [ ] '58 Jennie Lee
- [ ] '63 Linda
- [ ] '64 Little Old Lady (From Pasadena) ★
- [ ] '64 New Girl In School, The
- [ ] '66 Popsicle
- [ ] '64 Ride The Wild Surf
- [ ] '64 Sidewalk Surfin'
- [ ] '63 Surf City ★
- [ ] '62 Tennessee
- [ ] '60 We Go Together
- [ ] '65 You Really Know How To Hurt A Guy

JANE'S ADDICTION
- [ ] '90 Been Caught Stealing
- [ ] '88 Jane Says
- [ ] '03 Just Because
- [ ] '90 Stop!

JANKOWSKI, Horst
- [ ] '65 Walk In The Black Forest, A ★

JARMELS, The
- [ ] '61 Little Bit Of Soap, A

JARREAU, Al
- [ ] '87 Moonlighting (Theme)
- [ ] '83 Mornin'
- [x] '88 So Good
- [x] '81 We're In This Love Together

JARS OF CLAY
- [ ] '96 Flood
- [x] '02 I Need You
- [ ] '95 Love Song For A Savior

JA RULE
- [x] '01 Always On Time ★
- [x] '00 Between Me And You
- [x] '02 Down A** Chick
- [ ] '99 Holla Holla
- [ ] '01 I Cry
- [x] '01 Livin' It Up ★
- [x] '02 Mesmerize ★
- [ ] '04 New York
- [x] '00 Put It On Me
- [x] '04 Wonderful ★

JAYA
- [x] '90 If You Leave Me Now

JAY & THE AMERICANS
- [ ] '65 Cara, Mia
- [ ] '64 Come A Little Bit Closer
- [ ] '66 Crying
- [ ] '64 Let's Lock The Door (And Throw Away The Key)
- [ ] '63 Only In America
- [ ] '62 She Cried
- [ ] '65 Some Enchanted Evening
- [ ] '65 Sunday And Me
- [ ] '68 This Magic Moment
- [ ] '69 Walkin' In The Rain

JAY & THE TECHNIQUES
- ☐ '67 Apples, Peaches, Pumpkin Pie
- ☐ '67 Keep The Ball Rollin'
- ☐ '68 Strawberry Shortcake

JAYE, Jerry
- ☐ '67 My Girl Josephine

JAYHAWKS, The
- ☐ '56 Stranded In The Jungle

JAYNETTS, The
- ☐ '63 Sally, Go 'Round The Roses ★

JAY-Z
- ☐ '96 Ain't No Nigga
- ☐ '04 Big Chips [w/ R. Kelly]
- ■ '00 Big Pimpin' [w/ UGK]
- ■ '98 Can I Get A...
- ■ '03 Change Clothes
- ■ '04 Dirt Off Your Shoulder
- ■ '03 Excuse Me Miss
- ☐ '01 Girls, Girls, Girls
- ■ '98 Hard Knock Life (Ghetto Anthem)
- ☐ '00 I Just Wanna Love U (Give It 2 Me)
- ☐ '01 Izzo (H.O.V.A.) ★
- ■ '99 Jigga My Nigga
- ■ '04 99 Problems
- ■ '04 Numb/Encore [w/ Linkin Park]
- ■ '02 '03 Bonnie & Clyde ★
- ☐ '06 Show Me What You Got

JB's, The
- ☐ '73 Doing It To Death [w/ Fred Wesley]

JEAN, Wyclef
- ☐ '98 Gone Till November
- ☐ '00 911
- ☐ '02 Two Wrongs
- ☐ '97 We Trying To Stay Alive

JEFFERSON
- ■ '69 Baby Take Me In Your Arms

JEFFERSON AIRPLANE/STARSHIP
- ■ '82 Be My Lady
- ☐ '78 Count On Me
- ☐ '68 Crown Of Creation
- ☐ '81 Find Your Way Back
- ☐ '68 Greasy Heart
- ☐ '89 It's Not Enough
- ■ '87 It's Not Over ('Til It's Over)
- ☐ '79 Jane
- ☐ '75 Miracles
- ☐ '84 No Way Out
- ■ '87 Nothing's Gonna Stop Us Now ★
- ☐ '67 Plastic Fantastic Lover
- ☐ '75 Play On Love
- ☐ '71 Pretty As You Feel
- ☐ '74 Ride The Tiger
- ☐ '78 Runaway
- ■ '85 Sara
- ■ '67 Somebody To Love
- ☐ '86 Tomorrow Doesn't Matter Tonight
- ☐ '69 Volunteers
- ■ '85 We Built This City ★
- ☐ '67 White Rabbit ★

JEFFREY, Joe, Group
- ☐ '83 Winds Of Change
- ■ '76 With Your Love

JEFFREY, Joe, Group
- ☐ '69 My Pledge Of Love

JELLYBEAN
- ☐ '85 Sidewalk Talk
- ☐ '87 Who Found Who [w/ Elisa Fiorillo]

JELLY BEANS, The
- ☐ '64 I Wanna Love Him So Bad

JENNINGS, Lyfe
- ■ '05 Must Be Nice
- ■ '06 S.E.X.

JENNINGS, Waylon
- ■ '76 Good Hearted Woman [w/ Willie Nelson]
- ☐ '85 Highwayman [w/ Willie Nelson, Johnny Cash & Kris Kristofferson]
- ☐ '82 Just To Satisfy You [w/ Willie Nelson]
- ☐ '77 Luckenbach, Texas (Back to the Basics of Love)
- ■ '78 Mammas Don't Let Your Babies Grow Up To Be Cowboys [w/ Willie Nelson]
- ■ '80 Theme From The Dukes Of Hazzard (Good Ol' Boys)

JENSEN, Kris
- ☐ '62 Torture

JESUS & MARY CHAIN, The
- ☐ '89 Blues From A Gun
- ☐ '90 Head On

JESUS JONES
- ☐ '91 Real, Real, Real
- ■ '91 Right Here, Right Now ★

JET
- ☐ '03 Are You Gonna Be My Girl
- ☐ '04 Cold Hard Bitch
- ☐ '04 Look What You've Done

JETHRO TULL
- ■ '71 Aqualung
- ☐ '69 Bouree
- ☐ '74 Bungle In The Jungle
- ☐ '71 Cross-Eyed Mary
- ☐ '71 Hymn 43
- ☐ '72 Living In The Past
- ☐ '71 Locomotive Breath
- ☐ '75 Minstrel In The Gallery
- ☐ '69 New Day Yesterday
- ☐ '74 Skating Away On The Thin Ice Of A New Day
- ☐ '70 Teacher
- ☐ '72 Thick As A Brick
- ☐ '76 Too Old To Rock 'N' Roll: Too Young To Die

JETS, The
- ☐ '87 Cross My Broken Heart
- ■ '86 Crush On You
- ■ '87 I Do You
- ☐ '88 Make It Real

JETS, The — cont'd
- ☐ '88 Rocket 2 U
- ☒ '86 You Got It All

JETT, Joan, & The Blackhearts
- ☒ '82 Crimson And Clover
- ☐ '90 Dirty Deeds
- ☒ '82 Do You Wanna Touch Me (Oh Yeah)
- ☐ '83 Everyday People
- ☐ '83 Fake Friends
- ☒ '88 I Hate Myself For Loving You
- ☒ '81 I Love Rock 'N Roll ★
- ☐ '87 Light Of Day
- ☐ '88 Little Liar

JEWEL
- ☒ '97 Foolish Games
- ☒ '98 Hands ★
- ☐ '03 Intuition
- ☐ '01 Standing Still
- ☒ '96 Who Will Save Your Soul
- ☒ '96 You Were Meant For Me ★

JEWELL, Buddy
- ☐ '03 Help Pour Out The Rain (Lacey's Song)
- ☐ '03 Sweet Southern Comfort

JIBBS
- ☒ '06 Chain Hang Low ★

JIGSAW
- ☐ '76 Love Fire
- ☐ '75 Sky High

JIMENEZ, Jose
- ☐ '61 Astronaut, The

JIMMY EAT WORLD
- ☒ '01 Middle, The ★
- ☐ '04 Pain
- ☒ '02 Sweetness

JINKINS, Gus, & Orchestra
- ☒ '56 Tricky

JIVE BOMBERS, The
- ☒ '57 Bad Boy

JIVE BUNNY & THE MASTERMIXERS
- ☐ '89 Swing The Mood

JIVE FIVE, The
- ☐ '65 I'm A Happy Man
- ☐ '61 My True Story ★

J.J. FAD
- ☐ '88 Supersonic

J-KWON
- ☒ '04 Tipsy ★

JoBOXERS
- ☐ '83 Just Got Lucky

JODECI
- ☒ '92 Come & Talk To Me
- ☒ '93 Cry For You
- ☒ '94 Feenin'
- ☒ '91 Forever My Lady

- ☒ '95 Freek 'n You
- ☐ '96 Get On Up
- ☒ '93 Lately ★
- ☒ '95 Love U 4 Life
- ☒ '91 Stay

JOE
- ☐ '96 All The Things (Your Man Won't Do)
- ☒ '97 Don't Wanna Be A Player
- ☐ '98 Faded Pictures *[w/ Case]*
- ☒ '00 I Wanna Know ★
- ☒ '01 Stutter ★

JOEL, Billy
- ☐ '93 All About Soul
- ☐ '80 All For Leyna
- ☐ '82 Allentown
- ☐ '90 And So It Goes
- ☐ '87 Baby Grand *[w/ Ray Charles]*
- ☐ '74 Ballad Of Billy The Kid
- ☒ '79 Big Shot
- ☐ '74 Captain Jack
- ☐ '80 Close To The Borderline
- ☐ '80 Don't Ask Me Why
- ☐ '74 Entertainer, The
- ☐ '79 Honesty
- ☐ '90 I Go To Extremes
- ☐ '83 Innocent Man, An
- ☐ '80 It's Still Rock And Roll To Me ★
- ☒ '77 Just The Way You Are ★
- ☐ '85 Keeping The Faith
- ☐ '84 Leave A Tender Moment Alone
- ☒ '84 Longest Time, The
- ☐ '86 Matter Of Trust, A
- ☐ '86 Modern Woman
- ☒ '78 Movin' Out (Anthony's Song)
- ☒ '78 My Life ★
- ☒ '76 New York State Of Mind
- ☐ '85 Night Is Still Young, The
- ☒ '78 Only The Good Die Young
- ☒ '74 Piano Man
- ☐ '82 Pressure
- ☐ '93 River Of Dreams, The ★
- ☐ '78 Rosalinda's Eyes
- ☐ '81 Say Goodbye To Hollywood
- ☐ '77 Scenes From An Italian Restaurant
- ☐ '78 She's Always A Woman
- ☒ '81 She's Got A Way
- ☐ '80 Sometimes A Fantasy
- ☐ '77 Stranger, The
- ☒ '83 Tell Her About It ★
- ☐ '86 This Is The Time
- ☒ '83 Uptown Girl ★
- ☒ '89 We Didn't Start The Fire ★
- ☐ '80 You May Be Right
- ☐ '85 You're Only Human (Second Wind)

JOE PUBLIC
- ☐ '92 Live And Learn ★

JOHN, Elton
- ☐ '95 Believe
- ☒ '74 Bennie And The Jets ★
- ☐ '74 Bitch Is Back, The
- ☐ '77 Bite Your Lip (Get up and dance!)
- ☐ '95 Blessed

☐	'82	Blue Eyes
☐	'70	Border Song
☐	'71	Burn Down The Mission
▨	'94	Can You Feel The Love Tonight ★
▨	'73	Candle In The Wind
☐	'87	Candle In The Wind [live]
☐	'97	Candle In The Wind 1997 ★
☐	'81	Chloe
▨	'94	Circle Of Life
☐	'90	Club At The End Of The Street
▨	'72	Crocodile Rock ★
▨	'73	Daniel ★
▨	'76	Don't Go Breaking My Heart
		[w/ Kiki Dee] ★
▨	'74	Don't Let The Sun Go Down On Me ★
☐	'91	Don't Let The Sun Go Down On Me
		[live] [w/ George Michael] ★
☐	'78	Ego
☐	'82	Empty Garden (Hey Hey Johnny)
☐	'87	Flames Of Paradise [w/ Jennifer Rush]
☐	'71	Friends
☐	'73	Funeral For A Friend/Love Lies
		Bleeding
▨	'73	Goodbye Yellow Brick Road ★
☐	'76	Grow Some Funk Of Your Own
☐	'73	Harmony
☐	'89	Healing Hands
☐	'72	Honky Cat
☐	'88	I Don't Wanna Go On With You Like
		That
▨	'83	I Guess That's Why They Call It The
		Blues
▨	'83	I'm Still Standing
☐	'84	In Neon
☐	'75	Island Girl ★
▨	'83	Kiss The Bride
☐	'92	Last Song, The
☐	'71	Levon
☐	'80	Little Jeannie ★
☐	'74	Lucy In The Sky With Diamonds ★
☐	'71	Madman Across The Water
☐	'79	Mama Can't Buy You Love
☐	'72	Mona Lisas And Mad Hatters
☐	'86	Nikita
☐	'81	Nobody Wins
▨	'92	One, The
☐	'78	Part-Time Love
☐	'75	Philadelphia Freedom ★
☐	'75	Pinball Wizard
▨	'72	Rocket Man ★
☐	'90	Sacrifice
☐	'84	Sad Songs (Say So Much)
☐	'80	(Sartorial Eloquence) Don't Ya Wanna
		Play This Game No More?
▨	'73	Saturday Night's Alright For Fighting
☐	'93	Simple Life
☐	'75	Someone Saved My Life Tonight
▨	'97	Something About The Way You Look
		Tonight ★
▨	'76	Sorry Seems To Be The Hardest Word
☐	'73	Step Into Christmas
☐	'70	Take Me To The Pilot
☐	'89	Through The Storm [w/ Aretha Franklin]
▨	'71	Tiny Dancer

☐	'79	Victim Of Love
☐	'84	Who Wears These Shoes?
☐	'88	Word In Spanish, A
☐	'85	Wrap Her Up
☐	'99	Written In The Stars [w/ LeAnn Rimes]
▨	'90	You Gotta Love Someone
▨	'70	Your Song ★

JOHN, Little Willie
☐	'60	Cottage For Sale, A
☐	'56	Fever
☐	'60	Heartbreak (It's Hurtin' Me)
☐	'59	Leave My Kitten Alone
☐	'60	Sleep
☐	'58	Talk To Me, Talk To Me

JOHN, Robert
▨	'80	Hey There Lonely Girl
▨	'72	Lion Sleeps Tonight, The
☐	'79	Sad Eyes

JOHN & ERNEST
☐	'73	Super Fly Meets Shaft

JOHNNIE & JOE
☐	'57	Over The Mountain; Across The Sea

JOHNNY & THE HURRICANES
☐	'60	Beatnik Fly
☐	'59	Crossfire
☐	'60	Down Yonder
☐	'59	Red River Rock ★
☐	'59	Reveille Rock
☐	'60	Rocking Goose

JOHNNY HATES JAZZ
☐	'88	I Don't Want To Be A Hero
☐	'88	Shattered Dreams

JOHNS, Sammy
☐	'75	Chevy Van

JOHNSON, Betty
☐	'58	Dream
☐	'56	I Dreamed
☐	'58	Little Blue Man, The
☐	'57	Little White Lies

JOHNSON, Carolyn Dawn
☐	'01	Complicated

JOHNSON, Don
☐	'86	Heartbeat
☐	'88	Till I Loved You [w/ Barbra Streisand]

JOHNSON, Jack
☐	'05	Sitting, Waiting, Wishing
☐	'06	Upside Down

JOHNSON, Jesse
☐	'86	Crazay [w/ Sly Stone]

JOHNSON, Marv
☐	'59	Come To Me
▨	'60	I Love The Way You Love
☐	'59	You Got What It Takes
☐	'60	(You've Got To) Move Two Mountains

JOHNSON, Michael
- ☐ '78 Almost Like Being In Love
- ☐ '78 Bluer Than Blue
- ☐ '79 This Night Won't Last Forever

JOHNSTON, Tom
- ☐ '79 Savannah Nights

JOJO
- ☐ '04 Baby It's You
- ☐ '04 Leave (Get Out)
- ☐ '06 Too Little Too Late ★

JO JO GUNNE
- ☐ '72 Run Run Run

JOLI, France
- ☐ '79 Come To Me

JOMANDA
- ☐ '91 Got A Love For You

JON & ROBIN & The In Crowd
- ☐ '67 Do It Again A Little Bit Slower

JONAS BROTHERS
- ☐ '07 S.O.S.
- ☐ '07 Year 3000

JON B
- ☐ '98 Are U Still Down
- ☐ '95 Pretty Girl
- ☐ '95 Someone To Love
- ☐ '98 They Don't Know

JONES, Donell
- ☐ '97 Knocks Me Off My Feet
- ☐ '99 U Know What's Up
- ☐ '00 Where I Wanna Be

JONES, Etta
- ☐ '60 Don't Go To Strangers

JONES, George
- ☐ '80 He Stopped Loving Her Today ★
- ☐ '69 I'll Share My World With You
- ☐ '62 She Thinks I Still Care
- ☐ '61 Tender Years
- ☐ '67 Walk Through This World With Me
- ☐ '73 We're Gonna Hold On [w/ Tammy Wynette]
- ☐ '74 (We're Not) The Jet Set [w/ Tammy Wynette]
- ☐ '59 White Lightning

JONES, Glenn
- ☐ '92 Here I Go Again
- ☐ '84 Show Me
- ☐ '87 We've Only Just Begun (The Romance Is Not Over)

JONES, Howard
- ☐ '89 Everlasting Love
- ☐ '85 Life In One Day
- ☐ '92 Lift Me Up
- ☐ '84 New Song
- ☐ '86 No One Is To Blame
- ☐ '89 Prisoner, The

- ☐ '85 Things Can Only Get Better
- ☐ '84 What Is Love?
- ☐ '86 You Know I Love You...Don't You?

JONES, Jack
- ☐ '63 Call Me Irresponsible
- ☐ '66 Day In The Life Of A Fool, A
- ☐ '64 Dear Heart
- ☐ '66 Impossible Dream, The
- ☐ '67 Lady
- ☐ '62 Lollipops And Roses
- ☐ '67 Now I Know
- ☐ '65 Race Is On, The
- ☐ '63 Wives And Lovers

JONES, Jim
- ☐ '07 We Fly High ★

JONES, Jimmy
- ☐ '60 Good Timin' ★
- ☐ '59 Handy Man ★

JONES, Joe
- ☐ '60 You Talk Too Much

JONES, Linda
- ☐ '67 Hypnotized

JONES, Mike
- ☐ '05 Back Then

JONES, Norah
- ☐ '02 Don't Know Why
- ☐ '04 Here We Go Again [w/ Ray Charles]
- ☐ '04 Sunrise
- ☐ '02 Turn Me On

JONES, Oran "Juice"
- ☐ '86 Rain, The

JONES, Quincy
- ☐ '81 Ai No Corrida (I-No-Ko-ree-da)
- ☐ '89 I'll Be Good To You [w/ Ray Charles & Chaka Khan]
- ☐ '81 Just Once
- ☐ '81 One Hundred Ways [w/ James Ingram]
- ☐ '90 Secret Garden (Sweet Seduction Suite) [w/ Al B. Sure!, James Ingram, El DeBarge & Barry White]
- ☐ '78 Stuff Like That
- ☐ '90 Tomorrow (A Better You, Better Me) [w/ Tevin Campbell]

JONES, Rickie Lee
- ☐ '79 Chuck E.'s In Love
- ☐ '79 Young Blood

JONES, Shirley
- ☐ '86 Do You Get Enough Love

JONES, Tom
- ☐ '70 Can't Stop Loving You
- ☐ '81 Darlin'
- ☐ '70 Daughter Of Darkness
- ☐ '68 Delilah
- ☐ '67 Detroit City
- ☐ '66 Green, Green Grass Of Home
- ☐ '68 Help Yourself

- ☐ '70 I (Who Have Nothing)
- ☐ '67 I'll Never Fall In Love Again
- ☒ '65 It's Not Unusual
- ☐ '69 Love Me Tonight
- ☐ '71 Puppet Man
- ☐ '71 Resurrection Shuffle
- ☐ '77 Say You'll Stay Until Tomorrow
- ☒ '71 She's A Lady ★
- ☐ '65 Thunderball
- ☒ '65 What's New Pussycat? ★
- ☐ '65 With These Hands
- ☐ '69 Without Love (There Is Nothing)

JONES GIRLS, The
- ☐ '79 You Gonna Make Me Love Somebody Else

JOPLIN, Janis/BIG BROTHER & THE HOLDING COMPANY
- ☐ '68 Ball And Chain
- ☐ '68 Coo Coo
- ☐ '71 Cry Baby
- ☐ '68 Down On Me
- ☐ '71 Get It While You Can
- ☐ '69 Kozmic Blues
- ☐ '69 Maybe
- ☒ '71 Me And Bobby McGee ★
- ☐ '71 Mercedes Benz
- ☐ '71 Move Over
- ☒ '68 Piece Of My Heart ★
- ☐ '69 Try (Just A Little Bit Harder)

JORDAN, Jeremy
- ☒ '92 Right Kind Of Love, The
- ☐ '93 Wannagirl

JORDAN, Montell
- ☒ '96 Falling
- ☒ '99 Get It On...Tonite ★
- ☒ '98 I Can Do That
- ☐ '96 I Like
- ☒ '98 Let's Ride ★
- ☐ '95 Somethin' 4 Da Honeyz
- ☒ '95 This Is How We Do It ★
- ☐ '97 What's On Tonight

JOURNEY
- ☒ '83 After The Fall
- ☒ '80 Any Way You Want It
- ☒ '78 Anytime
- ☐ '83 Ask The Lonely
- ☐ '86 Be Good To Yourself
- ☒ '81 Don't Stop Believin'
- ☒ '83 Faithfully
- ☒ '86 Girl Can't Help It
- ☐ '86 I'll Be Alright Without You
- ☒ '79 Just The Same Way
- ☒ '78 Lights
- ☒ '79 Lovin', Touchin', Squeezin'
- ☐ '85 Only The Young
- ☒ '82 Open Arms ★
- ☒ '81 Party's Over (Hopelessly In Love)
- ☐ '83 Send Her My Love
- ☒ '83 Separate Ways (Worlds Apart)
- ☐ '82 Still They Ride
- ☒ '86 Suzanne

- ☒ '80 Walks Like A Lady
- ☒ '78 Wheel In The Sky
- ☒ '96 When You Love A Woman
- ☒ '81 Who's Crying Now

JOY DIVISION
- ☐ '80 Love Will Tear Us Apart

J-SHIN
- ☐ '99 One Night Stand

JUDAS PRIEST
- ☒ '80 Breaking The Law
- ☐ '80 Living After Midnight
- ☒ '82 You've Got Another Thing Comin'

JUDDS, The
- ☒ '88 Give A Little Love
- ☒ '86 Grandpa (Tell Me 'Bout The Good Old Days)
- ☐ '85 Have Mercy
- ☐ '84 Why Not Me
- ☒ '89 Young Love

JUMP 'N THE SADDLE
- ☐ '83 Curly Shuffle, The

JUNIOR
- ☐ '82 Mama Used To Say ━

JUNIOR M.A.F.I.A.
- ☐ '96 Get Money
- ☒ '95 Player's Anthem

JUSTIS, Bill
- ☐ '57 Raunchy ★

JUST US
- ☐ '66 I Can't Grow Peaches On A Cherry Tree

JUVENILE
- ☒ '99 Back That Azz Up
- ☐ '04 Nolia Clap [w/ Wacko & Skip]
- ☒ '04 Slow Motion

K

KADISON, Joshua
- ☐ '94 Beautiful In My Eyes
- ☐ '93 Jessie

KAEMPFERT, Bert, & His Orchestra
- ☐ '62 Afrikaan Beat
- ☐ '65 Moon Over Naples
- ☐ '65 Red Roses For A Blue Lady
- ☐ '61 Tenderly
- ☐ '65 Three O'Clock In The Morning
- ☐ '60 Wonderland By Night ★

KAJAGOOGOO
- ☐ '83 Too Shy

KALIN TWINS
- ☐ '58 Forget Me Not
- ☐ '59 It's Only The Beginning
- ☐ '58 When

KALLEN, Kitty
- ☐ '56 Go On With The Wedding *[w/ Georgie Shaw]*
- ☐ '59 If I Give My Heart To You
- ☐ '62 My Coloring Book
- ☐ '60 That Old Feeling

KALLMANN, Gunter, Chorus
- ☐ '66 Wish Me A Rainbow

KAMOZE, Ini
- ☐ '94 Here Comes The Hotstepper ★

KANDI
- ☐ '00 Don't Think I'm Not

KANE, Big Daddy
- ☐ '88 Ain't No Half-Steppin'
- 🔳 '93 Very Special

KANE, Madleen
- ☐ '81 You Can

KANE GANG, The
- ☐ '87 Motortown

KANSAS
- ☐ '86 All I Wanted
- 🔳 '76 Carry On Wayward Son
- 🔳 '78 Dust In The Wind
- ☐ '83 Fight Fire With Fire
- ☐ '80 Hold On
- ☐ '79 People Of The South Wind
- ☐ '82 Play The Game Tonight
- ☐ '77 Point Of Know Return
- ☐ '77 Portait (He Knew)

KASENETZ-KATZ SINGING ORCHESTRAL CIRCUS
- ☐ '68 Quick Joey Small (Run Joey Run)

KASHIF
- ☐ '87 Love Changes *[w/ Meli'sa Morgan]*

KATRINA & THE WAVES
- ☐ '85 Do You Want Crying
- ☐ '89 That's The Way
- 🔳 '85 Walking On Sunshine

KC & THE SUNSHINE BAND
- 🔳 '76 Boogie Shoes
- 🔳 '75 Get Down Tonight ★
- ☐ '83 Give It Up
- ☐ '76 I Like To Do It
- 🔳 '77 I'm Your Boogie Man ★
- ☐ '78 It's The Same Old Song
- ☐ '77 Keep It Comin' Love
- 🔳 '79 Please Don't Go ★
- 🔳 '76 (Shake, Shake, Shake) Shake Your Booty ★
- 🔳 '75 That's The Way (I Like It) ★
- ☐ '79 Yes, I'm Ready *[w/ Teri DeSario]*

K-CI & JOJO
- 🔳 '98 All My Life ★
- 🔳 '00 Crazy
- 🔳 '95 If You Think You're Lonely Now
- 🔳 '97 Last Night's Letter

[K-CI & JOJO cont.]
- 🔳 '99 Tell Me It's Real ★
- 🔳 '97 You Bring Me Up

K-DOE, Ernie
- ☐ '61 Mother-In-Law ★

KEANE
- ☐ '05 Somewhere Only We Know

KEARNEY, Mat
- ☐ '07 Nothing Left To Lose

KEEDY
- ☐ '91 Save Some Love

KEITH
- ☐ '66 Ain't Gonna Lie
- ☐ '66 98.6
- ☐ '67 Tell Me To My Face

KEITH, Lisa
- ☐ '93 Better Than You

KEITH, Toby
- ☐ '03 American Soldier
- 🔳 '05 As Good As I Once Was
- ☐ '02 Beer For My Horses *[w/ Willie Nelson]*
- ☐ '02 Courtesy Of The Red, White And Blue (The Angry American)
- ☐ '96 Does That Blue Moon Ever Shine On You
- ☐ '05 Get Drunk And Be Somebody
- 🔳 '07 High Maintenance Woman
- 🔳 '00 How Do You Like Me Now?!
- 🔳 '03 I Love This Bar
- 🔳 '01 I Wanna Talk About Me
- ☐ '01 I'm Just Talkin' About Tonight
- ☐ '97 I'm So Happy I Can't Stop Crying *[w/ Sting]*
- 🔳 '93 Little Less Talk And A Lot More Action
- 🔳 '06 Little Too Late, A
- ☐ '07 Love Me If You Can
- ☐ '96 Me Too
- ☐ '02 My List
- ☐ '93 Should've Been A Cowboy
- ☐ '04 Stays In Mexico
- ☐ '97 We Were In Love
- ☐ '04 Whiskey Girl
- ☐ '94 Who's That Man
- ☐ '02 Who's Your Daddy?
- ☐ '94 Wish I Didn't Know Now
- ☐ '95 You Ain't Much Fun
- 🔳 '00 You Shouldn't Kiss Me Like This

KELIS
- 🔳 '06 Bossy ★
- 🔳 '03 Milkshake ★

KELLER, Jerry
- ☐ '59 Here Comes Summer

KELLY, Monty, & His Orchestra
- ☐ '60 Summer Set

KELLY, R.
- ☐ '04 Big Chips *[w/ Jay-Z]*
- 🔳 '94 Bump N' Grind ★
- ☐ '93 Dedicated

- ☐ '99 Did You Ever Think
- ☐ '96 Down Low (Nobody Has To Know)
- ☑ '01 Feelin' On Yo Booty
- ☑ '01 Fiesta Remix ★
- ☐ '97 Gotham City
- ☐ '04 Happy People
- ☐ '92 Honey Love
- ☑ '96 I Believe I Can Fly ★
- ☐ '96 I Can't Sleep Baby (If I) ★
- ☑ '00 I Wish
- ☑ '07 I'm A Flirt
- ☑ '98 I'm Your Angel *[w/ Celine Dion]* ★
- ☑ '99 If I Could Turn Back The Hands Of Time ★
- ☑ '02 Ignition ★
- ☐ '07 Same Girl
- ☐ '93 Sex Me
- ☐ '92 Slow Dance (Hey Mr. DJ)
- ☐ '03 Snake
- ☑ '03 Step In The Name Of Love
- ☐ '03 Thoia Thoing
- ☐ '05 Trapped In The Closet
- ☑ '98 When A Woman's Fed Up
- ☑ '01 World's Greatest, The
- ☐ '95 You Remind Me Of Something
- ☑ '94 Your Body's Callin'

KEMP, Johnny
- ☐ '89 Birthday Suit
- ☐ '88 Just Got Paid

KEMP, Tara
- ☑ '91 Hold You Tight ★
- ☑ '91 Piece Of My Heart

KENDALLS, The
- ☐ '77 Heaven's Just A Sin Away

KENDRICKS, Eddie
- ☐ '74 Boogie Down ★
- ☐ '76 He's A Friend
- ☐ '73 Keep On Truckin' ★
- ☐ '75 Shoeshine Boy
- ☐ '74 Son Of Sagittarius

KENNEDY, Joyce — see OSBORNE, Jeffrey

KENNER, Chris
- ☑ '61 I Like It Like That ★

KENNY G
- ☐ '99 Auld Lang Syne
- ☐ '93 By The Time This Night Is Over *[w/ Peabo Bryson]*
- ☐ '87 Don't Make Me Wait For Love
- ☐ '92 Forever In Love
- ☐ '88 Silhouette
- ☐ '87 Songbird

KERSH, David
- ☐ '97 Another You
- ☐ '97 If I Never Stop Loving You

KERSHAW, Sammy
- ☐ '91 Cadillac Style
- ☐ '94 I Can't Reach Her Anymore
- ☑ '97 Love Of My Life

- ☐ '94 National Working Woman's Holiday
- ☑ '93 She Don't Know She's Beautiful
- ☐ '94 Third Rate Romance

KETCHUM, Hal
- ☐ '93 Hearts Are Gonna Roll
- ☐ '92 Past The Point Of Rescue
- ☐ '91 Small Town Saturday Night
- ☐ '92 Sure Love

KEYS, Alicia
- ☑ '04 Diary ★
- ☑ '01 Fallin'
- ☑ '04 If I Ain't Got You ★
- ☐ '05 Karma
- ☑ '04 My Boo *[w/ Usher]* ★
- ☑ '07 No One ★
- ☑ '05 Unbreakable
- ☑ '01 Woman's Worth, A
- ☑ '03 You Don't Know My Name ★

KHAN, Chaka/RUFUS
- ☐ '83 Ain't Nobody ⇒
- ☑ '84 I Feel For You ★ ⎯
- ☑ '78 I'm Every Woman
- ☑ '96 Missing You *[w/ Brandy, Tamia & Gladys Knight]*
- ☐ '75 Once You Get Started
- ☐ '76 Sweet Thing
- ☑ '74 Tell Me Something Good
- ☐ '81 What Cha' Gonna Do For Me
- ☑ '74 You Got The Love

KHIA
- ☑ '02 My Neck, My Back (Lick It)

KIARA
- ☐ '88 This Time *[w/ Shanice]*

KID FROST
- ☐ '90 La Raza

KID ROCK
- ☐ '99 Bawitdaba
- ☐ '99 Cowboy
- ☑ '00 Only God Knows Why
- ☑ '02 Picture *[w/ Sheryl Crow]* ★

KIHN, Greg, Band
- ☐ '81 Breakup Song (They Don't Write 'Em)
- ☐ '83 Jeopardy ★
- ☐ '85 Lucky

KILGORE, Theola
- ☐ '63 Love Of My Man, The

KILLERS, The
- ☐ '05 All These Things That I've Done
- ☐ '06 Great Big Sled, A
- ☑ '05 Mr. Brightside ★
- ☑ '04 Somebody Told Me
- ☑ '06 When You Were Young ★

KIM, Andy
- ☑ '69 Baby, I Love You
- ☑ '70 Be My Baby
- ☐ '74 Fire, Baby I'm On Fire
- ☐ '68 How'd We Ever Get This Way

KIM, Andy — cont'd
- '74 Rock Me Gently ★
- ☐ '68 Shoot'em Up, Baby
- ☐ '69 So Good Together

KIMBERLY, Adrian
- ☐ '61 The Graduation Song... Pomp And Circumstance

KING, Albert
- ☐ '67 Born Under A Bad Sign

KING, B.B.
- ☐ '71 Ask Me No Questions
- ☐ '56 Bad Luck
- ☐ '66 Don't Answer The Door
- ☐ '55 Every Day I Have The Blues
- ☐ '73 I Like To Live The Love
- ☐ '56 On My Word Of Honor
- ☐ '68 Paying The Cost To Be The Boss
- ☐ '58 Please Accept My Love
- ☐ '64 Rock Me Baby
- '60 Sweet Sixteen
- '69 Thrill Is Gone, The ★
- '73 To Know You Is To Love You
- ☐ '88 When Love Comes To Town *[w/ U2]*

KING, Ben E.
- ☐ '61 Amor
- ☐ '62 Don't Play That Song (You Lied)
- ☐ '63 I (Who Have Nothing)
- '60 Spanish Harlem
- '61 Stand By Me ★
- ☐ '75 Supernatural Thing

KING, Carole
- ☐ '72 Been To Canaan
- ☐ '73 Believe In Humanity
- ☐ '73 Corazón
- ☐ '77 Hard Rock Cafe
- ☐ '71 I Feel The Earth Move
- ☐ '62 It Might As Well Rain Until September
- '71 It's Too Late ★
- ☐ '74 Jazzman
- ☐ '75 Nightingale
- ☐ '80 One Fine Day
- ☐ '76 Only Love Is Real
- ☐ '71 So Far Away
- ☐ '72 Sweet Seasons
- '71 You've Got A Friend

KING, Claude
- ☐ '62 Wolverton Mountain

KING, Diana
- ☐ '97 I Say A Little Prayer
- ☐ '95 Shy Guy

KING, Evelyn "Champagne"
- ☐ '82 Betcha She Don't Love You
- ☐ '88 Flirt
- ☐ '79 I Don't Know If It's Right
- '81 I'm In Love
- '82 Love Come Down
- ☐ '78 Shame

KING, Freddy
- ☐ '61 Hide Away

KING, Jonathan
- ☐ '65 Everyone's Gone To The Moon

KING, Teddi
- ☐ '56 Mr. Wonderful

KING CRIMSON
- ☐ '69 Court Of The Crimson King

KING CURTIS
- ☐ '67 Memphis Soul Stew
- ☐ '67 Ode To Billie Joe
- ☐ '62 Soul Twist

KING HARVEST
- ☐ '72 Dancing In The Moonlight

KINGS, The
- ☐ '80 Switchin' To Glide/This Beat Goes On ★

KINGSMEN, The
- ☐ '65 Jolly Green Giant, The
- ☐ '63 Louie Louie ★
- ☐ '64 Money

KINGSTON, Sean
- '07 Beautiful Girls ★
- '07 Me Love

KINGSTON TRIO, The
- ☐ '60 Bad Man Blunder
- ☐ '63 Desert Pete
- ☐ '60 El Matador
- ☐ '60 Everglades
- ☐ '63 Greenback Dollar
- ☐ '59 M.T.A.
- ☐ '63 Reverend Mr. Black
- ☐ '62 Scotch And Soda
- ☐ '59 Tijuana Jail, The
- ☐ '58 Tom Dooley ★
- ☐ '62 Where Have All The Flowers Gone
- ☐ '59 Worried Man, A

KINKS, The
- ☐ '64 All Day And All Of The Night
- ☐ '70 Apeman
- ☐ '72 Celluloid Heroes
- '83 Come Dancing ★
- ☐ '66 Dedicated Follower Of Fashion
- ☐ '81 Destroyer
- ☐ '85 Do It Again
- ☐ '83 Don't Forget To Dance
- ☐ '77 Father Christmas
- ☐ '85 Living On A Thin Line
- '70 Lola ★
- ☐ '79 Low Budget
- ☐ '78 Rock 'N' Roll Fantasy, A
- ☐ '65 Set Me Free
- ☐ '77 Sleepwalker
- ☐ '66 Sunny Afternoon
- ☐ '65 Tired Of Waiting For You
- ☐ '70 Victoria
- ☐ '68 Waterloo Sunset

☐	'65	Well Respected Man, A
☐	'65	Who'll Be The Next In Line
☐	'79	(Wish I Could Fly Like) Superman
■	'64	You Really Got Me ★

KISS
☐	'76	Beth
☐	'77	Calling Dr. Love
☐	'77	Christine Sixteen
☐	'74	Cold Gin
☐	'76	Detroit Rock City
☐	'74	Deuce
☐	'76	Flaming Youth
☐	'90	Forever
☐	'76	Hard Luck Woman
☐	'74	Hotter Than Hell
☐	'79	I Was Made For Lovin' You
☐	'77	Love Gun
☐	'74	Nothin' To Lose
☐	'98	Psycho Circus
■	'75	Rock And Roll All Nite [live] ★
☐	'78	Rocket Ride
■	'76	Shout It Out Loud
☐	'74	Strutter
☐	'79	Sure Know Something

KISSOON, Mac & Katie
☐	'71	Chirpy Chirpy Cheep Cheep

KIX
■	'89	Don't Close Your Eyes

KLF, The
☐	'92	Justified & Ancient *[w/ Tammy Wynette]* ★
☐	'91	3 A.M. Eternal

KLIQUE
☐	'83	Stop Doggin' Me Around

KLYMAXX
■	'85	I Miss You
■	'87	I'd Still Say Yes
☐	'86	Man Size Love
☐	'84	Men All Pause, The

KNACK, The
☐	'80	Baby Talks Dirty
☐	'79	Frustrated
☐	'79	Good Girls Don't
■	'79	My Sharona ★

KNICKERBOCKERS, The
☐	'65	Lies

KNIGHT, Frederick
☐	'72	I've Been Lonely For So Long

KNIGHT, Gladys, & The Pips
☐	'74	Best Thing That Ever Happened To Me
☐	'73	Daddy Could Swear, I Declare
☐	'68	End Of Our Road, The
■	'61	Every Beat Of My Heart
■	'67	Everybody Needs Love
☐	'69	Friendship Train
☐	'64	Giving Up
☐	'72	Help Me Make It Through The Night
■	'71	I Don't Want To Do Wrong
☐	'74	I Feel A Song (In My Heart)
■	'67	I Heard It Through The Grapevine
☐	'73	I've Got To Use My Imagination
☐	'70	If I Were Your Woman
☐	'68	It Should Have Been Me
☐	'80	Landlord
☐	'61	Letter Full Of Tears
☐	'75	Love Finds It's Own Way
☐	'88	Love Overboard
☐	'88	Lovin' On Next To Nothin'
☐	'71	Make Me The Woman That You Go Home To
☐	'91	Men
■	'73	Midnight Train To Georgia ★
☐	'96	Missing You *[w/ Brandy, Tamia & Chaka Khan]*
☐	'73	Neither One Of Us (Wants To Be The First To Say Goodbye)
☐	'69	Nitty Gritty, The
☐	'74	On And On
☐	'75	Part Time Love
☐	'83	Save The Overtime (For Me)
☐	'76	So Sad The Song
☐	'75	Way We Were/Try To Remember
☐	'73	Where Peaceful Waters Flow
■	'70	You Need Love Like I Do (Don't You)

KNIGHT, Jean
■	'71	Mr. Big Stuff ★

KNIGHT, Jordan
☐	'99	Give It To You

KNIGHT, Robert
■	'67	Everlasting Love

KNIGHT, Sonny
☐	'56	Confidential

KNOBLOCK, Fred
☐	'80	Killin' Time *[w/ Susan Anton]*
☐	'80	Why Not Me

KNOCKOUTS, The
☐	'59	Darling Lorraine

KNOX, Buddy
☐	'57	Hula Love
☐	'59	I Think I'm Gonna Kill Myself
☐	'61	Ling-Ting-Tong
☐	'60	Lovey Dovey
☐	'57	Party Doll ★
☐	'57	Rock Your Little Baby To Sleep
☐	'58	Somebody Touched Me
■	'59	Teasable, Pleasable You

KOFFMAN, Moe, Quartette
☐	'58	Swingin' Shepherd Blues, The

KOKOMO
☐	'61	Asia Minor

KON KAN
☐	'88	I Beg Your Pardon

KOOL & THE GANG
☐	'82	Big Fun
■	'80	Celebration ★
■	'85	Cherish ★

KOOL & THE GANG — cont'd

- ☐ '85 Emergency
- ☐ '85 Fresh
- ☐ '73 Funky Stuff
- ▣ '82 Get Down On It
- ☐ '74 Higher Plane
- ☐ '74 Hollywood Swinging
- ▣ '83 Joanna ★
- ☐ '81 Jones Vs. Jones
- ▣ '73 Jungle Boogie
- ▣ '79 Ladies Night
- ▣ '82 Let's Go Dancin' (Ooh La, La, La)
- ☐ '84 Misled
- ▣ '75 Rhyme Tyme People
- ▣ '75 Spirit Of The Boogie
- ☐ '87 Stone Love
- ☐ '75 Summer Madness
- ▣ '81 Take My Heart (You Can Have It If You Want It)
- ☐ '84 Tonight
- ☐ '80 Too Hot
- ☐ '86 Victory

KOOL MOE DEE

- ☐ '89 They Want Money

KORGIS, The

- ☐ '80 Everybody's Got To Learn Sometime

KORN

- ▣ '06 Coming Undone
- ☐ '03 Did My Time
- ☐ '07 Evolution
- ☐ '05 Twisted Transistor

K.P. & ENVYI

- ☐ '97 Swing My Way

KRAFTWERK

- ☐ '75 Autobahn

KRAMER, Billy J.

- ☐ '64 Bad To Me
- ☐ '64 From A Window
- ☐ '64 I'll Keep You Satisfied
- ☐ '64 Little Children

KRANZ, George

- ☐ '85 Trommeltanz (Din Daa Daa)

KRAUSS, Alison, & Union Station

- ▣ '95 Baby Now That I've Found You
- ☐ '96 High Lonesome Sound [w/ Vince Gill]
- ▣ '95 When You Say Nothing At All
- ▣ '04 Whiskey Lullaby [w/ Brad Paisley]

KRAVITZ, Lenny

- ▣ '00 Again ★
- ▣ '99 American Woman
- ☐ '93 Are You Gonna Go My Way
- ☐ '01 Dig In
- ☐ '98 Fly Away
- ▣ '91 It Ain't Over 'Til It's Over ★
- ☐ '04 Lady

KRIS KROSS

- ☐ '93 Alright
- ▣ '92 Jump ★

KRISTOFFERSON, Kris

- ☐ '85 Highwayman [w/ Waylon Jennings, Willie Nelson & Johnny Cash]
- ☐ '71 Loving Her Was Easier (Than Anything I'll Ever Do Again)
- ☐ '73 Why Me

KROEGER, Chad

- ☐ '02 Hero ★
- ☐ '03 Why Don't You & I [w/ Alex Band or Chad Kroeger]

KROKUS

- ☐ '84 Midnite Maniac

K7

- ☐ '93 Come Baby Come

KUBAN, Bob, & The In-Men

- ☐ '66 Cheater, The

KUT KLOSE

- ☐ '95 I Like

K.W.S.

- ▣ '92 Please Don't Go

KYPER

- ☐ '90 Tic-Tac-Toe

L

LaBELLE, Patti/THE BLUE-BELLES

- ☐ '63 Down The Aisle (Wedding Song)
- ☐ '62 I Sold My Heart To The Junkman
- ☐ '83 If Only You Knew
- ☐ '75 Lady Marmalade ★
- ☐ '84 Love Has Finally Come At Last [w/ Bobby Womack]
- ▣ '85 New Attitude
- ☐ '86 Oh, People
- ☐ '86 On My Own [w/ Michael McDonald] ★
- ▣ '91 Somebody Loves You Baby (You Know Who It Is)
- ☐ '64 You'll Never Walk Alone

LA BOUCHE

- ▣ '95 Be My Lover ★
- ☐ '96 Fallin' In Love
- ▣ '96 Sweet Dreams

LACHEY, Nick

- ▣ '06 What's Left Of Me

LADD, Cheryl

- ▣ '78 Think It Over

LADY FLASH

- ☐ '76 Street Singin'

L.A. GUNS

- ☐ '90 Ballad of Jayne, The

LAI, Francis, & His Orchestra

- ☐ '71 Theme From Love Story

LAID BACK
- ☐ '84 White Horse

LAINE, Frankie
- ☐ '55 Humming Bird
- ☐ '67 I'll Take Care Of Your Cares
- ☐ '57 Love Is A Golden Ring
- ☐ '67 Making Memories
- ☐ '56 Moonlight Gambler ★
- ☐ '68 To Each His Own
- ☐ '55 Woman In Love, A
- ☐ '69 You Gave Me A Mountain

LAKESIDE
- ☑ '80 Fantastic Voyage

LAMBERT, Miranda
- ☐ '06 Kerosene

LaMOND, George
- ☐ '90 Bad Of The Heart

LANCE, Major
- ☐ '65 Come See
- ☐ '63 Hey Little Girl
- ☐ '64 Matador, The
- ☐ '63 Monkey Time, The
- ☐ '64 Rhythm
- ☐ '64 Um, Um, Um, Um, Um, Um

LANE, Mickey Lee
- ☐ '64 Shaggy Dog

lang, k.d.
- ☐ '93 Calling All Angels *[w/ Jane Siberry]*
- ☐ '92 Constant Craving

LARKS, The
- ☐ '64 Jerk, The

LaROSA, Julius
- ☐ '55 Domani (Tomorrow)
- ☐ '56 Lipstick And Candy And Rubbersole Shoes
- ☐ '55 Suddenly There's A Valley
- ☐ '58 Torero

LARSEN-FEITEN BAND
- ☐ '80 Who'll Be The Fool Tonight

LARSON, Nicolette
- ☐ '80 Let Me Go, Love
- ☑ '78 Lotta Love

LA'S, The
- ☐ '91 There She Goes

LaSALLE, Denise
- ☐ '72 Now Run And Tell That
- ☐ '71 Trapped By A Thing Called Love

LASGO
- ☐ '02 Something

LASLEY, David
- ☐ '82 If I Had My Wish Tonight

LAST, James, Band
- ☐ '80 Seduction (Love Theme)

- ☐ '72 Music From Across The Way

LATIMORE
- ☐ '74 Let's Straighten It Out
- ☐ '77 Somethin' 'Bout 'Cha

LaTOUR
- ☐ '91 People Are Still Having Sex

LATTIMORE, Kenny
- ☐ '97 For You

LATTISAW, Stacy
- ☐ '80 Let Me Be Your Angel
- ☐ '81 Love On A Two Way Street
- ☐ '83 Miracles
- ☐ '89 Where Do We Go From Here *[w/ Johnny Gill]*

LAUPER, Cyndi
- ☐ '84 All Through The Night
- ☐ '86 Change Of Heart
- ☑ '83 Girls Just Want To Have Fun ★
- ☐ '85 Goonies 'R' Good Enough, The
- ☐ '89 I Drove All Night
- ☑ '84 Money Changes Everything
- ☐ '84 She Bop
- ☑ '84 Time After Time ★
- ☑ '86 True Colors ★
- ☐ '87 What's Going On

LAUREN, Rod
- ☐ '59 If I Had A Girl

LAURIE, Annie
- ☐ '57 It Hurts To Be In Love

LAURIE SISTERS, The
- ☐ '55 Dixie Danny

LAVIGNE, Avril
- ☑ '02 Complicated ★
- ☐ '04 Don't Tell Me
- ☑ '07 Girlfriend ★
- ☑ '02 I'm With You ★
- ☑ '06 Keep Holding On
- ☐ '04 My Happy Ending
- ☐ '05 Nobody's Home
- ☑ '02 Sk8er Boi
- ☑ '07 When You're Gone

LAW, The
- ☐ '91 Laying Down The Law

LAWRENCE, Billy
- ☐ '97 Come On

LAWRENCE, Eddie
- ☐ '56 Old Philosopher, The

LAWRENCE, Joey
- ☐ '93 Nothin' My Love Can't Fix

LAWRENCE, Steve
- ☐ '57 Banana Boat Song, The
- ☐ '63 Don't Be Afraid, Little Darlin'
- ☐ '60 Footsteps
- ☐ '62 Go Away Little Girl ★

LAWRENCE, Steve — cont'd
- ☐ '63 I Can't Stop Talking About You
  [w/ Eydie Gorme]
- ☐ '63 I Want To Stay Here *[w/ Eydie Gorme]*
- ☐ '57 Party Doll
- ☐ '63 Poor Little Rich Girl
- ☐ '61 Portrait Of My Love
- ☐ '59 Pretty Blue Eyes
- ☐ '63 Walking Proud

LAWRENCE, Tracy
- ☐ '93 Alibis
- ☐ '94 As Any Fool Can See
- ☐ '97 Better Man, Better Off
- ☐ '93 Can't Break It To My Heart
- ☐ '07 Find Out Who Your Friends Are
- ☐ '94 I See It Now
- ☐ '94 If The Good Die Young
- ☐ '95 If The World Had A Front Porch
- ☐ '96 Is That A Tear
- ☐ '00 Lessons Learned
- ☐ '93 My Second Home
- ☐ '96 Stars Over Texas
- ☐ '91 Sticks And Stones
- ☐ '95 Texas Tornado
- ☐ '96 Time Marches On

LAWRENCE, Vicki
- ☒ '73 Night The Lights Went Out In Georgia ★

LAYNE, Joy
- ☐ '57 Your Wild Heart

LEAPY LEE
- ☐ '68 Little Arrows

LEAVES, The
- ☐ '66 Hey Joe

LeBLANC & CARR
- ☐ '77 Falling

LE CLICK
- ☐ '97 Call Me

LED ZEPPELIN
- ☒ '79 All My Love
- ☐ '69 Babe I'm Gonna Leave You
- ☐ '71 Black Dog
- ☐ '69 Communication Breakdown
- ☐ '73 Crunge, The
- ☐ '73 Dancing Days
- ☐ '69 Dazed And Confused
- ☐ '73 D'yer Mak'er
- ☐ '79 Fool In The Rain ★
- ☐ '70 Gallows Pole
- ☐ '71 Going To California
- ☐ '69 Good Times Bad Times
- ☐ '69 Heartbreaker
- ☐ '79 Hot Dog
- ☐ '75 Houses Of The Holy
- ☐ '69 How Many More Times
- ☒ '69 I Can't Quit You Baby
- ☐ '70 Immigrant Song ★
- ☐ '79 In The Evening
- ☒ '75 Kashmir

- ☐ '69 Living Loving Maid (She's Just A Woman)
- ☐ '71 Misty Mountain Hop
- ☐ '76 Nobody's Fault But Mine
- ☐ '73 Ocean, The
- ☐ '73 Over The Hills And Far Away
- ☐ '73 Rain Song
- ☐ '69 Ramble On
- ☐ '71 Rock And Roll
- ☐ '70 Since I've Been Loving You
- ☐ '73 Song Remains The Same
- ☒ '71 Stairway To Heaven ★
- ☐ '69 Thank You
- ☐ '75 Trampled Under Foot
- ☐ '69 What Is And What Should Never Be
- ☐ '71 When The Levee Breaks
- ☒ '69 Whole Lotta Love ★

LEE, Brenda
- ☐ '62 All Alone Am I
- ☐ '61 Anybody But Me
- ☐ '63 As Usual
- ☐ '62 Break It To Me Gently
- ☐ '66 Coming On Strong
- ☐ '61 Dum Dum
- ☐ '60 Emotions
- ☐ '62 Everybody Loves Me But You
- ☐ '61 Fool #1
- ☐ '63 Grass Is Greener, The
- ☐ '62 Heart In Hand
- ☒ '60 I Want To Be Wanted ★
- ☐ '63 I Wonder
- ☐ '61 I'm Learning About Love
- ☒ '60 I'm Sorry ★
- ☐ '64 Is It True
- ☐ '62 It Started All Over Again
- ☐ '69 Johnny One Time
- ☐ '60 Just A Little
- ☐ '63 Losing You
- ☐ '63 My Whole World Is Falling Down
- ☐ '67 Ride, Ride, Ride
- ☐ '60 Rockin' Around The Christmas Tree
- ☐ '65 Rusty Bells
- ☐ '62 So Deep
- ☐ '59 Sweet Nothin's
- ☐ '60 That's All You Gotta Do
- ☐ '64 Think
- ☐ '65 Too Many Rivers
- ☐ '61 You Can Depend On Me
- ☐ '63 Your Used To Be

LEE, Curtis
- ☒ '61 Pretty Little Angel Eyes

LEE, Dickey
- ☐ '62 I Saw Linda Yesterday
- ☐ '65 Laurie (Strange Things Happen)
- ☐ '62 Patches

LEE, Jackie
- ☐ '65 Duck, The

LEE, Johnny
- ☐ '82 Cherokee Fiddle
- ☒ '80 Lookin' For Love

LEE, Laura
- ☐ '72 Rip Off
- ☐ '71 Women's Love Rights

LEE, Murphy
- ☐ '03 Shake Ya Tailfeather *[w/ Nelly & P. Diddy]* ★
- ☐ '03 Wat Da Hook Gon Be

LEE, Peggy
- ☐ '58 Fever ★
- ☐ '69 Is That All There Is
- ☐ '56 Mr. Wonderful

LEFEVRE, Raymond, & His Orchestra
- ☐ '68 Ame Caline (Soul Coaxing)
- ☐ '58 Day The Rains Came, The

LEFT BANKE, The
- ☐ '67 Pretty Ballerina
- ☐ '66 Walk Away Renee

LEGEND, John
- ☐ '05 Ordinary People

LEKAKIS, Paul
- ☐ '87 Boom Boom (Let's Go Back To My Room)

LEMONHEADS, The
- ☐ '93 Into Your Arms

LEMON PIPERS, The
- ☐ '67 Green Tambourine ★

LEN
- ☐ '99 Steal My Sunshine

LENNON, John
- ☐ '80 Beautiful Boy (Darling Boy)
- ☐ '69 Cold Turkey
- ☐ '69 Give Peace A Chance
- ☐ '70 God
- ☐ '71 Happy Xmas (War Is Over)
- ☐ '71 Imagine ★
- ☐ '70 Instant Karma (We All Shine On) ★
- ☐ '80 (Just Like) Starting Over ★
- ☐ '70 Love
- ☐ '73 Mind Games
- ☐ '70 Mother
- ☐ '84 Nobody Told Me
- ☐ '74 #9 Dream
- ☐ '71 Power To The People
- ☐ '75 Stand By Me
- ☐ '81 Watching The Wheels
- ☐ '74 Whatever Gets You Thru The Night ★
- ☐ '81 Woman ★
- ☐ '72 Woman Is The Nigger Of The World
- ☐ '70 Working Class Hero

LENNON, Julian
- ☐ '89 Now You're In Heaven
- ☐ '85 Say You're Wrong
- ☐ '86 Stick Around
- ☐ '85 Too Late For Goodbyes
- ☐ '84 Valotte

LENNON SISTERS, The
- ☐ '56 Tonight You Belong To Me

LENNOX, Annie
- ☐ '03 Into The West
- ☐ '93 Little Bird
- ☐ '95 No More "I Love You's"
- ☐ '88 Put A Little Love In Your Heart *[w/ Al Green]*
- ☐ '92 Walking On Broken Glass ★
- ☐ '92 Why

LEONETTI, Tommy
- ☐ '56 Free
- ☐ '69 Kum Ba Yah

LE ROUX
- ☐ '82 Nobody Said It Was Easy (Lookin' For The Lights)

LESTER, Ketty
- ☐ '62 Love Letters

LeTOYA
- ☐ '06 Torn

LETTERMEN, The
- ☐ '62 Come Back Silly Girl
- ☐ '67 Goin' Out Of My Head/Can't Take My Eyes Off You
- ☐ '62 How Is Julie?
- ☐ '69 Hurt So Bad
- ☐ '71 Love
- ☐ '65 Theme From "A Summer Place"
- ☐ '69 Traces/Memories Medley
- ☐ '61 Way You Look Tonight, The
- ☐ '61 When I Fall In Love

LEVEL 42
- ☐ '87 Lessons In Love
- ☐ '86 Something About You

LEVERT
- ☐ '88 Addicted To You
- ☐ '91 Baby I'm Ready
- ☐ '87 Casanova
- ☐ '89 Just Coolin'
- ☐ '87 My Forever Love
- ☐ '86 (Pop, Pop, Pop, Pop) Goes My Mind
- ☐ '88 Pull Over

LEVERT, Gerald
- ☐ '92 Baby Hold On To Me
- ☐ '94 I'd Give Anything
- ☐ '91 Private Line
- ☐ '92 School Me
- ☐ '99 Taking Everything
- ☐ '98 Thinkin' Bout It

LEWIS, Aaron
- ☐ '00 Outside *[w/ Fred Durst]*

LEWIS, Barbara
- ☐ '65 Baby, I'm Yours
- ☐ '63 Hello Stranger
- ☐ '66 Make Me Belong To You
- ☐ '65 Make Me Your Baby
- ☐ '64 Puppy Love

LEWIS, Blake
- [ ] '07 You Give Love A Bad Name

LEWIS, Bobby
- [ ] '61 One Track Mind
- [ ] '61 Tossin' And Turnin' ★

LEWIS, Donna
- [x] '97 At The Beginning [w/ Richard Marx]
- [x] '96 I Love You Always Forever ★

LEWIS, Gary, & The Playboys
- [ ] '65 Count Me In
- [ ] '65 Everybody Loves A Clown
- [ ] '67 Girls In Love
- [ ] '66 Green Grass
- [ ] '66 My Heart's Symphony
- [ ] '65 Save Your Heart For Me
- [ ] '68 Sealed With A Kiss
- [x] '65 She's Just My Style ★
- [ ] '66 Sure Gonna Miss Her
- [ ] '65 This Diamond Ring ★
- [ ] '66 Where Will The Words Come From
- [ ] '66 (You Don't Have To) Paint Me A Picture

LEWIS, Glenn
- [ ] '01 Don't You Forget It

LEWIS, Huey, & The News
- [ ] '85 Back In Time
- [ ] '91 Couple Days Off
- [ ] '00 Cruisin' [w/ Gwyneth Paltrow]
- [ ] '82 Do You Believe In Love
- [ ] '87 Doing It All For My Baby
- [ ] '83 Heart And Soul
- [ ] '84 Heart Of Rock & Roll, The
- [ ] '86 Hip To Be Square
- [ ] '82 Hope You Love Me Like You Say You Do
- [ ] '87 I Know What I Like
- [ ] '84 I Want A New Drug
- [ ] '84 If This Is It
- [ ] '91 It Hit Me Like A Hammer
- [ ] '93 It's Alright
- [ ] '87 Jacob's Ladder ★
- [ ] '88 Perfect World
- [ ] '85 Power Of Love, The ★
- [ ] '88 Small World
- [ ] '86 Stuck With You
- [ ] '84 Walking On A Thin Line
- [ ] '82 Workin' For A Livin'

LEWIS, Jerry
- [ ] '56 Rock-A-Bye Your Baby With A Dixie Melody

LEWIS, Jerry Lee
- [ ] '58 Breathless
- [ ] '72 Chantilly Lace
- [ ] '73 Drinking Wine Spo-Dee O'Dee
- [x] '57 Great Balls Of Fire ★
- [ ] '58 High School Confidential
- [ ] '71 Me And Bobby McGee
- [ ] '61 What'd I Say
- [ ] '68 What's Made Milwaukee Famous (Has Made A Loser Out Of Me)

- [x] '57 Whole Lot Of Shakin' Going On ★
- [ ] '58 You Win Again

LEWIS, Ramsey
- [ ] '65 Hang On Sloopy
- [ ] '66 Hard Day's Night, A
- [ ] '65 "In" Crowd, The
- [ ] '66 Wade In The Water

LEWIS, Smiley
- [ ] '55 I Hear You Knocking

LFO
- [ ] '99 Girl On TV
- [ ] '99 Summer Girls ★

LIA, Orsa
- [ ] '79 I Never Said I Love You

LIFEHOUSE
- [ ] '07 First Time
- [x] '00 Hanging By A Moment ★
- [x] '05 You And Me ★

LIGHTER SHADE OF BROWN, A
- [ ] '91 On A Sunday Afternoon

LIGHTFOOT, Gordon
- [ ] '82 Baby Step Back
- [ ] '67 Canadian Railroad Trilogy
- [ ] '74 Carefree Highway
- [ ] '78 Circle Is Small (I Can See It In Your Eyes)
- [ ] '78 Daylight Katy
- [x] '70 If You Could Read My Mind
- [ ] '75 Rainy Day People
- [x] '74 Sundown ★
- [ ] '76 Wreck Of The Edmund Fitzgerald ★

LIGHTHOUSE
- [ ] '71 One Fine Morning
- [ ] '72 Sunny Days

LIGHTNING SEEDS, The
- [ ] '92 Life Of Riley, The
- [ ] '90 Pure

LIL' BOOSIE
- [ ] '07 Wipe Me Down

LIL' FLIP
- [ ] '04 Game Over (Flip)
- [ ] '04 Sunshine ★

LIL JON (& THE EAST SIDE BOYZ)
- [x] '03 Get Low ★
- [x] '05 Lovers And Friends ★
- [x] '06 Snap Yo Fingers ★
- [x] '04 What U Gon' Do

LIL' KIM
- [ ] '03 Jump Off, The
- [ ] '01 Lady Marmalade [w/ Christina Aguilera, Mya & P!nk] ★
- [x] '05 Lighters Up
- [x] '03 Magic Stick ★
- [ ] '96 No Time
- [ ] '97 Not Tonight

LIL MAMA
- ☑ '07 Lip Gloss

LIL' MO
- ☐ '03 4 Ever
- ☐ '01 Superwoman

LIL ROB
- ☐ '05 Summer Nights

LIL' ROMEO
- ☑ '01 My Baby ★

LIL SCRAPPY
- ☐ '06 Money In The Bank
- ☐ '04 No Problem

LIL WAYNE
- ☑ '05 Fireman
- ☐ '04 Go D.J.
- ☐ '06 Stuntin' Like My Daddy [w/ Birdman]

LIL' ZANE
- ☑ '00 Callin' Me [w/ 112]

LIMAHL
- ☐ '85 Never Ending Story

LIMP BIZKIT
- ☐ '04 Behind Blue Eyes
- ☐ '01 My Way
- ☐ '99 Nookie
- ☐ '99 Re-Arranged
- ☑ '00 Rollin'

LIND, Bob
- ☐ '66 Elusive Butterfly

LINDEN, Kathy
- ☐ '58 Billy
- ☐ '59 Goodbye Jimmy, Goodbye

LINDISFARNE
- ☐ '78 Run For Home

LINDSAY, Mark
- ☐ '69 Arizona
- ☐ '70 Silver Bird

LINEAR
- ☐ '90 Sending All My Love
- ☐ '92 T.L.C.

LINES, Aaron
- ☐ '02 You Can't Hide Beautiful

LINK
- ☐ '98 Whatcha Gone Do?

LINKIN PARK
- ☑ '07 Bleed It Out
- ☐ '04 Breaking The Habit
- ☐ '01 Crawling
- ☐ '03 Faint
- ☑ '01 In The End ★
- ☐ '04 Lying From You
- ☑ '03 Numb
- ☑ '04 Numb/Encore [w/ Jay-Z]
- ☐ '01 One Step Closer
- ☐ '03 Somewhere I Belong
- ☐ '07 What I've Done

LIPPS, INC.
- ☑ '80 Funkytown ★

LISA LISA & CULT JAM
- ☐ '86 All Cried Out
- ☐ '87 Head To Toe ★
- ☐ '85 I Wonder If I Take You Home
- ☐ '91 Let The Beat Hit 'Em
- ☐ '89 Little Jackie Wants To Be A Star
- ☐ '87 Lost In Emotion ★

LIT
- ☐ '99 Miserable
- ☐ '99 My Own Worst Enemy

LITTLE ANTHONY & THE IMPERIALS
- ☐ '64 Goin' Out Of My Head
- ☐ '65 Hurt So Bad
- ☐ '65 I Miss You So
- ☐ '64 I'm On The Outside (Looking In)
- ☐ '59 Shimmy, Shimmy, Ko-Ko-Bop
- ☐ '65 Take Me Back
- ☑ '58 Tears On My Pillow ★

LITTLE BEAVER
- ☐ '74 Party Down

LITTLE BIG TOWN
- ☑ '06 Boondocks
- ☑ '06 Bring It On Home

LITTLE CAESAR & THE ROMANS
- ☐ '61 Those Oldies But Goodies (Remind Me Of You)

LITTLE DIPPERS, The
- ☐ '60 Forever

LITTLE EVA
- ☐ '62 Keep Your Hands Off My Baby
- ☐ '63 Let's Turkey Trot
- ☑ '62 Loco-Motion, The ★
- ☐ '63 Swinging On A Star [w/ Big Dee Irwin]

LITTLE FEAT
- ☐ '78 Dixie Chicken
- ☐ '88 Hate To Lose Your Lovin'
- ☐ '88 Let It Roll
- ☐ '90 Texas Twister

LITTLE JOE & THE THRILLERS
- ☐ '57 Peanuts

LITTLE JOEY & THE FLIPS
- ☐ '62 Bongo Stomp

LITTLE MERMAID SOUNDTRACK
- ☑ '89 Kiss The Girl
- ☐ '89 Under The Sea

LITTLE MILTON
- ☐ '65 We're Gonna Make It

LITTLE RICHARD
- '58 Baby Face
- '57 Girl Can't Help It, The
- '58 Good Golly, Miss Molly ★
- '56 Heeby Jeebies
- '57 Jenny, Jenny
- '57 Keep A Knockin'
- '56 Long Tall Sally ★
- '57 Lucille ★
- '57 Miss Ann
- '58 Ooh! My Soul
- '56 Ready Teddy
- '56 Rip It Up
- '57 Send Me Some Lovin'
- '56 Slippin' And Slidin'
- '56 Tutti-Frutti ★

LITTLE RIVER BAND
- '79 Cool Change
- '77 Happy Anniversary
- '77 Help Is On Its Way
- '76 It's A Long Way There
- '79 Lady
- '79 Lonesome Loser
- '82 Man On Your Mind
- '81 Night Owls, The
- '82 Other Guy, The
- '78 Reminiscing
- '78 So Many Paths
- '81 Take It Easy On Me
- '83 We Two
- '83 You're Driving Me Out Of My Mind

LITTLE SISTER
- '70 Somebody's Watching You
- '70 You're The One

LITTLE TEXAS
- '93 God Blessed Texas
- '94 Kick A Little
- '94 My Love
- '93 What Might Have Been

LITTLE WALTER & HIS JUKES
- '55 My Babe

LIVE
- '95 All Over You
- '99 Dolphin's Cry, The
- '03 Heaven
- '94 I Alone
- '97 Lakini's Juice
- '95 Lightning Crashes
- '94 Selling The Drama
- '97 Turn My Head

LIVING COLOUR
- '89 Cult Of Personality
- '89 Glamour Boys
- '90 Type

LIVING IN A BOX
- '87 Living In A Box

LL COOL J
- '90 Around The Way Girl
- '06 Control Myself ★
- '96 Doin It
- '98 Father
- '88 Going Back To Cali
- '04 Headsprung
- '95 Hey Lover
- '04 Hush
- '87 I Need Love ——
- '89 I'm That Type Of Guy
- '96 Loungin ★
- '02 Luv U Better
- '91 Mama Said Knock You Out
- '02 Paradise
- '86 Rock The Bells

LLOYD
- '07 Get It Shawty
- '04 Southside
- '07 You

LOBO
- '72 Don't Expect Me To Be Your Friend
- '75 Don't Tell Me Goodnight
- '73 How Can I Tell Her
- '72 I'd Love You To Want Me ★
- '73 It Sure Took A Long, Long Time
- '71 Me And You And A Dog Named Boo
- '74 Standing At The End Of The Line
- '73 There Ain't No Way
- '79 Where Were You When I Was Falling In Love

LOCKE, Kimberley
- '04 8th World Wonder
- '05 Up On The Housetop

LOCKLIN, Hank
- '60 Please Help Me, I'm Falling

LODGE, John — see HAYWARD, Justin

LOEB, Lisa
- '95 Do You Sleep?
- '97 I Do
- '94 Stay (I Missed You) ★

LOGGINS, Dave
- '74 Please Come To Boston

LOGGINS, Kenny
- '77 Celebrate Me Home
- '86 Danger Zone ★
- '82 Don't Fight It [w/ Steve Perry]
- '84 Footloose ★
- '97 For The First Time
- '85 Forever
- '82 Heart To Heart
- '80 I'm Alright
- '84 I'm Free (Heaven Helps The Man)
- '80 Keep The Fire
- '87 Meet Me Half Way
- '88 Nobody's Fool
- '79 This Is It
- '85 Vox Humana
- '83 Welcome To Heartlight
- '78 Whenever I Call You "Friend"

LOGGINS & MESSINA
- ☐ '72 Danny's Song
- ☐ '72 House At Pooh Corner
- ☐ '73 My Music
- ☒ '73 Thinking Of You
- ☒ '72 Your Mama Don't Dance

LO-KEY?
- ☐ '92 I Got A Thang 4 Ya!

LOLITA
- ☐ '60 Sailor (Your Home Is The Sea)

LONDON, Julie
- ☐ '55 Cry Me A River

LONDON, Laurie
- ☐ '58 He's Got The Whole World (In His Hands) ★

LONDONBEAT
- ☐ '91 Better Love, A
- ☒ '91 I've Been Thinking About You ★

LONESTAR
- ☒ '99 Amazed ★
- ☐ '97 Come Cryin' To Me
- ☐ '98 Everything's Changed
- ☒ '01 I'm Already There
- ☐ '04 Let's Be Us Again
- ☐ '04 Mr. Mom
- ☐ '03 My Front Porch Looking In
- ☐ '96 No News
- ☒ '02 Not A Day Goes By
- ☒ '99 Smile
- ☒ '00 Tell Her
- ☒ '00 What About Now

LONG, Shorty
- ☐ '68 Here Comes The Judge

LOOKING GLASS
- ☐ '72 Brandy (You're A Fine Girl) ★
- ☐ '73 Jimmy Loves Mary-Anne

LOOSE ENDS
- ☐ '85 Hangin' On A String (Contemplating)
- ☐ '86 Slow Down
- ☐ '88 Watching You

LOPEZ, Denise
- ☐ '88 Sayin' Sorry (Don't Make It Right) ⎯

LOPEZ, Jennifer
- ☐ '01 Ain't It Funny
- ☒ '02 All I Have ★
- ☐ '05 Get Right
- ☐ '03 I'm Glad
- ☐ '02 I'm Gonna Be Alright
- ☐ '01 I'm Real ★
- ☒ '99 If You Had My Love ★
- ☒ '02 Jenny From The Block ★
- ☒ '00 Love Don't Cost A Thing
- ☐ '01 Play
- ☒ '99 Waiting For Tonight

LOPEZ, Trini
- ☐ '66 I'm Comin' Home, Cindy

- ☐ '63 If I Had A Hammer
- ☐ '63 Kansas City
- ☐ '65 Lemon Tree

LORAIN, A'Me
- ☐ '90 Whole Wide World

LORBER, Jeff
- ☐ '86 Facts Of Love *[w/ Karyn White]*

LORD TARIQ & PETER GUNZ
- ☐ '97 Deja Vu (Uptown Baby)

LORENZ, Trey
- ☐ '92 Someone To Hold

LORING, Gloria
- ☐ '86 Friends And Lovers *[w/ Carl Anderson]*

LOS BRAVOS
- ☐ '66 Black Is Black
- ☐ '68 Bring A Little Lovin'

LOS DEL RIO
- ☒ '95 Macarena (bayside boys mix) ★

LOS INDIOS TABAJARAS
- ☐ '63 Maria Elena

LOS LOBOS
- ☐ '87 Come On, Let's Go
- ☒ '87 La Bamba ★

LOS LONELY BOYS
- ☒ '04 Heaven

LOST BOYZ
- ☐ '96 Renee

LOST GENERATION, The
- ☐ '70 Sly, Slick, And The Wicked, The

LOSTPROPHETS
- ☐ '03 Last Train Home

LOUDERMILK, John D.
- ☐ '61 Language Of Love
- ☐ '57 Sittin' In The Balcony

LOUIE LOUIE
- ☐ '90 Sittin' In The Lap Of Luxury

LOVE
- ☐ '68 Alone Again Or
- ☐ '66 My Little Red Book
- ☐ '66 7 And 7 Is

LOVE, Darlene
- ☐ '63 (Today I Met) The Boy I'm Gonna Marry
- ☐ '63 Wait Til' My Bobby Gets Home

LOVE, Monie
- ☐ '91 It's A Shame (My Sister)

LOVE & KISSES
- ☒ '78 Thank God It's Friday

LOVE & ROCKETS
- ☒ '89 So Alive

LOVELESS, Patty
- ☐ '93 Blame It On Your Heart
- ☐ '90 Chains
- ☐ '94 I Try To Think About Elvis
- ☐ '96 Lonely Too Long
- ☐ '89 Timber, I'm Falling In Love
- ☐ '95 You Can Feel Bad

LOVERBOY
- ☐ '86 Heaven In Your Eyes
- ☐ '83 Hot Girls In Love
- ☐ '85 Lovin' Every Minute Of It
- ☐ '82 Lucky Ones
- ☐ '87 Notorious
- ☐ '83 Queen Of The Broken Hearts
- ☐ '86 This Could Be The Night
- ☐ '81 Turn Me Loose
- ☐ '82 When It's Over
- ☐ '81 Working For The Weekend ★

LOVETT, Lyle
- ☐ '86 Cowboy Man
- ☐ '86 Farther Down The Line
- ☐ '94 Funny How Time Slips Away
  [w/ Al Green]

LOVE UNLIMITED
- ☐ '74 I Belong To You
- ☐ '72 Walkin' In The Rain With The One I
  Love

LOVE UNLIMITED ORCHESTRA
- ☐ '73 Love's Theme ★
- ☐ '75 Satin Soul

LOVIN' SPOONFUL, The
- ☐ '67 Darling Be Home Soon
- ☐ '66 Daydream ★
- ☐ '66 Did You Ever Have To Make Up Your
  Mind?
- ☐ '65 Do You Believe In Magic ★
- ☐ '66 Nashville Cats
- ☐ '66 Rain On The Roof
- ☐ '67 She Is Still A Mystery
- ☐ '67 Six O'Clock
- ☐ '66 Summer In The City ★
- ☐ '65 You Didn't Have To Be So Nice

LOWE, Jim
- ☐ '57 Four Walls
- ☐ '56 Green Door, The ★
- ☐ '57 Talkin' To The Blues

LOWE, Nick
- ☐ '79 Cruel To Be Kind

LOX, The
- ☐ '98 If You Think I'm Jiggy
- ☐ '98 Money, Power & Respect

LSG
- ☐ '97 My Body ★

L.T.D.
- ☐ '77 (Every Time I Turn Around) Back In
  Love Again
- ☐ '78 Holding On (When Love Is Gone)
- ☐ '76 Love Ballad

- ☐ '80 Shine On

LUCAS
- ☐ '94 Lucas With The Lid Off

LUCY PEARL
- ☐ '00 Dance Tonight

LUDACRIS
- ☐ '03 Act A Fool
- ☐ '01 Area Codes
- ☐ '06 Georgia *[w/ Field Mob]*
- ☐ '04 Get Back
- ☐ '06 Money Maker ★
- ☐ '02 Move B***h
- ☐ '05 Number One Spot
- ☐ '05 Pimpin' All Over The World
- ☐ '01 Rollout (My Business)
- ☐ '07 Runaway Love ★
- ☐ '02 Saturday (Oooh! Ooooh!)
- ☐ '01 Southern Hospitality
- ☐ '04 Splash Waterfalls
- ☐ '03 Stand Up ★
- ☐ '01 Welcome To Atlanta *[w/ Jermaine Dupri]*
- ☐ '00 What's Your Fantasy

LUHRMANN, Baz
- ☐ '99 Everybody's Free (To Wear Sunscreen)
  The Speech Song

LUKE, Robin
- ☐ '58 Susie Darlin'

LULU
- ☐ '67 Best Of Both Worlds
- ☐ '68 Morning Dew
- ☐ '81 I Could Never Miss You (More Than I
  Do)
- ☐ '69 Oh Me Oh My (I'm A Fool For You
  Baby)
- ☐ '67 To Sir With Love ★

LUMAN, Bob
- ☐ '60 Let's Think About Living

LUMIDEE
- ☐ '03 Never Leave You - Uh Oooh, Uh
  Oooh! ★

LUNDBERG, Victor
- ☐ '67 Open Letter To My Teenage Son, An

LUNIZ
- ☐ '95 I Got 5 On It

LUSCIOUS JACKSON
- ☐ '96 Naked Eye

LYMAN, Arthur, Group
- ☐ '61 Yellow Bird ★

LYMON, Frankie, & The Teenagers
- ☐ '57 Goody Goody
- ☐ '56 I Want You To Be My Girl
- ☐ '57 I'm Not A Juvenile Delinquent
- ☐ '56 Why Do Fools Fall In Love ★

LYNN, Barbara
- ☐ '62 You'll Lose A Good Thing

LYNN, Cheryl
☐ '83 Encore
☒ '78 Got To Be Real

LYNN, Loretta
☐ '71 After The Fire Is Gone *[w/ Conway Twitty]*
☐ '70 Coal Miner's Daughter
☐ '71 One's On The Way

LYNNE, Gloria
☐ '64 I Wish You Love

LYNYRD SKYNYRD
☐ '74 Call Me The Breeze
☐ '74 Don't Ask Me No Questions
☐ '76 Double Trouble
☐ '74 Free Bird ★
☐ '76 Gimme Back My Bullets
☐ '73 Gimme Three Steps
☐ '73 I Ain't The One
☐ '75 Saturday Night Special
☐ '91 Smokestack Lightning
☐ '74 Sweet Home Alabama ★
☐ '77 That Smell
☐ '77 What's Your Name
☐ '74 Workin' For MCA
☐ '77 You Got That Right

LYTTLE, Kevin
☐ '04 Turn Me On ★

M

M
☐ '79 Pop Muzik ★

MABLEY, Moms
☐ '69 Abraham, Martin And John

MacGREGOR, Byron
☐ '74 Americans

MacGREGOR, Mary
☐ '79 Good Friend
☐ '76 Torn Between Two Lovers ★

MACK, Craig
☐ '94 Flava In Ya Ear
☐ '94 Get Down

MACK, Lonnie
☐ '63 Memphis
☐ '63 Wham!

MACK 10
☐ '97 Backyard Boogie
☐ '96 Nothin' But The Cavi Hit *[w/ Dogg Pound]*

MacKENZIE, Gisele
☐ '55 Hard To Get

MacRAE, Gordon
☐ '55 Oklahoma!
☐ '58 Secret, The

MAD COBRA
☐ '92 Flex

MADDOX, Johnny
☐ '55 Crazy Otto, The

MADIGAN, Betty
☐ '58 Dance Everyone Dance

MADNESS
☐ '83 It Must Be Love
☐ '83 Our House

MADONNA
☐ '03 American Life
☐ '00 American Pie
☐ '85 Angel
☐ '93 Bad Girl
☐ '99 Beautiful Stranger
☐ '84 Borderline
☐ '87 Causing A Commotion ★
☐ '89 Cherish
☐ '85 Crazy For You ★
☐ '92 Deeper And Deeper
☐ '02 Die Another Day
☐ '97 Don't Cry For Me Argentina
☐ '00 Don't Tell Me
☐ '86 Dress You Up
☐ '92 Erotica
☐ '89 Express Yourself ★
☐ '98 Frozen
☐ '90 Hanky Panky
☐ '83 Holiday
☐ '05 Hung Up ★
☐ '94 I'll Remember
☐ '85 Into The Groove
☐ '90 Justify My Love ★
☐ '90 Keep It Together
☐ '87 La Isla Bonita
☐ '89 Like A Prayer ★
☐ '84 Like A Virgin ★
☐ '86 Live To Tell
☐ '84 Lucky Star
☐ '85 Material Girl ★
☐ '03 Me Against The Music
☐ '00 Music ★
☐ '89 Oh Father
☐ '86 Open Your Heart
☐ '86 Papa Don't Preach ★
☐ '98 Power Of Good-Bye, The
☐ '93 Rain
☐ '98 Ray Of Light ★
☐ '91 Rescue Me
☐ '94 Secret
☐ '88 Spotlight
☐ '94 Take A Bow ★
☐ '92 This Used To Be My Playground ★
☐ '86 True Blue
☐ '90 Vogue ★
☐ '01 What It Feels Like For A Girl
☐ '87 Who's That Girl
☐ '96 You Must Love Me
☐ '95 You'll See

MAD SEASON
☐ '95 River Of Deceit

MAGGARD, Cledus
☐ '75 White Knight, The

MAGIC LANTERNS
☐ '68 Shame, Shame

MAHARIS, George
☐ '62 Teach Me Tonight

MAIN INGREDIENT, The
☐ '72 Everybody Plays The Fool
☐ '74 Happiness Is Just Around The Bend
☐ '74 Just Don't Want To Be Lonely

MAJORS, The
☐ '62 Wonderful Dream, A

MAKEBA, Miriam
☐ '67 Pata Pata

MALO
☐ '72 Suavecito

MALTBY, Richard, & His Orchestra
☐ '56 Themes From "The Man With The Golden Arm"

MAMA CASS
☐ '68 Dream A Little Dream Of Me
☐ '69 It's Getting Better
☐ '69 Make Your Own Kind Of Music

MAMAS & THE PAPAS, The
☐ '66 California Dreamin' ★
☐ '67 Creeque Alley
☐ '67 Dedicated To The One I Love
☐ '67 Glad To Be Unhappy
☐ '66 Go Where You Wanna Go
☐ '66 I Saw Her Again
☐ '66 Look Through My Window
☐ '66 Monday, Monday ★
☐ '66 No Salt On Her Tail
☐ '67 Twelve Thirty (Young Girls Are Coming To The Canyon)
☐ '66 Words Of Love

MANCHESTER, Melissa
☐ '78 Don't Cry Out Loud
☐ '80 Fire In The Morning
☐ '75 Just Too Many People
☐ '76 Just You And I
☐ '75 Midnight Blue
☐ '79 Pretty Girls
☐ '82 You Should Hear How She Talks About You ★

MANCINI, Henry, & His Orchestra
☐ '62 Baby Elephant Walk
☐ '63 Charade
☐ '63 Days Of Wine And Roses
☐ '64 Dear Heart
☐ '69 Love Theme From Romeo & Juliet ★
☐ '61 Moon River ★
☐ '60 Mr. Lucky
☐ '64 Pink Panther Theme, The
☐ '71 Theme From Love Story

MANDRELL, Barbara
☐ '81 I Was Country When Country Wasn't Cool

☐ '79 (If Loving You Is Wrong) I Don't Want To Be Right
☐ '78 Sleeping Single In A Double Bed

MANFRED MANN
☐ '76 Blinded By The Light ★
☐ '64 Do Wah Diddy Diddy ★
☐ '81 For You
☐ '68 Mighty Quinn (Quinn The Eskimo)
☐ '66 Pretty Flamingo
☐ '84 Runner
☐ '64 Sha La La
☐ '77 Spirit In The Night

MANGIONE, Chuck
☐ '78 Feels So Good
☐ '80 Give It All You Got
☐ '71 Hill Where The Lord Hides

MANHATTANS, The
☐ '75 Don't Take Your Love
☐ '76 Kiss And Say Goodbye ★
☐ '72 One Life To Live
☐ '80 Shining Star ★
☐ '73 There's No Me Without You

MANHATTAN TRANSFER, The
☐ '79 Birdland
☐ '81 Boy From New York City
☐ '75 Operator
☐ '83 Spice Of Life
☐ '80 Trickle Trickle
☐ '80 Twilight Zone/Twilight Tone

MANILOW, Barry
☐ '75 Bandstand Boogie
☐ '78 Can't Smile Without You
☐ '78 Copacabana (At The Copa)
☐ '75 Could It Be Magic
☐ '77 Daybreak
☐ '78 Even Now
☐ '80 I Don't Want To Walk Without You
☐ '80 I Made It Through The Rain
☐ '75 I Write The Songs ★
☐ '75 It's A Miracle
☐ '76 Jump Shout Boogie
☐ '89 Keep Each Other Warm
☐ '82 Let's Hang On
☐ '77 Looks Like We Made It
☐ '74 Mandy ★
☐ '82 Memory
☐ '82 Oh Julie
☐ '81 Old Songs, The
☐ '83 Read 'Em And Weep
☐ '78 Ready To Take A Chance Again
☐ '79 Ships
☐ '83 Some Kind Of Friend
☐ '81 Somewhere Down The Road
☐ '78 Somewhere In The Night
☐ '76 This One's For You
☐ '76 Tryin' To Get The Feeling Again
☐ '76 Weekend In New England
☐ '79 When I Wanted You

MANN, Barry
- ☐ '61 Who Put The Bomp (In The Bomp, Bomp, Bomp)

MANN, Carl
- ☐ '59 Mona Lisa

MANN, Gloria
- ☐ '55 Earth Angel Will You Be Mine
- ☐ '55 Teen Age Prayer

MANN, Herbie
- ☐ '75 Hijack
- ☐ '69 Memphis Underground
- ☐ '79 Superman

MANTOVANI & His Orchestra
- ☐ '57 Around The World
- ☐ '60 Jamaica Farewell
- ☐ '60 Main Theme from Exodus

MARATHONS, The
- ☐ '61 Peanut Butter

MARCELS, The
- ☐ '61 Blue Moon ★
- ☐ '61 Heartaches

MARCH, Little Peggy
- ☐ '63 Hello Heartache, Goodbye Love
- ☐ '63 I Will Follow Him ★
- ☐ '63 I Wish I Were A Princess

MARCHAN, Bobby
- ☐ '60 There's Something On Your Mind

MARCY PLAYGROUND
- ☐ '97 Sex and Candy

MARDONES, Benny
- ☐ '80 Into The Night

MARESCA, Ernie
- ☐ '62 Shout! Shout! (Knock Yourself Out)

MARÍ, Teairra
- ☐ '05 Make Her Feel Good

MARIE, Teena
- ☐ '80 I Need Your Lovin'
- ☐ '84 Lovergirl
- ☐ '88 Ooo La La La
- ☐ '81 Square Biz

MARIO
- ☐ '02 Just A Friend 2002 ★
- ☐ '05 Let Me Love You ★

MARKETTS, The
- ☐ '62 Balboa Blue
- ☐ '66 Batman Theme
- ☐ '63 Out Of Limits ★
- ☐ '62 Surfer's Stomp

MAR-KEYS
- ☐ '61 Last Night

MARKHAM, Pigmeat
- ☐ '68 Here Comes The Judge

MARK IV, The
- ☐ '59 I Got A Wife

MARKS, Guy
- ☐ '68 Loving You Has Made Me Bananas

MARKY MARK & The Funky Bunch
- ☐ '91 Good Vibrations ★
- ☐ '91 Wildside

MARLEY, Bob
- ☐ '78 Buffalo Soldier
- ☐ '80 Could You Be Loved
- ☐ '77 Exodus
- ☐ '75 Get Up, Stand Up ★
- ☐ '73 I Shot The Sheriff
- ☐ '78 Is This Love
- ☐ '77 Jamming
- ☐ '75 Lively Up Yourself
- ☐ '75 No Woman No Cry [live] ★
- ☐ '77 One Love/People Get Ready
- ☐ '80 Redemption Song ★
- ☐ '76 Roots, Rock, Reggae
- ☐ '73 Stir It Up
- ☐ '78 Sun Is Shining
- ☐ '77 Three Little Birds
- ☐ '77 Waiting In Vain

MARLEY, Ziggy, & The Melody Makers
- ☐ '88 Tomorrow People
- ☐ '88 Tumblin' Down

MARLOWE, Marion
- ☐ '55 Man In The Raincoat, The

MARMALADE, The
- ☐ '70 Reflections Of My Life

MAROON5
- ☐ '03 Harder To Breathe
- ☐ '07 Makes Me Wonder ★
- ☐ '04 She Will Be Loved ★
- ☐ '05 Sunday Morning
- ☐ '04 This Love ★
- ☐ '07 Wake Up Call ★

M/A/R/R/S
- ☐ '87 Pump Up The Volume ★

MARSHALL, Amanda
- ☐ '96 Birmingham

MARSHALL TUCKER BAND, The
- ☐ '73 Can't You See
- ☐ '75 Fire On The Mountain
- ☐ '77 Heard It In A Love Song

MARTERIE, Ralph, & His Orchestra
- ☐ '57 Shish-Kebab
- ☐ '57 Tricky

MARTHA & THE VANDELLAS
- ☐ '63 Come And Get These Memories
- ☐ '64 Dancing In The Street ★
- ☐ '63 Heat Wave
- ☐ '67 Honey Chile
- ☐ '66 I'm Ready For Love
- ☐ '67 Jimmy Mack

MARTHA & THE VANDELLAS — cont'd
- ☐ '67 Love Bug Leave My Heart Alone
- ☐ '66 My Baby Loves Me
- ☐ '65 Nowhere To Run
- ☐ '63 Quicksand
- ☐ '64 Wild One
- ☐ '65 You've Been In Love Too Long

MARTIKA
- ☐ '89 I Feel The Earth Move
- ☐ '91 Love...Thy Will Be Done
- ☐ '88 More Than You Know
- ☐ '89 Toy Soldiers ★

MARTIN, Billie Ray
- ☒ '96 Your Loving Arms

MARTIN, Bobbi
- ☐ '64 Don't Forget I Still Love You
- ☐ '70 For The Love Of Him

MARTIN, Dean
- ☐ '58 Angel Baby
- ☐ '66 Come Running Back
- ☐ '64 Door Is Still Open To My Heart, The
- ☒ '64 Everybody Loves Somebody ★
- ☐ '65 Houston
- ☐ '65 I Will
- ☐ '67 In The Chapel In The Moonlight
- ☐ '67 In The Misty Moonlight
- ☐ '56 Innamorata
- ☐ '67 Little Ole Wine Drinker, Me
- ☒ '55 Memories Are Made Of This ★
- ☐ '68 Not Enough Indians
- ☐ '65 (Remember Me) I'm The One Who Loves You
- ☐ '58 Return To Me
- ☐ '65 Send Me The Pillow You Dream On
- ☐ '66 Somewhere There's A Someone
- ☐ '56 Standing On The Corner
- ☐ '58 Volare (Nel Blu Dipinto Di Blu)
- ☐ '64 You're Nobody Till Somebody Loves You

MARTIN, Marilyn
- ☐ '86 Night Moves
- ☐ '85 Separate Lives *[w/ Phil Collins]* ★

MARTIN, Moon
- ☐ '79 Rolene

MARTIN, Ricky
- ☐ '98 Cup Of Life, The
- ☐ '99 Livin' La Vida Loca ★
- ☐ '01 Nobody Wants To Be Lonely
  [w/ Christina Aguilera]
- ☐ '99 Shake Your Bon-Bon
- ☐ '00 She Bangs
- ☒ '99 She's All I Ever Had ★

MARTIN, Steve
- ☐ '78 King Tut

MARTIN, Tony
- ☐ '56 Walk Hand In Hand

MARTIN, Trade
- ☐ '62 That Stranger Used To Be My Girl

MARTIN, Vince
- ☐ '56 Cindy, Oh Cindy

MARTINDALE, Wink
- ☐ '59 Deck Of Cards

MARTINEZ, Angie
- ☐ '02 If I Could Go!

MARTINEZ, Nancy
- ☐ '86 For Tonight

MARTINO, Al
- ☐ '64 Always Together
- ☐ '67 Daddy's Little Girl
- ☐ '63 I Love You Because
- ☐ '64 I Love You More And More Every Day
- ☐ '63 Living A Lie
- ☐ '68 Love Is Blue
- ☐ '67 Mary In The Morning
- ☐ '67 More Than The Eye Can See
- ☐ '63 Painted, Tainted Rose
- ☐ '65 Spanish Eyes
- ☐ '64 Tears And Roses
- ☐ '66 Think I'll Go Somewhere And Cry Myself To Sleep
- ☐ '74 To The Door Of The Sun
- ☐ '75 Volare
- ☐ '66 Wiederseh'n

MARVELETTES, The
- ☐ '63 As Long As I Know He's Mine
- ☐ '62 Beechwood 4-5789
- ☐ '66 Don't Mess With Bill
- ☐ '67 Hunter Gets Captured By The Game
- ☐ '65 I'll Keep Holding On
- ☐ '67 My Baby Must Be A Magician
- ☐ '62 Playboy
- ☐ '61 Please Mr. Postman ★
- ☐ '64 Too Many Fish In The Sea
- ☐ '62 Twistin' Postman
- ☐ '67 When You're Young And In Love

MARVELOWS, The
- ☐ '65 I Do

MARX, Richard
- ☐ '89 Angelia
- ☐ '97 At The Beginning *[w/ Donna Lewis]*
- ☐ '90 Children Of The Night
- ☐ '87 Don't Mean Nothing
- ☐ '88 Endless Summer Nights
- ☒ '92 Hazard ★
- ☒ '88 Hold On To The Nights ★
- ☐ '91 Keep Coming Back
- ☒ '94 Now and Forever ★
- ☒ '89 Right Here Waiting ★
- ☐ '89 Satisfied
- ☐ '87 Should've Known Better
- ☐ '92 Take This Heart
- ☐ '90 Too Late To Say Goodbye
- ☐ '97 Until I Find You Again
- ☒ '94 Way She Loves Me, The

MARY JANE GIRLS
- ☐ '85 In My House —

MARYMARY
- ☐ '00 Shackles (Praise You)

MASE
- 🎵 '04 Breathe, Stretch, Shake
- 🎵 '97 Feel So Good ★
- ☐ '98 Lookin' At Me
- ☐ '04 Welcome Back
- ☐ '98 What You Want

MASEKELA, Hugh
- ☐ '68 Grazing In The Grass ★

MASHMAKHAN
- ☐ '70 As The Years Go By

MASON, Barbara
- ☐ '74 From His Woman To You
- ☐ '73 Give Me Your Love
- ☐ '65 Sad, Sad Girl
- ☐ '65 Yes, I'm Ready

MASON, Dave
- ☐ '77 Let It Go, Let It Flow
- ☐ '70 Only You Know And I Know
- ☐ '77 So High (Rock Me Baby And Roll Me Away)
- ☐ '77 We Just Disagree
- ☐ '78 Will You Still Love Me Tomorrow

MASON, Vaughan
- ☐ '80 Bounce, Rock, Skate, Roll

MASTA ACE INCORPORATED
- ☐ '94 Born To Roll

MASTER P
- ☐ '98 Goodbye To My Homies
- ☐ '98 I Got The Hook Up!
- ☐ '97 I Miss My Homies
- ☐ '98 Make Em' Say Uhh!

MATCHBOX TWENTY
- ☐ '98 Back 2 Good
- 🎵 '00 Bent ★
- ☐ '03 Bright Lights
- ☐ '02 Disease
- ☐ '07 How Far We've Come ★
- 🎵 '00 If You're Gone ★
- 🎵 '97 Push ★
- ☐ '98 Real World ★
- 🎵 '97 3 AM ★
- 🎵 '03 Unwell ★

MATHEWS, Tobin
- ☐ '60 Ruby Duby Du

MATHIS, Johnny
- ☐ '58 All The Time
- ☐ '58 Call Me
- ☐ '58 Certain Smile, A
- 🎵 '57 Chances Are ★
- ☐ '58 Come To Me
- ☐ '63 Every Step Of The Way
- ☐ '82 Friends In Love *[w/ Dionne Warwick]*
- ☐ '62 Gina
- ☐ '73 I'm Coming Home
- ☐ '57 It's Not For Me To Say

- ☐ '60 Maria
- ☐ '59 Misty
- 🎵 '60 My Love For You
- 🎵 '57 No Love (But Your Love)
- ☐ '59 Small World
- ☐ '59 Someone
- ☐ '60 Starbright
- ☐ '58 Teacher, Teacher
- ☐ '78 Too Much, Too Little, Too Late
  - *[w/ Deniece Williams]* ★
- ☐ '57 Twelfth Of Never, The
- ☐ '63 What Will Mary Say
- ☐ '57 When Sunny Gets Blue
- ☐ '57 Wild Is The Wind
- 🎵 '57 Wonderful! Wonderful! ★

MATISYAHU
- ☐ '06 King Without A Crown

MATTEA, Kathy
- ☐ '88 Eighteen Wheels And A Dozen Roses
- ☐ '94 Walking Away A Winner

MATTHEWS, Dave, Band
- ☐ '05 American Baby ★
- ☐ '95 Ants Marching
- 🎵 '97 Crash Into Me ★
- ☐ '99 Crush
- ☐ '98 Don't Drink The Water
- ☐ '03 Gravedigger
- ☐ '02 Grey Street
- ☐ '01 I Did It
- ☐ '94 Jimi Thing
- 🎵 '96 Satellite
- ☐ '96 So Much To Say
- 🎵 '01 Space Between, The
- ☐ '98 Stay (Wasting Time)
- ☐ '96 Too Much
- ☐ '96 Two Step
- ☐ '95 What Would You Say
- 🎵 '02 Where Are You Going

MATTHEWS, Ian
- ☐ '78 Shake It
- ☐ '71 Woodstock

MATYS BROS., The
- ☐ '63 Who Stole The Keeshka?

MAURIAT, Paul, & His Orchestra
- ☐ '68 Love Is Blue ★

MAXWELL
- ☐ '96 Ascension (Don't Ever Wonder)
- ☐ '99 Fortunate
- ☐ '01 Lifetime

MAXWELL, Robert, Orchestra
- ☐ '59 Little Dipper *[MICKEY MOZARD QUINTET]*
- ☐ '64 Shangri-La

MAYALL, John
- ☐ '70 Don't Waste My Time
- ☐ '69 Room To Move

MAYE, Marilyn
- ☐ '67 Step To The Rear

MAYER, John
- ☐ '03 Bigger Than My Body
- ☒ '05 Daughters ★
- ☐ '02 No Such Thing
- ☒ '07 Waiting On The World To Change ★
- ☒ '02 Your Body Is A Wonderland

MAYER, Nathaniel
- ☐ '62 Village Of Love

MAYFIELD, Curtis
- ☐ '70 (Don't Worry) If There's A Hell Below We're All Going To Go
- ☐ '72 Freddie's Dead (Theme From "Superfly")
- ☐ '73 Future Shock
- ☐ '74 Kung Fu
- ☐ '72 Superfly

MAZE Featuring Frankie Beverly
- ☐ '85 Back In Stride
- ☐ '89 Can't Get Over You

MC BRAINS
- ☐ '92 Oochie Coochie

MC5
- ☐ '69 Kick Out The Jams

M.C. HAMMER
- ☐ '91 Addams Groove
- ☐ '90 Have You Seen Her
- ☐ '90 Pray ★
- ☐ '94 Pumps And A Bump
- ☐ '91 2 Legit 2 Quit ★
- ☒ '90 U Can't Touch This ★

MC LYTE
- ☐ '96 Cold Rock A Party
- ☐ '96 Keep On, Keepin' On
- ☐ '93 RuffNeck

McANALLY, Mac
- ☐ '77 It's A Crazy World

McBRIDE, Martina
- ☐ '07 Anyway
- ☐ '02 Blessed
- ☐ '97 Broken Wing, A
- ☒ '03 Concrete Angel
- ☐ '05 God's Will
- ☐ '98 Happy Girl
- ☒ '99 I Love You
- ☐ '04 In My Daughter's Eyes
- ☐ '94 Independence Day
- ☐ '99 Love's The Only House
- ☒ '93 My Baby Loves Me
- ☐ '00 There You Are
- ☒ '03 This One's For The Girls
- ☐ '97 Valentine
- ☐ '99 Whatever You Say
- ☐ '01 When God Fearin' Women Get The Blues
- ☐ '02 Where Would You Be
- ☐ '95 Wild Angels
- ☐ '98 Wrong Again

McCAIN, Edwin
- ☒ '99 I Could Not Ask For More
- ☒ '98 I'll Be

McCALL, C.W.
- ☐ '75 Convoy ★

McCANN, Lila
- ☐ '97 I Wanna Fall In Love

McCANN, Peter
- ☐ '77 Do You Wanna Make Love

McCARTNEY, Jesse
- ☒ '05 Beautiful Soul
- ☒ '06 Right Where You Want Me

McCARTNEY, Paul/Wings
- ☐ '71 Another Day
- ☐ '79 Arrow Through Me
- ☒ '74 Band On The Run ★
- ☐ '71 Bip Bop/Hey Diddle
- ☐ '80 Coming Up (Live At Glasgow) ★
- ☐ '82 Ebony And Ivory [w/ Stevie Wonder] ★
- ☐ '79 Getting Closer
- ☐ '82 Girl Is Mine, The [w/ Michael Jackson] ★
- ☐ '77 Girls' School
- ☐ '72 Give Ireland Back To The Irish
- ☐ '79 Goodnight Tonight
- ☐ '73 Helen Wheels
- ☐ '72 Hi, Hi, Hi
- ☐ '78 I've Had Enough
- ☐ '74 Jet
- ☐ '74 Junior's Farm ★
- ☐ '76 Let 'Em In
- ☐ '75 Letting Go
- ☐ '75 Listen To What The Man Said ★
- ☐ '73 Live And Let Die ★
- ☐ '78 London Town
- ☐ '72 Mary Had A Little Lamb
- ☐ '70 Maybe I'm Amazed
- ☐ '77 Maybe I'm Amazed [live]
- ☐ '77 Mull Of Kintyre
- ☐ '89 My Brave Face
- ☒ '73 My Love ★
- ☐ '74 Nineteen Hundred And Eighty Five
- ☐ '84 No More Lonely Nights
- ☐ '86 Press
- ☐ '74 Sally G
- ☐ '83 Say Say Say [w/ Michael Jackson] ★
- ☒ '76 Silly Love Songs ★
- ☐ '83 So Bad
- ☐ '85 Spies Like Us
- ☐ '82 Take It Away
- ☐ '82 Tug Of War
- ☐ '71 Uncle Albert/Admiral Halsey ★
- ☐ '75 Venus And Mars Rock Show
- ☐ '78 With A Little Luck ★

McCLAIN, Alton, & Destiny
- ☒ '79 It Must Be Love

McCLINTON, Delbert
- ☐ '80 Giving It Up For Your Love

McCLURE, Bobby
- ☐ '65 Don't Mess Up A Good Thing *[w/ Fontella Bass]*

McCOO, Marilyn, & Billy Davis, Jr.
- ☐ '76 You Don't Have To Be A Star (To Be In My Show)
- ▣ '77 Your Love

McCOY, Neal
- ☐ '93 No Doubt About It
- ☐ '97 Shake, The
- ☐ '94 Wink

McCOY, Van
- ▣ '75 Hustle, The ★

McCOYS, The
- ☐ '66 Come On Let's Go
- ☐ '65 Fever
- ☐ '65 Hang On Sloopy ★

McCRACKLIN, Jimmy
- ☐ '61 Just Got To Know
- ☐ '58 Walk, The

McCRAE, George
- ☐ '75 I Get Lifted
- ▣ '74 Rock Your Baby ★

McCRAE, Gwen
- ☐ '75 Rockin' Chair

McCREADY, Mindy
- ☐ '97 Girl's Gotta Do (What A Girl's Gotta Do)
- ☐ '96 Guys Do It All The Time

McDANIELS, Gene
- ☐ '62 Chip Chip
- ☐ '61 Hundred Pounds Of Clay, A ★
- ☐ '62 Point Of No Return
- ☐ '62 Spanish Lace
- ☐ '61 Tear, A
- ☐ '61 Tower Of Strength

McDEVITT, Chas., Skiffle Group
- ☐ '57 Freight Train

McDONALD, Michael
- ☐ '82 I Keep Forgettin' (Every Time You're Near)
- ☐ '85 No Lookin' Back
- ☐ '86 On My Own *[w/ Patti LaBelle]* ★
- ☐ '86 Sweet Freedom
- ☐ '83 Yah Mo B There *[w/ James Ingram]*

McDOWELL, Ronnie
- ☐ '77 King Is Gone, The

McENTIRE, Reba
- ☐ '95 And Still
- ☐ '07 Because Of You *[w/ Kelly Clarkson]*
- ☐ '93 Does He Love You *[w/ Linda Davis]*
- ▣ '91 Fancy
- ☐ '96 Fear Of Being Alone, The
- ☐ '91 For My Broken Heart
- ☐ '92 Greatest Man I Never Knew, The
- ☐ '95 Heart Is A Lonely Hunter, The
- ☐ '93 Heart Won't Lie, The *[w/ Vince Gill]*
- ☐ '96 How Was I To Know
- ☐ '97 I'd Rather Ride Around With You
- ☐ '01 I'm A Survivor
- ▣ '98 If You See Him/If You See Her *[w/ Brooks & Dunn]*
- ☐ '92 Is There Life Out There
- ☐ '86 Little Rock
- ☐ '90 Rumor Has It
- ☐ '04 Somebody
- ☐ '94 Till You Love Me
- ☐ '90 Walk On
- ☐ '99 What Do You Say
- ☐ '86 Whoever's In New England
- ☐ '90 You Lie

McFADDEN, Bob, & Dor
- ☐ '59 Mummy, The

McFADDEN & WHITEHEAD
- ▣ '79 Ain't No Stoppin' Us Now

McFERRIN, Bobby
- ▣ '88 Don't Worry Be Happy ★

McGOVERN, Maureen
- ☐ '79 Can You Read My Mind
- ☐ '79 Different Worlds
- ☐ '73 Morning After, The
- ☐ '75 We May Never Love Like This Again

McGRAW, Tim
- ☐ '01 Angry All The Time
- ☐ '04 Back When
- ☐ '01 Bring On The Rain *[w/ Jo Dee Messina]*
- ☐ '02 Cowboy In Me, The
- ▣ '05 Do You Want Fries With That
- ▣ '94 Don't Take The Girl ★
- ☐ '94 Down On The Farm
- ☐ '97 Everywhere
- ☐ '99 For A Little While
- ☐ '01 Grown Men Don't Cry
- ▣ '95 I Like It, I Love It
- ▣ '94 Indian Outlaw ★
- ▣ '97 It's Your Love *[w/ Faith Hill]* ★
- ▣ '98 Just To Hear You Say That You Love Me *[w/ Faith Hill]*
- ▣ '97 Just To See You Smile
- ☐ '07 Last Dollar (Fly Away)
- ▣ '00 Let's Make Love *[w/ Faith Hill]*
- ▣ '05 Like We Never Loved At All *[w/ Faith Hill]*
- ▣ '04 Live Like You Were Dying ★
- ▣ '99 My Best Friend
- ☐ '06 My Little Girl
- ▣ '00 My Next Thirty Years
- ☐ '94 Not A Moment Too Soon
- ▣ '98 One Of These Days
- ▣ '99 Please Remember Me ★
- ☐ '03 Real Good Man
- ☐ '02 Red Rag Top
- ▣ '96 She Never Lets It Go To Her Heart
- ▣ '02 She's My Kind Of Rain
- ▣ '99 Something Like That
- ☐ '02 Unbroken
- ☐ '03 Watch The Wind Blow By

McGRAW, Tim — cont'd
- ☐ '06 When The Stars Go Blue
- ◼ '98 Where The Green Grass Grows

McGRIFF, Jimmy
- ☐ '62 I've Got A Woman

McGUINN, CLARK & HILLMAN
- ☐ '79 Don't You Write Her Off

McGUIRE, Barry
- ☐ '65 Eve Of Destruction ★

McGUIRE SISTERS, The
- ☐ '56 Delilah Jones
- ☐ '58 Ding Dong
- ☐ '56 Ev'ry Day Of My Life
- ☐ '56 Goodnight My Love, Pleasant Dreams
- ☐ '55 He
- ☐ '56 In The Alps *[w/ Lawrence Welk]*
- ☐ '55 It May Sound Silly
- ☐ '61 Just For Old Time's Sake
- ☐ '59 May You Always
- ☐ '55 No More
- ☐ '56 Picnic
- ☐ '55 Sincerely
- ☐ '55 Something's Gotta Give
- ☐ '57 Sugartime ★
- ☐ '59 Summer Dreams
- ☐ '56 Weary Blues

McINTYRE, Joey
- ☐ '99 Stay The Same

McKENNITT, Loreena
- ☐ '98 Mummers' Dance, The

McKENZIE, Bob & Doug
- ☐ '82 Take Off *[w/ Geddy Lee]*

McKENZIE, Scott
- ☐ '67 Like An Old Time Movie
- ☐ '67 San Francisco (Be Sure To Wear Flowers In Your Hair)

McKNIGHT, Brian
- ◼ '98 Anytime
- ◼ '99 Back At One ★
- ☐ '98 Hold Me
- ◼ '93 Love Is *[w/ Vanessa Williams]* ★
- ☐ '93 One Last Cry
- ☐ '97 You Should Be Mine (Don't Waste Your Time)

McLACHLAN, Sarah
- ☐ '98 Adia ★
- ◼ '98 Angel ★
- ☐ '97 Building A Mystery
- ☐ '04 Fallen
- ◼ '99 I Will Remember You [live] ★
- ☐ '98 Sweet Surrender

McLAIN, Tommy
- ☐ '66 Sweet Dreams

McLEAN, Don
- ◼ '71 American Pie ★
- ☐ '72 Castles In The Air

McLEAN, Phil
- ☐ '81 Crying
- ☐ '72 Dreidel
- ☐ '81 It's Just The Sun
- ☐ '81 Since I Don't Have You
- ☐ '72 Vincent
- ☐ '75 Wonderful Baby

McLEAN, Phil
- ☐ '61 Small Sad Sam

McNAMARA, Robin
- ☐ '70 Lay A Little Lovin' On Me

McPHATTER, Clyde
- ☐ '58 Come What May
- ☐ '57 Just To Hold My Hand
- ☐ '62 Little Bitty Pretty One
- ☐ '57 Long Lonely Nights
- ☐ '62 Lover Please
- ☐ '58 Lover's Question, A ★
- ☐ '56 Seven Days
- ☐ '59 Since You've Been Gone
- ☐ '60 Ta Ta
- ☐ '56 Treasure Of Love
- ☐ '57 Without Love (There Is Nothing)

McPHEE, Katharine
- ☐ '07 Over It
- ☐ '06 Somewhere Over The Rainbow

McSHANN, Jay, Orchestra
- ☐ '55 Hands Off

McVIE, Christine
- ☐ '84 Got A Hold On Me
- ☐ '84 Love Will Show Us How

MEAD, Sister Janet
- ☐ '74 Lord's Prayer, The

MEAT LOAF
- ☐ '77 Bat Out Of Hell
- ◼ '93 I'd Do Anything For Love (But I Won't Do That)
- ☐ '95 I'd Lie For You (And That's The Truth)
- ☐ '94 Objects In The Rear View Mirror May Appear Closer Than They Are
- ◼ '78 Paradise By The Dashboard Light
- ☐ '94 Rock And Roll Dreams Come Through
- ◼ '78 Two Out Of Three Ain't Bad
- ☐ '78 You Took The Words Right Out Of My Mouth

MEAT PUPPETS
- ☐ '94 Backwater

MECO
- ☐ '80 Empire Strikes Back (Medley)
- ☐ '82 Pop Goes The Movies
- ☐ '77 Star Wars Theme/Cantina Band ★
- ☐ '78 Theme From Close Encounters
- ☐ '78 Themes From The Wizard Of Oz

MEDEIROS, Glenn
- ☐ '90 All I'm Missing Is You *[w/ Ray Parker Jr.]*
- ☐ '87 Nothing's Gonna Change My Love For You
- ☐ '90 She Ain't Worth It *[w/ Bobby Brown]* ★

MEDLEY, Bill
- ☐ '68 Brown Eyed Woman
- ☑ '87 (I've Had) The Time Of My Life
  [w/ Jennifer Warnes] ★
- ☐ '68 Peace Brother Peace

MEGADETH
- ☐ '88 In My Darkest Hour
- ☐ '86 Peace Sells
- ☐ '92 Symphony Of Destruction

MEGATRONS, The
- ☐ '59 Velvet Waters

MEISNER, Randy
- ☐ '80 Deep Inside My Heart
- ☐ '81 Hearts On Fire
- ☐ '82 Never Been In Love

MEL & TIM
- ☐ '69 Backfield In Motion
- ☐ '72 Starting All Over Again

MELANIE
- ☐ '73 Bitter Bad
- ☐ '71 Brand New Key ★
- ☐ '70 Lay Down (Candles In The Rain)
  [w/ Edwin Hawkins Singers]
- ☐ '72 Nickel Song, The
- ☐ '70 Peace Will Come (According To Plan)
- ☐ '72 Ring The Living Bell

MELENDEZ, Lisette
- ☐ '91 Together Forever

MELLENCAMP, John Cougar
- ☐ '92 Again Tonight
- ☐ '81 Ain't Even Done With The Night
- ☐ '84 Authority Song
- ☐ '88 Check It Out
- ☐ '87 Cherry Bomb
- ☐ '83 Crumblin' Down
- ☐ '91 Get A Leg Up
- ☐ '82 Hand To Hold On To
- ☐ '93 Human Wheels
- ☑ '82 Hurts So Good ★
- ☐ '79 I Need A Lover
- ☐ '99 I'm Not Running Anymore
- ☑ '82 Jack & Diane ★
- ☐ '96 Key West Intermezzo (I Saw You First)
- ☐ '85 Lonely Ol' Night
- ☐ '92 Now More Than Ever
- ☐ '87 Paper In Fire
- ☐ '01 Peaceful World
- ☐ '83 Pink Houses
- ☐ '89 Pop Singer
- ☐ '86 R.O.C.K. In The U.S.A. (A Salute To 60's Rock) ★
- ☐ '86 Rain On The Scarecrow
- ☐ '87 Real Life, The
- ☐ '86 Rumbleseat
- ☐ '85 Small Town
- ☐ '80 This Time
- ☐ '93 What If I Came Knocking
- ☐ '94 Wild Night *[w/ Me'shell Ndegéocello]* ★

MELLO-KINGS, The
- ☐ '57 Tonite, Tonite

MELLO-TONES, The
- ☐ '57 Rosie Lee

MELLOW MAN ACE
- ☐ '90 Mentirosa

MELVIN, Harold, & The Blue Notes
- ☐ '75 Bad Luck
- ☐ '75 Hope That We Can Be Together Soon
- ☑ '72 If You Don't Know Me By Now ★
- ☐ '73 Love I Lost, The
- ☐ '75 Wake Up Everybody

MEN AT LARGE
- ☐ '93 So Alone

MEN AT WORK
- ☐ '83 Be Good Johnny
- ☐ '82 Down Under ★
- ☐ '83 Dr. Heckyll & Mr. Jive
- ☐ '83 It's A Mistake
- ☐ '83 Overkill
- ☐ '82 Who Can It Be Now? ★

MENDES, Sergio
- ☐ '84 Alibis
- ☐ '68 Fool On The Hill, The
- ☐ '68 Look Of Love, The
- ☐ '66 Mas Que Nada
- ☐ '83 Never Gonna Let You Go
- ☐ '68 Scarborough Fair

MEN WITHOUT HATS
- ☐ '87 Pop Goes The World
- ☐ '83 Safety Dance, The ★

MERCHANT, Natalie
- ☐ '95 Carnival
- ☐ '96 Jealousy
- ☐ '98 Kind & Generous
- ☐ '95 Wonder

MERCY
- ☐ '69 Love (Can Make You Happy)

MERCYME
- ☐ '04 Here With Me
- ☐ '01 I Can Only Imagine
- ☐ '06 So Long Self
- ☐ '04 Word Of God Speak

MESSINA, Jo Dee
- ☐ '01 Bring On The Rain *[w/ Tim McGraw]*
- ☐ '00 Burn
- ☐ '98 Bye-Bye
- ☑ '96 Heads Carolina, Tails California
- ☐ '98 I'm Alright
- ☐ '99 Lesson In Leavin'
- ☐ '05 My Give A Damn's Busted
- ☑ '98 Stand Beside Me
- ☐ '00 That's The Way

MELLO-KINGS, The [continuation reference]
- ☐ '98 Your Life Is Now

METALLICA
- '91 Enter Sandman
- '96 Hero Of The Day
- '00 I Disappear
- '86 Master Of Puppets
- '97 Memory Remains, The
- '99 No Leaf Clover
- '92 Nothing Else Matters
- '89 One
- '98 Turn The Page
- '91 Unforgiven, The
- '97 Unforgiven II, The
- '96 Until It Sleeps
- '92 Wherever I May Roam
- '99 Whiskey In The Jar

METERS, The
- '69 Cissy Strut
- '69 Sophisticated Cissy

METHOD MAN
- '94 Bring The Pain
- '95 How High [w/ Redman]
- '95 I'll Be There For You/You're All I Need To Get By ★

MFSB
- '74 TSOP (The Sound Of Philadelphia) [w/ The Three Degrees] ★

MICHAEL, George/Wham!
- '84 Careless Whisper ★ ▬
- '86 Different Corner, A
- '91 Don't Let The Sun Go Down On Me [live] [w/ Elton John] ★
- '86 Edge Of Heaven, The
- '85 Everything She Wants ★
- '87 Faith ★
- '96 Fastlove
- '88 Father Figure ★
- '85 Freedom
- '90 Freedom ★
- '87 I Knew You Were Waiting (For Me) [w/ Aretha Franklin] ★
- '87 I Want Your Sex
- '85 I'm Your Man
- '96 Jesus To A Child
- '88 Kissing A Fool
- '88 Monkey ★
- '88 One More Try ★
- '90 Praying For Time ★
- '93 Somebody To Love [w/ Queen]
- '92 Too Funky
- '91 Waiting For That Day
- '84 Wake Me Up Before You Go-Go ★

MICHAELS, Lee
- '71 Can I Get A Witness
- '71 Do You Know What I Mean

MICHEL, Pras
- '98 Ghetto Supastar (That Is What You Are)

MICHEL'LE
- '90 Nicety
- '89 No More Lies

MICKEY & SYLVIA
- '57 Love Is Strange ★

MIDLER, Bette
- '73 Boogie Woogie Bugle Boy
- '72 Do You Want To Dance?
- '73 Friends
- '90 From A Distance ★
- '79 Married Men
- '80 My Mother's Eyes
- '80 Rose, The ★
- '80 When A Man Loves A Woman
- '89 Wind Beneath My Wings ★

MIDNIGHT OIL
- '88 Beds Are Burning
- '90 Blue Sky Mine

MIDNIGHT STAR
- '88 Don't Rock The Boat
- '83 Freak-A-Zoid
- '86 Headlines
- '84 Operator

MIGHTY CLOUDS OF JOY
- '76 Mighty High

MIGHTY MIGHTY BOSSTONES, The
- '97 Impression That I Get, The

MIKAILA
- '00 So In Love With Two

MIKE + THE MECHANICS
- '86 All I Need Is A Miracle
- '89 Living Years, The ★
- '88 Nobody's Perfect
- '85 Silent Running (On Dangerous Ground)
- '86 Taken In

MILES, Garry
- '60 Look For A Star

MILES, John
- '77 Slowdown

MILES, Robert
- '96 Children

MILESTONE
- '97 I Care 'Bout You

MILIAN, Christina
- '01 AM To PM
- '04 Dip It Low
- '06 Say I [w/ Young Jeezy]

MILLER, Chuck
- '55 House Of Blue Lights, The

MILLER, Jody
- '71 He's So Fine
- '65 Home Of The Brave
- '65 Queen Of The House

MILLER, Mitch, Orchestra
- '59 Children's Marching Song (Nick Nack Paddy Whack)

- ☐ '56 Lisbon Antigua (In Old Lisbon)
- ☐ '56 Madeira
- ☐ '58 March From The River Kwai and Colonel Bogey
- ☐ '56 Theme Song From "Song For A Summer Night"
- ☐ '55 Yellow Rose Of Texas, The ★

MILLER, Ned
- ☐ '62 From A Jack To A King

MILLER, Roger
- ☐ '64 Chug-A-Lug
- ☐ '64 Dang Me
- ☐ '64 Do-Wacka-Do
- ☐ '65 Engine Engine #9
- ☐ '65 England Swings
- ☐ '66 Husbands And Wives
- ☐ '65 Kansas City Star
- ☐ '65 King Of The Road ★
- ☐ '68 Little Green Apples
- ☐ '65 One Dyin' And A Buryin'
- ☐ '67 Walkin' In The Sunshine
- ☐ '66 You Can't Roller Skate In A Buffalo Herd

MILLER, Steve, Band
- ☐ '82 Abracadabra ★
- ☐ '76 Dance, Dance, Dance
- ☐ '76 Fly Like An Eagle ★
- ☐ '68 Gangster Of Love
- ☐ '70 Going To The Country
- ☐ '81 Heart Like A Wheel
- ☐ '86 I Want To Make The World Turn Around
- ☐ '77 Jet Airliner
- ☐ '73 Joker, The ★
- ☐ '77 Jungle Love
- ☐ '68 Living In The U.S.A.
- ☐ '76 Rock'n Me ★
- ☐ '69 Space Cowboy
- ☐ '77 Swingtown
- ☐ '76 Take The Money And Run ★
- ☐ '93 Wide River
- ☐ '73 Your Cash Ain't Nothin' But Trash

MILLI VANILLI
- ☐ '90 All Or Nothing
- ☐ '89 Baby Don't Forget My Number ★
- ☐ '89 Blame It On The Rain ★
- ☐ '89 Girl I'm Gonna Miss You ★
- ☐ '89 Girl You Know It's True

MILLS, Frank
- ☐ '79 Music Box Dancer ★

MILLS, Garry
- ☐ '60 Look For A Star

MILLS, Hayley
- ☐ '62 Johnny Jingo
- ☐ '61 Let's Get Together

MILLS, Stephanie
- ☐ '89 Home
- ☐ '87 I Feel Good All Over

- ☐ '86 I Have Learned To Respect The Power Of Love
- ☐ '80 Never Knew Love Like This Before ★
- ☐ '89 Something In The Way (You Make Me Feel)
- ☐ '80 Sweet Sensation
- ☐ '81 Two Hearts [w/ Teddy Pendergrass]
- ☐ '79 What Cha Gonna Do With My Lovin'
- ☐ '87 (You're Puttin') A Rush On Me

MILLS BROTHERS, The
- ☐ '68 Cab Driver
- ☐ '58 Get A Job
- ☐ '57 Queen Of The Senior Prom

MILSAP, Ronnie
- ☐ '82 Any Day Now
- ☐ '81 I Wouldn't Have Missed It For The World
- ☐ '77 It Was Almost Like A Song
- ☐ '85 Lost In The Fifties Tonight (In The Still Of The Night)
- ☐ '88 Old Folks [w/ Mike Reid]
- ☐ '74 Pure Love
- ☐ '80 Smoky Mountain Rain
- ☐ '83 Stranger In My House
- ☐ '81 (There's) No Gettin' Over Me

MIMMS, Garnet, & The Enchanters
- ☐ '63 Baby Don't You Weep
- ☐ '63 Cry Baby
- ☐ '63 For Your Precious Love
- ☐ '66 I'll Take Good Care Of You

MIMS
- ☐ '07 Like This
- ☐ '07 This Is Why I'm Hot ★

MINDBENDERS, The
- ☐ '65 Game Of Love ★
- ☐ '66 Groovy Kind Of Love, A ★

MINEO, Sal
- ☐ '57 Lasting Love
- ☐ '57 Start Movin' (In My Direction)

MINIATURE MEN
- ☐ '62 Baby Elephant Walk

MINOGUE, Kylie
- ☐ '02 Can't Get You Out Of My Head
- ☐ '88 I Should Be So Lucky
- ☐ '88 It's No Secret
- ☐ '88 Loco-Motion, The
- ☐ '02 Love At First Sight

MINT CONDITION
- ☐ '92 Breakin' My Heart (Pretty Brown Eyes)
- ☐ '99 If You Love Me
- ☐ '94 U Send Me Swingin'
- ☐ '96 What Kind Of Man Would I Be
- ☐ '97 You Don't Have To Hurt No More

MIRACLES, The
- ☐ '69 Abraham, Martin And John
- ☐ '69 Baby, Baby Don't Cry
- ☐ '66 (Come 'Round Here) I'm The One You Need

MIRACLES, The — cont'd
- ☐ '74 Do It Baby
- ☐ '69 Doggone Right
- ☐ '65 Going To A Go-Go
- ☐ '69 Here I Go Again
- ☐ '71 I Don't Blame You At All
- ☐ '63 I Gotta Dance To Keep From Crying
- ☒ '64 I Like It Like That
- ☐ '67 I Second That Emotion
- ☐ '62 I'll Try Something New
- ☐ '68 If You Can Want
- ☐ '67 Love I Saw In You Was Just A Mirage
- ☒ '75 Love Machine ★
- ☐ '63 Love She Can Count On, A
- ☐ '63 Mickey's Monkey
- ☒ '67 More Love
- ☐ '65 My Girl Has Gone
- ☒ '65 Ooo Baby Baby
- ☐ '69 Point It Out
- ☐ '60 Shop Around ★
- ☐ '68 Special Occasion
- ☐ '70 Tears Of A Clown, The ★
- ☐ '64 That's What Love Is Made Of
- ☐ '65 Tracks Of My Tears, The
- ☐ '62 What's So Good About Good-by
- ☐ '68 Yester Love
- ☒ '62 You've Really Got A Hold On Me

MISSING PERSONS
- ☐ '82 Destination Unknown
- ☐ '82 Words

MIS-TEEQ
- ☐ '04 Scandalous

MR. BIG
- ☐ '92 Just Take My Heart
- ☒ '91 To Be With You ★
- ☐ '93 Wild World

MR. CHEEKS
- ☐ '01 Lights, Camera, Action!

MR. MISTER
- ☒ '85 Broken Wings ★
- ☐ '86 Is It Love
- ☒ '85 Kyrie ★
- ☐ '87 Something Real (Inside Me/Inside You)

MR. PRESIDENT
- ☐ '97 Coco Jamboo

MITCHELL, Guy
- ☐ '59 Heartaches By The Number
- ☐ '57 Knee Deep In The Blues
- ☐ '56 Ninety Nine Years (Dead Or Alive)
- ☐ '57 Rock-A-Billy
- ☐ '56 Singing The Blues ★

MITCHELL, Joni
- ☐ '70 Big Yellow Taxi
- ☐ '74 Big Yellow Taxi [live]
- ☐ '69 Both Sides Now
- ☐ '71 Carey
- ☐ '69 Chelsea Morning
- ☐ '70 Circle Game, The
- ☐ '74 Free Man In Paris

- ☐ '74 Help Me
- ☐ '70 Woodstock
- ☐ '72 You Turn Me On, I'm A Radio

MITCHELL, Kim
- ☐ '85 Go For Soda

MITCHELL, Willie
- ☐ '68 Soul Serenade
- ☐ '64 20-75

MITCHUM, Robert
- ☐ '58 Ballad Of Thunder Road, The

MOBY
- ☐ '99 Natural Blues
- ☐ '00 South Side

MOBY GRAPE
- ☐ '67 Hey Grandma
- ☐ '67 Omaha

MOCEDADES
- ☐ '74 Eres Tu (Touch The Wind)

MODELS
- ☐ '86 Out Of Mind Out Of Sight

MODERN ENGLISH
- ☒ '83 I Melt With You ★

MODERN LOVERS, The
- ☐ '76 Roadrunner

MODEST MOUSE
- ☐ '04 Float On

MODUGNO, Domenico
- ☐ '58 Nel Blu Dipinto Di Blu (Volaré) ★

MOJO MEN, The
- ☐ '67 Sit Down, I Think I Love You

MOKENSTEF
- ☐ '95 He's Mine

MOLLY HATCHET
- ☐ '79 Flirtin' With Disaster

MOMENTS, The
- ☒ '75 Look At Me (I'm In Love)
- ☒ '70 Love On A Two-Way Street ★
- ☒ '74 Sexy Mama
- ☒ '80 Special Lady [RAY, GOODMAN & BROWN]

MONEY, Eddie
- ☐ '78 Baby Hold On
- ☐ '87 Endless Nights
- ☐ '79 Gimme Some Water
- ☐ '86 I Wanna Go Back
- ☐ '91 I'll Get By
- ☒ '88 Love In Your Eyes, The
- ☐ '79 Maybe I'm A Fool
- ☐ '89 Peace In Our Time
- ☐ '82 Shakin'
- ☒ '86 Take Me Home Tonight
- ☐ '82 Think I'm In Love
- ☒ '78 Two Tickets To Paradise
- ☐ '88 Walk On Water

MONEY, JT
- ☐ '99 Who Dat *[w/ Solé]* ★

MONICA
- ☐ '96 Ain't Nobody
- ♫ '98 Angel Of Mine ★
- ☐ '95 Before You Walk Out Of My Life
- ▣ '98 Boy Is Mine, The *[w/ Brandy]* ★
- ☐ '95 Don't Take It Personal (just one of dem days) ★
- ▣ '98 First Night, The ★
- ▣ '97 For You I Will
- ▣ '95 Like This And Like That
- ☐ '03 So Gone
- ☐ '04 U Should've Known Better
- ▣ '96 Why I Love You So Much

MONIFAH
- ▣ '98 Touch It
- ▣ '96 You

MONKEES, The
- ☐ '68 D. W. Washburn
- ☐ '67 Daydream Believer ★
- ☐ '67 Girl I Knew Somewhere, The
- ▣ '66 I'm A Believer ★
- ☐ '66 (I'm Not Your) Steppin' Stone
- ☐ '68 It's Nice To Be With You
- ☐ '66 Last Train To Clarksville ★
- ☐ '69 Listen To The Band
- ☐ '67 Little Bit Me, A Little Bit You, A
- ☐ '67 Mary, Mary
- ☐ '67 Pleasant Valley Sunday
- ☐ '67 Randy Scouse Git
- ☐ '67 She
- ☐ '68 Tapioca Tundra
- ☐ '86 That Was Then, This Is Now
- ☐ '66 Theme From The Monkees
- ☐ '68 Valleri
- ☐ '67 Words

MONOTONES, The
- ▣ '58 Book Of Love ★

MONRO, Matt
- ▣ '61 My Kind Of Girl
- ☐ '64 Walk Away

MONROE, Vaughn
- ☐ '56 Don't Go To Strangers
- ☐ '56 In The Middle Of The House

MONROES, The
- ☐ '82 What Do All The People Know

MONSTER MAGNET
- ☐ '98 Space Lord

MONTANA, Hannah
- ☐ '06 If We Were A Movie
- ☐ '07 Life's What You Make It
- ☐ '07 Nobody's Perfect

MONTE, Lou
- ☐ '58 Lazy Mary
- ☐ '62 Pepino The Italian Mouse

MONTENEGRO, Hugo, Orchestra
- ☐ '68 Good, The Bad And The Ugly, The ★

MONTEZ, Chris
- ☐ '66 Call Me
- ☐ '62 Let's Dance ★
- ☐ '66 More I See You, The
- ☐ '66 There Will Never Be Another You
- ☐ '66 Time After Time

MONTGOMERY, John Michael
- ☐ '94 Be My Baby Tonight
- ▣ '98 Cover You In Kisses
- ▣ '98 Hold On To Me
- ☐ '99 Home To You
- ☐ '97 How Was I To Know
- ▣ '95 I Can Love You Like That
- ▣ '93 I Love The Way You Love Me
- ▣ '93 I Swear
- ☐ '94 If You've Got Love
- ☐ '04 Letters From Home
- ☐ '92 Life's A Dance
- ☐ '00 Little Girl, The
- ☐ '95 Sold (The Grundy County Auction Incident)

MONTGOMERY, Melba
- ☐ '74 No Charge

MONTGOMERY, Wes
- ☐ '67 Windy

MONTGOMERY GENTRY
- ☐ '05 Gone
- ▣ '04 If You Ever Stop Loving Me
- ☐ '99 Lonely And Gone
- ▣ '07 Lucky Man
- ☐ '02 My Town
- ☐ '01 She Couldn't Change Me
- ▣ '06 She Don't Tell Me To
- ☐ '05 Something To Be Proud Of

MOODY BLUES, The
- ☐ '78 Driftwood
- ☐ '70 Eyes Of A Child
- ☐ '81 Gemini Dream
- ☐ '65 Go Now!
- ☐ '75 I Dreamed Last Night *[JUSTIN HAYWARD & JOHN LODGE]*
- ☐ '88 I Know You're Out There Somewhere
- ☐ '73 I'm Just A Singer (In A Rock And Roll Band)
- ☐ '72 Isn't Life Strange
- ☐ '68 Legend Of A Mind
- ☐ '69 Never Comes The Day
- ▣ '72 Nights In White Satin ★
- ☐ '70 Question
- ☐ '68 Ride My See-Saw
- ☐ '83 Sitting At The Wheel
- ☐ '78 Steppin' In A Slide Zone
- ☐ '71 Story In Your Eyes, The
- ☐ '68 Tuesday Afternoon (Forever Afternoon)
- ☐ '81 Voice, The
- ▣ '86 Your Wildest Dreams

MOONEY, Art, & His Orchestra
- [ ] '55 Honey-Babe

MOONGLOWS, The
- [ ] '56 See Saw
- [ ] '55 Sincerely ★
- [ ] '58 Ten Commandments Of Love
- [ ] '56 We Go Together

MOORE, Bob, & His Orch.
- [ ] '61 Mexico

MOORE, Bobby, & The Rhythm Aces
- [ ] '66 Searching For My Love

MOORE, Chanté
- [ ] '99 Chanté's Got A Man

MOORE, Dorothy
- [ ] '77 I Believe You
- [ ] '76 Misty Blue

MOORE, Jackie
- [ ] '70 Precious, Precious
- [ ] '73 Sweet Charlie Babe

MOORE, Mandy
- ■ '99 Candy
- ■ '00 I Wanna Be With You

MOORE, Melba
- [ ] '86 Falling
- [ ] '86 Little Bit More, A

MORALES, Michael
- [ ] '89 What I Like About You
- [ ] '89 Who Do You Give Your Love To?

MORGAN, Craig
- [ ] '02 Almost Home
- [ ] '05 Redneck Yacht Club
- [ ] '05 That's What I Love About Sunday

MORGAN, Debelah
- [ ] '00 Dance With Me ★

MORGAN, Jane
- [ ] '58 Day The Rains Came, The
- [ ] '57 Fascination
- [ ] '59 With Open Arms

MORGAN, Jaye P.
- [ ] '55 Danger! Heartbreak Ahead
- [ ] '55 If You Don't Want My Love
- [ ] '55 Longest Walk, The
- [ ] '55 Pepper-Hot Baby
- [ ] '55 Softly, Softly
- [ ] '55 That's All I Want From You

MORGAN, Lorrie
- [ ] '90 Five Minutes
- [ ] '97 Go Away
- [ ] '95 I Didn't Know My Own Strength
- [ ] '92 Watch Me
- [ ] '92 What Part Of No

MORGAN, Meli'sa
- [ ] '85 Do Me Baby
- [ ] '87 If You Can Do It: I Can Too!!

- [ ] '87 Love Changes *[w/ Kashif]*

MORGAN, Russ, & His Orchestra
- [ ] '55 Dogface Soldier
- [ ] '56 Poor People Of Paris, The

MORISSETTE, Alanis
- ■ '95 Hand In My Pocket
- [ ] '02 Hands Clean
- [ ] '96 Head Over Feet
- ■ '96 Ironic ★
- ■ '98 Thank U ★
- [ ] '98 Uninvited
- ■ '96 You Learn
- ■ '95 You Oughta Know ★

MORMON TABERNACLE CHOIR
- [ ] '59 Battle Hymn Of The Republic

MORODER, Giorgio
- [ ] '79 Chase
- [ ] '72 Son Of My Father

MORRISON, Mark
- [ ] '97 Return Of The Mack ★

MORRISON, Van
- [ ] '71 Blue Money
- ■ '67 Brown Eyed Girl ★
- [ ] '71 Call Me Up In Dreamland
- [ ] '70 Come Running
- [ ] '70 Crazy Love
- [ ] '70 Domino
- [ ] '70 Into The Mystic
- [ ] '72 Jackie Wilson Said (I'm In Heaven When You Smile)
- [ ] '70 Moondance
- [ ] '72 Redwood Tree
- [ ] '71 Tupelo Honey
- [ ] '78 Wavelength
- [ ] '71 Wild Night

MORRISSEY
- [ ] '89 Last Of The Famous International Playboys, The
- [ ] '94 More You Ignore Me, The Closer I Get
- [ ] '89 Ouija Board, Ouija Board
- [ ] '91 Our Frank
- [ ] '90 Piccadilly Palare
- [ ] '92 Tomorrow
- [ ] '92 We Hate It When Our Friends Become Successful

MOTELS, The
- [ ] '82 Only The Lonely
- [ ] '83 Remember The Nights
- [ ] '85 Shame
- [ ] '83 Suddenly Last Summer

MOTHERLODE
- [ ] '69 When I Die

MÖTLEY CRÜE
- [ ] '90 Don't Go Away Mad (Just Go Away)
- [ ] '89 Dr. Feelgood
- ■ '87 Girls, Girls, Girls
- [ ] '85 Home Sweet Home
- [ ] '89 Kickstart My Heart

- 🔲 '85 Smokin' In The Boys Room
- ☐ '90 Without You

MOTT THE HOOPLE
- ☐ '72 All The Young Dudes
- ☐ '74 Golden Age Of Rock 'N' Roll, The

MOUNTAIN
- ☐ '70 Mississippi Queen

MOUTH & MACNEAL
- ☐ '72 How Do You Do?

MOVING PICTURES
- ☐ '82 What About Me

MOYET, Alison
- ☐ '85 Invisible

M PEOPLE
- ☐ '94 Moving On Up

MRAZ, Jason
- 🔲 '03 Remedy (I Won't Worry)

MTUME
- 🔲 '83 Juicy Fruit ━━

M2M
- ☐ '99 Don't Say You Love Me
- ☐ '00 Mirror Mirror

MUDVAYNE
- ☐ '06 Fall Into Sleep
- ☐ '05 Happy?

MULDAUR, Maria
- ☐ '74 I'm A Woman
- ☐ '74 Midnight At The Oasis

MULLINS, Rich
- ☐ '88 Awesome God
- ☐ '98 My Deliverer
- ☐ '92 Sometimes By Step

MULLINS, Shawn
- ☐ '98 Lullaby ★

MUMBA, Samantha
- ☐ '00 Gotta Tell You ★

MUNGO JERRY
- ☐ '70 In The Summertime ★

MURDOCK, Shirley
- ☐ '87 As We Lay

MURMAIDS, The
- ☐ '63 Popsicles And Icicles ★

MURPHEY, Michael
- ☐ '75 Carolina In The Pines
- ☐ '72 Geronimo's Cadillac
- ☐ '76 Renegade
- ☐ '82 What's Forever For
- ☐ '75 Wildfire

MURPHY, David Lee
- 🔲 '95 Dust On The Bottle
- ☐ '04 Loco

MURPHY, Eddie
- ☐ '85 Party All The Time
- ☐ '89 Put Your Mouth On Me

MURPHY, Peter
- ☐ '90 Cuts You Up

MURPHY, Walter
- ☐ '76 Fifth Of Beethoven, A

MURRAY, Anne
- ☐ '81 Blessed Are The Believers
- ☐ '79 Broken Hearted Me
- ☐ '80 Could I Have This Dance
- ☐ '73 Danny's Song
- ☐ '79 Daydream Believer
- ☐ '79 I Just Fall In Love Again
- ☐ '83 Little Good News, A
- ☐ '73 Love Song
- ☐ '79 Shadows In The Moonlight
- ☐ '70 Snowbird
- ☐ '78 You Needed Me ★
- ☐ '74 You Won't See Me

MURRAY, Keith
- ☐ '94 Most Beautifullest Thing In This World, The

MUSE
- ☐ '07 Starlight

MUSICAL YOUTH
- ☐ '82 Pass The Dutchie

MUSIC EXPLOSION, The
- ☐ '67 Little Bit O' Soul ★

MUSIC MACHINE, The
- ☐ '66 Talk Talk

MUSIQ
- ☐ '07 Buddy
- ☐ '02 Dontchange
- ☐ '02 Halfcrazy
- ☐ '00 Just Friends (Sunny)
- 🔲 '01 Love
- ☐ '07 Teachme

MYA
- ☐ '00 Case Of The Ex (Whatcha Gonna Do) ★
- ☐ '98 It's All About Me [w/ Sisqo]
- ☐ '01 Lady Marmalade [w/ Christina Aguilera, Lil' Kim & P!nk] ★
- ☐ '98 Movin' On
- 🔲 '99 My First Night With You
- 🔲 '03 My Love Is Like...WO
- 🔲 '98 Take Me There [w/ BlackSTREET]

MY CHEMICAL ROMANCE
- ☐ '05 Helena (So Long & Goodnight)
- 🔲 '07 Welcome To The Black Parade ★

MYERS, Billie
- ☐ '97 Kiss The Rain

MYLES, Alannah
- 🔲 '89 Black Velvet ★

MYLES, Billy
- ☐ '57 Joker (That's What They Call Me)

MYSTICS, The
- ☐ '59 Hushabye

MYSTIKAL
- ☐ '01 Bouncin' Back (Bumpin' Me Against The Wall)
- ☐ '00 Danger (Been So Long)
- ☐ '99 It Ain't My Fault 2 [w/ Silkk The Shocker]
- ◼ '00 Shake Ya Ass

N

NAKED EYES
- ☐ '83 Always Something There To Remind Me
- ☐ '83 Promises, Promises
- ☐ '84 (What) In The Name Of Love
- ☐ '83 When The Lights Go Out

NALICK, Anna
- ☐ '06 Breathe (2 AM)

NAPOLEON XIV
- ☐ '66 They're Coming To Take Me Away, Ha-Haaa!

NAPPY ROOTS
- ☐ '02 Po' Folks

NAS
- ☐ '07 Hip Hop Is Dead
- ☐ '03 I Can
- ☐ '02 Made You Look
- ☐ '96 Street Dreams

NASH, Graham
- ☐ '71 Chicago
- ☐ '72 Immigration Man [w/ David Crosby]

NASH, Johnny
- ☐ '69 Cupid
- ☐ '68 Hold Me Tight
- ◼ '72 I Can See Clearly Now ★
- ☐ '73 Stir It Up
- ◼ '57 Very Special Love, A

NASHVILLE TEENS, The
- ☐ '64 Tobacco Road

NATALIE
- ◼ '05 Goin' Crazy

NATE DOGG
- ☐ '96 Never Leave Me Alone
- ☐ '98 Nobody Does It Better
- ☐ '94 Regulate [w/ Warren G.] ★

NATURAL FOUR
- ☐ '74 Can This Be Real

NATURAL SELECTION
- ☐ '91 Do Anything ★
- ☐ '91 Hearts Don't Think (They Feel)!

NAUGHTON, David
- ☐ '79 Makin' It

NAUGHTY BY NATURE
- ☐ '95 Feel Me Flow
- ☐ '93 Hip Hop Hooray
- ☐ '99 Jamboree
- ☐ '91 O.P.P. ★

NAZARETH
- ☐ '75 Hair Of The Dog
- ☐ '75 Love Hurts
- ☐ '74 This Flight Tonight

NAZZ
- ☐ '69 Hello It's Me

NDEGÉOCELLO, Me'Shell — see MELLENCAMP, JoHN

NEELY, Sam
- ☐ '72 Loving You Just Crossed My Mind
- ☐ '74 You Can Have Her

NEIGHBORHOOD, The
- ☐ '70 Big Yellow Taxi

NELLY
- ◼ '02 Air Force Ones ★
- ☐ '06 Call On Me [w/ Janet Jackson]
- ◼ '02 Dilemma ★
- ◼ '00 E.I.
- ☐ '05 Errtime
- ◼ '06 Grillz ★
- ◼ '02 Hot In Herre ★
- ◼ '00 (Hot S**t) Country Grammar
- ◼ '04 My Place
- ◼ '01 #1
- ◼ '04 Over And Over [w/ Tim McGraw] ★
- ☐ '01 Ride Wit Me ★
- ◼ '03 Shake Ya Tailfeather [w/ P. Diddy & Murphy Lee] ★

NELSON
- ☐ '90 After The Rain
- ◼ '90 (Can't Live Without Your) Love And Affection ★
- ☐ '91 More Than Ever
- ☐ '91 Only Time Will Tell

NELSON, Marc
- ☐ '99 15 Minutes

NELSON, Ricky
- ☐ '57 Be-Bop Baby
- ☐ '58 Believe What You Say ★
- ☐ '61 Everlovin'
- ☐ '63 Fools Rush In
- ☐ '63 For You
- ☐ '72 Garden Party
- ☐ '61 Hello Mary Lou ★
- ☐ '58 I Got A Feeling
- ☐ '59 I Wanna Be Loved
- ☐ '60 I'm Not Afraid
- ☐ '57 I'm Walking
- ☐ '59 It's Late
- ☐ '62 It's Up To You
- ☐ '59 Just A Little Too Much
- ☐ '58 Lonesome Town
- ☐ '59 Long Vacation, A

☐ '58 My Bucket's Got A Hole In It
☐ '59 Never Be Anyone Else But You
☐ '58 Poor Little Fool ★
☐ '69 She Belongs To Me
☐ '57 Stood Up ★
☐ '63 String Along
☐ '59 Sweeter Than You
☐ '62 Teen Age Idol
☐ '57 Teenager's Romance, A
☐ '61 Travelin' Man ★
☐ '57 Waitin' In School
☐ '61 Wonder Like You, A
☐ '60 You Are The Only One
☐ '57 You're My One And Only Love
☐ '60 Young Emotions
☐ '62 Young World

NELSON, Sandy
☐ '61 Let There Be Drums
☐ '59 Teen Beat

NELSON, Willie
☐ '82 Always On My Mind ★
☐ '02 Beer For My Horses [w/ Toby Keith]
☐ '75 Blue Eyes Crying In The Rain ★
☐ '84 City Of New Orleans
☐ '78 Georgia On My Mind
☐ '76 Good Hearted Woman [w/ Waylon Jennings]
☐ '85 Highwayman [w/ Waylon Jennings, Johnny Cash & Kris Kristofferson]
☐ '82 Just To Satisfy You [w/ Waylon Jennings]
☐ '82 Let It Be Me
☐ '78 Mammas Don't Let Your Babies Grow Up To Be Cowboys [w/ Waylon Jennings]
☐ '80 My Heroes Have Always Been Cowboys
☐ '76 Night Life
☐ '80 On The Road Again ★
☐ '83 Pancho And Lefty [w/ Merle Haggard]
☐ '67 Party's Over, The
☐ '85 Seven Spanish Angels [w/ Ray Charles]
☐ '84 To All The Girls I've Loved Before [w/ Julio Iglesias] ★

NENA
☐ '83 99 Luftballons ★

NEON PHILHARMONIC, The
☐ '69 Morning Girl

NERO, Peter
☐ '71 Theme From "Summer Of '42"

NERVOUS NORVUS
☐ '56 Ape Call
☐ '56 Transfusion

NESMITH, Michael
☐ '70 Joanne

NEVIL, Robbie
☐ '88 Back On Holiday
☐ '86 C'est La Vie
☐ '87 Dominoes
☐ '91 Just Like You
☐ '87 Wot's It To Ya

NEVILLE, Aaron
☐ '90 All My Life [w/ Linda Ronstadt]
☐ '89 Don't Know Much [w/ Linda Ronstadt] ★
☐ '91 Everybody Plays The Fool
☐ '67 Tell It Like It Is ★

NEVILLE, Ivan
☐ '88 Not Just Another Girl

NEWBEATS, The
☐ '64 Bread And Butter ★
☐ '64 Everything's Alright
☐ '65 Run, Baby Run (Back Into My Arms)

NEW BIRTH, The
☐ '75 Dream Merchant
☐ '73 I Can Understand It

NEWBURY, Mickey
☐ '71 American Trilogy, An

NEW CHRISTY MINSTRELS, The
☐ '63 Green, Green
☐ '63 Saturday Night
☐ '64 Today

NEW COLONY SIX, The
☐ '66 I Confess
☐ '68 I Will Always Think About You
☐ '68 Things I'd Like To Say

NEW EDITION
☐ '88 Can You Stand The Rain
☐ '83 Candy Girl
☐ '84 Cool It Now
☐ '85 Count Me Out
☐ '86 Earth Angel
☐ '96 Hit Me Off
☐ '96 I'm Still In Love With You
☐ '88 If It Isn't Love ⎯
☐ '86 Little Bit Of Love (Is All It Takes) ⎯
☐ '85 Lost In Love
☐ '84 Mr. Telephone Man

NEW ENGLAND
☐ '79 Don't Ever Wanna Lose Ya

NEW KIDS ON THE BLOCK
☐ '89 Cover Girl
☐ '89 Didn't I (Blow Your Mind)
☐ '89 Hangin' Tough ★
☐ '89 I'll Be Loving You (Forever) ★
☐ '92 If You Go Away
☐ '88 Please Don't Go Girl
☐ '90 Step By Step ★
☐ '89 This One's For The Children
☐ '90 Tonight
☐ '88 You Got It (The Right Stuff)

NEWMAN, Jimmy
☐ '57 Fallen Star, A

NEWMAN, Randy
☐ '88 It's Money That Matters
☐ '72 Political Science
☐ '72 Sail Away
☐ '77 Short People ★

NEW ORDER
- ☐ '86 Bizarre Love Triangle
- ☐ '83 Blue Monday
- ☐ '85 Perfect Kiss
- ☐ '93 Regret
- ☐ '87 True Faith

NEW RADICALS
- ☐ '98 You Get What You Give

NEWSBOYS
- ☐ '98 Entertaining Angels
- ☐ '03 He Reigns
- ☐ '02 It Is You
- ☐ '01 Joy
- ☐ '96 Reality
- ☐ '94 Shine
- ☐ '96 Take Me To Your Leader
- ☐ '03 You Are My King (Amazing Love)

NEW SEEKERS, The
- ☐ '71 I'd Like To Teach The World To Sing (In Perfect Harmony)
- ☐ '70 Look What They've Done To My Song Ma
- ☐ '73 Pinball Wizard/See Me, Feel Me

NEWSONG
- ☐ '00 Christmas Shoes, The

NEWTON, Juice
- ☐ '81 Angel Of The Morning
- ☐ '82 Break It To Me Gently
- ☐ '82 Heart Of The Night
- ☐ '82 Love's Been A Little Bit Hard On Me
- ☐ '81 Queen Of Hearts ★
- ☐ '81 Sweetest Thing (I've Ever Known)
- ☐ '83 Tell Her No

NEWTON, Wayne
- ☐ '72 Can't You Hear The Song?
- ☐ '72 Daddy Don't You Walk So Fast
- ☐ '63 Danke Schoen
- ☐ '65 Red Roses For A Blue Lady
- ☐ '80 Years

NEWTON-JOHN, Olivia
- ☐ '76 Come On Over
- ☐ '79 Deeper Than The Night
- ☐ '76 Don't Stop Believin'
- ☐ '96 Grease Megamix, The [w/ John Travolta]
- ☐ '75 Have You Never Been Mellow ★
- ☐ '82 Heart Attack
- ☐ '78 Hopelessly Devoted To You ★
- ☐ '80 I Can't Help It [w/ Andy Gibb]
- ☐ '74 I Honestly Love You ★
- ☐ '71 If Not For You
- ☐ '74 If You Love Me (Let Me Know)
- ☐ '75 Let It Shine
- ☐ '73 Let Me Be There
- ☐ '78 Little More Love, A
- ☐ '84 Livin' In Desperate Times
- ☐ '80 Magic ★
- ☐ '82 Make A Move On Me
- ☐ '81 Physical ★
- ☐ '75 Please Mr. Please

- ☐ '77 Sam
- ☐ '75 Something Better To Do
- ☐ '85 Soul Kiss
- ☐ '80 Suddenly [w/ Cliff Richard]
- ☐ '78 Summer Nights [w/ John Travolta]
- ☐ '83 Twist Of Fate
- ☐ '80 Xanadu [w/ Electric Light Orchestra] ★
- ☐ '78 You're The One That I Want [w/ John Travolta] ★

NEW VAUDEVILLE BAND, The
- ☐ '66 Winchester Cathedral ★

NEW YORK CITY
- ☐ '73 I'm Doin' Fine Now

NEW YORK DOLLS
- ☐ '73 Personality Crisis

NEXT
- ☐ '97 Butta Love
- ☐ '98 I Still Love You
- ☐ '98 Too Close ★
- ☐ '00 Wifey

NE-YO
- ☐ '07 Because Of You ★
- ☐ '07 Do You
- ☐ '06 Sexy Love ★
- ☐ '06 So Sick ★
- ☐ '06 When You're Mad

NICHOLAS, Paul
- ☐ '77 Heaven On The 7th Floor

NICHOLS, Joe
- ☐ '02 Brokenheartsville
- ☐ '02 Impossible, The
- ☐ '05 Tequila Makes Her Clothes Fall Off
- ☐ '05 What's A Guy Gotta Do

NICKELBACK
- ☐ '05 Animals
- ☐ '06 Far Away ★
- ☐ '04 Feelin' Way Too Damn Good
- ☐ '03 Figured You Out
- ☐ '01 How You Remind Me ★
- ☐ '07 If Everyone Cared
- ☐ '02 Never Again
- ☐ '05 Photograph ★
- ☐ '07 Rockstar ★
- ☐ '06 Savin' Me ★
- ☐ '03 Someday ★
- ☐ '01 Too Bad

NICKS, Stevie
- ☐ '82 After The Glitter Fades
- ☐ '82 Edge Of Seventeen (Just Like The White Winged Dove)
- ☐ '86 I Can't Wait
- ☐ '83 If Anyone Falls
- ☐ '81 Leather And Lace [w/ Don Henley]
- ☐ '86 Needles And Pins [w/ Tom Petty]
- ☐ '83 Nightbird [w/ Sandy Stewart]
- ☐ '89 Rooms On Fire
- ☐ '83 Stand Back

□ '81 Stop Draggin' My Heart Around *[w/ Tom Petty]* ★
□ '85 Talk To Me

NICOLE
□ '98 Make It Hot

NIELSEN/PEARSON
□ '80 If You Should Sail

NIGHT
□ '79 Hot Summer Nights
□ '79 If You Remember Me *[w/ Chris Thompson]*

NIGHTINGALE, Maxine
□ '79 Lead Me On
□ '76 Right Back Where We Started From ★

NIGHT RANGER
□ '83 Don't Tell Me You Love Me
□ '85 Four In The Morning (I Can't Take Any More)
□ '85 Goodbye
□ '85 Sentimental Street
□ '84 Sister Christian ★
□ '84 When You Close Your Eyes

NIKKI
□ '90 Notice Me

NILSSON
□ '72 Coconut
□ '74 Daybreak
□ '69 Everybody's Talkin'
□ '69 I Guess The Lord Must Be In New York City
□ '72 Jump Into The Fire
□ '71 Me And My Arrow
□ '72 Spaceman
□ '71 Without You ★

NINA SKY
□ '04 Move Ya Body ★

NINEDAYS
□ '00 Absolutely (Story Of A Girl) ★

NINE INCH NAILS
□ '94 Closer
□ '99 Day The World Went Away, The
□ '05 Every Day Is Exactly The Same
□ '05 Hand That Feeds, The
□ '95 Hurt
□ '94 March Of The Pigs
□ '05 Only
□ '07 Survivalism

1910 FRUITGUM CO.
□ '69 Indian Giver
□ '68 1, 2, 3, Red Light
□ '68 Simon Says

98°
□ '98 Because Of You ★
□ '00 Give Me Just One Night (Una Noche) ★
□ '99 Hardest Thing, The
□ '99 I Do (Cherish You)
□ '97 Invisible Man

□ '00 My Everything

95 SOUTH
□ '93 Whoot, There It Is

NIRVANA
□ '94 About A Girl
□ '93 All Apologies
□ '92 Come As You Are
□ '93 Heart-Shaped Box
□ '91 In Bloom
□ '95 Man Who Sold The World, The
□ '91 Smells Like Teen Spirit ★
□ '02 You Know You're Right

NITEFLYTE
□ '79 If You Want It

NITTY GRITTY DIRT BAND
□ '79 American Dream, An
□ '87 Fishin' In The Dark
□ '80 Make A Little Magic
□ '70 Mr. Bojangles ★

NITZSCHE, Jack
□ '63 Lonely Surfer, The

NIVEA
□ '02 Don't Mess With My Man
□ '05 Okay

NOBLE, Nick
□ '55 Bible Tells Me So, The
□ '57 Fallen Star, A
□ '57 Moonlight Swim
□ '56 To You, My Love

NOBLES, Cliff, & Co.
□ '68 Horse, The ★

NO DOUBT
□ '96 Don't Speak ★
□ '00 Ex-Girlfriend
□ '02 Hella Good
□ '01 Hey Baby ★
□ '03 It's My Life
□ '95 Just A Girl
□ '00 Simple Kind Of Life
□ '96 Spiderwebs
□ '02 Underneath It All ★

NOGUEZ, Jacky, & His Orchestra
□ '59 Ciao, Ciao Bambina

NOLAN, Kenny
□ '76 I Like Dreamin'
□ '77 Love's Grown Deep

NO MERCY
□ '97 Please Don't Go
□ '96 Where Do You Go ★

NONCHALANT
□ '96 5 O'Clock

N.O.R.E. /NOREAGA
□ '02 Nothin'
□ '04 Oye Mi Canto
□ '98 SuperThug (What What)

NORTH, Freddie
- ☐ '71 She's All I Got

NOTORIOUS B.I.G., The
- ☐ '95 Big Poppa ★
- ☐ '97 Going Back To Cali
- ☐ '97 Hypnotize ★
- ☐ '94 Juicy
- ☐ '97 Mo Money Mo Problems ★
- ☐ '95 One More Chance/Stay With Me ★

NOVA, Aldo
- ☐ '82 Fantasy

*NSYNC
- ☐ '00 Bring It All To Me [w/ Blaque] ★
- ☐ '00 Bye Bye Bye ★
- ☐ '02 Girlfriend ★
- ☐ '98 (God Must Have Spent) A Little More Time On You ★
- ☐ '01 Gone
- ☐ '98 I Want You Back
- ☐ '00 It's Gonna Be Me ★
- ☐ '99 Music Of My Heart [w/ Gloria Estefan] ★
- ☐ '01 Pop
- ☐ '98 Tearin' Up My Heart
- ☐ '00 This I Promise You ★

N2DEEP
- ☐ '92 Back To The Hotel

NIIU
- ☐ '94 I Miss You

NU FLAVOR
- ☐ '97 Heaven

NUGENT, Ted
- ☐ '77 Cat Scratch Fever
- ☐ '76 Dog Eat Dog
- ☐ '95 Fred Bear
- ☐ '76 Free-For-All
- ☐ '75 Hey Baby
- ☐ '77 Home Bound
- ☐ '78 Need You Bad
- ☐ '77 Wang Dang Sweet Poontang
- ☐ '80 Wango Tango
- ☐ '78 Yank Me, Crank Me

NUMAN, Gary
- ☐ '80 Cars ★

NU SHOOZ
- ☐ '86 I Can't Wait ⟵
- ☐ '86 Point Of No Return

NUTMEGS, The
- ☐ '55 Story Untold

NU TORNADOS, The
- ☐ '58 Philadelphia U.S.A.

NUTTY SQUIRRELS, The
- ☐ '59 Uh! Oh!

N.W.A.
- ☐ '89 F*** Tha Police

NYLONS, The
- ☐ '87 Kiss Him Goodbye

NYRO, Laura
- ☐ '68 Stoned Soul Picnic
- ☐ '66 Wedding Bell Blues

O

OAK RIDGE BOYS
- ☐ '83 American Made
- ☐ '82 Bobbie Sue
- ☐ '81 Elvira ★

OASIS
- ☐ '96 Champagne Supernova
- ☐ '97 Don't Go Away
- ☐ '95 Live Forever
- ☐ '95 Wonderwall

O'BANION, John
- ☐ '81 Love You Like I Never Loved Before

O'BRYAN
- ☐ '82 Gigolo, The
- ☐ '84 Lovelite

OCASEK, Ric
- ☐ '86 Emotion In Motion
- ☐ '86 Something To Grab For

OCEAN
- ☐ '71 Put Your Hand In The Hand ★

OCEAN, Billy
- ☐ '84 Caribbean Queen (No More Love On The Run) ★
- ☐ '88 Colour Of Love, The
- ☐ '88 Get Outta My Dreams, Get Into My Car ★
- ☐ '89 Licence To Chill
- ☐ '86 Love Is Forever
- ☐ '76 Love Really Hurts Without You
- ☐ '86 Love Zone
- ☐ '84 Loverboy ★
- ☐ '85 Mystery Lady
- ☐ '85 Suddenly
- ☐ '86 There'll Be Sad Songs (To Make You Cry) ★
- ☐ '85 When The Going Gets Tough, The Tough Get Going

OCEAN BLUE, The
- ☐ '91 Ballerina Out Of Control
- ☐ '89 Between Something And Nothing
- ☐ '93 Sublime

OCHS, Phil
- ☐ '65 I Ain't Marchin' Anymore

O'CONNOR, Sinéad
- ☐ '90 Emperor's New Clothes, The
- ☐ '90 Nothing Compares 2 U ★

O'DAY, Alan
- ☐ '77 Undercover Angel ★

O'DELL, Kenny
- ☐ '67 Beautiful People

ODYSSEY
- ☐ '77 Native New Yorker

OFFSPRING, The
- ☐ '94 Come Out And Play
- ☐ '97 Gone Away
- ☐ '03 Hit That
- ☐ '00 Original Prankster
- ☐ '98 Pretty Fly (For A White Guy)
- ☐ '94 Self Esteem
- ☐ '99 Why Don't You Get A Job?

OHIO EXPRESS
- ☐ '67 Beg, Borrow And Steal
- ☐ '68 Chewy Chewy
- ☐ '68 Down At Lulu's
- ☐ '68 Yummy Yummy Yummy

OHIO PLAYERS
- ☐ '73 Ecstasy
- ☐ '74 Fire
- ☐ '76 Fopp
- ☐ '73 Funky Worm
- ☐ '75 Love Rollercoaster ★
- ☐ '74 Skin Tight
- ☐ '75 Sweet Sticky Thing
- ☐ '76 Who'd She Coo?

O'JAYS, The
- ☐ '72 Back Stabbers ★
- ☐ '76 Darlin' Darlin' Baby (Sweet, Tender, Love)
- ☐ '74 For The Love Of Money
- ☐ '79 Forever Mine
- ☐ '80 Girl, Don't Let It Get You Down
- ☐ '75 Give The People What They Want
- ☐ '89 Have You Had Your Love Today
- ☐ '75 I Love Music
- ☐ '76 Livin' For The Weekend
- ☐ '73 Love Train ★
- ☐ '87 Lovin' You
- ☐ '76 Message In Our Music
- ☐ '73 Put Your Hands Together
- ☐ '73 Time To Get Down
- ☐ '78 Use Ta Be My Girl

O'KAYSIONS, The
- ☐ '68 Girl Watcher

O'KEEFE, Danny
- ☐ '72 Good Time Charlie's Got The Blues

OK GO
- ☐ '06 Here It Goes Again

OLDFIELD, Mike
- ☐ '74 Tubular Bells

OL DIRTY BASTARD
- ☐ '99 Got Your Money *[w/ Kelis]*

OLEANDER
- ☐ '99 Why I'm Here

OLIVER
- ☐ '69 Good Morning Starshine ★
- ☐ '69 Jean

OLIVIA
- ☐ '06 Best Friend *[w/ 50 Cent]*
- ☐ '01 Bizounce

OLLIE & JERRY
- ☐ '84 Breakin'...There's No Stopping Us

OL SKOOL
- ☐ '98 Am I Dreaming

OLSSON, Nigel
- ☐ '78 Dancin' Shoes
- ☐ '79 Little Bit Of Soap

OLYMPICS, The
- ☐ '60 Big Boy Pete
- ☐ '63 Bounce, The
- ☐ '58 Western Movies

OMARION
- ☐ '07 Ice Box
- ☐ '05 O

OMC
- ☐ '97 How Bizarre ★

O'NEAL, Alexander
- ☐ '87 Fake
- ☐ '88 Never Knew Love Like This *[w/ Cherrelle]*
- ☐ '86 Saturday Love *[w/ Cherrelle]*

O'NEAL, Jamie
- ☐ '00 There Is No Arizona
- ☐ '01 When I Think About Angels

O'NEAL, Shaquille
- ☐ '93 (I Know I Got) Skillz
- ☐ '94 I'm Outstanding
- ☐ '93 What's Up Doc? (Can We Rock?)
  [w/ Fu-Schnickens]

100 PROOF AGED IN SOUL
- ☐ '70 Somebody's Been Sleeping

ONE 2 MANY
- ☐ '89 Downtown

112
- ☐ '99 Anywhere
- ☐ '96 Come See Me
- ☐ '97 Cupid
- ☐ '01 Dance With Me
- ☐ '00 It's Over Now
- ☐ '98 Love Me
- ☐ '96 Only You
- ☐ '01 Peaches & Cream ★
- ☐ '05 U Already Know

ONYX
- ☐ '93 Slam

OPUS
- ☐ '86 Live Is Life

ORBISON, Roy
- ☐ '60 Blue Angel
- ☐ '63 Blue Bayou
- ☐ '66 Breakin' Up Is Breakin' My Heart
- ☐ '61 Candy Man

ORBISON, Roy — cont'd

- ☐ '62 Crowd, The
- ☐ '61 Crying ★
- ☐ '62 Dream Baby (How Long Must I Dream)
- ☐ '63 Falling
- ☐ '65 Goodnight
- ☐ '60 I'm Hurtin'
- ☐ '63 In Dreams
- ☐ '64 Indian Wedding
- ☐ '64 It's Over
- ☐ '62 Léah
- ☐ '63 Mean Woman Blues
- ☐ '64 Oh, Pretty Woman ★
- ☐ '60 Only The Lonely ★
- ☐ '56 Ooby Dooby
- ☐ '63 Pretty Paper
- ☐ '65 Ride Away
- ☐ '61 Running Scared ★
- ☐ '65 (Say) You're My Girl
- ☐ '80 That Lovin' You Feelin' Again
  [w/ Emmylou Harris]
- ☐ '66 Twinkle Toes
- ☐ '60 Up Town
- ☐ '62 Workin' For The Man
- ☐ '89 You Got It

ORCHESTRAL MANOEUVRES IN THE DARK

- ☐ '88 Dreaming
- ☐ '86 (Forever) Live And Die
- ☐ '86 If You Leave ★
- ☐ '85 So In Love

ORIGINAL CASTE, The

- ☐ '69 One Tin Soldier

ORIGINALS, The

- ☐ '69 Baby, I'm For Real
- ☐ '70 Bells, The

ORLANDO, Tony (& DAWN)

- ☐ '61 Bless You
- ☐ '70 Candida
- ☐ '76 Cupid
- ☐ '61 Halfway To Paradise
- ☐ '75 He Don't Love You (Like I Love You) ★
- ☐ '71 I Play And Sing
- ☐ '70 Knock Three Times ★
- ☐ '74 Look In My Eyes Pretty Woman
- ☐ '69 Make Believe *[WIND]*
- ☐ '75 Mornin' Beautiful
- ☐ '73 Say, Has Anybody Seen My Sweet Gypsy Rose
- ☐ '74 Steppin' Out (Gonna Boogie Tonight)
- ☐ '71 Summer Sand
- ☐ '73 Tie A Yellow Ribbon Round The Ole Oak Tree ★
- ☐ '73 Who's In The Strawberry Patch With Sally

ORLEANS

- ☐ '75 Dance With Me
- ☐ '79 Love Takes Time
- ☐ '76 Still The One

ORLONS, The

- ☐ '63 Cross Fire!
- ☐ '62 Don't Hang Up
- ☐ '63 Not Me
- ☐ '63 South Street
- ☐ '62 Wah Watusi, The ★

ORR, Benjamin

- ☐ '86 Stay The Night

ORRICO, Stacie

- ☐ '03 (there's gotta be) More To Life

OSBORNE, Jeffrey

- ☐ '85 Borderlines, The
- ☐ '83 Don't You Get So Mad
- ☐ '82 I Really Don't Need No Light
- ☐ '84 Last Time I Made Love, The *[w/ Joyce Kennedy]*
- ☐ '87 Love Power *[w/ Dionne Warwick]*
- ☐ '82 On The Wings Of Love
- ☐ '90 Only Human
- ☐ '88 She's On The Left
- ☐ '83 Stay With Me Tonight
- ☐ '86 You Should Be Mine (The Woo Woo Song)

OSBORNE, Joan

- ☐ '95 One Of Us ★

OSBOURNE, Ozzy

- ☐ '89 Close My Eyes Forever *[w/ Lita Ford]*
- ☐ '81 Crazy Train
- ☐ '81 Flying High Again
- ☐ '01 Gets Me Through
- ☐ '07 I Don't Wanna Stop
- ☐ '91 Mama, I'm Coming Home
- ☐ '95 Perry Mason
- ☐ '92 Road To Nowhere
- ☐ '86 Shot In The Dark

OSLIN, K.T.

- ☐ '90 Come Next Monday
- ☐ '87 Do Ya'
- ☐ '87 80's Ladies

OSMOND, Donny

- ☐ '73 Are You Lonesome Tonight
- ☐ '76 C'mon Marianne
- ☐ '71 Go Away Little Girl
- ☐ '71 Hey Girl
- ☐ '73 Million To One, A
- ☐ '90 My Love Is A Fire
- ☐ '72 Puppy Love
- ☐ '89 Sacred Emotion
- ☐ '89 Soldier Of Love
- ☐ '71 Sweet And Innocent
- ☐ '72 Too Young
- ☐ '73 Twelfth Of Never, The
- ☐ '72 Why
- ☐ '73 Young Love

OSMOND, Donny & Marie

- ☐ '76 Ain't Nothing Like The Real Thing
- ☐ '75 Deep Purple
- ☐ '74 I'm Leaving It (All) Up To You
- ☐ '74 Morning Side Of The Mountain

□ '78 On The Shelf
□ '77 (You're My) Soul And Inspiration

OSMOND, Little Jimmy
□ '72 Long Haired Lover From Liverpool

OSMOND, Marie
□ '85 Meet Me In Montana *[w/ Dan Seals]*
□ '73 Paper Roses
□ '77 This Is The Way That I Feel
□ '75 Who's Sorry Now

OSMONDS, The
□ '72 Crazy Horses
□ '71 Double Lovin'
□ '72 Down By The Lazy River
□ '72 Hold Her Tight
□ '74 Love Me For A Reason
□ '71 One Bad Apple ★
□ '75 Proud One, The
□ '71 Yo-Yo

O'SULLIVAN, Gilbert
□ '72 Alone Again (Naturally) ★
□ '72 Clair
□ '73 Get Down
□ '73 Ooh Baby
□ '73 Out Of The Question

OTHER ONES, The
□ '87 Holiday

OTIS, Johnny, Show
□ '58 Willie And The Hand Jive

O-TOWN
□ '01 All Or Nothing ★
□ '00 Liquid Dreams

OUR LADY PEACE
□ '02 Somewhere Out There

OUTFIELD, The
□ '86 All The Love In The World
□ '90 For You
□ '85 Say It Isn't So
□ '87 Since You've Been Gone
□ '89 Voices Of Babylon
□ '86 Your Love

OUTKAST
□ '96 ATLiens
□ '96 Elevators (me & you)
□ '03 Hey Ya! ★
□ '00 Ms. Jackson ★
□ '94 Player's Ball
□ '04 Roses ★
□ '01 So Fresh, So Clean
□ '03 Way You Move, The ★
□ '01 Whole World, The

OUTLAWS
□ '80 (Ghost) Riders In The Sky
□ '75 Green Grass & High Tides
□ '75 There Goes Another Love Song

OUTSIDERS, The
□ '66 Girl In Love

□ '66 Help Me Girl
□ '66 Respectable
□ '66 Time Won't Let Me

OVERSTREET, Paul
□ '90 Daddy's Come Around
□ '90 Seein' My Father In Me

OWEN, Reg, & His Orchestra
□ '58 Manhattan Spiritual

OWENS, Buck
□ '63 Act Naturally
□ '65 Buckaroo
□ '65 Cryin' Time
□ '65 I've Got A Tiger By The Tail
□ '63 Love's Gonna Live Here
□ '64 My Heart Skips A Beat
□ '88 Streets Of Bakersfield *[w/ Dwight Yoakam]*
□ '64 Together Again

OWENS, Donnie
□ '58 Need You

OXO
□ '83 Whirly Girl

OZARK MOUNTAIN DAREDEVILS
□ '74 If You Wanna Get To Heaven
□ '75 Jackie Blue

O-ZONE
□ '04 Dragostea Din Tei (Ma Ya Hi)

P

PABLO, Petey
□ '04 Freek-A-Leek ★
□ '01 Raise Up

PABLO CRUISE
□ '81 Cool Love
□ '78 Don't Want To Live Without It
□ '79 I Go To Rio
□ '79 I Want You Tonight
□ '78 Love Will Find A Way
□ '77 Whatcha Gonna Do?

PACIFIC GAS & ELECTRIC
□ '70 Are You Ready?

PACKERS, The
□ '65 Hole In The Wall

PAGE, Jimmy
□ '94 Gallows Pole *[w/ Robert Plant]*
□ '98 Most High *[w/ Robert Plant]*
□ '93 Pride And Joy *[w/ David Coverdale]*

PAGE, Martin
□ '94 In The House Of Stone And Light

PAGE, Patti
□ '56 Allegheny Moon ★
□ '58 Another Time, Another Place
□ '58 Belonging To Someone
□ '55 Croce Di Oro (Cross Of Gold)
□ '56 Go On With The Wedding

PAGE, Patti — cont'd
- ☐ '65 Hush, Hush, Sweet Charlotte ★
- ☐ '57 I'll Remember Today
- ☐ '58 Left Right Out Of Your Heart
- ☐ '55 Let Me Go, Lover!
- ☐ '56 Mama From The Train
- ☐ '62 Most People Get Married
- ☐ '57 Old Cape Cod ★
- ☐ '60 One Of Us (Will Weep Tonight)
- ☐ '57 Poor Man's Roses (Or A Rich Man's Gold)
- ☐ '57 Wondering

PAGE, Tommy
- ☐ '90 I'll Be Your Everything ★
- ☐ '89 Shoulder To Cry On, A

PAIGE, Jennifer
- ☐ '98 Crush ★

PAIGE, Kevin
- ☐ '90 Anything I Want
- ☐ '89 Don't Shut Me Out

PAISLEY, Brad
- ☐ '05 Alcohol
- ☐ '03 Celebrity
- ☐ '99 He Didn't Have To Be
- ☐ '02 I'm Gonna Miss Her (The Fishin' Song)
- ☐ '03 Little Moments
- ☐ '05 Mud On The Tires
- ☐ '06 She's Everything
- ☐ '07 Ticks
- ☐ '01 Two People Fell In Love
- ☐ '00 We Danced
- ☐ '06 When I Get Where I'm Going *[w/ Dolly Parton]*
- ☐ '04 Whiskey Lullaby *[w/ Alison Krauss]*
- ☐ '06 World, The
- ☐ '01 Wrapped Around

PALMER, Robert
- ☐ '86 Addicted To Love ★
- ☐ '79 Bad Case Of Loving You (Doctor, Doctor)
- ☐ '79 Can We Still Be Friends
- ☐ '88 Early In The Morning
- ☐ '78 Every Kinda People
- ☐ '86 Hyperactive
- ☐ '86 I Didn't Mean To Turn You On
- ☐ '91 Mercy Mercy Me (The Ecology)/I Want You
- ☐ '88 Simply Irresistible ★
- ☐ '90 You're Amazing

PANIC! AT THE DISCO
- ☐ '06 I Write Sins Not Tragedies ★
- ☐ '06 Only Difference Between Martyrdom And Suicide Is Press Coverage, The

PAN'JABI MC
- ☐ '03 Beware Of The Boys

PAPA ROACH
- ☐ '07 Forever
- ☐ '04 Getting Away With Murder
- ☐ '00 Last Resort

- ☐ '04 Scars ★
- ☐ '02 She Loves Me Not

PAPERBOY
- ☐ '92 Ditty

PAPER LACE
- ☐ '74 Night Chicago Died, The ★

PARADE, The
- ☐ '67 Sunshine Girl

PARADONS, The
- ☐ '60 Diamonds And Pearls

PARAMORE
- ☐ '07 Misery Business

PARIS, Twila
- ☐ '91 Cry For The Desert
- ☐ '94 God Is In Control
- ☐ '86 He Is Exalted
- ☐ '91 I See You Standing

PARIS SISTERS, The
- ☐ '61 Be My Boy
- ☐ '62 He Knows I Love Him Too Much
- ☐ '61 I Love How You Love Me ★

PARKER, Fess
- ☐ '55 Ballad Of Davy Crockett
- ☐ '57 Wringle Wrangle

PARKER, Graham
- ☐ '77 Hold Back The Night
- ☐ '85 Wake Up (Next To You) *[w/ The Shot]*

PARKER, Ray Jr./Raydio
- ☐ '82 Bad Boy
- ☐ '84 Ghostbusters ★
- ☐ '85 Girls Are More Fun
- ☐ '83 I Still Can't Get Over Loving You
- ☐ '78 Jack And Jill
- ☐ '84 Jamie
- ☐ '82 Other Woman, The
- ☐ '81 That Old Song
- ☐ '80 Two Places At The Same Time
- ☐ '81 Woman Needs Love (Just Like You Do)
- ☐ '79 You Can't Change That

PARKER, Robert
- ☐ '66 Barefootin'

PARKS, Michael
- ☐ '70 Long Lonesome Highway

PARLIAMENT
- ☐ '78 Aqua Boogie (A Psychoalphadisco-betabioaquadoloop)
- ☐ '78 Flash Light ⌐
- ☐ '67 (I Wanna) Testify *[THE PARLIAMENTS]*
- ☐ '76 Tear The Roof Off The Sucker (Give Up The Funk)

PARR, John
- ☐ '84 Naughty Naughty
- ☐ '85 St. Elmo's Fire (Man In Motion) ★

PARSONS, Alan, Project
- ☐ '77 Breakdown
- ☐ '79 Damned If I Do
- ☐ '84 Don't Answer Me
- ☐ '77 Don't Let It Show
- ☐ '82 Eye In The Sky ★
- ☐ '80 Games People Play
- ☐ '77 I Robot
- ☐ '77 I Wouldn't Want To Be Like You
- ☐ '84 Prime Time
- ☐ '76 Raven, The
- ☐ '87 Standing On Higher Ground
- ☐ '76 (System Of) Doctor Tarr And Professor Fether
- ☐ '81 Time
- ☐ '78 What Goes Up

PARSONS, Bill — see BARE, Bobby

PARTLAND BROTHERS
- ☐ '87 Soul City

PARTNERS IN KRYME
- ☐ '90 Turtle Power!

PARTON, Dolly
- ☐ '78 Baby I'm Burnin'
- ☐ '04 Baby, It's Cold Outside
- ☐ '81 But You Know I Love You
- ☐ '71 Coat Of Many Colors
- ☐ '78 Heartbreaker
- ☐ '77 Here You Come Again ★
- ☐ '74 I Will Always Love You
- ☐ '95 I Will Always Love You [w/ Vince Gill]
- ☐ '83 Islands In The Stream [w/ Kenny Rogers] ★
- ☐ '74 Jolene
- ☐ '70 Joshua
- ☐ '80 9 To 5 ★
- ☐ '91 Rockin' Years [w/ Ricky Van Shelton]
- ☐ '80 Starting Over Again
- ☐ '78 Two Doors Down
- ☐ '06 When I Get Where I'm Going [w/ Brad Paisley]

PARTRIDGE FAMILY, The
- ☐ '72 Breaking Up Is Hard To Do
- ☐ '71 Doesn't Somebody Want To Be Wanted
- ☐ '70 I Think I Love You ★
- ☐ '71 I Woke Up In Love This Morning
- ☐ '71 I'll Meet You Halfway
- ☐ '71 It's One Of Those Nights (Yes Love)
- ☐ '72 Looking Through The Eyes Of Love

PARTY, The
- ☐ '91 In My Dreams
- ☐ '90 Summer Vacation

PASTELS, The
- ☐ '58 Been So Long

PASTEL SIX, The
- ☐ '62 Cinnamon Cinder (It's A Very Nice Dance)

PATIENCE & PRUDENCE
- ☐ '56 Gonna Get Along Without Ya Now
- ☐ '56 Tonight You Belong To Me

PATTON, Robbie
- ☐ '81 Don't Give It Up
- ☐ '83 Smiling Islands

PATTY, Sandi
- ☐ '90 Another Time, Another Place [w/ Wayne Watson]
- ☐ '83 Upon This Rock
- ☐ '85 Via Dolorosa
- ☐ '81 We Shall Behold Him

PATTY & THE EMBLEMS
- ☐ '64 Mixed-Up, Shook-Up, Girl

PAUL, Billy
- ☐ '72 Me And Mrs. Jones ★ ━
- ☐ '74 Thanks For Saving My Life

PAUL, Les, & Mary Ford
- ☐ '55 Amukiriki (The Lord Willing)
- ☐ '57 Cinco Robles (Five Oaks)
- ☐ '55 Hummingbird
- ☐ '61 Jura (I Swear I Love You)
- ☐ '58 Put A Ring On My Finger

PAUL, Sean
- ☐ '07 Break It Off [w/ Rihanna]
- ☐ '03 Get Busy ★
- ☐ '02 Gimme The Light ★
- ☐ '04 I'm Still In Love With You
- ☐ '03 Like Glue
- ☐ '06 Temperature ★
- ☐ '05 We Be Burnin' ★
- ☐ '06 When You Gonna (Give It Up To Me) ★

PAUL & PAULA
- ☐ '63 First Quarrel
- ☐ '62 Hey Paula ★
- ☐ '63 Young Lovers

PAVEMENT
- ☐ '97 Shady Lane
- ☐ '92 Summer Babe

PAVONE, Rita
- ☐ '64 Remember Me

PAYNE, Freda
- ☐ '70 Band Of Gold ★
- ☐ '71 Bring The Boys Home
- ☐ '70 Deeper & Deeper

PEACHES & HERB
- ☐ '67 Close Your Eyes
- ☐ '67 For Your Love
- ☐ '80 I Pledge My Love
- ☐ '66 Let's Fall In Love
- ☐ '67 Love Is Strange
- ☐ '79 Reunited ★
- ☐ '78 Shake Your Groove Thing ━
- ☐ '67 Two Little Kids

PEACH UNION
- ☐ '97 On My Own

PEARL, Leslie
- ☐ '82 If The Love Fits Wear It

PEARL JAM
- ☐ '92 Alive
- ☐ '94 Better Man ★
- ☐ '92 Black
- ☐ '95 Corduroy
- ☐ '93 Daughter
- ☐ '94 Dissident
- ☐ '92 Even Flow
- ☐ '98 Given To Fly
- ☐ '93 Go
- ☐ '96 Hail, Hail
- ☐ '95 I Got Id
- ☐ '92 Jeremy ★
- ☐ '99 Last Kiss ★
- ☐ '00 Nothing As It Seems
- ☐ '94 Spin The Black Circle
- ☐ '94 Tremor Christ
- ☐ '96 Who You Are
- ☐ '06 World Wide Suicide
- ☐ '94 Yellow Ledbetter

PEBBLES
- ☐ '88 Girlfriend
- ☐ '90 Giving You The Benefit
- ☐ '90 Love Makes Things Happen
- ☐ '88 Mercedes Boy ★
- ☐ '88 Take Your Time

PEEBLES, Ann
- ☐ '73 I Can't Stand The Rain

PEEPLES, Nia
- ☐ '91 Street Of Dreams
- ☐ '88 Trouble

PENDERGRASS, Teddy
- ☐ '80 Can't We Try
- ☐ '78 Close The Door
- ☐ '91 It Should've Been You
- ☐ '88 Joy
- ☐ '80 Love T.K.O.
- ☐ '79 Turn Off The Lights
- ☐ '88 2 A.M.
- ☐ '81 Two Hearts *[w/ Stephanie Mills]*

PENGUINS, The
- ☐ '55 Earth Angel ★

PENISTON, Ce Ce
- ☐ '91 Finally
- ☐ '94 I'm In The Mood
- ☐ '92 Keep On Walkin'
- ☐ '92 We Got A Love Thang

PENN, Michael
- ☐ '90 No Myth

PEOPLE
- ☐ '68 I Love You

PEOPLE'S CHOICE
- ☐ '75 Do It Any Way You Wanna

(continued)
- ☐ '71 I Likes To Do It

PEPPERMINT RAINBOW, The
- ☐ '69 Will You Be Staying After Sunday

PEREZ, Amanda
- ☐ '03 Angel

PERFECT CIRCLE, A
- ☐ '00 Judith
- ☐ '03 Outsider, The
- ☐ '03 Weak And Powerless

PERFECT GENTLEMEN
- ☐ '90 Ooh La La (I Can't Get Over You)

PERICOLI, Emilio
- ☐ '62 Al Di La'

PERKINS, Carl
- ☐ '56 Blue Suede Shoes ★
- ☐ '56 Boppin' The Blues
- ☐ '56 Honey Don't
- ☐ '57 Matchbox

PERKINS, Tony
- ☐ '57 Moon-Light Swim

PERRY, Phil
- ☐ '91 Call Me

PERRY, Steve
- ☐ '82 Don't Fight It *[w/ Kenny Loggins]*
- ☐ '84 Foolish Heart
- ☐ '84 Oh Sherrie ★
- ☐ '84 She's Mine
- ☐ '84 Strung Out
- ☐ '94 You Better Wait

PERSUADERS, The
- ☐ '73 Some Guys Have All The Luck
- ☐ '71 Thin Line Between Love & Hate

PETER & GORDON
- ☐ '64 I Don't Want To See You Again
- ☐ '65 I Go To Pieces
- ☐ '66 Knight In Rusty Armour
- ☐ '66 Lady Godiva
- ☐ '64 Nobody I Know
- ☐ '67 Sunday For Tea
- ☐ '65 To Know You Is To Love You
- ☐ '65 True Love Ways
- ☐ '66 Woman
- ☐ '64 World Without Love, A ★

PETER, PAUL & MARY
- ☐ '63 Blowin' In The Wind
- ☐ '69 Day Is Done
- ☐ '63 Don't Think Twice, It's All Right
- ☐ '65 For Lovin' Me
- ☐ '67 I Dig Rock And Roll Music
- ☐ '62 If I Had A Hammer
- ☐ '69 Leaving On A Jet Plane ★
- ☐ '62 Lemon Tree
- ☐ '63 Puff (The Magic Dragon) ★
- ☐ '63 Stewball
- ☐ '67 Too Much Of Nothing

PETERS, Bernadette
- ☐ '80 Gee Whiz

PETERSEN, Paul
- ☐ '62 My Dad
- ☐ '62 She Can't Find Her Keys

PETERSON, Michael
- ☐ '97 Drink, Swear, Steal & Lie
- ☐ '97 From Here To Eternity

PETERSON, Ray
- ☐ '60 Corinna, Corinna
- ☐ '59 Goodnight My Love
- ☐ '61 Missing You
- ☐ '60 Tell Laura I Love Her ★
- ☐ '59 Wonder Of You, The

PETS, The
- ☐ '58 Cha-Hua-Hua

PET SHOP BOYS
- ☐ '88 Always On My Mind
- ☐ '88 Domino Dancing
- ☐ '87 It's A Sin
- ☐ '86 Opportunities (Let's Make Lots Of Money)
- ☐ '86 West End Girls ★ ——
- ☐ '87 What Have I Done To Deserve This? [w/ Dusty Springfield] ★

PETTY, Tom, & The Heartbreakers
- ☐ '77 American Girl
- ☐ '77 Breakdown
- ☐ '83 Change Of Heart
- ☐ '85 Don't Come Around Here No More ★
- ☐ '79 Don't Do Me Like That
- ☐ '79 Even The Losers
- ☐ '89 Free Fallin' ★
- ☐ '79 Here Comes My Girl
- ☐ '78 I Need To Know
- ☐ '89 I Won't Back Down
- ☐ '91 Into The Great Wide Open
- ☐ '87 Jammin' Me
- ☐ '91 Learning To Fly
- ☐ '78 Listen To Her Heart
- ☐ '93 Mary Jane's Last Dance
- ☐ '86 Needles And Pins [w/ Stevie Nicks]
- ☐ '91 Out In The Cold
- ☐ '80 Refugee
- ☐ '89 Runnin' Down A Dream
- ☐ '81 Stop Draggin' My Heart Around [w/ Stevie Nicks] ★
- ☐ '81 Waiting, The
- ☐ '94 You Don't Know How It Feels
- ☐ '82 You Got Lucky
- ☐ '94 You Wreck Me

PHAIR, Liz
- ☐ '94 Supernova
- ☐ '03 Why Can't I?

PHARRELL
- ☐ '03 Frontin' [w/ Jay-Z] ★

PHILLIPS, Little Esther
- ☐ '62 Release Me

- ☐ '75 What A Diff'rence A Day Makes

PHILLIPS, John
- ☐ '70 Mississippi

PHILLIPS, Phil, With The Twilights
- ☐ '59 Sea Of Love ★

PHOTOGLO, Jim
- ☐ '81 Fool In Love With You
- ☐ '80 We Were Meant To Be Lovers

PICKETT, Bobby "Boris", & The Crypt-Kickers
- ☐ '62 Monster Mash ★
- ☐ '62 Monsters' Holiday

PICKETT, Wilson
- ☐ '71 Don't Knock My Love
- ☐ '71 Don't Let The Green Grass Fool You
- ☐ '70 Engine Number 9
- ☐ '67 Everybody Needs Somebody To Love
- ☐ '71 Fire And Water
- ☐ '67 Funky Broadway
- ☐ '68 Hey Jude
- ☐ '67 I Found A Love
- ☐ '68 I'm A Midnight Mover
- ☐ '65 In The Midnight Hour ★
- ☐ '66 Land Of 1000 Dances
- ☐ '66 Mustang Sally
- ☐ '68 She's Lookin' Good
- ☐ '66 634-5789 (Soulsville, U.S.A.)
- ☐ '67 Stag-O-Lee
- ☐ '70 Sugar Sugar

PIERCE, Webb
- ☐ '59 I Ain't Never
- ☐ '55 In The Jailhouse Now
- ☐ '55 Love, Love, Love

PILOT
- ☐ '75 Magic

P!NK
- ☐ '02 Don't Let Me Get Me
- ☐ '02 Family Portrait
- ☐ '01 Get The Party Started ★
- ☐ '02 Just Like A Pill
- ☐ '01 Lady Marmalade [w/ Christina Aguilera, Lil' Kim & Mya] ★
- ☐ '00 Most Girls ★
- ☐ '06 Stupid Girls ★
- ☐ '00 There You Go ★
- ☐ '07 U + Ur Hand ★
- ☐ '07 Who Knew ★
- ☐ '01 You Make Me Sick

PINK FLOYD
- ☐ '80 Another Brick In The Wall ★
- ☐ '73 Brain Damage/Eclipse
- ☐ '80 Comfortably Numb
- ☐ '73 Great Gig In The Sky
- ☐ '75 Have A Cigar
- ☐ '80 Hey You
- ☐ '94 Keep Talking
- ☐ '87 Learning To Fly
- ☐ '73 Money ★

PINK FLOYD — cont'd
- ☐ '87 On The Turning Away
- ☐ '71 One Of These Days
- ☐ '80 Run Like Hell
- ☐ '67 See Emily Play
- ☐ '75 Shine On You Crazy Diamond
- ☐ '75 Speak To Me/Breathe
- ☐ '73 Time
- ☐ '73 Us And Them
- ☐ '75 Welcome To The Machine
- ☐ '75 Wish You Were Here
- ☐ '80 Young Lust

PINK LADY
- ☐ '79 Kiss In The Dark

PIPKINS, The
- ☐ '70 Gimme Dat Ding

PITBULL
- ☐ '04 Culo *[w/ Lil Jon]*

PITNEY, Gene
- ☐ '66 Backstage
- ☐ '61 Every Breath I Take
- ☐ '62 Half Heaven - Half Heartache
- ☐ '65 I Must Be Seeing Things
- ☐ '61 (I Wanna) Love My Life Away
- ☐ '64 I'm Gonna Be Strong
- ☐ '62 If I Didn't Have A Dime (To Play The Jukebox)
- ☐ '64 It Hurts To Be In Love
- ☐ '65 Last Chance To Turn Around
- ☐ '65 Looking Through The Eyes Of Love
- ☐ '62 (Man Who Shot) Liberty Valance ★
- ☐ '63 Mecca
- ☐ '62 Only Love Can Break A Heart ★
- ☐ '68 She's A Heartbreaker
- ☐ '61 Town Without Pity
- ☐ '63 True Love Never Runs Smooth
- ☐ '63 Twenty Four Hours From Tulsa

PIXIES
- ☐ '89 Here Comes Your Man
- ☐ '89 Monkey Gone To Heaven

PIXIES THREE, The
- ☐ '63 Birthday Party

PLAIN WHITE T'S
- ☐ '07 Hey There Delilah ★

PLANET SOUL
- ☐ '95 Set U Free

PLANT, Robert
- ☐ '83 Big Log
- ☐ '82 Burning Down One Side
- ☐ '93 Calling To You
- ☐ '94 Gallows Pole *[w/ Jimmy Page]*
- ☐ '88 Heaven Knows
- ☐ '90 Hurting Kind (I've Got My Eyes On You)
- ☐ '83 In The Mood
- ☐ '85 Little By Little
- ☐ '98 Most High *[w/ Jimmy Page]*
- ☐ '83 Other Arms
- ☐ '88 Ship Of Fools

- ☐ '88 Tall Cool One

PLATTERS, The
- ☐ '59 Enchanted
- ☐ '55 Great Pretender, The ★
- ☐ '60 Harbor Lights
- ☐ '57 He's Mine
- ☐ '66 I Love You 1000 Times
- ☐ '61 I'll Never Smile Again
- ☐ '57 I'm Sorry
- ☐ '61 If I Didn't Care
- ☐ '56 It Isn't Right
- ☐ '57 My Dream
- ☐ '56 My Prayer ★
- ☐ '56 On My Word Of Honor
- ☐ '56 One In A Million
- ☐ '55 Only You (And You Alone) ★
- ☐ '60 Red Sails In The Sunset
- ☐ '59 Remember When
- ☐ '58 Smoke Gets In Your Eyes ★
- ☐ '60 To Each His Own
- ☐ '58 Twilight Time ★
- ☐ '59 Where
- ☐ '67 With This Ring
- ☐ '56 You'll Never Never Know
- ☐ '56 (You've Got) The Magic Touch

PLAYA
- ☐ '98 Cheers 2 U

PLAYER
- ☐ '77 Baby Come Back ★ ▬
- ☐ '78 Prisoner Of Your Love
- ☐ '78 This Time I'm In It For Love

PLAYMATES, The
- ☐ '58 Beep Beep
- ☐ '58 Don't Go Home
- ☐ '58 Jo-Ann
- ☐ '60 Wait For Me
- ☐ '59 What Is Love?

PLIES
- ☐ '07 Shawty ★

PLIMSOULS, The
- ☐ '83 Million Miles Away, A

PM DAWN
- ☐ '92 I'd Die Without You ★
- ☐ '93 Looking Through Patient Eyes ★
- ☐ '92 Paper Doll
- ☐ '91 Set Adrift On Memory Bliss ★

POCO
- ☐ '89 Call It Love
- ☐ '79 Crazy Love
- ☐ '79 Heart Of The Night
- ☐ '89 Nothin' To Hide

P.O.D.
- ☐ '01 Alive
- ☐ '99 Set Your Eyes To Zion
- ☐ '01 Youth Of The Nation

POETS, The
- ☐ '66 She Blew A Good Thing

POINDEXTER, Buster
- ☐ '88 Hot Hot Hot

POINT BLANK
- ☐ '81 Nicole

POINTER, Bonnie
- ☐ '79 Heaven Must Have Sent You
- ☐ '79 I Can't Help Myself (Sugar Pie, Honey Bunch)

POINTER SISTERS
- ☐ '82 American Music
- ☐ '84 Automatic
- ☐ '85 Dare Me
- ☐ '74 Fairytale
- ☐ '78 Fire ★
- ☐ '86 Goldmine
- ☐ '79 Happiness
- ☐ '80 He's So Shy ★ ⚊
- ☐ '75 How Long (Betcha' Got A Chick On The Side)
- ☐ '82 I'm So Excited
- ☐ '84 Jump (For My Love) ★
- ☐ '84 Neutron Dance
- ☐ '82 Should I Do It
- ☐ '81 Slow Hand ★
- ☐ '73 Yes We Can Can

POISON
- ☐ '88 Every Rose Has Its Thorn ★
- ☐ '88 Fallen Angel
- ☐ '87 I Won't Forget You
- ☐ '91 Life Goes On
- ☐ '88 Nothin' But A Good Time
- ☐ '91 Ride The Wind
- ☐ '90 Something To Believe In
- ☐ '87 Talk Dirty To Me
- ☐ '90 Unskinny Bop ★
- ☐ '89 Your Mama Don't Dance

POLECATS
- ☐ '83 Make A Circuit With Me

POLICE, The
- ☐ '80 De Do Do Do, De Da Da Da ★
- ☐ '81 Don't Stand So Close To Me
- ☐ '83 Every Breath You Take ★
- ☐ '81 Every Little Thing She Does Is Magic ★
- ☐ '83 King Of Pain ★
- ☐ '79 Message In A Bottle
- ☐ '79 Roxanne ★
- ☐ '82 Spirits In The Material World
- ☐ '83 Synchronicity II
- ☐ '84 Wrapped Around Your Finger

PONI-TAILS
- ☐ '58 Born Too Late

POP, Iggy
- ☐ '90 Candy
- ☐ '90 Home
- ☐ '69 I Wanna Be Your Dog *[THE STOOGES]*
- ☐ '77 Lust For Life
- ☐ '86 Real Wild Child (Wild One)
- ☐ '73 Search And Destroy *[IGGY & THE STOOGES]*

POPPY FAMILY, The
- ☐ '70 That's Where I Went Wrong
- ☐ '70 Which Way You Goin' Billy? ★

PORNO FOR PYROS
- ☐ '93 Pets

PORTRAIT
- ☐ '92 Here We Go Again!

POSEY, Sandy
- ☐ '66 Born A Woman
- ☐ '67 I Take It Back
- ☐ '66 Single Girl
- ☐ '67 What A Woman In Love Won't Do

POSITIVE K
- ☐ '92 I Got A Man

POST, Mike
- ☐ '75 Rockford Files, The
- ☐ '81 Theme From Hill Street Blues, The
- ☐ '82 (Theme From) Magnum P.I.

POURCEL, Franck
- ☐ '59 Only You

POWELL, Jane
- ☐ '56 True Love

POWELL, Jesse
- ☐ '99 You

POWERS, Joey
- ☐ '63 Midnight Mary

POWER STATION, The
- ☐ '85 Communication
- ☐ '85 Get It On
- ☐ '85 Some Like It Hot ⚊

POWTER, Daniel
- ☐ '06 Bad Day ★

POZO-SECO SINGERS
- ☐ '66 I Can Make It With You
- ☐ '66 Look What You've Done
- ☐ '66 Time

PRADO, Perez, & His Orchestra
- ☐ '55 Cherry Pink And Apple Blossom White ★
- ☐ '58 Patricia ★

PRATT & McCLAIN
- ☐ '76 Happy Days

PRELUDE
- ☐ '74 After The Goldrush

PREMIERS, The
- ☐ '64 Farmer John

PRESIDENTS, The
- ☐ '70 5-10-15-20 (25-30 Years Of Love)

PRESIDENTS OF THE UNITED STATES OF AMERICA, The
- ☐ '95 Lump
- ☐ '96 Peaches

PRESLEY, Elvis

- ☐ '64 Ain't That Loving You Baby
- ☐ '57 All Shook Up ★
- ☐ '72 American Trilogy, An
- ☐ '62 Anything That's Part Of You
- ☐ '56 Anyway You Want Me (That's How I Will Be)
- ☐ '60 Are You Lonesome To-night? ★
- ☐ '64 Ask Me
- ☐ '67 Big Boss Man
- ☐ '59 Big Hunk O' Love, A ★
- ☐ '57 Blue Christmas
- ☐ '61 Blue Hawaii
- ☐ '56 Blue Suede Shoes
- ☐ '63 Bossa Nova Baby
- ☐ '72 Burning Love ★
- ☐ '61 Can't Help Falling In Love ★
- ☐ '69 Clean Up Your Own Back Yard
- ☐ '65 Crying In The Chapel ★
- ☐ '65 Do The Clam
- ☐ '58 Don't ★
- ☐ '58 Don't Ask Me Why
- ☐ '56 Don't Be Cruel ★
- ☐ '69 Don't Cry Daddy
- ☐ '58 Doncha' Think It's Time
- ☐ '60 Fame And Fortune
- ☐ '61 Flaming Star
- ☐ '62 Follow That Dream
- ☐ '59 Fool Such As I, A
- ☐ '66 Frankie And Johnny
- ☐ '62 Good Luck Charm ★
- ☐ '68 Guitar Man
- ☐ '58 Hard Headed Woman ★
- ☐ '56 Heartbreak Hotel ★
- ☐ '56 Hound Dog ★
- ☐ '76 Hurt
- ☐ '58 I Beg Of You
- ☐ '61 I Feel So Bad
- ☐ '58 I Got Stung
- ☐ '60 I Gotta Know
- ☐ '59 I Need Your Love Tonight
- ☐ '70 I Really Don't Want To Know
- ☐ '56 I Want You, I Need You, I Love You
- ☐ '56 I Was The One
- ☐ '65 I'm Yours
- ☐ '74 I've Got A Thing About You Baby
- ☐ '70 I've Lost You
- ☐ '66 If Every Day Was Like Christmas
- ☐ '68 If I Can Dream
- ☐ '74 If You Talk In Your Sleep
- ☐ '69 In The Ghetto ★
- ☐ '67 Indescribably Blue
- ☐ '64 It Hurts Me
- ☐ '60 It's Now Or Never ★
- ☐ '57 Jailhouse Rock ★
- ☐ '70 Kentucky Rain
- ☐ '58 King Creole
- ☐ '62 King Of The Whole Wide World
- ☐ '64 Kiss Me Quick
- ☐ '64 Kissin' Cousins
- ☐ '68 Little Less Conversation, A
- ☐ '61 Little Sister
- ☐ '61 Lonely Man
- ☐ '66 Love Letters

- ☐ '56 Love Me ★
- ☐ '56 Love Me Tender ★
- ☐ '57 Loving You
- ☐ '61 (Marie's the Name) His Latest Flame
- ☐ '69 Memories
- ☐ '60 Mess Of Blues, A
- ☐ '76 Moody Blue
- ☐ '56 My Baby Left Me
- ☐ '75 My Boy
- ☐ '77 My Way
- ☐ '59 My Wish Came True
- ☐ '55 Mystery Train ★
- ☐ '63 One Broken Heart For Sale
- ☐ '58 One Night
- ☐ '57 Peace In The Valley
- ☐ '57 Playing For Keeps
- ☐ '56 Poor Boy
- ☐ '74 Promised Land
- ☐ '65 Puppet On A String
- ☐ '62 Return To Sender ★
- ☐ '61 Rock-A-Hula Baby
- ☐ '69 Rubberneckin'
- ☐ '61 Sentimental Me
- ☐ '72 Separate Ways
- ☐ '62 She's Not You
- ☐ '66 Spinout
- ☐ '73 Steamroller Blues
- ☐ '60 Stuck On You ★
- ☐ '64 Such A Night
- ☐ '65 (Such An) Easy Question
- ☐ '61 Surrender ★
- ☐ '62 Suspicion
- ☐ '69 Suspicious Minds ★
- ☐ '57 Teddy Bear ★
- ☐ '66 Tell Me Why
- ☐ '54 That's All Right
- ☐ '57 That's When Your Heartaches Begin
- ☐ '70 There Goes My Everything
- ☐ '57 Too Much ★
- ☐ '57 Treat Me Nice
- ☐ '75 T-R-O-U-B-L-E
- ☐ '68 U.S. Male
- ☐ '72 Until It's Time For You To Go
- ☐ '64 Viva Las Vegas
- ☐ '77 Way Down
- ☐ '58 Wear My Ring Around Your Neck
- ☐ '64 What'd I Say
- ☐ '56 When My Blue Moon Turns To Gold Again
- ☐ '71 Where Did They Go, Lord
- ☐ '61 Wild In The Country
- ☐ '63 Witchcraft
- ☐ '70 Wonder Of You, The
- ☐ '60 Wooden Heart
- ☐ '70 You Don't Have To Say You Love Me
- ☐ '63 (You're the) Devil In Disguise ★
- ☐ '68 Your Time Hasn't Come Yet, Baby

PRESSHA

- ☐ '98 Splackavellie

PRESTON, Billy

- ☐ '74 Nothing From Nothing ★
- ☐ '72 Outa-Space
- ☐ '73 Space Race

136

- ☐ '74 Struttin'
- ☐ '73 Will It Go Round In Circles ★
- ☐ '79 With You I'm Born Again *[w/ Syreeta]*

PRESTON, Johnny
- ☐ '60 Cradle Of Love
- ☐ '60 Feel So Fine
- ☐ '59 Running Bear ★

PRESTON, Robert
- ☐ '62 Seventy Six Trombones

PRETENDERS, The
- ☐ '82 Back On The Chain Gang ★
- ☐ '80 Brass In Pocket (I'm Special)
- ☐ '86 Don't Get Me Wrong
- ☐ '94 I'll Stand By You ★
- ☐ '81 Message Of Love
- ☐ '83 Middle Of The Road
- ☐ '86 My Baby
- ☐ '82 My City Was Gone
- ☐ '94 Night In My Velns
- ☐ '84 Show Me
- ☐ '80 Stop Your Sobbing
- ☐ '84 2000 Miles

PRETTY POISON
- ☐ '87 Catch Me (I'm Falling)
- ☐ '88 Nightime

PRETTY RICKY
- ☐ '05 Grind With Me ★
- ☐ '07 On The Hotline
- ☐ '05 Your Body

PRICE, Kelly
- ☐ '98 Friend of Mine

PRICE, Lloyd
- ☐ '59 Come Into My Heart
- ☐ '59 I'm Gonna Get Married ★
- ☐ '57 Just Because
- ☐ '60 Lady Luck
- ☐ '63 Misty
- ☐ '59 Personality ★
- ☐ '60 Question
- ☐ '58 Stagger Lee ★
- ☐ '59 Where Were You (On Our Wedding Day)?

PRICE, Ray
- ☐ '58 City Lights
- ☐ '56 Crazy Arms
- ☐ '67 Danny Boy
- ☐ '70 For The Good Times

PRIDE, Charley
- ☐ '67 Crystal Chandelier
- ☐ '67 Does My Ring Hurt Your Finger
- ☐ '68 Easy Part's Over, The
- ☐ '70 Is Anybody Goin' To San Antone
- ☐ '69 Kaw-Liga [live]
- ☐ '71 Kiss An Angel Good Mornin'
- ☐ '70 Wonder Could I Live There Anymore

PRIEST, Maxi
- ☐ '90 Close To You ★
- ☐ '91 Set The Night To Music *[w/ Roberta Flack]*

- ☐ '96 That Girl
- ☐ '88 Wild World

PRIMA, Louis, & Keely Smith
- ☐ '56 Just A Gigolo/I Ain't Got Nobody
- ☐ '58 That Old Black Magic
- ☐ '60 Wonderland By Night *[LOUIS PRIMA]*

PRIMITIVE RADIO GODS
- ☐ '96 Standing Outside A Broken Phone Booth With Money In My Hand

PRINCE
- ☐ '88 Alphabet St.
- ☐ '89 Arms Of Orion, The *[w/ Sheena Easton]*
- ☐ '89 Batdance ★
- ☐ '81 Controversy
- ☐ '91 Cream ★
- ☐ '83 Delirious
- ☐ '91 Diamonds And Pearls ★
- ☐ '91 Gett Off
- ☐ '87 I Could Never Take The Place Of Your Man
- ☐ '95 I Hate U
- ☐ '79 I Wanna Be Your Lover ⎯
- ☐ '84 I Would Die 4 U
- ☐ '86 Kiss ★
- ☐ '84 Let's Go Crazy ★
- ☐ '94 Letitgo
- ☐ '83 Little Red Corvette ★
- ☐ '92 Money Don't Matter 2 Night
- ☐ '94 Most Beautiful Girl In The World, The ★
- ☐ '86 Mountains
- ☐ '92 My Name Is Prince
- ☐ '82 **1999**
- ☐ '89 Partyman
- ☐ '85 Pop Life ⎯
- ☐ '84 Purple Rain ★ ⎯
- ☐ '85 Raspberry Beret ★⎯
- ☐ '92 7 ★
- ☐ '87 Sign 'O' The Times
- ☐ '85 Take Me With U
- ☐ '90 Thieves In The Temple
- ☐ '87 U Got The Look
- ☐ '84 When Doves Cry ★ ⎯

PRISM
- ☐ '82 Don't Let Him Know

PROBY, P.J.
- ☐ '67 Niki Hoeky

PROCLAIMERS, The
- ☐ '93 I'm Gonna Be (500 Miles) ★

PROCOL HARUM
- ☐ '72 Conquistador [live]
- ☐ '67 Homburg
- ☐ '72 Salty Dog, A [live]
- ☐ '67 Whiter Shade Of Pale, A ★

PRODIGY
- ☐ '97 Firestarter

PRODUCERS, The
- ☐ '81 What's He Got?

PRODUCT G&B, The — see SANTANA

PROFYLE
- ☐ '00 Liar

PRUETT, Jeanne
- ☐ '73 Satin Sheets

PRYSOCK, Arthur
- ☐ '68 Working Man's Prayer, A

PSEUDO ECHO
- ☐ '87 Funky Town

PSYCHEDELIC FURS
- ☐ '88 All That Money Wants
- ☐ '84 Ghost In You
- ☐ '87 Heartbreak Beat
- ☐ '89 House
- ☐ '83 Love My Way
- ☐ '81 Pretty In Pink
- ☐ '91 Until She Comes

PUBLIC ANNOUNCEMENT
- ☐ '98 Body Bumpin' Yippie-Yi-Yo
- ☐ '00 Mamacita

PUBLIC ENEMY
- ☐ '88 Bring The Noise
- ☐ '91 Can't Truss It
- ☐ '88 Don't Believe The Hype
- ☐ '89 Fight The Power
- ☐ '94 Give It Up
- ☐ '90 911 Is A Joke

PUBLIC IMAGE LTD.
- ☐ '89 Disappointed
- ☐ '90 Don't Ask Me
- ☐ '84 This Is Not A Love Song

PUCKETT, Gary, & The Union Gap
- ☐ '69 Don't Give In To Him
- ☐ '68 Lady Willpower
- ☐ '68 Over You
- ☐ '69 This Girl Is A Woman Now
- ☐ '67 Woman, Woman ★
- ☐ '68 Young Girl

PUDDLE OF MUDD
- ☐ '03 Away From Me
- ☐ '01 Blurry ★
- ☐ '01 Control
- ☐ '02 Drift & Die
- ☐ '07 Famous
- ☐ '02 She Hates Me

PUFF DADDY/P. DIDDY/DIDDY
- ☐ '01 Bad Boy For Life [w/ Black Rob & Mark Curry]
- ☐ '98 Been Around The World
- ☐ '02 Bump, Bump, Bump [w/ B2K] ★
- ☐ '97 Can't Nobody Hold Me Down ★
- ☐ '06 Come To Me ★
- ☐ '98 Come With Me ★
- ☐ '02 I Need A Girl (Part One) ★
- ☐ '02 I Need A Girl (Part Two) [w/ Ginuwine] ★
- ☐ '97 I'll Be Missing You [w/ Faith Evans] ★
- ☐ '97 It's All About The Benjamins ★
- ☐ '07 Last Night

- ☐ '99 Satisfy You ★
- ☐ '03 Shake Ya Tailfeather [w/ Nelly & Murphy Lee] ★
- ☐ '98 Victory

PUPPIES, The
- ☐ '94 Funky Y-2-C

PURE PRAIRIE LEAGUE
- ☐ '75 Amie
- ☐ '80 I'm Almost Ready
- ☐ '80 Let Me Love You Tonight
- ☐ '81 Still Right Here In My Heart

PURIFY, James & Bobby
- ☐ '66 I'm Your Puppet
- ☐ '67 Let Love Come Between Us
- ☐ '67 Shake A Tail Feather

PURPLE RIBBON ALL-STARS
- ☐ '05 Kryptonite (I'm On It)

PURSELL, Bill
- ☐ '63 Our Winter Love

PUSSYCAT DOLLS, The
- ☐ '06 Beep ★
- ☐ '06 Buttons ★
- ☐ '05 Don't Cha ★
- ☐ '05 Stickwitu ★
- ☐ '07 Wait A Minute

PYRAMIDS, The
- ☐ '64 Penetration

Q

Q
- ☐ '77 Dancin' Man

QB FINEST
- ☐ '01 Oochie Wally

Q-TIP
- ☐ '99 Vivrant Thing

QUAD CITY DJ'S
- ☐ '96 C'Mon N' Ride It (The Train) ★
- ☐ '96 Space Jam

QUARTERFLASH
- ☐ '82 Find Another Fool
- ☐ '81 Harden My Heart ★
- ☐ '83 Take Me To Heart

QUATRO, Suzi
- ☐ '79 Stumblin' In [w/ Chris Norman]

QUEEN
- ☐ '80 Another One Bites The Dust ★
- ☐ '78 Bicycle Race
- ☐ '82 Body Language
- ☐ '76 Bohemian Rhapsody ★
- ☐ '79 Crazy Little Thing Called Love ★
- ☐ '78 Don't Stop Me Now
- ☐ '80 Don't Try Suicide
- ☐ '78 Fat Bottomed Girls
- ☐ '89 I Want It All
- ☐ '75 Killer Queen

- ☐ '80 Play The Game
- ☐ '84 Radio Ga-Ga
- ☐ '76 Somebody To Love
- ☐ '93 Somebody To Love [live] *[w/ George Michael]*
- ☐ '77 Tie Your Mother Down
- ☐ '81 Under Pressure *[w/ David Bowie]* ★
- ☐ '77 We Will Rock You/We Are The Champions ★
- ☐ '76 You're My Best Friend

QUEEN LATIFAH
- ☐ '90 Ladies First
- ☐ '93 U.N.I.T.Y.

QUEEN PEN
- ☐ '98 All My Love

QUEENS OF THE STONE AGE
- ☐ '05 Little Sister
- ☐ '02 No One Knows

QUEENSRYCHE
- ☐ '93 Real World
- ☐ '97 Sign Of The Times
- ☐ '91 Silent Lucidity

? & THE MYSTERIANS
- ☐ '66 96 Tears ★
- ☐ '66 I Need Somebody

QUICKSILVER MESSENGER SERVICE
- ☐ '70 Fresh Air

QUIET RIOT
- ☐ '84 Bang Your Head (Metal Health)
- ☐ '83 Cum On Feel The Noize ★

QUIN-TONES, The
- ☐ '58 Down The Aisle Of Love

R

RABBITT, Eddie
- ☐ '80 Drivin' My Life Away ★
- ☐ '79 Every Which Way But Loose ★
- ☐ '77 I Can't Help Myself
- ☐ '82 I Don't Know Where To Start
- ☐ '80 I Love A Rainy Night ★
- ☐ '89 On Second Thought
- ☐ '81 Someone Could Lose A Heart Tonight
- ☐ '81 Step By Step
- ☐ '79 Suspicions
- ☐ '82 You And I *[w/ Crystal Gayle]*
- ☐ '83 You Can't Run From Love

RACONTEURS
- ☐ '06 Steady, As She Goes

RADIOHEAD
- ☐ '93 Creep
- ☐ '95 Fake Plastic Trees
- ☐ '97 Paranoid Android

RAEKWON
- ☐ '95 Glaciers Of Ice
- ☐ '95 Ice Cream

RAFFERTY, Gerry
- ☐ '78 Baker Street ★
- ☐ '79 Days Gone Down (Still Got The Light In Your Eyes)
- ☐ '79 Get It Right Next Time
- ☐ '78 Home And Dry
- ☐ '78 Right Down The Line

RAGE AGAINST THE MACHINE
- ☐ '96 Bulls On Parade

RAINBOW
- ☐ '79 Since You Been Gone
- ☐ '82 Stone Cold
- ☐ '83 Street Of Dreams

RAINDROPS, The
- ☐ '63 Kind Of Boy You Can't Forget, The
- ☐ '63 What A Guy

RAINWATER, Marvin
- ☐ '57 Gonna Find Me A Bluebird

RAITT, Bonnie
- ☐ '90 Have A Heart
- ☐ '91 I Can't Make You Love Me
- ☐ '94 Love Sneakin' Up On You
- ☐ '92 Not The Only One
- ☐ '91 Something To Talk About ★
- ☐ '95 You Got It

RAMBEAU, Eddie
- ☐ '65 Concrete And Clay

RAM JAM
- ☐ '77 Black Betty

RAMONES
- ☐ '76 Blitzkrieg Bop ★
- ☐ '80 Do You Remember Rock 'N' Roll Radio
- ☐ '78 Do You Wanna Dance
- ☐ '95 I Don't Want To Grow Up
- ☐ '78 I Wanna Be Sedated
- ☐ '80 Rock 'N' Roll High School
- ☐ '78 Rockaway Beach
- ☐ '77 Sheena Is A Punk Rocker

RAMPAGE
- ☐ '97 Take It To The Streets

RAMRODS
- ☐ '61 (Ghost) Riders In The Sky

RANDAZZO, Teddy
- ☐ '63 Big Wide World
- ☐ '60 Way Of A Clown, The

RAN-DELLS, The
- ☐ '63 Martian Hop

RANDOLPH, Boots
- ☐ '63 Yakety Sax

RANDY & THE RAINBOWS
- ☐ '63 Denise

RANKS, Shabba
- ☐ '91 Housecall (Your Body Can't Lie To Me)
- ☐ '92 Mr. Loverman
- ☐ '92 Slow And Sexy [w/ Johnny Gill]

RAPPIN' 4-TAY
- ☐ '95 I'll Be Around
- ☐ '94 Playaz Club

RARE EARTH
- ☐ '70 Born To Wander
- ☐ '70 Get Ready
- ☐ '71 Hey Big Brother
- ☐ '71 I Just Want To Celebrate
- ☐ '70 (I Know) I'm Losing You
- ☐ '78 Warm Ride

RASCAL FLATTS
- ☐ '05 Bless The Broken Road ★
- ☐ '05 Fast Cars And Freedom
- ☐ '03 I Melt
- ☐ '06 Life Is A Highway ★
- ☐ '03 Love You Out Loud
- ☐ '04 Mayberry
- ☐ '06 My Wish
- ☐ '00 Prayin' For Daylight
- ☐ '05 Skin (Sarabeth)
- ☐ '07 Stand
- ☐ '07 Take Me There
- ☐ '02 These Days
- ☐ '06 What Hurts The Most ★

RASCALS, The
- ☐ '68 Beautiful Morning, A
- ☐ '69 Carry Me Back
- ☐ '67 Girl Like You, A
- ☐ '66 Good Lovin' ★
- ☐ '67 Groovin' ★
- ☐ '69 Heaven
- ☐ '67 How Can I Be Sure
- ☐ '66 I Ain't Gonna Eat Out My Heart Anymore
- ☐ '67 I've Been Lonely Too Long
- ☐ '67 It's Wonderful
- ☐ '68 People Got To Be Free ★
- ☐ '68 Ray Of Hope, A
- ☐ '69 See
- ☐ '66 You Better Run

RASPBERRIES
- ☐ '72 Go All The Way ★
- ☐ '72 I Wanna Be With You
- ☐ '73 Let's Pretend
- ☐ '74 Overnight Sensation (Hit Record)

RATT
- ☐ '85 Lay It Down
- ☐ '84 Round And Round

RAVEN, Eddy
- ☐ '88 I'm Gonna Get You

RAWLS, Lou
- ☐ '67 Dead End Street
- ☐ '78 Lady Love
- ☐ '66 Love Is A Hurtin' Thing
- ☐ '71 Natural Man, A
- ☐ '66 Tobacco Road [live]

- ☐ '76 You'll Never Find Another Love Like Mine ★
- ☐ '69 Your Good Thing (Is About To End)

RAY, Diane
- ☐ '63 Please Don't Talk To The Lifeguard

RAY, James
- ☐ '61 If You Gotta Make A Fool Of Somebody

RAY, Jimmy
- ☐ '98 Are You Jimmy Ray?

RAY, Johnnie
- ☐ '57 Build Your Love (On A Strong Foundation)
- ☐ '56 Just Walking In The Rain ★
- ☐ '57 Look Homeward, Angel
- ☐ '57 Yes Tonight, Josephine
- ☐ '57 You Don't Owe Me A Thing

RAYBON BROS.
- ☐ '97 Butterfly Kisses

RAYBURN, Margie
- ☐ '57 I'm Available

RAYE, Collin
- ☐ '99 Anyone Else
- ☐ '00 Couldn't Last A Moment
- ☐ '97 Gift, The
- ☐ '98 I Can Still Feel You
- ☐ '92 In This Life
- ☐ '97 Little Red Rodeo
- ☐ '94 Little Rock
- ☐ '91 Love, Me
- ☐ '94 My Kind Of Girl
- ☐ '95 Not That Different
- ☐ '95 One Boy, One Girl
- ☐ '94 That's My Story

RAYE, Susan
- ☐ '71 L.A. International Airport

RAY, GOODMAN & BROWN — see MOMENTS

RAY J
- ☐ '97 Let It Go
- ☐ '06 One Wish ★
- ☐ '01 Wait A Minute [w/ Lil' Kim]

RAYS, The
- ☐ '57 Silhouettes ★

REA, Chris
- ☐ '78 Fool (If You Think It's Over)

READY FOR THE WORLD
- ☐ '85 Digital Display
- ☐ '86 Love You Down ⬛
- ☐ '85 Oh Sheila ★

REAL LIFE
- ☐ '84 Catch Me I'm Falling
- ☐ '83 Send Me An Angel

REAL McCOY
- ☐ '94 Another Night ★

- ☐ '95 Come And Get Your Love
- ☐ '97 One More Time
- ☐ '95 Run Away ★

REBELS, The
- ☐ '62 Wild Weekend

REDBONE
- ☐ '74 Come And Get Your Love
- ☐ '71 Maggie
- ☐ '71 Witch Queen Of New Orleans, The

REDDING, Gene
- ☐ '74 This Heart

REDDING, Otis
- ☐ '68 Amen
- ☐ '66 Fa-Fa-Fa-Fa-Fa (Sad Song)
- ☐ '68 Happy Song, The
- ☐ '65 I Can't Turn You Loose
- ☐ '65 I've Been Loving You Too Long
- ☐ '67 Knock On Wood [w/ Carla Thomas]
- ☐ '63 Pain In My Heart
- ☐ '68 Papa's Got A Brand New Bag
- ☐ '65 Respect
- ☐ '66 Satisfaction
- ☐ '65 Shake
- ☐ '68 (Sittin' On) The Dock Of The Bay ★
- ☐ '63 These Arms Of Mine
- ☐ '67 Tramp [w/ Carla Thomas]
- ☐ '66 Try A Little Tenderness

REDDY, Helen
- ☐ '75 Ain't No Way To Treat A Lady
- ☐ '74 Angie Baby ★
- ☐ '75 Bluebird
- ☐ '73 Delta Dawn
- ☐ '75 Emotion
- ☐ '72 I Am Woman ★
- ☐ '76 I Can't Hear You No More
- ☐ '71 I Don't Know How To Love Him
- ☐ '74 Keep On Singing
- ☐ '73 Leave Me Alone (Ruby Red Dress)
- ☐ '73 Peaceful
- ☐ '75 Somewhere In The Night
- ☐ '74 You And Me Against The World
- ☐ '77 You're My World

REDEYE
- ☐ '70 Games

RED HOT CHILI PEPPERS
- ☐ '96 Aeroplane
- ☐ '02 By The Way
- ☐ '00 Californication
- ☐ '02 Can't Stop
- ☐ '06 Dani California ★
- ☐ '91 Give It Away
- ☐ '89 Higher Ground
- ☐ '96 Love Rollercoaster
- ☐ '95 My Friends
- ☐ '00 Otherside
- ☐ '99 Scar Tissue ★
- ☐ '07 Snow ((Hey Oh)) ★
- ☐ '93 Soul To Squeeze
- ☐ '06 Tell Me Baby
- ☐ '92 Under The Bridge ★

- ☐ '95 Warped
- ☐ '02 Zephyr Song, The

RED JUMPSUIT APPARATUS, The
- ☐ '07 Face Down

REDMAN
- ☐ '95 How High [w/ Method Man]

REDNEX
- ☐ '95 Cotton Eye Joe ★

REED, Dan, Network
- ☐ '88 Ritual

REED, Jerry
- ☐ '70 Amos Moses
- ☐ '71 When You're Hot, You're Hot

REED, Jimmy
- ☐ '56 Ain't That Lovin' You Baby
- ☐ '60 Baby What You Want Me To Do
- ☐ '61 Big Boss Man
- ☐ '61 Bright Lights Big City
- ☐ '57 Honest I Do
- ☐ '56 You Got Me Dizzy

REED, Lou
- ☐ '76 Coney Island Baby
- ☐ '89 Dirty Blvd.
- ☐ '72 Perfect Day
- ☐ '74 Sally Can't Dance
- ☐ '73 Satellite Of Love
- ☐ '78 Street Hassle
- ☐ '74 Sweet Jane
- ☐ '73 Walk On The Wild Side
- ☐ '74 White Light/White Heat

REESE, Della
- ☐ '57 And That Reminds Me
- ☐ '59 Don't You Know ★
- ☐ '59 Not One Minute More

REEVES, Jim
- ☐ '62 Adios Amigo
- ☐ '60 Am I Losing You
- ☐ '58 Billy Bayou
- ☐ '66 Distant Drums
- ☐ '57 Four Walls
- ☐ '59 He'll Have To Go ★
- ☐ '60 I Missed Me
- ☐ '60 I'm Gettin' Better

REFLECTIONS, The
- ☐ '64 (Just Like) Romeo & Juliet

RE-FLEX
- ☐ '83 Politics Of Dancing, The

REGENTS, The
- ☐ '61 Barbara-Ann
- ☐ '61 Runaround

REGINA
- ☐ '86 Baby Love

REID, Clarence
- ☐ '69 Nobody But You Babe

REID, Mike
- ☐ '88 Old Folks *[w/ Ronnie Milsap]*
- ☐ '90 Walk On Faith

R.E.M.
- ☐ '94 Bang And Blame
- ☐ '92 Drive
- ☐ '96 E-Bow The Letter
- ☐ '93 Everybody Hurts
- ☐ '91 Losing My Religion ★
- ☐ '93 Man On The Moon
- ☐ '87 One I Love, The
- ☐ '88 Orange Crush
- ☐ '83 Radio Free Europe
- ☐ '91 Shiny Happy People
- ☐ '88 Stand
- ☐ '94 What's The Frequency, Kenneth?

REMBRANDTS, The
- ☐ '95 I'll Be There For You (Theme from "Friends")
- ☐ '91 Just The Way It Is, Baby

RENAY, Diane
- ☐ '64 Kiss Me Sailor
- ☐ '64 Navy Blue

RENÉ & ANGELA
- ☐ '85 Save Your Love (For #1)
- ☐ '86 You Don't Have To Cry
- ☐ '85 Your Smile

RENE & RENE
- ☐ '68 Lo Mucho Que Te Quiero

RENO, Mike
- ☐ '84 Almost Paradise...Love Theme From Footloose *[w/ Ann Wilson]*

REO SPEEDWAGON
- ☐ '85 Can't Fight This Feeling ★
- ☐ '81 Don't Let Him Go
- ☐ '88 Here With Me
- ☐ '84 I Do'wanna Know
- ☐ '87 In My Dreams
- ☐ '81 In Your Letter
- ☐ '80 Keep On Loving You ★
- ☐ '82 Keep The Fire Burnin'
- ☐ '85 Live Every Moment
- ☐ '85 One Lonely Night
- ☐ '74 Ridin' The Storm Out
- ☐ '78 Roll With The Changes
- ☐ '82 Sweet Time
- ☐ '81 Take It On The Run ★
- ☐ '87 That Ain't Love
- ☐ '78 Time For Me To Fly

REPLACEMENTS, The
- ☐ '84 I Will Dare
- ☐ '89 I'll Be You
- ☐ '90 Merry Go Round

RESTLESS HEART
- ☐ '87 I'll Still Be Loving You
- ☐ '93 Tell Me What You Dream
- ☐ '92 When She Cries
- ☐ '91 You Can Depend On Me

REUNION
- ☐ '74 Life Is A Rock (But The Radio Rolled Me)

REVELS, The
- ☐ '59 Midnight Stroll

REVERE, Paul, & The Raiders
- ☐ '71 Birds Of A Feather
- ☐ '68 Don't Take It So Hard
- ☐ '66 Good Thing
- ☐ '66 Great Airplane Strike, The
- ☐ '67 Him Or Me - What's It Gonna Be?
- ☐ '66 Hungry
- ☐ '67 I Had A Dream
- ☐ '71 Indian Reservation ★
- ☐ '65 Just Like Me
- ☐ '66 Kicks ★
- ☐ '69 Let Me
- ☐ '61 Like, Long Hair
- ☐ '69 Mr. Sun, Mr. Moon
- ☐ '68 Too Much Talk
- ☐ '67 Ups And Downs

REYNOLDS, Debbie
- ☐ '60 Am I That Easy To Forget
- ☐ '57 Tammy ★
- ☐ '58 Very Special Love, A

REYNOLDS, Jody
- ☐ '58 Endless Sleep ★

REYNOLDS, Lawrence
- ☐ '69 Jesus Is A Soul Man

RHYTHM HERITAGE
- ☐ '76 Baretta's Theme ("Keep Your Eye On The Sparrow")
- ☐ '75 Theme From S.W.A.T. ★

RHYTHM SYNDICATE
- ☐ '91 Hey Donna
- ☐ '91 P.A.S.S.I.O.N

RICE, Chris
- ☐ '06 When Did You Fall (In Love With Me)

RICH, Charlie
- ☐ '73 Behind Closed Doors
- ☐ '75 Every Time You Touch Me (I Get High)
- ☐ '74 I Love My Friend
- ☐ '60 Lonely Weekends
- ☐ '65 Mohair Sam
- ☐ '73 Most Beautiful Girl, The ★
- ☐ '77 Rollin' With The Flow
- ☐ '74 There Won't Be Anymore
- ☐ '74 Very Special Love Song, A

RICH, Tony, Project
- ☐ '95 Nobody Knows ★

RICHARD, Cliff
- ☐ '80 Carrie
- ☐ '82 Daddy's Home
- ☐ '76 Devil Woman
- ☐ '80 Dreaming
- ☐ '63 It's All In The Game
- ☐ '80 Little In Love, A

☐ '59 Living Doll *[w/ The Drifters]*
☐ '58 Move It
☐ '80 Suddenly *[w/ Olivia Newton-John]*
☐ '79 We Don't Talk Anymore

RICHARDS, Keith
☐ '88 Take It So Hard
☐ '92 Wicked As It Seems

RICH BOY
☐ '07 Throw Some D's

RICHIE, Lionel
☐ '83 All Night Long (All Night) ★
☐ '86 Ballerina Girl
☐ '86 Dancing On The Ceiling ★
☐ '92 Do It To Me
☐ '96 Don't Wanna Lose You
☐ '81 Endless Love *[w/ Diana Ross]* ★
☐ '84 Hello
☐ '86 Love Will Conquer All
☐ '83 My Love
☐ '84 Penny Lover
☐ '83 Running With The Night
☐ '85 Say You, Say Me ★
☐ '87 Se La
☐ '84 Stuck On You
☐ '82 Truly ★
☐ '83 You Are

RICOCHET
☐ '96 Daddy's Money

RIDDLE, Nelson, & His Orchestra
☐ '55 Lisbon Antigua ★
☐ '56 Port Au Prince
☐ '62 Route 66 Theme
☐ '56 Theme From "The Proud Ones"

RIFF
☐ '91 My Heart Is Failing Me

RIGHTEOUS BROTHERS, The
☐ '74 Dream On
☐ '65 Ebb Tide
☐ '74 Give It To The People
☐ '66 Go Ahead And Cry
☐ '66 He
☐ '65 Hung On You
☐ '65 Just Once In My Life
☐ '63 Little Latin Lupe Lu
☐ '74 Rock And Roll Heaven
☐ '65 Unchained Melody ★
☐ '66 (You're My) Soul And Inspiration ★
☐ '64 You've Lost That Lovin' Feelin' ★

RIGHT SAID FRED (R*S*F)
☐ '91 I'm Too Sexy ★

RIHANNA
☐ '07 Break It Off *[w/ Sean Paul]*
☐ '05 If It's Lovin' That You Want
☐ '05 Pon De Replay ★
☐ '06 SOS ★
☐ '07 Shut Up And Drive
☐ '07 Umbrella ★
☐ '06 Unfaithful ★

RILEY, Cheryl Pepsii
☐ '88 Thanks For My Child

RILEY, Jeannie C.
☐ '68 Harper Valley P.T.A. ★

RILEY, Teddy
☐ '89 My Fantasy

RIMES, LeAnn
☐ '99 Big Deal
☐ '96 Blue
☐ '02 Can't Fight The Moonlight
☐ '98 Commitment
☐ '97 How Do I Live ★
☐ '00 I Need You
☐ '98 Looking Through Your Eyes
☐ '96 One Way Ticket (Because I Can)
☐ '06 Probably Wouldn't Be This Way
☐ '06 Something's Gotta Give
☐ '96 Unchained Melody
☐ '99 Written In The Stars *[w/ Elton John]*
☐ '97 You Light Up My Life

RINGS, The
☐ '81 Let Me Go

RIOS, Miguel
☐ '70 Song Of Joy, A

RIP CHORDS, The
☐ '63 Hey Little Cobra ★
☐ '64 Three Window Coupe

RIPERTON, Minnie
☐ '75 Lovin' You ★

RITCHIE FAMILY, The
☐ '76 Best Disco In Town, The
☐ '75 Brazil

RITENOUR, Lee
☐ '81 Is It You

RITTER, Tex
☐ '61 I Dreamed Of A Hill-Billy Heaven

RIVERA, Chita
☐ '61 America

RIVERS, Johnny
☐ '67 Baby I Need Your Lovin'
☐ '73 Blue Suede Shoes
☐ '75 Help Me Rhonda
☐ '66 (I Washed My Hands In) Muddy Water
☐ '64 Maybelline
☐ '64 Memphis ★
☐ '65 Midnight Special
☐ '64 Mountain Of Love
☐ '69 Muddy River
☐ '66 Poor Side Of Town ★
☐ '72 Rockin' Pneumonia - Boogie Woogie Flu
☐ '66 Secret Agent Man ★
☐ '65 Seventh Son
☐ '67 Summer Rain
☐ '77 Swayin' To The Music (Slow Dancin')
☐ '67 Tracks Of My Tears, The

RIVERS, Johnny — cont'd
- ☐ '65 Under Your Spell Again
- ☐ '65 Where Have All The Flowers Gone

RIVIERAS, The
- ☐ '64 California Sun

RIVINGTONS, The
- ☐ '62 Papa-Oom-Mow-Mow

ROACHFORD
- ☐ '89 Cuddly Toy (Feel For Me)

ROAD APPLES, The
- ☐ '75 Let's Live Together

ROB BASE & D.J. E-Z ROCK
- ☐ '88 It Takes Two

ROBBINS, Marty
- ☐ '60 Ballad Of The Alamo
- ☐ '60 Big Iron
- ☐ '62 Devil Woman
- ☐ '61 Don't Worry ★
- ☐ '59 El Paso ★
- ☐ '76 El Paso City
- ☐ '59 Hanging Tree, The
- ☐ '60 Is There Any Chance
- ☐ '58 Just Married
- ☐ '65 Ribbon Of Darkness
- ☐ '62 Ruby Ann
- ☐ '58 She Was Only Seventeen (He Was One Year More)
- ☐ '56 Singing The Blues
- ☐ '57 Story Of My Life, The
- ☐ '55 That's All Right
- ☐ '67 Tonight Carmen
- ☐ '57 White Sport Coat (And A Pink Carnation) ★

ROBERT & JOHNNY
- ☐ '58 We Belong Together

ROBERTS, Austin
- ☐ '75 Rocky
- ☐ '72 Something's Wrong With Me

ROBERTSON, Don
- ☐ '56 Happy Whistler, The

ROBERTSON, Robbie
- ☐ '87 Showdown At Big Sky

ROBIC, Ivo
- ☐ '59 Morgen

ROBIN S
- ☐ '93 Show Me Love ★

ROBINS, The
- ☐ '55 Smokey Joe's Café

ROBINSON, Floyd
- ☐ '59 Makin' Love

ROBINSON, Smokey
- ☐ '75 Agony And The Ecstasy, The
- ☐ '73 Baby Come Close
- ☐ '75 Baby That's Backatcha
- ☐ '81 Being With You
- ☐ '79 Cruisin'
- ☐ '87 Just To See Her
- ☐ '80 Let Me Be The Clock
- ☐ '87 One Heartbeat
- ☐ '82 Tell Me Tomorrow

ROBINSON, Vicki Sue
- ☐ '76 Turn The Beat Around

ROBYN
- ☐ '97 Do You Know (What It Takes)
- ☐ '98 Do You Really Want Me (Show Respect)
- ☐ '97 Show Me Love

ROCHELL & THE CANDLES
- ☐ '61 Once Upon A Time

ROCK & ROLL TRIO — see BURNETTE, Johnny

ROCK-A-TEENS
- ☐ '59 Woo-Hoo

ROCKETS
- ☐ '79 Oh Well

ROCKPILE
- ☐ '81 Teacher Teacher

ROCKWELL
- ☐ '84 Obscene Phone Caller
- ☐ '84 Somebody's Watching Me

ROCKY FELLERS, The
- ☐ '63 Killer Joe

RODGERS, Eileen
- ☐ '56 Miracle Of Love
- ☐ '58 Treasure Of Your Love

RODGERS, Jimmie
- ☐ '58 Are You Really Mine
- ☐ '58 Bimbombey
- ☐ '67 Child Of Clay
- ☐ '57 Honeycomb ★
- ☐ '59 I'm Never Gonna Tell
- ☐ '66 It's Over
- ☐ '57 Kisses Sweeter Than Wine ★
- ☐ '58 Make Me A Miracle
- ☐ '58 Oh-Oh, I'm Falling In Love Again
- ☐ '59 Ring-A-Ling-A-Lario
- ☐ '58 Secretly
- ☐ '60 T.L.C. Tender Love And Care
- ☐ '59 Tucumcari
- ☐ '60 Waltzing Matilda

ROE, Tommy
- ☐ '64 Come On
- ☐ '69 Dizzy ★
- ☐ '63 Everybody
- ☐ '69 Heather Honey
- ☐ '66 Hooray For Hazel
- ☐ '66 It's Now Winters Day
- ☐ '69 Jam Up Jelly Tight
- ☐ '62 Sheila ★
- ☐ '71 Stagger Lee

☐ '62 Susie Darlin'
☐ '66 Sweet Pea

ROGER
☐ '81 I Heard It Through The Grapevine
☐ '87 I Want To Be Your Man

ROGERS, Julie
☐ '64 Wedding, The

ROGERS, Kenny/First Edition
☐ '83 All My Life
☐ '69 But You Know I Love You
☐ '00 Buy Me A Rose *[w/ Alison Krauss & Billy Dean]*
☐ '79 Coward Of The County ★
☐ '77 Daytime Friends
☐ '80 Don't Fall In Love With A Dreamer *[w/ Kim Carnes]*
☐ '78 Gambler, The
☐ '99 Greatest, The
☐ '70 Heed The Call
☐ '81 I Don't Need You
☐ '83 Islands In The Stream *[w/ Dolly Parton]* ★
☐ '68 Just Dropped In (To See What Condition My Condition Was In)
☐ '80 Lady ★
☐ '78 Love Or Something Like It
☐ '80 Love The World Away
☐ '82 Love Will Turn You Around
☐ '77 Lucille ★
☐ '69 Reuben James
☐ '69 Ruby, Don't Take Your Love To Town
☐ '81 Share Your Love With Me
☐ '79 She Believes In Me
☐ '70 Something's Burning
☐ '78 Sweet Music Man
☐ '70 Tell It All Brother
☐ '84 This Woman
☐ '81 Through The Years
☐ '83 We've Got Tonight *[w/ Sheena Easton]*
☐ '84 What About Me? *[w/ Kim Carnes & James Ingram]*
☐ '81 What Are We Doin' In Love *[w/ Dottie West]*
☐ '79 You Decorated My Life

ROLLING STONES, The
☐ '74 Ain't Too Proud To Beg
☐ '90 Almost Hear You Sigh
☐ '73 Angie ★
☐ '97 Anybody Seen My Baby?
☐ '65 As Tears Go By
☐ '78 Beast Of Burden
☐ '71 Bitch
☐ '71 Brown Sugar ★
☐ '67 Dandelion
☐ '74 Doo Doo Doo Doo Doo (Heartbreaker)
☐ '80 Emotional Rescue ★
☐ '78 Far Away Eyes
☐ '76 Fool To Cry
☐ '65 Get Off Of My Cloud ★
☐ '69 Gimme Shelter
☐ '82 Going To A Go-Go
☐ '81 Hang Fire
☐ '72 Happy

☐ '86 Harlem Shuffle
☐ '66 Have You Seen Your Mother, Baby, Standing In The Shadow?
☐ '65 Heart Of Stone
☐ '91 Highwire
☐ '69 Honky Tonk Women ★
☐ '65 (I Can't Get No) Satisfaction ★
☐ '64 It's All Over Now
☐ '74 It's Only Rock 'N Roll (But I Like It)
☐ '68 Jumpin' Jack Flash ★
☐ '66 Lady Jane
☐ '65 Last Time, The
☐ '67 Let's Spend The Night Together
☐ '94 Love Is Strong
☐ '78 Miss You ★
☐ '89 Mixed Emotions
☐ '66 Mothers Little Helper
☐ '66 19th Nervous Breakdown ★
☐ '64 Not Fade Away
☐ '86 One Hit (To The Body)
☐ '66 Paint It, Black ★
☐ '89 Rock And A Hard Place
☐ '67 Ruby Tuesday ★
☐ '78 Shattered
☐ '67 She's A Rainbow
☐ '80 She's So Cold
☐ '81 Start Me Up ★
☐ '68 Street Fighting Man
☐ '68 Sympathy For The Devil ★
☐ '64 Tell Me (You're Coming Back)
☐ '64 Time Is On My Side
☐ '72 Tumbling Dice
☐ '66 Under My Thumb
☐ '83 Undercover Of The Night
☐ '81 Waiting On A Friend
☐ '71 Wild Horses
☐ '69 You Can't Always Get What You Want
☐ '94 You Got Me Rocking

ROMANTICS, The
☐ '84 One In A Million
☐ '83 Talking In Your Sleep ★
☐ '80 What I Like About You

ROME
☐ '97 Do You Like This
☐ '97 I Belong To You (Every Time I See Your Face)

ROMEO VOID
☐ '84 Girl In Trouble (Is A Temporary Thing)

RONDO, Don
☐ '56 Two Different Worlds
☐ '57 White Silver Sands

RONETTES, The
☐ '63 Baby, I Love You
☐ '63 Be My Baby ★
☐ '64 (Best Part Of) Breaking Up, The
☐ '64 Do I Love You?
☐ '64 Walking In The Rain

RONNIE & THE HI-LITES
☐ '62 I Wish That We Were Married

RONNY & THE DAYTONAS
- ☐ '64 G.T.O. ★
- ☐ '65 Sandy

RONSTADT, Linda
- ☐ '90 All My Life [w/ Aaron Neville]
- ☐ '78 Back In The U.S.A.
- ☐ '77 Blue Bayou
- ☐ '67 Different Drum
- ☐ '89 Don't Know Much [w/ Aaron Neville] ★
- ☐ '82 Get Closer
- ☐ '75 Heat Wave
- ☐ '80 How Do I Make You
- ☐ '80 Hurt So Bad
- ☐ '80 I Can't Let Go
- ☐ '82 I Knew You When
- ☐ '77 It's So Easy
- ☐ '70 Long Long Time
- ☐ '78 Ooh Baby Baby
- ☐ '78 Poor Poor Pitiful Me
- ☐ '86 Somewhere Out There [w/ James Ingram]
  ★
- ☐ '76 That'll Be The Day
- ☐ '75 Tracks Of My Tears
- ☐ '78 Tumbling Dice
- ☐ '75 When Will I Be Loved ★
- ☐ '74 You're No Good ★

ROOFTOP SINGERS, The
- ☐ '63 Tom Cat
- ☐ '63 Walk Right In ★

ROOTS, The
- ☐ '97 What They Do
- ☐ '99 You Got Me [w/ Erykah Badu]

ROSE, David, & His Orchestra
- ☐ '62 Stripper, The ★

ROSE GARDEN, The
- ☐ '67 Next Plane To London

ROSE ROYCE
- ☐ '76 Car Wash ★
- ☐ '77 I Wanna Get Next To You
- ☐ '78 Love Don't Live Here Anymore
- ☐ '77 Ooh Boy

ROSIE & THE ORIGINALS
- ☐ '60 Angel Baby

ROSS, Diana
- ☐ '70 Ain't No Mountain High Enough ★
- ☐ '84 All Of You [w/ Julio Iglesias]
- ☐ '79 Boss, The
- ☐ '81 Endless Love [w/ Lionel Richie] ★
- ☐ '77 Gettin' Ready For Love
- ☐ '73 Good Morning Heartache
- ☐ '80 I'm Coming Out
- ☐ '80 It's My Turn
- ☐ '74 Last Time I Saw Him
- ☐ '76 Love Hangover ★
- ☐ '82 Mirror, Mirror
- ☐ '84 Missing You
- ☐ '82 Muscles
- ☐ '74 My Mistake (Was To Love You) [w/ Marvin Gaye]

- ☐ '76 One Love In My Lifetime
- ☐ '83 Pieces Of Ice
- ☐ '70 Reach Out And Touch (Somebody's Hand)
- ☐ '71 Reach Out I'll Be There
- ☐ '70 Remember Me
- ☐ '71 Surrender
- ☐ '84 Swept Away
- ☐ '75 Theme From Mahogany (Do You Know Where You're Going To) ★
- ☐ '73 Touch Me In The Morning
- ☐ '80 Upside Down ★
- ☐ '81 Why Do Fools Fall In Love
- ☐ '73 You're A Special Part Of Me [w/ Diana Ross]

ROSS, Jack
- ☐ '62 Cinderella

ROSS, Jackie
- ☐ '64 Selfish One

ROSS, Spencer
- ☐ '60 Tracy's Theme

ROTH, David Lee
- ☐ '85 California Girls
- ☐ '85 Just A Gigolo/I Ain't Got Nobody
- ☐ '88 Just Like Paradise
- ☐ '86 Yankee Rose

ROUTERS, The
- ☐ '62 Let's Go

ROVER BOYS, The
- ☐ '56 Graduation Day

ROWLAND, Kelly
- ☐ '07 Like This
- ☐ '02 Stole

ROXETTE
- ☐ '92 Church Of Your Heart
- ☐ '89 Dangerous ★
- ☐ '89 Dressed For Success
- ☐ '91 Fading Like A Flower (Every Time You Leave)
- ☐ '90 It Must Have Been Love ★
- ☐ '91 Joyride ★
- ☐ '89 Listen To Your Heart ★
- ☐ '89 Look, The ★
- ☐ '91 Spending My Time

ROXY MUSIC
- ☐ '82 Avalon
- ☐ '75 Love Is The Drug
- ☐ '83 More Than This

ROYAL, Billy Joe
- ☐ '69 Cherry Hill Park
- ☐ '65 Down In The Boondocks
- ☐ '65 I Knew You When
- ☐ '65 I've Got To Be Somebody

ROYAL GUARDSMEN, The
- ☐ '68 Baby Let's Wait
- ☐ '67 Return Of The Red Baron, The
- ☐ '66 Snoopy Vs. The Red Baron ★

- ☐ '67 Snoopy's Christmas

ROYAL PHILHARMONIC ORCHESTRA
- ☐ '81 Hooked On Classics

ROYAL SCOTS DRAGOON GUARDS
- ☐ '72 Amazing Grace

ROYAL TEENS
- ☐ '59 Believe Me
- ☐ '58 Short Shorts ★

ROYALTONES, The
- ☐ '58 Poor Boy

ROZALLA
- ☐ '92 Everybody's Free (To Feel Good)

RTZ
- ☐ '92 Until Your Love Comes Back Around

RUBETTES, The
- ☐ '74 Sugar Baby Love

RUBICON
- ☐ '78 I'm Gonna Take Care Of Everything

RUBY & THE ROMANTICS
- ☐ '63 Hey There Lonely Boy
- ☐ '63 My Summer Love
- ☐ '63 Our Day Will Come ★

RUDE BOYS
- ☐ '91 Are You Lonely For Me
- ☐ '91 Written All Over Your Face

RUFF ENDZ
- ☐ '00 No More

RUFFIN, David
- ☐ '69 My Whole World Ended (The Moment You Left Me)
- ☐ '75 Walk Away From Love

RUFFIN, Jimmy
- ☐ '67 Gonna Give Her All The Love I've Got
- ☐ '80 Hold On To My Love
- ☐ '66 I've Passed This Way Before
- ☐ '66 What Becomes Of The Brokenhearted

RUFUS — see KHAN, Chaka

RUGBYS, The
- ☐ '69 You, I

RUNDGREN, Todd
- ☐ '83 Bang The Drum All Day
- ☐ '78 Can We Still Be Friends
- ☐ '76 Good Vibrations
- ☐ '73 Hello It's Me
- ☐ '72 I Saw The Light
- ☐ '70 We Gotta Get You A Woman *[RUNT]*

RUN-D.M.C.
- ☐ '93 Down With The King
- ☐ '84 It's Like That
- ☐ '85 King Of Rock
- ☐ '86 My Adidas
- ☐ '86 Walk This Way ★
- ☐ '86 You Be Illin'

RUPEE
- ☐ '04 Tempted To Touch

RUSH
- ☐ '85 Big Money, The
- ☐ '77 Closer To The Heart
- ☐ '93 Cold Fire
- ☐ '84 Distant Early Warning
- ☐ '91 Dreamline
- ☐ '75 Fly By Night
- ☐ '80 Freewill
- ☐ '91 Ghost Of A Chance
- ☐ '81 Limelight
- ☐ '82 New World Man
- ☐ '81 Red Barchetta
- ☐ '89 Show Don't Tell
- ☐ '80 Spirit Of Radio
- ☐ '93 Stick It Out
- ☐ '96 Test For Echo
- ☐ '81 Tom Sawyer

RUSH, Jennifer
- ☐ '87 Flames Of Paradise *[w/ Elton John]*

RUSH, Merrilee
- ☐ '68 Angel Of The Morning

RUSHEN, Patrice
- ☐ '84 Feels So Real (Won't Let Go)
- ☐ '82 Forget Me Nots ◄━

RUSSELL, Andy
- ☐ '67 It's Such A Pretty World Today

RUSSELL, Bobby
- ☐ '68 1432 Franklin Pike Circle Hero
- ☐ '71 Saturday Morning Confusion

RUSSELL, Brenda
- ☐ '88 Piano In The Dark ◄━
- ☐ '79 So Good, So Right

RUSSELL, Leon
- ☐ '76 Back To The Island
- ☐ '75 Lady Blue
- ☐ '72 Tight Rope

RYAN, Charlie
- ☐ '60 Hot Rod Lincoln

RYDELL, Bobby
- ☐ '63 Butterfly Baby
- ☐ '62 Cha-Cha-Cha, The
- ☐ '60 Ding-A-Ling
- ☐ '61 Fish, The
- ☐ '63 Forget Him
- ☐ '61 Good Time Baby
- ☐ '61 I Wanna Thank You
- ☐ '62 I'll Never Dance Again
- ☐ '62 (I've Got) Bonnie
- ☐ '61 Jingle Bell Rock *[w/ Chubby Checker]*
- ☐ '59 Kissin' Time
- ☐ '60 Little Bitty Girl
- ☐ '60 Sway
- ☐ '60 Swingin' School
- ☐ '61 That Old Black Magic
- ☐ '60 Volare

RYDELL, Bobby — cont'd
- ☐ '59 We Got Love
- ☐ '60 Wild One ★
- ☐ '63 Wildwood Days

RYDER, John & Anne
- ☐ '69 I Still Believe In Tomorrow

RYDER, Mitch, & The Detroit Wheels
- ☐ '66 Devil With A Blue Dress On & Good Golly Miss Molly ★
- ☐ '65 Jenny Take A Ride!
- ☐ '66 Little Latin Lupe Lu ★
- ☐ '67 Sock It To Me-Baby!
- ☐ '67 Too Many Fish In The Sea & Three Little Fishes

S

SAADIQ, Raphael
- ☐ '95 Ask Of You

SADE
- ☐ '86 Never As Good As The First Time
- ☐ '92 No Ordinary Love
- ☐ '88 Nothing Can Come Between Us
- ☐ '88 Paradise ⌐
- ☐ '85 Smooth Operator ★
- ☐ '85 Sweetest Taboo, The ⌐

SADLER, SSgt Barry
- ☐ '66 Ballad Of The Green Berets, The ★

SAFARIS
- ☐ '60 Image Of A Girl

SA-FIRE
- ☐ '89 Thinking Of You

SAGA
- ☐ '82 On The Loose
- ☐ '83 Wind Him Up

SAGER, Carole Bayer
- ☐ '81 Stronger Than Before

SAIGON KICK
- ☐ '92 Love Is On The Way

SAILCAT
- ☐ '72 Motorcycle Mama

SAINTE-MARIE, Buffy
- ☐ '72 Mister Can't You See

ST. JAMES, Rebecca
- ☐ '05 Alive
- ☐ '02 Breathe
- ☐ '96 God
- ☐ '03 I Thank You
- ☐ '99 Pray
- ☐ '01 Wait For Me

ST. PETERS, Crispian
- ☐ '66 Pied Piper, The ★
- ☐ '67 You Were On My Mind

SAKAMOTO, Kyu
- ☐ '63 Sukiyaki ★

SALIVA
- ☐ '02 Always
- ☐ '07 Ladies And Gentlemen
- ☐ '01 Your Disease

SALSOUL ORCHESTRA, The
- ☐ '76 Nice 'N' Naasty
- ☐ '76 Tangerine

SALT-N-PEPA
- ☐ '95 Ain't Nuthin' But A She Thing
- ☐ '91 Do You Want Me
- ☐ '90 Expression
- ☐ '91 Let's Talk About Sex
- ☐ '94 None Of Your Business
- ☐ '87 Push It
- ☐ '93 Shoop ★
- ☐ '94 Whatta Man [w/ En Vogue] ★

SAM & DAVE
- ☐ '66 Hold On! I'm A Comin'
- ☐ '68 I Thank You
- ☐ '67 Soul Man ★
- ☐ '67 When Something Is Wrong With My Baby

SAMI JO
- ☐ '74 Tell Me A Lie

SAMMIE
- ☐ '00 I Like It

SAM THE SHAM & THE PHARAOHS
- ☐ '66 Hair On My Chinny Chin Chin, The
- ☐ '66 How Do You Catch A Girl
- ☐ '65 Ju Ju Hand
- ☐ '66 Lil' Red Riding Hood ★
- ☐ '65 Ring Dang Doo
- ☐ '65 Wooly Bully ★

SAMUELLE
- ☐ '90 So You Like What You See

SANDLER, Adam
- ☐ '95 Chanukah Song, The

SANDPEBBLES, The
- ☐ '67 Love Power

SANDPIPERS, The
- ☐ '69 Come Saturday Morning
- ☐ '67 Cuando Sali De Cuba
- ☐ '66 Guantanamera
- ☐ '66 Louie, Louie

SANDS, Jodie
- ☐ '57 With All My Heart

SANDS, Tommy
- ☐ '57 Goin' Steady
- ☐ '58 Sing Boy Sing
- ☐ '57 Teen-Age Crush ★
- ☐ '59 Worryin' Kind, The

SANFORD/TOWNSEND BAND, The
- ☐ '77 Smoke From A Distant Fire

SANG, Samantha
- ☐ '77 Emotion

SANTA ESMERALDA
- ☐ '77 Don't Let Me Be Misunderstood

SANTAMARIA, Mongo
- ☐ '63 Watermelon Man

SANTANA
- ☐ '70 Black Magic Woman/Gypsy Queen ★
- ☐ '71 Everybody's Everything
- ☐ '70 Evil Ways
- ☐ '02 Game Of Love, The *[w/ Michelle Branch]* ★
- ☐ '82 Hold On
- ☐ '06 I'm Feeling You *[w/ Michelle Branch]*
- ☐ '69 Jingo
- ☐ '76 Let It Shine
- ☐ '00 Maria Maria *[w/ The Product G&B]* ★
- ☐ '72 No One To Depend On
- ☐ '78 One Chain (Don't Make No Prison)
- ☐ '71 Oye Como Va
- ☐ '77 She's Not There
- ☐ '99 Smooth *[w/ Rob Thomas]* ★
- ☐ '79 Stormy
- ☐ '03 Why Don't You & I *[w/ Alex Band or Chad Kroeger]*
- ☐ '81 Winning
- ☐ '79 You Know That I Love You

SANTANA, Juelz
- ☐ '06 There It Go! (The Whistle Song) ★

SANTO & JOHNNY
- ☐ '59 Sleep Walk ★
- ☐ '59 Tear Drop

SANTOS, Larry
- ☐ '76 We Can't Hide It Anymore

SANZ, Alejandro — see SHAKIRA

SAPPHIRES, The
- ☐ '64 Who Do You Love

SATRIANI, Joe
- ☐ '92 Summer Song

SAVAGE, Chantay
- ☐ '96 I Will Survive

SAVAGE GARDEN
- ☐ '99 Animal Song, The
- ☐ '00 Crash And Burn
- ☐ '99 I Knew I Loved You ★
- ☐ '97 I Want You ★
- ☐ '97 To The Moon And Back
- ☐ '97 Truly Madly Deeply ★

SAVING JANE
- ☐ '06 Girl Next Door

SAWYER BROWN
- ☐ '91 Dirt Road, The
- ☐ '89 Race Is On, The
- ☐ '97 Six Days On The Road
- ☐ '92 Some Girls Do
- ☐ '85 Step That Step
- ☐ '93 Thank God For You

- ☐ '97 This Night Won't Last Forever
- ☐ '94 This Time
- ☐ '96 Treat Her Right
- ☐ '91 Walk, The

SAYER, Leo
- ☐ '77 Easy To Love
- ☐ '77 How Much Love
- ☐ '81 Living In A Fantasy
- ☐ '75 Long Tall Glasses (I Can Dance)
- ☐ '80 More Than I Can Say ★
- ☐ '77 Thunder In My Heart
- ☐ '77 When I Need You ★
- ☐ '76 You Make Me Feel Like Dancing ★

SCAGGS, Boz
- ☐ '80 Breakdown Dead Ahead
- ☐ '72 Dinah Flo
- ☐ '76 Georgia
- ☐ '88 Heart Of Mine
- ☐ '76 It's Over
- ☐ '80 JoJo
- ☐ '77 Lido Shuffle
- ☐ '80 Look What You've Done To Me
- ☐ '76 Lowdown
- ☐ '80 Miss Sun

SCANDAL
- ☐ '84 Warrior, The

SCARBURY, Joey
- ☐ '81 Theme From "Greatest American Hero" (Believe It or Not)

SCARFACE
- ☐ '94 I Never Seen A Man Cry (aka I Seen A Man Die)
- ☐ '97 Smile

SCARLETT & BLACK
- ☐ '88 You Don't Know

SCHIFRIN, Lalo
- ☐ '68 Mission-Impossible

SCHILLING, Peter
- ☐ '83 Major Tom (Coming Home)

SCHMIT, Timothy B.
- ☐ '87 Boys Night Out

SCHNEIDER, John
- ☐ '81 It's Now Or Never

SCHWARTZ, Eddie
- ☐ '81 All Our Tomorrows

S CLUB 7
- ☐ '01 Never Had A Dream Come True

SCORPIONS
- ☐ '82 No One Like You
- ☐ '84 Rock You Like A Hurricane
- ☐ '91 Wind Of Change

SCOTT, Bobby
- ☐ '56 Chain Gang

SCOTT, Freddie
- ☐ '66 Are You Lonely For Me
- ☐ '63 Hey, Girl

SCOTT, Jack
- ☐ '60 Burning Bridges ★
- ☐ '58 Goodbye Baby
- ☐ '60 It Only Happened Yesterday
- ☐ '58 Leroy
- ☐ '58 My True Love ★
- ☐ '60 Oh, Little One
- ☐ '59 Way I Walk, The
- ☐ '60 What In The World's Come Over You ★
- ☐ '58 With Your Love

SCOTT, Linda
- ☐ '61 Don't Bet Money Honey
- ☐ '61 I Don't Know Why
- ☐ '61 I've Told Every Little Star ★
- ☐ '61 It's All Because

SCOTT, Peggy, & Jo Jo Benson
- ☐ '68 Lover's Holiday
- ☐ '68 Pickin' Wild Mountain Berries
- ☐ '69 Soulshake

SCRITTI POLITTI
- ☐ '85 Perfect Way

SEA, Johnny
- ☐ '66 Day For Decision

SEAL
- ☐ '91 Crazy ★
- ☐ '96 Don't Cry
- ☐ '96 Fly Like An Eagle
- ☐ '95 Kiss From A Rose ★
- ☐ '04 Love's Divine
- ☐ '94 Prayer For The Dying

SEALS, Dan
- ☐ '86 Bop
- ☐ '90 Good Times
- ☐ '90 Love On Arrival
- ☐ '85 Meet Me In Montana *[w/ Marie Osmond]*

SEALS & CROFTS
- ☐ '73 Diamond Girl
- ☐ '76 Get Closer
- ☐ '73 Hummingbird
- ☐ '75 I'll Play For You
- ☐ '77 My Fair Share
- ☐ '72 Summer Breeze
- ☐ '73 We May Never Pass This Way (Again)
- ☐ '78 You're The Love

SEARCHERS, The
- ☐ '65 Bumble Bee
- ☐ '64 Don't Throw Your Love Away
- ☐ '64 Love Potion Number Nine
- ☐ '64 Needles And Pins
- ☐ '64 Some Day We're Gonna Love Again
- ☐ '65 What Have They Done To The Rain
- ☐ '64 When You Walk In The Room

SEBASTIAN, John
- ☐ '76 Welcome Back ★

SECADA, Jon
- ☐ '93 Angel
- ☐ '92 Do You Believe In Us
- ☐ '05 Feliz Navidad
- ☐ '93 I'm Free
- ☐ '94 If You Go
- ☐ '92 Just Another Day ★
- ☐ '94 Mental Picture
- ☐ '06 Window To My Heart

SECRETS, The
- ☐ '63 Boy Next Door, The

SEDAKA, Neil
- ☐ '63 Alice In Wonderland
- ☐ '75 Bad Blood
- ☐ '63 Bad Girl
- ☐ '62 Breaking Up Is Hard To Do ★
- ☐ '75 Breaking Up Is Hard To Do [slow version]
- ☐ '60 Calendar Girl
- ☐ '58 Diary, The
- ☐ '61 Happy Birthday, Sweet Sixteen
- ☐ '75 Immigrant, The
- ☐ '74 Laughter In The Rain ★
- ☐ '63 Let's Go Steady Again
- ☐ '61 Little Devil
- ☐ '76 Love In The Shadows
- ☐ '62 Next Door To An Angel
- ☐ '59 Oh! Carol
- ☐ '60 Run Samson Run
- ☐ '80 Should've Never Let You Go *[w/ Dara Sedaka]*
- ☐ '74 Solitaire
- ☐ '60 Stairway To Heaven
- ☐ '76 Steppin' Out
- ☐ '75 That's When The Music Takes Me
- ☐ '60 You Mean Everything To Me

SEDUCTION
- ☐ '90 Could This Be Love
- ☐ '90 Heartbeat
- ☐ '89 Two To Make It Right ★
- ☐ '89 You're My One And Only (True Love)

SEEDS, The
- ☐ '66 Pushin' Too Hard

SEEKERS, The
- ☐ '66 Georgy Girl ★
- ☐ '65 I'll Never Find Another You
- ☐ '65 World Of Our Own, A

SEETHER
- ☐ '04 Broken
- ☐ '02 Fine Again

SEGER, Bob
- ☐ '80 Against The Wind ★
- ☐ '86 American Storm
- ☐ '75 Beautiful Loser
- ☐ '80 Betty Lou's Gettin' Out Tonight
- ☐ '83 Even Now
- ☐ '78 Feel Like A Number
- ☐ '77 Fire Down Below
- ☐ '80 Fire Lake

- ☐ '76 Get Out Of Denver
- ☐ '80 Her Strut
- ☐ '78 Hollywood Nights
- ☐ '80 Horizontal Bop
- ☐ '75 Katmandu
- ☐ '86 Like A Rock
- ☐ '77 Mainstreet
- ☐ '76 Night Moves ★
- ☐ '79 Old Time Rock & Roll
- ☐ '68 Ramblin' Gamblin' Man
- ☐ '91 Real Love, The
- ☐ '77 Rock And Roll Never Forgets
- ☐ '83 Roll Me Away
- ☐ '87 Shakedown ★
- ☐ '82 Shame On The Moon ★
- ☐ '78 Still The Same
- ☐ '75 Travelin' Man
- ☐ '81 Tryin' To Live My Life Without You
- ☐ '76 Turn The Page
- ☐ '84 Understanding
- ☐ '78 We've Got Tonite
- ☐ '80 You'll Accomp'ny Me

SELENA
- ☐ '95 Dreaming Of You
- ☐ '95 I Could Fall In Love ★

SELF, Ronnie
- ☐ '58 Bop-A-Lena

SELLARS, Marilyn
- ☐ '74 One Day At A Time

SEMBELLO, Michael
- ☐ '83 Automatic Man
- ☐ '83 Maniac ★

SEMISONIC
- ☐ '98 Closing Time

SENATOR BOBBY
- ☐ '67 Wild Thing

SENSATIONS, The
- ☐ '62 Let Me In

SERENDIPITY SINGERS, The
- ☐ '64 Beans In My Ears
- ☐ '64 Don't Let The Rain Come Down (Crooked Little Man)

SERMON, Erick
- ☐ '01 Music [w/ Marvin Gaye]
- ☐ '02 React

SETZER, Brian, Orchestra
- ☐ '98 Jump Jive An' Wail

SEVEN MARY THREE
- ☐ '95 Cumbersome

702
- ☐ '97 All I Want
- ☐ '97 Get It Together
- ☐ '96 Steelo
- ☐ '99 Where My Girls At? ★

SEVILLE, David
- ☐ '58 Bird On My Head, The

- ☐ '58 Witch Doctor ★

SEX PISTOLS
- ☐ '77 Anarchy In The U.K.
- ☐ '77 God Save The Queen
- ☐ '77 Pretty Vacant

SEXTON, Charlie
- ☐ '85 Beat's So Lonely

SEYMOUR, Phil
- ☐ '81 Precious To Me

SHADES OF BLUE
- ☐ '66 Oh How Happy

SHADOWS OF KNIGHT, The
- ☐ '66 Gloria
- ☐ '66 Oh Yeah

SHAGGY
- ☐ '00 Angel ★
- ☐ '95 Boombastic ★
- ☐ '00 It Wasn't Me ★
- ☐ '95 Summer Time

SHAI
- ☐ '93 Baby I'm Yours
- ☐ '93 Comforter
- ☐ '92 If I Ever Fall In Love ★
- ☐ '94 Place Where You Belong, The

SHAKESPEAR'S SISTER
- ☐ '92 Stay ★

SHAKIRA
- ☐ '07 Beautiful Liar ★ [w/ Beyoncé]
- ☐ '06 Hips Don't Lie ★
- ☐ '05 La Tortura [w/ Alejandro Sanz]
- ☐ '02 Underneath Your Clothes
- ☐ '01 Whenever, Wherever ★

SHALAMAR
- ☐ '84 Dancing In The Sheets
- ☐ '83 Dead Giveaway
- ☐ '79 Second Time Around, The
- ☐ '77 Uptown Festival

SHAMEN, The
- ☐ '91 Move Any Mountain (Progen 91)

SHANA
- ☐ '89 I Want You

SHANGRI-LAS, The
- ☐ '64 Give Him A Great Big Kiss
- ☐ '65 Give Us Your Blessings
- ☐ '65 I Can Never Go Home Anymore
- ☐ '64 Leader Of The Pack ★
- ☐ '66 Long Live Our Love
- ☐ '64 Remember (Walkin' in the Sand)

SHANICE
- ☐ '91 I Love Your Smile ★
- ☐ '92 Saving Forever For You
- ☐ '92 Silent Prayer [w/ Johnny Gill]
- ☐ '99 When I Close My Eyes

SHANNON
- ☐ '83 Let The Music Play ~
  ~~GIMME TONIGHT~~

SHANNON, Del
- ☐ '63 From Me To You
- ☐ '64 Handy Man
- ☐ '61 Hats Off To Larry
- ☐ '61 Hey! Little Girl
- ☐ '64 Keep Searchin' (We'll Follow The Sun)
- ☐ '62 Little Town Flirt
- ☐ '61 Runaway ★
- ☐ '81 Sea Of Love
- ☐ '61 So Long Baby
- ☐ '65 Stranger In Town
- ☐ '62 Swiss Maid, The
- ☐ '63 Two Kinds Of Teardrops

SHAREEFA
- ☐ '06 Need A Boss

SHARP, Dee Dee
- ☐ '63 Do The Bird
- ☐ '62 Gravy (For My Mashed Potatoes)
- ☐ '62 Mashed Potato Time ★
- ☐ '62 Ride!
- ☐ '62 Slow Twistin' [w/ Chubby Checker]
- ☐ '63 Wild!

SHARP, Kevin
- ☐ '96 Nobody Knows

SHARPE, Ray
- ☐ '59 Linda Lu

SHAW, Tommy
- ☐ '84 Girls With Guns

SHAWNNA
- ☐ '06 Gettin' Some

SHeDAISY
- ☐ '00 I Will...But
- ☐ '99 Little Good-Byes
- ☐ '04 Passenger Seat

SHEIK, Duncan
- ☐ '96 Barely Breathing

SHEILA E.
- ☐ '84 Belle Of St. Mark, The
- ☐ '84 Glamorous Life, The
- ☐ '85 Love Bizarre, A

SHELLS, The
- ☐ '60 Baby Oh Baby

SHELTON, Blake
- ☐ '01 Austin
- ☐ '02 Baby, The
- ☐ '06 Nobody But Me
- ☐ '02 Ol' Red
- ☐ '04 Some Beach

SHELTON, Ricky Van
- ☐ '91 I Am A Simple Man
- ☐ '88 I'll Leave This World Loving You
- ☐ '90 I've Cried My Last Tear For You
- ☐ '91 Keep It Between The Lines

- ☐ '88 Life Turned Her That Way
- ☐ '91 Rockin' Years [w/ Dolly Parton]

SHE MOVES
- ☐ '97 Breaking All The Rules

SHENANDOAH
- ☐ '89 Church On Cumberland Road, The
- ☐ '94 If Bubba Can Dance (I Can Too)
- ☐ '90 Next To You, Next To Me

SHEP & THE LIMELITES
- ☐ '61 Daddy's Home ★

SHEPARD, Vonda
- ☐ '87 Can't We Try [w/ Dan Hill]
- ☐ '98 Searchin' My Soul (Theme from "Ally McBeal")

SHEPHERD, Kenny Wayne
- ☐ '98 Blue On Black

SHEPHERD SISTERS
- ☐ '57 Alone (Why Must I Be Alone)

SHEPPARD, T.G.
- ☐ '75 Devil In The Bottle
- ☐ '81 I Loved 'Em Every One
- ☐ '79 Last Cheater's Waltz
- ☐ '81 Party Time
- ☐ '82 War Is Hell (On The Homefront Too)

SHERIFF
- ☐ '83 When I'm With You ★

SHERMAN, Allan
- ☐ '63 Hello Mudduh, Hello Fadduh! ★

SHERMAN, Bobby
- ☐ '71 Cried Like A Baby
- ☐ '71 Drum, The
- ☐ '70 Easy Come, Easy Go
- ☐ '70 Hey, Mister Sun
- ☐ '70 Julie, Do Ya Love Me
- ☐ '69 La La La (If I Had You)
- ☐ '69 Little Woman

SHERRYS, The
- ☐ '62 Pop Pop Pop - Pie

SHIELDS, The
- ☐ '58 You Cheated

SHINEDOWN
- ☐ '04 Burning Bright
- ☐ '03 45
- ☐ '06 I Dare You
- ☐ '05 Save Me

SHIRELLES, The
- ☐ '61 Baby It's You
- ☐ '61 Big John
- ☐ '59 Dedicated To The One I Love ★
- ☐ '63 Don't Say Goodnight And Mean Goodbye
- ☐ '62 Everybody Loves A Lover
- ☐ '63 Foolish Little Girl
- ☐ '58 I Met Him On A Sunday
- ☐ '61 Mama Said

□ '62 Soldier Boy ★
□ '62 Stop The Music
□ '60 Tonights The Night
□ '62 Welcome Home Baby
□ '60 Will You Love Me Tomorrow ★

SHIRLEY, Don, Trio
□ '61 Water Boy

SHIRLEY (& COMPANY)
□ '75 Shame, Shame, Shame

SHIRLEY & LEE
□ '55 Feel So Good
□ '56 I Feel Good
□ '56 Let The Good Times Roll

SHOCKING BLUE, The
□ '69 Venus ★

SHONDELL, Troy
□ '61 This Time

SHOP BOYZ
□ '07 Party Like A Rock Star ★

SHORE, Dinah
□ '57 Chantez-Chantez
□ '57 Fascination
□ '55 Love And Marriage
□ '55 Whatever Lola Wants (Lola Gets)

SHOWMEN, The
□ '61 It Will Stand

SHUST, Aaron
□ '06 My Savior, My God

SIBERRY, Jane
□ '93 Calling All Angels [w/ k.d. lang]
□ '89 Everything Reminds Me Of My Dog

SIGLER, Bunny
□ '67 Let The Good Times Roll & Feel So Good

SILHOUETTES, The
□ '58 Get A Job ★

SILK
□ '93 Freak Me
□ '93 Girl U For Me
□ '99 If You (Lovin' Me)

SILKIE, The
□ '65 You've Got To Hide Your Love Away

SILKK THE SHOCKER
□ '99 It Ain't My Fault 2 [w/ Mystikal]

SILVER
□ '76 Wham Bam (Shang-A-Lang)

SILVERCHAIR
□ '95 Tomorrow

SILVER CONDOR
□ '81 You Could Take My Heart Away

SILVER CONVENTION
□ '75 Fly, Robin, Fly ★ 〰

□ '76 Get Up And Boogie (That's Right)

SIMEONE, Harry, Chorale
□ '58 Little Drummer Boy, The

SIMMONS, Gene
□ '64 Haunted House

SIMMONS, Patrick
□ '83 So Wrong

SIMON, Carly
□ '71 Anticipation
□ '75 Attitude Dancing
□ '86 Coming Around Again
□ '78 Devoted To You [w/ James Taylor]
□ '74 Haven't Got Time For The Pain
□ '80 Jesse
□ '89 Let The River Run
□ '74 Mockingbird [w/ James Taylor]
□ '77 Nobody Does It Better ★
□ '73 Right Thing To Do, The
□ '71 That's The Way I've Always Heard It Should Be
□ '78 You Belong To Me
□ '72 You're So Vain ★

SIMON, Joe
□ '69 Chokin' Kind, The
□ '71 Drowning In The Sea Of Love
□ '75 Get Down, Get Down (Get On The Floor)
□ '72 Power Of Love
□ '73 Step By Step
□ '73 Theme From Cleopatra Jones
□ '68 (You Keep Me) Hangin' On
□ '70 Your Time To Cry

SIMON, Paul
□ '73 American Tune
□ '86 Diamonds On The Soles Of Her Shoes
□ '75 50 Ways To Leave Your Lover ★
□ '75 Gone At Last [w/ Phoebe Snow]
□ '87 Graceland ★
□ '73 Kodachrome ★
□ '80 Late In The Evening
□ '73 Loves Me Like A Rock [w/ The Dixie Hummingbirds]
□ '72 Me And Julio Down By The Schoolyard
□ '72 Mother And Child Reunion
□ '80 One-Trick Pony
□ '77 Slip Slidin' Away
□ '76 Still Crazy After All These Years
□ '86 Under African Skies
□ '78 (What A) Wonderful World [w/ Art Garfunkel & James Taylor]
□ '86 You Can Call Me Al

SIMON & GARFUNKEL
□ '68 America
□ '67 At The Zoo
□ '69 Boxer, The
□ '70 Bridge Over Troubled Water ★
□ '70 Cecilia
□ '66 Dangling Conversation, The
□ '70 El Condor Pasa
□ '67 Fakin' It

SIMON & GARFUNKEL — cont'd
- ☐ '66 Hazy Shade Of Winter, A
- ☐ '66 Homeward Bound
- ☐ '66 I Am A Rock
- ☐ '68 Mrs. Robinson ★
- ☐ '75 My Little Town
- ☐ '68 Scarborough Fair
- ☐ '65 Sound Of Silence, The ★
- ☐ '82 Wake Up Little Susie

SIMONE, Nina
- ☐ '59 I Loves You, Porgy

SIMPLE MINDS
- ☐ '85 Alive & Kicking
- ☐ '86 All The Things She Said
- ☐ '85 Don't You (Forget About Me) ★
- ☐ '85 Sanctify Yourself
- ☐ '91 See The Lights

SIMPLE PLAN
- ☐ '03 Perfect
- ☐ '04 Welcome To My Life

SIMPLY RED
- ☐ '86 Holding Back The Years ★
- ☐ '89 If You Don't Know Me By Now ★
- ☐ '86 Money$ Too Tight (To Mention)
- ☐ '87 Right Thing, The
- ☐ '91 Something Got Me Started

SIMPSON, Ashlee
- ☐ '05 Boyfriend
- ☐ '06 Invisible
- ☐ '06 L.O.V.E.
- ☐ '04 Pieces Of Me ★

SIMPSON, Jessica
- ☐ '00 I Think I'm In Love With You
- ☐ '99 I Wanna Love You Forever ★
- ☐ '01 Irresistible
- ☐ '06 Public Affair, A
- ☐ '04 Take My Breath Away
- ☐ '05 These Boots Are Made For Walkin'
- ☐ '03 With You

SIMPSONS, The
- ☐ '90 Do The Bartman

SIMS TWINS
- ☐ '61 Soothe Me

SINATRA, Frank
- ☐ '57 All The Way ★
- ☐ '64 Best Is Yet To Come, The
- ☐ '57 Chicago
- ☐ '57 Can I Steal A Little Love
- ☐ '58 Come Fly With Me
- ☐ '68 Cycles
- ☐ '64 Fly Me To The Moon
- ☐ '56 Hey! Jealous Lover ★
- ☐ '59 High Hopes
- ☐ '56 (How Little It Matters) How Little We Know
- ☐ '75 I Believe I'm Gonna Love You
- ☐ '62 I Get A Kick Out Of You
- ☐ '56 I've Got The World On A String

- ☐ '56 I've Got You Under My Skin
- ☐ '65 It Was A Very Good Year
- ☐ '55 Learnin' The Blues ★
- ☐ '55 Love And Marriage ★
- ☐ '55 (Love Is) The Tender Trap
- ☐ '65 My Kind Of Town
- ☐ '69 My Way
- ☐ '60 Nice 'N' Easy
- ☐ '58 One For My Baby
- ☐ '61 Pocketful Of Miracles
- ☐ '58 Put Your Dreams Away
- ☐ '68 Rain In My Heart
- ☐ '55 Same Old Saturday Night
- ☐ '61 Second Time Around, The
- ☐ '64 Softly, As I Leave You
- ☐ '67 Somethin' Stupid *[w/ Nancy Sinatra]* ★
- ☐ '64 Somewhere In Your Heart
- ☐ '66 Strangers In The Night ★
- ☐ '66 Summer Wind
- ☐ '59 Talk To Me
- ☐ '66 That's Life
- ☐ '80 Theme From New York, New York ★
- ☐ '58 Witchcraft
- ☐ '67 World We Knew (Over And Over)
- ☐ '56 You Make Me Feel So Young

SINATRA, Nancy
- ☐ '66 Friday's Child
- ☐ '66 How Does That Grab You, Darlin'?
- ☐ '67 Jackson *[w/ Lee Hazlewood]*
- ☐ '67 Lady Bird *[w/ Lee Hazlewood]*
- ☐ '67 Lightning's Girl
- ☐ '67 Love Eyes
- ☐ '68 Some Velvet Morning *[w/ Lee Hazlewood]*
- ☐ '67 Somethin' Stupid *[w/ Frank Sinatra]* ★
- ☐ '66 Sugar Town
- ☐ '69 Summer Wine *[w/ Lee Hazlewood]*
- ☐ '66 These Boots Are Made For Walkin' ★
- ☐ '67 You Only Live Twice

SINCLAIR, Gordon
- ☐ '74 Americans (A Canadian's Opinion)

SINGING DOGS, The
- ☐ '55 Oh! Susanna
- ☐ '55 Jingle Bells

SINGING NUN, The
- ☐ '63 Dominique ★

SIOUXSIE & THE BANSHEES
- ☐ '91 Kiss Them For Me
- ☐ '88 Peek-A-Boo

SIR DOUGLAS QUINTET
- ☐ '69 Mendocino
- ☐ '66 Rains Came, The
- ☐ '65 She's About A Mover

SIR MIX-A-LOT
- ☐ '92 Baby Got Back ★

SISQÓ
- ☐ '99 Got To Get It
- ☐ '00 Incomplete ★
- ☐ '98 It's All About Me *[w/ Mya]*
- ☐ '00 Thong Song ★

SISTER HAZEL
- ☐ '97 All For You

SISTER SLEDGE
- ☐ '81 All American Girls
- ☐ '79 He's The Greatest Dancer
- ☐ '82 My Guy
- ☐ '79 We Are Family ★

SIXPENCE NONE THE RICHER
- ☐ '02 Breathe Your Name
- ☐ '98 Kiss Me ★
- ☐ '99 There She Goes

SIX TEENS, The
- ☐ '56 Casual Look, A

69 BOYZ
- ☐ '94 Tootsee Roll
- ☐ '98 Woof Woof

SKEE-LO
- ☐ '95 I Wish

SKID ROW
- ☐ '89 18 And Life
- ☐ '89 I Remember You

SKIP & FLIP
- ☐ '60 Cherry Pie
- ☐ '59 It Was I

SKYLARK
- ☐ '73 Wildflower

SKYLINERS, The
- ☐ '59 It Happened Today
- ☐ '60 Pennies From Heaven
- ☐ '59 Since I Don't Have You
- ☐ '59 This I Swear

SKYY
- ☐ '82 Call Me
- ☐ '89 Real Love
- ☐ '89 Start Of A Romance

SLADE
- ☐ '73 Cum On Feel The Noize
- ☐ '72 Mama Weer All Crazee Now
- ☐ '84 My Oh My
- ☐ '84 Run Runaway

SLADES, The
- ☐ '58 You Cheated

SLAUGHTER
- ☐ '90 Fly To The Angels
- ☐ '90 Spend My Life
- ☐ '90 Up All Night

SLAVE
- ☐ '77 Slide

SLEDGE, Percy
- ☐ '66 It Tears Me Up
- ☐ '67 Love Me Tender
- ☐ '68 Take Time To Know Her
- ☐ '66 Warm And Tender Love
- ☐ '66 When A Man Loves A Woman ★

SLY & THE FAMILY STONE
- ☐ '68 Dance To The Music ★
- ☐ '68 Everyday People ★
- ☐ '71 Family Affair ★
- ☐ '69 Hot Fun In The Summertime ★
- ☐ '70 I Want To Take You Higher
- ☐ '73 If You Want Me To Stay
- ☐ '72 Runnin' Away
- ☐ '69 Stand!
- ☐ '70 Thank You (Falettinme Be Mice Elf Agin) ★
- ☐ '74 Time For Livin'

SLY FOX
- ☐ '85 Let's Go All The Way

SMALL, Millie
- ☐ '64 My Boy Lollipop ★

SMALL FACES
- ☐ '67 Itchycoo Park

SMASHING PUMPKINS, The
- ☐ '98 Ava Adore
- ☐ '95 Bullet With Butterfly Wings
- ☐ '94 Landslide
- ☐ '95 1979
- ☐ '98 Perfect
- ☐ '00 Stand Inside Your Love
- ☐ '07 Tarantula
- ☐ '96 Thirty-Three
- ☐ '93 Today
- ☐ '96 Tonight, Tonight

SMASH MOUTH
- ☐ '99 All Star ★
- ☐ '98 Can't Get Enough Of You Baby
- ☐ '01 I'm A Believer
- ☐ '99 Then The Morning Comes
- ☐ '97 Walkin' On The Sun ★

SMILEZ & SOUTHSTAR
- ☐ '03 Tell Me (What's Goin' On)

SMITH
- ☐ '69 Baby It's You

SMITH, Cal
- ☐ '74 Country Bumpkin

SMITH, Connie
- ☐ '64 Once A Day

SMITH, Frankie
- ☐ '81 Double Dutch Bus

SMITH, Huey (Piano)
- ☐ '58 Don't You Just Know It
- ☐ '57 Rocking Pneumonia And The Boogie Woogie Flu

SMITH, Hurricane
- ☐ '72 Oh, Babe, What Would You Say?

SMITH, Jimmy
- ☐ '66 Got My Mojo Working
- ☐ '62 Walk On The Wild Side

SMITH, Michael W.
- ☐ '03 Above All
- ☐ '92 Friends
- ☐ '92 I Will Be Here For You
- ☐ '04 Lord Have Mercy
- ☐ '98 Love Me Good
- ☐ '91 Place In This World
- ☐ '99 This Is Your Time

SMITH, O.C.
- ☐ '69 Daddy's Little Man
- ☐ '68 Little Green Apples
- ☐ '68 Son Of Hickory Holler's Tramp, The

SMITH, Patti, Group
- ☐ '78 Because The Night
- ☐ '79 Dancing Barefoot
- ☐ '75 Gloria
- ☐ '88 People Have The Power

SMITH, Ray
- ☐ '60 Rockin' Little Angel

SMITH, Rex
- ☐ '81 Everlasting Love *[w/ Rachel Sweet]*
- ☐ '79 You Take My Breath Away

SMITH, Sammi
- ☐ '71 Help Me Make It Through The Night

SMITH, Somethin', & The Redheads
- ☐ '56 In A Shanty In Old Shanty Town
- ☐ '55 It's A Sin To Tell A Lie

SMITH, Verdelle
- ☐ '66 Tar And Cement

SMITH, Whistling Jack
- ☐ '67 I Was Kaiser Bill's Batman

SMITH, Will
- ☐ '98 Gettin' Jiggy Wit It ★
- ☐ '98 Just The Two Of Us
- ☐ '97 Men In Black ★
- ☐ '98 Miami
- ☐ '05 Switch ★
- ☐ '99 Wild Wild West ★
- ☐ '99 Will 2K

SMITHEREENS, The
- ☐ '87 Behind The Wall Of Sleep
- ☐ '89 Girl Like You, A
- ☐ '88 House We Used To Live In
- ☐ '88 Only A Memory
- ☐ '92 Too Much Passion
- ☐ '91 Top Of The Pops

SMITHS, The
- ☐ '84 Heaven Knows I'm Miserable Now
- ☐ '85 How Soon Is Now?
- ☐ '84 William, It Was Really Nothing

SMOKIE
- ☐ '76 Living Next Door To Alice

SMYTH, Patty
- ☐ '92 No Mistakes

- ☐ '92 Sometimes Love Just Ain't Enough
  [w/ Don Henley] ★

SNAP!
- ☐ '90 Ooops Up
- ☐ '90 Power, The ★
- ☐ '92 Rhythm Is A Dancer ★

SNEAKER
- ☐ '81 More Than Just The Two Of Us

SNIFF 'N' THE TEARS
- ☐ '79 Driver's Seat

SNOOP DOGG
- ☐ '03 Beautiful
- ☐ '93 Dre Day *[w/ Dr. Dre]*
- ☐ '04 Drop It Like It's Hot ★
- ☐ '94 Gin & Juice
- ☐ '93 Next Episode, The *[w/ Dr. Dre]*
- ☐ '93 Nuthin' But A "G" Thang *[w/ Dr. Dre]* ★
- ☐ '98 Still A G Thang
- ☐ '06 That's That
- ☐ '93 What's My Name?

SNOW
- ☐ '93 Girl, I've Been Hurt
- ☐ '93 Informer ★

SNOW, Hank
- ☐ '62 I've Been Everywhere

SNOW, Phoebe
- ☐ '75 Gone At Last *[w/ Paul Simon]*
- ☐ '75 Poetry Man

SNOW PATROL
- ☐ '06 Chasing Cars ★

SOFT CELL
- ☐ '82 Tainted Love ★

SOHO
- ☐ '90 Hippychick ★

SOLÉ
- ☐ '99 4,5,6

SOMETHIN' FOR THE PEOPLE
- ☐ '97 My Love Is The Shhh! ★

SOMMERS, Joanie
- ☐ '62 Johnny Get Angry

SON BY FOUR
- ☐ '00 Purest Of Pain (A Puro Dolor)

SONIC YOUTH
- ☐ '88 Teen Age Riot

SONIQUE
- ☐ '00 It Feels So Good

SONNY & CHER
- ☐ '71 All I Ever Need Is You
- ☐ '65 Baby Don't Go
- ☐ '67 Beat Goes On, The
- ☐ '65 But You're Mine
- ☐ '72 Cowboys Work Is Never Done, A
- ☐ '65 I Got You Babe ★

☐ '65 Just You
☐ '65 Laugh At Me *[SONNY]*
☐ '66 Little Man
☐ '66 What Now My Love
☐ '72 When You Say Love

SOPWITH "CAMEL", The
☐ '66 Hello Hello

S.O.S. BAND, The
☐ '86 Finest, The
☐ '83 Just Be Good To Me ⬅
☐ '80 Take Your Time (Do It Right) ★ ⬅

SOUL, David
☐ '77 Don't Give Up On Us

SOUL, Jimmy
☐ '63 If You Wanna Be Happy ★
☐ '62 Twistin' Matilda

SOUL ASYLUM
☐ '95 Misery
☐ '93 Runaway Train ★
☐ '92 Somebody To Shove

SOUL CHILDREN, The
☐ '74 I'll Be The Other Woman

SOULDECISION
☐ '00 Faded

SOUL FOR REAL
☐ '95 Candy Rain ★
☐ '95 Every Little Thing I Do

SOULJA BOY
☐ '07 Crank That (Soulja Boy) ★

SOUL SURVIVORS
☐ '67 Explosion In Your Soul
☐ '67 Expressway To Your Heart

S.O.U.L. S.Y.S.T.E.M., The
☐ '92 It's Gonna Be A Lovely Day

SOUL II SOUL
☐ '89 Back To Life ★ ⬅
☐ '89 Keep On Movin' ⬅

SOUNDGARDEN
☐ '94 Black Hole Sun
☐ '96 Blow Up The Outside World
☐ '96 Burden In My Hand
☐ '94 Fell On Black Days
☐ '96 Pretty Noose
☐ '94 Spoonman

SOUNDS OF BLACKNESS
☐ '94 I Believe
☐ '91 Optimistic

SOUNDS OF SUNSHINE
☐ '71 Love Means (You Never Have To Say You're Sorry)

SOUNDS ORCHESTRAL
☐ '65 Cast Your Fate To The Wind

SOUP DRAGONS, The
☐ '92 Divine Thing
☐ '90 I'm Free

SOUTH, Joe
☐ '69 Don't It Make You Want To Go Home
☐ '69 Games People Play
☐ '70 Walk A Mile In My Shoes

SOUTHER, J.D.
☐ '74 Fallin' In Love *[SOUTHER, HILLMAN, FURAY BAND]*
☐ '81 Her Town Too *[w/ James Taylor]*
☐ '79 You're Only Lonely

SOVINE, Red
☐ '65 Giddyup Go
☐ '76 Teddy Bear

SPACEHOG
☐ '95 In The Meantime

SPACEMEN, The
☐ '59 Clouds, The

SPANDAU BALLET
☐ '83 Gold
☐ '84 Only When You Leave
☐ '83 True ★

SPANIELS, The
☐ '53 Baby It's You
☐ '54 Goodnite Sweetheart, Goodnite

SPANKY & OUR GANG
☐ '67 Lazy Day
☐ '68 Like To Get To Know You
☐ '67 Making Every Minute Count
☐ '68 Sunday Mornin'
☐ '67 Sunday Will Never Be The Same

SPARKLE
☐ '98 Be Careful *[w/ R. Kelly]*

SPARKS, Jordin
☐ '07 This Is My Now

SPARXXX, Bubba
☐ '06 Ms. New Booty
☐ '01 Ugly

SPEARS, Billie Jo
☐ '75 Blanket On The Ground

SPEARS, Britney
☐ '98 ...Baby One More Time ★
☐ '04 Everytime
☐ '00 From The Bottom Of My Broken Heart
☐ '01 I'm A Slave 4 U
☐ '00 Lucky
☐ '03 Me Against The Music
☐ '00 Oops!...I Did It Again
☐ '99 Sometimes
☐ '00 Stronger
☐ '04 Toxic ★
☐ '99 (You Drive Me) Crazy

SPENCE, Judson
☐ '88 Yeah, Yeah, Yeah

SPENCER, Tracie
- ☐ '99 It's All About You (Not About Me)
- ☐ '92 Love Me
- ☐ '88 Symptoms Of True Love
- ☐ '91 Tender Kisses ⎯⎯
- ☐ '90 This House

SPICE GIRLS
- ☐ '98 Goodbye
- ☐ '97 Say You'll Be There
- ☐ '97 Spice Up Your Life
- ☐ '98 Stop
- ☐ '98 Too Much
- ☐ '97 2 Become 1 ★
- ☐ '97 Wannabe ★

SPIDER
- ☐ '80 New Romance (It's A Mystery)

SPIN DOCTORS
- ☐ '92 Little Miss Can't Be Wrong
- ☐ '93 Two Princes

SPINNERS
- ☐ '72 Could It Be I'm Falling In Love ⎯⎯
- ☐ '80 Cupid/I've Loved You For A Long Time
- ☐ '73 Ghetto Child
- ☐ '65 I'll Always Love You
- ☐ '72 I'll Be Around
- ☐ '74 I'm Coming Home
- ☐ '70 It's A Shame
- ☐ '75 Living A Little, Laughing A Little
- ☐ '74 Love Don't Love Nobody
- ☐ '75 Love Or Leave
- ☐ '74 Mighty Love
- ☐ '73 One Of A Kind (Love Affair)
- ☐ '76 Rubberband Man, The ★
- ☐ '61 That's What Girls Are Made For
- ☐ '74 Then Came You [w/ Dionne Warwick] ★
- ☐ '75 "They Just Can't Stop It" the (Games People Play)
- ☐ '79 Working My Way Back To You/Forgive Me, Girl

SPIRAL STARECASE
- ☐ '69 More Today Than Yesterday

SPIRIT
- ☐ '69 I Got A Line On You
- ☐ '71 Nature's Way

SPLIT ENZ
- ☐ '80 I Got You
- ☐ '82 Six Months In A Leaky Boat

SPOKESMEN, The
- ☐ '65 Dawn Of Correction, The

SPONGE
- ☐ '95 Molly (Sixteen Candles)

SPORTY THIEVZ
- ☐ '99 No Pigeons

SPRINGFIELD, Dusty
- ☐ '66 All I See Is You
- ☐ '69 Brand New Me, A
- ☐ '64 I Only Want To Be With You
- ☐ '67 I'll Try Anything
- ☐ '67 Look Of Love, The
- ☐ '62 Silver Threads And Golden Needles
  [THE SPRINGFIELDS]
- ☐ '68 Son-Of-A Preacher Man
- ☐ '64 Stay Awhile
- ☐ '87 What Have I Done To Deserve This?
  [w/ Pet Shop Boys] ★
- ☐ '69 Windmills Of Your Mind, The
- ☐ '64 Wishin' And Hopin'
- ☐ '66 You Don't Have To Say You Love Me

SPRINGFIELD, Rick
- ☐ '83 Affair Of The Heart
- ☐ '84 Bop 'Til You Drop
- ☐ '84 Bruce
- ☐ '85 Celebrate Youth
- ☐ '82 Don't Talk To Strangers ★
- ☐ '84 Don't Walk Away
- ☐ '83 Human Touch
- ☐ '82 I Get Excited
- ☐ '81 I've Done Everything For You
- ☐ '81 Jessie's Girl ★
- ☐ '81 Love Is Alright Tonite
- ☐ '84 Love Somebody
- ☐ '88 Rock Of Life
- ☐ '83 Souls
- ☐ '72 Speak To The Sky
- ☐ '85 State Of The Heart
- ☐ '82 What Kind Of Fool Am I

SPRINGSTEEN, Bruce
- ☐ '78 Badlands
- ☐ '92 Better Days
- ☐ '73 Blinded By The Light
- ☐ '84 Born In The U.S.A. ★
- ☐ '75 Born To Run ★
- ☐ '87 Brilliant Disguise
- ☐ '81 Cadillac Ranch
- ☐ '84 Cover Me
- ☐ '84 Dancing In The Dark ★
- ☐ '78 Darkness On The Edge Of Town
- ☐ '05 Devils & Dust
- ☐ '81 Fade Away
- ☐ '73 For You
- ☐ '73 4th Of July, Asbury Park (Sandy)
- ☐ '85 Glory Days
- ☐ '92 Human Touch
- ☐ '80 Hungry Heart ★
- ☐ '85 I'm Goin' Down
- ☐ '85 I'm On Fire
- ☐ '75 Jungleland
- ☐ '85 My Hometown ★
- ☐ '87 One Step Up
- ☐ '84 Pink Cadillac
- ☐ '78 Promised Land
- ☐ '78 Prove It All Night
- ☐ '02 Rising, The
- ☐ '73 Rosalita (Come Out Tonight)
- ☐ '75 Santa Claus Is Comin' To Town
- ☐ '95 Secret Garden
- ☐ '73 Spirit In The Night
- ☐ '94 Streets Of Philadelphia ★
- ☐ '75 Tenth Avenue Freeze-Out
- ☐ '75 Thunder Road ★

- ☐ '85 Trapped
- ☐ '87 Tunnel Of Love
- ☐ '86 War [live]

SPYRO GYRA
- ☐ '79 Morning Dance

SQUEEZE
- ☐ '82 Black Coffee In Bed
- ☐ '87 853-5937
- ☐ '87 Hourglass
- ☐ '81 Tempted

SQUIER, Billy
- ☐ '82 Everybody Wants You
- ☐ '81 In The Dark
- ☐ '84 Rock Me Tonite
- ☐ '81 Stroke, The

SR-71
- ☐ '00 Right Now

STACEY Q
- ☐ '86 Two Of Hearts
- ☐ '86 We Connect

STAFFORD, Jim
- ☐ '75 I Got Stoned And I Missed It
- ☐ '74 My Girl Bill
- ☐ '73 Spiders & Snakes
- ☐ '73 Swamp Witch
- ☐ '74 Wildwood Weed
- ☐ '74 Your Bulldog Drinks Champagne

STAFFORD, Jo
- ☐ '55 It's Almost Tomorrow
- ☐ '56 On London Bridge
- ☐ '55 Suddenly There's A Valley
- ☐ '55 Teach Me Tonight
- ☐ '57 Wind In The Willow

STAFFORD, Terry
- ☐ '64 I'll Touch A Star
- ☐ '64 Suspicion ★

STAIND
- ☐ '01 Fade
- ☐ '01 For You
- ☐ '01 It's Been Awhile ★
- ☐ '03 Price To Play
- ☐ '05 Right Here
- ☐ '03 So Far Away

STALLION
- ☐ '77 Old Fashioned Boy (You're The One)

STALLONE, Frank
- ☐ '83 Far From Over

STAMPEDERS
- ☐ '76 Hit The Road Jack
- ☐ '71 Sweet City Woman

STAMPLEY, Joe
- ☐ '73 Soul Song

STANDELLS, The
- ☐ '66 Dirty Water

STANLEY, Michael, Band
- ☐ '80 He Can't Love You
- ☐ '83 My Town

STANSFIELD, Lisa
- ☐ '90 All Around The World
- ☐ '92 All Woman
- ☐ '91 Change
- ☐ '90 This Is The Right Time
- ☐ '90 You Can't Deny It

STAPLE SINGERS, The
- ☐ '71 Heavy Makes You Happy (Sha-Na-Boom Boom)
- ☐ '72 I'll Take You There ★
- ☐ '73 If You're Ready (Come Go With Me)
- ☐ '75 Let's Do It Again ★
- ☐ '73 Oh La De Da
- ☐ '71 Respect Yourself
- ☐ '72 This World
- ☐ '74 Touch A Hand, Make A Friend
- ☐ '56 Uncloudy Day

STAPLETON, Cyril, & His Orchestra
- ☐ '59 Children's Marching Song, The
- ☐ '56 Italian Theme, The

STARBUCK
- ☐ '77 Everybody Be Dancin'
- ☐ '76 Moonlight Feels Right

STARCHER, Buddy
- ☐ '66 History Repeats Itself

STARGARD
- ☐ '78 Theme Song From "Which Way Is Up"

STARLAND VOCAL BAND
- ☐ '76 Afternoon Delight ★

STARLETS, The
- ☐ '61 Better Tell Him No

STARPOINT
- ☐ '85 Object Of My Desire

STARR, Brenda K.
- ☐ '88 I Still Believe
- ☐ '88 What You See Is What You Get

STARR, Edwin
- ☐ '65 Agent Double-O-Soul
- ☐ '70 Stop The War Now
- ☐ '69 Twenty-Five Miles
- ☐ '70 War ★

STARR, Kay
- ☐ '57 My Heart Reminds Me
- ☐ '55 Rock And Roll Waltz ★
- ☐ '56 Second Fiddle

STARR, Randy
- ☐ '57 After School

STARR, Ringo
- ☐ '72 Back Off Boogaloo
- ☐ '76 Dose Of Rock 'N' Roll, A
- ☐ '71 Early 1970
- ☐ '71 It Don't Come Easy

STARR, Ringo — cont'd
- ☐ '75 It's All Down To Goodnight Vienna
- ☐ '75 No No Song
- ☐ '74 Oh My My
- ☐ '74 Only You
- ☐ '73 Photograph ★
- ☐ '81 Wrack My Brain
- ☐ '73 You're Sixteen ★

STARS on 45
- ☐ '81 Medley

STARSHIP — see JEFFERSON AIRPLANE

STARZ
- ☐ '77 Cherry Baby

STATLER BROTHERS, The
- ☐ '71 Bed Of Roses
- ☐ '72 Class Of '57, The
- ☐ '78 Do You Know You Are My Sunshine
- ☐ '72 Do You Remember These
- ☐ '65 Flowers On The Wall

STATON, Candi
- ☐ '70 Stand By Your Man
- ☐ '76 Young Hearts Run Free

STATUS QUO, The
- ☐ '68 Pictures Of Matchstick Men

STEALERS WHEEL
- ☐ '74 Star
- ☐ '73 Stuck In The Middle With You

STEAM
- ☐ '69 Na Na Hey Hey Kiss Him Goodbye ★

STEEL BREEZE
- ☐ '83 Dreamin' Is Easy
- ☐ '82 You Don't Want Me Anymore

STEELHEART
- ☐ '91 I'll Never Let You Go (Angel Eyes) ★

STEELY DAN
- ☐ '77 Aja
- ☐ '74 Any Major Dude Will Tell You
- ☐ '80 Babylon Sisters
- ☐ '77 Black Cow
- ☐ '75 Black Friday
- ☐ '73 Bodhisattva
- ☐ '00 Cousin Dupree
- ☐ '78 Deacon Blues
- ☐ '72 Dirty Work
- ☐ '72 Do It Again
- ☐ '78 FM (No Static At All)
- ☐ '76 Fez, The
- ☐ '80 Hey Nineteen
- ☐ '78 Josie
- ☐ '76 Kid Charlemagne
- ☐ '73 My Old School
- ☐ '77 Peg
- ☐ '74 Pretzel Logic
- ☐ '73 Reeling In The Years
- ☐ '74 Rikki Don't Lose That Number
- ☐ '81 Time Out Of Mind

STEFANI, Gwen
- ☐ '05 Cool
- ☐ '01 Let Me Blow Ya Mind *[w/ Eve]* ★
- ☐ '05 Luxurious
- ☐ '05 Hollaback Girl ★
- ☐ '05 Rich Girl ★
- ☐ '07 Sweet Escape, The ★
- ☐ '06 Wind It Up ★

STEINER, Tommy Shane
- ☐ '01 What If She's An Angel

STEINMAN, Jim
- ☐ '81 Rock And Roll Dreams Come Through

STEPHENSON, Van
- ☐ '84 Modern Day Delilah

STEPPENWOLF
- ☐ '68 Born To Be Wild ★
- ☐ '70 Hey Lawdy Mama
- ☐ '68 Magic Carpet Ride
- ☐ '69 Monster
- ☐ '69 Move Over
- ☐ '68 Pusher, The
- ☐ '69 Rock Me
- ☐ '74 Straight Shootin' Woman

STEREO MC'S
- ☐ '93 Connected
- ☐ '91 Elevate My Mind

STEREOS, The
- ☐ '61 I Really Love You

STEVENS, Cat
- ☐ '74 Another Saturday Night
- ☐ '71 Father & Son
- ☐ '68 First Cut Is The Deepest, The
- ☐ '73 Hurt, The
- ☐ '71 Moon Shadow
- ☐ '72 Morning Has Broken ★
- ☐ '74 Oh Very Young
- ☐ '71 Peace Train
- ☐ '74 Ready
- ☐ '77 (Remember The Days Of The) Old Schoolyard
- ☐ '72 Sitting
- ☐ '75 Two Fine People
- ☐ '71 Wild World

STEVENS, Connie
- ☐ '59 Kookie, Kookie (Lend Me Your Comb)
  [w/ Connie Stevens]
- ☐ '60 Sixteen Reasons

STEVENS, Dodie
- ☐ '59 Pink Shoe Laces ★

STEVENS, Ray
- ☐ '62 Ahab, The Arab
- ☐ '69 Along Came Jones
- ☐ '70 Everything Is Beautiful ★
- ☐ '69 Gitarzan
- ☐ '63 Harry The Hairy Ape
- ☐ '77 In The Mood

- ☐ '61 Jeremiah Peabody's Poly Unsaturated Quick Dissolving Fast Acting Pleasant Tasting Green And Purple Pills
- ☐ '75 Misty
- ☐ '68 Mr. Businessman
- ☐ '74 Streak, The ★
- ☐ '88 Surfin' U.S.S.R.

STEVENSON, B.W.
- ☐ '73 My Maria

STEVIE B
- ☐ '90 Because I Love You (The Postman Song) ★
- ☐ '95 Dream About You
- ☐ '89 I Wanna Be The One ---
- ☐ '91 I'll Be By Your Side
- ☐ '89 In My Eyes
- ☐ '90 Love & Emotion
- ☐ '90 Love Me For Life

STEWART, Al
- ☐ '80 Midnight Rocks
- ☐ '77 On The Border
- ☐ '79 Song On The Radio
- ☐ '78 Time Passages
- ☐ '76 Year Of The Cat

STEWART, Amii
- ☐ '79 Knock On Wood ★

STEWART, Billy
- ☐ '65 I Do Love You
- ☐ '66 Secret Love
- ☐ '65 Sitting In The Park
- ☐ '66 Summertime

STEWART, David A.
- ☐ '91 Lily Was Here

STEWART, Jermaine
- ☐ '88 Say It Again
- ☐ '86 We Don't Have To Take Our Clothes Off

STEWART, John
- ☐ '79 Gold
- ☐ '79 Lost Her In The Sun
- ☐ '79 Midnight Wind

STEWART, Rod
- ☐ '79 Ain't Love A Bitch
- ☐ '93 All For Love [w/ Bryan Adams & Sting] ★
- ☐ '72 Angel
- ☐ '04 Baby, It's Cold Outside
- ☐ '83 Baby Jane
- ☐ '91 Broken Arrow
- ☐ '89 Crazy About Her
- ☐ '70 Cut Across Shorty
- ☐ '78 Da Ya Think I'm Sexy? ★
- ☐ '89 Downtown Train ★
- ☐ '71 Every Picture Tells A Story
- ☐ '77 First Cut Is The Deepest, The
- ☐ '88 Forever Young
- ☐ '69 Handbags And Gladrags
- ☐ '93 Have I Told You Lately [live] ★
- ☐ '94 Having A Party [w/ Ronnie Wood]

- ☐ '78 Hot Legs
- ☐ '71 (I Know) I'm Losing You [w/ Faces]
- ☐ '78 I Was Only Joking
- ☐ '84 Infatuation
- ☐ '77 Killing Of Georgie, The
- ☐ '88 Lost In You
- ☐ '86 Love Touch
- ☐ '71 Maggie May ★
- ☐ '74 Mine For Me
- ☐ '91 Motown Song, The [w/ The Temptations]
- ☐ '88 My Heart Can't Tell You No
- ☐ '80 Passion
- ☐ '85 People Get Ready [w/ Jeff Beck]
- ☐ '71 Reason To Believe
- ☐ '93 Reason To Believe [live] [w/ Ronnie Wood]
- ☐ '91 Rhythm Of My Heart ★
- ☐ '75 Sailing
- ☐ '96 So Far Away
- ☐ '84 Some Guys Have All The Luck
- ☐ '90 This Old Heart Of Mine (1989 Version) [w/ Ronald Isley]
- ☐ '82 Tonight I'm Yours (Don't Hurt Me)
- ☐ '76 Tonight's The Night (Gonna Be Alright) ★
- ☐ '83 What Am I Gonna Do (I'm So In Love With You)
- ☐ '72 You Wear It Well
- ☐ '77 You're In My Heart (The Final Acclaim) ★
- ☐ '81 Young Turks ★

STEWART, Sandy
- ☐ '62 My Coloring Book

STIGERS, Curtis
- ☐ '91 I Wonder Why

STILLS, Stephen
- ☐ '71 Change Partners
- ☐ '70 Love The One You're With
- ☐ '71 Sit Yourself Down

STING
- ☐ '93 All For Love [w/ Bryan Adams & Rod Stewart] ★
- ☐ '91 All This Time
- ☐ '06 Always On Your Side [w/ Sheryl Crow]
- ☐ '88 Be Still My Beating Heart
- ☐ '00 Desert Rose
- ☐ '93 Fields Of Gold ★
- ☐ '85 Fortress Around Your Heart
- ☐ '87 Fragile
- ☐ '96 I'm So Happy I Can't Stop Crying
- ☐ '93 If I Ever Lose My Faith In You
- ☐ '85 If You Love Somebody Set Them Free ★
- ☐ '85 Love Is The Seventh Wave
- ☐ '86 Russians
- ☐ '87 We'll Be Together
- ☐ '94 When We Dance

STITES, Gary
- ☐ '59 Lonely For You

STOLOFF, Morris
- ☐ '56 Moonglow and Theme From "Picnic" ★

STONE, Cliffie, & His Orchestra
- ☐ '55 Popcorn Song, The

STONE, Doug
- ☐ '93 I Never Knew Love
- ☐ '91 In A Different Light
- ☐ '91 Jukebox With A Country Song, A
- ☐ '92 Too Busy Being In Love
- ☐ '93 Why Didn't I Think Of That

STONE, Joss
- ☐ '05 Cry Baby/Piece Of My Heart

STONE, Kirby, Four
- ☐ '58 Baubles, Bangles And Beads

STONEBOLT
- ☐ '78 I Will Still Love You

STONE ROSES, The
- ☐ '94 Love Spreads

STONE SOUR
- ☐ '02 Bother
- ☐ '07 Sillyworld
- ☐ '07 Through Glass

STONE TEMPLE PILOTS
- ☐ '96 Big Bang Baby
- ☐ '94 Big Empty
- ☐ '93 Creep
- ☐ '95 Dancing Days
- ☐ '94 Interstate Love Song
- ☐ '96 Lady Picture Show
- ☐ '93 Plush
- ☐ '00 Sour Girl
- ☐ '96 Trippin' On A Hole In A Paper Heart
- ☐ '94 Vasoline

STOOGES, The — see POP, Iggy

STOOKEY, Paul
- ☐ '71 Wedding Song (There Is Love)

STORIES
- ☐ '73 Brother Louie ★

STORM, The
- ☐ '91 I've Got A Lot To Learn About Love

STORM, Billy
- ☐ '59 I've Come Of Age

STORM, Gale
- ☐ '57 Dark Moon
- ☐ '55 I Hear You Knocking
- ☐ '56 Ivory Tower
- ☐ '55 Memories Are Made Of This
- ☐ '55 Teen Age Prayer
- ☐ '56 Why Do Fools Fall In Love

STRAIT, George
- ☐ '87 All My Ex's Live In Texas
- ☐ '87 Am I Blue
- ☐ '00 Best Day, The
- ☐ '94 Big One, The
- ☐ '96 Blue Clear Sky
- ☐ '96 Carried Away
- ☐ '97 Carrying Your Love With Me
- ☐ '95 Check Yes Or No
- ☐ '03 Cowboys Like Us
- ☐ '84 Does Fort Worth Ever Cross Your Mind
- ☐ '93 Easy Come, Easy Go
- ☐ '06 Give It Away
- ☐ '93 Heartland
- ☐ '92 I Cross My Heart
- ☐ '04 I Hate Everything
- ☐ '98 I Just Want To Dance With You
- ☐ '90 I've Come To Expect It From You
- ☐ '91 If I Know Me
- ☐ '07 It Just Comes Natural
- ☐ '02 Living And Living Well
- ☐ '90 Love Without End, Amen
- ☐ '87 Ocean Front Property
- ☐ '97 One Night At A Time
- ☐ '84 Right Or Wrong
- ☐ '97 Round About Way
- ☐ '01 Run
- ☐ '06 Seashores Of Mexico, The
- ☐ '06 She Let Herself Go
- ☐ '02 She'll Leave You With A Smile
- ☐ '07 Wrapped
- ☐ '99 Write This Down
- ☐ '94 You Can't Make A Heart Love Somebody
- ☐ '91 You Know Me Better Than That

STRANGELOVES, The
- ☐ '65 Cara-Lin
- ☐ '65 I Want Candy
- ☐ '66 Night Time

STRAWBERRY ALARM CLOCK
- ☐ '67 Incense And Peppermints ★
- ☐ '67 Tomorrow

STRAY CATS
- ☐ '83 I Won't Stand In Your Way
- ☐ '82 Rock This Town ★
- ☐ '83 (She's) Sexy + 17
- ☐ '82 Stray Cat Strut ★

STREET PEOPLE
- ☐ '70 Jennifer Tomkins

STREISAND, Barbra
- ☐ '81 Comin' In And Out Of Your Life
- ☐ '64 Don't Rain On My Parade
- ☐ '64 Funny Girl
- ☐ '80 Guilty [w/ Barry Gibb]
- ☐ '63 Happy Days Are Here Again
- ☐ '65 He Touched Me
- ☐ '96 I Finally Found Someone [w/ Bryan Adams]
- ☐ '80 Kiss Me In The Rain
- ☐ '76 Love Theme From "A Star Is Born" (Evergreen) ★
- ☐ '78 Love Theme From "Eyes Of Laura Mars" (Prisoner)
- ☐ '79 Main Event/Fight, The
- ☐ '82 Memory
- ☐ '77 My Heart Belongs To Me
- ☐ '65 My Man
- ☐ '79 No More Tears (Enough Is Enough) [w/ Donna Summer] ★

- ☐ '83 Papa, Can You Hear Me?
- ☐ '64 People
- ☐ '65 Second Hand Rose
- ☐ '85 Somewhere
- ☐ '78 Songbird
- ☐ '70 Stoney End
- ☐ '67 Stout-Hearted Men
- ☐ '72 Sweet Inspiration/Where You Lead
- ☐ '88 Till I Loved You [w/ Don Johnson]
- ☐ '71 Time And Love
- ☐ '83 Way He Makes Me Feel, The
- ☐ '73 Way We Were, The ★
- ☐ '81 What Kind Of Fool [w/ Barry Gibb]
- ☐ '71 Where You Lead
- ☐ '80 Woman In Love ★
- ☐ '78 You Don't Bring Me Flowers [w/ Neil Diamond] ★

STRING-A-LONGS, The
- ☐ '61 Wheels ★

STROKES, The
- ☐ '01 Last Nite

STRONG, Barrett
- ☐ '60 Money (That's what I want)

STRUNK, Jud
- ☐ '75 Biggest Parakeets In Town, The
- ☐ '73 Daisy A Day

STRYPER
- ☐ '87 Honestly

STUDDARD, Ruben
- ☐ '03 Flying Without Wings ★
- ☐ '04 Sorry 2004
- ☐ '03 Superstar

STYLE COUNCIL, The
- ☐ '84 My Ever Changing Moods

STYLES
- ☐ '02 Good Times

STYLISTICS, The
- ☐ '72 Betcha By Golly, Wow
- ☐ '73 Break Up To Make Up
- ☐ '72 I'm Stone In Love With You
- ☐ '74 Let's Put It All Together
- ☐ '72 People Make The World Go Round
- ☐ '73 Rockin' Roll Baby
- ☐ '71 Stop, Look, Listen (To Your Heart)
- ☐ '71 You Are Everything
- ☐ '74 You Make Me Feel Brand New ★
- ☐ '73 You'll Never Get To Heaven (If You Break My Heart)

STYX
- ☐ '79 Babe ★
- ☐ '81 Best Of Times, The ★
- ☐ '78 Blue Collar Man (Long Nights)
- ☐ '77 Come Sail Away
- ☐ '76 Crystal Ball
- ☐ '83 Don't Let It End
- ☐ '78 Fooling Yourself (The Angry Young Man)
- ☐ '77 Grand Illusion, The

- ☐ '74 Lady
- ☐ '76 Lorelei
- ☐ '91 Love At First Sight
- ☐ '76 Mademoiselle
- ☐ '83 Mr. Roboto ★
- ☐ '79 Renegade
- ☐ '90 Show Me The Way ★
- ☐ '78 Sing For The Day
- ☐ '76 Suite Madame Blue
- ☐ '81 Too Much Time On My Hands
- ☐ '79 Why Me

SUAVE'
- ☐ '88 My Girl

SUBLIME
- ☐ '97 Santeria
- ☐ '96 What I Got
- ☐ '97 Wrong Way

SUBWAY
- ☐ '95 This Lil' Game We Play [w/ 702]

SUGARCUBES, The
- ☐ '88 Coldsweat
- ☐ '92 Hit
- ☐ '89 Regina

SUGARHILL GANG
- ☐ '79 Rapper's Delight ★

SUGARLAND
- ☐ '05 Baby Girl
- ☐ '06 Just Might (Make Me Believe)
- ☐ '07 Settlin'
- ☐ '05 Something More
- ☐ '06 Want To

SUGARLOAF
- ☐ '74 Don't Call Us, We'll Call You
- ☐ '70 Green-Eyed Lady ★

SUGAR RAY
- ☐ '98 Every Morning ★
- ☐ '00 Falls Apart (Run Away)
- ☐ '97 Fly ★
- ☐ '99 Someday
- ☐ '01 When It's Over

SUM 41
- ☐ '01 Fat Lip

SUMMER, Donna
- ☐ '79 Bad Girls ★
- ☐ '80 Cold Love
- ☐ '79 Dim All The Lights
- ☐ '79 Heaven Knows [w/ Brooklyn Dreams] ★
- ☐ '79 Hot Stuff ★
- ☐ '77 I Feel Love
- ☐ '77 I Love You
- ☐ '78 Last Dance ★
- ☐ '82 Love Is In Control (Finger On The Trigger)
- ☐ '75 Love To Love You Baby ★
- ☐ '78 MacArthur Park ★
- ☐ '79 No More Tears (Enough Is Enough) [w/ Barbra Streisand] ★
- ☐ '80 On The Radio

SUMMER, Donna — cont'd
- ☑ '83 She Works Hard For The Money ★
- ☐ '82 State Of Independence
- ☐ '84 There Goes My Baby
- ☐ '89 This Time I Know It's For Real
- ☐ '80 Walk Away
- ☐ '80 Wanderer, The ★
- ☐ '82 Woman In Me, The

SUMMER, Henry Lee
- ☐ '89 Hey Baby
- ☐ '88 I Wish I Had A Girl

SUNDAYS, The
- ☐ '90 Here's Where The Story Ends
- ☐ '92 Love

SUNNY & THE SUNGLOWS
- ☐ '63 Talk To Me

SUNNYSIDERS, The
- ☐ '55 Hey, Mr. Banjo

SUNSCREEM
- ☐ '92 Love U More

SUNSHINE COMPANY, The
- ☐ '67 Back On The Street Again

SUPERNAW, Doug
- ☐ '93 I Don't Call Him Daddy

SUPERTRAMP
- ☐ '75 Bloody Well Right
- ☐ '79 Breakfast In America
- ☐ '85 Cannonball
- ☐ '75 Dreamer
- ☐ '80 Dreamer [live]
- ☐ '77 Give A Little Bit
- ☐ '79 Goodbye Stranger
- ☐ '82 It's Raining Again ★
- ☐ '79 Logical Song, The ★
- ☐ '83 My Kind Of Lady
- ☐ '75 Rudy
- ☐ '75 School
- ☐ '79 Take The Long Way Home

SUPREMES, The
- ☑ '64 Baby Love ★
- ☐ '65 Back In My Arms Again
- ☐ '64 Come See About Me ★
- ☐ '69 Composer, The
- ☐ '70 Everybody's Got The Right To Love
- ☐ '72 Floy Joy
- ☐ '68 Forever Came Today
- ☐ '67 Happening, The
- ☐ '65 I Hear A Symphony
- ☐ '69 I'll Try Something New [w/ The Temptations]
- ☐ '68 I'm Gonna Make You Love Me [w/ The Temptations]
- ☐ '69 I'm Livin' In Shame
- ☐ '67 In And Out Of Love
- ☐ '68 Love Child ★
- ☐ '67 Love Is Here And Now You're Gone
- ☐ '66 Love Is Like An Itching In My Heart
- ☐ '66 My World Is Empty Without You

- ☐ '71 Nathan Jones
- ☐ '69 No Matter What Sign You Are
- ☐ '65 Nothing But Heartaches
- ☐ '67 Reflections
- ☐ '70 River Deep - Mountain High [w/ the Four Tops]
- ☐ '68 Some Things You Never Get Used To
- ☐ '69 Someday We'll Be Together
- ☐ '70 Stoned Love
- ☑ '65 Stop! In The Name Of Love ★
- ☐ '70 Up The Ladder To The Roof
- ☐ '63 When The Lovelight Starts Shining Through His Eyes
- ☐ '64 Where Did Our Love Go ★
- ☐ '66 You Can't Hurry Love ★
- ☑ '66 You Keep Me Hangin' On ★

SURFACE
- ☐ '89 Closer Than Friends
- ☐ '90 First Time, The ★
- ☐ '87 Happy
- ☑ '91 Never Gonna Let You Down
- ☑ '89 Shower Me With Your Love
- ☑ '89 You Are My Everything

SURFARIS, The
- ☐ '63 Wipe Out ★

SURVIVOR
- ☐ '82 American Heartbeat
- ☐ '85 Burning Heart
- ☑ '82 Eye Of The Tiger ★
- ☐ '85 High On You
- ☐ '84 I Can't Hold Back
- ☑ '86 Is This Love
- ☐ '81 Poor Man's Son
- ☐ '85 Search Is Over, The

SWAN, Billy
- ☐ '74 I Can Help ★

SWANN, Bettye
- ☐ '69 Don't Touch Me
- ☐ '67 Make Me Yours

SWAYZE, Patrick
- ☑ '87 She's Like The Wind

SWEAT, Keith
- ☐ '98 Come And Get With Me
- ☑ '88 I Want Her
- ☑ '90 I'll Give All My Love To You
- ☐ '99 I'm Not Ready
- ☐ '91 Keep It Comin'
- ☑ '88 Make It Last Forever
- ☐ '90 Make You Sweat
- ☐ '90 Merry Go Round
- ☑ '96 Nobody ★
- ☐ '88 Something Just Ain't Right
- ☑ '96 Twisted ★
- ☐ '92 Why Me Baby?

SWEATHOG
- ☐ '71 Hallelujah

SWEET
- ☐ '76 Action

- ☐ '75 Ballroom Blitz
- ☐ '75 Fox On The Run ★
- ☐ '73 Little Willy
- ☐ '78 Love Is Like Oxygen

SWEET, Matthew
- ☐ '95 Sick Of Myself

SWEET INSPIRATIONS, The
- ☐ '68 Sweet Inspiration

SWEET SENSATION
- ☐ '75 Sad Sweet Dreamer

SWEET SENSATION
- ☒ '89 Hooked On You [remix]
- ☒ '90 If Wishes Came True ★
- ☐ '90 Love Child
- ☐ '89 Sincerely Yours

SWIFT, Taylor
- ☒ '07 Teardrops On My Guitar
- ☒ '07 Tim McGraw

SWINGING BLUE JEANS, The
- ☒ '64 Hippy Hippy Shake

SWINGIN' MEDALLIONS
- ☐ '66 Double Shot (Of My Baby's Love)

SWING OUT SISTER
- ☐ '92 Am I The Same Girl
- ☐ '87 Breakout
- ☐ '87 Twilight World

SWITCH
- ☐ '78 There'll Never Be

SWITCHFOOT
- ☐ '04 Dare You To Move
- ☐ '04 Meant To Live
- ☐ '04 This Is Your Life

SWV (Sisters With Voices)
- ☐ '94 Anything
- ☐ '93 Downtown
- ☒ '93 I'm So Into You
- ☐ '98 Rain
- ☐ '93 Right Here/Human Nature ★
- ☐ '97 Someone
- ☐ '96 Use Your Heart
- ☒ '93 Weak ★
- ☒ '96 You're The One

SYBIL
- ☐ '89 Don't Make Me Over
- ☐ '89 Walk On By

SYLK-E. FYNE
- ☐ '98 Romeo And Juliet

SYLVERS, Foster
- ☐ '73 Misdemeanor

SYLVERS, The
- ☐ '76 Boogie Fever ★
- ☐ '77 High School Dance
- ☐ '76 Hot Line

SYLVESTER
- ☐ '78 Dance (Disco Heat)
- ☐ '79 I (Who Have Nothing)
- ☐ '79 You Make Me Feel (Mighty Real)

SYLVIA [Disco]
- ☐ '73 Pillow Talk

SYLVIA [Country]
- ☐ '82 Nobody

SYMS, Sylvia
- ☐ '56 English Muffins And Irish Stew
- ☐ '56 I Could Have Danced All Night

SYNCH
- ☐ '86 Where Are You Now?

SYNDICATE OF SOUND
- ☐ '66 Little Girl ★

SYSTEM, The
- ☐ '87 Don't Disturb This Groove

SYSTEM OF A DOWN
- ☐ '02 Aerials
- ☐ '05 B.Y.O.B.
- ☐ '02 Chop Suey
- ☐ '05 Hypnotize
- ☐ '02 Toxicity

T

TACO
- ☒ '83 Puttin' On The Ritz ★

TAG TEAM
- ☒ '93 Whoomp! (There It Is) ★

TAKE THAT
- ☐ '95 Back For Good ★

TALKING HEADS
- ☒ '85 And She Was
- ☒ '83 Burning Down The House ★
- ☐ '79 Life During Wartime
- ☐ '80 Once In A Lifetime
- ☐ '77 Psycho Killer
- ☐ '85 Road To Nowhere
- ☐ '91 Sax And Violins
- ☒ '78 Take Me To The River ★
- ☐ '86 Wild Wild Life

TALK TALK
- ☒ '84 It's My Life

TA MARA & THE SEEN
- ☐ '85 Everybody Dance

TAMIA
- ☐ '98 Imagination
- ☐ '96 Missing You [w/ Brandy, Gladys Knight & Chaka Khan]
- ☐ '98 So Into You
- ☐ '01 Stranger In My House

TAMI SHOW
- ☐ '91 Truth, The

TAMS, The
- ☒ '63 What Kind Of Fool (Do You Think I Am)

TANEGA, Norma
- ☐ '66 Walkin' My Cat Named Dog

TANK
- ☐ '01 Maybe I Deserve
- ☒ '07 Please Don't Go

TANTRIC
- ☐ '01 Breakdown

TARRIERS, The
- ☐ '56 Banana Boat Song, The ★
- ☐ '56 Cindy, Oh Cindy

TASTE OF HONEY, A
- ☒ '78 Boogie Oogie Oogie ★━━
- ☐ '81 Sukiyaki ★

t.A.T.u.
- ☒ '03 All The Things She Said

TAVARES
- ☐ '73 Check It Out
- ☐ '76 Don't Take Away The Music
- ☒ '76 Heaven Must Be Missing An Angel
- ☐ '75 It Only Takes A Minute
- ☒ '77 More Than A Woman
- ☐ '82 Penny For Your Thoughts, A
- ☐ '75 Remember What I Told You To Forget
- ☐ '74 She's Gone
- ☐ '77 Whodunit

TAYLOR, Andy
- ☐ '86 Take It Easy

TAYLOR, Bobby, & The Vancouvers
- ☐ '68 Does Your Mama Know About Me

TAYLOR, James
- ☐ '69 Carolina In My Mind
- ☐ '71 Country Road
- ☒ '78 Devoted To You *[w/ Carly Simon]*
- ☐ '72 Don't Let Me Be Lonely Tonight
- ☐ '85 Everyday
- ☒ '70 Fire And Rain ★
- ☐ '77 Handy Man
- ☐ '81 Her Town Too *[w/ J.D. Souther]*
- ☒ '75 How Sweet It Is (To Be Loved By You)
- ☐ '97 Little More Time With You
- ☐ '71 Long Ago And Far Away
- ☒ '74 Mockingbird *[w/ Carly Simon]*
- ☐ '88 Never Die Young
- ☐ '76 Shower The People
- ☐ '70 Sweet Baby James
- ☐ '79 Up On The Roof
- ☒ '78 (What A) Wonderful World
  [w/ Art Garfunkel & Paul Simon]
- ☒ '71 You've Got A Friend ★
- ☐ '77 Your Smiling Face

TAYLOR, James "J.T."
- ☐ '89 All I Want Is Forever *[w/ Regina Belle]*

TAYLOR, Johnnie
- ☐ '73 Cheaper To Keep Her

- ☐ '76 Disco Lady ★
- ☐ '70 I Am Somebody
- ☐ '73 I Believe In You (You Believe In Me)
- ☐ '71 Jody's Got Your Girl And Gone
- ☐ '76 Somebody's Gettin' It
- ☐ '70 Steal Away
- ☐ '69 Take Care Of Your Homework
- ☐ '69 Testify (I Wonna)
- ☐ '74 We're Getting Careless With Our Love
- ☐ '68 Who's Making Love

TAYLOR, Little Johnny
- ☐ '63 Part Time Love

TAYLOR, Livingston
- ☐ '80 First Time Love
- ☒ '78 I Will Be In Love With You

TAYLOR, R. Dean
- ☐ '70 Indiana Wants Me

T-BONES, The
- ☐ '65 No Matter What Shape (Your Stomach's In)

TEARS FOR FEARS
- ☐ '93 Break It Down Again
- ☒ '85 Everybody Wants To Rule The World ★
- ☐ '85 Head Over Heels
- ☐ '86 Mothers Talk
- ☒ '85 Shout ★
- ☐ '89 Sowing The Seeds Of Love
- ☐ '89 Woman In Chains

TECHNIQUES
- ☐ '57 Hey! Little Girl

TECHNOTRONIC
- ☐ '90 Get Up! (Before The Night Is Over)
- ☒ '92 Move This
- ☒ '89 Pump Up The Jam ★

TEDDY BEARS, The
- ☒ '58 To Know Him, Is To Love Him ★

TEEGARDEN & VAN WINKLE
- ☐ '70 God, Love And Rock & Roll

TEEN QUEENS, The
- ☐ '56 Eddie My Love

TEE SET, The
- ☐ '70 Ma Belle Amie

TELEVISION
- ☐ '75 Little Johnny Jewel
- ☐ '77 Marquee Moon

TEMPO, Nino, & April Stevens
- ☐ '66 All Strung Out
- ☐ '63 Deep Purple
- ☐ '64 Stardust
- ☐ '63 Whispering

TEMPOS, The
- ☐ '59 See You In September

TEMPTATIONS, The
- ☐ '60 Barbara

TEMPTATIONS, The
- ⬛ '66 Ain't Too Proud To Beg
- ⬛ '67 All I Need
- ☐ '70 Ball Of Confusion (That's What The World Is Today)
- ☐ '66 Beauty Is Only Skin Deep
- ⬛ '68 Cloud Nine
- ☐ '69 Don't Let The Joneses Get You Down
- ☐ '66 Get Ready
- ☐ '64 Girl (Why You Wanna Make Me Blue)
- ☐ '74 Happy People
- ⬛ '73 Hey Girl (I Like Your Style)
- ⬛ '69 I Can't Get Next To You ★
- ⬛ '68 I Could Never Love Another (After Loving You)
- ☐ '66 (I Know) I'm Losing You
- ⬛ '68 I Wish It Would Rain
- ☐ '69 I'll Try Something New *[w/ The Supremes]*
- ☐ '68 I'm Gonna Make You Love Me *[w/ The Supremes]*
- ☐ '65 It's Growing
- ⬛ '71 Just My Imagination (Running Away With Me) ★
- ☐ '76 Keep Holding On
- ☐ '73 Let Your Hair Down
- ☐ '67 (Loneliness Made Me Realize) It's You That I Need
- ☐ '73 Masterpiece
- ☐ '91 Motown Song, The *[w/ Rod Stewart]*
- ☐ '65 My Baby
- ⬛ '65 My Girl ★
- ⬛ '72 Papa Was A Rollin' Stone ★
- ☐ '68 Please Return Your Love To Me
- ☐ '70 Psychedelic Shack
- ☐ '69 Run Away Child, Running Wild
- ☐ '75 Shakey Ground
- ☐ '65 Since I Lost My Baby
- ☐ '71 Superstar (Remember How You Got Where You Are)
- ⬛ '84 Treat Her Like A Lady
- ⬛ '64 Way You Do The Things You Do, The
- ⬛ '67 You're My Everything

10cc
- ⬛ '75 I'm Not In Love ★
- ⬛ '77 Things We Do For Love, The

10,000 MANIACS
- ☐ '93 Because The Night
- ☐ '97 More Than This
- ☐ '92 These Are Days
- ☐ '89 Trouble Me

10 YEARS
- ☐ '05 Wasteland

TEN YEARS AFTER
- ☐ '71 I'd Love To Change The World

TEPPER, Robert
- ☐ '86 No Easy Way Out

TERRELL, Tammi — see GAYE, Marvin

TERROR SQUAD
- ⬛ '04 Lean Back ★

TERRY, Tony
- ⬛ '91 With You

TESLA
- ⬛ '89 Love Song
- ☐ '90 Signs

TEX, Joe
- ☐ '77 Ain't Gonna Bump No More (With No Big Fat Woman)
- ☐ '64 Hold What You've Got
- ☐ '72 I Gotcha ★
- ⬛ '65 I Want To (Do Everything For You)
- ☐ '66 Love You Save (May Be Your Own)
- ☐ '68 Men Are Gettin' Scarce
- ☐ '66 S.Y.S.L.J.F.M. (The Letter Song)
- ☐ '67 Show Me
- ☐ '67 Skinny Legs And All
- ⬛ '65 Sweet Woman Like You, A

THALIA
- ⬛ '03 I Want You *[w/ Fat Joe]*

THEM
- ☐ '65 Gloria ★
- ☐ '65 Here Comes The Night
- ☐ '65 Mystic Eyes

THEY MIGHT BE GIANTS
- ☐ '88 Ana Ng
- ☐ '90 Birdhouse In Your Soul
- ☐ '87 Don't Let's Start

THICKE, Robin
- ⬛ '07 Lost Without U

THINK
- ☐ '71 Once You Understand

THIN LIZZY
- ⬛ '76 Boys Are Back In Town, The

3RD BASS
- ☐ '91 Pop Goes The Weasel

THIRD DAY
- ☐ '05 Cry Out To Jesus
- ☐ '00 My Hope Is In You
- ☐ '03 Show Me Your Glory
- ☐ '99 Your Love Oh Lord

THIRD EYE BLIND
- ⬛ '97 How's It Going To Be ★
- ⬛ '98 Jumper ★
- ⬛ '00 Never Let You Go
- ⬛ '97 Semi-Charmed Life ★

THIRD WORLD
- ⬛ '79 Now That We Found Love

38 SPECIAL
- ☐ '84 Back Where You Belong
- ☐ '82 Caught Up In You
- ⬛ '81 Hold On Loosely
- ☐ '83 If I'd Been The One
- ☐ '86 Like No Other Night
- ☐ '80 Rockin' Into The Night
- ⬛ '89 Second Chance

38 SPECIAL — cont'd
- [ ] '91 Sound Of Your Voice, The
- [x] '84 Teacher Teacher
- [ ] '82 You Keep Runnin' Away

30 SECONDS TO MARS
- [x] '07 From Yesterday
- [ ] '06 Kill (Bury Me), The

THOMAS, B.J.
- [ ] '66 Billy And Sue
- [ ] '77 Don't Worry Baby
- [ ] '78 Everybody Loves A Rain Song
- [ ] '70 Everybody's Out Of Town
- [ ] '68 Eyes Of A New York Woman, The
- [x] '75 (Hey Won't You Play) Another Somebody Done Somebody Wrong Song
- [x] '68 Hooked On A Feeling
- [ ] '70 I Just Can't Help Believing
- [x] '66 I'm So Lonesome I Could Cry
- [ ] '66 Mama
- [ ] '71 Mighty Clouds Of Joy
- [ ] '71 No Love At All
- [x] '69 Raindrops Keep Fallin' On My Head ★
- [ ] '72 Rock And Roll Lullaby

THOMAS, Carl
- [ ] '00 I Wish

THOMAS, Carla
- [ ] '66 B-A-B-Y
- [ ] '61 Gee Whiz (Look At His Eyes)
- [ ] '67 Knock On Wood [w/ Otis Redding]
- [ ] '67 Tramp [w/ Otis Redding]

THOMAS, Ian
- [ ] '73 Painted Ladies

THOMAS, Irma
- [ ] '64 Time Is On My Side
- [ ] '64 Wish Someone Would Care

THOMAS, Rob
- [x] '06 Ever The Same
- [ ] '07 Little Wonders
- [x] '05 Lonely No More ★
- [x] '99 Smooth [w/ Santana] ★
- [x] '07 Streetcorner Symphony
- [x] '05 This Is How A Heart Breaks

THOMAS, Rufus
- [ ] '71 Breakdown, The
- [ ] '70 Do The Funky Chicken
- [ ] '70 (Do The) Push And Pull
- [ ] '63 Walking The Dog

THOMAS, Timmy
- [ ] '72 Why Can't We Live Together

THOMPSON, Kay
- [ ] '56 Eloise

THOMPSON, Sue
- [ ] '62 Have A Good Time
- [ ] '62 James (Hold The Ladder Steady)
- [ ] '61 Norman
- [ ] '65 Paper Tiger
- [ ] '61 Sad Movies (Make Me Cry)

THOMPSON TWINS
- [ ] '84 Doctor! Doctor!
- [ ] '87 Get That Love
- [ ] '84 Hold Me Now ★
- [ ] '86 King For A Day
- [ ] '85 Lay Your Hands On Me
- [ ] '83 Lies
- [ ] '89 Sugar Daddy

THOMSON, Ali
- [ ] '80 Take A Little Rhythm

THOMSON, Cyndi
- [ ] '01 What I Really Meant To Say

THOROGOOD, George/The Destroyers
- [x] '82 Bad To The Bone
- [ ] '85 Gear Jammer
- [ ] '93 Get A Haircut
- [ ] '85 I Drink Alone
- [ ] '78 Madison Blues
- [x] '78 Move It On Over
- [x] '77 One Bourbon, One Scotch, One Beer
- [x] '78 Who Do You Love?

THREE DAYS GRACE
- [ ] '06 Animal I Have Become
- [ ] '05 Home
- [x] '03 (I Hate) Everything About You
- [ ] '04 Just Like You
- [ ] '07 Never Too Late
- [x] '07 Pain

THREE DEGREES, The
- [ ] '70 Maybe
- [ ] '74 TSOP (The Sound Of Philadelphia) [w/ MFSB] ★
- [x] '74 When Will I See You Again

THREE DOG NIGHT
- [x] '72 Black & White ★
- [x] '70 Celebrate
- [ ] '69 Easy To Be Hard
- [ ] '69 Eli's Coming
- [ ] '72 Family Of Man, The
- [ ] '71 Joy To The World ★
- [ ] '73 Let Me Serenade You
- [ ] '71 Liar
- [ ] '70 Mama Told Me (Not To Come) ★
- [ ] '71 Never Been To Spain
- [x] '71 Old Fashioned Love Song, An
- [ ] '69 One
- [ ] '70 One Man Band
- [ ] '70 Out In The Country
- [ ] '72 Pieces Of April
- [ ] '73 Shambala
- [ ] '74 Show Must Go On, The
- [ ] '74 Sure As I'm Sittin' Here
- [x] '69 Try A Little Tenderness

3 DOORS DOWN
- [ ] '04 Away From The Sun
- [ ] '01 Be Like That
- [ ] '01 Duck And Run
- [x] '03 Here Without You ★
- [x] '00 Kryptonite ★

- ☐ '05 Let Me Go ★
- ☐ '00 Loser
- ▣ '02 When I'm Gone ★

311
- ☐ '96 All Mixed Up
- ☐ '03 Creatures (For A While)
- ☐ '05 Don't Tread On Me
- ☐ '96 Down
- ▣ '04 Love Song

3LW
- ☐ '00 No More (Baby I'ma Do Right)

THREE 6 MAFIA
- ▣ '06 Poppin' My Collar
- ▣ '05 Stay Fly

3T
- ☐ '95 Anything

THUNDER, Johnny
- ☐ '62 Loop De Loop

THUNDERCLAP NEWMAN
- ☐ '69 Something In The Air

T.I.
- ☐ '07 Big Things Poppin' (Do It)
- ☐ '05 Bring Em Out
- ☐ '04 Let's Get Away
- ▣ '04 Rubber Band Man
- ☐ '07 Top Back
- ▣ '05 U Don't Know Me
- ▣ '06 What You Know ★
- ▣ '06 Why You Wanna
- ☐ '07 You Know What It Is

TIERRA
- ☐ '80 Together

TIFFANY
- ☐ '88 All This Time
- ☐ '87 Could've Been
- ☐ '88 I Saw Him Standing There
- ▣ '87 I Think We're Alone Now ★
- ☐ '89 Radio Romance

TILLIS, Pam
- ☐ '91 Maybe It Was Memphis
- ☐ '94 Mi Vida Loca (My Crazy Life)
- ☐ '94 When You Walk In The Room

TILLOTSON, Johnny
- ☐ '58 Dreamy Eyes
- ☐ '65 Heartaches By The Number
- ☐ '62 I Can't Help It (If I'm Still In Love With You)
- ☐ '64 I Rise, I Fall
- ☐ '62 It Keeps Right On A-Hurtin'
- ☐ '61 Jimmy's Girl
- ☐ '63 Out Of My Mind
- ☐ '60 Poetry In Motion ★
- ☐ '62 Send Me The Pillow You Dream On
- ☐ '64 She Understands Me
- ☐ '63 Talk Back Trembling Lips
- ☐ '60 Why Do I Love You So
- ☐ '61 Without You

- ☐ '64 Worried Guy
- ☐ '63 You Can Never Stop Me Loving You

'TIL TUESDAY
- ☐ '85 Voices Carry
- ☐ '86 What About Love

TIMBALAND
- ▣ '07 Apologize ★
- ▣ '07 Give It To Me ★
- ▣ '07 Way I Are, The ★

TIMBALAND & MAGOO
- ☐ '98 Clock Strikes
- ☐ '98 Luv 2 Luv U
- ☐ '97 Up Jumps Da Boogie

TIMBERLAKE, Justin
- ▣ '02 Cry Me A River ★
- ▣ '02 Like I Love You
- ▣ '07 LoveStoned ★
- ▣ '06 My Love ★
- ▣ '03 Rock Your Body
- ☐ '03 Señorita
- ▣ '06 SexyBack ★
- ▣ '07 Summer Love ★
- ▣ '07 What Goes Around...Comes Around ★

TIMBUK 3
- ☐ '86 Future's So Bright, I Gotta Wear Shades, The

TIME, The
- ☐ '85 Bird, The
- ☐ '90 Jerk-Out
- ▣ '84 Jungle Love
- ☐ '82 777-9311

TIMES TWO
- ☐ '88 Strange But True

TIMEX SOCIAL CLUB
- ☐ '86 Rumors

TIMMY -T-
- ▣ '90 One More Try ★
- ▣ '90 Time After Time

TIN MACHINE
- ☐ '91 Baby Universal
- ☐ '91 One Shot

TIN TIN
- ☐ '71 Toast And Marmalade For Tea

TINY TIM
- ☐ '68 Tip-Toe Thru' The Tulips With Me

TIPPIN, Aaron
- ☐ '00 Kiss This
- ▣ '95 That's As Close As I'll Get To Loving You
- ▣ '92 There Ain't Nothin' Wrong With The Radio
- ▣ '01 Where The Stars And Stripes And The Eagle Fly
- ☐ '90 You've Got To Stand For Something

TLC
- ■ '92 Ain't 2 Proud 2 Beg
- ■ '92 Baby-Baby-Baby ★
- ■ '94 Creep ★
- ☐ '95 Diggin' On You
- ☐ '02 Girl Talk
- ☐ '93 Hat 2 Da Back
- ■ '99 No Scrubs ★
- ■ '95 Red Light Special
- ■ '99 Unpretty ★
- ■ '95 Waterfalls ★
- ☐ '92 What About Your Friends

TOADIES
- ☐ '95 Possum Kingdom

TOAD THE WET SPROCKET
- ☐ '92 All I Want
- ☐ '94 Fall Down
- ☐ '95 Good Intentions
- ☐ '94 Something's Always Wrong
- ☐ '92 Walk On The Ocean

TOBY BEAU
- ■ '78 My Angel Baby

TODAY
- ■ '89 Girl I Got My Eyes On You

TODD, Art & Dotty
- ☐ '58 Chanson D'Amour (Song Of Love)

TOKENS, The
- ☐ '66 I Hear Trumpets Blow
- ■ '61 Lion Sleeps Tonight, The ★
- ☐ '67 Portrait Of My Love
- ■ '61 Tonight I Fell In Love

TOMMY TUTONE
- ☐ '80 Angel Say No
- ■ '81 867-5309/Jenny ★

TOM TOM CLUB
- ☐ '82 Genius Of Love

TONE LOC
- ☐ '89 Funky Cold Medina
- ☐ '88 Wild Thing ★

TONEY, Oscar Jr.
- ☐ '67 For Your Precious Love

TONIC
- ☐ '97 If You Could Only See
- ☐ '96 Open Up Your Eyes

TONY & JOE
- ☐ '58 Freeze, The

TONY! TONI! TONÉ!
- ☐ '93 Anniversary ⟶
- ☐ '90 Blues, The
- ☐ '90 Feels Good
- ☐ '93 If I Had No Loot ★
- ☐ '90 It Never Rains (In Southern California)
- ☐ '94 (Lay Your Head On My) Pillow
- ☐ '96 Let's Get Down
- ☐ '88 Little Walter

TOOL
- ☐ '97 Thinking Of You
- ☐ '91 Whatever You Want

TOOL
- ☐ '96 Aenima
- ☐ '06 Pot, The
- ☐ '01 Schism
- ☐ '06 Vicarious

TOO $HORT
- ☐ '91 Ghetto, The

TOOTS & THE MAYTALS
- ☐ '73 Pressure Drop

TOPOL
- ■ '71 If I Were A Rich Man

TORME, Mel
- ☐ '62 Comin' Home Baby
- ☐ '56 Foggy Day, A
- ☐ '56 Lullaby Of Birdland
- ☐ '63 Sunday In New York

TORNADOES, The
- ■ '62 Telstar ★

TOROK, Mitchell
- ☐ '59 Caribbean
- ☐ '60 Pink Chiffon
- ■ '57 Pledge Of Love

TOSH, Peter
- ■ '83 Johnny B. Goode
- ☐ '73 Stepping Razor

TOTAL
- ☐ '95 Can't You See
- ■ '96 Kissin' You
- ☐ '95 No One Else
- ☐ '98 Trippin'
- ☐ '97 What About Us

TOTAL COELO
- ☐ '83 I Eat Cannibals

TOTO
- ■ '82 Africa ★
- ☐ '78 Hold The Line
- ☐ '83 I Won't Hold You Back
- ☐ '86 I'll Be Over You
- ■ '78 I'll Supply The Love
- ☐ '82 Make Believe
- ■ '79 99
- ☐ '88 Pamela
- ■ '82 Rosanna ★
- ☐ '84 Stranger In Town
- ■ '86 Without Your Love

TOWER OF POWER
- ☐ '74 Don't Change Horses (In The Middle Of A Stream)
- ☐ '73 So Very Hard To Go
- ☐ '72 You're Still A Young Man

TOWNSELL, Lidell, & M.T.F.
- ☐ '92 Nu Nu

TOWNSEND, Ed
- '58 For Your Love

TOWNSHEND, Pete
- '85 Face The Face
- '89 Friend Is A Friend, A
- '80 Let My Love Open The Door
- '80 Rough Boys

TOYA
- '01 I Do!!

TOYS, The
- '65 Attack
- '65 Lover's Concerto, A ★

T-PAIN
- '07 Bartender ★
- '07 Buy U A Drank (Shawty Snappin') ★
- '06 I'm N Luv (Wit A Stripper) ★
- '05 I'm Sprung ★

T'PAU
- '87 Heart And Soul

TQ
- '98 Westside

TRADE WINDS, The
- '65 New York's A Lonely Town

TRAFFIC
- '68 Dear Mr. Fantasy
- '70 Empty Pages
- '68 Feelin' Alright?
- '68 Forty Thousand Headmen
- '70 Freedom Rider
- '68 Hole In My Shoe
- '70 John Barleycorn
- '71 Low Spark Of High Heeled Boys
- '68 Paper Sun
- '71 Rock & Roll Stew
- '68 You Can All Join In

TRAIN
- '03 Calling All Angels
- '01 Drops Of Jupiter (Tell Me) ★
- '99 Meet Virginia

TRAMMPS, The
- '78 Disco Inferno ▬
- '76 Hold Back The Night
- '76 That's Where The Happy People Go

TRANS-SIBERIAN ORCHESTRA
- '95 Christmas Eve (Sarajevo 12/24)

TRAPT
- '02 Headstrong
- '05 Stand Up
- '03 Still Frame

TRASHMEN, The
- '64 Bird Dance Beat
- '63 Surfin' Bird

TRAVELING WILBURYS
- '89 End Of The Line
- '88 Handle With Care

- '90 She's My Baby

TRAVERS, Pat
- '79 Boom Boom (Out Go The Lights)

TRAVIS, Randy
- '94 Before You Kill Us All
- '91 Better Class Of Losers
- '88 Deeper Than The Holler
- '87 Forever And Ever, Amen
- '91 Forever Together
- '90 Hard Rock Bottom Of Your Heart
- '90 He Walked On Water
- '92 If I Didn't Have You
- '92 Look Heart, No Hands
- '86 On The Other Hand
- '98 Out Of My Bones
- '98 Spirit Of A Boy - Wisdom Of A Man
- '02 Three Wooden Crosses
- '94 Whisper My Name

TRAVIS & BOB
- '59 Tell Him No

TRAVOLTA, John
- '77 All Strung Out On You
- '96 Grease Megamix, The *[w/ Olivia Newton-John]*
- '76 Let Her In
- '78 Summer Nights *[w/ Olivia Newton-John]*
- '78 You're The One That I Want *[w/ Olivia Newton John]* ★

TREMELOES, The
- '67 Even The Bad Times Are Good
- '67 Here Comes My Baby
- '67 Silence Is Golden

TRESVANT, Ralph
- '92 Money Can't Buy You Love
- '90 Sensitivity
- '91 Stone Cold Gentleman

TREVINO, Rick
- '96 Running Out Of Reasons To Run

T. REX
- '72 Bang A Gong (Get It On)

TRIBE CALLED QUEST, A
- '94 Award Tour
- '92 Scenario

TRICK DADDY
- '01 I'm A Thug
- '04 Let's Go
- '05 Sugar (Gimme Some)

TRILLVILLE
- '05 Some Cut

TRINA
- '05 Here We Go *[w/ Kelly Rowland]*

TRIO
- '82 Da Da Da I Don't Love You You Don't Love Me

TRIPLETS, The
- [ ] '91 You Don't Have To Go Home Tonight

TRITT, Travis
- [x] '91 Anymore
- [x] '00 Best Of Intentions
- [ ] '92 Can I Trust You With My Heart
- [x] '94 Foolish Pride
- [ ] '90 Help Me Hold On
- [ ] '91 Here's A Quarter (Call Someone Who Cares)
- [x] '01 It's A Great Day To Be Alive
- [x] '01 Love Of A Woman
- [ ] '93 Take It Easy

TRIUMPH
- [ ] '83 All The Way
- [ ] '79 Hold On
- [ ] '80 I Can Survive
- [ ] '80 I Live For The Weekend
- [ ] '79 Lay It On The Line
- [ ] '78 Rock & Roll Machine
- [ ] '86 Somebody's Out There

TROCCOLI, Kathy
- [ ] '92 Everything Changes

TROGGS, The
- [ ] '68 Love Is All Around
- [x] '66 Wild Thing ★
- [x] '66 With A Girl Like You

TROOP
- [x] '90 All I Do Is Think Of You
- [ ] '88 Mamacita
- [ ] '90 Spread My Wings
- [ ] '92 Sweet November

TROOPER
- [ ] '78 Raise A Little Hell

TROWER, Robin
- [ ] '74 Bridge Of Sighs
- [ ] '76 Caledonia
- [ ] '74 Day Of The Eagle
- [ ] '74 Little Bit Of Sympathy
- [ ] '74 Too Rolling Stoned
- [ ] '80 Victims Of The Fury

TROY, Doris
- [x] '63 Just One Look

TRUE, Andrea, Connection
- [x] '76 More, More, More
- [ ] '77 N.Y., You Got Me Dancing

TRUTH HURTS
- [x] '02 Addictive ★

TUBES, The
- [ ] '81 Don't Want To Wait Anymore
- [x] '83 She's A Beauty
- [ ] '81 Talk To Ya Later

TUCKER, Tanya
- [ ] '73 Blood Red And Goin' Down
- [x] '72 Delta Dawn
- [ ] '91 Down To My Last Teardrop

- [ ] '93 It's A Little Too Late
- [ ] '75 Lizzie And The Rainman
- [ ] '93 Soon
- [ ] '92 Two Sparrows In A Hurricane
- [ ] '73 What's Your Mama's Name
- [ ] '91 (Without You) What Do I Do With Me
- [ ] '74 Would You Lay With Me (In A Field Of Stone)

TUCKER, Tommy
- [ ] '64 Hi-Heel Sneakers

TUNE WEAVERS, The
- [x] '57 Happy, Happy Birthday Baby ★

TUNSTALL, KT
- [x] '06 Black Horse & The Cherry Tree ★
- [x] '07 Suddenly I See

TURBANS, The
- [ ] '55 When You Dance

TURNER, Big Joe
- [x] '51 Chains Of Love
- [x] '56 Corrine Corrina
- [ ] '55 Flip Flop And Fly
- [ ] '55 Hide And Seek
- [x] '54 Shake, Rattle & Roll
- [x] '52 Sweet Sixteen

TURNER, Ike & Tina
- [ ] '60 Fool In Love, A
- [ ] '70 I Want To Take You Higher
- [ ] '61 It's Gonna Work Out Fine
- [ ] '73 Nutbush City Limits
- [ ] '61 Poor Fool
- [x] '71 Proud Mary ★
- [x] '66 River Deep-Mountain High ★

TURNER, Jesse Lee
- [ ] '59 Little Space Girl, The

TURNER, Josh
- [ ] '04 Long Black Train
- [x] '06 Would You Go With Me
- [x] '06 Your Man

TURNER, Mary Lou — see ANDERSON, Bill

TURNER, Ruby
- [ ] '89 It's Gonna Be Alright

TURNER, Sammy
- [ ] '59 Always
- [ ] '59 Lavender-Blue

TURNER, Spyder
- [x] '66 Stand By Me

TURNER, Tina
- [ ] '89 Best, The
- [ ] '84 Better Be Good To Me
- [ ] '84 I Can't Stand The Rain
- [ ] '93 I Don't Wanna Fight
- [x] '85 It's Only Love *[w/ Bryan Adams]*
- [ ] '84 Let's Stay Together
- [ ] '85 One Of The Living
- [ ] '85 Private Dancer
- [ ] '85 Show Some Respect

- ☐ '89 Steamy Windows
- ☐ '86 Two People
- ☐ '86 Typical Male
- ☐ '85 We Don't Need Another Hero (Thunderdome) ★
- ☐ '87 What You Get Is What You See
- ▣ '84 What's Love Got To Do With It ★

TURTLES, The
- ☐ '68 Elenore
- ▣ '67 Happy Together ★
- ☐ '65 It Ain't Me Babe
- ☐ '65 Let Me Be
- ▣ '67 She'd Rather Be With Me
- ▣ '67 She's My Girl
- ☐ '66 You Baby
- ☐ '67 You Know What I Mean
- ▣ '69 You Showed Me

TUXEDO JUNCTION
- ☐ '78 Chattanooga Choo Choo

TWAIN, Shania
- ▣ '95 Any Man Of Mine
- ▣ '99 Come On Over
- ▣ '97 Don't Be Stupid (You Know I Love You)
- ▣ '03 Forever And For Always
- ▣ '98 From This Moment On ★
- ☐ '97 Honey, I'm Home
- ☐ '02 I'm Gonna Getcha Good!
- ☐ '95 (If You're Not In It For Love) I'm Outta Here!
- ▣ '97 Love Gets Me Every Time
- ▣ '99 Man! I Feel Like A Woman!
- ☐ '96 No One Needs To Know
- ▣ '99 That Don't Impress Me Much
- ▣ '95 Whose Bed Have Your Boots Been Under?
- ☐ '96 You Win My Love
- ▣ '98 You're Still The One ★

TWEET
- ▣ '02 Call Me
- ▣ '02 Oops (Oh My)

12 GAUGE
- ☐ '94 Dunkie Butt (Please Please Please)

TWENNYNINE
- ☐ '79 Peanut Butter

20 FINGERS FEAT. GILLETTE
- ▣ '94 Short Dick Man

TWILLEY, Dwight
- ☐ '84 Girls
- ☐ '75 I'm On Fire

TWISTA
- ▣ '05 Girl Tonite [w/ Trey Songz]
- ☐ '05 Hope [w/ Faith Evans]
- ▣ '04 Overnight Celebrity
- ▣ '03 Slow Jamz ★
- ▣ '04 So Sexy [w/ R. Kelly]

TWISTED SISTER
- ▣ '84 We're Not Gonna Take It

TWITTY, Conway
- ▣ '71 After The Fire Is Gone [w/ Loretta Lynn]
- ▣ '60 C'est Si Bon (It's So Good)
- ☐ '59 Danny Boy
- ▣ '70 Hello Darlin'
- ☐ '84 I Don't Know A Thing About Love (The Moon Song)
- ☐ '60 Is A Blue Bird Blue
- ▣ '58 It's Only Make Believe ★
- ☐ '59 Lonely Blue Boy
- ☐ '59 Mona Lisa
- ▣ '82 Slow Hand
- ▣ '59 Story Of My Love, The
- ☐ '87 That's My Job
- ▣ '60 What Am I Living For
- ▣ '73 You've Never Been This Far Before

2 IN A ROOM
- ▣ '90 Wiggle It

2 LIVE CREW/LUKE
- ☐ '90 Banned In The U.S.A.
- ▣ '89 Me So Horny
- ▣ '98 Raise The Roof

2PAC
- ▣ '96 California Love ★
- ▣ '98 Changes
- ▣ '95 Dear Mama
- ☐ '98 Do For Love
- ▣ '96 How Do U Want It ★
- ▣ '93 I Get Around
- ▣ '93 Keep Ya Head Up
- ☐ '03 Runnin (Dying To Live)
- ☐ '02 Thugz Mansion

2 UNLIMITED
- ☐ '92 Get Ready For This
- ☐ '92 Twilight Zone

TYCOON
- ☐ '79 Such A Woman

TYLER, Bonnie
- ☐ '84 Holding Out For A Hero
- ▣ '78 It's A Heartache ★
- ▣ '83 Total Eclipse Of The Heart ★

TYMES, The
- ☐ '68 People
- ☐ '63 So Much In Love ★
- ☐ '63 Somewhere
- ☐ '63 Wonderful! Wonderful!
- ☐ '74 You Little Trustmaker

TYRESE
- ☐ '03 How You Gonna Act Like That
- ▣ '98 Nobody Else
- ▣ '99 Sweet Lady

U

UB40
- ■ '93 Can't Help Falling In Love ★
- ☐ '91 Here I Am (Come And Take Me)
- ■ '85 I Got You Babe *[w/ Chrissie Hynde]*
- ■ '88 Red Red Wine [rap by Astro] ★
- ■ '90 Way You Do The Things You Do, The

UGLY KID JOE
- ☐ '93 Cats In The Cradle
- ☐ '92 Everything About You ★

U-KREW, The
- ☐ '90 If U Were Mine

ULLMAN, Tracey
- ☐ '84 They Don't Know

ULTRAVOX
- ☐ '83 Reap The Wild Wind

UNCLE KRACKER
- ■ '03 Drift Away *[w/ Dobie Gray]* ★
- ■ '01 Follow Me ★
- ■ '04 When The Sun Goes Down *[w/ Kenny Chesney]*

UNCLE SAM
- ☐ '97 I Don't Ever Want To See You Again

UNDERGROUND SUNSHINE
- ☐ '69 Birthday

UNDERWOOD, Carrie
- ■ '07 Before He Cheats ★
- ■ '06 Don't Forget To Remember Me
- ■ '07 I'll Stand By You ★
- ☐ '05 Inside Your Heaven
- ■ '06 Jesus, Take The Wheel ★
- ☐ '07 So Small
- ■ '07 Wasted

UNDISPUTED TRUTH, The
- ☐ '71 Smiling Faces Sometimes ★ ━

UNIFICS, The
- ☐ '68 Beginning Of My End, The
- ■ '68 Court Of Love

UNIT FOUR Plus TWO
- ☐ '65 Concrete And Clay

UNK
- ■ '07 2 Step
- ■ '07 Walk It Out

UNKNOWNS, The
- ☐ '66 Melody For An Unknown Girl

UNV
- ☐ '93 Something's Goin' On

UNWRITTEN LAW
- ☐ '02 Seein' Red

UPCHURCH, Philip, Combo
- ☐ '61 You Can't Sit Down

URBAN, Keith
- ■ '05 Better Life
- ☐ '00 But For The Grace Of God
- ■ '04 Days Go By
- ■ '07 I Told You So
- ■ '05 Making Memories Of Us
- ☐ '06 Once In A Lifetime
- ☐ '02 Raining On Sunday
- ■ '02 Somebody Like You
- ■ '07 Stupid Boy
- ■ '06 Tonight I Wanna Cry
- ☐ '01 Where The Blacktop Ends
- ☐ '03 Who Wouldn't Wanna Be Me
- ■ '03 You'll Think Of Me
- ■ '04 You're My Better Half

URBAN DANCE SQUAD
- ☐ '90 Deeper Shade Of Soul

URIAH HEEP
- ☐ '72 Easy Livin'
- ☐ '73 Stealin'

USA FOR AFRICA
- ■ '85 We Are The World ★

USHER
- ■ '04 Burn ★
- ■ '05 Caught Up ★
- ■ '04 Confessions Part II ★
- ■ '04 My Boo *[w/ Alicia Keys]* ★
- ■ '98 My Way ★
- ■ '98 Nice & Slow ★
- ■ '02 U Don't Have To Call
- ■ '01 U Got It Bad ★
- ■ '01 U Remind Me ★
- ■ '04 Yeah! ★
- ■ '97 You Make Me Wanna... ★

US3
- ☐ '93 Cantaloop

UTFO
- ☐ '85 Roxanne, Roxanne

UTOPIA
- ☐ '80 Set Me Free

U2
- ☐ '05 All Because Of You
- ☐ '89 All I Want Is You
- ☐ '88 Angel Of Harlem
- ☐ '00 Beautiful Day ★
- ☐ '87 Bullet The Blue Sky
- ☐ '05 City Of Blinding Lights
- ☐ '88 Desire
- ☐ '97 Discothéque
- ☐ '92 Even Better Than The Real Thing
- ☐ '91 Fly, The
- ☐ '83 40
- ☐ '95 Hold Me, Thrill Me, Kiss Me, Kill Me
- ☐ '87 I Still Haven't Found What I'm Looking For ★
- ☐ '81 I Will Follow
- ☐ '83 I Will Follow [live]
- ☐ '88 In God's Country
- ☐ '97 Last Night On Earth

- ☐ '91 Mysterious Ways
- ☐ '83 New Year's Day ★
- ☐ '90 Night And Day
- ☐ '93 Numb
- ☐ '92 One ★
- ☐ '84 Pride (In The Name Of Love)
- ☐ '06 Saints Are Coming, The *[w/ Green Day]*
- ☐ '05 Sometimes You Can't Make It On Your Own
- ☐ '97 Staring At The Sun
- ☐ '94 Stay (Faraway, So Close!)
- ☐ '01 Stuck In A Moment You Can't Get Out Of
- ☐ '83 Sunday Bloody Sunday
- ☐ '98 Sweetest Thing
- ☐ '83 Two Hearts Beat As One
- ☐ '05 Vertigo
- ☐ '88 When Love Comes To Town *[w/ B.B. King]*
- ☐ '87 Where The Streets Have No Name
- ☐ '92 Who's Gonna Ride Your Wild Horses
- ☐ '87 With Or Without You ★

V

VALE, Jerry
- ☐ '58 Go Chase A Moonbeam
- ☐ '64 Have You Looked Into Your Heart
- ☐ '56 Innamorata (Sweetheart)
- ☐ '57 Pretend You Don't See Her
- ☐ '56 You Don't Know Me

VALENS, Ritchie
- ☐ '58 Come On Let's Go
- ☐ '58 Donna ★
- ☐ '58 La Bamba ★
- ☐ '59 That's My Little Suzie

VALENTE, Caterina
- ☐ '55 Breeze And I, The

VALENTINE, Brooke
- ☐ '05 Girlfight

VALENTINO, Bobby
- ☐ '05 Slow Down ★

VALENTINO, Mark
- ☐ '62 Push And Kick, The

VALINO, Joe
- ☐ '56 Garden Of Eden

VALJEAN
- ☐ '62 Theme From Ben Casey

VALLI, Frankie
- ☐ '67 Can't Take My Eyes Off You
- ☐ '76 Fallen Angel
- ☐ '78 Grease ★
- ☐ '67 I Make A Fool Of Myself
- ☐ '74 My Eyes Adored You ★
- ☐ '75 Our Day Will Come
- ☐ '75 Swearin' To God
- ☐ '67 To Give (The Reason I Live)

VALLI, June
- ☐ '60 Apple Green

VANDENBERG
- ☐ '83 Burning Heart

VANDROSS, Luther
- ☐ '88 Any Love
- ☐ '82 Bad Boy/Having A Party
- ☐ '92 Best Things In Life Are Free, The *[w/ Janet Jackson]*
- ☐ '03 Dance With My Father
- ☐ '91 Don't Want To Be A Fool
- ☐ '94 Endless Love *[w/ Mariah Carey]*
- ☐ '86 Give Me The Reason
- ☐ '89 Here And Now
- ☐ '83 How Many Times Can We Say Goodbye *[w/ Dionne Warwick]*
- ☐ '81 Never Too Much
- ☐ '91 Power Of Love/Love Power
- ☐ '86 Stop To Love
- ☐ '01 Take You Out
- ☐ '87 There's Nothing Better Than Love *[w/ Gregory Hines]*
- ☐ '85 'Til My Baby Comes Home

VAN DYKE, Leroy
- ☐ '56 Auctioneer
- ☐ '61 Walk On By ★

VANGELIS
- ☐ '81 Chariots Of Fire ★
- ☐ '87 Hymne

VAN HALEN
- ☐ '78 Ain't Talkin' 'Bout Love
- ☐ '80 And The Cradle Will Rock...
- ☐ '79 Beautiful Girls
- ☐ '86 Best Of Both Worlds
- ☐ '88 Black And Blue
- ☐ '95 Can't Stop Lovin' You
- ☐ '79 Dance The Night Away
- ☐ '82 Dancing In The Street
- ☐ '95 Don't Tell Me (What Love Can Do)
- ☐ '86 Dreams
- ☐ '89 Feels So Good
- ☐ '88 Finish What Ya Started
- ☐ '84 Hot For Teacher
- ☐ '96 Humans Being
- ☐ '84 I'll Wait
- ☐ '78 Ice Cream Man
- ☐ '78 Jamie's Cryin'
- ☐ '84 Jump ★
- ☐ '86 Love Walks In
- ☐ '96 Me Wise Magic
- ☐ '82 (Oh) Pretty Woman
- ☐ '84 Panama
- ☐ '91 Poundcake
- ☐ '91 Right Now
- ☐ '91 Runaround
- ☐ '78 Runnin' With The Devil
- ☐ '91 Top Of The World
- ☐ '81 Unchained
- ☐ '88 When It's Love
- ☐ '86 Why Can't This Be Love ★
- ☐ '78 You Really Got Me

VANILLA FUDGE
- ☐ '68 Take Me For A Little While
- ◼ '68 You Keep Me Hangin' On

VANILLA ICE
- ◼ '90 Ice Ice Baby ★
- ◼ '90 Play That Funky Music

VANITY FARE
- ◼ '69 Early In The Morning
- ☐ '70 Hitchin' A Ride

VANNELLI, Gino
- ☐ '85 Black Cars
- ◼ '78 I Just Wanna Stop
- ☐ '81 Living Inside Myself
- ☐ '74 People Gotta Move
- ◼ '87 Wild Horses

VANWARMER, Randy
- ◼ '79 Just When I Needed You Most ★

VAPORS, The
- ◼ '80 Turning Japanese

VARIOUS ARTISTS
- ☐ '05 Across The Universe

VASSAR, Phil
- ◼ '04 In A Real Love
- ◼ '00 Just Another Day In Paradise
- ☐ '06 Last Day Of My Life
- ☐ '01 Six-Pack Summer
- ◼ '02 That's When I Love You

VAUGHAN, Sarah
- ☐ '56 Banana Boat Song, The
- ☐ '59 Broken-Hearted Melody
- ☐ '55 C'est La Vie
- ◼ '60 Eternally
- ☐ '55 Experience Unnecessary
- ☐ '56 Fabulous Character
- ☐ '55 How Important Can It Be?
- ☐ '55 Make Yourself Comfortable
- ☐ '59 Misty
- ◼ '56 Mr. Wonderful
- ◼ '59 Smooth Operator
- ☐ '55 Whatever Lola Wants

VAUGHAN, Stevie Ray
- ☐ '84 Cold Shot
- ☐ '89 Crossfire
- ◼ '83 Pride And Joy
- ☐ '91 Sky Is Crying, The
- ◼ '87 Superstition
- ☐ '87 Willie The Wimp

VAUGHN, Billy, & His Orchestra
- ☐ '58 Blue Hawaii
- ☐ '58 Cimarron (Roll On)
- ☐ '58 La Paloma
- ◼ '60 Look For A Star
- ◼ '55 Melody Of Love
- ☐ '57 Raunchy
- ☐ '57 Sail Along Silvery Moon
- ☐ '55 Shifting Whispering Sands, The ★
- ☐ '62 Swingin' Safari, A

- ☐ '58 Tumbling Tumbleweeds
- ☐ '56 When The White Lilacs Bloom Again

VAZQUEZ, Mario
- ◼ '06 Gallery

VEE, Bobby
- ◼ '67 Beautiful People
- ☐ '63 Charms
- ☐ '67 Come Back When You Grow Up
- ☐ '60 Devil Or Angel
- ☐ '66 Look At Me Girl
- ☐ '62 Night Has A Thousand Eyes, The
- ☐ '62 Please Don't Ask About Barbara
- ☐ '62 Punish Her
- ☐ '60 Rubber Ball
- ☐ '61 Run To Him
- ☐ '62 Sharing You
- ☐ '61 Stayin' In
- ☐ '59 Suzie Baby
- ☐ '61 Take Good Care Of My Baby ★
- ☐ '61 Walkin' With My Angel

VEGA, Suzanne
- ◼ '87 Luka ★
- ☐ '90 Tom's Diner [D.N.A. Feat. SUZANNE VEGA]

VELVET REVOLVER
- ☐ '04 Fall To Pieces
- ☐ '07 She Builds Quick Machines
- ☐ '04 Slither

VELVETS, The
- ◼ '61 Tonight (Could Be The Night)

VELVET UNDERGROUND, The
- ☐ '67 Heroin
- ☐ '67 I'm Waiting For The Man
- ◼ '69 Pale Blue Eyes
- ☐ '69 Rock 'N' Roll
- ☐ '67 Sunday Morning
- ☐ '70 Sweet Jane
- ☐ '68 White Light/White Heat

VENGABOYS
- ◼ '99 We Like To Party!

VENTURES, The
- ☐ '66 Blue Star
- ☐ '65 Diamond Head
- ☐ '69 Hawaii Five-O
- ◼ '64 Journey To The Stars
- ☐ '61 Lullaby Of The Leaves
- ☐ '63 Ninth Wave, The
- ☐ '60 Perfidia
- ☐ '61 Ram-Bunk-Shush
- ☐ '64 Rap City
- ◼ '66 Secret Agent Man
- ☐ '64 Slaughter On Tenth Avenue
- ◼ '60 Walk -- Don't Run ★
- ☐ '64 Walk-Don't Run '64

VERA, Billy, & The Beaters
- ☐ '81 At This Moment ★
- ☐ '68 Country Girl - City Man [w/ Judy Clay]
- ☐ '81 I Can Take Care Of Myself

VERNE, Larry
☐ '60 Mr. Custer ★

VERTICAL HORIZON
▨ '00 Everything You Want ★
☐ '00 You're A God

VERVE, The
▨ '98 Bitter Sweet Symphony

VERVE PIPE, The
▨ '97 Freshmen, The ★

VIBRATIONS, The
☐ '64 My Girl Sloopy
☐ '61 Watusi, The

VILLAGE PEOPLE
☐ '79 Go West
▨ '79 In The Navy ★
▨ '78 Macho Man ★
▨ '78 Y.M.C.A. ★

VILLAGE STOMPERS, The
☐ '63 Washington Square ★

VINCENT, Gene, & His Blue Caps
▨ '56 Be-Bop-A-Lula ★
☐ '56 Bluejean Bop
☐ '57 Dance To The Bop
▨ '57 Lotta Lovin'
☐ '56 Race With The Devil

VINTON, Bobby
☐ '75 Beer Barrel Polka
▨ '63 Blue Moon
☐ '63 Blue On Blue
▨ '63 Blue Velvet ★
☐ '64 Clinging Vine
☐ '66 Coming Home Soldier
☐ '69 Days Of Sand And Shovels, The
☐ '72 Every Day Of My Life
☐ '68 Halfway To Paradise
▨ '68 I Love How You Love Me
☐ '67 Just As Much As Ever
☐ '65 L-O-N-E-L-Y
☐ '65 Long Lonely Nights
▨ '64 Mr. Lonely ★
▨ '64 My Heart Belongs To Only You
☐ '74 My Melody Of Love
☐ '63 Over The Mountain (Across The Sea)
▨ '67 Please Love Me Forever
☐ '62 Rain Rain Go Away
▨ '62 Roses Are Red (My Love) ★
☐ '65 Satin Pillows
▨ '72 Sealed With A Kiss
☐ '68 Take Good Care Of My Baby
☐ '64 Tell Me Why
☐ '63 There! I've Said It Again
▨ '69 To Know You Is To Love You
▨ '68 When I Fall In Love

VIOLENT FEMMES
☐ '91 American Music
☐ '82 Blister In The Sun
☐ '82 Gone Daddy Gone
☐ '89 Nightmares

VIRTUES, The
☐ '59 Guitar Boogie Shuffle

VISCOUNTS, The
☐ '59 Harlem Nocturne

VITAMIN C
▨ '00 Graduation (Friends Forever)
▨ '99 Smile [w/ Lady Saw]

VIXEN
▨ '89 Cryin'
▨ '88 Edge Of A Broken Heart

VOGUES, The
☐ '65 Five O'Clock World
☐ '66 Land Of Milk And Honey, The
☐ '66 Magic Town
▨ '68 My Special Angel
☐ '69 No, Not Much
☐ '68 Till
☐ '68 Turn Around, Look At Me
▨ '65 You're The One

VOICES OF THEORY
☐ '98 Say It
☐ '98 Wherever You Go

VOICES THAT CARE
☐ '91 Voices That Care

VOLUME'S, The
▨ '62 I Love You

VOUDOURIS, Roger
☐ '79 Get Used To It

VOXPOPPERS, The
▨ '58 Wishing For Your Love

W

WADE, Adam
☐ '61 As If I Didn't Know
☐ '61 Take Good Care Of Her
☐ '61 Writing On The Wall, The

WADSWORTH MANSION
☐ '70 Sweet Mary

WAGNER, Jack
▨ '84 All I Need ★

WAGONER, Porter
☐ '69 Carroll County Accident, The
☐ '67 Cold Hard Facts Of Life, The
☐ '62 Misery Loves Company
☐ '55 Satisfied Mind, A
☐ '66 Skid Row Joe

WAIKIKIS, The
☐ '64 Hawaii Tattoo

WAILERS, The
☐ '59 Tall Cool One

WAINWRIGHT, Loudon III
☐ '73 Dead Skunk

WAITE, John
☑ '85 Every Step Of The Way
☑ '84 Missing You ★
☐ '84 Tears

WAKELIN, Johnny
☐ '75 Black Superman - "Muhammad Ali"

WALKER, Chris
☑ '92 Take Time

WALKER, Clay
☑ '99 Chain Of Love, The
☐ '94 Dreaming With My Eyes Open
☐ '96 Hypnotize The Moon
☑ '94 If I Could Make A Living
☐ '93 Live Until I Die
☐ '97 Rumor Has It
☐ '97 Then What?
☐ '95 This Woman And This Man
☐ '93 What's It To You
☐ '98 You're Beginning To Get To Me

WALKER, Jr., & The All Stars
☐ '67 Come See About Me
☐ '65 Do The Boomerang
☑ '70 Do You See My Love (For You Growing)
☐ '70 Gotta Hold On To This Feeling
☐ '68 Hip City
☑ '66 How Sweet It Is (To Be Loved By You)
☐ '66 (I'm A) Road Runner
☑ '67 Pucker Up Buttercup
☐ '65 Shake And Fingerpop
☐ '65 Shotgun
☑ '69 These Eyes
☑ '69 What Does It Take (To Win Your Love)

WALKER BROS., The
☐ '65 Make It Easy On Yourself
☐ '66 Sun Ain't Gonna Shine (Anymore)

WALL, Paul
☑ '06 Girl

WALLACE, Jerry
☐ '58 How The Time Flies
☑ '72 If You Leave Me Tonight I'll Cry
☐ '64 In The Misty Moonlight
☐ '60 Little Coco Palm
☐ '59 Primrose Lane
☐ '62 Shutters And Boards
☑ '60 There She Goes

WALLFLOWERS, The
☐ '97 Difference, The
☐ '98 Heroes
☑ '96 One Headlight ★
☐ '96 6th Avenue Heartache

WALL OF VOODOO
☐ '83 Mexican Radio

WALSH, Joe
☐ '80 All Night Long
☐ '81 Life Of Illusion, A
☐ '78 Life's Been Good

☐ '73 Meadows
☐ '73 Rocky Mountain Way

WALTERS, Jamie
☐ '95 Hold On

WAMMACK, Travis
☐ '64 Scratchy
☐ '75 (Shu-Doo-Pa-Poo-Poop) Love Being Your Fool

WANDERLEY, Walter
☐ '66 Summer Samba (So Nice)

WANG CHUNG
☑ '84 Dance Hall Days ★
☐ '84 Don't Let Go
☑ '86 Everybody Have Fun Tonight ★
☐ '87 Hypnotize Me
☑ '87 Let's Go!

WAR
☐ '71 All Day Music
☐ '74 Ballero
☐ '73 Cisco Kid, The ★
☐ '73 Gypsy Man
☐ '77 L.A. Sunshine
☑ '75 Low Rider
☐ '73 Me And Baby Brother
☐ '72 Slippin' Into Darkness
☐ '70 Spill The Wine [w/ Eric Burdon] ★
☐ '76 Summer
☑ '75 Why Can't We Be Friends? ★
☐ '72 World Is A Ghetto, The

WARD, Anita
☑ '79 Ring My Bell ★ ⬿

WARD, Billy, & His Dominoes
☐ '57 Deep Purple
☐ '56 St. Therese Of The Roses
☐ '57 Star Dust

WARD, Dale
☐ '63 Letter From Sherry

WARD, Joe
☐ '55 Nuttin For Xmas

WARD, Robin
☐ '63 Wonderful Summer

WARINER, Steve
☐ '98 Holes In The Floor Of Heaven
☐ '99 I'm Already Taken
☐ '99 Two Teardrops
☐ '97 What If I Said [w/ Anita Cochran]

WARNES, Jennifer
☐ '79 I Know A Heartache When I See One
☑ '87 (I've Had) The Time Of My Life [w/ Bill Medley] ★
☐ '77 Right Time Of The Night
☑ '82 Up Where We Belong [w/ Joe Cocker] ★

WARRANT
☑ '90 Cherry Pie
☐ '89 Down Boys
☑ '89 Heaven

- ☐ '90 I Saw Red
- ☐ '90 Sometimes She Cries

WARREN G
- ▣ '97 I Shot The Sheriff
- ▣ '99 I Want It All
- ☐ '94 Regulate [w/ Nate Dogg] ★
- ☐ '97 Smokin' Me Out
- ☐ '94 This DJ
- ▣ '96 What's Love Got To Do With It

WARWICK, Dionne
- ▣ '67 Alfie
- ☐ '63 Anyone Who Had A Heart
- ☐ '79 Deja Vu
- ☐ '68 Do You Know The Way To San José
- ☐ '62 Don't Make Me Over
- ☐ '82 Friends In Love [w/ Johnny Mathis]
- ☐ '70 Green Grass Starts To Grow, The
- ☐ '82 Heartbreaker
- ☐ '83 How Many Times Can We Say Goodbye [w/ Luther Vandross]
- ☐ '66 I Just Don't Know What To Do With Myself
- ☐ '67 I Say A Little Prayer
- ☐ '69 I'll Never Fall In Love Again
- ☐ '79 I'll Never Love This Way Again
- ☐ '87 Love Power [w/ Jeffrey Osborne]
- ☐ '70 Make It Easy On Yourself
- ☐ '66 Message To Michael
- ☐ '80 No Night So Long
- ☐ '68 Promises, Promises
- ☐ '64 Reach Out For Me
- ▣ '85 That's What Friends Are For ★
- ☐ '68 (Theme From) Valley Of The Dolls ★
- ▣ '74 Then Came You [w/ the Spinners] ★
- ▣ '69 This Girl's In Love With You
- ☐ '66 Trains And Boats And Planes
- ▣ '64 Walk On By ★
- ☐ '67 Windows Of The World, The
- ☐ '64 You'll Never Get To Heaven (If You Break My Heart)
- ☐ '69 You've Lost That Lovin' Feeling

WASHINGTON, Baby
- ☐ '63 That's How Heartaches Are Made

WASHINGTON, Dinah
- ▣ '60 Baby (You've Got What It Takes) [w/ Brook Benton] ★
- ▣ '60 Love Walked In
- ☐ '60 Rockin' Good Way (To Mess Around And Fall In Love) [w/ Brook Benton]
- ☐ '61 September In The Rain
- ☐ '60 This Bitter Earth
- ☐ '59 Unforgettable
- ☐ '59 What A Diff'rence A Day Makes
- ☐ '62 Where Are You

WASHINGTON, Grover Jr.
- ☐ '81 Just The Two Of Us [w/ Bill Withers] ★

WASHINGTON, Keith
- ▣ '91 Kissing You

WAS (NOT WAS)
- ☐ '88 Spy In The House Of Love

- ☐ '89 Walk The Dinosaur

WATERBOYS, The
- ☐ '88 Fisherman's Blues

WATERFRONT
- ☐ '89 Cry

WATERS, Crystal
- ☐ '91 Gypsy Woman (She's Homeless)
- ▣ '94 100% Pure Love
- ☐ '97 Say...If You Feel Alright

WATERS, Muddy
- ☐ '53 Baby Please Don't Go
- ☐ '57 Got My Mojo Working
- ☐ '54 Hoochie Coochie Man
- ☐ '51 Louisiana Blues
- ☐ '55 Mannish Boy
- ☐ '50 Rollin' Stone
- ☐ '50 Rollin' & Tumblin'

WATLEY, Jody
- ▣ '87 Don't You Want Me
- ☐ '89 Everything
- ☐ '89 Friends [w/ Eric B. & Rakim]
- ☐ '92 I'm The One You Need
- ☐ '87 Looking For A New Love ★
- ▣ '89 Real Love
- ▣ '88 Some Kind Of Lover
- ☐ '87 Still A Thrill

WATSON, Wayne — see PATTY, Sandi

WA WA NEE
- ☐ '87 Sugar Free

WAYNE, Jimmy
- ☐ '03 Stay Gone

WAYNE, Thomas
- ☐ '59 Tragedy

WEATHER GIRLS, The
- ▣ '83 It's Raining Men

WEATHERLY, Jim
- ☐ '74 Need To Be, The

WEBER, Joan
- ☐ '55 Let Me Go, Lover! ★

WEBSTAR & YOUNG B
- ☐ '06 Chicken Noodle Soup

WEEZER
- ▣ '05 Beverly Hills ★
- ▣ '94 Buddy Holly ★
- ☐ '01 Hash Pipe
- ☐ '05 Perfect Situation
- ▣ '95 Say It Ain't So
- ☐ '94 Undone-The Sweater Song

WE FIVE
- ▣ '65 Let's Get Together
- ▣ '65 You Were On My Mind ★

WEISSBERG, Eric, & Steve Mandell
- ▣ '73 Dueling Banjos ★

WELCH, Bob
- ☐ '78 Ebony Eyes
- ☐ '78 Hot Love, Cold World
- ☒ '79 Precious Love
- ☐ '77 Sentimental Lady

WELCH, Lenny
- ☒ '70 Breaking Up Is Hard To Do
- ☐ '64 Ebb Tide
- ☒ '63 Since I Fell For You
- ☐ '60 You Don't Know Me

WELK, Lawrence, & His Orchestra
- ☐ '60 Calcutta
- ☐ '56 In The Alps [w/ McGuire Sisters]
- ☐ '60 Last Date
- ☐ '56 Moritat (A Theme From "The Threepenny Opera")
- ☐ '56 Poor People Of Paris, The

WELLS, Mary
- ☐ '64 Ain't It The Truth
- ☐ '61 I Don't Want To Take A Chance
- ☐ '63 Laughing Boy
- ☒ '64 My Guy ★
- ☐ '64 Once Upon A Time [w/ Marvin Gaye]
- ☒ '62 One Who Really Loves You, The
- ☒ '62 Two Lovers
- ☐ '65 Use Your Head
- ☐ '63 What's Easy For Two Is So Hard For One
- ☐ '64 What's The Matter With You Baby [w/ Marvin Gaye]
- ☐ '62 You Beat Me To The Punch
- ☐ '63 You Lost The Sweetest Boy
- ☐ '63 Your Old Stand By

WESLEY, Fred — see J.B.'s

WEST, Dottie
- ☐ '81 What Are We Doin' In Love [w/ Kenny Rogers]

WEST, Kanye
- ☐ '04 All Falls Down
- ☒ '05 Diamonds From Sierra Leone
- ☒ '05 Gold Digger ★
- ☒ '07 Good Life ★
- ☐ '05 Heard 'Em Say
- ☒ '04 Jesus Walks
- ☐ '07 Stronger ★
- ☒ '03 Through The Wire
- ☐ '06 Touch The Sky

WEST COAST RAP ALL-STARS, The
- ☐ '90 We're All In The Same Gang

WESTLIFE
- ☐ '00 Swear It Again

WESTON, Kim — see GAYE, Marvin

WESTSIDE CONNECTION
- ☐ '96 Bow Down
- ☐ '03 Gangsta Nation
- ☐ '97 Gangstas Make The World Go Round

WET WILLIE
- ☒ '74 Keep On Smilin'
- ☐ '77 Street Corner Serenade
- ☐ '79 Weekend

WHEN IN ROME
- ☐ '88 Promise, The

WHISPERS, The
- ☐ '80 And The Beat Goes On —
- ☒ '81 It's A Love Thing ⌐
- ☐ '80 Lady
- ☐ '87 Rock Steady ⌐

WHISTLE
- ☐ '90 Always And Forever

WHITCOMB, Ian
- ☒ '65 You Turn Me On

WHITE, Barry
- ☒ '74 Can't Get Enough Of Your Love, Babe ★
- ☒ '75 I'll Do For You Anything You Want Me To
- ☐ '73 I'm Gonna Love You Just A Little More Baby
- ☒ '73 I've Got So Much To Give
- ☒ '77 It's Ecstasy When You Lay Down Next To Me
- ☐ '75 Let The Music Play
- ☒ '73 Never, Never Gonna Give Ya Up
- ☐ '78 Oh What A Night For Dancing
- ☐ '94 Practice What You Preach
- ☒ '75 What Am I Gonna Do With You
- ☒ '74 You're The First, The Last, My Everything ★
- ☒ '78 Your Sweetness Is My Weakness

WHITE, Bryan
- ☐ '95 Rebecca Lynn
- ☐ '97 Sittin' On Go
- ☐ '96 So Much For Pretending
- ☐ '95 Someone Else's Star

WHITE, Karyn
- ☒ '86 Facts Of Love [w/ Jeff Lorber]
- ☒ '89 Love Saw It
- ☒ '91 Romantic
- ☐ '89 Secret Rendezvous
- ☐ '89 Superwoman
- ☒ '91 Way I Feel About You, The
- ☒ '88 Way You Love Me, The

WHITE, Tony Joe
- ☐ '69 Polk Salad Annie

WHITE LION
- ☒ '88 Wait
- ☒ '88 When The Children Cry

WHITE PLAINS
- ☒ '70 My Baby Loves Lovin'

WHITESNAKE
- ☒ '90 Deeper The Love, The
- ☐ '89 Fool For Your Loving
- ☒ '87 Here I Go Again ★

☒ '87 Is This Love

WHITE STRIPES, The
- ☐ '06 Denial Twist, The
- ☐ '07 Icky Thump
- ☐ '03 Seven Nation Army
- ☐ '02 We're Going To Be Friends

WHITE TOWN
- ☐ '97 Your Woman

WHITING, Margaret
- ☐ '56 Money Tree, The
- ☐ '66 Wheel Of Hurt, The

WHITLEY, Keith
- ☐ '89 I'm No Stranger To The Rain
- ☒ '88 When You Say Nothing At All

WHITTAKER, Roger
- ☐ '75 Last Farewell, The ★

WHO, The
- ☐ '82 Athena
- ☐ '71 Baba O'Riley
- ☐ '71 Bargain
- ☐ '71 Behind Blue Eyes
- ☐ '67 Boris The Spider
- ☐ '68 Call Me Lightning
- ☐ '83 Eminence Front
- ☐ '73 5:15
- ☐ '71 Goin' Mobile
- ☐ '67 Happy Jack
- ☐ '67 I Can See For Miles ★
- ☐ '65 I Can't Explain
- ☐ '69 I'm Free
- ☐ '72 Join Together
- ☐ '71 Kids Are Alright
- ☐ '79 Long Live Rock
- ☐ '73 Love, Reign, O'er Me
- ☐ '68 Magic Bus
- ☐ '66 My Generation ★
- ☒ '71 My Wife
- ☐ '67 Pictures Of Lily
- ☐ '69 Pinball Wizard
- ☐ '73 Real Me, The
- ☐ '72 Relay, The
- ☐ '70 See Me, Feel Me
- ☐ '70 Seeker, The
- ☐ '75 Squeeze Box
- ☐ '66 Substitute
- ☐ '70 Summertime Blues
- ☒ '69 We're Not Gonna Take It
- ☒ '78 Who Are You
- ☐ '71 Won't Get Fooled Again ★
- ☐ '81 You Better You Bet

WIEDLIN, Jane
- ☐ '88 Rush Hour

WILCOX, Harlow, & The Oakies
- ☐ '69 Groovy Grubworm

WILD CHERRY
- ☒ '76 Play That Funky Music ★

WILDE, Eugene
- ☐ '85 Don't Say No Tonight
- ☐ '84 Gotta Get You Home Tonight

WILDE, Kim
- ☐ '82 Kids In America
- ☐ '87 You Keep Me Hangin' On

WILDER, Matthew
- ☒ '83 Break My Stride
- ☒ '84 Kid's American, The

WILKINSONS, The
- ☐ '98 26¢

will.i.am
- ☐ '07 I Got It From My Mama

WILLIAMS, Andy
- ☐ '65 And Roses And Roses
- ☐ '58 Are You Sincere
- ☐ '56 Baby Doll
- ☐ '68 Battle Hymn Of The Republic
- ☐ '61 Bilbao Song, The
- ☐ '57 Butterfly
- ☐ '63 Can't Get Used To Losing You ★
- ☐ '56 Canadian Sunset
- ☐ '63 Days Of Wine And Roses
- ☐ '64 Dear Heart
- ☐ '62 Don't You Believe It
- ☐ '64 Fool Never Learns, A
- ☒ '69 Happy Heart
- ☐ '58 Hawaiian Wedding Song, The
- ☐ '63 Hopeless
- ☒ '57 I Like Your Kind Of Love
- ☒ '66 In The Arms Of Love
- ☐ '57 Lips Of Wine
- ☐ '59 Lonely Street
- ☐ '72 Love Theme From "The Godfather"
- ☐ '63 May Each Day
- ☐ '62 Moon River
- ☒ '67 More And More
- ☐ '67 Music To Watch Girls By
- ☐ '64 On The Street Where You Live
- ☐ '70 One Day Of Your Life
- ☒ '58 Promise Me, Love
- ☐ '62 Stranger On The Shore
- ☐ '59 Village Of St. Bernadette, The
- ☒ '71 (Where Do I Begin) Love Story

WILLIAMS, Billy
- ☐ '56 Crazy Little Palace, A
- ☐ '57 I'm Gonna Sit Right Down And Write Myself A Letter ★

WILLIAMS, Christopher
- ☐ '91 I'm Dreamin'

WILLIAMS, Danny
- ☐ '64 White On White

WILLIAMS, Deniece
- ☐ '76 Free
- ☒ '82 It's Gonna Take A Miracle
- ☒ '84 Let's Hear It For The Boy ★
- ☐ '78 Too Much, Too Little, Too Late
  [w/ Johnny Mathis] ★

WILLIAMS, Don
- ■ '80 I Believe In You
- ☐ '78 Tulsa Time

WILLIAMS, Hank Jr.
- ■ '84 All My Rowdy Friends Are Coming Over Tonight
- ☐ '87 Born To Boogie
- ■ '82 Country Boy Can Survive, A
- ■ '79 Family Tradition
- ☐ '82 Honky Tonkin'
- ☐ '86 Mind Your Own Business
- ■ '89 There's A Tear In My Beer [w/ Hank Williams, Sr.]

WILLIAMS, John
- ☐ '75 Main Title (Theme From "Jaws")
- ☐ '77 Star Wars (Main Title)
- ☐ '77 Theme From "Close Encounters Of The Third Kind"
- ☐ '79 Theme From Superman

WILLIAMS, Larry
- ☐ '57 Bony Moronie
- ☐ '57 Short Fat Fannie

WILLIAMS, Mason
- ☐ '68 Classical Gas ★

WILLIAMS, Maurice, & The Zodiacs
- ■ '60 Stay ★

WILLIAMS, Robbie
- ☐ '00 Angels
- ☐ '99 Millennium

WILLIAMS, Roger
- ☐ '57 Almost Paradise
- ☐ '55 Autumn Leaves ★
- ☐ '66 Born Free
- ☐ '56 La Mer (Beyond The Sea)
- ☐ '66 Lara's Theme From "Dr. Zhivago"
- ■ '67 Love Me Forever
- ■ '67 More Than A Miracle
- ☐ '58 Near You
- ☐ '57 Till
- ■ '55 Wanting You

WILLIAMS, Vanessa
- ■ '95 Colors Of The Wind ★
- ☐ '91 Comfort Zone, The
- ■ '89 Dreamin' ➡
- ☐ '92 Just For Tonight
- ■ '93 Love Is [w/ Brian McKnight] ★
- ■ '91 Running Back To You
- ■ '92 Save The Best For Last ★
- ☐ '94 Sweetest Days, The

WILLIAMSON, "Sonny Boy"
- ☐ '55 Don't Start Me Talkin'

WILLIS, Bruce
- ☐ '87 Respect Yourself

WILLIS, Chuck
- ☐ '58 Betty And Dupree
- ☐ '57 C. C. Rider
- ☐ '58 Hang Up My Rock And Roll Shoes
- ☐ '56 It's Too Late
- ☐ '52 My Story
- ☐ '58 What Am I Living For

WILLS, Mark
- ☐ '00 Back At One
- ☐ '98 Don't Laugh At Me
- ■ '98 I Do [Cherish You]
- ☐ '02 19 Somethin'
- ☐ '99 Wish You Were Here

WILL TO POWER
- ■ '88 Baby, I Love Your Way/Freebird Medley (Free Baby) ★
- ☐ '90 I'm Not In Love

WILSON, Al
- ☐ '76 I've Got A Feeling (We'll Be Seeing Each Other Again)
- ☐ '74 La La Peace Song
- ☐ '73 Show And Tell
- ☐ '68 Snake, The

WILSON, Ann
- ■ '84 Almost Paradise...Love Theme From Footloose [w/ Mike Reno]
- ☐ '88 Surrender To Me [w/ Robin Zander]

WILSON, Gretchen
- ☐ '05 All Jacked Up
- ☐ '04 Here For The Party
- ☐ '05 Homewrecker
- ■ '04 Redneck Woman
- ☐ '04 When I Think About Cheatin'

WILSON, J. Frank, & The Cavaliers
- ■ '64 Last Kiss ★

WILSON, Jackie
- ☐ '60 Alone At Last
- ☐ '60 Am I The Man
- ☐ '63 Baby Workout
- ☐ '60 Doggin' Around
- ☐ '59 I'll Be Satisfied
- ☐ '61 I'm Comin' On On Back To You
- ☐ '58 Lonely Teardrops ★
- ☐ '61 My Empty Arms
- ☐ '60 Night ★
- ☐ '61 Please Tell Me Why
- ☐ '57 Reet Petite
- ■ '63 Shake! Shake! Shake!
- ☐ '59 Talk That Talk
- ■ '59 That's Why (I Love You So)
- ■ '58 To Be Loved
- ☐ '66 Whispers (Gettin' Louder)
- ■ '60 Woman, A Lover, A Friend, A
- ☐ '59 You Better Know It
- ■ '60 (You Were Made For) All My Love
- ■ '67 (Your Love Keeps Lifting Me) Higher And Higher ★

WILSON, Meri
- ☐ '77 Telephone Man

WILSON, Nancy
- ☐ '68 Face It Girl, It's Over
- ☐ '64 (You Don't Know) How Glad I Am

WILSON PHILLIPS
- ☐ '91 Dream Is Still Alive, The
- ☐ '92 Give It Up
- ▨ '90 Hold On ★
- ☐ '90 Impulsive
- ☐ '90 Release Me ★
- ☐ '92 You Won't See Me Cry
- ▨ '91 You're In Love ★

WILTON PLACE STREET BAND
- ☐ '77 Disco Lucy (I Love Lucy Theme)

WINANS, BeBe & CeCe
- ▨ '91 Addictive Love
- ▨ '89 Heaven
- ☐ '91 I'll Take You There

WINANS, CeCe
- ☐ '96 Count On Me [w/ Whitney Houston]

WINANS, Mario
- ▨ '04 I Don't Wanna Know [w/ P. Diddy] ★

WINBUSH, Angela
- ☐ '87 Angel
- ☐ '89 It's The Real Thing

WINCHESTER, Jesse
- ☐ '81 Say What

WIND — see ORLANDO, Tony

WINDING, Kai, & Orchestra
- ☐ '63 More

WINEHOUSE, Amy
- ▨ '07 Rehab ★

WING & A PRAYER FIFE & DRUM CORPS.
- ☐ '75 Baby Face

WINGER
- ☐ '89 Headed For A Heartbreak
- ☐ '90 Miles Away
- ▨ '89 Seventeen

WINGFIELD, Pete
- ☐ '75 Eighteen With A Bullet

WINSTONS, The
- ☐ '69 Color Him Father

WINTER, Edgar, Group
- ☐ '73 Frankenstein ★
- ☐ '73 Free Ride
- ☐ '74 River's Risin'

WINTERHALTER, Hugo, & His Orchestra with Eddie Heywood
- ☐ '56 Canadian Sunset ★

WINWOOD, Steve
- ▨ '87 Back In The High Life Again
- ☐ '88 Don't You Know What The Night Can Do?
- ☐ '87 Finer Things, The
- ☐ '86 Freedom Overspill
- ▨ '86 Higher Love ★

- ☐ '88 Holding On
- ☐ '90 One And Only Man
- ▨ '88 Roll With It ★
- ☐ '86 Split Decision
- ☐ '87 Valerie [remix]
- ☐ '81 While You See A Chance

WISEGUYS, The
- ☐ '01 Start The Commotion

WITHERS, Bill
- ▨ '71 Ain't No Sunshine ★ ▬
- ☐ '81 Just The Two Of Us [w/ Grover Washington, Jr.] ★
- ▨ '73 Kissing My Love
- ▨ '72 Lean On Me ★
- ☐ '77 Lovely Day
- ☐ '72 Use Me

WOLF, Peter
- ▨ '87 Come As You Are
- ▨ '84 I Need You Tonight
- ☐ '84 Lights Out

WOMACK, Bobby
- ☐ '72 Harry Hippie
- ☐ '85 I Wish He Didn't Trust Me So Much
- ☐ '81 If You Think You're Lonely Now
- ☐ '74 Lookin' For A Love
- ☐ '84 Love Has Finally Come At Last [w/ Patti LaBelle]
- ☐ '73 Nobody Wants You When You're Down And Out
- ☐ '71 That's The Way I Feel About Cha
- ☐ '72 Woman's Gotta Have It

WOMACK, Lee Ann
- ☐ '97 Fool, The
- ▨ '00 I Hope You Dance ★
- ☐ '99 I'll Think Of A Reason Later
- ☐ '98 Little Past Little Rock, A
- ▨ '97 You've Got To Talk To Me

WONDER, Stevie
- ☐ '66 Blowin In The Wind
- ☐ '74 Boogie On Reggae Woman
- ☐ '82 Do I Do
- ▨ '74 Don't You Worry 'Bout A Thing
- ▨ '82 Ebony And Ivory [w/ Paul McCartney] ★
- ▨ '63 Fingertips ★
- ▨ '68 For Once In My Life ★
- ▨ '95 For Your Love
- ☐ '85 Go Home
- ☐ '70 Heaven Help Us All
- ☐ '64 Hey Harmonica Man
- ☐ '73 Higher Ground
- ☐ '80 I Ain't Gonna Stand For It
- ▨ '84 I Just Called To Say I Love You ★
- ▨ '67 I Was Made To Love Her
- ☐ '76 I Wish
- ☐ '67 I'm Wondering
- ☐ '71 If You Really Love Me
- ▨ '77 Isn't She Lovely
- ☐ '73 Living For The City
- ☐ '84 Love Light In Flight
- ☐ '80 Master Blaster (Jammin') ★

WONDER, Stevie — cont'd
- '69 My Cherie Amour
- '70 Never Had A Dream Come True
- '66 Nothing's Too Good For My Baby
- '86 Overjoyed
- '85 Part-Time Lover ★
- '66 Place In The Sun, A
- '79 Send One Your Love ★
- '68 Shoo-Be-Doo-Be-Doo-Da-Day
- '70 Signed, Sealed, Delivered I'm Yours ★
- '77 Sir Duke ★
- '87 Skeletons
- '72 Superstition ★
- '72 Superwoman (Where Were You When I Needed You)
- '82 That Girl
- '65 Uptight (Everything's Alright)
- '71 We Can Work It Out
- '69 Yester-Me, Yester-You, Yesterday
- '73 You Are The Sunshine Of My Life ★
- '74 You Haven't Done Nothin
- '68 You Met Your Match
- '88 You Will Know

WONDER, Wayne
- '03 No Letting Go

WONDERS, The
- '96 That Thing You Do!

WOOD, Brenton
- '67 Gimme Little Sign
- '67 Oogum Boogum Song, The

WOOD, Lauren
- '79 Please Don't Leave

WOODS, Stevie
- '82 Just Can't Win 'Em All
- '81 Steal The Night

WOOLEY, Sheb
- '58 Purple People Eater, The ★

WORLD PARTY
- '87 Ship Of Fools (Save Me From Tomorrow)

WORLEY, Darryl
- '05 Awful, Beautiful Life
- '03 Have You Forgotten?
- '02 I Miss My Friend

WRAY, Link, & His Ray Men
- '59 Raw-Hide
- '58 Rumble

WRECKERS, The
- '06 Leave The Pieces

WRECKX-N-EFFECT
- '92 Rump Shaker ★

WRIGHT, Betty
- '71 Clean Up Woman
- '78 Dance With Me *[w/ Peter Brown]*
- '68 Girls Can't Do What The Guys Do

WRIGHT, Charles, & The Watts 103rd Street Rhythm Band
- '69 Do Your Thing
- '70 Express Yourself
- '70 Love Land

WRIGHT, Chely
- '99 Single White Female

WRIGHT, Dale
- '58 She's Neat

WRIGHT, Gary
- '76 Dream Weaver ★
- '76 Love Is Alive
- '81 Really Wanna Know You

WRIGHT, Priscilla
- '55 Man In The Raincoat, The

WU-TANG CLAN
- '94 C.R.E.A.M.
- '93 Method Man

WYATT, Keke
- '02 Nothing In This World *[w/ Avant]*

WYNETTE, Tammy
- '68 D-I-V-O-R-C-E
- '67 I Don't Wanna Play House
- '67 My Elusive Dreams *[w/ David Houston]*
- '68 Stand By Your Man ★
- '73 We're Gonna Hold On *[w/ George Jones]*
- '74 (We're Not) The Jet Set *[w/ George Jones]*

WYNONNA
- '93 Bad Goodbye, A *[w/ Clint Black]*
- '92 I Saw The Light
- '92 No One Else On Earth
- '94 Rock Bottom
- '92 She Is His Only Need
- '96 To Be Loved By You

X

X
- '85 Burning House Of Love
- '87 4th Of July

XSCAPE
- '98 Arms Of The One Who Loves You, The
- '95 Feels So Good
- '93 Just Kickin' It
- '98 My Little Secret
- '93 Understanding
- '95 Who Can I Run To?

XTC
- '92 Ballad Of Peter Pumpkinhead, The
- '89 Mayor Of Simpleton, The

Y

YAMIN, Elliott
- '07 Wait For You

YANKOVIC, "Weird Al"
- '84 Eat It
- '85 Like A Surgeon

- ☐ '92 Smells Like Nirvana
- ☐ '06 White & Nerdy ★

YARBROUGH, Glenn
- ☐ '65 Baby The Rain Must Fall

YARBROUGH & PEOPLES
- ☐ '81 Don't Stop The Music
- ☐ '84 Don't Waste Your Time

YARDBIRDS, The
- ▨ '65 For Your Love
- ☐ '66 Happenings Ten Years Time Ago
- ☐ '65 Heart Full Of Soul
- ☐ '65 I'm A Man
- ☐ '67 Little Games
- ☐ '66 Over Under Sideways Down
- ☐ '66 Shapes Of Things
- ☐ '65 Train Kept A-Rollin'

YAZ
- ☐ '82 Only You
- ☐ '82 Situation

YEARWOOD, Trisha
- ☐ '96 Believe Me Baby (I Lied)
- ▨ '97 How Do I Live
- ☐ '97 In Another's Eyes *[w/ Garth Brooks]*
- ▨ '98 Perfect Love, A
- ▨ '91 She's In Love With The Boy
- ☐ '93 Song Remembers When, The
- ☐ '98 There Goes My Baby
- ▨ '95 Thinkin' About You
- ☐ '92 Walkaway Joe *[w/ Don Henley]*
- ☐ '94 XXX's And OOO's (An American Girl)

YELLO
- ☐ '87 Oh Yeah

YELLOW BALLOON, The
- ☐ '67 Yellow Balloon

YELLOWCARD
- ☐ '06 Lights And Sounds
- ☐ '04 Ocean Avenue

YES
- ☐ '72 America
- ▨ '72 And You And I
- ☐ '72 Close To The Edge
- ☐ '69 Every Little Thing
- ☐ '77 Going For The One
- ☐ '84 Leave It
- ▨ '91 Lift Me Up
- ☐ '72 Long Distance Runaround
- ▨ '87 Love Will Find A Way
- ▨ '83 Owner Of A Lonely Heart ★
- ▨ '87 Rhythm Of Love
- ☐ '72 Roundabout
- ☐ '71 Starship Trooper
- ☐ '71 Your Move/All Good People
- ☐ '71 Yours Is No Disgrace

YING YANG TWINS
- ▨ '05 Badd
- ▨ '03 Salt Shaker
- ☐ '05 Shake
- ▨ '05 Wait (The Whisper Song)

- ☐ '04 Whats Happnin!

YOAKAM, Dwight
- ☐ '93 Ain't That Lonely Yet
- ☐ '93 Fast As You
- ☐ '86 Guitars, Cadillacs
- ☐ '86 Honky Tonk Man
- ☐ '88 Streets Of Bakersfield *[w/ Buck Owens]*
- ▨ '93 Thousand Miles From Nowhere, A

YOUNG, Barry
- ▨ '65 One Has My Name (The Other Has My Heart)

YOUNG, Faron
- ☐ '58 Alone With You
- ☐ '61 Hello Walls
- ☐ '71 It's Four In The Morning

YOUNG, John Paul
- ☐ '78 Love Is In The Air

YOUNG, Kathy, with The Innocents
- ☐ '61 Happy Birthday Blues
- ☐ '60 Thousand Stars, A ★

YOUNG, Neil
- ☐ '70 After The Gold Rush
- ☐ '69 Cinnamon Girl
- ☐ '78 Comes A Time
- ☐ '75 Cortez The Killer
- ▨ '69 Cowgirl In The Sand
- ☐ '69 Down By The River
- ☐ '78 Four Strong Winds
- ▨ '72 Heart Of Gold ★
- ▨ '77 Like A Hurricane
- ☐ '72 Needle And The Damage Done
- ☐ '72 Old Man
- ☐ '70 Only Love Can Break Your Heart
- ▨ '89 Rockin' In The Free World
- ☐ '79 Hey Hey, My My (Into The Black)
- ☐ '70 Southern Man
- ☐ '74 Walk On
- ▨ '70 When You Dance I Can Really Love

YOUNG, Paul
- ☐ '84 Come Back And Stay
- ▨ '85 Everytime You Go Away ★
- ☐ '85 I'm Gonna Tear Your Playhouse Down
- ▨ '90 Oh Girl
- ☐ '92 What Becomes Of The Brokenhearted

YOUNG, Victor, & His Singing Strings
- ☐ '57 Around The World (Main Theme)

YOUNGBLOODS, The
- ☐ '68 Get Together

YOUNGBLOODZ
- ☐ '03 Damn! *[w/ Lil' Jon]*

YOUNG BUCK
- ☐ '04 Let Me In
- ☐ '04 Shorty Wanna Ride

YOUNG DRO
- ☐ '06 Shoulder Lean ★

YOUNG GUNZ
- ☐ '03 Can't Stop, Won't Stop
- ☐ '04 No Better Love *[w/ Rell]*

YOUNG-HOLT UNLIMITED
- ☐ '68 Soulful Strut
- ☐ '66 Wack Wack

YOUNG JEEZY
- ▣ '07 Go Getta
- ☐ '06 I Luv It
- ▣ '05 Soul Survivor ★

YOUNG M.C.
- ☐ '89 Bust A Move ★
- ☐ '89 Principal's Office

YOUNG RASCALS — see RASCALS

YO-YO
- ☐ '91 You Can't Play With My Yo-Yo

YUNG BERG
- ▣ '07 Sexy Lady

YUNG JOC
- ▣ '06 I Know You See It
- ▣ '06 It's Goin' Down ★

YURO, Timi
- ☐ '61 Hurt
- ☐ '63 Make The World Go Away
- ☐ '62 What's A Matter Baby (Is It Hurting You)

Z

ZACHARIAS, Helmut
- ☐ '56 When The White Lilacs Bloom Again

ZACHERLE, John, "The Cool Ghoul"
- ☐ '58 Dinner With Drac

ZAGER, Michael, Band
- ☐ '78 Let's All Chant

ZAGER & EVANS
- ☐ '69 In The Year 2525 ★

ZAHND, Ricky, & The Blue Jeaners
- ☐ '55 (I'm Gettin') Nuttin' For Christmas

ZAPP
- ☐ '82 Dance Floor
- ☐ '80 More Bounce To The Ounce

ZAPPA, Frank
- ☐ '74 Cosmik Debris
- ▣ '79 Dancin' Fool
- ☐ '74 Don't Eat The Yellow Snow
- ☐ '79 Joe's Garage
- ☐ '73 Montana
- ☐ '70 My Guitar Wants To Kill Your Mama
- ☐ '69 Peaches En Regalia
- ☐ '70 Transylvania Boogie
- ▣ '82 Valley Girl

ZEVON, Warren
- ▣ '80 Certain Girl, A
- ☐ '78 Excitable Boy
- ☐ '78 Lawyers, Guns And Money
- ☐ '78 Werewolves Of London ★

ZHANÉ
- ☐ '94 Groove Thang
- ▣ '93 Hey Mr. D.J. ★
- ☐ '97 Request Line
- ▣ '94 Sending My Love
- ☐ '94 Shame

Z'LOOKE
- ☐ '88 Can U Read My Lips

ZOMBIES, The
- ☐ '64 She's Not There ★
- ☐ '65 Tell Her No
- ☐ '69 Time Of The Season ★

ZZ TOP
- ☐ '77 Arrested For Driving While Blind
- ▣ '80 Cheap Sunglasses
- ☐ '90 Concrete And Steel
- ☐ '90 Doubleback
- ☐ '72 Francene
- ☐ '83 Gimme All Your Lovin
- ☐ '90 Give It Up
- ☐ '75 Heard It On The X
- ☐ '80 I Thank You
- ☐ '80 I'm Bad, I'm Nationwide
- ☐ '77 It's Only Love
- ▣ '73 La Grange
- ▣ '84 Legs
- ☐ '90 My Head's In Mississippi
- ☐ '94 Pincushion
- ☐ '86 Rough Boy
- ▣ '83 Sharp Dressed Man
- ☐ '85 Sleeping Bag
- ☐ '85 Stages
- ☐ '81 Tube Snake Boogie
- ☐ '75 Tush
- ☐ '86 Velcro Fly
- ▣ '92 Viva Las Vegas
- ☐ '72 Waitin' For The Bus/Jesus Just Left Chicago

SONG TITLE SECTION

Following are some basic guidelines for using this section:

> All titles are listed in alphabetical order and are in bold type.
> The year is listed to the left of the title.
> The artist name is listed in italics to the right (or below) the title.

In this book, **songs with identical titles are listed together even if they are different compositions**. Listed below the song title, in chronological order, are the artists' names. The following artists recorded songs with the <u>same title</u>, but they are <u>not</u> the <u>same composition</u>:

> **My First Love**
> '89 *Atlantic Starr*
> '00 *Avant*

Most of the listings in this book mirror the following:

> '93 **All About Soul** *Billy Joel*

Abbreviated titles such as "C.C. Rider" and "S.O.S." are listed at the beginning of their respective first letters. Conversely, abbreviated titles which spell out a word, such as "T-R-O-U-B-L-E" and "D-I-V-O-R-C-E" are sorted along with the regular spellings of these words.

If any of the articles "A," "An," "The" or "Tha" is the first word of a title, it is not shown. However, if a title is made up of only <u>one other</u> word, then it is shown as follows:

> '77 **Pride, The** *Isley Brothers*

On occasion, similar titles are combined. Examples:

Tonight, Tonight [Tonite, Tonite]
'57   *Mello-Kings*
'96   *Smashing Pumpkins*

In the above case, one artist spelled the title "Tonight, Tonight" and the other artist spelled it as "Tonite, Tonite."

I Saw Her [Him] Standing There
'64   *Beatles*
'88   *Tiffany*

In the above case, one artist recorded the title "I Saw Her Standing There" and the other artist as "I Saw Him Standing There."

If [medley] follows either a title or an artist's name, that indicates that the title is part of a medley. Go to the artist section to find out the other part of the medley.

A

'70 **ABC** Jackson 5
'01 **AM To PM** Christina Milian
'96 **ATLiens** OutKast
'00 **Aaron's Party (Come Get It)** Aaron Carter
'81 **Abacab** Genesis
'64 **Abigail Beecher** Freddy Cannon
'63 **Abilene** George Hamilton IV
'94 **About A Girl** Nirvana
'60 **About This Thing Called Love** Fabian
'06 **About Us** Brooke Hogan
'03 **Above All** Michael W. Smith
Abracadabra
'73 DeFranco Family
'82 Steve Miller Band
Abraham, Martin And John
'68 Dion
'69 Moms Mabley
'69 Miracles
'71 Tom Clay [medley]
'71 **Absolutely Right** Five Man Electrical Band
'00 **Absolutely (Story Of A Girl)** Ninedays
'04 **Accidentally In Love** Counting Crows
'79 **Accidents Will Happen** Elvis Costello
'92 **Achy Breaky Heart** Billy Ray Cyrus
'90 **Across The River** Bruce Hornsby
Across The Universe
'70 Beatles
'05 Various Artists
'03 **Act A Fool** Ludacris
Act Naturally
'63 Buck Owens
'65 Beatles
Action
'65 Freddy Cannon
'76 Sweet
'60 **Adam And Eve** Paul Anka
'00 **Adam's Song** Blink 182
'91 **Addams Groove** Hammer
'86 **Addicted To Love** Robert Palmer
'88 **Addicted To You** Levert
'02 **Addictive** Truth Hurts
'91 **Addictive Love** BeBe & CeCe Winans
'98 **Adia** Sarah McLachlan
'62 **Adios Amigo** Jim Reeves
'55 **Adorable** Drifters
'84 **Adult Education** Daryl Hall - John Oates
'06 **Adventure, The** Angels & Airwaves
'88 **Ae, Ao** Julio Iglesias
'96 **Aenima** Tool
'02 **Aerials** System Of A Down
'96 **Aeroplane** Red Hot Chili Peppers
'83 **Affair Of The Heart** Rick Springfield
'57 **Affair To Remember (Our Love Affair)** Vic Damone
'82 **Africa** Toto
'61 **African Waltz** "Cannonball" Adderley
'62 **Afrikaan Beat** Bert Kaempfert
'89 **After All** Cher & Peter Cetera
After Midnight
'70 Eric Clapton
'72 J.J. Cale
'57 **After School** Randy Starr
'91 **After The Dance** Fourplay
'83 **After The Fall** Journey
'85 **After The Fire** Roger Daltrey
'71 **After The Fire Is Gone** Conway Twitty & Loretta Lynn
'82 **After The Glitter Fades** Stevie Nicks
After The Gold Rush
'70 Neil Young
'74 Prelude
'56 **After The Lights Go Down Low** Al Hibbler
'77 **After The Love Has Gone** Earth, Wind & Fire

'76 **After The Lovin'** Engelbert Humperdinck
'90 **After The Rain** Nelson
'75 **After The Thrill Is Gone** Eagles
'76 **Afternoon Delight** Starland Vocal Band
Again
'93 Janet Jackson
'96 Alice In Chains
'00 Lenny Kravitz
'05 Faith Evans
'92 **Again Tonight** John Mellencamp
'84 **Against All Odds (Take A Look At Me Now)** Phil Collins
'80 **Against The Wind** Bob Seger
'65 **Agent Double-O-Soul** Edwin Starr
'75 **Agony And The Ecstasy** Smokey Robinson
'80 **Ah! Leah!** Donnie Iris
'62 **Ahab, The Arab** Ray Stevens
'81 **Ai No Corrida** Quincy Jones
'81 **Ain't Even Done With The Night** John Cougar Mellencamp
'93 **Ain't Going Down (Til The Sun Comes Up)** Garth Brooks
'77 **Ain't Gonna Bump No More (With No Big Fat Woman)** Joe Tex
'66 **Ain't Gonna Lie** Keith
Ain't Got No Home
'56 Clarence Henry
'73 Band
'94 **Ain't Got Nothing If You Ain't Got Love** Michael Bolton
'69 **Ain't It Funky Now** James Brown
'01 **Ain't It Funny** Jennifer Lopez
'64 **Ain't It The Truth** Mary Wells
'79 **Ain't Love A Bitch** Rod Stewart
'88 **Ain't No Half-Steppin'** Big Daddy Kane
Ain't No Mountain High Enough
'67 Marvin Gaye & Tammi Terrell
'70 Diana Ross
'96 **Ain't No Nigga** Jay-Z
'06 **Ain't No Other Man** Christina Aguilera
'79 **Ain't No Stoppin' Us Now** McFadden & Whitehead
'71 **Ain't No Sunshine** Bill Withers
'68 **Ain't No Way** Aretha Franklin
'75 **Ain't No Way To Treat A Lady** Helen Reddy
'73 **Ain't No Woman (Like The One I've Got)** Four Tops
Ain't Nobody
'83 Rufus & Chaka Khan
'96 Monica
'92 **Ain't Nobody Like You** Miki Howard
'86 **Ain't Nothin' Goin' On But The Rent** Gwen Guthrie
'01 **Ain't Nothing 'Bout You** Brooks & Dunn
Ain't Nothing Like The Real Thing
'68 Marvin Gaye & Tammi Terrell
'76 Donny & Marie Osmond
'64 **Ain't Nothing You Can Do** Bobby Bland
'95 **Ain't Nuthin' But A She Thing** Salt-N-Pepa
'89 **Ain't Nuthin' In The World** Miki Howard
'64 **Ain't She Sweet** Beatles
'78 **Ain't Talkin' 'Bout Love** Van Halen
Ain't That A Shame
'55 Pat Boone
'55 Fats Domino
'63 4 Seasons
'79 Cheap Trick
'61 **Ain't That Just Like A Woman** Fats Domino
'93 **Ain't That Lonely Yet** Dwight Yoakam
'56 **Ain't That Lovin' You Baby** Jimmy Reed
'64 **Ain't That Loving You Baby** Elvis Presley
'65 **Ain't That Peculiar** Marvin Gaye

Ain't Too [2] Proud [2] Beg
'66 Temptations
'74 Rolling Stones
'92 TLC
'71 **Ain't Understanding Mellow** Jerry Butler & Brenda Lee Eager
'72 **Ain't Wastin' Time No More** Allman Brothers Band
'02 **Air Force Ones** Nelly
'74 **Air That I Breathe** Hollies
'70 **Airport Love Theme** Vincent Bell
'77 **Aja** Steely Dan
'71 **Ajax Liquor Store** Hudson & Landry
Al Di La'
'62 Emilio Pericoli
'64 Ray Charles Singers
'80 **Alabama Getaway** Grateful Dead
'55 **Alabama Jubilee** Ferko String Band
'67 **Alabama Song (Whiskey Bar)** Doors
'69 **Albatross** Fleetwood Mac
'05 **Alcohol** Brad Paisley
'71 **Albert Flasher** Guess Who
Alfie
'66 Cher
'67 Dionne Warwick
Alibis
'84 Sergio Mendes
'93 Tracy Lawrence
'63 **Alice In Wonderland** Neil Sedaka
'68 **Alice Long (You're Still My Favorite Girlfriend)** Tommy Boyce & Bobby Hart
'69 **Alice's Restaurant Massacre** Arlo Guthrie
'81 **Alien** Atlanta Rhythm Section
'77 **Alison** Elvis Costelly
Alive
'72 Bee Gees
'92 Pearl Jam
'01 P.O.D.
'05 Rebecca St. James
'78 **Alive Again** Chicago
'85 **Alive & Kicking** Simple Minds
'67 **All** James Darren
'03 **All About Love** Steven Curtis Chapman
'93 **All About Soul** Billy Joel
'62 **All Alone Am I** Brenda Lee
All Along The Watchtower
'68 Jimi Hendrix
'68 Bob Dylan
'58 **All American Boy** Bill Parsons
'81 **All American Girls** Sister Sledge
'93 **All Apologies** Nirvana
'90 **All Around The World** Lisa Stansfield
'55 **All At Once You Love Her** Perry Como
'05 **All Because Of You** U2
All By Myself
'55 Fats Domino
'75 Eric Carmen
'97 Celine Dion
All Cried Out
'86 Lisa Lisa & Cult Jam
'97 Allure
'64 **All Day And All Of The Night** Kinks
'71 **All Day Music** War
'04 **All Falls Down** Kanye West
'88 **All Fired Up** Pat Benatar
'80 **All For Leyna** Billy Joel
All For [4] Love
'91 Color Me Badd
'93 Bryan Adams/Rod Stewart/Sting
All For You
'97 Sister Hazel
'01 Janet Jackson
'71 **All Good People** [medley] Yes
'60 **All I Could Do Was Cry** Etta James
'90 **All I Do Is Think Of You** Troop
'71 **All I Ever Need Is You** Sonny & Cher
'02 **All I Have** Jennifer Lopez

All I Have To Do Is Dream
'58 *Everly Brothers*
'63 *Richard Chamberlain*
'70 *Bobbie Gentry & Glen Campbell*
'99 **All I Have To Give** *Backstreet Boys*
'73 **All I Know** *Garfunkel*
All I Need
'67 *Temptations*
'84 *Jack Wagner*
'86 **All I Need Is A Miracle**
Mike + The Mechanics
All I Really Want To Do
'64 *Bob Dylan*
'65 *Byrds*
'65 *Cher*
'66 **All I See Is You** *Dusty Springfield*
'94 **All I Wanna Do** *Sheryl Crow*
'90 **All I Wanna Do Is Make Love To**
You *Heart*
All I Want
'92 *Toad The Wet Sprocket*
'97 *702*
'94 **All I Want For Christmas Is You**
Mariah Carey
'89 **All I Want Is Forever** *James*
"J.T." Taylor & Regina Belle
'89 **All I Want Is You** *U2*
'86 **All I Wanted** *Kansas*
'90 **All I'm Missing Is You**
Glenn Medeiros w/ Ray Parker Jr.
'60 **All In My Mind** *Maxine Brown*
'05 **All Jacked Up** *Gretchen Wilson*
'96 **All Mixed Up** *311*
'87 **All My Ex's Live In Texas**
George Strait
All My Life
'83 *Kenny Rogers*
'90 *Linda Ronstadt/Aaron Neville*
'98 *K-Ci & JoJo*
'02 *Foo Fighters*
All My Love
'79 *Led Zeppelin*
'98 *Queen Pen*
'64 **All My Loving** *Beatles*
'84 **All My Rowdy Friends Are Coming**
Over Tonight *Hank Williams Jr.*
All Night Long
'80 *Joe Walsh*
'99 *Faith Evans*
'83 **All Night Long (All Night)**
Lionel Richie
'58 **(All of a Sudden) My Heart Sings**
Paul Anka
'89 **All Of My Love** *Gap Band*
'84 **All Of You**
Julio Iglesias & Diana Ross
All Or Nothing
'90 *Milli Vanilli*
'01 *O-Town*
'81 **All Our Tomorrows** *Eddie Schwartz*
'80 **All Out Of Love** *Air Supply*
'58 **All Over Again** *Johnny Cash*
'80 **All Over The World**
Electric Light Orchestra
'95 **All Over You** *Live*
'83 **All Right** *Christopher Cross*
'70 **All Right Now** *Free*
'88 **All She Wants Is** *Duran Duran*
'85 **All She Wants To Do Is Dance**
Don Henley
'57 **All Shook Up** *Elvis Presley*
'99 **All Star** *Smash Mouth*
All Strung Out
'66 *Nino Tempo & April Stevens*
'77 *John Travolta*
'88 **All That Money Wants**
Psychedelic Furs
'93 **All That She Wants** *Ace Of Base*
All The King's Horses
'72 *Aretha Franklin*
'86 *Firm*
'86 **All The Love In The World** *Outfield*
'90 **All The Man That I Need**
Whitney Houston
'98 **All The Places (I Will Kiss You)**
Aaron Hall

'99 **All The Small Things** *Blink 182*
All The Things She Said
'86 *Simple Minds*
'03 *t.A.T.u.*
'96 **All The Things (Your Man Won't Do)**
Joe
'58 **All The Time** *Johnny Mathis*
All The Way
'57 *Frank Sinatra*
'83 *Triumph*
'72 **All The Young Dudes**
Mott The Hoople
'05 **All These Things That I've Done**
Killers
'04 **All Things New**
Steven Curtis Chapman
'83 **All This Love** *DeBarge*
All This Time
'88 *Tiffany*
'91 *Sting*
'81 **All Those Years Ago**
George Harrison
'84 **All Through The Night** *Cyndi Lauper*
'83 **All Time High** *Rita Coolidge*
'92 **All Woman** *Lisa Stansfield*
'77 **All You Get From Love Is A Love**
Song *Carpenters*
'67 **All You Need Is Love** *Beatles*
'02 **All You Wanted** *Michelle Branch*
'85 **All You Zombies** *Hooters*
'56 **Allegheny Moon** *Patti Page*
'82 **Allentown** *Billy Joel*
'62 **Alley Cat** *Bent Fabric*
Alley-Oop
'60 *Danté & the Evergreens*
'60 *Hollywood Argyles*
'94 **Allison Road** *Gin Blossoms*
'05 **Almost** *Bowling For S oup*
'70 **Almost Cut My Hair**
Crosby, Stills, Nash & Young
'99 **Almost Doesn't Count** *Brandy*
'93 **Almost Goodbye** *Mark Chesnutt*
'59 **Almost Grown** *Chuck Berry*
'90 **Almost Hear You Sigh**
Rolling Stones
'02 **Almost Home** *Craig Morgan*
'78 **Almost Like Being In Love**
Michael Johnson
'83 **Almost Over You** *Sheena Easton*
'57 **Almost Paradise** *Roger Williams*
'84 **Almost Paradise...Love Theme**
From Footloose
Mike Reno & Ann Wilson
'66 **Almost Persuaded** *David Houston*
'75 **Almost Saturday Night**
John Fogerty
'78 **Almost Summer** *Celebration*
Alone
'87 *Heart*
'97 *Bee Gees*
'85 **Alone Again** *Dokken*
'72 **Alone Again (Naturally)**
Gilbert O'Sullivan
'68 **Alone Again Or** *Love*
'60 **Alone At Last** *Jackie Wilson*
Alone (Why Must I Be Alone)
'57 *Shepherd Sisters*
'64 *4 Seasons*
Alone With You
'58 *Faron Young*
'92 *Tevin Campbell*
Along Came Jones
'59 *Coasters*
'59 *Ray Stevens*
'85 **Along Comes A Woman** *Chicago*
'66 **Along Comes Mary** *Association*
'88 **Alphabet St.** *Prince*
'74 **Already Gone** *Eagles*
Alright
'90 *Janet Jackson*
'93 *Kris Kross*
'73 **Also Sprach Zarathustra (2001)**
Deodato
'62 **Alvin Twist** *Chipmunks*
'59 **Alvin's Harmonica** *Chipmunks*
'60 **Alvin's Orchestra** *Chipmunks*

Always
'59 *Sammy Turner*
'87 *Atlantic Starr*
'94 *Bon Jovi*
'94 *Erasure*
'02 *Saliva*
Always And Forever
'78 *Heatwave*
'90 *Whistle*
'96 **Always Be My Baby** *Mariah Carey*
'94 **Always In My Heart** *Tevin Campbell*
'60 **Always It's You** *Everly Brothers*
Always On My Mind
'82 *Willie Nelson*
'88 *Pet Shop Boys*
'01 **Always On Time** *Ja Rule*
'06 **Always On Your Side**
Sheryl Crow & Sting
'92 **Always The Last To Know**
Del Amitri
Always Together
'64 *Al Martino*
'68 *Dells*
'07 **Alyssa Lies** *Jason Michael Carroll*
'87 **Am I Blue** *George Strait*
'98 **Am I Dreaming** *Ol' Skool*
'60 **Am I Losing You** *Jim Reeves*
Am I That Easy To Forget
'60 *Debbie Reynolds*
'67 *Engelbert Humperdinck*
'60 **Am I The Man** *Jackie Wilson*
'92 **Am I The Same Girl**
Swing Out Sister
'86 **Amanda** *Boston*
'06 **Amarillo Sky** *Jason Aldean*
'99 **Amazed** *Lonestar*
'93 **Amazing** *Aerosmith*
Amazing Grace
'70 *Judy Collins*
'72 *Royal Scots Dragoon Guards*
'68 **Ame Caline (Soul Coaxing)**
Raymond Lefevre
Amen
'64 *Impressions*
'68 *Otis Redding*
America
'61 *Chita Rivera*
'68 *Simon & Garfunkel*
'72 *Yes*
'81 *Neil Diamond*
'72 **America The Beautiful** *Ray Charles*
'05 **American Baby**
Dave Matthews Band
'72 **American City Suite**
Cashman & West
American Dream
'79 *Dirt Band*
'88 *Crosby, Stills, Nash & Young*
'77 **American Girl** *Tom Petty*
'82 **American Heartbeat** *Survivor*
'93 **American Honky-Tonk Bar**
Association *Garth Brooks*
'04 **American Idiot** *Green Day*
'03 **American Life** *Madonna*
'83 **American Made** *Oak Ridge Boys*
American Music
'82 *Pointer Sisters*
'91 *Violent Femmes*
American Pie
'71 *Don McLean*
'00 *Madonna*
'03 **American Soldier** *Toby Keith*
'86 **American Storm** *Bob Seger*
American Trilogy
'71 *Mickey Newbury*
'72 *Elvis Presley*
'73 **American Tune** *Paul Simon*
American Woman
'70 *Guess Who*
'99 *Lenny Kravitz*
Americans
'74 *Byron MacGregor*
'74 *Gordon Sinclair*
'75 **Amie** *Pure Prairie League*

'59 **Among My Souvenirs**
    Connie Francis
'61 **Amor** *Ben E. King*
'70 **Amos Moses** *Jerry Reed*
'55 **Amukiriki (The Lord Willing)**
    Les Paul & Mary Ford
'88 **Ana Ng** *They Might Be Giants*
'77 **Anarchy In The U.K.**
    Sex Pistols
'57 **Anastasia** *Pat Boone*
'95 **And Fools Shine On** *Brother Cane*
'67 **And Get Away** *Esquires*
'82 **And I Am Telling You I'm Not Going**
    Jennifer Holliday
'64 **And I Love Her** *Beatles*
'73 **And I Love You So** *Perry Como*
'94 **And On And On** *Janet Jackson*
'94 **And Our Feelings** *Babyface*
'65 **And Roses And Roses**
    Andy Williams
'85 **And She Was** *Talking Heads*
'90 **And So It Goes** *Billy Joel*
'95 **And Still** *Reba McEntire*
    And That Reminds Me
'57   *Della Reese*
'57   *Kay Starr*
'80 **And The Beat Goes On** *Whispers*
'80 **And The Cradle Will Rock...**
    Van Halen
'85 **And We Danced** *Hooters*
'69 **And When I Die**
    Blood, Sweat & Tears
'72 **And You And I** *Yes*
    Angel
'71   *Jimi Hendrix*
'72   *Rod Stewart*
'73   *Aretha Franklin*
'85   *Madonna*
'87   *Angela Winbush*
'88   *Aerosmith*
'93   *Jon Secada*
'98   *Sarah McLachlan*
'00   *Shaggy*
'03   *Amanda Perez*
    Angel Baby
'58   *Dean Martin*
'60   *Rosie & The Originals*
'91   *Angelica*
'89 **Angel Eyes** *Jeff Healey Band*
'82 **Angel In Blue** *J. Geils Band*
'77 **Angel In Your Arms** *Hot*
'88 **Angel Of Harlem** *U2*
'98 **Angel Of Mine** *Monica*
    Angel Of The Morning
'68   *Merrilee Rush*
'81   *Juice Newton*
'60 **Angel On My Shoulder** *Shelby Flint*
'80 **Angel Say No** *Tommy Tutone*
'58 **Angel Smile** *Nat "King" Cole*
'89 **Angel Song** *Great White*
'60 **Angela Jones** *Johnny Ferguson*
'89 **Angelia** *Richard Marx*
    Angels
'85   *Amy Grant*
'00   *Robbie Williams*
'93 **Angels Among Us** *Alabama*
'55 **Angels In The Sky** *Crew Cuts*
'59 **Angels Listened In** *Crests*
'96 **Angels Of The Silences**
    Counting Crows
'73 **Angie** *Rolling Stones*
'74 **Angie Baby** *Helen Reddy*
'01 **Angry All The Time** *Tim McGraw*
'87 **Animal** *Def Leppard*
'06 **Animal I Have Become**
    Three Days Grace
'99 **Animal Song** *Savage Garden*
'05 **Animals** *Nickelback*
'62 **Anna (Go To Him)**
    Arthur Alexander
'06 **Anna-Molly** *Incubus*
'74 **Annie's Song** *John Denver*
'93 **Anniversary** *Tony Toni Tone*
'80 **Another Brick In The Wall**
    Pink Floyd

'71 **Another Day** *Paul McCartney*
'89 **Another Day In Paradise** *Phil Collins*
'00 **Another Dumb Blonde** *Hoku*
'88 **Another Lover** *Giant Steps*
    Another Night
'86   *Aretha Franklin*
'94   *Real McCoy*
'80 **Another One Bites The Dust** *Queen*
'74 **Another Park, Another Sunday**
    Doobie Brothers
'88 **Another Part Of Me** *Michael Jackson*
'93 **Another Sad Love Song**
    Toni Braxton
    Another Saturday Night
'63   *Sam Cooke*
'74   *Cat Stevens*
'60 **Another Sleepless Night**
    Jimmy Clanton
    Another Time, Another Place
'58   *Patti Page*
'90   *Sandi Patty w/ Wayne Watson*
'97 **Another You** *David Kersh*
'80 **Answering Machine** *Rupert Holmes*
'03 **Anthem, The** *Good Charlotte*
'71 **Anticipation** *Carly Simon*
'95 **Ants Marching** *Dave Matthews Band*
    Any Day Now
'62   *Chuck Jackson*
'82   *Ronnie Milsap*
'88 **Any Love** *Luther Vandross*
'74 **Any Major Dude Will Tell You**
    Steely Dan
'95 **Any Man Of Mine** *Shania Twain*
'94 **Any Time, Any Place** *Janet Jackson*
    Any Way You Want It
'64   *Dave Clark Five*
'80   *Journey*
'61 **Anybody But Me** *Brenda Lee*
'97 **Anybody Seen My Baby?**
    Rolling Stones
    Anymore
'60   *Teresa Brewer*
'91   *Travis Tritt*
'99 **Anyone Else** *Collin Raye*
'63 **Anyone Who Had A Heart**
    Dionne Warwick
    Anything
'94   *SWV*
'95   *3T*
'02   *Jaheim w/ Next*
'05 **Anything But Mine** *Kenny Chesney*
'88 **Anything For You** *Gloria Estefan*
'90 **Anything I Want** *Kevin Paige*
'90 **Anything Is Possible** *Debbie Gibson*
'62 **Anything That's Part Of You**
    Elvis Presley
    Anytime
'78   *Journey*
'98   *Brian McKnight*
'94 **Anytime You Need A Friend**
    Mariah Carey
'07 **Anyway** *Martina McBride*
'56 **Anyway You Want Me (That's How I**
    Will Be) *Elvis Presley*
'99 **Anywhere** *112*
'61 **Apache** *Jorgen Ingmann*
'56 **Ape Call** *Nervous Norvus*
'70 **Apeman** *Kinks*
'07 **Apologize** *Timbaland*
'60 **Apple Green** *June Valli*
'65 **Apple Of My Eye** *Roy Head*
'67 **Apples, Peaches, Pumpkin Pie**
    Jay & The Techniques
'56 **April In Paris** *Count Basie*
'57 **April Love** *Pat Boone*
'78 **Aqua Boogie** *Parliament*
'71 **Aqualung** *Jethro Tull*
'69 **Aquarius/Let The Sunshine In**
    5th Dimension
'98 **Are U Still Down** *Jon B.*
'84 **Are We Ourselves?** *Fixx*
'65 **Are You A Boy Or Are You A Girl**
    Barbarians
'67 **Are You Experienced?**
    Jimi Hendrix
'03 **Are You Gonna Be My Girl** *Jet*

'93 **Are You Gonna Go My Way**
    Lenny Kravitz
'68 **Are You Happy** *Jerry Butler*
'03 **Are You Happy Now?**
    Michelle Branch
'98 **Are You Jimmy Ray?** *Jimmy Ray*
    Are You Lonely For Me
'66   *Freddy Scott*
'91   *Rude Boys*
'60 **Are You Lonesome To-night?**
'60   *Elvis Presley*
'73   *Donny Osmond*
'73 **Are You Man Enough** *Four Tops*
'70 **Are You Ready?**
    Pacific Gas & Electric
'58 **Are You Really Mine**
    Jimmie Rodgers
'55 **Are You Satisfied?** *Rusty Draper*
'82 **Are You Serious** *Tyrone Davis*
'58 **Are You Sincere** *Andy Williams*
'98 **Are You That Somebody?** *Aaliyah*
'01 **Area Codes** *Ludacris*
'77 **Ariel** *Dean Friedman*
'69 **Arizona** *Mark Lindsay*
'88 **Armageddon It** *Def Leppard*
'73 **Armed And Extremely Dangerous**
    First Choice
'89 **Arms Of Orion**
    Prince w/ Sheena Easton
'98 **Arms Of The One Who Loves You**
    Xscape
'90 **Around The Way Girl** *LL Cool J*
    Around The World
'57   *Bing Crosby*
'57   *Mantovani*
'57   *Victor Young*
'01 **Around The World (La La La La La)**
    ATC
'77 **Arrested For Driving While Blind**
    ZZ Top
'79 **Arrow Through Me** *Wings*
'81 **Arthur's Theme (Best That You Can**
    Do) *Christopher Cross*
'60 **Artificial Flowers** *Bobby Darin*
'94 **As Any Fool Can See**
    Tracy Lawrence
'05 **As Good As I Once Was** *Toby Keith*
'95 **As I Lay Me Down**
    Sophie B. Hawkins
'61 **As If I Didn't Know** *Adam Wade*
'63 **As Long As I Know He's Mine**
    Marvelettes
'88 **As Long As You Follow**
    Fleetwood Mac
'97 **As Long As You Love Me**
    Backstreet Boys
    As Tears Go By
'64   *Marianne Faithfull*
'65   *Rolling Stones*
'70 **As The Years Go By** *Mashmakhan*
'63 **As Usual** *Brenda Lee*
'87 **As We Lay** *Shirley Murdock*
'96 **Ascension (Don't Ever Wonder)**
    Maxwell
'80 **Ashes By Now** *Rodney Crowell*
'80 **Ashes To Ashes** *David Bowie*
'61 **Asia Minor** *Kokomo*
    Ask Me
'56   *Nat "King" Cole*
'64   *Elvis Presley*
'71 **Ask Me No Questions** *B.B. King*
'72 **Ask Me What You Want**
    Millie Jackson
'95 **Ask Of You** *Raphael Saadiq*
    Ask The Lonely
'65   *Four Tops*
'83   *Journey*
'61 **Astronaut, The** *Jose Jimenez*
'61 **At Last** *Etta James*
    At My Front Door
'55   *Pat Boone*
'55   *El Dorados*
'75 **At Seventeen** *Janis Ian*
'97 **At The Beginning**
    Donna Lewis & Richard Marx
'57 **At The Hop** *Danny & The Juniors*

'66 **At The Scene** *Dave Clark Five*
'67 **At The Zoo** *Simon & Garfunkel*
'81 **At This Moment**
    Billy Vera & The Beaters
'94 **At Your Best (You Are Love)**
    Aaliyah
'82 **Athena** *Who*
'81 **Atlanta Lady (Something About**
    Your Love) *Marty Balin*
'69 **Atlantis** *Donovan*
'80 **Atomic** *Blondie*
'83 **Atomic Dog** *George Clinton*
'65 **Attack** *Toys*
'85 **Attack Me With Your Love** *Cameo*
'75 **Attitude Dancing** *Carly Simon*
'73 **Aubrey** *Bread*
'56 **Auctioneer** *Leroy Van Dyke*
'99 **Auld Lang Syne** *Kenny G*
'01 **Austin** *Blake Shelton*
'84 **Authority Song**
    John Cougar Mellencamp
'75 **Autobahn** *Kraftwerk*
'84 **Automatic** *Pointer Sisters*
'83 **Automatic Man** *Michael Sembello*
'55 **Autumn Leaves**
    Roger Williams
'68 **Autumn Of My Life**
    Bobby Goldsboro
'56 **Autumn Waltz** *Tony Bennett*
'98 **Ava Adore** *Smashing Pumpkins*
'82 **Avalon** *Roxy Music*
'00 **Awake** *Godsmack*
'94 **Award Tour** *Tribe Called Quest*
'03 **Away From Me** *Puddle Of Mudd*
'04 **Away From The Sun** *3 Doors Down*
'88 **Awesome God** *Rich Mullins*
'04 **Awful, Beautiful Life** *Darryl Worley*
' **Axel F**
'85 *Harold Faltermeyer*
'05 *Crazy Frog*
'07 **Ayo Technology** *50 Cent*

B

'90 **B.B.D. (I Thought It Was Me)?**
    Bell Biv DeVoe
'05 **B.Y.O.B.** *System Of A Down*
'71 **Baba O'Riley** *Who*
'79 **Babe** *Styx*
'69 **Babe I'm Gonna Leave You**
    Led Zeppelin
'66 **B-A-B-Y** *Carla Thomas*
    Baby
'95 *Brandy*
'02 *Ashanti*
'02 **Baby, The** *Blake Shelton*
'91 **Baby Baby** *Amy Grant*
'92 **Baby-Baby-Baby** *TLC*
'69 **Baby, Baby Don't Cry** *Miracles*
'69 **Baby, Baby (I Know You're A Lady)**
    David Houston
    Baby Blue
'61 *Echoes*
'72 *Badfinger*
'03 **Baby Boy** *Beyoncé*
'88 **Baby Can I Hold You**
    Tracy Chapman
    Baby, Come Back
'68 *Equals*
'77 *Player*
'73 **Baby Come Close**
    Smokey Robinson
    Baby, Come To Me
'82 *Patti Austin w/ James Ingram*
'89 *Regina Belle*
'94 **Baby Did A Bad Bad Thing**
    Chris Isaak
'56 **Baby Doll** *Andy Williams*
'89 **Baby Don't Forget My Number**
    Milli Vanilli
'72 **Baby Don't Get Hooked On Me**
    Mac Davis
'65 **Baby Don't Go** *Sonny & Cher*
'72 **Baby Don't You Do It** *Band*
'63 **Baby Don't You Weep**
    Garnet Mimms

    Baby Elephant Walk
'62 *Henry Mancini*
'62 *Miniature Men*
    Baby Face
'58 *Little Richard*
'75 *Wing & Prayer Fife & Drum Corps*
'05 **Baby Girl** *Sugarland*
'92 **Baby Got Back** *Sir Mix-A-Lot*
'87 **Baby Grand** *Billy Joel & Ray Charles*
    Baby Hold On
'70 *Grass Roots*
'78 *Eddie Money*
'92 **Baby Hold On To Me**
    Gerald Levert w/ Eddie Levert
'83 **Baby I Lied** *Deborah Allen*
    Baby, I Love You
'63 *Ronettes*
'67 *Aretha Franklin*
'69 *Andy Kim*
    Baby, I Love Your Way
'76 *Peter Frampton*
'88 *Will To Power [medley]*
'94 *Big Mountain*
    Baby I Need Your Loving
'64 *Four Tops*
'67 *Johnny Rivers*
'71 **Baby I'm - A Want You** *Bread*
'05 **Baby I'm Back** *Baby Bash*
'78 **Baby I'm Burnin'** *Dolly Parton*
'69 **Baby, I'm For Real** *Originals*
'91 **Baby I'm Ready** *Levert*
    Baby, I'm Yours
'65 *Barbara Lewis*
'93 *Shai*
'04 **Baby, It's Cold Outside**
    Rod Stewart w/ Dolly Parton
'90 **Baby, It's Tonight** *Jude Cole*
    Baby It's You
'53 *Spaniels*
'61 *Shirelles*
'69 *Smith*
'04 *JoJo*
'83 **Baby Jane** *Rod Stewart*
'71 **Baby Let Me Kiss You** *King Floyd*
'72 **Baby Let Me Take You (In My Arms)**
    Detroit Emeralds
'68 **Baby Let's Wait** *Royal Guardsmen*
    Baby Love
'64 *Supremes*
'86 *Regina*
'82 **Baby Makes Her Blue Jeans Talk**
    Dr. Hook
    Baby, Now That I've Found You
'67 *Foundations*
'95 *Alison Krauss*
'60 **Baby Oh Baby** *Shells*
'98 **Baby One More Time** *Britney Spears*
'53 **Baby Please Don't Go**
    Muddy Waters
'66 **Baby Scratch My Back** *Slim Harpo*
'61 **Baby Sittin' Boogie** *Buzz Clifford*
'82 **Baby Step Back** *Gordon Lightfoot*
'69 **Baby Take Me In Your Arms**
    Jefferson
'59 **Baby Talk** *Jan & Dean*
'80 **Baby Talks Dirty** *Knack*
'75 **Baby That's Backatcha**
    Smokey Robinson
'65 **Baby The Rain Must Fall**
    Glenn Yarbrough
'91 **Baby Universal** *Tin Machine*
'77 **Baby, What A Big Surprise** *Chicago*
'60 **Baby What You Want Me To Do**
    Jimmy Reed
'63 **Baby Workout** *Jackie Wilson*
'67 **Baby You're A Rich Man** *Beatles*
'61 **Baby, You're Right** *James Brown*
'60 **Baby (You've Got What It Takes)**
    Dinah Washington & Brook Benton
'61 **Baby's First Christmas**
    Connie Francis
'80 **Babylon Sisters** *Steely Dan*
    Back And Forth
'87 *Cameo*
'94 *Aaliyah*

    Back At One
'99 *Brian McKnight*
'00 *Mark Wills*
    Back Door Man
'61 *Howlin' Wolf*
'67 *Doors*
'95 **Back For Good** *Take That*
'00 **Back Here** *BBMak*
'74 **Back Home Again** *John Denver*
'80 **Back In Black** *AC/DC*
'65 **Back In My Arms Again** *Supremes*
'85 **Back In Stride**
    Maze Feat. Frankie Beverly
'94 **Back In The Day** *Ahmad*
'87 **Back In The High Life Again**
    Steve Winwood
'77 **Back In The Saddle** *Aerosmith*
    Back In The U.S.A.
'59 *Chuck Berry*
'78 *Linda Ronstadt*
'68 **Back In The U.S.S.R.** *Beatles*
'85 **Back In Time** *Huey Lewis*
'72 **Back Off Boogaloo** *Ringo Starr*
'88 **Back On Holiday** *Robbie Nevil*
'80 **Back On My Feet Again** *Babys*
'82 **Back On The Chain Gang**
    Pretenders
'67 **Back On The Street Again**
    Sunshine Company
'72 **Back Stabbers** *O'Jays*
'99 **Back That Azz Up** *Juvenile*
'05 **Back Then** *Mike Jones*
'98 **Back 2 Good** *Matchbox 20*
'89 **Back To Life** *Soul II Soul*
'92 **Back To The Hotel** *N2Deep*
'76 **Back To The Island** *Leon Russell*
'77 **Back Together Again**
    Daryl Hall & John Oates
'04 **Back When** *Tim McGraw*
'73 **Back When My Hair Was Short**
    Gunhill Road
'84 **Back Where You Belong** *38 Special*
'69 **Backfield In Motion** *Mel & Tim*
'66 **Backstage** *Gene Pitney*
'80 **Backstrokin'** *Fatback*
'94 **Backwater** *Meat Puppets*
'97 **Backyard Boogie** *Mack 10*
'87 **Bad** *Michael Jackson*
'73 **Bad, Bad Leroy Brown** *Jim Croce*
'75 **Bad Blood** *Neil Sedaka*
    Bad Boy
'57 *Jive Bombers*
'82 *Ray Parker Jr.*
'82 *Luther Vandross [medley]*
'86 *Miami Sound Machine*
'01 **Bad Boy For Life**
    P. Diddy, Black Rob & Mark Curry
'93 **Bad Boys** *Inner Circle*
'79 **Bad Case Of Loving You (Doctor,**
    Doctor) *Robert Palmer*
'74 **Bad Company** *Bad Company*
    Bad Girl
'63 *Neil Sedaka*
'93 *Madonna*
    Bad Day
'01 *Fuel*
'06 *Daniel Powter*
'79 **Bad Girls** *Donna Summer*
'93 **Bad Goodbye**
    Clint Black w/ Wynonna
'89 **Bad Love** *Eric Clapton*
    Bad Luck
'56 *B.B. King*
'75 *Harold Melvin*
'60 **Bad Man Blunder** *Kingston Trio*
'88 **Bad Medicine** *Bon Jovi*
'69 **Bad Moon Rising**
    Creedence Clearwater Revival
'90 **Bad Of The Heart** *George LaMond*
'75 **Bad Time** *Grand Funk*
'64 **Bad To Me** *Billy J. Kramer*
    w/ The Dakotas
'82 **Bad To The Bone**
    George Thorogood
'05 **Badd** *Ying Yang Twins*
'69 **Badge** *Cream*

'78 **Badlands** *Bruce Springsteen*
'63 **Bag Lady** *Erykah Badu*
'99 **Bailamos** *Enrique Iglesias*
'63 **Baja** *Astronauts*
'78 **Baker Street** *Gerry Rafferty*
'62 **Balboa Blue** *Marketts*
'68 **Ball And Chain** *Big Brother & The Holding Company*
'70 **Ball Of Confusion (That's What The World Is Today)** *Temptations*
'69 **Ball Of Fire** *Tommy James*
'04 **Balla Baby** *Chingy*
'58 **Ballad Of A Teenage Queen** *Johnny Cash*
'65 **Ballad Of A Thin Man** *Bob Dylan*
'74 **Ballad Of Billy The Kid** *Billy Joel*
'68 **Ballad Of Bonnie And Clyde** *Georgie Fame*
Ballad Of Davy Crockett
'55 *"Tennessee" Ernie Ford*
'55 *Bill Hayes*
'55 *Fess Parker*
'66 **Ballad Of Irving** *Frank Gallop*
'90 **Ballad of Jayne** *L.A. Guns*
'63 **Ballad Of Jed Clampett** *Flatt & Scruggs*
'69 **Ballad Of John And Yoko** *Beatles*
'62 **Ballad Of Paladin** *Duane Eddy*
'92 **Ballad Of Peter Pumpkinhead** *XTC*
'60 **Ballad Of The Alamo** *Marty Robbins*
'66 **Ballad Of The Green Berets** *SSgt Barry Sadler*
'58 **Ballad Of Thunder Road** *Robert Mitchum*
'57 **Ballerina** *Nat "King" Cole*
'86 **Ballerina Girl** *Lionel Richie*
'91 **Ballerina Out Of Control** *Ocean Blue*
'74 **Ballero** *War*
'75 **Ballroom Blitz** *Sweet*
Banana Boat Song
'56 *Fontane Sisters*
'56 *Tarriers*
'56 *Sarah Vaughan*
'57 *Harry Belafonte*
'57 *Stan Freberg*
'57 *Steve Lawrence*
Band Of Gold
'55 *Kit Carson*
'55 *Don Cherry*
'66 *Mel Carter*
'70 *Freda Payne*
'74 **Band On The Run** *Paul McCartney*
'67 **Banda, A** *Herb Alpert*
'55 **Bandit, The** *Eddie Barclay*
'75 **Bandstand Boogie** *Barry Manilow*
Bang A Gong (Get It On)
'72 *T. Rex*
'85 *Power Station*
'94 **Bang And Blame** *R.E.M.*
'66 **Bang Bang (My Baby Shot Me Down)** *Cher*
'68 **Bang-Shang-A-Lang** *Archies*
'83 **Bang The Drum All Day** *Todd Rundgren*
'84 **Bang Your Head (Metal Health)** *Quiet Riot*
'71 **Bangla-Desh** *George Harrison*
'55 **Banjo's Back In Town** *Teresa Brewer*
'90 **Banned In The U.S.A.** *Luke Feat. 2 Live Crew*
'60 **Barbara** *Temptations*
Barbara-Ann
'61 *Regents*
'66 *Beach Boys*
'97 **Barbie Girl** *Aqua*
'66 **Barefootin'** *Robert Parker*
'96 **Barely Breathing** *Duncan Sheik*
'76 **Baretta's Theme ("Keep Your Eye On The Sparrow")** *Rhythm Heritage*
'71 **Bargain** *Who*
'77 **Barracuda** *Heart*

'07 **Bartender** *T-Pain*
'94 **Basket Case** *Green Day*
'73 **Basketball Jones Featuring Tyrone Shoelaces** *Cheech & Chong*
'06 **Bat Country** *Avenged Sevenfold*
'77 **Bat Out Of Hell** *Meat Loaf*
'89 **Batdance** *Prince*
'66 **Batman & His Grandmother** *Dickie Goodman*
Batman Theme
'66 *Neal Hefti*
'66 *Marketts*
'71 **Battle Hymn Of Lt. Calley** *C Company*
Battle Hymn Of The Republic
'59 *Mormon Tabernacle Choir*
'68 *Andy Williams*
'59 **Battle Of Kookamonga** *Homer & Jethro*
'59 **Battle Of New Orleans** *Johnny Horton*
'58 **Baubles, Bangles And Beads** *Kirby Stone Four*
'99 **Bawitdaba** *Kid Rock*
'07 **Bay Bay** *Hurricane Chris*
'73 **Be** *Neil Diamond*
'56 **Be-Bop-A-Lula** *Gene Vincent*
'57 **Be-Bop Baby** *Ricky Nelson*
'98 **Be Careful** *Sparkle w/ R. Kelly*
'63 **Be Careful Of Stones That You Throw** *Dion*
'83 **Be Good Johnny** *Men At Work*
'86 **Be Good To Yourself** *Journey*
'94 **Be Happy** *Mary J. Blige*
'01 **Be Like That** *3 Doors Down*
Be My Baby
'63 *Ronettes*
'70 *Andy Kim*
'94 **Be My Baby Tonight** *John Michael Montgomery*
'61 **Be My Boy** *Paris Sisters*
'76 **Be My Girl** *Dramatics*
'59 **Be My Guest** *Fats Domino*
'82 **Be My Lady** *Jefferson Starship*
Be My Lover
'72 *Alice Cooper*
'95 *La Bouche*
'85 **Be Near Me** *ABC*
'88 **Be Still My Beating Heart** *Sting*
'74 **Be Thankful For What You Got** *William DeVaughn*
'63 **Be True To Your School** *Beach Boys*
Be With You
'89 *Bangles*
'00 *Enrique Iglesias*
'06 **Be Without You** *Mary J. Blige*
'05 **Be Yourself** *Audioslave*
'74 **Beach Baby** *First Class*
'81 **Beach Boys Medley** *Beach Boys*
'64 **Beach Girl** *Pat Boone*
'95 **Beaches Of Cheyenne** *Garth Brooks*
'64 **Beans In My Ears** *Serendipity Singers*
'78 **Beast Of Burden** *Rolling Stones*
'67 **Beat Goes On** *Sonny & Cher*
'83 **Beat It** *Michael Jackson*
'85 **Beat's So Lonely** *Charlie Sexton*
'82 **Beatles' Movie Medley** *Beatles*
'60 **Beatnik Fly** *Johnny & The Hurricanes*
Beautiful
'02 *Christina Aguilera*
'03 *Snoop Dogg*
'05 *Jim Brickman w/ Wayne Brady*
'80 **Beautiful Boy (Darling Boy)** *John Lennon*
'00 **Beautiful Day** *U2*
Beautiful Girls
'79 *Van Halen*
'07 *Sean Kingston*
'94 **Beautiful In My Eyes** *Joshua Kadison*
'07 **Beautiful Liar** *Beyoncé & Shakira*
'95 **Beautiful Life** *Ace Of Base*
'75 **Beautiful Loser** *Bob Seger*

'02 **Beautiful Mess** *Diamond Rio*
'68 **Beautiful Morning** *Rascals*
'76 **Beautiful Noise** *Neil Diamond*
Beautiful People
'67 *Kenny O'Dell*
'67 *Bobby Vee*
'05 **Beautiful Soul** *Jesse McCartney*
'99 **Beautiful Stranger** *Madonna*
'72 **Beautiful Sunday** *Daniel Boone*
'92 **Beauty And The Beast** *Celine Dion & Peabo Bryson*
'66 **Beauty Is Only Skin Deep** *Temptations*
'64 **Because** *Dave Clark Five*
'01 **Because I Got High** *Afroman*
'90 **Because I Love You (The Postman Song)** *Stevie B*
'94 **Because Of Love** *Janet Jackson*
Because Of You
'87 *Cover Girls*
'98 *98°*
'05 *Kelly Clarkson*
'07 *Ne-Yo*
'07 *Reba McEntire & Kelly Clarkson*
Because The Night
'78 *Patti Smith Group*
'93 *10,000 Maniacs*
'60 **Because They're Young** *Duane Eddy*
'96 **Because You Loved Me** *Celine Dion*
'68 **Beck's Bolero** *Jeff Beck*
'07 **Bed** *J. Holiday*
'71 **Bed Of Rose's** *Statler Brothers*
'93 **Bed Of Roses** *Bon Jovi*
'88 **Beds Are Burning** *Midnight Oil*
'62 **Beechwood 4-5789** *Marvelettes*
'98 **Been Around The World** *Puff Daddy*
'90 **Been Caught Stealing** *Jane's Addiction*
'58 **Been So Long** *Pastels*
'00 **Been There** *Clint Black*
'72 **Been To Canaan** *Carole King*
'06 **Beep** *Pussycat Dolls*
'84 **Beep A Freak** *Gap Band*
'58 **Beep Beep** *Playmates*
'75 **Beer Barrel Polka** *Bobby Vinton*
'03 **Beer For My Horses** *Toby Keith w/ Willie Nelson*
'07 **Beer In Mexico** *Kenny Chesney*
'65 **Before And After** *Chad & Jeremy*
'07 **Before He Cheats** *Carrie Underwood*
'94 **Before I Let You Go** *BLACKstreet*
'78 **Before My Heart Finds Out** *Gene Cotton*
'75 **Before The Next Teardrop Falls** *Freddy Fender*
'94 **Before You Kill Us All** *Randy Travis*
'95 **Before You Walk Out Of My Life** *Monica*
'67 **Beg, Borrow And Steal** *Ohio Express*
'64 **Beg Me** *Chuck Jackson*
'67 **Beggin'** *4 Seasons*
'68 **Beginning Of My End** *Unifics*
'71 **Beginnings** *Chicago*
Behind Blue Eyes
'71 *Who*
'04 *Limp Bizkit*
'73 **Behind Closed Doors** *Charlie Rich*
'65 **Behind The Tear** *Sonny James*
'87 **Behind The Wall Of Sleep** *Smithereens*
'05 **Behind These Hazel Eyes** *Kelly Clarkson*
'81 **Being With You** *Smokey Robinson*
Believe
'95 *Elton John*
'98 *Cher*
'04 *Josh Groban*
'73 **Believe In Humanity** *Carole King*
'84 **Believe In Me** *Dan Fogelberg*
'59 **Believe Me** *Royal Teens*
'96 **Believe Me Baby (I Lied)** *Trisha Yearwood*
'58 **Believe What You Say** *Ricky Nelson*

'70 **Bell Bottom Blues**
  Derek & The Dominos
'68 **Bella Linda** *Grassroots*
'84 **Belle Of St. Mark** *Sheila E.*
'70 **Bells, The** *Originals*
'05 **Belly Dancer (Bananza)** *Akon*
'58 **Belonging To Someone** *Patti Page*
'72 **Ben** *Michael Jackson*
'67 **Bend Me, Shape Me**
  American Breed
'74 **Bennie And The Jets** *Elton John*
'00 **Bent** *Matchbox Twenty*
'67 **Bernadette** *Four Tops*
'57 **Bernardine** *Pat Boone*
'71 **Bertha** *Grateful Dead*
'75 **Bertha Butt Boogie**
  Jimmy Castor Bunch
'89 **Best, The** *Tina Turner*
'00 **Best Day** *George Strait*
'76 **Best Disco In Town** *Ritchie Family*
Best Friend
'95   *Brandy*
'06   *50 Cent & Olivia*
Best Is Yet To Come
'60   *Tony Bennett*
'64   *Frank Sinatra*
Best Of Both Worlds
'67   *Lulu*
'86   *Van Halen*
'00 **Best Of Intentions** *Travis Tritt*
Best Of My Love
'74   *Eagles*
'77   *Emotions*
'81 **Best Of Times** *Styx*
'05 **Best Of You** *Foo Fighters*
'64 **(Best Part Of) Breaking Up**
  Ronettes
'74 **Best Thing That Ever Happened To
  Me** *Gladys Knight*
'92 **Best Things In Life Are Free**
  Luther Vandross & Janet Jackson
'72 **Betcha By Golly, Wow** *Stylistics*
'87 **Betcha Say That** *Gloria Estefan*
'82 **Betcha She Don't Love You**
  Evelyn King
'76 **Beth** *Kiss*
'81 **Bette Davis Eyes** *Kim Carnes*
'84 **Better Be Good To Me** *Tina Turner*
'91 **Better Class Of Losers**
  Randy Travis
Better Days
'92   *Bruce Springsteen*
'05   *Goo Goo Dolls*
'99 **Better Days (And The Bottom
  Drops Out)** *Citizen King*
'05 **Better Life** *Keith Urban*
'91 **Better Love** *Londonbeat*
'79 **Better Love Next Time** *Dr. Hook*
Better Man
'89   *Clint Black*
'94   *Pearl Jam*
'97 **Better Man, Better Off**
  Tracy Lawrence
'00 **Better Off Alone** *Alice Deejay*
'61 **Better Tell Him No** *Starlets*
'07 **Better Than Me** *Hinder*
'93 **Better Than You** *Lisa Keith*
'95 **Better Things To Do** *Terri Clark*
'58 **Betty And Dupree** *Chuck Willis*
'58 **Betty Lou Got A New Pair Of Shoes**
  Bobby Freeman
'80 **Betty Lou's Gettin' Out Tonight** *Bob
  Seger*
'00 **Between Me And You** *Ja Rule*
'89 **Between Something And Nothing**
  Ocean Blue
'97 **Between The Devil And Me**
  Alan Jackson
'83 **Between The Sheets** *Isley Brothers*
'05 **Beverly Hills** *Weezer*
'03 **Beware Of The Boys (Mundian To
  Bach Ke)** *Pan'jabi MC*
'61 **Bewildered** *James Brown*
Beyond The Sea
'56   *Roger Williams*
'60   *Bobby Darin*

Bible Tells Me So
'55   *Don Cornell*
'55   *Nick Noble*
'78 **Bicycle Race** *Queen*
'61 **Big Bad John** *Jimmy Dean*
'96 **Big Bang Baby** *Stone Temple Pilots*
'57 **Big Beat** *Fats Domino*
'58 **Big Bopper's Wedding** *Big Bopper*
Big Boss Man
'61   *Jimmy Reed*
'67   *Elvis Presley*
'60 **Big Boy Pate** *Olympics*
'04 **Big Chips** *R. Kelly & Jay-Z*
'72 **Big City Miss Ruth Ann** *Gallery*
'61 **Big Cold Wind** *Pat Boone*
'97 **Big Daddy** *Heavy D*
'99 **Big Deal** *LeAnn Rimes*
'62 **Big Draft** *Four Preps*
'94 **Big Empty** *Stone Temple Pilots*
'82 **Big Fun** *Kool & The Gang*
Big Girls Don't Cry
'62   *4 Seasons*
'07   *Fergie*
'58 **Big Guitar** *Owen Bradley Quintet*
'93 **Big Gun** *AC/DC*
'59 **Big Hunk O' Love** *Elvis Presley*
'59 **Big Hurt** *Miss Toni Fisher*
'60 **Big Iron** *Marty Robbins*
'61 **Big John** *Shirelles*
'83 **Big Log** *Robert Plant*
Big Love
'87   *Fleetwood Mac*
'96   *Tracy Byrd*
'58 **Big Man** *Four Preps*
'64 **Big Man In Town** *4 Seasons*
'96 **Big Me** *Foo Fighters*
'85 **Big Money** *Rush*
'94 **Big One** *George Strait*
'00 **Big Pimpin'** *Jay-Z w/ UGK*
'95 **Big Poppa** *Notorious B.I.G.*
'79 **Big Shot** *Billy Joel*
'03 **Big Star** *Kenny Chesney*
'75 **Big Ten Inch Record** *Aerosmith*
'07 **Big Things Poppin' (Do It)** *T.I.*
'86 **Big Time** *Peter Gabriel*
'94 **Big Time Sensuality** *Björk*
'63 **Big Wide World** *Teddy Randazzo*
Big Yellow Taxi
'70   *Joni Mitchell*
'70   *Neighborhood*
'74   *Joni Mitchell [live]*
'03   *Counting Crows*
'03 **Bigger Than My Body** *John Mayer*
'95 **Bigger Than The Beatles** *Joe Diffie*
'75 **Biggest Parakeets In Town**
  Jud Strunk
'80 **Biggest Part Of Me** *Ambrosia*
'80 **Biko** *Peter Gabriel*
'61 **Bilbao Song** *Andy Williams*
'83 **Billie Jean** *Michael Jackson*
'73 **Billion Dollar Babies**
  Alice Cooper
'99 **Bills, Bills, Bills** *Destiny's Child*
'58 **Billy** *Kathy Linden*
'66 **Billy And Sue** *B.J. Thomas*
'58 **Billy Bayou** *Jim Reeves*
'74 **Billy, Don't Be A Hero**
  Bo Donaldson
'58 **Bimbombey** *Jimmie Rodgers*
'71 **Bip Bop** *Paul McCartney*
'85 **Bird, The** *Time*
'64 **Bird Dance Beat** *Trashmen*
'58 **Bird Dog** *Everly Brothers*
'90 **Bird On My Head** *David Seville*
'90 **Birdhouse In Your Soul**
  They Might Be Giants
Birdland
'63   *Chubby Checker*
'79   *Manhattan Transfer*
'65 **Birds And The Bees** *Jewel Akens*
'71 **Birds Of A Feather** *Raiders*
'96 **Birmingham** *Amanda Marshall*
'55 **Birth Of The Boogie** *Bill Haley*

Birthday
'68   *Beatles*
'69   *Underground Sunshine*
'63 **Birthday Party** *Pixies Three*
'89 **Birthday Suit** *Johnny Kemp*
Bitch
'71   *Rolling Stones*
'97   *Meredith Brooks*
'74 **Bitch Is Back** *Elton John*
'77 **Bite Your Lip (Get up and dance!)**
  Elton John
'64 **Bits And Pieces** *Dave Clark Five*
'73 **Bitter Bad** *Melanie*
'98 **Bitter Sweet Symphony** *Verve*
Bizarre Love Triangle
'86   *New Order*
'94   *Frente!*
'01 **Bizounce** *Olivia*
'92 **Black** *Pearl Jam*
'88 **Black And Blue** *Van Halen*
'72 **Black & White** *Three Dog Night*
'99 **Black Balloon** *Goo Goo Dolls*
'77 **Black Betty** *Ram Jam*
'85 **Black Cars** *Gino Vannelli*
'90 **Black Cat** *Janet Jackson*
'82 **Black Coffee In Bed** *Squeeze*
'77 **Black Cow** *Steely Dan*
'55 **Black Denim Trousers** *Cheers*
'71 **Black Dog** *Led Zeppelin*
'75 **Black Friday** *Steely Dan*
'94 **Black Hole Sun** *Soundgarden*
'06 **Black Horse & The Cherry Tree**
  KT Tunstall
'66 **Black Is Black** *Los Bravos*
'74 **Black Lassie** *Cheech & Chong*
Black Magic Woman
'69   *Fleetwood Mac*
'70   *Santana [medley]*
'70 **Black Night** *Deep Purple*
'91 **Black Or White** *Michael Jackson*
'69 **Black Pearl** *Sonny Charles
  & The Checkmates, Ltd.*
'70 **Black Sabbath** *Black Sabbath*
'57 **Black Slacks** *Joe Bennett*
'75 **Black Superman - "Muhammad Ali"**
  Johnny Wakelin
'89 **Black Velvet** *Alannah Myles*
'74 **Black Water** *Doobie Brothers*
'68 **Blackbird** *Beatles*
'78 **Blame It On The Boogie** *Jacksons*
'63 **Blame It On The Bossa Nova**
  Eydie Gorme
'89 **Blame It On The Rain** *Milli Vanilli*
'93 **Blame It On Your Heart**
  Patty Loveless
'75 **Blanket On The Ground**
  Billie Jo Spears
'90 **Blaze Of Glory** *Jon Bon Jovi*
'07 **Bleed It Out** *Linkin Park*
'64 **Bless Our Love** *Gene Chandler*
'05 **Bless The Broken Road**
  Rascal Flatts
'61 **Bless You** *Tony Orlando*
Blessed
'95   *Elton John*
'02   *Martina McBride*
'81 **Blessed Are The Believers**
  Anne Murray
'69 **Blessed Is The Rain** *Brooklyn Bridge*
'94 **Blind Man** *Aerosmith*
Blinded By The Light
'73   *Bruce Springsteen*
'76   *Manfred Mann*
'99 **Bling Bling** *B.G.*
'82 **Blister In The Sun** *Violent Femmes*
'76 **Blitzkrieg Bop** *Ramones*
'78 **Bloat On** *Cheech & Chong*
'58 **Blob, The** *Five Blobs*
'73 **Blood Red And Goin' Down**
  Tanya Tucker
'75 **Bloody Well Right** *Supertramp*
'55 **Blossom Fell** *Nat "King" Cole*
'79 **Blow Away** *George Harrison*
'96 **Blow Up The Outside World**
  Soundgarden

Blowin' In The Wind *Bob Dylan*
'63   *Bob Dylan*
'63   *Peter, Paul & Mary*
'66   *Stevie Wonder*
'03   **Blowin' Me Up (With Her Love)**
       JC Chasez
'70   **Blowing Away** *5th Dimension*
'91   **Blowing Kisses In The Wind**
       Paula Abdul
'96   **Blue** *LeAnn Rimes*
'60   **Blue Angel** *Roy Orbison*
'66   **Blue Autumn** *Bobby Goldsboro*
       Blue Bayou
'63   *Roy Orbison*
'77   *Linda Ronstadt*
'58   **Blue Blue Day** *Don Gibson*
'57   **Blue Christmas** *Elvis Presley*
'96   **Blue Clear Sky** *George Strait*
'73   **Blue Collar**
       Bachman-Turner Overdrive
'78   **Blue Collar Man (Long Nights)** *Styx*
'99   **Blue (Da Ba Dee)** *Eiffel 65*
'82   **Blue Eyes** *Elton John*
'75   **Blue Eyes Crying In The Rain**
       Willie Nelson
       Blue Hawaii
'58   *Billy Vaughn*
'61   *Elvis Presley*
'84   **Blue Jean** *David Bowie*
       Blue Monday
'57   *Fats Domino*
'83   *New Order*
'71   **Blue Money** *Van Morrison*
       Blue Moon
'61   *Marcels*
'63   *Bobby Vinton*
'78   **Blue Morning, Blue Day** *Foreigner*
'98   **Blue On Black**
       Kenny Wayne Shepherd Band
'63   **Blue On Blue** *Bobby Vinton*
'72   **Blue Sky** *Allman Brothers Band*
'90   **Blue Sky Mine** *Midnight Oil*
       Blue Star
'55   *Les Baxter*
'66   *Ventures*
       Blue Suede Shoes
'56   *Carl Perkins*
'56   *Elvis Presley*
'73   *Johnny Rivers*
'60   **Blue Tango** *Bill Black's Combo*
'63   **Blue Velvet** *Bobby Vinton*
'64   **Blue Winter** *Connie Francis*
'67   **Blue's Theme** *Davie Allan*
       Blueberry Hill
'56   *Louis Armstrong*
'56   *Fats Domino*
       Bluebird
'67   *Buffalo Springfield*
'75   *Helen Reddy*
'56   **Bluejean Bop** *Gene Vincent*
'78   **Bluer Than Blue** *Michael Johnson*
'90   **Blues, The** *Tony! Toni! Toné!*
'89   **Blues From A Gun**
       Jesus & Mary Chain
'70   **Blues Power** *Eric Clapton*
'62   **Blues (Stay Away From Me)**
       Ace Cannon
'01   **Blurry** *Puddle Of Mudd*
'55   **Bo Diddley** *Bo Diddley*
       Bo Weevil
'56   *Teresa Brewer*
'56   *Fats Domino*
'79   **Boat Drinks** *Jimmy Buffett*
'82   **Bobbie Sue** *Oak Ridge Boys*
'59   **Bobby Sox To Stockings**
       Frankie Avalon
'62   **Bobby's Girl** *Marcie Blane*
'73   **Bodhisattva** *Steely Dan*
'94   **Body & Soul** *Anita Baker*
'98   **Body Bumpin' Yippie-Yi-Yo**
       Public Announcement
'82   **Body Language** *Queen*
'83   **Body Talk** *Deele*
'76   **Bohemian Rhapsody** *Queen*
'68   **Bold As Love** *Jimi Hendrix*

'61   **Boll Weevil Song** *Brook Benton*
'61   **Bonanza** *Al Caiola*
'59   **Bongo Rock** *Preston Epps*
'62   **Bongo Stomp** *Little Joey & The Flips*
'59   **Bonnie Came Back** *Duane Eddy*
'57   **Bony Moronie** *Larry Williams*
'59   **Boo Boo Stick Beat** *Chet Atkins*
'67   **Boogaloo Down Broadway**
       Fantastic Johnny C
'77   **Boogie Child** *Bee Gees*
'74   **Boogie Down** *Eddie Kendricks*
'76   **Boogie Fever** *Sylvers*
'77   **Boogie Nights** *Heatwave*
'74   **Boogie On Reggae Woman**
       Stevie Wonder
'78   **Boogie Oogie Oogie**
       Taste Of Honey
'76   **Boogie Shoes**
       KC & The Sunshine Band
'79   **Boogie Wonderland** *Earth,*
       Wind & Fire/The Emotions
'73   **Boogie Woogie Bugle Boy**
       Bette Midler
'58   **Book Of Love** *Monotones*
       Boom Boom
'62   *John Lee Hooker*
'64   *Animals*
'55   **Boom Boom Boomerang**
       DeCastro Sisters
'87   **Boom Boom (Let's Go Back To My**
       Room) *Paul Lekakis*
'79   **Boom Boom (Out Go The Lights)**
       Pat Travers
'93   **Boom! Shake The Room**
       Jazzy Jeff & Fresh Prince
'95   **Boombastic** *Shaggy*
'06   **Boondocks** *Little Big Town*
'92   **Boot Scootin' Boogie**
       Brooks & Dunn
'94   **Booti Call** *BLACKstreet*
'71   **Booty Butt** *Ray Charles*
'01   **Bootylicious** *Destiny's Child*
'78   **Bootzilla** *Bootsy's Rubber Band*
'86   **Bop** *Dan Seals*
'58   **Bop-A-Lena** *Ronnie Self*
'84   **Bop 'Til You Drop** *Rick Springfield*
'55   **Bop-Ting-A-Ling** *LaVern Baker*
'56   **Boppin' The Blues** *Carl Perkins*
'83   **Border, The** *America*
'70   **Border Song** *Elton John*
'84   **Borderline** *Madonna*
'85   **Borderlines, The** *Jeffrey Osborne*
'67   **Boris The Spider** *Who*
'66   **Born A Woman** *Sandy Posey*
'92   **Born Country** *Alabama*
       Born Free
'66   *Roger Williams*
'68   *Hesitations*
'85   **Born In East L.A.** *Cheech & Chong*
'84   **Born In The U.S.A.**
       Bruce Springsteen
'69   **Born On The Bayou** *Creedence*
       Clearwater Revival
'79   **Born To Be Alive** *Patrick Hernandez*
'88   **Born To Be My Baby** *Bon Jovi*
'68   **Born To Be Wild** *Steppenwolf*
'56   **Born To Be With You** *Chordettes*
'87   **Born To Boogie** *Hank Williams Jr.*
'00   **Born To Fly** *Sara Evans*
'62   **Born To Lose** *Ray Charles*
'94   **Born To Roll**
       Masta Ace Incorporated
'75   **Born To Run** *Bruce Springsteen*
'70   **Born To Wander** *Rare Earth*
'58   **Born Too Late** *Poni-Tails*
'67   **Born Under A Bad Sign** *Albert King*
'79   **Boss, The** *Diana Ross*
'63   **Boss Guitar** *Duane Eddy*
'63   **Bossa Nova Baby** *Elvis Presley*
'06   **Bossy** *Kelis*
'06   **Boston** *Augustana*
       Both Sides Now
'68   *Judy Collins*
'69   *Joni Mitchell*
'93   **Both Sides Of The Story** *Phil Collins*
'02   **Bother** *Stone Sour*

'66   **Bottle Let Me Down** *Merle Haggard*
'67   **Bottle Of Wine** *Fireballs*
'75   **Boulder To Birmingham**
       Emmylou Harris
'80   **Boulevard** *Jackson Browne*
'05   **Boulevard Of Broken Dreams**
       Green Day
'63   **Bounce, The** *Olympics*
'80   **Bounce, Rock, Skate, Roll**
       Vaughan Mason
'00   **Bounce With Me** *Lil Bow Wow*
'01   **Bouncin' Back (Bumpin' Me Against**
       The Wall) *Mystikal*
'69   **Bouree** *Jethro Tull*
'96   **Bow Down** *Westside Connection*
'00   **Bow Wow (That's My Name)**
       Lil Bow Wow
'67   **Bowling Green** *Everly Brothers*
'70   **Box Of Rain** *Grateful Dead*
'69   **Boxer, The** *Simon & Garfunkel*
       Boy From New York City
'65   *Ad Libs*
'81   *Manhattan Transfer*
'85   **Boy In The Box** *Corey Hart*
'98   **Boy Is Mine** *Brandy & Monica*
'69   **Boy Named Sue** *Johnny Cash*
'63   **Boy Next Door** *Secrets*
'59   **Boy Without A Girl** *Frankie Avalon*
'05   **Boyfriend** *Ashlee Simpson*
'76   **Boys Are Back In Town** *Thin Lizzy*
'84   **Boys Do Fall In Love** *Robin Gibb*
'85   **Boys Don't Cry** *Cure*
'87   **Boys Night Out** *Timothy B. Schmit*
       Boys Of Summer
'84   *Don Henley*
'03   *Ataris*
'73   **Brain Damage [medley]**
       Pink Floyd
'95   **Brain Stew [medley]** *Green Day*
'06   **Brand New Girlfriend** *Steve Holy*
'71   **Brand New Key** *Melanie*
'86   **Brand New Lover** *Dead Or Alive*
'91   **Brand New Man** *Brooks & Dunn*
'69   **Brand New Me** *Dusty Springfield*
'72   **Brandy (You're A Fine Girl)**
       Looking Glass
'80   **Brass In Pocket (I'm Special)**
       Pretenders
'75   **Brazil** *Ritchie Family*
'64   **Bread And Butter** *Newbeats*
'75   **Break Away** *Art Garfunkel*
'93   **Break It Down again**
       Tears For Fears
'07   **Break It Off** *Rihanna & Sean Paul*
       Break It To Me Gently
'62   *Brenda Lee*
'77   *Aretha Franklin*
'82   *Juice Newton*
'82   **Break It Up** *Foreigner*
'83   **Break My Stride** *Matthew Wilder*
'67   **Break On Through (To The Other**
       Side) *Doors*
'73   **Break Up To Make Up** *Stylistics*
'01   **Break Ya Neck** *Busta Rhymes*
'68   **Break Your Promise** *Delfonics*
'04   **Breakaway** *Kelly Clarkson*
'84   **Breakdance** *Irene Cara*
       Breakdown
'77   *Tom Petty*
'77   *Alan Parsons Project*
'01   *Tantric*
'71   **Breakdown, The** *Rufus Thomas*
'80   **Breakdown Dead Ahead**
       Boz Scaggs
'95   **Breakfast At Tiffany's**
       Deep Blue Something
'79   **Breakfast In America** *Supertramp*
       (also see: Cupid's Chokehold)
'61   **Breakin' In A Brand New Broken**
       Heart *Connie Francis*
'92   **Breakin' My Heart (Pretty Brown**
       Eyes) *Mint Condition*
'84   **Breakin'...There's No Stopping Us**
       Ollie & Jerry
'66   **Breakin' Up Is Breakin' My Heart**
       Roy Orbison

'97 **Breaking All The Rules** *She Moves*
'81 **Breaking Away** *Balance*
'06 **Breaking Free**
      High School Musical Cast
'83 **Breaking The Chains** *Dokken*
'04 **Breaking The Habit** *Linkin Park*
'80 **Breaking The Law** *Judas Priest*
     Breaking Up Is Hard To Do
'62   *Neil Sedaka*
'70   *Lenny Welch*
'72   *Partridge Family*
'75   *Neil Sedaka [slow version]*
'83 **Breaking Us In Two** *Joe Jackson*
'87 **Breakout** *Swing Out Sister*
'80 **Breaks, The** *Kurtis Blow*
'81 **Breakup Song (They Don't Write
      'Em)** *Greg Kihn Band*
'07 **Breath** *Breaking Benjamin*
     Breathe
'73   *Pink Floyd [medley]*
'99   *Faith Hill*
'02   *Rebecca St. James*
'03   *Michelle Branch*
'04   *Fabolous*
'93 **Breathe Again** *Toni Braxton*
'04 **Breathe, Stretch, Shake** *Mase*
'06 **Breathe (2 AM)** *Anna Nalick*
'02 **Breathe Your Name**
      Sixpence None The Richer
     Breathless
'58   *Jerry Lee Lewis*
'01   *Corrs*
'55 **Breeze And I** *Caterina Valente*
'97 **Brick** *Ben Folds Five*
'77 **Brick House** *Commodores*
'74 **Bridge Of Sighs** *Robin Trower*
     Bridge Over Troubled Water
'70   *Simon & Garfunkel*
'71   *Aretha Franklin*
'03 **Bright Lights** *Matchbox Twenty*
'61 **Bright Lights Big City** *Jimmy Reed*
'87 **Brilliant Disguise** *Bruce Springsteen*
'68 **Bring A Little Lovin'** *Los Bravos*
'05 **Bring Em Out** *T.I.*
'99 **Bring It All To Me**
      *Blaque Feat. *NSYNC*
'06 **Bring It On Home** *Little Big Town*
     Bring It On Home To Me
'62   *Sam Cooke*
'65   *Animals*
'68   *Eddie Floyd*
'67 **Bring It Up** *James Brown*
'03 **Bring Me To Life** *Evanescence*
'86 **Bring On The Dancing Horses**
      Echo & The Bunnymen
'01 **Bring On The Rain** *Jo Dee
      Messina w/ Tim McGraw*
'71 **Bring The Boys Home** *Freda Payne*
'88 **Bring The Noise** *Public Enemy*
'94 **Bring The Pain** *Method Man*
'84 **Bringin' On The Heartbreak** *Def
      Leppard*
'61 **Bristol Stomp** *Dovells*
'62 **Bristol Twistin' Annie** *Dovells*
'00 **Broadway** *Goo Goo Dolls*
'04 **Broken** *Seether*
'91 **Broken Arrow** *Rod Stewart*
'79 **Broken Hearted Me** *Anne Murray*
'59 **Broken-Hearted Melody**
      Sarah Vaughan
'97 **Broken Wing** *Martina McBride*
'85 **Broken Wings** *Mr. Mister*
'95 **Brokenhearted** *Brandy*
'03 **Brokenheartsville** *Joe Nichols*
'68 **Brooklyn Roads** *Neil Diamond*
'90 **Brother Jukebox** *Mark Chesnutt*
'73 **Brother Louie** *Stories*
'69 **Brother Love's Travelling Salvation
      Show** *Neil Diamond*
'70 **Brother Rapp** *James Brown*
'67 **Brown Eyed Girl** *Van Morrison*
'56 **Brown Eyed Handsome Man**
      Chuck Berry
'68 **Brown Eyed Woman** *Bill Medley*

     Brown Sugar
'71   *Rolling Stones*
'95   *D'Angelo*
'84 **Bruce** *Rick Springfield*
'92 **Bubba Shot The Jukebox**
      Mark Chesnutt
'07 **Bubbly** *Colbie Caillat*
'65 **Buckaroo** *Buck Owens*
'07 **Buddy** *Musiq Soulchild*
'94 **Buddy Holly** *Weezer*
'78 **Buffalo Soldier** *Bob Marley*
'89 **Buffalo Stance** *Neneh Cherry*
'99 **Bug A Boo** *Destiny's Child*
'69 **Build Me Up Buttercup** *Foundations*
'57 **Build Your Love (On A Strong
      Foundation)** *Johnnie Ray*
'97 **Building A Mystery**
      Sarah McLachlan
'06 **Building Bridges** *Brooks & Dunn*
'60 **Bulldog** *Fireballs*
'87 **Bullet The Blue Sky** *U2*
'95 **Bullet With Butterfly Wings**
      Smashing Pumpkins
'96 **Bulls On Parade**
      Rage Against The Machine
     Bumble Bee
'60   *LaVern Baker*
'65   *Searchers*
'61 **Bumble Boogie**
      B. Bumble & The Stingers
'02 **Bump, Bump, Bump** *B2K & P. Diddy*
'94 **Bump N' Grind** *R. Kelly*
'74 **Bungle In The Jungle** *Jethro Tull*
'96 **Burden In My Hand** *Soundgarden*
     Burn
'00   *Jo Dee Messina*
'04   *Usher*
'71 **Burn Down The Mission**
      Elton John
'80 **Burn Rubber (Why You Wanna Hurt
      Me)** *Gap Band*
'55 **Burn That Candle** *Bill Haley*
'81 **Burnin' For You** *Blue Öyster Cult*
'77 **Burnin' Sky** *Bad Company*
     Burning Bridges
'60   *Jack Scott*
'70   *Mike Curb Congregation*
'04 **Burning Bright** *Shinedown*
'82 **Burning Down One Side**
      Robert Plant
'83 **Burning Down The House**
      Talking Heads
     Burning Heart
'83   *Vandenberg*
'85   *Survivor*
'85 **Burning House Of Love** *X*
'72 **Burning Love** *Elvis Presley*
'68 **Burning Of The Midnight Lamp**
      Jimi Hendrix
'66 **Bus Stop** *Hollies*
'56 **Bus Stop Song (A Paper Of Pins)**
      Four Lads
'89 **Bust A Move** *Young MC*
'63 **Bust Out** *Busters*
'79 **Bustin' Loose** *Chuck Brown*
'98 **Busy Man** *Billy Ray Cyrus*
'96 **But Anyway** *Blues Traveler*
'00 **But For The Grace Of God**
      Keith Urban
'61 **But I Do** *Clarence Henry*
'66 **But It's Alright** *J.J. Jackson*
     But You Know I Love You
'69   *First Edition*
'81   *Dolly Parton*
'65 **But You're Mine** *Sonny & Cher*
'97 **Butta Love** *Next*
'75 **Butter Boy** *Fanny*
'01 **Butterflies** *Michael Jackson*
     Butterfly
'57   *Charlie Gracie*
'57   *Andy Williams*
'97   *Mariah Carey*
'01   *Crazy Town*
'63 **Butterfly Baby** *Bobby Rydell*

     Butterfly Kisses
'97   *Bob Carlisle*
'97   *Raybon Bros.*
'06 **Buttons** *Pussycat Dolls*
'00 **Buy Me A Rose** *Kenny Rogers*
'07 **Buy U A Drank** *T-Pain*
'61 **Buzz Buzz A-Diddle-It**
      Freddy Cannon
'57 **Buzz-Buzz-Buzz** *Hollywood Flames*
     By The Time I Get To Phoenix
'67   *Glen Campbell*
'69   *Isaac Hayes*
'93 **By The Time This Night Is Over**
      Kenny G w/ Peabo Bryson
'02 **By The Way** *Red Hot Chili Peppers*
'98 **Bye-Bye** *Jo Dee Messina*
'65 **Bye, Bye, Baby (Baby, Goodbye)**
      4 Seasons
'00 **Bye Bye Bye** *NSYNC*
     Bye Bye Love
'57   *Everly Brothers*
'78   *Cars*

C

'97 **C U When U Get There** *Coolio*
     C.C. Rider
'57   *Chuck Willis*
'62   *LaVern Baker*
'66   *Animals*
     C'est La Vie
'55   *Sarah Vaughan*
'86   *Robbie Nevil*
'99   *B*Witched*
'60 **C'est Si Bon (It's So Good)**
      Conway Twitty
'57 **Ca, C'est L'amour** *Tony Bennett*
'78 **Ca Plane Pour Moi** *Plastic Bertrand*
'68 **Cab Driver** *Mills Brothers*
'81 **Cadillac Ranch**
      Bruce Springsteen
'62 **Cadillac Style** *Sammy Kershaw*
'60 **Cajun Queen** *Jimmy Dean*
'60 **Calcutta** *Lawrence Welk*
'76 **Caledonia** *Robin Trower*
'60 **Calendar Girl** *Neil Sedaka*
'66 **California Dreamin'** *Mamas & Papas*
     California Girls
'65   *Beach Boys*
'85   *David Lee Roth*
'96 **California Love** *2 Pac*
'67 **California Nights** *Lesley Gore*
'68 **California Soul** *5th Dimension*
'64 **California Sun** *Rivieras*
'00 **Californication**
      Red Hot Chili Peppers
'89 **Call It Love** *Poco*
     Call Me
'58   *Johnny Mathis*
'66   *Chris Montez*
'70   *Aretha Franklin*
'80   *Blondie*
'82   *Skyy*
'91   *Phil Perry*
'97   *Le Click*
'02   *Tweet*
'73 **Call Me (Come Back Home)**
      Al Green
'63 **Call Me Irresponsible** *Jack Jones*
'68 **Call Me Lightning** *Who*
'62 **Call Me Mr. In-Between** *Burl Ives*
'74 **Call Me The Breeze**
      Lynyrd Skynyrd
'77 **Call Me Up In Dreamland**
      Van Morrison
'06 **Call Me When You're Sober**
      Evanescence
     Call On Me
'63   *Bobby Bland*
'74   *Chicago*
'06   *Janet Jackson w/ Nelly*
'84 **Call To The Heart** *Giuffria*
'94 **Callin' Baton Rouge** *Garth Brooks*
'00 **Callin' Me** *Lil' Zane w/ 112*

196

'03 **Change Clothes** *Jay-Z*
'00 **Change (In The House Of Flies)**
Deftones
'86 **Change In The Weather**
John Fogerty
'65 **Change Is Gonna Come** *Sam Cooke*
Change Of Heart
'78 *Eric Carmen*
'83 *Tom Petty*
'86 *Cyndi Lauper*
'71 **Change Partners** *Stephen Stills*
'96 **Change The World** *Eric Clapton*
'97 **Change Would Do You Good**
Sheryl Crow
Changes
'72 *David Bowie*
'98 *2Pac*
'77 **Changes In Latitudes, Changes In
Attitudes** *Jimmy Buffett*
'89 **Channel Z** *B-52's*
Chanson D'Amour (Song Of Love)
'58 *Fontane Sisters*
'58 *Art & Dotty Todd*
'99 **Chanté's Got A Man** *Chanté Moore*
'57 **Chantez-Chantez** *Dinah Shore*
Chantilly Lace
'58 *Big Bopper*
'72 *Jerry Lee Lewis*
'95 **Chanukah Song** *Adam Sandler*
Chapel In The Moonlight
'65 *Bachelors*
'67 *Dean Martin*
'64 **Chapel Of Love** *Dixie Cups*
'63 **Charade** *Henry Mancini*
'05 **Chariot** *Gavin DeGraw*
'81 **Chariots Of Fire** *Vangelis*
'71 **Charity Ball** *Fanny*
'04 **Charlene** *Anthony Hamilton*
'59 **Charlie Brown** *Coasters*
'63 **Charms** *Bobby Vee*
'79 **Chase** *Giorgio Moroder*
'90 **Chasin' That Neon Rainbow**
Alan Jackson
'06 **Chasing Cars** *Snow Patrol*
'93 **Chattahoochee** *Alan Jackson*
Chattanooga Choo Choo
'62 *Floyd Cramer*
'67 *Harpers Bizarre*
'78 *Tuxedo Junction*
'60 **Chattanooga Shoe Shine Boy**
Freddy Cannon
'80 **Cheap Sunglasses** *ZZ Top*
'73 **Cheaper To Keep Her**
Johnnie Taylor
'66 **Cheater, The** *Bob Kuban*
Check It Out
'73 *Tavares*
'88 *John Cougar Mellencamp*
'06 **Check On It** *Beyoncé*
'70 **Check Out Your Mind** *Impressions*
'95 **Check Yes Or No** *George Strait*
'93 **Check Yo Self** *Ice Cube*
'98 **Cheers 2 U** *Playa*
'78 **Cheeseburger In Paradise**
Jimmy Buffett
'69 **Chelsea Morning** *Joni Mitchell*
'99 **Chemicals Between Us** *Bush*
'06 **Chemicals React** *Aly & AJ*
'76 **Cherchez La Femme [medley]**
*Dr. Buzzard's Original "Savannah"
Band*
Cherish
'66 *Association*
'71 *David Cassidy*
'85 *Kool & The Gang*
'89 *Madonna*
'82 **Cherokee Fiddle** *Johnny Lee*
'77 **Cherry Baby** *Starz*
'87 **Cherry Bomb**
John Cougar Mellencamp
Cherry, Cherry
'66 *Neil Diamond*
'73 *Neil Diamond [live]*
'69 **Cherry Hill Park** *Billy Joe Royal*

Cherry Pie
'60 *Skip & Flip*
'90 *Warrant*
**Cherry Pink (And Apple Blossom
White)**
'55 *Alan Dale*
'55 *Perez Prado*
'59 **Cherrystone** *Addrisi Brothers*
'68 **Chest Fever** *Band*
'70 **Chestnut Mare** *Byrds*
**(Chestnuts Roasting On An Open
Fire) ..see: Christmas Song**
'75 **Chevy Van** *Sammy Johns*
'68 **Chewy Chewy** *Ohio Express*
Chicago
'57 *Frank Sinatra*
'71 *Graham Nash*
'71 **Chick-A-Boom (Don't Ya Jes' Love
It)** *Daddy Dewdrop*
'06 **Chicken Noodle Soup**
Webstar & Young B
'67 **Child Of Clay** *Jimmie Rodgers*
'96 **Children** *Robert Miles*
'71 **Children Of The Grave**
Black Sabbath
'90 **Children Of The Night** *Richard Marx*
Children's Marching Song
'59 *Mitch Miller*
'59 *Cyril Stapleton*
'65 **Chimes Of Freedom** *Byrds*
'60 **China Doll** *Ames Brothers*
'83 **China Girl** *David Bowie*
'73 **China Grove** *Doobie Brothers*
'62 **Chip Chip** *Gene McDaniels*
'58 **Chipmunk Song** *Chipmunks*
'79 **Chiquitita** *Abba*
'71 **Chirpy Chirpy Cheep Cheep**
Mac & Katie Kissoon
'81 **Chloe** *Elton John*
'69 **Choice Of Colors** *Impressions*
'69 **Chokin' Kind** *Joe Simon*
'68 **Choo Choo Train** *Box Tops*
'94 **Choose** *Color Me Badd*
'55 **Chop Chop Boom** *Crew-Cuts*
'02 **Chop Suey** *System Of A Down*
'77 **Christine Sixteen** *Kiss*
'95 **Christmas Eve (Sarajevo 12/24)**
Trans-Siberian Orchestra
'00 **Christmas Shoes** *Newsong*
'99 **Christmas Song (Chestnuts
Roasting On An Open Fire)**
Christina Aguilera
'79 **Chuck E.'s In Love** *Rickie Lee Jones*
'64 **Chug-A-Lug** *Roger Miller*
'56 **Church Bells May Ring** *Diamonds*
'83 **Church Of The Poison Mind**
Culture Club
'92 **Church Of Your Heart** *Roxette*
'89 **Church On Cumberland Road**
Shenandoah
'59 **Ciao, Ciao Bambina** *Jacky Noguez*
'93 **Cielito Lindo** *Brave Combo*
'58 **Cimarron (Roll On)** *Billy Vaughn*
'68 **Cinnamon** *Derek*
'70 **Cinnamon Girl** *Gentrys*
Cinco Robles (Five Oaks)
'57 *Russell Arms*
'57 *Les Paul & Mary Ford*
Cinderella
'62 *Jack Ross*
'77 *Firefall*
Cindy, Oh Cindy
'56 *Eddie Fisher*
'56 *Vince Martin/The Tarriers*
'62 **Cindy's Birthday** *Johnny Crawford*
'62 **Cinnamon Cinder (It's A Very Nice
Dance)** *Pastel Six*
'69 **Cinnamon Girl** *Neil Young*
'70 **Circle Game** *Joni Mitchell*
'88 **Circle In The Sand** *Belinda Carlisle*
'78 **Circle Is Small (I Can See It In Your
Eyes)** *Gordon Lightfoot*
'94 **Circle Of Life** *Elton John*
'82 **Circles** *Atlantic Starr*
'73 **Cisco Kid** *War*
'69 **Cissy Strut** *Meters*

'85 **C-I-T-Y** *John Cafferty*
'58 **City Lights** *Ray Price*
'56 **City Of Angels** *Highlights*
'05 **City Of Blinding Lights** *U2*
City Of New Orleans
'72 *Arlo Guthrie*
'84 *Willie Nelson*
'72 **Clair** *Gilbert O'Sullivan*
'74 **Clap For The Wolfman** *Guess Who*
'65 **Clapping Song** *Shirley Ellis*
'59 **Class, The** *Chubby Checker*
'72 **Class of '57** *Statler Brothers*
'68 **Classical Gas** *Mason Williams*
'58 **Claudette** *Everly Brothers*
'71 **Clean Up Woman** *Betty Wright*
'69 **Clean Up Your Own Back Yard**
Elvis Presley
'02 **Cleanin' Out My Closet** *Eminem*
'60 **Clementine** *Bobby Darin*
'98 **Cleopatra's Theme** *Cleopatra*
'58 **Click-Clack** *Dickey Doo & The Don'ts*
'60 **Climb Ev'ry Mountain** *Tony Bennett*
'64 **Clinging Vine** *Bobby Vinton*
'01 **Clint Eastwood** *Gorillaz*
'98 **Clock Strikes** *Timbaland & Magoo*
'03 **Clocks** *Coldplay*
'80 **Clones (We're All)** *Alice Cooper*
'89 **Close My Eyes Forever**
Lita Ford/Ozzy Osbourne
'78 **Close The Door** *Teddy Pendergrass*
'62 **Close To Cathy** *Mike Clifford*
'80 **Close To The Borderline**
Billy Joel
'72 **Close To The Edge** *Yes*
'90 **Close To You** *Maxi Priest*
Close Your Eyes
'67 *Peaches & Herb*
'73 *Edward Bear*
'94 **Closer** *Nine Inch Nails*
'78 **Closer I Get To You** *Roberta Flack
w/ Donny Hathaway*
'86 **Closer Than Close** *Jean Carne*
'89 **Closer Than Friends** *Surface*
'89 **Closer To Fine** *Indigo Girls*
'96 **Closer To Free** *BoDeans*
'70 **Closer To Home [medley]**
Grand Funk Railroad
'77 **Closer To The Heart** *Rush*
'83 **Closer You Get** *Alabama*
'98 **Closing Time** *Semisonic*
'68 **Cloud Nine** *Temptations*
'85 **Cloudbusting** *Kate Bush*
'73 **Clouds** *David Gates*
'59 **Clouds, The** *Spacemen*
'90 **Club At The End Of The Street**
Elton John
'03 **Clubbin** *Marques Houston*
'70 **Coal Miner's Daughter** *Loretta Lynn*
'71 **Coat Of Many Colors** *Dolly Parton*
Cocaine
'77 *Eric Clapton*
'80 *Eric Clapton [live]*
'02 **Cochise** *Audioslave*
'97 **Coco Jamboo** *Mr. President*
'72 **Coconut** *Nilsson*
'57 **Cocoanut Woman** *Harry Belafonte*
Cold
'67 *John Gary*
'04 *Crossfade*
'77 **Cold As Ice** *Foreigner*
'83 **Cold Blooded** *Rick James*
'93 **Cold Fire** *Rush*
'74 **Cold Gin** *Kiss*
'04 **Cold Hard Bitch** *Jet*
'67 **Cold Hard Facts Of Life**
Porter Wagoner
'89 **Cold Hearted** *Paula Abdul*
'80 **Cold Love** *Donna Summer*
'96 **Cold Rock A Party** *MC Lyte*
'84 **Cold Shot** *Stevie Ray Vaughan*
'67 **Cold Sweat** *James Brown*
'88 **Coldsweat** *Sugarcubes*
'69 **Cold Turkey** *Plastic Ono Band*
'05 **Collide** *Howie Day*
'69 **Color Him Father** *Winstons*

'66 **Color My World** *Petula Clark*
'95 **Colors Of The Wind**
  Vanessa Williams
'71 **Colour My World** *Chicago*
'88 **Colour Of Love** *Billy Ocean*
'64 **Come A Little Bit Closer**
  Jay & The Americans
'05 **Come A Little Closer** *Dierks Bentley*
'70 **Come And Get It** *Badfinger*
'63 **Come And Get These Memories**
  Martha & The Vandellas
'98 **Come And Get With Me** *Keith Sweat*
Come And Get Your Love
'74 *Redbone*
'95 *Real McCoy*
'65 **Come And Stay With Me**
  Marianne Faithfull
'92 **Come & Talk To Me** *Jodeci*
'89 **Come Anytime** *Hoodoo Gurus*
Come As You Are
'87 *Peter Wolf*
'92 *Nirvana*
'93 **Come Baby Come** *K7*
Come Back
'60 *Jimmy Clanton*
'80 *J. Geils Band*
'81 **Come Back And Stay** *Paul Young*
'62 **Come Back Silly Girl** *Lettermen*
'90 **Come Back To Me** *Janet Jackson*
'67 **Come Back When You Grow Up**
  Bobby Vee
'04 **Come Clean** *Hilary Duff*
'58 **Come Closer To Me** *Nat "King" Cole*
'97 **Come Cryin' To Me** *Lonestar*
'83 **Come Dancing** *Kinks*
'58 **Come Fly With Me** *Frank Sinatra*
'73 **Come Get To This** *Marvin Gaye*
Come Go With Me
'57 *Dell-Vikings*
'81 *Beach Boys*
'87 *Exposé*
'65 **Come Home** *Dave Clark Five*
'93 **Come Inside** *Intro*
'59 **Come Into My Heart** *Lloyd Price*
'73 **Come Live With Me** *Roy Clark*
'74 **Come Monday** *Jimmy Buffett*
'90 **Come Next Monday** *K.T. Oslin*
Come On
'64 *Tommy Roe*
'97 *Billy Lawrence*
'59 **Come On And Get Me** *Fabian*
'89 **C'mon And Get My Love**
  D Mob/Cathy Dennis
'64 **C'mon And Swim** *Bobby Freeman*
'90 **Come On Back** *Carlene Carter*
'67 **Come On Down To My Boat**
  Every Mothers' Son
'83 **Come On Eileen**
  Dexys Midnight Runners
'58 **C'mon Everybody** *Eddie Cochran*
Come On Let's Go
'58 *Ritchie Valens*
'66 *McCoys*
'87 *Los Lobos*
'62 **Come On Little Angel** *Belmonts*
'99 **Come On Over** *Shania Twain*
C'mon Marianne
'67 *4 Seasons*
'76 *Donny Osmond*
'96 **C'Mon N' Ride It (The Train)**
  Quad City DJ's
'76 **Come On Over** *Olivia Newton-John*
'00 **Come On Over Baby (all I want is
  you)** *Christina Aguilera*
'94 **Come Out And Play** *Offspring*
'03 **Come Over** *Aaliyah*
'66 **(Come 'Round Here) I'm The One
  You Need** *Miracles*
'70 **Come Running** *Van Morrison*
'66 **Come Running Back** *Dean Martin*
'77 **Come Sail Away** *Styx*
'69 **Come Saturday Morning**
  Sandpipers
'65 **Come See** *Major Lance*

Come See About Me
'64 *Supremes*
'67 *Jr. Walker*
'96 **Come See Me** *112*
'59 **Come Softly To Me** *Fleetwoods*
Come To Me
'58 *Johnny Mathis*
'59 *Marv Johnson*
'79 *France Joli*
'06 *Diddy*
'94 **Come To My Window**
  Melissa Etheridge
'67 **Come To The Sunshine**
  Harpers Bizarre
Come Together
'69 *Beatles*
'78 *Aerosmith*
'93 **Come Undone** *Duran Duran*
'58 **Come What May** *Clyde McPhatter*
'98 **Come With Me** *Puff Daddy*
'95 **Comedown** *Bush*
'78 **Comes A Time** *Neil Young*
'91 **Comfort Zone** *Vanessa Williams*
'80 **Comfortably Numb** *Pink Floyd*
'93 **Comforter** *Shai*
'70 **Comin' Home**
  Delaney & Donnie
'62 **Comin' Home Baby** *Mel Torme*
'67 **Comin' In And Out Of Your Life**
  Barbra Streisand
'66 **Coming On Strong** *Brenda Lee*
'86 **Coming Around Again** *Carly Simon*
'89 **Coming Home** *Cinderella*
'66 **Coming Home Soldier** *Bobby Vinton*
'90 **Coming Of Age** *Damn Yankees*
'91 **Coming Out Of The Dark**
  Gloria Estefan
'06 **Coming Undone** *Korn*
'80 **Coming Up** *Paul McCartney*
'98 **Commitment** *LeAnn Rimes*
'69 **Commotion**
  Creedence Clearwater Revival
'85 **Communication** *Power Station*
'69 **Communication Breakdown** *Led
  Zeppelin*
'79 **Complete Control** *Clash*
'94 **Completely** *Michael Bolton*
Complicated
'01 *Carolyn Dawn Johnson*
'02 *Avril Lavigne*
'69 **Composer, The** *Supremes*
'80 **Concerto In D** *Steve Howe*
Concrete And Clay
'65 *Eddie Rambeau*
'65 *Unit Four Plus Two*
'90 **Concrete And Steel** *ZZ Top*
'03 **Concrete Angel** *Martina McBride*
'76 **Coney Island Baby** *Lou Reed*
'04 **Confessions Part II** *Usher*
'56 **Confidential** *Sonny Knight*
'79 **Confusion** *Electric Light Orchestra*
'85 **Conga** *Miami Sound Machine*
'93 **Connected** *Stereo MC's*
'95 **Connection** *Elastica*
'72 **Conquistador** *Procol Harum [live]*
'62 **Conscience** *James Darren*
'92 **Constant Craving** *k.d. lang*
'94 **Constantly** *Immature*
'01 **Contagious** *Isley Brothers*
'61 **Continental Walk** *Hank Ballard*
Control
'86 *Janet Jackson*
'01 *Puddle Of Mudd*
'06 **Control Myself** *LL Cool J*
'81 **Controversy** *Prince*
'72 **Convention '72** *Delegates*
'75 **Convoy** *C.W. McCall*
'68 **Coo Coo** *Janis Joplin*
'73 **Cook With Honey** *Judy Collins*
'05 **Cool** *Gwen Stefani*
'71 **Cool Aid** *Paul Humphrey*
'79 **Cool Change** *Little River Band*
'84 **Cool It Now** *New Edition*
'66 **Cool Jerk** *Capitols*
'81 **Cool Love** *Pablo Cruise*

'81 **Cool Night** *Paul Davis*
'57 **Cool Shake** *Del Vikings*
'78 **Copacabana (At The Copa)**
  Barry Manilow
'73 **Corazón** *Carole King*
'95 **Corduroy** *Pearl Jam*
'60 **Corinna, Corinna** *Ray Peterson*
'72 **Corner Of The Sky** *Jackson 5*
'94 **Cornflake Girl** *Tori Amos*
'56 **Corrine Corrina** *Big Joe Turner*
'75 **Cortez The Killer** *Neil Young*
'74 **Cosmik Debris** *Frank Zappa*
'60 **Cottage For Sale** *Little Willie John*
'64 **Cotton Candy** *Al Hirt*
'95 **Cotton Eye Joe** *Rednex*
'61 **Cotton Fields** *Highwaymen*
'80 **Could I Have This Dance**
  Anne Murray
'01 **Could It Be** *Jaheim*
'72 **Could It Be Forever** *David Cassidy*
'72 **Could It Be I'm Falling In Love**
  Spinners
'75 **Could It Be Magic** *Barry Manilow*
'90 **Could This Be Love** *Seduction*
'57 **Could This Be Magic** *Dubs*
'80 **Could You Be Loved** *Bob Marley*
'07 **Could've Been** *Tiffany*
'92 **Could've Been Me** *Billy Ray Cyrus*
'77 **Couldn't Get It Right**
  Climax Blues Band
'00 **Couldn't Last A Moment**
  Collin Raye
'61 **Count Every Star**
  Donnie & The Dreamers
'65 **Count Me In** *Gary Lewis*
'85 **Count Me Out** *New Edition*
Count On Me
'78 *Jefferson Starship*
'96 *Whitney Houston & CeCe Winans*
'96 **Counting Blue Cars** *Dishwalla*
'60 **Country Boy** *Fats Domino*
'82 **Country Boy Can Survive**
  Hank Williams Jr.
'75 **Country Boy (You Got Your Feet In
  L.A.)** *Glen Campbell*
'74 **Country Bumpkin** *Cal Smith*
'68 **Country Girl - City Man**
  Billy Vera & Judy Clay
'71 **Country Road** *James Taylor*
'91 **Couple Days Off** *Huey Lewis*
'68 **Court Of Love** *Unifics*
'69 **Court Of The Crimson King**
  King Crimson
'02 **Courtesy Of The Red, White And
  Blue (The Angry American)**
  Toby Keith
'00 **Cousin Dupree** *Steely Dan*
'64 **Cousin Of Mine** *Sam Cooke*
'89 **Cover Girl** *New Kids On The Block*
'84 **Cover Me** *Bruce Springsteen*
'89 **Cover Of Love** *Michael Damian*
'72 **Cover Of "Rolling Stone"** *Dr. Hook*
'98 **Cover You In Kisses**
  John Michael Montgomery
'79 **Coward Of The County**
  Kenny Rogers
'99 **Cowboy** *Kid Rock*
'02 **Cowboy In Me** *Tim McGraw*
'86 **Cowboy Man** *Lyle Lovett*
'99 **Cowboy Take Me Away** *Dixie Chicks*
'03 **Cowboys Like Us** *George Strait*
'68 **Cowboys To Girls** *Intruders*
'72 **Cowboys Work Is Never Done**
  Sonny & Cher
'69 **Cowgirl In The Sand**
  Neil Young
'77 **Crackerbox Palace** *George Harrison*
'70 **Cracklin' Rosie** *Neil Diamond*
Cradle Of Love
'60 *Johnny Preston*
'90 *Billy Idol*
'07 **Crank That** *Soulja Boy*
'00 **Crash And Burn** *Savage Garden*
'97 **Crash Into Me** *Dave Matthews Band*
'01 **Crawling** *Linkin Park*
'01 **Crawling In The Dark** *Hoobastank*

'86 **Crazay** *Jesse Johnson w/ Sly Stone*
Crazy
'61 *Patsy Cline*
'87 *Icehouse*
'90 *Boys*
'91 *Seal*
'94 *Aerosmith*
'00 *K-Ci & JoJo*
'06 *Gnarls Barkley*
'89 **Crazy About Her** *Rod Stewart*
Crazy Arms
'56 *Ray Price*
'60 *Bob Beckham*
'06 **Crazy Bitch** *Buckcherry*
'58 **Crazy Eyes For You** *Bobby Hamilton*
'00 **Crazy For This Girl** *Evan & Jaron*
'85 **Crazy For You** *Madonna*
'72 **Crazy Horses** *Osmonds*
'03 **Crazy In Love** *Beyoncé*
'85 **Crazy In The Night (Barking At Airplanes)** *Kim Carnes*
'56 **Crazy Little Palace** *Billy Williams*
'79 **Crazy Little Thing Called Love** *Queen*
Crazy Love
'58 *Paul Anka*
'70 *Van Morrison*
'79 *Poco*
'79 *Allman Brothers Band*
'72 **Crazy Mama** *J.J. Cale*
'53 **Crazy Man, Crazy** *Bill Haley*
'76 **Crazy On You** *Heart*
'55 **Crazy Otto [medley]** *Johnny Maddox*
'81 **Crazy Train** *Ozzy Osbourne*
'94 **C.R.E.A.M.** *Wu-Tang Clan*
'91 **Cream** *Prince & The N.P.G.*
'03 **Creatures (For A While)** *311*
Creep
'93 *Radiohead*
'93 *Stone Temple Pilots*
'94 *TLC*
'67 **Creeque Alley** *Mamas & Papas*
'71 **Cried Like A Baby** *Bobby Sherman*
'97 **Criminal** *Fiona Apple*
Crimson And Clover
'68 *Tommy James*
'82 *Joan Jett*
'55 **Croce Di Oro (Cross Of Gold)** *Patti Page*
'72 **Crocodile Rock** *Elton John*
'71 **Cross-Eyed Mary** *Jethro Tull*
'87 **Cross My Broken Heart** *Jets*
Cross Fire!
'63 *Orlons*
'89 *Stevie Ray Vaughan*
'59 **Crossfire** *Johnny & The Hurricanes*
'69 **Crossroads** *Cream*
'96 **Crossroads, Tha** *Bone Thugs-N-Harmony*
'68 **Crosstown Traffic** *Jimi Hendrix*
'62 **Crowd, The** *Roy Orbison*
'68 **Crown Of Creation** *Jefferson Airplane*
Cruel Summer
'84 *Bananarama*
'98 *Ace Of Base*
'79 **Cruel To Be Kind** *Nick Lowe*
Cruisin'
'79 *Smokey Robinson*
'95 *D'Angelo*
'00 *Huey Lewis & Gwyneth Paltrow*
'90 **Cruising For Bruising** *Basia*
'83 **Crumblin' Down** *John Cougar Mellencamp*
'73 **Crunge, The** *Led Zeppelin*
Crush
'98 *Jennifer Paige*
'99 *Dave Matthews Band*
'86 **Crush On You** *Jets*
Cry
'66 *Ronnie Dove*
'85 *Godley & Creme*
'89 *Waterfront*
'02 *Faith Hill*

Cry Baby
'56 *Bonnie Sisters*
'63 *Garnet Mimms*
'71 *Janis Joplin*
'05 *Melissa Etheridge & Joss Stone [medley]*
'62 **Cry Baby Cry** *Angels*
'55 **Cry! Cry! Cry!** *Johnny Cash*
'91 **Cry For Help** *Rick Astley*
'91 **Cry For The Desert** *Twila Paris*
'93 **Cry For You** *Jodeci*
'68 **Cry Like A Baby** *Box Tops*
Cry Me A River
'55 *Julie London*
'70 *Joe Cocker*
'02 *Justin Timberlake*
'05 **Cry Out To Jesus** *Third Day*
Cry To Me
'62 *Solomon Burke*
'63 *Betty Harris*
'00 **Crybaby** *Mariah Carey*
Cryin'
'89 *Vixen*
'93 *Aerosmith*
'65 **Cryin' Time** *Buck Owens*
Crying
'61 *Roy Orbison*
'66 *Jay & The Americans*
'81 *Don McLean*
'93 **Crying Game** *Boy George*
'65 **Crying In The Chapel** *Elvis Presley*
'62 **Crying In The Rain** *Everly Brothers*
'65 **Crying Time** *Ray Charles*
'76 **Crystal Ball** *Styx*
'69 **Crystal Blue Persuasion** *Tommy James*
'67 **Crystal Chandelier** *Charley Pride*
'67 **Crystal Ship** *Doors*
'67 **Cuando Sali De Cuba** *Sandpipers*
'89 **Cuddly Toy (Feel For Me)** *Roachford*
'04 **Culo** *Pitbull w/ Lil Jon*
'89 **Cult Of Personality** *Living Colour*
Cum On Feel The Noize
'73 *Slade*
'83 *Quiet Riot*
'95 **Cumbersome** *7 Mary 3*
'98 **Cup Of Life** *Ricky Martin*
Cupid
'61 *Sam Cooke*
'69 *Johnny Nash*
'76 *Tony Orlando & Dawn*
'80 *Spinners [medley]*
'97 *112*
'07 **Cupid's Chokehold/Breakfast In America** *Gym Class Heroes*
'83 **Curly Shuffle** *Jump 'N The Saddle*
Cut Across Shorty
'59 *Eddie Cochran*
'70 *Rod Stewart*
'75 **Cut The Cake** *AWB*
'90 **Cuts Both Ways** *Gloria Estefan*
'83 **Cuts Like A Knife** *Bryan Adams*
'90 **Cuts You Up** *Peter Murphy*
'68 **Cycles** *Frank Sinatra*
'07 **Cyclone** *Baby Bash*

D

'68 **D. W. Washburn** *Monkees*
'73 **D'yer Mak'er** *Led Zeppelin*
'06 **DJ Play A Love Song** *Jamie Foxx*
D.O.A. [DOA]
'71 *Bloodrock*
'05 *Foo Fighters*
'88 **Da'Butt** *E.U.*
'82 **Da Da Da I Don't Love You You Don't Love Me** *Trio*
'97 **Da' Dip** *Freak Nasty*
Da Doo Ron Ron
'63 *Crystals*
'77 *Shaun Cassidy*
'78 **Da Ya Think I'm Sexy?** *Rod Stewart*
'73 **Daddy Could Swear, I Declare** *Gladys Knight*

'72 **Daddy Don't You Walk So Fast** *Wayne Newton*
Daddy-O
'55 *Bonnie Lou*
'55 *Fontane Sisters*
'69 **Daddy Sang Bass** *Johnny Cash*
'74 **Daddy What If** *Bobby Bare*
'90 **Daddy's Come Around** *Paul Overstreet*
'86 **Daddy's Hands** *Holly Dunn*
Daddy's Home
'61 *Shep & The Limelites*
'72 *Jermaine Jackson*
'82 *Cliff Richard*
'67 **Daddy's Little Girl** *Al Martino*
'69 **Daddy's Little Man** *O.C. Smith*
'96 **Daddy's Money** *Ricochet*
'73 **Daisy A Day** *Jud Strunk*
'75 **Daisy Jane** *America*
'63 **Daisy Petal Pickin'** *Jimmy Gilmer/Fireballs*
'92 **Dallas** *Alan Jackson*
'03 **Damn!** *Youngbloodz w/ Lil' Jon*
'92 **Damn I Wish I Was Your Lover** *Sophie B. Hawkins*
'79 **Damned If I Do** *Alan Parsons Project*
'90 **Dance, The** *Garth Brooks*
'78 **Dance Across The Floor** *Jimmy "Bo" Horne*
'06 **Dance, Dance** *Fall Out Boy*
Dance, Dance, Dance
'64 *Beach Boys*
'76 *Steve Miller Band*
'77 **Dance, Dance, Dance (Yowsah, Yowsah, Yowsah)** *Chic*
'78 **Dance (Disco Heat)** *Sylvester*
'58 **Dance Everyone Dance** *Betty Madigan*
'82 **Dance Floor** *Zapp*
'84 **Dance Hall Days** *Wang Chung*
'88 **Dance Little Sister** *Terence Trent D'Arby*
'61 **Dance On Little Girl** *Paul Anka*
'61 **(Dance The) Mess Around** *Chubby Checker*
'79 **Dance The Night Away** *Van Halen*
'79 **Dance This Mess Around** *B-52s*
'57 **Dance To The Bop** *Gene Vincent*
'68 **Dance To The Music** *Sly & The Family Stone*
'00 **Dance Tonight** *Lucy Pearl*
'82 **Dance Wit' Me** *Rick James*
Dance With Me
'59 *Drifters*
'75 *Orleans*
'78 *Peter Brown w/ Betty Wright*
'00 *Debelah Morgan*
'01 *112*
'55 **Dance With Me Henry (Wallflower)** *Georgia Gibbs*
'03 **Dance With My Father** *Luther Vandross*
'62 **(Dance With The) Guitar Man** *Duane Eddy*
'99 **Dancin'** *Guy*
Dancin' Fool
'74 *Guess Who*
'79 *Frank Zappa*
'77 **Dancin' Man** *Q*
'62 **Dancin' Party** *Chubby Checker*
'97 **Dancin', Shaggin' On The Boulevard** *Alabama*
'78 **Dancin' Shoes** *Nigel Olsson*
'79 **Dancing Barefoot** *Patti Smith*
Dancing Days
'73 *Led Zeppelin*
'95 *Stone Temple Pilots*
'84 **Dancing In The Dark** *Bruce Springsteen*
'72 **Dancing In The Moonlight** *King Harvest*
'84 **Dancing In The Sheets** *Shalamar*
Dancing In The Street
'64 *Martha & The Vandellas*
'82 *Van Halen*
'85 *Mick Jagger & David Bowie*

'74 Dancing Machine *Jackson 5*
'86 Dancing On The Ceiling
    Lionel Richie
'76 Dancing Queen *Abba*
'58 Dancing With My Shadow
    Four Voices
'81 Dancing With Myself *Billy Idol*
'67 Dandelion *Rolling Stones*
'66 Dandy *Herman's Hermits*
'64 Dang Me *Roger Miller*
'00 Danger (Been So Long) *Mystikal*
'55 Danger! Heartbreak Ahead
    Jaye P. Morgan
'86 Danger Zone *Kenny Loggins*
Dangerous
'89   *Roxette*
'91   *Doobie Brothers*
'98   *Busta Rhymes*
'79 Dangerous Type *Cars*
'66 Dangling Conversation
    Simon & Garfunkel
'06 Dani California
    Red Hot Chili Peppers
'73 Daniel *Elton John*
'63 Danke Schoen *Wayne Newton*
Danny Boy
'59   *Conway Twitty*
'67   *Ray Price*
Danny's Song
'72   *Loggins & Messina*
'73   *Anne Murray*
'85 Dare Me *Pointer Sisters*
'90 Dare To Fall In Love
    Brent Bourgeois
'04 Dare You To Move *Switchfoot*
'74 Dark Horse *George Harrison*
'74 Dark Lady *Cher*
Dark Moon
'57   *Bonnie Guitar*
'57   *Gale Storm*
Dark Star
'70   *Grateful Dead*
'77   *Crosby, Stills & Nash*
'78 Darkness On The Edge Of Town
    Bruce Springsteen
Darlin'
'67   *Beach Boys*
'81   *Tom Jones*
'76 Darlin' Darlin' Baby (Sweet, Tender,
    Love) *O'Jays*
'67 Darling Be Home Soon
    Lovin' Spoonful
'55 Darling Je Vous Aime Beaucoup
    Nat "King" Cole
'59 Darling Lorraine *Knockouts*
Daughter
'63   *Blenders*
'93   *Pearl Jam*
'70 Daughter Of Darkness *Tom Jones*
'05 Daughters *John Mayer*
'71 Dave *Cheech & Chong*
'64 Dawn (Go Away) *Four Seasons*
'65 Dawn Of Correction *Spokesmen*
'71 Day After Day *Badfinger*
Day By Day
'72   *Godspell*
'85   *Hooters*
'72 Day Dreaming *Aretha Franklin*
'66 Day For Decision *Johnny Sea*
'72 Day I Found Myself *Honey Cone*
'87 Day-In Day-Out *David Bowie*
'67 Day In The Life *Beatles*
'66 Day In The Life Of A Fool *Jack Jones*
'69 Day Is Done *Peter, Paul & Mary*
'74 Day Of The Eagle *Robin Trower*
Day The Rains Came
'58   *Raymond Lefevre*
'58   *Jane Morgan*
'99 Day The World Went Away
    Nine Inch Nails
'65 Day Tripper *Beatles*
Daybreak
'74   *Nilsson*
'77   *Barry Manilow*
'66 Daydream *Lovin' Spoonful*

Daydream Believer
'67   *Monkees*
'79   *Anne Murray*
'98 Daydreamin' *Tatyana Ali*
'78 Daylight Katy *Gordon Lightfoot*
Days Go By
'02   *Dirty Vegas*
'04   *Keith Urban*
'79 Days Gone Down (Still Got The
    Light In Your Eyes)
    Gerry Rafferty
'90 Days Like These *Asia*
'96 Days Of Our Livez
    Bone Thugs-N-Harmony
'69 Days Of Sand And Shovels
    Bobby Vinton
Days Of Wine And Roses
'63   *Henry Mancini*
'63   *Andy Williams*
'77 Daytime Friends *Kenny Rogers*
'69 Dazed And Confused
    Led Zeppelin
'76 Dazz *Brick*
'93 Dazzey Duks *Duice*
'80 De Do Do Do, De Da Da Da *Police*
'78 Deacon Blues *Steely Dan*
'67 Dead End Street *Lou Rawls*
'83 Dead Giveaway *Shalamar*
'64 Dead Man's Curve *Jan & Dean*
'73 Dead Skunk *Loudon Wainwright III*
'90 Deadbeat Club *B-52's*
Dear Heart
'64   *Jack Jones*
'64   *Henry Mancini*
'64   *Andy Williams*
'62 Dear Ivan *Jimmy Dean*
'61 Dear Lady Twist *Gary (U.S.) Bonds*
'62 Dear Lonely Hearts *Nat King Cole*
'95 Dear Mama *2Pac*
'68 Dear Mr. Fantasy *Traffic*
'62 Dear One *Larry Finnegan*
'68 Dear Prudence *Beatles*
'95 December *Collective Soul*
'75 December, 1963 (Oh, What a Night)
    4 Seasons
'59 Deck Of Cards *Wink Martindale*
'59 DeDe Dinah *Frankie Avalon*
'93 Dedicated *R. Kelly*
'66 Dedicated Follower Of Fashion
    Kinks
Dedicated To The One I Love
'59   *Shirelles*
'67   *Mamas & Papas*
'66 Dedication Song *Freddy Cannon*
'80 Deep Inside My Heart
    Randy Meisner
Deep Purple
'57   *Billy Ward*
'63   *Nino Tempo & April Stevens*
'76   *Donny & Marie Osmond*
Deeper And [&] Deeper
'70   *Freda Payne*
'84   *Fixx*
'92   *Madonna*
'90 Deeper Shade Of Soul
    Urban Dance Squad
'88 Deeper Than The Holler
    Randy Travis
'79 Deeper Than The Night
    Olivia Newton-John
'90 Deeper The Love *Whitesnake*
Deja Vu
'79   *Dionne Warwick*
'06   *Beyoncé*
'97 Deja Vu (Uptown Baby)
    Lord Tariq & Peter Gunz
'60 Delaware *Perry Como*
'58 Delicious! *Jim Backus*
'68 Delilah *Tom Jones*
'83 Delirious *Prince*
Delta Dawn
'72   *Tanya Tucker*
'73   *Helen Reddy*
'69 Delta Lady *Joe Cocker*
'06 Denial Twist *White Stripes*
'63 Denise *Randy & The Rainbows*

'79 Dependin' On You *Doobie Brothers*
'83 Der Kommissar *After The Fire*
'62 Desafinado *Stan Getz/Charlie Byrd*
'84 Desert Moon *Dennis DeYoung*
'63 Desert Pete *Kingston Trio*
'00 Desert Rose *Sting*
'71 Desiderata *Les Crane*
Desire
'80   *Andy Gibb*
'88   *U2*
'77 Desirée *Neil Diamond*
'65 Desolation Row *Bob Dylan*
'73 Desperado *Eagles*
'97 Desperately Wanting
    Better Than Ezra
'82 Destination Unknown
    Missing Persons
'81 Destroyer *Kinks*
Detroit City
'63   *Bobby Bare*
'67   *Tom Jones*
'76 Detroit Rock City *Kiss*
'74 Deuce *Kiss*
'94 Deuces Are Wild *Aerosmith*
'75 Devil In The Bottle *T.G. Sheppard*
'87 Devil Inside *INXS*
Devil Or Angel
'56   *Clovers*
'60   *Bobby Vee*
'79 Devil Went Down To Georgia
    Charlie Daniels Band
'66 Devil With A Blue Dress On
    [medley] *Mitch Ryder*
Devil Woman
'62   *Marty Robbins*
'76   *Cliff Richard*
'77 Devil's Gun *C.J. & Co.*
'05 Devils & Dust *Bruce Springsteen*
Devoted To You
'58   *Everly Brothers*
'78   *Carly Simon & James Taylor*
'74 Devotion *Earth, Wind & Fire*
'88 Dial My Heart *Boys*
'72 Dialogue *Chicago*
'74 Diamond Dogs *David Bowie*
'73 Diamond Girl *Seals & Crofts*
'65 Diamond Head *Ventures*
'87 Diamonds *Herb Alpert w/
    Janet Jackson*
Diamonds And Pearls
'60   *Paradons*
'91   *Prince*
'75 Diamonds And Rust *Joan Baez*
'05 Diamonds From Sierra Leone
    Kanye West
'86 Diamonds On The Soles Of Her
    Shoes *Paul Simon*
'57 Diana *Paul Anka*
'64 Diane *Bachelors*
Diary
'72   *Bread*
'04   *Alicia Keys*
'58 Diary, The *Neil Sedaka*
'06 Diary Of Jane *Breaking Benjamin*
'82 Did It In A Minute
    Daryl Hall & John Oates
'03 Did My Time *Korn*
'76 Did You Boogie (With Your Baby)
    *Flash Cadillac &
    The Continental Kids*
'66 Did You Ever Have To Make Up
    Your Mind? *Lovin' Spoonful*
'99 Did You Ever Think *R. Kelly*
'69 Did You See Her Eyes *Illusion*
'55 Diddley Daddy *Bo Diddley*
Didn't I (Blow Your Mind This Time)
'70   *Delfonics*
'89   *New Kids On The Block*
'87 Didn't We Almost Have It All
    Whitney Houston
'02 Die Another Day *Madonna*
'97 Difference, The *Wallflowers*
'01 Differences *Ginuwine*
'86 Different Corner *George Michael*
'67 Different Drum *Linda Ronstadt*

'79 **Different Worlds** *Maureen McGovern*
'01 **Dig In** *Lenny Kravitz*
'95 **Diggin' On You** *TLC*
'92 **Digging In The Dirt** *Peter Gabriel*
'86 **Digging Your Scene** *Blow Monkeys*
'85 **Digital Display** *Ready For The World*
'02 **Dilemma** *Nelly*
'79 **Dim All The Lights** *Donna Summer*
'55 **Dim, Dim, The Lights** *Bill Haley*
'72 **Dinay Flo** *Boz Scaggs*
'60 **Ding-A-Ling** *Bobby Rydell*
'58 **Ding Dong** *McGuire Sisters*
'75 **Ding Dong; Ding Dong**
   George Harrison
'67 **Ding Dong! The Witch Is Dead**
   Fifth Estate
'58 **Dinner With Drac** *John Zacherle*
'04 **Dip It Low** *Christina Milian*
'04 **Dirt Off Your Shoulder** *Jay-Z*
'91 **Dirt Road** *Sawyer Brown*
'89 **Dirty Blvd.** *Lou Reed*
'90 **Dirty Cash (Money Talks)**
   Adventures Of Stevie V
'90 **Dirty Deeds** *Joan Jett*
'76 **Dirty Deeds Done Dirt Cheap**
   AC/DC
'88 **Dirty Diana** *Michael Jackson*
'82 **Dirty Laundry** *Don Henley*
'06 **Dirty Little Secret**
   All-American Rejects
'66 **Dirty Water** *Standells*
'79 **Dirty White Boy** *Foreigner*
'72 **Dirty Work** *Steely Dan*
'67 **Dis-Advantages Of You** *Brass Ring*
'90 **Disappear** *INXS*
'89 **Disappointed** *Public Image Ltd.*
'76 **Disco Duck** *Rick Dees*
   Disco Inferno
'78   *Trammps*
'05   *50 Cent*
'76 **Disco Lady** *Johnnie Taylor*
'77 **Disco Lucy (I Love Lucy Theme)**
   Wilton Place Street Band
'79 **Disco Nights (Rock-Freak)** *GQ*
'75 **Disco Queen** *Hot Chocolate*
'97 **Discothéque** *U2*
'02 **Disease** *Matchbox Twenty*
'94 **Dissident** *Pearl Jam*
'96 **Distance, The** *Cake*
'66 **Distant Drums** *Jim Reeves*
'84 **Distant Early Warning** *Rush*
'74 **Distant Lover** *Marvin Gaye*
'66 **Distant Shores** *Chad & Jeremy*
'92 **Ditty** *Paperboy*
'99 **Dive** *Steven Curtis Chapman*
'92 **Divine Thing** *Soup Dragons*
'68 **D-I-V-O-R-C-E** *Tammy Wynette*
'78 **Dixie Chicken** *Little Feat*
'55 **Dixie Danny** *Laurie Sisters*
'83 **Dixieland Delight** *Alabama*
'69 **Dizzy** *Tommy Roe*
'91 **Do Anything** *Natural Selection*
'98 **Do For Love** *2Pac*
'82 **Do I Do** *Stevie Wonder*
'92 **Do I Have To Say The Words?**
   Bryan Adams
'64 **Do I Love You?** *Ronettes*
'06 **Do I Make You Proud** *Taylor Hicks*
'70 **Do It** *Neil Diamond*
   Do It Again
'68   *Beach Boys*
'72   *Steely Dan*
'85   *Kinks*
'67 **Do It Again A Little Bit Slower**
   Jon & Robin & The In Crowd
'75 **Do It Any Way You Wanna**
   People's Choice
'74 **Do It Baby** *Miracles*
   Do It For Love
'85   *Sheena Easton*
'02   *Daryl Hall & John Oates*
'79 **Do It Or Die** *Atlanta Rhythm Section*
'74 **Do It ('Til You're Satisfied)**
   B.T. Express

'06 **Do It To It** *Cherish*
'92 **Do It To Me** *Lionel Richie*
'90 **Do Me!** *Bell Biv DeVoe*
'91 **Do Me Again** *Freddie Jackson*
'85 **Do Me Baby** *Meli'sa Morgan*
   Do Me Right
'71   *Detroit Emeralds*
'91   *Guy*
'61 **Do-Re-Mi** *Lee Dorsey*
'80 **Do Right** *Paul Davis*
'67 **Do Right Woman-Do Right Man**
   Aretha Franklin
'68 **Do Something To Me** *Tommy James*
'02 **Do That...** *Baby*
'79 **Do That To Me One More Time**
   Captain & Tennille
'90 **Do The Bartman** *Simpsons*
'63 **Do The Bird** *Dee Dee Sharp*
'65 **Do The Boomerang** *Jr. Walker*
'65 **Do The Clam** *Elvis Presley*
'65 **Do The Freddie**
   Freddie & The Dreamers
'70 **Do The Funky Chicken**
   Rufus Thomas
'62 **(Do The New) Continental** *Dovells*
'70 **(Do The) Push And Pull**
   Rufus Thomas
'84 **Do They Know It's Christmas?**
   Band Aid
   Do-Wacka-Do *Roger Miller*
'64 **Do Wah Diddy Diddy** *Manfred Mann*
'84 **Do What You Do** *Jermaine Jackson*
'70 **Do What You Wanna Do**
   Five Flights Up
'76 **Do What You Want, Be What You
   Are** *Daryl Hall & John Oates*
   Do Ya
'77   *Electric Light Orchestra*
'87   *K.T. Oslin*
'77 **Do Ya Wanna Get Funky With Me**
   Peter Brown
'07 **Do You** *Ne-Yo*
'82 **Do You Believe In Love** *Huey Lewis*
   Do You Believe In Magic
'65   *Lovin' Spoonful*
'78   *Shaun Cassidy*
'92 **Do You Believe In Us** *Jon Secada*
'76 **Do You Feel Like We Do**
   Peter Frampton
'86 **Do You Get Enough Love**
   Shirley Jones
'07 **Do You Know? (The Ping Pong
   Song)** *Enrique Iglesias*
'68 **Do You Know The Way To San José**
   Dionne Warwick
'78 **Do You Know You Are My Sunshine**
   Statler Brothers
'71 **Do You Know What I Mean**
   Lee Michaels
'97 **Do You Know (What It Takes)**
   Robyn
'97 **Do You Like This** *Rome*
   Do You Love Me
'62   *Contours*
'64   *Dave Clark Five*
'96 **Do You Miss Me** *Jocelyn Enriquez*
'98 **Do You Really Want Me (Show
   Respect)** *Robyn*
'82 **Do You Really Want To Hurt Me**
   Culture Club
'90 **Do You Remember?** *Phil Collins*
'80 **Do You Remember Rock 'N' Roll
   Radio** *Ramones*
'72 **Do You Remember These**
   Statler Brothers
'70 **Do You See My Love (For You
   Growing)** *Jr. Walker*
'95 **Do You Sleep?** *Lisa Loeb*
'94 **Do You Wanna Get Funky**
   C+C Music Factory
'78 **Do You Wanna Dance** *Ramones*
'77 **Do You Wanna Make Love**
   Peter McCann
'82 **Do You Wanna Touch Me (Oh Yeah)**
   Joan Jett
'85 **Do You Want Crying**
   Katrina & The Waves

'05 **Do You Want Fries With That**
   Tim McGraw
'91 **Do You Want Me** *Salt-N-Pepa*
   Do You Want To Dance
'58   *Bobby Freeman*
'65   *Beach Boys*
'72   *Bette Midler*
'64 **Do You Want To Know A Secret**
   Beatles
   Do Your Thing
'69   *Watts 103rd Street Rhythm Band*
'72   *Isaac Hayes*
'89 **Doctor, The** *Doobie Brothers*
'84 **Doctor! Doctor!** *Thompson Twins*
'89 **Dr. Feelgood** *Mötley Crüe*
'83 **Dr. Heckyll & Mr. Jive** *Men At Work*
'77 **Doctor Love** *First Choice*
'72 **Doctor My Eyes** *Jackson Browne*
'74 **Doctor's Orders** *Carol Douglas*
'68 **Does Anybody Know I'm Here** *Dells*
'70 **Does Anybody Really Know What
   Time It Is?** *Chicago*
'84 **Does Fort Worth Ever Cross Your
   Mind** *George Strait*
   Does He Love You
'93   *Reba McEntire w/ Linda Davis*
'82 **Does It Make You Remember**
   Kim Carnes
'67 **Does My Ring Hurt Your Finger**
   Charley Pride
'96 **Does That Blue Moon Ever Shine
   On You** *Toby Keith*
'61 **Does Your Chewing Gum Lose It's
   Flavor (On The Bedpost Over
   Night)** *Lonnie Donegan*
'68 **Does Your Mama Know About Me**
   Bobby Taylor
'79 **Does Your Mother Know** *Abba*
'00 **Doesn't Really Matter** *Janet Jackson*
'05 **Doesn't Remind Me** *Audioslave*
'71 **Doesn't Somebody Want To Be
   Wanted** *Partridge Family*
'79 **Dog & Butterfly** *Heart*
'76 **Dog Eat Dog** *Ted Nugent*
'55 **Dogface Soldier** *Russ Morgan*
'60 **Doggin' Around** *Jackie Wilson*
'69 **Doggone Right** *Miracles*
'96 **Doin It** *LL Cool J*
'87 **Doing It All For My Baby**
   Huey Lewis
'73 **Doing It To Death** *JB's*
'06 **Doing Too Much** *Paula DeAnda*
'60 **Doll House** *Donnie Brooks*
'94 **Doll Parts** *Hole*
'71 **Dolly Dagger** *Jimi Hendrix*
'99 **Dolphin's Cry** *Live*
'55 **Domani (Tomorrow)** *Julius LaRosa*
'63 **Dominique** *Singing Nun*
'70 **Domino** *Van Morrison*
'88 **Domino Dancing** *Pet Shop Boys*
'87 **Dominoes** *Robbie Nevil*
'58 **Don't** *Elvis Presley*
'84 **Don't Answer Me**
   Alan Parsons Project
'66 **Don't Answer The Door** *B.B. King*
'90 **Don't Ask Me** *Public Image Ltd.*
'74 **Don't Ask Me No Questions**
   Lynyrd Skynyrd
   Don't Ask Me Why
'58   *Elvis Presley*
'80   *Billy Joel*
'89   *Eurythmics*
'92 **Don't Be Afraid** *Aaron Hall*
'63 **Don't Be Afraid, Little Darlin'**
   Steve Lawrence
   Don't Be Angry
'55   *Nappy Brown*
'55   *Crew-Cuts*
   Don't Be Cruel
'56   *Elvis Presley*
'60   *Bill Black's Combo*
'88   *Cheap Trick*
'88   *Bobby Brown*
'97 **Don't Be Stupid (You Know I Love
   You)** *Shania Twain*

'88 **Don't Believe The Hype**
Public Enemy
'61 **Don't Bet Money Honey** Linda Scott
'61 **Don't Blame Me** Everly Brothers
'67 **Don't Blame The Children**
Sammy Davis, Jr.
'07 **Don't Blink** Kenny Chesney
'62 **Don't Break The Heart That Loves
You** Connie Francis
Don't Bring Me Down
'66 Animals
'79 Electric Light Orchestra
'74 **Don't Call Us, We'll Call You**
Sugarloaf/Jerry Corbetta
'05 **Don't Cha** Pussycat Dolls
Don't Change [Dontchange]
'83 INXS
'02 Musiq
'74 **Don't Change Horses (In The
Middle Of A Stream)**
Tower Of Power
'71 **Don't Change On Me** Ray Charles
'89 **Don't Close Your Eyes** Kix
'85 **Don't Come Around Here No More**
Tom Petty
'60 **Don't Come Knockin'** Fats Domino
'73 **Don't Cross The River** America
Don't Cry
'83 Asia
'91 Guns N' Roses
'96 Seal
'61 **Don't Cry, Baby** Etta James
'69 **Don't Cry Daddy** Elvis Presley
'97 **Don't Cry For Me Argentina**
Madonna
'61 **Don't Cry No More** Bobby Bland
'78 **Don't Cry Out Loud**
Melissa Manchester
'87 **Don't Disturb This Groove** System
'79 **Don't Do Me Like That** Tom Petty
'87 **Don't Dream It's Over**
Crowded House
'98 **Don't Drink The Water**
Dave Matthews Band
'74 **Don't Eat The Yellow Snow**
Frank Zappa
'72 **Don't Ever Be Lonely (A Poor Little
Fool Like Me)** Cornelius
Brothers & Sister Rose
'57 **Don't Ever Love Me** Harry Belafonte
'79 **Don't Ever Wanna Lose Ya**
New England
'72 **Don't Expect Me To Be Your Friend**
Lobo
'80 **Don't Fall In Love With A Dreamer**
Kenny Rogers w/ Kim Carnes
'76 **(Don't Fear) The Reaper**
Blue Öyster Cult
'82 **Don't Fight It**
Kenny Loggins/Steve Perry
'56 **Don't Forbid Me** Pat Boone
'05 **Don't Forget About Us**
Mariah Carey
'64 **Don't Forget I Still Love You**
Bobbi Martin
'86 **Don't Forget Me (When I'm Gone)**
Glass Tiger
'83 **Don't Forget To Dance** Kinks
'69 **Don't Forget To Remember**
Bee Gees
'06 **Don't Forget To Remember Me**
Carrie Underwood
'96 **Don't Get Me Started** Rhett Akins
'86 **Don't Get Me Wrong** Pretenders
'69 **Don't Give In To Him** Gary Puckett
'81 **Don't Give It Up** Robbie Patton
Don't Give Up
'68 Petula Clark
'87 Peter Gabriel & Kate Bush
'77 **Don't Give Up On Us** David Soul
'91 **Don't Go** En Vogue
'97 **Don't Go Away** Oasis
'90 **Don't Go Away Mad (Just Go Away)**
Mötley Crüe
'76 **Don't Go Breaking My Heart**
Elton John & Kiki Dee
'58 **Don't Go Home** Playmates

'62 **Don't Go Near The Indians**
Rex Allen
'67 **Don't Go Out Into The Rain (You're
Going To Melt)** Herman's Hermits
Don't Go To Strangers
'56 Vaughn Monroe
'60 Etta Jones
'62 **Don't Hang Up** Orlons
'01 **Don't Happen Twice**
Kenny Chesney
'78 **Don't Hold Back** Chanson
'77 **Don't It Make My Brown Eyes Blue**
Crystal Gayle
'69 **Don't It Make You Want To Go
Home** Joe South
'65 **Don't Just Stand There** Patty Duke
'71 **Don't Knock My Love** Wilson Pickett
'89 **Don't Know Much**
Linda Ronstadt/Aaron Neville
'88 **Don't Know What You Got (Till It's
Gone)** Cinderella
'02 **Don't Know Why** Norah Jones
'98 **Don't Laugh At Me** Mark Wills
'97 **Don't Leave Me** BLACKstreet
'76 **Don't Leave Me This Way**
Thelma Houston
Don't Let Go
'58 Roy Hamilton
'79 Isaac Hayes
'84 Wang Chung
'96 **Don't Let Go (Love)** En Vogue
'77 **Don't Let It Show**
Alan Parsons Project
'81 **Don't Let Him Go** REO Speedwagon
'82 **Don't Let Him Know** Prism
'83 **Don't Let It End** Styx
'72 **Don't Let Me Be Lonely Tonight**
James Taylor
Don't Let Me Be Misunderstood
'65 Animals
'77 Santa Esmeralda
'69 **Don't Let Me Down** Beatles
'02 **Don't Let Me Get Me** P!nk
'92 **Don't Let Our Love Start Slippin'
Away** Vince Gill
'71 **Don't Let The Green Grass Fool
You** Wilson Pickett
'69 **Don't Let The Joneses Get You
Down** Temptations
'64 **Don't Let The Rain Come Down
(Crooked Little Man)**
Serendipity Singers
'67 **Don't Let The Rain Fall Down On
Me** Critters
'64 **Don't Let The Sun Catch You
Crying** Gerry & The Pacemakers
Don't Let The Sun Go Down On Me
'74 Elton John
'91 George Michael/Elton John [live]
'87 **Don't Let's Start**
They Might Be Giants
'05 **Don't Lie** Black Eyed Peas
'84 **Don't Look Any Further**
Dennis Edwards
Don't Look Back
'78 Boston
'89 Fine Young Cannibals
'87 **Don't Look Down - The Sequel**
Go West
'85 **Don't Lose My Number** Phil Collins
Don't Make Me Over
'62 Dionne Warwick
'89 Sybil
'87 **Don't Make Me Wait For Love**
Kenny G
'07 **Don't Matter** Akon
'87 **Don't Mean Nothing** Richard Marx
'65 **Don't Mess Up A Good Thing**
Fontella Bass & Bobby McClure
'66 **Don't Mess With Bill** Marvelettes
'02 **Don't Mess With My Man** Nivea
'87 **Don't Need A Gun** Billy Idol
'83 **Don't Pay The Ferryman**
Chris DeBurgh
'05 **Don't Phunk With My Heart**
Black Eyed Peas
'58 **Don't Pity Me** Dion & The Belmonts

Don't Play That Song
'62 Ben E. King
'70 Aretha Franklin
'71 **Don't Pull Your Love**
Hamilton, Joe Frank & Reynolds
'80 **Don't Push It Don't Force It**
Leon Haywood
'64 **Don't Rain On My Parade**
Barbra Streisand
'88 **Don't Rock The Boat** Midnight Star
'91 **Don't Rock The Jukebox**
Alan Jackson
'88 **Don't Rush Me** Taylor Dayne
'63 **Don't Say Goodnight And Mean
Goodbye** Shirelles
'80 **Don't Say Goodnight (It's Time For
Love)** Isley Brothers
'85 **Don't Say No Tonight** Eugene Wilde
'63 **Don't Say Nothin' Bad (About My
Baby)** Cookies
'71 **Don't Say You Don't Remember**
Beverly Bremers
'99 **Don't Say You Love Me** M2M
'63 **Don't Set Me Free** Ray Charles
'87 **Don't Shed A Tear** Paul Carrack
'89 **Don't Shut Me Out** Kevin Paige
'67 **Don't Sleep In The Subway**
Petula Clark
'96 **Don't Speak** No Doubt
'81 **Don't Stand So Close To Me** Police
'55 **Don't Start Me Talkin'**
"Sonny Boy" Williamson
'77 **Don't Stop** Fleetwood Mac
Don't Stop Believin'
'76 Olivia Newton-John
'81 Journey
'78 **Don't Stop Me Now** Queen
'81 **Don't Stop The Music**
Yarbrough & Peoples
'79 **Don't Stop 'Til You Get Enough**
Michael Jackson
'76 **Don't Take Away The Music**
Tavares
'89 **Don't Take It Personal**
Jermaine Jackson
'95 **Don't Take It Personal (just one of
dem days)** Monica
'68 **Don't Take It So Hard**
Paul Revere & The Raiders
'94 **Don't Take The Girl** Tim McGraw
'59 **Don't Take Your Guns To Town**
Johnny Cash
'75 **Don't Take Your Love** Manhattans
'04 **Don't Take Your Love Away** Avant
'82 **Don't Talk To Strangers**
Rick Springfield
'93 **Don't Tear Me Up** Mick Jagger
Don't Tell Me
'00 Madonna
'04 Avril Lavigne
'75 **Don't Tell Me Goodnight** Lobo
'89 **Don't Tell Me Lies** Breathe
'95 **Don't Tell Me (What Love Can Do)**
Van Halen
'83 **Don't Tell Me You Love Me**
Night Ranger
'00 **Don't Think I'm Not** Kandi
Don't Think Twice, It's All Right
'63 Bob Dylan
'63 Peter, Paul & Mary
'65 4 Seasons
'60 **Don't Throw Away All Those
Teardrops** Frankie Avalon
'64 **Don't Throw Your Love Away**
Searchers
'69 **Don't Touch Me** Bettye Swann
Don't Tread On Me
'92 Damn Yankees
'05 311
'91 **Don't Treat Me Bad** Firehouse
'80 **Don't Try Suicide** Queen
'94 **Don't Turn Around** Ace Of Base
Don't Walk Away
'84 Rick Springfield
'92 Jade
'97 **Don't Wanna Be A Player** Joe

'91 **Don't Wanna Change The World**
   Phyllis Hyman
'90 **Don't Wanna Fall In Love**
   Jane Child
   Don't Wanna Lose You
'89 *Gloria Estefan*
'96 *Lionel Richie*
'03 **Don't Wanna Try** *Frankie J.*
'91 **Don't Want To Be A Fool**
   Luther Vandross
'78 **Don't Want To Live Without It**
   Pablo Cruise
'81 **Don't Want To Wait Anymore** *Tubes*
'70 **Don't Waste My Time**
   John Mayall
'84 **Don't Waste Your Time**
   Yarbrough & Peoples
'61 **Don't Worry** *Marty Robbins*
   Don't Worry Baby
'64 *Beach Boys*
'77 *B.J. Thomas*
'88 **Don't Worry Be Happy**
   Bobby McFerrin
'70 **(Don't Worry) If There's A Hell**
   Below We're All Going To Go
   Curtis Mayfield
'62 **Don't You Believe It** *Andy Williams*
'67 **Don't You Care** *Buckinghams*
'85 **Don't You (Forget About Me)**
   Simple Minds
'01 **Don't You Forget It** *Glenn Lewis*
'83 **Don't You Get So Mad**
   Jeffrey Osborne
'58 **Don't You Just Know It**
   Huey (Piano) Smith
'59 **Don't You Know** *Della Reese*
'88 **Don't You Know What The Night**
   Can Do? *Steve Winwood*
   Don't You Want Me
'82 *Human League*
'87 *Jody Watley*
'74 **Don't You Worry 'Bout A Thing**
   Stevie Wonder
'79 **Don't You Write Her Off**
   McGuinn, Clark & Hillman
'58 **Doncha' Think It's Time**
   Elvis Presley
'71 **Done Too Soon** *Neil Diamond*
'58 **Donna** *Ritchie Valens*
'63 **Donna The Prima Donna** *Dion*
'64 **Donnie** *Bermudas*
'74 **Doo Doo Doo Doo Doo**
   (Heartbreaker) *Rolling Stones*
'98 **Doo Wop (That Thing)** *Lauryn Hill*
'73 **Doolin'-Dalton** *Eagles*
'64 **Door Is Still Open To My Heart**
   Dean Martin
'74 **Doraville** *Atlanta Rhythm Section*
'76 **Dose Of Rock 'N' Roll** *Ringo Starr*
'58 **Dottie** *Danny & The Juniors*
'71 **Double Barrel** *Dave & Ansil Collins*
'81 **Double Dutch Bus** *Frankie Smith*
'71 **Double Lovin'** *Osmonds*
'66 **Double Shot (Of My Baby's Love)**
   Swingin' Medallions
'76 **Double Trouble** *Lynyrd Skynyrd*
'78 **Double Vision** *Foreigner*
'90 **Doubleback** *ZZ Top*
'96 **Down** *311*
'02 **Down A** Chick** *Ja Rule*
'68 **Down At Lulu's** *Ohio Express*
'63 **(Down At) Papa Joe's** *Dixiebelles*
'91 **Down At The Twist And Shout**
   Mary-Chapin Carpenter
'89 **Down Boys** *Warrant*
'72 **Down By The Lazy River** *Osmonds*
'69 **Down By The River** *Neil Young*
'59 **Down By The Station** *Four Preps*
'95 **Down By The Water** *PJ Harvey*
'02 **Down 4 U** *Inc.*
'91 **Down Home** *Alabama*
'65 **Down In The Boondocks**
   Billy Joe Royal
'81 **Down In The Silvermine** *Diesel*
'96 **Down Low (Nobody Has To Know)**
   R. Kelly

'68 **Down On Me** *Big Brother & The*
   Holding Company
'69 **Down On The Corner**
   Creedence Clearwater Revival
'94 **Down On The Farm** *Tim McGraw*
'58 **Down The Aisle Of Love**
   Quin-Tones
'63 **Down The Aisle (Wedding Song)**
   Patti LaBelle
'91 **Down To My Last Teardrop**
   Tanya Tucker
'98 **Down Town** *Days Of The New*
'82 **Down Under** *Men At Work*
'93 **Down With The King** *Run-D.M.C.*
'60 **Down Yonder**
   Johnny & The Hurricanes
   Downtown
'64 *Petula Clark*
'89 *One 2 Many*
'93 *SWV*
'88 **Downtown Life**
   Daryl Hall/John Oates
'89 **Downtown Train** *Rod Stewart*
'63 **Drag City** *Jan & Dean*
'71 **Draggin' The Line** *Tommy James*
'04 **Dragostea Din Tei (Ma Ya Hi)**
   O-Zone
'81 **Draw Of The Cards** *Kim Carnes*
'77 **Draw The Line** *Aerosmith*
'93 **Dre Day** *Dr. Dre/Snoop Dogg*
'58 **Dream** *Betty Johnson*
'68 **Dream A Little Dream Of Me**
   Mama Cass
'95 **Dream About You** *Stevie B*
'56 **Dream Along With Me** *Perry Como*
   Dream Baby (How Long Must I
   Dream)
'62 *Roy Orbison*
'71 *Glen Campbell*
'91 **Dream Is Still Alive** *Wilson Phillips*
'59 **Dream Lover** *Bobby Darin*
   Dream Merchant
'67 *Jerry Butler*
'75 *New Birth*
   Dream On
'73 *Aerosmith*
'74 *Righteous Brothers*
'65 **Dream On Little Dreamer**
   Perry Como
'79 **Dream Police** *Cheap Trick*
'76 **Dream Weaver** *Gary Wright*
'76 **Dreamboat Annie** *Heart*
   Dreamer
'75 *Supertramp*
'80 *Supertramp [live]*
   Dreamin'
'60 *Johnny Burnette*
'89 *Vanessa Williams*
'83 **Dreamin' Is Easy** *Steel Breeze*
   Dreaming
'79 *Blondie*
'80 *Cliff Richard*
'88 *Orchestral Manoeuvres In The Dark*
'95 **Dreaming Of You** *Selena*
'94 **Dreaming With My Eyes Open**
   Clay Walker
'91 **Dreamline** *Rush*
'93 **Dreamlover** *Mariah Carey*
   Dreams
'70 *Allman Brothers Band*
'77 *Fleetwood Mac*
'86 *Van Halen*
'93 *Gabrielle*
'04 *Diana DeGarmo*
'05 *Game*
'68 **Dreams Of The Everyday**
   Housewife *Glen Campbell*
'86 **Dreamtime** *Daryl Hall*
   Dreamy Eyes
'56 *Four Preps*
'58 *Johnny Tillotson*
'72 **Dreidel** *Don McLean*
'85 **Dress You Up** *Madonna*
'89 **Dressed For Success** *Roxette*
'02 **Drift & Die** *Puddle Of Mudd*

   Drift Away
'73 *Dobie Gray*
'03 *Uncle Kracker w/ Dobie Gray*
'70 **Drifting** *Jimi Hendrix*
'78 **Driftwood** *Moody Blues*
'97 **Drink, Swear, Steal & Lie**
   Michael Peterson
'73 **Drinking Wine Spo-Dee O'Dee**
   Jerry Lee Lewis
'63 **Drip Drop** *Dion*
   Drive
'84 *Cars*
'92 *R.E.M.*
'00 *Incubus*
'02 **Drive (For Daddy Gene)**
   Alan Jackson
'57 **Drive In Show** *Eddie Cochran*
'66 **Drive My Car** *Beatles*
'92 **Drive South** *Suzy Bogguss*
'89 **Driven Out** *Fixx*
'79 **Driver's Seat** *Sniff 'n' the Tears*
'80 **Drivin' My Life Away** *Eddie Rabbitt*
'76 **Drivin' Wheel** *Foghat*
'04 **Drop It Like It's Hot** *Snoop Dogg*
'01 **Drops Of Jupiter (Tell Me)** *Train*
'56 **Drown In My Own Tears**
   Ray Charles
'01 **Drowning** *Backstreet Boys*
'71 **Drowning In The Sea Of Love**
   Joe Simon
'71 **Drum, The** *Bobby Sherman*
'67 **Dry Your Eyes**
   Brenda & The Tabulations
'65 **Duck, The** *Jackie Lee*
'01 **Duck And Run** *3 Doors Down*
'04 **Dude** *Beenie Man*
'87 **Dude (Looks Like A Lady)**
   Aerosmith
'73 **Dueling Banjos** *Eric Weissberg &*
   Steve Mandell
'62 **Duke Of Earl** *Gene Chandler*
'61 **Dum Dum** *Brenda Lee*
'55 **Dungaree Doll** *Eddie Fisher*
'94 **Dunkie Butt (Please Please Please)**
   12 Gauge
'77 **Dusic** *Brick*
'78 **Dust In The Wind** *Kansas*
'95 **Dust On The Bottle**
   David Lee Murphy
'60 **Dutchman's Gold** *Walter Brennan*
'84 **Dynamite** *Jermaine Jackson*
'75 **Dynamite** *Bazuka*

E

'96 **E-Bow The Letter** *R.E.M.*
'05 **E-Pro** *Beck*
'00 **E.I.** *Nelly*
'74 **Earache My Eye (Featuring Alice**
   Bowie) *Cheech & Chong*
   Early In The Morning
'58 *Bobby Darin*
'58 *Buddy Holly*
'69 *Vanity Fare*
'82 *Gap Band*
'88 *Robert Palmer*
'71 **Early 1970** *Ringo Starr*
   Earth Angel
'55 *Penguins*
'55 *Crew-Cuts*
'55 *Gloria Mann*
'86 *New Edition*
'96 **Earth, The Sun, The Rain**
   Color Me Badd
'63 **Easier Said Than Done** *Essex*
'66 **East West** *Herman's Hermits*
'77 **Easy** *Commodores*
   Easy Come, Easy Go
'70 *Bobby Sherman*
'93 *George Strait*
'72 **Easy Livin** *Uriah Heep*
'84 **Easy Lover**
   Philip Bailey w/ Phil Collins
'71 **Easy Loving** *Freddie Hart*
'68 **Easy Part's Over** *Charley Pride*
'69 **Easy To Be Hard** *Three Dog Night*

'77 **Easy To Love** *Leo Sayer*
'84 **Eat It** *Weird Al Yankovic*
'93 **Eat The Rich** *Aerosmith*
Ebb Tide
'64 *Lenny Welch*
'65 *Righteous Brothers*
'82 **Ebony And Ivory** *Paul McCartney*
 (w/ Stevie Wonder)
Ebony Eyes
'61 *Everly Brothers*
'78 *Bob Welch*
'69 **Echo Park** *Keith Barbour*
'73 **Eclipse [medley]** *Pink Floyd*
'73 **Ecstasy** *Ohio Players*
Eddie My Love
'56 *Chordettes*
'56 *Fontane Sisters*
'56 *Teen Queens*
'87 **Edge Of A Broken Heart**
'87 *Bon Jovi*
'88 *Vixen*
'86 **Edge Of Heaven** *Wham!*
'82 **Edge Of Seventeen (Just Like The**
 White Winged Dove) *Stevie Nicks*
'77 **Edge Of The Universe** *Bee Gees*
'78 **Ego** *Elton John*
'65 **Eight Days A Week** *Beatles*
'87 **853-5937** *Squeeze*
'66 **Eight Miles High** *Byrds*
'99 **808** *Blaque*
'81 **867-5309/Jenny** *Tommy Tutone*
'71 **Eighteen** *Alice Cooper*
'89 **18 And Life** *Skid Row*
'63 **8 X 10** *Bill Anderson*
'88 **Eighteen Wheels And A Dozen**
 Roses *Kathy Mattea*
'75 **Eighteen With A Bullet**
 Pete Wingfield
'63 **18 Yellow Roses** *Bobby Darin*
'87 **80's Ladies** *K.T. Oslin*
'04 **8th World Wonder** *Kimberley Locke*
'94 **Einstein On The Beach (For An**
 Eggman) *Counting Crows*
'75 **El Bimbo** *Bimbo Jet*
'70 **El Condor Pasa** *Simon & Garfunkel*
'60 **El Matador** *Kingston Trio*
'59 **El Paso** *Marty Robbins*
'76 **El Paso City** *Marty Robbins*
'58 **El Rancho Rock** *Champs*
'82 **El Shaddai** *Amy Grant*
'63 **El Watusi** *Ray Barretto*
Eleanor Rigby
'66 *Beatles*
'68 *Ray Charles*
'69 *Aretha Franklin*
'72 **Elected** *Alice Cooper*
'85 **Election Day** *Arcadia*
'83 **Electric Avenue** *Eddy Grant*
'88 **Electric Blue** *Icehouse*
'89 **Electric Slide (Boogie)**
 Marcia Griffiths
'89 **Electric Youth** *Debbie Gibson*
'82 **Electricland** *Bad Company*
'97 **Elegantly Wasted** *INXS*
'68 **Elenore** *Turtles*
'91 **Elevate My Mind** *Stereo MC's*
'96 **Elevators (me & you)** *OutKast*
11th Hour Melody
'56 *Lou Busch*
'56 *Al Hibbler*
'69 **Eli's Coming** *Three Dog Night*
'56 **Eloise** *Kay Thompson*
'66 **Elusive Butterfly** *Bob Lind*
'81 **Elvira** *Oak Ridge Boys*
'85 **Emergency** *Kool & The Gang*
'83 **Eminence Front** *Who*
'75 **Emma** *Hot Chocolate*
Emotion
'75 *Helen Reddy*
'77 *Samantha Sang*
'01 *Destiny's Child*
'86 **Emotion In Motion** *Ric Ocasek*
'97 **Emotional Girl** *Terri Clark*
'80 **Emotional Rescue** *Rolling Stones*

'03 **Emotional Rollercoaster**
 Vivian Green
Emotions
'60 *Brenda Lee*
'91 *Mariah Carey*
'90 **Emperor's New Clothes**
 Sinéad O'Connor
'80 **Empire Strikes Back [medley]** *Meco*
Empty Arms
'57 *Teresa Brewer*
'57 *Ivory Joe Hunter*
'82 **Empty Garden (Hey Hey Johnny)**
 Elton John
'70 **Empty Pages** *Traffic*
'59 **Enchanted** *Platters*
'58 **Enchanted Island** *Four Lads*
Enchanted Sea
'59 *Martin Denny*
'59 *Islanders*
Encore
'83 *Cheryl Lynn*
'05 *Eminem*
 (also see: Numb)
End, The
'58 *Earl Grant*
'67 *Doors*
'69 *Beatles [medley]*
'76 **End Is Not In Sight (The Cowboy**
 Tune) *Amazing Rhythm Aces*
'68 **End Of Our Road** *Gladys Knight*
'89 **End Of The Innocence** *Don Henley*
End Of The Line
'89 *Traveling Wilburys*
'91 *Allman Brothers Band*
'92 **End of the Road** *Boyz II Men*
'63 **End Of The World** *Skeeter Davis*
Endless Love
'81 *Diana Ross & Lionel Richie*
'94 *Luther Vandross & Mariah Carey*
'87 **Endless Nights** *Eddie Money*
'58 **Endless Sleep** *Jody Reynolds*
'88 **Endless Summer Nights**
 Richard Marx
'59 **Endlessly** *Brook Benton*
'99 **Enemy** *Days Of The New*
'74 **Energy Crisis '74** *Dickie Goodman*
'89 **Engine Engine #9** *Roger Miller*
'70 **Engine Number 9** *Wilson Pickett*
'65 **England Swings** *Roger Miller*
'56 **English Muffins And Irish Stew**
 Sylvia Syms
'90 **Enjoy The Silence** *Depeche Mode*
'76 **Enjoy Yourself** *Jacksons*
'06 **Enough Cryin** *Mary J. Blige*
'82 **Enough Is Enough** *April Wine*
'91 **Enter Sandman** *Metallica*
Entertainer, The
'65 *Tony Clarke*
'74 *Marvin Hamlisch/"The Sting"*
'74 *Billy Joel*
'98 **Entertaining Angels** *Newsboys*
'90 **Epic** *Faith No More*
'67 **Epistle To Dippy** *Donovan*
'74 **Eres Tu (Touch The Wind)**
 Mocedades
'92 **Erotica** *Madonna*
'05 **Errtime** *Nelly*
'90 **Escapade** *Janet Jackson*
'02 **Escape** *Enrique Iglesias*
'80 **Escape (The Pina Colada Song)**
 Rupert Holmes
'71 **Escape-ism** *James Brown*
'62 **Eso Beso (That Kiss!)** *Paul Anka*
'89 **Eternal Flame** *Bangles*
'60 **Eternally** *Sarah Vaughan*
'65 **Eve Of Destruction** *Barry McGuire*
'93 **Even A Fool Can See** *Peter Cetera*
'92 **Even Better Than The Real Thing**
 U2
'92 **Even Flow** *Pearl Jam*
'80 **Even It Up** *Heart*
Even Now
'78 *Barry Manilow*
'83 *Bob Seger*
'67 **Even The Bad Times Are Good**
 Tremeloes

'79 **Even The Losers** *Tom Petty*
'82 **Even The Nights Are Better**
 Air Supply
'78 **Ever Fallen In Love** *Buzzcocks*
'06 **Ever The Same** *Rob Thomas*
'60 **Everglades** *Kingston Trio*
Everlasting Love
'67 *Robert Knight*
'74 *Carl Carlton*
'78 *Andy Gibb*
'81 *Rex Smith/Rachel Sweet*
'89 *Howard Jones*
'97 **Everlong** *Foo Fighters*
'61 **Everlovin'** *Rick Nelson*
'61 **Every Beat Of My Heart** *Pips*
Every Breath You Take
'61 *Gene Pitney*
'83 *Police*
Every Day I Have The Blues
'55 *Count Basie*
'55 *B.B. King*
'75 **Every Day I Have To Cry Some**
 Arthur Alexander
'05 **Every Day Is Exactly The Same**
 Nine Inch Nails
Every Day Of My Life
'56 *McGuire Sisters*
'72 *Bobby Vinton*
'94 **Every Day Of The Week** *Jade*
'91 **Every Heartbeat** *Amy Grant*
'78 **Every Kinda People** *Robert Palmer*
'96 **Every Light In The House**
 Trace Adkins
'64 **Every Little Bit Hurts**
 Brenda Holloway
'86 **Every Little Kiss** *Bruce Hornsby*
'89 **Every Little Step** *Bobby Brown*
Every Little Thing
'69 *Yes*
'93 *Carlene Carter*
Every Little Thing I Do
'59 *Dion & The Belmonts*
'95 *Soul For Real*
'81 **Every Little Thing She Does Is**
 Magic *Police*
'06 **Every Mile A Memory** *Dierks Bentley*
'98 **Every Morning** *Sugar Ray*
'58 **Every Night (I Pray)** *Chantels*
'94 **Every Once In A While** *BlackHawk*
'78 **Every 1's A Winner** *Hot Chocolate*
'71 **Every Picture Tells A Story**
 Rod Stewart
'88 **Every Rose Has Its Thorn** *Poison*
Every Step Of The Way
'63 *Johnny Mathis*
'85 *John Waite*
'97 **Every Time I Close My Eyes**
 Babyface
'79 **Every Time I Think Of You** *Babys*
'77 **(Every Time I Turn Around) Back In**
 Love Again *L.T.D.*
'75 **Every Time You Touch Me (I Get**
 High) *Charlie Rich*
'79 **Every Which Way But Loose**
 Eddie Rabbitt
'80 **Every Woman In The World**
 Air Supply
'63 **Everybody** *Tommy Roe*
'98 **Everybody (Backstreet's Back)**
 Backstreet Boys
'77 **Everybody Be Dancin'** *Starbuck*
'85 **Everybody Dance**
 Ta Mara & The Seen
'90 **Everybody Everybody** *Black Box*
'86 **Everybody Have Fun Tonight**
 Wang Chung
'93 **Everybody Hurts** *R.E.M.*
'67 **Everybody Knows** *Dave Clark Five*
'64 **Everybody Knows (I Still Love You)**
 Dave Clark Five
'93 **Everybody Lay Down** *Pat Benatar*
'59 **Everybody Likes To Cha Cha Cha**
 Sam Cooke
'65 **Everybody Loves A Clown**
 Gary Lewis

Everybody Loves A Lover
'58   *Doris Day*
'62   *Shirelles*
'78   **Everybody Loves A Rain Song**
     B.J. Thomas
'62   **Everybody Loves Me But You**
     Brenda Lee
'64   **Everybody Loves Somebody**
     Dean Martin
     Everybody Needs Love
'67   *Gladys Knight*
'78   *Stephen Bishop*
     Everybody Needs Somebody To Love
'64   *Solomon Burke*
'67   *Wilson Pickett*
     Everybody Plays The Fool
'72   *Main Ingredient*
'91   *Aaron Neville*
'85   **Everybody Wants To Rule The World** *Tears For Fears*
'82   **Everybody Wants You** *Billy Squier*
'71   **Everybody's Everything** *Santana*
'92   **Everybody's Free (To Feel Good)** *Rozalla*
'99   **Everybody's Free (To Wear Sunscreen) The Speech Song** *Baz Luhrmann*
'55   **Everybody's Got A Home But Me** *Eddie Fisher*
'70   **Everybody's Got The Right To Love** *Supremes*
'80   **Everybody's Got To Learn Sometime** *Korgis*
'70   **Everybody's Out Of Town** *B.J. Thomas*
'60   **Everybody's Somebody's Fool** *Connie Francis*
'69   **Everybody's Talkin'** *Nilsson*
     Everyday
'57   *Buddy Holly*
'85   *James Taylor*
'94   *Phil Collins*
'83   **Everyday I Write The Book** *Elvis Costello*
'97   **Everyday Is A Winding Road** *Sheryl Crow*
     Everyday People
'68   *Sly & The Family Stone*
'83   *Joan Jett*
'69   **Everyday With You Girl** *Classics IV*
'65   **Everyone's Gone To The Moon** *Jonathan King*
     Everything
'89   *Jody Watley*
'97   *Mary J. Blige*
'97   *Michael Bublé*
'70   **Everything A Man Could Ever Need** *Glen Campbell*
'92   **Everything About You** *Ugly Kid Joe*
'92   **Everything Changes** *Kathy Troccoli*
'96   **Everything Falls Apart** *Dog's Eye View*
'91   **(Everything I Do) I Do It For You** *Bryan Adams*
'88   **Everything I Miss At Home** *Cherrelle*
'72   **Everything I Own** *Bread*
'85   **Everything In My Heart** *Corey Hart*
'70   **Everything Is Beautiful** *Ray Stevens*
'89   **Everything Is Broken** *Bob Dylan*
'99   **Everything Is Everything** *Lauryn Hill*
'89   **Everything Reminds Me Of My Dog** *Jane Siberry*
'85   **Everything She Wants** *Wham!*
'68   **Everything That Touches You** *Association*
'97   **Everything To Everyone** *Everclear*
'00   **Everything You Want** *Vertical Horizon*
'88   **Everything Your Heart Desires** *Daryl Hall & John Oates*
'94   **Everything Zen** *Bush*
'64   **Everything's Alright** *Newbeats*
'98   **Everything's Changed** *Lonestar*

'92   **Everything's Gonna Be Alright** *Father MC*
'70   **Everything's Tuesday** *Chairman Of The Board*
'04   **Everytime** *Britney Spears*
'06   **Everytime We Touch** *Cascada*
'85   **Everytime You Go Away** *Paul Young*
     Everywhere
'87   *Fleetwood Mac*
'97   *Tim McGraw*
'01   *Michelle Branch*
'70   **Evil Ways** *Santana*
'75   **Evil Woman** *Electric Light Orchestra*
'69   **Evil Woman Don't Play Your Games With Me** *Crow*
'66   **Evol-Not Love** *Five Americans*
'07   **Evolution** *Korn*
'99   **Ex-Factor** *Lauryn Hill*
'00   **Ex-Girlfriend** *No Doubt*
'78   **Excitable Boy** *Warren Zevon*
'91   **Exclusivity** *Damian Dame*
'03   **Excuse Me Miss** *Jay-Z*
'95   **Exhale (Shoop Shoop)** *Whitney Houston*
     Exodus
'48   *Pat Boone [This Land Is Mine]*
'60   *Ferrante & Teicher*
'60   *Mantovani*
'61   *Eddie Harris*
'77   *Bob Marley*
'55   **Experience Unnecessary** *Sarah Vaughan*
'67   **Explosion (In Your Soul)** *Soul Survivors*
'75   **Express** *B.T. Express*
     Express Yourself
'70   *Charles Wright*
'89   *Madonna*
'90   **Expression** *Salt-N-Pepa*
'67   **Expressway (To Your Heart)** *Soul Survivors*
'82   **Eye In The Sky** *Alan Parsons Project*
'82   **Eye Of The Tiger** *Survivor*
'86   **Eye Of The Zombie** *John Fogerty*
'70   **Eyes Of A Child** *Moody Blues*
'68   **Eyes Of A New York Woman** *B.J. Thomas*
'74   **Eyes Of Silver** *Doobie Brothers*
'84   **Eyes Without A Face** *Billy Idol*

F

'78   **FM (No Static At All)** *Steely Dan*
'94   **Fa All Y'all** *Da Brat*
'66   **Fa-Fa-Fa-Fa-Fa (Sad Song)** *Otis Redding*
     Fabulous
'57   *Charlie Gracie*
'02   *Jaheim w/ Tha Rayne*
'56   **Fabulous Character** *Sarah Vaughan*
'68   **Face Down** *Jumpsuit Apparatus*
'68   **Face It Girl, It's Over** *Nancy Wilson*
'85   **Face The Face** *Pete Townshend*
'86   **Facts Of Love** *Jeff Lorber Feat. Karyn White*
'01   **Fade** *Staind*
'81   **Fade Away** *Bruce Springsteen*
'94   **Fade Into You** *Mazzy Star*
'86   **Fadeaway** *BoDeans*
'00   **Faded** *SoulDecision*
'98   **Faded Pictures** *Case & Joe*
'91   **Fading Like A Flower (Every Time You Leave)** *Roxette*
'03   **Faint** *Linkin Park*
'77   **Fair Game** *Crosby, Stills & Nash*
'90   **Fairweather Friend** *Johnny Gill*
'74   **Fairytale** *Pointer Sisters*
'92   **Faith** *George Michael*
'92   **Faithful** *Go West*
'83   **Faithfully** *Journey*
'87   **Fake** *Alexander O'Neal*
'83   **Fake Friends** *Joan Jett*
'95   **Fake Plastic Trees** *Radiohead*
'67   **Fakin' It** *Simon & Garfunkel*

'94   **Fall Down** *Toad The Wet Sprocket*
'83   **Fall In Love With Me** *Earth, Wind & Fire*
'02   **Fall Into Me** *Emerson Drive*
'06   **Fall Into Sleep** *Mudvayne*
'04   **Fall To Pieces** *Velvet Revolver*
'04   **Fallen** *Sarah McLachlan*
     Fallen Angel
'76   *Frankie Valli*
'88   *Poison*
     Fallen Star
'57   *Jimmy Newman*
'57   *Nick Noble*
'01   **Fallin'** *Alicia Keys*
     Fallin' In Love
'74   *Souther, Hillman, Furay Band*
'75   *Hamilton, Joe Frank & Reynolds*
'96   *La Bouche*
     Falling
'63   *Roy Orbison*
'77   *LeBlanc & Carr*
'86   *Melba Moore*
'96   *Montell Jordan*
'97   **Falling In Love (Is Hard On The Knees)** *Aerosmith*
'86   **Falling In Love (Uh-Oh)** *Miami Sound Machine*
'00   **Falls Apart (Run Away)** *Sugar Ray*
     Fame
'75   *David Bowie*
'80   *Irene Cara*
'60   **Fame And Fortune** *Elvis Presley*
     Family Affair
'71   *Sly & The Family Stone*
'01   *Mary J. Blige*
'83   **Family Man** *Daryl Hall & John Oates*
'72   **Family Of Man** *Three Dog Night*
'02   **Family Portrait** *P!nk*
'79   **Family Tradition** *Hank Williams Jr.*
'07   **Famous** *Puddle Of Mudd*
'83   **Fanatic, The** *Felony*
     Fancy
'69   *Bobbie Gentry*
'91   *Reba McEntire*
'77   **Fanfare For The Common Man** *Emerson, Lake & Palmer*
'60   **Fannie Mae** *Buster Brown*
'75   **Fanny (Be Tender With My Love)** *Bee Gees*
     Fantastic Voyage
'80   *Lakeside*
'94   *Coolio*
     Fantasy
'78   *Earth, Wind & Fire*
'82   *Aldo Nova*
'95   *Mariah Carey*
'06   **Far Away** *Nickelback*
'78   **Far Away Eyes** *Rolling Stones*
'94   **Far Behind** *Candlebox*
'60   **Far, Far Away** *Don Gibson*
'83   **Far From Over** *Frank Stallone*
'84   **Farewell My Summer Love** *Michael Jackson*
'64   **Farmer John** *Premiers*
'86   **Farther Down The Line** *Lyle Lovett*
'57   **Farther Up The Road** *Bobby "Blue" Bland*
'87   **Fascinated** *Company B*
     Fascination
'57   *Dick Jacobs*
'57   *Jane Morgan*
'57   *Dinah Shore*
'89   **Fascination Street** *Cure*
'80   **Fashion** *David Bowie*
'93   **Fast As You** *Dwight Yoakam*
'88   **Fast Car** *Tracy Chapman*
'05   **Fast Cars And Freedom** *Rascal Flatts*
'96   **Fastlove** *George Michael*
'78   **Fat Bottomed Girls** *Queen*
'01   **Fat Lip** *Sum 41*
'98   **Father** *LL Cool J*
'71   **Father & Son** *Cat Stevens*
'77   **Father Christmas** *Kinks*
'88   **Father Figure** *George Michael*

'98 **Father Of Mine** *Everclear*
'96 **Fear Of Being Alone** *Reba McEntire*
'93 **Feed The Tree** *Belly*
'05 **Feel Good Inc** *Gorillaz/De La Soul*
'61 **Feel It** *Sam Cooke*
'86 **Feel It Again** *Honeymoon Suite*
'02 **Feel It Boy** *Beenie Man*
'78 **Feel Like A Number** *Bob Seger*
    Feel Like Makin' Love
'74   *Roberta Flack*
'75   *Bad Company*
'95 **Feel Me Flow** *Naughty By Nature*
'60 **Feel So Fine** *Johnny Preston*
    Feel So Good
'55   *Shirley & Lee*
'97   *Mase*
'94 **Feel The Pain** *Dinosaur Jr.*
'68 **Feelin' Alright?** *Traffic*
'01 **Feelin' On Yo Booty** *R. Kelly*
'78 **Feelin' Satisfied** *Boston*
'73 **Feelin' Stronger Every Day** *Chicago*
'04 **Feelin' Way Too Damn Good**
    Nickelback
'72 **Feeling Alright** *Joe Cocker*
'03 **Feeling This** *Blink-182*
'75 **Feelings** *Morris Albert*
'90 **Feels Good** *Tony! Toni! Toné!*
'77 **Feels Like The First Time** *Foreigner*
    Feels So Good
'67   *Bunny Sigler [medley]*
'78   *Chuck Mangione*
'89   *Van Halen*
'95   *Xscape*
'84 **Feels So Real (Won't Let Go)**
    Patrice Rushen
'81 **Feels So Right** *Alabama*
'94 **Feenin'** *Jodeci*
    Feliz Navidad
'70   *José Feliciano*
'05   *Jon Secada*
'61 **Fell In Love On Monday**
    Fats Domino
'94 **Fell On Black Days** *Soundgarden*
'07 **Fergalicious** *Fergie*
'76 **Fernando** *Abba*
'65 **Ferry Cross The Mersey**
    Gerry & The Pacemakers
    Fever
'56   *Little Willie John*
'58   *Peggy Lee*
'65   *McCoys*
'76 **Fez, The** *Steely Dan*
'77 **Ffun** *Con Funk Shun*
'93 **Fields Of Gold** *Sting*
'01 **Fiesta Remix** *R. Kelly*
'99 **15 Minutes** *Marc Nelson*
'76 **Fifth Of Beethoven** *Walter Murphy*
'67 **59th Street Bridge Song (Feelin' Groovy)** *Harpers Bizarre*
'75 **50 Ways To Leave Your Lover**
    Paul Simon
'83 **Fight Fire With Fire** *Kansas*
    Fight The Power
'75   *Isley Brothers*
'89   *Public Enemy*
'03 **Fighter** *Christina Aguilera*
'03 **Figured You Out** *Nickelback*
'01 **Fill Me In** *Craig David*
'87 **Final Countdown** *Europe*
'91 **Finally** *Ce Ce Peniston*
'74 **Finally Got Myself Together (I'm A Changed Man)** *Impressions*
'85 **Find A Way** *Amy Grant*
'82 **Find Another Fool** *Quarterflash*
'61 **Find Another Girl** *Jerry Butler*
'07 **Find Out Who Your Friends Are**
    Tracy Lawrence
'81 **Find Your Way Back**
    Jefferson Starship
'02 **Fine Again** *Seether*
'84 **Fine Fine Day** *Tony Carey*
'87 **Finer Things** *Steve Winwood*
'86 **Finest, The** *S.O.S. Band*
'60 **Finger Poppin' Time** *Hank Ballard*

'00 **Fingerprints Of God**
    Steven Curtis Chapman
'63 **Fingertips** *Stevie Wonder*
'88 **Finish What Ya Started** *Van Halen*
'79 **Fins** *Jimmy Buffett*
    Fire
'67   *Jimi Hendrix*
'68   *Arthur Brown*
'74   *Ohio Players*
'78   *Pointer Sisters*
'81 **Fire And Ice** *Pat Benatar*
'70 **Fire And Rain** *James Taylor*
'71 **Fire And Water** *Wilson Pickett*
'74 **Fire, Baby I'm On Fire** *Andy Kim*
'77 **Fire Down Below** *Bob Seger*
'80 **Fire In The Morning**
    Melissa Manchester
    Fire It Up ..see: Turn It Up
'80 **Fire Lake** *Bob Seger*
'75 **Fire On High**
    Electric Light Orchestra
'75 **Fire On The Mountain**
    Marshall Tucker Band
'89 **Fire Woman** *Cult*
'58 **Firefly** *Tony Bennett*
'05 **Fireman** *Lil Wayne*
'97 **Firestarter** *Prodigy*
    First Cut Is The Deepest
'68   *Cat Stevens*
'77   *Rod Stewart*
'03   *Sheryl Crow*
'57 **First Date, First Kiss, First Love**
    Sonny James
'84 **First Day Of Summer** *Tony Carey*
'59 **First Name Initial** *Annette*
'98 **First Night** *Monica*
'69 **First Of May** *Bee Gees*
'95 **1st Of Tha Month**
    Bone Thugs-N-Harmony
'63 **First Quarrel** *Paul & Paula*
    First Time
'90   *Surface*
'07   *Lifehouse*
'72 **First Time Ever I Saw Your Face**
    Roberta Flack
'80 **First Time Love** *Livingston Taylor*
'61 **Fish, The** *Bobby Rydell*
'74 **Fish Ain't Bitin'** *Lamont Dozier*
'88 **Fisherman's Blues** *Waterboys*
'87 **Fishin' In The Dark**
    Nitty Gritty Dirt Band
'88 **Fishnet** *Morris Day*
'73 **5:15** *Who*
'63 **500 Miles Away From Home**
    Bobby Bare
'97 **5 Miles To Empty** *Brownstone*
'90 **Five Minutes** *Lorrie Morgan*
'96 **5 O'Clock** *Nonchalant*
'65 **Five O'Clock World** *Vogues*
'78 **5.7.0.5.** *City Boy*
'70 **5-10-15-20 (25-30 Years Of Love)**
    Presidents
'68 **Five To One** *Doors*
'98 **Flagpole Sitta** *Harvey Danger*
'88 **Flame, The** *Cheap Trick*
'87 **Flames Of Paradise**
    Jennifer Rush (w/ Elton John)
'81 **Flamethrower** *J. Geils Band*
'61 **Flaming Star** *Elvis Presley*
'76 **Flaming Youth** *Kiss*
'66 **Flamingo** *Herb Alpert*
'78 **Flash Light** *Parliament*
'83 **Flashdance...What A Feeling**
    Irene Cara
'94 **Flava In Ya Ear** *Craig Mack*
'84 **Flesh For Fantasy** *Billy Idol*
'92 **Flex** *Mad Cobra*
'55 **Flip Flop And Fly** *Big Joe Turner*
'88 **Flirt** *Evelyn King*
'79 **Flirtin' With Disaster**
    Molly Hatchet
    Float On
'77   *Floaters*
'04   *Modest Mouse*
'96 **Flood** *Jars Of Clay*

    Flowers On The Wall
'65   *Statler Brothers*
'00   *Eric Heatherly*
'72 **Floy Joy** *Supremes*
    Fly, The
'61   *Chubby Checker*
'91   *U2*
    Fly Away
'75   *John Denver*
'98   *Lenny Kravitz*
'75 **Fly By Night** *Rush*
    Fly Like An Eagle
'76   *Steve Miller*
'96   *Seal*
    Fly Me To The Moon
'62   *Joe Harnell [Bossa Nova]*
'64   *Frank Sinatra*
'65   *Tony Bennett*
'75 **Fly, Robin, Fly** *Silver Convention*
'90 **Fly To The Angels** *Slaughter*
'81 **Flying High Again** *Ozzy Osbourne*
'56 **Flying Saucer**
    Buchanan & Goodman
'57 **Flying Saucer The 2nd**
    Buchanan & Goodman
'03 **Flying Without Wings**
    Ruben Studdard
'56 **Foggy Day** *Mel Torme*
'68 **Foggy Mountain Breakdown (Theme From Bonnie & Clyde)**
    Flatt & Scruggs
'01 **Follow Me** *Uncle Kracker*
'62 **Follow That Dream** *Elvis Presley*
'63 **Follow The Boys** *Connie Francis*
'96 **Follow You Down** *Gin Blossoms*
'78 **Follow You Follow Me** *Genesis*
    Folsom Prison Blues
'56   *Johnny Cash*
'68   *Johnny Cash [live]*
    Fool, The
'56   *Sanford Clark*
'97   *Lee Ann Womack*
'75 **Fool For The City** *Foghat*
    Fool For You
'55   *Ray Charles*
'68   *Impressions*
'89 **Fool For Your Loving** *Whitesnake*
'78 **Fool (If You Think It's Over)**
    Chris Rea
'60 **Fool In Love** *Ike & Tina Turner*
'81 **Fool In Love With You** *Jim Photoglo*
'79 **Fool In The Rain** *Led Zeppelin*
'64 **Fool Never Learns** *Andy Williams*
'61 **Fool #1** *Brenda Lee*
    Fool On The Hill
'67   *Beatles*
'68   *Sergio Mendes*
    Fool Such As I
'59   *Elvis Presley*
'73   *Bob Dylan*
'76 **Fool To Cry** *Rolling Stones*
'76 **Fooled Around And Fell In Love**
    Elvin Bishop
'83 **Foolin'** *Def Leppard*
'94 **Foolin' Around** *Changing Faces*
'78 **Fooling Yourself (The Angry Young Man)** *Styx*
'02 **Foolish** *Ashanti*
'88 **Foolish Beat** *Debbie Gibson*
'97 **Foolish Games** *Jewel*
'84 **Foolish Heart** *Steve Perry*
'63 **Foolish Little Girl** *Shirelles*
    Foolish Pride
'86   *Daryl Hall*
'94   *Travis Tritt*
'59 **Fools Hall Of Fame** *Pat Boone*
    Fools Rush In
'60   *Brook Benton*
'63   *Rick Nelson*
'61 **Foot Stomping** *Flares*
'84 **Footloose** *Kenny Loggins*
'60 **Footsteps** *Steve Lawrence*
'72 **Footstompin' Music**
    Grand Funk Railroad
'76 **Fopp** *Ohio Players*

'99 **For A Little While** _Tim McGraw_
'59 **For A Penny** _Pat Boone_
'83 **For A Rocker** _Jackson Browne_
'71 **For All We Know** _Carpenters_
'86 **For America** _Jackson Browne_
'71 **(For God's Sake) Give More Power To The People** _Chi-Lites_
'65 **For Lovin' Me** _Peter, Paul & Mary_
'67 **For Loving You**
    Bill Anderson & Jan Howard
'61 **For Me And My Gal**
    Judy Garland [live]
'61 **For My Baby** _Brook Benton_
'91 **For My Broken Heart** _Reba McEntire_
'58 **For My Good Fortune** _Pat Boone_
    For Once In My Life
'67   _Tony Bennett_
'68   _Stevie Wonder_
'97 **For The First Time** _Kenny Loggins_
'70 **For The Good Times** _Ray Price_
'70 **For The Love Of Him** _Bobbi Martin_
'74 **For The Love Of Money** _O'Jays_
'75 **For The Love Of You** _Isley Brothers_
'91 **For The Sake Of The Call**
    Steven Curtis Chapman
'81 **For Those About To Rock (We Salute You)** _AC/DC_
'86 **For Tonight** _Nancy Martinez_
'67 **For What It's Worth**
    Buffalo Springfield
    For You
'63   _Rick Nelson_
'73   _Bruce Springsteen_
'81   _Manfred Mann_
'90   _Outfield_
'97   _Kenny Lattimore_
'01   _Staind_
'97 **For You I Will** _Monica_
'06 **For You I Will (Confidence)**
    Teddy Geiger
'81 **For Your Eyes Only** _Sheena Easton_
    For Your Love
'58   _Ed Townsend_
'65   _Yardbirds_
'67   _Peaches & Herb_
'95   _Stevie Wonder_
    For Your Precious Love
'58   _Jerry Butler & The Impressions_
'63   _Garnet Mimms_
'67   _Oscar Toney, Jr._
    Forever [4 Ever]
'60   _Little Dippers_
'64   _Peter Drake_
'85   _Kenny Loggins_
'90   _Kiss_
'96   _Mariah Carey_
'03   _Lil' Mo_
'07   _Papa Roach_
'87 **Forever And Ever, Amen**
    Randy Travis
'03 **Forever And For Always**
    Shania Twain
'78 **Forever Autumn** _Justin Hayward_
'68 **Forever Came Today** _Supremes_
'56 **Forever Darling** _Ames Brothers_
'79 **Forever In Blue Jeans** _Neil Diamond_
'92 **Forever In Love** _Kenny G_
'86 **(Forever) Live And Die**
    Orchestral Manoeuvres In The Dark
'92 **Forever Love** _Color Me Badd_
'85 **Forever Man** _Eric Clapton_
'79 **Forever Mine** _O'Jays_
'91 **Forever My Lady** _Jodeci_
'91 **Forever Together** _Randy Travis_
    Forever Young
'74   _Bob Dylan_
'88   _Rod Stewart_
'89 **Forever Your Girl** _Paula Abdul_
'90 **Forever's As Far As I'll Go** _Alabama_
'63 **Forget Him** _Bobby Rydell_
    Forget Me Not
'58   _Kalin Twins_
'89   _Bad English_
'82 **Forget Me Nots** _Patrice Rushen_
'79 **Forgive Me Girl [medley]** _Spinners_

'55 **Forgive My Heart** _Nat "King" Cole_
'00 **Forgot About Dre** _Dr. Dre_
'85 **Fortress Around Your Heart** _Sting_
'99 **Fortunate** _Maxwell_
'69 **Fortunate Son**
    Creedence Clearwater Revival
'62 **Fortuneteller** _Bobby Curtola_
'83 **40** _U2_
'59 **Forty Days** _Ronnie Hawkins_
'03 **45** _Shinedown_
'85 **Forty Hour Week (For A Livin')**
    Alabama
'59 **Forty Miles Of Bad Road**
    Duane Eddy
'68 **Forty Thousand Headmen** _Traffic_
'79 **Found A Cure** _Ashford & Simpson_
'93 **Found Out About You**
    Gin Blossoms
'74 **Fountain Of Sorrow** _Jackson Browne_
'99 **4,5,6** _Solé_
'85 **Four In The Morning (I Can't Take Any More)** _Night Ranger_
'06 **4 Minutes** _Avant_
'62 **409** _Beach Boys_
'97 **4 Seasons Of Loneliness**
    Boyz II Men
'78 **Four Strong Winds** _Neil Young_
    Four Walls
'57   _Jim Lowe_
'57   _Jim Reeves_
'68 **1432 Franklin Pike Circle Hero**
    Bobby Russell
'87 **4th Of July** _X_
'73 **4th Of July, Asbury Park (Sandy)**
    Bruce Springsteen
'75 **Fox On The Run** _Sweet_
'67 **Foxey Lady** _Jimi Hendrix_
'87 **Fragile** _Sting_
'76 **Framed** _Cheech & Chong_
'72 **Francene** _ZZ Top_
'73 **Frankenstein** _Edgar Winter Group_
'59 **Frankie** _Connie Francis_
    Frankie And Johnny
'61   _Brook Benton_
'63   _Sam Cooke_
'66   _Elvis Presley_
'75 **Franklin's Tower** _Grateful Dead_
'57 **Fraulein** _Bobby Helms_
'83 **Freak-A-Zoid** _Midnight Star_
'95 **Freak Like Me** _Adina Howard_
'93 **Freak Me** _Silk_
'84 **Freakshow On The Dance Floor**
    Bar-Kays
'81 **Freaky Dancin'** _Cameo_
'95 **Fred Bear** _Ted Nugent_
'72 **Freddie's Dead** _Curtis Mayfield_
    Free
'56   _Tommy Leonetti_
'71   _Chicago_
'76   _Deniece Williams_
'95 **Free As A Bird** _Beatles_
    Free Bird
'74   _Lynyrd Skynyrd_
'88   _Will To Power [medley]_
'73 **Free Electric Band** _Albert Hammond_
'89 **Free Fallin'** _Tom Petty_
'76 **Free-For-All** _Ted Nugent_
'74 **Free Man In Paris** _Joni Mitchell_
'73 **Free Ride** _Edgar Winter Group_
'92 **Free Your Mind** _En Vogue_
'05 **Free Yourself** _Fantasia_
    Freedom
'71   _Jimi Hendrix_
'85   _George Michael_
'90   _George Michael_
'86 **Freedom Overspill** _Steve Winwood_
'70 **Freedom Rider** _Traffic_
'04 **Freek-A-Leek** _Petey Pablo_
'95 **Freek 'n You** _Jodeci_
'85 **Freeway Of Love** _Aretha Franklin_
'80 **Freewill** _Rush_
'58 **Freeze, The** _Tony & Joe_
'82 **Freeze-Frame** _J. Geils Band_

    Freight Train
'57   _Rusty Draper_
'57   _Chas. McDevitt_
'85 **Fresh** _Kool & The Gang_
'70 **Fresh Air**
    Quicksilver Messenger Service
'06 **Fresh Azimiz** _Bow Wow_
'97 **Freshmen, The** _Verve Pipe_
'92 **Friday I'm In Love** _Cure_
'66 **Friday On My Mind** _Easybeats_
'66 **Friday's Child** _Nancy Sinatra_
'89 **Friend Is A Friend** _Pete Townshend_
'67 **Friend of Mine** _Kelly Price_
'70 **Friend Of The Devil** _Grateful Dead_
    Friendly Persuasion (Thee I Love)
'56   _Pat Boone_
'56   _Four Aces_
    Friends
'68   _Beach Boys_
'71   _Elton John_
'73   _Bette Midler_
'89   _Jody Watley_
'92   _Michael W. Smith_
'86 **Friends And Lovers**
    Gloria Loring & Carl Anderson
'82 **Friends In Love**
    Dionne Warwick & Johnny Mathis
'90 **Friends In Low Places** _Garth Brooks_
'69 **Friendship Train** _Gladys Knight_
'61 **Frogg** _Brothers Four_
'90 **From A Distance** _Bette Midler_
'62 **From A Jack To A King** _Ned Miller_
'64 **From A Window**
    Billy J. Kramer w/ The Dakotas
'97 **From Here To Eternity**
    Michael Peterson
'74 **From His Woman To You**
    Barbara Mason
    From Me To You
'63   _Del Shannon_
'64   _Beatles_
'72 **From The Beginning**
    Emerson, Lake & Palmer
'00 **From The Bottom Of My Broken Heart** _Britney Spears_
'56 **From The Candy Store On The Corner To The Chapel On The Hill** _Tony Bennett_
'98 **From This Moment On**
    Shania Twain
'07 **From Yesterday** _30 Seconds To Mars_
'03 **Frontin'** _Pharrell w/ Jay-Z_
'98 **Frozen** _Madonna_
'79 **Frustrated** _Knack_
'03 **F**k It (I Don't Want You Back)**
    Eamon
'89 **F*** Tha Police** _N.W.A._
'95 **Fu-Gee-La** _Fugees_
'66 **Fugitive, The** _Merle Haggard_
'02 **Full Moon** _Brandy_
'75 **Full Of Fire** _Al Green_
'64 **Fun, Fun, Fun** _Beach Boys_
'73 **Funeral For A Friend [medley]**
    Elton John
'70 **Funk #49** _James Gang_
'94 **Funkdafied** _Da Brat_
'80 **Funkin' For Jamaica (N.Y.)**
    Tom Browne
'67 **Funky Broadway** _Wilson Pickett_
'89 **Funky Cold Medina** _Tone Loc_
'71 **Funky Nassau**
    Beginning Of The End
'68 **Funky Street** _Arthur Conley_
'73 **Funky Stuff** _Kool & The Gang_
'73 **Funky Worm** _Ohio Players_
'94 **Funky Y-2-C** _Puppies_
    Funkytown
'80   _Lipps, Inc._
'87   _Pseudo Echo_
'61 **Funny** _Maxine Brown_
'72 **Funny Face** _Donna Fargo_
'64 **Funny Girl** _Barbra Streisand_
    Funny How Time Slips Away
'61   _Jimmy Elledge_
'64   _Joe Hinton_
'94   _Lyle Lovette & Al Green_

'62 **Funny Way Of Laughin'** *Burl Ives*
'73 **Future Shock** *Curtis Mayfield*
'86 **Future's So Bright, I Gotta Wear
   Shades** *Timbuk 3*

G

'97 **G.H.E.T.T.O.U.T.** *Changing Faces*
'64 **G.T.O.** *Ronny & The Daytonas*
'66 **Gallant Men** *Senator Everett
   McKinley Dirksen*
'06 **Gallery** *Mario Vazquez*
Gallows Pole
'70   *Led Zeppelin*
'94   *Jimmy Page & Robert Plant*
'69 **Galveston** *Glen Campbell*
'78 **Gambler, The** *Kenny Rogers*
Game Of Love
'65   *Wayne Fontana & The Mindbenders*
'02   *Santana feat. Michelle Branch*
'04 **Game Over (Flip)** *Lil' Flip*
Games
'70   *Redeye*
'92   *Chuckii Booker*
Games People Play
'69   *Joe South*
'80   *Alan Parsons Project*
'66 **Games That Lovers Play**
   Eddie Fisher
'80 **Games Without Frontiers**
   Peter Gabriel
'92 **Gangsta** *Bell Biv DeVoe*
'93 **Gangsta Lean** *D.R.S.*
'02 **Gangsta Lovin'** *Eve*
'03 **Gangsta Nation**
   Westside Connection
'95 **Gangsta's Paradise** *Coolio*
'97 **Gangstas Make The World Go
   Round** *Westside Connection*
'68 **Gangster Of Love**
   Steve Miller Band
'56 **Garden Of Eden** *Joe Valino*
'72 **Garden Party** *Rick Nelson*
'04 **Gasolina** *Daddy Yankee*
'85 **Gear Jammer** *George Thorogood*
'58 **Gee, But It's Lonely** *Pat Boone*
'55 **Gee Whittakers!** *Pat Boone*
'60 **Gee Whiz** *Innocents*
Gee Whiz (Look At His Eyes)
'61   *Carla Thomas*
'80   *Bernadette Peters*
'95 **Geek Stink Breath** *Green Day*
'95 **Gel** *Collective Soul*
'81 **Gemini Dream** *Moody Blues*
'99 **Genie In A Bottle** *Christina Aguilera*
'82 **Genius Of Love** *Tom Tom Club*
'90 **Gentle** *Dino*
'67 **Gentle On My Mind** *Glen Campbell*
'71 **George Jackson** *Bob Dylan*
Georgia
'78   *Boz Scaggs*
'06   *Ludacris & Field Mob*
Georgia On My Mind
'60   *Ray Charles*
'78   *Willie Nelson*
'90   *Michael Bolton*
'66 **Georgy Girl** *Seekers*
'72 **Geronimo's Cadillac**
   Michael Murphey
'93 **Get A Haircut** *George Thorogood*
Get A Job
'58   *Mills Brothers*
'58   *Silhouettes*
'91 **Get A Leg Up** *John Mellencamp*
'98 **Get At Me Dog** *DMX*
'93 **Get Away** *Bobby Brown*
Get Back
'69   *Beatles w/ Billy Preston*
'04   *Ludacris*
'03 **Get Busy** *Sean Paul*
Get Closer
'76   *Seals & Crofts*
'82   *Linda Ronstadt*
'74 **Get Dancin'**
   Disco-Tex & The Sex-O-Lettes

Get Down
'73   *Gilbert O'Sullivan*
'78   *Gene Chandler*
'94   *Craig Mack*
'75 **Get Down, Get Down (Get On The
   Floor)** *Joe Simon*
'82 **Get Down On It** *Kool & The Gang*
'75 **Get Down Tonight**
   KC & The Sunshine Band
'05 **Get Drunk And Be Somebody**
   Toby Keith
'99 **Get Gone** *Ideal*
'90 **Get Here** *Oleta Adams*
'71 **Get It On** *Chase*
'99 **Get It On...Tonite** *Montell Jordan*
'05 **Get It Poppin'** *Fat Joe*
'83 **Get It Right** *Aretha Franklin*
'79 **Get It Right Next Time**
   Gerry Rafferty
'07 **Get It Shawty** *Lloyd*
Get It Together
'73   *Jackson 5*
'97   *702*
'71 **Get It While You Can**
   Janis Joplin
'03 **Get Low**
   Lil Jon & The East Side Boyz
'07 **Get Me Bodied** *Beyoncé*
'97 **Get Me Home** *Foxy Brown*
'67 **Get Me To The World On Time**
   Electric Prunes
'96 **Get Money** *Junior M.A.F.I.A.*
'78 **Get Off** *Foxy*
'65 **Get Off Of My Cloud** *Rolling Stones*
'72 **Get On The Good Foot**
   James Brown
Get On Up
'67   *Esquires*
'96   *Jodeci*
'89 **Get On Your Feet** *Gloria Estefan*
'76 **Get Out Of Denver** *Bob Seger*
'88 **Get Outta My Dreams, Get Into My
   Car** *Billy Ocean*
'94 **Get Over It** *Eagles*
'01 **Get Over Yourself** *Eden's Crush*
Get Ready
'66   *Temptations*
'70   *Rare Earth*
'92 **Get Ready For This** *2 Unlimited*
'56 **Get Rhythm** *Johnny Cash*
'06 **Get Right** *Jennifer Lopez*
'06 **Get Stoned** *Hinder*
'87 **Get That Love** *Thompson Twins*
'76 **Get The Funk Out Ma Face**
   Brothers Johnson
'91 **Get The Message** *Electronic*
'01 **Get The Party Started** *P!nk*
Get Together
'65   *We Five*
'68   *Youngbloods*
'96   *Big Mountain*
'06 **Get Up** *Ciara*
'76 **Get Up And Boogie (That's Right)**
   Silver Convention
'90 **Get Up! (Before The Night Is Over)**
   Technotronic
'71 **Get Up, Get Into It, Get Involved**
   James Brown
'70 **Get Up (I Feel Like Being Like A)
   Sex Machine** *James Brown*
'75 **Get Up, Stand Up** *Bob Marley*
'01 **Get Ur Freak On** *Missy Elliott*
'79 **Get Used To It** *Roger Voudouris*
'76 **Getaway** *Earth, Wind & Fire*
'85 **Getcha Back** *Beach Boys*
'06 **Get'cha Head In The Game**
   High School Musical Cast
'01 **Gets Me Through** *Ozzy Osbourne*
'91 **Gett Off** *Prince*
'98 **Gettin' Jiggy Wit It** *Will Smith*
'77 **Gettin' Ready For Love** *Diana Ross*
'06 **Gettin' Some** *Shawnna*
'67 **Gettin' Together** *Tommy James*
'90 **Getting Away With It** *Electronic*
'04 **Getting Away With Murder**
   Papa Roach

'79 **Getting Closer** *Wings*
'93 **Getto Jam** *Domino*
'91 **Ghetto, The** *Too $hort*
'73 **Ghetto Child** *Spinners*
'98 **Ghetto Cowboy** *Mo Thugs Family &
   Bone Thugs-N-Harmony*
'97 **Ghetto Love** *Da Brat*
'98 **Ghetto Supastar (That Is What You
   Are)** *Pras Michel*
'84 **Ghost In You** *Psychedelic Furs*
'91 **Ghost Of A Chance** *Rush*
(Ghost) Riders In The Sky
'61   *Ramrods*
'79   *Johnny Cash*
'80   *Outlaws*
Ghost Town
'56   *Don Cherry*
'88   *Cheap Trick*
'84 **Ghostbusters** *Ray Parker Jr.*
'65 **Giddyup Go** *Red Sovine*
'59 **Gidget** *James Darren*
'97 **Gift, The** *Jim Brickman w/ Collin
   Raye & Susan Ashton*
'03 **Gigolo** *Nick Cannon*
'82 **Gigolo, The** *O'Bryan*
'83 **Gimme All Your Lovin** *ZZ Top*
'76 **Gimme Back My Bullets** *Lynyrd
   Skynyrd*
'70 **Gimme Dat Ding** *Pipkins*
'80 **Gimme! Gimme! Gimme!** *Abba*
'69 **Gimme Gimme Good Lovin'**
   Crazy Elephant
'67 **Gimme Little Sign** *Brenton Wood*
'69 **Gimme Shelter** *Rolling Stones*
Gimme Some Lovin'
'66   *Spencer Davis Group*
'80   *Blues Brothers*
'79 **Gimme Some Water**
   Eddie Money
'06 **Gimme That** *Chris Brown*
'02 **Gimme The Light** *Sean Paul*
'73 **Gimme Three Steps**
   Lynyrd Skynyrd
'94 **Gin & Juice** *Snoop Doggy Dogg*
'62 **Gina** *Johnny Mathis*
'58 **Ginger Bread** *Frankie Avalon*
'61 **Ginnie Bell** *Paul Dino*
'62 **Ginny Come Lately** *Brian Hyland*
Girl
'05   *Destiny's Child*
'06   *Paul Wall*
Girl Can't Help It
'57   *Little Richard*
'86   *Journey*
'80 **Girl, Don't Let It Get You Down**
   O'Jays
'64 **Girl From Ipanema**
   Stan Getz/Astrud Gilberto
'89 **Girl I Got My Eyes On You** *Today*
'67 **Girl I Knew Somewhere** *Monkees*
'89 **Girl I'm Gonna Miss You** *Milli Vanilli*
'93 **Girl, I've Been Hurt** *Snow*
'66 **Girl In Love** *Outsiders*
'84 **Girl In Trouble (Is A Temporary
   Thing)** *Romeo Void*
'82 **Girl Is Mine**
   Michael Jackson/Paul McCartney
Girl Like You
'67   *Young Rascals*
'89   *Smithereens*
'95   *Edwyn Collins*
'06 **Girl Next Door** *Saving Jane*
'61 **Girl Of My Best Friend** *Ral Donner*
'79 **Girl Of My Dreams**
   Bram Tchaikovsky
'66 **Girl On A Swing**
   Gerry & The Pacemakers
'99 **Girl On TV** *LFO*
'02 **Girl Talk** *TLC*
'05 **Girl Tonite** *Twista w/ Trey Songz*
'68 **Girl Watcher** *O'Kaysions*
'64 **Girl (Why You Wanna Make Me
   Blue)** *Temptations*
'57 **Girl With The Golden Braids**
   Perry Como
'93 **Girl U For Me** *Silk*

209

'89 **Girl You Know It's True** *Milli Vanilli*
'67 **Girl, You'll Be A Woman Soon**
       Neil Diamond
'97 **Girl's Gotta Do (What A Girl's Gotta
       Do)** *Mindy cCready*
'05 **Girlfight** *Brooke Valentine*
Girlfriend
'86   *Bobby Brown*
'88   *Pebbles*
'02   **NSYNC*
'03   *B2K*
'07   *Avril Lavigne*
'84 **Girls** *Dwight Twilley*
'94 **Girls & Boys** *Blur*
'03 **Girls And Boys** *Good Charlotte*
'85 **Girls Are More Fun** *Ray Parker Jr.*
'80 **Girls Can Get It** *Dr. Hook*
'68 **Girls Can't Do What The Guys Do**
       Betty Wright
Girls, Girls, Girls
'87   *Mötley Crüe*
'01   *Jay-Z*
'62 **(Girls, Girls, Girls) Made To Love**
       Eddie Hodges
'63 **Girls Grow Up Faster Than Boys**
       Cookies
'67 **Girls In Love** *Gary Lewis*
'83 **Girls Just Want To Have Fun**
       Cyndi Lauper
'04 **Girls Lie Too** *Terri Clark*
'90 **Girls Nite Out** *Tyler Collins*
'83 **Girls On Film** *Duran Duran*
'77 **Girls' School** *Wings*
'84 **Girls With Guns** *Tommy Shaw*
'69 **Gitarzan** *Ray Stevens*
Give A Little Bit
'77   *Supertramp*
'04   *Goo Goo Dolls*
'88 **Give A Little Love** *Judds*
'64 **Give Him A Great Big Kiss**
       Shangri-Las
'72 **Give Ireland Back To The Irish**
       Wings
'80 **Give It All You Got** *Chuck Mangione*
Give It Away
'91   *Red Hot Chili Peppers*
'06   *George Strait*
Give It To Me
'73   *J. Geils Band*
'07   *Timbaland*
'81 **Give It To Me Baby** *Rick James*
'74 **Give It To The People**
       Righteous Brothers
Give It To [2] You
'95   *Da Brat*
'99   *Jordan Knight*
Give It Up
'83   *KC*
'90   *ZZ Top*
'92   *Wilson Phillips*
'94   *Public Enemy*
'69 **Give It Up Or Turnit A Loose**
       James Brown
Give It Up, Turn It Loose
'76   *Tyrone Davis*
'92   *En Vogue*
'75 **Give It What You Got** *B.T. Express*
'70 **Give Me Just A Little More Time**
       Chairmen Of The Board
'00 **Give Me Just One Night (Una
       Noche)** *98°*
'73 **Give Me Love - (Give Me Peace On
       Earth)** *George Harrison*
'96 **Give Me One Reason**
       Tracy Chapman
'80 **Give Me The Night** *George Benson*
'86 **Give Me The Reason**
       Luther Vandross
'57 **Give My Love To Rose** *Johnny Cash*
'73 **Give Me Your Love** *Barbara Mason*
'58 **Give Myself A Party** *Don Gibson*
'69 **Give Peace A Chance**
       Plastic Ono Band
'75 **Give The People What They Want**
       O'Jays
'87 **Give To Live** *Sammy Hagar*

'92 **Give U My Heart** *Babyface*
'56 **Give Us This Day** *Joni James*
'65 **Give Us Your Blessings**
       Shangri-Las
'73 **Give Your Baby A Standing Ovation**
       Dells
'98 **Given To Fly** *Pearl Jam*
'80 **Giving It Up For Your Love**
       Delbert McClinton
'64 **Giving Up** *Gladys Knight*
'89 **Giving Up On Love** *Rick Astley*
'90 **Giving You The Benefit** *Pebbles*
'88 **Giving You The Best That I Got**
       Anita Baker
'95 **Glaciers Of Ice** *Raekwon*
'64 **Glad All Over** *Dave Clark Five*
'67 **Glad To Be Unhappy**
       Mamas & Papas
'07 **Glamorous** *Fergie*
'84 **Glamorous Life** *Sheila E.*
'89 **Glamour Boys** *Living Colour*
'68 **Glass Onion** *Beatles*
'56 **Glendora** *Perry Como*
'91 **Globe, The** *Big Audio Dynamite II*
Gloria
'65   *Them*
'66   *Shadows Of Knight*
'75   *Patti Smith*
'77   *Enchantment*
'82   *Laura Branigan*
'72 **Glory Bound** *Grass Roots*
'85 **Glory Days** *Bruce Springsteen*
'86 **Glory Of Love** *Peter Cetera*
'96 **Glycerine** *Bush*
'93 **Go** *Pearl Jam*
'66 **Go Ahead And Cry**
       Righteous Brothers
'72 **Go All The Way** *Raspberries*
'97 **Go Away** *Lorrie Morgan*
Go Away Little Girl
'62   *Steve Lawrence*
'66   *Happenings*
'71   *Donny Osmond*
'70 **Go Back** *Crabby Appleton*
'58 **Go Chase A Moonbeam** *Jerry Vale*
'04 **Go D.J.** *Lil Wayne*
'98 **Go Deep** *Janet Jackson*
'71 **Go Down Gamblin'**
       Blood, Sweat & Tears
'85 **Go For Soda** *Kim Mitchell*
'07 **Go Getta** *Young Jeezy*
'85 **Go Home** *Stevie Wonder*
'84 **Go Insane** *Lindsey Buckingham*
'59 **Go, Jimmy, Go** *Jimmy Clanton*
'65 **Go Now!** *Moody Blues*
Go On With The Wedding
'56   *Kitty Kallen & Georgie Shaw*
'56   *Patti Page*
'95 **Go Rest High On That Mountain**
       Vince Gill
'97 **Go The Distance** *Michael Bolton*
'79 **Go West** *Village People*
Go Where You Wanna Go
'66   *Mamas & Papas*
'67   *5th Dimension*
'77 **Go Your Own Way** *Fleetwood Mac*
God
'70   *John Lennon*
'94   *Tori Amos*
'96   *Rebecca St. James*
'59 **God Bless America** *Connie Francis*
'69 **God Bless The Child**
       Blood, Sweat & Tears
God Bless The USA
'84   *Lee Greenwood*
'03   *American Idol*
'93 **God Blessed Texas** *Little Texas*
'61 **God, Country And My Baby**
       Johnny Burnette
'94 **God Is In Control** *Twila Paris*
'70 **God, Love And Rock & Roll**
       Teegarden & Van Winkle

**(God Must Have Spent) A Little
    More Time On You**
'98   **NSYNC*
'99   *Alabama (w/ *NSYNC)*
'66 **God Only Knows** *Beach Boys*
'77 **God Save The Queen**
       Sex Pistols
'05 **God's Will** *Martina McBride*
'77 **Godzilla** *Blue Öyster Cult*
'05 **Goin' Crazy** *Natalie*
'82 **Goin' Down** *Greg Guidry*
'71 **Goin' Mobile** *Who*
Goin' Out Of My Head
'64   *Little Anthony & The Imperials*
'67   *Lettermen [medley]*
'57 **Goin' Steady** *Tommy Sands*
'94 **Goin' Through The Big D**
       Mark Chesnutt
Going Back To Cali
'88   *LL Cool J*
'97   *Notorious B.I.G.*
'77 **Going For The One** *Yes*
'64 **Going Going Gone** *Brook Benton*
Going In Circles
'69   *Friends Of Distinction*
'86   *Gap Band*
Going To A Go-Go
'65   *Miracles*
'82   *Rolling Stones*
'71 **Going To California**
       Led Zeppelin
'70 **Going To The Country**
       Steve Miller Band
'68 **Going Up The Country**
       Canned Heat
Gold
'79   *John Stewart*
'83   *Spandau Ballet*
'05 **Gold Digger** *Kanye West*
'77 **Gold Dust Woman**
       Fleetwood Mac
'74 **Golden Age Of Rock 'N' Roll**
       Mott The Hoople
'69 **Golden Slumbers [medley]** *Beatles*
'75 **Golden Years** *David Bowie*
'65 **Goldfinger** *Shirley Bassey*
'86 **Goldmine** *Pointer Sisters*
Gone
'57   *Ferlin Husky*
'72   *Joey Heatherton*
'01   **NSYNC*
'05   *Montgomery Gentry*
'75 **Gone At Last**
       Paul Simon/Phoebe Snow
'97 **Gone Away** *Offspring*
'94 **Gone Country** *Alan Jackson*
'82 **Gone Daddy Gone** *Violent Femmes*
'64 **Gone, Gone, Gone** *Everly Brothers*
'98 **Gone Till November** *Wyclef Jean*
'77 **Gone Too Far** *England Dan &
       John Ford Coley*
'57 **Gonna Find Me A Bluebird**
       Marvin Rainwater
**Gonna Fly Now (Theme From
    'Rocky')**
'77   *Bill Conti*
'77   *Maynard Ferguson*
'95 **Gonna Get A Life** *Mark Chesnutt*
'56 **Gonna Get Along Without Ya Now**
       Patience & Prudence
'67 **Gonna Give Her All The Love I've
       Got** *Jimmy Ruffin*
'90 **Gonna Make You Sweat (Everybody
       Dance Now)** *C & C Music Factory*
'60 **Gonzo** *James Booker*
'69 **Goo Goo Barabajagal (Love Is Hot)**
       Donovan w/ The Jeff Beck Group
'95 **Good** *Better Than Ezra*
'90 **Good Clean Fun**
       Allman Brothers Band
'66 **Good Day Sunshine** *Beatles*
'07 **Good Directions** *Billy Currington*
'92 **Good Enough** *Bobby Brown*
'92 **Good For Me** *Amy Grant*
'79 **Good Friend** *Mary MacGregor*
'79 **Good Girls Don't** *Knack*

Good Golly, Miss Molly
'58 *Little Richard*
'66 *Mitch Ryder [medley]*
'76 **Good Hearted Woman**
      Waylon Jennings & Willie Nelson
'95 **Good Intentions**
      Toad The Wet Sprocket
      Good Life
'63 *Tony Bennett*
'07 *Kanye West*
'66 **Good Lovin'** *Young Rascals*
'69 **Good Lovin' Ain't Easy To Come By**
      Marvin Gaye & Tammi Terrell
'75 **Good Lovin' Gone Bad**
      Bad Company
'62 **Good Luck Charm** *Elvis Presley*
'01 **Good Morning Beautiful** *Steve Holy*
'73 **Good Morning Heartache**
      Diana Ross
'69 **Good Morning Starshine** *Oliver*
'64 **Good News** *Sam Cooke*
'69 **Good Old Rock 'N Roll** *Cat Mother*
      & the All Night News Boys
'97 **Good Riddance (Time Of Your Life)**
      Green Day
'05 **Good Ride Cowboy** *Garth Brooks*
'55 **Good Rockin' Daddy** *Etta James*
'94 **Good Run Of Bad Luck** *Clint Black*
      Good Stuff
'92 *B-52's*
'02 *Kenny Chesney*
'68 **Good, The Bad And The Ugly**
      Hugo Montenegro
      Good Thing
'66 *Paul Revere & The Raiders*
'89 *Fine Young Cannibals*
'91 **Good Things** *BoDeans*
'61 **Good Time Baby** *Bobby Rydell*
'72 **Good Time Charlie's Got The Blues**
      Danny O'Keefe
      Good Times
'64 *Sam Cooke*
'79 *Chic*
'87 *INXS & Jimmy Barnes*
'90 *Dan Seals*
'02 *Styles*
'69 **Good Times Bad Times**
      Led Zeppelin
'78 **Good Times Roll** *Cars*
      Good Timin'
'60 *Jimmy Jones*
'79 *Beach Boys*
      Good Vibrations
'66 *Beach Boys*
'76 *Todd Rundgren*
'91 *Marky Mark & The Funky Bunch*
      Goodbye
'69 *Mary Hopkin*
'85 *Night Ranger*
'92 *Tevin Campbell*
'98 *Spice Girls*
'06 *Army Of Anyone*
'58 **Goodbye Baby** *Jack Scott*
'64 **Goodbye Baby (Baby Goodbye)**
      Solomon Burke
'61 **Goodbye Cruel World**
      James Darren
'00 **Goodbye Earl** *Dixie Chicks*
'77 **Goodbye Girl** *David Gates*
'86 **Goodbye Is Forever** *Arcadia*
'59 **Goodbye Jimmy, Goodbye**
      Kathy Linden
'79 **Goodbye Stranger** *Supertramp*
'72 **Goodbye To Love** *Carpenters*
'98 **Goodbye To My Homies** *Master P*
'02 **Goodbye To You** *Michelle Branch*
'73 **Goodbye Yellow Brick Road**
      Elton John
'04 **Goodies** *Ciara*
'65 **Goodnight** *Roy Orbison*
      Goodnight My Love
'56 *Jesse Belvin*
'56 *McGuire Sisters*
'56 *Ray Peterson*
'63 *Fleetwoods*
'69 *Paul Anka*

'79 **Goodnight Tonight** *Wings*
'54 **Goodnite Sweeheart, Goodnite**
      Spaniels
'57 **Goody Goody** *Frankie Lymon*
'82 **Goody Two Shoes** *Adam Ant*
'85 **Goonies 'R' Good Enough**
      Cyndi Lauper
'02 **Gossip Folks** *Missy Elliott*
'60 **Got A Girl** *Four Preps*
'84 **Got A Hold On Me** *Christine McVie*
'91 **Got A Love For You** *Jomanda*
'58 **Got A Match?** *Daddy-O's*
'88 **Got It Bad**
      Crosby, Stills, Nash & Young
'94 **Got Me Waiting**
      Heavy D & The Boyz
'87 **Got My Mind Set On You**
      George Harrison
      Got My Mojo Working
'57 *Muddy Waters*
'66 *Jimmy Smith*
'93 **Got No Shame** *Brother Cane*
'97 **Got 'Til It's Gone** *Janet Jackson*
'02 **Got To Be Real** *Cheryl Lynn*
'78 **Got To Be There** *Michael Jackson*
'91 **Got To Get It** *Sisqó*
      Got To Get You Into My Life
'76 *Beatles*
'78 *Earth, Wind & Fire*
'65 **Got To Get You Off My Mind**
      Solomon Burke
'77 **Got To Give It Up** *Marvin Gaye*
'99 **Got Your Money**
      Ol' Dirty Bastard w/ Kelis
'97 **Gotham City** *R. Kelly*
'02 **Gots Ta Be** *B2K*
'98 **Gotta Be** *Jagged Edge*
'02 **Gotta Get Thru This**
      Daniel Bedingfield
'84 **Gotta Get You Home Tonight**
      Eugene Wilde
'07 **Gotta Go My Own Way**
      High School Musical Cast
'70 **Gotta Hold On To This Feeling**
      Jr. Walker
'99 **Gotta Man** *Eve*
'79 **Gotta Serve Somebody** *Bob Dylan*
'00 **Gotta Tell You** *Samantha Mumba*
'58 **Gotta Travel On** *Billy Grammer*
'86 **Graceland** *Paul Simon*
      Graduation Day
'56 *Four Freshmen*
'56 *Rover Boys*
'00 **Graduation (Friends Forever)**
      Vitamin C
'61 **Graduation Song... Pomp And
      Circumstance** *Adrian Kimberly*
'59 **Graduation's Here** *Fleetwoods*
'77 **Grand Illusion** *Styx*
'86 **Grandpa (Tell Me 'Bout The Good
      Old Days)** *Judds*
'78 **Grapefruit/Juicy Fruit** *Jimmy Buffett*
'63 **Grass Is Greener** *Brenda Lee*
'03 **Gravedigger** *Dave Matthews Band*
'62 **Gravy (For My Mashed Potatoes)**
      Dee Dee Sharp
      Grazing In The Grass
'68 *Hugh Masekela*
'69 *Friends Of Distinction*
'78 **Grease** *Frankie Valli*
'96 **Grease Megamix** *John Travolta &*
      Olivia Newton-John
'68 **Greasy Heart** *Jefferson Airplane*
'92 **Great Adventure**
      Steven Curtis Chapman
'66 **Great Airplane Strike**
      Paul Revere & The Raiders
'57 **Great Balls Of Fire** *Jerry Lee Lewis*
'06 **Great Big Sled** *Killers*
'88 **Great Commandment** *Camouflage*
'07 **Great Escape** *Boys Like Girls*
'73 **Great Gig In The Sky**
      Pink Floyd
'55 **Great Pretender** *Platters*
'99 **Greatest, The** *Kenny Rogers*

      Greatest Love Of All
'77 *George Benson*
'86 *Whitney Houston*
'92 **Greatest Man I Never Knew**
      Reba McEntire
'01 **Greed** *Godsmack*
'96 **Greedy Fly** *Bush*
'56 **Green Door** *Jim Lowe*
'70 **Green-Eyed Lady** *Sugarloaf*
'66 **Green Grass** *Gary Lewis*
'75 **Green Grass & High Tides** *Outlaws*
'70 **Green Grass Starts To Grow**
      Dionne Warwick
'63 **Green, Green** *New Christy Minstrels*
'66 **Green, Green Grass Of Home**
      Tom Jones
'68 **Green Light** *American Breed*
'62 **Green Onions** *Booker T. & The MG's*
'69 **Green River**
      Creedence Clearwater Revival
'67 **Green Tambourine** *Lemon Pipers*
'63 **Greenback Dollar** *Kingston Trio*
'60 **Greenfields** *Brothers Four*
'02 **Grey Street** *Dave Matthews Band*
'06 **Grillz** *Nelly*
'05 **Grind With Me** *Pretty Ricky*
'02 **Grindin'** *Clipse*
'90 **Groove Is In The Heart** *Deee-Lite*
'78 **Groove Line** *Heatwave*
'70 **Groove Me** *King Floyd*
'94 **Groove Thang** *Zhané*
      Groovin'
'67 *Booker T. & The M.G.'s*
'67 *Young Rascals*
'69 **Groovy Grubworm** *Harlow Wilcox*
      Groovy Kind Of Love
'66 *Mindbenders*
'88 *Phil Collins*
'70 **Groovy Situation** *Gene Chandler*
'76 **Grow Some Funk Of Your Own**
      Elton John
'01 **Grown Men Don't Cry** *Tim McGraw*
'66 **Guantanamera** *Sandpipers*
'58 **Guess Things Happen That Way**
      Johnny Cash
'59 **Guess Who** *Jesse Belvin*
'80 **Guilty** *Barbra Streisand & Barry Gibb*
'59 **Guitar Boogie Shuffle** *Virtues*
      Guitar Man
'68 *Elvis Presley*
'72 *Bread*
'86 **Guitar Town** *Steve Earle*
'86 **Guitars, Cadillacs** *Dwight Yoakam*
'55 **Gum Drop** *Crew-Cuts*
'96 **Guys Do It All The Time**
      Mindy McCready
'82 **Gypsy** *Fleetwood Mac*
'63 **Gypsy Cried** *Lou Christie*
'73 **Gypsy Man** *War*
'70 **Gypsy Queen [medley]** *Santana*
      Gypsy Woman
'61 *Impressions*
'63 *Brian Hyland*
'91 **Gypsy Woman (She's Homeless)**
      Crystal Waters
'71 **Gypsys, Tramps & Thieves** *Cher*

H

'96 **Hail, Hail** *Pearl Jam*
'69 **Hair** *Cowsills*
'75 **Hair Of The Dog** *Nazareth*
'66 **Hair On My Chinny Chin Chin**
      Sam The Sham & The Pharoahs
'73 **Half-Breed** *Cher*
'02 **Halfcrazy** *Musiq*
'62 **Half Heaven - Half Heartache**
      Gene Pitney
'79 **Half The Way** *Crystal Gayle*
      Halfway To Paradise
'61 *Tony Orlando*
'68 *Bobby Vinton*
      Hallelujah
'71 *Sweathog*
'94 *Jeff Buckley*

'73 **Hallelujah Day** *Jackson 5*
'95 **Hand In My Pocket** *Alanis Morissette*
'70 **Hand Me Down World** *Guess Who*
'05 **Hand That Feeds** *Nine Inch Nails*
'82 **Hand To Hold On To**
   John Cougar Mellencamp
'69 **Handbags And Gladrags**
   Rod Stewart
'88 **Handle With Care** *Traveling Wilburys*
'98 **Hands** *Jewel*
'02 **Hands Clean** *Alanis Morissette*
'55 **Hands Off** *Jay McShann*
'88 **Hands To Heaven** *Breathe*
   Handy Man
'59   *Jimmy Jones*
'64   *Del Shannon*
'77   *James Taylor*
'68 **Hang 'Em High**
   Booker T. & The MG's
'82 **Hang Fire** *Rolling Stones*
'90 **Hang In Long Enough** *Phil Collins*
'74 **Hang On In There Baby**
   Johnny Bristol
   Hang On Sloopy
'64   *Vibrations [My Girl]*
'65   *Ramsey Lewis Trio*
'65   *McCoys*
'58 **Hang Up My Rock And Roll Shoes**
   Chuck Willis
'99 **Hanginaround** *Counting Crows*
'85 **Hangin' On A String**
   (Contemplating) *Loose Ends*
'89 **Hangin' Tough**
   New Kids On The Block
'01 **Hanging By A Moment** *Lifehouse*
'86 **Hanging On A Heart Attack** *Device*
'59 **Hanging Tree** *Marty Robbins*
   Hanky Panky
'66   *Tommy James*
'90   *Madonna*
   Happening
'67   *Herb Alpert*
'67   *Supremes*
'66 **Happenings Ten Years Time Ago**
   Yardbirds
'72 **Happiest Girl In The Whole U.S.A.**
   Donna Fargo
'99 **Happily Ever After** *Case*
'79 **Happiness** *Pointer Sisters*
'74 **Happiness Is Just Around The**
   Bend *Main Ingredient*
   Happiness Street (Corner Sunshine
   Square)
'56   *Tony Bennett*
'56   *Georgia Gibbs*
   Happy
'72   *Rolling Stones*
'87   *Surface*
'02   *Ashanti*
'05   *Mudvayne*
'77 **Happy Anniversary** *Little River Band*
'61 **Happy Birthday Blues** *Kathy Young*
'61 **Happy Birthday, Sweet Sixteen**
   Neil Sedaka
'76 **Happy Days** *Pratt & McClain*
'63 **Happy Days Are Here Again**
   Barbra Streisand
'98 **Happy Girl** *Martina McBride*
'60 **Happy-Go-Lucky-Me** *Paul Evans*
'57 **Happy, Happy Birthday Baby**
   Tune Weavers
'69 **Happy Heart** *Andy Williams*
'67 **Happy Jack** *Who*
'76 **Happy Music** *Blackbyrds*
'59 **Happy Organ** *Dave 'Baby' Cortez*
   Happy People
'74   *Temptations*
'04   *R. Kelly*
'59 **Happy Reindeer**
   Dancer, Prancer & Nervous
'68 **Happy Song (Dum-Dum)**
   Otis Redding
'66 **Happy Summer Days** *Ronnie Dove*
'67 **Happy Together** *Turtles*
'87 **Happy Wanderer** *Brave Combo*
'56 **Happy Whistler** *Don Robertson*

'71 **Happy Xmas (War Is Over)** *John*
   Lennon
'60 **Harbor Lights** *Platters*
'95 **Hard As A Rock** *AC/DC*
   Hard Day's Night
'64   *Beatles*
'66   *Ramsey Lewis Trio*
'84 **Hard Habit To Break** *Chicago*
'58 **Hard Headed Woman** *Elvis Presley*
'98 **Hard Knock Life (Ghetto Anthem)**
   Jay-Z
   Hard Luck Woman
'76   *Kiss*
'94   *Garth Brooks*
'63 **Hard Rain's-A-Gonna Fall**
   Bob Dylan
'90 **Hard Rock Bottom Of Your Heart**
   Randy Travis
'77 **Hard Rock Cafe** *Carole King*
'55 **Hard To Get** *Gisele MacKenzie*
'90 **Hard To Handle** *Black Crowes*
'81 **Hard To Say** *Dan Fogelberg*
   Hard To Say I'm Sorry
'82   *Chicago*
'97   *Az Yet*
'81 **Harden My Heart** *Quarterflash*
'75 **Harder They Come** *Jimmy Cliff*
'03 **Harder To Breathe** *Maroon5*
'99 **Hardest Thing** *98°*
'59 **Harlem Nocturne** *Viscounts*
   Harlem Shuffle
'63   *Bob & Earl*
'86   *Rolling Stones*
'73 **Harmony** *Elton John*
'68 **Harper Valley P.T.A.**
   Jeannie C. Riley
'72 **Harry Hippie** *Bobby Womack*
'63 **Harry The Hairy Ape** *Ray Stevens*
'75 **Harry Truman** *Chicago*
'01 **Hash Pipe** *Weezer*
'93 **Hat 2 Da Back** *TLC*
'05 **Hate It Or Love It** *Game*
'06 **Hate Me** *Blue October*
'88 **Hate To Lose Your Lovin'** *Little Feat*
'61 **Hats Off To Larry** *Del Shannon*
'64 **Haunted House** *Gene Simmons*
'76 **Havana Daydreamin'** *Jimmy Buffett*
'75 **Have A Cigar** *Pink Floyd*
'62 **Have A Good Time** *Sue Thompson*
'90 **Have A Heart** *Bonnie Raitt*
'64 **Have I The Right?** *Honeycombs*
'93 **Have I Told You Lately**
   Rod Stewart [live]
'85 **Have Mercy** *Judds*
98 **Have You Ever?** *Brandy*
'03 **Have You Ever Been In Love**
   Celine Dion
'86 **Have You Ever Loved Somebody**
   Freddie Jackson
'92 **Have You Ever Needed Someone**
   So Bad *Def Leppard*
'95 **Have You Ever Really Loved A**
   Woman? *Bryan Adams*
'71 **Have You Ever Seen The Rain**
   Creedence Clearwater Revival
'03 **Have You Forgotten?** *Darryl Worley*
'89 **Have You Had Your Love Today**
   O'Jays
'63 **Have You Heard** *Duprees*
'64 **Have You Looked Into Your Heart**
   Jerry Vale
'75 **Have You Never Been Mellow**
   Olivia Newton-John
   Have You Seen Her
'71   *Chi-Lites*
'90   *M.C. Hammer*
'66 **Have You Seen Your Mother, Baby,**
   Standing In The Shadow?
   Rolling Stones
'74 **Haven't Got Time For The Pain**
   Carly Simon
'79 **Haven't Stopped Dancing Yet**
   Gonzalez
'61 **Havin' Fun** *Dion*

   Having A Party
'62   *Sam Cooke*
'82   *Luther Vandross [medley]*
'94   *Rod Stewart w/ Ronnie Wood*
'69 **Hawaii Five-O** *Ventures*
'64 **Hawaii Tattoo** *Waikikis*
'58 **Hawaiian Wedding Song**
   Andy Williams
'96 **Hay** *Crucial Conflict*
'92 **Hazard** *Richard Marx*
   Hazy Shade Of Winter
'66   *Simon & Garfunkel*
'87   *Bangles*
   He
'55   *Al Hibbler*
'55   *McGuire Sisters*
'66   *Righteous Brothers*
   He Ain't Heavy, He's My Brother
'69   *Hollies*
'70   *Neil Diamond*
   He Can't Love You [U]
'80   *Michael Stanley Band*
'99   *Jagged Edge*
'99 **He Didn't Have To Be** *Brad Paisley*
   He Don't Love You (Like I Love
   You)
'60   *Jerry Butler*
'75   *Tony Orlando & Dawn*
'86 **He Is Exalted** *Twila Paris*
'62 **He Knows I Love Him Too Much**
   Paris Sisters
'00 **He Loves U Not** *Dream*
'03 **He Reigns** *Newsboys*
'80 **He Stopped Loving Her Today**
   George Jones
'93 **He Thinks He'll Keep Her**
   Mary Chapin Carpenter
'65 **He Touched Me** *Barbra Streisand*
'90 **He Walked On Water** *Randy Travis*
'65 **He Was A Friend Of Mine** *Byrds*
'00 **He Wasn't Man Enough**
   Toni Braxton
   He Will Break Your Heart ..see: He
   Don't Love You (Like I Love You)
   He'll Have To Go [Stay]
'59   *Jim Reeves*
'60   *Jeanne Black*
'85 **He'll Never Love You (Like I Do)**
   Freddie Jackson
'76 **He's A Friend** *Eddie Kendricks*
'81 **He's A Liar** *Bee Gees*
'62 **He's A Rebel** *Crystals*
'57 **He's Gone** *Chantels*
'58 **He's Got The Whole World (In His**
   Hands) *Laurie London*
'97 **He's Got You** *Brooks & Dunn*
   He's Mine
'57   *Platters*
'95   *MoKenStef*
'61 **(He's My) Dreamboat**
   Connie Francis
   He's So Fine
'63   *Chiffons*
'71   *Jody Miller*
'80 **He's So Shy** *Pointer Sisters*
'62 **He's Sure The Boy I Love** *Crystals*
'61 **(He's) The Great Impostor**
   Fleetwoods
'79 **He's The Greatest Dancer**
   Sister Sledge
'79 **Head Games** *Foreigner*
'90 **Head On** *Jesus & Mary Chain*
'96 **Head Over Feet** *Alanis Morissette*
   Head Over Heels
'84   *Go-Go's*
'85   *Tears For Fears*
'97   *Allure*
'87 **Head To Toe** *Lisa Lisa & Cult Jam*
'80 **Headed For A Fall** *Firefall*
'89 **Headed For A Heartbreak** *Winger*
'86 **Headlines** *Midnight Star*
'96 **Heads Carolina, Tails California**
   Jo Dee Messina
'04 **Headsprung** *LL Cool J*
'02 **Headstrong** *Trapt*
'92 **Heal The World** *Michael Jackson*

'89 **Healing Hands** *Elton John*
'70 **Hear My Train A Comin'** *Jimi Hendrix*
'05 **Heard 'Em Say** *Kanye West*
'01 **Heard It All Before**
    Sunshine Anderson
'77 **Heard It In A Love Song**
    Marshall Tucker Band
'75 **Heard It On The X** *ZZ Top*
Heart
'55   *Eddie Fisher*
'55   *Four Aces*
Heart And Soul
'61   *Cleftones*
'61   *Jan & Dean*
'83   *Huey Lewis*
'87   *T'Pau*
'82 **Heart Attack** *Olivia Newton-John*
'65 **Heart Full Of Soul** *Yardbirds*
'80 **Heart Hotels** *Dan Fogelberg*
'62 **Heart In Hand** *Brenda Lee*
'95 **Heart Is A Lonely Hunter**
    Reba McEntire
Heart Like A Wheel
'81   *Steve Miller Band*
'90   *Human League*
'79 **Heart Of Glass** *Blondie*
'72 **Heart Of Gold** *Neil Young*
'88 **Heart Of Mine** *Boz Scaggs*
'84 **Heart Of Rock & Roll** *Huey Lewis*
Heart Of Stone
'65   *Rolling Stones*
'90   *Taylor Dayne*
'90   *Cher*
'90 **Heart Of The Matter** *Don Henley*
Heart Of The Night
'79   *Poco*
'82   *Juice Newton*
'93 **Heart-Shaped Box** *Nirvana*
'82 **Heart To Heart** *Kenny Loggins*
'93 **Heart Won't Lie**
    Reba McEntire & Vince Gill
'79 **Heartache Tonight** *Eagles*
'61 **Heartaches** *Marcels*
Heartaches By The Number
'59   *Guy Mitchell*
'65   *Johnny Tillotson*
Heartbeat
'58   *Buddy Holly*
'86   *Don Johnson*
'90   *Seduction*
'73 **Heartbeat - It's A Lovebeat**
    DeFranco Family
'87 **Heartbreak Beat** *Psychedelic Furs*
Heartbreak Hotel
'56   *Elvis Presley*
'56   *Stan Freberg*
'80   *Jacksons*
'98   *Whitney Houston*
'60 **Heartbreak (It's Hurtin' Me)**
    Little Willie John
'74 **Heartbreak Kid** *Bo Donaldson*
Heartbreaker
'69   *Led Zeppelin*
'78   *Dolly Parton*
'79   *Pat Benatar*
'82   *Dionne Warwick*
'99   *Mariah Carey*
'93 **Heartland** *George Strait*
'78 **Heartless** *Heart*
'82 **Heartlight** *Neil Diamond*
'81 **Hearts** *Marty Balin*
'93 **Hearts Are Gonna Roll** *Hal Ketchum*
'91 **Hearts Don't Think (They Feel)!**
    Natural Selection
Hearts Of Stone
'55   *Fontane Sisters*
'56   *Charms*
'61   *Bill Black's Combo*
'73   *John Fogerty*
Hearts On Fire
'81   *Randy Meisner*
'87   *Bryan Adams*
'84 **Heat Is On** *Glenn Frey*

Heat Of The Moment
'82   *Asia*
'89   *After 7*
'87 **Heat Of The Night** *Bryan Adams*
Heat Wave
'63   *Martha & The Vandellas*
'75   *Linda Ronstadt*
'69 **Heather Honey** *Tommy Roe*
'88 **Heatseeker** *AC/DC*
Heaven
'69   *Rascals*
'85   *Bryan Adams*
'89   *Warrant*
'89   *BeBe & CeCe Winans*
'97   *Nu Flavor*
'02   *DJ Sammy & Yanou*
'03   *Live*
'04   *Los Lonely Boys*
'95 **Heaven Beside You** *Alice In Chains*
'89 **Heaven Help Me** *Deon Estus*
'70 **Heaven Help Us All** *Stevie Wonder*
'86 **Heaven In Your Eyes** *Loverboy*
'87 **Heaven Is A Place On Earth**
    Belinda Carlisle
Heaven Knows
'69   *Grass Roots*
'79   *Donna Summer*
'88   *Robert Plant*
'90   *Lalah Hathaway*
'84 **Heaven Knows I'm Miserable Now**
    Smiths
'76 **Heaven Must Be Missing An Angel**
    Tavares
'79 **Heaven Must Have Sent You**
    Bonnie Pointer
'77 **Heaven On The 7th Floor**
    Paul Nicholas
'68 **Heaven Says Hello** *Sonny James*
'92 **Heaven Sent** *INXS*
'77 **Heaven's Just A Sin Away** *Kendalls*
'98 **Heaven's What I Feel** *Gloria Estefan*
'99 **Heavy** *Collective Soul*
'91 **Heavy Fuel** *Dire Straits*
'71 **Heavy Makes You Happy**
    (Sha-Na-Boom Boom)
    Staple Singers
'81 **Heavy Metal (Takin' A Ride)**
    Don Felder
'56 **Heeby Jeebies** *Little Richard*
'70 **Heed The Call** *Kenny Rogers &*
    The First Edition
'73 **Helen Wheels** *Paul McCartney*
'05 **Helena (So Long & Goodnight)**
    My Chemical Romance
'87 **Hell In A Bucket** *Grateful Dead*
'80 **Hell Is For Children**
    Pat Benatar
'03 **Hell Yeah** *Ginuwine*
'02 **Hella Good** *No Doubt*
'84 **Hello** *Lionel Richie*
Hello Again
'81   *Neil Diamond*
'84   *Cars*
'70 **Hello Darlin'** *Conway Twitty*
'64 **Hello, Dolly!** *Louis Armstrong*
'67 **Hello Goodbye** *Beatles*
'63 **Hello Heartache, Goodbye Love**
    Little Peggy March
'66 **Hello Hello** *Sopwith "Camel"*
'73 **Hello Hurray** *Alice Cooper*
'68 **Hello, I Love You** *Doors*
Hello It's Me
'69   *Nazz*
'73   *Todd Rundgren*
'61 **Hello Mary Lou** *Ricky Nelson*
'63 **Hello Mudduh, Hello Fadduh!**
    Allan Sherman
'76 **Hello Old Friend** *Eric Clapton*
Hello Stranger
'63   *Barbara Lewis*
'77   *Yvonne Elliman*
'61 **Hello Walls** *Faron Young*
'60 **Hello Young Lovers** *Paul Anka*
'80 **Hells Bells** *AC/DC*
'65 **Help!** *Beatles*
'77 **Help Is On Its Way** *Little River Band*

'74 **Help Me** *Joni Mitchell*
Help Me Girl
'66   *Animals*
'66   *Outsiders*
'90 **Help Me Hold On** *Travis Tritt*
Help Me Make It Through The Night
'71   *Sammi Smith*
'72   *Gladys Knight*
Help Me, Rhonda
'65   *Beach Boys*
'75   *Johnny Rivers*
'03 **Help Pour Out The Rain (Lacey's**
    Song) *Buddy Jewell*
'68 **Help Yourself** *Tom Jones*
'70 **Helpless**
    Crosby, Stills, Nash & Young
'69 **Helplessly Hoping**
    Crosby, Stills, Nash & Young
'68 **Helter Skelter** *Beatles*
'00 **Hemorrhage (In My Hands)** *Fuel*
'58 **Henrietta** *Jimmy Dee*
'69 **Her Majesty [medley]** *Beatles*
'62 **Her Royal Majesty** *James Darren*
'80 **Her Strut** *Bob Seger*
'81 **Her Town Too**
    James Taylor & J.D. Souther
'09 **Here And Now** *Luther Vandross*
'77 **Here Come Those Tears Again**
    Jackson Browne
'67 **Here Comes My Baby** *Tremeloes*
'79 **Here Comes My Girl** *Tom Petty*
'59 **Here Comes Summer** *Jerry Keller*
'71 **Here Comes That Rainy Day**
    Feeling Again *Fortunes*
'94 **Here Comes The Hotstepper**
    Ini Kamoze
Here Comes The Judge
'68   *Shorty Long*
'68   *Pigmeat Markham*
'65 **Here Comes The Night** *Them*
'84 **Here Comes The Rain Again**
    Eurythmics
Here Comes The Sun
'69   *Beatles*
'71   *Richie Havens*
'89 **Here Comes Your Man** *Pixies*
'04 **Here For The Party** *Gretchen Wilson*
Here I Am (Come And Take Me)
'73   *Al Green*
'91   *UB40*
'81 **Here I Am (Just When I Thought I**
    Was Over You) *Air Supply*
Here I Go Again
'69   *Miracles*
'87   *Whitesnake*
'92   *Glenn Jones*
'97 **Here In My Heart** *Chicago*
'90 **Here In The Real World**
    Alan Jackson
'07 **Here (In Your Arms)** *HelloGoodbye*
'02 **Here Is Gone** *Goo Goo Dolls*
'65 **Here It Comes Again** *Fortunes*
'06 **Here It Goes Again** *OK Go*
Here We Are
'89   *Gloria Estefan*
'91   *Alabama*
Here We Go
'91   *C + C Music Factory*
'05   *Trina w/ Kelly Rowland*
Here We Go Again
'67   *Ray Charles*
'92   *Portrait*
'92   *Norah Jones w/ Ray Charles*
Here With Me
'88   *REO Speedwagon*
'04   *MercyMe*
'03 **Here Without You** *3 Doors Down*
'77 **Here You Come Again** *Dolly Parton*
'91 **Here's A Quarter (Call Someone**
    Who Cares) *Travis Tritt*
'01 **Here's To The Night** *Eve 6*
'90 **Here's Where The Story Ends**
    Sundays
'97 **Here's Your Sign**
    Bill Engvall w/ Travis Tritt

Hero
'93 *Mariah Carey*
'93 *David Crosby & Phil Collins*
'01 *Enrique Iglesias*
'02 *Chad Kroeger*
'96 Hero Of The Day *Metallica*
Heroes
'77 *David Bowie*
'98 *Wallflowers*
'67 Heroes And Villains *Beach Boys*
'67 Heroin *Velvet Underground*
Hey Baby
'62 *Bruce Channel*
'75 *Ted Nugent*
'89 *Henry Lee Summer*
'01 *No Doubt*
'67 Hey Baby (They're Playing Our Song) *Buckinghams*
'79 Hey Bartender *Blues Brothers*
'71 Hey Big Brother *Rare Earth*
'57 Hey Bo Diddley *Bo Diddley*
'64 Hey, Bobba Needle *Chubby Checker*
'77 Hey Deanie *Shaun Cassidy*
'71 Hey Diddle *Paul McCartney*
'91 Hey Donna *Rythm Syndicate*
Hey, Girl
'63 *Freddie Scott*
'71 *Donny Osmond*
'73 Hey Girl (I Like Your Style) *Temptations*
'67 Hey Grandma *Moby Grape*
'64 Hey Harmonica Man *Stevie Wonder*
'79 Hey Hey, My My (Into The Black) *Neil Young*
'56 Hey! Jealous Lover *Frank Sinatra*
'93 Hey Jealousy *Gin Blossoms*
'64 Hey Jean, Hey Dean *Dean & Jean*
Hey Joe
'66 *Leaves*
'67 *Jimi Hendrix*
Hey Jude
'68 *Beatles*
'68 *Wilson Pickett*
'89 Hey Ladies *Beastie Boys*
'70 Hey Lawdy Mama *Steppenwolf*
'99 Hey Leonardo (she likes me for me) *Blessid Union Of Souls*
'66 Hey, Leroy, Your Mama's Callin' You *Jimmy Castor*
'62 Hey, Let's Twist *Joey Dee*
'63 Hey Little Cobra *Rip Chords*
Hey Little Girl
'57 *Techniques*
'59 *Dee Clark*
'61 *Del Shannon*
'63 *Major Lance*
Hey Lover
'88 *Freddie Jackson*
'95 *LL Cool J*
'02 Hey Ma *Cam'ron*
'04 Hey Mama *Black Eyed Peas*
'95 Hey Man Nice Shot *Filter*
'55 Hey, Mr. Banjo *Sunnysiders*
'93 Hey Mr. D.J. *Zhané*
'70 Hey, Mister Sun *Bobby Sherman*
'80 Hey Nineteen *Steely Dan*
'62 Hey Paula *Paul & Paula*
'54 Hey There *Rosemary Clooney*
'07 Hey There Delilah *Plain White T's*
Hey There Lonely Girl [Boy]
'63 *Ruby & The Romantics*
'69 *Eddie Holman*
'80 *Robert John*
'71 Hey Tonight *Creedence Clearwater Revival*
'68 Hey, Western Union Man *Jerry Butler*
'75 (Hey Won't You Play) Another Somebody Done Somebody Wrong Song *B.J. Thomas*
'03 Hey Ya! *OutKast*
Hey You
'75 *Bachman-Turner Overdrive*
'80 *Pink Floyd*

'73 Hey You! Get Off My Mountain *Dramatics*
'70 Hi-De-Ho *Blood, Sweat & Tears*
Hi-Heel Sneakers
'64 *Tommy Tucker*
'68 *José Feliciano*
'72 Hi, Hi, Hi *Wings*
'68 Hickory Wood *Byrds*
'05 Hicktown *Jason Aldean*
'62 Hide & Go Seek *Bunker Hill*
'55 Hide And Seek *Big Joe Turner*
'61 Hide Away *Freddy King*
'62 Hide 'Nor Hair *Ray Charles*
'58 Hideaway *Four Esquires*
'92 High *Cure*
'89 High Cotton *Alabama*
'90 High Enough *Damn Yankees*
'59 High Hopes *Frank Sinatra*
'96 High Lonesome Sound *Vince Gill w/ Alison Krauss*
'07 High Maintenance Woman *Toby Keith*
'84 High On Emotion *Chris DeBurgh*
'85 High On You *Survivor*
'58 High School Confidential *Jerry Lee Lewis*
'77 High School Dance *Sylvers*
'59 High School U.S.A. *Tommy Facenda*
'58 High Sign *Diamonds*
'71 High Time We Went *Joe Cocker*
'85 Highwayman *Waylon Jennings/ Willie Nelson/Johnny Cash/ Kris Kristofferson*
'91 Highwire *Rolling Stones*
'99 Higher *Creed*
Higher Ground
'73 *Stevie Wonder*
'89 *Red Hot Chili Peppers*
'86 Higher Love *Steve Winwood*
'74 Higher Plane *Kool & The Gang*
'65 Highway 61 Revisited *Bob Dylan*
'79 Highway Song *Blackfoot*
'72 Highway Star *Deep Purple*
'79 Highway To Hell *AC/DC*
'75 Hijack *Herbie Mann*
'71 Hill Where The Lord Hides *Chuck Mangione*
'80 Him *Rupert Holmes*
'67 Him Or Me - What's It Gonna Be? *Paul Revere & The Raiders*
'68 Hip City *Jr. Walker*
'93 Hip Hop Hooray *Naughty By Nature*
'07 Hip Hop Is Dead *Nas*
'67 Hip Hug-Her *Booker T. & The M.G.'s*
'86 Hip To Be Square *Huey Lewis*
'64 Hippy Hippy Shake *Swinging Blue Jeans*
'90 Hippychick *Soho*
'06 Hips Don't Lie *Shakira*
'66 History Repeats Itself *Buddy Starcher*
'92 Hit *Sugarcubes*
'01 Hit 'Em Up Style (Oops!) *Blu Cantrell*
'96 Hit Me Off *New Edition*
'80 Hit Me With Your Best Shot *Pat Benatar*
'62 Hit Record *Brook Benton*
'03 Hit That *Offspring*
'86 Hit That Perfect Beat *Bronski Beat*
Hit The Road Jack
'61 *Ray Charles*
'76 *Stampeders*
'76 Hitch A Ride *Boston*
'63 Hitch Hike *Marvin Gaye*
'68 Hitch It To The Horse *Fantastic Johnny C*
'70 Hitchin' A Ride *Vanity Fare*
'60 Hither And Thither And Yon *Brook Benton*
'73 Hocus Pocus *Focus*
'72 Hoedown *Emerson, Lake & Palmer*

'76 Hold Back The Night *Trammps*
'77 *Graham Parker*
'72 Hold Her Tight *Osmonds*
'58 Hold It *Bill Doggett*
Hold Me
'82 *Fleetwood Mac*
'98 *Brian McKnight*
'84 Hold Me Now *Thompson Twins*
'65 Hold Me, Thrill Me, Kiss Me *Mel Carter*
'95 Hold Me, Thrill Me, Kiss Me, Kill Me *U2*
'68 Hold Me Tight *Johnny Nash*
'83 Hold Me 'Til The Mornin' Comes *Paul Anka*
'94 Hold My Hand *Hootie & The Blowfish*
Hold On
'79 *Ian Gomm*
'79 *Triumph*
'80 *Kansas*
'82 *Santana*
'90 *Wilson Phillips*
'90 *En Vogue*
'95 *Jamie Walters*
'80 Hold On Hold Out *Jackson Browne*
'66 Hold On! I'm A Comin' *Sam & Dave*
'81 Hold On Loosely *.38 Special*
'92 Hold On My Heart *Genesis*
'81 Hold On Tight *ELO*
'98 Hold On To Me *John Michael Montgomery*
'80 Hold On To My Love *Jimmy Ruffin*
'88 Hold On To The Nights *Richard Marx*
'78 Hold The Line *Toto*
'64 Hold What You've Got *Joe Tex*
'91 Hold You Tight *Tara Kemp*
'72 Hold Your Head Up *Argent*
'93 Holdin' Heaven *Tracy Byrd*
'75 Holdin' On To Yesterday *Ambrosia*
'86 Holding Back The Years *Simply Red*
'88 Holding On *Steve Winwood*
'78 Holding On (When Love Is Gone) *L.T.D.*
'84 Holding Out For A Hero *Bonnie Tyler*
'91 Hole Hearted *Extreme*
'68 Hole In My Shoe *Traffic*
'98 Holes In The Floor Of Heaven *Steve Wariner*
'65 Hole In The Wall *Packers*
'03 Holidae In *Chingy*
Holiday
'67 *Bee Gees*
'83 *Madonna*
'87 *Other Ones*
'05 *Green Day*
'83 Holiday Road *Lindsey Buckingham*
'99 Holla Holla *Ja Rule*
'05 Hollaback Girl *Gwen Stefani*
'69 Holly Holy *Neil Diamond*
'78 Hollywood Nights *Bob Seger*
'74 Hollywood Swinging *Kool & The Gang*
'66 Holy Cow *Lee Dorsey*
'90 Holy Water *Bad Company*
'67 Homburg *Procol Harum*
Home
'89 *Stephanie Mills*
'90 *Joe Diffie*
'90 *Iggy Pop*
'96 *Alan Jackson*
'05 *Three Days Grace*
'05 *Michael Bublé*
'07 *Daughtry*
'78 Home And Dry *Gerry Rafferty*
'77 Home Bound *Ted Nugent*
'65 Home Of The Brave *Jody Miller*
'85 Home Sweet Home *Mötley Crüe*
'99 Home To You *John Michael Montgomery*

'76 **Homecoming, The** *Hagood Hardy*
'66 **Homeward Bound**
    Simon & Garfunkel
'05 **Homewrecker** *Gretchen Wilson*
    Honest I Do
'57 *Jimmy Reed*
'60 *Innocents*
'87 **Honestly** *Stryper*
'79 **Honesty** *Billy Joel*
'03 **Honesty (Write Me A List)**
    Rodney Atkins
    Honey
'68 *Bobby Goldsboro*
'97 *Mariah Carey*
'55 **Honey-Babe** *Art Mooney*
    Honey Chile
'56 *Fats Domino*
'67 *Martha & The Vandellas*
'70 **Honey Come Back** *Glen Campbell*
'56 **Honey Don't** *Carl Perkins*
'74 **Honey, Honey** *Abba*
'97 **Honey, I'm Home** *Shania Twain*
'92 **Honey Love** *R. Kelly*
'57 **Honeycomb** *Jimmie Rodgers*
'87 **Honeythief, The** *Hipsway*
'72 **Honky Cat** *Elton John*
'56 **Honky Tonk** *Bill Doggett*
'06 **Honky Tonk Badonkadonk**
    Trace Adkins
'86 **Honky Tonk Man** *Dwight Yoakam*
'97 **Honky Tonk Truth** *Brooks & Dunn*
'69 **Honky Tonk Women** *Rolling Stones*
'82 **Honky Tonkin'** *Hank Williams Jr.*
'63 **Honolulu Lulu** *Jan & Dean*
'98 **Hooch** *Everything*
'60 **Hoochi Coochi Coo** *Hank Ballard*
'54 **Hoochie Coochie Man**
    Muddy Waters
'95 **Hook** *Blues Traveler*
'63 **Hooka Tooka** *Chubby Checker*
    Hooked On A Feeling
'68 *B.J. Thomas*
'74 *Blue Swede*
'81 **Hooked On Classics**
    Royal Philharmonic Orchestra
'82 **Hooked On Swing [medley]**
    Larry Elgart
    Hooked On You
'77 *Bread*
'89 *Sweet Sensation [remix]*
'66 **Hooray For Hazel** *Tommy Roe*
'63 **Hootenanny** *Glencoves*
'05 **Hope** *Twista w/ Faith Evans*
'75 **Hope That We Can Be Together**
    Soon *Sharon Paige/Harold Melvin*
'82 **Hope You Love Me Like You Say**
    You Do *Huey Lewis*
'63 **Hopeless** *Andy Williams*
'93 **Hopelessly** *Rick Astley*
'78 **Hopelessly Devoted To You**
    Olivia Newton-John
'80 **Horizontal Bop** *Bob Seger*
'68 **Horse, The** *Cliff Nobles & Co.*
'98 **Horse & Carriage** *Cam'ron*
'72 **Horse With No Name** *America*
'78 **Hot Blooded** *Foreigner*
'99 **Hot Boyz**
    Missy "Misdemeanor" Elliott
'69 **Hot Burrito #1** *Flying Burrito Brothers*
'78 **Hot Child In The City** *Nick Gilder*
'56 **Hot Diggity (Dog Ziggity Boom)**
    Perry Como
'79 **Hot Dog** *Led Zeppelin*
'84 **Hot For Teacher** *Van Halen*
'69 **Hot Fun In The Summertime**
    Sly & The Family Stone
'83 **Hot Girls In Love** *Loverboy*
'88 **Hot Hot Hot** *Buster Poindexter*
'02 **Hot In Herre** *Nelly*
'82 **Hot In The City** *Billy Idol*
'78 **Hot Legs** *Rod Stewart*
'76 **Hot Line** *Sylvers*
'78 **Hot Love, Cold World** *Bob Welch*
'83 **Hot 'N' Nasty** *Humble Pie*
'79 **Hot Number** *Foxy*
'71 **Hot Pants** *James Brown*

'63 **Hot Pastrami** *Dartells*
'63 **Hot Pastrami With Mashed**
    Potatoes *Joey Dee*
'80 **Hot Rod Hearts** *Robbie Dupree*
    Hot Rod Lincoln
'60 *Johnny Bond*
'60 *Charlie Ryan*
'72 *Commander Cody*
'00 **(Hot S**t) Country Grammar** *Nelly*
'69 **Hot Smoke & Sasafrass**
    Bubble Puppy
'79 **Hot Stuff** *Donna Summer*
'79 **Hot Summer Nights** *Night*
'03 **Hotel** *Cassidy*
'77 **Hotel California** *Eagles*
'62 **Hotel Happiness** *Brook Benton*
'92 **Hotel Illness** *Black Crowes*
'74 **Hotter Than Hell** *Kiss*
'56 **Hound Dog** *Elvis Presley*
'59 **Hound Dog Man** *Fabian*
'85 **Hounds Of Love** *Kate Bush*
'87 **Hourglass** *Squeeze*
'89 **House** *Psychedelic Furs*
'72 **House At Pooh Corner**
    Loggins & Messina
'55 **House Of Blue Lights** *Chuck Miller*
'94 **House Of Love**
    Amy Grant w/ Vince Gill
'90 **House Of Pain** *Faster Pussycat*
    House Of The Rising Sun
'64 *Animals*
'70 *Frijid Pink*
'68 **House That Jack Built**
    Aretha Franklin
'88 **House We Used To Live In**
    Smithereens
'56 **House With Love In It** *Four Lads*
'91 **Housecall (Your Body Can't Lie To**
    Me) *Shabba Ranks*
'75 **Houses Of The Holy**
    Led Zeppelin
'65 **Houston** *Dean Martin*
    How About That
'59 *Dee Clark*
'92 *Bad Company*
    How Am I Supposed To Live
    Without You
'83 *Laura Branigan*
'89 *Michael Bolton*
'97 **How Bizarre** *OMC*
'81 **How 'Bout Us** *Champaign*
    How Can I Be Sure
'67 *Young Rascals*
'72 *David Cassidy*
'91 **How Can I Ease The Pain**
    Lisa Fischer
'88 **How Can I Fall?** *Breathe*
'77 **How Can I Leave You Again**
    John Denver
'83 **How Can I Refuse** *Heart*
'73 **How Can I Tell Her** *Lobo*
'90 **How Can We Be Lovers**
    Michael Bolton
'71 **How Can You Mend A Broken Heart**
    Bee Gees
'04 **How Come** *D12*
    How Deep Is Your Love
'77 *Bee Gees*
'98 *Dru Hill*
'97 **How Do I Get There** *Deana Carter*
    How Do I Live
'97 *LeAnn Rimes*
'97 *Trisha Yearwood*
'80 **How Do I Make You** *Linda Ronstadt*
'80 **How Do I Survive** *Amy Holland*
'96 **How Do U Want It** *2 Pac*
'66 **How Do You Catch A Girl**
    Sam The Sham & The Pharoahs
'72 **How Do You Do?** *Mouth & MacNeal*
'64 **How Do You Do It?**
    Gerry & The Pacemakers
'98 **How Do You Fall In Love** *Alabama*
'86 **How Do You Keep The Music**
    Tony Bennett
'00 **How Do You Like Me Now?!**
    Toby Keith

'92 **How Do You Talk To An Angel**
    Heights
'80 **How Does It Feel To Be Back**
    Daryl Hall & John Oates
'66 **How Does That Grab You, Darlin'?**
    Nancy Sinatra
'07 **How Far We've Come**
    Matchbox Twenty
'99 **How Forever Feels** *Kenny Chesney*
'95 **How High** *Redman/Method Man*
'60 **How High The Moon** *Ella Fitzgerald*
    How Important Can It Be?
'55 *Joni James*
'55 *Sarah Vaughan*
'62 **How Is Julie?** *Lettermen*
'56 **(How Little It Matters) How Little We**
    Know *Frank Sinatra*
'75 **How Long** *Ace*
'75 **How Long (Betcha' Got A Chick On**
    The Side) *Pointer Sisters*
'98 **How Long Gone** *Brooks & Dunn*
'69 **How Many More Times**
    Led Zeppelin
'83 **How Many Times Can We Say**
    Goodbye
    Dionne Warwick & Luther Vandross
'94 **How Many Ways** *Toni Braxton*
'78 **How Much I Feel** *Ambrosia*
'91 **How Much Is Enough** *Fixx*
'77 **How Much Love** *Leo Sayer*
'85 **How Soon Is Now?** *Smiths*
    How Sweet It Is (To Be Loved By
    You)
'64 *Marvin Gaye*
'66 *Jr. Walker*
'75 *James Taylor*
'58 **How The Time Flies** *Jerry Wallace*
'86 **(How To Be A) Millionaire** *ABC*
'91 **How To Dance** *Bingoboys/Princessa*
'05 **How To Deal** *Frankie J*
'06 **How To Save A Life** *Fray*
    How Was I To Know
'96 *Reba McEntire*
'97 *John Michael Montgomery*
'05 **How We Do** *Game*
'85 **How Will I Know** *Whitney Houston*
'03 **How You Gonna Act Like That**
    Tyrese
'78 **How You Gonna See Me Now**
    Alice Cooper
'01 **How You Remind Me** *Nickelback*
'97 **How Your Love Makes Me Feel**
    Diamond Rio
'68 **How'd We Ever Get This Way**
    Andy Kim
'97 **How's It Going To Be**
    Third Eye Blind
'60 **Hucklebuck, The** *Chubby Checker*
    Hula Hoop Song
'58 *Teresa Brewer*
'58 *Georgia Gibbs*
'57 **Hula Love** *Buddy Knox*
'62 **Hully Gully Baby** *Dovells*
'86 **Human** *Human League*
'93 **Human Behaviour** *Björk*
'83 **Human Nature** *Michael Jackson*
    (also see: Right Here)
    Human Touch
'83 *Rick Springfield*
'92 *Bruce Springsteen*
'93 **Human Wheels** *John Mellencamp*
'96 **Humans Being** *Van Halen*
    Humming Bird
'55 *Frankie Laine*
'55 *Les Paul & Mary Ford*
'73 **Hummingbird** *Seals & Crofts*
'92 **Humpin' Around** *Bobby Brown*
'90 **Humpty Dance** *Digital Underground*
'61 **Hundred Pounds Of Clay**
    Gene McDaniels
'65 **Hung On You** *Righteous Brothers*
'05 **Hung Up** *Madonna*
'66 **Hungry** *Paul Revere & The Raiders*
'87 **Hungry Eyes** *Eric Carmen*
'80 **Hungry Heart** *Bruce Springsteen*
'82 **Hungry Like The Wolf** *Duran Duran*

'60 **(I Do The) Shimmy Shimmy**
  Bobby Freeman
'84 **I Do'wanna Know** *REO Speedwagon*
'87 **I Do You** *Jets*
'71 **I Don't Blame You At All** *Miracles*
'93 **I Don't Call Him Daddy**
  Doug Supernaw
'95 **I Don't Even Know Your Name** *Alan Jackson*
'97 **I Don't Ever Want To See You Again**
  Uncle Sam
'90 **I Don't Have The Heart**
  James Ingram
'02 **I Don't Have To Be Me ('Til Monday)**
  Steve Azar
'84 **I Don't Know A Thing About Love**
  (The Moon Song) *Conway Twitty*
'90 **I Don't Know Anybody Else**
  Black Box
  I Don't Know How To Love Him
'71   *Yvonne Elliman*
'71   *Helen Reddy*
'79 **I Don't Know If It's Right**
  Evelyn "Champagne" King
'82 **I Don't Know Where To Start**
  Eddie Rabbitt
'61 **I Don't Know Why** *Linda Scott*
'80 **I Don't Like Mondays**
  Boomtown Rats
'75 **I Don't Like To Sleep Alone**
  Paul Anka/Odia Coates
'87 **I Don't Mind At All** *Bourgeois Tagg*
'71 **I Don't Need No Doctor** *Humble Pie*
'81 **I Don't Need You** *Kenny Rogers*
'00 **I Don't Wanna** *Aaliyah*
'64 **I Don't Wanna Be A Loser**
  Lesley Gore
'91 **I Don't Wanna Cry** *Mariah Carey*
'93 **I Don't Wanna Fight** *Tina Turner*
'88 **I Don't Wanna Go On With You Like**
  That *Elton John*
'04 **I Don't Wanna Know**
  Mario Winans w/ P. Diddy
'88 **I Don't Wanna Live Without Your**
  Love *Chicago*
'65 **I Don't Wanna Lose You Baby** *Chad*
  & Jeremy
'67 **I Don't Wanna Play House**
  Tammy Wynette
'07 **I Don't Wanna Stop**
  Ozzy Osbourne
'95 **I Don't Want To Grow Up** *Ramones*
'91 **I Don't Want To Lose Your Love**
  B Angie B
'69 **I Don't Want Nobody To Give Me**
  Nothing *James Brown*
'97 **I Don't Want To** *Toni Braxton*
'05 **I Don't Want To Be** *Gavin DeGraw*
'88 **I Don't Want To Be A Hero**
  Johnny Hates Jazz
'64 **I Don't Want To Be Hurt Anymore**
  Nat King Cole
'61 **I Don't Want To Cry** *Chuck Jackson*
'71 **I Don't Want To Do Wrong**
  Gladys Knight
'77 **I Don't Want To Know** *Fleetwood*
  Mac
'88 **I Don't Want To Live Without You**
  Foreigner
'87 **I Don't Want To Lose Your Love**
  Freddie Jackson
  I Don't Want To Miss A Thing
'98   *Aerosmith*
'98   *Mark Chesnutt*
'64 **I Don't Want To See Tomorrow**
  Nat King Cole
'64 **I Don't Want To See You Again**
  Peter & Gordon
'65 **I Don't Want To Spoil The Party**
  Beatles
'61 **I Don't Want To Take A Chance**
  Mary Wells
'97 **I Don't Want To Wait** *Paula Cole*
'80 **I Don't Want To Walk Without You**
  Barry Manilow
'88 **I Don't Want Your Love**
  Duran Duran
'56 **I Dreamed** *Betty Johnson*

'75 **I Dreamed Last Night**
  Justin Hayward & John Lodge
'75 **I Dreamed Blues** *Moody Blues*
'61 **I Dreamed Of A Hill-Billy Heaven**
  Tex Ritter
'85 **I Drink Alone**
  George Thorogood
'89 **I Drove All Night** *Cyndi Lauper*
'83 **I Eat Cannibals** *Total Coelo*
'61 **I Fall To Pieces** *Patsy Cline*
'74 **I Feel A Song (In My Heart)**
  Gladys Knight
'64 **I Feel Fine** *Beatles*
'84 **I Feel For You** *Chaka Khan*
'67 **I Feel Free** *Cream*
'56 **I Feel Good** *Shirley & Lee*
'87 **I Feel Good All Over** *Stephanie Mills*
'67 **I-Feel-Like-I'm-Fixin'-To-Die-**
  Rag *Country Joe & The Fish*
'77 **I Feel Love** *Donna Summer*
'92 **I Feel Lucky** *Mary Chapin Carpenter*
'61 **I Feel So Bad** *Elvis Presley*
  I Feel The Earth Move
'71   *Carole King*
'89   *Martika*
'93 **I Feel You** *Depeche Mode*
'90 **I Fell In Love** *Carlene Carter*
'96 **I Finally Found Someone**
  Barbra Streisand & Bryan Adams
'66 **I Fooled You This Time**
  Gene Chandler
'66 **I Fought The Law** *Bobby Fuller Four*
'65 **I Found A Girl** *Jan & Dean*
'67 **I Found A Love** *Wilson Pickett*
'82 **I Found Somebody** *Glenn Frey*
'87 **I Found Someone** *Cher*
'62 **I Get A Kick Out Of You**
  Frank Sinatra
  I Get Around
'64   *Beach Boys*
'93   *2Pac*
'82 **I Get Excited** *Rick Springfield*
'75 **I Get Lifted** *George McCrae*
'98 **I Get Lonely** *Janet Jackson*
'66 **I Get The Fever** *Bill Anderson*
'88 **I Get Weak** *Belinda Carlisle*
'04 **I Go Back** *Kenny Chesney*
'96 **I Go Blind** *Hootie & The Blowfish*
'77 **I Go Crazy** *Paul Davis*
'90 **I Go To Extremes** *Billy Joel*
'65 **I Go To Pieces** *Peter & Gordon*
'79 **I Go To Rio** *Pablo Cruise*
'72 **I Got A Bag Of My Own**
  James Brown
'58 **I Got A Feeling** *Ricky Nelson*
'69 **I Got A Line On You** *Spirit*
'92 **I Got A Man** *Positive K*
'73 **I Got A Name** *Jim Croce*
'92 **I Got A Thang 4 Ya!** *Lo-Key?*
'59 **I Got A Wife** *Mark IV*
'62 **I Got A Woman** *Jimmy McGriff*
'73 **I Got Ants In My Pants**
  James Brown
'95 **I Got 5 On It** *Luniz*
'95 **I Got Id** *Pearl Jam*
'07 **I Got It From My Mama** *will.i.am*
'79 **I Got My Mind Made Up (You Can**
  Get It Girl) *Instant Funk*
'67 **I Got Rhythm** *Happenings*
'75 **I Got Stoned And I Missed It**
  Jim Stafford
'59 **I Got Stripes** *Johnny Cash*
'58 **I Got Stung** *Elvis Presley*
'68 **I Got The Feelin'** *James Brown*
'66 **I Got The Feelin' (Oh No No)**
  Neil Diamond
'98 **I Got The Hook Up!** *Master P*
'63 **I Got What I Wanted** *Brook Benton*
'80 **I Got You** *Split Enz*
'65 **I Got You Babe** *Sonny & Cher*
'65 **I Got You (I Feel Good)**
  James Brown
'72 **I Gotcha** *Joe Tex*
'63 **I Gotta Dance To Keep From Crying**
  Miracles
'60 **I Gotta Know** *Elvis Presley*

'83 **I Guess That's Why They Call It The**
  Blues *Elton John*
'69 **I Guess The Lord Must Be In New**
  York City *Nilsson*
'67 **I Had A Dream**
  Paul Revere & The Raiders
'64 **I Had A Talk With My Man**
  Mitty Collier
'66 **I Had Too Much To Dream (Last**
  Night) *Electric Prunes*
'04 **I Hate Everything** *George Strait*
'03 **(I Hate) Everything About You**
  Three Days Grace
'88 **I Hate Myself For Loving You**
  Joan Jett
'95 **I Hate U** *Prince*
'63 **I Have A Boyfriend** *Chiffons*
'79 **I Have A Dream** *Abba*
'86 **I Have Learned To Respect The**
  Power Of Love *Stephanie Mills*
'93 **I Have Nothing** *Whitney Houston*
'65 **I Hear A Symphony** *Supremes*
'66 **I Hear Trumpets Blow** *Tokens*
  I Hear You Knocking
'55   *Smiley Lewis*
'55   *Gale Storm*
'70   *Dave Edmunds*
'87 **I Heard A Rumour** *Bananarama*
  I Heard It Through The Grapevine
'67   *Gladys Knight*
'68   *Marvin Gaye*
'70   *Creedence Clearwater Revival*
'81   *Roger*
'74 **I Honestly Love You**
  Olivia Newton-John
'00 **I Hope You Dance** *Lee Ann Womack*
'84 **I Just Called To Say I Love You**
  Stevie Wonder
'70 **I Just Can't Help Believing**
  B.J. Thomas
'87 **I Just Can't Stop Loving You**
  Michael Jackson w/ Siedah Garrett
'87 **(I Just) Died In Your Arms**
  Cutting Crew
'57 **I Just Don't Know** *Four Lads*
'66 **I Just Don't Know What To Do With**
  Myself *Dionne Warwick*
'61 **I Just Don't Understand**
  Ann-Margret
'79 **I Just Fall In Love Again**
  Anne Murray
'02 **I Just Wanna Be Mad** *Terri Clark*
'05 **I Just Wanna Live** *Good Charlotte*
'00 **I Just Wanna Love U (Give It 2 Me)**
  Jay-Z
'78 **I Just Wanna Stop** *Gino Vannelli*
'79 **I Just Want To Be** *Cameo*
'77 **I Just Want To Be Your Everything**
  Andy Gibb
'71 **I Just Want To Celebrate** *Rare Earth*
'98 **I Just Want To Dance With You**
  George Strait
'77 **I Just Want To Make Love To You**
  Foghat [live]
'93 **I Just Wanted You To Know**
  Mark Chesnutt
'82 **I Keep Forgettin' (Every Time**
  You're Near) *Michael McDonald*
'02 **I Keep Looking** *Sara Evans*
'99 **I Knew I Loved You** *Savage Garden*
'87 **I Knew You Were Waiting (For Me)**
  Aretha Franklin & George Michael
  I Knew You When
'65   *Billy Joe Royal*
'82   *Linda Ronstadt*
'95 **I Know** *Dionne Farris*
'79 **I Know A Heartache When I See**
  One *Jennifer Warnes*
'65 **I Know A Place** *Petula Clark*
'93 **(I Know I Got) Skillz**
  Shaquille O'Neal
  (I Know) I'm Losing You
'66   *Temptations*
'70   *Rare Earth*
'71   *Rod Stewart w/ Faces*
'82 **I Know There's Something Going**
  On *Frida*

I Think We're Alone Now
'67   *Tommy James*
'87   *Tiffany*
'69   **I Threw It All Away** *Bob Dylan*
'07   **I Told You So** *Keith Urban*
'91   **I Touch Myself** *Divinyls*
'07   **I Tried** *Bone Thugs-N-Harmony*
'00   **I Try** *Macy Gray*
'94   **I Try To Think About Elvis**
     Patty Loveless
'00   **I Turn To You** *Christina Aguilera*
'69   **I Turned You On** *Isley Brothers*
     I Understand (Just How You Feel)
'61   *G-Clefs*
'65   *Freddie & The Dreamers*
'59   **I Waited Too Long** *LaVern Baker*
'56   **I Walk The Line** *Johnny Cash*
'86   **I Wanna Be A Cowboy**
     Boys Don't Cry
'63   **I Wanna Be Around** *Tony Bennett*
'01   **I Wanna Be Bad** *Willa Ford*
'94   **I Wanna Be Down** *Brandy*
'59   **I Wanna Be Loved** *Ricky Nelson*
'90   **I Wanna Be Rich** *Calloway*
'78   **I Wanna Be Sedated** *Ramones*
'89   **I Wanna Be The One** *Stevie B*
'97   **I Wanna Be There**
     Blessid Union Of Souls
'72   **I Wanna Be Where You Are**
     Michael Jackson
     I Wanna Be With You
'72   *Raspberries*
'79   *Isley Brothers*
'00   *Mandy Moore*
'69   **I Wanna Be Your Dog** *Stooges*
'92   **I Wanna Be Your Girl** *Icy Blu*
'79   **I Wanna Be Your Lover** *Prince*
'75   **I Wanna Dance Wit' Choo**
     Disco Tex & The Sex-O-Lettes
'87   **I Wanna Dance With Somebody**
     (Who Loves Me) *Whitney Houston*
'03   **I Wanna Do It All** *Terri Clark*
'97   **I Wanna Fall In Love** *Lila McCann*
'77   **I Wanna Get Next To You**
     Rose Royce
'86   **I Wanna Go Back** *Eddie Money*
'88   **I Wanna Have Some Fun**
     Samantha Fox
'85   **I Wanna Hear It From Your Lips**
     Eric Carmen
'00   **I Wanna Know** *Joe*
'68   **I Wanna Live** *Glen Campbell*
'64   **I Wanna Love Him So Bad**
     Jelly Beans
'61   **(I Wanna) Love My Life Away**
     Gene Pitney
     I Wanna Love You
'92   *Jade*
'06   *Akon*
'92   **I Wanna Love You** *Jade*
'99   **I Wanna Love You Forever**
     Jessica Simpson
'91   **I Wanna Sex You Up** *Color Me Badd*
'01   **I Wanna Talk About Me** *Toby Keith*
     (I Wanna) Testify
'67   *Parliaments*
'69   *Johnnie Taylor*
'61   **I Wanna Thank You** *Bobby Rydell*
'84   **I Want A New Drug** *Huey Lewis*
     I Want Candy
'65   *Strangeloves*
'82   *Bow Wow Wow*
'88   **I Want Her** *Keith Sweat*
     I Want It All
'89   *Queen*
'99   *Warren G*
'99   **I Want It That Way** *Backstreet Boys*
'60   **I Want To Be Wanted** *Brenda Lee*
'87   **I Want To Be Your Man** *Roger*
'96   **I Want To Come Over**
     Melissa Etheridge
'65   **I Want To (Do Everything For You)**
     Joe Tex
'55   **I Want To Do More** *Ruth Brown*
'66   **I Want To Go With You** *Eddy Arnold*
'64   **I Want To Hold Your Hand** *Beatles*

'84   **I Want To Know What Love Is**
     Foreigner
'86   **I Want To Make The World Turn**
     Around *Steve Miller Band*
'63   **I Want To Stay Here** *Steve & Eydie*
     I Want To Take You Higher
'70   *Sly & The Family Stone*
'70   *Ike & Tina Turner*
'59   **I Want To Walk You Home**
     Fats Domino
     I Want You
'66   *Bob Dylan*
'76   *Marvin Gaye*
'89   *Shana*
'91   *Robert Palmer [medley]*
'97   *Savage Garden*
'03   *Thalia w/ Fat Joe*
     I Want You Back
'69   *Jackson 5*
'98   *'N Sync*
'81   **I Want You, I Need You**
     Chris Christian
'56   **I Want You, I Need You, I Love You**
     Elvis Presley
'55   **I Want You To Be My Baby**
     Georgia Gibbs
'56   **I Want You To Be My Girl**
     Frankie Lymon
'57   **I Want You To Know** *Fats Domino*
'55   **I Want You To Be My Baby**
     Lillian Briggs
'64   **I Want You To Meet My Baby**
     Eydie Gorme
'79   **I Want You To Want Me** *Cheap Trick*
'79   **I Want You Tonight** *Pablo Cruise*
'79   **I Want Your Love** *Chic*
'87   **I Want Your Sex** *George Michael*
'75   **I Want'a Do Something Freaky To**
     You *Leon Haywood*
'62   **(I Was) Born To Cry** *Dion*
'73   **I Was Checkin' Out She Was**
     Checkin' In *Don Covay*
'81   **I Was Country When Country**
     Wasn't Cool *Barbara Mandrell*
'67   **I Was Kaiser Bill's Batman**
     Whistling Jack Smith
'78   **I Was Made For Dancin'** *Leif Garrett*
'79   **I Was Made For Lovin' You** *Kiss*
'67   **I Was Made To Love Her**
     Stevie Wonder
'78   **I Was Only Joking** *Rod Stewart*
'56   **I Was The One** *Elvis Presley*
'66   **(I Washed My Hands In) Muddy**
     Water *Johnny Rivers*
     I (Who Have Nothing)
'63   *Ben E. King*
'70   *Tom Jones*
'79   *Sylvester*
'65   **I Will** *Dean Martin*
     I Will Always Love You
'74   *Dolly Parton*
'92   *Whitney Houston*
'95   *Dolly Parton w/ Vince Gill*
'68   **I Will Always Think About You**
     New Colony Six
'92   **I Will Be Here For You**
     Michael W. Smith
'78   **I Will Be In Love With You**
     Livingston Taylor
'87   **I Will Be There** *Glass Tiger*
'00   **I Will...But** *SheDaisy*
'98   **I Will Buy You A New Life** *Everclear*
'97   **I Will Come To You** *Hanson*
'84   **I Will Dare** *Replacements*
     I Will Follow
'81   *U2*
'83   *U2 [live]*
'63   **I Will Follow Him** *Little Peggy March*
'99   **I Will Get There** *Boyz II Men*
'00   **I Will Love Again** *Lara Fabian*
'89   **I Will Not Go Quietly** *Don Henley*
     I Will Remember You
'92   *Amy Grant*
'99   *Sarah McLachlan [live]*
'78   **I Will Still Love You** *Stonebolt*

'78   **I Will Survive**
'78   *Gloria Gaynor*
'96   *Chantay Savage*
'98   **I Will Wait** *Hootie & The Blowfish*
     I Wish
'76   *Stevie Wonder*
'95   *Skee-Lo*
'00   *R. Kelly*
'00   *Carl Thomas*
'85   **I Wish He Didn't Trust Me So Much**
     Bobby Womack
'88   **I Wish I Had A Girl**
     Henry Lee Summer
'03   **I Wish I Wasn't** *Heather Headley*
'63   **I Wish I Were A Princess**
     Little Peggy March
'68   **I Wish It Would Rain** *Temptations*
'90   **I Wish It Would Rain Down**
     Phil Collins
'62   **I Wish That We Were Married**
     Ronnie & The Hi-Lites
'92   **I Wish The Phone Would Ring**
     Exposé
'64   **I Wish You Love** *Gloria Lynne*
'71   **I Woke Up In Love This Morning**
     Partridge Family
'89   **I Won't Back Down** *Tom Petty*
'87   **I Won't Forget You** *Poison*
'83   **I Won't Hold You Back** *Toto*
'74   **I Won't Last A Day Without You**
     Carpenters
'83   **I Won't Stand In Your Way**
     Stray Cats
'63   **I Wonder** *Brenda Lee*
'85   **I Wonder If I Take You Home**
     Lisa-Lisa & Cult Jam
     I Wonder What She's Doing Tonight
     [Tonite]
'63   *Barry & The Tamerlanes*
'67   *Tommy Boyce & Bobby Hart*
     I Wonder Why
'58   *Dion & The Belmonts*
'91   *Curtis Stigers*
'84   **I Would Die 4 U** *Prince*
'81   **I Wouldn't Have Missed It For The**
     World *Ronnie Milsap*
'74   **I Wouldn't Treat A Dog (The Way**
     You Treated Me) *Bobby Bland*
'77   **I Wouldn't Want To Be Like You**
     Alan Parsons
'06   **I Write Sins Not Tragedies**
     Panic! At The Disco
'75   **I Write The Songs** *Barry Manilow*
'92   **I'd Die Without You** *PM Dawn*
'93   **I'd Do Anything For Love (But I**
     Won't Do That) *Meat Loaf*
'94   **I'd Give Anything** *Gerald Levert*
'95   **I'd Lie For You (And That's The**
     Truth) *Meat Loaf*
     I'd Like To Teach The World To
     Sing
'71   *Hillside Singers*
'71   *New Seekers*
'71   **I'd Love To Change The World**
     Ten Years After
'91   **I'd Love You All Over Again**
     Alan Jackson
'72   **I'd Love You To Want Me** *Lobo*
'79   **I'd Rather Leave While I'm In Love**
     Rita Coolidge
'97   **I'd Rather Ride Around With You**
     Reba McEntire
'76   **I'd Really Love To See You Tonight**
     England Dan & John Ford Coley
'87   **I'd Still Say Yes** *Klymaxx*
'69   **I'd Wait A Million Years** *Grass Roots*
'97   **I'll Always Be Right There**
     Bryan Adams
'73   **I'll Always Love My Mama** *Intruders*
     I'll Always Love You
'65   *Spinners*
'88   *Taylor Dayne*
     I'll Be
'97   *Foxy Brown*
'98   *Edwin McCain*
'86   **I'll Be Alright Without You** *Journey*

'06 **I'm N Luv (Wit A Stripper)** *T-Pain*
'72 **I'm Never Gonna Be Alone Anymore** *Cornelius Brothers & Sister Rose*
'59 **I'm Never Gonna Tell** *Jimmie Rodgers*
'87 **I'm No Angel** *Gregg Allman Band*
'89 **I'm No Stranger To The Rain** *Keith Whitley*
'57 **I'm Not A Juvenile Delinquent** *Frankie Lymon*
'97 **I'm Not A Player** *Big Punisher*
'60 **I'm Not Afraid** *Ricky Nelson*
'96 **I'm Not Giving You Up** *Gloria Estefan*
'78 **I'm Not Gonna Let It Bother Me Tonight** *Atlanta Rhythm Section*
I'm Not In Love
'75 *10cc*
'90 *Will To Power*
'75 **I'm Not Lisa** *Jessi Colter*
'70 **I'm Not My Brothers Keeper** *Flaming Ember*
'99 **I'm Not Ready** *Keith Sweat*
'99 **I'm Not Running Anymore** *John Mellencamp*
'95 **I'm Not Strong Enough To Say No** *BlackHawk*
'86 **I'm Not The One** *Cars*
'88 **I'm Not Your Man** *Tommy Conwell*
'66 **(I'm Not Your) Steppin' Stone** *Monkees*
I'm On Fire
'75 *Dwight Twilley Band*
'75 *5000 Volts*
'85 *Bruce Springsteen*
'64 **I'm On The Outside (Looking In)** *Little Anthony & The Imperials*
'94 **I'm Outstanding** *Shaquille O'Neal*
I'm Ready
'59 *Fats Domino*
'94 *Tevin Campbell*
'66 **I'm Ready For Love** *Martha & The Vandellas*
I'm Real
'88 *James Brown*
'01 *Jennifer Lopez*
'82 **I'm So Excited** *Pointers Sisters*
I'm So Happy I Can't Stop Crying
'96 *Sting*
'97 *Toby Keith w/ Sting*
I'm So Into You
'78 *Peabo Bryson*
'93 *SWV*
'66 **I'm So Lonesome I Could Cry** *B.J. Thomas*
'64 **I'm So Proud** *Impressions*
I'm Sorry
'57 *Platters*
'60 *Brenda Lee*
'75 *John Denver*
'05 **I'm Sprung** *T-Pain*
'57 **I'm Stickin' With You** *Jimmy Bowen*
I'm Still In Love With You
'72 *Al Green*
'96 *New Edition*
'04 *Sean Paul*
'88 **I'm Still Searching** *Glass Tiger*
'83 **I'm Still Standing** *Elton John*
'72 **I'm Stone In Love With You** *Stylistics*
'65 **I'm Telling You Now** *Freddie & The Dreamers*
'89 **I'm That Type Of Guy** *LL Cool J*
'62 **(I'm The Girl On) Wolverton Mountain** *Jo Ann Campbell*
'92 **I'm The One You Need** *Jody Watley*
'94 **I'm The Only One** *Melissa Etheridge*
'91 **I'm Too Sexy** *R*S*F (Right Said Fred)*
'67 **I'm Waiting For The Man** *Velvet Underground*
'57 **I'm Waiting Just For You** *Pat Boone*
I'm Walkin'
'57 *Fats Domino*
'57 *Ricky Nelson*

'02 **I'm With You** *Avril Lavigne*
'67 **I'm Wondering** *Stevie Wonder*
'98 **I'm Your Angel** *R. Kelly & Celine Dion*
'90 **I'm Your Baby Tonight** *Whitney Houston*
'77 **I'm Your Boogie Man** *KC & The Sunshine Band*
'70 **I'm Your Captain [medley]** *Grand Funk Railroad*
'85 **I'm Your Man** *Wham!*
'66 **I'm Your Puppet** *James & Bobby Purify*
'65 **I'm Yours** *Elvis Presley*
'62 **I've Been Everywhere** *Hank Snow*
'69 **I've Been Hurt** *Bill Deal*
'87 **I've Been In Love Before** *Cutting Crew*
'72 **I've Been Lonely For So Long** *Frederick Knight*
'67 **I've Been Lonely Too Long** *Young Rascals*
'65 **I've Been Loving You Too Long (To Stop Now)** *Otis Redding*
'74 **(I've Been) Searchin' So Long** *Chicago*
'91 **I've Been Thinking About You** *Londonbeat*
'75 **I've Been This Way Before** *Neil Diamond*
'81 **I've Been Waiting For You All Of My Life** *Paul Anka*
'59 **I've Come Of Age** *Billy Storm*
'90 **I've Come To Expect It From You** *George Strait*
'90 **I've Cried My Last Tear For You** *Ricky Van Shelton*
'81 **I've Done Everything For You** *Rick Springfield*
'71 **I've Found Someone Of My Own** *Free Movement*
'76 **I've Got A Feeling (We'll Be Seeing Each Other Again)** *Al Wilson*
'91 **I've Got A Lot To Learn About Love** *Storm*
'83 **I've Got A Rock N' Roll Heart** *Eric Clapton*
'74 **I've Got A Thing About You Baby** *Elvis Presley*
'65 **I've Got A Tiger By The Tail** *Buck Owens*
'55 **I've Got A Woman** *Ray Charles*
'62 **(I've Got) Bonnie** *Bobby Rydell*
'77 **I've Got Love On My Mind** *Natalie Cole*
'64 **I've Got Sand In My Shoes** *Drifters*
'73 **I've Got So Much To Give** *Barry White*
'74 **I've Got The Music In Me** *Kiki Dee Band*
'56 **I've Got The World On A String** *Frank Sinatra*
'65 **I've Got To Be Somebody** *Billy Joe Royal*
'73 **I've Got To Use My Imagination** *Gladys Knight*
I've Got You Under My Skin
'56 *Frank Sinatra*
'66 *4 Seasons*
'68 **I've Gotta Be Me** *Sammy Davis, Jr.*
'68 **I've Gotta Get A Message To You** *Bee Gees*
'78 **I've Had Enough** *Wings*
'59 **I've Had It** *Bell Notes*
'87 **(I've Had) The Time Of My Life** *Bill Medley & Jennifer Warnes*
'70 **I've Lost You** *Elvis Presley*
'80 **I've Loved You For A Long Time [medley]** *Spinners*
'82 **I've Never Been To Me** *Charlene*
'68 **I've Never Found A Girl (To Love Me Like You Do)** *Eddie Floyd*
'66 **I've Passed This Way Before** *Jimmy Ruffin*
'61 **I've Told Every Little Star** *Linda Scott*
'07 **Ice Box** *Omarion*
'95 **Ice Cream** *Raekwon*

'78 **Ice Cream Man** *Van Halen*
'90 **Ice Ice Baby** *Vanilla Ice*
'07 **Icky Thump** *White Stripes*
'91 **Iesha** *Another Bad Creation*
If
'71 *Bread*
'93 *Janet Jackson*
'62 **If A Man Answers** *Bobby Darin*
'83 **If Anyone Falls** *Stevie Nicks*
'94 **If Bubba Can Dance (I Can Too)** *Shenandoah*
'58 **If Dreams Came True** *Pat Boone*
'78 **If Ever I See You Again** *Roberta Flack*
'84 **If Ever You're In My Arms Again** *Peabo Bryson*
'66 **If Every Day Was Like Christmas** *Elvis Presley*
'07 **If Everyone Cared** *Nickelback*
'04 **If I Ain't Got You** *Alicia Keys*
'68 **If I Can Dream** *Elvis Presley*
If I Can't Have You
'77 *Bee Gees*
'78 *Yvonne Elliman*
'67 **If I Could Build My Whole World Around You** *Marvin Gaye & Tammi Terrell*
'02 **If I Could Go!** *Angie Martinez*
'94 **If I Could Make A Living** *Clay Walker*
'75 **If I Could Only Win Your Love** *Emmylou Harris*
'72 **If I Could Reach You** *5th Dimension*
'97 **If I Could Teach The World** *Bone Thugs-N-Harmony*
'99 **If I Could Turn Back The Hands Of Time** *R. Kelly*
'89 **If I Could Turn Back Time** *Cher*
If I Didn't Care
'59 *Connie Francis*
'61 *Platters*
'62 **If I Didn't Have A Dime (To Play The Jukebox)** *Gene Pitney*
'92 **If I Didn't Have You** *Randy Travis*
'92 **If I Ever Fall In Love** *Shai*
'93 **If I Ever Lose My Faith In You** *Sting*
'75 **If I Ever Lose This Heaven** *AWB*
'01 **If I Fall You're Going Down With Me** *Dixie Chicks*
'64 **If I Fell** *Beatles*
'59 **If I Give My Heart To You** *Kitty Kallen*
'59 **If I Had A Girl** *Rod Lauren*
If I Had A Hammer
'62 *Peter, Paul & Mary*
'63 *Trini Lopez*
'82 **If I Had My Wish Tonight** *David Lasley*
'93 **If I Had No Loot** *Tony Toni Tone*
'05 **If Heaven** *Andy Griggs*
'91 **If I Know Me** *George Strait*
'65 **If I Loved You** *Chad & Jeremy*
'55 **If I May** *Nat "King" Cole/Four Knights*
'70 **If I Never Knew Your Name** *Vic Dana*
'97 **If I Never Stop Loving You** *David Kersh*
'65 **If I Ruled The World** *Tony Bennett*
'79 **If I Said You Have A Beautiful Body Would You Hold It Against Me** *Bellamy Brothers*
'95 **If I Wanted To** *Melissa Etheridge*
If I Were A Carpenter
'66 *Bobby Darin*
'68 *Four Tops*
'70 *Johnny Cash & June Carter*
'71 **If I Were A Rich Man** *Topol*
'70 **If I Were Your Woman** *Gladys Knight*
'83 **If I'd Been The One** *38 Special*
'89 **If I'm Not Your Lover** *Al B. Sure!*
'82 **If It Ain't One Thing...It's Another** *Richard "Dimples" Fields*
'88 **If It Isn't Love** *New Edition*
'96 **If It Makes You Happy** *Sheryl Crow*
'05 **If It's Lovin' That You Want** *Rihanna*

(If Loving You Is Wrong) I Don't Want To Be Right
'72 Luther Ingram
'79 Barbara Mandrell
'01 If My Heart Had Wings Faith Hill
'63 If My Pillow Could Talk Connie Francis
If Not For You
'70 Bob Dylan
'71 Olivia Newton-John
'83 If Only You Knew Patti LaBelle
'86 If She Knew What She Wants Bangles
'87 If She Would Have Been Faithful... Chicago
'68 If 6 Was 9 Jimi Hendrix
'91 If The Devil Danced (In Empty Pockets) Joe Diffie
'94 If The Good Die Young Tracy Lawrence
'82 If The Love Fits Wear It Leslie Pearl
'95 If The World Had A Front Porch Tracy Lawrence
'92 If There Hadn't Been You Billy Dean
'91 (If There Was) Any Other Way Celine Dion
'84 If This Is It Huey Lewis
'93 If Tomorrow Never Comes Garth Brooks
'90 If U Were Mine U-Krew
'73 If We Make It Through December Merle Haggard
'88 If We Never Meet Again Tommy Conwell
'06 If We Were A Movie Hannah Montana
'90 If Wishes Came True Sweet Sensation
'92 If You Asked Me To Celine Dion
'87 If You Can Do It: I Can Too!! Meli'sa Morgan
'68 If You Can Want Miracles
'97 If You Could Only See Tonic
'70 If You Could Read My Mind Gordon Lightfoot
'59 (If You Cry) True Love, True Love Drifters
If You Don't Know Me By Now
'72 Harold Melvin & The Bluenotes
'89 Simply Red
'55 If You Don't Want My Love Jaye P. Morgan
'04 If You Ever Stop Loving Me Montgomery Gentry
'94 If You Go Jon Secada
'92 If You Go Away NKOTB
'61 If You Gotta Make A Fool Of Somebody James Ray
'99 If You Had My Love Jennifer Lopez
'76 If You Know What I Mean Neil Diamond
'86 If You Leave Orchestral Manoeuvres In The Dark
If You Leave Me Now
'76 Chicago
'90 Jaya
'72 If You Leave Me Tonight I'll Cry Jerry Wallace
'70 (If You Let Me Make Love To You Then) Why Can't I Touch You? Ronnie Dyson
If You Love Me
'94 Brownstone
'99 Mint Condition
'74 If You Love Me (Let Me Know) Olivia Newton-John
'85 If You Love Somebody Set Them Free Sting
'99 If You (Lovin' Me) Silk
'63 If You Need Me Solomon Burke
'90 If You Needed Somebody Bad Company
'71 If You Really Love Me Stevie Wonder
'79 If You Remember Me Chris Thompson & Night
'98 If You See Him/If You See Her Reba McEntire/Brooks & Dunn

'80 If You Should Sail Nielsen/Pearson
'74 If You Talk In Your Sleep Elvis Presley
'98 If You Think I'm Jiggy Lox
If You Think You're Lonely Now
'81 Bobby Womack
'95 K-Ci Hailey
'63 If You Wanna Be Happy Jimmy Soul
'74 If You Wanna Get To Heaven Ozark Mountain Daredevils
'79 If You Want It Niteflyte
'90 If You Want Me To Joe Diffie
'73 If You Want Me To Stay Sly & The Family Stone
'71 If You Were Mine Ray Charles
'06 If You're Going Through Hell (Before The Devil Even Knows) Rodney Atkins
'00 If You're Gone Matchbox Twenty
'84 If You're Gonna Play In Texas (You Gotta Have A Fiddle In The Band) Alabama
'95 (If You're Not In It For Love) I'm Outta Here! Shania Twain
'03 If You're Not The One Daniel Bedingfield
'73 If You're Ready (Come Go With Me) Staple Singers
'94 If You've Got Love John Michael Montgomery
'96 If Your Girl Only Knew Aaliyah
'02 Ignition R. Kelly
Iko Iko
'65 Dixie Cups
'89 Belle Stars
'60 Image Of A Girl Safaris
'78 Imaginary Lover Atlanta Rhythm Section
'98 Imagination Tamia
'71 Imagine John Lennon
'98 Imagine That Diamond Rio
'75 Immigrant, The Neil Sedaka
'70 Immigrant Song Led Zeppelin
'72 Immigration Man Graham Nash & David Crosby
'02 Impossible, The Joe Nichols
'66 Impossible Dream Jack Jones
'97 Impression That I Get Mighty Mighty Bosstones
'90 Impulsive Wilson Phillips
'83 In A Big Country Big Country
'91 In A Different Light Doug Stone
'68 In-A-Gadda-Da-Vida Iron Butterfly
'69 In A Moment Intrigues
'04 In A Real Love Phil Vassar
'56 In A Shanty In Old Shanty Town Somethin' Smith & The Redheads
'92 In A Week Or Two Diamond Rio
'80 In America Charlie Daniels Band
'67 In And Out Of Love Supremes
'97 In Another's Eyes Trisha Yearwood & Garth Brooks
'85 In Between Days Cure
'91 In Bloom Nirvana
"In" Crowd
'65 Dobie Gray
'65 Ramsey Lewis Trio
'03 In Da Club 50 Cent
'63 In Dreams Roy Orbison
'88 In God's Country U2
'72 In Heaven There Is No Beer Clean Living
'03 In Love Wit Chu Da Brat
'70 In Memory Of Elizabeth Reed Allman Brothers Band
'97 In My Bed Dru Hill
'88 In My Darkest Hour Megadeth
'04 In My Daughter's Eyes Martina McBride
In My Dreams
'87 REO Speedwagon
'91 Party
'89 In My Eyes Stevie B
'85 In My House Mary Jane Girls
'65 In My Life Beatles
'60 In My Little Corner Of The World Anita Bryant

'63 In My Room Beach Boys
'84 In Neon Elton John
'81 In The Air Tonight Phil Collins
'56 In The Alps McGuire Sisters w/ Lawrence Welk
'66 In The Arms Of Love Andy Williams
'95 In The Blood Better Than Ezra
In The City
'79 Eagles
'83 Jam
'92 In The Closet Michael Jackson
'81 In The Dark Billy Squier
'01 In The End Linkin Park
'79 In The Evening Led Zeppelin
'69 In The Ghetto Elvis Presley
'93 In The Heart Of A Woman Billy Ray Cyrus
'67 In The Heat Of The Night Ray Charles
'94 In The House Of Stone And Light Martin Page
'55 In The Jailhouse Now Webb Pierce
'95 In The Meantime Spacehog
'61 In The Middle Of A Heartache Wanda Jackson
In The Middle Of An Island
'57 Tony Bennett
'57 Tennessee Ernie Ford
In The Middle Of The House
'56 Rusty Draper
'56 Vaughn Monroe
In The Midnight Hour
'65 Wilson Pickett
'73 Cross Country
In The Misty Moonlight
'64 Jerry Wallace
'67 Dean Martin
In The Mood
'59 Ernie Fields
'77 Henhouse Five Plus Too
'83 Robert Plant
'79 In The Navy Village People
'72 In The Rain Dramatics
'86 In The Shape Of A Heart Jackson Browne
In The Still Of The Night [Nite]
'56 Five Satins
'60 Dion & The Belmonts
'92 Boyz II Men
In The Summertime
'70 Mungo Jerry
'95 Shaggy
'69 In The Year 2525 Zager & Evans
'79 In Thee Blue Öyster Cult
'93 In These Arms Bon Jovi
'92 In This Life Collin Raye
'03 In Those Jeans Ginuwine
'87 In Too Deep Genesis
'86 In Your Eyes Peter Gabriel
'81 In Your Letter REO Speedwagon
'88 In Your Room Bangles
'88 In Your Soul Corey Hart
'67 Incense And Peppermints Strawberry Alarm Clock
Incomplete
'00 Sisqó
'05 Backstreet Boys
'94 Independence Day Martina McBride
'00 Independent Women Destiny's Child
'67 Indescribably Blue Elvis Presley
'88 Indestructible Four Tops
'69 Indian Giver 1910 Fruitgum Co.
'68 Indian Lake Cowsills
'94 Indian Outlaw Tim McGraw
Indian Reservation
'68 Don Fardon
'71 Paul Revere & The Raiders
'70 Indiana Wants Me R. Dean Taylor
'84 Infatuation Rod Stewart
'93 Informer Snow
Innamorata
'56 Dean Martin
'56 Jerry Vale
'71 Inner City Blues (Make Me Wanna Holler) Marvin Gaye

'83 **Innocent Man** *Billy Joel*
'93 **Insane In The Brain** *Cypress Hill*
'96 **Insensitive** *Jann Arden*
'75 **Inseparable** *Natalie Cole*
Inside Looking Out
'66 *Animals*
'70 *Grand Funk Railroad*
'83 **Inside Love (So Personal)**
George Benson
'98 **Inside Out** *Eve 6*
Inside Your Heaven
'05 *Bo Bice*
'05 *Carrie Underwood*
'70 **Instant Karma** *John Ono Lennon*
'78 **Instant Replay** *Dan Hartman*
'98 **Intergalactic** *Beastie Boys*
'94 **Interstate Love Song**
Stone Temple Pilots
'91 **Into The Great Wide Open**
Tom Petty
'85 **Into The Groove** *Madonna*
'70 **Into The Mystic** *Van Morrison*
'80 **Into The Night** *Benny Mardones*
'07 **Into The Ocean** *Blue October*
'03 **Into The West** *Annie Lennox*
'03 **Into You** *Fabolous*
'93 **Into Your Arms** *Lemonheads*
'03 **Intuition** *Jewel*
'85 **Invincible** *Pat Benatar*
Invisible
'85 *Alison Moyet*
'03 *Clay Aiken*
'06 *Ashlee Simpson*
'97 **Invisible Man** *98°*
'86 **Invisible Touch** *Genesis*
'98 **Iris** *Goo Goo Dolls*
'71 **Iron Man** *Black Sabbath*
'96 **Ironic** *Alanis Morissette*
'06 **Irreplaceable** *Beyoncé*
'01 **Irresistible** *Jessica Simpson*
'61 **Irresistible You** *Bobby Darin*
'60 **Is A Blue Bird Blue** *Conway Twitty*
'70 **Is Anybody Goin' To San Antone**
Charley Pride
'91 **Is It Good To You**
Heavy D & The Boyz
'86 **Is It Love** *Mr. Mister*
'69 **Is It Something You've Got**
Tyrone Davis
'64 **Is It True** *Brenda Lee*
'81 **Is It You** *Lee Ritenour*
'79 **Is She Really Going Out With Him?**
Joe Jackson
'96 **Is That A Tear** *Tracy Lawrence*
'69 **Is That All There Is** *Peggy Lee*
'60 **Is There Any Chance** *Marty Robbins*
'92 **Is There Life Out There**
Reba McEntire
'83 **Is There Something I Should Know**
Duran Duran
Is This Love
'78 *Bob Marley*
'86 *Survivor*
'87 *Whitesnake*
'76 **Isis** *Bob Dylan*
'75 **Island Girl** *Elton John*
'57 **Island In The Sun** *Harry Belafonte*
'82 **Island Of Lost Souls** *Blondie*
'83 **Islands In The Stream** *Kenny*
Rogers w/ Dolly Parton
'70 **Isn't It A Pity** *George Harrison*
'77 **Isn't It Time** *Babys*
'72 **Isn't Life Strange** *Moody Blues*
'77 **Isn't She Lovely** *Stevie Wonder*
'69 **Israelites** *Desmond Dekker*
'84 **It Ain't Enough** *Corey Hart*
It Ain't Me Babe
'64 *Bob Dylan*
'65 *Turtles*
'99 **It Ain't My Fault 2**
Silkk The Shocker & Mystikal
'91 **It Ain't Over 'Til It's Over**
Lenny Kravitz
'59 **It Doesn't Matter Anymore**
Buddy Holly
'71 **It Don't Come Easy** *Ringo Starr*

'70 **It Don't Matter To Me** *Bread*
'07 **It Ends Tonight**
All-American Rejects
'00 **It Feels So Good** *Sonique*
'59 **It Happened Today** *Skyliners*
'91 **It Hit Me Like A Hammer**
Huey Lewis
'64 **It Hurts Me** *Elvis Presley*
It Hurts To Be In Love
'57 *Annie Laurie*
'64 *Gene Pitney*
'02 **It Is You** *Newsboys*
'56 **It Isn't Right** *Platters*
'07 **It Just Comes Natural** *George Strait*
'61 **It Keeps Rainin'** *Fats Domino*
'62 **It Keeps Right On A-Hurtin'**
Johnny Tillotson
'76 **It Keeps You Runnin'**
Doobie Brothers
'95 **It Matters To Me** *Faith Hill*
'55 **It May Sound Silly** *McGuire Sisters*
'62 **It Might As Well Rain Until**
September *Carole King*
'83 **It Might Be You** *Stephen Bishop*
'67 **It Must Be Him** *Vikki Carr*
It Must Be Love
'79 *Alton McClain & Destiny*
'83 *Madness*
'98 *Ty Herndon*
'00 *Alan Jackson*
'90 **It Must Have Been Love** *Roxette*
It Never Rains In Southern California
'72 *Albert Hammond*
'90 *Tony! Toni! Toné!*
'60 **It Only Happened Yesterday**
Jack Scott
'56 **It Only Hurts For A Little While**
Ames Brothers
'75 **It Only Takes A Minute** *Tavares*
'78 **It Seems To Hang On**
Ashford & Simpson
'68 **It Should Have Been Me**
Gladys Knight
'91 **It Should've Been You**
Teddy Pendergrass
'62 **It Started All Over Again**
Brenda Lee
'93 **It Sure Is Monday** *Mark Chesnutt*
'73 **It Sure Took A Long, Long Time**
Lobo
It Takes Two
'67 *Marvin Gaye & Kim Weston*
'88 *Rob Base & D.J. E-Z Rock*
'66 **It Tears Me Up** *Percy Sledge*
'93 **It Was A Good Day** *Ice Cube*
'63 **It Was A Very Good Year**
Frank Sinatra
'77 **It Was Almost Like A Song**
Ronnie Milsap
'19 **It Was I** *Skip & Flip*
'00 **It Wasn't Me** *Shaggy*
'61 **It Will Stand** *Showmen*
'88 **It Would Take A Strong Strong Man**
Rick Astley
'77 **It's A Crazy World** *Mac McAnally*
'01 **It's A Great Day To Be Alive**
Travis Tritt
'78 **It's A Heartache** *Bonnie Tyler*
'78 **It's A Laugh** *Daryl Hall & John Oates*
It's A Little Too Late
'93 *Tanya Tucker*
'96 *Mark Chesnutt*
'76 **It's A Long Way There**
Little River Band
'81 **It's A Love Thing** *Whispers*
'66 **It's A Man's Man's Man's World**
James Brown
It's A Miracle
'75 *Barry Manilow*
'84 *Culture Club*
'83 **It's A Mistake** *Men At Work*
'70 **It's A New Day** *James Brown*
'70 **It's A Shame** *Spinners*
'91 **It's A Shame (My Sister)** *Monie Love*
'87 **It's A Sin** *Pet Shop Boys*

'55 **It's A Sin To Tell A Lie**
Somethin' Smith & The Redheads
'98 **It's All About Me** *Mya w/ Sisqo*
'97 **It's All About The Benjamins**
Puff Daddy
'99 **It's All About You (Not About Me)**
Tracie Spencer
'61 **It's All Because** *Linda Scott*
'99 **It's All Been Done** *Barenaked Ladies*
'96 **It's All Coming Back To Me Now**
Celine Dion
'75 **It's All Down To Goodnight Vienna**
Ringo Starr
'79 **It's All I Can Do** *Cars*
It's All In The Game
'58 *Tommy Edwards*
'63 *Cliff Richard*
'70 *Four Tops*
'64 **It's All Over Now** *Rolling Stones*
'65 **It's All Over Now, Baby Blue**
Bob Dylan
It's All Right
'63 *Impressions*
'93 *Huey Lewis*
'98 *Candlebox*
'96 **It's All The Way Live (Now)** *Coolio*
It's Almost Tomorrow
'55 *David Carroll*
'55 *Dream Weavers*
'55 *Jo Stafford*
'65 **It's Alright** *Adam Faith*
'00 **It's Always Somethin'** *Joe Diffie*
'58 **(It's Been A Long Time) Pretty Baby**
Gino & Gina
'01 **It's Been Awhile** *Staind*
'77 **It's Ecstasy When You Lay Down**
Next To Me *Barry White*
'03 **It's Five O'Clock Somewhere**
Alan Jackson & Jimmy Buffett
'71 **It's Four In The Morning**
Faron Young
'69 **It's Getting Better** *Mama Cass*
'05 **It's Getting Better All The Time**
Brooks & Dunn
'06 **It's Goin' Down** *Yung Joc*
'72 **It's Going To Take Some Time**
Carpenters
'92 **It's Gonna Be A Lovely Day**
S.O.U.L. S.Y.S.T.E.M.
It's Gonna Be Alright
'65 *Gerry & The Pacemakers*
'89 *Ruby Turner*
'00 **It's Gonna Be Me** **NSYNC*
'82 **It's Gonna Take A Miracle**
Deniece Williams
'61 **It's Gonna Work Out Fine**
Ike & Tina Turner
'66 **It's Good News Week**
Hedgehoppers Anonymous
'65 **It's Growing** *Temptations*
'80 **It's Hard To Be Humble** *Mac Davis*
'70 **It's Impossible** *Perry Como*
'86 **It's In The Way That You Use It**
Eric Clapton
'83 **It's Inevitable** *Charlie*
'59 **It's Just A Matter Of Time**
Brook Benton
'81 **It's Just The Sun** *Don McLean*
'89 **(It's Just) The Way That You Love**
Me *Paula Abdul*
'59 **It's Late** *Ricky Nelson*
It's Like That
'84 *Run-D.M.C.*
'05 *Mariah Carey*
'55 **It's Love Baby (24 Hours A Day)**
Louis Brooks
'96 **It's Midnight Cinderella** *Garth Brooks*
'88 **It's Money That Matters**
Randy Newman
It's My Life
'65 *Animals*
'84 *Talk Talk*
'00 *Bon Jovi*
'03 *No Doubt*
'63 **It's My Party** *Lesley Gore*
'80 **It's My Turn** *Diana Ross*
'68 **It's Nice To Be With You** *Monkees*

'89 **It's No Crime** *Babyface*
'97 **It's No Good** *Depeche Mode*
'88 **It's No Secret** *Kylie Minogue*
'89 **It's Not Enough** *Starship*
'57 **It's Not For Me To Say**
    Johnny Mathis
'07 **It's Not Over** *Daughtry*
'87 **It's Not Over ('Til It's Over)** *Starship*
'99 **It's Not Right But It's Okay**
    Whitney Houston
'65 **It's Not Unusual** *Tom Jones*
It's Now Or Never
'60   *Elvis Presley*
'81   *John Schneider*
'66 **It's Now Winters Day** *Tommy Roe*
'76 **It's O.K.** *Beach Boys*
'71 **It's One Of Those Nights (Yes Love)**
    Partridge Family
It's Only Love
'66   *Tommy James*
'77   *ZZ Top*
'85   *Bryan Adams/Tina Turner*
It's Only Make Believe
'58   *Conway Twitty*
'70   *Glen Campbell*
'74 **It's Only Rock 'N Roll (But I Like It)**
    Rolling Stones
'59 **It's Only The Beginning** *Kalin Twins*
It's Over
'64   *Roy Orbison*
'66   *Jimmie Rodgers*
'76   *Boz Scaggs*
'00 **It's Over Now** *112*
'82 **It's Raining Again** *Supertramp*
'83 **It's Raining Men** *Weather Girls*
'77 **It's Sad To Belong**
    England Dan & John Ford Coley
It's So Easy
'58   *Crickets*
'77   *Linda Ronstadt*
'91 **It's So Hard To Say Goodbye To**
    Yesterday *Boyz II Men*
'80 **It's Still Rock And Roll To Me**
    Billy Joel
'67 **It's Such A Pretty World Today**
    Andy Russell
'67 **It's The Little Things** *Sonny James*
'89 **It's The Real Thing** *Angela Winbush*
It's The Same Old Song
'65   *Four Tops*
'78   *KC & The Sunshine Band*
'59 **It's Time To Cry** *Paul Anka*
It's Too Late
'56   *Chuck Willis*
'66   *Bobby Goldsboro*
'71   *Carole King*
'58 **It's Too Soon To Know** *Pat Boone*
'62 **It's Up To You** *Rick Nelson*
'67 **It's Wonderful** *Young Rascals*
'57 **It's You I Love** *Fats Domino*
'78 **It's You That I Need** *Enchantment*
'97 **It's Your Love**
    Tim McGraw w/ Faith Hill
'69 **It's Your Thing** *Isley Brothers*
'82 **Italian Girls**
    Daryl Hall & John Oates
'56 **Italian Theme** *Cyril Stapleton*
'58 **Itchy Twitchy Feeling**
    Bobby Hendricks
'67 **Itchycoo Park** *Small Faces*
'60 **Itsy Bitsy Teenie Weenie Yellow**
    Polkadot Bikini *Brian Hyland*
Ivory Tower
'56   *Cathy Carr*
'56   *Otis Williams/Charms*
'56   *Gale Storm*
'57 **Ivy Rose** *Perry Como*
'01 **Izzo (H.O.V.A.)** *Jay-Z*

J

'95 **J.A.R. (Jason Andrew Relva)**
    Green Day
'78 **Jack, The** *AC/DC*
'82 **Jack & Diane**
    John Cougar Mellencamp

'78 **Jack And Jill** *Raydio*
'97 **Jack-Ass** *Beck*
'75 **Jackie Blue**
    Ozark Mountain Daredevils
'72 **Jackie Wilson Said (I'm In Heaven**
    When You Smile) *Van Morrison*
Jackson
'67   *Johnny Cash & June Carter*
'67   *Nancy Sinatra & Lee Hazlewood*
'87 **Jacob's Ladder** *Huey Lewis*
Jaded
'95   *Green Day [medley]*
'01   *Aerosmith*
'84 **Jail House Rap** *Fat Boys*
'57 **Jailhouse Rock** *Elvis Presley*
'92 **Jam** *Michael Jackson*
'62 **Jam, The** *Bobby Gregg*
'87 **Jam Tonight** *Freddie Jackson*
'69 **Jam Up Jelly Tight** *Tommy Roe*
Jamaica Farewell
'56   *Harry Belafonte*
'60   *Mantovani*
'72 **Jambalaya (On The Bayou)**
    John Fogerty
'99 **Jamboree** *Naughty By Nature*
'89 **James Brown** *Big Audio Dynamite*
'74 **James Dean** *Eagles*
'62 **James (Hold The Ladder Steady)**
    Sue Thompson
Jamie
'62   *Eddie Holland*
'84   *Ray Parker Jr.*
'78 **Jamie's Cryin'** *Van Halen*
'87 **Jammin' Me** *Tom Petty*
'77 **Jamming** *Bob Marley*
'79 **Jane** *Jefferson Starship*
'88 **Jane Says** *Jane's Addiction*
'89 **Janie's Got A Gun** *Aerosmith*
'64 **Java** *Al Hirt*
'74 **Jazzman** *Carole King*
'90 **Jealous** *Gene Loves Jezebel*
'69 **Jealous Kind Of Fella**
    Garland Green
'60 **Jealous Of You** *Connie Francis*
'96 **Jealousy** *Natalie Merchant*
'69 **Jean** *Oliver*
'72 **Jean Genie** *David Bowie*
'58 **Jeannie Jeannie Jeannie**
    Eddie Cochran
'76 **Jeans On** *David Dundas*
'58 **Jennie Lee** *Jan & Dean*
'68 **Jennifer Eccles** *Hollies*
'68 **Jennifer Juniper** *Donovan*
'70 **Jennifer Tomkins** *Street People*
'02 **Jenny From The Block**
    Jennifer Lopez
'57 **Jenny, Jenny** *Little Richard*
'65 **Jenny Take A Ride!** *Mitch Ryder*
'83 **Jeopardy** *Greg Kihn Band*
'61 **Jeremiah Peabody's Poly**
    Unsaturated Pills *Ray Stevens*
'92 **Jeremy** *Pearl Jam*
'64 **Jerk, The** *Larks*
'90 **Jerk-Out** *Time*
Jesse
'73   *Roberta Flack*
'80   *Carly Simon*
'73 **Jessica** *Allman Brothers Band*
'93 **Jessie** *Joshua Kadison*
'81 **Jessie's Girl** *Rick Springfield*
'95' **Jesus Freak** *DC Talk*
'92 **Jesus He Knows Me** *Genesis*
'69 **Jesus Is A Soul Man**
    Lawrence Reynolds
'72 **Jesus Is Just Alright**
    Doobie Brothers
'72 **Jesus Just Left Chicago [medley]**
    ZZ Top
'06 **Jesus, Take The Wheel**
    Carrie Underwood
'96 **Jesus To A Child** *George Michael*
'04 **Jesus Walks** *Kanye West*
'74 **Jet** *Paul McCartney*
'77 **Jet Airliner** *Steve Miller Band*
'99 **Jigga My Nigga** *Jay-Z*

'00 **Jim Dandy**
'56   *LaVern Baker*
'73   *Black Oak Arkansas*
'57 **Jim Dandy Got Married**
    LaVern Baker
'94 **Jimi Thing** *Dave Matthews Band*
'86 **Jimmy Lee** *Aretha Franklin*
'73 **Jimmy Loves Mary-Anne**
    Looking Glass
'67 **Jimmy Mack**
    Martha & The Vandellas
'61 **Jimmy's Girl** *Johnny Tillotson*
Jingle Bell Rock
'57   *Bobby Helms*
'61   *Bobby Rydell/Chubby Checker*
'55 **Jingle Bells** *Singing Dogs*
'69 **Jingle Jangle** *Archies*
'69 **Jingo** *Santana*
'75 **Jive Talkin'** *Bee Gees*
'58 **Jo-Ann** *Playmates*
'80 **JoJo** *Boz Scaggs*
'83 **Joanna** *Kool & The Gang*
'70 **Joanne** *Michael Nesmith*
'97 **Jock Jam** *ESPN Presents*
'71 **Jody's Got Your Girl And Gone**
    Johnnie Taylor
'79 **Joe's Garage** *Frank Zappa*
'90 **Joey** *Concrete Blonde*
'62 **John Barleycorn** *Traffic*
'62 **Johnny Angel** *Shelley Fabares*
'87 **Johnny B** *Hooters*
Johnny B. Goode
'58   *Chuck Berry*
'83   *Peter Tosh*
'62 **Johnny Get Angry** *Joanie Sommers*
'62 **Johnny Jingo** *Hayley Mills*
'62 **Johnny Loves Me** *Shelley Fabares*
'69 **Johnny One Time** *Brenda Lee*
'61 **Johnny Will** *Pat Boone*
'72 **Join Together** *Who*
'73 **Joker, The** *Steve Miller Band*
Joker (That's What They Call Me)
'57   *Hilltoppers*
'57   *Billy Myles*
'66 **Joker Went Wild** *Brian Hyland*
'74 **Jolene** *Dolly Parton*
'65 **Jolly Green Giant** *Kingsmen*
'85 **Jolly Mon Sing** *Jimmy Buffett*
'81 **Jones Vs. Jones** *Kool & The Gang*
'60 **Josephine** *Bill Black's Combo*
'70 **Joshua** *Dolly Parton*
'78 **Josie** *Steely Dan*
'68 **Journey To The Center Of The Mind**
    Amboy Dukes
'64 **Journey To The Stars** *Ventures*
Joy
'72   *Apollo 100*
'73   *Isaac Hayes*
'88   *Teddy Pendergrass*
'01   *Newsboys*
'89 **Joy And Pain** *Donna Allen*
'71 **Joy To The World** *Three Dog Night*
'91 **Joyride** *Roxette*
'65 **Ju Ju Hand** *Sam The Sham &*
    the Pharaohs
'00 **Judith** *Perfect Circle*
'67 **Judy In Disguise (With Glasses)**
    John Fred
'75 **Judy Mae** *Boomer Castleman*
'62 **Judy's Turn To Cry** *Lesley Gore*
'94 **Juicy** *Notorious B.I.G.*
'83 **Juicy Fruit** *Mtume*
'56 **Juke Box Baby** *Perry Como*
'81 **Juke Box Hero** *Foreigner*
'90 **Jukebox In My Mind** *Alabama*
'91 **Jukebox With A Country Song**
    Doug Stone
'70 **Julie, Do Ya Love Me**
    Bobby Sherman
'81 **Julie Don't Live Here**
    Electric Light Orchestra
Jump
'84   *Van Halen*
'92   *Kris Kross*
'92 **Jump Around** *House Of Pain*

'84 **Jump (For My Love)** *Pointer Sisters*
'72 **Jump Into The Fire** *Nilsson*
'98 **Jump Jive An' Wail**
   Brian Setzer Orchestra
'03 **Jump Off** *Lil' Kim*
'60 **Jump Over** *Freddy Cannon*
'76 **Jump Shout Boogie** *Barry Manilow*
'87 **Jump Start** *Natalie Cole*
'82 **Jump To It** *Aretha Franklin*
'98 **Jumper** *Third Eye Blind*
   Jumpin' Jack Flash
'68   *Rolling Stones*
'86   *Aretha Franklin*
'00 **Jumpin', Jumpin'** *Destiny's Child*
'57 **June Night** *Jimmy Dorsey*
'73 **Jungle Boogie** *Kool & The Gang*
'86 **Jungle Boy** *John Eddie*
'72 **Jungle Fever** *Chakachas*
   Jungle Love
'77   *Steve Miller Band*
'84   *Time*
'75 **Jungleland** *Bruce Springsteen*
'74 **Junior's Farm** *Paul McCartney*
'76 **Junk Food Junkie** *Larry Groce*
'61 **Jura (I Swear I Love You)**
   Les Paul & Mary Ford
'58 **Just A Dream** *Jimmy Clanton*
'90 **Just A Friend** *Biz Markie*
'02 **Just A Friend 2002** *Mario*
   Just A Gigolo [medley]
'56   *Louis Prima & Keely Smith*
'85   *David Lee Roth*
'95 **Just A Girl** *No Doubt*
'83 **Just A Job To Do** *Genesis*
'05 **Just A Lil Bit** *50 Cent*
   Just A Little
'60   *Brenda Lee*
'65   *Beau Brummels*
   Just A Little Bit
'60   *Rosco Gordon*
'65   *Roy Head*
'65 **Just A Little Bit Better**
   Herman's Hermits
'75 **Just A Little Bit Of You**
   Michael Jackson
'59 **Just A Little Too Much**
   Ricky Nelson
'77 **Just A Song Before I Go**
   Crosby, Stills & Nash
'92 **Just Another Day** *Jon Secada*
'00 **Just Another Day In Paradise**
   Phil Vassar
'90 **Just Another Dream** *Cathy Dennis*
'85 **Just Another Night** *Mick Jagger*
'85 **Just As I Am** *Air Supply*
   Just As Much As Ever
'59   *Bob Beckham*
'67   *Bobby Vinton*
'59 **Just Ask Your Heart** *Frankie Avalon*
'00 **Just Be A Man About It**
   Toni Braxton
'83 **Just Be Good To Me** *S.O.S. Band*
'64 **Just Be True** *Gene Chandler*
   Just Because
'57   *Lloyd Price*
'89   *Anita Baker*
'03   *Jane's Addiction*
   Just Between You And Me
'57   *Chordettes*
'81   *April Wine*
'89   *Lou Gramm*
'96   *DC Talk*
'57 **Just Born (To Be Your Baby)**
   Perry Como
'82 **Just Can't Win 'Em All**
   Stevie Woods
'59 **Just Come Home** *Hugo & Luigi*
'89 **Just Coolin'** *Levert*
'74 **Just Don't Want To Be Lonely**
   Main Ingredient
'68 **Just Dropped In (To See What**
   Condition My Condition Was In)
   First Edition
'61 **Just For Old Time's Sake**
   McGuire Sisters
'92 **Just For Tonight** *Vanessa Williams*

'00 **Just Friends (Sunny)** *Musiq*
'83 **Just Got Lucky** *JoBoxers*
'88 **Just Got Paid** *Johnny Kemp*
'61 **Just Got To Know**
   Jimmy McCracklin
'56 **Just In Time** *Tony Bennett*
'59 **Just Keep It Up** *Dee Clark*
'93 **Just Kickin' It** *Xscape*
'02 **Just Like A Pill** *P!nk*
'66 **Just Like A Woman** *Bob Dylan*
'87 **Just Like Heaven** *Cure*
'89 **Just Like Jesse James** *Cher*
'65 **Just Like Me**
   Paul Revere & The Raiders
'88 **Just Like Paradise** *David Lee Roth*
'64 **(Just Like) Romeo & Juliet**
   Reflections
'80 **(Just Like) Starting Over**
   John Lennon
   Just Like You
'91   *Robbie Nevil*
'04   *Three Days Grace*
'04 **Just Lose It** *Eminem*
'58 **Just Married** *Marty Robbins*
'06 **Just Might (Make Me Believe)**
   Sugarland
'71 **Just My Imagination** *Temptations*
'81 **Just Once**
   Quincy Jones/James Ingram
'65 **Just Once In My Life**
   Righteous Brothers
   Just One Look
'63   *Doris Troy*
'64   *Hollies*
'60 **Just One Time** *Don Gibson*
'61 **Just Out Of Reach (Of My Two**
   Open Arms) *Solomon Burke*
'88 **Just Play Music!**
   Big Audio Dynamite
'77 **Just Remember I Love You** *Firefall*
'06 **Just Stop** *Disturbed*
'92 **Just Take My Heart** *Mr. Big*
'05 **Just The Girl** *Click Five*
'79 **Just The Same Way** *Journey*
   Just The Two Of Us
'81   *Grover Washington, Jr. w/ Bill*
     Withers
'98   *Will Smith*
'91 **Just The Way It Is, Baby**
   Rembrandts
'77 **Just The Way You Are** *Billy Joel*
'76 **Just To Be Close To You**
   Commodores
'98 **Just To Hear You Say That You**
   Love Me
   Faith Hill (w/ Tim McGraw)
'57 **Just To Hold My Hand**
   Clyde McPhatter
'82 **Just To Satisfy You**
   Waylon Jennings & Willie Nelson
'87 **Just To See Her** *Smokey Robinson*
'97 **Just To See You Smile** *Tim McGraw*
'75 **Just Too Many People**
   Melissa Manchester
'56 **Just Walking In The Rain**
   Johnnie Ray
'91 **Just Want To Hold You**
   Jasmine Guy
'78 **Just What I Needed** *Cars*
'79 **Just When I Needed You Most**
   Randy Vanwarmer
'65 **Just You** *Sonny & Cher*
'76 **Just You And I** *Melissa Manchester*
'73 **Just You 'N' Me** *Chicago*
'92 **Justified & Ancient** *KLF*
'90 **Justify My Love** *Madonna*

K

   Ka-Ding-Dong
'56   *Diamonds*
'56   *G-Clefs*
'56   *Hilltoppers*
   Kansas City
'59   *Wilbert Harrison*
'63   *Trini Lopez*

'65 **Kansas City Star** *Roger Miller*
   Karma
'05   *Lloyd Banks*
'05   *Alicia Keys*
'83 **Karma Chameleon** *Culture Club*
'73 **Karn Evil 9**
   Emerson, Lake & Palmer
'75 **Kashmir** *Led Zeppelin*
'75 **Katmandu** *Bob Seger*
'58 **Kathy-O** *Diamonds*
'69 **Kaw-Liga** *Charley Pride [live]*
'69 **Keem-O-Sabe** *Electric Indian*
'57 **Keep A Knockin'** *Little Richard*
'91 **Keep Coming Back** *Richard Marx*
'89 **Keep Each Other Warm**
   Barry Manilow
'83 **(Keep Feeling) Fascination**
   Human League
   Keep Holding On
'76   *Temptations*
'06   *Avril Lavigne*
'91 **Keep It Between The Lines**
   Ricky Van Shelton
'91 **Keep It Comin'** *Keith Sweat*
'77 **Keep It Comin' Love**
   KC & The Sunshine Band
'90 **Keep It Together** *Madonna*
'76 **Keep Me Cryin'** *Al Green*
'65 **Keep On Dancing** *Gentrys*
'96 **Keep On, Keepin' On** *MC Lyte*
'68 **Keep On Lovin' Me Honey**
   Marvin Gaye & Tammi Terrell
'80 **Keep On Loving You**
   REO Speedwagon
'89 **Keep On Movin'** *Soul II Soul*
'64 **Keep On Pushing** *Impressions*
'74 **Keep On Singing** *Helen Reddy*
'74 **Keep On Smilin'** *Wet Willie*
'73 **Keep On Truckin'** *Eddie Kendricks*
'92 **Keep On Walkin'** *Ce Ce Peniston*
'64 **Keep Searchin'** *Del Shannon*
'94 **Keep Talking** *Pink Floyd*
'67 **Keep The Ball Rollin'**
   Jay & The Techniques
'07 **Keep The Car Running** *Arcade Fire*
'92 **Keep The Faith** *Bon Jovi*
'80 **Keep The Fire** *Kenny Loggins*
'82 **Keep The Fire Burnin'**
   REO Speedwagon
'95 **Keep Their Heads Ringin'** *Dr. Dre*
'93 **Keep Ya Head Up** *2Pac*
'87 **Keep Your Eye On Me** *Herb Alpert*
'75 **Keep Your Eye On The Sparrow**
   Merry Clayton
'62 **Keep Your Hands Off My Baby**
   Little Eva
'86 **Keep Your Hands To Yourself**
   Georgia Satellites
'72 **Keeper Of The Castle** *Four Tops*
'95 **Keeper Of The Stars** *Tracy Byrd*
'78 **Keeping The Faith** *Billy Joel*
'55 **Kentuckian Song** *Hilltoppers*
'70 **Kentucky Rain** *Elvis Presley*
   Kentucky Woman
'67   *Neil Diamond*
'68   *Deep Purple*
'85 **Kern River** *Merle Haggard*
'06 **Kerosene** *Miranda Lambert*
'58 **Kewpie Doll** *Perry Como*
'81 **Key Largo** *Bertie Higgins*
'96 **Key West Intermezzo (I Saw You**
   First) *John Mellencamp*
'94 **Kick A Little** *Little Texas*
'77 **Kick It Out** *Heart*
'69 **Kick Out The Jams** *MC5*
'98 **Kicking My Heart Around**
   Black Crowes
'66 **Kicks** *Paul Revere & The Raiders*
'89 **Kickstart My Heart** *Mötley Crüe*
'76 **Kid Charlemagne** *Steely Dan*
'84 **Kid's American** *Matthew Wilder*
'60 **Kiddio** *Brook Benton*
'71 **Kids Are Alright** *Who*
'82 **Kids In America** *Kim Wilde*
'84 **Kids Wanna Rock** *Bryan Adams*
'63 **Killer Joe** *Rocky Fellers*

'75 **Killer Queen** *Queen*
     Killin' Time
'80   *Fred Knoblock & Susan Anton*
'89   *Clint Black*
'65 **Killing Floor** *Howlin' Wolf*
     Killing Me Softly With His Song
'73   *Roberta Flack*
'96   *Fugees*
'84 **Killing Moon** *Echo & The Bunnymen*
'77 **Killing Of Georgie** *Rod Stewart*
'98 **Kind & Generous** *Natalie Merchant*
'66 **Kind Of A Drag** *Buckinghams*
'63 **Kind Of Boy You Can't Forget**
        Raindrops
'58 **King Creole** *Elvis Presley*
'86 **King For A Day** *Thompson Twins*
'72 **King Heroin** *James Brown*
'77 **King Is Gone** *Ronnie McDowell*
'83 **King Of Pain** *Police*
'85 **King Of Rock** *Run-D.M.C.*
'65 **King Of The Road** *Roger Miller*
'62 **King Of The Whole Wide World**
        Elvis Presley
'90 **King Of Wishful Thinking** *Go West*
'78 **King Tut** *Steve Martin*
'06 **King Without A Crown** *Matisyahu*
'77 **Kings And Queens** *Aerosmith*
'74 **Kings Of The Party**
        Brownsville Station
     Kiss
'86   *Prince*
'88   *Art Of Noise*
'71 **Kiss An Angel Good Mornin'**
        Charley Pride
'76 **Kiss And Say Goodbye** *Manhattans*
'88 **Kiss And Tell** *Bryan Ferry*
'65 **Kiss Away** *Ronnie Dove*
'95 **Kiss From A Rose** *Seal*
'79 **Kiss In The Dark** *Pink Lady*
'98 **Kiss Me** *Sixpence None The Richer*
'56 **Kiss Me Another** *Georgia Gibbs*
'88 **Kiss Me Deadly** *Lita Ford*
'68 **Kiss Me Goodbye** *Petula Clark*
'80 **Kiss Me In The Rain**
        Barbra Streisand
'64 **Kiss Me Quick** *Elvis Presley*
'64 **Kiss Me Sailor** *Diane Renay*
'81 **Kiss On My List**
        Daryl Hall & John Oates
'83 **Kiss The Bride** *Elton John*
'89 **Kiss The Girl**
        Little Mermaid Soundtrack
'97 **Kiss The Rain** *Billie Myers*
'91 **Kiss Them For Me**
        Siouxsie & The Banshees
'00 **Kiss This** *Aaron Tippin*
'90 **Kiss This Thing Goodbye** *Del Amitri*
'78 **Kiss You All Over** *Exile*
'91 **Kiss You Back** *Digital Underground*
'89 **Kisses On The Wind** *Neneh Cherry*
'57 **Kisses Sweeter Than Wine**
        Jimmie Rodgers
'64 **Kissin' Cousins** *Elvis Presley*
'61 **Kissin' On The Phone** *Paul Anka*
'59 **Kissin' Time** *Bobby Rydell*
'96 **Kissin' You** *Total*
'91 **Kissing You** *Keith Washington*
'88 **Kissing A Fool** *George Michael*
'73 **Kissing My Love** *Bill Withers*
'57 **Knee Deep In The Blues**
        Guy Mitchell
'66 **Knight In Rusty Armour**
        Peter & Gordon
     Knock On Wood
'66   *Eddie Floyd*
'67   *Otis Redding & Carla Thomas*
'79   *Amii Stewart*
'70 **Knock Three Times** *Dawn*
'88 **Knocked Out** *Paula Abdul*
'90 **Knockin' Boots** *Candyman*
'93 **Knockin' Da Boots** *H-Town*
     Knockin' On Heaven's Doo
'73   *Bob Dylan*
'90   *Guns N' Roses*
'97 **Knocks Me Off My Feet**
        Donell Jones

'77 **Knowing Me, Knowing You** *Abba*
     Ko Ko Mo (I Love You So)
'55   *Perry Como*
'55   *Crew-Cuts*
'73 **Kodachrome** *Paul Simon*
'88 **Kokomo** *Beach Boys*
'59 **Kookie, Kookie (Lend Me Your**
        Comb) *Edward Byrnes &*
        Connie Stevens
'60 **Kookie Little Paradise**
        Jo Ann Campbell
'69 **Kozmic Blues** *Janis Joplin*
'00 **Kryptonite** *3 Doors Down*
'05 **Kryptonite (I'm On It)**
        Purple Ribbon All-Stars
'69 **Kum Ba Yah** *Tommy Leonetti*
'74 **Kung Fu** *Curtis Mayfield*
'74 **Kung Fu Fighting** *Carl Douglas*
'85 **Kyrie** *Mr. Mister*

L

'71 **L.A. International Airport**
        Susan Raye
'77 **L.A. Sunshine** *War*
'71 **L.A. Woman** *Doors*
     La Bamba
'58   *Ritchie Valens*
'87   *Los Lobos*
'58 **La Dee Dah** *Billy & Lillie*
'58 **La-Do-Dada** *Dale Hawkins*
'73 **La Grange** *ZZ Top*
'87 **La Isla Bonita** *Madonna*
'69 **La La La (If I Had You)**
        Bobby Sherman
'68 **La-La Means I Love You** *Delfonics*
'74 **La La Peace Song** *Al Wilson*
'58 **La Paloma** *Billy Vaughn*
'90 **La Raza** *Kid Frost*
'05 **La Tortura**
        Shakira w/ Alejandro Sanz
'07 **Ladies And Gentlemen** *Saliva*
'90 **Ladies First** *Queen Latifah*
'07 **Ladies Love Country Boys**
        Trace Adkins
'79 **Ladies Night** *Kool & The Gang*
     Lady
'67   *Jack Jones*
'74   *Styx*
'79   *Little River Band*
'80   *Kenny Rogers*
'80   *Whispers*
'96   *D'Angelo*
'04   *Lenny Kravitz*
'67 **Lady Bird** *Nancy Sinatra &*
        Lee Hazlewood
'75 **Lady Blue** *Leon Russell*
'66 **Lady Godiva** *Peter & Gordon*
'87 **Lady In Red** *Chris DeBurgh*
'66 **Lady Jane** *Rolling Stones*
'78 **Lady Love** *Lou Rawls*
'83 **Lady Love Me (One More Time)**
        George Benson
'60 **Lady Luck** *Lloyd Price*
'68 **Lady Madonna** *Beatles*
     Lady Marmalade
'75   *LaBelle*
'01   *Christina Aguilera, Lil' Kim, Mya &*
        P!nk
'96 **Lady Picture Show**
        Stone Temple Pilots
'68 **Lady Willpower** *Gary Puckett*
'79 **Lady Writer** *Dire Straits*
'81 **Lady (You Bring Me Up)**
        Commodores
'06 **Laffy Taffy** *D4L*
'93 **Laid** *James*
'97 **Lakini's Juice** *Live*
'68 **Lalena** *Donovan*
'75 **Lamb Lies Down On Broadway**
        Genesis
     Land Of Confusion
'86   *Genesis*
'07   *Disturbed*
'66 **Land Of Milk And Honey** *Vogues*

     Land Of 1000 Dances
'65   *Cannibal & The Headhunters*
'66   *Wilson Pickett*
'80 **Landlord** *Gladys Knight*
     Landslide
'75   *Fleetwood Mac*
'94   *Smashing Pumpkins*
'02   *Dixie Chicks*
     Language Of Love
'61   *John D. Loudermilk*
'84   *Dan Fogelberg*
'66 **Lara's Theme From "Dr. Zhivago"**
        Roger Williams
'99 **Larger Than Life** *Backstreet Boys*
'65 **Last Chance To Turn Around**
        Gene Pitney
'79 **Last Cheater's Waltz** *T.G. Sheppard*
'76 **Last Child** *Aerosmith*
'78 **Last Dance** *Donna Summer*
     Last Date
'60   *Floyd Cramer*
'60   *Lawrence Welk*
'06 **Last Day Of My Life** *Phil Vassar*
'07 **Last Dollar (Fly Away)** *Tim McGraw*
'75 **Last Farewell** *Roger Whittaker*
'75 **Last Game Of The Season (A Blind**
        Man In The Bleachers)
        David Geddes
     Last Kiss
'64   *J. Frank Wilson*
'99   *Pearl Jam*
'63 **Last Leaf** *Cascades*
'89 **Last Mile** *Cinderella*
     Last Night [Nite]
'61   *Mar-Keys*
'96   *Az Yet*
'01   *Strokes*
'07   *Diddy*
'72 **(Last Night) I Didn't Get To Sleep At**
        All *5th Dimension*
'97 **Last Night On Earth** *U2*
'97 **Last Night's Letter** *K-Ci & JoJo*
'89 **Last Of The Famous International**
        Playboys *Morrissey*
'00 **Last Resort** *Papa Roach*
     Last Song
'72   *Edward Bear*
'92   *Elton John*
'65 **Last Time** *Rolling Stones*
'84 **Last Time I Made Love**
        Joyce Kennedy & Jeffrey Osborne
'74 **Last Time I Saw Him** *Diana Ross*
'03 **Last Train Home** *Lostprophets*
'66 **Last Train To Clarksville** *Monkees*
'79 **Last Train To London**
        Electric Light Orchestra
'67 **Last Waltz** *Engelbert Humperdinck*
'66 **Last Word In Lonesome Is Me**
        Eddy Arnold
'89 **Last Worthless Evening**
        Don Henley
'57 **Lasting Love** *Sal Mineo*
'74 **Late For The Sky**
        Jackson Browne
'80 **Late In The Evening** *Paul Simon*
     Lately
'93   *Jodeci*
'98   *Divine*
'65 **Laugh At Me** *Sonny*
'65 **Laugh, Laugh** *Beau Brummels*
'69 **Laughing** *Guess Who*
'63 **Laughing Boy** *Mary Wells*
'74 **Laughter In The Rain** *Neil Sedaka*
'65 **Laurie (Strange Things Happen)**
        Dickey Lee
'59 **Lavender-Blue** *Sammy Turner*
'78 **Lawyers, Guns And Money**
        Warren Zevon
'83 **Lawyers In Love** *Jackson Browne*
'70 **Lay A Little Lovin' On Me**
        Robin McNamara
'81 **Lay All Your Love On Me** *Abba*
'70 **Lay Down (Candles In The Rain)**
        Melanie/Edwin Hawkins Singers
'78 **Lay Down Sally** *Eric Clapton*
'56 **Lay Down Your Arms** *Chordettes*

226

'58 **Letter To An Angel** *Jimmy Clanton*
'92 **Letter To Elise** *Cure*
'73 **Letter To Myself** *Chi-Lites*
'04 **Letters From Home**
    John Michael Montgomery
'75 **Letting Go** *Wings*
'71 **Levon** *Elton John*
Liar
'71   *Three Dog Night*
'00   *Profyle*
'65 **Liar, Liar** *Castaways*
'89 **Licence To Chill** *Billy Ocean*
'68 **Licking Stick - Licking Stick**
    James Brown
'77 **Lido Shuffle** *Boz Scaggs*
'62 **Lie To Me** *Brook Benton*
'57 **Liechtensteiner Polka** *Will Glahé*
Lies
'65   *Knickerbockers*
'83   *Thompson Twins*
'87   *Jonathan Butler*
'90   *En Vogue*
'91   *EMF*
'06 **Life Ain't Always Beautiful**
    Gary Allan
'79 **Life During Wartime**
    Talking Heads
'91 **Life Goes On** *Poison*
'85 **Life In A Northern Town**
    Dream Academy
'85 **Life In One Day** *Howard Jones*
'77 **Life In The Fast Lane** *Eagles*
'71 **Life Is A Carnival** *Band*
Life Is A Highway
'92   *Tom Cochrane*
'06   *Rascal Flatts*
'74 **Life Is A Rock (But The Radio**
    Rolled Me) *Reunion*
'55 **Life Is But A Dream** *Harptones*
'81 **Life Of Illusion** *Joe Walsh*
'92 **Life Of Riley** *Lightning Seeds*
'88 **Life Turned Her That Way**
    Ricky Van Shelton
'92 **Life's A Dance**
    John Michael Montgomery
'78 **Life's Been Good** *Joe Walsh*
'07 **Life's What You Make It**
    Hannah Montana
'02 **Lifestyles Of The Rich And Famous**
    Good Charlotte
'01 **Lifetime** *Maxwell*
Lift Me Up
'91   *Yes*
'92   *Howard Jones*
'00 **Light, The** *Common*
Light My Fire
'67   *Doors*
'68   *Jose Feliciano*
'87 **Light Of Day** *Joan Jett*
'05 **Lighters Up** *Lil' Kim*
'65 **Lightnin' Strikes** *Lou Christie*
'95 **Lightning Crashes** *Live*
'67 **Lightning's Girl** *Nancy Sinatra*
'78 **Lights** *Journey*
'06 **Lights And Sounds** *Yellowcard*
'01 **Lights, Camera, Action!** *Mr. Cheeks*
'84 **Lights Out** *Peter Wolf*
'67 **(Lights Went Out In) Massachusetts**
    Bee Gees
'66 **Like A Baby** *Len Barry*
'07 **Like A Boy** *Ciara*
'77 **Like A Hurricane** *Neil Young*
'89 **Like A Prayer** *Madonna*
'86 **Like A Rock** *Bob Seger*
'65 **Like A Rolling Stone** *Bob Dylan*
'03 **Like A Stone** *Audioslave*
'78 **Like A Sunday In Salem (The Amos**
    & Andy Song) *Gene Cotton*
'85 **Like A Surgeon** *"Weird Al" Yankovic*
'84 **Like A Virgin** *Madonna*
'67 **Like An Old Time Movie**
    Scott McKenzie
'03 **Like Glue** *Sean Paul*
'02 **Like I Love You** *Justin Timberlake*
'61 **Like, Long Hair**
    Paul Revere & The Raiders

'86 **Like No Other Night** *38 Special*
'60 **Like Strangers** *Everly Brothers*
'96 **Like The Rain** *Clint Black*
'95 **Like There Ain't No Yesterday**
    BlackHawk
Like This
'07   *Kelly Rowland*
'07   *Mims*
'95 **Like This And Like That** *Monica*
'68 **Like To Get To Know You**
    Spanky & Our Gang
'05 **Like Toy Soldiers** *Eminem*
'05 **Like We Never Loved At All**
    Faith Hill w/ Tim McGraw
'91 **Like You** *Bow Wow*
'91 **Lily Was Here** *David A. Stewart*
    & Candy Dulfer
Limbo Rock
'62   *Champs*
'62   *Chubby Checker*
'81 **Limelight** *Rush*
'63 **Linda** *Jan & Dean*
'59 **Linda Lu** *Ray Sharpe*
Ling, Ting, Tong
'55   *Charms*
'55   *Five Keys*
'61   *Buddy Knox*
'93 **Linger** *Cranberries*
'87 **Linus And Lucy** *Vince Guaraldi Trio*
Lion Sleeps Tonight
'61   *Tokens*
'72   *Robert John*
'07 **Lip Gloss** *Lil Mama*
'06 **Lips Of An Angel** *Hinder*
'57 **Lips Of Wine** *Andy Williams*
'56 **Lipstick And Candy And**
    Rubbersole Shoes *Julius LaRosa*
'59 **Lipstick On Your Collar**
    Connie Francis
'00 **Liquid Dreams** *O-Town*
Lisbon Antigua
'55   *Nelson Riddle*
'56   *Mitch Miller*
'97 **Listen** *Collective Soul*
'85 **Listen Like Thieves** *INXS*
'66 **Listen People** *Herman's Hermits*
'78 **Listen To Her Heart** *Tom Petty*
'69 **Listen To The Band** *Monkees*
'72 **Listen To The Music**
    Doobie Brothers
'75 **Listen To What The Man Said**
    Wings
Listen To Your Heart
'89   *Roxette*
'05   *D.H.T.*
'99 **Lit Up** *Buckcherry*
'61 **Little Altar Boy** *Vic Dana*
'68 **Little Arrows** *Leapy Lee*
'63 **Little Band Of Gold** *James Gilreath*
'93 **Little Bird** *Annie Lennox*
'67 **Little Bit Me, A Little Bit You**
    Monkees
Little Bit More
'76   *Dr. Hook*
'86   *Melba Moore w/ Freddie Jackson*
'67 **Little Bit O' Soul** *Music Explosion*
'65 **Little Bit Of Heaven** *Ronnie Dove*
'86 **Little Bit Of Love (Is All It Takes)**
    New Edition
Little Bit Of Soap
'61   *Jarmels*
'79   *Nigel Olsson*
'74 **Little Bit Of Sympathy**
    Robin Trower
'96 **Little Bitty** *Alan Jackson*
'60 **Little Bitty Girl** *Bobby Rydell*
Little Bitty Pretty One
'57   *Thurston Harris*
'62   *Clyde McPhatter*
'72   *Jackson 5*
'61 **Little Bitty Tear** *Burl Ives*
'62 **Little Black Book** *Jimmy Dean*
'58 **Little Blue Man** *Betty Johnson*
'61 **Little Boy Sad** *Johnny Burnette*

Little By Little
'57   *Nappy Brown*
'85   *Robert Plant*
'64 **Little Children** *Billy J. Kramer*
    w/ The Dakotas
'60 **Little Coco Palm** *Jerry Wallace*
Little Darlin'
'57   *Diamonds*
'57   *Gladiolas*
'63 **Little Deuce Coupe** *Beach Boys*
'61 **Little Devil** *Neil Sedaka*
'62 **Little Diane** *Dion*
'59 **Little Dipper** *Mickey Mozart Quintet*
'58 **Little Drummer Boy**
    Harry Simeone Chorale
'61 **Little Egypt (Ying-Yang)** *Coasters*
'67 **Little Games** *Yardbirds*
Little Girl
'66   *Syndicate Of Sound*
'00   *John Michael Montgomery*
'65 **Little Girl I Once Knew** *Beach Boys*
'56 **Little Girl Of Mine** *Cleftones*
'99 **Little Good-Byes** *SheDaisy*
'83 **Little Good News** *Anne Murray*
Little Green Apples
'68   *Roger Miller*
'68   *O.C. Smith*
'70 **Little Green Bag**
    George Baker Selection
Little Honda
'64   *Beach Boys*
'64   *Hondells*
'80 **Little In Love** *Cliff Richard*
'89 **Little Jackie Wants To Be A Star**
    Lisa Lisa & Cult Jam
'80 **Little Jeannie** *Elton John*
'75 **Little Johnny Jewel** *Television*
Little Latin Lupe Lu
'63   *Righteous Brothers*
'66   *Mitch Ryder*
'68 **Little Less Conversation**
    Elvis Presley
'93 **Little Less Talk And A Lot More**
    Action *Toby Keith*
'88 **Little Liar** *Joan Jett*
'87 **Little Lies** *Fleetwood Mac*
'90 **Little Love** *Corey Hart*
Little Man
'66   *Sonny & Cher*
'99   *Alan Jackson*
'72 **Little Martha** *Allman Brothers Band*
'92 **Little Miss Can't Be Wrong**
    Spin Doctors
'95 **Little Miss Honky Tonk**
    Brooks & Dunn
'03 **Little Moments** *Brad Paisley*
Little More Love
'78   *Olivia Newton-John*
'97   *Vince Gill*
'97 **Little More Time With You**
    James Taylor
'64 **Little Old Lady (From Pasadena)**
    Jan & Dean
'67 **Little Old Wine Drinker, Me**
    Dean Martin
'67 **Little Ole Man (Uptight- Every-**
    thing's Alright) *Bill Cosby*
'98 **Little Past Little Rock**
    Lee Ann Womack
'77 **Little Queen** *Heart*
'83 **Little Red Corvette** *Prince*
'62 **Little Red Rented Rowboat**
    Joe Dowell
'66 **Lil' Red Riding Hood** *Sam The*
    Sham & The Pharoahs
'97 **Little Red Rodeo** *Collin Raye*
'63 **Little Red Rooster** *Sam Cooke*
'88 **Little Respect** *Erasure*
Little Rock
'86   *Reba McEntire*
'94   *Collin Raye*
'63 **Little Saint Nick** *Beach Boys*
Little Sister
'61   *Elvis Presley*
'05   *Queens Of The Stone Age*
'59 **Little Space Girl** *Jesse Lee Turner*

'58 **Little Star** *Elegants*
Little Things
'65   *Bobby Goldsboro*
'02   *India.Arie*
'59 **Little Things Mean A Lot**
      Joni James
Little Too Late
'83   *Pat Benatar*
'06   *Toby Keith*
'62 **Little Town Flirt** *Del Shannon*
'88 **Little Walter** *Tony! Toni! Toné!*
'97 **Little White Lie** *Sammy Hagar*
'57 **Little White Lies** *Betty Johnson*
'73 **Little Willy** *Sweet*
'68 **Little Wing** *Jimi Hendrix*
'07 **Little Wonders** *Rob Thomas*
'92 **Live And Learn** *Joe Public*
Live And Let Die
'73   *Wings*
'91   *Guns N' Roses*
'85 **Live Every Moment**
      REO Speedwagon
'91 **Live For Loving You** *Gloria Estefan*
'95 **Live Forever** *Oasis*
'86 **Live Is Life** *Opus*
'04 **Live Like You Were Dying**
      Tim McGraw
'87 **Live My Life** *Boy George*
'01 **Live Out Loud**
      Steven Curtis Chapman
'86 **Live To Tell** *Madonna*
'93 **Live Until I Die** *Clay Walker*
'75 **Lively Up Yourself** *Bob Marley*
'76 **Livin' For The Weekend** *O'Jays*
'73 **Livin' For You** *Al Green*
'84 **Livin' In Desperate Times**
      Olivia Newton-John
'77 **Livin' In The Life** *Isley Brothers*
'01 **Livin' It Up** *Ja Rule*
'79 **Livin' It Up (Friday Night)**
      Bell & James
'99 **Livin' La Vida Loca** *Ricky Martin*
'86 **Livin' On A Prayer** *Bon Jovi*
'94 **Livin' On Love** *Alan Jackson*
'93 **Livin' On The Edge** *Aerosmith*
'76 **Livin' Thing** *Electric Light Orchestra*
'63 **Living A Lie** *Al Martino*
'75 **Living A Little, Laughing A Little**
      Spinners
'80 **Living After Midnight**
      Judas Priest
'02 **Living And Living Well**
      George Strait
'59 **Living Doll** *Cliff Richard*
'73 **Living For The City** *Stevie Wonder*
'87 **Living In A Box** *Living In A Box*
'81 **Living In A Fantasy** *Leo Sayer*
'72 **Living In A House Divided** *Cher*
'96 **Living In A Moment** *Ty Herndon*
'85 **Living In America** *James Brown*
'94 **Living In Danger** *Ace Of Base*
'06 **Living In Fast Forward**
      Kenny Chesney
'89 **Living In Sin** *Bon Jovi*
'72 **Living In The Past** *Jethro Tull*
'68 **Living In The U.S.A.**
      Steve Miller Band
'81 **Living Inside Myself** *Gino Vannelli*
'69 **Living Loving Maid (She's Just A
      Woman)** *Led Zeppelin*
'76 **Living Next Door To Alice** *Smokie*
'85 **Living On A Thin Line** *Kinks*
'83 **Living On The Edge**
      Jim Capaldi
'73 **Living Together, Growing Together**
      5th Dimension
'89 **Living Years** *Mike & The Mechanics*
'75 **Lizzie And The Rainman**
      Tanya Tucker
'68 **Lo Mucho Que Te Quiero**
      Rene & Rene
'78 **Load-Out, The [medley]**
      Jackson Browne
'04 **Locked Up** *Akon*
'04 **Loco** *David Lee Murphy*

Loco-Motion, The
'62   *Little Eva*
'74   *Grand Funk*
'88   *Kylie Minogue*
'71 **Locomotive Breath** *Jethro Tull*
'63 **Loddy Lo** *Chubby Checker*
'69 **Lodi**
      Creedence Clearwater Revival
'79 **Logical Song** *Supertramp*
'58 **Lola** *Kinks*
'58 **Lollipop** *Chordettes*
'62 **Lollipops And Roses** *Jack Jones*
'97 **Lollipop (Candyman)** *Aqua*
'06 **London Bridge** *Fergie*
'80 **London Calling** *Clash*
'78 **London Town** *Wings*
'67 **(Loneliness Made Me Realize) It's
      You That I Need** *Temptations*
'65 **L-O-N-E-L-Y** *Bobby Vinton*
'05 **Lonely** *Akon*
'99 **Lonely And Gone**
      Montgomery Gentry
Lonely Boy
'59   *Paul Anka*
'59   *Conway Twitty*
'77   *Andrew Gold*
'62 **Lonely Bull (El Solo Torro)**
      Herb Alpert
'70 **Lonely Days** *Bee Gees*
'59 **Lonely For You** *Gary Stites*
'59 **Lonely Guitar** *Annette*
'87 **Lonely In Love** *Dan Fogelberg*
'58 **Lonely Island** *Sam Cooke*
'62 **Lonely Man** *Elvis Presley*
'76 **Lonely Night (Angel Face)**
      Captain & Tennille
'82 **Lonely Nights** *Bryan Adams*
'05 **Lonely No More** *Rob Thomas*
'85 **Lonely Ol' Night**
      John Cougar Mellencamp
'70 **Lonely One** *Duane Eddy*
'74 **Lonely People** *America*
'59 **Lonely Saturday Night** *Don French*
'59 **Lonely Street** *Andy Williams*
'63 **Lonely Surfer** *Jack Nitzsche*
'58 **Lonely Teardrops** *Jackie Wilson*
'63 **Lonely Teenager** *Dion*
'96 **Lonely Too Long** *Patty Loveless*
'60 **Lonely Weekends** *Charlie Rich*
'79 **Lonesome Loser** *Little River Band*
'61 **Lonesome Number One** *Don Gibson*
'58 **Lonesome Old House** *Don Gibson*
'58 **Lonesome Town** *Ricky Nelson*
'71 **Long Ago And Far Away**
      James Taylor
'70 **Long And Winding Road** *Beatles*
'70 **Long As I Can See The Light**
      Creedence Clearwater Revival
'04 **Long Black Train** *Josh Turner*
'72 **Long Cool Woman (In A Black
      Dress)** *Hollies*
'72 **Long Dark Road** *Hollies*
'96 **Long December** *Counting Crows*
'72 **Long Distance Runaround** *Yes*
'01 **Long Goodbye** *Brooks & Dunn*
'75 **Long Haired Country Boy** *Charlie
      Daniels Band*
'72 **Long Haired Lover From Liverpool**
      Little Jimmy Osmond
'66 **Long Live Our Love** *Shangri-Las*
'79 **Long Live Rock** *Who*
Long Lonely Nights
'57   *America*
'57   *Lee Andrews*
'57   *Clyde McPhatter*
'65   *Bobby Vinton*
'70 **Long Lonesome Highway**
      Michael Parks
'70 **Long Long Time** *Linda Ronstadt*
'77 **Long, Long Way From Home**
      Foreigner
'79 **Long Run** *Eagles*
'75 **Long Tall Glasses (I Can Dance)**
      Leo Sayer

Long Tall Sally
'56   *Pat Boone*
'56   *Little Richard*
'77 **Long Time** *Boston*
'02 **Long Time Gone** *Dixie Chicks*
'73 **Long Train Runnin'** *Doobie Brothers*
'59 **Long Vacation** *Ricky Nelson*
'94 **Long View** *Green Day*
'79 **Longer** *Dan Fogelberg*
'84 **Longest Time** *Billy Joel*
'55 **Longest Walk** *Jaye P. Morgan*
'74 **Longfellow Serenade** *Neil Diamond*
'97 **Longneck Bottle** *Garth Brooks*
'89 **Look, The** *Roxette*
'66 **Look At Me Girl** *Bobby Vee*
'75 **Look At Me (I'm In Love)** *Moments*
'88 **Look Away** *Chicago*
Look For A Star
'60   *Garry Miles*
'60   *Billy Vaughn*
'92 **Look Heart, No Hands** *Randy Travis*
Look Homeward, Angel
'56   *Four Esquires*
'57   *Johnnie Ray*
'61 **Look In My Eyes** *Chantels*
'74 **Look In My Eyes Pretty Woman**
      Tony Orlando & Dawn
'97 **Look Into My Eyes**
      Bone Thugs-N-Harmony
Look Of Love
'64   *Lesley Gore*
'67   *Dusty Springfield*
'68   *Sergio Mendes*
'82   *ABC*
'88 **Look Out Any Window**
      Bruce Hornsby
'65 **Look Through Any Window** *Hollies*
'66 **Look Through My Window**
      Mamas & Papas
'70 **Look What They've Done To My
      Song Ma** *New Seekers*
'72 **Look What You Done For Me**
      Al Green
Look What You've Done
'66   *Pozo Seco Singers*
'04   *Jet*
'80 **Look What You've Done To Me**
      Boz Scaggs
'98 **Lookin' At Me** *Mase*
Lookin' For A Love
'71   *J. Geils Band*
'74   *Bobby Womack*
Lookin' For Love
'66   *Ray Conniff*
'80   *Johnny Lee*
'70 **Lookin' Out My Back Door**
      Creedence Clearwater Revival
'72 **Lookin' Through The Windows**
      Jackson 5
'58 **Looking Back** *Nat "King" Cole*
'68 **Looking For A Fox** *Clarence Carter*
'87 **Looking For A New Love**
      Jody Watley
'83 **Looking For A Stranger** *Pat Benatar*
'76 **Looking For Space** *John Denver*
'06 **Looking For You** *Kirk Franklin*
'93 **Looking Through Patient Eyes**
      PM Dawn
Looking Through The Eyes Of Love
'65   *Gene Pitney*
'72   *Partridge Family*
'98 **Looking Through Your Eyes**
      LeAnn Rimes
'77 **Looks Like We Made It**
      Barry Manilow
'62 **Loop De Loop** *Johnny Thunder*
'88 **Loosey's Rap** *Rick James*
'04 **Lord Have Mercy** *Michael W. Smith*
'96 **Lord Of The Dance**
      Steven Curtis Chapman
'74 **Lord Of The Thighs** *Aerosmith*
'74 **Lord's Prayer** *Sister Janet Mead*
'76 **Lorelei** *Styx*
'05 **Lose Control** *Missy Elliott*
'04 **Lose My Breath** *Destiny's Child*
'02 **Lose Yourself** *Eminem*

	Loser	'84	**Love Has Finally Come At Last**		**Love Makes The World Go 'Round**
'93	*Beck*		*Bobby Womack & Patti LaBelle*	'58	*Perry Como*
'00	*3 Doors Down*	'71	**Love Her Madly** *Doors*	'63	*Paul Anka*
'91	**Losing My Religion** *R.E.M.*		**Love Hurts**	'66	*Deon Jackson*
'63	**Losing You** *Brenda Lee*	'60	*Everly Brothers*	'90	**Love Makes Things Happen**
'79	**Lost Her In The Sun** *John Stewart*	'75	*Nazareth*		*Pebbles*
'87	**Lost In Emotion**	'73	**Love I Lost** *Harold Melvin*		**Love Me**
	Lisa Lisa & Cult Jam	'67	**Love I Saw In You Was Just A**	'56	*Elvis Presley*
	Lost In Love		**Mirage** *Miracles*	'76	*Yvonne Elliman*
'80	*Air Supply*	'89	**Love In An Elevator** *Aerosmith*	'91	*Collin Raye*
'85	*New Edition*	'77	**Love In 'C' Minor** *Cerrone*	'92	*Tracie Spencer*
'85	**Lost In The Fifties Tonight (In The**	'82	**Love In Store** *Fleetwood Mac*	'98	*112*
	Still Of The Night) *Ronnie Milsap*		**Love In The First Degree**	'91	**Love Me All Up** *Stacy Earl*
'07	**Lost In This Moment** *Big & Rich*	'81	*Alabama*	'64	**Love Me Do** *Beatles*
	Lost In You	'88	*Bananarama*	'90	**Love Me Down** *Freddie Jackson*
'88	*Rod Stewart*	'76	**Love In The Shadows** *Neil Sedaka*	'74	**Love Me For A Reason** *Osmonds*
'99	*Garth Brooks As Chris Gaines*	'89	**Love In Your Eyes** *Eddie Money*	'90	**Love Me For Life** *Stevie B*
'89	**Lost In Your Eyes** *Debbie Gibson*	'93	**Love Is** *Vanessa Williams &*		**Love Me Forever**
'61	**Lost Love** *H.B. Barnum*		*Brian McKnight*	'57	*Four Esquires*
'61	**Lost Someone** *James Brown*	'83	**Love Is A Battlefield** *Pat Benatar*	'57	*Eydie Gorme*
'07	**Lost Without U** *Robin Thicke*	'57	**Love Is A Golden Ring**	'67	*Roger Williams*
'76	**Lost Without Your Love** *Bread*		*Frankie Laine*	'98	**Love Me Good** *Michael W. Smith*
'05	**Lot Of Leavin' Left To Do**	'87	**Love Is A House** *Force M.D.'s*	'07	**Love Me If You Can** *Toby Keith*
	Dierks Bentley	'66	**Love Is A Hurtin' Thing** *Lou Rawls*		**Love Me Or Leave Me**
'78	**Lotta Love** *Nicolette Larson*		**Love Is A Many-Splendored Thing**	'55	*Sammy Davis, Jr.*
'57	**Lotta Lovin'** *Gene Vincent*	'55	*Don Cornell*	'55	*Lena Horne*
	Louie Louie	'55	*Four Aces*	'55	*Doris Day*
'63	*Kingsmen*	'83	**Love Is A Stranger** *Eurythmics*		**Love Me Tender**
'66	*Sandpipers*	'91	**Love Is A Wonderful Thing**	'56	*Elvis Presley*
'51	**Louisiana Blues** *Muddy Waters*		*Michael Bolton*	'62	*Richard Chamberlain*
'96	**Loungin** *LL Cool J*	'76	**Love Is Alive** *Gary Wright*	'67	*Percy Sledge*
	Love [L.O.V.E.]	'68	**Love Is All Around** *Troggs*	'57	**Love Me To Pieces** *Jill Corey*
'70	*John Lennon*	'58	**Love Is All We Need**	'82	**Love Me Tomorrow** *Chicago*
'71	*Lettermen*		*Tommy Edwards*	'69	**Love Me Tonight** *Tom Jones*
'92	*Sundays*	'81	**Love Is Alright Tonite**	'67	**Love Me Two Times** *Doors*
'01	*Musiq Soulchild*		*Rick Springfield*	'62	**Love Me Warm And Tender**
'06	*Keyshia Cole*	'00	**Love Is Blind** *Eve*		*Paul Anka*
'06	*Ashlee Simpson*		**Love Is Blue**		**Love Me With All Your Heart**
'94	**Love A Little Stronger** *Diamond Rio*	'68	*Al Martino*	'64	*Ray Charles Singers*
'57	**Love Affair** *Sal Mineo*	'68	*Paul Mauriat*	'66	*Bachelors*
'89	**Love And Anger** *Kate Bush*	'69	*Dells [medley]*	'71	**Love Means (You Never Have To**
'90	**Love & Emotion** *Stevie B*	'86	**Love Is Forever** *Billy Ocean*		**Say You're Sorry)**
'72	**Love And Happiness** *Al Green*	'67	**Love Is Here And Now You're Gone**		*Sounds Of Sunshine*
	Love And Marriage		*Supremes*	'83	**Love My Way** *Psychedelic Furs*
'55	*Dinah Shore*	'82	**Love Is In Control (Finger On The**	'91	**Love Of A Lifetime** *Firehouse*
'55	*Frank Sinatra*		**Trigger)** *Donna Summer*	'01	**Love Of A Woman** *Travis Tritt*
'91	**Love And Understanding** *Cher*	'78	**Love Is In The Air** *John Paul Young*		**Love Of My Life**
	Love At [@] First [1st] Sight	'68	**(Love Is Like A) Baseball Game**	'58	*Everly Brothers*
'91	*Styx*		*Intruders*	'97	*Sammy Kershaw*
'02	*Kylie Minogue*	'81	**Love Is Like A Rock** *Donnie Iris*	'02	**Love Of My Life (An Ode To Hip**
'03	*Mary J. Blige*	'66	**Love Is Like An Itching In My Heart**		**Hop)** *Erykah Badu*
	Love Ballad		*Supremes*	'63	**Love Of My Man** *Theola Kilgore*
'76	*L.T.D.*	'78	**Love Is Like Oxygen** *Sweet*	'91	**Love On A Rooftop** *Desmond Child*
'79	*George Benson*	'92	**Love Is On The Way** *Saigon Kick*		**Love On A Two-Way Street**
'88	**Love Bites** *Def Leppard*		**Love Is Strange**	'70	*Moments*
'85	**Love Bizarre** *Sheila E.*	'57	*Mickey & Sylvia*	'81	*Stacy Lattisaw*
'67	**Love Bug Leave My Heart Alone**	'67	*Peaches & Herb*	'90	**Love On Arrival** *Dan Seals*
	Martha & The Vandellas	'94	**Love Is Strong** *Rolling Stones*	'80	**Love On The Rocks** *Neil Diamond*
'62	**Love Came To Me** *Dion*	'79	**Love Is The Answer**	'75	**Love Or Leave** *Spinners*
'69	**Love (Can Make You Happy)** *Mercy*		*England Dan & John Ford Coley*	'70	**Love Or Let Me Be Lonely**
'92	**Love Can Move Mountains**	'75	**Love Is The Drug** *Roxy Music*		*Friends Of Distinction*
	Celine Dion	'85	**Love Is The Seventh Wave** *Sting*	'78	**Love Or Something Like It**
'87	**Love Changes**	'55	**(Love Is) The Tender Trap**		*Kenny Rogers*
	Kashif & Meli'sa Morgan		*Frank Sinatra*	'88	**Love Overboard** *Gladys Knight*
'88	**Love Changes (Everything)**	'77	**(Love Is) Thicker Than Water**	'79	**Love Pains** *Yvonne Elliman*
	Climie Fisher		*Andy Gibb*	'86	**Love Parade** *Dream Academy*
	Love Child	'72	**Love Jones**	'82	**Love Plus One** *Haircut One Hundred*
'68	*Supremes*		*Brighter Side Of Darkness*		**Love Potion Number Nine**
'90	*Sweet Sensation*	'70	**Love Land** *Charles Wright*	'59	*Clovers*
'82	**Love Come Down** *Evelyn King*		**Love Letters**	'64	*Searchers*
'00	**Love Don't Cost A Thing**	'62	*Ketty Lester*	'72	*Coasters*
	Jennifer Lopez	'66	*Elvis Presley*		**Love Power**
'78	**Love Don't Live Here Anymore**	'57	**Love Letters In The Sand**	'67	*Sandpebbles*
	Rose Royce		*Pat Boone*	'87	*Dionne Warwick & Jeffrey Osborne*
'74	**Love Don't Love Nobody** *Spinners*	'73	**Love Lies Bleeding [medley]**	'91	*Luther Vandross [medley]*
'93	**Love Don't Love You** *En Vogue*		*Elton John*	'76	**Love Really Hurts Without You**
'67	**Love Eyes** *Nancy Sinatra*	'84	**Love Light In Flight** *Stevie Wonder*		*Billy Ocean*
'75	**Love Finds It's Own Way**	'98	**Love Like This** *Faith Evans*	'73	**Love, Reign, O'er Me** *Who*
	Gladys Knight	'75	**L-O-V-E (Love)** *Al Green*		**Love Rollercoaster**
'76	**Love Fire** *Jigsaw*		**Love, Love, Love**	'75	*Ohio Players*
'97	**Love Gets Me Every Time**	'55	*Webb Pierce*	'96	*Red Hot Chili Peppers*
	Shania Twain	'56	*Clovers*	'89	**Love Saw It** *Karyn White*
'70	**Love Grows (Where My Rosemary**	'56	*Diamonds*	'89	**Love Shack** *B-52's*
	Goes) *Edison Lighthouse*	'75	**Love Machine** *Miracles*	'63	**Love She Can Count On** *Miracles*
'77	**Love Gun** *Kiss*	'68	**Love Makes A Woman**		
'76	**Love Hangover** *Diana Ross*		*Barbara Acklin*		

230

'92 **Love Shoulda Brought You Home**
    Toni Braxton
'94 **Love Sneakin' Up On You**
    Bonnie Raitt
'63 **Love So Fine** *Chiffons*
'76 **Love So Right** *Bee Gees*
'84 **Love Somebody** *Rick Springfield*
Love Song
'73   *Anne Murray*
'89   *Cure*
'89   *Tesla*
'04   *311*
'95 **Love Song For A Savior** *Jars Of Clay*
'94 **Love Spreads** *Stone Roses*
'80 **Love Stinks** *J. Geils Band*
'07 **LoveStoned** *Justin Timberlake*
'80 **Love T.K.O.** *Teddy Pendergrass*
Love Takes Time
'79   *Orleans*
'90   *Mariah Carey*
Love The One You're With
'70   *Stephen Stills*
'71   *Isley Brothers*
'80 **Love The World Away**
    Kenny Rogers
'76 **Love Theme From A Star Is Born**
    (Evergreen) *Barbra Streisand*
'78 **Love Theme From Eyes Of Laura**
    Mars (Prisoner) *Barbra Streisand*
'61 **(Love Theme From) One Eyed**
    Jacks *Ferrante & Teicher*
'69 **Love Theme From Romeo & Juliet**
    Henry Mancini
'85 **Love Theme From St. Elmo's Fire**
    David Foster
'72 **Love Theme From The Godfather**
    Andy Williams
'91 **Love...Thy Will Be Done** *Martika*
'75 **Love To Love You Baby**
    Donna Summer
'86 **Love Touch** *Rod Stewart*
'73 **Love Train** *O'Jays*
'95 **Love U 4 Life** *Jodeci*
'92 **Love U More** *Sunscreem*
'90 **Love Under New Management**
    Miki Howard
'60 **Love Walked In** *Dinah Washington*
'86 **Love Walks In** *Van Halen*
'71 **Love We Had (Stays On My Mind)**
    Dells
'86 **Love Will Conquer All** *Lionel Richie*
Love Will Find A Way
'69   *Jackie DeShannon*
'78   *Pablo Cruise*
'87   *Yes*
'94 **Love Will Keep Us Alive** *Eagles*
'75 **Love Will Keep Us Together**
    Captain & Tennille
'90 **Love Will Lead You Back**
    Taylor Dayne
'90 **Love Will Never Do (Without You)**
    Janet Jackson
'88 **Love Will Save The Day**
    Whitney Houston
'84 **Love Will Show Us How**
    Christine McVie
'80 **Love Will Tear Us Apart**
    Joy Division
'82 **Love Will Turn You Around**
    Kenny Rogers
'90 **Love Without End, Amen**
    George Strait
'75 **Love Won't Let Me Wait**
    Major Harris
Love You Down
'86   *Ready For The World*
'98   *Inoj*
'79 **Love You Inside Out** *Bee Gees*
'81 **Love You Like I Never Loved Before**
    John O'Banion
'58 **Love You Most Of All** *Sam Cooke*
'03 **Love You Out Loud** *Rascal Flatts*
'70 **Love You Save** *Jackson 5*
'66 **Love You Save (May Be Your Own)**
    Joe Tex
'60 **Love You So** *Ron Holden*
'86 **Love Zone** *Billy Ocean*

'82 **Love's Been A Little Bit Hard On Me**
    Juice Newton
'04 **Love's Divine** *Seal*
'63 **Love's Gonna Live Here**
    Buck Owens
"92 **Love's Got A Hold On You**
    Alan Jackson
'77 **Love's Grown Deep** *Kenny Nolan*
'71 **Love's Lines, Angles And Rhymes**
    5th Dimension
'66 **Love's Made A Fool Of You**
    Bobby Fuller Four
'99 **Love's The Only House**
    Martina McBride
'73 **Love's Theme**
    Love Unlimited Orchestra
'97 **Loved Too Much** *Ty Herndon*
'96 **Lovefool** *Cardigans*
'84 **Lovelite** *O'Bryan*
'77 **Lovely Day** *Bill Withers*
Lovely One
'56   *Four Voices*
'80   *Jacksons*
'67 **Lovely Rita** *Beatles*
'88 **Lover In Me** *Sheena Easton*
'62 **Lover Please** *Clyde McPhatter*
'65 **Lover's Concerto** *Toys*
Lover's Holiday
'68   *Peggy Scott & Jo Jo Benson*
'80   *Change*
'61 **Lover's Island** *Blue Jays*
'58 **Lover's Question** *Clyde McPhatter*
Loverboy
'84   *Billy Ocean*
'01   *Mariah Carey*
'84 **Lovergirl** *Teena Marie*
'05 **Lovers And Friends**
    Lil Jon & The East Side Boyz
'62 **Lovers By Night, Strangers By Day**
    Fleetwoods
'59 **Lovers Never Say Goodbye**
    Flamingos
'62 **Lovers Who Wander** *Dion*
'73 **Loves Me Like A Rock** *Paul Simon*
'60 **Lovey Dovey** *Buddy Knox*
'85 **Lovin' Every Minute Of It** *Loverboy*
'88 **Lovin' On Next To Nothin'**
    Gladys Knight
'79 **Lovin', Touchin', Squeezin'** *Journey*
Lovin' You
'75   *Minnie Riperton*
'87   *O'Jays*
'91 **Loving Blind** *Clint Black*
'71 **Loving Her Was Easier (Than**
    Anything I'll Ever Do Again)
    Kris Kristofferson
'57 **Loving You** *Elvis Presley*
'68 **Loving You Has Made Me Bananas**
    Guy Marks
'72 **Loving You Just Crossed My Mind**
    Sam Neely
'93 **Low** *Cracker*
'79 **Low Budget** *Kinks*
'75 **Low Rider** *War*
'71 **Low Spark Of High Heeled Boys**
    Traffic
Lowdown
'71   *Chicago*
'76   *Boz Scaggs*
'94 **Lucas With The Lid Off** *Lucas*
Lucille
'57   *Little Richard*
'60   *Everly Brothers*
'77   *Kenny Rogers*
'77 **Luckenbach, Texas**
    Waylon Jennings
Lucky
'85   *Greg Kihn*
'00   *Britney Spears*
'89 **Lucky Charm** *Boys*
'59 **Lucky Devil** *Carl Dobkins, Jr.*
'85 **Lucky In Love** *Mick Jagger*
'58 **Lucky Ladybug** *Billy & Lillie*
'57 **Lucky Lips** *Ruth Brown*
'96 **Lucky Love** *Ace Of Base*

Lucky Man
'71   *Emerson, Lake & Palmer*
'07   *Montgomery Gentry*
Lucky One
'84   *Laura Branigan*
'94   *Amy Grant*
'06   *Faith Hill*
'82 **Lucky Ones** *Loverboy*
'84 **Lucky Star** *Madonna*
'70 **Lucretia Mac Evil**
    Blood, Sweat & Tears
Lucy In The Sky With Diamonds
'67   *Beatles*
'74   *Elton John*
'87 **Luka** *Suzanne Vega*
'98 **Lullaby** *Shawn Mullins*
Lullaby Of Birdland
'55   *Blue Stars*
'56   *Mel Torme*
'61 **Lullaby Of Love** *Frank Gari*
'61 **Lullaby Of The Leaves** *Ventures*
'95 **Lump** *Presidents Of The*
    United States Of America
'77 **Lust For Life** *Iggy Pop*
'98 **Luv 2 Luv U** *Timbaland & Magoo*
'02 **Luv U Better** *LL Cool J*
'05 **Luxurious** *Gwen Stefani*
'75 **Lyin' Eyes** *Eagles*
'90 **Lyin' To Myself** *David Cassidy*
'04 **Lying From You** *Linkin Park*

M

'97 **MMMBop** *Hanson*
'59 **M.T.A.** *Kingston Trio*
'70 **Ma Belle Amie** *Tee Set*
MacArthur Park
'68   *Richard Harris*
'78   *Donna Summer*
'95 **Macarena (bayside boys mix)**
    Los Del Rio
'74 **Machine Gun** *Commodores*
'96 **Machinehead** *Bush*
'78 **Macho Man** *Village People*
    Mack The Knife ..see: Moritat
'86 **Mad About You** *Belinda Carlisle*
'02 **Made You Look** *Nas*
'56 **Madeira** *Mitch Miller*
'76 **Mademoiselle** *Styx*
'60 **Madison, The** *Al Brown*
'78 **Madison Blues** *George Thorogood*
'60 **Madison Time** *Ray Bryant Combo*
'71 **Madman Across The Water**
    Elton John
'89 **Madonna Of The Wasps**
    Robyn Hitchcock/Egyptians
'71 **Maggie** *Redbone*
'71 **Maggie May** *Rod Stewart*
'65 **Maggie's Farm** *Bob Dylan*
'71 **Maggot Brain** *Funkadelic*
Magic
'75   *Pilot*
'80   *Olivia Newton-John*
'84   *Cars*
'68 **Magic Bus** *Who*
'68 **Magic Carpet Ride** *Steppenwolf*
'76 **Magic Man** *Heart*
'58 **Magic Moments** *Perry Como*
'03 **Magic Stick** *Lil' Kim*
'66 **Magic Town** *Vogues*
Magical Mystery Tour
'67   *Beatles*
'77   *Ambrosia*
'78 **Magnet And Steel** *Walter Egan*
'60 **Magnificent Seven** *Al Caiola*
'91 **Main Course** *Freddie Jackson*
'79 **Main Event/Fight** *Barbra Streisand*
'77 **Mainstreet** *Bob Seger*
'61 **Majestic, The** *Dion*
'83 **Major Tom (Coming Home)**
    Peter Schilling
'83 **Make A Circuit With Me** *Polecats*
'80 **Make A Little Magic** *Dirt Band*
'82 **Make A Move On Me**
    Olivia Newton-John

Make Believe
'69 *Wind*
'82 *Toto*
'98 **Make Em' Say Uhh!** *Master P*
'05 **Make Her Feel Good** *Teairra Marí*
Make It Easy On Yourself
'62 *Jerry Butler*
'65 *Walker Bros.*
'70 *Dionne Warwick*
'71 **Make It Funky** *James Brown*
'92 **Make It Happen** *Mariah Carey*
'98 **Make It Hot** *Nicole*
'88 **Make It Last Forever** *Keith Sweat*
'89 **Make It Like It Was** *Regina Belle*
'07 **Make It Rain** *Fat Joe*
'88 **Make It Real** *Jets*
'70 **Make It With You** *Bread*
'92 **Make Love Like A Man** *Def Leppard*
'83 **Make Love Stay** *Dan Fogelberg*
'58 **Make Me A Miracle** *Jimmie Rodgers*
'66 **Make Me Belong To You**
     Barbara Lewis
'07 **Make Me Better** *Fabolous*
'88 **Make Me Lose Control** *Eric Carmen*
'70 **Make Me Smile** *Chicago*
'71 **Make Me The Woman That You Go
     Home To** *Gladys Knight*
'65 **Make Me Your Baby** *Barbara Lewis*
'67 **Make Me Yours** *Bettye Swann*
Make The World Go Away
'63 *Timi Yuro*
'65 *Eddy Arnold*
'90 **Make You Sweat** *Keith Sweat*
'69 **Make Your Own Kind Of Music**
     Mama Cass Elliot
'55 **Make Yourself Comfortable**
     Sarah Vaughan
'07 **Makes Me Wonder** *Maroon 5*
'02 **Makin' Good Love** *Avant*
'79 **Makin' It** *David Naughton*
'59 **Makin' Love** *Floyd Robinson*
'67 **Making Every Minute Count**
     Spanky & Our Gang
'82 **Making Love** *Roberta Flack*
'87 **Making Love In The Rain**
     Herb Alpert
'83 **Making Love Out Of Nothing At All**
     Air Supply
'67 **Making Memories** *Frankie Laine*
'05 **Making Memories Of Us** *Keith Urban*
'76 **Making Our Dreams Come True**
     Cyndi Grecco
'98 **Malibu** *Hole*
Mama
'60 *Connie Francis*
'66 *B.J. Thomas*
'83 *Genesis*
'79 **Mama Can't Buy You Love**
     Elton John
'63 **Mama Didn't Lie** *Jan Bradley*
'56 **Mama From The Train** *Patti Page*
'91 **Mama, I'm Coming Home**
     Ozzy Osbourne
'73 **Mama Kin** *Aerosmith*
'57 **Mama Look At Bubu**
     Harry Belafonte
'61 **Mama Said** *Shirelles*
'91 **Mama Said Knock You Out**
     LL Cool J
'56 **Mama, Teach Me To Dance**
     Eydie Gorme
'70 **Mama Told Me (Not To Come)**
     Three Dog Night
'68 **Mama Tried** *Merle Haggard*
'82 **Mama Used To Say** *Junior*
'72 **Mama Weer All Crazee Now** *Slade*
'71 **Mama's Pearl** *Jackson 5*
Mamacita
'88 *Troop*
'00 *Public Announcement*
'54 **Mambo Italiano** *Rosemary Clooney*
'99 **Mambo No. 5 (A Little Bit Of...)**
     Lou Bega
'55 **Mambo Rock** *Bill Haley*

Mame
'66 *Herb Alpert*
'66 *Bobby Darin*
'76 **Mamma Mia** *Abba*
'87 **Mammas Don't Let Your Babies
     Grow Up To Be Cowboys**
     Waylon Jennings & Willie Nelson
'55 **Man Chases A Girl** *Eddie Fisher*
'99 **Man! I Feel Like A Woman!**
     Shania Twain
'78 **Man I'll Never Be** *Boston*
'71 **Man In Black** *Johnny Cash*
'91 **Man In The Box** *Alice In Chains*
'88 **Man In The Mirror** *Michael Jackson*
Man In The Raincoat
'55 *Marion Marlowe*
'55 *Priscilla Wright*
'82 **Man On The Corner** *Genesis*
'93 **Man On The Moon** *R.E.M.*
'82 **Man On Your Mind** *Little River Band*
'00 **Man Overboard** *Blink-182*
'86 **Man Size Love** *Klymaxx*
'96 **Man This Lonely** *Brooks & Dunn*
'03 **Man To Man** *Gary Allan*
'62 **(Man Who Shot) Liberty Valance**
     Gene Pitney
'95 **Man Who Sold The World** *Nirvana*
'79 **Man With The Child In His Eyes**
     Kate Bush
Man With The Golden Arm
'56 *Dick Jacobs [Main Title/Molly-O]*
'56 *Richard Maltby*
'56 *McGuire Sisters*
'68 **Man Without Love**
     Engelbert Humperdinck
'78 **Mañana** *Jimmy Buffett*
'87 **Mandolin Rain** *Bruce Hornsby*
'74 **Mandy** *Barry Manilow*
Maneater
'82 *Daryl Hall & John Oates*
'06 *Nelly Furtado*
'57 **Mangos** *Rosemary Clooney*
'58 **Manhattan Spiritual** *Reg Owen*
'83 **Maniac** *Michael Sembello*
'67 **Manic Depression** *Jimi Hendrix*
'86 **Manic Monday** *Bangles*
'55 **Mannish Boy** *Muddy Waters*
'69 **Many Rivers To Cross**
     Jimmy Cliff
'60 **Many Tears Ago** *Connie Francis*
'58 **March From The River Kwai and
     Colonel Bogey** *Mitch Miller*
'94 **March Of The Pigs** *Nine Inch Nails*
'97 **Marching To Mars** *Sammy Hagar*
'77 **Margaritaville** *Jimmy Buffett*
Maria
'60 *Johnny Mathis*
'99 *Blondie*
'62 **Maria Elena** *Los Indios Tabajaras*
'00 **Maria Maria**
     Santana Feat. The Product G&B
Marianne
'57 *Terry Gilkyson & The Easy Riders*
'57 *Hilltoppers*
'65 **Marie** *Bachelors*
'74 **Marie Laveau** *Bobby Bare*
'61 **(Marie's the Name) His Latest Flame**
     Elvis Presley
'63 **Marina** *Rocco Granata*
'63 **Marlena** *Four Seasons*
'77 **Marquee Moon** *Television*
'69 **Marrakesh Express**
     Crosby, Stills & Nash
'79 **Married Men** *Bette Midler*
'62 **Martian Hop** *Ran-Dells*
'62 **Mary Ann Regrets** *Burl Ives*
'72 **Mary Had A Little Lamb** *Wings*
'61 **Mary In The Morning** *Al Martino*
'78 **Mary Jane** *Rick James*
'93 **Mary Jane's Last Dance** *Tom Petty*
'55 **Mary Lou** *Ronnie Hawkins*
'67 **Mary, Mary** *Monkees*

Mary's Boy Child
'56 *Harry Belafonte*
'78 *Boney M [medley]*
'62 **Mary's Little Lamb** *James Darren*
'87 **Mary's Prayer** *Danny Wilson*
'66 **Mas Que Nada** *Sergio Mendes*
'99 **Mas Tequila** *Sammy Hagar*
'62 **Mashed Potato Time**
     Dee Dee Sharp
'80 **Master Blaster (Jammin')**
     Stevie Wonder
'68 **Master Jack** *Four Jacks & A Jill*
'86 **Master Of Puppets** *Metallica*
Masterpiece
'73 *Temptations*
'92 *Atlantic Starr*
'63 **Masters Of War** *Bob Dylan*
'64 **Matador, The** *Major Lance*
Matchbox
'57 *Carl Perkins*
'64 *Beatles*
'85 **Material Girl** *Madonna*
'86 **Matter Of Trust** *Billy Joel*
'69 **Maxwell's Silver Hammer** *Beatles*
'63 **May Each Day** *Andy Williams*
'69 **May I** *Bill Deal*
'65 **May The Bird Of Paradise Fly Up
     Your Nose** *"Little" Jimmy Dickens*
'59 **May You Always** *McGuire Sisters*
Maybe
'58 *Chantels*
'69 *Janis Joplin*
'70 *Three Degrees*
'58 **Maybe Baby** *Crickets*
'01 **Maybe I Deserve** *Tank*
'64 **Maybe I Know** *Lesley Gore*
'79 **Maybe I'm A Fool** *Eddie Money*
Maybe I'm Amazed
'70 *Paul McCartney*
'77 *Wings [live]*
'91 **Maybe It Was Memphis** *Pam Tillis*
'71 **Maybe Tomorrow** *Jackson 5*
Maybellene
'55 *Chuck Berry*
'64 *Johnny Rivers*
'04 **Mayberry** *Rascal Flatts*
'89 **Mayor Of Simpleton** *XTC*
'98 **Me** *Paula Cole*
'03 **Me Against The Music**
     Britney Spears
'92 **Me And A Gun** *Tori Amos*
'73 **Me And Baby Brother** *War*
Me And Bobby McGee
'71 *Janis Joplin*
'71 *Jerry Lee Lewis*
'72 **Me And Julio Down By The
     Schoolyard** *Paul Simon*
'72 **Me And Mrs. Jones** *Billy Paul*
'71 **Me And My Arrow** *Nilsson*
Me And You [U]
'96 *Kenny Chesney*
'06 *Cassie*
'71 **Me And You And A Dog Named Boo**
     Lobo
'07 **Me Love** *Sean Kingston*
Me, Myself And I
'89 *De La Soul*
'03 *Beyoncé*
'89 **Me So Horny** *2 Live Crew*
'96 **Me Too** *Toby Keith*
'96 **Me Wise Magic** *Van Halen*
'73 **Meadows** *Joe Walsh*
'63 **Mean Woman Blues** *Roy Orbison*
'04 **Meant To Live** *Switchfoot*
'63 **Mecca** *Gene Pitney*
'69 **Medicine Man** *Buchanan Brothers*
'81 **Medley** *Stars On 45*
'91 **Meet In The Middle** *Diamond Rio*
'87 **Meet Me Half Way** *Kenny Loggins*
'85 **Meet Me In Montana**
     Marie Osmond w/ Dan Seals
'99 **Meet Virginia** *Train*
'04 **Megalomaniac** *Incubus*
'72 **Melissa** *Allman Brothers Band*
'66 **Mellow Yellow** *Donovan*

233

'56 **Money Tree** *Margaret Whiting*
'86 **Money$ Too Tight (To Mention)**
   Simply Red
'90 **Moneytalks** *AC/DC*
'70 **Mongoose** *Elephant's Memory*
'88 **Monkey** *George Michael*
'89 **Monkey Gone To Heaven** *Pixies*
'63 **Monkey Time** *Major Lance*
'69 **Monster** *Steppenwolf*
'62 **Monster Mash** *Bobby "Boris" Pickett*
'62 **Monsters' Holiday**
   Bobby "Boris" Pickett
'73 **Montana** *Frank Zappa*
'70 **Montego Bay** *Bobby Bloom*
'67 **Monterey** *Animals*
Mony Mony
'68   *Tommy James*
'81   *Billy Idol*
'87   *Billy Idol [live]*
'76 **Moody Blue** *Elvis Presley*
'61 **Moody River** *Pat Boone*
'69 **Moody Woman** *Jerry Butler*
'65 **Moon Over Naples** *Bert Kaempfert*
Moon River
'61   *Jerry Butler*
'61   *Henry Mancini*
'62   *Andy Williams*
'71 **Moon Shadow** *Cat Stevens*
'58 **Moon Talk** *Perry Como*
'70 **Moondance** *Van Morrison*
Moonglow And Theme From
   "Picnic"
'56   *George Cates*
'56   *McGuire Sisters [Picnic]*
'56   *Morris Stoloff*
'67 **Moonlight Drive** *Doors*
'76 **Moonlight Feels Right** *Starbuck*
'56 **Moonlight Gambler** *Frankie Laine*
Moonlight Swim
'57   *Nick Noble*
'57   *Tony Perkins*
'87 **Moonlighting (Theme)** *Al Jarreau*
More
'56   *Perry Como*
'63   *Kai Winding*
More And More
'67   *Andy Williams*
'93   *Captain Hollywood Project*
'80 **More Bounce To The Ounce** *Zapp*
'66 **More I See You** *Chris Montez*
More Love
'67   *Miracles*
'80   *Kim Carnes*
'61 **More Money For You And Me**
   Four Preps
'76 **More, More, More**
   Andrea True Connection
'76 **More Than A Feeling** *Boston*
'07 **More Than A Memory** *Garth Brooks*
'67 **More Than A Miracle** *Roger Williams*
More Than A Woman
'77   *Tavares*
'78   *Bee Gees*
'02   *Aaliyah*
'91 **More Than Ever** *Nelson*
'80 **More Than I Can Say** *Leo Sayer*
'81 **More Than Just The Two Of Us**
   Sneaker
'01 **More Than That** *Backstreet Boys*
'67 **More Than The Eye Can See**
   Al Martino
More Than This
'83   *Roxy Music*
'97   *10,000 Maniacs*
More Than Words
'91   *Extreme*
'05   *Frankie J*
'90 **More Than Words Can Say** *Alias*
'88 **More Than You Know** *Martika*
'89 **More To This Life**
   Steven Curtis Chapman
'69 **More Today Than Yesterday**
   Spiral Starecase
'94 **More You Ignore Me, The Closer
   I Get** *Morrissey*

'59 **Morgen** *Ivo Robic*
'59 **Moritat (Theme From The
   Threepenny Opera)**
'56   *Louis Armstrong*
'56   *Richard Hayman & Jan August*
'56   *Dick Hyman*
'56   *Lawrence Welk*
'59   *Bobby Darin [Mack The Knife]*
'60   *Ella Fitzgerald*
'83 **Mornin'** *Al Jarreau*
'75 **Mornin' Beautiful**
   Tony Orlando & Dawn
'73 **Morning After** *Maureen McGovern*
'79 **Morning Dance** *Spyro Gyra*
'68 **Morning Dew** *Lulu*
'69 **Morning Girl** *Neon Philharmonic*
'72 **Morning Has Broken** *Cat Stevens*
Morning Side Of The Mountain
'59   *Tommy Edwards*
'74   *Donny & Marie Osmond*
'81 **Morning Train (Nine To Five)**
   Sheena Easton
'72 **Morningside** *Neil Diamond*
'73 **Most Beautiful Girl** *Charlie Rich*
'94 **Most Beautiful Girl In The World**
   Prince
'94 **Most Beautifullest Thing In This
   World** *Keith Murray*
'00 **Most Girls** *P!nk*
'98 **Most High**
   Jimmy Page & Robert Plant
'74 **Most Likely You Go Your Way (And
   I'll Go Mine)** *Bob Dylan*
'55 **Most Of All** *Don Cornell*
'62 **Most People Get Married** *Patti Page*
'55 **Mostly Martha** *Crew Cuts*
'70 **Mother** *John Lennon*
'72 **Mother And Child Reunion**
   Paul Simon
'71 **Mother Freedom** *Bread*
'61 **Mother-In-Law** *Ernie K-Doe*
'96 **Mother Mother** *Tracy Bonham*
'69 **Mother Popcorn** *James Brown*
'66 **Mothers Little Helper** *Rolling Stones*
'86 **Mothers Talk** *Tears For Fears*
'72 **Motorcycle Mama** *Sailcat*
'87 **Motortown** *Kane Gang*
'91 **Motown Song** *Rod Stewart w/
   The Temptations*
'91 **Motownphilly** *Boyz II Men*
'66 **Moulty** *Barbarians*
'67 **Mount Harissa** *Duke Ellington*
'82 **Mountain Music** *Alabama*
Mountain Of Love
'60   *Harold Dorman*
'64   *Johnny Rivers*
'61 **Mountain's High** *Dick & DeeDee*
'86 **Mountains** *Prince*
'96 **Mouth** *Merril Bainbridge*
'02 **Move Along** *All-American Rejects*
'91 **Move Any Mountain** *Shamen*
'86 **Move Away** *Culture Club*
'02 **Move B***h** *Ludacris*
'58 **Move It** *Cliff Richard*
'78 **Move It On Over** *George Thorogood*
Move Over
'69   *Steppenwolf*
'71   *Janis Joplin*
'92 **Move This** *Technotronic*
'04 **Move Ya Body** *Nina Sky*
'79 **Move Your Boogie Body** *Bar-Kays*
'76 **Movin'** *Brass Construction*
'58 **Movin' N' Groovin'** *Duane Eddy*
Movin' On
'75   *Bad Company*
'98   *Mya*
'78 **Movin' Out (Anthony's Song)**
   Billy Joel
'78 **Moving In Stereo** *Cars*
'94 **Moving On Up** *M People*
'76 **Mozambique** *Bob Dylan*
'63 **Mr. Bass Man** *Johnny Cymbal*
'71 **Mr. Big Stuff** *Jean Knight*
'59 **Mr. Blue** *Fleetwoods*
'78 **Mr. Blue Sky** *Electric Light Orchestra*

'70 **Mr. Bojangles** *Nitty Gritty Dirt Band*
'05 **Mr. Brightside** *Killers*
'68 **Mr. Businessman** *Ray Stevens*
'72 **Mister Can't You See**
   Buffy Sainte-Marie
'60 **Mr. Custer** *Larry Verne*
'89 **Mr. D.J.** *Joyce "Fenderella" Irby*
'66 **Mr. Dieingly Sad** *Critters*
'75 **Mr. Jaws** *Dickie Goodman*
'93 **Mr. Jones** *Counting Crows*
'57 **Mr. Lee** *Bobbettes*
'64 **Mr. Lonely** *Bobby Vinton*
'92 **Mr. Loverman** *Shabba Ranks*
'60 **Mr. Lucky** *Henry Mancini*
'04 **Mr. Mom** *Lonestar*
'92 **Mister Please** *Damn Yankees*
'83 **Mr. Roboto** *Styx*
Mister Sandman
'55   *Chordettes*
'55   *Four Aces*
'81   *Emmylou Harris*
'67 **Mr. Soul** *Buffalo Springfield*
'66 **Mr. Spaceman** *Byrds*
'69 **Mr. Sun, Mr. Moon**
   Paul Revere & The Raiders
Mr. Tambourine Man
'65   *Byrds*
'65   *Bob Dylan*
'84 **Mr. Telephone Man** *New Edition*
'93 **Mr. Vain** *Culture Beat*
'92 **Mr. Wendal** *Arrested Development*
Mr. Wonderful
'56   *Teddi King*
'56   *Peggy Lee*
'56   *Sarah Vaughan*
'65 **Mrs. Brown You've Got A Lovely
   Daughter** *Herman's Hermits*
Mrs. Robinson
'68   *Simon & Garfunkel*
'69   *Booker T. & The M.G.'s*
'00 **Ms. Jackson** *OutKast*
'06 **Ms. New Booty** *Bubba Sparxxx*
'89 **Much Too Young (To Feel This
   Damn Old)** *Garth Brooks*
'05 **Mud On The Tires** *Brad Paisley*
'69 **Muddy River** *Johnny Rivers*
'60 **Mule Skinner Blues** *Fendermen*
'77 **Mull Of Kintyre** *Paul McCartney*
'61 **Multiplication** *Bobby Darin*
'98 **Mummers' Dance**
   Loreena McKennitt
'59 **Mummy, The** *Bob McFadden & Dor*
'82 **Muscles** *Diana Ross*
Music
'00   *Madonna*
'01   *Eric Sermon w/ Marvin Gaye*
'79 **Music Box Dancer** *Frank Mills*
'72 **Music From Across The Way**
   James Last
'75 **Music Never Stopped**
   Grateful Dead
'99 **Music Of My Heart**
   **NSYNC & Gloria Estefan*
Music To Watch Girls By
'66   *Bob Crewe Generation*
'67   *Andy Williams*
'76 **Muskrat Love** *Captain & Tennille*
'05 **Must Be Doin' Somethin' Right**
   Billy Currington
'74 **Must Be Love** *James Gang*
'05 **Must Be Nice** *Lyfe Jennings*
'74 **Must Of Got Lost** *J. Geils Band*
'65 **Must To Avoid** *Herman's Hermits*
'66 **Mustang Sally** *Wilson Pickett*
'56 **Mutual Admiration Society**
   Teresa Brewer
'86 **My Adidas** *Run-D.M.C.*
'98 **My All** *Mariah Carey*
'78 **My Angel Baby** *Toby Beau*

My Babe
'55 Little Walter
'58 Dale Hawkins
My Baby
'65 Temptations
'86 Pretenders
'01 Lil' Romeo
'97 MyBabyDaddy B-Rock & The Bizz
'55 (My Baby Don't Love Me) No More
    DeJohn Sisters
'56 My Baby Left Me Elvis Presley
'70 My Baby Loves Lovin' White Plains
My Baby Loves Me
'66 Martha & The Vandellas
'93 Martina McBride
'67 My Baby Must Be A Magician
    Marvelettes
My Back Pages
'64 Bob Dylan
'67 Byrds
'04 My Band D12
'99 My Best Friend Tim McGraw
'78 My Best Friend's Love Cars
'56 My Blue Heaven Fats Domino
'97 My Body LSG
'55 My Bonnie Lassie Ames Brothers
'64 My Bonnie (My Bonnie Lies Over
    The Ocean) Beatles
My Boo
'96 Ghost Town DJ's
'04 Usher & Alicia Keys
'62 My Boomerang Won't Come Back
    Charlie Drake
'75 My Boy Elvis Presley
My Boy-Flat Top
'55 Boyd Bennett
'55 Dorothy Collins
'64 My Boy Lollipop Millie Small
'63 My Boyfriend's Back Angels
'89 My Brave Face Paul McCartney
'58 My Bucket's Got A Hole In It
    Ricky Nelson
'69 My Cherie Amour Stevie Wonder
'82 My City Was Gone Pretenders
My Coloring Book
'62 Kitty Kallen
'62 Sandy Stewart
'67 My Cup Runneth Over Ed Ames
'62 My Dad Paul Petersen
'60 My Dearest Darling Etta James
'98 My Deliverer Rich Mullins
'72 My Ding-A-Ling Chuck Berry
'57 My Dream Platters
'61 My Elusive Dreams
    David Houston & Tammy Wynette
'61 My Empty Arms Jackie Wilson
'84 My Ever Changing Moods
    Style Council
'00 My Everything 98°
'74 My Eyes Adored You Frankie Valli
'77 My Fair Share Seals & Crofts
'89 My Fantasy Teddy Riley
'98 My Father's Eyes Eric Clapton
'99 My Favorite Girl Dave Hollister
'98 My Favorite Mistake Sheryl Crow
My Favorite Things
'65 Julie Andrews
'68 Tony Bennett
My First Love
'89 Atlantic Starr
'00 Avant
'99 My First Night With You Mya
'87 My Forever Love Levert
'95 My Friends Red Hot Chili Peppers
'03 My Front Porch Looking In
    Lonestar
'66 My Generation Who
My Girl
'65 Temptations
'82 Donnie Iris
'85 Daryl Hall & John Oates/David
    Ruffin/ Eddie Kendrick [medley]
'88 Suave'
'74 My Girl Bill Jim Stafford

'81 My Girl (Gone, Gone, Gone)
    Chilliwack
'65 My Girl Has Gone Miracles
My Girl Josephine
'60 Fats Domino
'67 Jerry Jaye
'05 My Give A Damn's Busted
    Jo Dee Messina
'70 My Guitar Wants To Kill Your Mama
    Frank Zappa
My Guy
'64 Mary Wells
'82 Sister Sledge
'58 My Happiness Connie Francis
'04 My Happy Ending Avril Lavigne
'90 My Head's In Mississippi ZZ Top
'77 My Heart Belongs To Me
    Barbra Streisand
'64 My Heart Belongs To Only You
    Bobby Vinton
'91 My Heart Belongs To You
    Russ Irwin
'88 My Heart Can't Tell You No
    Rod Stewart
'64 My Heart Cries For You
    Ray Charles
'60 My Heart Has A Mind Of Its Own
    Connie Francis
'59 My Heart Is An Open Book
    Carl Dobkins, Jr.
'91 My Heart Is Failing Me Riff
My Heart Skips A Beat
'64 Buck Owens
'89 Cover Girls
'98 My Heart Will Go On (Love Theme
    From 'Titanic') Celine Dion
'66 My Heart's Symphony Gary Lewis
'80 My Heroes Have Always Been
    Cowboys Willie Nelson
'60 My Home Town Paul Anka
'85 My Hometown Bruce Springsteen
'80 My Home's In Alabama Alabama
'00 My Hope Is In You Third Day
'05 My Humps Black Eyed Peas
'04 My Immortal Evanescence
My Kind Of Girl
'61 Matt Monro
'94 Collin Raye
'83 My Kind Of Lady Supertramp
'65 My Kind Of Town Frank Sinatra
'90 My Kinda Girl Babyface
My Last Date (With You)
'60 Skeeter Davis
'60 Joni James
'78 My Life Billy Joel
'69 My Life (Throw It Away If I Want To)
    Bill Anderson
'02 My List Toby Keith
'56 My Little Angel Four Lads
'82 My Little Girl Tim McGraw
'66 My Little Red Book Love
'98 My Little Secret Xscape
'75 My Little Town Simon & Garfunkel
My Love
'65 Petula Clark
'73 Paul McCartney
'83 Lionel Richie
'94 Little Texas
'06 Justin Timberlake
'60 My Love For You Johnny Mathis
'64 My Love, Forgive Me Robert Goulet
'90 My Love Is A Fire Donny Osmond
'95 My Love Is For Real Paula Abdul
'03 My Love Is Like...WO Mya
'97 My Love Is The Shhh!
    Somethin' For The People
'99 My Love Is Your Love
    Whitney Houston
'92 My Lovin' (You're Never Gonna Get
    It) En Vogue
'67 My Mammy Happenings
'65 My Man Barbra Streisand
My Maria
'73 B.W. Stevenson
'96 Brooks & Dunn
'70 My Marie Engelbert Humperdinck

'59 My Melancholy Baby Tommy Edwards
'74 My Melody Of Love Bobby Vinton
'74 My Mistake (Was To Love You)
    Diana Ross & Marvin Gaye
'80 My Mother's Eyes Bette Midler
'73 My Music Loggins & Messina
'90 My, My, My Johnny Gill
'99 My Name Is Eminem
'91 My Name Is Not Susan
    Whitney Houston
'92 My Name Is Prince Prince
'02 My Neck, My Back (Lick It) Khia
'91 My Next Broken Heart
    Brooks & Dunn
'00 My Next Thirty Years Tim McGraw
'84 My Oh My Slade
'73 My Old School Steely Dan
'57 My One Sin Four Coins
'97 My Own Prison Creed
My Own True Love
'59 Jimmy Clanton
'62 Duprees
'99 My Own Worst Enemy Lit
'57 My Personal Possession
    Nat "King" Cole/Four Knights
'04 My Place Nelly
'69 My Pledge Of Love
    Joe Jeffrey Group
'56 My Prayer Platters
'88 My Prerogative Bobby Brown
'01 My Sacrifice Creed
'06 My Savior, My God Aaron Shust
'93 My Second Home Tracy Lawrence
'79 My Sharona Knack
'93 My Sister Juliana Hatfield Three
My Special Angel
'57 Bobby Helms
'68 Vogues
'52 My Story Chuck Willis
'63 My Summer Love
    Ruby & The Romantics
My Sweet Lady
'74 Cliff DeYoung
'77 John Denver
'70 My Sweet Lord George Harrison
'60 My Tani Brothers Four
'74 My Thang James Brown
My Town
'83 Michael Stanley Band
'02 Montgomery Gentry
'65 My Town, My Guy And Me
    Lesley Gore
'55 My Treasure Hilltoppers
'63 My True Confession Brook Benton
'58 My True Love Jack Scott
'61 My True Story Jive Five
My Way
'69 Frank Sinatra
'72 Paul Anka
'77 Elvis Presley
'98 Usher
'01 Limp Bizkit
'69 My Whole World Ended (The
    Moment You Left Me)
    David Ruffin
'63 My Whole World Is Falling Down
    Brenda Lee
'71 My Wife Who
'06 My Wish Rascal Flatts
'59 My Wish Came True Elvis Presley
'72 My World Bee Gees
'66 My World Is Empty Without You
    Supremes
'91 Mysterious Ways U2
'85 Mystery Lady Billy Ocean
'55 Mystery Train Elvis Presley
'65 Mystic Eyes Them

N

'70 N.I.B. Black Sabbath
Na Na Hey Hey Kiss Him Goodbye
'69 Steam
'87 Nylons

'76 **Nadia's Theme (The Young And The Restless)**
 Barry DeVorzon & Perry Botkin, Jr.
'64 **Nadine (Is It You?)** *Chuck Berry*
'61 **"Nag"** *Halos*
'96 **Naked Eye** *Luscious Jackson*
'95 **Name** *Goo Goo Dolls*
'64 **Name Game** *Shirley Ellis*
'77 **Name Of The Game** *Abba*
'66 **Nashville Cats** *Lovin' Spoonful*
'86 **Nasty** *Janet Jackson*
'71 **Nathan Jones** *Supremes*
'94 **National Working Woman's Holiday**
 Sammy Kershaw
'77 **Native New Yorker** *Odyssey*
'99 **Natural Blues** *Moby*
'60 **Natural Born Lover** *Fats Domino*
'73 **Natural High** *Bloodstone*
'71 **Natural Man** *Lou Rawls*
'95 **Natural One** *Folk Implosion*
'67 **Natural Woman** *Aretha Franklin*
'68 **Naturally Stoned** *Avant-Garde*
'61 **Nature Boy** *Bobby Darin*
'71 **Nature's Way** *Spirit*
'04 **Naughty Girl** *Beyoncé*
'88 **Naughty Girls (Need Love Too)**
 Samantha Fox
'54 **Naughty Lady Of Shady Lane, The**
 Ames Brothers
'84 **Naughty Naughty** *John Parr*
'64 **Navy Blue** *Diane Renay*
'70 **Neanderthal Man** *Hotlegs*
'58 **Near You** *Roger Williams*
'58 **Nee Nee Na Na Na Na Nu Nu**
 Dicky Doo & The Don'ts
'06 **Need A Boss** *Shareefa*
'89 **Need A Little Taste Of Love**
 Doobie Brothers
'74 **Need To Be** *Jim Weatherly*
'63 **Need To Belong** *Jerry Butler*
'58 **Need You** *Donnie Owens*
'78 **Need You Bad** *Ted Nugent*
'87 **Need You Tonight** *INXS*
'72 **Needle And The Damage Done**
 Neil Young
 Needles And Pins
'64 *Searchers*
'86 *Tom Petty/Stevie Nicks*
'73 **Neither One Of Us (Wants To Be The First To Say Goodbye)**
 Gladys Knight
'92 **Neon Moon** *Brooks & Dunn*
'67 **Neon Rainbow** *Box Tops*
'77 **Nether Lands** *Dan Fogelberg*
'84 **Neutron Dance** *Pointer Sisters*
'85 **Never** *Heart*
'92 **Never A Time** *Genesis*
 Never Again
'02 *Nickelback*
'07 *Kelly Clarkson*
'86 **Never As Good As The First Time**
 Sade
'59 **Never Be Anyone Else But You**
 Ricky Nelson
'80 **Never Be The Same**
 Christopher Cross
'75 **Never Been Any Reason**
 Head East
'82 **Never Been In Love** *Randy Meisner*
'71 **Never Been To Spain**
 Three Dog Night
 Never Can Say Goodbye
'71 *Isaac Hayes*
'71 *Jackson 5*
'74 *Gloria Gaynor*
'87 *Communards*
'69 **Never Comes The Day**
 Moody Blues
'88 **Never Die Young** *James Taylor*
'71 **Never Ending Song Of Love**
 Delaney & Bonnie
'85 **Never Ending Story** *Limahl*
'90 **Never Enough** *Cure*
'98 **Never Ever** *All Saints*
'68 **Never Give You Up** *Jerry Butler*

'77 **Never Going Back Again**
 Fleetwood Mac
'76 **Never Gonna Fall In Love Again**
 Eric Carmen
'87 **Never Gonna Give You Up**
 Rick Astley
'91 **Never Gonna Let You Down**
 Surface
 Never Gonna Let You Go
'83 *Sergio Mendes*
'99 *Faith Evans*
 Never Had A Dream Come True
'70 *Stevie Wonder*
'01 *S Club 7*
'93 **Never Keeping Secrets** *Babyface*
'90 **Never Knew Lonely** *Vince Gill*
'88 **Never Knew Love Like This**
 Alexander O'Neal/Cherrelle
'80 **Never Knew Love Like This Before**
 Stephanie Mills
'96 **Never Leave Me Alone** *Nate Dogg*
'03 **Never Leave You - Uh Ooh, Uh Oooh!** *Lumidee*
'75 **Never Let Her Go** *David Gates*
'87 **Never Let Me Down** *David Bowie*
'87 **Never Let Me Down Again**
 Depeche Mode
'00 **Never Let You Go** *Third Eye Blind*
'94 **Never Lie** *Immature*
'97 **Never Make A Promise** *Dru Hill*
 Never My Love
'67 *Association*
'71 *5th Dimension*
'74 *Blue Swede*
'73 **Never, Never Gonna Give Ya Up**
 Barry White
 Never On Sunday
'60 *Don Costa*
'61 *Chordettes*
'87 **Never Say Goodbye** *Bon Jovi*
'03 **Never Scared** *Bone Crusher*
'93 **Never Should've Let You Go**
 Hi-Five
'91 **Never Stop** *Brand New Heavies*
'85 **Never Surrender** *Corey Hart*
'88 **Never Tear Us Apart** *INXS*
'98 **Never There** *Cake*
'87 **Never Thought (That I Could Love)**
 Dan Hill
'04 **Never Too Late** *Three Days Grace*
'81 **Never Too Much** *Luther Vandross*
'56 **Never Turn Back** *Al Hibbler*
'07 **Never Wanted Nothing More**
 Kenny Chesney
'94 **New Age Girl** *Deadeye Dick*
'85 **New Attitude** *Patti LaBelle*
'02 **New Day Has Come** *Celine Dion*
'69 **New Day Yesterday** *Jethro Tull*
'83 **New Frontier** *Donald Fagen*
'64 **New Girl In School** *Jan & Dean*
'76 **New Kid In Town** *Eagles*
'63 **New Mexican Rose** *Four Seasons*
'84 **New Moon On Monday** *Duran Duran*
'60 **New Orleans** *U.S. Bonds*
'80 **New Romance (It's A Mystery)**
 Spider
'76 **New Rose** *Damned*
'88 **New Sensation** *INXS*
'84 **New Song** *Howard Jones*
'91 **New Way (To Light Up An Old Flame)** *Joe Diffie*
'82 **New World Man** *Rush*
'83 **New Year's Day** *U2*
'04 **New York** *Ja Rule*
'78 **New York Groove** *Ace Frehley*
'67 **New York Mining Disaster 1941**
 Bee Gees
'90 **New York Minute** *Don Henley*
'76 **New York State Of Mind**
 Billy Joel
'77 **New York, You Got Me Dancing**
 Andrea True Connection
'65 **New York's A Lonely Town**
 Trade Winds
'62 **Next Door To An Angel** *Neil Sedaka*
'00 **Next Episode** *Dr. Dre/Snoop Dogg*

'97 **Next Lifetime** *Erykah Badu*
'67 **Next Plane To London** *Rose Garden*
'86 **Next Time I Fall**
 Peter Cetera w/ Amy Grant
'90 **Next To You, Next To Me**
 Shenandoah
'98 **Nice & Slow** *Usher*
'82 **Nice Girls** *Eye To Eye*
'60 **Nice 'N' Easy** *Frank Sinatra*
'76 **Nice 'N' Naasty** *Salsoul Orchestra*
'88 **Nice 'N' Slow** *Freddie Jackson*
'72 **Nice To Be With You** *Gallery*
'90 **Nicety** *Michel'le*
'72 **Nickel Song** *Melanie*
'81 **Nicole** *Point Blank*
'60 **Night** *Jackie Wilson*
 Night [Nite] And Day
'88 *Al B. Sure!*
'90 *U2*
'70 **Night Bird Flying** *Jimi Hendrix*
'74 **Night Chicago Died** *Paper Lace*
'78 **Night Fever** *Bee Gees*
'62 **Night Has A Thousand Eyes**
 Bobby Vee
'94 **Night In My Veins** *Pretenders*
'85 **Night Is Still Young** *Billy Joel*
'76 **Night Life** *Willie Nelson*
'56 **Night Lights** *Nat "King" Cole*
 Night Moves
'76 *Bob Seger*
'86 *Marilyn Martin*
'81 **Night Owls** *Little River Band*
'73 **Night The Lights Went Out In Georgia** *Vicki Lawrence*
 Night They Drove Old Dixie Down
'69 *Band*
'71 *Joan Baez*
'66 **Night Time** *Strangeloves*
'99 **Night To Remember** *Joe Diffie*
'62 **Night Train** *James Brown*
'83 **Nightbird**
 Stevie Nicks/Sandy Stewart
'88 **Nightime** *Pretty Poison*
'75 **Nightingale** *Carole King*
'88 **Nightmare On My Street** *DJ Jazzy Jeff & The Fresh Prince*
'89 **Nightmares** *Violent Femmes*
'76 **Nights Are Forever Without You**
 England Dan & John Ford Coley
'72 **Nights In White Satin** *Moody Blues*
'91 **Nights Like This** *After 7*
'75 **Nights On Broadway** *Bee Gees*
'85 **Nightshift** *Commodores*
'67 **Niki Hoeky** *P.J. Proby*
'86 **Nikita** *Elton John*
'00 **911** *Wyclef Jean*
'90 **911 Is A Joke** *Public Enemy*
'80 **9 To 5** *Dolly Parton*
'85 **19** *Paul Hardcastle*
'04 **1985** *Bowling For Soup*
'74 **Nineteen Hundred And Eighty Five**
 Paul McCartney
'70 **1900 Yesterday**
 Liz Damon's Orient Express
'82 ****1999**** *Prince*
'96 **1979** *Smashing Pumpkins*
'02 **19 Somethin'** *Mark Wills*
'66 **19th Nervous Breakdown**
 Rolling Stones
'66 **98.6** *Keith*
'79 **99** *Toto*
'83 **99 Luftballons** *Nena*
'75 **99 Miles From L.A.** *Albert Hammond*
'04 **99 Problems** *Jay-Z*
'57 **Ninety-Nine Ways** *Tab Hunter*
'56 **Ninety Nine Years (Dead Or Alive)**
 Guy Mitchell
'66 **96 Tears** *? & The Mysterians*
'63 **Ninth Wave** *Ventures*
 Nitty Gritty
'63 *Shirley Ellis*
'69 *Gladys Knight*
 No Arms Can Ever Hold You
'55 *Georgie Shaw*
'64 *Bachelors*

'04 **No Better Love** *Young Gunz w/ Rell*
'91 **No Better Place**
    Steven Curtis Chapman
No Charge
'74 *Melba Montgomery*
'75 *Shirley Caesar*
'58 **No Chemise, Please**
    Gerry Granahan
'96 **No Diggity** *BLACKstreet*
'93 **No Doubt About It** *Neal McCoy*
'86 **No Easy Way Out** *Robert Tepper*
'94 **No Excuses** *Alice In Chains*
'93 **No Future In The Past** *Vince Gill*
'99 **No Leaf Clover** *Metallica*
'03 **No Letting Go** *Wayne Wonder*
'85 **No Lookin' Back** *Michael McDonald*
'71 **No Love At All** *B.J. Thomas*
'57 **No Love (But Your Love)**
    Johnny Mathis
'70 **No Matter What** *Badfinger*
'65 **No Matter What Shape (Your**
    Stomach's In) *T-Bones*
'69 **No Matter What Sign You Are**
    Supremes
'67 **No Milk Today** *Herman's Hermits*
'92 **No Mistakes** *Patty Smyth*
No More
'55 *McGuire Sisters*
'00 *Ruff Endz*
'00 **No More (Baby I'ma Do Right)** *3LW*
'05 **No More Cloudy Days** *Eagles*
'01 **No More Drama** *Mary J. Blige*
'95 **No More "I Love You's"**
    Annie Lennox
'89 **No More Lies** *Michel'le*
'84 **No More Lonely Nights**
    Paul McCartney
'73 **No More Mr. Nice Guy** *Alice Cooper*
'89 **No More Rhyme** *Debbie Gibson*
'79 **No More Tears (Enough Is Enough)**
    Barbra Streisand/Donna Summer
'84 **No More Words** *Berlin*
'90 **No Myth** *Michael Penn*
'96 **No News** *Lonestar*
'80 **No Night So Long** *Dionne Warwick*
'97 **No, No, No** *Destiny's Child*
'75 **No No Song** *Ringo Starr*
No, Not Much!
'56 *Four Lads*
'69 *Vogues*
No One
'63 *Ray Charles*
'07 *Alicia Keys*
'95 **No One Else** *Total*
'92 **No One Else On Earth** *Wynonna*
'86 **No One Is To Blame** *Howard Jones*
No One Knows
'58 *Dion & The Belmonts*
'02 *Queens Of The Stone Age*
'82 **No One Like You** *Scorpions*
'96 **No One Needs To Know**
    Shania Twain
'72 **No One To Depend On** *Santana*
'92 **No Ordinary Love** *Sade*
'59 **No Other Arms, No Other Lips**
    Chordettes
'64 **No Particular Place To Go**
    Chuck Berry
'99 **No Pigeons** *Sporty Thievz*
'98 **No Place That Far** *Sara Evans*
'04 **No Problem** *Lil Scrappy*
'93 **No Rain** *Blind Melon*
'92 **No Regrets** *Tom Cochrane*
'65 **No Reply** *Beatles*
'81 **No Reply At All** *Genesis*
'66 **No Salt On Her Tail** *Mamas & Papas*
'99 **No Scrubs** *TLC*
'03 **No Shoes, No Shirt, No Problems**
    Kenny Chesney
'88 **No Smoke Without A Fire**
    Bad Company
'91 **No Son Of Mine** *Genesis*
'02 **No Such Thing** *John Mayer*
'70 **No Sugar Tonight** *Guess Who*
'78 **No Tell Lover** *Chicago*

No Time
'69 *Guess Who*
'96 *Lil' Kim*
'06 **No Way Back** *Foo Fighters*
'84 **No Way Out** *Jefferson Starship*
No Woman, No Cry
'75 *Bob Marley*
'96 *Fugees*
Nobody
'82 *Sylvia*
'96 *Keith Sweat*
Nobody But Me
'67 *Human Beinz*
'06 *Blake Shelton*
'58 **Nobody But You** *Dee Clark*
'69 **Nobody But You Babe**
    Clarence Reid
Nobody Does It Better
'77 *Carly Simon*
'98 *Nate Dogg*
'98 **Nobody Else** *Tyrese*
'64 **Nobody I Know** *Peter & Gordon*
Nobody Knows
'95 *Tony Rich Project*
'96 *Kevin Sharp*
'60 **Nobody Loves Me Like You**
    Flamingos
'82 **Nobody Said It Was Easy** *Le Roux*
'84 **Nobody Told Me** *John Lennon*
'01 **Nobody Wants To Be Lonely**
    Ricky Martin w/ Christina Aguilera
'73 **Nobody Wants You When You're**
    Down And Out *Bobby Womack*
Nobody Wins
'81 *Elton John*
'93 *Radney Foster*
'76 **Nobody's Fault But Mine**
    Led Zeppelin
Nobody's Fool
'86 *Cinderella*
'88 *Kenny Loggins*
Nobody's Home
'90 *Clint Black*
'05 *Avril Lavigne*
Nobody's Perfect
'88 *Mike + The Mechanics*
'07 *Hannah Montana*
'98 **Nobody's Supposed To Be Here**
    Deborah Cox
'04 **Nolia Clap** *Juvenile • Wacko • Skip*
'94 **None Of Your Business**
    Salt-N-Pepa
'99 **Nookie** *Limp Bizkit*
'92 **Norma Jean Riley** *Diamond Rio*
'61 **Norman** *Sue Thompson*
'60 **North To Alaska** *Johnny Horton*
'65 **Norwegian Wood (This Bird Has**
    Flown) *Beatles*
'02 **Not A Day Goes By** *Lonestar*
'94 **Not A Moment Too Soon**
    Tim McGraw
'90 **Not Counting You** *Garth Brooks*
'68 **Not Enough Indians** *Dean Martin*
'85 **Not Enough Love In The World**
    Don Henley
'92 **Not Enough Time** *INXS*
Not Fade Away
'57 *Buddy Holly*
'64 *Rolling Stones*
'96 **Not Gon' Cry** *Mary J. Blige*
'88 **Not Just Another Girl** *Ivan Neville*
'79 **(not just) Knee Deep** *Funkadelic*
'63 **Not Me** *Orlons*
'95 **Not On Your Love** *Jeff Carson*
'94 **Not One Minute More** *Della Reese*
'07 **Not Ready To Make Nice**
    Dixie Chicks
'67 **Not So Sweet Martha Lorraine**
    Country Joe & The Fish
'95 **Not That Different** *Collin Raye*
'65 **Not The Lovin' Kind**
    Dino, Desi & Billy
'92 **Not The Only One** *Bonnie Raitt*
'04 **Not Today** *Mary J. Blige*
'97 **Not Tonight** *Lil' Kim*
'02 **Nothin'** *N.O.R.E.*

'86 **Nothin' At All** *Heart*
'88 **Nothin' But A Good Time** *Poison*
'96 **Nothin' But The Cavi Hit**
    Mack 10 & Tha Dogg Pound
'97 **Nothin' But The Taillights**
    Clint Black
'93 **Nothin' My Love Can't Fix**
    Joey Lawrence
'89 **Nothin' To Hide** *Poco*
Nothin' To Lose
'74 *Kiss*
'04 *Josh Gracin*
'00 **Nothing As It Seems** *Pearl Jam*
'92 **Nothing Broken But My Heart**
    Celine Dion
'69 **Nothing But A Heartache** *Flirtations*
'65 **Nothing But Heartaches** *Supremes*
'62 **Nothing Can Change This Love**
    Sam Cooke
'88 **Nothing Can Come Between Us**
    Sade
'65 **Nothing Can Stop Me**
    Gene Chandler
'90 **Nothing Compares 2 U**
    Sinéad O'Connor
'92 **Nothing Else Matters** *Metallica*
'74 **Nothing From Nothing** *Billy Preston*
'02 **Nothing In This World**
    Keke Wyatt w/ Avant
'07 **Nothing Left To Lose** *Mat Kearney*
'04 **Nothing On But The Radio**
    Gary Allan
'87 **Nothing's Gonna Change My Love**
    For You *Glenn Medeiros*
'87 **Nothing's Gonna Stop Us Now**
    Starship
'66 **Nothing's Too Good For My Baby**
    Stevie Wonder
'90 **Notice Me** *Nikki*
Notorious
'86 *Duran Duran*
'87 *Loverboy*
'92 **November Rain** *Guns N' Roses*
'96 **Novocaine For The Soul** *Eels*
'58 **Now And For Always**
    George Hamilton IV
'94 **Now and Forever** *Richard Marx*
'67 **Now I Know** *Jack Jones*
'92 **Now More Than Ever**
    John Mellencamp
'72 **Now Run And Tell That**
    Denise LaSalle
'98 **Now That I Found You** *Terri Clark*
Now That We Found Love
'79 *Third World*
'91 *Heavy D & The Boyz*
'89 **Now You're In Heaven**
    Julian Lennon
'66 **Nowhere Man** *Beatles*
'96 **Nowhere To Go** *Melissa Etheridge*
Nowhere To Run
    Martha & The Vandellas
'92 **Nu Nu** *Lidell Townsell & M.T.F.*
Numb
'93 *U2*
'03 *Linkin Park*
'04 **Numb/Encore** *Jay-Z/Linkin Park*
'74 **#9 Dream** *John Lennon*
'01 **#1** *Nelly*
'96 **#1 Crush** *Garbage*
'05 **Number One Spot** *Ludacris*
'73 **Nutbush City Limits**
    Ike & Tina Turner
'93 **Nuthin' But A "G" Thang**
    Dr. Dre/Snoop Dogg
'62 **Nutrocker** *B. Bumble & The Stingers*
'94 **Nuttin' But Love**
    Heavy D & The Boyz
Nuttin' For Christmas
'55 *Barry Gordon*
'55 *Joe Ward*
'55 *Ricky Zahnd*

O

'05 **O** *Omarion*
'60 **O Dio Mio** *Annette*

'02 **O Holy Night** *Josh Groban*
'82 **O Superman (For Massenet)**
Laurie Anderson
'02 **'03 Bonnie & Clyde** *Jay-Z*
'91 **O.P.P.** *Naughty By Nature*
'85 **Oak Tree** *Morris Day*
'88 **Oasis** *Roberta Flack*
'85 **Object Of My Desire** *Starpoint*
'94 **Objects In The Rear View Mirror
May Appear Closer Than They
Are** *Meat Loaf*
'68 **Ob-La-Di, Ob-La-Da** *Beatles*
'84 **Obscene Phone Caller** *Rockwell*
'85 **Obsession** *Animotion*
'05 **Obsession [No Es Amor]** *Frankie J*
'73 **Ocean, The** *Led Zeppelin*
'04 **Ocean Avenue** *Yellowcard*
'87 **Ocean Front Property** *George Strait*
'69 **Octopus's Garden** *Beatles*
Ode To Billie Joe
'67 *Bobbie Gentry*
'67 *Kingpins*
'95 **Ode To My Family** *Cranberries*
'88 **Off On Your Own (Girl)** *Al B. Sure!*
'80 **Off The Wall** *Michael Jackson*
'05 **Oh** *Ciara*
'72 **Oh, Babe, What Would You Say?**
Hurricane Smith
'64 **Oh Baby Don't You Weep**
James Brown
Oh Boy
'57 *Crickets*
'02 *Cam'ron*
'59 **Oh! Carol** *Neil Sedaka*
'89 **Oh Daddy** *Adrian Belew*
Oh! Darling
'69 *Beatles*
'78 *Robin Gibb*
'89 **Oh Father** *Madonna*
Oh Girl
'72 *Chi-Lites*
'90 *Paul Young*
Oh Happy Day
'69 *Edwin Hawkins' Singers*
'70 *Glen Campbell*
'66 **Oh How Happy** *Shades Of Blue*
Oh Julie
'58 *Crescendos*
'82 *Barry Manilow*
'73 **Oh La De Da** *Staple Singers*
'60 **Oh, Little One** *Jack Scott*
'58 **Oh Lonesome Me** *Don Gibson*
'69 **Oh Me Oh My (I'm A Fool For You
Baby)** *Lulu*
'78 **Oh My Lord [medley]** *Boney M*
'74 **Oh My My** *Ringo Starr*
'81 **Oh No** *Commodores*
Oh No Not My Baby
'64 *Maxine Brown*
'73 *Merry Clayton*
'58 **Oh-Oh, I'm Falling In Love Again**
Jimmie Rodgers
'86 **Oh, People** *Patti LaBelle*
Oh, Pretty Woman
'64 *Roy Orbison*
'82 *Van Halen*
'85 **Oh Sheila** *Ready For The World*
'84 **Oh Sherrie** *Steve Perry*
'55 **Oh! Susanna** *Singing Dogs*
'74 **Oh Very Young** *Cat Stevens*
Oh Well
'70 *Fleetwood Mac*
'79 *Rockets*
'69 **Oh, What A Night** *Dells*
'78 **Oh What A Night For Dancing**
Barry White
Oh Yeah
'66 *Shadows Of Knight*
'87 *Yello*
'70 **Ohio** *Crosby, Stills, Nash & Young*
'94 **Oíche Chiún (Silent Night)** *Enya*
'05 **Okay** *Nivea*
'69 **Okie From Muskogee**
Merle Haggard
'55 **Oklahoma!** *Gordon MacRae*

'02 **Ol' Red** *Blake Shelton*
'69 **Old Brown Shoe** *Beatles*
'57 **Old Cape Cod** *Patti Page*
'75 **Old Days** *Chicago*
'94 **Old Enough To Know Better**
Wade Hayes
'80 **Old-Fashion Love** *Commodores*
'77 **Old Fashioned Boy (You're The
One)** *Stallion*
'71 **Old Fashioned Love Song**
Three Dog Night
'88 **Old Folks**
Ronnie Milsap & Mike Reid
'85 **Old Hippie** *Bellamy Brothers*
'60 **Old Lamplighter** *Browns*
'72 **Old Man** *Neil Young*
'96 **Old Man & Me (When I Get To
Heaven)** *Hootie & The Blowfish*
'84 **Old Man Down The Road**
John Fogerty
'56 **Old Philosopher** *Eddie Lawrence*
'62 **Old Rivers** *Walter Brennan*
'81 **Old Songs** *Barry Manilow*
'79 **Old Time Rock & Roll** *Bob Seger*
'61 **Ole Buttermilk Sky**
Bill Black's Combo
'79 **Oliver's Army** *Elvis Costello*
'67 **Omaha** *Moby Grape*
'96 **On A Good Night** *Wade Hayes*
'74 **On A Night Like This**
Bob Dylan
'91 **On A Sunday Afternoon**
Lighter Shade Of Brown
On And [&] On
'74 *Gladys Knight*
'77 *Stephen Bishop*
'97 *Erykah Badu*
'94 **On Bended Knee** *Boyz II Men*
On Broadway
'63 *Drifters*
'78 *George Benson*
'04 **On Fire** *Lloyd Banks*
'56 **On London Bridge** *Jo Stafford*
On My Own
'86 *Patti LaBelle & Michael McDonald*
'97 *Peach Union*
On My Word Of Honor
'56 *B.B. King*
'56 *Platters*
'89 **On Our Own** *Bobby Brown*
'89 **On Second Thought** *Eddie Rabbitt*
'77 **On The Border** *Al Stewart*
'84 **On The Dark Side**
John Cafferty
'07 **On The Hotline** *Pretty Ricky*
'82 **On The Loose** *Saga*
'86 **On The Other Hand** *Randy Travis*
'80 **On The Radio** *Donna Summer*
'61 **On The Rebound** *Floyd Cramer*
On The Road Again
'68 *Canned Heat*
'80 *Willie Nelson*
'78 **On The Shelf**
Donny & Marie Osmond
On The Street Where You Live
'56 *Vic Damone*
'56 *Eddie Fisher*
'64 *Andy Williams*
'78 **On The Turning Away** *Pink Floyd*
'04 **On The Way Down** *Ryan Cabrera*
'82 **On The Way To The Sky**
Neil Diamond
'90 **On The Way Up** *Elisa Fiorillo*
'82 **On The Wings Of Love**
Jeffrey Osborne
'63 **On Top Of Spaghetti** *Tom Glazer*
'64 **Once A Day** *Connie Smith*
'89 **Once Bitten Twice Shy** *Great White*
Once In A Lifetime
'80 *Talking Heads*
'06 *Keith Urban*
'79 **Once In Awhile** *Chimes*
Once Upon A Time
'63 *Rochell & The Candles*
'64 *Marvin Gaye & Mary Wells*

'75 **Once You Get Started**
Rufus Feat. Chaka Khan
'71 **Once You Understand** *Think*
One
'69 *Three Dog Night*
'89 *Bee Gees*
'89 *Metallica*
'92 *U2*
'98 *Creed*
One, The
'92 *Elton John*
'00 *Backstreet Boys*
'02 *Gary Allan*
'91 **One And Only** *Chesney Hawkes*
'90 **One And Only Man** *Steve Winwood*
'71 **One Bad Apple** *Osmonds*
'77 **One Bourbon, One Scotch, One
Beer** *George Thorogood*
'95 **One Boy, One Girl** *Collin Raye*
'63 **One Broken Heart For Sale**
Elvis Presley
'04 **One Call Away** *Chingy*
One Chain Don't Make No Prison
'74 *Four Tops*
'78 *Santana*
'74 **One Day At A Time** *Marilyn Sellars*
'70 **One Day Of Your Life** *Andy Williams*
'65 **One Dyin' And A Buryin'**
Roger Miller
'95 **One Emotion** *Clint Black*
One Fine Day
'63 *Chiffons*
'80 *Carole King*
'71 **One Fine Morning** *Lighthouse*
One For My Baby
'57 *Tony Bennett*
'58 *Frank Sinatra*
'87 **One For The Mockingbird**
Cutting Crew
'88 **One Good Reason** *Paul Carrack*
'88 **One Good Woman** *Peter Cetera*
'65 **One Has My Name (The Other Has
My Heart)** *Barry Young*
'96 **One Headlight** *Wallflowers*
'87 **One Heartbeat** *Smokey Robinson*
'74 **One Hell Of A Woman** *Mac Davis*
'86 **One Hit (To The Body)**
Rolling Stones
'94 **100% Pure Love** *Crystal Waters*
'81 **One Hundred Ways**
Quincy Jones/James Ingram
'04 **100 Years** *Five For Fighting*
'97 **One I Gave My Heart To** *Aaliyah*
'87 **One I Love** *R.E.M.*
One In A Million
'56 *Platters*
'84 *Romantics*
'96 *Aaliyah*
'80 **One In A Million You** *Larry Graham*
'65 **One Kiss For Old Times' Sake**
Ronnie Dove
'02 **One Last Breath** *Creed*
'93 **One Last Cry** *Brian McKnight*
'78 **One Last Kiss** *J. Geils Band*
'70 **One Less Bell To Answer**
5th Dimension
'73 **One Less Set Of Footsteps**
Jim Croce
'72 **One Life To Live** *Manhattans*
'85 **One Lonely Night**
REO Speedwagon
One Love
'77 *Bob Marley*
'06 *Hootie & The Blowfish*
'76 **One Love In My Lifetime**
Diana Ross
'70 **One Man Band** *Three Dog Night*
'73 **One Man Band (Plays All Alone)**
Ronnie Dyson
'74 **One Man Woman/One Woman Man**
Paul Anka/Odia Coates
'61 **One Mint Julep** *Ray Charles*
'01 **One Minute Man** *Missy Elliott*
'88 **One Moment In Time**
Whitney Houston

'71 **One Monkey Don't Stop No Show** *Honey Cone*
'95 **One More Chance/Stay With Me** *Notorious B.I.G.*
'01 **One More Day** *Diamond Rio*
'93 **One More Last Chance** *Vince Gill*
'85 **One More Night** *Phil Collins*
'72 **One More Saturday Night [live]** *Grateful Dead*
'97 **One More Time** *Real McCoy*
One More Try
'88 *George Michael*
'90 *Timmy -T-*
'99 *Divine*
One Nation Under A Groove
'78 *Funkadelic*
'94 *Ice Cube [Bop Gun]*
'58 **One Night** *Elvis Presley*
'97 **One Night At A Time** *George Strait*
'85 **One Night In Bangkok** *Murray Head*
'85 **One Night Love Affair** *Bryan Adams*
'99 **One Night Stand** *J-Shin*
'73 **One Of A Kind (Love Affair)** *Spinners*
'85 **One Of The Living** *Tina Turner*
One Of These Days
'71 *Pink Floyd*
'75 *Emmylou Harris*
'98 *Tim McGraw*
'75 **One Of These Nights** *Eagles*
'95 **One Of Us** *Joan Osborne*
'60 **One Of Us (Will Weep Tonight)** *Patti Page*
'83 **One On One** *Daryl Hall & John Oates*
'83 **One Particular Harbor** *Jimmy Buffett*
'76 **One Piece At A Time** *Johnny Cash*
'91 **One Shot** *Tin Machine*
One Step Closer
'80 *Doobie Brothers*
'01 *Linkin Park*
'86 **One Step Closer To You** *Gavin Christopher*
'87 **One Step Up** *Bruce Springsteen*
One Summer Night
'58 *Danleers*
'61 *Diamonds*
'95 **One Sweet Day** *Mariah Carey & Boyz II Men*
'81 **One That You Love** *Air Supply*
One [1] Thing
'83 *INXS*
'04 *Finger Eleven*
'05 *Amerie*
'83 **One Thing Leads To Another** *Fixx*
One Tin Soldier (The Legend Of Billy Jack)
'69 *Original Caste*
'71 *Coven*
'71 **One Toke Over The Line** *Brewer & Shipley*
'61 **One Track Mind** *Bobby Lewis*
'80 **One-Trick Pony** *Paul Simon*
'05 **1,2 Step** *Ciara*
1-2-3
'65 *Len Barry*
'88 *Gloria Estefan*
'07 **1, 2, 3, 4** *Feist*
'96 **1,2,3,4 (Sumpin' New)** *Coolio*
'68 **1, 2, 3, Red Light** *1910 Fruitgum Co.*
'00 **One Voice** *Billy Gilman*
'79 **One Way Or Another** *Blondie*
'72 **One Way Out** *Allman Brothers Band*
'96 **One Way Ticket (Because I Can)** *LeAnn Rimes*
'98 **One Week** *Barenaked Ladies*
'62 **One Who Really Loves You** *Mary Wells*
'06 **One Wish** *Ray J*
'93 **One Woman** *Jade*
'01 **One Woman Man** *Dave Hollister*
'82 **One You Love** *Glenn Frey*
'71 **One's On The Way** *Loretta Lynn*
'05 **Only** *Nine Inch Nails*
'80 **Only A Lonely Heart Sees** *Felix Cavaliere*

'88 **Only A Memory** *Smithereens*
'06 **Only Difference Between Martyrdom And Suicide Is Press Coverage** *Panic! At The Disco*
'00 **Only God Knows Why** *Kid Rock*
'90 **Only Here For A Little While** *Billy Dean*
'90 **Only Human** *Jeffrey Osborne*
Only In America
'63 *Jay & The Americans*
'01 *Brooks & Dunn*
'87 **Only In My Dreams** *Debbie Gibson*
'62 **Only Love Can Break A Heart** *Gene Pitney*
'70 **Only Love Can Break Your Heart** *Neil Young*
'76 **Only Love Is Real** *Carole King*
'57 **Only One Love** *George Hamilton IV*
Only Sixteen
'59 *Sam Cooke*
'76 *Dr. Hook*
'78 **Only The Good Die Young** *Billy Joel*
Only The Lonely
'60 *Roy Orbison*
'82 *Motels*
'69 **Only The Strong Survive** *Jerry Butler*
'85 **Only The Young** *Journey*
'01 **Only Time** *Enya*
Only Time Will Tell
'82 *Asia*
'91 *Nelson*
'95 **Only Wanna Be With You** *Hootie & The Blowfish*
'84 **Only When You Leave** *Spandau Ballet*
'75 **Only Women** *Alice Cooper*
'75 **Only Yesterday** *Carpenters*
Only You [U]
'55 *Hilltoppers*
'55 *Platters*
'59 *Franck Pourcel*
'74 *Ringo Starr*
'82 *Yaz*
'96 *112*
'04 *Ashanti*
Only You Know And I Know
'70 *Dave Mason*
'71 *Delaney & Bonnie*
'65 **Oo Wee Baby, I Love You** *Fred Hughes*
'56 **Ooby Dooby** *Roy Orbison*
'92 **Oochie Coochie** *MC Brains*
'01 **Oochie Wally** *QB Finest*
Oogum Boogum Song
Brenton Wood
'03 **Ooh!** *Mary J. Blige*
'96 **Ooh Aah...Just A Little Bit** *Gina G*
'73 **Ooh Baby** *Gilbert O'Sullivan*
Ooh Baby Baby
'65 *Miracles*
'78 *Linda Ronstadt*
'77 **Ooh Boy** *Rose Royce*
O-o-h Child
'70 *5 Stairsteps*
'93 *Dino*
'73 **Ooh La La** *Faces*
'90 **Ooh La La (I Can't Get Over You)** *Perfect Gentlemen*
'58 **Ooh! My Soul** *Little Richard*
'85 **Ooh Ooh Song** *Pat Benatar*
'60 **Ooh Poo Pah Doo** *Jessie Hill*
'88 **Ooo La La La** *Teena Marie*
'90 **Ooops Up** *Snap!*
'00 **Oops!...I Did It Again** *Britney Spears*
'02 **Oops (Oh My)** *Tweet*
'82 **Open Arms** *Journey*
'67 **Open Letter To My Teenage Son** *Victor Lundberg*
'66 **Open The Door To Your Heart** *Darrell Banks*
'96 **Open Up Your Eyes** *Tonic*
'55 **Open Up Your Heart (And Let The Sunshine In)** *Cowboy Church Sunday School*
'04 **Open Your Eyes** *Alter Bridge*

'86 **Open Your Heart** *Madonna*
Operator
'75 *Manhattan Transfer*
'84 *Midnight Star*
'72 **Operator (That's Not the Way it Feels)** *Jim Croce*
'76 **Ophelia** *Band*
'86 **Opportunities (Let's Make Lots Of Money)** *Pet Shop Boys*
'89 **Opposites Attract** *Paula Abdul*
'91 **Optimistic** *Sounds Of Blackness*
'66 **Opus 17 (Don't You Worry 'Bout Me)** *4 Seasons*
'88 **Orange Crush** *R.E.M.*
'02 **Ordinary Day** *Vanessa Carlton*
'99 **Ordinary Life** *Chad Brock*
'05 **Ordinary People** *John Legend*
'93 **Ordinary World** *Duran Duran*
'06 **Original Fire** *Audioslave*
'00 **Original Prankster** *Offspring*
'89 **Orinoco Flow (Sail Away)** *Enya*
'83 **Other Arms** *Robert Plant*
'82 **Other Guy** *Little River Band*
'67 **Other Man's Grass Is Always Greener** *Petula Clark*
Other Side
'90 *Aerosmith*
'00 *Red Hot Chili Peppers*
'91 **Other Side Of Summer** *Elvis Costello*
'82 **Other Woman** *Ray Parker Jr.*
'89 **Ouija Board, Ouija Board** *Morrissey*
Our Day Will Come
'63 *Ruby & The Romantics*
'75 *Frankie Valli*
'91 **Our Frank** *Morrissey*
Our House
'70 *Crosby, Stills, Nash & Young*
'83 *Madness*
'81 **Our Lips Are Sealed** *Go-Go's*
'78 **Our Love** *Natalie Cole*
'78 **(Our Love) Don't Throw It All Away** *Andy Gibb*
'63 **Our Winter Love** *Bill Pursell*
'80 **Out Here On My Own** *Irene Cara*
'91 **Out In The Cold** *Tom Petty*
'70 **Out In The Country** *Three Dog Night*
'63 **Out Of Limits** *Marketts*
'86 **Out Of Mind Out Of Sight** *Models*
'98 **Out Of My Bones** *Randy Travis*
'99 **Out Of My Head** *Fastball*
'63 **Out Of My Mind** *Johnny Tillotson*
'64 **Out Of Sight** *James Brown*
'56 **Out Of Sight, Out Of Mind** *Five Keys*
'88 **Out Of The Blue** *Debbie Gibson*
'73 **Out Of The Question** *Gilbert O'Sullivan*
'84 **Out Of Touch** *Daryl Hall & John Oates*
'82 **Out Of Work** *Gary U.S. Bonds*
'72 **Outa-Space** *Billy Preston*
'73 **Outlaw Man** *Eagles*
'00 **Outside** *Aaron Lewis w/ Fred Durst*
'60 **Outside My Window** *Fleetwoods*
'74 **Outside Woman** *Bloodstone*
'03 **Outsider, The** *Perfect Circle*
'82 **Outstanding** *Gap Band*
'02 **Outta Control (Remix)** *50 Cent w/ Mobb Deep*
'07 **Outta My System** *Bow Wow*
Over And Over
'58 *Bobby Day*
'65 *Dave Clark Five*
'04 *Nelly w/ Tim McGraw*
'07 **Over It** *Katharine McPhee*
'75 **Over My Head** *Fleetwood Mac*
'06 **Over My Head (Cable Car)** *Fray*
'73 **Over The Hills And Far Away** *Led Zeppelin*
Over The Mountain; Across The Sea
'57 *Johnnie & Joe*
'63 *Bobby Vinton*

Over The Rainbow
'60 *Demensions*
'61 *Judy Garland [live]*
'66 **Over Under Sideways Down**
Yardbirds
Over You
'68 *Gary Puckett*
'07 *Daughtry*
'86 **Overjoyed** *Stevie Wonder*
'83 **Overkill** *Men At Work*
'04 **Overnight Celebrity** *Twista*
'74 **Overnight Sensation (Hit Record)**
Raspberries
'70 **Overture From Tommy (A Rock
Opera)** *Assembled Multitude*
'83 **Owner Of A Lonely Heart** *Yes*
'71 **Oye Como Va** *Santana*
'04 **Oye Mi Canto** *N.O.R.E.*

P

'03 **P.I.M.P.** *50 Cent*
'64 **P.S. I Love You** *Beatles*
'62 **P.T. 109** *Jimmy Dean*
'83 **P.Y.T. (Pretty Young Thing)**
Michael Jackson
'82 **Pac-Man Fever** *Buckner & Garcia*
'58 **Padre** *Toni Arden*
'88 **Paid In Full** *Eric B & Rakim*
Pain
'04 *Jimmy Eat World*
'07 *Three Days Grace*
'63 **Pain In My Heart** *Otis Redding*
'66 **Paint It, Black** *Rolling Stones*
'73 **Painted Ladies** *Ian Thomas*
'63 **Painted, Tainted Rose** *Al Martino*
'69 **Pale Blue Eyes** *Velvet Underground*
'62 **Palisades Park** *Freddy Cannon*
'75 **Paloma Blanca**
George Baker Selection
'88 **Pamela** *Toto*
'84 **Panama** *Van Halen*
'83 **Pancho And Lefty**
Willie Nelson & Merle Haggard
'66 **Pandora's Golden Heebie Jeebies**
Association
'83 **Papa, Can You Hear Me?**
Barbra Streisand
'86 **Papa Don't Preach** *Madonna*
'74 **Papa Don't Take No Mess**
James Brown
'92 **Papa Loved Mama** *Garth Brooks*
'54 **Papa Loves Mambo** *Perry Como*
'62 **Papa-Oom-Mow-Mow** *Rivingtons*
'72 **Papa Was A Rollin' Stone**
Temptations
Papa's Got A Brand New Bag
'65 *James Brown*
'68 *Otis Redding*
'67 **Paper Cup** *5th Dimension*
'92 **Paper Doll** *PM Dawn*
'87 **Paper In Fire**
John Cougar Mellencamp
Paper Roses
'60 *Anita Bryant*
'73 *Marie Osmond*
'68 **Paper Sun** *Traffic*
'65 **Paper Tiger** *Sue Thompson*
'66 **Paperback Writer** *Beatles*
'82 **Paperlate** *Genesis*
Paradise
'88 *Sade*
'02 *LL Cool J*
'78 **Paradise By The Dashboard Light**
Meat Loaf
'89 **Paradise City** *Guns N' Roses*
'07 **Paralyzer** *Finger Eleven*
'71 **Paranoid** *Black Sabbath*
'97 **Paranoid Andoid** *Radiohead*
'86 **Paranoimia** *Art Of Noise*
'99 **Pardon Me** *Incubus*
'88 **Parents Just Don't Understand**
D.J. Jazzy Jeff & The Fresh Prince
'58 **Part Of Me** *Jimmy Clanton*
'75 **Part Of The Plan** *Dan Fogelberg*

Part Time Love
'63 *Little Johnny Taylor*
'75 *Gladys Knight*
'78 *Elton John*
'85 **Part-Time Lover** *Stevie Wonder*
'85 **Party All The Time** *Eddie Murphy*
'98 **Party Continues** *JD & Da Brat*
Party Doll
'57 *Buddy Knox*
'57 *Steve Lawrence*
'74 **Party Down** *Little Beaver*
'62 **Party Lights** *Claudine Clark*
'07 **Party Like A Rock Star** *Shop Boyz*
'81 **Party Time** *T.G. Sheppard*
'83 **Party Train** *Gap Band*
'00 **Party Up (Up In Here)** *DMX*
'67 **Party's Over** *Willie Nelson*
'81 **Party's Over (Hopelessly In Love)**
Journey
'89 **Partyman** *Prince*
'90 **Pass It On Down** *Alabama*
'03 **Pass That Dutch** *Missy Elliott*
'02 **Pass The Courvoisier**
Busta Rhymes
'82 **Pass The Dutchie** *Musical Youth*
'04 **Passenger Seat** *SheDaisy*
'91 **P.A.S.S.I.O.N** *Rythm Syndicate*
'80 **Passion** *Rod Stewart*
'93 **Passionate Kisses**
Mary Chapin Carpenter
'92 **Past The Point Of Rescue**
Hal Ketchum
'67 **Pata Pata** *Miriam Makeba*
Patches
'62 *Dickey Lee*
'70 *Clarence Carter*
'89 **Patience** *Guns N' Roses*
'58 **Patricia** *Perez Prado*
'74 **Payback, The** *James Brown*
'70 **Pay To The Piper**
Chairmen Of The Board
'67 **Pay You Back With Interest** *Hollies*
'68 **Paying The Cost To Be The Boss**
B.B. King
'68 **Peace Brother Peace** *Bill Medley*
'89 **Peace In Our Time** *Eddie Money*
'57 **Peace In The Valley** *Elvis Presley*
'77 **Peace Of Mind** *Boston*
'75 **Peace Pipe** *B.T. Express*
'86 **Peace Sells** *Megadeth*
'71 **Peace Train** *Cat Stevens*
'70 **Peace Will Come (According To
Plan)** *Melanie*
'73 **Peaceful** *Helen Reddy*
'72 **Peaceful Easy Feeling** *Eagles*
'01 **Peaceful World**
John Mellencamp
'96 **Peaches** *Presidents Of The
United States Of America*
'01 **Peaches & Cream** *112*
'69 **Peaches En Regalia**
Frank Zappa
'65 **Peaches "N" Cream** *Ikettes*
'79 **Peanut Butter** *Twennynine*
'57 **Peanuts** *Little Joe & The Thrillers*
Peek-A-Boo
'58 *Cadillacs*
'88 *Siouxsie & The Banshees*
'77 **Peg** *Steely Dan*
'57 **Peggy Sue** *Buddy Holly*
'74 **Pencil Thin Mustache** *Jimmy Buffett*
'64 **Penetration** *Pyramids*
'60 **Pennies From Heaven** *Skyliners*
'82 **Penny For Your Thoughts** *Tavares*
'81 **Penny Lane** *Beatles*
'84 **Penny Lover** *Lionel Richie*
People
'64 *Barbra Streisand*
'68 *Tymes*
'85 **People Are People** *Depeche Mode*
'91 **People Are Still Having Sex** *LaTour*
'67 **People Are Strange** *Doors*
'92 **People Everyday**
Arrested Development

People Get Ready
'65 *Impressions*
'77 *Bob Marley*
'85 *Jeff Beck & Rod Stewart*
'68 **People Got To Be Free** *Rascals*
'74 **People Gotta Move** *Gino Vannelli*
'88 **People Have The Power** *Patti Smith*
'72 **People Make The World Go Round**
Stylistics
'79 **People Of The South Wind** *Kansas*
'64 **People Say** *Dixie Cups*
'60 **"Pepe"** *Duane Eddy*
'62 **Pepino The Italian Mouse**
Lou Monte
'96 **Pepper** *Butthole Surfers*
'55 **Pepper-Hot Baby** *Jaye P. Morgan*
'61 **Peppermint Twist**
Joey Dee & the Starliters
'62 **Percolator (Twist)**
Billy Joe & The Checkmates
Perfect
'98 *Smashing Pumpkins*
'03 *Sara Evans*
'03 *Simple Plan*
'72 **Perfect Day** *Lou Reed*
'85 **Perfect Kiss** *New Order*
'98 **Perfect Love** *Trisha Yearwood*
'05 **Perfect Situation** *Weezer*
'85 **Perfect Way** *Scritti Politti*
'88 **Perfect World** *Huey Lewis*
'60 **Perfidia** *Ventures*
'95 **Perry Mason** *Ozzy Osbourne*
'89 **Personal Jesus** *Depeche Mode*
'59 **Personality** *Lloyd Price*
'73 **Personality Crisis**
New York Dolls
'82 **Personally** *Karla Bonoff*
Peter Gunn
'59 *Ray Anthony*
'60 *Duane Eddy*
'86 *Art Of Noise*
'59 **Petite Fleur** *Chris Barber*
'93 **Pets** *Porno For Pyros*
'56 **Petticoats Of Portugal** *Dick Jacobs*
'75 **Philadelphia Freedom** *Elton John*
'58 **Philadelphia U.S.A.** *Nu Tornados*
'66 **Phoenix Love Theme (Senza Fine)**
Brass Ring
Photograph
'73 *Ringo Starr*
'83 *Def Leppard*
'05 *Nickelback*
'81 **Physical** *Olivia Newton-John*
'88 **Piano In The Dark** *Brenda Russell*
'74 **Piano Man** *Billy Joel*
'90 **Piccadilly Palare** *Morrissey*
'74 **Pick Up The Pieces** *AWB*
'68 **Pickin' Wild Mountain Berries**
Peggy Scott & Jo Jo Benson
'94 **Pickup Man** *Joe Diffie*
'02 **Picture** *Kid Rock Feat. Sheryl Crow*
'67 **Pictures Of Lily** *Who*
Pictures Of Matchstick Men
'68 *Status Quo*
'89 *Camper Van Beethoven*
'90 **Pictures Of You** *Cure*
Piece Of My Heart
'68 *Big Brother & The Holding Company*
'91 *Tara Kemp*
'94 *Faith Hill*
'05 *Melissa Etheridge & Joss Stone
[medley]*
'72 **Piece Of Paper** *Gladstone*
'72 **Pieces Of April** *Three Dog Night*
'83 **Pieces Of Ice** *Diana Ross*
'04 **Pieces Of Me** *Ashlee Simpson*
'66 **Pied Piper** *Crispian St. Peters*
'73 **Pillow Talk** *Sylvia*
'80 **Pilot Of The Airwaves** *Charlie Dore*
'05 **Pimpin' All Over The World** *Ludacris*
Pinball Wizard
'69 *Who*
'73 *New Seekers [medley]*
'75 *Elton John*
'00 **Pinch Me** *Barenaked Ladies*

'94	**Pincushion** *ZZ Top*	'68	**Please Return Your Love To Me**	'77	**Portrait (He Knew)** *Kansas*
'60	**Pineapple Princess** *Annette*		*Temptations*		**Portrait Of My Love**
'98	**Pink** *Aerosmith*	'61	**Please Stay** *Drifters*	'61	*Steve Lawrence*
	Pink Cadillac		**Please Tell Me Why**	'67	*Tokens*
'84	*Bruce Springsteen*	'61	*Jackie Wilson*	'56	**Portuguese Washerwomen**
'88	*Natalie Cole*	'66	*Dave Clark Five*		*Joe "Fingers" Carr*
'60	**Pink Chiffon** *Mitchell Torok*	'87	**Pleasure Principle** *Janet Jackson*	'65	**Positively 4th Street** *Bob Dylan*
'83	**Pink Houses**		**Pledge Of Love**	'90	**Possession** *Bad English*
	John Cougar Mellencamp	'57	*Ken Copeland*	'85	**Possession Obsession**
'64	**Pink Panther Theme** *Henry Mancini*	'57	*Mitchell Torok*		*Daryl Hall/John Oates*
'59	**Pink Shoe Laces** *Dodie Stevens*		**Pledging My Love**	'95	**Possum Kingdom** *Toadies*
'63	**Pipeline** *Chantay's*	'55	*Johnny Ace*	'06	**Pot, The** *Tool*
'75	**Pirate Looks At Forty** *Jimmy Buffett*	'55	*Teresa Brewer*	'07	**Potential Breakup Song** *Aly & AJ*
'66	**Place In The Sun** *Stevie Wonder*	'93	**Plush** *Stone Temple Pilots*	'91	**Poundcake** *Van Halen*
'91	**Place In This World**	'02	**Po' Folks** *Nappy Roots*	'88	**Pour Some Sugar On Me**
	Michael W. Smith	'96	**Po Pimp** *Do Or Die*		*Def Leppard*
'94	**Place Where You Belong** *Shai*	'61	**Pocketful Of Miracles** *Frank Sinatra*	'90	**Power, The** *Snap!*
'59	**Plain Jane** *Bobby Darin*	'59	**Poco-Loco** *Gene & Eunice*	'78	**Power Of Gold**
'82	**Planet Rock** *Afrika Bambaataa*	'60	**Poetry In Motion** *Johnny Tillotson*		*Dan Fogelberg/Tim Weisberg*
'55	**Plantation Boogie** *Lenny Dee*	'75	**Poetry Man** *Phoebe Snow*	'98	**Power Of Good-Bye** *Madonna*
'67	**Plastic Fantastic Lover**	'69	**Point It Out** *Miracles*		**Power Of Love**
	Jefferson Airplane	'77	**Point Of Know Return** *Kansas*	'72	*Joe Simon*
	Play		**Point Of No Return**	'85	*Huey Lewis*
'01	*Jennifer Lopez*	'62	*Gene McDaniels*	'87	*Laura Branigan*
'05	*David Banner*	'86	*Nu Shooz*	'91	*Luther Vandross [medley]*
'55	**Play It Fair** *LaVern Baker*	'87	*Exposé*	'93	*Celine Dion*
'72	**Play Me** *Neil Diamond*		**Poison**	'71	**Power To The People** *John Lennon*
'55	**Play Me Hearts And Flowers**	'89	*Alice Cooper*	'91	**Power Windows** *Billy Falcon*
	(I Wanna Cry) *Johnny Desmond*	'90	*Bell Biv DeVoe*	'88	**Powerful Stuff**
'75	**Play On Love** *Jefferson Starship*	'83	**Poison Arrow** *ABC*		*Fabulous Thunderbirds*
'05	**Play Something Country**	'59	**Poison Ivy** *Coasters*	'94	**Practice What You Preach**
	Brooks & Dunn	'90	**Policy Of Truth** *Depeche Mode*		*Barry White*
	Play That Funky Music	'72	**Political Science**	'99	**Praise You** *Fatboy Slim*
'76	*Wild Cherry*		*Randy Newman*	'05	**Praise You In This Storm**
'90	*Vanilla Ice*	'83	**Politics Of Dancing** *Re-Flex*		*Casting Crowns*
'80	**Play The Game** *Queen*	'69	**Polk Salad Annie** *Tony Joe White*		**Pray**
'82	**Play The Game Tonight** *Kansas*	'05	**Pon De Replay** *Rihanna*	'90	*M.C. Hammer*
'94	**Playaz Club** *Rappin' 4-Tay*	'96	**Pony** *Ginuwine*	'99	*Rebecca St. James*
	Playboy	'61	**Pony Time** *Chubby Checker*	'02	**Prayer** *Disturbed*
'62	*Marvelettes*		**Poor Boy**	'94	**Prayer For The Dying** *Seal*
'68	*Gene & Debbe*	'56	*Elvis Presley*	'00	**Prayin' For Daylight** *Rascal Flatts*
'95	**Player's Anthem** *Junior M.A.F.I.A.*	'58	*Royaltones*	'90	**Praying For Time** *George Michael*
'94	**Player's Ball** *OutKast*	'61	**Poor Fool** *Ike & Tina Turner*	'72	**Precious And Few** *Climax*
'91	**Playground** *Another Bad Creation*	'59	**Poor Jenny** *Everly Brothers*	'97	**Precious Declaration**
'73	**Playground In My Mind**	'58	**Poor Little Fool** *Ricky Nelson*		*Collective Soul*
	Clint Holmes	'63	**Poor Little Rich Girl**	'79	**Precious Love** *Bob Welch*
'57	**Playing For Keeps** *Elvis Presley*		*Steve Lawrence*	'70	**Precious, Precious** *Jackie Moore*
'71	**Playing In The Band**	'57	**Poor Man's Roses (Or A Rich Man's**	'81	**Precious To Me** *Phil Seymour*
	Grateful Dead		**Gold)** *Patti Page*	'69	**Presence Of The Lord** *Blind Faith*
'67	**Pleasant Valley Sunday** *Monkees*	'81	**Poor Man's Son** *Survivor*	'86	**Press** *Paul McCartney*
'58	**Please Accept My Love** *B.B. King*	'55	**Poor Me** *Fats Domino*	'82	**Pressure** *Billy Joel*
	Please Come Home For Christmas		**Poor People Of Paris**	'73	**Pressure Drop**
'60	*Charles Brown*	'56	*Les Baxter*		*Toots & The Maytals*
'78	*Eagles*	'56	*Russ Morgan*	'57	**Pretend You Don't See Her**
'74	**Please Come To Boston**	'56	*Lawrence Welk*		*Jerry Vale*
	Dave Loggins		**Poor Poor Pitiful Me**		**Pretender, The**
'62	**Please Don't Ask About Barbara**	'78	*Linda Ronstadt*	'76	*Jackson Browne*
	Bobby Vee	'96	*Terri Clark*	'07	*Foo Fighters*
	Please Don't Go	'66	**Poor Side Of Town** *Johnny Rivers*	'89	**Pretending** *Eric Clapton*
'61	*Ral Donner*	'01	**Pop** **NSYNC*	'71	**Pretty As You Feel**
'79	*KC & The Sunshine Band*	'99	**Pop A Top** *Alan Jackson*		*Jefferson Airplane*
'92	*K.W.S.*	'82	**Pop Goes The Movies** *Meco*	'67	**Pretty Ballerina** *Left Banke*
'96	*Immature*	'91	**Pop Goes The Weasel** *3rd Bass*	'59	**Pretty Blue Eyes** *Steve Lawrence*
'97	*No Mercy*	'87	**Pop Goes The World**	'66	**Pretty Flamingo** *Manfred Mann*
'07	*Tank*		*Men Without Hats*	'98	**Pretty Fly (For A White Guy)**
'88	**Please Don't Go Girl**	'85	**Pop Life** *Prince*		*Offspring*
	New Kids On The Block	'07	**Pop, Lock And Drop It** *Huey*	'95	**Pretty Girl** *Jon B.*
'79	**Please Don't Leave** *Lauren Wood*	'79	**Pop Muzik** *M*	'79	**Pretty Girls** *Melissa Manchester*
'63	**Please Don't Talk To The Lifeguard**	'62	**Pop Pop Pop - Pie** *Sherrys*	'58	**Pretty Girls Everywhere**
	Diane Ray	'86	**(Pop, Pop, Pop, Pop) Goes My Mind**		*Eugene Church*
'93	**Please Forgive Me** *Bryan Adams*		*Levert*	'81	**Pretty In Pink** *Psychedelic Furs*
'60	**Please Help Me, I'm Falling**	'89	**Pop Singer**	'96	**Pretty Little Adriana** *Vince Gill*
	Hank Locklin		*John Cougar Mellencamp*	'61	**Pretty Little Angel Eyes** *Curtis Lee*
	Please Love Me Forever	'72	**Pop That Thang** *Isley Brothers*	'96	**Pretty Noose** *Soundgarden*
'61	*Cathy Jean & The Roommates*	'72	**Popcorn** *Hot Butter*	'63	**Pretty Paper** *Roy Orbison*
'67	*Bobby Vinton*	'69	**Popcorn, The** *James Brown*	'90	**Pretty Pink Rose**
'75	**Please Mr. Please**	'55	**Popcorn Song** *Cliffie Stone*		*Adrian Belew & David Bowie*
	Olivia Newton-John	'62	**Popeye (The Hitchhiker)**	'77	**Pretty Vacant** *Sex Pistols*
	Please Mr. Postman		*Chubby Checker*	'05	**Pretty Vegas** *INXS*
'61	*Marvelettes*	'07	**Poppin'** *Chris Brown*	'74	**Pretzel Logic** *Steely Dan*
'74	*Carpenters*	'66	**Poppin' My Collar** *Three 6 Mafia*	'89	**Price Of Love** *Bad English*
'59	**Please Mr. Sun** *Tommy Edwards*	'66	**Popsicle** *Jan & Dean*	'03	**Price To Play** *Staind*
'64	**Please Please Me** *Beatles*	'76	**Popsicle Toes** *Michael Franks*	'77	**Pride, The** *Isley Brothers*
'56	**Please, Please, Please**	'63	**Popsicles And Icicles** *Murmaids*		
	James Brown	'56	**Port Au Prince** *Nelson Riddle*		
'99	**Please Remember Me** *Tim McGraw*				

Pride And Joy
'63 Marvin Gaye
'83 Stevie Ray Vaughan
'93 Coverdale-Page
'84 **Pride (In The Name Of Love)** U2
'84 **Prime Time** Alan Parsons Project
'59 **Primrose Lane** Jerry Wallace
'61 **Princess** Frank Gari
'89 **Principal's Office** Young M.C.
'56 **Priscilla** Eddie Cooley
'89 **Prisoner, The** Howard Jones
'63 **Prisoner Of Love** James Brown
'78 **Prisoner Of Your Love** Player
'85 **Private Dancer** Tina Turner
'81 **Private Eyes**
        Daryl Hall & John Oates
'80 **Private Idaho** B-52's
'91 **Private Line** Gerald Levert
'06 **Probably Wouldn't Be This Way**
        LeAnn Rimes
'58 **Problems** Everly Brothers
'06 **Promiscuous** Nelly Furtado
Promise
'00 Eve 6
'00 Jagged Edge
'06 Ciara
'88 **Promise, The** When In Rome
'88 **Promise Me** Cover Girls
'58 **Promise Me, Love** Andy Williams
'91 **Promise Of A New Day** Paula Abdul
Promised Land
'74 Elvis Presley
'78 Bruce Springsteen
Promises
'78 Eric Clapton
'99 Def Leppard
'81 **Promises In The Dark** Pat Benatar
Promises, Promises
'68 Dionne Warwick
'83 Naked Eyes
'93 **Prop Me Up Beside The Jukebox
        (If I Die)** Joe Diffie
'63 **Proud** Johnny Crawford
Proud Mary
'69 Creedence Clearwater Revival
'71 Ike & Tina Turner
'07 **Proud Of The House We Built**
        Brooks & Dunn
'75 **Proud One** Osmonds
'78 **Prove It All Night** Bruce Springsteen
'88 **Prove Your Love** Taylor Dayne
'70 **Psychedelic Shack** Temptations
'98 **Psycho Circus** Kiss
'77 **Psycho Killer** Talking Heads
'98 **Psycho Man** Black Sabbath
'66 **Psychotic Reaction** Count Five
'06 **Public Affair** Jessica Simpson
'67 **Pucker Up Buttercup** Jr. Walker
'63 **Puff (The Magic Dragon)**
        Peter, Paul & Mary
'88 **Pull Over** Levert
'06 **Pullin' Me Back** Chingy
'80 **Pump, The** Jeff Beck
'06 **Pump It** Black Eyed Peas
Pump It Up
'78 Elvis Costello
'03 Joe Budden
'89 **Pump Up The Jam** Technotronic
'87 **Pump Up The Volume** M/A/R/R/S
'94 **Pumps And A Bump** Hammer
'62 **Punish Her** Bobby Vee
Puppet Man
'70 5th Dimension
'71 Tom Jones
'65 **Puppet On A String** Elvis Presley
Puppy Love
'60 Paul Anka
'64 Barbara Lewis
'72 Donny Osmond
'90 **Pure** Lightning Seeds
'74 **Pure Love** Ronnie Milsap
'00 **Purest Of Pain (A Puro Dolor)**
        Son By Four

Purple Haze
'67 Jimi Hendrix
'93 Cure
'01 **Purple Hills [Pills]** D-12
'58 **Purple People Eater** Sheb Wooley
'84 **Purple Rain** Prince
'97 **Push** Matchbox 20
'62 **Push And Kick** Mark Valentino
'87 **Push It** Salt-N-Pepa
'07 **Push It To The Limit** Corbin Bleu
'68 **Pusher, The** Steppenwolf
'66 **Pushin' Too Hard** Seeds
'98 **Pushin' Weight** Ice Cube
'63 **Pushover** Etta James
'58 **Pussy Cat** Ames Brothers
'57 **Put A Light In The Window**
        Four Lads
Put A Little Love In Your Heart
'69 Jackie DeShannon
'88 Annie Lennox & Al Green
'58 **Put A Ring On My Finger**
        Les Paul & Mary Ford
'83 **Put It In A Magazine** Sonny Charles
'00 **Put It On Me** Ja Rule
'03 **Put That Woman First** Jaheim
'88 **Put This Love To The Test**
        Jon Astley
'60 **Put Your Arms Around Me Honey**
        Fats Domino
'58 **Put Your Dreams Away**
        Frank Sinatra
'71 **Put Your Hand In The Hand** Ocean
'73 **Put Your Hands Together** O'Jays
'97 **Put Your Hands Where My Eyes
        Could See** Busta Rhymes
'59 **Put Your Head On My Shoulder**
        Paul Anka
'89 **Put Your Mouth On Me**
        Eddie Murphy
'06 **Put Your Records On**
        Corinne Bailey Rae
'83 **Puttin' On The Ritz** Taco

Q

'92 **Quality Time** Hi-Five
'68 **Quando, Quando, Quando**
        Engelbert Humperdinck
'61 **Quarter To Three** U.S. Bonds
'56 **Que Sera, Sera (Whatever Will Be,
        Will Be)** Doris Day
'81 **Queen Of Hearts** Juice Newton
'92 **Queen Of Memphis**
        Confederate Railroad
'76 **Queen Of My Soul**
        Average White Band
'83 **Queen Of The Broken Hearts**
        Loverboy
'58 **Queen Of The Hop** Bobby Darin
'65 **Queen Of The House** Jody Miller
'93 **Queen Of The Night**
        Whitney Houston
'57 **Queen Of The Senior Prom**
        Mills Brothers
'69 **Quentin's Theme** Charles
        Randolph Grean Sounde
Question
'60 Lloyd Price
'70 Moody Blues
'68 **Question Of Temperature**
        Balloon Farm
'71 **Questions 67 And 68** Chicago
'68 **Quick Joey Small (Run Joey Run)**
        Kasenetz-Katz Singing Orchestral
        Circus
'63 **Quicksand** Martha & The Vandellas
'59 **Quiet Village** Martin Denny
'79 **Quinn The Eskimo ..see: Mighty
        Quinn**
'97 **Quit Playing Games (With My Heart)**
        Backstreet Boys
'61 **Quite A Party** Fireballs

R

Race Is On
'65 Jack Jones
'89 Sawyer Brown
'56 **Race With The Devil** Gene Vincent
'74 **Radar Love** Golden Earring
'83 **Radio Free Europe** R.E.M.
'84 **Radio Ga-Ga** Queen
'78 **Radio, Radio** Elvis Costello
'89 **Radio Romance** Tiffany
'85 **Radioactive** Firm
Rag Doll
'64 4 Seasons
'88 Aerosmith
'69 **Rag Mama Rag** Band
'59 **Ragtime Cowboy Joe** Chipmunks
Rain
'66 Beatles
'90 Dan Fogelberg [medley]
'93 Madonna
'98 SWV
'86 **Rain, The** Oran "Juice" Jones
'71 **Rain Dance** Guess Who
'68 **Rain In My Heart** Frank Sinatra
'03 **Rain On Me** Ashanti
'66 **Rain On The Roof** Lovin' Spoonful
'86 **Rain On The Scarecrow**
        John Cougar Mellencamp
'62 **Rain Rain Go Away** Bobby Vinton
'73 **Rain Song** Led Zeppelin
'97 **Rain (Supa Dupa Fly)** Missy Elliott
'67 **Rain, The Park & Other Things**
        Cowsills
Rainbow
'57 Russ Hamilton
'63 Gene Chandler
'65 Gene Chandler ['65]
'79 **Rainbow Connection**
        Kermit (Jim Henson)
'61 **Raindrops** Dee Clark
'69 **Raindrops Keep Fallin' On My Head**
        B.J. Thomas
Raining In My Heart
'59 Buddy Holly
'61 Slim Harpo
'03 **Raining On Sunday** Keith Urban
'66 **Rains Came** Sir Douglas Quintet
'75 **Rainy Day People** Gordon Lightfoot
'66 **Rainy Day Women #12 & 35**
        Bob Dylan
'71 **Rainy Days And Mondays**
        Carpenters
'02 **Rainy Dayz** Mary J. Blige
'70 **Rainy Night In Georgia**
        Brook Benton
'78 **Riase A Little Hell** Trooper
'98 **Raise The Roof** Luke
'01 **Raise Up** Petey Pablo
'61 **Ram-Bunk-Shush** Ventures
'61 **Rama Lama Ding Dong** Edsels
'69 **Ramble On** Led Zeppelin
'68 **Ramblin' Gamblin' Man** Bob Seger
'73 **Ramblin Man** Allman Brothers Band
'62 **Ramblin' Rose** Nat King Cole
'58 **Ramrod** Duane Eddy
'67 **Randy Scouse Git** Monkees
'80 **Ranking Full Stop** English Beat
'70 **Rapper, The** Jaggerz
'79 **Rapper's Delight** Sugarhill Gang
'97 **Rappers' Ball** E-40
'81 **Rapture** Blondie
'85 **Raspberry Beret** Prince
Raunchy
'57 Ernie Freeman
'57 Bill Justis
'57 Billy Vaughn
'58 **Rave On** Buddy Holly
'76 **Raven, The**
        Alan Parsons Project
'59 **Raw-Hide** Link Wray
'68 **Ray Of Hope** Rascals
'98 **Ray Of Light** Madonna
'55 **Razzle-Dazzle** Bill Haley
'03 **Re-Align** Godsmack

242

'99 **Re-Arranged** *Limp Bizkit*
'77 **Reach For It** *George Duke*
'70 **Reach Out And Touch (Somebody's Hand)** *Diana Ross*
'64 **Reach Out For Me** *Dionne Warwick*
Reach Out I'll Be There
'66 *Four Tops*
'71 *Diana Ross*
'68 **Reach Out Of The Darkness** *Friend & Lover*
'02 **React** *Erick Sermon*
'83 **Read 'Em And Weep** *Barry Manilow*
'03 **Read Your Mind** *Avant*
'74 **Ready** *Cat Stevens*
'74 **Ready For Love** *Bad Company*
'78 **Ready For The Times To Get Better** *Crystal Gayle*
Ready Or Not
'90 *After 7*
'96 *Fugees*
'68 **Ready Or Not Here I Come (Can't Hide From Love)** *Delfonics*
'56 **Ready Teddy** *Little Richard*
'99 **Ready To Run** *Dixie Chicks*
'78 **Ready To Take A Chance Again** *Barry Manilow*
'05 **Real Fine Place To Start** *Sara Evans*
'03 **Real Good Man** *Tim McGraw*
'87 **Real Life** *John Cougar Mellencamp*
Real Love
'80 *Doobie Brothers*
'89 *Jody Watley*
'89 *Skyy*
'91 *Bob Seger*
'92 *Mary J. Blige*
'96 *Beatles*
'73 **Real Me** *Who*
'91 **Real, Real, Real** *Jesus Jones*
'00 **Real Slim Shady** *Eminem*
'58 **Real Wild Child** *Ivan*
'86 **Real Wild Child (Wild One)** *Iggy Pop*
Real World
'93 *Queensryche*
'98 *Matchbox 20*
'96 **Reality** *Newsboys*
'81 **Really Wanna Know You** *Gary Wright*
'83 **Reap The Wild Wind** *Ultravox*
'04 **Reason, The** *Hoobastank*
Reason To Believe
'71 *Rod Stewart*
'93 *Rod Stewart w/ Ronnie Wood [live]*
'95 **Rebecca Lynn** *Bryan Wahl*
'65 **Rebel Kind** *Dino, Desi & Billy*
'74 **Rebel Rebel** *David Bowie*
'58 **Rebel-'Rouser** *Duane Eddy*
'83 **Rebel Yell** *Billy Idol*
'04 **Rebellion (Lies)** *Arcade Fire*
'93 **Rebirth Of Slick (Cool Like Dat)** *Digable Planets*
'93 **Reckless** *Alabama*
Reconsider Me
'69 *Johnny Adams*
'75 *Narvel Felts*
'65 **Recovery** *Fontella Bass*
'02 **Red, The** *Chevelle*
'81 **Red Barchetta** *Rush*
'03 **Red Dirt Road** *Brooks & Dunn*
'67 **Red House** *Jimi Hendrix*
'80 **Red Light** *Linda Clifford*
'95 **Red Light Special** *TLC*
'02 **Red Rag Top** *Tim McGraw*
'86 **Red Rain** *Peter Gabriel*
Red Red Wine
'68 *Neil Diamond*
'70 *Vic Dana*
'88 *UB40 [rap by Astro]*
'59 **Red River Rock** *Johnny & The Hurricanes*
'58 **Red River Rose** *Ames Brothers*
'58 **Red Rooster** *Howling' Wolf*

Red Roses For A Blue Lady
'65 *Vic Dana*
'65 *Bert Kaempfert*
'65 *Wayne Newton*
'66 **Red Rubber Ball** *Cyrkle*
Red Sails In The Sunset
'60 *Platters*
'63 *Fats Domino*
'80 **Redemption Song** *Bob Marley*
'72 **Redneck Friend** *Jackson Browne*
'82 **Redneck Girl** *Bellamy Brothers*
'04 **Redneck Woman** *Gretchen Wilson*
'05 **Redneck Yacht Club** *Craig Morgan*
'72 **Redwood Tree** *Van Morrison*
Reelin' And Rockin'
'58 *Chuck Berry*
'65 *Dave Clark Five*
'72 *Chuck Berry [live]*
'73 **Reeling In The Years** *Steely Dan*
'57 **Reet Petite** *Jackie Wilson*
'67 **Reflections** *Supremes*
'70 **Reflections Of My Life** *Marmalade*
'84 **Reflex, The** *Duran Duran*
'82 **Refugee** *Tom Petty*
'89 **Regina** *Sugarcubes*
'93 **Regret** *New Order*
'94 **Regulate** *Warren G. & Nate Dogg*
'07 **Rehab** *Amy Winehouse*
'84 **Relax** *Frankie Goes To Hollywood*
'72 **Relay, The** *Who*
Release Me
'62 *Little Esther Phillips*
'67 *Engelbert Humperdinck*
'90 *Wilson Phillips*
'92 **Remedy** *Black Crowes*
'03 **Remedy (I Won't Worry)** *Jason Mraz*
Remember Me
'64 *Rita Pavone*
'70 *Diana Ross*
'65 **(Remember Me) I'm The One Who Loves You** *Dean Martin*
'77 **(Remember The Days Of The) Old Schoolyard** *Cat Stevens*
'89 **Remember (The First Time)** *Eric Gable*
'83 **Remember The Nights** *Motels*
'92 **Remember The Time** *Michael Jackson*
'62 **Remember Then** *Earls*
Remember (Walkin' In The Sand)
'64 *Shangri-Las*
'79 *Aerosmith*
'75 **Remember What I Told You To Forget** *Tavares*
Remember When
'59 *Platters*
'03 *Alan Jackson*
'57 **Remember You're Mine** *Pat Boone*
'78 **Reminiscing** *Little River Band*
'75 **Rendezvous** *Hudson Brothers*
'96 **Renee** *Lost Boyz*
Renegade
'76 *Michael Murphey*
'79 *Styx*
'97 **Request Line** *Zhané*
Rescue Me
'65 *Fontella Bass*
'88 *Al B. Sure!*
'91 *Madonna*
Respect
'65 *Otis Redding*
'67 *Aretha Franklin*
Respect Yourself
'71 *Staple Singers*
'87 *Bruce Willis*
'66 **Respectable** *Outsiders*
'92 **Rest In Peace** *Extreme*
'92 **Restless Heart** *Peter Cetera*
Resurrection Shuffle
'71 *Ashton, Gardner & Dyke*
'71 *Tom Jones*
'97 **Return Of The Mack** *Mark Morrison*
'67 **Return Of The Red Baron** *Royal Guardsmen*

'94 **Return To Innocence** *Enigma*
'58 **Return To Me** *Dean Martin*
'62 **Return To Sender** *Elvis Presley*
'69 **Reuben James** *Kenny Rogers & The First Edition*
'79 **Reunited** *Peaches & Herb*
'59 **Reveille Rock** *Johnny & The Hurricanes*
'61 **Revenge** *Brook Benton*
'63 **Reverend Mr. Black** *Kingston Trio*
'70 **Revival (Love Is Everywhere** *Allman Brothers Band*
'68 **Revolution** *Beatles*
'66 **Rhapsody In The Rain** *Lou Christie*
'76 **Rhiannon (Will You Ever Win)** *Fleetwood Mac*
'75 **Rhinestone Cowboy** *Glen Campbell*
'74 **Rhyme Tyme People** *Kool & The Gang*
'64 **Rhythm** *Major Lance*
'99 **Rhythm Divine** *Enrique Iglesias*
'92 **Rhythm Is A Dancer** *Snap!*
'87 **Rhythm Is Gonna Get You** *Gloria Estefan*
'89 **Rhythm Nation** *Janet Jackson*
'87 **Rhythm Of Love** *Yes*
'91 **Rhythm Of My Heart** *Rod Stewart*
Rhythm Of The Night
'85 *DeBarge*
'94 *Corona*
Rhythm Of The Rain
'63 *Cascades*
'90 *Dan Fogelberg [medley]*
'65 **Ribbon Of Darkness** *Marty Robbins*
Rich Girl
'77 *Daryl Hall & John Oates*
'05 *Gwen Stefani*
'91 **Rico Suave** *Gerardo*
'06 **Riddle, The** *Five For Fighting*
'62 **Ride!** *Dee Dee Sharp*
'65 **Ride Away** *Roy Orbison*
'70 **Ride Captain Ride** *Blues Image*
'74 **Ride 'Em Cowboy** *Paul Davis*
'80 **Ride Like The Wind** *Christopher Cross*
'68 **Ride My See-Saw** *Moody Blues*
'67 **Ride, Ride, Ride** *Brenda Lee*
'74 **Ride The Tiger** *Jefferson Starship*
'64 **Ride The Wild Surf** *Jan & Dean*
'91 **Ride The Wind** *Poison*
'01 **Ride Wit Me** *Nelly*
'65 **Ride Your Pony** *Lee Dorsey*
'71 **Riders On The Storm** *Doors*
'05 **Ridin'** *Chamillionaire*
'74 **Ridin' The Storm Out** *REO Speedwagon*
'01 **Riding With Private Malone** *David Ball*
'76 **Right Back Where We Started From** *Maxine Nightingale*
'84 **Right By Your Side** *Eurythmics*
'78 **Right Down The Line** *Gerry Rafferty*
'91 **Right Down To It** *Damian Dame*
Right Here
'93 *SWV [Human Nature]*
'05 *Staind*
'91 **Right Here, Right Now** *Jesus Jones*
'89 **Right Here Waiting** *Richard Marx*
'92 **Right Kind Of Love** *Jeremy Jordan*
Right Now
'91 *Van Halen*
'92 *Al B. Sure!*
'00 *SR-71*
'98 **Right On The Money** *Alan Jackson*
'71 **Right On The Tip Of My Tongue** *Brenda & The Tabulations*
'87 **Right On Track** *Breakfast Club*
Right Or Wrong
'61 *Wanda Jackson*
'64 *Ronnie Dove*
'84 *George Strait*
'73 **Right Place Wrong Time** *Dr. John*
'87 **Right Thing** *Simply Red*
'73 **Right Thing To Do** *Carly Simon*
'03 **Right Thurr** *Chingy*

'77 **Right Time Of The Night**
   Jennifer Warnes
'06 **Right Where You Want Me**
   Jesse McCartney
'74 **Rikki Don't Lose That Number**
   Steely Dan
'59 **Ring-A-Ling-A-Lario**
   Jimmie Rodgers
'65 **Ring Dang Doo** *Sam The Sham*
   & The Pharoahs
   Ring My Bell
'79 *Anita Ward*
'91 *D.J. Jazzy Jeff & The Fresh Prince*
   Ring Of Fire
'61 *Duane Eddy*
'63 *Johnny Cash*
'06 **Ring The Alarm** *Beyoncé*
'72 **Ring The Living Bell** *Melanie*
'64 **Ringo** *Lorne Greene*
'71 **Rings** *Cymarron*
'62 **Rinky Dink** *Baby Cortez*
'83 **Rio** *Duran Duran*
   Rip It Up
'56 *Bill Haley*
'56 *Little Richard*
'72 **Rip Off** *Laura Lee*
'64 **Rip Van Winkle** *Devotions*
'70 **Ripple** *Grateful Dead*
'79 **Rise** *Herb Alpert*
'02 **Rising, The** *Bruce Springsteen*
'88 **Ritual** *Dan Reed Network*
   River, The
'92 *Garth Brooks*
'07 *Good Charlotte*
   River Deep - Mountain High
'66 *Ike & Tina Turner*
'69 *Deep Purple*
'70 *Supremes & Four Tops*
'69 **River Is Wide** *Grassroots*
'95 **River Of Deceit** *Mad Season*
'93 **River Of Dreams** *Billy Joel*
'74 **River's Risin'** *Edgar Winter*
'78 **Rivers Of Babylon** *Boney M*
'60 **Road Runner** *Bo Diddley*
   Road To Nowhere
'85 *Talking Heads*
'92 *Ozzy Osbourne*
'70 **Roadhouse Blues** *Doors*
'76 **Roadrunner** *Modern Lovers*
'89 **Roam** *B-52's*
'84 **Robert DeNiro's Waiting**
   Bananarama
'59 **Robbin' The Cradle** *Tony Bellus*
'56 **R-O-C-K** *Bill Haley*
'55 **Rock-A-Beatin' Boogie** *Bill Haley*
'57 **Rock-A-Billy** *Guy Mitchell*
   Rock-A-Bye Your Baby With A Dixie
   Melody
'56 *Jerry Lewis*
'61 *Aretha Franklin*
'61 **Rock-A-Hula Baby** *Elvis Presley*
'89 **Rock And A Hard Place**
   Rolling Stones
   Rock And Roll
'71 *Led Zeppelin*
'72 *Gary Glitter*
'75 **Rock And Roll All Nite** *Kiss [live]*
'76 **Rock & Roll Band** *Boston*
   Rock And Roll Dreams Come
   Through
'81 *Jim Steinman*
'94 *Meat Loaf*
'85 **Rock And Roll Girls** *John Fogerty*
'74 **Rock And Roll Heaven**
   Righteous Brothers
'74 **Rock And Roll, Hoochie Koo**
   Rick Derringer
'58 **Rock And Roll Is Here To Stay**
   Danny & The Juniors
'76 **Rock And Roll Love Letter**
   Bay City Rollers
'72 **Rock And Roll Lullaby** *B.J. Thomas*
'78 **Rock & Roll Machine** *Triumph*

   Rock And Roll Music
'57 *Chuck Berry*
'64 *Beatles*
'76 *Beach Boys*
'77 **Rock And Roll Never Forgets**
   Bob Seger
'71 **Rock & Roll Stew** *Traffic*
'55 **Rock And Roll Waltz** *Kay Starr*
'68 **Rock And Soul Music**
   Country Joe & The Fish
'55 **Rock Around The Clock** *Bill Haley*
'94 **Rock Bottom** *Wynonna*
'86 **R.O.C.K. In The U.S.A. (A Salute To**
   60's Rock)
   John Cougar Mellencamp
'56 **Rock Island Line** *Lonnie Donegan*
'79 **Rock Lobster** *B-52's*
'55 **Rock Love** *Fontane Sisters*
'69 **Rock Me** *Steppenwolf*
'86 **Rock Me Amadeus** *Falco*
   Rock Me Baby
'64 *B.B. King*
'72 *David Cassidy*
'74 **Rock Me Gently** *Andy Kim*
'85 **Rock Me Tonight (For Old Times**
   Sake) *Freddie Jackson*
'84 **Rock Me Tonite** *Billy Squier*
'93 **Rock My World (Little Country Girl)**
   Brooks & Dunn
'69 **Rock 'N' Roll** *Velvet Underground*
   Rock 'N' Roll Fantasy
'78 *Kinks*
'79 *Bad Company*
'80 **Rock 'N' Roll High School** *Ramones*
'74 **Rock N' Roll (I Gave You The Best**
   Years Of My Life) *Mac Davis*
'83 **Rock 'N' Roll Is King** *ELO*
'72 **Rock 'N Roll Soul**
   Grand Funk Railroad
'67 **Rock 'N' Roll Woman**
   Buffalo Springfield
'83 **Rock Of Ages** *Def Leppard*
'88 **Rock Of Life** *Rick Springfield*
   Rock On
'73 *David Essex*
'89 *Michael Damian*
'72 **Rock Me On The Water**
   Jackson Browne
'56 **Rock Right** *Georgia Gibbs*
'01 **Rock Show** *Blink-182*
   Rock Steady
'71 *Aretha Franklin*
'87 *Whispers*
'86 **Rock The Bells** *LL Cool J*
   Rock The Boat
'74 *Hues Corporation*
'01 *Aaliyah*
'82 **Rock The Casbah** *Clash*
'02 **Rock The Mic** *Freeway*
'87 **Rock The Night** *Europe*
'82 **Rock This Town** *Stray Cats*
'03 **Rock Wit U (Awww Baby)** *Ashanti*
'89 **Rock Wit'cha** *Bobby Brown*
'79 **Rock With You** *Michael Jackson*
'07 **Rock Yo Hips** *Crime Mob*
'84 **Rock You Like A Hurricane**
   Scorpions
'74 **Rock Your Baby** *George McCrae*
'03 **Rock Your Body** *Justin Timberlake*
'57 **Rock Your Little Baby To Sleep**
   Buddy Knox
'58 **Rocka-Conga** *Applejacks*
'98 **Rockafeller Skank** *Fatboy Slim*
'78 **Rockaway Beach** *Ramones*
'57 **Rockbilly Boogie**
   Johnny Burnette [Rock & Roll Trio]
'89 **Rocket** *Def Leppard*
'72 **Rocket Man** *Elton John*
'78 **Rocket Ride** *Kiss*
'88 **Rocket 2 U** *Jets*
'75 **Rockford Files** *Mike Post*
'75 **Rockin' All Over The World**
   John Fogerty
'60 **Rockin' Around The Christmas Tree**
   Brenda Lee
'85 **Rockin' At Midnight** *Honeydrippers*

'75 **Rockin' Chair** *Gwen McCrae*
'72 **Rockin' Down The Highway**
   Doobie Brothers
'60 **Rockin' Good Way (To Mess**
   Around And Fall In Love)
   Dinah Washington & Brook Benton
'89 **Rockin' In The Free World**
   Neil Young
'80 **Rockin' Into The Night** *38 Special*
'60 **Rockin' Little Angel** *Ray Smith*
'76 **Rockin' Me** *Steve Miller*
   Rockin' Robin
'58 *Bobby Day*
'72 *Michael Jackson*
'73 **Rockin' Roll Baby** *Stylistics*
'74 **Rockin' Soul** *Hues Corporation*
'91 **Rockin' Years** *Dolly Parton*
   w/ Ricky Van Shelton
'60 **Rocking Goose**
   Johnny & The Hurricanes
   Rocking Pneumonia And The
   Boogie Woogie Flu
'57 *Huey Smith*
'72 *Johnny Rivers*
'83 **Rockit** *Herbie Hancock*
'07 **Rockstar** *Nickelback*
'75 **Rocky** *Austin Roberts*
'72 **Rocky Mountain High** *John Denver*
'73 **Rocky Mountain Way** *Joe Walsh*
'68 **Rocky Raccoon** *Beatles*
'91 **Rodeo** *Garth Brooks*
'79 **Rolene** *Moon Martin*
'83 **Roll Me Away** *Bob Seger*
'75 **Roll On Down The Highway**
   Bachman-Turner Overdrive
'84 **Roll On (Eighteen Wheeler)**
   Alabama
   Roll Over Beethoven
'56 *Chuck Berry*
'64 *Beatles*
'73 *Electric Light Orchestsra*
'95 **Roll To Me** *del Amitri*
'88 **Roll With It** *Steve Winwood*
'78 **Roll With The Changes**
   REO Speedwagon
'79 **Roller** *April Wine*
'00 **Rollin'** *Limp Bizkit*
'50 **Rollin' & Tumblin'** *Muddy Waters*
   Rollin' Stone
'50 *Muddy Waters*
'55 *Fontane Sisters*
'77 **Rollin' With The Flow** *Charlie Rich*
'01 **Rollout (My Business)** *Ludacris*
'84 **Romancing The Stone** *Eddy Grant*
'91 **Romantic** *Karyn White*
'90 **Romeo** *Dino*
   Romeo And [&] Juliet
'92 *Stacy Earl*
'98 *Sylk-E. Fyne*
'79 **Romeo's Tune** *Steve Forbert*
'06 **Rompe** *Daddy Yankee*
'89 **Roni** *Bobby Brown*
'64 **Ronnie** *4 Seasons*
'90 **Room At The Top** *Adam Ant*
   Room To Move
'69 *John Mayall*
'89 *Animotion*
'89 **Rooms On Fire** *Stevie Nicks*
'93 **Rooster** *Alice In Chains*
'76 **Roots, Rock, Reggae** *Bob Marley*
'78 **Rosalinda's Eyes** *Billy Joel*
'73 **Rosalita (Come Out Tonight)**
   Bruce Springsteen
'82 **Rosanna** *Toto*
'80 **Rose, The** *Bette Midler*
'56 **Rose And A Baby Ruth**
   George Hamilton IV
'70 **Rose Garden** *Lynn Anderson*
'98 **Rose Is Still A Rose** *Aretha Franklin*
'04 **Roses** *OutKast*
'62 **Roses Are Red (My Love)**
   Bobby Vinton
'57 **Rosie Lee** *Mello-Tones*
'79 **Rotation** *Herb Alpert*
'86 **Rough Boy** *ZZ Top*
'80 **Rough Boys** *Pete Townshend*

'97 **Round About Way** *George Strait*
Round And Round
'57   *Perry Como*
'84   *Ratt*
'90   *Tevin Campbell*
'65 **Round Every Corner** *Petula Clark*
'94 **Round Here** *Counting Crows*
'72 **Roundabout** *Yes*
'82 **Route 101** *Herb Alpert*
'62 **Route 66 Theme** *Nelson Riddle*
'79 **Roxanne** *Police*
'85 **Roxanne, Roxanne** *UTFO*
'74 **Rub It In** *Billy "Crash" Craddock*
'90 **Rub You The Right Way** *Johnny Gill*
'60 **Rubber Ball** *Bobby Vee*
'04 **Rubber Band Man** *T.I.*
'79 **Rubber Biscuit** *Blues Brothers*
'70 **Rubber Duckie** *Ernie (Jim Henson)*
'76 **Rubberband Man** *Spinners*
'69 **Rubberneckin'** *Elvis Presley*
'60 **Ruby** *Ray Charles*
'62 **Ruby Ann** *Marty Robbins*
Ruby Baby
'63   *Dion*
'74   *Billy "Crash" Craddock*
'69 **Ruby, Don't Take Your Love To
    Town** *Kenny Rogers & The
    First Edition*
'60 **Ruby Duby Du** *Tobin Mathews*
'67 **Ruby Tuesday** *Rolling Stones*
'60 **Rudolph The Red Nosed Reindeer**
    Chipmunks
'75 **Rudy** *Supertramp*
'56 **Rudy's Rock** *Bill Haley*
'99 **Ruff Ryders' Anthem** *DMX*
'93 **RuffNeck** *MC Lyte*
'58 **Rumble** *Link Wray*
'86 **Rumbleseat**
    John Cougar Mellencamp
Rumor Has It
'90   *Reba McEntire*
'97   *Clay Walker*
Rumors
'62   *Johnny Crawford*
'86   *Timex Social Club*
'92 **Rump Shaker** *Wreckx-N-Effect*
'01 **Run** *George Strait*
'95 **Run Away** *Real McCoy*
'69 **Run Away Child, Running Wild**
    Temptations
'65 **Run, Baby Run (Back Into My
    Arms)** *Newbeats*
'78 **Run For Home** *Lindisfarne*
'82 **Run For The Roses** *Dan Fogelberg*
'05 **Run It!** *Chris Brown*
'75 **Run Joey Run** *David Geddes*
'80 **Run Like Hell** *Pink Floyd*
'59 **Run Red Run** *Coasters*
'66 **Run, Run, Look And See**
    Brian Hyland
'72 **Run Run Run** *Jo Jo Gunne*
'84 **Run Runaway** *Slade*
'60 **Run Samson Run** *Neil Sedaka*
'70 **Run Through The Jungle**
    Creedence Clearwater Revival
'61 **Run To Him** *Bobby Vee*
'72 **Run To Me** *Bee Gees*
Run To You
'84   *Bryan Adams*
'93   *Whitney Houston*
'76 **Run With The Pack**
    Bad Company
'95 **Run-Around** *Blues Traveler*
Runaround
'60   *Fleetwoods*
'61   *Regents*
'91   *Van Halen*
Runaround Sue
'61   *Dion*
'77   *Leif Garrett*
Runaway
'61   *Del Shannon*
'78   *Jefferson Starship*
'84   *Bon Jovi*
'95   *Janet Jackson*

Runaway Love
'78   *Linda Clifford*
'07   *Ludacris*
'93 **Runaway Train** *Soul Asylum*
'84 **Runner** *Manfred Mann*
'72 **Runnin' Away**
    Sly & The Family Stone
'89 **Runnin' Down A Dream** *Tom Petty*
'03 **Runnin (Dying To Live)** *2Pac*
'78 **Runnin' With The Devil**
    Van Halen
'02 **Running Away** *Hoobastank*
'91 **Running Back To You**
    Vanessa Williams
'59 **Running Bear** *Johnny Preston*
'08 **Running Blind** *Godsmack*
'78 **Running On Empty** *Jackson Browne*
'96 **Running Out Of Reasons To Run**
    Rick Trevino
'61 **Running Scared** *Roy Orbison*
'85 **Running Up That Hill** *Kate Bush*
'83 **Running With The Night**
    Lionel Richie
'72 **Runway, The** *Grass Roots*
Rush
'91   *Big Audio Dynamite*
'06   *Aly & AJ*
'88 **Rush Hour** *Jane Wiedlin*
'91 **Rush, Rush** *Paula Abdul*
'86 **Russians** *Sting*
'65 **Rusty Bells** *Brenda Lee*

S

S.O.S. [SOS]
'75   *Abba*
'06   *Rihanna*
'07   *Jonas Brothers*
'66 **S.Y.S.L.J.F.M. (The Letter Song)**
    Joe Tex
'94 **Sabotage** *Beastie Boys*
'61 **Sacred** *Castells*
'89 **Sacred Emotion** *Donny Osmond*
'90 **Sacrifice** *Elton John*
'79 **Sad Café** *Eagles*
'79 **Sad Eyes** *Robert John*
'97 **Sad Lookin' Moon** *Alabama*
'60 **Sad Mood** *Sam Cooke*
'61 **Sad Movies (Make Me Cry)**
    Sue Thompson
'65 **Sad, Sad Girl** *Barbara Mason*
'84 **Sad Songs (Say So Much)**
    Elton John
'75 **Sad Sweet Dreamer**
    Sweet Sensation
'91 **Sadeness** *Enigma*
'83 **Safety Dance** *Men Without Hats*
'93 **Said I Loved You...But I Lied**
    Michael Bolton
'57 **Sail Along Silvery Moon**
    Billy Vaughn
'72 **Sail Away** *Randy Newman*
'79 **Sail On** *Commodores*
'73 **Sail On Sailor** *Beach Boys*
Sailing
'75   *Rod Stewart*
'80   *Christopher Cross*
'60 **Sailor (Your Home Is The Sea)**
    Lolita
'06 **Saints Are Coming** *U2 & Green Day*
'74 **Sally Can't Dance** *Lou Reed*
'74 **Sally G** *Paul McCartney*
'63 **Sally, Go 'Round The Roses**
    Jaynetts
'83 **Salt In My Tears** *Martin Briley*
'03 **Salt Shaker** *Ying Yang Twins*
'72 **Salty Dog** *Procol Harum [live]*
'96 **Salvation** *Cranberries*
'77 **Sam** *Olivia Newton-John*
'07 **Same Girl** *R. Kelly & Usher*
'80 **Same Old Lang Syne**
    Dan Fogelberg
'55 **Same Old Saturday Night**
    Frank Sinatra
'74 **Same Old Song And Dance**
    Aerosmith

'60 **Same One** *Brook Benton*
'75 **Same Thing It Took** *Impressions*
'61 **San Antonio Rose** *Floyd Cramer*
'67 **San Franciscan Nights** *Animals*
'67 **San Francisco (Be Sure To Wear
    Flowers In Your Hair)**
    Scott McKenzie
'68 **San Francisco Girls (Return Of The
    Native)** *Fever Tree*
'82 **San Jacinto** *Peter Gabriel*
'85 **Sanctified Lady** *Marvin Gaye*
'86 **Sanctify Yourself** *Simple Minds*
'55 **Sand And The Sea** *Nat "King" Cole*
'72 **Sandman** *America*
'01 **Sandstorm** *Darude*
Sandy
'59   *Larry Hall*
'63   *Dion*
'65   *Ronny & The Daytonas*
'57 **Santa And The Satellite**
    Buchanan & Goodman
Santa Claus Is Coming To Town
'62   *4 Seasons*
'75   *Bruce Springsteen*
'95 **Santa Monica (Watch The World
    Die)** *Everclear*
'97 **Santeria** *Sublime*
Sara
'79   *Fleetwood Mac*
'85   *Starship*
'76 **Sara Smile** *Daryl Hall & John Oates*
'80 **(Sartorial Eloquence) Don't Ya
    Wanna Play This Game No More?**
    Elton John
'96 **Satellite** *Dave Matthews Band*
'73 **Satellite Of Love** *Lou Reed*
'65 **Satin Pillows** *Bobby Vinton*
'73 **Satin Sheets** *Jeanne Pruett*
'75 **Satin Soul** *Love Unlimited Orchestra*
'02 **Satisfaction** *Eve*
'89 **Satisfied** *Richard Marx*
Satisfied Mind
'55   *Porter Wagoner*
'66   *Bobby Hebb*
'99 **Satisfy You** *Puff Daddy*
'72 **Saturday In The Park** *Chicago*
'86 **Saturday Love**
    Cherrelle/Alexander O'Neal
'71 **Saturday Morning Confusion**
    Bobby Russell
Saturday Night [Nite]
'63   *New Christy Minstrels*
'75   *Bay City Rollers*
'76   *Earth, Wind & Fire*
'64 **Saturday Night At The Movies**
    Drifters
'75 **Saturday Night Special**
    Lynyrd Skynyrd
'79 **Saturday Night, Sunday Morning**
    Thelma Houston
'73 **Saturday Night's Alright For
    Fighting** *Elton John*
'02 **Saturday (Oooh! Ooooh!)** *Ludacris*
'81 **Sausalito Summernight** *Diesel*
'79 **Savannah Nights** *Tom Johnston*
'04 **Save A H orse (Ride A Cowboy)**
    Big & Rich
'85 **Save A Prayer** *Duran Duran*
'76 **Save It For A Rainy Day**
    Stephen Bishop
'82 **Save It For Later** *English Beat*
'64 **Save It For Me** *4 Seasons*
Save Me
'90   *Fleetwood Mac*
'05   *Shinedown*
'91 **Save Some Love** *Keedy*
'92 **Save The Best For Last**
    Vanessa Williams
'70 **Save The Country** *5th Dimension*
Save The Last Dance For Me
'60   *Drifters*
'74   *DeFranco Family*
'06   *Michael Bublé*
'83 **Save The Overtime (For Me)**
    Gladys Knight
'98 **Save Tonight** *Eagle-Eye Cherry*

'65 **Save Your Heart For Me** *Gary Lewis*
'76 **Save Your Kisses For Me**
   Brotherhood Of Man
'85 **Save Your Love (For #1)**
   René & Angela
'61 **Saved** *LaVern Baker*
'83 **Saved By Zero** *Fixx*
'06 **Savin' Me** *Nickelback*
'85 **Saving All My Love For You**
   Whitney Houston
'92 **Saving Forever For You** *Shanice*
'91 **Sax And Violins** *Talking Heads*
'90 **Say A Prayer** *Breathe*
'06 **Say Goodbye** *Chris Brown*
'81 **Say Goodbye To Hollywood**
   Billy Joel
'73 **Say, Has Anybody Seen My Sweet**
   Gypsy Rose *Dawn*
'06 **Say I** *Christina Milian w/ Young Jeezy*
'66 **Say I Am (What I Am)**
   Tommy James
'97 **Say...If You Feel Alright**
   Crystal Waters
'98 **Say It** *Voices Of Theory*
'88 **Say It Again** *Jermaine Stewart*
'95 **Say It Ain't So** *Weezer*
    Say It Isn't So
'83 *Daryl Hall & John Oates*
'85 *Outfield*
'68 **Say It Loud - I'm Black And I'm**
   Proud *James Brown*
'07 **Say It Right** *Nelly Furtado*
'59 **Say Man** *Bo Diddley*
'79 **Say Maybe** *Neil Diamond*
'99 **Say My Name** *Destiny's Child*
'83 **Say Say Say**
   Paul McCartney & Michael Jackson
'65 **Say Something Funny** *Patty Duke*
'81 **Say What** *Jesse Winchester*
'06 **Say What You Will** *Eric Clapton*
'03 **Say Yes** *Floetry*
'64 **Say You** *Ronnie Dove*
'76 **Say You Love Me** *Fleetwood Mac*
'85 **Say You, Say Me** *Lionel Richie*
'87 **Say You Will** *Foreigner*
'81 **Say You'll Be Mine**
   Christopher Cross
'97 **Say You'll Be There** *Spice Girls*
'77 **Say You'll Stay Until Tomorrow**
   Tom Jones
'65 **(Say) You're My Girl** *Roy Orbison*
'85 **Say You're Wrong** *Julian Lennon*
'88 **Sayin' Sorry (Don't Make It Right)**
   Denise Lopez
'04 **Scandalous** *Mis-Teeq*
'99 **Scar Tissue** *Red Hot Chili Peppers*
    Scarborough Fair
'68 *Sergio Mendes*
'68 *Simon & Garfunkel*
'59 **Scarlet Ribbons (For Her Hair)**
   Browns
'04 **Scars** *Papa Roach*
'92 **Scenario** *Tribe Called Quest*
'77 **Scenes From An Italian Restaurant**
   Billy Joel
'01 **Schism** *Tool*
'75 **School** *Supertramp*
'75 **School Boy Crush** *AWB*
'57 **School Day** *Chuck Berry*
'61 **School Is In** *Gary (U.S.) Bonds*
'61 **School Is Out** *Gary (U.S.) Bonds*
'92 **School Me** *Gerald Levert*
'72 **School's Out** *Alice Cooper*
'71 **Scorpio** *Dennis Coffey*
'62 **Scotch And Soda** *Kingston Trio*
'64 **Scratchy** *Travis Wammack*
'95 **Scream**
   Michael Jackson & Janet Jackson
'87 **Se La** *Lionel Richie*
'76 **Se Si Bon [medley]** *Dr. Buzzard's*
   Original "Savannah" Band
'59 **Sea Cruise** *Frankie Ford*
'61 **Sea Of Heartbreak** *Don Gibson*
'69 **Sea Of Joy** *Blind Faith*

    Sea Of Love
'59 *Phil Phillips w/ The Twilights*
'81 *Del Shannon*
'84 *Honeydrippers*
    Sealed With A Kiss
'62 *Brian Hyland*
'68 *Gary Lewis*
'72 *Bobby Vinton*
'73 **Search And Destroy** *Iggy & The*
   Stooges
'85 **Search Is Over** *Survivor*
'57 **Searchin'** *Coasters*
'98 **Searchin' My Soul** *Vonda Shepard*
'66 **Searching For My Love**
   Bobby Moore
'06 **Seashores Of Mexico** *George Strait*
'81 **Seasons** *Charles Fox*
'87 **Seasons Change** *Exposé*
'74 **Seasons In The Sun** *Terry Jacks*
'05 **Seasons Of Love** *Cast Of Rent*
'74 **Seasons Of Wither** *Aerosmith*
'69 **Seattle** *Perry Como*
'74 **Second Avenue** *Garfunkel*
'89 **Second Chance** *Thirty Eight Special*
'56 **Second Fiddle** *Kay Starr*
'62 **Second Hand Love** *Connie Francis*
'77 **Second Hand News**
   Fleetwood Mac
'65 **Second Hand Rose**
   Barbra Streisand
'85 **Second Nature** *Dan Hartman*
'98 **Second Round K.O.** *Canibus*
    Second Time Around
'61 *Frank Sinatra*
'79 *Shalamar*
'94 **Secret** *Madonna*
'87 **Secret, The** *Gordon MacRae*
    Secret Agent Man
'66 *Johnny Rivers*
'66 *Ventures*
'95 **Secret Garden** *Bruce Springsteen*
'90 **Secret Garden (Sweet Seduction**
   Suite) *Quincy Jones/Al B. Sure!/*
   James Ingram/El DeBarge/
   Barry White
    Secret Love
'66 *Billy Stewart*
'75 *Freddy Fender*
'85 **Secret Lovers** *Atlantic Starr*
'89 **Secret Rendezvous** *Karyn White*
'86 **Secret Separation** *Fixx*
'68 **Secretly** *Jimmie Rodgers*
'68 **Security** *Etta James*
    Seduction, The *James Last Band*
'69 **See** *Rascals*
'67 **See Emily Play** *Pink Floyd*
    See Me, Feel Me
'70 *Who*
'73 *New Seekers [medley]*
    See Saw
'56 *Moonglows*
'68 *Aretha Franklin*
'64 **See The Funny Little Clown**
   Bobby Goldsboro
'91 **See The Lights** *Simple Minds*
'85 **See What Love Can Do** *Eric Clapton*
    See You In September
'59 *Tempos*
'66 *Happenings*
'56 **See You Later, Alligator** *Bill Haley*
'90 **Seein' My Father In Me**
   Paul Overstreet
'02 **Seein' Red** *Unwritten Law*
'91 **Seeing Things** *Black Crowes*
'70 **Seeker, The** *Who*
'84 **Self Control** *Laura Branigan*
'94 **Self Esteem** *Offspring*
'64 **Selfish One** *Jackie Ross*
'94 **Selling The Drama** *Live*
'97 **Semi-Charmed Life** *Third Eye Blind*
'94 **Seminole Wind** *John Anderson*
'57 **Send For Me** *Nat "King" Cole*
'83 **Send Her My Love** *Journey*
'75 **Send In The Clowns** *Judy Collins*
'83 **Send Me An Angel** *Real Life*

    Send Me Some Lovin'
'57 *Little Richard*
'63 *Sam Cooke*
    Send Me The Pillow You Dream On
'62 *Johnny Tillotson*
'65 *Dean Martin*
'79 **Send One Your Love** *Stevie Wonder*
'03 **Send The Pain Below** *Chevelle*
'90 **Sending All My Love** *Linear*
'94 **Sending My Love** *Zhané*
'03 **Señorita** *Justin Timberlake*
'90 **Sensitivity** *Ralph Tresvant*
'95 **Sentimental** *Deborah Cox*
'77 **Sentimental Lady** *Bob Welch*
'61 **Sentimental Me** *Elvis Presley*
'85 **Sentimental Street** *Night Ranger*
'85 **Separate Lives**
   Phil Collins & Marilyn Martin
'72 **Separate Ways** *Elvis Presley*
'83 **Separate Ways (Worlds Apart)**
   Journey
'00 **Separated** *Avant*
'78 **September** *Earth, Wind & Fire*
'74 **September Gurls** *Big Star*
'61 **September In The Rain**
   Dinah Washington
'79 **September Morn'** *Neil Diamond*
'80 **Sequel** *Harry Chapin*
'87 **Serious** *Donna Allen*
'77 **Serpentine Fire** *Earth, Wind & Fire*
'91 **Set Adrift On Memory Bliss**
   PM Dawn
    Set Me Free
'65 *Kinks*
'80 *Utopia*
'91 **Set The Night To Music**
   Roberta Flack w/ Maxi Priest
'95 **Set U Free** *Planet Soul*
'99 **Set Your Eyes To Zion** *P.O.D.*
'59 **Settin' The Woods On Fire**
   Johnny Burnette
'06 **Settle For A Slowdown**
   Dierks Bentley
'07 **Settlin'** *Sugarland*
'92 **7** *Prince*
'66 **7 And 7 Is** *Love*
'80 **Seven Bridges Road** *Eagles*
'62 **Seven Day Weekend**
   Gary (US) Bonds
    Seven [7] Days
'56 *Dorothy Collins*
'56 *Crew Cuts*
'56 *Clyde McPhatter*
'97 *Mary J. Blige*
'01 *Craig David*
'58 **"7-11" (Mambo No. 5)**
   Gone All Stars
'59 **(Seven Little Girls) Sitting In The**
   Back Seat *Paul Evans*
'03 **Seven Nation Army** *White Stripes*
'67 **7 Rooms Of Gloom** *Four Tops*
'82 **777-9311** *Time*
'85 **Seven Spanish Angels**
   Ray Charles & Willie Nelson
'93 **Seven Whole Days** *Toni Braxton*
'87 **Seven Wonders** *Fleetwood Mac*
'81 **Seven Year Ache** *Rosanne Cash*
'65 **Seventh Son** *Johnny Rivers*
    Seventeen [17]
'55 *Boyd Bennett*
'55 *Rusty Draper*
'55 *Fontane Sisters*
'84 *Rick James*
'89 *Winger*
'62 **Seventy Six Trombones**
   Robert Preston
'06 **S.E.X.** *Lyfe Jennings*
'98 **Sex and Candy** *Marcy Playground*
'85 **Sex As A Weapon** *Pat Benatar*
    Sex Machine ..see: Get Up
'93 **Sex Me** *R. Kelly*
'82 **Sexual Healing** *Marvin Gaye*
'99 **Sexual (Li Da Di)** *Amber*
'80 **Sexy Eyes** *Dr. Hook*
'84 **Sexy Girl** *Glenn Frey*
'07 **Sexy Lady** *Yung Berg*

'06 **Sexy Love** *Ne-Yo*
'74 **Sexy Mama** *Moments*
'06 **SexyBack** *Justin Timberlake*
'67 **Sgt. Pepper's Lonely Hearts Club Band** *Beatles*
'64 **Sha La La** *Manfred Mann*
'74 **Sha-La-La (Make Me Happy)** *Al Green*
'00 **Shackles (Praise You)** *Mary Mary*
'78 **Shadow Dancing** *Andy Gibb*
'65 **Shadow Of Your Smile** *Tony Bennett*
'79 **Shadows In The Moonlight** *Anne Murray*
'82 **Shadows Of The Night** *Pat Benatar*
'62 **Shadrack** *Brook Benton*
'97 **Shady Lane** *Pavement*
'64 **Shaggy Dog** *Mickey Lee Lane*
Shake
'65   *Sam Cooke*
'65   *Otis Redding*
'05   *Ying Yang Twins*
'97 **Shake, The** *Neal McCoy*
'67 **Shake A Tail Feather** *James & Bobby Purify*
'65 **Shake And Fingerpop** *Jr. Walker*
'88 **Shake For The Sheik** *Escape Club*
'78 **Shake It** *Ian Matthews*
'05 **Shake It Off** *Mariah Carey*
'81 **Shake It Up** *Cars*
'66 **Shake Me, Wake Me (When It's Over)** *Four Tops*
Shake, Rattle & Roll
'54   *Bill Haley*
'54   *Big Joe Turner*
'67   *Arthur Conley*
'63 **Shake! Shake! Shake!** *Jackie Wilson*
'76 **(Shake, Shake, Shake) Shake Your Booty** *KC & The Sunshine Band*
'06 **Shake That** *Eminem*
'00 **Shake Ya Ass** *Mystikal*
'03 **Shake Ya Tailfeather** *Nelly/P. Diddy/Murphy Lee*
'86 **Shake You Down** *Gregory Abbott*
'79 **Shake Your Body (Down To The Ground)** *Jacksons*
'99 **Shake Your Bon-Bon** *Ricky Martin*
'78 **Shake Your Groove Thing** *Peaches & Herb*
'87 **Shake Your Love** *Debbie Gibson*
'61 **Shake Your Moneymaker** *Elmore James*
'76 **Shake Your Rump To The Funk** *Bar-Kays*
'87 **Shakedown** *Bob Seger*
'79 **Shakedown Cruise** *Jay Ferguson*
'78 **Shakedown Street** *Grateful Dead*
'75 **Shakey Ground** *Temptations*
'82 **Shakin'** *Eddie Money*
'65 **Shakin' All Over** *Guess Who?*
'56 **Shall We Dance** *Yul Brynner & Deborah Kerr*
'73 **Shambala** *Three Dog Night*
Shame
'78   *Evelyn "Champagne" King*
'85   *Motels*
'94   *Zhané*
'62 **Shame On Me** *Bobby Bare*
'82 **Shame On The Moon** *Bob Seger*
'97 **Shame On You** *Indigo Girls*
'68 **Shame, Shame** *Magic Lanterns*
'75 **Shame, Shame, Shame** *Shirley (& Company)*
'91 **Shameless** *Garth Brooks*
'82 **Shanghai Breezes** *John Denver*
Shangri-La
'57   *Four Coins*
'64   *Vic Dana*
'64   *Robert Maxwell*
'76 **Shannon** *Henry Gross*
'70 **Shape I'm In** *Band*
'00 **Shape Of My Heart** *Backstreet Boys*
'68 **Shape Of Things To Come** *Max Frost*

Shapes Of Things
'66   *Yardbirds*
'68   *Jeff Beck*
'70 **Share The Land** *Guess Who*
Share Your Love With Me
'69   *Aretha Franklin*
'81   *Kenny Rogers*
'78 **Sharing The Night Together** *Dr. Hook*
'62 **Sharing You** *Bobby Vee*
'84 **Sharkey's Day** *Laurie Anderson*
'83 **Sharp Dressed Man** *ZZ Top*
'78 **Shattered** *Rolling Stones*
'88 **Shattered Dreams** *Johnny Hates Jazz*
'75 **Shaving Cream** *Benny Bell*
'07 **Shawty** *Plies*
'60 **Shazam!** *Duane Eddy*
Sh'Boom
'54   *Chords*
'54   *Crew-Cuts*
She
'67   *Monkees*
'69   *Tommy James*
'90 **She Ain't Worth It** *Glenn Medeiros w/ Bobby Brown*
'95 **She Ain't Your Ordinary Girl** *Alabama*
'00 **She Bangs** *Ricky Martin*
'79 **She Believes In Me** *Kenny Rogers*
She Belongs To Be
'65   *Bob Dylan*
'69   *Rick Nelson*
'66 **She Blew A Good Thing** *Poets*
'83 **She Blinded Me With Science** *Thomas Dolby*
'84 **She Bop** *Cyndi Lauper*
'07 **She Builds Quick Machines** *Velvet Revolver*
She Came In Through The Bathroom Window
'69   *Beatles*
'69   *Joe Cocker*
'62 **She Can't Find Her Keys** *Paul Petersen*
'01 **She Couldn't Change Me** *Montgomery Gentry*
'62 **She Cried** *Jay & The Americans*
'77 **She Did It** *Eric Carmen*
'93 **She Don't Know She's Beautiful** *Sammy Kershaw*
'06 **She Don't Tell Me To** *Montgomery Gentry*
'94 **She Don't Use Jelly** *Flaming Lips*
'89 **She Drives Me Crazy** *Fine Young Cannibals*
'02 **She Hates Me** *Puddle Of Mudd*
'92 **She Is His Only Need** *Wynonna*
'67 **She Is Still A Mystery** *Lovin' Spoonful*
'06 **She Let Herself Go** *George Strait*
'02 **She Loves Me Not** *Papa Roach*
'64 **She Loves You** *Beatles*
'96 **She Never Lets It Go To Her Heart** *Tim McGraw*
'59 **She Say (Oom Dooby Doom)** *Diamonds*
'91 **She Talks To Angels** *Black Crowes*
'62 **She Thinks I Still Care** *George Jones*
'00 **She Thinks My Tractor's Sexy** *Kenny Chesney*
'04 **She Thinks She Needs Me** *Andy Griggs*
'64 **She Understands Me** *Johnny Tillotson*
'93 **She Used To Be Mine** *Brooks & Dunn*
'88 **She Wants To Dance With Me** *Rick Astley*
'58 **She Was Only Seventeen (He Was One Year More)** *Marty Robbins*
'04 **She Will Be Loved** *Maroon5*
'83 **She Works Hard For The Money** *Donna Summer*
'67 **She'd Rather Be With Me** *Turtles*

'02 **She'll Leave You With A Smile** *George Strait*
'81 **She's A Bad Mama Jama (She's Built, She's Stacked)** *Carl Carlton*
'83 **She's A Beauty** *Tubes*
'63 **She's A Fool** *Lesley Gore*
'68 **She's A Heartbreaker** *Gene Pitney*
'71 **She's A Lady** *Tom Jones*
'67 **She's A Rainbow** *Rolling Stones*
'64 **She's A Woman** *Beatles*
'65 **She's About A Mover** *Sir Douglas Quintet*
'99 **She's All I Ever Had** *Ricky Martin*
She's All I Got
'71   *Freddie North*
'01   *Jimmy Cozier*
'78 **She's Always A Woman** *Billy Joel*
'95 **She's Every Woman** *Garth Brooks*
'06 **She's Everything** *Brad Paisley*
'61 **She's Everything (I Wanted You To Be)** *Ral Donner*
She's Gone
'74   *Tavares*
'74   *Daryl Hall & John Oates*
'97 **She's Gonna Make It** *Garth Brooks*
'81 **She's Got A Way** *Billy Joel*
'97 **She's Got It All** *Kenny Chesney*
'92 **She's Got The Rhythm (And I Got The Blues)** *Alan Jackson*
'62 **She's Got You** *Patsy Cline*
'91 **She's In Love With The Boy** *Trisha Yearwood*
'65 **She's Just My Style** *Gary Lewis*
'67 **She's Leaving Home** *Beatles*
'87 **She's Like The Wind** *Patrick Swayze*
'68 **She's Lookin' Good** *Wilson Pickett*
'84 **She's Mine** *Steve Perry*
'00 **She's More** *Andy Griggs*
'90 **She's My Baby** *Traveling Wilburys*
'67 **She's My Girl** *Turtles*
'03 **She's My Kind Of Rain** *Tim McGraw*
'58 **She's Neat** *Dale Wright*
'71 **She's Not Just Another Woman** *8th Day*
'94 **She's Not The Cheatin' Kind** *Brooks & Dunn*
She's Not There
'64   *Zombies*
'77   *Santana*
'62 **She's Not You** *Elvis Presley*
'88 **She's On The Left** *Jeffrey Osborne*
'80 **She's Out Of My Life** *Michael Jackson*
'92 **She's Playing Hard To Get** *Hi-Five*
'83 **(She's) Sexy + 17** *Stray Cats*
'80 **She's So Cold** *Rolling Stones*
'99 **She's So High** *Tal Bachman*
'84 **She's Strange** *Cameo*
'96 **She's Taken A Shine** *John Berry*
'64 **She's The One** *Chartbusters*
'85 **She's Waiting** *Eric Clapton*
'77 **Sheena Is A Punk Rocker** *Ramones*
'62 **Sheila** *Tommy Roe*
'98 **Shelf In The Room** *Days Of The New*
'90 **Shelter Me** *Cinderella*
'63 **Shelter Of Your Arms** *Sammy Davis Jr.*
'62 **Sherry** *4 Seasons*
Shifting, Whispering Sands
'55   *Rusty Draper*
'55   *Billy Vaughn*
'70 **Shilo** *Neil Diamond*
'98 **Shimmer** *Fuel*
'59 **Shimmy, Shimmy, Ko-Ko-Bop** *Little Anthony & The Imperials*
Shine
'94   *Collective Soul*
'94   *Newsboys*
'79 **Shine A Little Love** *Electric Light Orchestra*
'80 **Shine On** *L.T.D.*
'75 **Shine On You Crazy Diamond** *Pink Floyd*
'74 **Shinin' On** *Grand Funk*

247

Shining Star
'75 *Earth, Wind & Fire*
'80 *Manhattans*
'91 **Shiny Happy People** *R.E.M.*
'88 **Ship Of Fools** *Robert Plant*
'87 **Ship Of Fools (Save Me From Tomorrow)** *World Party*
'79 **Ships** *Barry Manilow*
'57 **Shish-Kebab** *Ralph Marterie*
'82 **Shock The Monkey** *Peter Gabriel*
'98 **Shoes You're Wearing** *Clint Black*
'75 **Shoeshine Boy** *Eddie Kendricks*
'68 **Shoo-Be-Doo-Be-Doo-Da-Day** *Stevie Wonder*
'93 **Shoop** *Salt-N-Pepa*
Shoop Shoop Song (It's In His Kiss)
'64 *Betty Everett*
'90 *Cher*
'68 **Shoot'em Up, Baby** *Andy Kim*
'75 **Shooting Star** *Bad Company*
Shop Around
'60 *Miracles*
'76 *Captain & Tennille*
'57 **Short Fat Fannie** *Larry Williams*
'77 **Short People** *Randy Newman*
'58 **Short Shorts** *Royal Teens*
'06 **Shortie Like Mine** *Bow Wow*
'04 **Shorty Wanna Ride** *Young Buck*
'98 **Shorty (You Keep Playin' With My Mind)** *Imajin w/ Keith Murray*
'86 **Shot In The Dark** *Ozzy Osbourne*
'65 **Shotgun** *Jr. Walker*
'82 **Should I Do It** *Pointer Sisters*
'82 **Should I Stay Or Should I Go** *Clash*
'95 **Should've Asked Her Faster** *Ty England*
'93 **Should've Been A Cowboy** *Toby Keith*
'87 **Should've Known Better** *Richard Marx*
'80 **Should've Never Let You Go** *Neil Sedaka & Dara Sedaka*
'06 **Shoulder Lean** *Young Dro*
'89 **Shoulder To Cry On** *Tommy Page*
Shout
'59 *Isley Brothers*
'62 *Joey Dee*
'85 *Tears For Fears*
'76 **Shout It Out Loud** *Kiss*
'62 **Shout! Shout! (Knock Yourself Out)** *Ernie Maresca*
Show And Tell
'73 *Al Wilson*
'89 *Peabo Bryson*
'89 **Show Don't Tell** *Rush*
Show Me
'67 *Joe Tex*
'84 *Glenn Jones*
'84 *Pretenders*
'90 *Howard Hewett*
'03 **Show Me How To Live** *Audioslave*
Show Me Love
'93 *Robin S*
'97 *Robyn*
'00 **Show Me The Meaning Of Being Lonely** *Backstreet Boys*
Show Me The Way
'76 *Peter Frampton*
'87 *Regina Belle*
'90 *Styx*
'06 **Show Me What You Got** *Jay-Z*
'03 **Show Me Your Glory** *Third Day*
'74 **Show Must Go On** *Three Dog Night*
'85 **Show Some Respect** *Tina Turner*
'06 **Show Stopper** *Danity Kane*
'77 **Show You The Way To Go** *Jacksons*
'73 **Showdown** *Electric Light Orchestra*
'87 **Showdown At Big Sky** *Robbie Robertson*
'89 **Shower Me With Your Love** *Surface*
'76 **Shower The People** *James Taylor*
'75 **(Shu-Doo-Pa-Poo-Poop) Love Being Your Fool** *Travis Wammack*

'61 **Shu Rah** *Fats Domino*
'63 **Shut Down** *Beach Boys*
'07 **Shut Up And Drive** *Rihanna*
'94 **Shut Up And Kiss Me** *Mary Chapin Carpenter*
'62 **Shutters And Boards** *Jerry Wallace*
'95 **Shy Guy** *Diana King*
'58 **Sick And Tired** *Fats Domino*
'02 **Sick Of Being Lonely** *Field Mob*
'95 **Sick Of Myself** *Matthew Sweet*
'74 **Sideshow** *Blue Magic*
'64 **Sidewalk Surfin'** *Jan & Dean*
'85 **Sidewalk Talk** *Jellybean*
'02 **Scientist, The** *Coldplay*
'94 **Sign, The** *Ace Of Base*
'83 **Sign Of Fire** *Fixx*
'81 **Sign Of The Gypsy Queen** *April Wine*
Sign 'O' The Times
'87 *Prince*
'97 *Queensrÿche*
'66 **Sign Of The Times** *Petula Clark*
'88 **Sign Your Name** *Terence Trent D'Arby*
Signed, Sealed, Delivered I'm Yours
'70 *Stevie Wonder*
'77 *Peter Frampton*
Signs
'71 *Five Man Electrical Band*
'91 *Tesla*
Silence Is Golden
'64 *4 Seasons*
'67 *Tremeloes*
'92 **Silent All These Years** *Tori Amos*
'04 **Silent Lucidity** *Queensrÿche*
'04 **Silent Night** *Five For Fighting*
'92 **Silent Prayer** *Shanice feat. Johnny Gill*
'85 **Silent Running (On Dangerous Ground)** *Mike + The Mechanics*
'88 **Silhouette** *Kenny G*
Silhouettes
'57 *Diamonds*
'57 *Rays*
'65 *Herman's Hermits*
'76 **Silly Love Songs** *Wings*
'07 **Sillyworld** *Stone Sour*
'70 **Silver Bird** *Mark Lindsay*
'76 **Silver, Blue & Gold** *Bad Company*
'55 **Silver Dollar** *Teresa Brewer*
'77 **Silver Springs** *Fleetwood Mac*
'62 **Silver Threads And Golden Needles** *Springfields*
'68 **Simon Says** *1910 Fruitgum Co.*
'00 **Simple Kind Of Life** *No Doubt*
'93 **Simple Life** *Elton John*
'01 **Simple Things** *Jim Brickman*
'88 **Simply Irresistible** *Robert Palmer*
'69 **Sin City** *Flying Burrito Brothers*
Since I Don't Have You
'59 *Skyliners*
'81 *Don McLean*
'63 **Since I Fell For You** *Lenny Welch*
'65 **Since I Lost My Baby** *Temptations*
'56 **Since I Met You Baby** *Ivory Joe Hunter*
'70 **Since I've Been Loving You** *Led Zeppelin*
Since You [U] Been Gone
'78 *Head East*
'79 *Rainbow*
'05 *Kelly Clarkson*
'82 **Since You're Gone** *Cars*
Since You've Been Gone
'59 *Clyde McPhatter*
'87 *Outfield*
Sincerely
'55 *McGuire Sisters*
'55 *Moonglow's*
'89 **Sincerely Yours** *Sweet Sensation*
'73 **Sing** *Carpenters*
'73 **Sing A Song** *Earth, Wind & Fire*
'58 **Sing Boy Sing** *Tommy Sands*
'78 **Sing For The Day** *Styx*

'03 **Sing For The Moment** *Eminem*
Singing The Blues
'56 *Guy Mitchell*
'56 *Marty Robbins*
'66 **Single Girl** *Sandy Posey*
'85 **Single Life** *Cameo*
'99 **Single White Female** *Chely Wright*
'60 **Sink The Bismarck** *Johnny Horton*
'84 **Sir Duke** *Stevie Wonder*
'84 **Sister Christian** *Night Ranger*
'75 **Sister Golden Hair** *America*
'73 **Sister Mary Elephant (Shudd-Up!)** *Cheech & Chong*
'85 **Sisters Are Doin' It For Themselves** *Eurythmics & Aretha Franklin*
'67 **Sit Down, I Think I Love You** *Mojo Men*
'71 **Sit Yourself Down** *Stephen Stills*
Sittin' In The Balcony
'57 *Eddie Cochran*
'57 *Johnny Dee*
'90 **Sittin' In The Lap Of Luxury** *Louie Louie*
'97 **Sittin' On Go** *Bryan White*
(Sittin' On) The Dock Of The Bay
'68 *Otis Redding*
'87 *Michael Bolton*
'96 **Sittin' On Top Of The World** *Da Brat*
'95 **Sittin' Up In My Room** *Brandy*
'72 **Sitting** *Cat Stevens*
'83 **Sitting At The Wheel** *Moody Blues*
'67 **Sitting In The Park** *Billy Stewart*
'05 **Sitting, Waiting, Wishing** *Jack Johnson*
'82 **Situation** *Yaz*
Six Days On The Road
'63 *Dave Dudley*
'97 *Sawyer Brown*
'86 **Six Feet Deep** *Geto Boys*
'82 **Six Months In A Leaky Boat** *Split Enz*
'59 **Six Nights A Week** *Crests*
'67 **Six O'Clock** *Lovin' Spoonful*
'01 **Six-Pack Summer** *Phil Vassar*
'66 **634-5789 (Soulsville, U.S.A.)** *Wilson Pickett*
'58 **16 Candles** *Crests*
'60 **Sixteen Reasons** *Connie Stevens*
Sixteen Tons
'55 *Johnny Desmond*
'55 *"Tennessee" Ernie Ford*
'96 **6th Avenue Heartache** *Wallflowers*
'82 **'65 Love Affair** *Paul Davis*
'02 **Sk8er Boi** *Avril Lavigne*
'74 **Skating Away On The Thin Ice Of A New Day** *Jethro Tull*
'87 **Skeletons** *Stevie Wonder*
'59 **Ski King** *E.C. Beatty*
'66 **Skid Row Joe** *Porter Wagoner*
'05 **Skin (Sarabeth)** *Hascal Flatts*
'74 **Skin Tight** *Ohio Players*
'87 **Skin Trade** *Duran Duran*
'67 **Skinny Legs And All** *Joe Tex*
'58 **Skinny Minnie** *Bill Haley*
'67 **Skip A Rope** *Henson Cargill*
'75 **Sky High** *Jigsaw*
'91 **Sky Is Crying** *Stevie Ray Vaughan*
'68 **Sky Pilot** *Animals*
'93 **Slam** *Onyx*
'64 **Slaughter On Tenth Avenue** *Ventures*
'85 **Slave To Love** *Bryan Ferry*
'86 **Sledgehammer** *Peter Gabriel*
'60 **Sleep** *Little Willie John*
'59 **Sleep Walk** *Santo & Johnny*
'85 **Sleeping Bag** *ZZ Top*
'93 **Sleeping Satellite** *Tasmin Archer*
'78 **Sleeping Single In A Double Bed** *Barbara Mandrell*
'77 **Sleepwalker** *Kinks*
Slide
'77 *Slave*
'98 *Goo Goo Dolls*
'68 **Slip Away** *Clarence Carter*
'77 **Slip Slidin' Away** *Paul Simon*

'75 **Slippery When Wet** *Commodores*
'56 **Slippin' And Slidin'** *Little Richard*
'72 **Slippin' Into Darkness** *War*
'83 **Slipping Away** *Dave Edmunds*
'04 **Slither** *Velvet Revolver*
'66 **Sloop John B** *Beach Boys*
'92 **Slow And Sexy**
      Shabba Ranks feat. Johnny Gill
'92 **Slow Dance (Hey Mr. DJ)** *R. Kelly*
'77 **Slow Dancin' Don't Turn Me On**
      Addrisi Bros.
'77 **Slow Dancin' (Swayin' To The**
      Music) *Johnny Rivers*
   Slow Down
'64   *Beatles*
'86   *Loose Ends*
'05   *Bobby Valentino*
   Slow Hand
'81   *Pointer Sisters*
'82   *Conway Twitty*
'03 **Slow Jamz** *Twista*
   Slow Motion
'90   *Gerald Alston*
'92   *Color Me Badd*
'04   *Juvenile*
'75 **Slow Ride** *Foghat*
'62 **Slow Twistin'** *Chubby Checker*
      (w/ Dee Dee Sharp)
   Slow Walk
'56   *Sil Austin*
'56   *Bill Doggett*
'77 **Slowdown** *John Miles*
'70 **Sly, Slick, And The Wicked**
      Lost Generation
'06 **Smack That** *Akon*
'72 **Small Beginnings** *Flash*
'61 **Small Sad Sam** *Phil McLean*
'85 **Small Town**
      John Cougar Mellencamp
'91 **Small Town Saturday Night**
      Hal Ketchum
   Small World
'59   *Johnny Mathis*
'88   *Huey Lewis*
'85 **Smalltown Boys** *Bronski Beat*
'95 **Smashing Young Man**
      Collective Soul
'92 **Smells Like Nirvana**
      "Weird Al" Yankovic
'91 **Smells Like Teen Spirit** *Nirvana*
   Smile
'59   *Tony Bennett*
'97   *Scarface*
'99   *Vitamin C w/ Lady Saw*
'99   *Lonestar*
'69 **Smile A Little Smile For Me**
      Flying Machine
'83 **Smile Has Left Your Eyes** *Asia*
'71 **Smiling Faces Sometimes**
      Undisputed Truth
'83 **Smiling Islands** *Robbie Patton*
'77 **Smoke From A Distant Fire**
      Sanford/Townsend Band
   Smoke Gets In Your Eyes
'58   *Platters*
'72   *Blue Haze*
'73 **Smoke On The Water** *Deep Purple*
   Smoke Stack Lightnin'
'56   *Howlin' Wolf*
'91   *Lynyrd Skynyrd*
'55 **Smokey Joe's Cafe** *Robins*
'59 **Smokie** *Bill Black's Combo*
'76 **Smokin'** *Boston*
   Smokin' In The Boy's Room
'73   *Brownsville Station*
'85   *Mötley Crüe*
'97 **Smokin' Me Out** *Warren G*
'86 **Smoking Gun** *Robert Cray Band*
'80 **Smoky Mountain Rain**
      Ronnie Milsap
'61 **Smoky Places** *Corsairs*
'99 **Smooth** *Santana Feat. Rob Thomas*
   Smooth Criminal
'88   *Michael Jackson*
'01   *Alien Ant Farm*

   Smooth Operator
'59   *Sarah Vaughan*
'85   *Sade*
'85 **Smuggler's Blues** *Glenn Frey*
'03 **Snake** *R. Kelly*
'68 **Snake, The** *Al Wilson*
'06 **Snap Yo Fingers** *Lil Jon*
'62 **Snap Your Fingers** *Joe Henderson*
'69 **Snatching It Back** *Clarence Carter*
'66 **Snoopy Vs. The Red Baron**
      Royal Guardsmen
'67 **Snoopy's Christmas**
      Royal Guardsmen
'07 **Snow ((Hey Oh))**
      Red Hot Chili Peppers
'70 **Snowbird** *Anne Murray*
'89 **So Alive** *Love & Rockets*
'93 **So Alone** *Men At Large*
'99 **So Anxious** *Ginuwine*
'83 **So Bad** *Paul McCartney*
   So Close
'59   *Brook Benton*
'90   *Daryl Hall/John Oates*
'04 **So Cold** *Breaking Benjamin*
'62 **So Deep** *Brenda Lee*
'87 **So Emotional** *Whitney Houston*
   So Far Away
'71   *Carole King*
'86   *Dire Straits*
'96   *Rod Stewart*
'03   *Staind*
'59 **So Fine** *Fiestas*
'01 **So Fresh, So Clean** *OutKast*
'03 **So Gone** *Monica*
'88 **So Good** *Al Jarreau*
'79 **So Good, So Right** *Brenda Russell*
'69 **So Good Together** *Andy Kim*
'95 **So Help Me Girl** *Joe Diffie*
'77 **So High (Rock Me Baby And Roll**
      Me Away) *Dave Mason*
'69 **So I Can Love You** *Emotions*
'85 **So In Love** *Orchestral*
      Manoeuvres In The Dark
'00 **So In Love With Two** *Mikaila*
'77 **So In To You**
      Atlanta Rhythm Section
'98 **So Into You** *Tamia*
'61 **So Long Baby** *Del Shannon*
'06 **So Long Self** *MercyMe*
'78 **So Many Paths** *Little River Band*
'59 **So Many Ways** *Brook Benton*
'96 **So Much For Pretending**
      Bryan White
   So Much In Love
'63   *Tymes*
'94   *All-4-One*
'91 **So Much Love** *B Angie B*
'96 **So Much To Say**
      Dave Matthews Band
'57 **So Rare** *Jimmy Dorsey*
'76 **So Sad The Song** *Gladys Knight*
'60 **So Sad (To Watch Good Love Go**
      Bad) *Everly Brothers*
'04 **So Sexy** *Twista w/ R. Kelly*
'06 **So Sick** *Ne-Yo*
'07 **So Small** *Carrie Underwood*
'62 **So This Is Love** *Castells*
'73 **So Very Hard To Go**
      Tower Of Power
'06 **So What** *Field Mob*
'83 **So Wrong** *Patrick Simmons*
'03 **So Yesterday** *Hilary Duff*
'74 **So You Are A Star** *Hudson Brothers*
'90 **So You Like What You See**
      Samuelle
'91 **So You Think You're In Love**
      Robyn Hitchcock/Egyptians
'67 **So You Want To Be A Rock 'N' Roll**
      Star *Byrds*
'77 **So You Win Again** *Hot Chocolate*
'02 **Soak Up The Sun** *Sheryl Crow*
'67 **Society's Child (Baby I've Been**
      Thinking) *Janis Ian*
'97 **Sock It 2 Me**
      Missy "Misdemeanor" Elliott
'67 **Sock It To Me-Baby!** *Mitch Ryder*

'57 **Soft** *Bill Doggett*
   Soft Summer Breeze
'56   *Diamonds*
'56   *Eddie Heywood*
'64 **Softly, As I Leave You** *Frank Sinatra*
'55 **Softly, Softly** *Jaye P. Morgan*
'72 **Softly Whispering I Love You**
      English Congregation
'89 **Sold Me Down The River** *Alarm*
'95 **Sold (The Grundy County Auction**
      Incident)
      John Michael Montgomery
'05 **Soldier** *Destiny's Child*
'62 **Soldier Boy** *Shirelles*
'89 **Soldier Of Love** *Donny Osmond*
'84 **Solid** *Ashford & Simpson*
   Solitaire
'74   *Neil Sedaka*
'75   *Carpenters*
'83   *Laura Branigan*
'04   *Clay Aiken*
'66 **Solitary Man** *Neil Diamond*
'77 **Solsbury Hill** *Peter Gabriel*
'04 **Some Beach** *Blake Shelton*
'05 **Some Cut** *Trillville*
'64 **Some Day We're Gonna Love Again**
      Searchers
'81 **Some Days Are Diamonds (Some**
      Days Are Stone) *John Denver*
'65 **Some Enchanted Evening**
      Jay & The Americans
'92 **Some Girls Do** *Sawyer Brown*
   Some Guys Have All The Luck
'73   *Persuaders*
'84   *Rod Stewart*
'59 **Some Kind-A Earthquake**
      Duane Eddy
'83 **Some Kind Of Friend** *Barry Manilow*
'88 **Some Kind Of Lover** *Jody Watley*
   Some Kind Of Wonderful
'61   *Drifters*
'74   *Grand Funk*
'85 **Some Like It Hot** *Power Station*
'85 **Some Things Are Better Left**
      Unsaid *Daryl Hall/John Oates*
'68 **Some Things You Never Get Used**
      To *Supremes*
'68 **Some Velvet Morning**
      Nancy Sinatra & Lee Hazlewood
   Somebody
'85   *Bryan Adams*
'04   *Reba McEntire*
'84 **Somebody Else's Guy**
      Jocelyn Brown
'62 **Somebody Have Mercy** *Sam Cooke*
'66 **Somebody Like Me** *Eddy Arnold*
'02 **Somebody Like You** *Keith Urban*
'91 **Somebody Loves You Baby (You**
      Know Who It Is) *Patti LaBelle*
   Somebody To Love
'67   *Jefferson Airplane*
'76   *Queen*
'93   *George Michael & Queen [live]*
'92 **Somebody To Know** *Soul Asylum*
'04 **Somebody Told Me** *Killers*
'58 **Somebody Touched Me**
      Buddy Knox
'56 **Somebody Up There Likes Me**
      Perry Como
'82 **Somebody's Baby** *Jackson Browne*
'70 **Somebody's Been Sleeping**
      100 Proof Aged in Soul
'95 **Somebody's Crying** *Chris Isaak*
'76 **Somebody's Gettin' It**
      Johnnie Taylor
'81 **Somebody's Knockin'** *Terri Gibbs*
'86 **Somebody's Out There** *Triumph*
'84 **Somebody's Watching Me** *Rockwell*
'70 **Somebody's Watching You**
      Little Sister

Someday
'86 *Glass Tiger*
'91 *Alan Jackson*
'91 *Mariah Carey*
'96 *All-4-One*
'99 *Sugar Ray*
'03 *Nickelback*
'72 **Someday Never Comes**
     Creedence Clearwater Revival
'82 **Someday, Someway**
     Marshall Crenshaw
'69 **Someday We'll Be Together**
     Supremes
Someone
'59 *Johnny Mathis*
'97 *SWV*
'81 **Someone Could Lose A Heart**
     Tonight *Eddie Rabbitt*
'96 **Someone Else's Dream** *Faith Hill*
'95 **Someone Else's Star** *Bryan White*
'75 **Someone Saved My Life Tonight**
     Elton John
'80 **Someone That I Used To Love**
     Natalie Cole
'01 **Someone To Call My Lover**
     Janet Jackson
'92 **Someone To Hold** *Trey Lorenz*
'95 **Someone To Love** *Jon B.*
'55 **Someone You Love** *Nat "King" Cole*
'77 **Somethin' 'Bout 'Cha** *Latimore*
'59 **Somethin Else** *Eddie Cochran*
'95 **Somethin' 4 Da Honeyz**
     Montell Jordan
'67 **Somethin' Stupid**
     Nancy Sinatra & Frank Sinatra
Something
'69 *Beatles*
'02 *Lasgo*
'97 **Something About The Way You**
     Look Tonight *Elton John*
Something About You
'65 *Four Tops*
'76 *Boston*
'86 *Level 42*
'75 **Something Better To Do**
     Olivia Newton-John
'91 **Something Got Me Started**
     Simply Red
'60 **Something Happened** *Paul Anka*
'90 **Something Happened On The Way**
     To Heaven *Phil Collins*
'92 **Something He Can Feel** *En Vogue*
'93 **Something In Common** *Bobby*
     Brown w/ Whitney Houston
'91 **Something In My Heart** *Michel'le*
'69 **Something In The Air**
     Thunderclap Newman
'89 **Something In The Way (You Make**
     Me Feel) *Stephanie Mills*
'93 **Something In Your Eyes**
     Bell Biv DeVoe
'88 **Something Just Ain't Right**
     Keith Sweat
'99 **Something Like That** *Tim McGraw*
'05 **Something More** *Sugarland*
'87 **Something Real (Inside Me/Inside**
     You) *Mr. Mister*
'87 **Something So Strong**
     Crowded House
'97 **Something That We Do** *Clint Black*
'05 **Something To Be Proud Of**
     Montgomery Gentry
'90 **Something To Believe In** *Poison*
'86 **Something To Grab For** *Ric Ocasek*
'91 **Something To Talk About**
     Bonnie Raitt
'94 **Something's Always Wrong**
     Toad The Wet Sprocket
'70 **Something's Burning**
     Kenny Rogers & The First Edition
'93 **Something's Goin' On** *U.N.V.*
'62 **Something's Got A Hold On Me**
     Etta James
Something's Gotta Give
'55 *Sammy Davis, Jr.*
'55 *McGuire Sisters*
'06 *LeAnn Rimes*

'72 **Something's Wrong With Me**
     Austin Roberts
Sometimes
'75 *Bill Anderson & Mary Lou Turner*
'77 *Facts Of Life*
'99 *Britney Spears*
'80 **Sometimes A Fantasy** *Billy Joel*
'92 **Sometimes By Step** *Rich Mullins*
'92 **Sometimes Love Just Ain't Enough**
     Patty Smyth w/ Don Henley
'90 **Sometimes She Cries** *Warrant*
'77 **Sometimes When We Touch**
     Dan Hill
'05 **Sometimes You Can't Make It On**
     Your Own *U2*
Somewhere
'63 *Tymes*
'64 *Len Barry*
'85 *Barbra Streisand*
'81 **Somewhere Down The Road**
     Barry Manilow
'03 **Somewhere I Belong** *Linkin Park*
'91 **Somewhere In My Broken Heart**
     Billy Dean
Somewhere In The Night
'75 *Helen Reddy*
'78 *Barry Manilow*
'64 **Somewhere In Your Heart**
     Frank Sinatra
'66 **Somewhere, My Love** *Ray Conniff*
'05 **Somewhere Only We Know** *Keane*
'92 **Somewhere Other Than The Night**
     Garth Brooks
Somewhere Out There
'86 *Linda Ronstadt & James Ingram*
'02 *Our Lady Peace*
'06 **Somewhere Over The Rainbow**
     Katharine McPhee
'66 **Somewhere There's A Someone**
     Dean Martin
'01 **Son Of A Gun (I Betcha Think This**
     Song Is About You)
     Janet Jackson
'68 **Son Of A Preacher Man**
     Dusty Springfield
'78 **Son Of A Son Of A Sailor**
     Jimmy Buffett
'68 **Son Of Hickory Holler's Tramp**
     O.C. Smith
'72 **Son Of My Father** *Giorgio Moroder*
'74 **Son Of Sagittarius** *Eddie Kendricks*
'56 **Song For A Summer Night**
     Mitch Miller
'97 **Song For Mama** *Boyz II Men*
'70 **Song From M*A*S*H** *Al DeLory*
'70 **Song Of Joy** *Miguel Rios*
     (Song Of Love) ..see: Chanson
     D'Amour
'55 **Song Of The Dreamer** *Eddie Fisher*
'79 **Song On The Radio** *Al Stewart*
'89 **Song Of The South** *Alabama*
'73 **Song Remains The Same**
     Led Zeppelin
'93 **Song Remembers When**
     Trisha Yearwood
'72 **Song Sung Blue** *Neil Diamond*
'97 **Song 2** *Blur*
Songbird
'78 *Barbra Streisand*
'87 *Kenny G*
'70 **Soolaimón (African Trilogy II)**
     Neil Diamond
'93 **Soon** *Tanya Tucker*
'95 **Soon As I Get Home** *Faith Evans*
Sooner Or Later
'71 *Grass Roots*
'75 *Impressions*
'05 *Breaking Benjamin*
'61 **Soothe Me** *Sims Twins*
'69 **Sophisticated Cissy** *Meters*
'76 **Sophisticated Lady (She's A**
     Different Lady) *Natalie Cole*
'07 **Sorry, Blame It On Me** *Akon*
'59 **Sorry (I Ran All The Way Home)**
     Impalas
'76 **Sorry Seems To Be The Hardest**
     Word *Elton John*

'04 **Sorry 2004** *Ruben Studdard*
'87 **Soul City** *Partland Brothers*
'69 **Soul Deep** *Box Tops*
'67 **Soul Finger** *Bar-Kays*
'85 **Soul Kiss** *Olivia Newton-John*
'68 **Soul-Limbo** *Booker T. & The M.G.'s*
'73 **Soul Makossa** *Manu Dibango*
Soul Man
'67 *Sam & Dave*
'78 *Blues Brothers*
'06 **Soul Meets Body**
     Death Cab For Cutie
'71 **Soul Power** *James Brown*
'89 **Soul Provider** *Michael Bolton*
'68 **Soul Serenade** *Willie Mitchell*
'70 **Soul Shake** *Delaney & Bonnie*
'73 **Soul Song** *Joe Stampley*
'05 **Soul Survivor** *Young Jeezy w/ Akon*
'93 **Soul To Squeeze**
     Red Hot Chili Peppers
'62 **Soul Twist** *King Curtis*
'68 **Soulful Strut** *Young-Holt Unlimited*
'83 **Souls** *Rick Springfield*
'69 **Soulshake**
     Peggy Scott & Jo Jo Benson
'67 **Sound Of Love** *Five Americans*
'65 **Sound Of Music** *Julie Andrews*
'65 **Sound Of Silence**
     Simon & Garfunkel
'91 **Sound Of Your Voice** *38 Special*
'00 **Sour Girl** *Stone Temple Pilots*
'73 **South City Midnight Lady** *Doobie*
     Brothers
'00 **South Side** *Moby*
'63 **South Street** *Orlons*
'75 **South's Gonna Do It**
     Charlie Daniels Band
'82 **Southern Cross**
     Crosby, Stills & Nash
'01 **Southern Hospitality** *Ludacris*
'70 **Southern Man** *Neil Young*
'77 **Southern Nights** *Glen Campbell*
'04 **Southside** *Lloyd*
'64 **Southtown, U.S.A.** *Dixiebelles*
'89 **Sowing The Seeds Of Love**
     Tears For Fears
'82 **Space Age Love Song**
     Flock Of Seagulls
'01 **Space Between**
     Dave Matthews Band
'73 **Space Cowboy**
     Steve Miller Band
'96 **Space Jam** *Quad City DJ's*
'98 **Space Lord** *Monster Magnet*
'73 **Space Oddity** *David Bowie*
'73 **Space Race** *Billy Preston*
'72 **Space Truckin'** *Deep Purple*
'72 **Spaceman** *Nilsson*
'68 **Spanish Castle Magic** *Jimi Hendrix*
'85 **Spanish Eddie** *Laura Branigan*
'65 **Spanish Eyes** *Al Martino*
'66 **Spanish Flea** *Herb Alpert*
Spanish Harlem
'60 *Ben E. King*
'71 *Aretha Franklin*
'62 **Spanish Lace** *Gene McDaniels*
'98 **Spark** *Tori Amos*
'06 **Speak** *Godsmack*
'73 **Speak To Me [medley]**
     Pink Floyd
'72 **Speak To The Sky** *Rick Springfield*
'80 **Special Lady**
     Ray, Goodman, & Brown
'68 **Special Occasion** *Miracles*
'99 **Speechless** *Steven Curtis Chapman*
'05 **Speed Of Sound** *Coldplay*
'55 **Speedoo** *Cadillacs*
'62 **Speedy Gonzales** *Pat Boone*
'90 **Spend My Life** *Slaughter*
'99 **Spend My Life With You** *Eric Benét*
'91 **Spending My Time** *Roxette*
'83 **Spice Of Life** *Manhattan Transfer*
'97 **Spice Up Your Life** *Spice Girls*
'73 **Spiders & Snakes** *Jim Stafford*
'96 **Spiderwebs** *No Doubt*
'85 **Spies Like Us** *Paul McCartney*

250

'70 **Spill The Wine** *Eric Burdon & War*
'94 **Spin The Black Circle** *Pearl Jam*
'69 **Spinning Wheel**
    Blood, Sweat & Tears
'66 **Spinout** *Elvis Presley*
'70 **Spirit In The Dark** *Aretha Franklin*
    Spirit In The Night
'73   *Bruce Springsteen*
'77   *Manfred Mann*
'70 **Spirit In The Sky**
    Norman Greenbaum
'98 **Spirit Of A Boy - Wisdom Of A Man**
    Randy Travis
'80 **Spirit Of Radio** *Rush*
'75 **Spirit Of The Boogie**
    Kool & The Gang
'82 **Spirits In The Material World** *Police*
'98 **Splackavellie** *Pressha*
'04 **Splash Waterfalls** *Ludacris*
'58 **Splish Splash** *Bobby Darin*
'86 **Split Decision** *Steve Winwood*
    Spooky
'67   *Classics IV*
'79   *Atlanta Rhythm Section*
    Spoonful
'60   *Howlin' Wolf*
'68   *Cream*
'65 **Spoonful Of Sugar** *Julie Andrews*
'94 **Spoonman** *Soundgarden*
'88 **Spotlight** *Madonna*
'90 **Spread My Wings** *Troop*
'76 **Springtime Mama** *Henry Gross*
'88 **Spy In The House Of Love**
    Was (Not Was)
'81 **Square Biz** *Teena Marie*
'75 **Squeeze Box** *Who*
'85 **St. Elmo's Fire (Man In Motion)**
    John Parr
'69 **St. Stephen** *Grateful Dead*
'56 **St. Therese Of The Roses**
    Billy Ward
'03 **Stacy's Mom** *Fountains Of Wayne*
'86 **Stages** *ZZ Top*
    Stagger Lee
'58   *Lloyd Price*
'67   *Wilson Pickett*
'71   *Tommy Roe*
    Stairway To Heaven
'60   *Neil Sedaka*
'71   *Led Zeppelin*
'00 **Stan** *Eminem*
    Stand
'69   *Sly & The Family Stone*
'88   *R.E.M.*
'07   *Rascal Flatts*
'83 **Stand Back** *Stevie Nicks*
'98 **Stand Beside Me** *Jo Dee Messina*
    Stand By Me
'61   *Ben E. King*
'66   *Spyder Turner*
'75   *John Lennon*
'80   *Mickey Gilley*
    Stand By Your Man
'68   *Tammy Wynette*
'70   *Candi Staton*
'00 **Stand Inside Your Love**
    Smashing Pumpkins
'76 **Stand Tall** *Burton Cummings*
    Stand Up
'03   *Ludacris*
'05   *Trapt*
'92 **Stand Up (Kick Love Into Motion)**
    Def Leppard
'74 **Standing At The End Of The Line**
    Lobo
'66 **Standing In The Shadows Of Love**
    Four Tops
'87 **Standing On Higher Ground**
    Alan Parsons Project
    Standing On The Corner
'56   *Four Lads*
'56   *Dean Martin*
'95 **Standing On The Edge Of Goodbye**
    John Berry

'96 **Standing Outside A Broken Phone Booth With Money In My Hand**
    Primitive Radio Gods
'93 **Standing Outside The Fire**
    Garth Brooks
'01 **Standing Still** *Jewel*
'74 **Star** *Stealers Wheel*
'74 **Star Baby** *Guess Who*
    Star Spangled Banner
'69   *Jimi Hendrix [live]*
'91   *Whitney Houston*
    Star Wars Theme
'77   *Meco*
'77   *John Williams*
'60 **Starbright** *Johnny Mathis*
    Stardust
'57   *Billy Ward*
'57   *Nat "King" Cole*
'64   *Nino Tempo & April Stevens*
'07 **Starlight** *Muse*
'72 **Starman** *David Bowie*
'97 **Staring At The Sun** *U2*
'06 **Stars Are Blind** *Paris Hilton*
'96 **Stars Over Texas** *Tracy Lawrence*
'71 **Starship Trooper** *Yes*
'81 **Start Me Up** *Rolling Stones*
'57 **Start Movin' (In My Direction)**
    Sal Mineo
'89 **Start Of A Romance** *Skyy*
'06 **Start Of Something New**
    High School Musical Cast
'92 **Start The Car** *Jude Cole*
'01 **Start The Commotion** *Wiseguys*
'72 **Starting All Over Again** *Mel & Tim*
'80 **Starting Over Again** *Dolly Parton*
'82 **State Of Independence**
    Donna Summer
'93 **State Of Mind** *Clint Black*
'84 **State Of Shock** *Jacksons*
'85 **State Of The Heart** *Rick Springfield*
'91 **State Of The World** *Janet Jackson*
'71 **Statesboro Blues**
    Allman Brothers Band
    Stay
'60   *Maurice Williams*
'64   *4 Seasons*
'78   *Jackson Browne [medley]*
'91   *Jodeci*
'92   *Shakespear's Sister*
'94   *Eternal*
'98 **Stay (Awasting Time)**
    Dave Matthews Band
    Stay Awhile
'64   *Dusty Springfield*
'71   *Bells*
'94 **Stay (Faraway, So Close!)** *U2*
'05 **Stay Fly** *Three 6 Mafia*
'03 **Stay Gone** *Jimmy Wayne*
'94 **Stay (I Missed You)** *Lisa Loeb*
'68 **Stay In My Corner** *Dells*
    Stay The Night
'84   *Chicago*
'86   *Benjamin Orr*
'99   *Immature*
'99 **Stay The Same** *Joey McIntyre*
    Stay With Me
'66   *Lorraine Ellison*
'72   *Faces*
    (also see: One More Chance)
'83 **Stay With Me Tonight**
    Jeffrey Osborne
'77 **Stayin' Alive** *Bee Gees*
'61 **Stayin' In** *Bobby Vee*
'88 **Staying Together** *Debbie Gibson*
'81 **Staying With It** *Firefall*
'04 **Stays In Mexico** *Toby Keith*
'06 **Steady, As She Goes** *Raconteurs*
    Steal Away
'64   *Jimmy Hughes*
'70   *Johnnie Taylor*
'80   *Robbie Dupree*
'77 **Steal My Sunshine** *Len*
'81 **Steal The Night** *Stevie Woods*
'73 **Stealin'** *Uriah Heep*
'92 **Steam** *Peter Gabriel*

'73 **Steamroller Blues** *Elvis Presley*
'89 **Steamy Windows** *Tina Turner*
'92 **Steel Bars** *Michael Bolton*
'62 **Steel Guitar And A Glass Of Wine**
    Paul Anka
'62 **Steel Men** *Jimmy Dean*
'96 **Steelo** *702*
'00 **Stellar** *Incubus*
    Step By Step
'60   *Crests*
'73   *Joe Simon*
'81   *Eddie Rabbitt*
'90   *New Kids On The Block*
'97   *Whitney Houston*
'03 **Step In The Name Of Love** *R. Kelly*
'73 **Step Into Christmas**
    Elton John
'67 **Step Out Of Your Mind**
    American Breed
'85 **Step That Step** *Sawyer Brown*
'67 **Step To The Rear** *Marilyn Maye*
'78 **Steppin' In A Slide Zone**
    Moody Blues
    Steppin' Out
'76   *Neil Sedaka*
'82   *Joe Jackson*
'74 **Steppin' Out (Gonna Boogie Tonight)** *Tony Orlando & Dawn*
'93 **Steppin' Out With My Baby**
    Tony Bennett
'73 **Stepping Razor** *Peter Tosh*
'02 **Steve McQueen** *Sheryl Crow*
'63 **Stewball** *Peter, Paul & Mary*
'86 **Stick Around** *Julian Lennon*
'93 **Stick It Out** *Rush*
'61 **Stick Shift** *Duals*
'71 **Stick-Up** *Honey Cone*
'61 **Stick With Me Baby** *Everly Brothers*
'91 **Sticks And Stones** *Tracy Lawrence*
'05 **Stickwitu** *Pussycat Dolls*
'00 **Stiff Upper Lip** *AC/DC*
    Still
'63   *Bill Anderson*
'79   *Commodores*
'98 **Still A G Thang** *Snoop Dogg*
'87 **Still A Thrill** *Jody Watley*
'76 **Still Crazy After All These Years**
    Paul Simon
'02 **Still Fly** *Big Tymers*
'03 **Still Frame** *Trapt*
'87 **Still In Love [medley]** *Boston*
'82 **Still In Saigon** *Charlie Daniels Band*
'98 **Still Not A Player** *Big Punisher*
'81 **Still Right Here In My Heart**
    Pure Prairie League
'76 **Still The One** *Orleans*
'78 **Still The Same** *Bob Seger*
'82 **Still They Ride** *Journey*
'70 **Still Water (Love)** *Four Tops*
'92 **Sting Me** *Black Crowes*
'02 **Stingy** *Ginuwine*
    Stir It Up
'73   *Bob Marley*
'73   *Johnny Nash*
'02 **Stole** *Kelly Rowland*
    Stomp
'80   *Brothers Johnson*
'97   *God's Property*
'78 **Stone Blue** *Foghat*
'82 **Stone Cold** *Rainbow*
'71 **Stone Cold Fever** *Jimi Hendrix*
'91 **Stone Cold Gentleman**
    Ralph Tresvant
'66 **Stone Free** *Jimi Hendrix*
'87 **Stone Love** *Kool & The Gang*
'70 **Stoned Love** *Supremes*
'73 **Stoned Out Of My Mind** *Chi-Lites*
    Stoned Soul Picnic
'68   *5th Dimension*
'68   *Laura Nyro*
'71 **Stones** *Neil Diamond*
'70 **Stoney End** *Barbra Streisand*
'57 **Stood Up** *Ricky Nelson*

Stop!
'90   *Jane's Addiction*
'98   *Spice Girls*
'74 **Stop And Smell The Roses**
      Mac Davis
Stop And Think It Over
'64   *Dale & Grace*
'67   *Perry Como*
'83 **Stop Doggin' Me Around** *Klique*
'81 **Stop Draggin' My Heart Around**
      Stevie Nicks (w/ Tom Petty)
Stop! In The Name Of Love
'65   *Supremes*
'83   *Hollies*
'71 **Stop, Look, Listen (To Your Heart)**
      Stylistics
'66 **Stop Stop Stop** *Hollies*
'62 **Stop The Music** *Shirelles*
'70 **Stop The War Now** *Edwin Starr*
'62 **Stop The Wedding** *Etta James*
'86 **Stop To Love** *Luther Vandross*
'80 **Stop Your Sobbing** *Pretenders*
Stormy
'68   *Classics IV*
'79   *Santana*
'71 **Story In Your Eyes** *Moody Blues*
'57 **Story Of My Life** *Marty Robbins*
Story Of My Love
'59   *Conway Twitty*
'61   *Paul Anka*
Story Untold
'55   *Crew-Cuts*
'55   *Nutmegs*
'67 **Stout-Hearted Men** *Barbra Streisand*
Straight From The Heart
'81   *Allman Brothers Band*
'83   *Bryan Adams*
'68 **Straight Life** *Bobby Goldsboro*
'78 **Straight On** *Heart*
'03 **Straight Out Of Line** *Godsmack*
'74 **Straight Shootin' Woman**
      Steppenwolf
'91 **Straight Tequila Night**
      John Anderson
'88 **Straight Up** *Paula Abdul*
'90 **Stranded** *Heart*
Stranded In The Jungle
'56   *Cadets*
'56   *Gadabouts*
'56   *Jayhawks*
'67 **Strange Brew** *Cream*
'88 **Strange But True** *Times Two*
'67 **Strange Days** *Doors*
'71 **Strange Kind Of Woman**
      Deep Purple
'76 **Strange Magic**
      Electric Light Orchestra
'78 **Strange Way** *Firefall*
'87 **Strangelove** *Depeche Mode*
'77 **Stranger, The** *Billy Joel*
Stranger In My House
'83   *Ronnie Milsap*
'01   *Tamia*
Stranger In Town
'65   *Del Shannon*
'84   *Toto*
Stranger On The Shore
'62   *Mr. Acker Bilk*
'62   *Andy Williams*
'66 **Strangers In The Night**
      Frank Sinatra
'67 **Strawberry Fields Forever** *Beatles*
'77 **Strawberry Letter 23**
      Brothers Johnson
'68 **Strawberry Shortcake**
      Jay & The Techniques
'96 **Strawberry Wine** *Deana Carter*
'82 **Stray Cat Strut** *Stray Cats*
'74 **Streak, The** *Ray Stevens*
'77 **Street Corner Serenade** *Wet Willie*
'96 **Street Dreams** *Nas*
'68 **Street Fighting Man**
      Rolling Stones
'78 **Street Hassle** *Lou Reed*
'79 **Street Life** *Crusaders*

Street Of Dreams
'83   *Rainbow*
'91   *Nia Peeples*
'76 **Street Singin'** *Lady Flash*
'07 **Streetcorner Symphony**
      Rob Thomas
'88 **Streets Of Bakersfield**
      Dwight Yoakam & Buck Owens
'94 **Streets Of Philadelphia**
      Bruce Springsteen
'05 **Stricken** *Disturbed*
'91 **Strike It Up** *Black Box*
String Along
'60   *Fabian*
'63   *Rick Nelson*
'84 **Strip** *Adam Ant*
'62 **Stripper, The** *David Rose*
'81 **Stroke, The** *Billy Squier*
'94 **Stroke You Up** *Changing Faces*
'89 **Strokin'** *Clarence Carter*
'57 **Stroll, The** *Diamonds*
'94 **Strong Enough** *Sheryl Crow*
Stronger
'00   *Britney Spears*
'07   *Kanye West*
'81 **Stronger Than Before**
      Carole Bayer Sager
'84 **Strung Out** *Steve Perry*
'84 **Strut** *Sheena Easton*
'74 **Strutter** *Kiss*
'74 **Struttin'** *Billy Preston*
'62 **Stubborn Kind Of Fellow**
      Marvin Gaye
'01 **Stuck In A Moment You Can't Get**
      Out Of *U2*
'73 **Stuck In The Middle With You**
      Stealers Wheel
'66 **Stuck Inside Of Mobile With The**
      Memphis Blues Again *Bob Dylan*
Stuck On You
'60   *Elvis Presley*
'84   *Lionel Richie*
'86 **Stuck With You** *Huey Lewis*
'78 **Stuff Like That** *Quincy Jones*
'79 **Stumblin' In**
      Suzi Quatro & Chris Norman
'03 **Stunt 101** *G-Unit*
'06 **Stuntin' Like My Daddy**
      Birdman & Lil Wayne
'07 **Stupid Boy** *Keith Urban*
'58 **Stupid Cupid** *Connie Francis*
'96 **Stupid Girl** *Garbage*
'06 **Stupid Girls** *P!nk*
'01 **Stutter** *Joe*
'72 **Suavecito** *Malo*
'93 **Sublime** *Ocean Blue*
'66 **Substitute** *Who*
'65 **Subterranean Homesick Blues**
      Bob Dylan
'64 **Such A Night** *Elvis Presley*
'79 **Such A Woman** *Tycoon*
'65 **(Such An) Easy Question**
      Elvis Presley
Suddenly
'80   *Olivia Newton-John & Cliff Richard*
'85   *Billy Ocean*
'07 **Suddenly I See** *KT Tunstall*
'83 **Suddenly Last Summer** *Motels*
Suddenly There's A Valley
'55   *Gogi Grant*
'55   *Julius LaRosa*
'55   *Jo Stafford*
'04 **Suds In The Bucket** *Sara Evans*
'72 **Suffragette City** *David Bowie*
'03 **Suga Suga** *Baby Bash*
'66 **Sugar And Spice** *Cryan' Shames*
'74 **Sugar Baby Love** *Rubettes*
Sugar Daddy
'71   *Jackson 5*
'89   *Thompson Twins*
'84 **Sugar Don't Bite** *Sam Harris*
'63 **Sugar Dumpling** *Sam Cooke*
'87 **Sugar Free** *Wa Wa Nee*
'05 **Sugar (Gimme Some)** *Trick Daddy*
'95 **Sugar Hill** *AZ*
'64 **Sugar Lips** *Al Hirt*

'70 **Sugar Magnolia** *Grateful Dead*
'58 **Sugar Moon** *Pat Boone*
'69 **Sugar On Sunday** *Clique*
'63 **Sugar Shack** *Jimmy Gilmer/Fireballs*
Sugar, Sugar
'69   *Archies*
'70   *Wilson Pickett*
'66 **Sugar Town** *Nancy Sinatra*
'84 **Sugar Walls** *Sheena Easton*
'05 **Sugar, We're Goin' Down**
      Fall Out Boy
'57 **Sugartime** *McGuire Sisters*
'90 **Suicide Blonde** *INXS*
'69 **Suite: Judy Blue Eyes**
      Crosby, Stills & Nash
'76 **Suite Madame Blue** *Styx*
Sukiyaki
'63   *Kyu Sakamoto*
'81   *Taste Of Honey*
'94   *4 P.M. (For Positive Music)*
'79 **Sultans Of Swing** *Dire Straits*
'76 **Summer** *War*
'92 **Summer Babe** *Pavement*
'72 **Summer Breeze** *Seals & Crofts*
'59 **Summer Dreams** *McGuire Sisters*
'99 **Summer Girls** *LFO*
'66 **Summer In The City** *Lovin' Spoonful*
'07 **Summer Love** *Justin Timberlake*
'75 **Summer Madness** *Kool & The Gang*
Summer Nights
'65   *Marianne Faithfull*
'78   *John Travolta & Olivia Newton-John*
'05   *Lil Rob*
'85 **Summer Of Love** *B-52' s*
'85 **Summer Of '69** *Bryan Adams*
Summer Rain
'67   *Johnny Rivers*
'90   *Belinda Carlisle*
'66 **Summer Samba (So Nice)**
      Walter Wanderley
'71 **Summer Sand** *Dawn*
'60 **Summer Set** *Monty Kelly*
Summer Song
'64   *Chad & Jeremy*
'92   *Joe Satriani*
'61 **Summer Souvenirs** *Karl Hammel Jr.*
'73 **Summer (The First Time)**
      Bobby Goldsboro
'90 **Summer Vacation** *Party*
'66 **Summer Wind** *Frank Sinatra*
'69 **Summer Wine**
      Nancy Sinatra w/ Lee Hazelwood
'95 **Summer's Comin'** *Clint Black*
'60 **Summer's Gone** *Paul Anka*
Summertime
'57   *Sam Cooke*
'66   *Billy Stewart*
'91   *D.J. Jazzy Jeff & The Fresh Prince*
'05   *Kenny Chesney*
Summertime Blues
'58   *Eddie Cochran*
'68   *Blue Cheer*
'70   *Who*
'94   *Alan Jackson*
'58 **Summertime, Summertime** *Jamies*
'66 **Sun Ain't Gonna Shine (Anymore)**
      Walker Bros.
'85 **Sun Always Shines On T.V.** *A-Ha*
'85 **Sun City**
      Artists United Against Apartheid
'78 **Sun Is Shining** *Bob Marley*
'65 **Sunday And Me**
      Jay & The Americans
'83 **Sunday Bloody Sunday** *U2*
'67 **Sunday For Tea** *Peter & Gordon*
'63 **Sunday In New York** *Mel Torme*
'53 **Sunday Kind Of Love** *Harptones*
'68 **Sunday Mornin'** *Spanky & Our Gang*
Sunday Morning
'67   *Velvet Underground*
'05   *Maroon5*
'70 **Sunday Morning Coming Down**
      Johnny Cash
'67 **Sunday Will Never Be The Same**
      Spanky & Our Gang

'74 **Sundown** *Gordon Lightfoot*
'77 **Sunflower** *Glen Campbell*
'84 **Sunglasses At Night** *Corey Hart*
'66 **Sunny** *Bobby Hebb*
'66 **Sunny Afternoon** *Kinks*
'97 **Sunny Came Home** *Shawn Colvin*
'72 **Sunny Days** *Lighthouse*
Sunrise
'76   *Eric Carmen*
'04   *Norah Jones*
'85 **Sunset Grill** *Don Henley*
Sunshine
'71   *Jonathan Edwards*
'75   *O'Jays*
'77   *Enchantment*
'89   *Dino*
'04   *Lil' Flip*
'67 **Sunshine Girl** *Parade*
'65 **Sunshine, Lollipops And Rainbows**
   Lesley Gore
'68 **Sunshine Of Your Love** *Cream*
'74 **Sunshine On My Shoulders**
   John Denver
'66 **Sunshine Superman** *Donovan*
'70 **Super Bad** *James Brown*
'73 **Super Fly Meets Shaft**
   John & Ernest
'81 **Super Freak** *Rick James*
'98 **SuperThug (What What)** *Noreaga*
'86 **Superbowl Shuffle**
   Chicago Bears Shufflin' Crew
'65 **Super-cali-fragil-istic-expi-ali-docious** *Julie Andrews*
'72 **Superfly** *Curtis Mayfield*
Superman
'79   *Herbie Mann*
'03   *Eminem*
'01 **Superman (It's Not Easy)**
   Five For Fighting
'75 **Supernatural Thing** *Ben E. King*
'94 **Supernova** *Liz Phair*
'88 **Supersonic** *J.J. Fad*
Superstar
'70   *Murray Head*
'71   *Carpenters*
'76   *Paul Davis*
'03   *Ruben Studdard*
'71 **Superstar (Remember How You Got Where You Are)** *Temptations*
Superstition
'72   *Stevie Wonder*
'87   *Stevie Ray Vaughan*
'88 **Superstitious** *Europe*
Superwoman
'89   *Karyn White*
'01   *Lil' Mo*
'72 **Superwoman (Where Were You When I Needed You)**
   Stevie Wonder
'74 **Sure As I'm Sittin' Here**
   Three Dog Night
'66 **Sure Gonna Miss Her** *Gary Lewis*
'79 **Sure Know Something** *Kiss*
'92 **Sure Love** *Hal Ketchum*
'62 **Surf Beat** *Dick Dale*
'63 **Surf City** *Jan & Dean*
'63 **Surfer Girl** *Beach Boys*
'62 **Surfer's Stomp** *Mar-Kets*
'63 **Surfin' Bird** *Trashmen*
'63 **Surfin' Hootenanny** *Al Casey*
'62 **Surfin' Safari** *Beach Boys*
Surfin' U.S.A.
'63   *Beach Boys*
'77   *Leif Garrett*
'88 **Surfin' U.S.S.R.** *Ray Stevens*
Surrender
'61   *Elvis Presley*
'71   *Diana Ross*
'78   *Cheap Trick*
'88 **Surrender To Me**
   Ann Wilson & Robin Zander
'07 **Survivalism** *Nine Inch Nails*
'01 **Survivor** *Destiny's Child*
'67 **Susan** *Buckinghams*

Susie Darlin'
'58   *Robin Luke*
'62   *Tommy Roe*
Suspicion
'62   *Elvis Presley*
'64   *Terry Stafford*
'79 **Suspicions** *Eddie Rabbitt*
'69 **Suspicious Minds** *Elvis Presley*
'85 **Sussudio** *Phil Collins*
'86 **Suzanne** *Journey*
'59 **Suzie Baby** *Bobby Vee*
Suzie-Q
'57   *Dale Hawkins*
'68   *Creedence Clearwater Revival*
'96 **Swallowed** *Bush*
'73 **Swamp Witch** *Jim Stafford*
'55 **Swanee** *Jaye P. Morgan*
'57 **Swanee River Rock (Talkin' 'Bout That River)** *Ray Charles*
'60 **Sway** *Bobby Rydell*
'00 **Swear It Again** *Westlife*
'75 **Swearin' To God** *Frankie Valli*
'93 **Sweat (A La La La La Long)**
   Inner Circle
Sweet And Gentle
'55   *Alan Dale*
'55   *Georgia Gibbs*
'71 **Sweet And Innocent** *Donny Osmond*
'81 **Sweet Baby**
   Stanley Clarke/George Duke
'70 **Sweet Baby James** *James Taylor*
'68 **Sweet Blindness** *5th Dimension*
'69 **Sweet Caroline** *Neil Diamond*
'73 **Sweet Charlie Babe** *Jackie Moore*
'69 **Sweet Cherry Wine** *Tommy James*
'88 **Sweet Child O' Mine** *Guns N' Roses*
'71 **Sweet City Woman** *Stampeders*
'68 **Sweet Cream Ladies, Forward March** *Box Tops*
Sweet Dreams
'66   *Tommy McLain*
'81   *Air Supply*
'96   *La Bouche*
'83 **Sweet Dreams (Are Made of This)**
   Eurythmics
'63 **Sweet Dreams (Of You)** *Patsy Cline*
'75 **Sweet Emotion** *Aerosmith*
'07 **Sweet Escape** *Gwen Stefani*
'86 **Sweet Freedom** *Michael McDonald*
'71 **Sweet Hitch-Hiker**
   Creedence Clearwater Revival
'74 **Sweet Home Alabama**
   Lynyrd Skynyrd
Sweet Inspiration
'68   *Sweet Inspirations*
'72   *Barbra Streisand [medley]*
Sweet Jane
'70   *Velvet Underground*
'74   *Lou Reed*
'94   *Cowboy Junkies*
'99 **Sweet Lady** *Tyrese*
'78 **Sweet Life** *Paul Davis*
'58 **Sweet Little Sixteen** *Chuck Berry*
Sweet Love
'75   *Commodores*
'86   *Anita Baker*
'79 **Sweet Lui-Louise** *Ironhorse*
'70 **Sweet Mary** *Wadsworth Mansion*
'75 **Sweet Maxine** *Doobie Brothers*
'78 **Sweet Music Man** *Kenny Rogers*
'59 **Sweet Nothin's** *Brenda Lee*
'92 **Sweet November** *Troop*
'56 **Sweet Old Fashioned Girl**
   Teresa Brewer
'66 **Sweet Pea** *Tommy Roe*
'94 **Sweet Potatoe Pie** *Domino*
'72 **Sweet Seasons** *Carole King*
'80 **Sweet Sensation** *Stephanie Mills*
Sweet Sixteen
'52   *Big Joe Turner*
'60   *B.B. King*
'87   *Billy Idol*
'67 **Sweet Soul Music** *Arthur Conley*
'03 **Sweet Southern Comfort**
   Buddy Jewell

'75 **Sweet Sticky Thing** *Ohio Players*
Sweet Surrender
'72   *Bread*
'74   *John Denver*
'98   *Sarah McLachlan*
'68 **(Sweet Sweet Baby) Since You've Been Gone** *Aretha Franklin*
'66 **Sweet Talkin' Guy** *Chiffons*
'78 **Sweet Talkin' Woman**
   Electric Light Orchestra
Sweet Thing
'76   *Rufus Feat. Chaka Khan*
'93   *Mary J. Blige*
'82 **Sweet Time** *REO Speedwagon*
'73 **Sweet Understanding Love**
   Four Tops
'64 **Sweet William** *Millie Small*
'65 **Sweet Woman Like You** *Joe Tex*
'59 **Sweeter Than You** *Ricky Nelson*
'94 **Sweetest Days** *Vanessa Williams*
'85 **Sweetest Taboo** *Sade*
Sweetest Thing
'97   *Fugees*
'98   *U2*
'81 **Sweetest Thing (I've Ever Known)**
   Juice Newton
'67 **Sweetest Thing This Side Of Heaven** *Chris Bartley*
Sweetheart
'70   *Engelbert Humperdinck*
'81   *Franke & The Knockouts*
'84 **Sweetheart Like You** *Bob Dylan*
'02 **Sweetness** *Jimmy Eat World*
'61 **Sweets For My Sweet** *Drifters*
'84 **Swept Away** *Diana Ross*
'97 **Swing My Way** *K.P. & Envyi*
'89 **Swing The Mood [medley]**
   Jive Bunny & the Mastermixers
'83 **Swingin'** *John Anderson*
'62 **Swingin' Gently** *Earl Grant*
'62 **Swingin' Safari** *Billy Vaughn*
'60 **Swingin' School** *Bobby Rydell*
'58 **Swingin' Shepherd Blues**
   Moe Koffman Quartette
'66 **Swinging Doors** *Merle Haggard*
'63 **Swinging On A Star**
   Big Dee Irwin/Little Eva
'77 **Swingtown** *Steve Miller Band*
'62 **Swiss Maid** *Del Shannon*
'05 **Switch** *Will Smith*
'61 **Switch-A-Roo, The** *Hank Ballard*
'80 **Switchin' To Glide [medley]** *Kings*
'72 **Sylvia's Mother** *Dr. Hook*
'68 **Sympathy For The Devil**
   Rolling Stones
'66 **Symphony For Susan** *Arbors*
'92 **Symphony Of Destruction**
   Megadeth
'88 **Symptoms Of True Love**
   Tracie Spencer
'83 **Synchronicity II** *Police*
'76 **(System Of) Doctor Tarr And Professor Fether**
   Alan Parsons Project
'87 **System Of Survival**
   Earth, Wind & Fire

T

'92 **T.L.C.** *Linear*
'60 **T.L.C. Tender Love And Care**
   Jimmie Rodgers
'76 **T.N.T.** *AC/DC*
'74 **TSOP (The Sound Of Philadelphia)**
   MFSB feat. The Three Degrees
'82 **TV Party** *Black Flag*
'76 **TVC 15** *David Bowie*
'60 **Ta Ta** *Clyde McPhatter*
'82 **Tainted Love** *Soft Cell*
'94 **Take A Bow** *Madonna*
'78 **Take A Chance On Me** *Abba*
'69 **Take A Letter Maria** *R.B. Greaves*
'80 **Take A Little Rhythm** *Ali Thomson*
'59 **Take A Message To Mary**
   Everly Brothers
'99 **Take A Picture** *Filter*

253

'69	Take Care Of Your Homework
	Johnnie Taylor
'61	Take Five *Dave Brubeck Quartet*
'61	Take Good Care Of Her *Adam Wade*
	Take Good Care Of My Baby
'61	*Bobby Vee*
'68	*Bobby Vinton*
'82	Take It Away *Paul McCartney*
	Take It Easy
'72	*Eagles*
'86	*Andy Taylor*
'93	*Travis Tritt*
'81	Take It Easy On Me *Little River Band*
'76	Take It Like A Man
	Bachman-Turner Overdrive
'81	Take It On The Run
	REO Speedwagon
'88	Take It So Hard *Keith Richards*
'75	Take It To The Limit *Eagles*
'97	Take It To The Streets *Rampage*
	Take Me As I Am
'94	*Faith Hill*
'06	*Mary J. Blige*
'65	Take Me Back
	Little Anthony & The Imperials
'82	Take Me Down *Alabama*
'68	Take Me For A Little While
	Vanilla Fudge
	Take Me Home
'79	*Cher*
'86	*Phil Collins*
'71	Take Me Home, Country Roads
	John Denver
'86	Take Me Home Tonight
	Eddie Money
'78	Take Me I'm Yours
	Michael Henderson
'75	Take Me In Your Arms (Rock Me)
	Doobie Brothers
'04	Take Me Out *Franz Ferdinand*
	Take Me There
'98	*BLACstreet & Mya*
'07	*Rascal Flatts*
'83	Take Me To Heart *Quarterflash*
'78	Take Me To The Next Phase
	Isley Brothers
'70	Take Me To The Pilot
	Elton John
	Take Me To The River
'74	*Al Green*
'78	*Talking Heads*
'96	Take Me To Your Leader *Newsboys*
'85	Take Me With U *Prince*
	Take My Breath Away
'86	*Berlin*
'04	*Jessica Simpson*
'81	Take My Heart (You Can Have It If
	You Want It) *Kool & The Gang*
'82	Take Off *Bob & Doug McKenzie*
	w/ Geddy Lee
'85	Take On Me *A-Ha*
'79	Take The Long Way Home
	Supertramp
'76	Take The Money And Run
	Steve Miller
'63	Take These Chains From My Heart
	Ray Charles
'92	Take This Heart *Richard Marx*
'92	Take Time *Chris Walker*
'68	Take Time To Know Her
	Percy Sledge
'01	Take You Out *Luther Vandross*
'92	Take Your Memory With You
	Vince Gill
	Take Your Time (Do It Right)
'80	*S.O.S. Band*
'88	*Pebbles*
'86	Taken In *Mike + The Mechanics*
'97	Takes A Little Time *Amy Grant*
'74	Takin' Care Of Business
	Bachman-Turner Overdrive
'76	Takin' It To The Streets
	Doobie Brothers
'99	Taking Everything *Gerald Levert*
'00	Taking You Home *Don Henley*
'06	Talk *Coldplay*
'04	Talk About Our Love *Brandy*

'63	Talk Back Trembling Lips
	Johnny Tillotson
'87	Talk Dirty To Me *Poison*
'89	Talk It Over *Grayson Hugh*
'04	Talk Shows On Mute *Incubus*
'66	Talk Talk *Music Machine*
'59	Talk That Talk *Jackie Wilson*
	Talk To Me
'59	*Frank Sinatra*
'85	*Stevie Nicks*
'86	*Chico DeBarge*
'90	*Anita Baker*
	Talk To Me, Talk To Me
'58	*Little Willie John*
'63	*Sunny & The Sunglows*
81	Talk To Ya Later *Tubes*
'57	Talkin' To The Blues *Jim Lowe*
'64	Talking About My Baby *Impressions*
	Talking In Your Sleep
'78	*Crystal Gayle*
'83	*Romantics*
'72	Talking Loud And Saying Nothing
	James Brown
	Tall Cool One
'59	*Wailers*
'88	*Robert Plant*
'59	Tall Paul *Annette*
'95	Tall, Tall Trees *Alan Jackson*
'59	Tallahassee Lassie *Freddy Cannon*
'07	Tambourine *Eve*
	Tammy
'57	*Ames Brothers*
'57	*Debbie Reynolds*
'76	Tangerine *Salsoul Orchestra*
'75	Tangled Up In Blue *Bob Dylan*
'68	Tapioca Tundra *Monkees*
'66	Tar And Cement *Verdelle Smith*
'07	Tarantula *Smashing Pumpkins*
'85	Tarzan Boy *Baltimora*
'65	Taste Of Honey *Herb Alpert*
'97	Taste Of India *Aerosmith*
'86	Tasty Love *Freddie Jackson*
'72	Taurus *Dennis Coffey*
'72	Taxi *Harry Chapin*
'66	Taxman *Beatles*
'58	Tchaikovsky: Piano Concerto No. 1
	Van Cliburn
'58	Tea For Two (Cha Cha)
	Tommy Dorsey Orchestra
'07	Teachme *Musiq Soulchild*
	Teach Me Tonight
'55	*DeCastro Sisters*
'55	*Jo Stafford*
'62	*George Maharis*
'70	Teach Your Children
	Crosby, Stills, Nash & Young
'70	Teacher *Jethro Tull*
	Teacher, Teacher
'58	*Johnny Mathis*
'81	*Rockpile*
'84	*38 Special*
'61	Tear, A *Gene McDaniels*
'59	Tear Drop *Santo & Johnny*
'57	Tear Drops *Lee Andrews*
'56	Tear Fell *Teresa Brewer*
'59	Tear The Roof Off The Sucker (Give
	Up The Funk) *Parliament*
'07	Teardrops On My Guitar
	Taylor Swift
'98	Tearin' Up My Heart **NSYNC*
'84	Tears *John Waite*
'64	Tears And Roses *Al Martino*
'92	Tears In Heaven *Eric Clapton*
'70	Tears Of A Clown *Miracles*
'58	Tears On My Pillow
	Little Anthony & The Imperials
'59	Teasable, Pleasable You
	Buddy Knox
'60	Teddy *Connie Francis*
	Teddy Bear
'57	*Elvis Presley*
'76	*Red Sovine*
'73	Teddy Bear Song *Barbara Fairchild*
'57	Teen-Age Crush *Tommy Sands*
'62	Teen Age Idol *Rick Nelson*

	Teen Age Prayer
'55	*Gloria Mann*
'55	*Gale Storm*
'88	Teen Age Riot *Sonic Youth*
'59	Teen Angel *Mark Dinning*
'59	Teen Beat *Sandy Nelson*
'59	Teenager In Love
	Dion & The Belmonts
	Teenage Heaven
'59	*Eddie Cochran*
'63	*Johnny Cymbal*
'57	Teenager's Romance *Ricky Nelson*
'83	Telefone (Long Distance Love
	Affair) *Sheena Easton*
'77	Telephone Line
	Electric Light Orchestra
'77	Telephone Man *Meri Wilson*
'69	Tell All The People *Doors*
'00	Tell Her *Lonestar*
'83	Tell Her About It *Billy Joel*
	Tell Her No
'65	*Zombies*
'83	*Juice Newton*
'73	Tell Her She's Lovely *El Chicano*
	Tell Him
'62	*Exciters*
'67	*Patti Drew*
'63	Tell Him I'm Not Home
	Chuck Jackson
'59	Tell Him No *Travis & Bob*
'70	Tell It All Brother *Kenny Rogers &*
	The First Edition
	Tell It Like It Is
'67	*Aaron Neville*
'80	*Heart*
'87	Tell It To My Heart *Taylor Dayne*
'66	Tell It To The Rain *4 Seasons*
'60	Tell Laura I Love Her *Ray Peterson*
'67	Tell Mama *Etta James*
	Tell Me
'62	*Dick & DeeDee*
'95	*Groove Theory*
'96	*Dru Hill*
'74	Tell Me A Lie *Sami Jo*
'06	Tell Me Baby *Red Hot Chili Peppers*
'84	Tell Me I'm Not Dreamin' (Too Good
	To Be True) *Jermaine Jackson &*
	Michael Jackson
'99	Tell Me It's Real *K-Ci & JoJo*
'90	Tell Me Something
	Indecent Obsession
'74	Tell Me Something Good *Rufus*
'67	Tell Me To My Face *Keith*
'82	Tell Me Tomorrow
	Smokey Robinson
'93	Tell Me What You Dream
	Restless Heart
'91	Tell Me What You Want Me To Do
	Tevin Campbell
'03	Tell Me (What's Goin' On)
	Smilez & Southstar
'95	Tell Me When *Human League*
'06	Tell Me When To Go *E-40*
	Tell Me Why
'61	*Belmonts*
'64	*Bobby Vinton*
'66	*Elvis Presley*
'89	*Exposé*
'64	Tell Me (You're Coming Back)
	Rolling Stones
'62	Telstar *Tornadoes*
'70	Temma Harbour *Mary Hopkin*
'06	Temperature *Sean Paul*
	Temptation
'61	*Everly Brothers*
'91	*Corina*
'70	Temptation Eyes *Grass Roots*
'81	Tempted *Squeeze*
'04	Tempted To Touch *Rupee*
'58	Ten Commandments Of Love
	Harvey & The Moonglows
'63	Ten Little Indians *Beach Boys*
'84	10-9-8 *Face To Face*
'02	Ten Rounds With José Cuervo
	Tracy Byrd

254

'93 **Thousand Miles From Nowhere**
  Dwight Yoakam
'60 **Thousand Stars** *Kathy Young*
'97 **3 AM** *Matchbox 20*
'91 **3 A.M. Eternal** *KLF*
'59 **Three Bells** *Browns*
'61 **Three Hearts In A Tangle**
  Roy Drusky
'77 **Three Little Birds** *Bob Marley*
'67 **Three Little Fishes [medley]**
  Mitch Ryder
Three Little Pigs
'74   *Cheech & Chong*
'93   *Green Jelly*
'60 **Three Nights A Week** *Fats Domino*
'65 **Three O'Clock In The Morning**
  Bert Kaempfert
'74 **Three Ring Circus** *Blue Magic*
'59 **Three Stars**
  Tommy Dee w/ Carol Kay
'60 **Three Steps To Heaven**
  Eddie Cochran
'78 **Three Times A Lady** *Commodores*
'80 **Three Times In Love** *Tommy James*
'64 **Three Window Coupe** *Rip Chords*
'03 **Three Wooden Crosses**
  Randy Travis
'69 **Thrill Is Gone** *B.B. King*
'84 **Thriller** *Michael Jackson*
'07 **Through Glass** *Stone Sour*
'89 **Through The Storm**
  Aretha Franklin & Elton John
'03 **Through The Wire** *Kanye West*
'81 **Through The Years** *Kenny Rogers*
'07 **Throw Some D's** *Rich Boy*
'86 **Throwing It All Away** *Genesis*
'94 **thuggish-ruggish-Bone**
  Bone Thugs-N-Harmony
'02 **Thugz Mansion** *2Pac*
'72 **Thunder And Lightning**
  Chi Coltrane
'77 **Thunder In My Heart** *Leo Sayer*
'77 **Thunder Island** *Jay Ferguson*
'75 **Thunder Road**
  Bruce Springsteen
'91 **Thunder Rolls** *Garth Brooks*
'65 **Thunderball** *Tom Jones*
'90 **Thunderstruck** *AC/DC*
'85 **Thy Word** *Amy Grant*
'90 **Tic-Tac-Toe** *Kyper*
'65 **Ticket To Ride** *Beatles*
'07 **Ticks** *Brad Paisley*
'80 **Tide Is High** *Blondie*
'73 **Tie A Yellow Ribbon Round The Ole
  Oak Tree** *Dawn*
'63 **Tie Me Kangaroo Down, Sport**
  Rolf Harris
'77 **Tie Your Mother Down** *Queen*
'60 **Ties That Bind** *Brook Benton*
'59 **Tiger** *Fabian*
'72 **Tight Rope** *Leon Russell*
'68 **Tighten Up** *Archie Bell*
'70 **Tighter, Tighter** *Alive & Kicking*
'59 **Tijuana Jail** *Kingston Trio*
'65 **Tijuana Taxi** *Herb Alpert*
'96 **Til I Hear It From You** *Gin Blossoms*
'59 **('Til) I Kissed You** *Everly Brothers*
'85 **'Til My Baby Comes Home**
  Luther Vandross
'95 **'Til You Do Me Right** *After 7*
Till
'57   *Roger Williams*
'61   *Angels*
'68   *Vogues*
'62 **Till Death Do Us Part** *Bob Braun*
'88 **Till I Loved You**
  Barbra Streisand & Don Johnson
'63 **Till Then** *Classics*
'59 **Till There Was You** *Anita Bryant*
'94 **Till You Love Me** *Reba McEntire*
'07 **Tim McGraw** *Taylor Swift*
'89 **Timber, I'm Falling In Love**
  Patty Loveless

Time
'66   *Pozo-Seco Singers*
'73   *Pink Floyd*
'81   *Alan Parsons Project*
'95   *Hootie & The Blowfish*
Time After Time
'66   *Chris Montez*
'84   *Cyndi Lauper*
'90   *Timmy -T-*
'98   *Inoj*
'93 **Time And Chance** *Color Me Badd*
'71 **Time And Love** *Barbra Streisand*
'60 **Time And The River** *Nat King Cole*
'88 **Time And Tide** *Basia*
'83 **Time (Clock Of The Heart)**
  Culture Club
'90 **Time For Letting Go** *Jude Cole*
Time For Livin'
'68   *Association*
'74   *Sly & The Family Stone*
'66 **Time For Love** *Tony Bennett*
'79 **Time For Me To Fly**
  REO Speedwagon
'68 **Time Has Come Today**
  Chambers Brothers
'73 **Time In A Bottle** *Jim Croce*
Time Is On My Side
'64   *Rolling Stones*
'64   *Irma Thomas*
'69 **Time Is Tight**
  Booker T. & The M.G.'s
'80 **Time Is Time** *Andy Gibb*
'91 **Time, Love And Tenderness**
  Michael Bolton
'96 **Time Marches On** *Tracy Lawrence*
'69 **Time Of The Season** *Zombies*
'81 **Time Out Of Mind** *Steely Dan*
'78 **Time Passages** *Al Stewart*
'67 **Time, Time** *Ed Ames*
'73 **Time To Get Down** *O'Jays*
'70 **Time To Kill** *Band*
'83 **Time Will Reveal** *DeBarge*
'66 **Time Won't Let Me** *Outsiders*
'75 **Times Of Your Life** *Paul Anka*
'64 **Times They Are A-Changin'**
  Bob Dylan
'71 **Timothy** *Buoys*
'74 **Tin Man** *America*
'55 **Tina Marie** *Perry Como*
'71 **Tiny Dancer** *Elton John*
'68 **Tip-Toe Thru' The Tulips With Me**
  Tiny Tim
'66 **Tippy Toeing** *Harden Trio*
'04 **Tipsy** *J-Kwon*
'72 **Tired Of Being Alone** *Al Green*
'80 **Tired Of Toein' The Line**
  Rocky Burnette
'65 **Tired Of Waiting For You** *Kinks*
'62 **To A Sleeping Beauty** *Jimmy Dean*
'84 **To All The Girls I've Loved Before**
  Julio Iglesias & Willie Nelson
'86 **To Be A Lover** *Billy Idol*
'58 **To Be Loved** *Jackie Wilson*
'96 **To Be Loved By You** *Wynonna*
'91 **To Be With You** *Mr. Big*
To Each His Own
'60   *Platters*
'68   *Frankie Laine*
'75   *Faith Hope & Charity*
'67 **To Give (The Reason I Live)**
  Frankie Valli
**To Know You [Him] Is To Love You
  [Him]**
'58   *Teddy Bears*
'65   *Peter & Gordon*
'69   *Bobby Vinton*
'73   *B.B. King*
To Love Somebody
'67   *Bee Gees*
'92   *Michael Bolton*
'98 **To Love You More** *Celine Dion*
'98 **To Make You Feel My Love**
  Garth Brooks
'87 **To Prove My Love** *Michael Cooper*
'67 **To Sir With Love** *Lulu*

'69 **To Susan On The West Coast
  Waiting** *Donovan*
'57 **To The Aisle** *Five Satins*
'74 **To The Door Of The Sun** *Al Martino*
'56 **To The Ends Of The Earth**
  Nat "King" Cole
'97 **To The Moon And Back**
  Savage Garden
'68 **To Wait For Love** *Herb Alpert*
'02 **To Where You Are** *Josh Groban*
'56 **To You, My Love** *Nick Noble*
'71 **Toast And Marmalade For Tea**
  Tin Tin
Tobacco Road
'64   *Nashville Teens*
'66   *Lou Rawls [live]*
Today
'64   *New Christy Minstrels*
'93   *Smashing Pumpkins*
'63 **(Today I Met) The Boy I'm Gonna
  Marry** *Darlene Love*
'76 **Today's The Day** *America*
Together
'61   *Connie Francis*
'80   *Tierra*
Together Again
'64   *Buck Owens*
'66   *Ray Charles*
'76   *Emmylou Harris*
'97   *Janet Jackson*
Together Forever
'88   *Rick Astley*
'91   *Lisette Melendez*
'72 **Together Let's Find Love**
  5th Dimension
'60 **Togetherness** *Frankie Avalon*
'63 **Tom Cat** *Rooftop Singers*
'58 **Tom Dooley** *Kingston Trio*
'81 **Tom Sawyer** *Rush*
'90 **Tom's Diner**
  D.N.A. Feat. Suzanne Vega
Tomorrow
'67   *Strawberry Alarm Clock*
'92   *Morrissey*
'95   *Silverchair*
'90 **Tomorrow (A Better You, Better Me)**
  Quincy Jones/Tevin Campbell
'86 **Tomorrow Doesn't Matter Tonight**
  Starship
'88 **Tomorrow People** *Ziggy Marley*
Tonight
'61   *Ferrante & Teicher*
'84   *Kool & The Gang*
'90   *New Kids On The Block*
'67 **Tonight Carmen** *Marty Robbins*
'61 **Tonight (Could Be The Night)**
  Velvets
'83 **Tonight, I Celebrate My Love**
  Peabo Bryson/Roberta Flack
'61 **Tonight I Fell In Love** *Tokens*
'06 **Tonight I Wanna Cry** *Keith Urban*
'82 **Tonight I'm Yours (Don't Hurt Me)**
  Rod Stewart
'61 **Tonight My Love, Tonight**
  Paul Anka
'85 **Tonight She Comes** *Cars*
'90 **Tonight, Tonight [Tonite, Tonite]**
'57   *Mello-Kings*
'96   *Smashing Pumpkins*
'87 **Tonight, Tonight, Tonight** *Genesis*
Tonight You Belong To Me
'56   *Patience & Prudence*
'56   *Lennon Sisters*
Tonight's The [Tonite's Tha] Night
'60   *Shirelles*
'65   *Solomon Burke*
'76   *Rod Stewart*
'95 **Tonite's Tha Night** *Kris Kross*
'01 **Too Bad** *Nickelback*
'92 **Too Busy Being In Love**
  Doug Stone
'69 **Too Busy Thinking About My Baby**
  Marvin Gaye
'98 **Too Close** *Next*
'56 **Too Close For Comfort**
  Eydie Gorme

257

'90 **Too Cold At Home** *Mark Chesnutt*
'92 **Too Funky** *George Michael*
'97 **Too Gone, Too Long** *En Vogue*
Too Hot
'80 *Kool & The Gang*
'95 *Coolio*
'77 **Too Hot Ta Trot** *Commodores*
'85 **Too Late For Goodbyes**
 Julian Lennon
'90 **Too Late To Say Goodbye**
 Richard Marx
'72 **Too Late To Turn Back Now**
 Cornelius Brothers & Sister Rose
'91 **2 Legit 2 Quit** *Hammer*
'06 **Too Little Too Late** *JoJo*
Too Many Fish In The Sea
'64 *Marvelettes*
'67 *Mitch Ryder [medley]*
'65 **Too Many Rivers** *Brenda Lee*
'91 **Too Many Walls** *Cathy Dennis*
'92 **Too Many Ways To Fall** *Arc Angels*
Too Much
'57 *Elvis Presley*
'96 *Dave Matthews Band*
'98 *Spice Girls*
'88 **Too Much Ain't Enough Love**
 Jimmy Barnes
'78 **Too Much Heaven** *Bee Gees*
'56 **Too Much Monkey Business**
 Chuck Berry
'67 **Too Much Of Nothing**
 Peter, Paul & Mary
'92 **Too Much Passion** *Smithereens*
'68 **Too Much Talk**
 Paul Revere & The Raiders
'60 **Too Much Tequila** *Champs*
'81 **Too Much Time On My Hands** *Styx*
'78 **Too Much, Too Little, Too Late**
 Johnny Mathis/ Deniece Williams
'76 **Too Old To Rock 'N' Roll: Too
 Young To Die** *Jethro Tull*
'74 **Too Rolling Stoned**
 Robin Trower
'83 **Too Shy** *Kajagoogoo*
'81 **Too Tight** *Con Funk Shun*
'68 **Too Weak To Fight** *Clarence Carter*
'72 **Too Young** *Donny Osmond*
'56 **Too Young To Go Steady**
 Nat "King" Cole
'78 **Took The Last Train** *David Gates*
'94 **Tootsee Roll** *69 Boyz*
'07 **Top Back** *T.I.*
'91 **Top Of The Pops** *Smithereens*
Top Of The World
'73 *Carpenters*
'91 *Van Halen*
'58 **Topsy II** *Cozy Cole*
Torero
'58 *Renato Carosone*
'58 *Julius LaRosa*
Torn
'98 *Creed*
'98 *Natalie Imbruglia*
'06 *LeToya*
'76 **Torn Between Two Lovers**
 Mary MacGregor
'59 **Torquay** *Fireballs*
Torture
'62 *Kris Jensen*
'84 *Jacksons*
'61 **Tossin' And Turnin'** *Bobby Lewis*
Total Eclipse Of The Heart
'83 *Bonnie Tyler*
'95 *Nicki French*
'74 **Touch A Hand, Make A Friend**
 Staple Singers
'80 **Touch And Go** *Cars*
'98 **Touch It** *Monifah*
Touch It
'98 *Monifah*
'06 *Busta Rhymes*
Touch Me
'68 *Doors*
'74 *Fancy*
'91 **Touch Me (All Night Long)**
 Cathy Dennis

'86 **Touch Me (I Want Your Body)**
 Samantha Fox
'73 **Touch Me In The Morning**
 Diana Ross
'96 **Touch Me Tease Me** *Case*
'81 **Touch Me When We're Dancing**
 Carpenters
'87 **Touch Of Grey** *Grateful Dead*
'97 **Touch, Peel And Stand**
 Days Of The New
'06 **Touch The Sky** *Kanye West*
'61 **Touchables In Brooklyn**
 Dickie Goodman
'85 **Tough All Over** *John Cafferty*
'03 **Tough Little Boys** *Gary Allan*
'61 **Tower Of Strength** *Gene McDaniels*
'82 **Town Called Malice** *Jam*
'61 **Town Without Pity** *Gene Pitney*
'04 **Toxic** *Britney Spears*
'02 **Toxicity** *System Of A Down*
'89 **Toy Soldiers** *Martika*
'56 **Tra La La** *Georgia Gibbs*
'63 **Tra La La La Suzy** *Dean & Jean*
Traces
'69 *Classics IV*
'69 *Lettermen [medley]*
Tracks Of My Tears
'65 *Miracles*
'67 *Johnny Rivers*
'75 *Linda Ronstadt*
'69 **Tracy** *Cuff Links*
'60 **Tracy's Theme** *Spencer Ross*
'02 **Trade It All** *Fabolous*
Tragedy
'59 *Thomas Wayne*
'61 *Fleetwoods*
'79 *Bee Gees*
'84 *John Hunter*
'80 **Train In Vain (Stand By Me)** *Clash*
Train Kept A Rollin'
'56 *Rock & Roll Trio*
'65 *Yardbirds*
'74 *Aerosmith*
'60 **Train Of Love** *Annette*
'74 **Train Of Thought** *Cher*
'79 **Train, Train** *Blackfoot*
Trains And Boats And Planes
'66 *Dionne Warwick*
'67 **Tramp** *Otis Redding & Carla Thomas*
'75 **Trampled Under Foot** *Led Zeppelin*
'56 **Transfusion** *Nervous Norvus*
'70 **Transylvania Boogie**
 Frank Zappa
'61 **Transistor Sister** *Freddy Cannon*
'85 **Trapped** *Bruce Springsteen*
'71 **Trapped By A Thing Called Love**
 Denise LaSalle
'05 **Trapped In The Closet** *R. Kelly*
'93 **Trashy Woman**
 Confederate Railroad
'70 **Travelin' Band**
 Creedence Clearwater Revival
Travelin' Man
'61 *Ricky Nelson*
'75 *Bob Seger*
'02 **Travelin' Soldier** *Dixie Chicks*
'56 **Treasure Of Love** *Clyde McPhatter*
'58 **Treasure Of Your Love**
 Eileen Rodgers
Treat Her Like A Lady
'71 *Cornelius Brothers & Sister Rose*
'84 *Temptations*
Treat Her Right
'65 *Roy Head*
'96 *Sawyer Brown*
'57 **Treat Me Nice** *Elvis Presley*
'81 **Treat Me Right** *Pat Benatar*
'94 **Tremor Christ** *Pearl Jam*
'96 **Tres Delinquentes**
 Delinquent Habits
'61 **Triangle** *Janie Grant*
'80 **Trickle Trickle** *Manhattan Transfer*
Tricky
'56 *Gus Jinkins*
'57 *Ralph Marterie*
'98 **Trippin'** *Total*

'96 **Trippin' On A Hole In A Paper Heart**
 Stone Temple Pilots
'72 **Troglodyte (Cave Man)**
 Jimmy Castor Bunch
'61 **Trolley Song** *Judy Garland [live]*
'85 **Trommeltanz (Din Daa Daa)**
 George Kranz
'75 **T-R-O-U-B-L-E** *Elvis Presley*
Trouble
'81 *Lindsey Buckingham*
'88 *Nia Peeples*
'60 **Trouble In Paradise** *Crests*
'72 **Trouble Man** *Marvin Gaye*
'89 **Trouble Me** *10,000 Maniacs*
'70 **Truckin'** *Grateful Dead*
True
'83 *Spandau Ballet*
'04 *Ryan Cabrera*
'86 **True Blue** *Madonna*
'90 **True Blue Love** *Lou Gramm*
True Colors
'86 *Cyndi Lauper*
'98 *Phil Collins*
'87 **True Faith** *New Order*
'69 **True Grit** *Glen Campbell*
True Love
'56 *Bing Crosby & Grace Kelly*
'56 *Jane Powell*
'88 *Glenn Frey*
'63 **True Love Never Runs Smooth**
 Gene Pitney
True Love Ways
'59 *Buddy Holly*
'65 *Peter & Gordon*
'82 **Truly** *Lionel Richie*
'97 **Truly Madly Deeply** *Savage Garden*
'61 **Trust In Me** *Etta James*
'91 **Truth, The** *TAMI Show*
'05 **Truth Is** *Fantasia*
'69 **Try A Little Kindness**
 Glen Campbell
Try A Little Tenderness
'66 *Otis Redding*
'69 *Three Dog Night*
Try Again
'83 *Champaign*
'00 *Aaliyah*
'64 **Try It Baby** *Marvin Gaye*
'69 **Try (Just A Little Bit Harder)**
 Janis Joplin
'58 **Try Me** *James Brown*
'58 **Try The Impossible** *Lee Andrews*
Try To Remember
'65 *Ed Ames*
'65 *Brothers Four*
'75 *Gladys Knight [medley]*
'66 **Try Too Hard** *Dave Clark Five*
'94 **Tryin' To Get Over You** *Vince Gill*
'76 **Tryin' To Get The Feeling Again**
 Barry Manilow
'81 **Tryin' To Live My Life Without You**
 Bob Seger
'77 **Tryin' To Love Two** *William Bell*
'73 **Trying To Hold On To My Woman**
 Lamont Dozier
'70 **Trying To Make A Fool Of Me**
 Delfonics
'81 **Tube Snake Boogie** *ZZ Top*
'97 **Tubthumping** *Chumbawamba*
'74 **Tubular Bells** *Mike Oldfield*
'96 **Tucker's Town**
 Hootie & The Blowfish
'59 **Tucumcari** *Jimmie Rodgers*
'68 **Tuesday Afternoon (Forever
 Afternoon)** *Moody Blues*
'61 **Tuff** *Ace Cannon*
'86 **Tuff Enuff** *Fabulous Thunderbirds*
'82 **Tug Of War** *Paul McCartney*
Tulsa Time
'78 *Don Williams*
'80 *Eric Clapton*
'88 **Tumblin' Down** *Ziggy Marley*
Tumbling Dice
'72 *Rolling Stones*
'78 *Linda Ronstadt*

'58 **Tumbling Tumbleweeds**
   Billy Vaughn
   Tunnel Of Love
'80 *Dire Straits*
'87 *Bruce Springsteen*
'71 **Tupelo Honey** *Van Morrison*
'63 **Turn Around** *Dick & DeeDee*
'68 **Turn Around, Look At Me** *Vogues*
'70 **Turn Back The Hands Of Time**
   Tyrone Davis
'66 **Turn-Down Day** *Cyrkle*
'80 **Turn It On Again** *Genesis*
'06 **Turn It Up** *Chamillionaire*
'98 **Turn It Up [Remix]/Fire It Up**
   Busta Rhymes
   Turn Me Loose
'59 *Fabian*
'81 *Loverboy*
   Turn Me On
'02 *Norah Jones*
'04 *Kevin Lyttle*
'97 **Turn My Head** *Live*
'01 **Turn Off The Light** *Nelly Furtado*
'79 **Turn Off The Lights**
   Teddy Pendergrass
'84 **Turn On The News** *Hüsker Dü*
   Turn On Your Love Light
'61 *Bobby Bland*
'69 *Grateful Dead*
   Turn The Beat Around
'76 *Vicki Sue Robinson*
'94 *Gloria Estefan*
   Turn The Page
'76 *Bob Seger*
'98 *Metallica*
'67 **Turn The World Around**
   Eddy Arnold
'77 **Turn To Stone**
   Electric Light Orchestra
'84 **Turn To You** *Go-Go's*
'65 **Turn! Turn! Turn!** *Byrds*
'84 **Turn Up The Radio** *Autograph*
'81 **Turn Your Love Around**
   George Benson
'89 **Turned Away** *Chuckii Booker*
'80 **Turning Japanese** *Vapors*
'75 **Turning Point** *Tyrone Davis*
'90 **Turtle Power!** *Partners In Kryme*
'58 **Turvy II** *Cozy Cole*
'75 **Tush** *ZZ Top*
'79 **Tusk** *Fleetwood Mac*
   Tutti' Frutti
'56 *Pat Boone*
'56 *Little Richard*
   Tweedlee Dee
'55 *LaVern Baker*
'55 *Georgia Gibbs*
   Twelfth Of Never
'57 *Johnny Mathis*
'73 *Donny Osmond*
'67 **Twelve Thirty (Young Girls Are
   Coming To The Canyon)**
   Mamas & Papas
'69 **Twenty-Five Miles** *Edwin Starr*
'70 **25 Or 6 To 4** *Chicago*
'57 **Twenty Flight Rock** *Eddie Cochran*
'63 **Twenty Four Hours From Tulsa**
   Gene Pitney
   24/7
'89 *Dino*
'99 *Kevon Edmonds*
'63 **Twenty Miles** *Chubby Checker*
'03 **21 Questions** *50 Cent*
'64 **20-75** *Willie Mitchell*
'98 **26¢** *Wilkinsons*
'58 **26 Miles (Santa Catalina)**
   Four Preps
'81 **Twilight** *ELO*
'58 **Twilight Time** *Platters*
'87 **Twilight World** *Swing Out Sister*
   Twilight Zone
'82 *Golden Earring*
'92 *2 Unlimited*
'80 **Twilight Zone/Twilight Tone**
   Manhattan Transfer

'65 **Twine Time**
   Alvin Cash & The Crawlers
'66 **Twinkle Toes** *Roy Orbison*
   Twist, The
'60 *Chubby Checker*
'60 *Hank Ballard*
'88 *Fat Boys/Chubby Checker*
   [Yo, Twist!]
   Twist And Shout
'62 *Isley Brothers*
'64 *Beatles*
'62 **Twist-Her** *Bill Black's Combo*
'63 **Twist It Up** *Chubby Checker*
'83 **Twist Of Fate** *Olivia Newton-John*
'62 **Twist, Twist Senora**
   Gary (U.S.) Bonds
'96 **Twisted** *Keith Sweat*
'05 **Twisted Transistor** *Korn*
'62 **Twistin' Matilda** *Jimmy Soul*
'62 **Twistin' Postman** *Marvelettes*
'62 **Twistin' The Night Away**
   Sam Cooke
'60 **Twistin' U.S.A.** *Danny & The Juniors*
'59 **Twixt Twelve And Twenty**
   Pat Boone
'88 **2 A.M.** *Teddy Pendergrass*
'97 **2 Become 1** *Spice Girls*
'56 **Two Different Worlds** *Don Rondo*
'71 **Two Divided By Love** *Grass Roots*
'78 **Two Doors Down** *Dolly Parton*
'63 **Two Faces Have I** *Lou Christie*
'75 **Two Fine People** *Cat Stevens*
   Two Hearts
'55 *Pat Boone*
'81 *Stephanie Mills/Teddy Pendergrass*
'88 *Phil Collins*
'83 **Two Hearts Beat As One** *U2*
'63 **Two Kinds Of Teardrops**
   Del Shannon
'82 **Two Less Lonely People In The
   World** *Air Supply*
'67 **Two Little Kids** *Peaches & Herb*
'62 **Two Lovers** *Mary Wells*
'88 **Two Occasions** *Deele*
'91 **Two Of A Kind, Workin' On A Full
   House** *Garth Brooks*
'86 **Two Of Hearts** *Stacey Q*
'78 **Two Out Of Three Ain't Bad**
   Meat Loaf
'86 **Two People** *Tina Turner*
'01 **Two People Fell In Love**
   Brad Paisley
'97 **Two Piña Coladas** *Garth Brooks*
'80 **Two Places At The Same Time**
   Ray Parker Jr.
'93 **Two Princes** *Spin Doctors*
'84 **Two Sides Of Love** *Sammy Hagar*
'92 **Two Sparrows In A Hurricane**
   Tanya Tucker
   Two [2] Step
'96 *Dave Matthews Band*
'07 *Unk*
'93 **Two Steps Behind** *Def Leppard*
'99 **Two Teardrops** *Steve Wariner*
'84 **2000 Miles** *Pretenders*
   Two Tickets To Paradise
'63 *Brook Benton*
'78 *Eddie Money*
'89 **Two To Make It Right** *Seduction*
'84 **Two Tribes**
   Frankie Goes To Hollywood
'02 **Two Wrongs** *Wyclef Jean*
'90 **Type** *Living Colour*
'86 **Typical Male** *Tina Turner*
'97 **Tyrone** *Erykah Badu*

U

'05 **U Already Know** *112*
'06 **U And Dat** *E-40*
'90 **U Can't Touch This** *M.C. Hammer*
'02 **U Don't Have To Call** *Usher*
'05 **U Don't Know Me** *T.I.*
'01 **U Got It Bad** *Usher*
'87 **U Got The Look** *Prince*

'99 **U Know What's Up** *Donell Jones*
'04 **U Make Me Wanna** *Jadakiss*
'07 **U + Ur Hand** *P!nk*
'01 **U Remind Me** *Usher*
'94 **U Send Me Swingin'** *Mint Condition*
'04 **U Should've Known Better** *Monica*
'94 **U Will Know**
   BMU (Black Men United)
'68 **U.S. Male** *Elvis Presley*
'01 **Ugly** *Bubba Sparxxx*
'02 **Uh Huh** *B2K*
'59 **Uh! Oh!** *Nutty Squirrels*
'92 **Uhh Ahh** *Boyz II Men*
'64 **Um, Um, Um, Um, Um, Um**
   Major Lance
'07 **Umbrella** *Rihanna*
'90 **Unanswered Prayers** *Garth Brooks*
   Unbelievable
'91 *EMF*
'98 *Diamond Rio*
'89 **Unborn Heart** *Dan Hill*
'96 **Un-Break My Heart** *Toni Braxton*
'05 **Unbreakable** *Alicia Keys*
'02 **Unbroken** *Tim McGraw*
'61 **Unchain My Heart** *Ray Charles*
'81 **Unchained** *Van Halen*
   Unchained Melody
'55 *Les Baxter*
'55 *Roy Hamilton*
'55 *Al Hibbler*
'65 *Righteous Brothers*
'96 *LeAnn Rimes*
'71 **Uncle Albert/Admiral Halsey**
   Paul & Linda McCartney
'70 **Uncle John's Band**
   Grateful Dead
'56 **Uncloudy Day** *Staple Singers*
'00 **Unconditional** *Clay Davidson*
'86 **Under African Skies** *Paul Simon*
'66 **Under My Thumb**
   Rolling Stones
'72 **Under My Wheels** *Alice Cooper*
'81 **Under Pressure**
   Queen & David Bowie
'64 **Under The Boardwalk** *Drifters*
'92 **Under The Bridge**
   Red Hot Chili Peppers
'88 **Under The Milky Way** *Church*
'89 **Under The Sea**
   Little Mermaid Soundtrack
'65 **Under Your Spell Again**
   Johnny Rivers
'77 **Undercover Angel** *Alan O'Day*
'83 **Undercover Of The Night**
   Rolling Stones
'02 **Underneath It All** *No Doubt*
'02 **Underneath Your Clothes** *Shakira*
'64 **Understand Your Man** *Johnny Cash*
   Understanding
'84 *Bob Seger*
'93 *Xscape*
'61 **Underwater** *Frogmen*
'94 **Undone-The Sweather Song**
'69 **Undun** *Guess Who*
'73 **Uneasy Rider** *Charlie Daniels*
'06 **Unfaithful** *Rihanna*
   Unforgettable
'59 *Dinah Washington*
'91 *Natalie Cole w/ Nat "King" Cole*
'91 **Unforgiven, The** *Metallica*
'97 **Unforgiven II** *Metallica*
'68 **Unicorn, The** *Irish Rovers*
'98 **Uninvited** *Alanis Morissette*
'76 **Union Man** *Cate Bros.*
'83 **Union Of The Snake** *Duran Duran*
'80 **United Together** *Aretha Franklin*
'70 **United We Stand**
   Brotherhood Of Man
'93 **U.N.I.T.Y.** *Queen Latifah*
'65 **Universal Soldier** *Donovan*
'68 **Unknown Soldier** *Doors*
'06 **Unpredictable** *Jamie Foxx*
'99 **Unpretty** *TLC*
'90 **Unskinny Bop** *Poison*
'94 **Until I Fall Away** *Gin Blossoms*

'57 **Walkin' After Midnight** *Patsy Cline*
Walkin' Away
'90 *Clint Black*
'95 *Diamond Rio*
Walkin' In The Rain
'64 *Ronettes*
'69 *Jay & The Americans*
'72 **Walkin' In The Rain With The One I Love** *Love Unlimited*
'67 **Walkin' In The Sunshine**
Roger Miller
'63 **Walkin' Miracle** *Essex*
'66 **Walkin' My Cat Named Dog**
Norma Tanega
'97 **Walkin' On The Sun** *Smash Mouth*
'58 **Walkin' With Mr. Lee** *Lee Allen*
'61 **Walkin' With My Angel** *Bobby Vee*
'58 **Walking Along** *Diamonds*
'88 **Walking Away** *Information Society*
'94 **Walking Away A Winner**
Kathy Mattea
'87 **Walking Down Your Street** *Bangles*
'91 **Walking In Memphis** *Marc Cohn*
'93 **Walking In My Shoes**
Depeche Mode
'75 **Walking In Rhythm** *Blackbyrds*
'84 **Walking On A Thin Line** *Huey Lewis*
'92 **Walking On Broken Glass**
Annie Lennox
'85 **Walking On Sunshine**
Katrina & The Waves
'63 **Walking Proud** *Steve Lawrence*
'63 **Walking The Dog** *Rufus Thomas*
'60 **Walking To New Orleans**
Fats Domino
'80 **Walks Like A Lady** *Journey*
'55 **Wallflower, The** *Etta James*
'60 **Waltzing Matilda** *Jimmie Rodgers*
Wanderer, The
'61 *Dion*
'80 *Donna Summer*
'77 **Wang Dang Sweet Poontang**
Ted Nugent
'80 **Wango Tango** *Ted Nugent*
'02 **Wanksta** *50 Cent*
'83 **Wanna Be Startin' Somethin'**
Michael Jackson
'04 **Wanna Get To Know You** *G-Unit*
'97 **Wannabe** *Spice Girls*
'93 **Wannagirl** *Jeremy Jordan*
'71 **Want Ads** *Honey Cone*
'06 **Want To** *Sugarland*
'90 **Wanted** *Alan Jackson*
'87 **Wanted Dead Or Alive** *Bon Jovi*
'55 **Wanting You** *Roger Williams*
War
'70 *Edwin Starr*
'86 *Bruce Springsteen [live]*
'82 **War Is Hell (On The Homefront Too)**
T.G. Sheppard
'71 **War Pigs** *Black Sabbath*
'84 **War Song** *Culture Club*
'66 **Warm And Tender Love**
Percy Sledge
'92 **Warm It Up** *Kris Kross*
'78 **Warm Ride** *Rare Earth*
'62 **Warmed Over Kisses (Left Over Love)** *Brian Hyland*
Warning
'00 *Green Day*
'02 *Incubus*
'95 **Warped** *Red Hot Chili Peppers*
'84 **Warrior, The** *Scandal*
'89 **Was It Nothing At All**
Michael Damian
'63 **Washington Square**
Village Stompers
'81 **Wasn't That A Party** *Irish Rovers*
'07 **Wasted** *Carrie Underwood*
'75 **Wasted Days And Wasted Nights**
Freddy Fender
'82 **Wasted On The Way**
Crosby, Stills & Nash
'77 **Wasted Time** *Eagles*
'05 **Wasteland** *10 Years*
'01 **Wasting My Time** *Default*

'03 **Wat Da Hook Gon Be** *Murphy Lee*
'92 **Watch Me** *Lorrie Morgan*
'97 **Watch Me Do My Thing** *Immature*
'79 **Watch Out For Lucy** *Eric Clapton*
'67 **Watch The Flowers Grow**
4 Seasons
'03 **Watch The Wind Blow By**
Tim McGraw
'70 **Watching Scotty Grow**
Bobby Goldsboro
'77 **Watching The Detectives**
Elvis Costello
'71 **Watching The River Flow**
Bob Dylan
'81 **Watching The Wheels** *John Lennon*
Watching You
'88 *Loose Ends*
'07 *Rodney Atkins*
'61 **Water Boy** *Don Shirley Trio*
'95 **Water Runs Dry** *Boyz II Men*
'95 **Waterfalls** *TLC*
Waterloo
'59 *Stonewall Jackson*
'74 *Abba*
'68 **Waterloo Sunset** *Kinks*
'63 **Watermelon Man**
Mongo Santamaria Band
'61 **Watusi, The** *Vibrations*
'03 **Wave On Wave** *Pat Green*
'78 **Wavelength** *Van Morrison*
'98 **Way, The** *Fastball*
'77 **Way Down** *Elvis Presley*
'59 **Way Down Yonder In New Orleans**
Freddie Cannon
'83 **Way He Makes Me Feel**
Barbra Streisand
'07 **Way I Are** *Timbaland*
'91 **Way I Feel About You** *Karyn White*
'77 **Way I Feel Tonight** *Bay City Rollers*
'07 **Way I Live** *Baby Boy Da Prince*
'59 **Way I Walk** *Jack Scott*
'75 **Way I Want To Touch You**
Captain & Tennille
'86 **Way It Is** *Bruce Hornsby*
'60 **Way Of A Clown** *Teddy Randazzo*
'72 **Way Of Love** *Cher*
'94 **Way She Loves Me** *Richard Marx*
Way We Were
'73 *Barbra Streisand*
'75 *Gladys Knight [medley]*
Way You Do The Things You Do
'64 *Temptations*
'78 *Rita Coolidge*
'85 *Daryl Hall & John Oates/David Ruffin/ Eddie Kendrick [medley]*
'90 *UB40*
'61 **Way You Look Tonight** *Lettermen*
Way You Love Me
'88 *Karyn White*
'00 *Faith Hill*
'87 **Way You Make Me Feel**
Michael Jackson
'03 **Way You Move** *OutKast*
'58 **Ways Of A Woman In Love**
Johnny Cash
'56 **Wayward Wind** *Gogi Grant*
'66 **(We Ain't Got) Nothin' Yet**
Blues Magoos
'88 **We All Sleep Alone** *Cher*
'79 **We Are Family** *Sister Sledge*
'77 **We Are The Champions [medley]**
Queen
'85 **We Are The World** *USA for Africa*
'84 **We Are The Young** *Dan Hartman*
'05 **We Be Burnin'** *Sean Paul*
'98 **We Be Clubbin'** *Ice Cube*
'84 **We Belong** *Pat Benatar*
We Belong Together
'58 *Robert & Johnny*
'05 *Mariah Carey*
'06 *Gavin DeGraw*
'85 **We Built This City** *Starship*
'68 **We Can Fly** *Cowsills*
We Can Work It Out
'65 *Beatles*
'71 *Stevie Wonder*

'99 **We Can't Be Friends**
Deborah Cox w/ R.L.
'89 **We Can't Go Wrong** *Cover Girls*
'76 **We Can't Hide It Anymore**
Larry Santos
'85 **We Close Our Eyes** *Go West*
'86 **We Connect** *Stacey Q*
'00 **We Danced** *Brad Paisley*
'96 **We Danced Anyway** *Deana Carter*
'89 **We Didn't Start The Fire** *Billy Joel*
'86 **We Don't Have To Take Our Clothes Off** *Jermaine Stewart*
'85 **We Don't Need Another Hero (Thunderdome)** *Tina Turner*
'79 **We Don't Talk Anymore**
Cliff Richard
'07 **We Fly High** *Jim Jones*
We Go Together
'56 *Moonglows*
'60 *Jan & Dean*
'92 **We Got A Love Thang**
Ce Ce Peniston
'95 **We Got It** *Immature*
'59 **We Got Love** *Bobby Rydell*
'69 **We Got More Soul**
Dyke & The Blazers
'82 **We Got The Beat** *Go-Go's*
'65 **We Gotta Get Out Of This Place**
Animals
'70 **We Gotta Get You A Woman** *Runt*
'92 **We Hate It When Our Friends Become Successful** *Morrissey*
'77 **We Just Disagree** *Dave Mason*
'99 **We Like To Party!** *Vengaboys*
'80 **We Live For Love** *Pat Benatar*
'64 **We Love You Beatles** *Carefrees*
'75 **We May Never Love Like This Again**
Maureen McGovern
'73 **We May Never Pass This Way (Again)** *Seals & Crofts*
'81 **We Shall Behold Him** *Sandi Patty*
'63 **We Shall Overcome** *Joan Baez*
'07 **We Takin' Over** *DJ Khaled*
'92 **We Tell Ourselves** *Clint Black*
'01 **We Thuggin** *Fat Joe*
'97 **We Trying To Stay Alive**
Wyclef Jean
'83 **We Two** *Little River Band*
'91 **We Want The Funk** *Gerardo*
'97 **We Were In Love** *Toby Keith*
'80 **We Were Meant To Be Lovers**
Photoglo
'77 **We Will Rock You [medley]** *Queen*
'87 **We'll Be Together** *Sting*
'93 **We'll Burn That Bridge**
Brooks & Dunn
'78 **We'll Never Have To Say Goodbye Again**
England Dan & John Ford Coley
'64 **We'll Sing In The Sunshine**
Gale Garnett
'67 **We're A Winner** *Impressions*
'77 **We're All Alone** *Rita Coolidge*
'90 **We're All In The Same Gang**
West Coast Rap All-Stars
'06 **We're All In This Together**
High School Musical Cast
'73 **We're An American Band**
Grand Funk
'74 **We're Getting Careless With Our Love** *Johnnie Taylor*
'02 **We're Going To Be Friends**
White Stripes
'73 **We're Gonna Hold On**
George Jones & Tammy Wynette
'65 **We're Gonna Make It** *Little Milton*
'81 **We're In This Love Together**
Al Jarreau
We're Not Gonna Take It
'69 *Who*
'84 *Twisted Sister*
'97 **We're Not Making Love No More**
Dru Hill
'74 **(We're Not) The Jet Set**
George Jones & Tammy Wynette
'86 **We're Ready** *Boston*
'72 **We've Got To Get It On Again**
Addrisi Brothers

261

'62 **What's So Good About Good-by** *Miracles*
'94 **What's The Frequency, Kenneth?** *R.E.M.*
'64 **What's The Matter With You Baby** *Marvin Gaye & Mary Wells*
'69 **What's The Use Of Breaking Up** *Jerry Butler*
'98 **What's This Life For** *Creed*
'93 **What's Up** *4 Non Blondes*
'93 **What's Up Doc? (Can We Rock?)** *Fu-Schnickens w/ Shaquille O'Neal*
'00 **What's Your Fantasy** *Ludacris*
'73 **What's Your Mama's Name** *Tanya Tucker*
What's Your Name
'62 *Don & Juan*
'77 *Lynyrd Skynyrd*
'98 **Whatcha Gone Do?** *Link*
'77 **Whatcha Gonna Do** *Pablo Cruise*
'71 **Whatcha See Is Whatcha Get** *Dramatics*
'97 **Whatever** *En Vogue*
'74 **Whatever Gets You Thru The Night** *John Lennon*
Whatever Lola Wants (Lola Gets)
'55 *Dinah Shore*
'55 *Sarah Vaughan*
'74 **Whatever You Got, I Want** *Jackson 5*
'99 **Whatever You Say** *Martina McBride*
'91 **Whatever You Want** *Tony! Toni! Toné!*
'04 **Whats Happnin!** *Ying Yang Twins*
'94 **Whatta Man** *Salt 'N' Pepa w/ En Vogue*
'78 **Wheel In The Sky** *Journey*
'66 **Wheel Of Hurt** *Margaret Whiting*
'61 **Wheels** *String-A-Longs*
'96 **Wheelz Of Steel** *OutKast*
'58 **When** *Kalin Twins*
'63 **When A Boy Falls In Love** *Mel Carter*
When A Man Loves A Woman
'66 *Percy Sledge*
'80 *Bette Midler*
'91 *Michael Bolton*
'98 **When A Woman's Fed Up** *R. Kelly*
'82 **When All Is Said And Done** *Abba*
'95 **When Boy Meets Girl** *Terri Clark*
'94 **When Can I See You** *Babyface*
'06 **When Did You Fall (In Love With Me)** *Chris Rice*
'84 **When Doves Cry** *Prince*
'01 **When God-Fearin' Women Get The Blues** *Martina McBride*
'82 **When He Shines** *Sheena Easton*
'90 **When I Call Your Name** *Vince Gill*
When I Close My Eyes
'96 *Kenny Chesney*
'99 *Shanice*
'94 **When I Come Around** *Green Day*
'69 **When I Die** *Motherlode*
When I Fall In Love
'61 *Lettermen*
'68 *Bobby Vinton*
'93 *Celine Dion & Clive Griffin*
'06 **When I Get Where I'm Going** *Brad Paisley w/ Dolly Parton*
'64 **When I Grow Up (To Be A Man)** *Beach Boys*
'92 **When I Look Into Your Eyes** *Firehouse*
'89 **When I Looked At Him** *Exposé*
'77 **When I Need You** *Leo Sayer*
'99 **When I Said I Do** *Clint Black (w/Lisa Hartman Black)*
When I See You [U]
'57 *Fats Domino*
'07 *Fantasia*
'89 **When I See You Smile** *Bad English*
'01 **When I Think About Angels** *Jamie O'Neal*
'04 **When I Think About Cheatin'** *Gretchen Wilson*
'86 **When I Think Of You** *Janet Jackson*
'79 **When I Wanted You** *Barry Manilow*

'67 **When I Was Young** *Animals*
'90 **When I'm Back On My Feet Again** *Michael Bolton*
When I'm Gone
'65 *Brenda Holloway*
'02 *3 Doors Down*
'05 *Eminem*
'67 **When I'm Sixty-Four** *Beatles*
'83 **When I'm With You** *Sheriff*
'88 **When It's Love** *Van Halen*
When I'ts Over
'82 *Loverboy*
'01 *Sugar Ray*
'66 **When Liking Turns To Loving** *Ronnie Dove*
'88 **When Love Comes To Town** *U2 w/ B.B. King*
'94 **When Love Finds You** *Vince Gill*
'56 **When My Blue Moon Turns To Gold Again** *Elvis Presley*
'56 **When My Dreamboat Comes Home** *Fats Domino*
'73 **When My Little Girl Is Smiling** *Drifters*
'93 **When My Ship Comes In** *Clint Black*
'92 **When She Cries** *Restless Heart*
'66 **(When She Needs Good Lovin') She Comes To Me** *Chicago Loop*
'81 **When She Was My Girl** *Four Tops*
'87 **When Smokey Sings** *ABC*
'67 **When Something Is Wrong With My Baby** *Sam & Dave*
'57 **When Sunny Gets Blue** *Johnny Mathis*
'61 **When The Boy In Your Arms (Is The Boy In Your Heart)** *Connie Francis*
'58 **When The Boys Talk About The Girls** *Valerie Carr*
'88 **When The Children Cry** *White Lion*
'85 **When The Going Gets Tough, The Tough Get Going** *Billy Ocean*
'86 **When The Heart Rules The Mind** *GTR*
'02 **When The Last Time** *Clipse*
'71 **When The Levee Breaks** *Led Zeppelin*
When The Lights Go Out
'83 *Naked Eyes*
'98 *Five*
'63 **When The Lovelight Starts Shining Through His Eyes** *Supremes*
'67 **When The Music's Over** *Doors*
'89 **When The Night Comes** *Joe Cocker*
'56 **When The Saints Go Marching In** *Bill Haley*
'67 **When The Snow Is On The Roses** *Ed Ames*
'06 **When The Stars Go Blue** *Tim McGraw*
'04 **When The Sun Goes Down** *Kenny Chesney & Uncle Kracker*
When The White Lilacs Bloom Again
'56 *Billy Vaughn*
'56 *Helmut Zacharias*
'71 **When There's No You** *Engelbert Humperdinck*
'94 **When We Dance** *Sting*
'61 **When We Get Married** *Dreamlovers*
'88 **When We Kiss** *Bardeux*
'87 **When We Was Fab** *George Harrison*
When Will I Be Loved
'60 *Everly Brothers*
'75 *Linda Ronstadt*
'90 **When Will I See You Smile Again?** *Bell Biv DeVoe*
'74 **When Will I See You Again** *Three Degrees*
'98 **When You Believe** *Whitney Houston & Mariah Carey*
'84 **When You Close Your Eyes** *Night Ranger*
'55 **When You Dance** *Turbans*
'70 **When You Dance I Can Really Love** *Neil Young*
'06 **When You Gonna (Give It Up To Me)** *Sean Paul*

'96 **When You Love A Woman** *Journey*
'72 **When You Say Love** *Sonny & Cher*
When You Say Nothing At All
'88 *Keith Whitley*
'95 *Alison Krauss & Union Station*
'05 **When You Tell Me That You Love Me** *American Idol*
When You Walk In The Room
'64 *Searchers*
'94 *Pam Tillis*
'06 **When You Were Young** *Killers*
'60 **When You Wish Upon A Star** *Dion & The Belmonts*
When You're Gone
'96 *Cranberries*
'07 *Avril Lavigne*
'71 **When You're Hot, You're Hot** *Jerry Reed*
'79 **When You're In Love With A Beautiful Woman** *Dr. Hook*
'06 **When You're Mad** *Ne-Yo*
'67 **When You're Young And In Love** *Marvelettes*
'85 **When Your Heart Is Weak** *Cock Robin*
'64 **Whenever He Holds You** *Bobby Goldsboro*
'78 **Whenever I Call You "Friend"** *Kenny Loggins*
'01 **Whenever, Wherever** *Shakira*
'94 **Whenever You Come Around** *Vince Gill*
'59 **Where** *Platters*
Where Are You
'60 *Frankie Avalon*
'62 *Dinah Washington*
'02 **Where Are You Going** *Dave Matthews Band*
Where Are You Now?
'86 *Synch*
'91 *Clint Black*
'93 *Janet Jackson*
Where Did Our Love Go
'64 *Supremes*
'71 *Donnie Elbert*
'71 **Where Did They Go, Lord** *Elvis Presley*
'88 **Where Do Broken Hearts Go** *Whitney Houston*
'86 **Where Do The Children Go** *Hooters*
'89 **Where Do We Go From Here** *Stacy Lattisaw w/ Johnny Gill*
Where Do You Go
'65 *Cher*
'96 *No Mercy*
'90 **Where Does My Heart Beat Now** *Celine Dion*
'97 **Where Have All The Cowboys Gone?** *Paula Cole*
Where Have All The Flowers Gone
'62 *Kingston Trio*
'65 *Johnny Rivers*
'01 **Where I Come From** *Alan Jackson*
'00 **Where I Wanna Be** *Donell Jones*
Where Is The Love
'72 *Roberta Flack & Donny Hathaway*
'03 *Black Eyed Peas*
'96 **Where It's At** *Beck*
'99 **Where My Girls At?** *702*
'59 **Where Or When** *Dion & The Belmonts*
'73 **Where Peaceful Waters Flow** *Gladys Knight*
'01 **Where The Blacktop Ends** *Keith Urban*
'61 **Where The Boys Are** *Connie Francis*
'98 **Where The Green Grass Grows** *Tim McGraw*
'01 **Where The Party At** *Jagged Edge*
'96 **Where The River Flows** *Collective Soul*
'01 **Where The Stars And Stripes And The Eagle Fly** *Aaron Tippin*
'87 **Where The Streets Have No Name** *U2*
'89 **Where Were You** *Jeff Beck*

263

Wild Thing
'66 *Troggs*
'67 *Senator Bobby*
'74 *Fancy*
'88 *Tone Loc*
'62 **Wild Weekend** *Rebels*
'86 **Wild Wild Life** *Talking Heads*
Wild, Wild West
'88 *Escape Club*
'99 *Will Smith*
'90 **Wild Women Do** *Natalie Cole*
Wild World
'71 *Cat Stevens*
'88 *Maxi Priest*
'93 *Mr. Big*
'75 **Wildfire** *Michael Murphey*
'73 **Wildflower** *Skylark*
'91 **Wildside** *Marky Mark & The Funky Bunch*
'63 **Wildwood Days** *Bobby Rydell*
'74 **Wildwood Weed** *Jim Stafford*
'73 **Will It Go Round In Circles**
       Billy Preston
'99 **Will 2K** *Will Smith*
'69 **Will You Be Staying After Sunday**
       Peppermint Rainbow
'93 **Will You Be There** *Michael Jackson*
'93 **Will You Be There (In The Morning)**
       Heart
Will You Love Me Tomorrow
'60 *Shirelles*
'68 *4 Seasons*
'78 *Dave Mason*
'92 **Will You Marry Me?** *Paula Abdul*
'86 **Will You Still Love Me?** *Chicago*
'84 **William, It Was Really Nothing**
       Smiths
Willie And The Hand Jive
'58 *Johnny Otis Show*
'74 *Eric Clapton*
'94 **Willing To Forgive** *Aretha Franklin*
'64 **Willow Weep For Me**
       Chad & Jeremy
'58 **Win Your Love For Me** *Sam Cooke*
'66 **Winchester Cathedral**
       New Vaudeville Band
'89 **Wind Beneath My Wings**
       Bette Midler
'67 **Wind Cries Mary** *Jimi Hendrix*
'83 **Wind Him Up** *Saga*
'57 **Wind In The Willow** *Jo Stafford*
'06 **Wind It Up** *Gwen Stefani*
'91 **Wind Of Change** *Scorpions*
'69 **Windmills Of Your Mind**
       Dusty Springfield
'05 **Window Shopper** *50 Cent*
'06 **Window To My Heart** *Jon Secada*
'67 **Windows Of The World**
       Dionne Warwick
'83 **Winds Of Change** *Jefferson Starship*
Windy
'67 *Association*
'67 *Wes Montgomery*
'60 **Wings Of A Dove** *Ferlin Husky*
'94 **Wink** *Neal McCoy*
Winner Takes It All
'80 *Abba*
'87 *Sammy Hagar*
'75 **Winners And Losers**
       Hamilton, Joe Frank & Reynolds
'81 **Winning** *Santana*
'69 **Winter World Of Love**
       Engelbert Humperdinck
'07 **Wipe Me Down** *Lil' Boosie*
Wipe Out
'63 *Surfaris*
'87 *Fat Boys w/ The Beach Boys*
'56 **Wisdom Of A Fool** *Five Keys*
'79 **(Wish I Could Fly Like) Superman**
       Kinks
'94 **Wish I Didn't Know Now** *Toby Keith*
'66 **Wish Me A Rainbow**
       Gunter Kallmann Chorus
'64 **Wish Someone Would Care**
       Irma Thomas

Wish You Were Here
'75 *Pink Floyd*
'99 *Mark Wills*
'01 *Incubus*
'69 **Wishful Sinful** *Doors*
'64 **Wishin' And Hopin'**
       Dusty Springfield
'58 **Wishing For Your Love** *Voxpoppers*
'98 **Wishing I Was There**
       Natalie Imbruglia
'83 **Wishing (If I Had A Photograph Of You)** *Flock Of Seagulls*
'92 **Wishing On A Star** *Cover Girls*
'88 **Wishing Well** *Terence Trent D'Arby*
'74 **Wishing You Were Here** *Chicago*
'58 **Witch Doctor** *David Seville*
'71 **Witch Queen Of New Orleans**
       Redbone
Witchcraft
'58 *Frank Sinatra*
'63 *Elvis Presley*
'72 **Witchy Woman** *Eagles*
'66 **With A Girl Like You** *Troggs*
With A Little Help From My Friends
'67 *Beatles*
'69 *Joe Cocker*
'78 **With A Little Luck** *Wings*
'57 **With All My Heart** *Jodie Sands*
'00 **With Arms Wide Open** *Creed*
'89 **With Every Beat Of My Heart**
       Taylor Dayne
'07 **With Love** *Hilary Duff*
'59 **With Open Arms** *Jane Morgan*
'87 **With Or Without You** *U2*
'69 **With Pen In Hand** *Vikki Carr*
'59 **With The Wind And The Rain In Your Hair** *Pat Boone*
'65 **With These Hands** *Tom Jones*
'67 **With This Ring** *Platters*
With You
'91 *Tony Terry*
'03 *Jessica Simpson*
'79 **With You I'm Born Again**
       Billy Preston & Syreeta
'57 **With You On My Mind**
       Nat "King" Cole
With Your Love
'58 *Jack Scott*
'76 *Jefferson Starship*
'91 **Without Love (There Is Nothing)**
'57 *Clyde McPhatter*
'63 *Ray Charles*
'69 *Tom Jones*
'02 **Without Me** *Eminem*
Without You
'61 *Johnny Tillotson*
'71 *Nilsson*
'90 *Mötley Crüe*
'94 *Mariah Carey*
'00 *Dixie Chicks*
'82 **Without You (Not Another Lonely Night)** *Franke & The Knockouts*
'91 **(Without You) What Do I Do With Me** *Tanya Tucker*
Without Your Love
'80 *Roger Daltrey*
'86 *Toto*
'63 **Wives And Lovers** *Jack Jones*
'00 **Wobble Wobble** *504 Boyz*
'62 **Wolverton Mountain** *Claude King*
Woman
'66 *Peter & Gordon*
'81 *John Lennon*
'60 **Woman, A Lover, A Friend**
       Jackie Wilson
'72 **Woman Don't Go Astray** *King Floyd*
'73 **Woman From Tokyo**
       Deep Purple
'89 **Woman In Chains** *Tears For Fears*
Woman In Love
'55 *Four Aces*
'55 *Frankie Laine*
'80 *Barbra Streisand*
'82 **Woman In Me** *Donna Summer*
'83 **Woman In You** *Bee Gees*

'72 **Woman Is The Nigger Of The World**
       John Lennon
'81 **Woman Needs Love (Just Like You Do)** *Ray Parker Jr.*
'74 **Woman To Woman** *Shirley Brown*
'04 **Woman With You** *Kenny Chesney*
'67 **Woman, Woman**
       Union Gap feat. Gary Puckett
'65 **Woman's Got Soul** *Impressions*
'72 **Woman's Gotta Have It**
       Bobby Womack
'07 **Woman's Love** *Alan Jackson*
'01 **Woman's Worth** *Alicia Keys*
'71 **Women's Love Rights** *Laura Lee*
'71 **Won't Get Fooled Again** *Who*
'60 **Won't You Come Home Bill Bailey**
       Bobby Darin
'95 **Wonder** *Natalie Merchant*
'70 **Wonder Could I Live There Anymore** *Charley Pride*
'61 **Wonder Like You** *Rick Nelson*
Wonder Of You
'59 *Ray Peterson*
'70 *Elvis Presley*
Wonderful
'95 *Adam Ant*
'00 *Everclear*
'04 *Ja Rule*
'75 **Wonderful Baby** *Don McLean*
'62 **Wonderful Dream** *Majors*
'63 **Wonderful Summer** *Robin Ward*
'58 **Wonderful Time Up There**
       Pat Boone
'78 **Wonderful Tonight** *Eric Clapton*
       Wonderful! Wonderful!
'57 *Johnny Mathis*
'63 *Tymes*
Wonderful World
'60 *Sam Cooke*
'65 *Herman's Hermits*
'78 *Art Garfunkel w/ James Taylor & Paul Simon*
'69 **Wonderful World, Beautiful People**
       Jimmy Cliff
'57 **Wondering** *Patti Page*
'80 **Wondering Where The Lions Are**
       Bruce Cockburn
'79 **Wonderland** *Commodores*
       Wonderland By Night
'60 *Anita Bryant*
'60 *Bert Kaempfert*
'60 *Louis Prima*
'96 **Wonderwall** *Oasis*
'96 **Woo-Hah!! Got You All In Check**
       Busta Rhymes
'59 **Woo-Hoo** *Rock-A-Teens*
Wooden Heart
'60 *Elvis Presley*
'61 *Joe Dowell*
'69 **Wooden Ships**
       Crosby, Stills, Nash & Young
Woodstock
'70 *Crosby, Stills & Nash*
'70 *Joni Mitchell*
'71 *Matthews' Southern Comfort*
'98 **Woof Woof** *69 Boyz*
'65 **Wooly Bully**
       Sam The Sham & the Pharaohs
'88 **Word In Spanish** *Elton John*
'04 **Word Of God Speak** *MercyMe*
'91 **Word To The Mutha!** *Bell Biv DeVoe*
'86 **Word Up** *Cameo*
Words
'67 *Monkees*
'68 *Bee Gees*
'82 *Missing Persons*
'86 **Words Get In The Way**
       Miami Sound Machine
Words Of Love
'57 *Diamonds*
'57 *Buddy Holly*
'66 *Mamas & Papas*
'02 **Work In Progress** *Alan Jackson*
'02 **Work It** *Missy Elliott*
'66 **Work Song** *Herb Alpert*

'81 **You Could Have Been With Me**
Sheena Easton
'81 **You Could Take My Heart Away**
Silver Condor
'79 **You Decorated My Life**
Kenny Rogers
'65 **You Didn't Have To Be So Nice**
Lovin' Spoonful
'78 **You Don't Bring Me Flowers**
Barbra Streisand & Neil Diamond
'63 **You Don't Have To Be A Baby To Cry** *Caravelles*
'76 **You Don't Have To Be A Star**
Marilyn McCoo & Billy Davis, Jr.
'86 **You Don't Have To Cry**
René & Angela
'91 **You Don't Have To Go Home Tonight** *Triplets*
'97 **You Don't Have To Hurt No More**
Mint Condition
'66 **(You Don't Have To) Paint Me A Picture** *Gary Lewis*
You Don't Have To Say You Love Me
'66 *Dusty Springfield*
'70 *Elvis Presley*
'90 **You Don't Have To Worry** *En Vogue*
You Don't Know
'88 *Scarlett & Black*
'06 *Eminem*
'64 **(You Don't Know) How Glad I Am**
Nancy Wilson
'94 **You Don't Know How It Feels**
Tom Petty
You Don't Know Me
'56 *Jerry Vale*
'60 *Lenny Welch*
'62 *Ray Charles*
'03 **You Don't Know My Name**
Alicia Keys
'61 **You Don't Know What You've Got (Until You Lose It)** *Ral Donner*
'72 **You Don't Mess Around With Jim**
Jim Croce
'57 **You Don't Owe Me A Thing**
Johnnie Ray
'63 **You Don't Own Me** *Lesley Gore*
'82 **You Don't Want Me Anymore**
Steel Breeze
'99 **(You Drive Me) Crazy**
Britney Spears
'82 **You Dropped A Bomb On Me**
Gap Band
'69 **You Gave Me A Mountain**
Frankie Laine
'98 **You Get What You Give**
New Radicals
'01 **You Gets No Love** *Faith Evans*
'85 **You Give Good Love**
Whitney Houston
You Give Love A Bad Name
'86 *Bon Jovi*
'07 *Blake Lewis*
'79 **You Gonna Make Me Love Somebody Else** *Jones Girls*
You Got It
'89 *Roy Orbison*
'95 *Bonnie Raitt*
'86 **You Got It All** *Jets*
'88 **You Got It (The Right Stuff)**
New Kids On The Block
'82 **You Got Lucky** *Tom Petty*
'99 **You Got Me** *Roots w/ Erykah Badu*
'56 **You Got Me Dizzy** *Jimmy Reed*
'94 **You Got Me Rocking** *Rolling Stones*
'77 **You Got That Right**
Lynyrd Skynyrd
'74 **You Got The Love**
Rufus feat. Chaka Khan
'67 **You Got To Me** *Neil Diamond*
You Got What It Takes
'59 *Marv Johnson*
'67 *Dave Clark Five*
'69 **You Got Yours And I'll Get Mine**
Delfonics
'94 **You Gotta Be** *Des'ree*
'86 **(You Gotta) Fight For Your Right (To Party!)** *Beastie Boys*

'90 **You Gotta Love Someone**
Elton John
'99 **You Had Me From Hello**
Kenny Chesney
'74 **You Haven't Done Nothin**
Stevie Wonder
'69 **You, I** *Rugbys*
You Keep Me Hangin' On
'66 *Supremes*
'68 *Joe Simon*
'68 *Vanilla Fudge*
'87 *Kim Wilde*
'82 **You Keep Runnin' Away** *38 Special*
'67 **You Keep Running Away** *Four Tops*
'94 **You Know How We Do It** *Ice Cube*
'86 **You Know I Love You...Don't You?**
Howard Jones
'91 **You Know Me Better Than That**
George Strait
'79 **You Know That I Love You** *Santana*
'67 **You Know What I Mean** *Turtles*
'07 **You Know What It Is** *T.I.*
'02 **You Know You're Right** *Nirvana*
'96 **You Learn** *Alanis Morissette*
'90 **You Lie** *Reba McEntire*
'92 **You Lied To Me** *Cathy Dennis*
You Light Up My Life
'77 *Debby Boone*
'97 *LeAnn Rimes*
'74 **You Little Trustmaker** *Tymes*
'63 **You Lost The Sweetest Boy**
Mary Wells
'78 **You Love The Thunder**
Jackson Browne
'67 **You Made It That Way (Watermelon Summer)** *Perry Como*
'77 **You Made Me Believe In Magic**
Bay City Rollers
'61 **You Made Me Love You**
Judy Garland [live]
'77 **You Make Loving Fun**
Fleetwood Mac
'74 **You Make Me Feel Brand New**
Stylistics
'76 **You Make Me Feel Like Dancing**
Leo Sayer
'79 **You Make Me Feel (Mighty Real)**
Sylvester
'56 **You Make Me Feel So Young**
Frank Sinatra
'70 **You Make Me Real** *Doors*
'01 **You Make Me Sick** *P!nk*
'97 **You Make Me Wanna...** *Usher*
'81 **You Make My Dreams**
Daryl Hall & John Oates
'80 **You May Be Right** *Billy Joel*
'60 **You Mean Everything To Me**
Neil Sedaka
You Mean The World To Me
'67 *David Houston*
'94 *Toni Braxton*
'68 **You Met Your Match** *Stevie Wonder*
'84 **You Might Think** *Cars*
'98 **You Move Me** *Garth Brooks*
'64 **You Must Believe Me** *Impressions*
You Must Have Been A Beautiful Baby
'61 *Bobby Darin*
'67 *Dave Clark Five*
'96 **You Must Love Me** *Madonna*
'58 **You Need Hands** *Eydie Gorme*
'67 **You Need Love Like I Do (Don't You)** *Gladys Knight*
'78 **You Needed Me** *Anne Murray*
'64 **You Never Can Tell** *Chuck Berry*
'78 **You Never Done It Like That**
Captain & Tennille
'67 **You Only Live Twice** *Nancy Sinatra*
'72 **You Ought To Be With Me** *Al Green*
'95 **You Oughta Know** *Alanis Morissette*
'03 **You Raise Me Up** *Josh Groban*
You Really Got Me
'64 *Kinks*
'78 *Van Halen*
'90 **You Really Had Me Going**
Holly Dunn

'65 **You Really Know How To Hurt A Guy** *Jan & Dean*
'92 **You Remind Me** *Mary J. Blige*
'95 **You Remind Me Of Something**
R. Kelly
'01 **You Rock My World**
Michael Jackson
'00 **You Sang To Me** *Marc Anthony*
'06 **You Save Me** *Kenny Chesney*
'81 **You Saved My Soul**
Burton Cummings
You Send Me
'57 *Teresa Brewer*
'57 *Sam Cooke*
'75 **You Sexy Thing** *Hot Chocolate*
'80 **You Shook Me All Night Long**
AC/DC
'76 **You Should Be Dancing** *Bee Gees*
'97 **You Should Be Mine (Don't Waste Your Time)** *Brian McKnight*
'86 **You Should Be Mine (The Woo Woo Song)** *Jeffrey Osborne*
'64 **You Should Have Seen The Way He Looked At Me** *Dixie Cups*
'82 **You Should Hear How She Talks About You** *Melissa Manchester*
'57 **You Shouldn't Do That** *Sal Mineo*
'00 **You Shouldn't Kiss Me Like This**
Toby Keith
'69 **You Showed Me** *Turtles*
'85 **You Spin Me Round (Like A Record)** *Dead Or Alive*
'79 **You Take My Breath Away**
Rex Smith
'60 **You Talk Too Much** *Joe Jones*
'65 **You Tell Me Why** *Beau Brummels*
'92 **You Think You Know Her**
Cause & Effect
'78 **You Thrill Me** *Exile*
'78 **You Took The Words Right Out Of My Mouth** *Meat Loaf*
'65 **You Turn Me On** *Ian Whitcomb*
'72 **You Turn Me On, I'm A Radio**
Joni Mitchell
'95 **You Used To Love Me** *Faith Evans*
'72 **You Want It, You Got It**
Detroit Emeralds
'94 **You Want This** *Janet Jackson*
'07 **(You Want To) Make A Memory**
Bon Jovi
'72 **You Wear It Well** *Rod Stewart*
'60 **(You Were Made For) All My Love**
Jackie Wilson
You Were Made For Me
'58 *Sam Cooke*
'65 *Freddie & The Dreamers*
'96 **You Were Meant For Me** *Jewel*
You Were Mine
'59 *Fireflies*
'99 *Dixie Chicks*
You Were On My Mind
'65 *We Five*
'67 *Crispian St. Peters*
'65 **You Were Only Fooling (While I Was Falling In Love)** *Vic Damone*
'88 **You Will Know** *Stevie Wonder*
You Win Again
'58 *Jerry Lee Lewis*
'62 *Fats Domino*
'96 **You Win My Love** *Shania Twain*
'99 **You Won't Ever Be Lonely**
Andy Griggs
'74 **You Won't See Me** *Anne Murray*
'92 **You Won't See Me Cry**
Wilson Phillips
'94 **You Wreck Me** *Tom Petty*
'65 **You'd Better Come Home**
Petula Clark
'80 **You'll Accomp'ny Me** *Bob Seger*
'99 **You'll Be In My Heart** *Phil Collins*
You'll Lose A Good Thing
'62 *Barbara Lynn*
'76 *Freddy Fender*
'76 **You'll Never Find Another Love Like Mine** *Lou Rawls*

You'll Never Get To Heaven (If You Break My Heart)
'64 Dionne Warwick
'73 Stylistics
'56 You'll Never Never Know Platters
'64 You'll Never Walk Alone
Patti LaBelle
'95 You'll See Madonna
'03 You'll Think Of Me Keith Urban
'85 You're A Friend Of Mine Clarence Clemons & Jackson Browne
'00 You're A God Vertical Horizon
'78 You're A Part Of Me
Gene Cotton w/ Kim Carnes
'73 You're A Special Part Of Me
Diana Ross & Marvin Gaye
'64 You're A Wonderful One
Marvin Gaye
You're All I Need To Get By
'68 Marvin Gaye & Tammi Terrell
'71 Aretha Franklin
'95 Method Man ft. Mary J. Blige [medley]
'78 You're All I've Got Tonight Cars
'90 You're Amazing Robert Palmer
'06 You're Beautiful James Blunt
'98 You're Beginning To Get To Me
Clay Walker
'83 You're Driving Me Out Of My Mind
Little River Band
'98 You're Easy On The Eyes
Terri Clark
'65 You're Going To Lose That Girl
Beatles
'95 You're Gonna Miss Me When I'm Gone Brooks & Dunn
'63 You're Good For Me Solomon Burke
'74 (You're) Having My Baby
Paul Anka/Odia Coates
'91 You're In Love Wilson Phillips
'77 You're In My Heart (The Final Acclaim) Rod Stewart
'96 You're Makin' Me High Toni Braxton
'76 You're My Best Friend Queen
'04 You're My Better Half Keith Urban
'67 You're My Everything Temptations
'81 You're My Girl
Franke & The Knockouts
'57 You're My One And Only Love
Ricky Nelson
'89 You're My One And Only (True Love) Seduction
(You're My) Soul And Inspiration
'66 Righteous Brothers
'77 Donny & Marie Osmond
You're My World
'64 Cilla Black
'77 Helen Reddy
'74 You're No Good Linda Ronstadt
'64 You're Nobody Till Somebody Loves You Dean Martin
'89 You're Not Alone Chicago
'85 You're Only Human (Second Wind)
Billy Joel
'79 You're Only Lonely J.D. Souther
'87 (You're Puttin') A Rush On Me
Stephanie Mills
You're Sixteen
'60 Johnny Burnette
'73 Ringo Starr
'59 You're So Fine Falcons
'72 You're So Vain Carly Simon
'72 You're Still A Young Man
Tower Of Power
'98 You're Still The One Shania Twain
'80 You're Supposed To Keep Your Love For Me Jermaine Jackson
'63 (You're the) Devil In Disguise
Elvis Presley
'74 You're The First, The Last, My Everything Barry White

'84 You're The Inspiration Chicago
'78 You're The Love Seals & Crofts
You're The One
'65 Vogues
'70 Little Sister
'96 SWV
'78 You're The One That I Want John Travolta & Olivia Newton-John
'90 You're The Only Woman Brat Pack
'80 You're The Only Woman (You & I)
Ambrosia
'65 You're The Only World I Know
Sonny James
'61 You're The Reason Bobby Edwards
'63 You're The Reason I'm Living
Bobby Darin
'65 You've Been Cheatin' Impressions
'65 You've Been In Love Too Long
Martha & The Vandellas
You've Got A Friend
'71 Roberta Flack & Donny Hathaway
'71 Carole King
'71 James Taylor
'82 You've Got Another Thing Comin'
Judas Priest
'70 (You've Got Me) Dangling On A String Chairmen Of The Board
'76 You've Got Me Runnin' Gene Cotton
'56 (You've Got) The Magic Touch
Platters
'71 You've Got To Crawl (Before You Walk) 8th Day
You've Got To Hide Your Love Away
'65 Beatles
'65 Silkie
'60 (You've Got To) Move Two Mountains Marv Johnson
'90 You've Got To Stand For Something Aaron Tippin
'97 You've Got To Talk To Me
Lee Ann Womack
'65 You've Got Your Troubles Fortunes
You've Lost That Lovin' Feelin'
'64 Righteous Brothers
'69 Dionne Warwick
'80 Daryl Hall & John Oates
You've Made Me So Very Happy
'67 Brenda Holloway
'69 Blood, Sweat & Tears
'73 You've Never Been This Far Before
Conway Twitty
'62 You've Really Got A Hold On Me
Miracles
'02 Young Kenny Chesney
'55 Young Abe Lincoln Don Cornell
'75 Young Americans David Bowie
'63 Young And In Love Dick & DeeDee
'58 Young And Warm And Wonderful
Tony Bennett
Young Blood
'57 Coasters
'76 Bad Company
'79 Rickie Lee Jones
'60 Young Emotions Ricky Nelson
'68 Young Girl
Union Gap feat. Gary Puckett
'76 Young Hearts Run Free
Candi Staton
Young Love
'56 Sonny James
'57 Crew-Cuts
'57 Tab Hunter
'73 Donny Osmond
'82 Air Supply
'89 Judds
'63 Young Lovers Paul & Paula
'80 Young Lust Pink Floyd
'81 Young Turks Rod Stewart
'62 Young World Rick Nelson

'66 Younger Girl Critters
'01 Young'n (Holla Back) Fabolous
'90 Your Baby Never Looked Good In Blue Exposé
'05 Your Body Pretty Ricky
'02 Your Body Is A Wonderland
John Mayer
'94 Your Body's Callin' R. Kelly
'74 Your Bulldog Drinks Champagne
Jim Stafford
'73 Your Cash Ain't Nothin' But Trash
Steve Miller Band
'62 Your Cheating Heart Ray Charles
'01 Your Disease Saliva
'61 Your Friends Dee Clark
'69 Your Good Thing (Is About To End)
Lou Rawls
'82 Your Imagination
Daryl Hall & John Oates
'98 Your Life Is Now
John Mellencamp
Your Love
'77 Marilyn McCoo & Billy Davis Jr.
'86 Outfield
'94 Your Love Amazes Me John Berry
'91 Your Love Is A Miracle
Mark Chesnutt
'82 Your Love Is Driving Me Crazy
Sammy Hagar
(Your Love Keeps Lifting Me) Higher And Higher
'67 Jackie Wilson
'77 Rita Coolidge
'99 Your Love Oh Lord Third Day
'96 Your Loving Arms Billie Ray Martin
'61 Your Ma Said You Cried In Your Sleep Last Night Kenny Dino
Your Mama Don't Dance
'72 Loggins & Messina
'89 Poison
'06 Your Man Josh Turner
'71 Your Move [medley] Yes
'62 Your Nose Is Gonna Grow
Johnny Crawford
'63 Your Old Stand By Mary Wells
Your Other Love
'60 Flamingos
'63 Connie Francis
'67 Your Precious Love
Marvin Gaye & Tammi Terrell
'85 Your Smile René & Angela
'77 Your Smiling Face James Taylor
'70 Your Song Elton John
'78 Your Sweetness Is My Weakness
Barry White
'68 Your Time Hasn't Come Yet, Baby
Elvis Presley
'70 Your Time To Cry Joe Simon
'63 Your Used To Be Brenda Lee
'57 Your Wild Heart Joy Layne
'86 Your Wildest Dreams Moody Blues
'97 Your Woman White Town
'71 Yours Is No Disgrace Yes
'01 Youth Of The Nation P.O.D.
'68 Yummy Yummy Yummy
Ohio Express

Z

'02 Zephyr Song Red Hot Chili Peppers
'72 Ziggy Stardust David Bowie
'62 Zip-A-Dee Doo-Dah Bob B. Soxx & The Blue Jeans
'67 Zip Code Five Americans
'57 Zip Zip Diamonds
'94 Zombie Cranberries
'98 Zoot Suit Riot
Cherry Poppin' Daddies
'65 Zorba The Greek Herb Alpert
'58 Zorro Chordettes

CLASSIC SONGS BY HALF DECADE PLAYLISTS

1955-1959	1985-1989
1960-1964	1990-1994
1965-1969	1995-1999
1970-1974	2000-2004
1975-1979	2005-2007
1980-1984	

Each of the above playlists consists of 200 of the hottest hits of each half-decade of the rock era, except for 2005-2007. 2005 and 2006 covers those entire years, while 2007 covers the top hits for the first 8 months of the year.

Ain't That A Shame...*Fats Domino*
All American Boy, The...*Bill Parsons*
All I Have To Do Is Dream...*Everly Brothers*
All Shook Up...*Elvis Presley*
All The Way...*Frank Sinatra*
Allegheny Moon...*Patti Page*
April Love...*Pat Boone*
At The Hop...*Danny & The Juniors*
Autumn Leaves...*Roger Williams*
Ballad Of Davy Crockett, The...*Bill Hayes*
Banana Boat (Day-O)...*Harry Belafonte*
Band Of Gold...*Don Cherry*
Battle Of New Orleans, The...*Johnny Horton*
Be-Bop-A-Lula...*Gene Vincent*
Believe What You Say...*Ricky Nelson*
Big Hunk O' Love, A...*Elvis Presley*
Big Hurt, The...*Miss Toni Fisher*
Bird Dog...*Everly Brothers*
Black Denim Trousers...*Cheers*
Blossom Fell, A...*Nat "King" Cole*
Blue Monday...*Fats Domino*
Blue Suede Shoes...*Carl Perkins*
Blueberry Hill...*Fats Domino*
Bo Diddley...*Bo Diddley*
Book Of Love...*Monotones*
Butterfly...*Charlie Gracie*
Bye Bye Love...*Everly Brothers*
Canadian Sunset...*Hugo Winterhalter/Eddie Heywood*
Catch A Falling Star...*Perry Como*
Chances Are...*Johnny Mathis*
Chantilly Lace...*Big Bopper*
Charlie Brown'...*Coasters*
Cherry Pink And Apple Blossom White ...*Perez Prado*
C'mon Everybody...*Eddie Cochran*
Come Go With Me...*Dell-Vikings*
Come Softly To Me...*Fleetwoods*
Diana...*Paul Anka*
Donna...*Ritchie Valens*
Don't...*Elvis Presley*
Don't Be Cruel...*Elvis Presley*
Don't You Know...*Della Reese*
Dream Lover...*Bobby Darin*
Earth Angel...*Penguins*
Endless Sleep...*Jody Reynolds*
Fever...*Peggy Lee*
Fool, The...*Sanford Clark*
Get A Job...*Silhouettes*
Good Golly, Miss Molly...*Little Richard*
Great Balls Of Fire...*Jerry Lee Lewis*
Great Pretender, The...*Platters*
Green Door, The...*Jim Lowe*
Happy, Happy Birthday Baby...*Tune Weavers*
Happy Organ, The...*Dave 'Baby' Cortez*
Hard Headed Woman...*Elvis Presley*
Heartbreak Hotel...*Elvis Presley*

He's Got The Whole World (In His Hands) ...*Laurie London*
Hey! Jealous Lover...*Frank Sinatra*
Honeycomb...*Jimmie Rodgers*
Honky Tonk...*Bill Doggett*
Hot Diggity...*Perry Como*
Hound Dog...*Elvis Presley*
I Almost Lost My Mind...*Pat Boone*
I Only Have Eyes For You...*Flamingos*
I Walk The Line...*Johnny Cash*
I Want You, I Need You, I Love You...*Elvis Presley*
I'm Gonna Get Married...*Lloyd Price*
I'm Gonna Sit Right Down And Write Myself A Letter...*Billy Williams*
In The Still Of The Nite...*Five Satins*
It's All In The Game...*Tommy Edwards*
It's Just A Matter Of Time...*Brook Benton*
It's Only Make Believe...*Conway Twitty*
Ivory Tower...*Cathy Carr*
Jailhouse Rock...*Elvis Presley*
Jim Dandy...*LaVern Baker*
Johnny B. Goode...*Chuck Berry*
Just Walking In The Rain...*Johnnie Ray*
Kansas City...*Wilbert Harrison*
Kisses Sweeter Than Wine...*Jimmie Rodgers*
La Bamba...*Ritchie Valens*
La Dee Dah...*Billy & Lillie*
Learnin' The Blues...*Frank Sinatra*
(Let Me Be Your) Teddy Bear...*Elvis Presley*
Let Me Go Lover...*Joan Weber*
Lisbon Antigua...*Nelson Riddle*
Little Darlin'...*Diamonds*
Little Star...*Elegants*
Lollipop...*Chordettes*
Lonely Boy...*Paul Anka*
Lonely Teardrops...*Jackie Wilson*
Long Tall Sally...*Little Richard*
Love And Marriage...*Frank Sinatra*
Love Is A Many-Splendored Thing...*Four Aces*
Love Is Strange...*Mickey & Sylvia*
Love Letters In The Sand...*Pat Boone*
Love Me...*Elvis Presley*
Love Me Tender...*Elvis Presley*
Lover's Question, A...*Clyde McPhatter*
Lucille...*Little Richard*
Mack The Knife...*Bobby Darin*
Maybe...*Chantels*
Maybellene...*Chuck Berry*
Memories Are Made Of This...*Dean Martin*
Mr. Blue...*Fleetwoods*
Mr. Lee...*Bobbettes*
Mr. Sandman...*Chordettes*
Moments To Remember...*Four Lads*
Moonglow And Theme From "Picnic"...*Morris Stoloff/Columbia Pictures Orch.*
Moonlight Gambler...*Frankie Laine*

My Happiness...*Connie Francis*
My Prayer...*Platters*
My True Love...*Jack Scott*
Mystery Train...*Elvis Presley*
Nel Blu Dipinto Di Blu (Volaré)...*Domenico Modugno*
No, Not Much!...*Four Lads*
Oh, Boy!...*Buddy Holly & The Crickets*
Oh Lonesome Me...*Don Gibson*
Old Cape Cod...*Patti Page*
On The Street Where You Live...*Vic Damone*
Only You (And You Alone)...*Platters*
Party Doll...*Buddy Knox*
Patricia...*Perez Prado*
Peggy Sue...*Buddy Holly*
Personality...*Lloyd Price*
Pink Shoe Laces...*Dodie Stevens*
Please, Please, Please...*James Brown*
Poor Little Fool...*Ricky Nelson*
Poor People Of Paris, The...*Les Baxter*
Problems...*Everly Brothers*
Purple People Eater, The...*Sheb Wooley*
Put Your Head On My Shoulder...*Paul Anka*
Queen Of The Hop...*Bobby Darin*
Raunchy...*Bill Justis*
Rave On...*Buddy Holly*
Rebel-'Rouser...*Duane Eddy*
Red River Rock...*Johnny & The Hurricanes*
Rock & Roll Music...*Chuck Berry*
Rock And Roll Waltz...*Kay Starr*
Rock Around The Clock...*Bill Haley & His Comets*
Rock-In Robin...*Bobby Day*
Rock Island Line...*Lonnie Donegan*
Roll Over Beethoven...*Chuck Berry*
Round And Round...*Perry Como*
School Day...*Chuck Berry*
Sea Of Love...*Phil Phillips*
Searchin'...*Coasters*
See You Later, Alligator...*Bill Haley & His Comets*
Shifting Whispering Sands, The...*Billy Vaughn*
Short Shorts...*Royal Teens*
Shout...*Isley Brothers*
Silhouettes...*Rays*
Since I Met You Baby...*Ivory Joe Hunter*
Sincerely...*Moonglows*
Singing The Blues...*Guy Mitchell*
16 Candles...*Crests*
Sixteen Tons...*"Tennessee" Ernie Ford*

Sleep Walk...*Santo & Johnny*
Smoke Gets In Your Eyes...*Platters*
So Rare...*Jimmy Dorsey*
Sorry (I Ran All The Way Home)...*Impalas*
Splish Splash...*Bobby Darin*
Stagger Lee...*Lloyd Price*
Standing On The Corner...*Four Lads*
Stood Up...*Ricky Nelson*
Sugartime...*McGuire Sisters*
Summertime Blues...*Eddie Cochran*
Sweet Little Sixteen...*Chuck Berry*
Tammy...*Debbie Reynolds*
Tears On My Pillow...*Little Anthony & The Imperials*
Teen-Age Crush...*Tommy Sands*
Teenager In Love...*Dion & The Belmonts*
Tequila...*Champs*
That'll Be The Day...*Buddy Holly & The Crickets*
There Goes My Baby...*Drifters*
Three Bells, The...*Browns*
Tiger...*Fabian*
('Til) I Kissed You...*Everly Brothers*
To Know Him, Is To Love Him...*Teddy Bears*
Tom Dooley...*Kingston Trio*
Too Much...*Elvis Presley*
Topsy II...*Cozy Cole*
True Love...*Bing Crosby & Grace Kelly*
Tutti-Fruitti...*Little Richard*
26 Miles (Santa Catalina)...*Four Preps*
Twilight Time...*Platters*
Unchained Melody...*Al Hibbler*
Venus...*Frankie Avalon*
Wake Up Little Susie...*Everly Brothers*
Wayward Wind, The...*Gogi Grant*
What'd I Say...*Ray Charles*
Whatever Will Be, Will Be (Que Sera, Sera)...*Doris Day*
White Sport Coat (And A Pink Carnation)...*Marty Robbins*
Whole Lot Of Shakin' Going On...*Jerry Lee Lewis*
Why Do Fools Fall In Love...*Frankie Lymon & The Teenagers*
Witch Doctor...*David Seville*
Wonderful! Wonderful!...*Johnny Mathis*
Yakety Yak...*Coasters*
Yellow Rose Of Texas, The...*Mitch Miller*
You Send Me...*Sam Cooke*
Young Blood...*Coasters*
Young Love...*Sonny James*

Alley-Oop...*Hollywood Argyles*
Apache...*Jorgen Ingmann*
Are You Lonesome To-night?...*Elvis Presley*
Baby Love...*Supremes*
Baby (You've Got What It Takes)...*Dinah Washington & Brook Benton*
Be My Baby...*Ronettes*
Because They're Young...*Duane Eddy*
Big Bad John...*Jimmy Dean*
Big Girls Don't Cry...*4 Seasons*
Blowin' In The Wind...*Bob Dylan*
Blue Moon...*Marcels*
Blue Velvet...*Bobby Vinton*
Bobby's Girl...*Marcie Blane*
Bread And Butter...*Newbeats*
Breaking Up Is Hard To Do...*Neil Sedaka*
Bristol Stomp...*Dovells*
Burning Bridges...*Jack Scott*
Can't Buy Me Love...*Beatles*
Can't Get Used To Losing You...*Andy Williams*
Can't Help Falling In Love...*Elvis Presley*
Cathy's Clown...*Everly Brothers*
Chain Gang...*Sam Cooke*
Chapel Of Love...*Dixie Cups*
Come See About Me...*Supremes*
Crazy...*Patsy Cline*
Crying...*Roy Orbison*
Da Doo Ron Ron...*Crystals*
Daddy's Home...*Shep & The Limelites*
Dancing In The Street...*Martha & The Vandellas*
Dawn (Go Away)...*4 Seasons*
Dedicated To The One I Love...*Shirelles*
Do Wah Diddy Diddy...*Manfred Mann*
Do You Love Me...*Contours*
Do You Want To Know A Secret...*Beatles*
Dominique...*Singing Nun*
Don't Break The Heart That Loves You...*Connie Francis*
Don't Worry...*Marty Robbins*
Duke Of Earl...*Gene Chandler*
Easier Said Than Done...*Essex*
El Paso...*Marty Robbins*
End Of The World, The...*Skeeter Davis*
Everybody Loves Somebody...*Dean Martin*
Everybody's Somebody's Fool...*Connie Francis*
Exodus...*Ferrante & Teicher*
Fingertips...*Stevie Wonder*
Fun, Fun, Fun...*Beach Boys*
G.T.O....*Ronny & The Daytonas*
Georgia On My Mind...*Ray Charles*
Go Away Little Girl...*Steve Lawrence*
Good Luck Charm...*Elvis Presley*
Good Timin'...*Jimmy Jones*
Green Onions...*Booker T. & The MG's*

Greenfields...*Brothers Four*
Handy Man...*Jimmy Jones*
Hard Day's Night, A...*Beatles*
He'll Have To Go...*Jim Reeves*
Hello, Dolly!...*Louis Armstrong*
Hello Mary Lou...*Ricky Nelson*
Hello Mudduh, Hello Fadduh!...*Allan Sherman*
He's A Rebel...*Crystals*
He's So Fine...*Chiffons*
Hey! Baby...*Bruce Channel*
Hey Little Cobra...*Rip Chords*
Hey Paula...*Paul & Paula*
Hit The Road Jack...*Ray Charles*
House Of The Rising Sun, The...*Animals*
Hundred Pounds Of Clay, A...*Gene McDaniels*
I Can't Stop Loving You...*Ray Charles*
I Fall To Pieces...*Patsy Cline*
I Feel Fine...*Beatles*
I Get Around...*Beach Boys*
I Left My Heart In San Francisco...*Tony Bennett*
I Like It Like That...*Chris Kenner*
I Love How You Love Me...*Paris Sisters*
I Saw Her Standing There...*Beatles*
I Want To Be Wanted...*Brenda Lee*
I Want To Hold Your Hand...*Beatles*
I Will Follow Him...*Little Peggy March*
I'm Sorry...*Brenda Lee*
I've Told Every Little Star...*Linda Scott*
If You Wanna Be Happy...*Jimmy Soul*
In My Room...*Beach Boys*
It's My Party...*Lesley Gore*
It's Now Or Never...*Elvis Presley*
Itsy Bitsy Teenie Weenie Yellow Polkadot Bikini...*Brian Hyland*
Johnny Angel...*Shelley Fabares*
Last Date...*Floyd Cramer*
Last Kiss...*J. Frank Wilson & The Cavaliers*
Leader Of The Pack...*Shangri-Las*
Let's Dance...*Chris Montez*
Limbo Rock...*Chubby Checker*
Lion Sleeps Tonight, The...*Tokens*
Little Honda...*Hondells*
Little Old Lady (From Pasadena)...*Jan & Dean*
Loco-Motion, The...*Little Eva*
Louie Louie...*Kingsmen*
Love Me Do...*Beatles*
(Man Who Shot) Liberty Valance, The...*Gene Pitney*
Mashed Potato Time...*Dee Dee Sharp*
Memphis...*Johnny Rivers*
Michael...*Highwaymen*
Midnight In Moscow...*Kenny Ball*
Monster Mash...*Bobby "Boris" Pickett*
Moody River...*Pat Boone*
Moon River...*Henry Mancini*

Mother-In-Law...*Ernie K-Doe*
Mountain's High, The...*Dick & Dee Dee*
Mr. Custer...*Larry Verne*
Mr. Lonely...*Bobby Vinton*
Mule Skinner Blues...*Fendermen*
My Boy Lollipop...*Millie Small*
My Boyfriend's Back...*Angels*
My Guy...*Mary Wells*
My True Story...*Jive Five*
Night...*Jackie Wilson*
North To Alaska...*Johnny Horton*
Oh, Pretty Woman...*Roy Orbison*
Only Love Can Break A Heart...*Gene Pitney*
Only The Lonely...*Roy Orbison*
Our Day Will Come...*Ruby & The Romantics*
Out Of Limits...*Marketts*
Palisades Park...*Freddy Cannon*
Peppermint Twist...*Joey Dee & The Starliters*
Pipeline...*Chantay's*
Please Mr. Postman...*Marvelettes*
Please Please Me...*Beatles*
Poetry In Motion...*Johnny Tillotson*
Pony Time...*Chubby Checker*
Popsicles And Icicles...*Murmaids*
Puff (The Magic Dragon)...*Peter, Paul & Mary*
Puppy Love...*Paul Anka*
Quarter To Three...*Gary (U.S.) Bonds*
Rag Doll...*4 Seasons*
Raindrops...*Dee Clark*
Ramblin' Rose...*Nat King Cole*
Return To Sender...*Elvis Presley*
Rhythm Of The Rain...*Cascades*
Ring Of Fire...*Johnny Cash*
Roses Are Red (My Love)...*Bobby Vinton*
Ruby Baby...*Dion*
Runaround Sue...*Dion*
Runaway...*Del Shannon*
Running Bear...*Johnny Preston*
Running Scared...*Roy Orbison*
Sally, Go 'Round The Roses...*Jaynetts*
Save The Last Dance For Me...*Drifters*
She Loves You...*Beatles*
Sheila...*Tommy Roe*
Sherry...*4 Seasons*
She's Not There...*Zombies*
Shop Around...*Miracles*
So Much In Love...*Tymes*
Soldier Boy...*Shirelles*
Spanish Harlem...*Ben E. King*

Stand By Me...*Ben E. King*
Stay...*Maurice Williams & The Zodiacs*
Stranger On The Shore...*Mr. Acker Bilk*
Stripper, The...*David Rose*
Stuck On You...*Elvis Presley*
Sugar Shack...*Jimmy Gilmer & The Fireballs*
Sukiyaki...*Kyu Sakamoto*
Surf City...*Jan & Dean*
Surfin' U.S.A....*Beach Boys*
Surrender...*Elvis Presley*
Suspicion...*Terry Stafford*
Take Good Care Of My Baby...*Bobby Vee*
Teen Angel...*Mark Dinning*
Tell Laura I Love Her...*Ray Peterson*
Telstar...*Tornadoes*
Theme From "A Summer Place"...*Percy Faith*
There's A Moon Out Tonight...*Capris*
Thousand Stars, A...*Kathy Young w/ The Innocents*
Times They Are A-Changin', The...*Bob Dylan*
Tossin' And Turnin'...*Bobby Lewis*
Travelin' Man...*Ricky Nelson*
Twist, The...*Chubby Checker*
Twist And Shout...*Beatles*
Up On The Roof...*Drifters*
Wah Watusi, The...*Orlons*
Walk -- Don't Run...*Ventures*
Walk Like A Man...*4 Seasons*
Walk On By...*Dionne Warwick*
Walk On By...*Leroy Van Dyke*
Walk Right In...*Rooftop Singers*
Walking To New Orleans...*Fats Domino*
Wanderer, The...*Dion*
Washington Square...*Village Stompers*
What In The World's Come Over You...*Jack Scott*
Wheels...*String-A-Longs*
Where Did Our Love Go...*Supremes*
Wild One...*Bobby Rydell*
Will You Love Me Tomorrow...*Shirelles*
Wipe Out...*Surfaris*
Wonderland By Night...*Bert Kaempfert*
Wooden Heart...*Joe Dowell*
World Without Love, A...*Peter & Gordon*
Yellow Bird...*Arthur Lyman Group*
You Really Got Me...*Kinks*
You're Sixteen...*Johnny Burnette*
(You're The) Devil In Disguise...*Elvis Presley*

All Along The Watchtower...*Jimi Hendrix*
All You Need Is Love...*Beatles*
Aquarius/Let The Sunshine In...*5th Dimension*
Bad Moon Rising...*Creedence Clearwater Revival*
Ballad Of The Green Berets, The...*SSgt Barry Sadler*
Barbara Ann...*Beach Boys*
Birds And The Bees, The...*Jewel Akens*
Born To Be Wild...*Steppenwolf*
Boy From New York City, The...*Ad Libs*
Boy Named Sue, A...*Johnny Cash*
Brown Eyed Girl...*Van Morrison*
California Dreamin'...*Mamas & Papas*
California Girls...*Beach Boys*
Chain Of Fools...*Aretha Franklin*
Change Is Gonna Come, A...*Sam Cooke*
Cherish...*Association*
Classical Gas...*Mason Williams*
Come On Down To My Boat...*Every Mothers' Son*
Come Together...*Beatles*
Crimson And Clover...*Tommy James & The Shondells*
Cry Like A Baby...*Box Tops*
Crying In The Chapel...*Elvis Presley*
Dance To The Music...*Sly & The Family Stone*
Daydream...*Lovin' Spoonful*
Daydream Believer...*Monkees*
Devil With A Blue Dress On & Good Golly Miss Molly...*Mitch Ryder*
Dizzy...*Tommy Roe*
Do You Believe In Magic...*Lovin' Spoonful*
Down On The Corner...*Creedence Clearwater Revival*
Downtown...*Petula Clark*
Eight Days A Week...*Beatles*
Eight Miles High...*Byrds*
Eleanor Rigby...*Beatles*
Eve Of Destruction...*Barry McGuire*
Everyday People...*Sly & The Family Stone*
For Once In My Life...*Stevie Wonder*
For What It's Worth...*Buffalo Springfield*
Game Of Love...*Wayne Fontana & The Mindbenders*
Georgy Girl...*Seekers*
Get Back...*Beatles*
Get Off Of My Cloud...*Rolling Stones*
Gimme Some Lovin'...*Spencer Davis Group*
Gloria...*Them*
God Only Knows...*Beach Boys*
Good Lovin'...*Young Rascals*
Good Morning Starshine...*Oliver*
Good, The Bad And The Ugly, The...*Hugo Montenegro*
Good Vibrations...*Beach Boys*
Grazing In The Grass...*Hugh Masekela*

Green River...*Creedence Clearwater Revival*
Green Tambourine...*Lemon Pipers*
Groovin'...*Young Rascals*
Groovy Kind Of Love, A...*Mindbenders*
Hang On Sloopy...*McCoys*
Hanky Panky...*Tommy James & The Shondells*
Happy Together...*Turtles*
Harper Valley P.T.A....*Jeannie C. Riley*
Hello Goodbye...*Beatles*
Hello, I Love You...*Doors*
Help!...*Beatles*
Help Me, Rhonda...*Beach Boys*
Hey Jude...*Beatles*
Honey...*Bobby Goldsboro*
Honky Tonk Women...*Rolling Stones*
Horse, The...*Cliff Nobles*
Hot Fun In The Summertime...*Sly & The Family Stone*
Hush, Hush Sweet Charlotte...*Patti Page*
I Can See For Miles...*Who*
I Can't Get Next To You...*Temptations*
(I Can't Get No) Satisfaction...*Rolling Stones*
I Can't Help Myself...*Four Tops*
I Fought The Law...*Bobby Fuller Four*
I Got You Babe...*Sonny & Cher*
I Got You (I Feel Good)...*James Brown*
I Heard It Through The Grapevine...*Marvin Gaye*
I'm A Believer...*Monkees*
I'm Henry VIII, I Am...*Herman's Hermits*
I'm Telling You Now...*Freddie & The Dreamers*
In-A-Gadda-Da-Vida...*Iron Butterfly*
In My Life...*Beatles*
In The Ghetto...*Elvis Presley*
In The Midnight Hour...*Wilson Pickett*
In The Year 2525...*Zager & Evans*
Incense And Peppermints...*Strawberry Alarm Clock*
It's Your Thing...*Isley Brothers*
Judy In Disguise (With Glasses)...*John Fred & His Playboy Band*
Jumpin' Jack Flash...*Rolling Stones*
Kicks...*Paul Revere & The Raiders*
Kind Of A Drag...*Buckinghams*
King Of The Road...*Roger Miller*
Lady Madonna...*Beatles*
Last Train To Clarksville...*Monkees*
Leaving On A Jet Plane...*Peter, Paul & Mary*
Letter, The...*Box Tops*
Light My Fire...*Doors*
Lightnin' Strikes...*Lou Christie*
Like A Rolling Stone...*Bob Dylan*
Lil' Red Riding Hood...*Sam The Sham & The Pharaohs*
Little Bit O' Soul...*Music Explosion*
Little Girl...*Syndicate Of Sound*
Little Latin Lupe Lu...*Mitch Ryder*

Love Child...*Supremes*
Love Is Blue...*Paul Mauriat*
Love Theme From Romeo & Juliet...*Henry Mancini*
Lover's Concerto, A...*Toys*
Mellow Yellow...*Donovan*
Monday, Monday...*Mamas & Papas*
Mony Mony...*Tommy James & The Shondells*
Mr. Tambourine Man...*Byrds*
Mrs. Brown You've Got A Lovely Daughter ...*Herman's Hermits*
Mrs. Robinson...*Simon & Garfunkel*
My Generation...*Who*
My Girl...*Temptations*
My Love...*Petula Clark*
Na Na Hey Hey Kiss Him Goodbye...*Steam*
Never My Love...*Association*
19th Nervous Breakdown...*Rolling Stones*
96 Tears...*? & The Mysterians*
Nowhere Man...*Beatles*
Ode To Billie Joe...*Bobbie Gentry*
Over And Over...*Dave Clark Five*
Paint It, Black...*Rolling Stones*
Papa's Got A Brand New Bag...*James Brown*
Paperback Writer...*Beatles*
Penny Lane...*Beatles*
People Get Ready...*Impressions*
People Got To Be Free...*Rascals*
Piece Of My Heart...*Big Brother & The Holding Co. (Janis Joplin)*
Pied Piper, The...*Crispian St. Peters*
Poor Side Of Town...*Johnny Rivers*
Proud Mary...*Creedence Clearwater Revival*
Purple Haze...*Jimi Hendrix*
Rain, The Park & Other Things, The...*Cowsills*
Rainy Day Women #12 & 35...*Bob Dylan*
Reach Out I'll Be There...*Four Tops*
Red Rubber Ball...*Cyrkle*
Respect...*Aretha Franklin*
River Deep-Mountain High...*Ike & Tina Turner*
Ruby Tuesday...*Rolling Stones*
Secret Agent Man...*Johnny Rivers*
She's Just My Style...*Gary Lewis & The Playboys*
(Sittin' On) The Dock Of The Bay...*Otis Redding*
Sloop John B...*Beach Boys*
Snoopy Vs. The Red Baron...*Royal Guardsmen*
Somethin' Stupid...*Nancy Sinatra & Frank Sinatra*
Something...*Beatles*
Soul Man...*Sam & Dave*
Sounds Of Silence, The...*Simon & Garfunkel*
Spinning Wheel...*Blood, Sweat & Tears*
Spooky...*Classics IV*
Stand By Your Man...*Tammy Wynette*
Stop! In The Name Of Love...*Supremes*

Strangers In The Night...*Frank Sinatra*
Strawberry Fields Forever...*Beatles*
Sugar, Sugar...*Archies*
Summer In The City...*Lovin' Spoonful*
Sunny...*Bobby Hebb*
Sunshine Of Your Love...*Cream*
Sunshine Superman...*Donovan*
Suspicious Minds...*Elvis Presley*
Sweet Caroline...*Neil Diamond*
Sweet Soul Music...*Arthur Conley*
Sympathy For The Devil...*Rolling Stones*
Take A Letter Maria...*R.B. Greaves*
Tell It Like It Is...*Aaron Neville*
(Theme From) Valley Of The Dolls...*Dionne Warwick*
These Boots Are Made For Walkin'...*Nancy Sinatra*
This Diamond Ring...*Gary Lewis & The Playboys*
This Guy's In Love With You...*Herb Alpert*
Those Were The Days...*Mary Hopkin*
Ticket To Ride...*Beatles*
Tighten Up...*Archie Bell & The Drells*
Time Of The Season...*Zombies*
To Sir With Love...*Lulu*
Treat Her Right...*Roy Head*
Turn! Turn! Turn!...*Byrds*
Unchained Melody...*Righteous Brothers*
Walk In The Black Forest...*Horst Jankowski*
We Can Work It Out...*Beatles*
Wedding Bell Blues...*5th Dimension*
Weight, The...*Band*
What's New Pussycat?...*Tom Jones*
When A Man Loves A Woman...*Percy Sledge*
White Rabbit...*Jefferson Airplane*
Whiter Shade Of Pale...*Procol Harum*
Wichita Lineman...*Glen Campbell*
Wild Thing...*Troggs*
Winchester Cathedral...*New Vaudeville Band*
Windy...*Association*
Woman, Woman...*Gary Puckett & The Union Gap*
Wooly Bully...*Sam The Sham & The Pharaohs*
Yellow Submarine...*Beatles*
Yesterday...*Beatles*
You Can't Hurry Love...*Supremes*
You Keep Me Hangin' On...*Supremes*
You Were On My Mind...*We Five*
(You're My) Soul And Inspiration...*Righteous Brothers*
You've Lost That Lovin' Feelin'...*Righteous Brothers*
You've Made Me So Very Happy...*Blood, Sweat & Tears*
Your Love Keeps Lifting Me Higher And Higher...*Jackie Wilson*

ABC...*Jackson 5*
Ain't No Mountain High Enough...*Diana Ross*
Ain't No Sunshine...*Bill Withers*
Air That I Breathe...*Hollies*
Alone Again (Naturally)...*Gilbert O'Sullivan*
Amazing Grace...*Judy Collins*
American Pie...*Don McLean*
American Woman...*Guess Who*
Angie...*Rolling Stones*
Angie Baby...*Helen Reddy*
Annie's Song...*John Denver*
Baby Don't Get Hooked On Me...*Mac Davis*
Back Stabbers...*O'Jays*
Bad, Bad Leroy Brown...*Jim Croce*
Band Of Gold...*Freda Payne*
Band On The Run...*Paul McCartney*
Bennie And The Jets...*Elton John*
Billy, Don't Be A Hero...*Bo Donaldson*
Black & White...*Three Dog Night*
Black Magic Woman...*Santana*
Boogie Down...*Eddie Kendricks*
Brand New Key...*Melanie*
Brandy (You're A Fine Girl)...*Looking Glass*
Bridge Over Troubled Water...*Simon & Garfunkel*
Brother Louie...*Stories*
Brown Sugar...*Rolling Stones*
Burning Love...*Elvis Presley*
Candy Man, The...*Sammy Davis, Jr.*
Can't Get Enough Of Your Love, Babe...*Barry White*
Cat's In The Cradle...*Harry Chapin*
China Grove...*Doobie Brothers*
Cisco Kid, The...*War*
Cracklin' Rosie...*Neil Diamond*
Crocodile Rock...*Elton John*
Daniel...*Elton John*
Day After Day...*Badfinger*
Do It ('Til You're Satisfied)...*B.T. Express*
Don't Let The Sun Go Down On Me...*Elton John*
Dueling Banjos...*Eric Weissberg & Steve Mandell*
Everything Is Beautiful...*Ray Stevens*
Family Affair...*Sly & The Family Stone*
Fire And Rain...*James Taylor*
First Time Ever I Saw Your Face, The...*Roberta Flack*
Frankenstein...*Edgar Winter Group*
Free Bird...*Lynyrd Skynyrd*
Give Me Love - (Give Me Peace On Earth)...*George Harrison*
Go All The Way...*Raspberries*
Goodbye Yellow Brick Road...*Elton John*
Green-Eyed Lady...*Sugarloaf*
Gypsys, Tramps & Thieves...*Cher*
Have You Ever Seen The Rain...*Creedence Clearwater Revival*

Have You Seen Her...*Chi-Lites*
Heart Of Gold...*Neil Young*
Hey There Lonely Girl...*Eddie Holman*
Hold Your Head Up...*Argent*
Hooked On A Feeling...*Blue Swede*
Horse With No Name, A...*America*
How Can You Mend A Broken Heart...*Bee Gees*
I Am Woman...*Helen Reddy*
I Can Help...*Billy Swan*
I Can See Clearly Now...*Johnny Nash*
I Gotcha...*Joe Tex*
I Honestly Love You...*Olivia Newton-John*
I Shot The Sheriff...*Eric Clapton*
I Think I Love You...*Partridge Family*
I Want You Back...*Jackson 5*
I'd Love You To Want Me...*Lobo*
I'll Be There...*Jackson 5*
I'll Take You There...*Staple Singers*
If You Don't Know Me By Now...*Harold Melvin & The Bluenotes*
Imagine...*John Lennon*
Immigrant Song...*Led Zeppelin*
In The Summertime...*Mungo Jerry*
Indian Reservation...*Raiders*
Instant Karma (We All Shine On)...*John Lennon & Yoko Ono*
It's Too Late...*Carole King*
Joker, The...*Steve Miller Band*
Joy To The World...*Three Dog Night*
Just My Imagination (Running Away With Me)...*Temptations*
Keep On Truckin'...*Eddie Kendricks*
Killing Me Softly With His Song...*Roberta Flack*
King Fu Fighting...*Carl Douglas*
Knock Three Times...*Tony Orlando & Dawn*
Kodachrome...*Paul Simon*
Layla...*Derek & The Dominos (Eric Clapton)*
Lean On Me...*Bill Withers*
Let It Be...*Beatles*
Let's Get It On...*Marvin Gaye*
Let's Stay Together...*Al Green*
Live And Let Die...*Paul McCartney*
Lola...*Kinks*
Lonely Days...*Bee Gees*
Long And Winding Road, The...*Beatles*
Long Cool Woman (In A Black Dress)...*Hollies*
Lookin' Out My Back Door...*Creedence Clearwater Revival*
Love On A Two-Way Street...*Moments*
Love Train...*O'Jays*
Love You Save, The...*Jackson 5*
Love's Theme...*Love Unlimited Orchestra*
Maggie May...*Rod Stewart*
Make It With You...*Bread*
Mama Told Me (Not To Come)...*Three Dog Night*

Me And Bobby McGee...*Janis Joplin*
Me And Mrs. Jones...*Billy Paul*
Midnight Train To Georgia...*Gladys Knight & The Pips*
Money...*Pink Floyd*
Morning Has Broken...*Cat Stevens*
Most Beautiful Girl, The...*Charlie Rich*
Mr. Big Stuff...*Jean Knight*
Mr. Bojangles...*Nitty Gritty Dirt Band*
My Ding-A-Ling...*Chuck Berry*
My Love...*Paul McCartney*
My Sweet Lord...*George Harrison*
Night Chicago Died, The...*Paper Lace*
Night The Lights Went Out In Georgia, The...*Vicki Lawrence*
Night They Drove Old Dixie Down, The...*Joan Baez*
Nights In White Satin...*Moody Blues*
Nothing From Nothing...*Billy Preston*
Oh Girl...*Chi-Lites*
Ohio...*Crosby, Stills, Nash & Young*
One Bad Apple...*Osmonds*
One Less Bell To Answer...*5th Dimension*
O-o-h Child...*5 Stairsteps*
Papa Was A Rollin' Stone...*Temptations*
Patches...*Clarence Carter*
Photograph...*Ringo Starr*
Playground In My Mind...*Clint Holmes*
Proud Mary...*Ike & Tina Turner*
Put Your Hand In The Hand...*Ocean*
Raindrops Keep Fallin' On My Head...*B.J. Thomas*
Rainy Days And Mondays...*Carpenters*
Rainy Night In Georgia...*Brook Benton*
Ramblin Man...*Allman Brothers Band*
Rapper, The...*Jaggerz*
Ride Captain Ride...*Blues Image*
Rings...*Cymarron*
Rock And Roll Part 2...*Gary Glitter*
Rock Me Gently...*Andy Kim*
Rock The Boat...*Hues Corporation*
Rock Your Baby...*George McCrae*
Rocket Man...*Elton John*
Rose Garden...*Lynn Anderson*
Saturday In The Park...*Chicago*
Seasons In The Sun...*Terry Jacks*
She's A Lady...*Tom Jones*
Signed, Sealed, Delivered I'm Yours...*Stevie Wonder*
Signs...*Five Man Electrical Band*
Smiling Faces Sometimes...*Undisputed Truth*
Smoke On The Water...*Deep Purple*
Song Sung Blue...*Neil Diamond*
Spill The Wine...*Eric Burdon & War*
Spirit In The Sky...*Norman Greenbaum*
Stairway To Heaven...*Led Zeppelin*
Streak, The...*Ray Stevens*
Sundown...*Gordon Lightfoot*

Sunshine On My Shoulders...*John Denver*
Superstar...*Carpenters*
Superstition...*Stevie Wonder*
Sweet Home Alabama...*Lynyrd Skynyrd*
TSOP (The Sound Of Philadelphia)...*MFSB feat. The Three Degrees*
Take Me Home, Country Roads...*John Denver*
Tears Of A Clown, The...*Smokey Robinson & The Miracles*
Thank You (Falettinme Be Mice Elf Agin)...*Sly & The Family Stone*
Theme From Shaft...*Isaac Hayes*
Then Came You...*Dionne Warwicke & Spinners*
(They Long To Be) Close To You...*Carpenters*
Thrill Is Gone...*B.B. King*
Tie A Yellow Ribbon Round The Ole Oak Tree...*Tony Orlando & Dawn*
Time In A Bottle...*Jim Croce*
Too Late To Turn Back Now...*Cornelius Brothers & Sister Rose*
Top Of The World...*Carpenters*
Travelin' Band...*Creedence Clearwater Revival*
Treat Her Like A Lady...*Cornelius Brothers & Sister Rose*
25 Or 5 To 4...*Chicago*
Uncle Albert/Admiral Halsey...*Paul & Linda McCartney*
Up Around The Bend...*Creedence Clearwater Revival*
Vehicle...*Ides Of March*
Venus...*Shocking Blue*
Want Ads...*Honey Cone*
War...*Edwin Starr*
Way We Were, The...*Barbra Streisand*
We're An American Band...*Grand Funk*
We've Only Just Begun...*Carpenters*
Whatcha See Is Whatcha Get...*Dramatics*
Whatever Gets You Thru The Night...*John Lennon*
What's Going On...*Marvin Gaye*
Which Way You Goin' Billy?...*Poppy Family*
Who'll Stop The Rain...*Creedence Clearwater Revival*
Whole Lotta Love...*Led Zeppelin*
Will It Go Round In Circles...*Billy Preston*
Without You...*Nilsson*
Won't Get Fooled Again...*Who*
You Ain't Seen Nothing Yet...*Bachman-Turner Overdrive*
You Are The Sunshine Of My Life...*Stevie Wonder*
You Make Me Feel Brand New...*Stylistics*
(You're) Having My Baby...*Paul Anka w/ Odia Coates*
You're Sixteen...*Ringo Starr*
You're So Vain...*Carly Simon*
You've Got A Friend...*James Taylor*
Your Song...*Elton John*

After The Love Has Gone...*Earth, Wind & Fire*
Afternoon Delight...*Starland Vocal Band*
All By Myself...*Eric Carmen*
Babe...*Styx*
Baby Come Back...*Player*
Bad Blood...*Neil Sedaka*
Bad Girls...*Donna Summer*
Baker Street...*Gerry Rafferty*
Before The Next Teardrop Falls...*Freddy Fender*
Best Of My Love...*Eagles*
Best Of My Love...*Emotions*
Black Water...*Doobie Brothers*
Blinded By The Light...*Manfred Mann*
Blitzkrieg Bop...*Ramones*
Blue Eyes Crying In The Rain...*Willie Nelson*
Bohemian Rhapsody...*Queen*
Boogie Fever...*Sylvers*
Boogie Nights...*Heatwave*
Boogie Oogie Oogie...*Taste Of Honey*
Born To Be Alive...*Patrick Hernandez*
Born To Run...*Bruce Springsteen*
Car Wash...*Rose Royce*
Convoy...*C.W. McCall*
Da Ya Think I'm Sexy?...*Rod Stewart*
Dancing Queen...*Abba*
December, 1963 (Oh, What A Night) ...*4 Seasons*
Devil Went Down To Georgia, The...*Charlie Daniels Band*
Disco Lady...*Johnnie Taylor*
Don't Bring Me Down...*Electric Light Orchestra*
Don't Fear The Reaper...*Blue Öyster Cult*
Don't Go Breaking My Heart...*Elton John & Kiki Dee*
Don't It Make My Brown Eyes Blue...*Crystal Gayle*
Don't Leave Me This Way...*Thelma Houston*
Don't Stop...*Fleetwood Mac*
Don't Stop 'Til You Get Enough...*Michael Jackson*
Dream Weaver...*Gary Wright*
Dreams...*Fleetwood Mac*
Escape (The Pina Colada Song)...*Rupert Holmes*
Every Which Way But Loose...*Eddie Rabbitt*
Fallin' In Love...*Hamilton, Joe Frank & Reynolds*
Fame...*David Bowie*
50 Ways To Leave Your Lover...*Paul Simon*
Fire...*Pointer Sisters*
Float On...*Floaters*
Fly Like An Eagle...*Steve Miller*
Fly, Robin, Fly...*Silver Convention*
Fooled Around And Fell In Love...*Elvin Bishop*
Fox On The Run...*Sweet*
Get Down Tonight...*KC & The Sunshine Band*
Get Up, Stand Up...*Bob Marley*

Go Your Own Way...*Fleetwood Mac*
Good Times...*Chic*
Got To Give It Up...*Marvin Gaye*
Grease...*Frankie Valli*
Have You Never Been Mellow...*Olivia Newton-John*
He Don't Love You (Like I Love You)...*Tony Orlando & Dawn*
Heart Of Glass...*Blondie*
Heartache Tonight...*Eagles*
Heaven Knows...*Donna Summer & Brooklyn Dreams*
Here You Come Again...*Dolly Parton*
Heroes...*David Bowie*
Hopelessly Devoted To You...*Olivia Newton-John*
Hot Blooded...*Foreigner*
Hot Child In The City...*Nick Gilder*
Hot Stuff...*Donna Summer*
Hotel California...*Eagles*
How Deep Is Your Love...*Bee Gees*
Hustle, The...*Van McCoy*
I Just Want To Be Your Everything...*Andy Gibb*
I Want You To Want Me...*Cheap Trick*
I Will Survive...*Gloria Gaynor*
I Write The Songs...*Barry Manilow*
I'd Really Love To See You Tonight...*England Dan & John Ford Coley*
I'm In You...*Peter Frampton*
I'm Not In Love...*10cc*
I'm Your Boogie Man...*KC & The Sunshine Band*
If I Can't Have You...*Yvonne Elliman*
If You Leave Me Now...*Chicago*
In The Navy...*Village People*
Island Girl...*Elton John*
It's A Heartache...*Bonnie Tyler*
Jive Talkin'...*Bee Gees*
Junior's Farm...*Paul McCartney*
Just The Way You Are...*Billy Joel*
Just When I Needed You Most...*Randy Vanwarmer*
Kiss And Say Goodbye...*Manhattans*
Kiss You All Over...*Exile*
Knock On Wood...*Amii Stewart*
Lady Marmalade...*LaBelle*
Last Dance...*Donna Summer*
Last Farewell, The...*Roger Whittaker*
Laughter In The Rain...*Neil Sedaka*
Lay Down Sally...*Eric Clapton*
Le Freak...*Chic*
Let Your Love Flow...*Bellamy Brothers*
Let's Do It Again...*Staple Singers*
Let's Go...*The Cars*
Listen To What The Man Said...*Paul McCartney*
Logical Song, The...*Supertramp*

Love Hangover...*Diana Ross*
(Love Is) Thicker Than Water...*Andy Gibb*
Love Machine...*Miracles*
Love Rollercoaster...*Ohio Players*
Love Theme From "A Star Is Born" (Evergreen)...*Barbra Streisand*
Love To Love You Baby...*Donna Summer*
Love Will Keep Us Together...*Captain & Tennille*
Lovin' You...*Minnie Riperton*
Lucille...*Kenny Rogers*
Lucy In The Sky With Diamonds...*Elton John*
Lyin' Eyes...*Eagles*
MacArthur Park...*Donna Summer*
Macho Man...*Village People*
Mandy...*Barry Manilow*
Margaritaville...*Jimmy Buffett*
Miss You...*Rolling Stones*
More Than A Feeling...*Boston*
Music Box Dancer...*Frank Mills*
My Eyes Adored You...*Frankie Valli*
My Life...*Billy Joel*
My Sharona...*Knack*
New Kid In Town...*Eagles*
Night Fever...*Bee Gees*
Night Moves...*Bob Seger*
No More Tears (Enough Is Enough)...*Barbra Streisand & Donna Summer*
No Woman No Cry (live)...*Bob Marley*
Nobody Does It Better...*Carly Simon*
One Of These Nights...*Eagles*
Philadelphia Freedom...*Elton John*
Pick Up The Pieces...*AWB*
Play That Funky Music...*Wild Cherry*
Pop Muzik...*M*
Rapper's Delight...*Sugarhill Gang*
Reunited...*Peaches & Herb*
Rhinestone Cowboy...*Glen Campbell*
Rich Girl...*Daryl Hall & John Oates*
Right Back Where We Started From...*Maxine Nightingale*
Ring My Bell...*Anita Ward*
Rise...*Herb Alpert*
Rock & Roll All Nite (live)...*Kiss*
Rock'n Me...*Steve Miller*
Roxanne...*Police*
Rubberband Man, The...*Spinners*
Saturday Night...*Bay City Rollers*
Send One Your Love...*Stevie Wonder*
Shadow Dancing...*Andy Gibb*
(Shake, Shake, Shake) Shake Your Booty ...*KC & The Sunshine Band*
Shining Star...*Earth, Wind & Fire*
Short People...*Randy Newman*
Show Me The Way...*Peter Frampton*
Silly Love Songs...*Paul McCartney*
Sir Duke...*Stevie Wonder*
Sister Golden Hair...*America*

Sometimes When We Touch...*Dan Hill*
Southern Nights...*Glen Campbell*
Star Wars Theme/Cantina Band...*Meco*
Stayin' Alive...*Bee Gees*
Sultans Of Swing...*Dire Straits*
Sweet Emotion...*Aerosmith*
Take A Chance On Me...*Abba*
Take It To The Limit...*Eagles*
Take Me To The River...*Talking Heads*
Take The Money And Run...*Steve Miller Band*
Thank God I'm A Country Boy...*John Denver*
That's The Way (I Like It)...*KC & The Sunshine Band*
Theme From Mahogany (Do You Know Where You're Going To)...*Diana Ross*
Theme From S.W.A.T....*Rhythm Heritage*
Three Times A Lady...*Commodores*
Thunder Road...*Bruce Springsteen*
Tonight's The Night (Gonna Be Alright)...*Rod Stewart*
Too Much Heaven...*Bee Gees*
Too Much, Too Little, Too Late...*Johnny Mathis & Deniece Williams*
Torn Between Two Lovers...*Mary MacGregor*
Tragedy...*Bee Gees*
Tusk...*Fleetwood Mac*
Undercover Angel...*Alan O'Day*
Walk This Way...*Aerosmith*
Watching The Detectives...*Elvis Costello*
We Are Family...*Sister Sledge*
We Will Rock You/We Are The Champions ...*Queen*
Welcome Back...*John Sebastian*
Werewolves Of London...*Warren Zevon*
What A Fool Believes...*Doobie Brothers*
When I Need You...*Leo Sayer*
When Will I Be Loved...*Linda Ronstadt*
Who Loves You...*4 Seasons*
Why Can't We Be Friends...*War*
With A Little Luck...*Paul McCartney*
Wreck Of The Edmund Fitzgerald, The ...*Gordon Lightfoot*
Y.M.C.A....*Village People*
You Don't Bring Me Flowers...*Barbra Streisand & Neil Diamond*
You Light Up My Life...*Debby Boone*
You Make Me Feel Like Dancing...*Leo Sayer*
You Needed Me...*Anne Murray*
You Sexy Thing...*Hot Chocolate*
You Should Be Dancing...*Bee Gees*
You'll Never Find Another Love Like Mine...*Lou Rawls*
You're In My Heart...*Rod Stewart*
You're No Good...*Linda Ronstadt*
You're The First, The Last, My Everything ...*Barry White*
You're The One That I Want...*John Travolta & Olivia Newton-John*

Abracadabra...*Steve Miller Band*
Africa...*Toto*
Against All Odds (Take A Look At Me Now)...*Phil Collins*
Against The Wind...*Bob Seger*
All Night Long (All Night)...*Lionel Richie*
All Out Of Love...*Air Supply*
All Those Years Ago...*George Harrison*
Always On My Mind...*Willie Nelson*
Another Brick In The Wall...*Pink Floyd*
Another One Bites The Dust...*Queen*
Arthur's Theme (Best That You Can Do)...*Christopher Cross*
Baby, Come To Me...*Patti Austin w/ James Ingram*
Back On The Chain Gang...*Pretenders*
Beat It...*Michael Jackson*
Best Of Times, The...*Styx*
Bette Davis Eyes...*Kim Carnes*
Billie Jean...*Michael Jackson*
Burning Down The House...*Talking Heads*
Call Me...*Blondie*
Caribbean Queen (No More Love On The Run)...*Billy Ocean*
Cars...*Gary Numan*
Celebration...*Kool & The Gang*
Centerfold...*J. Geils Band*
Chariots Of Fire...*Vangelis*
Come Dancing...*Kinks*
Come On Eileen...*Dexys Midnight Runners*
Coming Up (Live At Glasgow)...*Paul McCartney*
Coward Of The County...*Kenny Rogers*
Crazy Little Thing Called Love...*Queen*
Cum On Feel The Noize...*Quiet Riot*
Dance Hall Days...*Wang Chung*
Dancing In The Dark...*Bruce Springsteen*
De Do Do Do, De Da Da Da...*Police*
Der Kommissar...*After The Fire*
Dirty Laundry...*Don Henley*
Do That To Me One More Time...*Captain & Tennille*
Do You Really Want To Hurt Me...*Culture Club*
Don't Talk To Strangers...*Rick Springfield*
Don't You Want Me...*Human League*
Down Under...*Men At Work*
Drive...*Cars*
Drivin' My Life Away...*Eddie Rabbitt*
Ebony And Ivory...*Paul McCartney w/ Stevie Wonder*
867-5309/Jenny...*Tommy Tutone*
Electric Avenue...*Eddy Grant*
Elvira...*Oak Ridge Boys*
Emotional Rescue...*Rolling Stones*
Endless Love...*Diana Ross & Lionel Richie*
Every Breath You Take...*Police*
Every Little Thing She Does Is Magic...*Police*

Eye In The Sky...*Alan Parsons Project*
Eye Of The Tiger...*Survivor*
Eyes Without A Face...*Billy Idol*
Fame...*Irene Cara*
Flashdance...What A Feeling...*Irene Cara*
Fool In The Rain...*Led Zeppelin*
Footloose...*Kenny Loggins*
For Your Eyes Only...*Sheena Easton*
Freeze-Frame...*J. Geils Band*
Funkytown...*Lipps, Inc.*
Ghostbusters...*Ray Parker Jr.*
Girl Is Mine, The...*Michael Jackson & Paul McCartney*
Girls Just Want To Have Fun...*Cyndi Lauper*
Gloria...*Laura Branigan*
Goody Two Shoes...*Adam Ant*
Hard To Say I'm Sorry...*Chicago*
Harden My Heart...*Quarterflash*
He Stopped Loving Her Today...*George Jones*
He's So Shy...*Pointer Sisters*
Heat Of The Moment...*Asia*
Here Comes The Rain Again...*Eurythmics*
Hit Me With Your Best Shot...*Pat Benatar*
Hold Me...*Fleetwood Mac*
Hold Me Now...*Thompson Twins*
Hungry Heart...*Bruce Springsteen*
Hungry Like The Wolf...*Duran Duran*
Hurts So Good...*John Cougar Mellencamp*
I Can't Tell You Why...*Eagles*
I Feel For You...*Chaka Khan*
I Just Called To Say I Love You...*Stevie Wonder*
I Love A Rainy Night...*Eddie Rabbitt*
I Love Rock 'N Roll...*Joan Jett & The Blackhearts*
I Melt With You...*Modern English*
I Ran (So Far Away)...*Flock Of Seagulls*
I Want Candy...*Bow Wow Wow*
Islands In The Stream...*Kenny Rogers w/ Dolly Parton*
It's Raining Again...*Supertramp*
It's Still Rock And Roll To Me...*Billy Joel*
Jack & Diane...*John Cougar Mellencamp*
Jeopardy...*Greg Kihn Band*
Jessie's Girl...*Rick Springfield*
Joanna...*Kool & The Gang*
Jump...*Van Halen*
Jump (For My Love)...*Pointer Sisters*
(Just Like) Starting Over...*John Lennon*
Just The Two Of Us...*Grover Washington, Jr. w/ Bill Withers*
Karma Chameleon...*Culture Club*
Keep On Loving You...*REO Speedwagon*
King Of Pain...*Police*
Kiss On My List...*Daryl Hall & John Oates*
Lady...*Kenny Rogers*
Let It Whip...*Dazz Band*

Let's Dance...*David Bowie*
Let's Go Crazy...*Prince*
Let's Groove...*Earth, Wind & Fire*
Let's Hear It For The Boy...*Deniece Williams*
Like A Virgin...*Madonna*
Little Jeannie...*Elton John*
Little Red Corvette...*Prince*
London Calling...*Clash*
Lost In Love...*Air Supply*
Love On The Rocks...*Neil Diamond*
Magic...*Olivia Newton-John*
Maneater...*Daryl Hall & John Oates*
Maniac...*Michael Sembello*
Master Blaster (Jammin')...*Stevie Wonder*
Message, The...*Grand Master Flash*
Mickey...*Toni Basil*
Missing You...*John Waite*
More Than I Can Say...*Leo Sayer*
Morning Train (Nine To Five)...*Sheena Easton*
Mr. Roboto...*Styx*
Never Knew Love Like This Before...*Stephanie Mills*
New Year's Day...*U2*
9 To 5...*Dolly Parton*
99 Luftballons...*Nena*
Oh Sherrie...*Steve Perry*
On The Road Again...*Willie Nelson*
One Thing Leads To Another...*Fixx*
Open Arms...*Journey*
Our Lips Are Sealed...*Go-Go's*
Out Of Touch...*Daryl Hall & John Oates*
Owner Of A Lonely Heart...*Yes*
Physical...*Olivia Newton-John*
Planet Rock...*Afrika Bambaataa*
Please Don't Go...*KC & The Sunshine Band*
Private Eyes...*Daryl Hall & John Oates*
Purple Rain...*Prince*
Puttin' On The Ritz...*Taco*
Queen Of Hearts...*Juice Newton*
Rapture...*Blondie*
Rebel Yell...*Billy Idol*
Redemption Song...*Bob Marley*
Reflex, The...*Duran Duran*
Relax...*Frankie Goes To Hollywood*
Ride Like The Wind...*Christopher Cross*
Rock The Casbah...*Clash*
Rock This Town...*Stray Cats*
Rock With You...*Michael Jackson*
Rosanna...*Toto*
Rose, The...*Bette Midler*
Safety Dance, The...*Men Without Hats*
Sailing...*Christopher Cross*
Say Say Say...*Paul McCartney & Michael Jackson*

Sexual Healing...*Marvin Gaye*
Shake It Up...*Cars*
Shame On The Moon...*Bob Seger*
She Works Hard For The Money...*Donna Summer*
Shining Star...*Manhattans*
Sister Christian...*Night Ranger*
Slow Hand...*Pointer Sisters*
Start Me Up...*Rolling Stones*
Stop Draggin' My Heart Around...*Stevie Nicks w/ Tom Petty*
Stray Cat Strut...*Stray Cats*
Sukiyaki...*Taste Of Honey*
Sweet Dreams (Are Made Of This)...*Eurythmics*
Switchin' To Glide...*The Kings*
Tainted Love...*Soft Cell*
Take It On The Run...*REO Speedwagon*
Take Your Time (Do It Right)...*S.O.S. Band*
Talking In Your Sleep...*Romantics*
Tell Her About It...*Billy Joel*
Theme From New York, New York...*Frank Sinatra*
Thriller...*Michael Jackson*
Tide Is High, The...*Blondie*
Time After Time...*Cyndi Lauper*
To All The Girls I've Loved Before...*Julio Iglesias & Willie Nelson*
Total Eclipse Of The Heart...*Bonnie Tyler*
True...*Spandau Ballet*
Truly...*Lionel Richie*
Under Pressure...*Queen & David Bowie*
Up Where We Belong...*Joe Cocker & Jennifer Warnes*
Upside Down...*Diana Ross*
Uptown Girl...*Billy Joel*
Waiting For A Girl Like You...*Foreigner*
Wake Me Up Before You Go-Go...*Wham!*
Wanderer, The...*Donna Summer*
We Got The Beat...*Go-Go's*
What's Love Got To Do With It...*Tina Turner*
When Doves Cry...*Prince*
Whip It...*Devo*
Who Can It Be Now?...*Men At Work*
Wild Boys, The...*Duran Duran*
Woman...*John Lennon*
Woman In Love...*Barbra Streisand*
Working For The Weekend...*Loverboy*
Xanadu...*Olivia Newton-John/Electric Light Orchestra*
You Shook Me All Night Long...*AC/DC*
You Should Hear How She Talks About You...*Melissa Manchester*
Young Turks...*Rod Stewart*

Addicted To Love...*Robert Palmer*
All I Need...*Jack Wagner*
Alone...*Heart*
Always...*Atlantic Starr*
Amanda...*Boston*
Another Day In Paradise...*Phil Collins*
Anything For You...*Gloria Estefan*
At This Moment...*Billy Vera & The Beaters*
Axel F...*Harold Faltermeyer*
Baby Don't Forget My Number...*Milli Vanilli*
Baby, I Love Your Way/Freebird Medley...*Will To Power*
Back To Life...*Soul II Soul*
Bad...*Michael Jackson*
Bad Medicine...*Bon Jovi*
Batdance...*Prince*
Blame It On The Rain...*Milli Vanilli*
Born In The U.S.A. ...*Bruce Springsteen*
Boys Of Summer, The...*Don Henley*
Broken Wings...*Mr. Mister*
Buffalo Stance...*Neneh Cherry*
Bust A Move...*Young MC*
Can't Fight This Feeling...*REO Speedwagon*
Careless Whisper...*Wham!/George Michael*
Causing A Commotion...*Madonna*
Cherish...*Kool & The Gang*
Crazy For You...*Madonna*
Dancing On The Ceiling...*Lionel Richie*
Danger Zone...*Kenny Loggins*
Devil Inside...*INXS*
Didn't We Almost Have It All...*Whitney Houston*
Dirty Diana...*Michael Jackson*
Don't Come Around Here No More...*Tom Petty*
Don't Dream It's Over...*Crowded House*
Don't Forget Me (When I'm Gone)...*Glass Tiger*
Don't Know Much...*Linda Ronstadt w/ Aaron Neville*
Don't Wanna Lose You...*Gloria Estefan*
Don't Worry Be Happy...*Bobby McFerrin*
Don't You (Forget About Me)...*Simple Minds*
Eternal Flame...*Bangles*
Every Rose Has Its Thorn...*Poison*
Everybody Have Fun Tonight...*Wang Chung*
Everybody Wants To Rule The World...*Tears For Fears*
Everything She Wants...*Wham!*
Everytime You Go Away...*Paul Young*
Express Yourself...*Madonna*
Faith...*George Michael*
Fast Car...*Tracy Chapman*
Father Figure...*George Michael*
Final Countdown, The...*Europe*
Flame, The...*Cheap Trick*
Forever Your Girl...*Paula Abdul*
Freedom...*Wham!/George Michael*
Get Outta My Dreams, Get Into My Car...*Billy Ocean*

Girl I'm Gonna Miss You...*Milli Vanilli*
Glory Of Love...*Peter Cetera*
Good Thing...*Fine Young Cannibals*
Got My Mind Set On You...*George Harrison*
Graceland...*Paul Simon*
Greatest Love Of All...*Whitney Houston*
Groovy Kind Of Love...*Phil Collins*
Hands To Heaven...*Breathe*
Hangin' Tough...*New Kids On The Block*
Hazy Shade Of Winter...*Bangles*
Head To Toe...*Lisa Lisa & Cult Jam*
Heat Is On, The...*Glenn Frey*
Heaven...*Bryan Adams*
Heaven Is A Place On Earth...*Belinda Carlisle*
Here I Go Again...*Whitesnake*
Higher Love...*Steve Winwood*
Hold On To The Nights...*Richard Marx*
Holding Back The Years...*Simply Red*
How Will I Know...*Whitney Houston*
Human...*Human League*
I Just Can't Stop Loving You...*Michael Jackson*
(I Just) Died In Your Arms...*Cutting Crew*
I Knew You Were Waiting (For Me)...*Aretha Franklin & George Michael*
I Still Haven't Found What I'm Looking For ...*U2*
I Think We're Alone Now...*Tiffany*
I Wanna Dance With Somebody (Who Loves Me)...*Whitney Houston*
I Want To Know What Love Is...*Foreigner*
(I've Had) The Time Of My Life...*Bill Medley & Jennifer Warnes*
I'll Be Loving You (Forever)...*New Kids On The Block*
I'll Be There For You...*Bon Jovi*
If I Could Turn Back Time...*Cher*
If You Don't Know Me By Now...*Simply Red*
If You Leave...*Orchestral Manoeuvres In The Dark*
If You Love Somebody Set Them Free...*Sting*
Invisible Touch...*Genesis*
Jacob's Ladder...*Huey Lewis*
Keep Your Hands To Yourself...*Georgia Satellites*
Kiss...*Prince*
Kokomo...*Beach Boys*
Kyrie...*Mr. Mister*
La Bamba...*Los Lobos*
Lady In Red, The...*Chris DeBurgh*
Lean On Me...*Club Nouveau*
Life In A Northern Town...*Dream Academy*
Like A Prayer...*Madonna*
Listen To Your Heart...*Roxette*
Livin' On A Prayer...*Bon Jovi*
Living Years, The...*Mike & The Mechanics*

Look, The...*Roxette*
Looking For A New Love...*Jody Watley*
Lost In Emotion...*Lisa Lisa & Cult Jam*
Lost In Your Eyes...*Debbie Gibson*
Love Shack...*B-52's*
Loverboy...*Billy Ocean*
Luka...*Suzanne Vega*
Man In The Mirror...*Michael Jackson*
Manic Monday...*Bangles*
Material Girl...*Madonna*
Mercedes Boy...*Pebbles*
Miami Vice Theme...*Jan Hammer*
Miss You Much...*Janet Jackson*
Money For Nothing...*Dire Straits*
Monkey...*George Michael*
Mony Mony "Live"...*Billy Idol*
My Hometown...*Bruce Springsteen*
My Prerogative...*Bobby Brown*
Need You Tonight...*INXS*
Never Gonna Give You Up...*Rick Astley*
Nothing's Gonna Stop Us Now...*Starship*
Notorious...*Duran Duran*
Oh Sheila...*Ready For The World*
On My Own...*Patti LaBelle & Michael McDonald*
On Our Own...*Bobby Brown*
One More Night...*Phil Collins*
One More Try...*George Michael*
One Night In Bangkok...*Murray Head*
Orinoco Flow (Sail Away)...*Enya*
Papa Don't Preach...*Madonna*
Part-Time Lover...*Stevie Wonder*
Patience...*Guns N' Roses*
People Are People...*Depeche Mode*
Pour Some Sugar On Me...*Def Leppard*
Power Of Love, The...*Huey Lewis*
Pump Up The Volume...*M/A/R/R/S*
Raspberry Beret...*Prince*
Red Red Wine...*UB40*
Rhythm Of The Night...*DeBarge*
Right Here Waiting...*Richard Marx*
R.O.C.K. In The U.S.A....*John Cougar Mellencamp*
Rock Me Amadeus...*Falco*
Roll With It...*Steve Winwood*
St. Elmo's Fire (Man In Motion)...*John Parr*
Saving All My Love For You...*Whitney Houston*
Say You, Say Me...*Lionel Richie*
Sea Of Love...*Honeydrippers*
Seasons Change...*Exposé*
Separate Lives...*Phil Collins & Marilyn Martin*
Shake You Down...*Gregory Abbott*
Shakedown...*Bob Seger*
She Drives Me Crazy...*Fine Young Cannibals*
Shout...*Tears For Fears*

Simply Irresistible...*Robert Palmer*
Sledgehammer...*Peter Gabriel*
Smooth Operator...*Sade*
Somewhere Out There...*Linda Ronstadt & James Ingram*
Straight Up...*Paula Abdul*
Summer Of '69...*Bryan Adams*
Sussudio...*Phil Collins*
Sweet Child O' Mine...*Guns N' Roses*
Take My Breath Away...*Berlin*
Take On Me...*A-Ha*
That's What Friends Are For...*Dionne Warwick & Friends*
There'll Be Sad Songs (To Make You Cry)...*Billy Ocean*
These Dreams...*Heart*
Touch Of Grey...*Grateful Dead*
Toy Soldiers...*Martika*
True Colors...*Cyndi Lauper*
Two Hearts...*Phil Collins*
Venus...*Bananarama*
View To A Kill, A...*Duran Duran*
Walk Like An Egyptian...*Bangles*
Walk Of Life...*Dire Straits*
Walk This Way...*Run-D.M.C.*
Way It Is, The...*Bruce Hornsby*
Way You Make Me Feel, The...*Michael Jackson*
We Are The World...*USA For Africa*
We Belong...*Pat Benatar*
We Built This City...*Starship*
We Didn't Start The Fire...*Billy Joel*
We Don't Need Another Hero (Thunderdome)...*Tina Turner*
West End Girls...*Pet Shop Boys*
What Have I Done To Deserve This?...*Pet Shop Boys & Dusty Springfield*
When I See You Smile...*Bad English*
When I Think Of You...*Janet Jackson*
When I'm With You...*Sheriff*
Where Do Broken Hearts Go...*Whitney Houston*
Why Can't This Be Love...*Van Halen*
Wild Thing...*Tone Loc*
Wild, Wild West...*Escape Club*
Wind Beneath My Wings...*Bette Midler*
Wishing Well...*Terence Trent D'Arby*
With Or Without You...*U2*
Word Up...*Cameo*
You Belong To The City...*Glenn Frey*
You Give Love A Bad Name...*Bon Jovi*
You Gotta Fight For Your Right To Party!...*Beastie Boys*
You're The Inspiration...*Chicago*

Achy Breaky Heart...*Billy Ray Cyrus*
Again...*Janet Jackson*
All 4 Love...*Color Me Badd*
All For Love...*Bryan Adams/Rod Stewart/Sting*
All I Wanna Do...*Sheryl Crow*
All I Wanna Do Is Make Love To You...*Heart*
All That She Wants...*Ace Of Base*
All The Man That I Need...*Whitney Houston*
Always...*Bon Jovi*
Another Night...*Real McCoy*
Baby Baby...*Amy Grant*
Baby-Baby-Baby...*TLC*
Baby Got Back...*Sir Mix-A-Lot*
Baby, I Love Your Way...*Big Mountain*
Back & Forth...*Aaliyah*
Bad Boys...*Inner Circle*
Beauty And The Beast...*Celine Dion & Peabo Bryson*
Because I Love You (The Postman Song) ...*Stevie B*
Black Cat...*Janet Jackson*
Black Or White...*Michael Jackson*
Black Velvet...*Alannah Myles*
Blaze Of Glory...*Jon Bon Jovi*
Boot Scootin' Boogie...*Brooks & Dunn*
Breathe Again...*Toni Braxton*
Bump N' Grind...*R. Kelly*
Can You Feel The Love Tonight...*Elton John*
Can't Help Falling In Love...*UB40*
(Can't Live Without Your) Love And Affection ...*Nelson*
Can't Stop This Thing We Started...*Bryan Adams*
Chattahoochee...*Alan Jackson*
Close To You...*Maxi Priest*
Coming Out Of The Dark...*Gloria Estefan*
Cradle Of Love...*Billy Idol*
Crazy...*Seal*
Cream...*Prince*
Dangerous...*Roxette*
Diamonds And Pearls...*Prince*
Do Anything...*Natural Selection*
Don't Let The Sun Go Down On Me...*George Michael & Elton John*
Don't Take The Girl...*Tim McGraw*
Downtown Train...*Rod Stewart*
Dreamlover...*Mariah Carey*
Electric Slide (Boogie)...*Marcia Griffiths*
Emotions...*Mariah Carey*
End Of The Road...*Boyz II Men*
Escapade...*Janet Jackson*
Every Heartbeat...*Amy Grant*
Everything About You...*Ugly Kid Joe*
(Everything I Do) I Do It For You...*Bryan Adams*
Fantastic Voyage...*Coolio*

Fields Of Gold...*Sting*
First Time, The...*Surface*
Free Fallin'...*Tom Petty*
Friends In Low Places...*Garth Brooks*
From A Distance...*Bette Midler*
Gonna Make You Sweat (Everybody Dance Now)...*C & C Music Factory*
Good Vibrations...*Marky Mark w/ Loleatta Holloway*
Have I Told You Lately...*Rod Stewart*
Hazard...*Richard Marx*
Here Come The Hotstepper...*Ini Kamoze*
Hero...*Mariah Carey*
Hey Mr. D.J....*Zhané*
High Enough...*Damn Yankees*
Hippychick...*Soho*
Hold On...*Wilson Phillips*
Hold You Tight...*Tara Kemp*
How Am I Supposed To Live Without You ...*Michael Bolton*
How Do You Talk To An Angel...*Heights*
Humpty Dance...*Digital Underground*
I Adore Mi Amor...*Color Me Badd*
I Don't Have The Heart...*James Ingram*
I Like The Way (The Kissing Game)...*Hi-Five*
I Love Your Smile...*Shanice*
I Swear...*All-4-One*
I Wanna Be Down...*Brandy*
I Wanna Be Rich...*Calloway*
I Will Always Love You...*Whitney Houston*
I Wish It Would Rain Down...*Phil Collins*
I'd Die Without You...*PM Dawn*
I'll Be There...*Mariah Carey*
I'll Be Your Everything...*Tommy Page*
I'll Make Love To You...*Boyz II Men*
I'll Never Let You Go (Angel Eyes)...*Steelheart*
I'll Stand By You...*Pretenders*
I'm Gonna Be (500 Miles)...*Proclaimers*
I'm Too Sexy...*R*S*F (Right Said Fred)*
I'm Your Baby Tonight...*Whitney Houston*
I've Been Thinking About You...*Londonbeat*
Ice Ice Baby...*Vanilla Ice*
If I Ever Fall In Love...*Shai*
If I Had No Loot...*Tony! Toni! Toné!*
If Wishes Came True...*Sweet Sensation*
If You Asked Me To...*Celine Dion*
Indian Outlaw...*Tim McGraw*
Informer...*Snow*
It Ain't Over 'Til It's Over...*Lenny Kravitz*
It Must Have Been Love...*Roxette*
It's So Hard To Say Goodbye To Yesterday ...*Boyz II Men*
Janie's Got A Gun...*Aerosmith*
Jeremy...*Pearl Jam*
Joey...*Concrete Blonde*
Joyride...*Roxette*

Jump...*Kris Kross*
Jump Around...*House Of Pain*
Just A Friend...*Biz Markie*
Just Another Day...*Jon Secada*
Justified & Ancient...*KLF w/ Tammy Wynette*
Justify My Love...*Madonna*
Lately...*Jodeci*
Let's Get Rocked...*Def Leppard*
Linger...*The Cranberries*
Live And Learn...*Joe Public*
Looking Through Patient Eyes...*PM Dawn*
Loser...*Beck*
Losing My Religion...*R.E.M.*
Love Is...*Vanessa Williams & Brian McKnight*
Love Takes Time...*Mariah Carey*
Love Will Lead You Back...*Taylor Dayne*
Love Will Never Do (Without You)...*Janet Jackson*
Masterpiece...*Atlantic Starr*
Mmm Mmm Mmm Mmm...*Crash Test Dummies*
More Than Words...*Extreme*
More Than Words Can Say...*Alias*
Most Beautiful Girl In The World, The...*Prince*
Mr. Jones...*Counting Crows*
Mr. Wendal...*Arrested Development*
My Lovin' (You're Never Gonna Get It)... *En Vogue*
Nothing Compares 2 U...*Sinéad O'Connor*
November Rain...*Guns N' Roses*
Now And Forever...*Richard Marx*
Nuthin' But A "G" Thang...*Dr. Dre*
On Bended Knee...*Boyz II Men*
One...*U2*
One More Try...*Timmy -T-*
O.P.P. ...*Naughty By Nature*
Opposites Attract...*Paula Abdul*
Ordinary World...*Duran Duran*
Personal Jesus...*Depeche Mode*
Poison...*Bell Biv DeVoe*
Power, The...*Snap!*
Power Of Love, The...*Celine Dion*
Pray...*MC Hammer*
Praying For Time...*George Michael*
Promise Of A New Day, The...*Paula Abdul*
Pump Up The Jam...*Technotronic*
Regulate...*Warren G. & Nate Dogg*
Release Me...*Wilson Phillips*
Remember The Time...*Michael Jackson*
Return To Innocence...*Enigma*
Rhythm Is A Dancer...*Snap!*
Rhythm Nation...*Janet Jackson*
Rhythm Of My Heart...*Rod Stewart*

Right Here/Human Nature...*SWV*
Right Here, Right Now...*Jesus Jones*
River Of Dreams, The...*Billy Joel*
Romantic...*Karyn White*
Rump Shaker...*Wreckx-N-Effect*
Runaway Train...*Soul Asylum*
Rush, Rush...*Paula Abdul*
Save The Best For Last...*Vanessa Williams*
Set Adrift On Memory Bliss...*PM Dawn*
7...*Prince*
She Ain't Worth It...*Glenn Medeiros*
Shoop...*Salt-N-Pepa*
Show Me Love...*Robin S*
Show Me The Way...*Styx*
Sign, The...*Ace Of Base*
Smells Like Teen Spirit...*Nirvana*
So Much In Love...*All-4-One*
Someday...*Mariah Carey*
Something To Talk About...*Bonnie Raitt*
Sometimes Love Just Ain't Enough...*Patty Smyth w/ Don Henley*
Stay...*Shakespear's Sister*
Stay (I Missed You)...*Lisa Loeb & Nine Stories*
Step By Step...*New Kids On The Block*
Streets Of Philadelphia...*Bruce Springsteen*
Tears In Heaven...*Eric Clapton*
Tennessee...*Arrested Development*
That's The Way Love Goes...*Janet Jackson*
This Used To Be My Playground...*Madonna*
To Be With You...*Mr. Big*
2 Legit 2 Quit...*MC Hammer*
Two To Make It Right...*Seduction*
U Can't Touch This...*M.C. Hammer*
Unbelievable...*EMF*
Under The Bridge...*Red Hot Chili Peppers*
Unskinny Bop...*Poison*
Vision Of Love...*Mariah Carey*
Vogue...*Madonna*
Walking On Broken Glass...*Annie Lennox*
Weak...*SWV*
What Is Love...*Haddaway*
What's Up...*4 Non Blondes*
Whatta Man...*Salt 'N' Pepa w/ En Vogue*
Where Does My Heart Beat Now...*Celine Dion*
Whole New World (Aladdin's Theme)...*Peabo Bryson & Regina Belle*
Whoomp! (There It Is)...*Tag Team*
Wicked Game...*Chris Isaak*
Wild Night...*John Mellencamp & Me'Shell Ndegéocello*
You're In Love...*Wilson Phillips*

Adia...*Sarah McLachlan*
All My Life...*K-Ci & JoJo*
All Star...*Smash Mouth*
Always Be My Baby...*Mariah Carey*
Angel...*Sarah McLachlan*
Angel Of Mine...*Monica*
Are You That Somebody?...*Aaliyah*
As I Lay Me Down...*Sophie B. Hawkins*
As Long As You Love Me...*Backstreet Boys*
Baby...*Brandy*
Baby One More Time...*Britney Spears*
Back At One...*Brian McKnight*
Back For Good...*Take That*
Bailamos...*Enrique Iglesias*
Basket Case...*Green Day*
Be My Lover...*La Bouche*
Because Of You...*98°*
Because You Loved Me...*Celine Dion*
Believe...*Cher*
Better Man...*Pearl Jam*
Big Poppa...*Notorious B.I.G.*
Bills, Bills, Bills...*Destiny's Child*
Bitch...*Meredith Brooks*
Boombastic...*Shaggy*
Boy Is Mine, The...*Brandy & Monica*
Breakfast At Tiffany's...*Deep Blue Something*
Buddy Holly...*Weezer*
Butterfly Kisses...*Bob Carlisle*
California Love...*2Pac*
Can't Nobody Hold Me Down...*Puff Daddy w/ Mase*
Candle In The Wind 1997...*Elton John*
Candy Rain...*Soul For Real*
Change The World...*Eric Clapton*
Colors Of The Wind...*Vanessa Williams*
C'Mon N' Ride It (The Train)...*Quad City DJ's*
Come With Me...*Puff Daddy*
Cotton Eye Joe...*Rednex*
Crash Into Me...*Dave Matthews Band*
Creep...*TLC*
Crossroads, Tha...*Bone Thugs-N-Harmony*
Crush...*Jennifer Paige*
Don't Let Go (Love)...*En Vogue*
Don't Speak...*No Doubt*
Don't Take It Personal...*Monica*
Doo Wop (That Thing)...*Lauryn Hill*
Every Morning...*Sugar Ray*
Everybody (Backstreet's Back)...*Backstreet Boys*
Exhale (Shoop Shoop)...*Whitney Houston*
Fantasy...*Mariah Carey*
Feel So Good...*Mase*
First Night, The...*Monica*
Fly...*Sugar Ray*
Follow You Down...*Gin Blossoms*
4 Seasons Of Loneliness...*Boyz II Men*
Freak Like Me...*Adina Howard*

Freshmen, The...*Verve Pipe*
From This Moment On...*Shania Twain*
Gangsta's Paradise...*Coolio*
Genie In A Bottle...*Christina Aguilera*
Gettin' Jiggy Wit It...*Will Smith*
Give Me One Reason...*Tracy Chapman*
Glycerine...*Bush*
God Must Have Spent A Little More Time On You...**NSYNC*
Hands...*Jewel*
Have You Ever?...*Brandy*
Have You Ever Really Loved A Woman?...*Bryan Adams*
Heartbreak Hotel...*Whitney Houston*
Hold My Hand...*Hootie & The Blowfish*
Honey...*Mariah Carey*
How Bizarre...*OMC*
How Deep Is Your Love...*Dru Hill w/ Redman*
How Do I Live...*LeAnn Rimes*
How Do U Want It...*2Pac w/ K-Ci & JoJo*
How's It Going To Be...*Third Eye Blind*
Hypnotize...*Notorious B.I.G.*
I Believe...*Blessid Union Of Souls*
I Believe I Can Fly...*R. Kelly*
I Can't Sleep Baby (If I)...*R. Kelly*
I Could Fall In Love...*Selena*
I Don't Want To Miss A Thing...*Aerosmith*
I Know...*Dionne Farris*
I Love You Always Forever...*Donna Lewis*
I Need To Know...*Marc Anthony*
I Wanna Love You Forever...*Jessica Simpson*
I Want It That Way...*Backstreet Boys*
I Want You...*Savage Garden*
I'll Be Missing You...*Puff Daddy & Faith Evans*
I'll Be There For You/You're All I Need To Get By...*Method Man w/ Mary J. Blige*
I'll Never Break Your Heart...*Backstreet Boys*
I'm The Only One...*Melissa Etheridge*
I'm Your Angel...*R. Kelly & Celine Dion*
If I Could Turn Back The Hands Of Time...*R. Kelly*
If It Makes You Happy...*Sheryl Crow*
If You Had My Love...*Jennifer Lopez*
Iris...*Goo Goo Dolls*
Ironic...*Alanis Morissette*
It's All About The Benjamins...*Puff Daddy*
It's All Coming Back To Me Now...*Celine Dion*
It's Not Right But It's Okay...*Whitney Houston*
It's Your Love...*Tim McGraw & Faith Hill*
Jumper...*Third Eye Blind*
Killing Me Softly...*Fugees feat. Lauryn Hill*
Kiss From A Rose...*Seal*
Kiss Me...*Sixpence None The Richer*
Last Kiss...*Pearl Jam*
Lately...*Divine*
Let's Ride...*Montell Jordan*
Livin' La Vida Loca...*Ricky Martin*

Long December, A...*Counting Crows*
Look Into My Eyes...*Bone Thugs-N-Harmony*
Loungin...*LL Cool J*
Lovefool...*Cardigans*
Lullaby...*Shawn Mullins*
Macarena...*Los Del Rio*
Mambo No. 5 (A Little Bit Of...)...*Lou Bega*
Men In Black...*Will Smith*
Missing...*Everything But The Girl*
MMMBop...*Hanson*
Mo Money Mo Problems...*Notorious B.I.G.*
Mouth...*Merril Bainbridge*
Music Of My Heart...**NSYNC & Gloria Estefan*
My All...*Mariah Carey*
My Body...*LSG*
My Heart Will Go On (Love Theme From 'Titanic')...*Celine Dion*
My Love Is The Shhh!...*Somethin' For The People*
My Way...*Usher*
Name...*Goo Goo Dolls*
Never Ever...*All Saints*
Nice & Slow...*Usher*
No Diggity...*Blackstreet w/ Dr. Dre*
No, No, No...*Destiny's Child w/ Wyclef Jean*
No Scrubs...*TLC*
Nobody...*Keith Sweat w/ Athena Cage*
Nobody Knows...*Tony Rich Project*
Nobody's Supposed To Be Here...*Deborah Cox*
Not Gon' Cry...*Mary J. Blige*
One Headlight...*Wallflowers*
One I Gave My Heart To...*Aaliyah*
One More Chance/Stay With Me...*Notorious B.I.G.*
One Of Us...*Joan Osborne*
One Sweet Day...*Mariah Carey & Boyz II Men*
One Week...*Barenaked Ladies*
Only Wanna Be With You...*Hootie & The Blowfish*
Please Remember Me...*Tim McGraw*
Pony...*Ginuwine*
Push...*Matchbox 20*
Quit Playing Games (With My Heart) ...*Backstreet Boys*
Ray Of Light...*Madonna*
Real World...*Matchbox 20*
Return Of The Mack...*Mark Morrison*
Rhythm Of The Night...*Corona*
Run-Around...*Blues Traveler*

Run Away...*Real McCoy*
Runaway...*Janet Jackson*
Satisfy You...*Puff Daddy w/ R. Kelly*
Save Tonight...*Eagle-Eye Cherry*
Scar Tissue...*Red Hot Chili Peppers*
Semi-Charmed Life...*Third Eye Blind*
She's All I Ever Had...*Ricky Martin*
Sittin' Up In My Room...*Brandy*
Slide...*Goo Goo Dolls*
Smooth...*Santana Feat. Rob Thomas*
Something About The Way You Look Tonight...*Elton John*
Strong Enough...*Sheryl Crow*
Summer Girls...*LFO*
Sunny Came Home...*Shawn Colvin*
Take A Bow...*Madonna*
Tell Me It's Real...*K-Ci & JoJo*
Thank U...*Alanis Morissette*
This Is For The Lover In You...*Babyface*
This Is How We Do It...*Montell Jordan*
This Kiss...*Faith Hill*
3 AM...*Matchbox 20*
Together Again...*Janet Jackson*
Too Close...*Next*
Torn...*Natalie Imbruglia*
Total Eclipse Of The Heart...*Nicki French*
Truly Madly Deeply...*Savage Garden*
Tubthumping...*Chumbawamba*
Twisted...*Keith Sweat*
2 Become 1...*Spice Girls*
Un-Break My Heart...*Toni Braxton*
Unpretty...*TLC*
Walkin' On The Sun...*Smash Mouth*
Wannabe...*Spice Girls*
Waterfalls...*TLC*
Way, The...*Fastball*
What's It Gonna Be?!...*Busta Rhymes w/ Janet Jackson*
When I Come Around...*Green Day*
Where Do You Go...*No Mercy*
Where My Girls At?...*702*
Who Dat...*JT Money*
Wild Wild West...*Will Smith*
Wonderwall...*Oasis*
You Gotta Be...*Des'ree*
You Make Me Wanna......*Usher*
You Oughta Know...*Alanis Morissette*
You Were Meant For Me...*Jewel*
You're Makin' Me High...*Toni Braxton*
You're Still The One...*Shania Twain*

Absolutely (Story Of A Girl)...*Ninedays*
Addictive...*Truth Hurts w/ Rakim*
Again...*Lenny Kravitz*
Air Force Ones...*Nelly*
All For You...*Janet Jackson*
All I Have...*Jennifer Lopez w/ LL Cool J*
All Or Nothing...*O-Town*
All The Small Things...*Blink 182*
All You Wanted...*Michelle Branch*
Always On Time...*Ja Rule w/ Ashanti*
Amazed...*Lonestar*
Angel...*Shaggy w/ Rayvon*
Baby Boy...*Beyoncé w/ Sean Paul*
Be With You...*Enrique Iglesias*
Beautiful...*Christina Aguilera*
Beautiful Day...*U2*
Bent...*Matchbox Twenty*
Blue (Da Ba Dee)...*Eiffel 65*
Blurry...*Puddle Of Mudd*
Bootylicious...*Destiny's Child*
Breakaway...*Kelly Clarkson*
Breathe...*Faith Hill*
Bring It All To Me...*Blaque w/ *NSYNC*
Bring Me To Life...*Evanescence*
Bump, Bump, Bump...*B2K & P. Diddy*
Burn...*Usher*
Butterfly...*Crazy Town*
Bye Bye Bye...**NSYNC*
Can't Let You Go...*Fabolous*
Case Of The Ex (Whatcha Gonna Do)...*Mya*
Cleanin' Out My Closet...*Eminem*
Clocks...*Coldplay*
Come On Over Baby (All I Want Is You)...
  Christina Aguilera
Complicated...*Avril Lavigne*
Confessions Part II...*Usher*
Crazy In Love...*Beyoncé w/ Jay-Z*
Cry Me A River...*Justin Timberlake*
Dance With Me...*Debelah Morgan*
Days Go By...*Dirty Vegas*
Dilemma...*Nelly w/ Kelly Rowland*
Doesn't Really Matter...*Janet Jackson*
Drift Away...*Uncle Kracker w/ Dobie Gray*
Drop It Like It's Hot...*Snoop Dogg w/ Pharrell*
Drops Of Jupiter (Tell Me)...*Train*
Everything You Want...*Vertical Horizon*
Fallin'...*Alicia Keys*
Family Affair...*Mary J. Blige*
Fiesta Remix...*R. Kelly w/ Jay-Z*
Flying Without Wings...*Ruben Studdard*
Follow Me...*Uncle Kracker*
Foolish...*Ashanti*
Freek-A-Leek...*Petey Pablo*
Frontin'...*Pharrell w/ Jay-Z*
Game Of Love, The...*Santana Feat. Michelle Branch*

Gangsta Lovin'...*Eve w/ Alicia Keys*
Get Busy...*Sean Paul*
Get It On...Tonite...*Montell Jordan*
Get Low...*Lil Jon & The East Side Boyz*
Get The Party Started...*P!nk*
Get Ur Freak On...*Missy "Misdemeanor" Elliott*
Gimme The Light...*Sean Paul*
Girlfriend...**NSYNC w/ Nelly*
Give Me Just One Night (Una Noche)...*98°*
Goodies...*Ciara w/ Petey Pablo*
Gotta Tell You...*Samantha Mumba*
Hanging By A Moment...*Lifehouse*
He Loves U Not...*Dream*
He Wasn't Man Enough...*Toni Braxton*
Heaven...*DJ Sammy & Yannou*
Here Without You...*3 Doors Down*
Hero...*Chad Kroeger w/ Josey Scott*
Hero...*Enrique Iglesias*
Hey Baby...*No Doubt w/ Bounty Killer*
Hey Ma...*Cam'ron*
Hey Ya!...*OutKast*
Higher...*Creed*
Hit 'Em Up Style (Oops!)...*Blu Cantrell*
Holidae In...*Chingy w/ Ludacris & Snoop Dogg*
Hot Boyz...*Missy "Misdemeanor" Elliott*
Hot In Herre...*Nelly*
Hotel...*Cassidy w/ R. Kelly*
How You Remind Me...*Nickelback*
I Believe...*Fantasia*
I Don't Wanna Know...*Mario Winans w/ Enya
  & P. Diddy*
I Hope You Dance...*Lee Ann Womack*
I Knew I Loved You...*Savage Garden*
I Know What You Want...*Busta Rhymes &
  Mariah Carey*
I Need A Girl (Part One)...*P. Diddy w/ Usher &
  Loon*
I Need A Girl (Part Two)...*P. Diddy & Ginuwine*
I Try...*Macy Gray*
I Wanna Know...*Joe*
I'm Real...*Jennifer Lopez w/ Ja Rule*
I'm With You...*Avril Lavigne*
If I Ain't Got You...*Alicia Keys*
If You're Gone...*Matchbox Twenty*
Ignition...*R. Kelly*
In Da Club...*50 Cent*
In The End...*Linkin Park*
Incomplete...*Sisqó*
Independent Women...*Destiny's Child*
Into You...*Fabolous*
It Wasn't Me...*Shaggy w/ Ricardo Ducent*
It's Been Awhile...*Staind*
It's Gonna Be Me...**NSYNC*
Izzo (H.O.V.A.)...*Jay-Z*
Jenny From The Block...*Jennifer Lopez*
Jesus Walks...*Kanye West*

Jumpin', Jumpin'...*Destiny's Child*
Just A Friend 2002...*Mario*
Just Lose It...*Eminem*
Kryptonite...*3 Doors Down*
Lady Marmalade...*Christina Aguilera, Lil' Kim, Mya & P!nk*
Lean Back...*Terror Squad w/ Fat Joe & Remy*
Let Me Blow Ya Mind...*Eve & Gwen Stefani*
Livin' It Up...*Ja Rule w/ Case*
Lose My Breath...*Destiny's Child*
Lose Yourself...*Eminem*
Magic Stick...*Lil' Kim w/ 50 Cent*
Maria Maria...*Santana Feat. The Product G&B*
Mesmerize...*Ja Rule w/ Ashanti*
Middle, The...*Jimmy Eat World*
Milkshake...*Kelis*
Miss You...*Aaliyah*
Missing You...*Case*
Moment Like This, A...*Kelly Clarkson*
Most Girls...*P!nk*
Move Ya Body...*Nina Sky w/ Jabba*
Ms. Jackson...*OutKast*
Music...*Madonna*
My Baby...*Lil' Romeo*
My Band...*D12*
My Boo...*Usher & Alicia Keys*
My Immortal...*Evanescence*
My Love Is Your Love...*Whitney Houston*
My Sacrifice...*Creed*
Naughty Girl...*Beyoncé*
Never Leave You – Uh Oooh, Uh Oooh!...*Lumidee*
'03 Bonnie & Clyde...*Jay-Z w/ Beyoncé*
Oh Boy...*Cam'ron w/ Juelz Santana*
One Call Away...*Chingy*
Only Time...*Enya*
Over And Over...*Nelly w/ Tim McGraw*
Peaches & Cream...*112*
Picture...*Kid Rock w/ Sheryl Crow*
Pieces Of Me...*Ashlee Simpson*
P.I.M.P.....*50 Cent*
Real Slim Shady, The...*Eminem*
Reason, The...*Hoobastank*
Ride Wit Me...*Nelly*
Right Thurr...*Chingy*
Rock Wit U (Awww Baby)...*Ashanti*
Roses...*OutKast*
Say My Name...*Destiny's Child*
Shake Ya Tailfeather...*Nelly/P. Diddy/Murphy Lee*

She Will Be Loved...*Maroon5*
Show Me The Meaning Of Being Lonely...*Backstreet Boys*
Slow Jamz...*Twista w/ Kanye West & Jamie Foxx*
Someday...*Nickelback*
Someone To Call My Lover...*Janet Jackson*
Stan...*Eminem w/ Dido*
Stand Up...*Ludacris w/ Shawnna*
Stutter...*Joe w/ Mystikal*
Sunshine...*Lil' Flip*
Survivor...*Destiny's Child*
Thank God I Found You...*Mariah Carey w/ Joe & 98°*
Thankyou...*Dido*
There You Go...*P!nk*
This I Promise You...**NSYNC*
This Is The Night...*Clay Aiken*
This Love...*Maroon5*
Thong Song...*Sisqó*
Thousand Miles, A...*Vanessa Carlton*
Tipsy...*J-Kwon*
Toxic...*Britney Spears*
Try Again...*Aaliyah*
Turn Me On...*Kevin Lyttle*
Turn Off The Light...*Nelly Furtado*
21 Questions...*50 Cent w/ Nate Dogg*
U Got It Bad...*Usher*
U Remind Me...*Usher*
Underneath It All...*No Doubt*
Unwell...*Matchbox Twenty*
Walked Outta Heaven...*Jagged Edge*
Way You Love Me, The...*Faith Hill*
Way You Move, The...*OutKast*
What A Girl Wants...*Christina Aguilera*
What's Luv?...*Fat Joe w/ Ashanti*
When I'm Gone...*3 Doors Down*
Whenever, Wherever...*Shakira*
Where Is The Love?...*Black Eyed Peas*
Where The Party At...*Jagged Edge w/ Nelly*
Wherever You Will Go...*Calling*
Who Let The Dogs Out...*Baha Men*
With Arms Wide Open...*Creed*
Without Me...*Eminem*
Wonderful...*Ja Rule w/ R. Kelly & Ashanti*
Work It...*Missy "Misdemeanor" Elliott*
Yeah!...*Usher w/ Lil' Jon & Ludacris*
You Don't Know My Name...*Alicia Keys*
You Sang To Me...*Marc Anthony*

Ain't No Other Man...*Christina Aguilera*
American Baby...*Dave Matthews Band*
Apologize...*Timbaland w/ OneRepublic*
Ayo Technology...*50 Cent w/ Justin Timberlake*
   & Timbaland
Bad Day...*Daniel Powter*
Bartender...*T-Pain w/ Akon*
Bay Bay, A...*Hurricane Chris*
Be Without You...*Mary J. Blige*
Beautiful Girls...*Sean Kingston*
Beautiful Liar...*Beyoncé & Shakira*
Because Of You...*Kelly Clarkson*
Because Of You...*Ne-Yo*
Bed...*J. Holiday*
Beep...*The Pussycat Dolls*
Before He Cheats...*Carrie Underwood*
Behind These Hazel Eyes...*Kelly Clarkson*
Best Of You...*Foo Fighters*
Beverly Hills...*Weezer*
Big Girls Don't Cry...*Fergie*
Black Horse & The Cherry Tree...*KT Tunstall*
Bless The Broken Road...*Rascal Flatts*
Bossy...*Kelis w/ Too Short*
Boston...*Augustana*
Boulevard Of Broken Dreams...*Green Day*
Breaking Free...*High School Musical Cast*
Bubbly...*Colbie Caillat*
Buttons...*The Pussycat Dolls w/ Snoop Dogg*
Buy You A Drank (Shawty Snappin')...*T-Pain*
   w/ Yung Joc
Call Me (When You're Sober) ...*Evanescence*
Candy Shop...*50 Cent w/ Olivia*
Caught Up...*Usher*
Chain Hang Low...*Jibbs*
Chariot...*Gavin DeGraw*
Chasing Cars...*Snow Patrol*
Check On It...*Beyoncé w/ Slim Thug & Bun B*
Come To Me...*Diddy w/ Nicole Scherzinger*
Control Myself...*LL Cool J w/ Jennifer Lopez*
Crank That (Soulja Boy) ...*Soulja Boy*
Crazy...*Gnarls Barkley*
Cupid's Chokehold/Breakfast In America...
   Gym Class Heroes
Cyclone...*Baby Bash w/ T-Pain*
Dance, Dance...*Fall Out Boy*
Dani California...*Red Hot Chili Peppers*
Daughters...*John Mayer*
Deja Vu...*Beyoncé w/ Jay-Z*
Dirty Little Secret...*All-American Rejects*
Disco Inferno...*50 Cent*
Don't Blink...*Kenny Chesney*
Don't Cha...*The Pussycat Dolls w/ Busta*
   Rhymes

Don't Forget About Us...*Mariah Carey*
Don't Matter...*Akon*
Don't Phunk With My Heart...*Black Eyed Peas*
Everytime We Touch...*Cascada*
Far Away...*Nickelback*
Feel Good Inc...*Gorillaz w/ De La Soul*
Fergalicious...*Fergie w/ will.i.am*
Gasolina...*Daddy Yankee*
Get It Poppin'...*Fat Joe w/ Nelly*
Girlfriend...*Avril Lavigne*
Give It To Me...*Timbaland w/ Nelly Furtado &*
   Justin Timberlake
Glamorous...*Fergie w/ Ludacris*
Gold Digger...*Kanye West w/ Jamie Foxx*
Good Life...*Kanye West w/ T-Pain*
Grillz...*Nelly w/ Paul Wall, Ali & Gipp*
Grind With Me...*Pretty Ricky*
Hate It Or Love It...*The Game w/ 50 Cent*
Hey There Delilah...*Plain White T's*
Hips Don't Lie...*Shakira w/ Wyclef Jean*
Holiday...*Green Day*
Hollaback Girl...*Gwen Stefani*
Home...*Michael Bublé*
Home...*Daughtry*
Honky Tonk Badonkadonk...*Trace Adkins*
How Far We've Come...*Matchbox Twenty*
How To Save A Life...*The Fray*
How We Do...*The Game w/ 50 Cent*
Hung Up...*Madonna*
I Don't Want To Be...*Gavin DeGraw*
I Wanna Love You...*Akon w/ Snoop Dogg*
I Write Sins Not Tragedies...*Panic! At The Disco*
I'll Stand By You...*Carrie Underwood*
I'm N Luv (Wit A Stripper) ...*T-Pain*
I'm Sprung...*T-Pain*
If You're Going Through Hell (Before The
   Devil Even Knows)...*Rodney Atkins*
Inside Your Heaven...*Carrie Underwood*
Irreplaceable...*Beyoncé*
It Ends Tonight...*All-American Rejects*
It's Goin' Down...*Yung Joc w/ Nitti*
It's Not Over...*Daughtry*
Jesus, Take The Wheel...*Carrie Underwood*
Just A Lil Bit...*50 Cent*
Just The Girl...*The Click Five*
Laffy Taffy...*D4L*
Lean Wit It, Rock Wit It...*Dem Franchize Boyz*
Let It Go...*Keyshia Cole w/ Missy Elliott & Lil Kim*
Let Me Go...*3 Doors Down*
Let Me Hold You...*Bow Wow w/ Omarion*
Let Me Love You...*Mario*
Life Is A Highway...*Rascal Flatts*
Like You...*Bow Wow w/ Ciara*

Lips Of An Angel...*Hinder*
Listen To Your Heart...*D.H.T.*
Live Like You Were Dying...*Tim McGraw*
London Bridge...*Fergie*
Lonely...*Akon*
Lonely No More...*Rob Thomas*
Lose Control...*Missy Elliott w/ Ciara*
Lovers And Friends...*Lil Jon w/ Usher & Ludacris*
LoveStoned...*Justin Timberlake*
Makes Me Wonder...*Maroon5*
Me & U...*Cassie*
Mockingbird...*Eminem*
Money Maker...*Ludacris w/ Pharrell*
Move Along...*All-American Rejects*
Mr. Brightside...*The Killers*
My Humps...*The Black Eyed Peas*
My Love...*Justin Timberlake w/ T.I.*
No One...*Alicia Keys*
Not Ready To Make Nice...*Dixie Chicks*
Obsession (No Es Amor) ...*Frankie J w/ Baby Bash*
Oh...*Ciara w/ Ludacris*
One Wish...*Ray J*
Over My Head (Cable Car) ...*The Fray*
1 Thing...*Amerie*
1, 2 Step...*Ciara w/ Missy Elliott*
1, 2, 3, 4...*Feist*
Party Like A Rockstar...*Shop Boyz*
Photograph...*Nickelback*
Pon De Replay...*Rihanna*
Pop, Lock & Drop It...*Huey*
Promiscuous...*Nelly Furtado w/ Timbaland*
Pump It...*The Black Eyed Peas*
Rehab...*Amy Winehouse*
Rich Girl...*Gwen Stefani w/ Eve*
Ridin'...*Chamillionaire w/ Krazie Bone*
Ring The Alarm...*Beyoncé*
Rockstar...*Nickelback*
Run It! ...*Chris Brown*
Runaway Love...*Ludacris w/ Mary J. Blige*
SOS...*Rihanna*
Savin' Me...*Nickelback*
Say Goodbye...*Chris Brown*
Say It Right...*Nelly Furtado*
Scars...*Papa Roach*
SexyBack...*Justin Timberlake w/ Timbaland*
Sexy Love...*Ne-Yo*
Shake It Off...*Mariah Carey*
Shake That...*Eminem w/ Nate Dogg*
Shawty...*Plies w/ T-Pain*
Shortie Like Mine...*Bow Wow w/ Chris Brown & Johnta Austin*
Shoulder Lean...*Young Dro w/ T.I.*

Since U Been Gone...*Kelly Clarkson*
Slow Down...*Bobby Valentino*
Smack That...*Akon w/ Eminem*
Snap Your Fingers...*Lil Jon w/ E40 & Sean Paul*
Snow ((Hey Oh))...*Red Hot Chili Peppers*
So Sick...*Ne-Yo*
So What...*Field Mob w/ Ciara*
Soldier...*Destiny's Child w/ T.I. & Lil Wayne*
Sorry, Blame It On Me...*Akon*
Soul Survivor...*Young Jeezy w/ Akon*
Speed Of Sound...*Coldplay*
Stickwitu...*The Pussycat Dolls*
Stronger...*Kanye West*
Stupid Girls...*Pink*
Sugar, We're Goin' Down...*Fall Out Boy*
Summer Love...*Justin Timberlake*
Sweet Escape, The...*Gwen Stefani w/ Akon*
Switch...*Will Smith*
Temperature...*Sean Paul*
Thnks Fr Th Mmrs...*Fall Out Boy*
There It Go (The Whistle Song)...*Juelz Santana*
This Ain't No Scene, It's An Arms Race...*Fall Out Boy*
This Is Why I'm Hot...*Mims*
Too Little Too Late...*JoJo*
U + Ur Hand...*P!nk*
Umbrella...*Rihanna w/ Jay-Z*
Unfaithful...*Rihanna*
Unpredictable...*Jamie Foxx w/ Ludacris*
Unwritten...*Natasha Bedingfield*
Waiting On The World To Change...*John Mayer*
Wake Me Up When September Ends...*Green Day*
Wake Up Call...*Maroon5*
Way I Are, The...*Timbaland w/ Keri Hilson*
We Be Burnin'...*Sean Paul*
We Belong Together...*Mariah Carey*
We Fly High...*Jim Jones*
Welcome To The Black Parade...*My Chemical Romance*
What Goes Around...Comes Around...*Justin Timberlake*
What Hurts The Most...*Rascal Flatts*
What You Know...*T.I.*
(When You Gonna) Give It Up To Me...*Sean Paul w/ Keyshia Cole*
When You Were Young...*The Killers*
Where'd You Go...*Fort Minor w/ Holly Brook*
White & Nerdy..."Weird Al" Yankovic
Who Knew...*P!nk*
Wind It Up...*Gwen Stefani*
Yo (Excuse Me Miss) ...*Chris Brown*
You And Me...*Lifehouse*
You're Beautiful...*James Blunt*

SPECIALTY PLAYLISTS

These songs are a representative sampling of the thousands that could be on these playlists. For example, of the scores of dance songs, the songs on the DANCE, DANCE, DANCE playlist are those that mention dancing or are dances themselves. Their inclusion on this list is to jog your memory.

Each music fan has their own definitive list of songs that fit these categories. Create your own playlists in the pages that follow this section. It's fun but we warn you, it can be addicting!

Roots Of Rock
The Country Road
Classic Rock
We Will Rock You

Road Trip
Rock & Roll — The '50s
Rhythm & Blues — The '50s

The British Invasion 1964-65
We're An American Band '60s & '70s
Retro Radio Early '80s
The Motown Sound Of The '60s

Super Country Hits '90s
Super Disco Hits '70s

Catch A Wave
Island In The Sun
Dance, Dance, Dance

Instrumentally Yours
More Cowbell!
Happy Anniversary
Big Boppers

It's A Disney World After All
Sing, Sing A Song
Foreign Language Hits
Big Bands 1935-1945

Spring Fever
Summertime
'Tis Autumn
Wintertime

Work Out!
Haunted House
Take It Easy
Sing Alleluia
(Contemporary Christian 2000-2007)

A Classic Christmas:
A Holly Jolly Christmas (Secular Songs)
Joy To The World (Sacred Songs)

'45 **Rock Me Mamma**...*Arthur "Big Boy" Crudup*
'45 **The Honeydripper**...*Joe Liggins*
'45 **Midnight Stomp**...*Jimmy Yancey*
'46 **Hillbilly Boogie**...*The Delmore Brothers*
'47 **Move It On Over**...*Hank Williams*
'48 **Write Me A Letter**...*The Ravens*
'48 **Rolling Stone**...*Muddy Waters*
'48 **Call It Stormy Monday**...*T-Bone Walker*
'48 **Good Rockin' Tonight**...*Wynonie Harris*
'48 **It's Too Soon To Know**...*The Orioles*
'49 **Boogie Chillen'**...*John Lee Hooker*
'49 **The Huckle-Buck**...*Paul Williams*
'49 **Lovesick Blues**...*Hank Williams*
'49 **Rockin' At Midnight**...*Roy Brown*
'49 **T-Bone Shuffle**...*T-Bone Walker*
'49 **Drinkin' Wine Spo-Dee-O-Dee**..."*Stick" McGhee*
'49 **All She Wants To Do Is Rock**...*Wynonie Harris*
'50 **I Almost Lost My Mind**...*Ivory Joe Hunter*
'50 **The Fat Man**...*Fats Domino*
'50 **We're Gonna Rock**...*Cecil Gant*
'50 **Birmingham Bounce**...*Red Foley*
'50 **Why Don't You Love Me**...*Hank Williams*
'50 **Blues Stay Away From Me**...*The Delmore Brothers*
'50 **Teardrops From My Eyes**...*Ruth Brown*
'51 **Rocket "88"**...*Jackie Brenston & His Delta Cats*
'51 **Sixty-Minute Man**...*The Dominoes*
'51 **Fool, Fool, Fool**...*The Clovers*
'52 **Dust My Broom**...*Elmore James*
'52 **Rock The Joint**...*Bill Haley & The Saddlemen*
'52 **Lawdy Miss Clawdy**...*Lloyd Price*
'52 **Ting-A-Ling**...*The Clovers*
'52 **Juke**...*Little Walter & His Night Cats*
'53 **Mama He Treats Your Daughter Mean**...*Ruth Brown*
'53 **Tipitina**...*Professor Longhair*
'53 **Mess Around**...*Ray Charles*
'53 **Hound Dog**..."*Big Mama" Thornton*
'53 **Bear Cat**...*Rufus Thomas*
'53 **Crazy Man, Crazy**...*Bill Haley & Haley's Comets*
'53 **Please Don't Leave Me**...*Fats Domino*
'53 **Honey Hush**...*Big Joe Turner*
'53 **Feelin' Good**...*Little Junior's Blue Flames*
'53 **Money Honey**...*Clyde McPhatter & The Drifters*
'54 **Work With Me Annie**...*The Midnighters*
'54 **Gee**...*The Crows*
'54 **Goodnite Sweetheart, Goodnite**...*The Spaniels*
'54 **Shake, Rattle And Roll**...*Big Joe Turner*
'54 **Honey Love**...*Clyde McPhatter & The Drifters*
'54 **Sh-Boom**...*The Chords*
'54 **Blue Moon Of Kentucky**...*Elvis Presley*
'54 **That's All Right**...*Elvis Presley*

'28 **Blue Yodel (T For Texas)**...*Jimmie Rodgers*
'28 **In The Jailhouse Now**...*Jimmie Rodgers*
'28 **Keep On The Sunny Side**...*The Carter Family*
'28 **Wildwood Flower**...*The Carter Family*
'34 **Tumbling Tumbleweeds**...*The Sons Of The Pioneers*
'35 **Can The Circle Be Unbroken**...*The Carter Family*
'36 **I Want To Be A Cowboy's Sweetheart**...*Patsy Montana*
'38 **Wabash Cannon Ball**...*Roy Acuff*
'39 **Back In The Saddle Again**...*Gene Autry*
'40 **You Are My Sunshine**...*Jimmie Davis*
'40 **New San Antonio Rose**...*Bob Wills & His Texas Playboys*
'41 **Cool Water**...*The Sons Of The Pioneers*
'41 **Walking The Floor Over You**...*Ernest Tubb*
'43 **Pistol Packin' Mama**...*Al Dexter*
'45 **Blue Moon Of Kentucky**...*Bill Monroe & His Blue Grass Boys*
'49 **I'm So Lonesome I Could Cry**...*Hank Williams*
'49 **Blues Stay Away From Me**...*The Delmore Brothers*
'49 **Foggy Mountain Breakdown**...*Flatt & Scruggs*
'50 **I'm Moving On**...*Hank Snow*
'50 **If You've Got The Money I've Got The Time**...*Lefty Frizzell*
'51 **Hey Good Lookin'**...*Hank Williams*
'52 **The Wild Side Of Life**...*Hank Thompson*
'52 **It Wasn't God Who Made Honky Tonk Angels**...*Kitty Wells*
'52 **Jambalaya (On The Bayou)**...*Hank Williams*
'55 **Sixteen Tons**...*Tennessee Ernie Ford*
'56 **Folsom Prison Blues**...*Johnny Cash*
'56 **Crazy Arms**...*Ray Price*
'56 **I Walk The Line**...*Johnny Cash*
'57 **Bye Bye Love**...*The Everly Brothers*
'59 **The Battle Of New Orleans**...*Johnny Horton*
'59 **El Paso**...*Marty Robbins*
'60 **He'll Have To Go**...*Jim Reeves*
'61 **Hello Walls**...*Faron Young*
'61 **I Fall To Pieces**...*Patsy Cline*
'61 **Crazy**...*Patsy Cline*
'63 **She Thinks I Still Care**...*George Jones*
'63 **Ring Of Fire**...*Johnny Cash*
'64 **Dang Me**...*Roger Miller*
'65 **I've Got A Tiger By The Tail**...*Buck Owens*
'65 **King Of The Road**...*Roger Miller*
'65 **Make The World Go Away**...*Eddy Arnold*
'67 **By The Time I Get To Phoenix**...*Glen Campbell*
'68 **Mama Tried**...*Merle Haggard*
'68 **Stand By Your Man**...*Tammy Wynette*
'70 **Hello Darlin'**...*Conway Twitty*
'70 **Coal Miner's Daughter**...*Loretta Lynn*
'71 **Help Me Make It Through The Night**...*Sammi Smith*
'73 **Behind Closed Doors**...*Charlie Rich*
'74 **I Will Always Love You**...*Dolly Parton*
'80 **He Stopped Loving Her Today**...*George Jones*

CLASSIC ROCK

All Right Now...*Free*
American Pie...*Don McLean*
American Woman...*The Guess Who*
Barracuda...*Heart*
Black Water...*Doobie Brothers*
Blinded By The Light...*Manfred Mann*
Bohemian Rhapsody...*Queen*
Born In The U.S.A. ...*Bruce Springsteen*
Casey Jones...*Grateful Dead*
Changes...*David Bowie*
Crocodile Rock...*Elton John*
Do You Feel Like We Do...*Peter Frampton*
Don't Stop...*Fleetwood Mac*
For What It's Worth...*Buffalo Springfield*
Free Bird...*Lynyrd Skynyrd*
Heart Of Gold...*Neil Young*
Hey Jude...*The Beatles*
Honky Tonk Women...*The Rolling Stones*
Hotel California...*Eagles*
Imagine...*John Lennon*
In-A-Gadda-Da-Vida...*Iron Butterfly*
Iron Man...*Black Sabbath*
La Grange...*ZZ Top*
Layla...*Derek & The Dominos*
Light My Fire...*The Doors*
Like A Rolling Stone...*Bob Dylan*
Maggie May...*Rod Stewart*
Magic Carpet Ride...*Steppenwolf*
Maybe I'm Amazed...*Paul McCartney*
Money...*Pink Floyd*
More Than A Feeling...*Boston*
Mr. Tambourine Man...*The Byrds*
Night Moves...*Bob Seger*
Nights In White Satin...*The Moody Blues*
Piece Of My Heart...*Big Brother & The Holding Company*
Proud Mary...*Creedence Clearwater Revival*
Purple Haze...*Jimi Hendrix*
Runnin' With The Devil...*Van Halen*
Slow Ride...*Foghat*
Smoke On The Water...*Deep Purple*
Somebody To Love...*Jefferson Airplane*
Stairway To Heaven...*Led Zeppelin*
Suite: Judy Blue Eyes...*Crosby, Stills & Nash*
Sunshine Of Your Love...*Cream*
Takin' Care Of Business...*Bachman-Turner Overdrive*
Tom Sawyer...*Rush*
Walk On The Wild Side...*Lou Reed*
Walk This Way...*Aerosmith*
Weight, The...*The Band*
Whiter Shade Of Pale, A...*Procol Harum*
With A Little Help From My Friends...*Joe Cocker*
Won't Get Fooled Again...*The Who*
You Shook Me All Night Long...*AC/DC*

WE WILL ROCK YOU (SPORTS ANTHEMS)

Alé, Alé, Alé, Alé (Soccer Anthem)...*The Crowd*
All Star...*Smash Mouth*
Bang The Drum All Day...*Todd Rundgren*
Blitzkrieg Bop...*Ramones*
Block Rockin' Beats...*The Chemical Brothers*
Boom Boom Boom...*The Outhere Brothers*
Bust A Move...*Young M.C.*
Can U Feel It...*3rd Party*
Can't Wait One Minute More...*CIV*
Centerfield...*John Fogerty*
Cup Of Life...*Ricky Martin*
C'mon N' Ride It (The Train)...*Quad City DJ's*
Doctorin' The Tardis...*The Timelords*
Everybody Everybody...*Black Box*
Get Ready For This...*2 Unlimited*
Get Ready To Bounce...*Brooklyn Bounce*
Get The Party Started...*P!nk*
Gettin' Jiggy Wit It...*Will Smith*
Gonna Make You Sweat...*C & C Music Factory*
Here It Goes Again...*OK Go*
I Like It...*Tito Nieves*
I Like To Move It...*Reel 2 Real*
Jump Around...*House Of Pain*
Kernkraft 400...*Zombie Nation*
Na Na Hey Hey Kiss Him Goodbye...*Steam*
Party Hard...*Andrew W.K.*
Power, The...*Snap!*
Pump It Up...*Elvis Costello*
Pump Up The Jam...*Technotronic*
Pump Up The Volume...*M/A/R/R/S*
Push It...*Salt-N-Pepa*
Raise The Roof...*Luke*
Rock And Roll Part 2...*Gary Glitter*
Rockafella Skank, The...*Fatboy Slim*
Sandstorm...*Darude*
Shout...*The Isley Brothers*
Sirius...*Alan Parsons Project*
Space Jam...*Quad City DJ's*
Start Me Up...*The Rolling Stones*
Start The Commotion...*The Wiseguys*
Strike It Up...*Black Box*
Take Me Out To The Ballgame...*Lonestar*
This Is Your Night...*Amber*
Tootsee Roll...*69 Boyz*
Tribal Dance...*2 Unlimited*
Tubthumping...*Chumbawamba*
Way You Move, The...*OutKast*
We Will Rock You/We Are The Champions...*Queen*
Welcome To The Jungle...*Guns N' Roses*
What's Up...*DJ Miko*
Who Let The Dogs Out...*Baha Men*
Whoomp! (There It Is)...*Tag Team*
Wipe Out...*The Surfaris*

ROAD TRIP!

Arrested For Driving While Blind...*ZZ Top*
Baby Please Don't Go...*Them*
Bad Case Of Loving You...*Robert Palmer*
Bad Moon Rising...*Creedence Clearwater Revival*
Barbara Ann...*The Beach Boys*
Barracuda...*Heart*
Be My Baby...*The Ronettes*
Beautiful Day...*U2*
Born To Be Wild...*Steppenwolf*
Born To Run...*Bruce Springsteen*
Brown Eyed Girl...*Van Morrison*
Burning Love...*Elvis Presley*
Call Me...*Blondie*
Chattahoochee...*Alan Jackson*
China Grove...*The Doobie Brothers*
Country Road...*James Taylor*
Crazy Little Thing Called Love...*Queen*
Da Doo Ron Ron...*The Crystals*
De Do Do Do, De Da Da Da...*The Police*
Desire...*U2*
Devil Went Down To Georgia...*Charlie Daniels Band*
Distance, The...*Cake*
Don't Get Me Wrong...*The Pretenders*
Don't Look Back...*Fine Young Cannibals*
Dream Police...*Cheap Trick*
Drive My Car...*The Beatles*
Driver's Seat...*Sniff 'N' The Tears*
Drivin' My Life Away...*Eddie Rabbitt*
Drops Of Jupiter (Tell Me)...*Train*
Electric Avenue...*Eddy Grant*
Escapade...*Janet Jackson*
Fly Away...*Lenny Kravitz*
Free Ride...*Edgar Winter Group*
Friends In Low Places...*Garth Brooks*
Fun, Fun, Fun...*The Beach Boys*
Gear Jammer...*George Thorogood*
Gimme Some Lovin'...*Spencer Davis Group*
Go Your Own Way...*Fleetwood Mac*
Goin' Back To Cali...*LL Cool J*
Good Lovin'...*The Young Rascals*
Great Balls Of Fire...*Jerry Lee Lewis*
Happy Wanderer...*Brave Combo*
Highway 61 Revisited...*Bob Dylan*
Hit The Road Jack...*Ray Charles*
Holiday...*Green Day*
Holiday Road...*Lindsey Buckingham*
Hollywood Nights...*Bob Seger*
I Can't Drive 55...*Sammy Hagar*
I Drove All Night...*Roy Orbison*
I Fought The Law...*Bobby Fuller Four*
I'm Alright...*Kenny Loggins*
I'm Gonna Be (500 Miles)...*The Proclaimers*
I've Been Everywhere...*Johnny Cash*
Interstate Love Song...*Stone Temple Pilots*
Johnny B. Goode...*Chuck Berry*
Jump...*Van Halen*

Kansas City...*Wilbert Harrison*
Keep Your Hands To Yourself...*Georgia Satellites*
King Of The Road...*Roger Miller*
Let's Go...*The Cars*
Letter, The...*The Box Tops*
Life In The Fast Lane...*Eagles*
Life Is A Highway...*Tom Cochrane*
Little Bit O' Soul...*The Music Explosion*
Logical Song, The...*Supertramp*
London Calling...*The Clash*
Love Train...*The O'Jays*
Low Rider...*War*
Margaritaville...*Jimmy Buffett*
Memphis...*Johnny Rivers*
Middle, The...*Jimmy Eat World*
Mustang Sally...*Wilson Pickett*
No Particular Place To Go...*Chuck Berry*
On The Road Again...*Willie Nelson*
One Headlight...*The Wallflowers*
Open Road Song...*Eve 6*
Pride And Joy...*Stevie Ray Vaughan*
Radar Love...*Golden Earring*
Ramblin' Man...*Allman Brothers Band*
Real Gone...*Sheryl Crow*
Rhythm Of My Heart...*Rod Stewart*
Road Runner...*Bo Diddley*
Road To Nowhere...*Talking Heads*
Road Trippin'...*Red Hot Chili Peppers*
Roadhouse Blues...*The Doors*
Roadrunner...*Modern Lovers*
R.O.C.K. In The U.S.A. ...*John Cougar Mellencamp*
Rock Of Ages...*Def Leppard*
Roll On Down The Highway...*Bachman-Turner Overdrive*
Route 66...*John Mayer*
Runaway...*Del Shannon*
Runnin' Down A Dream...*Tom Petty*
Running On Empty...*Jackson Browne*
Santa Monica...*Everclear*
Spirit In The Sky...*Norman Greenbaum*
Switchin' To Glide...*The Kings*
Take It Easy...*Eagles*
Take Me Home Country Roads...*Toots & The Maytals*
Take The Money And Run...*Steve Miller Band*
Truckin'...*Grateful Dead*
Vacation...*The Go-Go's*
Ventura Highway...*America*
Walk Of Life...*Dire Straits*
Watching The Detectives...*Elvis Costello*
What I Like About You...*The Romantics*
Whole Lotta Love...*Led Zeppelin*
Working For The Weekend...*Loverboy*
You Ain't Seen Nothing Yet...*Bachman-Turner Overdrive*

ROCK & ROLL THE '50s

All American Boy, The...*Bill Parsons*
All Shook Up...*Elvis Presley*
At The Hop...*Danny & The Juniors*
Be-Bop-A-Lula...*Gene Vincent*
Believe What You Say...*Ricky Nelson*
Blue Suede Shoes...*Carl Perkins*
Butterfly...*Charlie Gracie*
Bye Bye Love...*The Everly Brothers*
Chantilly Lace...*Big Bopper*
Come Go With Me...*The Dell-Vikings*
Don't Be Cruel...*Elvis Presley*
Good Golly, Miss Molly...*Little Richard*
Great Balls Of Fire...*Jerry Lee Lewis*
Hard Headed Woman...*Elvis Presley*
Heartbreak Hotel...*Elvis Presley*
Hound Dog...*Elvis Presley*
It's Only Make Believe...*Conway Twitty*
Jailhouse Rock...*Elvis Presley*
Johnny B. Goode...*Chuck Berry*
La Bamba...*Ritchie Valens*
Leroy...*Jack Scott*
Little Darlin'...*The Diamonds*
Long Tall Sally...*Little Richard*
Lucille...*Little Richard*
Maybellene...*Chuck Berry*
Mystery Train...*Elvis Presley*
Oh, Boy!...*Buddy Holly & The Crickets*
Ooby Dooby...*Roy Orbison*
Party Doll...*Buddy Knox*
Peggy Sue...*Buddy Holly*
Queen Of The Hop...*Bobby Darin*
Raunchy...*Bill Justis*
Rebel-'Rouser...*Duane Eddy*
Red River Rock...*Johnny & The Hurricanes*
Rock & Roll Music...*Chuck Berry*
Rock Around The Clock...*Bill Haley & His Comets*
Roll Over Beethoven...*Chuck Berry*
School Day...*Chuck Berry*
See You Later, Alligator...*Bill Haley & His Comets*
Short Shorts...*Royal Teens*
Stroll, The...*The Diamonds*
Summertime Blues...*Eddie Cochran*
Sweet Little Sixteen...*Chuck Berry*
Teenager In Love, A...*Dion & The Belmonts*
Tequila...*The Champs*
That'll Be The Day...*Buddy Holly & The Crickets*
Too Much...*Elvis Presley*
Tutti-Frutti...*Little Richard*
Wake Up Little Susie...*The Everly Brothers*
Whole Lot Of Shakin' Going On...*Jerry Lee Lewis*

RHYTHM & BLUES THE '50s

Ain't That A Shame...*Fats Domino*
At My Front Door...*The El Dorados*
Blueberry Hill...*Fats Domino*
Bo Diddley...*Bo Diddley*
Book Of Love...*The Monotones*
C.C. Rider...*Chuck Willis*
Earth Angel...*The Penguins*
Get A Job...*The Silhouettes*
Great Pretender, The...*The Platters*
Happy, Happy Birthday Baby...*The Tune Weavers*
Hearts Of Stone...*The Charms*
Honky Tonk...*Bill Doggett*
I Cried A Tear...*LaVern Baker*
I Hear You Knocking...*Smiley Lewis*
I Only Have Eyes For You...*The Flamingos*
I Put A Spell On You...*Screamin' Jay Hawkins*
I've Got A Woman...*Ray Charles*
In The Still Of The Nite...*The Five Satins*
Jim Dandy...*LaVern Baker*
Kansas City...*Wilbert Harrison*
La Dee Dah...*Billy & Lillie*
Little Bitty Pretty One...*Thurston Harris*
Lonely Teardrops...*Jackie Wilson*
Love Is Strange...*Mickey & Sylvia*
Lover's Question, A...*Clyde McPhatter*
Maybe...*The Chantels*
Mr. Lee...*The Bobbettes*
Only You (And You Alone)...*The Platters*
Over The Mountain; Across The Sea...*Johnnie & Joe*
Please, Please, Please...*James Brown*
Pledging My Love...*Johnny Ace*
Rock-In Robin...*Bobby Day*
Searchin'...*The Coasters*
Short Fat Fannie...*Larry Williams*
Silhouettes...*The Rays*
Since I Met You Baby...*Ivory Joe Hunter*
Sincerely...*The Moonglows*
Speedoo...*The Cadillacs*
Stagger Lee...*Lloyd Price*
Tears On My Pillow...*Little Anthony & The Imperials*
There Goes My Baby...*The Drifters*
Topsy II...*Cozy Cole*
Tweedlee Dee...*LaVern Baker*
Wallflower, The...*Etta James*
What'd I Say...*Ray Charles*
When You Dance...*The Turbans*
Why Do Fools Fall In Love...*Frankie Lymon & The Teenagers*
Yakety Yak...*The Coasters*
You Send Me...*Sam Cooke*
Young Blood...*The Coasters*

THE BRITISH INVASION 1964-65

All Day And All Of The Night...*The Kinks*
As Tears Go By...*Marianne Faithfull*
Bad To Me...*Billy J. Kramer*
Can't Buy Me Love...*The Beatles*
Catch The Wind...*Donovan*
Do Wah Diddy Diddy...*Manfred Mann*
Don't Let The Sun Catch You Crying...*Gerry & The Pacemakers*
Downtown...*Petula Clark*
Everyone's Gone To The Moon...*Jonathan King*
Ferry Cross The Mersey...*Gerry & The Pacemakers*
For Your Love...*The Yardbirds*
Game Of Love...*Wayne Fontana & The Mindbenders*
Girl Don't Come...*Sandie Shaw*
Glad All Over...*Dave Clark Five*
Go Now!...*The Moody Blues*
Goldfinger...*Shirley Bassey*
Have I The Right?...*The Honeycombs*
Heart Full Of Soul...*The Yardbirds*
Hippy Hippy Shake...*The Swinging Blue Jeans*
House Of The Rising Sun, The...*The Animals*
I Can't Explain...*The Who*
(I Can't Get No) Satisfaction...*The Rolling Stones*
I Go To Pieces...*Peter & Gordon*
I Want To Hold Your Hand...*The Beatles*
I'm Gonna Love You Too...*The Hullaballoos*
I'm Into Something Good...*Herman's Hermits*
I'm Telling You Now...*Freddie & The Dreamers*
It's Alright...*Adam Faith & The Roulettes*
It's Not Unusual...*Tom Jones*
Just One Look...*The Hollies*
Last Time, The...*The Rolling Stones*
Little Children...*Billy J. Kramer*
Mrs. Brown You've Got A Lovely Daughter...*Herman's Hermits*
My Generation...*The Who*
Needles And Pins...*The Searchers*
Over And Over...*Dave Clark Five*
She Loves You...*The Beatles*
She's Not There...*The Zombies*
Tobacco Road...*The Nashville Teens*
We Gotta Get Out Of This Place...*The Animals*
What's New Pussycat?...*Tom Jones*
Wishin' And Hopin'...*Dusty Springfield*
World Without Love, A...*Peter & Gordon*
Yeh, Yeh...*Georgie Fame*
Yesterday's Gone...*Chad & Jeremy*
You Really Got Me...*The Kinks*
You Turn Me On...*Ian Whitcomb & Bluesville*
You're My World...*Cilla Black*
You've Got To Hide Your Love Away...*The Silkie*
You've Got Your Troubles...*The Fortunes*

WE'RE AN AMERICAN BAND '60s & '70s

Along Comes Mary...*The Association*
And When I Die...*Blood, Sweat & Tears*
Black Magic Woman...*Santana*
Carry On Wayward Son...*Kansas*
Come Sail Away...*Styx*
Crazy Love...*Allman Brothers Band*
Cry Like A Baby...*The Box Tops*
Dance The Night Away...*Van Halen*
Do You Believe In Magic...*The Lovin' Spoonful*
Don't Look Back...*Boston*
Dream On...*Aerosmith*
Eight Miles High...*The Byrds*
Fire Lake...*Bob Seger*
Good Thing...*Paul Revere & The Raiders*
Green River...*Creedence Clearwater Revival*
Heart Of Glass...*Blondie*
Heart Of The Night...*Poco*
Hold The Line...*Toto*
I Get Around...*The Beach Boys*
I Was Made For Lovin' You...*Kiss*
Imaginary Lover...*Atlanta Rhythm Section*
It Don't Matter To Me...*Bread*
Jenny Take A Ride...*Mitch Ryder & The Detroit Wheels*
Kind Of A Drag...*The Buckinghams*
Last Train To Clarksville...*The Monkees*
Let's Go...*The Cars*
Let's Live For Today...*The Grass Roots*
Long Train Runnin'...*The Doobie Brothers*
Looking For A Love...*J. Geils Band*
Lovin', Touchin', Squeezin'...*Journey*
Make Me Smile...*Chicago*
Money...*The Kingsmen*
One...*Three Dog Night*
People Got To Be Free...*The Rascals*
Refugee...*Tom Petty & The Heartbreakers*
Riders On The Storm...*The Doors*
Rock Me...*Steppenwolf*
Rock 'N' Roll Woman...*The Buffalo Springfield*
Rockaway Beach...*Ramones*
Rock'n Me...*Steve Miller*
She'd Rather Be With Me...*The Turtles*
Sugar Magnolia...*Grateful Dead*
Surrender...*Cheap Trick*
Sweet Home Alabama...*Lynyrd Skynyrd*
Take It To The Limit...*Eagles*
Take Me To The River...*Talking Heads*
Time For Me To Fly...*REO Speedwagon*
Tush...*ZZ Top*
We're An American Band...*Grand Funk Railroad*
White Rabbit...*Jefferson Airplane*

RETRO RADIO EARLY '80s

Always Something There To Remind Me...*Naked Eyes*
Blister In The Sun...*Violent Femmes*
Blue Monday...*New Order*
Da Da Da I Don't Love You You Don't Love Me...*Trio*
Dancing With Myself...*Billy Idol*
Der Kommissar...*After The Fire*
Destination Unknown...*Missing Persons*
Doctor! Doctor!...*Thompson Twins*
Forever Mine...*The Motels*
Genius Of Love...*Tom Tom Club*
Goody Two Shoes...*Adam Ant*
I Melt With You...*Modern English*
I Want Candy...*Bow Wow Wow*
In A Big Country...*Big Country*
In Between Days (Without You)...*The Cure*
Just Can't Get Enough...*Depeche Mode*
Just Got Lucky...*JoBoxers*
(Keep Feeling) Fascination...*Human League*
Let Me Go...*Heaven 17*
Love My Way...*Psychedelic Furs*
Love Plus One...*Haircut 100*
Make A Circuit With Me...*The Polecats*
Metro, The...*Berlin*
Mexican Radio...*Wall Of Voodoo*
99 Luftballons...*Nena*
Our House...*Madness*
Politics Of Dancing, The...*Re-Flex*
Reap The Wild Wind...*Ultravox*
Red Skies...*The Fixx*
Rock Lobster...*The B-52's*
Safety Dance, The...*Men Without Hats*
Save It For Later...*English Beat*
She Blinded Me With Science...*Thomas Dolby*
Situation...*Yaz*
Six Months In A Leaky Boat...*Split Enz*
So In Love...*Orchestral Manoeuvres In The Dark*
Space Age Love Song...*A Flock Of Seagulls*
Tainted Love...*Soft Cell*
Tempted...*Squeeze*
Tenderness...*General Public*
Too Shy...*Kajagoogoo*
Trommeltanz (Din Daa Daa)...*George Kranz*
Turning Japanese...*The Vapors*
Up All Night...*The Boomtown Rats*
Weird Science...*Oingo Boingo*
What Do All The People Know...*The Monroes*
What I Like About You...*The Romantics*
What's He Got?...*The Producers*
Whip It...*Devo*
Whisper To A Scream (Birds Fly)...*Icicle Works*

THE MOTOWN SOUND OF THE '60s

Ain't Nothing Like The Real Thing...*Marvin Gaye & Tammi Terrell*
Ain't Too Proud To Beg...*The Temptations*
Baby I Need Your Loving...*Four Tops*
Baby Love...*The Supremes*
Beauty Is Only Skin Deep...*The Temptations*
Beechwood 4-5789...*The Marvelettes*
Bernadette...*Four Tops*
Cloud Nine...*The Temptations*
Dancing In The Street...*Martha & The Vandellas*
Do You Love Me...*The Contours*
Don't Mess With Bill...*The Marvelettes*
Every Little Bit Hurts...*Brenda Holloway*
Fingertips – Pt. 2...*Little Stevie Wonder*
For Once In My Life...*Stevie Wonder*
Heat Wave...*Martha & The Vandellas*
Hot Sweet It Is To Be Loved By You...*Marvin Gaye*
I Can't Help Myself...*Four Tops*
I Second That Emotion...*Smokey Robinson & The Miracles*
I Want You Back...*The Jackson 5*
I Was Made To Love Her...*Stevie Wonder*
I'll Be Doggone...*Marvin Gaye*
It Takes Two...*Marvin Gaye & Kim Weston*
Jimmy Mack...*Martha & The Vandellas*
Love Child...*Diana Ross & The Supremes*
Mickey's Monkey...*The Miracles*
My Girl...*The Temptations*
My Guy...*Mary Wells*
Nowhere To Run...*Martha & The Vandellas*
Opce Upon A Time...*Marvin Gaye & Mary Wells*
One Who Really Loves You, The...*Mary Wells*
Playboy...*The Marvelettes*
Please Mr. Postman...*The Marvelettes*
Pride And Joy...*Marvin Gaye*
Quicksand...*Martha & The Vandellas*
Reach Out I'll Be There...*Four Tops*
Shop Around...*The Miracles*
Stop! In The Name Of Love...*The Supremes*
This Old Heart Of Mine (Is Weak For You)...*The Isley Brothers*
Tracks Of My Tears...*The Miracles*
Twenty-Five Miles...*Edwin Starr*
Two Lovers...*Mary Wells*
Uptight (Everything's Alright)...*Stevie Wonder*
War...*Edwin Starr*
Way You Do The Things You Do, The...*The Temptations*
Where Did Our Love Go...*The Supremes*
You Beat Me To The Punch...*Mary Wells*
You Can't Hurry Love...*The Supremes*
You Keep Me Hangin' On...*The Supremes*
You've Really Got A Hold On Me...*The Miracles*
Your Precious Love...*Marvin Gaye & Tammi Terrell*

Achy Breaky Heart...*Billy Ray Cyrus*
Ain't Going Down (Til The Sun Comes Up)...
Garth Brooks
Ain't That Lonely Yet...*Dwight Yoakam*
Amazed...*Lonestar*
Any Man Of Mine...*Shania Twain*
Anymore...*Travis Tritt*
Be My Baby Tonight...*John Michael Montgomery*
Better Class Of Losers...*Randy Travis*
Blame It On Your Heart...*Patty Loveless*
Blue...*LeAnn Rimes*
Boot Scootin' Boogie...*Brooks & Dunn*
Brand New Man...*Brooks & Dunn*
Breathe...*Faith Hill*
Brother Jukebox...*Mark Chesnutt*
Carrying Your Love With Me...*George Strait*
Chattahoochee...*Alan Jackson*
Check Yes Or No...*George Strait*
Daddy's Money...*Ricochet*
Dance, The...*Garth Brooks*
Don't Let Our Love Start Slippin' Away...
Vince Gill
Don't Rock The Jukebox...*Alan Jackson*
Don't Take The Girl...*Tim McGraw*
Down At The Twist And Shout...*Mary Chapin Carpenter*
Down Home...*Alabama*
Every Little Thing...*Carlene Carter*
Five Minutes...*Lorrie Morgan*
Friends In Low Places...*Garth Brooks*
From This Moment On...*Shania Twain w/ Bryan White*
Happy Girl...*Martina McBride*
Hard Rock Bottom Of Your Heart...*Randy Travis*
Heads Carolina, Tails California...*Jo Dee Messina*
Holes In The Floor Of Heaven...*Steve Wariner*
How Do I Live...*Trisha Yearwood*
How Forever Feels...*Kenny Chesney*
How Was I To Know...*Reba McEntire*
I Can Love You Like That...*John Michael Montgomery*
I Just Want To Dance With You...*George Strait*
I Like It, I Love It...*Tim McGraw*
I Love The Way You Love Me...*John Michael Montgomery*
I Love You...*Martina McBride*
I Swear...*John Michael Montgomery*
I'll Think Of A Reason Later...*Lee Ann Womack*
I'm Alright...*Jo Dee Messina*
I've Come To Expect It From You...*George Strait*
If I Didn't Have You...*Randy Travis*
If You See Him/If You See Her...*Reba McEntire w/ Brooks & Dunn*
It Matters To Me...*Faith Hill*
It's A Little Too Late...*Tanya Tucker*
It's Your Love...*Tim McGraw & Faith Hill*
Jukebox In My Mind...*Alabama*

Just To See You Smile...*Tim McGraw*
Little Bitty...*Alan Jackson*
Longneck Bottle...*Garth Brooks*
Love Gets Me Every Time...*Shania Twain*
Love, Me...*Collin Raye*
Love Without End, Amen...*George Strait*
Meet In The Middle...*Diamond Rio*
Mercury Blues...*Alan Jackson*
Mi Vida Loca (My Crazy Life)...*Pam Tillis*
Neon Moon...*Brooks & Dunn*
No News...*Lonestar*
No One Else On Earth...*Wynonna*
No Time To Kill...*Clint Black*
Nobody Knows...*Kevin Sharp*
Not A Moment Too Soon...*Tim McGraw*
On Second Thought...*Eddie Rabbitt*
On The Verge...*Collin Raye*
One Night At A Time...*George Strait*
One Way Ticket (Because I Can)...*LeAnn Rimes*
Pickup Man...*Joe Diffie*
Please Remember Me...*Tim McGraw*
Prop Me Up Beside The Jukebox (If I Die)...
Joe Diffie
She Came From Fort Worth...*Kathy Mattea*
She Don't Know She's Beautiful...*Sammy Kershaw*
She's Got It All...*Kenny Chesney*
She's In Love With The Boy...*Trisha Yearwood*
Should've Been A Cowboy...*Toby Keith*
Small Town Saturday Night...*Hal Ketchum*
Sold (The Grundy County Auction Incident)...
John Michael Montgomery
Something Like That...*Tim McGraw*
Strawberry Wine...*Deana Carter*
Tall, Tall Trees...*Alan Jackson*
Thank God For You...*Sawyer Brown*
Then What? ...*Clay Walker*
There Ain't Nothin' Wrong With The Radio...
Aaron Tippin
Third Rock From The Sun...*Joe Diffie*
This Kiss...*Faith Hill*
This Woman And This Man...*Clay Walker*
Thunder Rolls, The...*Garth Brooks*
Time Marches On...*Tracy Lawrence*
26¢...*The Wilkinsons*
Unanswered Prayers...*Garth Brooks*
Walkaway Joe...*Trisha Yearwood*
What Part Of No...*Lorrie Morgan*
What She's Doing Now...*Garth Brooks*
When I Said I Do...*Clint Black w/ Lisa Hartman Black*
Where The Green Grass Grows...*Tim McGraw*
Wide Open Spaces...*Dixie Chicks*
Wild One...*Faith Hill*
Wink...*Neal MCoy*
Write This Down...*George Strait*
XXX's And OOO's (An American Girl)...*Trisha Yearwood*
You Know Me Better Than That...*George Strait*

Also Sprach Zarathustra...*Deodato*
Bad Girls...*Donna Summer*
Bad Luck...*Harold Melvin & The Blue Notes*
Best Disco In Town, The...*The Ritchie Family*
Boogie Fever...*The Sylvers*
Boogie Nights...*Heatwave*
Boogie Oogie Oogie...*A Taste Of Honey*
Boogie Wonderland...*Earth, Wind & Fire*
Born To Be Alive...*Patrick Hernandez*
Boss, The...*Diana Ross*
Brazil...*The Ritchie Family*
Brick House...*The Commodores*
Car Wash...*Rose Royce*
Cherchez La Femme...*Dr. Buzzard's Original Savannah Band*
Come To Me...*France Joli*
Dance (Disco Heat)...*Sylvester*
Dazz...*Brick*
Devil's Gun...*C.J. & Company*
Dance, Dance, Dance...*Chic*
Dance (Disco Heat)...*Sylvester*
Dance With Me...*Peter Brown w/ Betty Wright*
Dancer...*Gino Soccio*
Deputy Of Love...*Don Armando*
Disco Inferno...*The Trammps*
Disco Lady...*Johnnie Taylor*
Disco Nights (Rock Freak)...*G.Q.*
Disco Party...*The Trammps*
Da Ya Think I'm Sexy...*Rod Stewart*
Dancing Queen...*Abba*
Devil's Gun...*C.J. & Company*
Dim All The Lights...*Donna Summer*
Do What You Wanna Do...*T-Connection*
Don't Leave Me This Way...*Thelma Houston*
Don't Stop 'Til You Get Enough...*Michael Jackson*
Ease On Down The Road...*Consumer Rapport*
El Bimbo...*Bimbo Jet*
Express...*B.T. Express*
Fly, Robin, Fly...*Silver Convention*
Forever Came Today...*The Jackson 5*
From Here To Eternity...*Giorgio Moroder*
Get Dancin'...*Disco Tex & His Sex-O-Lettes*
Get Down Tonight...*KC & The Sunshine Band*
Get Up And Boogie (That's Right)...*Silver Convention*
Good Times...*Chic*
Got To Be Real...*Cheryl Lynn*
Got To Give It Up...*Marvin Gaye*
Grooveline...*Heatwave*
Heaven Must Be Missing An Angel...*Tavares*
He's The Greatest Dancer...*Sister Sledge*
Hot Stuff...*Donna Summer*
Hustle, The...*Van McCoy*
I Feel Love...*Donna Summer*
I Love Music...*The O'Jays*

I Love The Nightlife (Disco 'Round)...*Alicia Bridges*
I Need A Man...*Grace Jones*
I Will Survive...*Gloria Gaynor*
I'm Your Boogie Man...*KC & The Sunshine Band*
If My Friends Could See Me Now...*Linda Clifford*
In The Navy...*The Village People*
Instant Replay...*Dan Hartman*
Jive Talkin'...*Bee Gees*
Keep On Dancin'...*Gary's Gang*
Knock On Wood...*Amii Stewart*
Kung Fu Fighting...*Carl Douglas*
Ladies Night...*Kool & The Gang*
Lady Bump...*Penny McLean*
Last Dance...*Donna Summer*
Le Freak...*Chic*
Let's All Chant...*Michael Zager*
Let's Groove...*Archie Bell & The Drells*
Love Hangover...*Donna Summer*
Love To Love You Baby...*Donna Summer*
Macho Man...*Village People*
Makin' It...*David Naughton*
Mighty High...*Mighty Clouds Of Joy*
More, More, More Pt. 1...*Andrea True Connection*
More Than A Woman...*Bee Gees*
Move On Up...*Destination*
Never Can Say Goodbye...*Gloria Gaynor*
Night Fever...*Bee Gees*
No More Tears (Enough Is Enough)...*Donna Summer & Barbra Streisand*
Pick Up The Pieces...*Average White Band*
Pillow Talk...*Sylvia*
Right Back Where We Started From...*Maxine Nightingale*
Ring My Bell...*Anita Ward*
Second Time Around...*Shalamar*
(Shake, Shake, Shake) Shake Your Booty...*KC & The Sunshine Band*
Shake Your Body (Down To The Ground)...*The Jacksons*
Shake Your Groove Thing...*Peaches & Herb*
Shadow Dancing...*Andy Gibb*
Shame, Shame, Shame...*Shirley & Company*
Souvenirs...*Voyage*
Stayin' Alive...*Bee Gees*
Thank God It's Friday...*Love & Kisses*
That's The Way (I Like It)...*KC & The Sunshine Band*
Turn The Beat Around...*Vickie Sue Robinson*
We Are Family...*Sister Sledge*
You Make Me Feel (Mighty Real)...*Sylvester*
You Should Be Dancing...*Bee Gees*
Y.M.C.A....*Village People*

CATCH A WAVE

Baja...*The Astronauts*
Beach Girl...*Pat Boone*
Bustin' Surfboards...*The Tornadoes*
Catch A Wave...*The Beach Boys*
Diamond Head...*The Ventures*
Jezabel...*The Illusions*
King Of The Surf Guitar...*Dick Dale*
Latin'ia...*The Sentinals*
Let's Go Trippin'...*Dick Dale*
Lonely Surfer, The...*Jack Nitzsche*
Misirlou...*Dick Dale*
Mister Moto...*The Belairs*
Moon Dawg!...*The Gamblers*
Out Of Limits...*The Marketts*
Penetration...*The Pyramids*
Pipeline...*The Chantay's*
Point Panic...*The Surfaris*
Ride The Wild Surf...*Jan & Dean*
Rocking Surfer...*The Beach Boys*
Surf Beat...*Dick Dale*
Surf Buggy...*Dick Dale*
Surf City...*Jan & Dean*
Surf Dreams...*The Dartells*
Surf Party...*Chubby Checker*
Surf Rider...*The Lively Ones*
Surf Song...*Fenix Tx*
Surf Wax America...*Weezer*
Surfer Boy...*Jenny Mae*
Surfer Dan...*The Turtles*
Surfer Girl...*The Beach Boys*
Surfer Joe...*The Surfaris*
Surfer's Stomp...*The Mar-Kets*
Surfin'...*The Beach Boys*
Surfin' Bird...*The Trashmen*
Surfin' Cow...*The Dead Milkmen*
Surfin' Hootenanny...*Al Casey*
Surfin' In The Summertime...*Ronny & The Daytonas*
Surfin' Safari...*The Beach Boys*
Surfin' U.S.A....*The Beach Boys*
Surfin' U.S.S.R....*Ray Stevens*
Surfing With The Aliens...*Joe Satriani*
Surf's Up...*The Beach Boys*
Sweet Surf Music...*The Malibooz*
Tell 'Em I'm Surfing...*The Fantastic Baggies*
Theme From Endless Summer...*The Sandals*
Underwater...*The Frogmen*
Walk-Don't Run '64...*The Ventures*
Windsurfer...*Roy Orbison*
Wipe Out...*The Surfaris*
Your Baby's Gone Surfin'...*Duane Eddy*

ISLAND IN THE SUN

Almost Paradise...*Roger Williams*
Aloha Oe...*George Greeley*
American Dream, An...*Dirt Band*
Back To The Island...*Leon Russell*
Bali Ha'i...*Jo Stafford*
Beyond The Reef...*Andy Williams*
Blue Hawaii...*Elvis Presley*
Caribbean...*Mitchell Torok*
Caribbean Queen...*Billy Ocean*
Ebb Tide...*Frank Chacksfield*
Enchanted Island...*The Four Lads*
Gidget Goes Hawaiian...*Duane Eddy*
Harbor Lights...*Sammy Kaye w/ Tony Alamo*
Hawaii...*The Beach Boys*
Hawaii Five-O...*The Ventures*
Hawaii Tattoo...*The Waikikis*
Hawaiian Sunset...*Elvis Presley*
Hawaiian War Chant...*Billy Vaughn*
Hawaiian Wedding Song...*Andy Williams*
Hula Love...*Buddy Knox*
In The Middle Of An Island...*Tennessee Ernie Ford*
Island...*Jesse Colin Young*
Island Girl...*Elton John*
Island In The Sun...*Harry Belafonte*
Island Of Lost Souls...*Blondie*
Island Of Love...*Elvis Presley*
Island Woman...*Pablo Cruise*
Islands...*John Denver*
Jamaica Farewell...*Harry Belafonte*
Kokomo...*The Beach Boys*
La Isla Bonita...*Madonna*
Leah...*Roy Orbison*
Little Coco Palm...*Jerry Wallace*
Margaritaville...*Jimmy Buffett*
On An Island...*David Gilmour*
Paradise...*Third World*
Pearly Shells...*Burl Ives*
Pineapple Princess...*Annette*
Quiet Village...*Martin Denny*
Red Sails In The Sunset...*The Platters*
Rock-A-Hula Baby...*Elvis Presley*
Smiling Islands...*Robbie Patton*
Stranger In Paradise...*Tony Bennett*
Sweet Leilani...*Bing Crosby w/ Lani McIntyre*
Tamoure'...*Bill Justis*
Thunder Island...*Jay Ferguson*
Tiny Bubbles...*Don Ho*
Two Piña Coladas...*Garth Brooks*
Trade Winds...*Billy Vaughn*
White Silver Sands...*Don Rondo*

At The Hop...*Danny & The Juniors*
Bailamos...*Enrique Iglesias*
Ballroom Blitz...*Sweet*
Barefootin'...*Robert Parker*
Beer Barrel Polka...*Frankie Yankovic*
Bird, The...*Time*
Blue Tango...*Leroy Anderson*
Boogie Fever...*Sylvers*
Boogie Nights...*Heatwave*
Boogie Wonderland...*Earth, Wind & Fire w/ The Emotions*
Boot Scootin' Boogie...*Brooks & Dunn*
Breakin'...There's No Stopping Us...*Ollie & Jerry*
Bunny Hop...*Ray Anthony*
Bust A Move...*Young M.C.*
C'mon N' Ride It (The Train)...*Quad City DJ's*
Canned Heat...*Jamiroquai*
Cha Cha Slide...*Mr. C The Slide Man*
Chicken Dance (Dance Little Bird)...*Raymond Castoldi*
Conga...*Gloria Estefan*
Cotton Eye Joe...*Rednex*
Could I Have This Dance...*Anne Murray*
Crank That...*Soulja Boy*
Dance (Disco Heat)...*Sylvester*
Dancing In The Dark...*Bruce Springsteen*
Dancing Queen...*ABBA*
Dancing With Myself...*Billy Idol*
Disco Inferno...*Trammps*
Double Dutch Bus...*Frankie Smith*
Down At The Twist And Shout...*Mary-Chapin Carpenter*
Dragostea Din Tei (Ma Ya Hi)...*O-Zone*
Electric Slide (Electric Boogie)...*Marcia Griffiths*
Footloose...*Kenny Loggins*
Funkytown...*Lipps Inc.*
Gasolina...*Daddy Yankee*
Get Busy...*Sean Paul*
Get Down Tonight...*KC & The Sunshine Band*
Get Up And Boogie (That's Right)...*Silver Convention*
Get Up! (Before The Night Is Over)...*Technotronic*
Gonna Make You Sweat (Everybody Dance Now)...*C+C Music Factory f/ Freedom Williams*
Groove Line...*Heatwave*
Here Comes The Hotstepper...*Ini Kamoze*
Hey Mr. D.J....*Zhané*
Hokey Pokey...*Ray Anthony*
Hot, Hot, Hot...*Buster Poindexter*
Humpty Dance...*Digital Underground*
Hustle, The...*Van McCoy*
I Love The Nightlife (Disco 'Round)...*Alicia Bridges*
In Da Club...*50 Cent*

Into The Groove...*Madonna*
Jamming...*Bob Marley*
Jump Around...*House Of Pain*
Jungle Boogie...*Kool & The Gang*
Keep On Dancing...*Gentrys*
Kung Fu Fighting...*Carl Douglas*
La Bamba...*Ritchie Valens*
Lambada...*Kaoma*
Land Of 1000 Dances...*Wilson Pickett*
Last Dance...*Donna Summer*
Last Waltz, The...*Engelbert Humperdinck*
Le Freak...*Chic*
Let's Dance...*Chris Montez*
Let's Groove...*Earth, Wind & Fire*
Let The Music Play...*Shannon*
Liechtensteiner Polka...*Will Glahe*
Limbo Rock...*Chubby Checker*
Loco-Motion, The...*Little Eva*
Love Train...*O'Jays*
Macarena...*Los Del Rio*
Mambo Italiano...*Rosemary Clooney*
Mambo No. 5 ...*Lou Bega*
Monkey Time...*Major Lance*
Mony Mony...*Tommy James & The Shondells*
Moondance...*Van Morrison*
Night Fever...*Bee Gees*
1999...*Prince*
No Parking (On The Dance Floor)...*Midnight Star*
Nobody But Me...*Human Beinz*
1,2 Step...*Ciara*
1,2,3,4 (Sumpin' New)...*Coolio*
Peppermint Twist-Part I...*Joey Dee & The Starliters*
Pon De Replay...*Rihanna*
Quarter To Three...*Gary (U.S.) Bonds*
Rock Around the Clock...*Bill Haley & The Comets*
Rock Your Body...*Justin Timberlake*
Safety Dance, The...*Men Without Hats*
Save The Last Dance For Me...*Drifters*
Shake It Up...*Cars*
Shake Your Body (Down To The Ground)...*Jacksons*
Shout – Pts. 1 & 2...*Isley Brothers*
Stroll, The...*Diamonds*
Switch...*Will Smith*
Tea for Two Cha Cha ...*Tommy Dorsey*
Tennessee Waltz...*Patti Page*
Turn The Beat Around...*Vicki Sue Robinson*
Twist And Shout...*Beatles*
Twist, The...*Chubby Checker*
Vogue...*Madonna*
What I Like About You...*Romantics*
Who Let The Dogs Out...*Baha Men*
Willie And The Hand Jive ...*Johnny Otis Show*
Y.M.C.A....*Village People*
Zoot Suit Riot...*Cherry Poppin' Daddies*

INSTRUMENTALLY YOURS

SWINGIN' GENTLY:

Alley Cat...*Bent Fabric*
Autumn Leaves...*Roger Williams*
Calcutta...*Lawrence Welk*
Canadian Sunset...*Hugo Winterhalter/Eddie Heywood*
Cast Your Fate To The Wind...*Sounds Orchestral*
Chariots Of Fire – Titles...*Vangelis*
Cherry Pink & Apple Blossom White...*Perez Prado*
Classical Gas...*Mason Williams*
Dueling Banjos...*Eric Weissberg & Steve Mandell*
Entertainer, The...*Marvin Hamlisch*
Exodus...*Ferrante & Teicher*
Fly Me To The Moon – Bossa Nova...*Joe Harnell*
Good, The Bad And The Ugly...*Hugo Montenegro*
Java...*Al Hirt*
Last Date...*Floyd Cramer*
Lisbon Antigua...*Nelson Riddle*
Love Is Blue...*Paul Mauriat*
Love Theme From Romeo & Juliet...*Henry Mancini*
Maria Elena...*Los Indios Tabajaras*
Midnight Cowboy...*Ferrante & Teicher*
Midnight In Moscow...*Kenny Ball*
Moonglow And Theme From "Picnic"...*Morris Stoloff*
Mr. Lucky...*Henry Mancini*
Music Box Dancer...*Frank Mills*
Music To Watch Girls By...*Bob Crewe Generation*
Never On Sunday...*Don Costa*
Only You...*Franck Pourcel*
Patricia...*Perez Prado*
Petite Fleur...*Chris Barber*
Pink Panther Theme...*Henry Mancini*
Poor People Of Paris...*Les Baxter*
Quiet Village...*Martin Denny*
Sail Along Silvery Moon...*Billy Vaughn*
Sleep Walk...*Santo & Johnny*
Songbird...*Kenny G*
Star Wars Main Theme...*London Symphony Orchestra*
Stranger On The Shore...*Mr. Acker Bilk*
Stripper, The...*David Rose*
Swingin' Gently...*Earl Grant*
Swingin' Safari...*Billy Vaughn*
Take Five...*Dave Brubeck Quartet*
Taste Of Honey...*Herb Alpert/The Tijuana Brass*
Tea For Two Cha Cha...*Tommy Dorsey*
Theme From "A Summer Place"...*Percy Faith*
Theme From "Summer Of '42"...*Peter Nero*
Theme From The Apartment...*Ferrante & Teicher*
Walk In The Black Forest...*Horst Jankowski*
Washington Square...*The Village Stompers*
Wonderland By Night...*Bert Kaempfert*
Yellow Bird...*Arthur Lyman Group*

WILD WEEKEND:

Apache...*Jorgen Ingmann*
Asia Minor...*Kokomo*
Because They're Young...*Duane Eddy*
Bonanza...*Al Caiola*
Bongo Rock...*Preston Epps*
Frankenstein...*Edgar Winter Group*
Ghost Riders In The Sky...*The Ramrods*
Grazing In The Grass...*Hugh Masekela*
Green Onions...*Booker T. & The MG's*
Guitar Boogie Shuffle...*The Virtues*
Happy Organ, The...*Dave 'Baby' Cortez*
Harlem Nocturne...*The Viscounts*
Hawaii Five-O...*The Ventures*
Honky Tonk...*Bill Doggett*
Horse, The...*Cliff Nobles & Co.*
Keem-O-Sabe...*The Electric Indian*
Last Night...*Mar-Keys*
Let There Be Drums...*Sandy Nelson*
Let's Go...*The Routers*
Memphis...*Lonnie Mack*
Misirlou...*Dick Dale & The Del-Tones*
Mission: Impossible...*Adam Clayton & Larry Mullen*
No Matter What Shape...*The T-Bones*
Out Of Limits...*The Marketts*
Penetration...*The Pyramids*
Percolator Twist...*Billy Joe & The Checkmates*
Pipeline...*The Chantay's*
Poor Boy...*The Royaltones*
Popcorn...*Hot Butter*
Quite A Party...*The Fireballs*
Raunchy...*Bill Justis*
Rebel-'Rouser...*Duane Eddy*
Red River Rock...*Johnny & The Hurricanes*
Rinky Dink...*Baby Cortez*
Rumble...*Link Wray*
Smokie – Part 2...*Bill Black's Combo*
Soulful Strut...*Young-Holt Unlimited*
Tall Cool One...*The Wailers*
Teen Beat...*Sandy Nelson*
Telstar...*The Tornadoes*
Tequila...*The Champs*
Time Is Tight...*Booker T. & The MG's*
Topsy II...*Cozy Cole*
Torquay...*The Fireballs*
Walk—Don't Run...*The Ventures*
Watermelon Man...*Mongo Santamaria*
Wheels...*The String-A-Longs*
Wild Weekend...*The Rebels*
Wipe Out...*The Surfaris*
Woo-Hoo...*Rock-A-Teens*

MORE COWBELL!

Dance The Night Away...*Van Halen*
Don't Fear The Reaper...*Blue Oyster Cult*
Down On The Corner...*Creedence Clearwater Revival*
Evil Ways...*Santana*
Funkytown...*Lipps Inc.*
Grazing In The Grass...*Hugh Masekela*
Honky Tonk Women...*Rolling Stones*
It's So Easy...*Linda Ronstadt*
Jammin' Me...*Tom Petty*
Logical Song, The...*Supertramp*
Love Rollercoaster...*Ohio Players*
Low Rider...*War*
Mississippi Queen...*Mountain*
Never Been Any Reason...*Head East*
Oye Como Va...*Santana*
Susie-Q...*Dale Hawkins*
Teenagers...*My Chemical Romance*
Time Has Come Today...*Chambers Brothers*
We're An American Band...*Grand Funk Railroad*
Working For The Weekend...*Loverboy*
You Ain't Seen Nothin' Yet...*Bachman Turner Overdrive*

HAPPY ANNIVERSARY

Anniversary...*Tony! Toni! Toné!*
Anniversary Song...*Dinah Shore*
Anniversary Waltz...*Lawrence Welk*
As Time Goes By...*Jimmy Durante*
Because Of You...*Tony Bennett*
Celebration...*Kool & The Gang*
Could I Have This Dance...*Anne Murray*
Fly Me To The Moon...*Frank Sinatra*
How Sweet It Is (To Be Loved By You)...*Marvin Gaye*
I Love You Always Forever...*Donna Lewis*
If I Didn't Have You...*Randy Travis*
It Had To Be You...*Harry Connick, Jr.*
It's Your Love...*Tim McGraw & Faith Hill*
Longer...*Dan Fogelberg*
Look At Us...*Vince Gill*
L-O-V-E...*Michael Bublé'*
Love And Marriage...*Frank Sinatra*
Memories Are Made Of This...*Dean Martin*
On The Wings Of Love...*Jeffrey Osborne*
Round And Round...*Perry Como*
Sea Of Love...*The Honeydrippers*
Through The Years...*Kenny Rogers*
Times Of Your Life...*Paul Anka*
Unforgettable...*Natalie Cole w/ Nat "King" Cole*
We Are Family...*Sister Sledge*
When I Said I Do...*Clint Black w/ Lisa Hartman Black*
You're Still The One...*Shania Twain*

BIG BOPPERS

Ahab, The Arab...*Ray Stevens*
Ajax Liquor Store...*Hudson & Landry*
All American Boy, The...*Bill Parsons*
Alley-Oop...*Hollywood Argyles*
Along Came Jones...*The Coasters*
Astronaut, The...*Jose Jimenez*
Baby Sittin' Boogie...*Buzz Clifford*
Banana Boat (Day-O) ...*Stan Freberg*
Battle Of Kookamonga...*Homer & Jethro*
Beep Beep...*The Playmates*
Big Bopper's Wedding...*Big Bopper*
Boy Named Sue, A...*Johnny Cash*
Chantilly Lace...*Big Bopper*
Class, The...*Chubby Checker*
Curly Shuffle, The...*Jump 'N The Saddle*
Dang Me...*Roger Miller*
Delicious! ...*Jim Backus & Friend*
Disco Duck...*Rick Dees & His Cast Of Idiots*
Don't Go Near The Eskimos...*Ben Colder*
Flying Saucer, The...*Buchanan & Goodman*
Gitarzan...*Ray Stevens*
Heartbreak Hotel...*Stan Freberg*
Hello Mudduh, Hello Fadduh!...*Allan Sherman*
I Got A Wife...*The Mark IV*
King Tut...*Steve Martin*
Kookie, Kookie (Lend Me Your Comb)...*Edd Byrnes & Connie Stevens*
Leader Of The Laundromat...*The Detergents*
Little Blue Man, The...*Betty Johnson*
Little Space Girl, The...*Jesse Lee Turner*
Martian Hop...*The Ran-Dells*
Mr. Custer...*Larry Verne*
Mr. Jaws...*Dickie Goodman*
My Boomerang Won't Come Back...*Charlie Drake*
My Ding-A-Ling...*Chuck Berry*
Pepino The Italian Mouse...*Lou Monte*
Purple People Eater, The...*Sheb Wooley*
Rip Van Winkle...*The Devotions*
Snoopy Vs. The Red Baron...*The Royal Guardsmen*
Speedy Gonzales...*Pat Boone*
Stranded In The Jungle...*The Cadets*
Streak, The...*Ray Stevens*
Take Off...*Bob & Doug McKenzie*
They're Coming To Take Me Away, Ha-Haaa!...*Napoleon XIV*
Tie Me Kangaroo Down, Sport...*Rolf Harris*
Transfusion...*Nervous Norvus*
Western Movies...*The Olympics*
White & Nerdy..."*Weird Al*" *Yankovic*
Wild Thing...*Senator Bobby*
Witch Doctor...*David Seville*
Yogi...*The Ivy Three*

IT'S A DISNEY WORLD AFTER ALL

Amigas Cheetahs...*The Cheetah Girls* (TV)
Anytime You Need A Friend...*Home On The Range*
Baby Mine...*Dumbo*
Ballad Of Davy Crockett, The...*Disneyland's Davy Crockett* (TV)
Bare Necessities...*The Jungle Book*
Be Our Guest...*Beauty And The Beast*
Beauty And The Beast...*Beauty And The Beast*
Bibbidi-Bobbidi-Boo (The Magic Song)...*Cinderella*
Breaking Free...*High School Musical* (TV)
Call Me, Beep Me...*Kim Possible* (TV)
Can You Feel The Love Tonight...*The Lion King*
Candle On The Water...*Pete's Dragon*
Chim Chim Cheree...*Mary Poppins*
Circle Of Life...*The Lion King*
Colors Of The Wind...*Pocahontas*
Cruella De Ville...*101 Dalmatians*
Dream Is A Wish Your Heart Makes, A...*Cinderella*
Friend Like Me...*Aladdin*
Go The Distance...*Hercules*
Hakuna Matata...*The Lion King*
Hawaiian Roller Coaster Ride...*Lilo & Stitch*
Heigh-Ho...*Snow White*
I Just Can't Wait To Be King...*The Lion King*
It's A Small World (After All)...*Disneyworld* (attraction)
Just Around The River Bend...*Pocahontas*
Kiss The Girl...*The Little Mermaid*
Lavender Blue (Dilly Dilly)...*So Dear To My Heart*
Let's Get Together...*The Parent Trap*
Let's Go Fly A Kite...*Mary Poppins*
Life's What You Make It...*Hannah Montana* (TV)
Little April Shower...*Bambi*
Look Through My Eyes...*Brother Bear*
Mickey Mouse Club March...*Mickey Mouse Club* (TV)
Prince Ali...*Aladdin*
Real Gone...*Cars*
Reflection...*Mulan*
Someday My Prince Will Come...*Snow White*
Super-cali-fragil-istic-expi-ali-docious...*Mary Poppins*
Two Worlds...*Tarzan*
Under The Sea...*The Little Mermaid*
What Dreams Are Made Of...*The Lizzie McGuire Movie*
What Time Is It...*High School Musical 2* (TV)
When You Wish Upon A Star...*Pinocchio*
Whistle While You Work...*Snow White*
Who's Afraid Of The Big Bad Wolf...*The Three Little Pigs*
Whole New World, A...*Aladdin*
You Belong To My Heart...*The Three Caballeros*
You Can Fly! You Can Fly! You Can Fly!...*Peter Pan*
You've Got A Friend In Me...*Toy Story*
Zip-A-Dee-Doo-Dah...*Song Of The South*

SING, SING A SONG

American Pie
Amy
Banana Boat Song (Day-O
Beer Barrel Polka
Bicycle Built For Two
Brown-Eyed Girl
By The Light Of The Silvery Moon
Cecelia
Clementine
Dancing Queen
Danny Boy
Desperado
Dixie
Do-Re-Mi
Friends In Low Places
God Bless America
Hava Nagila
Home On The Range
I Am A Man Of Constant Sorrow
I Love Rock 'N' Roll
I've Been Working On The Railroad
Jamaica Farewell
Joy To The World (Jeremiah Was A Bullfrog)
Let Me Call You Sweetheart
Lion Sleeps Tonight, The
Lola
Macarena
Margaritaville
Michael (Row The Boat Ashore)
Mony Mony
Oh Susanna!
Over The River & Through The Woods
Puff The Magic Dragon
Saturday Night
She'll Be Coming 'Round The Mountain
Shine On Harvest Moon
Shout...
Sloop John B
Star Spangled Banner
Swanee
Sweet Caroline
Swing Low, Sweet Chariot
Take Me Home, Country Roads
Take Me Out To The Ballgame
This Land Is Your Land
This Little Light Of Mine
Too-Ra-Loo-Ra-Loo-Ral
Tubthumping
Walk On The Wild Side
We Will Rock You
What Shall We Do With The Drunken Sailor
When The Saints Go Marching In
Who Let The Dogs Out
Whoomp! (There It Is)
Wild Thing
Yankee Doodle
Y.M.C.A.
You Are My Sunshine
You've Lost That Lovin' Feelin'

FOREIGN LANGUAGE HITS

Al Di La'...*Emilio Pericoli*
Al Otro Lado Del Rio...*Jorge Dexter*
Amor...*Xavier Cugat*
Amor Eterno...*Christian Castro*
Anna (El Negro Zumbon)...*Silvana Mangano*
Bang Bang...*Joe Cuba*
Banjo Boy...*Jan & Kjeld*
C'est Si Bon...*Eartha Kitt*
Ca Plane Pour Moi...*Plastic Bertrand*
Cuando Caliente El Sol...*The Copacabana Trio*
Dimelo...*Enrique Iglesias*
Dominique...*Singing Nun*
Dragostea Din Tei (Ma Ya Hi)...*O-Zone*
Eh Cumpari...*Julius LaRosa*
El Watusi...*Ray Baretto*
Enamorado...*Keith Colley*
Eres Tu...*Mocedades*
French Song, The...*Lucille Starr*
Gasolina...*Daddy Yankee*
Guantanamera...*Sandpipers*
Je T'Aime.Moi Non Plus...*Jane Birkin & Serge Gainsbourg*
Jealous Of You...*Connie Francis*
La Bamba...*Ritchie Valens*
La Pachanga...*Audrey Arno*
La Tortura...*Shakira with Alejandro Sanz*
Lazy Mary...*Lou Monte*
Liechensteiner Polka...*Will Glahe*
Little Train, The...*Marianne Vasel & Erich Storz*
Lullaby Of Birdland...*Blue Stars*
Macarena...*Los Del Rio*
Marina...*Rocco Granata*
Mas Que Nada...*Sergio Mendes & Brasil '66*
Me Enamora...*Juanes*
Morgen...*Ivo Robic*
Mover, A (La Colita) ...*Artie The 1 Man Party*
99 Luftballons...*Nena*
Otro Dia Mas...*Jon Secada*
Oye Como Va...*Santana*
Oye Mi Canto...*N.O.R.E. w/ Daddy Yankee*
Pata Pata...*Miriam Makeba*
Que Hiciste...*Jennifer Lopez*
Quitame Ese Hombre...*Pilar Montenegro*
Sadeness Part 1...*Enigma*
Sailor (Your Home Is The Sea)...*Lolita*
Sie Liebt Dich (She Love You)...*Beatles*
Soul Makossa...*Afrique*
Suavemente...*Elvis Crespo*
Sukiyaki...*Kyu Sakamoto*
Torero...*Renato Carosone*
Volaré (Nel Blu Dipinto Di Blu)...*Domenico Modugno*
Wimoweh...*Weavers & Gordon Jenkins*

BIG BANDS
1935-1945

American Patrol...*Glenn Miller*
And Her Tears Flowed Like Wine...*Stan Kenton*
And The Angels Sing...*Benny Goodman*
Artistry In Rhythm...*Stan Kenton*
Begin The Beguine...*Artie Shaw*
Besame Mucho...*Jimmy Dorsey*
Blues In The Night...*Woody Herman*
Boogie Woogie...*Tommy Dorsey*
Brazil...*Xavier Cugat*
Breeze And I, The...*Jimmy Dorsey*
Bugle Call Rag...*Benny Goodman*
Chattanooga Choo Choo...*Glenn Miller*
Cherokee...*Charlie Barnet*
Daddy...*Sammy Kaye*
Don't Get Around Much Anymore...*Duke Ellington*
Elmer's Tune...*Glenn Miller*
For Dancer's Only...*Jimmie Lunceford*
Frenesi...*Artie Shaw*
Green Eyes...*Jimmy Dorsey*
I'm Beginning To See The Light...*Harry James*
I've Got A Gal In Kalamazoo...*Glenn Miller*
I've Heard That Song Before...*Harry James*
I Don't Want To Walk Without You...*Harry James*
In The Mood...*Glenn Miller*
It's Been A Long, Long Time...*Harry James*
Jingle Jangle Jingle...*Kay Kyser*
King Porter Stomp...*Benny Goodman*
Let's Dance...*Benny Goodman*
Marie...*Tommy Dorsey*
Moonglow...*Benny Goodman*
Moonlight Cocktail...*Glenn Miller*
Moonlight Serenade...*Glenn Miller*
Music Goes Round And Round, The...*Tommy Dorsey*
My Dreams Are Getting Better All The Time...*Les Brown*
One O'Clock Jump...*Count Basie*
Opus No. 1...*Tommy Dorsey*
Pennsylvania Six-Five Thousand...*Glenn Miller*
Perfidia...*Xavier Cugat*
Sentimental Journey...*Les Brown*
Sing, Sing, Sing (With A Swing)...*Benny Goodman*
South Rampart Street Parade...*Bob Crosby*
Star Dust...*Artie Shaw*
Stompin' At The Savoy...*Benny Goodman*
String Of Pearls, A...*Glenn Miller*
Summit Ridge Drive...*Artie Shaw*
Take The "A" Train...*Duke Ellington*
Taking A Chance On Love...*Benny Goodman*
Tampico...*Stan Kenton*
Tuxedo Junction...*Glenn Miller*
Woodchopper's Ball...*Woody Herman*

SPRING FEVER

Apple Blossom Wedding, An...*Sammy Kaye with Don Cornell*
April Come She Will...*Simon & Garfunkel*
April Fools...*Dionne Warwick*
April In Paris...*Count Basie*
April In Portugal...*Les Baxter*
April Joy...*Pat Metheny*
April Love...*Pat Boone*
April Showers...*Al Jolson*
April Skies...*Jesus & Mary Chain*
April Song...*John Tesh*
Blossom Fell, A...*Nat "King" Cole*
Cherry Pink & Apple Blossom White...*Perez Prado*
Day The Rains Came, The...*Jane Morgan*
First Day Of May...*James Taylor*
First Of May...*Bee Gees*
Here Comes The Sun...*Richie Havens*
I'll Be With You In Apple Blossom Time...*Andrews Sisters*
I'll Remember April...*Bobby Darin*
I've Got Spring Fever...*Little Willie John*
It Might As Well Be Spring...*Dick Haymes*
Late Winter, Early Spring...*John Denver*
Lusty Month Of May...*Julie Andrews*
New Day Has Come, A...*Celine Dion*
Paris In The Spring...*Ferrante & Teicher*
Pieces Of April...*Three Dog Night*
Please Come To Boston...*Dave Loggins*
So Early, Early In The Spring...*Judy Collins*
Somewhere, My Love...*Ray Conniff Singers*
Spring...*The Serendipity Singers*
Spring Affair...*Donna Summer*
Spring Again...*Lou Rawls*
Spring Can Really Hang You Up The Most...*Bette Midler*
Spring Concerto...*Peter Nero*
Spring Fever...*Elvis Presley*
Spring Haze...*Tori Amos*
Spring In Central Park...*Dave Brubeck Quartet*
Spring In Manhattan...*Tony Bennett*
Spring Is Here...*Carly Simon*
Spring Love...*The Cover Girls*
Spring Rain...*Silvetti*
Spring Vacation...*Black Oak Arkansas*
Springtime...*The New Christy Minstrels*
Springtime Mama...*Henry Gross*
Suddenly It's Spring...*Frank Sinatra*
Their Hearts Were Full Of Spring...*The Four Preps*
When It's Springtime In Alaska...*Johnny Horton*
When The White Lilacs Bloom Again...*Helmut Zacharias*
White Sport Coat And A Pink Carnation...*Marty Robbins*
Wildwood Days...*Bobby Rydell*
Younger Than Springtime...*John Gary*

SUMMERTIME

Beach Baby...*First Class*
California Sun...*The Rivieras*
Centerfield...*John Fogerty*
Endless Summer Nights...*Richard Marx*
First Day Of Summer, The...*Tony Carey*
Green Grass...*Gary Lewis & The Playboys*
Green Leaves Of Summer, The...*The Brothers Four*
Groovin'...*The Rascals*
Happy Summer Days...*Ronnie Dove*
Heat Wave...*Martha & The Vandellas*
Here Comes Summer...*Jerry Keller*
Hot Fun In The Summertime...*Sly & The Family Stone*
Hot Summer Nights...*Night*
In The Summertime...*Mungo Jerry*
It's Summer...*The Temptations*
Lazy Summer Night...*The Four Preps*
Magic...*Cars*
Moonglow and Theme from "Picnic"...*Morris Stoloff*
My Summer Love...*Ruby & The Romantics*
One Summer Night...*The Danleers*
Saturday In The Park...*Chicago*
Soft Summer Breeze...*Eddie Heywood*
Song For A Summer Night...*Mitch Miller*
Suddenly Last Summer...*The Motels*
Summer...*War*
Summer Breeze...*Seals & Crofts*
Summer Bunnies...*R. Kelly*
Summer In The City...*The Lovin' Spoonful*
Summer Love...*Roy Orbison*
Summer Madness...*Kool & The Gang*
Summer Nights...*John Travolta & Olivia Newton-John*
Summer Of '69...*Bryan Adams*
Summer Rain...*Johnny Rivers*
Summer Sand...*Dawn*
Summer Song...*Joe Satriani*
Summer Song, A...*Chad & Jeremy*
Summer Souvenirs...*Karl Hammel Jr.*
Summer Wind...*Frank Sinatra*
Summer Wine...*Nancy Sinatra & Lee Hazlewood*
Summertime...*Kenny Chesney*
Summertime...*Sam Cooke*
Summertime Blues...*Eddie Cochran*
Summertime, Summertime...*The Jamies*
Sunny Afternoon...*The Kinks*
That Sunday, That Summer...*Nat "King" Cole*
Theme From "A Summer Place"...*Percy Faith*
Those Lazy-Hazy-Crazy Days Of Summer...*Nat "King" Cole*
Vacation...*Connie Francis*
Walkin' In The Sunshine...*Roger Miller*
Wonderful Summer...*Robin Ward*

'TIS AUTUMN

Autumn...*Barbra Streisand*
Autumn Afternoon...*The Sandpipers*
Autumn Changes...*Donna Summer*
Autumn In New York...*Sarah Vaughan*
Autumn In Rome...*Robert Goulet*
Autumn Leaves...*Roger Williams*
Autumn Love Song...*Billy Vaughn*
Autumn Nocturne...*Henry Mancini*
Autumn Of My Life...*Bobby Goldsboro*
Autumn Rhapsody...*Ronnie Dove*
Autumn Serenade...*Les Elgart*
Autumn Song...*Van Morrison*
Autumn Waltz, The...*Tony Bennett*
Autumn Wind...*The Serendipity Singers*
Blue Autumn...*Bobby Goldsboro*
Chill Of An Early Fall...*George Strait*
Cool Change...*Little River Band*
Dark Moon...*Bonnie Guitar*
Early Autumn...*Woody Herman & Stan Getz*
Fall In Philadelphia...*Daryl Hall & John Oates*
Gone Till November...*Wyclef Jean*
Indian Summer...*Ella Fitzgerald*
It Might As Well Rain Until September...*Carole King*
Last Leaf, The...*The Cascades*
Lullaby Of The Leaves...*The Ventures*
Moments To Remember...*The Four Lads*
Moondance...*Van Morrison*
November Rain...*Guns N' Roses*
November Sky...*Yanni*
November Twilight...*Julie London*
October....*U2*
October Morning...*Fourplay*
Old Cape Cod...*Patti Page*
Seasons...*Charles Fox*
Seasons Change...*Exposé*
See You In September...*The Happenings*
September...*Earth, Wind & Fire*
September Gurls...*Big Star*
September In Seattle...*Shawn Mullins*
September In The Rain... *Dinah Washington*
September Morn'...*Neil Diamond*
September Of My Years...*Frank Sinatra*
September Skies...*Brian Setzer Orchestra*
September Song...*Jimmy Durante*
Shine On Harvest Moon...*The Four Aces*
Summer's Gone...*Paul Anka*
Sweet Seasons...*Carole King*
'Tis Autumn...*Ella Fitzgerald & Joe Pass*
Wake Me Up When September Ends...*Green Day*
When October Goes...*Barry Manilow*

WINTERTIME

Baby It's Cold Outside...*Dinah Shore & Buddy Clark*
Big Cold Wind...*Pat Boone*
Blizzard, The...*Jim Reeves*
California Dreamin'...*The Mamas & The Papas*
Cold As Ice...*Foreigner*
Cold Winter Day...*BoDeans*
December 1963 (Oh, What A Night)...*4 Seasons*
Fall Softly Snow...*Jim Ed Brown & Helen Cornelius*
Hazy Shade Of Winter, A...*Simon & Garfunkel*
I Am A Rock...*Simon & Garfunkel*
I'm Gonna Be Warm This Winter...*Connie Francis*
If We Make It Through December...*Merle Haggard*
In The Winter...*Janis Ian*
It's Cold Outside...*Choir*
It's Now Winter's Day...*Tommy Roe*
It May Be Winter Outside (But In My Heart It's Spring...*Felice Taylor*
Jingo Jango...*Bert Kaempfert*
Let It Snow...*Boyz II Men*
Let It Snow! Let It Snow! Let It Snow!...*Vaughn Monroe*
Life In A Northern Town...*Dream Academy*
Long Cold Winter...*Pure Prairie League*
Long December, A...*Counting Crows*
Our Winter Love...*Bill Pursell*
Snowbird...*Anne Murray*
Snowbound...*Genesis*
Snow Flake...*Jim Reeves*
Song For A Winter's Night...*Gordon Lightfoot*
When The Snow Is On The Roses...*Ed Ames*
Winter...*John Denver*
Winter Ballad...*Dave Brubeck Quartet*
Winter Blizzard...*Johnny Bond*
Winter Boy...*Buffy Sainte-Marie*
Winter Had Me In Its Grip...*Don McLean*
Winter In America...*Gil Scott-Heron & Brian Jackson*
Winter Light...*Linda Ronstadt*
Winterlude...*Bob Dylan*
Winter Marches On...*Duran Duran*
Winter Peace...*Jim Brickman*
Winter Sky...*Judy Collins*
Winter Song...*Barry DeVorzon*
Winter Symphony...*The Beach Boys*
Winter Time...*Steve Miller Band*
Wintertime Love...*The Doors*
Winter Weather...*Squirrel Nut Zippers*
Winter Wonderland...*Elvis Presley*
Winter World Of Love...*Engelbert Humperdinck*
Winter's Day...*Mannheim Steamroller*
Winter's Here Again...*The Ames Brothers*
Wintry Feeling...*Jesse Winchester*
Wizards In Winter...*Trans-Siberian Orchestra*

WORK OUT!

WARM UP:

Beautiful Day...*U2*
Clocks...*Coldplay*
Everybody Wants To Rule The World...*Tears For Fears*
Hippychick...*Soho*
Stop To Love...*Luther Vandross*
Word Up...*Cameo*

HIT IT:

Blue Monday...*New Order*
Brand New Lover...*Dead Or Alive*
Can't Get You Out Of My Head...*Kylie Minogue*
Da Funk...*Daft Punk*
Delirious...*Prince*
Don't Go...*Yaz*
Don't Leave Me This Way...*Communards w/ Sarah Jane Morris*
Everytime We Touch...*Cascada*
Firestarter...*Prodigy*
Funky Town...*Pseudo Echo*
Galvanize...*The Chemical Brothers*
Get The Party Started...*Pink*
I Beg Your Pardon...*Kon Kan*
It's My Life...*No Doubt*
It's The End Of The World As We Know It...*R.E.M.*
Knock On Wood...*Amii Stewart*
Little Bird...*Annie Lennox*
Little Less Conversation...*Elvis Presley vs JXL*
Move This...*Technotronic Featuring Ya Kid K*
100% Pure Love...*Crystal Waters*
Promise Of A New Day...*Paula Abdul*
Pump It...*Black Eyed Peas*
Ray Of Light...*Madonna*
Respectable...*Tipsy & Tipsy*
Rhythm Is A Dancer...*Snap!*
Rhythm Of The Night...*Corona*
Rockafeller Skank...*Fatboy Slim*
Set U Free...*Planet Soul*
Show Me Love...*Robin S*
Sk8ter Boi...*Avril Lavigne*
SOS...*Rihanna*
Step Into The Sun...*Solid State Revival*
Stupid Girl...*Garbage*
Take Me Out...*Franz Ferdinand*
Tall Cool One...*Robert Plant*
What Is Love...*Haddaway*

COOL DOWN:

Crazy...*Gnarls Barkley*
Feels So Good...*Chuck Mangione*
Fields Of Gold...*Sting*
Keep On Movin'...*Soul II Soul*
Lily Was Here...*David A. Stewart w/ Candy Dulfer*
Video...*India.Arie*

HAUNTED HOUSE

Addams Family...*TV Theme Song*
Bad Moon Rising...*Creedence Clearwater Revival*
Bark At The Moon...*Ozzy Osbourne*
Bela Lugosi's Dead...*Bauhaus*
Bigfoot...*Bro Smith*
Black Magic Woman...*Santana*
Blob, The...*Five Blobs*
Creature From The Black Lagoon, The...*Dave Edmunds*
Dead Man's Party...*Oingo Boingo*
Dinner With Drac...*Zacherle*
(Don't Fear) The Reaper...*Blue Oyster Cult*
Dragula...*Rob Zombie*
Frankenstein...*Edgar Winter Group*
(Ghost) Riders In The Sky...*Outlaws*
Ghost Town...*Specials*
Ghost Train...*Elvis Costello*
Ghostbusters...*Ray Parker Jr.*
Groovy Ghost Show...*Casper*
Halloween...*Helloween*
Halloween Americana...*Everclear*
Halloween Parade...*Lou Reed*
Haunted House...*Gene Simmons*
Haunted Mansion On The Hill...*San Sebastian Strings*
I Put A Spell On You...*Screamin' Jay Hawkins*
I Want My Baby Back...*Jimmy Cross*
Iron Man...*Black Sabbath*
(It's A) Monsters' Holiday...*Buck Owens*
Laurie (Strange Things Happening)...*Dickey Lee*
Legend Of Wooley Swamp, The...*Charlie Daniels Band*
Marie Laveau...*Bobby Bare*
Martian Boogie, The...*Brownsville Station*
Monster Mash...*Bobby "Boris" Pickett*
Mummy, The...*Bob McFadden & Dor*
Munsters, The...*TV Theme Song*
Nightmare On My Street...*D.J. Jazzy Jeff & The Fresh Prince*
Psycho Killer...*Talking Heads*
Purple People Eater, The...*Sheb Wooley*
Scary Monsters (And Super Creeps)...*David Bowie*
Spooky...*Classics IV*
Swamp Witch...*Jim Stafford*
This Is Halloween...*Danny Elfman*
Thriller...*Michael Jackson*
Twilight Zone/Twilight Tone...*Manhattan Transfer*
Welcome To My Nightmare...*Alice Cooper*
Werewolf...*Five Man Electrical Band*
Werewolves Of London...*Warren Zevon*
Witch Queen Of New Orleans, The...*Redbone*
Witches...*Cowboy Junkies*
Witchy Woman...*Eagles*
X-Files Theme...*Mark Snow*

TAKE IT EASY

Baker Street...*Gerry Rafferty*
Black Water...*Doobie Brothers*
Breathe Your Name...*Sixpence None The Richer*
Captain Of Her Heart...*Double*
Chuck E.'s In Love...*Rickie Lee Jones*
Crazy Love...*Poco*
Deacon Blues...*Steely Dan*
Don't Know Why...*Norah Jones*
Every Little Kiss...*Bruce Hornsby*
Everything Reminds Me Of My Dog...*Jane Siberry*
Fly Me To The Moon...*Tony Bennett*
Girl From Ipanema...*Stan Getz & Astrud Gilberto*
Giving You The Best That I Got...*Anita Baker*
Graceland...*Paul Simon*
I Love You...*Climax Blues Band*
I Try...*Macy Gray*
Is It Love...*Bob Marley*
Is It You...*Lee Ritenour*
Jazzman...*Carole King*
Killing Me Softly With His Song...*Roberta Flack*
Life In A Northern Town...*Dream Academy*
Lights...*Journey*
Linger...*Cranberries*
Lotta Love...*Nicolette Larson*
Mexico...*James Taylor*
Midnight At The Oasis...*Maria Muldaur*
Miss Sun...*Boz Scaggs*
Moondance...*Van Morrison*
Moonlight Feels Right...*Starbuck*
Mornin'...*Al Jarreau*
No Myth...*Michael Penn*
One Particular Harbour...*Jimmy Buffett*
Only Time...*Enya*
Overjoyed...*Stevie Wonder*
Paradise...*Sade*
Perfidia...*Nat "King" Cole*
Piano In The Dark...*Brenda Russell*
Sara...*Fleetwood Mac*
Southern Cross...*Crosby, Stills & Nash*
Sundown...*Gordon Lightfoot*
Take Five...*Dave Brubeck Quartet*
Take It Easy...*Eagles*
This Masquerade...*George Benson*
Touch Of Grey...*Grateful Dead*
Until You Come Back To Me...*Aretha Franklin*
What You Won't Do For Love...*Bobby Caldwell*
When Did You Fall...*Chris Rice*
Wicked Game...*Chris Isaak*
Wondering Where The Lions Are...*Bruce Cockburn*
You'll Never Find Another Love Like Mine...*Lou Rawls*

SING ALLELUIA
Contemporary Christian
2000-2007

Above All...*Michael W. Smith*
Alive...*Rebecca St. James*
All About Love...*Steven Curtis Chapman*
All I Need...*Bethany Dillon*
Beautiful...*Audio Adrenaline*
Beautiful One...*By The Tree*
Before There Was Time...*Caedmon's Call*
Better Is One Day...*FFH*
Blessed Be Your Name...*Tree 63*
Brave...*Nichole Nordeman*
Everlasting God...*Lincoln Brewster*
First Song That I Sing...*Sara Groves*
Forever...*Chris Tomlin*
Free...*Ginny Owens*
Getting Into You...*Relient K*
Gloria (All God's Children)...*Paul Colman*
Glory Defined...*Building 429*
Gone...*TobyMac*
Grace Like Rain...*Todd Agnew*
Gravity...*Shawn McDonald*
Great Light Of The World...*Bebo Norman*
Hallelujah...*Nicol Sponberg*
Hallelujah God Is Near...*Robbie Seay Band*
Happy Song, The...*delirious?*
He Reigns...*Newsboys*
Hide...*Joy Williams*
I Can Only Imagine...*MercyMe*
I Have Been There...*Mark Schultz*
I Need You...*Jars of Clay*
Lose This Life...*Tait*
Love, Peace & Happiness...*Out Of Eden*
More...*Matthew West*
My Savior My God...*Aaron Shust*
Nothing Left To Lose...*Matt Kearney*
Out Of My Hands...*The Turning*
Resurrection...*Nicol Sponberg*
Run...*Kutless*
Set Your Eyes To Zion...*P.O.D.*
Shine...*Salvador*
Sing Alleluia...*Jennifer Knapp & Mac Powell*
Smile (Just Want To Be With You)...*Chris Rice*
Take You Back...*Jeremy Camp*
(There's Gotta Be) More To Life...*Stacie Orrico*
This Is Your Life...*Switchfoot*
Until The World...*The Afters*
Voice of Truth...*Casting Crowns*
We Live...*Superchick*
Whatever It Takes...*Nate Sallie*
Where I Wanna Be...*V*Enna*
Wholly Yours...*David Crowder Band*
Witness...*Nicole C. Mullen*
Wonderful Cross, The...*Matt Redman*
You Are Holy...*Caleb Rowden*
You Get Me...*ZOEgirl*
You Raise Me Up...*Selah*
Your Love Oh Lord...*Third Day*

A CLASSIC CHRISTMAS

A HOLLY JOLLY CHRISTMAS:

All Alone On Christmas...*Darlene Love*
All I Want For Christmas Is You...*Mariah Carey*
Blue Christmas...*Elvis Presley*
Carol Of The Bells...*Johnny Mathis*
Chipmunk Song, The...*Chipmunks*
Christmas (Baby Please Come Home)...
  Darlene Love
Christmas Canon...*Trans-Siberian Orchestra*
Christmas Island...*Leon Redbone*
Christmas Song, The...*Nat "King" Cole*
Christmas Waltz, The...*Frank Sinatra*
Deck The Halls...*Mitch Miller*
Feliz Navidad...*Jose Feliciano*
Frosty The Snow Man...*Gene Autry*
Good King Wenceslas...*Judy Collins*
Happy Holiday...*Barry Manilow*
Happy Xmas (War Is Over)...*John & Yoko*
Have Yourself A Merry Little Christmas...*Judy Garland*
Here Comes Santa Claus...*Gene Autry*
Here We Come A-Caroling...*Ray Conniff Singers*
Holly Jolly Christmas, A...*Burl Ives*
Home For The Holidays...*Perry Como*
I'll Be Home For Christmas...*Bing Crosby*
If Every Day Was Like Christmas...*Elvis Presley*
It's Beginning To Look Like Christmas...*Perry Como*
It's The Most Wonderful Time Of The Year...
  Andy Williams
Jingle Bell Rock...*Bobby Helms*
Jingle Bells...*Bing Crosby & The Andrews Sisters*
Jolly Old St. Nicholas...*Chicago*

Let It Snow! Let It Snow! Let It Snow!...*Vaughn Monroe*
Little Saint Nick...*Beach Boys*
Marshmallow World, A...*Dean Martin*
Merry Christmas Baby...*Charles Brown*
Merry Christmas Darling...*Carpenters*
Mistletoe And Wine...*London Community Choir*
My Favorite Things...*Tony Bennett*
O Christmas Tree (O Tannenbaum)...*Aretha Franklin*
Please Come Home For Christmas...*Charles Brown*
Pretty Paper...*Roy Orbison*
Rockin' Around The Christmas Tree...*Brenda Lee*
Rudolph, The Red-Nosed Reindeer...*Gene Autry*
Santa Baby...*Eartha Kitt*
Santa Claus Is Comin' To Town...*Bruce Springsteen*
Silver Bells...*Bing Crosby & Carol Richards*
Sleigh Ride...*Boston Pops Orchestra*
Snoopy's Christmas...*Royal Guardsmen*
Someday At Christmas...*Stevie Wonder*
Step Into Christmas...*Elton John*
Stop The Cavalry...*London Community Choir*
'Twas The Night Before Christmas...*Harry Simeone Chorale*
Twelve Days Of Christmas...*Harry Belafonte*
Up On The Housetop...*Kimberley Locke*
We Wish You A Merry Christmas...*Andre Kostelanetz Orch.*
White Christmas...*Bing Crosby*
Winter Wonderland...*Perry Como*
Wonderful Christmastime...*Paul McCartney*

JOY TO THE WORLD:

Angels From The Realms Of Glory
Angels We Have Heard On High
Ave Maria (Schubert and Bach/Gounod versions)
Away In A Manger
Breath Of Heaven
Bring A Torch, Jeannette, Isabella
Caroling, Caroling
Coventry Carol
Ding Dong! Merrily On High
Do You Hear What I Hear
First Noel, The
Gesu Bambino
Go Tell It On The Mountain
God Rest Ye Merry Gentlemen
Good Christian Men, Rejoice
Hallelujah Chorus
Hark! The Herald Angels Sing
Holly And The Ivy, The
I Heard The Bells On Christmas Day

I Saw Three Ships
I Wonder As I Wander
It Came Upon A Midnight Clear
Jesu, Joy Of Man's Desiring
Joy To The World
Little Drummer Boy, The
Lo, How A Rose E'er Blooming
Mary, Did You Know?
Mary's Boy Child
O Come All Ye Faithful
O Come, O Come, Emmanuel
O Holy Night
O Little Town Of Bethlehem
Silent Night
Sweet Little Jesus Boy
We Three Kings Of Orient Are
Welcome To Our World
What Child Is This?
While By My Sheep (Joy, Joy, Joy)

Again And Again...*Jewel*
Ain't No Other Man...*Christina Aguilera*
All Because Of You...*Marques Houston*
All Good Things (Come To An End)...
    Nelly Furtado
Always On Your Side...*Sheryl Crow & Sting*
Amarillo Sky...*Jason Aldean*
American Baby...*Dave Matthews Band*
Amusement Park...*50 Cent*
And Then What...*Young Jeezy w/ Mannie Fresh*
Anonymous...*Bobby Valentino w/ Timbaland*
Anyway...*Martina McBride*
Ass Like That...*Eminem*
Back Like That...*Ghostface Killah w/ Ne-Yo*
Back Then...*Mike Jones*
Badd...*Ying Yang Twins w/ Mike Jones &*
    Mr. ColliPark
Bad Day...*Daniel Powter*
Bartender...*T-Pain w/ Akon*
Bat Country...*Avenged Sevenfold*
Bay Bay...*Hurricane Chris*
Be Without You...*Mary J. Blige*
Beautiful Girls...*Sean Kingston*
Beautiful Liar...*Beyoncé & Shakira*
Beautiful Love...*Afters*
Because Of You...*Kelly Clarkson*
Because Of You...*Ne-Yo*
Bed...*J. Holiday*
Beep...*Pussycat Dolls w/ will.i.am*
Before He Cheats...*Carrie Underwood*
Behind These Hazel Eyes...*Kelly Clarkson*
Believe...*Brooks & Dunn*
Best Friend...*50 Cent & Olivia*
Best Of You...*Foo Fighters*
Betcha Can't Do It Like Me...*D4L*
Better Life...*Keith Urban*
Beverly Hills...*Weezer*
Big Girls Don't Cry...*Fergie*
Big Things Poppin' (Do It)...*T.I.*
Black Horse & The Cherry Tree...*KT Tunstall*
Black Sweat...*Prince*
Bleed It Out...*Linkin Park*
Bleeding...*Prom Kings*
Bones...*Killers*
Bossy...*Kelis w/ Too $hort*
Boston...*Augustana*
Boyfriend...*Ashlee Simpson*
Breakout...*Sean Paul*
Buddy...*Musiq Soulchild*
Buttons...*Pussycat Dolls w/ Snoop Dogg*
Buy U A Drank (Shawty Snappin')...*T-Pain w/*
    Yung Joc
Cab...*Train*
Call Me When You're Sober...*Evanescence*
Call On Me...*Janet & Nelly*
Can I Have It Like That...*Pharrell w/ Gwen*
    Stefani

Can I Live? ...*Nick Cannon w/ Anthony Hamilton*
Can't Forget About You...*Nas*
Can't Leave 'Em Alone...*Ciara w/ 50 Cent*
Can't Tell Me Nothing...*Kanye West*
Candyman...*Christina Aguilera*
Cater 2 U...*Destiny's Child*
Chain Hang Low...*Jibbs*
Chasing Cars...*Snow Patrol*
Cheatin'...*Sara Evans*
Check On It...*Beyoncé w/ Bun B & Slim Thug*
Chemicals React...*Aly & AJ*
Chicken Noodle Soup...*Webstar & Young B*
Circle...*Marques Houston*
City Of Blinding Lights...*U2*
Clothes Off!! ...*Gym Class Heroes*
Coffee Shop...*Yung Joc w/ Gorilla Zoe*
Colony Of Birchmen...*Mastodon*
Colorful...*Rocco DeLuca & The Burden*
Come A Little Closer...*Dierks Bentley*
Come To Me...*Diddy w/ Nicole Scherzinger*
Come With Me...*Sammie*
Comin' To Your City...*Big & Rich*
Concentrate...*Xzibit*
Confessions Of A Broken Heart (Daughter To
    Father)...*Lindsay Lohan*
Control Myself...*LL Cool J w/ Jennifer Lopez*
Cool...*Gwen Stefani*
Crank That (Soulja Boy)...*Soulja Boy*
Crazy...*Gnarls Barkley*
Cupid's Chokehold...*Gym Class Heroes*
DJ Play A Love Song...*Jamie Foxx w/ Twista*
Dance, Dance...*Fall Out Boy*
Dani California...*Red Hot Chili Peppers*
Dem Boyz...*Boyz N Da Hood*
Dem Jeans...*Chingy w/ Jermaine Dupri*
Deja Vu...*Beyoncé w/ Jay-Z*
Diamonds From Sierra Leone...*Kanye West*
Dirty Little Secret...*All-American Rejects*
Do It...*Nelly Furtado*
Do It To It...*Cherish*
Do You...*Ne-Yo*
Doesn't Remind Me...*Audioslave*
Don't Bother...*Shakira*
Don't Cha...*Pussycat Dolls w/ Busta Rhymes*
Don't Forget About Us...*Mariah Carey*
Don't Forget To Remember Me...*Carrie*
    Underwood
Don't Lie...*Black Eyed Peas*
Don't Matter...*Akon*
Don't Phunk With My Heart...*Black Eyed Peas*
Dope Boy Magic...*Yung Joc*
Dreamin'...*Young Jeezy w/ Keyshia Cole*
Dreamgirl...*Dave Matthews Band*
Dreams.*Game*
Drivin' Me Wild...*Common*
Drugs Or Jesus...*Tim McGraw*
8th Of November...*Big & Rich*

Enough Cryin'...*Mary J. Blige*
Entourage...*Omarion*
Errtime...*Nelly*
Every Mile A Memory...*Dierks Bentley*
Everytime I Think About Her...*Jaheim w/ Jadakiss*
Everytime Tha Beat Drop...*Monica w/ Dem Franchize Boyz*
Famous Last Words...*My Chemical Romance*
Far Away...*Nickelback*
Feel Good Inc...*Gorillaz/De La Soul*
Fergalicious...*Fergie*
Fidelity...*Regina Spektor*
Fireman...*Lil' Wayne*
1st Time...*Yung Joc w/ Marques Houston & Trey Songz*
Fix You...*Coldplay*
Flathead...*Fratellis*
For You I Will (Confidence)...*Teddy Geiger*
4 In The Morning...*Gwen Stefani*
4 Minutes...*Avant*
Freak On A Leash (Unplugged)...*Korn w/ Amy Lee*
Free Yourself...*Fantasia*
From Yesterday...*30 Seconds To Mars*
Georgia...*Ludacris & Field Mob*
Get Buck...*Young Buck*
Get Drunk And Be Somebody...*Toby Keith*
Get It Poppin'...*Fat Joe w/ Nelly*
Get It Shawty...*Lloyd*
Get Up...*Ciara w/ Chamillionaire*
Gettin' Some...*Shawnna*
Ghetto Story (Chapter 2)...*Cham w/ Alicia Keys*
Ghost Of A Good Thing...*Dashboard Confessional*
Gimme Dat...*Big Ro*
Gimme That...*Chris Brown w/ Lil' Wayne*
Girl...*Beck*
Girl Tonite...*Twista w/ Trey Songz*
Girlfriend...*Avril Lavigne*
Give Me That...*Webbie w/ Bun-B*
Glamorous...*Fergie w/ Ludacris*
Go!...*Common*
Go Getta...*Young Jeezy w/ R. Kelly*
God's Gonna Cut You Down...*Johnny Cash*
Going Through Changes...*Army Of Me*
Gold Digger...*Kanye West w/ Jamie Foxx*
Golden Skans...*Klaxons*
Good Is Good...*Sheryl Crow*
Gotta Getcha...*Jermaine Dupri*
Great Escape...*Boys Like Girls*
Grillz...*Nelly w/ Paul Wall, Ali & Gipp*
Grind With Me...*Pretty Ricky*
Hang Me Up To Dry...*Cold War Kids*
Happy Hour...*Jazze Pha & Ceelo Green*
Hate It Or Love It...*Game w/ 50 Cent*
Have A Nice Day...*Bon Jovi*

Have A Party...*Mobb Deep w/ 50 Cent & Nate Dogg*
Heard 'Em Say...*Kanye West w/ Adam Levine*
Helena (So Long & Goodnight)...*My Chemical Romance*
Here It Goes Again...*OK Go*
Here We Go...*Trina w/ Kelly Rowland*
Hey There Delilah...*Plain White T's*
High Maintenance Woman...*Toby Keith*
Hip Hop Is Dead...*Nas w/ will.i.am*
Hip Hop Police...*Chamillionaire w/ Slick Rick*
Hips Don't Lie...*Shakira w/ Wyclef Jean*
Holiday...*Green Day*
Holla At Me...*DJ Khaled w/ Lil Wayne, Paul Wall, Fat Joe, Rick Ross & Pitbull*
Hollaback Girl...*Gwen Stefani*
Home...*Daughtry*
Honky Tonk Badonkadonk...*Trace Adkins*
Hood Boy...*Fantasia w/ Big Boi*
House Of Cards...*Madina Lake*
How Do I Breathe...*Mario*
How To Save A Life...*Fray*
Hung Up...*Madonna*
Hurt...*Christina Aguilera*
Hustler Muzik...*Lil Wayne*
Hustler's Ambition...*50 Cent*
Hustlin'...*Rick Ross*
I Ain't No Quitter...*Shania Twain*
I Get Money...*50 Cent*
I Know You Don't Love Me...*Tony Yayo*
I Know You See It...*Yung Joc*
I Love My B****...*Busta Rhymes w/ will.i.am & Kelis*
I Luv It...*Young Jeezy*
I Should Have Cheated...*Keyshia Cole*
I Think They Like Me...*Dem Franchize Boyz w/ Jermaine Dupri, Da Brat & Bow Wow*
I Told You So...*Keith Urban*
I Tried...*Bone Thugs-N-Harmony w/ Akon*
I Wanna Love You...*Akon w/ Snoop Dogg*
I Write Sins Not Tragedies...*Panic! At The Disco*
I'm A Flirt...*R. Kelly w/ T.I. & T-Pain*
I'm A Hustla...*Cassidy*
I'm A King...*P$C w/ T.I. & Lil' Scrappy*
I'm Sprung...*T-Pain*
I'm Tryna...*Omarion*
Ice Box...*Omarion*
Icky Thump...*White Stripes*
If Everyone Cared...*Nickelback*
If You Could See Into My Soul...*Silverstein*
If You're Going Through Hell (Before The Devil Even Knows)...*Rodney Atkins*
Illegal...*Shakira w/ Carlos Santana*
Int'l. Players Anthem (I Choose You)...*UGK w/ OutKast*
Invisible...*Ashlee Simpson*
Irreplaceable...*Beyoncé*

Is It Any Wonder?...*Keane*
It Ends Tonight...*All-American Rejects*
It's Goin' Down...*Yung Joc*
It's Me Snitches...*Swizz Beatz*
It's Not Over...*Daughtry*
It's Okay (One Blood)...*Game w/ Junior Reid*
Jesus, Take The Wheel...*Carrie Underwood*
Just A Lil' Bit...*50 Cent*
Kick Push...*Lupe Fiasco*
King Kong...*Jibbs w/ Chamillionaire*
King Without A Crown...*Matisyahu*
Kryptonite (I'm On It)...*Purple Ribbon All-Stars*
La Tortura...*Shakira w/ Alejandro Sanz*
Ladies Love Country Boys...*Trace Adkins*
Laffy Taffy...*D4L*
Last Night...*Diddy w/ Keyshia Cole*
Lazy Eye...*Silversun Pickups*
Lean Wit It, Rock Wit It...*Dem Franchize Boyz*
Leave The Pieces...*Wreckers*
Let It Go...*Keyshia Cole w/ Missy Elliott & Lil Kim*
Let Me Hold You...*Bow Wow w/ Omarion*
Let U Go...*Ashley Parker Angel*
Let's Ride...*Game*
Life Ain't Always Beautiful...*Gary Allan*
Lighters Up...*Lil' Kim*
Lights And Sounds...*Yellowcard*
Like A Boy...*Ciara*
Like Red On A Rose...*Alan Jackson*
Like That...*Memphis Bleek*
Like This...*Kelly Rowland w/ Eve*
Like We Never Loved At All...*Faith Hill w/ Tim McGraw*
Like You...*Bow Wow w/ Ciara*
Lip Gloss...*Lil Mama*
Lips Of An Angel...*Hinder*
Listen...*Beyoncé*
Lithium...*Evanescence*
Little Less Sixteen Candles, A Little More "Touch Me"...*Fall Out Boy*
Little Too Late...*Toby Keith*
Live In The Sky...*T.I. w/ Jamie Foxx*
London Bridge...*Fergie*
Long Trip Alone...*Dierks Bentley*
Long Way 2 Go...*Cassie*
Looking For You...*Kirk Franklin*
Lose Control...*Missy Elliott w/ Ciara & Fat Man Scoop*
Lost One...*Jay-Z*
Lost Without U...*Robin Thicke*
L.O.V.E.....*Ashlee Simpson*
Love...*Keyshia Cole*
Love Like Winter...*AFI*
Love Me Or Hate Me (F**k You!!!!)...*Lady Sovereign*
LoveStoned...*Justin Timberlake*
Lucky One...*Faith Hill*
Luxurious...*Gwen Stefani*

Make Her Feel Good...*Teairra Mari*
Make It Rain...*Fat Joe w/ Lil Wayne*
Make Me Better...*Fabolous w/ Ne-Yo*
Make This Go On Forever...*Snow Patrol*
Makes Me Wonder...*Maroon 5*
Maneater...*Nelly Furtado*
Me And My Gang...*Rascal Flatts*
Me & U...*Cassie*
Misery Business...*Paramore*
Miss Murder...*AFI*
Mr. Brightside...*Killers*
Money In The Bank...*Lil Scrappy w/ Young Buck*
Money In The Bank...*Swizz Beatz*
Money Maker...*Ludacris w/ Pharrell*
Monster...*Meg & Dia*
Morris Brown...*OutKast*
Move Along...*All-American Rejects*
My Give A Damn's Busted...*Jo Dee Messina*
My Hood...*Young Jeezy*
My Humps...*Black Eyed Peas*
My Love...*Justin Timberlake w/ T.I.*
My 64...*Mike Jones w/ Bun B & Snoop Dogg*
Naked...*Marques Houston*
Nasty Girl...*Notorious B.I.G. w/ Diddy, Nelly, Jagged Edge & Avery Storm*
Neck Of The Woods...*Baby w/ Lil' Wayne*
Need A Boss...*Shareefa w/ Ludacris*
Never Again...*Kelly Clarkson*
1973...*James Blunt*
Not Ready To Make Nice...*Dixie Chicks*
Nothing Left To Lose...*Mat Kearney*
Number One...*Pharrell w/ Kanye West*
Oh...*Ciara w/ Ludacris*
Oh Yes (aka 'Postman')...*Juelz Santana*
Old Blue Chair...*Kenny Chesney*
On And On...*Missy Elliott*
On The Hotline...*Pretty Ricky*
One...*Mary J. Blige & U2*
One...*Tyrese*
One Wish...*Ray J*
Original Of The Species...*U2*
Outta Control (Remix)...*50 Cent*
Outta My System...*Bow Wow w/ T-Pain & Johnta Austin*
Over My Head (Cable Car)...*Fray*
Party Like A Rockstar...*Shop Boyz*
People...*Common*
Perfect Situation...*Weezer*
Photograph...*Nickelback*
Pick Of Destiny...*Tenacious D*
Pimpin' All Over The World...*Ludacris w/ Bobby Valentino*
Play...*David Banner*
Pon De Replay...*Rihanna*
Pop Lock And Drop It...*Huey*
Poppin' My Collar...*Three 6 Mafia*
Presidential...*YoungBloodz*

Pretender, The...*Foo Fighters*
Pretty Vegas...*INXS*
Probably Wouldn't Be This Way...*LeAnn Rimes*
Promise...*Ciara*
Promise Ring...*Tiffany Evans w/ Ciara*
Promiscuous...*Nelly Furtado w/ Timbaland*
Pullin' Me Back...*Chingy w/ Tyrese*
Public Affair...*Jessica Simpson*
Pump It...*Black Eyed Peas*
Push It...*Rick Ross*
Push It Baby...*Pretty Ricky*
Put Your Records On...*Corinne Bailey Rae*
Read My Mind...*Killers*
Real Thing...*Bo Bice*
Red High Heels...*Kellie Pickler*
Rehab...*Amy Winehouse*
Reppin Time...*Jim Jones*
Riddle, The...*Five For Fighting*
Ridin'...*Chamillionaire w/ Krayzie Bone*
Ridin' Rims...*Dem Franchize Boyz*
Right Here In My Arms...*Him*
Ring The Alarm...*Beyoncé*
Rock Yo Hips...*Crime Mob w/ Lil Scrappy*
Rockstar...*Nickelback*
Rodeo...*Juvenile*
Rompe...*Daddy Yankee*
Rubberband Banks...*Young Dro*
Run It!...*Chris Brown*
Runaway Love...*Ludacris w/ Mary J. Blige*
SOS...*Rihanna*
Saints Are Coming...*U2 & Green Day*
Same Girl...*R. Kelly w/ Usher*
Save Room...*John Legend*
Savin' Me...*Nickelback*
Say Goodbye...*Chris Brown*
Say I...*Christina Milian w/ Young Jeezy*
Say It Right...*Nelly Furtado*
Say Somethin'...*Mariah Carey w/ Snoop Dogg*
Say This Sooner (No One Will See Things The Way I Do)...*Almost.*
Saying Sorry...*Hawthorne Heights*
Seashores Of Old Mexico...*George Strait*
Settle For A Slowdown...*Dierks Bentley*
Sex With You...*Marques Houston*
SexyBack...*Justin Timberlake w/ Timbaland*
Sexy Lady...*Yung Berg w/ Junior*
Sexy Love...*Ne-Yo*
Shake...*Ying Yang Twins w/ Pitbull*
Shake It Off...*Mariah Carey*
Shawty...*Plies w/ T-Pain*
She Don't...*LeToya*
She Don't Tell Me To...*Montgomery Gentry*
She's No You...*Jesse McCartney*
Shine On...*Jet*
Shortie Like Me...*Bow Wow w/ Chris Brown & Johnta Austin*
Shoulder Lean...*Young Dro w/ T.I.*
Show Me What You Got...*Jay-Z*

Show Stopper...*Danity Kane*
Shut Up And Drive...*Rihanna*
Side 2 Side...*Three 6 Mafia*
Since U Been Gone...*Kelly Clarkson*
Sittin' Sideways...*Paul Wall*
Slow Down...*Bobby Valentino*
Smack That...*Akon w/ Eminem*
Smile...*Lily Allen*
Snap Yo Fingers...*Lil Jon w/ E-40 & Sean Paul (of YoungBloodz)*
Snow ((Hey Oh))...*Red Hot Chili Peppers*
So Excited...*Janet w/ Khia*
So Seductive...*Tony Yayo w/ 50 Cent*
So Sick...*Ne-Yo*
So What...*Field Mob w/ Ciara*
Some People Change...*Montgomery Gentry*
Something To Be Proud Of...*Montgomery Gentry*
Sometimes You Can't Make It On Your Own...*U2*
Sorry...*Madonna*
Soul Survivor...*Young Jeezy w/ Akon*
Speed of Sound...*Coldplay*
Stand Up For Love...*Destiny's Child*
Stay...*Ne-Yo w/ Peedi Peedi*
Stay Fly...*Three 6 Mafia w/ Young Buck & 8Ball & MJG*
Stay With You...*Goo Goo Dolls*
Steady As She Goes...*Raconteurs*
Stickwitu...*Pussycat Dolls*
Still On It...*Ashanti w/ Paul Wall & Method Man*
Stolen...*Dashboard Confessional*
Stop Me...*Mark Ronson w/ Daniel Merriweather*
Straight To The Bank...*50 Cent*
Stronger...*Kanye West*
Stuntin' Like My Daddy...*Birdman & Lil Wayne*
Stupid Boy...*Keith Urban*
Stupid Girls...*P!nk*
Sugar, We're Goin' Down...*Fall Out Boy*
Surrender...*Camp Freddy*
Sweet Escape...*Gwen Stefani w/ Akon*
Swing...*Trace Adkins*
Switch...*Will Smith*
Take Me As I Am...*Mary J. Blige*
Take Over, The Breaks Over...*Fall Out Boy*
Taking Chances...*Platinum Weird*
Tambourine...*Eve*
Te Amo Corazon...*Prince*
Teary Eyed...*Missy Elliott*
Tell Me...*Diddy w/ Christina Aguilera*
Tell Me...*Bobby Valentino*
Tell Me Baby...*Red Hot Chili Peppers*
Tell Me 'Bout It...*Joss Stone*
Tell Me When To Go...*E-40*
Temperature...*Sean Paul*
Testify...*Common*

Thnks Fr Th Mmrs...*Fall Out Boy*
That's That...*Snoop Dogg w/ R. Kelly*
There It Go! (The Whistle Song)...*Juelz Santana*
These Boots Are Made For Walkin'...*Jessica Simpson*
These Words...*Natasha Bedingfield*
Thinking About You...*Norah Jones*
This Ain't A Scene, It's An Arms Race...*Fall Out Boy*
This Is Why I'm Hot...*Mims*
Throw Some D's...*Rich Boy*
Tim McGraw...*Taylor Swift*
Time Won't Let Me Go...*Bravery*
Top Back...*T.I.*
Today...*Junkie XL*
Torn...*LeToya*
Touch...*Omarion*
Touch It...*Busta Rhymes*
Touch The Sky...*Kanye West w/ Lupe Fiasco*
Trapped In The Closet...*R. Kelly*
Turn It Up...*Chamillionaire w/ Lil' Flip*
Twist It...*Olivia w/ Lloyd Banks*
2 Step...*Unk*
Typical...*Mutemath*
U And Dat...*E-40 w/ T-Pain & Kandi Girl*
U + Ur Hand...*P!nk*
Umbrella...*Rihanna w/ Jay-Z*
Unappreciated...*Cherish*
Unbreakable...*Alicia Keys*
Unchained Melody...*Righteous Brothers*
Unfaithful...*Rihanna*
Unpredictable...*Jamie Foxx w/ Ludacris*
Untitled (How Can This Happen To Me?)...*Simple Plan*
Unwritten...*Natasha Bedingfield*
Upgrade U...*Beyoncé w/ Jay-Z*
Vulnerable...*Secondhand Serenade*
Wait...*Ying Yang Twins*
Wait A Minute...*Pussycat Dolls*
Waiting On The World To Change...*John Mayer*
Wake Me Up When September Ends...*Green Day*
Wake Up Call...*Maroon 5*
Walk Away...*Kelly Clarkson*
Walk It Out...*Unk*
Wall To Wall...*Chris Brown*
Want To...*Sugarland*
Watching You...*Rodney Atkins*
Way Down In The Hole...*Blind Boys Of Alabama*
Way I Are...*Timbaland w/ Keri Hilson*
We Be Burnin'...*Sean Paul*
We Belong Together...*Mariah Carey*
We Fly High...*Jim Jones*

We Ride ((I See The Future))...*Mary J. Blige*
We Takin' Over...*DJ Khaled w/ T.I., Akon, Rick Ross, Fat Joe, Lil' Wayne & Baby*
Welcome To Jamrock...*Damian "Jr. Gong" Marley*
Welcome To The Black Parade...*My Chemical Romance*
What Goes Around...Comes Around...*Justin Timberlake*
What Hurts The Most...*Rascal Flatts*
What I've Done...*Linkin Park*
What It Do...*Lil' Flip w/ Mannie Fresh*
What You Know...*T.I.*
What's Left Of Me...*Nick Lachey*
When I Get Where I'm Going...*Brad Paisley w/ Dolly Parton*
When I See U...*Fantasia*
When I'm Gone...*Eminem*
(When You Gonna) Give It Up To Me...*Sean Paul w/ Keyshia Cole*
When You Were Young...*Killers*
When You're Gone...*Avril Lavigne*
When You're Mad...*Ne-Yo*
Where'd You Go...*Fort Minor w/ Holly Brook*
White & Nerdy..."Weird Al" Yankovic*
Who Knew...*P!nk*
Who Says You Can't Go Home...*Bon Jovi w/ Jennifer Nettles*
Who You'd Be Today...*Kenny Chesney*
Why You Wanna...*T.I.*
Wind It Up...*Gwen Stefani*
Window Shopper...*50 Cent*
Wipe Me Down...*Lil Boosie w/ Foxx & Webbie*
Working Class Hero...*Green Day*
World, The...*Brad Paisley*
World Wide Suicide...*Pearl Jam*
Would You Go With Me...*Josh Turner*
Wouldn't Get Far...*Game w/ Kanye West*
Yo (Excuse Me Miss)...*Chris Brown*
You...*Lloyd w/ Lil' Wayne*
You And Me...*Lifehouse*
You Don't Know...*Eminem, 50 Cent, Lloyd Banks & Cashis*
You Know I'm No Good...*Amy Winehouse w/ Ghostface Killah*
You Know What It Is...*T.I. w/ Wyclef Jean*
You Save Me...*Kenny Chesney*
You Should Be My Girl...*Sammie w/ Sean Paul (of YoungBloodz)*
(You Want To) Make A Memory...*Bon Jovi*
You'll Always Be My Baby...*Sara Evans*
You're Beautiful...*James Blunt*
Your Body...*Pretty Ricky*
Zoom...*Lil' Boosie w/ Yung Joc*

CREATE YOUR OWN PLAYLIST

☐ _____
☐ _____
☐ _____
☐ _____
☐ _____
☐ _____
☐ _____
☐ _____
☐ _____
☐ _____
☐ _____
☐ _____
☐ _____
☐ _____
☐ _____
☐ _____
☐ _____
☐ _____
☐ _____
☐ _____
☐ _____
☐ _____
☐ _____

☐ _____
☐ _____
☐ _____
☐ _____
☐ _____
☐ _____
☐ _____
☐ _____
☐ _____
☐ _____
☐ _____
☐ _____
☐ _____
☐ _____
☐ _____
☐ _____
☐ _____
☐ _____
☐ _____
☐ _____
☐ _____
☐ _____
☐ _____

CREATE YOUR OWN PLAYLIST

- ☐ _____
- ☐ _____
- ☐ _____
- ☐ _____
- ☐ _____
- ☐ _____
- ☐ _____
- ☐ _____
- ☐ _____
- ☐ _____
- ☐ _____
- ☐ _____
- ☐ _____
- ☐ _____
- ☐ _____
- ☐ _____
- ☐ _____
- ☐ _____
- ☐ _____
- ☐ _____
- ☐ _____
- ☐ _____
- ☐ _____
- ☐ _____
- ☐ _____
- ☐ _____
- ☐ _____
- ☐ _____
- ☐ _____
- ☐ _____
- ☐ _____
- ☐ _____
- ☐ _____
- ☐ _____
- ☐ _____
- ☐ _____
- ☐ _____
- ☐ _____
- ☐ _____
- ☐ _____

CREATE YOUR OWN PLAYLIST

- ☐ _____
- ☐ _____
- ☐ _____
- ☐ _____
- ☐ _____
- ☐ _____
- ☐ _____
- ☐ _____
- ☐ _____
- ☐ _____
- ☐ _____
- ☐ _____
- ☐ _____
- ☐ _____
- ☐ _____
- ☐ _____
- ☐ _____
- ☐ _____
- ☐ _____
- ☐ _____
- ☐ _____
- ☐ _____
- ☐ _____
- ☐ _____
- ☐ _____
- ☐ _____
- ☐ _____
- ☐ _____
- ☐ _____
- ☐ _____
- ☐ _____
- ☐ _____
- ☐ _____
- ☐ _____
- ☐ _____
- ☐ _____
- ☐ _____
- ☐ _____
- ☐ _____
- ☐ _____
- ☐ _____
- ☐ _____
- ☐ _____
- ☐ _____
- ☐ _____
- ☐ _____
- ☐ _____
- ☐ _____

CREATE YOUR OWN PLAYLIST

☐ _____   ☐ _____

☐ _____   ☐ _____

☐ _____   ☐ _____

☐ _____   ☐ _____

☐ _____   ☐ _____

☐ _____   ☐ _____

☐ _____   ☐ _____

☐ _____   ☐ _____

☐ _____   ☐ _____

☐ _____   ☐ _____

☐ _____   ☐ _____

☐ _____   ☐ _____

☐ _____   ☐ _____

☐ _____   ☐ _____

☐ _____   ☐ _____

☐ _____   ☐ _____

☐ _____   ☐ _____

☐ _____   ☐ _____

☐ _____   ☐ _____

☐ _____   ☐ _____

☐ _____   ☐ _____

☐ _____   ☐ _____

☐ _____   ☐ _____

☐ _____   ☐ _____

NOTES FOR YOUR PLAYLISTS

NOTES FOR YOUR PLAYLISTS

NOTES FOR YOUR PLAYLISTS

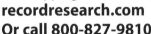

Joel Whitburn's
NEW Top Pop Singles
1955-2006

Our biggest bestseller…revised, revamped and re-energized like never before! Brimming with basic chart facts, plus detailed artist and song trivia, this comprehensive artist-by-artist arrangement contains the 26,000 songs and 6,200 artists that made Billboard's "Hot 100" and Pop music charts since 1955. Thousands of classic non-Hot 100 songs have now been added to the artist discographies! Rock and roll pioneers now listed with their pre-1955 hits that helped spark a musical revolution!

$79⁹⁵

1,184 PAGES
SIZE: 7" X 9"
HARDCOVER

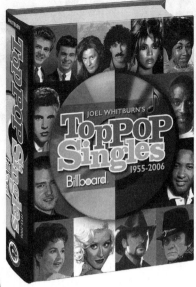

Billboard. DEBUT PEAK WKS	RIAA	ARTIST Song Title	Ⓐ=Album Cut Ⓖ=CD Ⓢ=Cassette ⓅPic. Slv. Ⓣ=12" Ⓥ='45'	B-side	Label & Number

DYLAN, Bob
Born Robert Zimmerman on 5/24/1941 in Duluth, Minnesota; raised in Hibbing, Minnesota. Highly influential, legendary singer/songwriter/guitarist/harmonica player. Innovator of folk-rock style. Took stage name from poet Dylan Thomas. To New York City in December 1960. Worked Greenwich Village folk clubs. Signed to Columbia Records in October 1961. Motorcycle crash on 7/29/1966 led to short retirement. Subject of documentaries *Don't Look Back* and *Eat The Document*. Acted in movies *Pat Garrett And Billy The Kid, Renaldo And Clara* (also directed) and *Hearts Of Fire*. Newly-found Christian faith reflected in his recordings of 1979-81. Member of the supergroup **Traveling Wilburys**. His son Jakob is lead singer of **The Wallflowers**.

AWARDS: Grammy: Lifetime Achievement 1991 ★ R&R Hall of Fame: 1988

TOP HITS: 1)Like A Rolling Stone   2)Rainy Day Women #12 & 35   3)Lay Lady Lay   4)Positively 4th Street   5)Knockin' On Heaven's Door

All-Time: #199

DEBUT	PEAK	WKS	#	Song Title	B-side		Label & Number
4/3/65	39	8	1	Subterranean Homesick Blues	She Belongs To Me	Ⓟ	Columbia 43242
				R&R Hall of Fame ★ RS500 #332			
				B-side was a #33 hit for Rick Nelson in 1969			
7/24/65	2²	12	2	Like A Rolling Stone	Gates Of Eden		Columbia 43346
				Grammy: Hall of Fame ★ R&R Hall of Fame ★ RS500 #1 ★ RIAA #92 ★ NPR 100			
				features Al Kooper (later of **Blood, Sweat & Tears**) on organ	From A Buick 6	Ⓟ	Columbia 43389
10/2/65	7	9	3	Positively 4th Street	Highway 61 Revisited		Columbia 43477
				RS500 #203			
1/1/66	58	6	4	Can You Please Crawl Out Your Window?	Pledging My Time		Columbia 43592
4/16/66	2¹	10	5	Rainy Day Women #12 & 35	Just Like Tom Thumb's Blues	Ⓟ	Columbia 43683
7/2/66	20	7	6	I Want You	Obviously 5 Believers		Columbia 43792
9/10/66	33	6	7	Just Like A Woman	Most Likely You Go Your Way And I'll Go Home		Columbia 44069
				RS500 #230			
5/20/67	81	4	8	Leopard-Skin Pill-Box Hat	Drifter's Escape		Columbia 44826
				above 4 from his album Blonde On Blonde			
5/17/69	85	5	9	I Threw It All Away	Peggy Day		Columbia 44926
7/12/69	7	14	10	Lay Lady Lay	Country Pie		Columbia 45004
				written for his wife Sarah Lowndes (married 1965-77)			
11/1/69	50	7	11	Tonight I'll Be Staying Here With You	Copper Kettle (The Pale Moonlight) [I]		Columbia 45199
7/25/70	41	7	12	Wigwam	Spanish Is The Loving Tongue		Columbia 45409
				#3-12: produced by Bob Johnston			
6/26/71	41	8	13	Watching The River Flow	(big band version)		Columbia 45516
				Leon Russell (piano)			
12/4/71+	33	8	14	George Jackson	Turkey Chase		Columbia 45913
				Jackson: black militant shot to death in a prison riot at San Quentin on 8/21/1971			
9/1/73	12	16	15	Knockin' On Heaven's Door	Lily Of The West		Columbia 45982
				RS500 #190			
				Roger McGuinn (of **The Byrds**; guitar); from the movie Pat Garrett And Billy The Kid starring Dylan			
12/15/73+	55	7	16	A Fool Such As I	You Angel You		Asylum 11033
				#3 Country hit for Hank Snow in 1953			
2/23/74	44	6	17	On A Night Like This	Stage Fright (The Band) [L]		Asylum 11043
				B-side was a hit for Manfred Mann in 1979			
8/10/74	66	5	18	Most Likely You Go Your Way (And I'll Go Mine) [w/ The Band]	If You See Her, Say Hello		Columbia 10106
				Dylan's studio version is on the B-side of #8 above			
3/8/75	31	7	19	Tangled Up In Blue	(Part II)	Ⓟ	Columbia 10245
				R&R Hall of Fame ★ RS500 #68			
'/29/75+	33	11	20	Hurricane (Part I)	Oh, Sister		Columbia 10298
				true story of boxer Rubin "Hurricane" Carter			
⟨76	54	5	21	Mozambique	Trouble In Mind		Columbia 11072
⟨9	24	12	22	Gotta Serve Somebody			

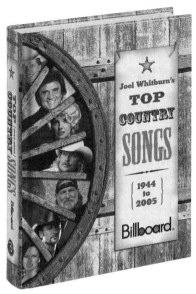

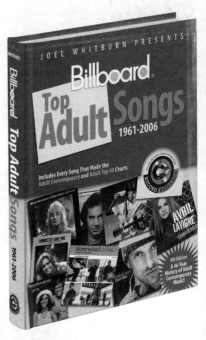

Joel Whitburn's
Top Adult Songs

It's strictly "Adults only" here—in the only comprehensive compilation of one of today's hottest music formats! Here's every song that ever made Billboard's "Adult Contemporary" and "Adult Top 40" charts—in one big book! It covers the complete history of the "Adult Top 40" chart—where modern rock, dance and R&B artists rub shoulders with traditional Adult Contemporary acts. And it includes essential chart data for every "Adult" song... features and facts on "Adult" songs and artists...and much more!

416 PAGES
SIZE: 7" X 9"
HARDCOVER

$49⁹⁵

Billboard				ARTIST	Ranking		
Debut	T40	Peak	Wks	Adult Chart Hit		Songwriter	Label & Number

MARX, Richard   1990s: #11 / All-Time: #36
Born on 9/16/1963 in Chicago, Illinois. Pop-rock singer/songwriter. Professional jingle singer since age five. Backing singer for **Lionel Richie**. Married Cynthia Rhodes (of **Animotion**) on 1/8/1989.

Debut	T40	Peak	Wks		Adult Chart Hit	Songwriter	Label & Number
11/7/87		20	15	1	Should've Known Better	Richard Marx	Manhattan 50083
					Fee Waybill (of The Tubes) and Timothy B. Schmit (backing vocals)		
2/6/88	2²		24	2	Endless Summer Nights	Richard Marx	EMI-Manhattan 50113
5/28/88	3		27	3	Hold On To The Nights	Richard Marx	EMI-Manhattan 50106
7/8/89	❶⁶		23 ▲	4	Right Here Waiting	Richard Marx	EMI 50219
10/14/89	2²		20	5	Angelia	Richard Marx/Fee Waybill	EMI 50218
3/10/90	47		2	6	Too Late To Say Goodbye	Richard Marx	EMI 50234
5/5/90	6		20	7	Children Of The Night	Richard Marx	EMI 50288
					tribute to the Los Angeles organization helping child prostitutes		
11/2/91	❶⁴		22	8	Keep Coming Back	Richard Marx	Capitol 44753
2/8/92	❶¹		32	9	Hazard	Richard Marx	Capitol 44796
6/13/92	4		37	10	Take This Heart	Richard Marx	Capitol 44782
10/17/92+	9		24	11	Chains Around My Heart	Richard Marx/Fee Waybill	Capitol 44848
1/1/94	❶¹¹		34	12	Now And Forever	Richard Marx	Capitol 58005
7/2/94	3¹		26	13	The Way She Loves Me	Richard Marx	Capitol 58167
11/26/94+	11		26	14	Nothing Left Behind Us	Richard Marx/Fee Waybill	album cut
					from the album Paid Vacation on Capitol 81232		
3/15/97	3¹		26	15	Until I Find You Again	Richard Marx	Capitol 58633
10/25/97	2⁶		35	16	At The Beginning	Lynn Ahrens/Stephen Flaherty	Atlantic 84037
					DONNA LEWIS & RICHARD MARX from the animated movie Anastasia		
11/11/00		25	12	17	Days In Avalon	Richard Marx	Manhattan 49472
					from the album Days In Avalon on Signal 21 10001		
6/26/04 (40)		20	16	18	When You're Gone	Richard Marx	album cut
11/20/04+		22	18	19	Ready To Fly	Richard Marx	album cut
11/20/04 (40)		29	13		above 2 from the album My Own Best Enemy on Manhattan 91719		

MATCHBOX TWENTY   T40: 1990s: #16 / 2000s: #7 / All-Time: #10
Pop-rock group from Orlando, Florida: **Rob Thomas** (vocals; born on 2/14/1972), Kyle Cook (guitar; born on 8/29/1975), Adam Gaynor (guitar; born on 11/26/1963), Brian Yale (bass; born on 10/24/1968) and Paul Doucette (drums; born on 8/22/1972).

Joel Whitburn's

Top R&B/Hip-Hop Singles

From R&B's early pioneers...to today's hottest Hip-Hop stars! Over 4,400 artists and nearly 20,000 song titles from Billboard's Rhythm & Blues/Soul/Black/Hip-Hop Singles charts from 1942-2004—all arranged by artist! With complete R&B chart data...R&B record and artist info... and much more.

816 PAGES
SIZE: 7" X 9"
HARDCOVER

Joel Whitburn's

Top R&B Albums

Covers every artist and album to appear on Billboard's "Top R&B Albums" chart from 1965-1998, with complete chart info...features highlighting each artist's hit albums and hot chart eras...complete track listings for Top 10 albums... and more!

360 PAGES
SIZE: 7" X 9"
HARDCOVER

Billboard "Hot 100" Singles Chart Books

Straight from the pages of Billboard -- each decade's "Hot 100" and Pop singles music charts, with every weekly chart reproduced in black and white at about 70% of its original size.
VARIOUS PAGE LENGTHS / SIZES: 50s, 60s, 90s: 9" x 12", 70s & 80s: 8½" x 11" / HARDCOVER

$59⁹⁵ $79⁹⁵ $79⁹⁵ $79⁹⁵ $79⁹⁵

Billboard Pop Charts 1955-1959

Billboard Hot 100 Charts The Sixties

Billboard Hot 100 Charts The Seventies

Billboard Hot 100 Charts The Eighties

Billboard Hot 100 Charts The Nineties

Mention this ad when you order by phone and get 10% off your first order!

Joel Whitburn's
Pop Hits Singles & Albums 1940-1954

The big bands. The classic crooners. The classy female vocalists. The smooth vocal groups. The dynamic duos. Here's the complete history of pre-Rock Pop in four big books in one! An artist-by-artist singles anthology; a year-by-year ranking of classic Pop hits; the complete story of early Pop albums; plus the weekly "Best Sellers" Top 10 singles charts of 1940-1954.

576 PAGES
SIZE: 7" X 9"
HARDCOVER

Joel Whitburn's
Country Annual

54 complete, year-by-year rankings of over 16,000 records that peaked on Billboard's Country singles charts from 1944-1997, with each song ranked according to its highest chart position.

704 PAGES
SIZE: 7" X 9"
HARDCOVER

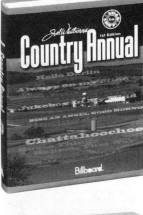

Joel Whitburn's
2005-2006 Music Yearbook

Our Yearbook is back...in a new combined edition covering both 2005 and 2006! Ten artist-by-artist sections listing every single, track and album that made these 2005-2006 major Billboard music charts:

SONGS & TRACKS	ALBUMS
The Billboard Hot 100	The Billboard 200
Bubbling Under The Hot 100	Top Country Albums
Hot Country Songs	Top R&B/Hip-Hop Albums
Hot R&B/Hip-Hop Songs	
Adult Contemporary/Adult Top 40	
Mainstream Rock Tracks	
Modern Rock Tracks	

336 PAGES
SIZE: 6" X 9"
SOFTCOVER

Visit www.recordresearch.com for book descriptions, sample pages and shipping terms.

Billboard Music Yearbooks 1983-2004

Each Yearbook is a comprehensive annual recap of each year's music, in complete artist-by-artist sections covering Billboard's major singles and albums charts. With complete chart data on every single, track and album that debuted during the year...plus artist biographical info, Time Capsules, entertainment obituaries and more!

OVER 200 PAGES EACH
SIZE: 6" X 9" SOFTCOVER

80s $14⁹⁵ each

90s $19⁹⁵ each

00s $24⁹⁵ each

Rock Tracks

Billboard's two greatest Rock charts—now covered individually in this one book! A total of 22 years of every track and every artist that ever hit Billboard's "Mainstream Rock Tracks" and "Modern Rock Tracks" charts, with comprehensive data on every track from 1981-2002!

$19⁹⁵

336 PAGES
SIZE: 7" X 9"
HARDCOVER

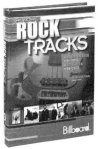

Christmas In the Charts

Charted holiday classics cover to cover—a jolly, joyous celebration of America's favorite holiday music from 1920-2004! This complete history of every charted Christmas single and album is drawn from a diversity of Billboard charts and music genres. Arranged by artist, with full chart data and all the trimmings for every Christmas hit!

$29⁹⁵

272 PAGES
SIZE: 7" X 9"
SOFTCOVER

Hot Dance/Disco

Lists every artist and hit to appear on Billboard's national "Dance/Disco Club Play" chart from 1974-2003. All charted titles, album cuts—even complete albums that made the Dance chart in their entirety. Loaded with basic chart facts...intriguing Info on artists and recordings...Top Artists' pix...plus much more!

$39⁹⁵

368 PAGES
SIZE: 7" X 9"
HARDCOVER

Top 1000 Hits of the Rock Era

The book worth a thousand pictures—showing, in full color, the original 45 RPM picture sleeve, cassette single box, CD single insert, sheet music or full-page Billboard ad for each and every recording ranked among the Top 1000 hits of the entire rock era.

200 PAGES   SIZE: 6" X 9"   SOFTCOVER

$14.95

Billboard Top 10 Singles Charts

Includes every weekly Top 10 chart from rock and roll's formative years on Billboard's "Best Sellers" charts (1955-1958), followed by weekly Top 10's drawn from the "Hot 100" (1958-2000).

712 PAGES   SIZE: 6" X 9"   HARDCOVER

$34.95

Billboard Top 10 Album Charts

More than 1800 individual Top 10 charts from over 35 years of weekly Billboard Top Album charts, beginning with the August 17, 1963 "Top LP's" chart right through "The Billboard 200" of December 26, 1998.

536 PAGES   SIZE: 6" X 9"   HARDCOVER

$34.95

#1 Pop Pix

Picture this: 1,045 full-color photos of picture sleeves, sheet music covers or Billboard ads representing every #1 Pop hit from Billboard's Pop/Hot 100 charts, with selected chart data, from 1953-2003.

112 PAGES   SIZE: 6" X 9"   SOFTCOVER

$14.95

#1 Album Pix

1,651 full-color photos—in three separate sections—of album covers of every #1 Pop, Country & R&B album in Billboard chart history, with selected chart data, from 1945-2004.

176 PAGES   SIZE: 6" X 9"   SOFTCOVER

$14.95

Visit www.recordresearch.com for book descriptions, sample pages and shipping terms.

Bubbling Under The Billboard Hot 100

Bursting with over 6,100 titles by more than 3,500 artists who appeared on Billboard's "Bubbling Under" chart—long the home to regional hits that lacked the sales and airplay to hit the Hot 100. Includes recordings by legendary artists before they hit the mainstream...rock's top stars...famous non-music celebrities...and classic one-shot "Bubbling"-only artists in this comprehensive chronology from 1959-2004.

352 PAGES   SIZE: 7" X 9"   HARDCOVER

A Century of Pop Music 1900-1999

100 rankings of the 40 biggest hits of each year of the past century, based on America's weekly popular record charts—with complete chart data on every hit!

256 PAGES   SIZE: 7" X 9"   SOFTCOVER

Pop Memories 1890-1954

An artist-by-artist account of the 65 formative years of recorded popular music—over 1,600 artists and 12,000 recordings in all—with data from popular music charts, surveys and listings.

660 PAGES   SIZE: 6" X 9"   HARDCOVER

Album Cuts

Nearly 1/4 million cuts from over 22,000 Pop albums that charted from 1955-2001, listed alphabetically, with the artist's name and chart debut year for each cut. The perfect partner for *Songs & Artists 2006*!

720 PAGES   SIZE: 7" X 9"   HARDCOVER

Billboard Pop Album Charts 1965-1969

A complete collection of actual reproductions of every weekly Billboard "Top LP's" Pop albums chart from January 2, 1965 through December 27, 1969— each shown in its entirety, in black-and-white, at about 70% of original size.

496 PAGES   SIZE: 9" X 12"   HARDCOVER

Billboard #1s

See in seconds which record held the top spot each and every week for 42 years (1950-1991) on Billboard's Pop, R&B and Country singles and albums charts and Adult Contemporary singles chart.

336 PAGES   SIZE: 7" X 9"   SOFTCOVER

ORDERING INFORMATION

Shipping/Handling Extra—If you do not order through our online Web site (see below), please contact us for shipping rates.

Order by:

U.S. Toll-Free: 1-800-827-9810
    (orders only please—Mon-Fri 8 AM-12 PM, 1 PM-5 PM CST)
Foreign Orders: 1-262-251-5408
Questions?: 1-262-251-5408 or **Email**: books@recordresearch.com
Mention this ad when you order by phone and get 10% off your first order.

Online at our Web site: www.recordresearch.com

Fax (24 hours): 1-262-251-9452

Mail: Record Research Inc.
    P.O. Box 200
    Menomonee Falls, WI 53052-0200
    U.S.A.

Payment methods accepted: MasterCard, VISA, American Express, Discover, Money Order, or Check (personal checks may be held up to 10 days for bank clearance).

U.S. orders are shipped **via UPS**; please allow **7-10 business days** for delivery. (If only a post office box number is given, it will be shipped 4th class media mail which can lengthen the delivery time.)

Canadian and foreign orders can be shipped by either surface M-Bag or airmail M-Bag through our third-party shipper. Call or email for a shipping/handling quote. Transit times vary. Orders must be paid in U.S. dollars and drawn on a U.S. bank."

Prices subject to change without notice.